Olympic Park Map —II-III.
Olympic Park
  Aquatics Centre —V. (4E 53)
  Basketball Arena —VI. (2D 53)
  BMX Track —VI. (2D 53)
  Copper Box —VI. (3C 52)
  Eton Manor —VII. (1D 53)
  Olympic Stadium —V. (4D 53)
  Riverbank Arena —XII. (2C 52)
  Velodrome —XII. (2D 53)
  Water Polo Arena —XIII. (4D 53)
Brands Hatch —VI.
Earls Court —VII. (1C 86)
Eton Dorney —VII.
ExCeL —VIII. (1D 83)
Greenwich Park —IX. (2F 95)
Hadleigh Farm —IX.
Hampton Court Palace —X.
Horse Guards Parade —X. (2C 22)
Hyde Park —X. (2B 74)
Lee Valley White Water
  Centre —X.

Lord's Cricket Ground —XI. (2F 59)
The Mall —XI. (3B 22)
North Greenwich Arena —XI. (2A 82)
The Royal Artillery Barracks —XII.
Wembley Arena —XIII.
Wembley Stadium —XIII.
Weymouth and Portland—XIV
Wimbledon —XIV. (3A 114)

London 2012 Shops —XIV
Live sites —XV
Transport —XV
Journey Planner —XVIII

This summer London and the UK will come alive with the world's largest sporting events when the Games begin.

The London 2012 Olympic and Paralympic Games will encompass 30 days of competition with 14,723 athletes and millions of people gathered here to enjoy the sporting and cultural action.

Olympic Heritage

The first ancient Olympic Games can be traced back to 776 BC. They were dedicated to the Olympian gods and staged on the plains of Olympia in Greece. The modern Olympic Games were founded by French-born athlete, poet and educator Pierre de Coubertin (1863–1937).

Olympic Games

In 2012 London will host a Games like never before, drawing on the UK's proud Olympic heritage. In 1908, London stood in as Host City for Rome after an eruption of Mount Vesuvius. It was the first time that the athletes paraded under national flags at the start of the Games and the Marathon was fixed at 42.195km (26.2 miles). In 1948, London again stepped in at the last minute to host the first Games after World War II. It was the first time that the Games were shown on home television.

Paralympic Games

The London 2012 Paralympic Games are being organised together with the Olympic Games. In 1948, Dr Ludwig Guttmann organised a sports competition that involved World War II soldiers with spinal cord injuries based at Stoke Mandeville Hospital. The competition took place between sports clubs and other hospitals on the same day as the Opening Ceremony of the London 1948 Olympic Games. Four years later, athletes from Holland joined in, creating the forerunner of the Paralympic Games. The first official Paralympic Games was that held in Rome in 1960.

Olympic Torch Relay

An important element of the Olympic Games of ancient Greece, the Flame is lit from the sun's rays at the Temple of Hera in Olympia. The Olympic Torch Relay route has been planned so that the Flame will come within 10 miles of 95% of people in the UK. The last Torchbearer lights the cauldron at the Olympic Games Opening Ceremony.

Cultural Olympiad

The London 2012 Festival, will bring leading artists from all over the world to create the UK's biggest ever festival; a chance for everyone to celebrate London 2012 through dance, music, theatre, the visual arts, film and digital innovation and leave a lasting legacy for the arts in the UK.

Legacy

For the first time, the Games are being planned hand-in-hand with the long-term improvement of the area. A new sustainable community will be integrated with the area surrounding the Olympic Park, with local people benefiting from a new park, homes and world-class sporting facilities.

Olympic Stadium

The Olympic Stadium will host the Athletics and Paralympic Athletics events at the London 2012 Games, as well as the Opening and Closing Ceremonies.

 ### Athletics

One of the most popular sports is also the biggest, with 2,000 athletes competing in 47 events. There are four main strands to the Athletics competition: track events, such as the 100m; field events, which include the High Jump and the Shot Put; combined events such as the Decathlon, a mix of track and field elements; and road events, among them the Marathon.

 ### Paralympic Athletics

Athletics will also be the largest sport at the Paralympic Games with 1,100 athletes competing. Some athletes compete in wheelchairs or throwing frames, others with prostheses, and others with the guidance of a sighted companion.

Aquatics Centre

The Aquatics Centre will be the venue for Swimming, Paralympic Swimming, Diving, Synchronised Swimming and the swimming element of the Modern Pentathlon. The venue features a spectacular wave-like roof that is 160m long and up to 80m wide.

 ### Diving

Diving requires acrobatic excellence and supreme coordination skills, as athletes dive from heights of up to 10m.

 ### Swimming

There are four strokes used in Olympic competition: Freestyle, Backstroke, Breaststroke and Butterfly. The 10km Marathon Swimming will be held in the Serpentine within Hyde Park.

 ### Synchronised Swimming

Synchronised Swimmers use pinpoint precision and immense stamina to deliver beautiful routines in the pool.

Modern Pentathlon

The venue for the swimming element of Modern Pentathlon. The fencing element takes place in Copper Box, riding and the combined event will be staged in Greenwich Park.

 ### Paralympic Swimming

Swimmers are classified according to their functional ability to perform each stroke, and compete against athletes in their own classification.

Basketball Arena

The fourth-largest venue on the Olympic Park and one of the largest ever temporary venues built for any Games.

 ### Basketball

Preliminaries and women's quarter-finals are held here at the Basketball Arena. All other rounds take place in the North Greenwich Arena.

 ### Handball

Venue for the Handball men's quarter-finals, all semi-finals and all medal matches. All other rounds take place in the Copper Box.

 ### Wheelchair Basketball

Preliminary games will be split between the Basketball Arena and North Greenwich Arena. All quarter-finals, semi-finals and medal games will take place at North Greenwich Arena.

 ### Wheelchair Rugby

Played indoors on a regulation-size basketball court by teams of four, contact between wheelchairs is permitted, but physical contact is outlawed.

BMX Track

The purpose built BMX Track will be reconfigured after the Games to form part of a new VeloPark with a mountain bike track and road-cycle circuit.

 ### BMX Racing

Inspired by motocross, BMX Racing is the most recent discipline to have been added to the Olympic programme.

Brands Hatch

Brands Hatch motor racing circuit in Kent is approximately 20 miles south-east of the Olympic Park.

 ### Paralympic Cycling - Road

Athletes with a visual impairment, cerebral palsy, amputations or other physical disabilities compete on bicycles, tricycles, tandems and hand cycles.

Copper Box

This Olympic Park venue will be adapted after the Games to

become a multi-use sports centre for community use, athlete training and small- to medium-sized events.

 ## Handball

Preliminary rounds of both the men's and women's competitions, as well as the women's quarter-finals, will take place here. The competition will then move to the Basketball Arena, also in the Olympic Park.

 ## Modern Pentathlon

Fencing, the first element of Modern Pentathlon takes place here. Swimming takes place in the Aquatics Centre, riding and the combined event will be staged in Greenwich Park.

 ## Goalball

Goalball is played by visually impaired athletes using a ball with bells inside. Athletes wear blackout masks on the playing court, which allows persons with varying degrees of vision to participate together.

Earls Court

A major west London venue for exhibitions, conferences and events. It first opened its doors in 1937, and now holds hundreds of events each year.

 ## Volleyball

The dynamic, competitive sport of Volleyball made its Olympic Games debut in 1964.

Eton Dorney

Eton Dorney is located near Windsor Castle, about 25 miles west of London.

 ## Canoe Sprint

Races will be held over three distances with the fastest races taking just 30 seconds to complete. Canoe Slalom takes place at Lee Valley White Water Centre.

 ## Rowing

The 14 Olympic Rowing events range from the Single Sculls, featuring solo rowers, to the Eights, contested by teams of eight rowers plus a cox.

 ## Paralympic Rowing

Appearing at the Paralympic Games for only the second time. Adaptive rowing boats are equipped with special seats, which vary according to the disability of the athlete.

Eton Manor

Eton Manor will be transformed after the Games into sporting facilities for local and regional communities.

 ## Wheelchair Tennis

First played in 1976, Wheelchair Tennis is one of the fastest-growing wheelchair sports in the world.

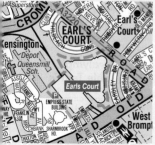

ExCeL

A London Docklands exhibition and conference centre, its arenas will host a range of Olympic and Paralympic sports.

Boxing

Men's Boxing events will be joined on the Olympic programme by a women's competition for the first time. Boxing featured at the original Olympic Games in the 7th century BC.

Fencing

Although sword fighting dates back thousands of years, Fencing really came of age as a sport in the 19th century.

Judo

Developed from jujitsu and established as a sport in the late 19th century, contests will be a five-minute whirlwind of combat, with athletes attempting a combination of throws and holds in a bid to defeat their opponents.

Table Tennis

Table tennis, based on the same basic principles as Tennis, is a spectacle that blends power, speed, skill and subtlety.

Taekwondo

'Taekwondo' translates into English as 'the way of foot and fist' – an accurate description of this martial art - with the aim being to land powerful kicks and punches on your opponent.

Weightlifting

The aim of Weightlifting is simple, to lift more weight than anyone else - resulting in pure sporting theatre. The strongest competitors may lift more than three times their body weight.

Wrestling

Recognised as one of the world's oldest sports, Wrestling was first held at the ancient Olympics Games in 708 BC.

Boccia

Boccia is a target sport that tests muscle control and accuracy, demanding extreme skill and concentration. Players must be in a seated position within a throwing box at one end of the playing court.

Paralympic Judo

Contested by visually impaired athletes, the mats have different textures to indicate the competition area and zones.

Paralympic Table Tennis

A permanent part of the Paralympic programme since the first Games in 1960, it is also one of the largest with 29 medal events and 300 athletes.

Powerlifting

Powerlifting is a bench-press competition – competitors are classified by bodyweight alone.

 ## Sitting Volleyball

Sitting Volleyball emerged in the Netherlands in the 1950s, a combination of Volleyball and a German game called Sitzbal.

Wheelchair Fencing

Athletes compete in wheelchairs fastened to the floor, resulting in a fierce, fast-moving battle of tactics and technique.

Greenwich Park

Greenwich Park will host the Olympic and Paralympic Equestrian competitions, plus the combined running and shooting element of the Modern Pentathlon. Situated on the south bank of the River Thames in south-east London.

Equestrian - Dressage

Dressage events will be a test of both athletic prowess and supreme elegance.

 ## Equestrian - Eventing

Featuring dressage, cross-country and a dramatic jumping finale, the Eventing competition showcases an all-encompassing test of Equestrian skill.

 ## Equestrian - Jumping

Known as 'show jumping' in the UK, the Jumping competition will require horse and rider to navigate a short course with precision, speed and perfect technique.

 ## Modern Pentathlon

Riding and combined running/shooting will be staged here in Greenwich Park. Fencing will be in the Copper Box, swimming in the Aquatics Centre - both venues in the Olympic Park.

 ## Paralympic Equestrian

Athletes with a disability have long taken part in Equestrian activities, originally as a means of rehabilitation and recreation. Classified across five grades to ensure that the tests can be judged on the skill of the rider, regardless of their disability.

Hadleigh Farm

Hadleigh Farm, with its ideal mountain biking terrain, is to the east of London in Essex.

 ## Cycling - Mountain Bike

Rocky paths, tricky climbs and technical descents will provide plenty of challenges for riders in the competition.

Hampton Court Palace

Hampton Court Palace is one of London's historic Royal Palaces. It is located in the London Borough of Richmond upon Thames in south-west London.

Cycling - Road

The Olympic Road Cycling programme includes two events. Time Trials begin and finish at Hampton Court Palace, Road Racing will begin and end on The Mall.

Horse Guards Parade

Horse Guards Parade is situated between Whitehall and St James's Park. A temporary beach will be created with 3,000 tonnes of imported sand.

Beach Volleyball

Beach Volleyball is similar to the indoor game, although it is played by teams of two, instead of teams of six.

Hyde Park

Within London's West End this extensive park abuts Mayfair and Knightsbridge.

Marathon Swimming 10km

This event takes place in the Serpentine lake. All other swimming events are held in the Olympic Park Aquatics Centre.

Triathlon

Triathlon races combine swimming, cycling and running, in that order. Events are conducted over a variety of distances: for the Olympic Games, the men's and women's Triathlons will consist of a 1,500m swim, a 40km bike ride and a 10km run.

Lee Valley White Water Centre

Lee Valley White Water Centre is located in the River Lee Country Park 30km north of the Olympic Park. After the Games this new centre will become a venue for canoeing, kayaking and white water rafting.

Canoe Slalom

Modelled on slalom skiing, the sport was first staged on flat water, but was later switched to white water rapids. The competitions consist of timed runs down a white water course with up to 25 gates. Canoe Sprint takes place at Eton Dorney.

Lord's Cricket Ground

Lord's is the home of cricket. It is located in St John's Wood, north-west London, near Regent's Park.

Archery

Archery dates back around 10,000 years; developed as a competitive activity in medieval England, it is now practised in more than 140 countries around the world.

The Mall

This famous ceremonial route connects Buckingham Palace and Trafalgar Square.

Athletics - Marathon and Race Walk

The start and finish points for the Olympic Marathon and Race Walk. At London 1908, the marathon distance was extended from around 25 miles to 26.2 miles (42.195 kilometres) so that it finished in front of the Royal Box.
This distance became standard for the Marathon and is still used today.

Cycling - Road Racing

The start and finish point for Cycling Road Racing events. There are two Road Cycling

events for both men and women. Time Trials take place at Hampton Court Palace.

Paralympic Athletics - Marathon

Men's and women's Marathons will be held on the streets of central London, starting and finishing on The Mall.

North Greenwich Arena

Built for the Millennium celebrations, and transformed into a sports and entertainment venue, the arena is sited on the south side of the River Thames.

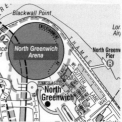

Basketball

Men's quarter-finals and women's semi-finals onwards are held here, preliminaries and women's quarter-finals are held at the Basketball Arena in the Olympic Park.

Gymnastics - Artistic

The grace, strength and skill of Olympic gymnasts have been astonishing audiences since the Games in ancient Greece.

Gymnastics - Trampoline

Trampoline is the newest of the

three Gymnastics disciplines making its Olympic debut at Sydney in 2000.

Wheelchair Basketball

Preliminary games will be split between the Olympic Park Basketball Arena and North Greenwich Arena. All quarter-finals, semi-finals and medal games will take place here.

Riverbank Arena

The Riverbank Arena is located in the Olympic Park.

Hockey

Until the 1970s, hockey was always played on grass. However, top-level matches now take place on water-based synthetic-turf pitches.

Paralympic 5-a-side Football

Played by visually impaired athletes plus a sighted goal-keeper using a ball with a noise-making device inside, the pitch is surrounded by a rebound wall. The sport is played with no throw-ins and no offside rule.

Paralympic 7-a-side Football

Follows modified FIFA rules; the playing field is smaller, as are the goals. Teams are made up of ambulant cerebral palsy athletes, featuring players with varying levels of disability.

The Royal Artillery Barracks

Located south of the River Thames in Woolwich, the Barracks are a historic military site dating from 1776.

Shooting

Olympic Shooting events fall broadly into three types: Pistol, Rifle and Shotgun events. Having been practised competitively for centuries, the sport of Shooting is now popular all over the world.

Paralympic Archery

Paralympic Archery consists of both standing and wheelchair events for individuals and teams.

Paralympic Shooting

Athletes with different disabilities compete together in two classes – for athletes who can support the weight of their firearm themselves, and for athletes who use a shooting stand to support their arm.

Velodrome

Purpose built within the Olympic Park the Velodrome features a distinctive sweeping roof design reflecting the geometry of the cycling track. After the Games a new mountain bike course and road-cycle circuit will be added to create a VeloPark for the local community, sports clubs and elite athletes.

Cycling - Track

Cycling has a long history in

the UK. As early as 1870, large crowds were drawn to races held on indoor wooden tracks. Track Cycling has featured at every Games but one since the first modern Olympic Games in 1896. There are ten Olympic Track Cycling events (five for men, five for women): Sprint, Keirin, Team Sprint, Team Pursuit and Omnium.

Paralympic Cycling - Track

The competition is for athletes with a visual impairment, cerebral palsy, amputations or other physical disabilities competing on bicycles, tricycles, tandems and hand cycles.

Water Polo Arena

A temporary Olympic Park venue adjacent to the Aquatics Centre.

Water Polo

Water Polo developed during the 19th century as an aquatic version of rugby, played informally in rivers and lakes. The version of the game that survives today is closer to handball.

Wembley Arena

A flagship live music and sport venue, in north-west London.

Badminton

One of the most dynamic Olympic sports, Badminton made its full Olympic debut at Barcelona 1992.

Gymnastics - Rhythmic

Rhythmic Gymnastics is a combination of gymnastics and dance. Scores are awarded for difficulty, artistry and execution.

Wembley Stadium

England's national stadium is situated in north-west London, it is the biggest of the six stadiums staging the London 2012 Olympic Games Football competition.

 Football

The five other co-Host City stadia are: **City of Coventry Stadium**, Glasgow's **Hampden Park**, Cardiff's **Millennium Stadium**, Manchester's **Old Trafford** and Newcastle upon Tyne's **St. James' Park**. The finals for both the men's and women's competitions will be played at Wembley.

Weymouth and Portland

This beautiful bay setting has some of the best natural sailing waters in the UK.

 Sailing

The competition will host 10 Sailing events featuring a variety of craft from dinghies and keelboats, to windsurfing boards.

 Paralympic Sailing

Paralympic Sailing will consist of three mixed events.

Wimbledon

The home of the All England Lawn Tennis and Croquet Club. Wimbledon staged the tennis competition for London's first Olympic Games in 1908.

 Tennis

The Tennis competition will feature five medal events including Mixed Doubles, making its first apperance since 1924. Situated in southwest London about 12 miles from the Olympic Park.

London 2012 Shops

Canary Wharf, Jubilee
  Place...2D 81 (Off Bank St.)
Heathrow Airport
  Terminal 3 (airside)
  Terminal 5 (airside)
Hyde Park.....................3A 74
John Lewis
  Brent Cross Shopping Centre
  .... 2E 29
  Kingston, Wood Street
  Oxford Street (fifth floor)
  ....3E 13
  Stratford City Shopping
  Centre.....................3E 53
Paddington Station.........5F 59
Peter Jones, Sloane Square
  ....5B 74
Royal Opera House........3E 15
St Pancras International... 1D 7
Stansted Airport, Essex
Team GB and ParalympicsGB
  Shop: Stratford City Shopping
  Centre....................... 3E 53

http://shop.london2012.com

Live Sites

Live Sites are big screen and event spaces in urban centres providing a unique combination of free sports screenings, cultural entertainment and ticketed concerts.

With the exception of the Hyde Park Opening and Closing Ceremony Celebrations (27 July and 12 August) entry will be free, though ticketed to control numbers, with daily guaranteed entry tickets available in advance.

All tickets via btlondonlive.com

BT London Live Sites:
Hyde Park (Olympic Games)
.................................2B 74
Trafalgar Square (Paralympic Games)....................1D 23
Victoria Park (Olympic Games)
.... 4B 52

Additional Live Sites include:
London Park (Olympic Games
& Paralympic Games)
.................................2E 27

Transport

Scan for up-to-date travel details and bookings

www.london2012.com/ getting-to-the-games

London 2012 is aiming for a 'public transport' Games, so please do not drive as there will be no parking at or around venues. You can travel to each competition venue using different types of public transport, or by walking or cycling.

Venues in London
London's transport system will be very busy, so you should allow plenty of time to travel to, from and between venues. Check the information on travelling to your event to find out where your venue is, the best way to get there and how long your journey will take between the recommended stations serving venues.
London is well-served by public transport with travel options including the London Underground, London Overground, Docklands Light Railway, National Rail, buses and river services.

Outer London venues
Some sporting events are being held in venues on the outskirts of London, including Eton Dorney, the Lee Valley White Water Centre and Hadleigh Farm. All of these venues are linked to London by National Rail.

Co-Host Cities and Towns
The co-Host Cities are Cardiff, Coventry, Glasgow, Manchester, Newcastle upon Tyne (all for Football) and Weymouth and Portland (Sailing). They all have National Rail stations with direct links to London, although some of these venues are significant distances from the capital.

Travel tickets
London 2012 ticket holders can benefit from a range of special travel tickets for the Games. Spectators with a ticket for a Games event in London will receive a one-day Games Travelcard for the day of that event, valid within zones 1 to 9. This includes London Underground (Tube), London Overground, Docklands Light Railway (DLR), buses, trams and National Rail services, including the Javelin® service between St Pancras and Stratford

International stations, but excluding the Heathrow, Stansted or Gatwick Express trains, or taxis and private hire vehicles.

Travel to outer London venues

Spectators with tickets for Games events at Eton Dorney, the Lee Valley White Water Centre and Hadleigh Farm will receive a Games Travelcard for use on public transport in London and National Rail between London and the recommended stations for those venues.

London Underground

The Underground is one of the main ways to travel around London. All of the London 2012 venues within London can be reached by London Underground, with the exception of ExCeL, Greenwich Park and The Royal Artillery Barracks.

Travel within zones 1 to 9 on London Underground for the day of your event is included with the Games Travelcard. Many of London Underground's stations have been improved to make them more accessible; details on www.tfl.gov.uk

London Buses

London has an extensive bus network and there are routes and stops close to all London 2012 venues. London's buses are a good travel option for people with accessibility needs. Most of London's 8,000 buses are low-floor with clearly marked priority seating next to doors for disabled people. There is room for one wheelchair space and assistance dogs are allowed on all buses. Travel on London's buses on the day of your event is included with the Games Travelcard. There are 24-hour bus routes providing travel options

all night in London.

Docklands Light Railway (DLR)

The DLR serves London 2012 venues at the Olympic Park, ExCeL, Greenwich Park and The Royal Artillery Barracks. The DLR is a step-free network and all DLR stations have lift or ramp access to all platforms. Travel on the DLR for the day of your event is included with the Games Travelcard.

London Overground

London Overground is a suburban network of rail services in London, managed by Transport for London. Travel on London Overground on the day of your event is included with the Games Travelcard. Passengers requiring assistance are recommended to give at least 24 hours notice by calling London Overground Customer Services on 0845 601 4867, 9am–5pm on weekdays.

Rail

The National Rail network connects London and all the co-Host Cities for the London 2012 venues. Extra Rail services will be provided to Games venues, and trains will run later from London to key destinations up to approximately two hours away, such as Birmingham, Manchester, Leeds and Cardiff.

Cycling

Cycling in London is an easy and convenient alternative to public transport. Free, secure, managed cycle parking will be provided at all London 2012 venues. Bicycle locks are not supplied. TfL cycle hire docking stations may be within walking distance of London 2012 venues, but you will not be able to dock your cycle hire bike at venues.

Shuttle Buses

Shuttle buses will be provided from some recommended stations to London 2012 and co-Host City venues, particularly where these stations are more than a short walk away from the venue entrance. These shuttles will be low-floor accessible buses and the service will be available for all spectators.

River services

Venues accessible by river include Greenwich Park, North Greenwich Arena, The Royal Artillery Barracks, Horse Guards Parade, The Mall and Eton Dorney. All passengers on boat services will have a seat or wheelchair space. Travel by scheduled river services on the Thames in London is not included with the Games Travelcard provided with your event tickets, but it does entitle spectators to a one third discount on the price of river service tickets.

Taxis

Taxis and private hire vehicles do not accept Oyster cards or travelcards and are not covered by the Games Travelcard that you will receive with your event ticket.
Only licensed taxis can pick up passengers on the street or at ranks without a booking. Minicabs and other private hire vehicles must be booked through a licensed operator (in person, over the phone or online) before the journey starts.
Unbooked minicabs are illegal. You may be approached by touts or minicab drivers seeking passengers or offering a service; these are unsafe, unlicensed and uninsured. You put yourself in danger if you use these services.

2012 Games coach services

- During the Olympic Games coach services will be provided to the Olympic Park, ExCeL, Greenwich Park (30 July only) and Weymouth and Portland from a range of locations outside the M25. Coaches will pick up from bus stops and bus stations throughout Great Britain.
- During the Paralympic Games, 2012 Games coach services will be provided to the Olympic Park and ExCeL.
- All passengers on the coach services will have a dedicated seat or wheelchair space.
- All seats and wheelchair spaces on the coach services must be booked in advance: www.firstgroupgamestravel
.com/direct-coaching

2012 Games park-and-ride

- Secure park-and-ride sites with limited space will be provided at convenient locations.
- Park-and-ride services must be booked in advance: www.firstgroupgamestravel
.com
- Venues with park-and-ride facilities during the Olympic Games include: the Olympic Park, ExCeL, Greenwich Park (30 July only), Eton Dorney, Hadleigh Farm, the Lee Valley White Water Centre and Weymouth and Portland.
- Venues with park-and-ride facilities during the Paralympic Games include: the Olympic Park, ExCeL, and Eton Dorney.

Blue Badge Parking

Blue Badge parking spaces are available for spectators who hold a valid Blue Badge or recognised national disability permit.
- Blue Badge parking spaces must be booked in advance: www.firstgroupgamestravel
.com

Scan for 2012 Games spectator journey planner

Plan your journey using the 2012 Games spectator journey planner. It will provide you with:
- Estimated journey times to and from Games venues from anywhere in Great Britain.
- Estimated walking and cycling times to and from recommended stations to Games venues.
- Timetable information to allow Games ticket holders to plan their travel.
- Links to travel booking sites (such as 2012 Games Rail services and 2012 Games coach services) to enable Games ticket holders to purchase travel tickets in advance of travel.
- Recommended routes to make your journey as easy as possible.

Useful websites

London 2012 Information
www.london2012.com

**2012 Games Travel Services
Rail:**
- www.nationalrailgames travel.co.uk

Eurostar:
- www.eurostar.com

**Coach, park-and-ride &
Blue Badge:**
- www.firstgroupgames travel.co.uk

River:
- www.citycruisesgames travel.co.uk
- https://booking.thames clippers.com/gamestravel

- www.frenchbrothers.co.uk /games travel
- www.water-chariots.co.uk /gamestravel

London Travel Information
- www.tfl.gov.uk

London Tourist Information
- www.visitlondon.com Hotels, places to visit, events, travel and other important information.

Accessibility Information
- www.london2012.com/ accessibility
- www.inclusivelondon.com

Picture credits:
© www.Bigstock.com: **I** (1.2.) **V** (2.) **IX XI XII XIII** (2.) **XIV** (2.)
© www.iStockphoto.com: **VI**
© www.Shutterstock.com: **XIV** (1.)
© ODA: **X XIII** (1.) **XIV** (3.)
© Populous: **V** (1.)

Every possible care has been taken to ensure that, to the best of our knowledge, the information contained in this atlas is accurate at the date of publication 03.2012.

MIX
Paper from responsible sources
FSC® C006021

![A-Z] LONDON
Mini Street Atlas

CONTENTS

Reference Page	1
Key to Map Pages	2-3
Large Scale Map Pages	4-27
Map Pages	28-125
Underground Map	126-127
Congestion Charging Information	128
Index to Streets, etc.	129-371
Index to Hospitals	372-376
Index to Stations	377-380

Direct
Customer Service

If you experience difficulty obtaining
any of our 300 titles, please contact
us direct for help and advice.

www./az.co.uk

Tel: 01732 783422   Fax: 01732 780677

Geographers' A-Z Map Company Ltd.

Fairfield Road, Borough Green, Sevenoaks, Kent TN15 8PP
Telephone : 01732 781000 (Enquiries & Trade Sales)
            01732 783422 (Retail Sales)

www.az.co.uk

Edition 9 2012
© Copyright of Geographers' A-Z Map Company Limited

Every possible care has been taken to ensure that, to the best of our
knowledge, the information contained in this atlas is accurate at the date of
publication. However, we cannot warrant that our work is entirely error free and
whilst we would be grateful to learn of any inaccuracies, we do not accept any
responsibility for loss or damage resulting from reliance on information
contained within this publication.

The representation on the maps of a road, track or footpath is no evidence of
the existence of a right of way.

The Grid on this map is the National Grid taken from Ordnance Survey
mapping with the permission of the Controller of Her Majesty's Stationery Office.

Ordnance Survey® This Product includes mapping data licensed from Ordnance Survey®
with the permission of the Controller of Her Majesty's Stationery Office.
© Crown Copyright 2011. All rights reserved. Licence Number 100017302

Safety camera information supplied by www.PocketGPSWorld.com
Speed Camera Location Database Copyright 2011 © PocketGPSWorld.com

Safety camera locations are publicised by the Safer Roads Partnership
which operates them in order to encourage drivers to comply with speed limits
at these sites. It is the drivers absolute responsibility to be aware of and to
adhere to speed limits at all times.

By showing this safety camera information it is the intention of
Geographers' A-Z Map Company Ltd., to encourage safe driving and
greater awareness of speed limits and vehicle speed.
Data accurate at time of printing.

The publishers are deeply grateful for the ready co-operation and valuable help
given to them in the production of this atlas. They would like to record their
obligation to: The Engineers and Surveyors Departments and Planning Offices
of all the Local Authorities covered in this atlas, The Department for Transport,
Highways Agency, Transport for London, The Post Office, Police Authorities,
Fire Brigades, London 2012, Taxi Drivers, Members of the Public.

Printed and bound in the United Kingdom by Polestar Wheatons Ltd., Exeter.

An AtoZ Publication

MIX
Paper from
responsible sources
FSC® C006021

REFERENCE

Motorway	**M1**
A Road	**A2**
B Road	**B519**
Dual Carriageway	
One-way Street Traffic flow on A Roads is also indicated by a heavy line on the driver's left.	
Junction Name	**MARBLE ARCH**
Restricted Access	
Pedestrianized Road	
Track & Footpath	
Residential Walkway	
Congestion Charging Zone	
Railway	Tunnel / Level Crossing

Stations:

National Rail Network and Overground	⇌
Docklands Light Railway	**DLR**
Overground	🚇 Super Scale Map Pages
Underground	● / ⊖

London Tramlink	Tunnel / Stop

The boarding of Tramlink trams at stops may be limited to a single direction, indicated by the arrow.

Built-up Area	BANK / STREET
Map Continuation	▲ 84 / Large Scale City Centre ▲ 8
Airport	✈

Car Park (selected)	**P**
Church or Chapel	†
Fire Station	■
Hospital	**H**
House Numbers (A & B Roads only)	40 / 23
Information Centre	🇮
National Grid Reference	539
Park & Ride	Cumberland Gate **P+R**
Police Station	▲
Post Office	★
River Bus Stop	**R**
Safety Camera with Speed Limit Fixed and long term road works cameras. Symbols do not indicate camera direction	**(30)**

Toilet:

without facilities for the Disabled	▽
with facilities for the Disabled	▽
Disabled use only	▽
Educational Establishment	
Hospital or Healthcare	
Industrial Building	
Leisure or Recreational Facility	
Place of Interest	
Public Building	
Shopping Centre or Market	
Other Selected Building	

SCALE

Map Pages 28-125	Map Pages 4-27
1:21,477 Approx. 3 inches to 1 mile	1:10,560 6 inches to 1 mile
0 ⅛ ¼ Mile	0 1/16 ⅛ Mile
0 100 200 300 Metres	0 100 200 Metres
4.66 cm to 1 km 7.49 cm to 1 mile	9.47 cm to 1km 15.24 cm to 1 mile

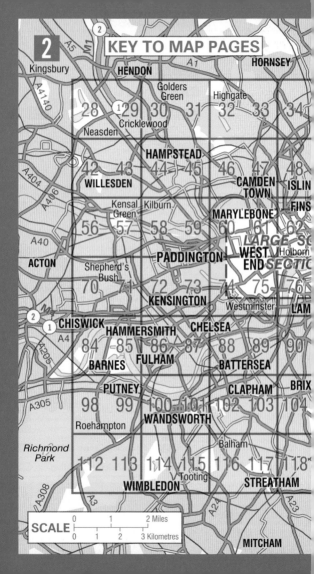

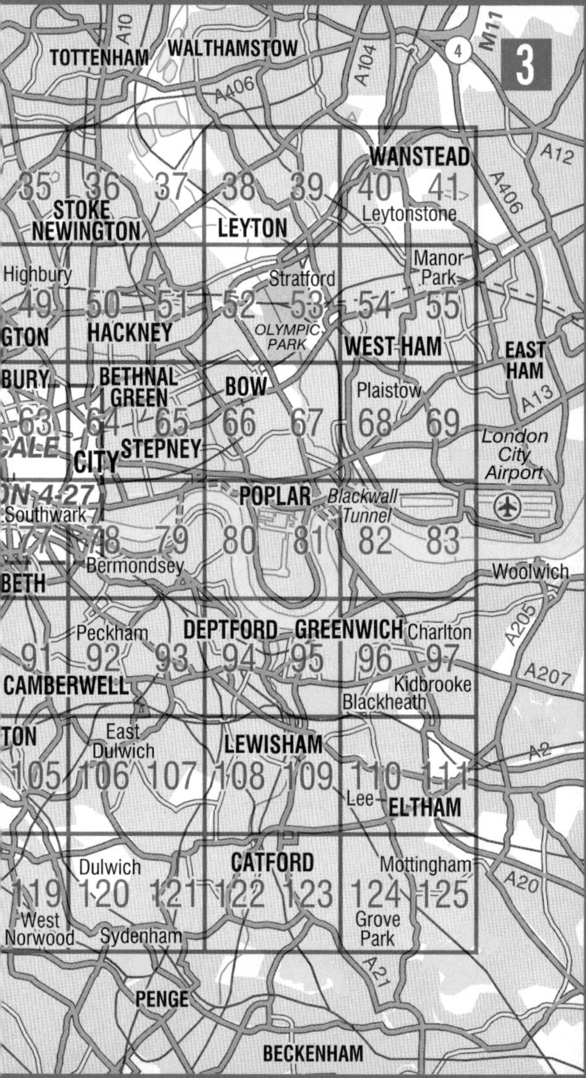

TOTTENHAM WALTHAMSTOW

A10 A406 A104 M11 4 A12

WANSTEAD

35 36 37 38 39 40 41

STOKE
NEWINGTON LEYTON Leytonstone

Highbury Stratford Manor Park

49 50 51 52 53 54 55

GTON HACKNEY OLYMPIC
PARK WEST HAM EAST
HAM

BURY BETHNAL
GREEN BOW Plaistow A13

63 64 65 66 67 68 69

CALE STEPNEY London
City
Airport

CITY

N 4:27) POPLAR Blackwall
Tunnel

Southwark

77 78 79 80 81 82 83

BETH Bermondsey Woolwich

A205

Peckham DEPTFORD GREENWICH Charlton A207

91 92 93 94 95 96 97

CAMBERWELL Kidbrooke
Blackheath

TON East
Dulwich LEWISHAM A2

105 106 107 108 109 110 111

Lee ELTHAM

Dulwich CATFORD Mottingham A20

119 120 121 122 123 124 125

West
Norwood Sydenham Grove
Park

PENGE A21

BECKENHAM

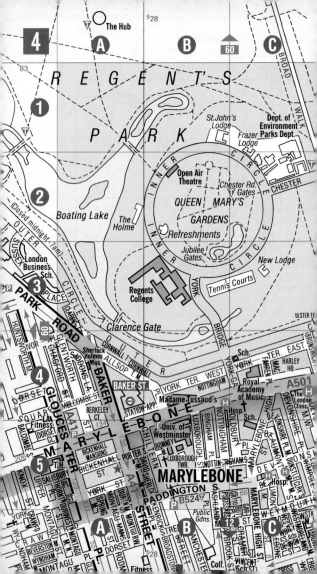

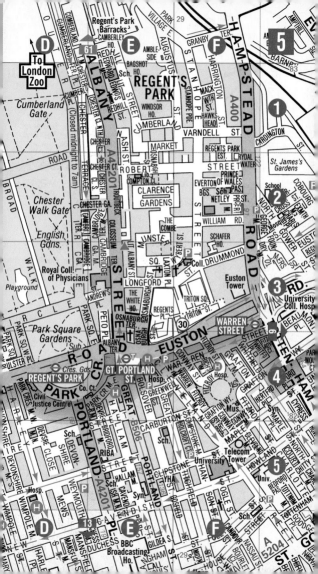

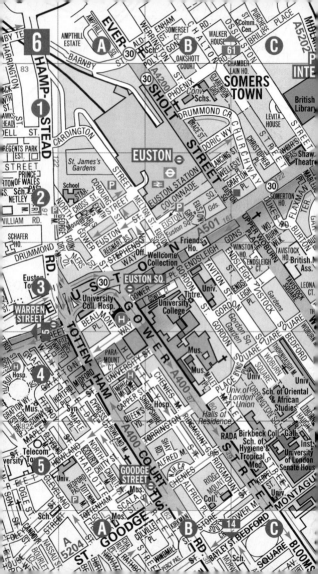

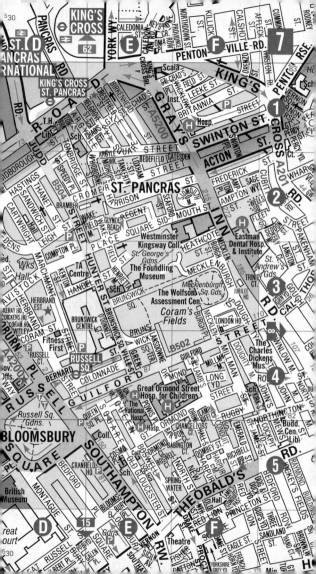

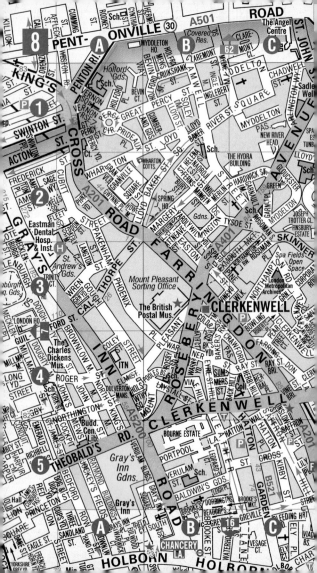

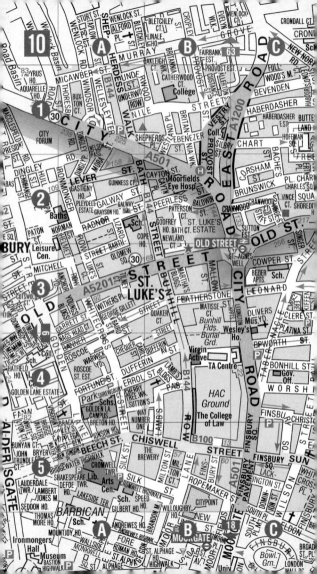

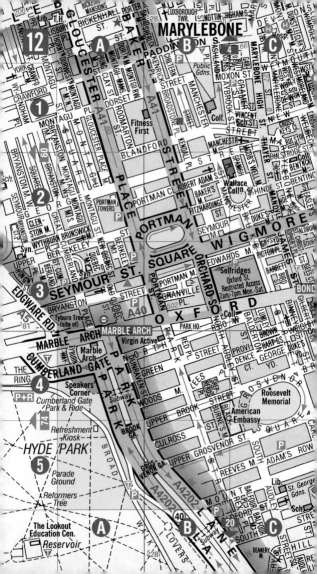

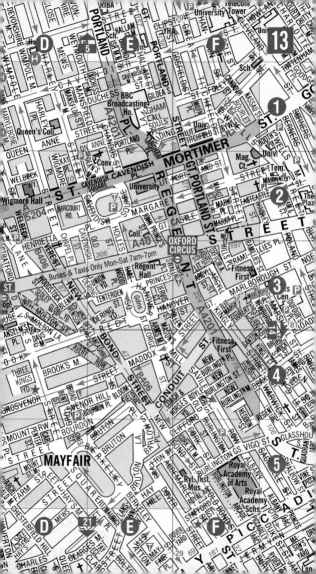

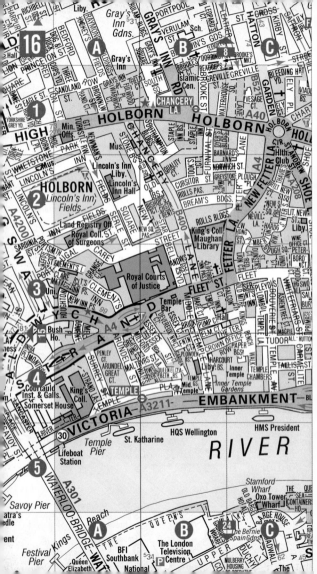

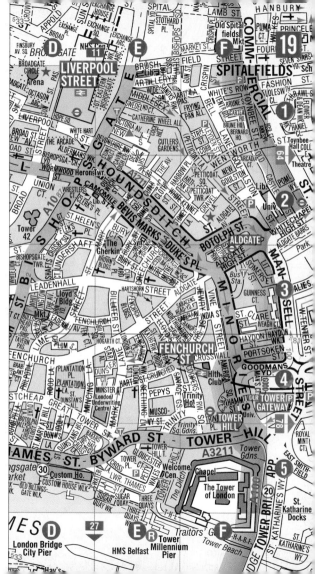

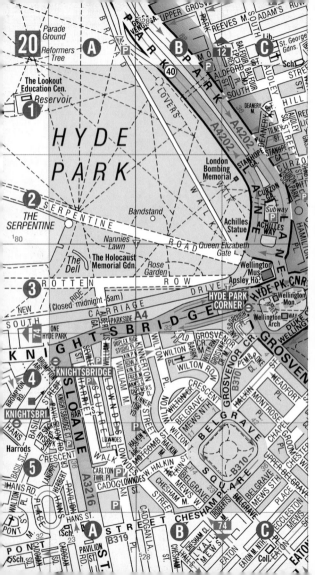

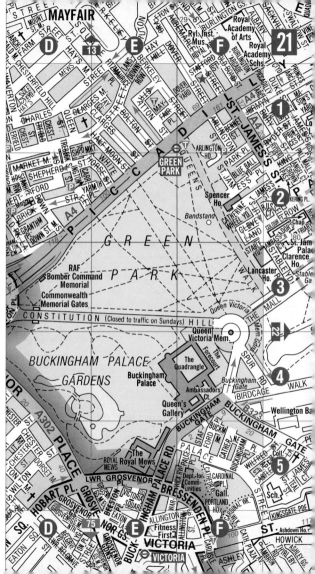

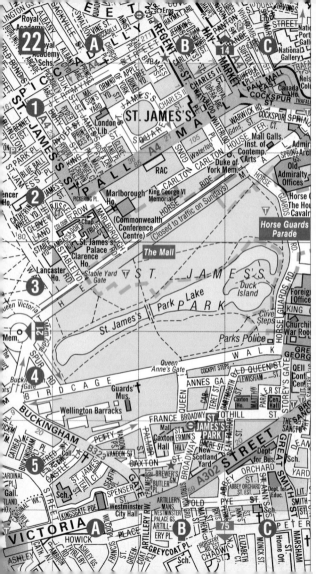

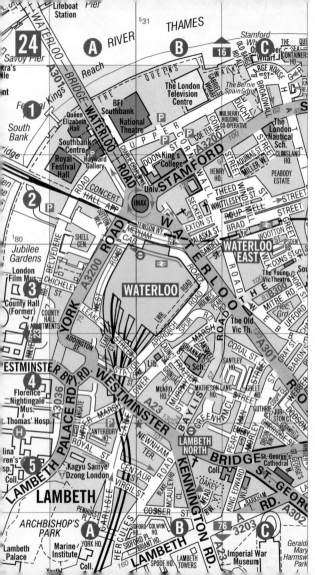

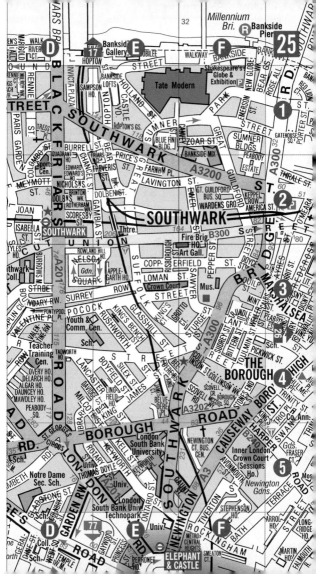

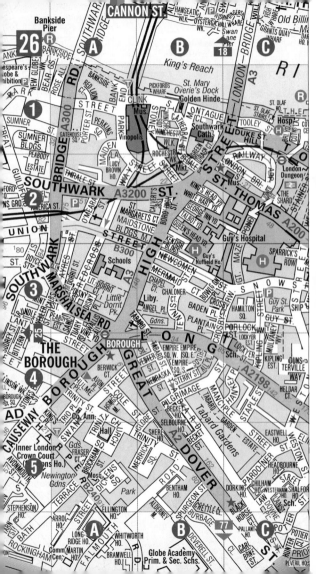

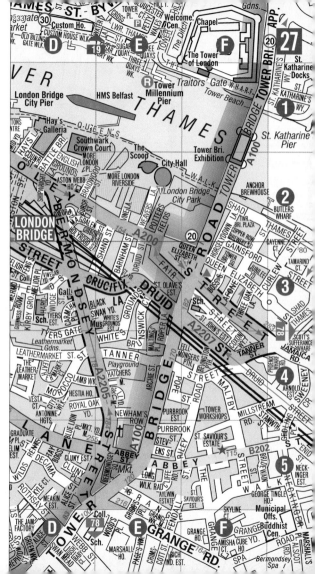

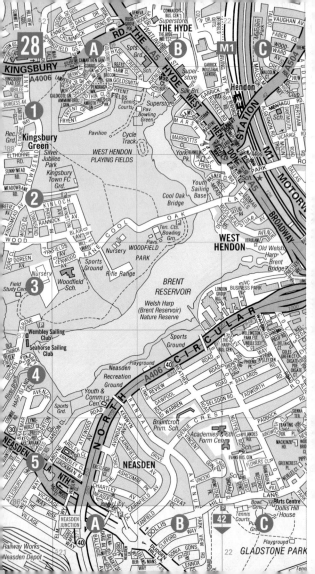

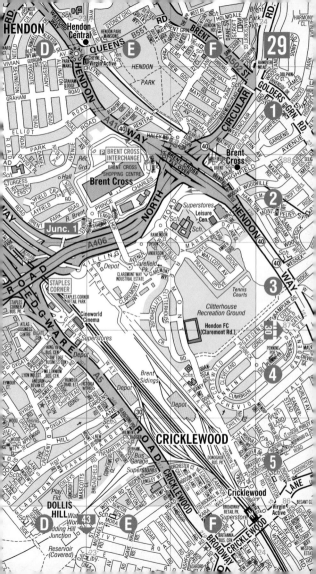

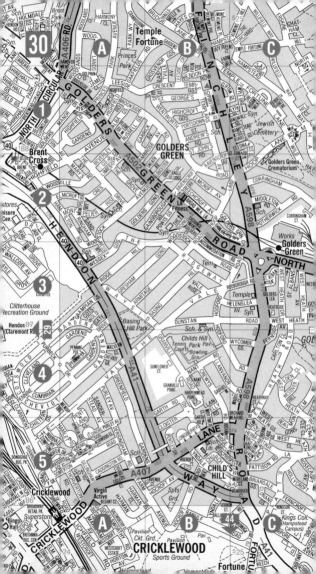

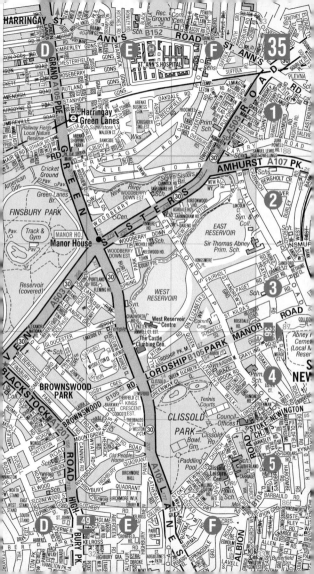

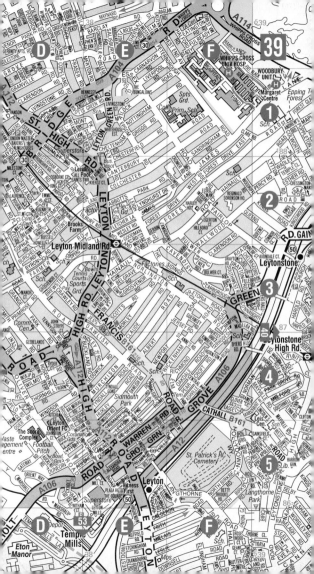

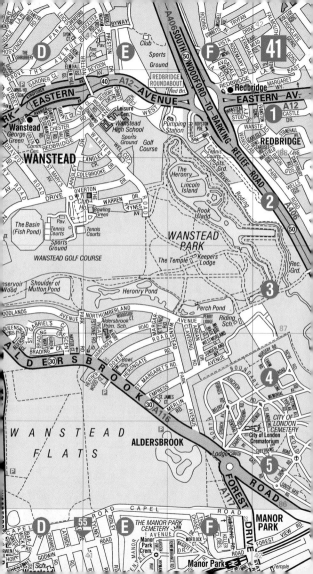

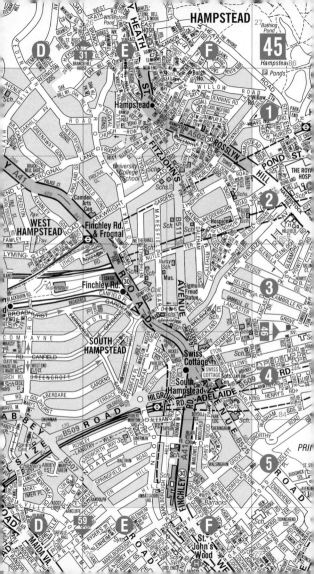

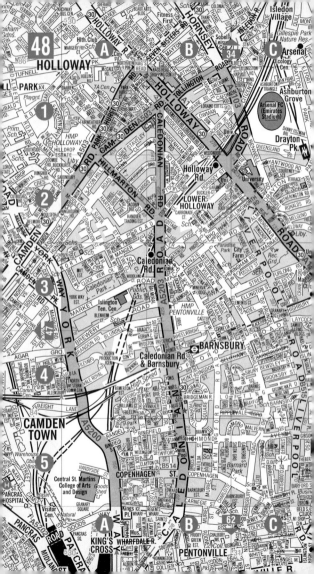

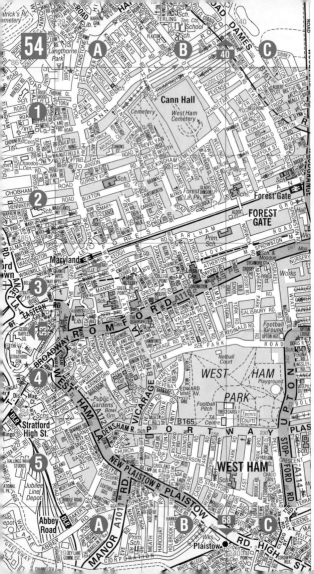

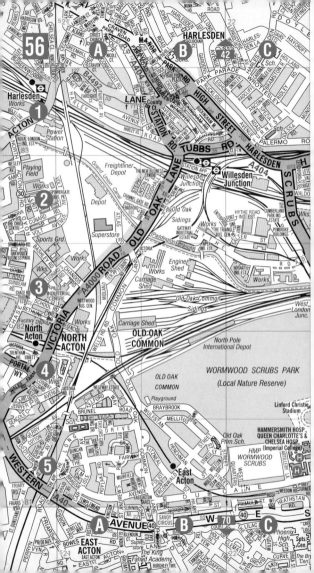

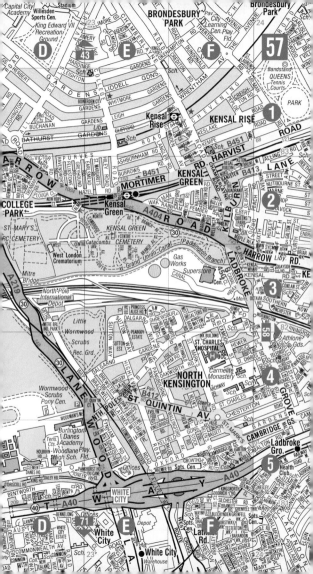

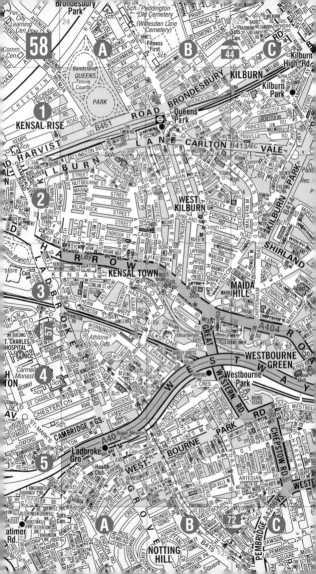

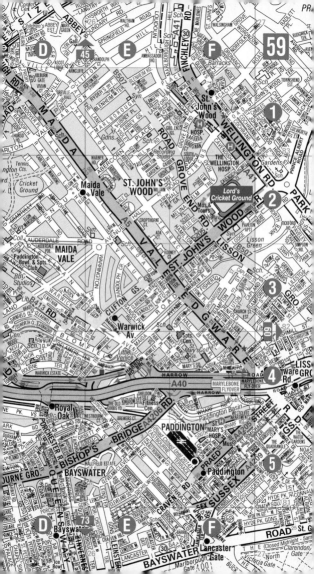

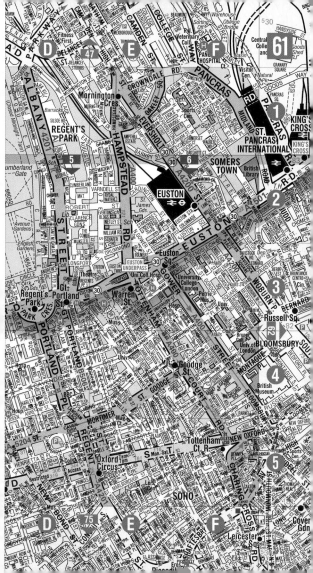

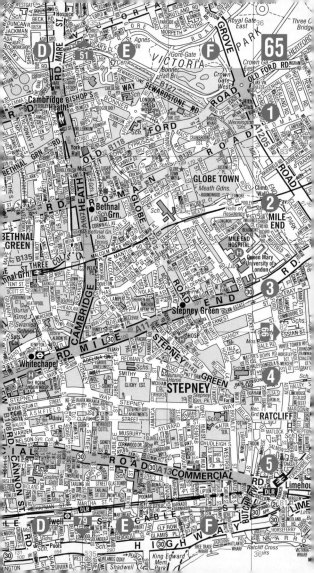

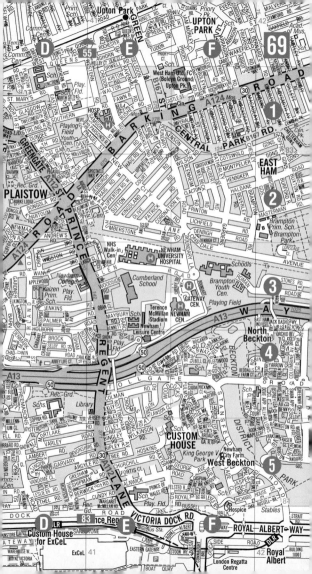

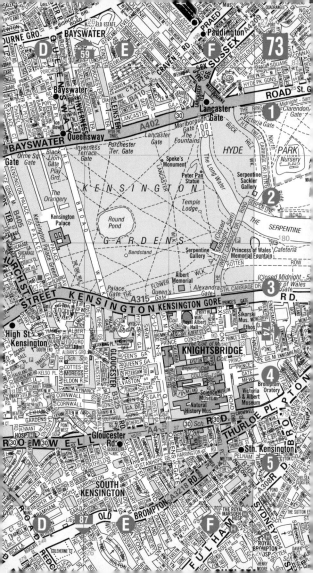

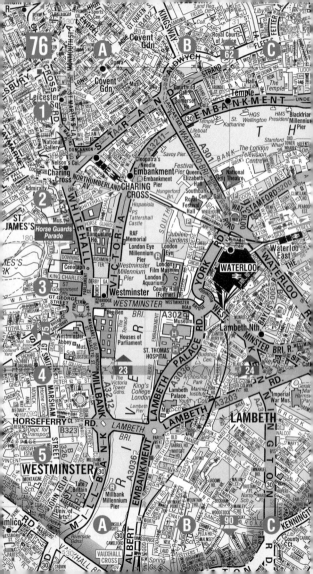

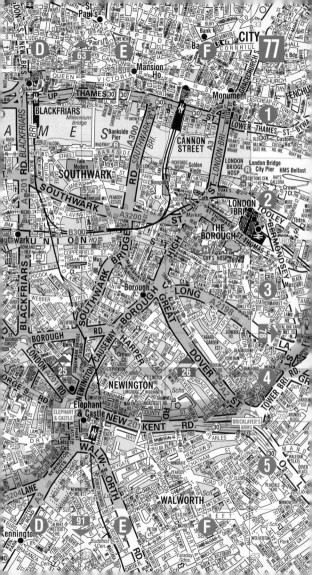

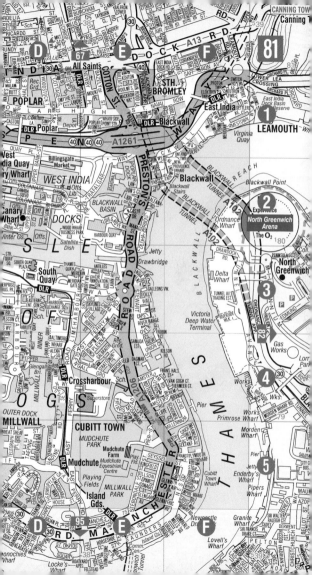

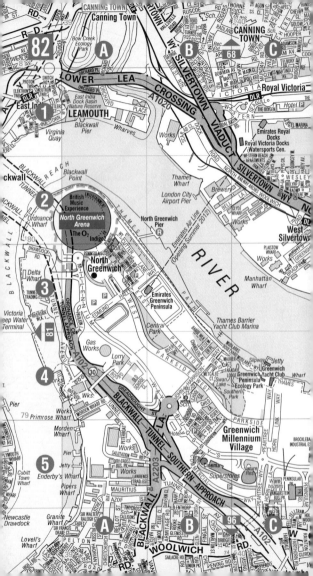

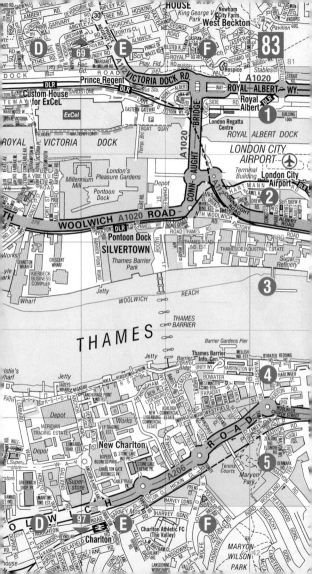

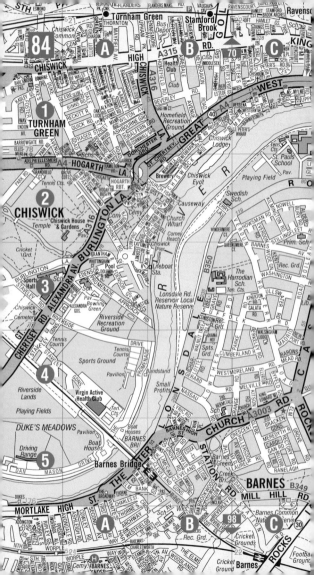

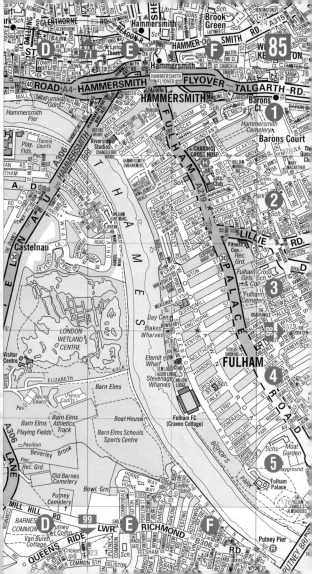

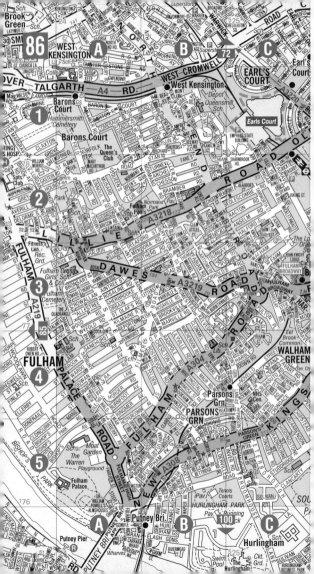

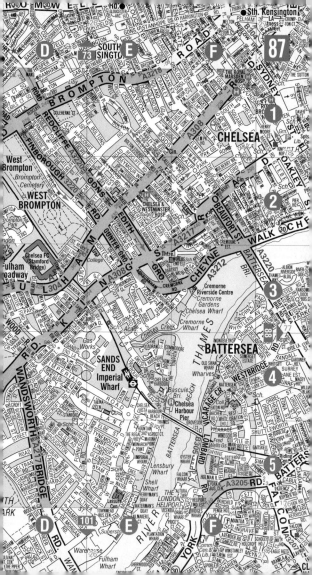

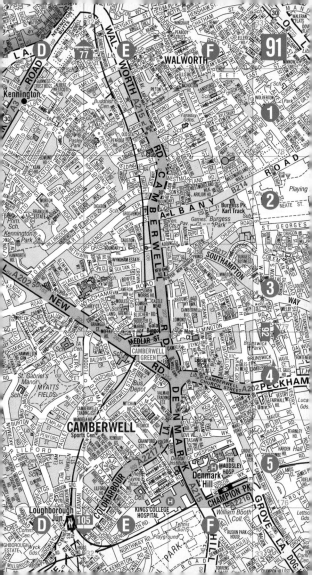

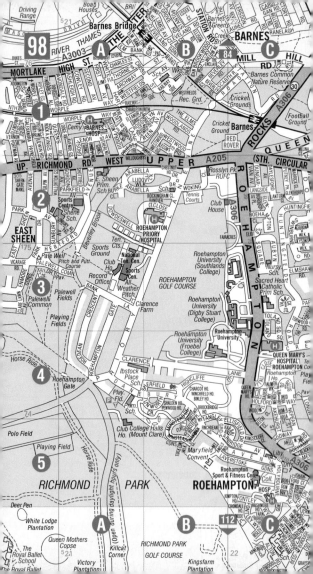

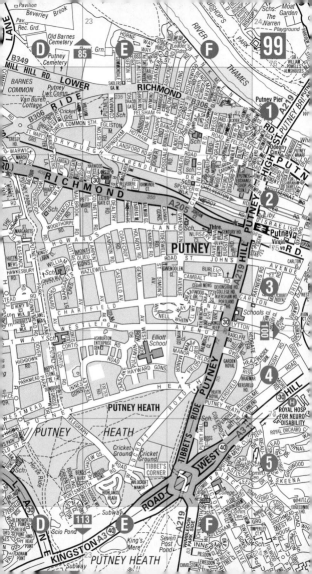

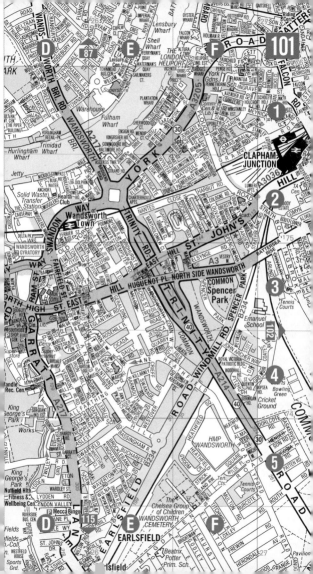

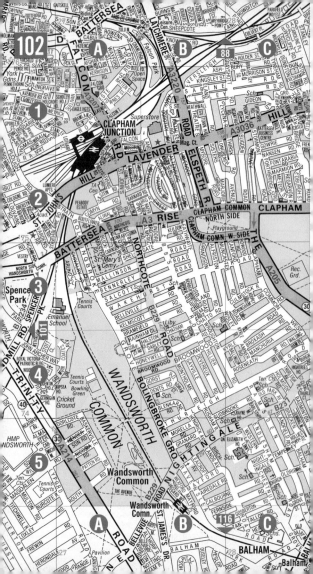

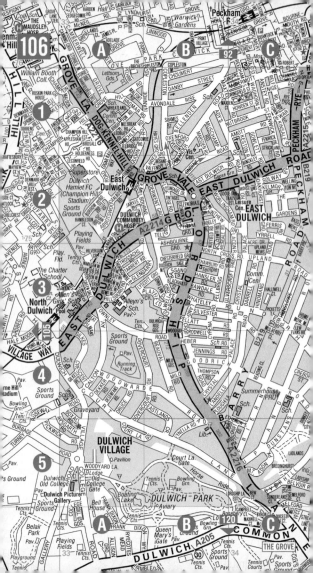

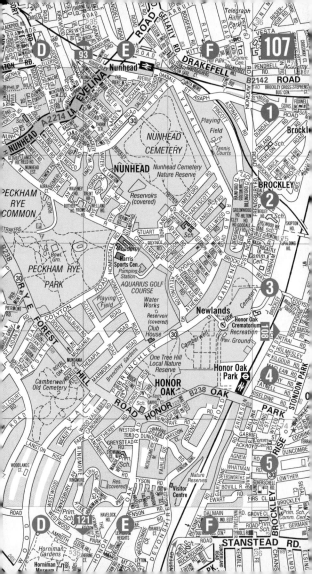

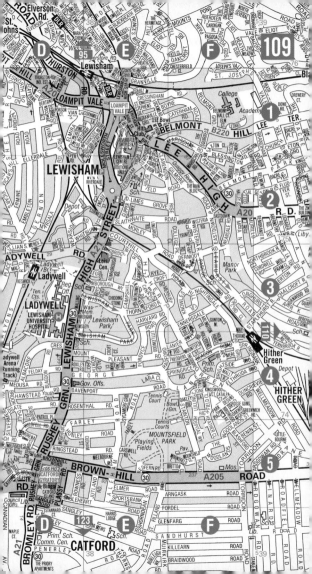

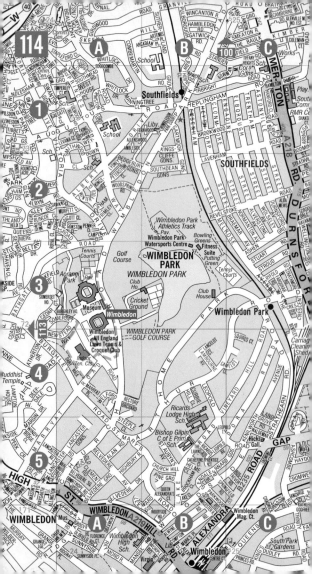

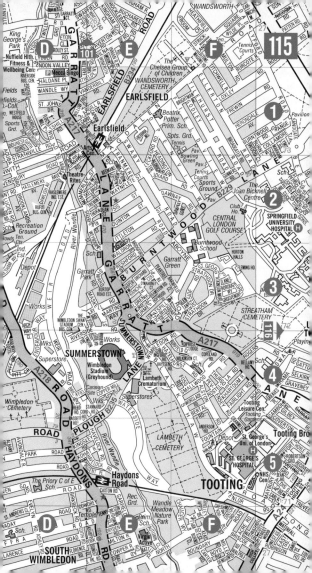

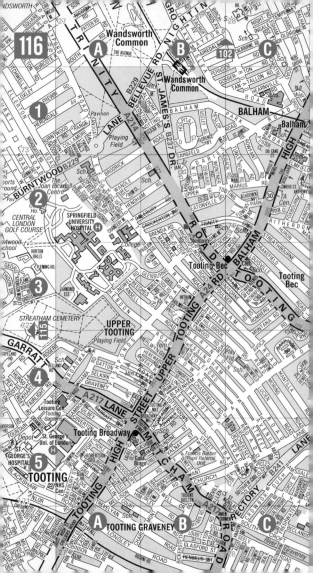

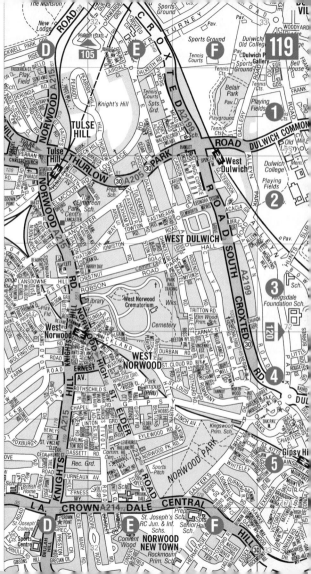

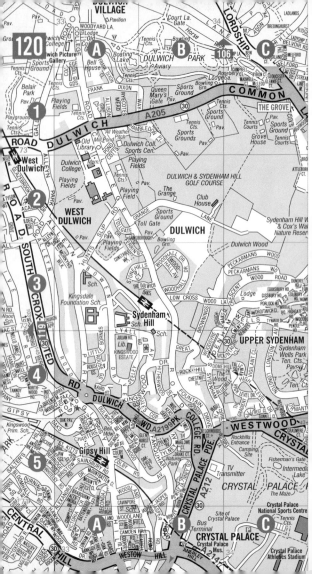

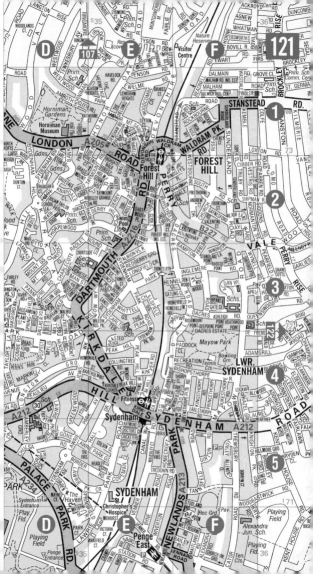

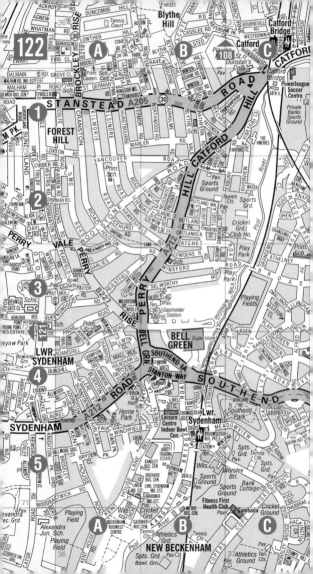

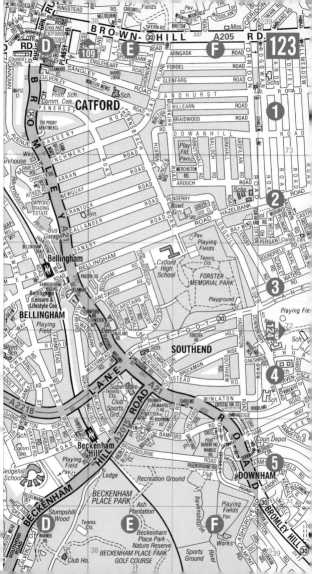

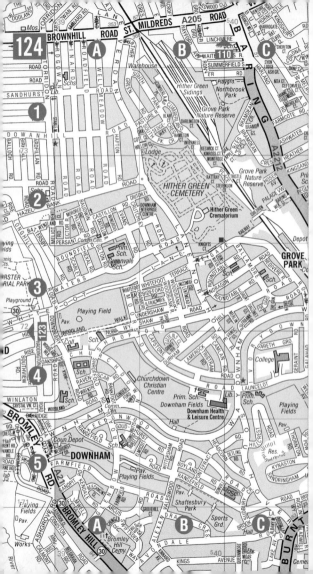

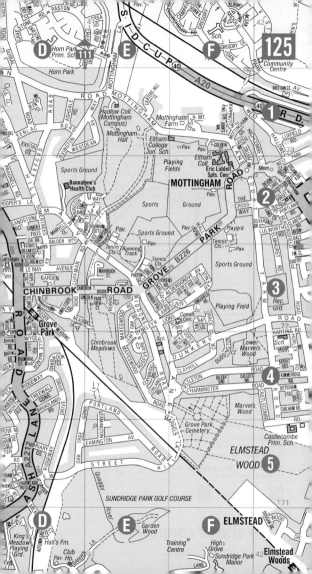

O Interchange stations
Ⓐ Step-free access from street to train
Ⓐ Step-free access from street to platform

Improvement works may affect your
journey, please check before you travel

Website
tfl.gov.uk

24 hour travel information
0843 222 1234*

*You pay no more than 5p per minute if calling
from a BT landline. There may be a connection charge.
Charges from mobiles or other landline providers may

MAYOR OF LONDON

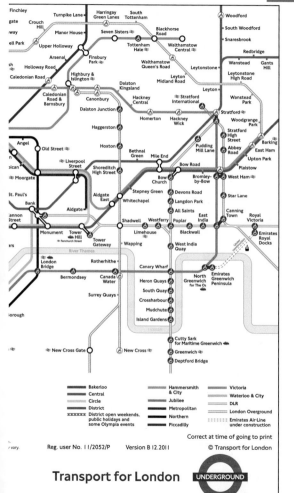

Bakerloo	Hammersmith & City	Victoria
Central	Jubilee	Waterloo & City
Circle	Metropolitan	DLR
District	Northern	London Overground
District open weekends, public holidays and some Olympia events	Piccadilly	Emirates Air-Line under construction

Correct at time of going to print

Reg. user No. 11/2052/P   Version B 12.2011   © Transport for London

Transport for London   UNDERGROUND

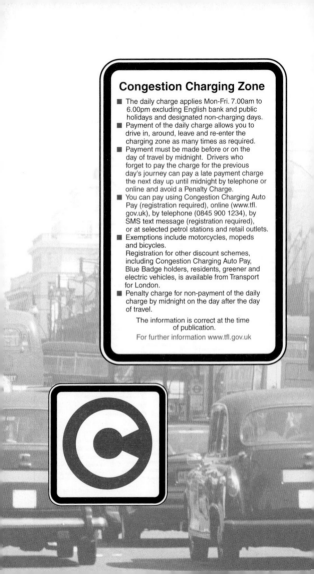

Congestion Charging Zone

- The daily charge applies Mon-Fri. 7.00am to 6.00pm excluding English bank and public holidays and designated non-charging days.
- Payment of the daily charge allows you to drive in, around, leave and re-enter the charging zone as many times as required.
- Payment must be made before or on the day of travel by midnight. Drivers who forget to pay the charge for the previous day's journey can pay a late payment charge the next day up until midnight by telephone or online and avoid a Penalty Charge.
- You can pay using Congestion Charging Auto Pay (registration required), online (www.tfl. gov.uk), by telephone (0845 900 1234), by SMS text message (registration required), or at selected petrol stations and retail outlets.
- Exemptions include motorcycles, mopeds and bicycles.
  Registration for other discount schemes, including Congestion Charging Auto Pay, Blue Badge holders, residents, greener and electric vehicles, is available from Transport for London.
- Penalty charge for non-payment of the daily charge by midnight on the day after the day of travel.

The information is correct at the time of publication.

For further information www.tfl.gov.uk

INDEX

Including Streets, Places & Areas, Industrial Estates,
Selected Flats & Walkways, Junction Names and Selected Places of Interest.

HOW TO USE THIS INDEX

1. Each street name is followed by its Postcode District (or, if outside the London Postcodes, by its Locality Abbreviation(s)) and then by its map reference;
   e.g. **Abbeville Rd.** SW4 . . . .4E **103** is in the SW4 Postcode District and is to be found in square 4E on page **103**. The page number is shown in bold type.

2. A strict alphabetical order is followed in which Av., Rd., St., etc. (though abbreviated) are read in full and as part of the street name; e.g. **Alder M.** appears after **Aldermans Wlk.** but before **Aldermoor Rd.**

3. Streets and a selection of flats and walkways that cannot be shown on the mapping, appear in the index with the thoroughfare to which they are connected shown in brackets;
   e.g. **Abady Ho.** SW1 . . . .5F **75** (off Page St.)

4. Addresses that are in more than one part are referred to as not continuous.

5. Places and areas are shown in the index in BLUE TYPE and the map reference is to the actual map square in which the town centre or area is located and not to the place name shown on the map; e.g. **BARNES** 5B **84**

6. An example of a selected place of interest is **Alexander Fleming Laboratory Mus.** 5F **59**

7. An example of a Park & Ride is **Cumberland Gate (Park & Ride)** 4A **12** (1B **74**)

8. Junction names are shown in the index in **BOLD CAPITAL TYPE**; e.g. **ANGEL** 1C **62**

9. Map references for entries that appear on large scale pages **4-27** are shown first, with small scale map references shown in brackets; e.g. **Abbey St.** SE1 . . . .5E **27** (4A **78**)

GENERAL ABBREVIATIONS

All. : Alley	**Emb.** : Embankment	**Nth.** : North
App. : Approach	**Ent.** : Enterprise	**Pal.** : Palace
Arc. : Arcade	**Est.** : Estate	**Pde.** : Parade
Av. : Avenue	**Fld.** : Field	**Pk.** : Park
Bk. : Back	**Flds.** : Fields	**Pas.** : Passage
Blvd. : Boulevard	**Gdn.** : Garden	**Pav.** : Pavilion
Bri. : Bridge	**Gdns.** : Gardens	**Pl.** : Place
B'way. : Broadway	**Gth.** : Garth	**Prom.** : Promenade
Bldg. : Building	**Ga.** : Gate	**Quad.** : Quadrant
Bldgs. : Buildings	**Gt.** : Great	**Ri.** : Rise
Bus. : Business	**Grn.** : Green	**Rd.** : Road
C'way. : Causeway	**Gro.** : Grove	**Rdbt.** : Roundabout
Cen. : Centre	**Hgts.** : Heights	**Shop.** : Shopping
Chu. : Church	**Ho.** : House	**Sth.** : South
Chyd. : Churchyard	**Ho's.** : Houses	**Sq.** : Square
Circ. : Circle	**Ind.** : Industrial	**Sta.** : Station
Cir. : Circus	**Info.** : Information	**St.** : Street
Cl. : Close	**Junc.** : Junction	**Ter.** : Terrace
Coll. : College	**La.** : Lane	**Twr.** : Tower
Comn. : Common	**Lit.** : Little	**Trad.** : Trading
Cnr. : Corner	**Lwr.** : Lower	**Up.** : Upper
Cott. : Cottage	**Mnr.** : Manor	**Va.** : Vale
Cotts. : Cottages	**Mans.** : Mansions	**Vw.** : View
Ct. : Court	**Mkt.** : Market	**Vs.** : Villas
Cres. : Crescent	**Mdw.** : Meadow	**Vis.** : Visitors
Cft. : Croft	**Mdws.** : Meadows	**Wlk.** : Walk
Dpt. : Depot	**M.** : Mews	**W.** : West
Dr. : Drive	**Mt.** : Mount	**Yd.** : Yard
E. : East	**Mus.** : Museum	

LOCALITY ABBREVIATIONS

Beck : **Beckenham**	Chst : **Chislehurst**	King T : **Kingston upon Thames**
Brom : **Bromley**	Ilf : **Ilford**	

LONDON 2012 OLYMPIC GAMES AND PARALYMPIC GAMES VENUES

Aquatics Centre, Olympic Park 4D **53**
Basketball Arena, Olympic Park . . .2D **53**
BMX Track, Olympic Park 2D **53**
Copper Box, Olympic Park 3C **52**
Earls Court 1C **86**
Eton Manor, Olympic Park 1D **53**
ExCeL 1D **83**
Greenwich Park 2F **95**
Horse Guards Parade 2C **22** (2F **75**)
Hyde Park 2A **74**

Lord's Cricket Ground 2F **59**
Mall, The 3B **22** (3F **75**)
North Greenwich Arena 2A **82**
Olympic Park 4D **53**
Olympic Stadium, Olympic Park 4D **53**
Riverbank Arena, Olympic Park 2C **52**
Velodrome, Olympic Park 2D **53**
Water Polo Arena, Olympic Park 4D **53**
Wimbledon 3A **114**

1st Bowl 1E **109**
2 Willow Road 1A **46**
60 St Martins La.
  WC2 . . . . .5F **7**
  (off St Martin's La.)
198 Contemporary Arts and
  Learning 4D **105**
  (off Railton Rd.)
201 Bishopsgate EC2 . . .5E **11**

A

Abady Ho. SW1 . . . . . . .5F **75**
  (off Page St.)
Abberley M. SW4 . . . . .1D **103**
Abbess Cl. SW2 . . . . . .1D **119**
Abbeville M. SW4 . . . . .2F **103**
Abbeville Rd. SW4 . . . .4E **103**
Abbey Bus. Cen.
  SW8 . . . . .4E **89**
Abbey Cl. E5 . . . . .1C **50**
  SW8 . . . . .4E **89**
Abbey Ct. NW8 . . . . . . .1E **59**
  (off Abbey Rd.)
  SE17 . . . . .1E **91**
  (off Macleod St.)
Abbey Dr. SW17 . . . . . .5C **116**
Abbey Est. NW8 . . . . . .5D **45**
Abbeyfield Est. SE16 . . .5E **79**
Abbeyfield Rd. SE16 . . .5E **79**
  (not continuous)
Abbey Gdns. NW8 . . . . .1C **59**
  SE16 . . . . .5C **78**
  W6 . . . . .2A **86**
Abbey Ho. E15 . . . . . . .1A **68**
  (off Baker's Row)
  NW8 . . . . .2E **59**
  (off Garden Rd.)
Abbey La. E15 . . . . . . .1E **67**
Abbey La. Commercial Est.
  E15 . . . . .1A **68**
Abbey Life Ct. E16 . . . .4D **69**
Abbey Lodge NW8 . . . . .2A **60**
  (off Park Rd.)
Abbey M. E17 . . . . .1C **38**
Abbey Orchard St.
  SW1 . . . . .5C **22** (4F **75**)
Abbey Orchard St. Est.
  SW1 . . . . .5C **22** (4F **75**)
  (not continuous)

Abbey Rd. E15 . . . . . . .1F **67**
  NW6 . . . . .4D **45**
  NW8 . . . . .4D **45**
Abbey Rd. Apartments
  NW8 . . . . .1E **59**
  (off Abbey Rd.)
Abbey St. E13 . . . . .3D **68**
  SE1 . . . . .5E **27** (4A **78**)
Abbey Trad. Est.
  SE26 . . . . .5B **122**
Abbot Ct. SW8 . . . . . . .3A **90**
  (off Hartington Rd.)
Abbot Ho. E14 . . . . . . .1D **81**
  (off Smythe St.)
Abbotsbury NW1 . . . . . .4F **47**
  (off Camley St.)
Abbotsbury Cl. E15 . . . .1E **67**
  W14 . . . . .3A **72**
Abbotsbury Ho. W14 . . .3A **72**
Abbotsbury M. SE15 . . .1E **107**
Abbotsbury Rd. W14 . . .3A **72**
Abbots Cl. W8 . . . . .3D **73**
  (off Thackeray St.)
Abbotshade Rd. SE16 . . .2F **79**
Abbotshall Rd. SE6 . . . .1F **123**
Abbot's Ho. W14 . . . . . .4B **72**
  (off St Mary Abbots Ter.)
Abbotsleigh Rd.
  SW16 . . . . .4E **117**
Abbots Mnr. SW1 . . . . .5D **75**
  (not continuous)
Abbots Pk. SW2 . . . . . .1C **118**
Abbot's Pl. NW6 . . . . . .5D **45**
Abbot's Rd. E6 . . . . .5F **55**
Abbots Ter. N8 . . . . . . .1A **34**
Abbotstone Rd.
  SW15 . . . . .1E **99**
Abbot St. E8 . . . . .3B **50**
Abbots Wlk. W8 . . . . . . .4D **73**
Abbotswell Rd. SE4 . . . .3B **108**
Abbotswood Rd.
  SE22 . . . . .2A **106**
  SW16 . . . . .3F **117**
Abbott Rd. E14 . . . . . . .4E **67**
  (not continuous)
Abbotts Cl. N1 . . . . .3E **49**
Abbotts Ho. SW1 . . . . . .1F **89**
  (off Aylesford St.)
Abbotts Pk. Rd.
  E10 . . . . .2E **39**
Abbott's Wharf E14 . . . .5C **66**
  (off Stainsby Pl.)
Abbotts Wharf Moorings
  E14 . . . . .5C **66**
  (off Stainsby Rd.)

Abchurch La.
  EC4 . . . . .4C **18** (1F **77**)
  (not continuous)
Abchurch Yd.
  EC4 . . . . .4B **18** (1F **77**)
Abdale Rd. W12 . . . . . . .2D **71**
Abel Ho. SE11 . . . . .2C **90**
  (off Kennington Rd.)
Aberavon Rd. E3 . . . . . .2A **66**
Abercorn Cl. NW8 . . . . .2E **59**
Abercorn Cotts. NW8 . . .2E **59**
  (off Abercorn Pl.)
Abercorn Mans. NW8 . . .1E **59**
  (off Abercorn Pl.)
Abercorn Pl. NW8 . . . . .2E **59**
Abercorn Wlk. NW8 . . . .2E **59**
Abercorn Way SE1 . . . .1C **92**
Abercrombie St.
  SW11 . . . . .5A **88**
Aberdale Cl. SE16 . . . . .3F **79**
  (off Garter Way)
Aberdare Gdns. NW6 . . .4D **45**
Aberdeen Ct. W9 . . . . . .3F **59**
  (off Maida Va.)
Aberdeen La. N5 . . . . . .2E **49**
Aberdeen Mans. WC1 . . .3D **7**
  (off Kenton St.)
Aberdeen Pk. N5 . . . . . .2E **49**
Aberdeen Pl. NW8 . . . . .3F **59**
  NW10 . . . . .2B **42**
Aberdeen Rd. N5 . . . . . .1E **49**
Aberdeen Sq. E14 . . . . .2B **80**
Aberdeen Ter. SE3 . . . . .5F **95**
Aberdeen Wharf E1 . . . .2D **79**
  (off Wapping High St.)
Aberdour St. SE1 . . . . . .5A **78**
Aberfeldy Ho. SE5 . . . . .3D **91**
  (not continuous)
Aberfeldy St. E14 . . . . . .4E **67**
  (not continuous)
Aberford Gdns. SE18 . . .4F **97**
Abergeldie Rd.
  SE12 . . . . .4D **111**
Abernethy Rd. SE13 . . . .2A **110**
Abersham Rd. E8 . . . . . .2B **50**
Ability Pl. E14 . . . . .3D **81**
Ability Towers EC1 . . . . .1F **9**
  (off Macclesfield St.)
Abingdon W14 . . . . .5B **72**
  (off Kensington Village)
Abingdon Cl. NW1 . . . . .3F **47**
  SE1 . . . . .5B **78**
  (off Bushwood Dr.)
Abingdon Ct. W8 . . . . . .4C **72**
  (off Abingdon Vs.)

Abingdon Gdns. W8 . . . .4C 72
Abingdon Ho. E2 . . . . . . .3F 11
    (off Boundary St.)
Abingdon Lodge W8 . . . .4C 72
Abingdon Mans. W8 . . . .4C 72
    (off Pater St.)
Abingdon Rd. W8 . . . . . .4C 72
Abingdon St.
   SW1 . . . . . .5D 23 (4A 76)
Abingdon Vs. W8 . . . . . . .4C 72
Abinger Gro. SE8 . . . . . . .2B 94
Abinger Ho. SE1 . . . . . .4B 26
    (off Gt. Dover St.)
Abinger M. W9 . . . . .3C 58
Abinger Rd. W4 . . . . .4A 70
Ablett St. SE16 . . . . .1E 93
Abney Gdns. N16 . . . . . . .4B 36
Abney Pk. Cemetery
  (Local Nature Reserve)
 . . . . .4A 36
Abney Pk. Ter. N16 . . . . .4B 36
    (off Cazenov Rd.)
Aborfield NW5 . . . . .2E 47
Aboyne Rd. NW10 . . . . .5A 28
   SW17 . . . . .3F 115
Abyssinia Cl. SW11 . . . .2A 102
Abyssinia Ct. N8 . . . . . .1B 34
Abyssinia Rd.
   SW11 . . . . .2A 102
Acacia Bus. Cen. E11 . . .5A 40
Acacia Cl. SE8 . . . . .5A 80
Acacia Gdns. NW8 . . . . .1F 59
Acacia Gro. SE21 . . . . .2F 119
Acacia Pl. NW8 . . . . .1F 59
Acacia Rd. E11 . . . . .4A 40
   E17 . . . . .1A 38
   NW8 . . . . .1F 59
Acacia Wlk. SW10 . . . . .3E 87
    (off Tadema Rd.)
Academy, The SW8 . . . . .2B 90
Academy Apartments
   E8 . . . . .2D 51
    (off Institute Pl.)
Academy Bldgs. N1 . . . .1D 11
    (off Fanshaw St.)
Academy Ct. E2 . . . . . . .2E 65
    (off Kirkwall Pl.)
   NW6 . . . . .5C 44
Academy Gdns. W8 . . . .3C 72
Academy Ho. E3 . . . . . .4D 67
    (off Violet Rd.)
Acanthus Dr. SE1 . . . . .1C 92
Acanthus Rd. SW11 . . . .1C 102
Accommodation Rd.
   NW11 . . . . .3B 30
Acer Rd. E8 . . . . .4B 50
Acfold Rd. SW6 . . . . . . .4D 87
Achilles Cl. SE1 . . . . . . .1C 92
Achilles Ho. E2 . . . . . . .1D 65
    (off Old Bethnal Grn. Rd.)
Achilles Rd. NW6 . . . . . .2C 44
Achilles Statue
 . . . . .2C 20 (2C 74)
Achilles St. SE14 . . . . . .3A 94
Achilles Way
   W1 . . . . . .2C 20 (2C 74)
Acklam Rd. W10 . . . . . . .4A 58
    (not continuous)
Ackmar Rd. SW6 . . . . . .4C 86
Ackroyd Dr. E3 . . . . .4B 66

Ackroyd Rd. SE23 . . . . .5F 107
Acland Cres. SE5 . . . . . .1F 105
Acland Ho. SW9 . . . . . . .4B 90
Acland Rd. NW2 . . . . . . .3D 43
Acme Studios E14 . . . . . .4E 67
    (Gillender St.)
   E14 . . . . .4E 67
    (off Leven Rd.)
Acol Ct. NW6 . . . . .4C 44
Acol Rd. NW6 . . . . .4C 44
Acorn Ct. E3 . . . . .1C 66
    (off Morville St.)
   E6 . . . . .4F 55
Acorn Gdns. W3 . . . . . . .4A 56
Acorn Pde. SE15 . . . . . . .3D 93
Acorn Production Cen.
   N7 . . . . .4A 48
Acorn Wlk. SE16 . . . . . . .2A 80
Acorn Way SE23 . . . . . . .3F 121
Acre Ct. SE22 . . . . .2C 106
Acre La. SW2 . . . . .2A 104
Acre Rd. SW19 . . . . .5F 115
Acris St. SW18 . . . . .3E 101
Acton Ho. E8 . . . . .5B 50
    (off Lee St.)
Acton La. NW10 . . . . . . .1A 56
Acton M. E8 . . . . .5B 50
Acton Pk. Est. W3 . . . . . .3A 70
Acton St. WC1 . . . .2F 7 (2B 62)
Acton W. Ind. Pk.
   W3 . . . . .3B 70
Acuba Rd. SW18 . . . . . . .2D 115
Ada Ct. N1 . . . . .1C 62
    (off Packington St.)
   W9 . . . . .2E 59
Ada Gdns. E14 . . . . .5F 67
   E15 . . . . .5B 54
Adagio Point SE8 . . . . . .2D 95
    (off Copperas St.)
Ada Ho. E2 . . . . .5C 50
    (off Ada Pl.)
Adair Ho. SW3 . . . . .2A 88
    (off Oakley St.)
Adair Rd. W10 . . . . .3A 58
Adair Twr. W10 . . . . .3A 58
    (off Appleford Rd.)
Ada Kennedy Ct.
   SE10 . . . . .3E 95
    (off Greenwich Sth. St.)
Adam & Eve Ct. W1 . . . .2A 14
Adam & Eve M. W8 . . . . .4C 72
Ada Maria Ct. E1 . . . . . .5D 65
    (off James Voller Way)
Adam Cl. SE6 . . . . .4B 122
Adam Ct. SE11 . . . . .5D 77
    (off Opal St.)
   SW7 . . . . .5E 73
    (off Gloucester Rd.)
Adams Ct. E17 . . . . .1A 38
   EC2 . . . . .2C 18 (5A 64)
Adams Gdns. Est.
   SE16 . . . . .3E 79
Adams Ho. E14 . . . . .5F 67
    (off Aberfeldy St.)
Adams M. SW17 . . . . . . .2B 116
Adamson Rd. E16 . . . . . .5C 68
   NW3 . . . . .4F 45
Adams Pl. E14 . . . . .2D 81
    (off The Nth. Colonnade)
   N7 . . . . .2B 48

Adamsrill Rd. SE26 . . . . .4F 121
Adam's Row
   W1 . . . . . .5C 12 (1C 74)
Adams Ter. E3 . . . . .2C 66
    (off Rainhill Way)
Adam St.
   WC2 . . . . . .5E 15 (1A 76)
Adam Wlk. SW6 . . . . . . .3E 85
Adana SE13 . . . . .5E 95
Adana Pl. E2 . . . . .5C 50
Adare Wlk. SW16 . . . . . .3B 118
Ada Rd. SE5 . . . . .3A 92
Adastral Ho. WC1 . . . . . .5F 7
    (off Harpur St.)
Ada St. E8 . . . . .5D 51
Ada Workshops E8 . . . . .5D 51
Adderley Gro.
   SW11 . . . . .3C 102
Adderley St. E14 . . . . . . .5E 67
Addey Ho. SE8 . . . . .3B 94
Addington St. SW14 . . . .1A 98
Addington Gro.
   SE26 . . . . .4A 122
Addington Ho. SW9 . . . .5B 90
    (off Stockwell Rd.)
Addington Lofts SE5 . . . .3E 91
    (off Wyndham Est.)
Addington Rd. E3 . . . . . .2C 66
   E16 . . . . .3A 68
   N4 . . . . .1C 34
Addington Sq. SE5 . . . . .2F 91
Addington St.
   SE1 . . . . . .4A 24 (3B 76)
Addis Ho. E1 . . . . .4E 65
    (off Lindley St.)
Addisland Ct. W14 . . . . .3A 72
    (off Holland Vs. Rd.)
Addison Av. W11 . . . . . . .2A 72
Addison Bri. Pl. W14 . . . .5B 72
Addison Cres. W14 . . . . .4A 72
    (not continuous)
Addison Dr. SE12 . . . . . .3D 111
Addison Gdns. W14 . . . . .4F 71
Addison Gro. W4 . . . . . . .4A 70
Addison Ho. NW8 . . . . . .2F 59
    (off Grove End Rd.)
Addison Pk. Mans.
   W14 . . . . .4F 71
    (off Richmond Way)
Addison Pl. W11 . . . . . . .2A 72
Addison Rd. E11 . . . . . . .1C 40
   W14 . . . . .3A 72
Addle Hill
   EC4 . . . . . .3E 17 (5D 63)
Addlestone Ho. W10 . . . .4E 57
    (off Sutton Way)
Addle St.
   EC2 . . . . . .2A 18 (5E 63)
Addy Ho. SE16 . . . . .5E 79
Adela Ho. W6 . . . . .1E 85
    (off Queen Caroline St.)
Adelaide Av. SE4 . . . . . . .2B 108
Adelaide Cl. SW9 . . . . . .2C 104
Adelaide Ct. E9 . . . . .2A 52
    (off Kenworthy Rd.)
   NW8 . . . . .1E 59
    (off Abbey Rd.)
Adelaide Gro. W12 . . . . .2C 70

Adelaide Ho. E15 . . . . .1B 68
  SE5 . . . . .5A 92
  W11 . . . . .5B 58
  (off Portobello Rd.)
Adelaide Rd. E10 . . . . .5D 39
  NW3 . . . . .4F 45
  SW18 . . . . .3C 100
Adelaide St.
  WC2 . . . . .5D 15 (1A 76)
  (not continuous)
Adela St. W10 . . . . .3A 58
Adelina Gro. E1 . . . . .4E 65
Adelina M. SW12 . . . . . . .1F 117
Adelina Yd. E1 . . . . .4E 65
  (off Adelina Gro.)
Adeline Pl.
  WC1 . . . . . . .1C 14 (4F 61)
Adelphi Ct. E8 . . . . .4B 50
  (off Celandine Dr.)
  SE16 . . . . .1E 79
  (off Garter Way)
  W4 . . . . .2A 84
Adelphi Ter.
  WC2 . . . . .5E 15 (1A 76)
  (off Strand)
Adelphi Theatre
  . . . . .5E 15
  (off Strand)
Adeney Cl. W6 . . . . .2F 85
Aden Gro. N16 . . . . .1F 49
Adenmore Rd.
  SE6 . . . . .5C 108
Aden Ter. N16 . . . . .1F 49
Adeyfield Ho. EC1 . . . . . .2C 10
  (off Cranwood St.)
Adie Rd. W6 . . . . .4E 71
Adine Rd. E13 . . . . .3D 69
Adler St. E1 . . . . .5C 64
Adley St. E5 . . . . .2A 52
Admiral Ct. SE5 . . . . .4A 92
  (off Havil St.)
  SW10 . . . . .4E 87
  (off Admiral Sq.)
  W1 . . . . .1B 12
  (off Blandford St.)
Admiral Ho. SW1 . . . . .5E 75
  (off Willow Pl.)
Admiral Hyson Ind. Est.
  SE16 . . . . .1D 93
Admiral M. W10 . . . . .3F 57
Admiral Pl. SE16 . . . . .2A 80
Admirals Ct. SE1 . . . . .2F 27
  (off Horselydown La.)
Admiral's Ga.
  SE10 . . . . .4D 95
Admiral Sq. SW10 . . . . . .4E 87
Admiral St. SE8 . . . . .5C 94
Admirals Wlk. NW3 . . . . . .5E 31
Admirals Way E14 . . . . . .3C 80
Admiralty Arch
  . . . . .1C 22 (2F 75)
Admiralty Cl. SE8 . . . . . . .3C 94
Admiral Wlk. W9 . . . . .4C 58
Adolf St. SE6 . . . . .4D 123
Adolphus Rd. N4 . . . . .4D 35
Adolphus St. SE8 . . . . . . .3B 94
Adpar St. W2 . . . . .4F 59
Adrian Av. NW2 . . . . .3D 29
Adrian Boult Ho. E2 . . . . .2D 65
  (off Mansford St.)
Adrian Ho. E15 . . . . .4F 53
  (off Jupp Rd.)

Adrian Ho. N1 . . . . .5B 48
  (off Barnsbury Est.)
  SW8 . . . . .3A 90
  (off Wyvil Rd.)
Adrian M. SW10 . . . . .2D 87
Adriatic Apartments
  E16 . . . . .1C 82
  (off Western Gateway)
Adriatic Bldg. E14 . . . . . . .1A 80
  (off Horseferry Rd.)
Adriatic Ho. E1 . . . . .3F 65
  (off Ernest St.)
Adron Ho. SE16 . . . . .5E 79
  (off Millender Wlk.)
Adstock Ho. N1 . . . . .4D 49
  (off The Sutton Est.)
Advance Rd. SE27 . . . . . .4E 119
Adventurers Ct. E14 . . . .1F 81
  (off Newport Av.)
Adys Lawn NW2 . . . . .3D 43
Ady's Rd. SE15 . . . . .1B 106
Aegean Apartments
  E16 . . . . .1C 82
  (off Western Gateway)
Aegon Ho. E14 . . . . .4D 81
  (off Lanark Sq.)
Affleck St.
  N1 . . . . .1F 7 (1B 62)
Afghan Rd. SW11 . . . . . . .5A 88
Afsil Ho. EC1 . . . . .1C 16
  (off Viaduct Bldgs.)
Aftab Ter. E1 . . . . .3D 65
  (off Tent St.)
Agamemnon Rd.
  NW6 . . . . .1B 44
Agar Gro. NW1 . . . . .4E 47
Agar Gro. Est.
  NW1 . . . . .4E 47
Agar Pl. NW1 . . . . .4E 47
Agar St.
  WC2 . . . . .5D 15 (1A 76)
Agate Cl. E16 . . . . .5F 69
Agate Rd. W6 . . . . .4E 71
Agatha Cl. E1 . . . . .2D 79
Agave Rd. NW2 . . . . .1E 43
Agdon St. EC1 . . .3D 9 (3D 63)
Age Exchange
  Reminiscence Cen.
  . . . . .1B 110
Agincourt Rd. NW3 . . . . . .1B 46
Agnes George Wlk.
  E16 . . . . .2F 83
Agnes Ho. W11 . . . . .1F 71
  (off St Ann's Rd.)
Agnes Rd. W3 . . . . .2B 70
Agnes St. E14 . . . . .5B 66
Agnew Rd. SE23 . . . . .5F 107
Agricola Ct. E3 . . . . .5B 52
  (off Parnell Rd.)
Ahoy Sailing Cen. 1C 94
  (off Stretton Mans.)
Aigburth Mans. SW9 . . . . .3C 90
  (off Mowll St.)
Aileen Wlk. E15 . . . . .4B 54
Ailsa St. E14 . . . . .4E 67
Ailsa Wlk. E14 . . . . .3C 80
  (off Alpha Gro.)
Ainger M. NW3 . . . . .4B 46
  (off Ainger Rd., not continuous)
Ainger Rd. NW3 . . . . .4B 46

Ainsdale NW1 . . . . .1F 5
  (off Harrington St.)
Ainsdale Dr. SE1 . . . . . . .1C 92
Ainsley St. E2 . . . . .2D 65
Ainslie Wlk. SW12 . . . . . .5D 103
Ainsty Est. SE16 . . . . . . .3F 79
Ainsty St. SE16 . . . . .3E 79
Ainsworth Cl. NW2 . . . . . .5C 28
  SE15 . . . . .5A 92
Ainsworth Ct. NW10 . . . . .2D 57
  (off Plough Cl.)
Ainsworth Ho. NW8 . . . . . .5D 45
  (off Ainsworth Way)
  W10 . . . . .2A 58
  (off Kilburn La.)
Ainsworth Rd. E9 . . . . . . .4E 51
Ainsworth Way NW8 . . . . .5E 45
Aintree Av. E6 . . . . .5F 55
Aintree Est. SW6 . . . . . . .3A 86
  (off Aintree St.)
Aintree St. SW6 . . . . .3A 86
Aird Ho. SE1 . . . . .5F 25
  (off Rockingham St.)
Airdrie Cl. N1 . . . . .4B 48
Airedale Av. W4 . . . . .5B 70
Airedale Av. Sth. W4 . . . . .1B 84
Airedale Rd. SW12 . . . . . .5B 102
Airedale Wlk. E15 . . . . . . .4A 54
  (off Maiden Rd.)
Airlie Gdns. W8 . . . . .2C 72
Air St. W1 . . . . . .5A 14 (1E 75)
Aisgill Av. W14 . . . . .1B 86
  (not continuous)
Aislibie Rd. SE12 . . . . . . .2A 110
Aiten Pl. W6 . . . . .5C 70
Aithan Ho. E14 . . . . .5B 66
  (off Copenhagen Pl.)
Aitken Cl. E8 . . . . .5C 50
Aitken Rd. SE6 . . . . .2D 123
Ajax Ho. E2 . . . . .1D 65
  (off Old Bethnal Grn. Rd.)
Ajax Rd. NW6 . . . . .1B 44
Akbar Ho. E14 . . . . .5D 81
  (off Cahir St.)
Akehurst St. SW15 . . . . . .4C 98
Akenside Rd. NW3 . . . . . .2F 45
Akerman Rd. SW9 . . . . . .5D 91
Akintaro Ho. SE8 . . . . . . .2B 94
  (off Alverton St.)
Alamaro Lodge SE10 . . . .4B 82
  (off Teal St.)
Aland Ct. SE16 . . . . .4A 80
Alan Hocken Way
  E15 . . . . .1A 68
Alan Preece Ct. NW6 . . . .4F 43
Alan Rd. SW19 . . . . .5A 114
Alanthus Cl. SE12 . . . . . . .4C 110
Alaska Apartments
  E16 . . . . .1C 82
  (off Western Gateway)
Alaska Bldg. SE10 . . . . . .4D 95
  (off Deal's Gateway)
Alaska Bldgs. SE1 . . . . . .4A 78
Alaska St.
  SE1 . . . . . . .2B 24 (2C 76)
Alastor Ho. E14 . . . . .4E 81
  (off Strattondale Rd.)
Albacore Cres.
  SE13 . . . . .4D 109
Alba Gdns. NW11 . . . . . .1A 30

Alba M. SW18 . . . . .2C 114
Alban Highwalk EC2 . . . .2A 18
(not continuous)
Albany, The 3C 94
Albany W1 . . . . . .5F 13 (1E 75)
Albany Ct. E1 . . . . .5C 64
(off Plumber's Row)
E10 . . . . .2C 38
NW8 . . . . .1F 59
(off Abbey Rd.)
NW10 . . . . .2D 57
(off Trenmar Gdns.)
Albany Courtyard
W1 . . . . .5A 14 (1E 75)
Albany Mans.
SW11 . . . . .3A 88
Albany M.
BR1: Brom 5C 124
N1 . . . . .4C 48
SE5 . . . . .2E 91
Albany Rd. E10 . . . . .2C 38
E12 . . . . .1F 55
E17 . . . . .1A 38
N4 . . . . .1C 34
SE5 . . . . .2F 91
SW19 . . . . .5D 115
Albany St.
NW1 . . . . .1E 5 (1D 61)
Albany Ter. NW1 . . . . .4E 5
Albany Works E3 . . . . . . .5A 52
(off Gunmakers La.)
Alba Pl. W11 . . . . .5B 58
Albatross Way SE16 . . . .3F 79
Albemarle SW19 . . . . . . .2F 113
Albemarle Ho. SE8 . . . . .5B 80
(off Foreshore)
SW9 . . . . .1C 104
Albemarle St.
W1 . . . . .5E 13 (1D 75)
Albemarle Way
EC1 . . . . . . .4D 9 (3D 63)
Alberta Est. SE17 . . . . . .1D 91
(off Alberta St.)
Alberta St. SE17 . . . . . . .1D 91
Albert Av. SW8 . . . . .3B 90
Albert Barnes Ho.
SE1 . . . . .4E 77
(off New Kent Rd.)
Albert Bigg Point E15 . . .1E 67
(off Godfrey St.)
Albert Bri. SW3 . . . . .2A 88
Albert Bri. Rd. SW11 . . . .3A 88
Albert Carr Gdns.
SW16 . . . . .5A 118
Albert Cl. E9 . . . . .5D 51
Albert Cotts. E1 . . . . .4C 64
(off Deal St.)
Albert Ct. E7 . . . . .1C 54
SW7 . . . . .4F 73
Albert Ct. Ga. SW1 . . . . .3B 74
(off Knightsbridge)
Albert Dr. SW19 . . . . .2A 114
Albert Emb.
SE1 . . . . . .5F 23 (4B 76)
(Lambeth Pal. Rd.)
SE1 . . . . .1A 90
(Vauxhall Bri.)
Albert Gdns. E1 . . . . .5F 65
Albert Ga.
SW1 . . . . .3A 20 (3B 74)

Albert Gray Ho.
SW10 . . . . .3F 87
(off Worlds End Est.)
Albert Hall Mans.
SW7 . . . . .3F 73
Albert Mans. SW11 . . . . .4B 88
(off Albert Bri. Rd.)
Albert Memorial
Knightsbridge 3F 73
Albert M. E14 . . . . .1A 80
(off Northey St.)
N4 . . . . .3B 34
SE4 . . . . .2A 108
W8 . . . . .4E 73
Albert Pal. Mans.
SW11 . . . . .4D 89
(off Lurline Gdns.)
Albert Pl. W8 . . . . .4D 73
Albert Rd. E10 . . . . .4E 39
E16 . . . . .2F 83
E17 . . . . .1C 38
N4 . . . . .3B 34
N15 . . . . .1A 36
NW6 . . . . .1B 58
Albert Rd. Cen. NW6 . . . .1B 58
(off Albert Rd.)
Alberts Ct. NW1 . . . . . . .3A 60
(off Palgrave Gdns.)
Albert Sq. E15 . . . . .2A 54
SW8 . . . . .3B 90
Albert Starr Ho. SE8 . . . .5F 79
(off Haddonfield)
Albert St. NW1 . . . . .5D 47
Albert Studios
SW11 . . . . .4B 88
Albert Ter. NW1 . . . . .5C 46
W6 . . . . .1C 84
(off Beavor La.)
Albert Ter. M. NW1 . . . . .5C 46
Albert Way SE15 . . . . . . .3D 93
Albert Westcott Ho.
SE17 . . . . .1D 91
Albery Ct. E8 . . . . .4B 50
(off Middleton Rd.)
Albion Av. SW8 . . . . .5F 89
Albion Bldgs. N1 . . . . . . .1A 62
(off Albion Yd.)
Albion Cl. W2 . . . . .1A 74
Albion Ct. SE10 . . . . .5A 82
(off Azof St.)
W6 . . . . .5D 71
(off Albion Pl.)
Albion Dr. E8 . . . . .4B 50
Albion Est. SE16 . . . . . . .3F 79
Albion Gdns. W6 . . . . . . .5D 71
Albion Ga. W2 . . . . .1A 74
(off Albion St., not continuous)
Albion Gro. N16 . . . . .1A 50
Albion Ho. SE8 . . . . .3C 94
(off Watsons St.)
Albion M. N1 . . . . .5C 48
NW6 . . . . .4B 44
W2 . . . . .1A 74
W6 . . . . .5D 71
Albion Pde. N16 . . . . .1F 49
Albion Pl. EC1 . . . .5D 9 (4D 63)
EC2 . . . . . .1C 18 (4F 63)
W6 . . . . .5D 71
Albion Riverside Bldg.
SW11 . . . . .3A 88

Albion Rd. N16 . . . . .1F 49
Albion Sq. E8 . . . . .4B 50
(not continuous)
Albion St. SE16 . . . . .3E 79
W2 . . . . .5A 60
Albion Ter. E8 . . . . .4B 50
Albion Vs. Rd. SE26 . . . .3E 121
Albion Wlk. N1 . . . . .1E 7
(off York Way)
Albion Way
EC1 . . . . . .1F 17 (4E 63)
SE13 . . . . .2E 109
Albion Yd. E1 . . . . .4D 65
N1 . . . . .1A 62
Albon Ho. SW18 . . . . . . .4D 101
(off Neville Gill Cl.)
Albrighton Rd.
SE22 . . . . .1A 106
Albury Ct. SE8 . . . . .2C 94
(off Albury St.)
Albury Ho. SE1 . . . . .4E 25
(off Boyfield St.)
Albury M. E12 . . . . .4E 41
Albury St. SE8 . . . . .2C 94
Albyn Rd. SE8 . . . . .4C 94
Alcester Cres. E5 . . . . . . .4D 37
Alconbury Rd. E5 . . . . . . .4C 36
Aldam Pl. N16 . . . . .4B 36
Aldbourne Rd. W12 . . . . .2B 70
Aldbridge St. SE17 . . . . . .1A 92
Aldburgh M.
W1 . . . . .2C 12 (5C 60)
Aldbury Ho. SW3 . . . . . . .5A 74
(off Cale St.)
Aldebert Ter. SW8 . . . . . .3A 90
Aldeburgh Cl. E5 . . . . . . .4D 37
Aldeburgh Pl. SE10 . . . . .5C 82
(off Aldeburgh St.)
Aldeburgh St. SE10 . . . . .1C 96
Alden Av. E15 . . . . .2B 68
Aldenham Ho. NW1 . . . . .1A 6
(off Aldenham St.)
Aldenham St.
NW1 . . . . .1A 6 (1E 61)
Aldensley Ho. E8 . . . . . . .5D 51
(off Duncan Rd.)
Aldensley Rd. W6 . . . . . . .4D 71
Alderbrook Rd.
SW12 . . . . .4D 103
Alderbury Rd. SW13 . . . .2C 84
Alder Cl. SE15 . . . . .2B 92
Alder Ct. E7 . . . . .2C 54
Alder Gro. NW2 . . . . .4C 28
Alder Ho. E3 . . . . .5B 52
(off Hornbeam Sq.)
NW3 . . . . .3B 46
SE4 . . . . .1C 108
SE15 . . . . .2B 92
(off Alder Cl.)
Alder Lodge SW6 . . . . . . .4E 85
Aldermanbury
EC2 . . . . .2A 18 (5E 63)
Aldermanbury Sq.
EC2 . . . . .1A 18 (4E 63)
Aldermans Wlk.
EC2 . . . . .1D 19 (4A 64)
Alder M. N19 . . . . .4E 33
Aldermoor Rd. SE6 . . . . . .3B 122
Alderney Ct. SE10 . . . . . .2F 95
(off Trafalgar Rd.)

Alderney Ho. *N1* *3E 49*
  (off Arran Wlk.)
Alderney M.
  SE1 . . . . . . .5B **26** (4F **77**)
Alderney Rd. *E1* *3F 65*
Alderney St. *SW1* 5D **75**
Alders, The *SW16* 4E **117**
ALDERSBROOK 4D **41**
Aldersbrook Rd. *E11* 4D **41**
  E12 . . . . .4D **41**
Alders Cl. *E11* 4D **41**
Aldersford Cl. *SE4* 3F **107**
Aldersgate Ct. *EC1* *1F 17*
  (off Bartholomew Cl.)
Aldersgate St.
  EC1 . . . . . . .5F **9** (4E **63**)
Aldersgrove Av. *SE9* *3F 125*
Aldershot Rd. *NW6* 5B **44**
Alderson St. *W10* 3A **58**
Alderton Cl. *NW10* 5A **28**
Alderton Cres. *NW4* 1D **29**
Alderton Rd. *SE24* 1E **105**
Alderton Way *NW4* 1D **29**
Alderville Rd. *SW6* 5B **86**
Alderwick Cl. *N7* *3B 48*
  (off Cornelia St.)
Aldford Ho. *W1* *1B 20*
  (off Park St.)
Aldford St.
  W1 . . . . . .1C **20** (2C **74**)
ALDGATE 5B **64**
Aldgate *E1* *5B 64*
  (off Whitechapel High St.)
  EC3 . . . . . . .3F **19** (5A **64**)
Aldgate Av.
  E1 . . . . . . .2F **19** (5B **64**)
Aldgate Barrs *E1* 2F **19**
Aldgate High St.
  EC3 . . . . . . .3F **19** (5B **64**)
Aldgate Twr. *E1* 5B **64**
Aldham Ho. *SE4* *5B 94*
  (off Malpas Rd.)
Aldine Ct. *W12* *3E 71*
  (off Aldine St.)
Aldine Pl. *W12* 3E **71**
Aldine St. *W12* 3E **71**
Aldington Ct. *E8* *4C 50*
  (off London Flds. W. Side)
Aldington Rd. *SE18* 4F **83**
Aldis M. *SW17* 3A **116**
Aldis St. *SW17* 5A **116**
Aldred Rd. *NW6* 2C **44**
Aldren Rd. *SW17* 3E **115**
Aldrich Ter. *SW18* 2E **115**
Aldrick Ho. *N1* *5B 48*
  (off Barnsbury Est.)
Aldridge Ct. *W11* *4B 58*
  (off Aldridge Rd. Vs.)
Aldridge Rd. Vs.
  W11 . . . . .4B **58**
Aldrington Rd.
  SW16 . . . . .5E **117**
Aldsworth Cl. *W9* 3D **59**
Aldworth Gro. *SE13* 4E **109**
Aldworth Rd. *E15* 4A **54**
Aldwych *WC2* . . .4F **15** (5B **62**)
Aldwych Bldgs. *WC2* *2C 15*
  (off Parker M.)
Aldwych Ct. *E8* *4B 50*
  (off Middleton Rd.)

Aldwych Theatre *3F 15*
  (off Aldwych)
Aldwyn Ho. *SW8* *3A 90*
  (off Davidson Gdns.)
Alestan Beck Rd.
  E16 . . . . .5F **69**
Alexa Ct. *W8* 5C **72**
Alexander Av. *NW10* 4D **43**
Alexander Evans M.
  SE23 . . . . .2F **121**
Alexander Fleming
  Laboratory Mus.
  . . . . .5F **59**
Alexander Ho. *E14* *4C 80*
  (off Tiller Rd.)
  SE15 . . . .*5D 93*
  (off Godman Rd.)
Alexander M. *SW16* 5E **117**
  W2 . . . . .5D **59**
Alexander Pl. *SW7* 5A **74**
Alexander Rd. *N19* 5A **34**
Alexander Sq. *SW3* 5A **74**
Alexander St. *W2* 5C **58**
Alexander Studios
  SW11 . . . .*2F 101*
  (off Haydon Way)
Alexandra Av. *SW11* 4C **88**
  W4 . . . . .3A **84**
Alexandra Cl. *SE8* 2B **94**
Alexandra Cotts.
  SE14 . . . . .4B **94**
Alexandra Ct. *SE5* *2E 91*
  (off Urlwin St.)
  SW7 . . . .*4E 73*
  (off Queen's Ga.)
  W2 . . . .*1D 73*
  (off Moscow Rd.)
  W9 . . . .*3E 59*
  (off Maida Va.)
Alexandra Cres.
  BR1: Brom 5B **124**
Alexandra Dr. *SE19* 5A **120**
Alexandra Gdns. *W4* 3A **84**
Alexandra Gro. *N4* 3D **35**
Alexandra Ho. *E16* *2D 83*
  (off Wesley Av.)
  W6 . . . .*1E 85*
  (off Queen Caroline St.)
Alexandra Mans.
  SW3 . . . .*2F 87*
  (off King's Rd.)
  W12 . . . .*2E 71*
  (off Stanlake Rd.)
Alexandra Mus. *SW19* . . .5B **114**
Alexandra National Ho.
  N4 . . . . .3D **35**
Alexandra Pl. *NW8* 5E **45**
Alexandra Rd. *E10* 5E **39**
  E17 . . . . .1B **38**
  NW8 . . . . .5E **45**
  SE26 . . . . .5F **121**
  SW14 . . . . .1A **98**
  SW19 . . . . .5B **114**
  W4 . . . . .3A **70**
Alexandra St. *E16* 4C **68**
  SE14 . . . . .3A **94**
Alexandra Ter. *E14* *1D 95*
  (off Westferry Rd.)
Alexandra Wlk.
  SE19 . . . . .5A **120**

Alexandra Wharf *E2* *5D 51*
  (off Darwen Pl.)
Alexandra Yd. *E9* *5F 51*
Alexandria Apartments
  SE17 . . . .*5A 78*
  (off Townsend St.)
Alexia Sq. *E14* 4D **81**
Alexis St. *SE16* 5C **78**
Alfearn Rd. *E5* 1E **51**
Alford Cl. *N1* *1A 10*
  (off Shepherdess Wlk.)
Alford Ho. *N6* 1E **33**
Alford Pl. *N1* 1A **10** (1E **63**)
Alfreda St. *SW11* 4D **89**
Alfred Cl. *SE16* *5D 79*
  (off Bombay St.)
Alfred Dickens Ho.
  E16 . . . .*5B 68*
  (off Hallsville Rd.)
Alfred Ho. *E9* *2A 52*
  (off Homerton Rd.)
  E12 . . . .*4F 55*
  (off Tennyson Av.)
Alfred M. *W1* 5B **6** (4F **61**)
Alfred Nunn Ho.
  NW10 . . . . .5B **42**
Alfred Pl. *WC1* 5B **6** (4F **61**)
Alfred Rd. *E15* 2B **54**
  W2 . . . . .4C **58**
Alfred Salter Ho. *SE1* *5B 78*
  (off Fort Rd.)
Alfred St. *E3* 2B **66**
Alfreton Cl. *SW19* *3F 113*
Alfriston Rd. *SW11* 3B **102**
Algar Ho. *SE1* 4D **25**
Algarve Rd. *SW18* 1D **115**
Algernon Rd. *NW4* 1C **28**
  NW6 . . . . .5C **44**
  SE13 . . . . .2D **109**
Algiers Rd. *SE13* 2C **108**
Alice Gilliatt Ct. *W14* *2B 86*
  (off Star Rd.)
Alice La. *E3* 5B **52**
Alice Owen Technology Cen.
  EC1 . . . .*1D 9*
  (off Goswell Rd.)
Alice Shepherd Ho.
  E14 . . . .*3E 81*
  (off Manchester Rd.)
Alice St. *SE1* 5D **27** (4A **78**)
  (not continuous)
Alice Thompson Cl.
  SE12 . . . . .2E **125**
Alice Walker Cl.
  SE24 . . . . .2D **105**
Alie St. *E1* 3F **19** (5B **64**)
Aliwal M. *SW11* 2A **102**
Aliwal Rd. *SW11* 2A **102**
Alkerden Rd. *W4* 1A **84**
Alkham Rd. *N16* 4B **36**
Allan Barclay Cl.
  N15 . . . . .1B **36**
Allanson Ct. *E10* *4C 38*
  (off Leyton Grange Est.)
Allard Gdns. *SW4* 3F **103**
Allardyce St. *SW4* 2B **104**
Allcroft Rd. *NW5* 2C **46**
Allenby Rd. *SE23* 3A **122**
Allen Ct. *E17* *1C 38*
  (off Yunus Khan Cl.)

Allendale Cl. SE5 . . . . .5F **91**
  SE26 . . . . .5F **121**
Allen Edwards Dr.
  SW8 . . . . .4A **90**
Allenford Ho. SW15 . . .4B **98**
  (off Tunworth Cres.)
Allen Ho. W8 . . . . .4C **72**
  (off Allen St.)
Allen Mans. W8 . . . . . .4C **72**
  (off Allen St.)
Allen Rd. E3 . . . . .1B **66**
  N16 . . . . .1A **50**
Allensbury Pl. NW1 . . . .4F **47**
Allen St. W8 . . . . .4C **72**
Allenswood SW19 . . . .1A **114**
Allerford Ho. SE6 . . . . .3D **123**
Allerton Ho. N1 . . . . . . .1B **10**
  (off Provost Est.)
Allerton Rd. N16 . . . . . .4E **35**
Allerton St.
  N1 . . . . . .1B **10** (2F **63**)
Allerton Wlk. N7 . . . . . .4B **34**
Allestree Rd. SW6 . . . . .3A **86**
Alleyn Cres. SE21 . . . .2F **119**
Alleyn Ho. SE1 . . . . . . .5C **26**
  (off Burbage Cl.)
Alleyn Pk. SE21 . . . . . .2F **119**
Alleyn Rd. SE21 . . . . . .3F **119**
Allfarthing La.
  SW18 . . . . .4D **101**
Allgood St. E2 . . . . . . .1B **64**
Allhallows La.
  EC4 . . . . . .5B **18** (1F **77**)
Allhallows Rd. E6 . . . . .4F **69**
Alliance Rd. E13 . . . . . .4E **69**
Allied Ct. N1 . . . . .4A **50**
  (off Enfield Rd.)
Allied Ind. Est. W3 . . . . .3A **70**
Allied Way W3 . . . . .3A **70**
Allingham M. N1 . . . . . .1E **63**
  (off Allingham St.)
Allingham St. N1 . . . . . .1E **63**
Allington Cl. SW19 . . . .5F **113**
Allington Ct. SW1 . . . . .5E **21**
  (off Allington St.)
  SW8 . . . . .5E **89**
Allington Rd. NW4 . . . . .1D **29**
  W10 . . . . .2A **58**
Allington St.
  SW1 . . . . . .5E **21** (4D **75**)
Allison Cl. SE10 . . . . . .4E **95**
Allison Gro. SE21 . . . . .1A **120**
Alliston Ho. E2 . . . . .2B **64**
  (off Gibraltar Wlk.)
Allitsen Rd. NW8 . . . . . .1A **60**
  (not continuous)
All Nations Ho. E8 . . . . .4D **51**
  (off Martello St.)
Allnutt Way SW4 . . . . . .3F **103**
Alloa Rd. SE8 . . . . .1F **93**
Allom Ho. W11 . . . . . . .1A **72**
  (off Clarendon Rd.)
Allonby Ho. E14 . . . . . . .4A **66**
  (off Aston St.)
Allotment Way NW2 . . . .5F **29**
Alloway Rd. E3 . . . . . . .2A **66**
Allport Ho. SE5 . . . . . . .1F **105**
  (off Champion Pk.)
Allport M. E1 . . . . .3E **65**
  (off Hayfield Pas.)

All Saints Cl. SW8 . . . . .4A **90**
All Saints Ct. E1 . . . . . . .1E **79**
  (off Johnson St.)
  SW11 . . . . .3D **89**
  (off Prince of Wales Dr.)
All Saints Dr. SE3 . . . . .5A **96**
  (not continuous)
All Saints Ho. W11 . . . . .4B **58**
  (off All Saints St.)
All Saints Pas.
  SW18 . . . . .3C **100**
All Saints Rd. W11 . . . . .4B **58**
All Saints St. N1 . . . . . . .1B **62**
All Saints Twr. E10 . . . . .2D **39**
Allsop Pl.
  NW1 . . . . . . .4A **4** (3B **60**)
All Souls Av. NW10 . . . .1D **57**
All Souls' Pl.
  W1 . . . . . . .1E **13** (4D **61**)
Alluvium St. SE1 . . . . . .5D **27**
  (off Long La.)
Alwood Cl. SE26 . . . . . .4F **121**
Alma Birk Ho. NW6 . . . .4A **44**
Almack Rd. E5 . . . . .1E **51**
Alma Gro. SE1 . . . . . . .5B **78**
Alma Pl. NW10 . . . . . . .2D **57**
Alma Rd. SW18 . . . . . . .2E **101**
Alma Sq. NW8 . . . . .1E **59**
Alma St. E15 . . . . .3F **53**
  NW5 . . . . .3D **47**
Alma Ter. E3 . . . . .5B **52**
  (off Beale Rd.)
  SW18 . . . . .5F **101**
  W8 . . . . .4C **72**
Almeida St. N1 . . . . .5D **49**
Almeida Theatre 5D **49**
  (off Almeida St.)
Almeric Rd. SW11 . . . . .2B **102**
Almington St. N4 . . . . . .3B **34**
Almond Cl. SE15 . . . . . .5C **92**
Almond Ho. E15 . . . . . . .2A **68**
  (off Teasel Way)
Almond Rd. SE16 . . . . . .5D **79**
Almorah Rd. N1 . . . . . . .4F **49**
Alnwick Rd. E16 . . . . . . .5E **69**
  SE12 . . . . .4D **111**
Alperton St. W10 . . . . . .3B **58**
Alphabet Sq. E3 . . . . . . .4C **66**
Alpha Bus. Cen. E17 . . .1B **38**
Alpha Cl. NW1 . . . . .3A **60**
Alpha Gro. E14 . . . . . . .3C **80**
Alpha Ho. NW6 . . . . . . .1C **58**
  NW8 . . . . .3A **60**
  (off Ashbridge St.)
  SW4 . . . . .2B **104**
Alpha Pl. NW6 . . . . .1C **58**
  SW3 . . . . .2A **88**
Alpha Rd. SE14 . . . . . . .4B **94**
Alpha St. SE15 . . . . . . .5C **92**
Alpine Gro. E9 . . . . .4E **51**
Alpine Rd. E10 . . . . .4D **39**
  SE16 . . . . .1F **93**
Alric Av. NW10 . . . . . . .4A **42**
Alroy Rd. N4 . . . . .2C **34**
Alsace Rd. SE17 . . . . . .1A **92**
Alscot Rd.
  SE1 . . . . . . .5F **27** (5B **78**)
Alscot Rd. Ind. Est.
  SE1 . . . . .4B **78**
Alscot Way SE1 . . . . . . .5B **78**

Alston Rd. SW17 . . . . . .4F **115**
Altenburg Gdns.
  SW11 . . . . .2B **102**
Althea St. SW6 . . . . . . .5D **87**
Althorpe M. SW11 . . . . .4F **87**
Althorp Rd. SW17 . . . . .1B **116**
Altima Ct. SE22 . . . . . . .2C **106**
  (off E. Dulwich Rd.)
Altior Ct. N6 . . . . .1E **33**
Altius Apartments E3 . . .1C **66**
  (off Wick La.)
Alton Ho. E3 . . . . .2D **67**
  (off Bromley High St.)
Alton Rd. SW15 . . . . . . .1C **112**
Alton St. E14 . . . . .4D **67**
Altura Twr. SW11 . . . . . .5F **87**
Aluna Ct. SE15 . . . . . . .1E **107**
Alvanley Gdns. NW6 . . . .2D **45**
Alverstone Av.
  SW19 . . . . .2C **114**
Alverstone Ho. SE11 . . .2C **90**
Alverstone Rd. NW2 . . . .4E **43**
Alverton St. SE8 . . . . . . .1B **94**
  (not continuous)
Alvey St. SE17 . . . . .1A **92**
Alvington Cres. E8 . . . . .2B **50**
Alwold Cres. SE12 . . . . .4D **111**
Alwyne La. N1 . . . . .4D **49**
Alwyne Pl. N1 . . . . .3E **49**
Alwyne Rd. N1 . . . . .4E **49**
  SW19 . . . . .5B **114**
Alwyne Sq. N1 . . . . .3E **49**
Alwyne Vs. N1 . . . . .4D **49**
Alyth Gdns. NW11 . . . . .1C **30**
Alzette Ho. E2 . . . . .1F **65**
  (off Mace St.)
Amazon St. E1 . . . . .5C **64**
Ambassador Ho.
  NW8 . . . . .2F **59**
  (off Holly St.)
Ambassadors Ct. E8 . . . .4B **50**
  (off Holly St.)
  SW1 . . . . .2A **22**
Ambassador Sq. E14 . . .5D **81**
Ambassadors Theatre
  . . . . .4C **14**
  (off West St.)
Amber Ct. E15 . . . . .5E **53**
  (off Warton Rd.)
  N7 . . . . .3C **48**
  (off Bride St.)
Ambergate St. SE17 . . .1D **91**
Amberley Gro. SE26 . . .5D **121**
Amberley Rd. E10 . . . . .2C **38**
  W9 . . . . .4C **58**
Amber Way W3 . . . . . . .3A **70**
Amber Wharf E2 . . . . . . .5B **50**
  (off Nursery La.)
Amblecote Cl. SE12 . . . .3D **125**
Amblecote Mdws.
  SE12 . . . . .3D **125**
Amblecote Rd.
  SE12 . . . . .3D **125**
Ambler Rd. N4 . . . . .5D **35**
Ambleside
  BR1: Brom 5F **123**
  NW1 . . . . .1E **5**
  SW19 . . . . .1A **114**

Ambleside Av.
  SW16 . . . . .4F 117
Ambleside Cl. E9 . . . . .2E 51
  E10 . . . . .2D 39
Ambleside Gdns.
  SW16 . . . . .5F 117
Ambleside Point
  SE15 . . . . .3E 93
  (off Tustin Est.)
Ambleside Rd. NW10 . .4B 42
Ambrosden Av.
  SW1 . . . . . .5A 22 (4E 75)
Ambrose Av. NW11 . . . .2A 30
Ambrose Ho. E14 . . . . .4C 66
  (off Selsey St.)
Ambrose M. SW11 . . . . .5B 88
Ambrose St. SE16 . . . . .5D 79
Ambrose Wlk. E3 . . . . .1C 66
Ambulance Rd. E11 . . .1F 39
Amelia Ho. W6 . . . . . . .1E 85
  (off Queen Caroline St.)
Amelia St. SE17 . . . . . .1E 91
Amen Cnr.
  EC4 . . . . .3E 17 (5D 63)
  SW17 . . . . .5B 116
Amen Ct.
  EC4 . . . . .3E 17 (5D 63)
American International
  University in London, The
  Kensington Campus:
  —Ansdell Street 4D 73
  St Albans Grove
   . . . . .4D 73
  —Young Street 3D 73
American University of
  London, The 5B 34
America Sq.
  EC3 . . . .4F 19 (1B 78)
America St.
  SE1 . . . . . . .2F 25 (2E 77)
Amerland Rd.
  SW18 . . . . .3B 100
Amersham Gro. SE14 . .3B 94
Amersham Rd. SE14 . . .4B 94
Amersham Va. SE14 . . .3B 94
Amery Gdns. NW10 . . . .5E 43
Amery Ho. SE17 . . . . . .1A 92
  (off Kinglake St.)
Amesbury Av. SW2 . . . .2A 118
Amesbury Twr. SW8 . . .5E 89
Ames Cotts. E14 . . . . . .4A 66
  (off Maroon St.)
Ames Ho. E2 . . . . .1F 65
  (off Mace St.)
Amethyst Rd. E15 . . . . .1F 53
Amherst Ho. SE16 . . . . .3F 79
  (off Wolfe Cres.)
Amhurst Pde. N16 . . . . .2B 36
  (off Amhurst Pk.)
Amhurst Pk. N16 . . . . . .2F 35
Amhurst Pas. E8 . . . . . .1C 50
Amhurst Rd. E8 . . . . . . .2D 51
  N16 . . . . .1B 50
Amhurst Ter. E8 . . . . . .1C 50
Amias Ho. EC1 . . . . . . .3F 9
  (off Central St.)
Amiel St. E1 . . . . .3E 65
Amies St. SW11 . . . . . .1B 102
Amigo Ho. SE1 . . . . . . .5C 24
  (off Morley St.)

Amina Way SE16 . . . . . .4C 78
Amisha Ct. SE1 . . . . . . .5F 27
Amity Rd. E15 . . . . .4B 54
Ammanford Grn.
  NW9 . . . . .1A 28
Ammonite Ho. E15 . . . . .4B 54
Amner Rd. SW11 . . . . . .4C 102
Amor Rd. W6 . . . . .4E 71
Amory Ho. N1 . . . . .5B 48
  (off Barnsbury Est.)
Amott Rd. SE15 . . . . . . .1C 106
Amoy Pl. E14 . . . . .1C 80
  (not continuous)
Ampthill Est.
  NW1 . . . . . .1A 6 (1E 61)
Ampthill Sq.
  NW1 . . . . . .1A 6 (1E 61)
Ampton Pl.
  WC1 . . . . . .2F 7 (2B 62)
Ampton St.
  WC1 . . . . . .2F 7 (2B 62)
Amroth Cl. SE23 . . . . . .1D 121
Amroth Grn. NW9 . . . . .1A 28
Amstel Ct. SE15 . . . . . .3B 92
Amsterdam Rd. E14 . . . .4E 81
Amundsen Ct. E14 . . . . .1C 94
  (off Napier Av.)
Amwell Ct. Est. N4 . . . .4E 35
Amwell St.
  EC1 . . . . . .1B 8 (2C 62)
Amyruth Rd. SE4 . . . . . .3C 108
Anatola Rd. N19 . . . . . .4E 33
Anchor SW18 . . . . .2D 101
Anchorage Cl.
  SW19 . . . . .5C 114
Anchorage Ho. E14 . . . .1F 81
  (off Clove Cres.)
Anchorage Point E14 . . .3B 80
  (off Cuba St.)
Anchorage Point Ind. Est.
  SE7 . . . . .4E 83
Anchor & Hope La.
  SE7 . . . . .4D 83
Anchor Brewhouse
  SE1 . . . . . .2F 27 (2B 78)
Anchor Ct. SW1 . . . . . .5F 75
  (off Vauxhall Bri. Rd.)
Anchor Ho. E16 . . . . . . .4B 68
  (off Barking Rd.)
  E16 . . . . .5E 69
  (off Prince Regent La.)
  EC1 . . . . .3F 9
  (off Old St.)
  SW10 . . . . .2F 87
  (off Cremorne Est.)
Anchor M. N1 . . . . .3A 50
  SW12 . . . . .4D 103
Anchor Retail Pk. E1 . . .3E 65
Anchor St. SE16 . . . . . .5D 79
Anchor Ter. E1 . . . . .3E 65
  SE1 . . . . .1A 26
  (off Southwark Bri. Rd.)
Anchor Wharf E3 . . . . . .4D 67
  (off Yeo St.)
Anchor Yd.
  EC1 . . . . . .3A 10 (3E 63)
Ancill Cl. W6 . . . . .2A 86
Ancona Rd. NW10 . . . . .1C 56
Andalus Rd. SW9 . . . . .1A 104
Anderson Cl. W3 . . . . . .5A 56

Anderson Ct. NW2 . . . . .3E 29
Anderson Ho. E14 . . . . .1E 81
  (off Woolmore St.)
  SW17 . . . . .5F 115
Anderson Rd. E9 . . . . . .3F 51
Anderson Sq. N1 . . . . . .5D 49
  (off Gaskin St.)
Anderson St. SW3 . . . . .1B 88
Anderton Cl. SE5 . . . . . .1F 105
Andora Ct. NW6 . . . . . .4A 44
  (off Brondesbury Pk.)
Andover Av. E16 . . . . . .5F 69
Andover Pl. NW6 . . . . . .1D 59
Andover Rd. N7 . . . . . . .4B 34
Andoversford Ct.
  SE15 . . . . .2A 92
  (off Bibury Cl.)
Andover Ter. W6 . . . . . .5D 71
  (off Raynham Rd.)
Andre St. E8 . . . . .2C 50
Andrew Ct. SE23 . . . . . .2F 121
Andrewes Gdns.
  E6 . . . . .5F 69
Andrewes Highwalk
  EC2 . . . . .1A 18
Andrewes Ho. EC2 . . . .1A 18
Andrew Gibb Memorial, The
   . . . . .4B 96
Andrew Pl. SW8 . . . . . .3F 89
Andrew Reed Ho.
  SW18 . . . . .5A 100
  (off Linstead Way)
Andrews Crosse WC2 . . .3B 16
Andrews Ho. NW3 . . . . .4B 46
  (off Fellows Rd.)
Andrew's Rd. E8 . . . . . .5D 51
Andrew St. E14 . . . . . . .5C 67
Andrews Wlk. SE17 . . . .2D 91
Anerley Hill SE19 . . . . . .5B 120
Aneurin Bevan Ct.
  NW2 . . . . .4D 29
Anfield Cl. SW12 . . . . . .5E 103
ANGEL 1C 62
Angela Carter Cl.
  SW9 . . . . .1C 104
Angela Davies Ind. Est.
  SE24 . . . . .2D 105
Angel All. E1 . . . . .5B 64
  (off Whitechapel High St.)
Angel Centre, The
  N1 . . . . .1C 8
Angel Ct. EC2 . .2C 18 (5F 63)
  SW1 . . . . .2A 22 (2E 75)
Angel Ga. EC1 . . . . .1E 9
  (not continuous)
Angelica Ho. E3 . . . . . . .5B 52
  (off Sycamore Av.)
Angelina Ho. SE15 . . . . .4C 92
  (off Goldsmith Rd.)
Angelis Apartments
  N1 . . . . .1E 9
  (off Graham St.)
Angel La. E15 . . . . .3F 53
  EC4 . . . . . .5B 18 (1F 77)
Angell Pk. Gdns.
  SW9 . . . . .1C 104
Angell Rd. SW9 . . . . . . .1C 104
ANGELL TOWN 4C 90
Angell Town Est.
  SW9 . . . . .5C 90

Angel M. E1 . . . . .1D 79
  N1 . . . . .1C 62
  SW15 . . . . .5C 98
Angel Pl.
  SE1 . . . . . .3B 26 (3F 77)
Angel Sq. EC1 . . . . . . .1D 63
Angel St. EC1 . . .2F 17 (5E 63)
Angel Wlk. W6 . . . . . . .5E 71
Angel Wharf N1 . . . . . . .1E 63
Angel Yd. N6 . . . . .3C 32
Angerstein Bus. Pk.
  SE10 . . . . .5C 82
Angerstein La. SE3 . . . .4B 96
Anglebury W2 . . . . .5C 58
    (off Talbot Rd.)
Angler's La. NW5 . . . . .3D 47
Anglesea Ter. W6 . . . . .4D 71
    (off Wellesley Av.)
Anglesey Ho. E14 . . . . .5C 66
    (off Lindfield St.)
Angles Rd. SW16 . . . . .4A 118
Anglia Ho. E14 . . . . . . .5A 66
    (off Salmon La.)
Anglian Rd. E11 . . . . . .5F 39
Anglo Rd. E3 . . . . .1B 66
Angrave Ct. E8 . . . . . . .5B 50
    (off Scriven St.)
Angrave Pas. E8 . . . . . .5B 50
Angus Ho. SW2 . . . . . .5F 103
Angus Rd. E13 . . . . . . .2E 69
Angus St. SE14 . . . . . . .3A 94
Anhalt Rd. SW11 . . . . . .3A 88
Anley Rd. W14 . . . . . . .3F 71
Annabel Cl. E14 . . . . . .5D 67
Anna Cl. E8 . . . . .5B 50
Annandale Rd. SE10 . . .2B 96
  W4 . . . . .1A 84
Anne Compton M.
  SE12 . . . . .5B 110
Anne Goodman Ho.
  E1 . . . . .5E 65
    (off Jubilee St.)
Annes Ct. NW1 . . . . . . .3A 60
    (off Palgrave Gdns.)
Annesley Cl. NW10 . . . .5A 28
Annesley Ho. SW9 . . . . .4C 90
Annesley Rd. SE3 . . . . .4D 97
Annesley Wlk. N19 . . . . .4E 33
Annesmere Gdns.
  SE3 . . . . .1F 111
Anne St. E13 . . . . .3C 68
Annette Cres. N1 . . . . . .4E 49
Annette Rd. N7 . . . . . . .5B 34
    (not continuous)
Annexe Mkt. E1 . . . . . . .5F 11
    (off Old Spitalfields Market)
Annie Besant Cl. E3 . . . .5B 52
Anning St.
  EC2 . . . . .3E 11 (3A 64)
Annis Rd. E9 . . . . .3A 52
Ann La. SW10 . . . . .2F 87
Ann Moss Way SE16 . . . .4E 79
Ann's Cl. SW1 . . . . .4A 20
Ann's Pl. E1 . . . . .1F 19
Ann Stroud Ct. SE12 . . .3D 110
Ansar Gdns. E17 . . . . . .1B 38
Ansdell Rd. SE15 . . . . . .5E 93
Ansdell St. W8 . . . . . . .4D 73
Ansdell Ter. W8 . . . . . .4D 73

Ansell Ho. E1 . . . . .4E 65
    (off Mile End Rd.)
Ansell Rd. SW17 . . . . . .3A 116
Anselm Rd.
  SW6 . . . . .2C 86
Ansford Rd.
  BR1: Brom 5E 123
Ansleigh Pl. W11 . . . . . .1F 71
Anson Ho. E1 . . . . .3A 66
    (off Shandy St.)
  SW1 . . . . .2E 89
    (off Churchill Gdns.)
Anson Rd. N7 . . . . .1E 47
  NW2 . . . . .1D 43
Anstey Ho. E9 . . . . .5E 51
    (off Templecombe Rd.)
Anstey Rd. SE15 . . . . . .1C 106
Anstice Cl. W4 . . . . .3A 84
Antenor Ho. E2 . . . . . . .1D 65
    (off Old Bethnal Grn. Rd.)
Anthony Cope Ct.
  N1 . . . . .1C 10
    (off Chart St.)
Anthony Ct. W3 . . . . . . .3A 70
Anthony Ho. NW8 . . . . . .3A 60
    (off Ashbridge St.)
Anthony St. E1 . . . . . . .5D 65
Antigua M. E13 . . . . . . .2D 69
Antigua Wlk. SE19 . . . . .5F 119
Antilles Bay E14 . . . . . .3E 81
Antill Rd. E3 . . . . .2A 66
Antill Ter. E1 . . . . .5F 65
Antoinette M. NW2 . . . . .3C 42
Antonine Hgts. SE1 . . . . .4D 27
Anton St. E8 . . . . .2C 50
Antony Ho. SE16 . . . . . .5E 79
    (off Raymouth Rd.)
Antrim Gro. NW3 . . . . . .3B 46
Antrim Ho. E3 . . . . .5B 52
    (off Birdsfield La.)
Antrim Rd. NW3 . . . . . . .3B 46
AOP Gallery 3D 11
    (off Leonard St.)
Apex Ho. E1 . . . . .3F 11
    (off Bacon St.)
Apex Ind. Est. NW10 . . .3B 56
Aphrodite Ct. E14 . . . . . .5C 80
    (off Homer Dr.)
  E15 . . . . .5E 53
    (off Warton St.)
Apollo Bldg. E14 . . . . . .5C 80
Apollo Bus. Cen. SE8 . . .1F 93
Apollo Ct. E1 . . . . .1C 78
    (off Thomas More St.)
  E15 . . . . .5E 53
    (off High St.)
  SW9 . . . . .4C 90
    (off Southey Rd.)
Apollo Ho. E2 . . . . .1D 65
    (off St Jude's Rd.)
  E3 . . . . .1C 66
    (off Garrison Rd.)
  N6 . . . . .2C 32
  SW10 . . . . .3F 87
    (off Milman's St.)
Apollo Pl. E11 . . . . .5A 40
  SW10 . . . . .3F 87
Apollo Theatre
  Soho 4B 14
    (off Shaftesbury Av.)

Apollo Victoria Theatre
  . . . . .4E 75
    (off Wilton Rd.)
Apollo West End Cinema
  . . . . .5B 14
    (off Regent St.)
Apostles, The SE23 . . . .2F 121
    (off Church Ri.)
Apothecary St.
  EC4 . . . . . . .3D 17 (5D 63)
Appach Rd. SW2 . . . . . .3C 104
Appian Ct. E3 . . . . .1B 66
    (off Parnell Rd.)
Apple Blossom Ct.
  SW8 . . . . .3F 89
    (off Pascal St.)
Appleby Cl. N15 . . . . . . .1F 35
Appleby Rd. E8 . . . . . . .4C 50
  E16 . . . . .5B 68
Appleby St. E2 . . . . .1B 64
Appledore Cl.
  SW17 . . . . .2B 116
Appleford Ho. W10 . . . . .3A 58
    (off Bosworth Rd.)
Appleford Rd. W10 . . . . .3A 58
Applegarth Ho. SE1 . . . .3E 25
  SE15 . . . . .3C 92
    (off Bird in Bush Rd.)
Applegarth Rd. W14 . . . .4F 71
Apple Rd. E11 . . . . .5A 40
Appleshaw Ho. SE5 . . . .1A 106
Appleton Rd. SE9 . . . . . .1F 111
Apple Tree Yd. E1 . . . . . .2F 65
    (off Longnor Rd.)
  SW1 . . . . . . .1A 22 (2E 75)
Applewood Cl. NW2 . . . .5D 29
Applewood Dr. E13 . . . . .3D 69
Appold St.
  EC2 . . . . . . .5D 11 (4A 64)
Apprentice Way
  E5 . . . . .1D 51
  W3 . . . . .5A 56
Approach, The NW4 . . . .1F 29
  W3 . . . . .5A 56
Approach Rd. N16 . . . . .1A 50
Approach Rd. E2 . . . . . .1E 65
April Ct. E2 . . . . .1C 64
    (off Teale St.)
April Glen SE23 . . . . . . .3F 121
April St. E8 . . . . .1B 50
Apsley Centre, The
  NW2 . . . . .4C 28
Apsley House
  . . . . .3C 20 (3C 74)
Apsley Ho. E1 . . . . .4E 65
    (off Stepney Way)
  NW8 . . . . .1F 59
    (off Finchley Rd.)
Apsley Way NW2 . . . . . .4C 28
  W1 . . . . . . .3C 20 (3C 74)
    (not continuous)
Aquarelle Ho.
  EC1 . . . . . . .1F 9 (2E 63)
Aquarius Bus. Pk.
  NW2 . . . . .3C 28
    (off Priestley Way)
Aquarius Golf Course
  . . . . .4E 107
Aquatics Centre, Olympic Pk.
  . . . . .4D 53
Aquila St. NW8 . . . . . . .1F 59

Aquinas St.
SE1 . . . . . . 2C **24** (2C **76**)
Arabella Ct. NW8 . . . . .1E **59**
(off Marlborough Pl.)
Arabella Dr.
SW15 . . . . .2A **98**
Arabian Ho. E1 . . . . . .3A **66**
(off Ernest St.)
Arabin Rd. SE4 . . . . . .2A **108**
Aragon Ct. SE11 . . . . . .1C **90**
(off Hotspur St.)
Aragon Ho. E16 . . . . . .2C **82**
(off Capulet M.)
Aragon Twr. SE8 . . . . . .5B **80**
Aral Ho. E1 . . . . .3F **65**
(off Ernest St.)
Aran Lodge NW6 . . . . . .4C **44**
(off Woodchurch Rd.)
Aran M. N7 . . . . .4C **48**
(off St Clements St.)
Arapiles Ho. E14 . . . . . .5F **67**
(off Blair St.)
Arbery Rd. E3 . . . . .2A **66**
Arbon Ct. N1 . . . . .5E **49**
(off Linton St.)
Arbor Ct. N16 . . . . .4F **35**
Arboretum Cl. SW2 . . . .3F **49**
(off Dove Rd.)
Arborfield Cl. SW2 . . .1B **118**
Arborfield Ho. E14 . . . . .1C **80**
(off E. India Dock Rd.)
Arbour Ho. E1 . . . . .5F **65**
(off Arbour Sq.)
Arbour Sq. E1 . . . . .5F **65**
Arbury Ter. SE26 . . . . . .3C **120**
Arbuthnot Rd. SE14 . . .5F **93**
Arbutus St. E8 . . . . .5B **50**
Arcade, The E20 . . . . . .3E **53**
*(within Westfield Stratford
City Shopping Cen.)*
EC2 . . . . .1D **19**
N7 . . . . .1A **48**
(off Macready Pl.)
Arcadia Ct. E1 . . . . .2F **19**
Arcadian Pl. SW18 . . . .5B **100**
Arcadia St. E14 . . . . . .5C **66**
Archangel St. SE16 . . . .3F **79**
Archbishop's Pl.
SW2 . . . . .5B **104**
Archdale Ct. W12 . . . . .2D **71**
Archdale Ho. SE1 . . . . .5D **27**
(off Long La.)
Archdale Rd. SE22 . . . .3B **106**
Archel Rd. W14 . . . . . . .2B **86**
Archer Apartments
N1 . . . . .1A **64**
(off Fern Cl.)
Archer Ho. N1 . . . . .5A **50**
(off Whitmore Est.)
SE14 . . . . .4A **94**
SW11 . . . . .4F **87**
W11 . . . . .1B **72**
(off Westbourne Gro.)
Archer M. SW9 . . . . . . .1A **104**
Archers Lodge SE16 . . .1C **92**
(off Culloden Cl.)
Archer Sq. SE14 . . . . . .2A **94**
Archer St.
W1 . . . .4B **14** (1B **75**)
Archery Cl. W2 . . . . . . .5A **60**

Archery Flds. Ho.
WC1 . . . . .1A **8**
(off Wharton St.)
Archery Steps W2 . . . . .1A **74**
(off St George's Flds.)
Arches, The E16 . . . . . .3A **68**
NW1 . . . . .4D **47**
SE8 . . . . .2A **94**
SW8 . . . . .3F **89**
WC2 . . . . .1E **23**
(off Villiers St.)
Arches Leisure Cen. . . .2A **96**
Archibald M.
W1 . . . . .5D **13** (1D **75**)
Archibald Rd. N7 . . . . . .1F **47**
Archibald St. E3 . . . . . .2C **66**
Archie St.
SE1 . . . . .4E **27** (3A **78**)
Arch St. SE1 . . . . .4E **77**
ARCHWAY 4E **33**
Archway Bus. Cen.
N19 . . . . .5F **33**
Archway Cl. N19 . . . . . .4E **33**
SW19 . . . . .3D **115**
W10 . . . . .4F **57**
Archway Leisure Cen.
. . . . .4E **33**
Archway Mall N19 . . . . .4E **33**
Archway M. SW15 . . . . .2A **100**
(off Putney Bri. Rd.)
Archway Rd. N6 . . . . . . .1C **32**
N19 . . . . .1C **32**
Archway St. SW13 . . . . .1A **98**
Arcola St. E8 . . . . .2B **50**
Arcola Theatre 2B **50**
Arctic St. NW5 . . . . .2D **47**
Arcus Rd.
BR1: Brom 5A **124**
Ardbeg Rd. SE24 . . . . . .3F **105**
Arden Ct. Gdns. N2 . . . .1F **31**
Arden Cres. E14 . . . . . .5C **80**
Arden Est. N1 . . . . .1A **64**
Arden Ho. N1 . . . . .1D **11**
SE11 . . . . .5B **76**
(off Black Prince Rd.)
SW9 . . . . .5A **90**
(off Grantham Rd.)
Ardent Ho. E3 . . . . .1A **66**
(off Roman Rd.)
Ardfillan Rd. SE6 . . . . . .1F **123**
Ardgowan Rd. SE6 . . . . .5A **110**
Ardilaun Rd. N5 . . . . . . .1E **49**
Ardleigh Rd. N1 . . . . . . .3A **50**
Ardley Cl. NW10 . . . . . . .5A **28**
SE6 . . . . .3A **122**
Ardlui Rd. SE27 . . . . . . .2E **119**
Ardmere Rd. SE13 . . . . .4F **109**
Ardoch Rd. SE6 . . . . . . .2F **123**
Ardshiel Cl. SW15 . . . . .1F **99**
Ardwell Rd. SW2 . . . . . .2A **118**
Ardwick Rd. NW2 . . . . . .1C **44**
Arena Bus. Cen. N4 . . . .1E **35**
Arena Ho. E3 . . . . .1C **66**
(off Lefevre Wlk.)
Arena Shop. Pk. N4 . . . .1D **35**
Ares Ct. E14 . . . . .5C **80**
(off Homer Dr.)
Arethusa Ho. E14 . . . . . .5C **80**
(off Cahir St.)

Argall Av. E10 . . . . .2F **37**
Argall Way E10 . . . . .3F **37**
Argent Ct. E14 . . . . .4C **66**
(off Thomas Rd.)
Argenton Twr.
SW18 . . . . .4D **101**
(off Mapleton Cres.)
Argo Bus. Cen. NW6 . . .2C **58**
Argon M. SW6 . . . . .3C **86**
Argos Ct. SW9 . . . . .4C **90**
(off Caldwell St.)
Argos Ho. E2 . . . . .1D **65**
(off Old Bethnal Grn. Rd.)
Argosy Ho. SE8 . . . . . . .5A **80**
Argyle Ho. E14 . . . . .4E **81**
Argyle Pl. W6 . . . . .5D **71**
Argyle Rd. E1 . . . . .3F **65**
E15 . . . . .1A **54**
E16 . . . . .5D **69**
Argyle Sq.
WC1 . . . . . . .1E **7** (2A **62**)
(not continuous)
Argyle St.
WC1 . . . . . . .1D **7** (2A **62**)
Argyle Wlk.
WC1 . . . . . . .2E **7** (2A **62**)
Argyle Way SE16 . . . . . .1C **92**
Argyll Cl. SW9 . . . . .1B **104**
Argyll Ct. SW2 . . . . .5A **104**
(off New Pk. Rd.)
Argyll Mans.
SW3 . . . . .2F **87**
W14 . . . . .5A **72**
(off Hammersmith Rd.)
Argyll Rd. W8 . . . . .3C **72**
Argyll St. W1 . . .3F **13** (5E **61**)
Arica Ho. SE16 . . . . .4D **79**
(off Slippers Pl.)
Arica Rd. SE4 . . . . .2A **108**
Ariel Apartments
E16 . . . . .5C **68**
Ariel Ct. SE11 . . . . .5D **77**
Ariel Rd. NW6 . . . . .3C **44**
Ariel Way W12 . . . . .2E **71**
Aristotle Rd. SW4 . . . . .1F **103**
Arizona Bldg. SE10 . . . .4D **95**
(off Deal's Gateway)
Ark, The W6 . . . . .1F **85**
(off Talgarth Rd.)
Arkindale Rd. SE6 . . . . .3E **123**
Arkley Cres. E17 . . . . . .1B **38**
Arkley Rd. E17 . . . . .1B **38**
Arklow Ho. SE17 . . . . . .2F **91**
Arklow Rd. SE14 . . . . . .2B **94**
Arklow Rd. Trad. Est.
SE14 . . . . .2A **94**
Arkwright Rd. NW3 . . . . .2E **45**
Arlesey Cl. SW15 . . . . . .3A **100**
Arlesford Rd. SW9 . . . . .1A **104**
Arlidge Ho. EC1 . . . . .5C **8**
(off Kirby St.)
Arlingford Rd. SW2 . . . .3C **104**
Arlington Av. N1 . . . . . . .5E **49**
(not continuous)
Arlington Bldg. E3 . . . . .1C **66**
Arlington Cl. SE13 . . . . .3F **109**
Arlington Ho. EC1 . . . . . . .1C **8**
(off Arlington Way)
SE8 . . . . .2B **94**
(off Evelyn St.)

Arlington Ho.
SW1 . . . . . .1F **21** (2E **75**)
W12 . . . . .2D **71**
(off Tunis Rd.)
Arlington Lodge
SW2 . . . . .2B **104**
Arlington Pl. SE10 . . . . . .3E **95**
Arlington Rd. NW1 . . . . .5D **47**
Arlington Sq. N1 . . . . . . .5E **49**
Arlington St.
SW1 . . . . . .1F **21** (2E **75**)
Arlington Way
EC1 . . . . . . .1C **8** (2C **62**)
Armada Ct. SE8 . . . . . . .2C **94**
Armadale Rd. SW6 . . . . .3C **86**
Armada St. SE8 . . . . . . .2C **94**
Armagh Rd. E3 . . . . .5B **52**
Arminger Rd. W12 . . . . . .2D **71**
Armitage Ho. NW1 . . . . . .4A **60**
(off Lisson Gro.)
Armitage Rd. NW11 . . . .3A **30**
SE10 . . . . .1B **96**
Armour Cl. N7 . . . . .3B **48**
Armoury Ho. E3 . . . . . .5A **52**
(off Gunmakers La.)
Armoury Rd. SE8 . . . . . .5D **95**
Armoury Way SW18 . . . .3C **100**
Armsby Ho. E1 . . . . .4E **65**
(off Stepney Way)
Armstrong Rd. NW10 . . . .4A **42**
SW7 . . . . .4F **73**
W3 . . . . .2B **70**
Arnal Cres. SW18 . . . . .5A **100**
Arncliffe NW6 . . . . .1D **59**
Arndale Wlk. SW18 . . .3D **101**
Arne Ho. SE11 . . . . .1B **90**
(off Tylers St.)
Arne St. WC2 . . . .3E **15** (5A **62**)
Arne Wlk. SE3 . . . . .2B **110**
Arneway St. SW1 . . . . . .4F **75**
Arnewood Ct. SW15 . . .1C **112**
Arngask Rd. SE6 . . . . . .5F **109**
Arnhem Pl. E14 . . . . . . .4C **80**
Arnhem Way SE22 . . . . .3A **106**
Arnhem Wharf E14 . . . .4B **80**
Arnold Cir. E2 . . .2F **11** (2B **64**)
Arnold Est.
SE1 . . . . . .4F **27** (3B **78**)
(not continuous)
Arnold Ho. SE3 . . . . . . .3E **97**
(off Shooters Hill Rd.)
SE17 . . . . .1D **91**
(off Doddington Gro.)
Arnold Mans. W14 . . . . .2B **86**
(off Queen's Club Gdns.)
Arnold Rd. E3 . . . . .2C **66**
Arnot Ho. SE5 . . . . .3E **91**
(off Comber Gro.)
Arnott Cl. W4 . . . . .5A **70**
Arnould Av. SE5 . . . . . .2F **105**
Arnside Ho. SE17 . . . . . .2F **91**
(off Arnside St.)
Arnside St. SE17 . . . . . .2F **91**
Arnulf St. SE6 . . . . .4D **123**
Arnulls Rd. SW16 . . . . .5D **119**
Arodene Rd. SW2 . . . . . .4B **104**
Arragon Rd. E6 . . . . . . .5F **55**
SW18 . . . . .1C **114**
Arran Ct. NW10 . . . . . . .5A **28**
Arran Dr. E12 . . . . .3F **41**

Arran Ho. E14 . . . . .2E **81**
(off Raleana Rd.)
Arran Rd. SE6 . . . . .2D **123**
Arran Wlk. N1 . . . . .4E **49**
Arrol Ho.
SE1 . . . . . .5A **26** (4E **77**)
Arrow Ct. SW5 . . . . .5C **72**
(off W. Cromwell Rd.)
Arrow Ho. N1 . . . . .5A **50**
(off Wilmer Gdns.)
Arrow Rd. E3 . . . . .2D **67**
Arrows Ho. SE15 . . . . . .3E **93**
(off Clifton Way)
Arrowsmith Ho. SE11 . . .1B **90**
(off Tylers St.)
Arsenal FC 1C **48**
Arta Ho. E1 . . . . .5E **65**
(off Devonport St.)
Artbrand Ho. SE1 . . . . . .4D **27**
(off Leathermarket St.)
Artemis SW11 . . . . .5B **88**
Artemis Ct. E14 . . . . . . .5C **80**
(off Homer Dr.)
Artemis Pl. SW18 . . . . .5B **100**
Artesian Cl. NW10 . . . . .4A **42**
Artesian Ho. SE1 . . . . . .4B **78**
(off Aslcot Rd.)
Artesian Rd. W2 . . . . . . .5C **58**
Artesian Wlk. E11 . . . . . .5A **40**
Arthingworth St. E15 . . .5A **54**
Arthur Ct. SW11 . . . . . . .4C **88**
W2 . . . . .5D **59**
(off Queensway)
W10 . . . . .5F **57**
(off Silchester Rd.)
Arthur Deakin Ho. E1 . . .4C **64**
(off Hunton St.)
Arthurdon Rd. SE4 . . . . .3C **108**
Arthur Henderson Ho.
SW6 . . . . .5B **86**
(off Fulham Rd.)
Arthur Horsley Wlk.
E7 . . . . .2B **54**
(off Tower Hamlets Rd.)
Arthur Ho. N1 . . . . .5A **50**
(off New Era Est.)
Arthur Newton Ho.
SW11 . . . . .1F **101**
(off Winstanley Est.)
Arthur Rd. N7 . . . . .1B **48**
SW19 . . . . .5B **114**
Arthur St.
EC4 . . . . . .4C **18** (1F **77**)
Arthur Wade Ho. E2 . . . .1F **11**
(off Baroness Rd.)
Artichoke Hill E1 . . . . . .1D **79**
Artichoke M. SE5 . . . . . .4F **91**
(off Artichoke Pl.)
Artichoke Pl. SE5 . . . . . .4F **91**
Artillery Building, The
E1 . . . . .1E **19**
(off Artillery La.)
Artillery Ho. E3 . . . . .5A **52**
(off Barge La.)
E15 . . . . .3A **54**
Artillery La.
E1 . . . . . .1E **19** (4A **64**)
W12 . . . . .5C **56**
Artillery Mans. SW1 . . . .5B **22**
Artillery Pas. E1 . . . . . . .1F **19**

Artillery Pl.
SW1 . . . . . .5B **22** (4F **75**)
Artillery Row
SW1 . . . . . .5B **22** (4F **75**)
Artisan Ct. E8 . . . . .3C **50**
Artisan M. NW10 . . . . . .2F **57**
(off Warfield Rd.)
Artisan Quarter
NW10 . . . . .2F **57**
(off Wellington Rd.)
Artizan St. E1 . . . . .2F **19**
Arts Theatre 4D **15**
(off Gt. Newport St.)
Arundel Bldgs. SE1 . . . .4A **78**
(off Swan Mead)
Arundel Ct. E15 . . . . .1A **54**
SW11 . . . . .3A **102**
Arundel Ct. SE16 . . . . . .1D **93**
(off Verney Rd.)
SW3 . . . . .1A **88**
(off Jubilee Pl.)
SW13 . . . . .2D **85**
(off Arundel Ter.)
W11 . . . . .1B **72**
(off Arundel Gdns.)
Arundel Gdns. W11 . . . .1B **72**
Arundel Gt. Ct.
WC2 . . . . . .4A **16** (1B **76**)
Arundel Gro. N16 . . . . . .2A **50**
Arundel Mans. SW6 . . . .4B **86**
(off Kelvedon Rd.)
Arundel Pl. N1 . . . . .3C **48**
Arundel Sq. N7 . . . . .3C **48**
Arundel St.
WC2 . . . . . .4A **16** (1B **76**)
Arundel Ter. SW13 . . . . .2D **85**
Arvon Rd. N5 . . . . .2C **48**
(not continuous)
Asbridge Ct. W6 . . . . . . .4D **71**
(off Dalling Rd.)
Ascalon Ho. SW8 . . . . . .3E **89**
(off Thessaly Rd.)
Ascalon St. SW8 . . . . . . .3E **89**
Ascensis Twr. SW18 . . . .2E **101**
Ascham St. NW5 . . . . . . .2E **47**
Ascot Ct. NW8 . . . . .2F **59**
(off Grove End Rd.)
Ascot Ho. NW1 . . . . .1E **5**
(off Redhill St.)
W9 . . . . .3C **58**
(off Harrow Rd.)
Ascot Lodge NW6 . . . . . .5D **45**
Ascot Rd. N15 . . . . .1F **35**
SW17 . . . . .5C **116**
Ashanti M. E8 . . . . .2E **51**
Ashbee Ho. E2 . . . . .2E **65**
(off Portman Pl.)
Ashbourne Ct. E5 . . . . . .1A **52**
Ashbourne Gro.
SE22 . . . . .2B **106**
W4 . . . . .1A **84**
Ashbridge Rd. E11 . . . . .2A **40**
Ashbridge St. NW8 . . . . .3A **60**
Ashbrook Rd. N19 . . . . . .3F **33**
Ashburn Gdns. SW7 . . . .5E **73**
Ashburnham Gro.
SE10 . . . . .3D **95**
Ashburnham Mans.
SW10 . . . . .3E **87**
(off Ashburnham Rd.)

Ashburnham Pl.
SE10 . . . . .3D **95**
Ashburnham Retreat
SE10 . . . . .3D **95**
Ashburnham Rd.
NW10 . . . . .2E **57**
SW10 . . . . .3E **87**
Ashburnham Twr.
SW10 . . . . .3F **87**
(off Worlds End Est.)
Ashburn Pl. SW7 . . . .5E **73**
Ashburton Ent. Cen.
SW15 . . . . .4E **99**
ASHBURTON GROVE . .1C **48**
Ashburton Ho.
W9 . . . . .3B **58**
(off Fernhead Rd.)
Ashburton Rd. E16 . . .5C **68**
Ashburton Ter. E13 . . .1C **68**
Ashburton Triangle
N7 . . . . .1C **48**
Ashbury Pl. SW19 . . .5E **115**
Ashbury Rd. SW11 . . .1B **102**
Ashby Ct. *NW8* 3F **59**
(off Pollitt Dr.)
Ashby Gro. N1 . . . . . .4E **49**
(not continuous)
Ashby Ho. *N1* 4E **49**
(off Essex Rd.)
SW9 . . . . .5D **91**
Ashby M. SE4 . . . . . . .5B **94**
SW2 . . . . .3A **104**
(off Prague Pl.)
Ashby Rd. SE4 . . . . . .5B **94**
Ashbys Ct. *E3* 1B **66**
(off Centurion La.)
Ashby St. EC1 . . .2E **9** (2D **63**)
Aschurch Gro. W12 . . .4C **70**
Aschurch Pk. Vs.
W12 . . . . .4C **70**
Aschurch Ter. W12 . . .4C **70**
Ashcombe Ho. *E3* 2D **67**
(off Bruce Rd.)
Ashcombe Pk. NW2 . . .5A **28**
Ashcombe Rd.
SW19 . . . . .5C **114**
Ashcombe St. SW6 . . .5D **87**
Ashcroft Ho. *SW8* 4E **89**
(off Wadhurst Rd.)
Ashcroft Sq. W6 . . . . .5E **71**
Ashdale Ho. N4 . . . . . .2F **35**
Ashdale Rd. SE12 . . . .1D **125**
Ashdene SE15 . . . . . .3D **93**
Ashdon Rd. NW10 . . . .5B **42**
Ashdown Cres. NW5 . . .2C **46**
Ashdown Ho. *SW1* 4E **75**
(off Victoria St.)
Ashdown Wlk. E14 . . . .5C **80**
Ashdown Way
SW17 . . . . .2C **116**
Ashenden *SE17* 5E **77**
(off Deacon Way)
Ashenden Rd. E5 . . . . .2A **52**
Ashen Gro. SW19 . . . .3C **114**
Ashentree Ct. EC4 . . . .3C **16**
Asher Way E1 . . . . . . .1C **78**
Ashfield Ct. *SW9* 5A **90**
(off Clapham Rd.)
Ashfield Ho. *W14* 1B **86**
(off W. Cromwell Rd.)

Ashfield Rd. N4 . . . . . .1E **35**
W3 . . . . .2B **70**
Ashfield St. E1 . . . . . .4D **65**
(not continuous)
Ashfield Yd. E1 . . . . . .4E **65**
Ashford Cl. E17 . . . . . .1B **38**
Ashford Ct. NW2 . . . . .1F **43**
Ashford Ho. SE8 . . . . .2B **94**
SW9 . . . . .2D **105**
Ashford Pas.
NW2 . . . . .1F **43**
Ashford Rd. NW2 . . . . .1F **43**
Ashford St.
N1 . . . . . .1D **11** (2A **64**)
Ash Gro. E8 . . . . .5D **51**
(not continuous)
NW2 . . . . .1F **43**
SE12 . . . . .1C **124**
Ashgrove Ct. *W9* 4C **58**
(off Elmfield Way)
Ashgrove Ho. *SW1* 1F **89**
(off Lindsay Sq.)
Ashgrove Rd.
BR1: Brom 5F **123**
Ash Ho. *E14* 3E **81**
(off E. Ferry Rd.)
SE1 . . . . .5B **78**
(off Longfield Est.)
W10 . . . . .3A **58**
(off Heather Wlk.)
Ashington Ho. *E1* 3D **65**
(off Barnsley St.)
Ashington Rd. SW6 . . . .5B **86**
Ashlake Rd. SW16 . . . .4A **118**
Ashland Pl.
W1 . . . . . .5B **4** (4C **60**)
Ashleigh Commercial Est.
SE7 . . . . .4E **83**
Ashleigh M. *SE15* 1B **106**
(off Oglander Rd.)
Ashleigh Point SE23 . .3F **121**
Ashleigh Rd. SW14 . . . .1A **98**
Ashley Ct. *SW1* 4E **75**
(off Morpeth Ter.)
Ashley Cres. SW11 . . . .1C **102**
Ashley Gdns.
SW1 . . . . .5A **22** (4E **75**)
(not continuous)
Ashley Pl.
SW1 . . . . . .5F **21** (4E **75**)
(not continuous)
Ashley Rd. E7 . . . . . . .4E **55**
N19 . . . . .3A **34**
SW19 . . . . .5D **115**
Ashlin Rd. E15 . . . . . .1F **53**
Ashlone Rd. SW15 . . . .1E **99**
Ashmead Bus. Cen.
E16 . . . . .3F **67**
Ashmead Ho. *E9* 2A **52**
(off Homerton Rd.)
Ashmead M. SE8 . . . . .5C **94**
Ashmead Rd. SE8 . . . .5C **94**
Ashmere Gro. SW2 . . . .2A **104**
Ash M. NW5 . . . . .2E **47**
Ashmill St. NW1 . . . . . .4A **60**
Ashmole Pl. SW8 . . . . .2B **90**
Ashmole St. SW8 . . . . .2B **90**
Ashmore NW1 . . . . . . .4F **47**
(off Agar Gro.)
Ashmore Cl. SE15 . . . .3B **92**

Ashmore Ho. *W14* 4A **72**
(off Russell Rd.)
Ashmore Rd. W9 . . . . .1B **58**
Ashmount Est. N19 . . . .2F **33**
Ashmount Rd. N19 . . . .2E **33**
Ashness Ho. SW11 . . . .3B **102**
Ashpark Ho. *E14* 5B **66**
(off Norbiton Rd.)
Ash Rd. E15 . . . . .2A **54**
Ashtead Rd. E5 . . . . . .2C **36**
Ashton Hgts. SE23 . . . .1E **121**
Ashton Ho. *SE11* 1D **91**
(off Cottington St.)
SW9 . . . . .3C **90**
Ashton Rd. E15 . . . . . .2F **53**
Ashton St. E14 . . . . . .1E **81**
Ash Tree Ho. *SE5* 3E **91**
(off Pitman St.)
Ashurst Gdns. SW2 . . . .1C **118**
Ashvale Ct. *E3* 1C **66**
(off Matilda Gdns.)
Ashvale Rd. SW17 . . . .5B **116**
Ashville Rd. E11 . . . . . .4F **39**
Ashwater Rd. SE12 . . . .1C **124**
Ashwin St. E8 . . . . . . .3B **50**
Ashworth Cl. SE5 . . . . .5F **91**
Ashworth Mans. *W9* 2D **59**
(off Elgin Av.)
Ashworth Rd. W9 . . . . .2D **59**
Aske Ho. N1 . . . . .1D **11**
Asker Ho. N7 . . . . .1A **48**
Aske St. N1 . . . .1D **11** (2A **64**)
Askew Cres. W12 . . . . .3B **70**
Askew Est. *W12* 2B **70**
(off Uxbridge Rd.)
Askew Rd. W12 . . . . . .3B **70**
Askham Ct. W12 . . . . . .2C **70**
Askham Rd. W12 . . . . . .2C **70**
Askill Dr. SW15 . . . . . .3A **100**
Asland Rd. E15 . . . . . .5A **54**
Aslett St. SW18 . . . . . .5D **101**
Asman Ho. *N1* 1D **63**
(off Colebrooke Rd.)
Asmara Rd. NW2 . . . . .2A **44**
Asmuns Hill NW11 . . . .1C **30**
Asmuns Pl. NW11 . . . . .1B **30**
Asolando Dr. SE17 . . . .5E **77**
Aspect Ct. *E14* 3E **81**
(off Manchester Rd.)
SW6 . . . . .5E **87**
Aspen Cl. N19 . . . . . . .4E **33**
Aspen Gdns. W6 . . . . . .1D **85**
Aspen Ho. *E15* 2A **68**
(off Teasel Way)
SE15 . . . . .2E **93**
(off Sharratt St.)
Aspenlea Rd. W6 . . . . . .2F **85**
Aspen Lodge *W8* 4D **73**
(off Abbots Wlk.)
Aspen Way E14 . . . . . .1D **81**
Aspern Gro. NW3 . . . . .2A **46**
Aspinall Rd. SE4 . . . . . .1F **107**
(not continuous)
Aspinden Rd. SE16 . . . .5D **79**
Aspley Rd. SW18 . . . . .3D **101**
Asquith Ho. *SW1* 4F **75**
(off Monck St.)
Assam St. *E1* 5C **64**
(off White Church La.)
Assata M. N1 . . . . .3D **49**

Assembly Apartments
SE15 . . . . .4E **93**
(off York Gro.)
Assembly Pas. E1 . . . . .4E **65**
Astbury Bus. Pk.
SE15 . . . . .4E **93**
Astbury Ho. SE11 . . .4C **76**
(off Lambeth Wlk.)
Astbury Rd. SE15 . . . .4E **93**
Astell Ho. SW3 . . . . .1A **88**
(off Astell St.)
Astell St. SW3 . . . . . .1A **88**
Aster Ct. E5 . . . . .4E **37**
(off Woodmill Rd.)
Aste St. E14 . . . . .3E **81**
Astey's Row N1 . . . . .4E **49**
Astle St. SW11 . . . . . .5C **88**
Astley Av. NW2 . . . . . .2E **43**
Astley Ho. SE1 . . . . . .1B **92**
(off Rowcross St.)
SW13 . . . . .2D **85**
(off Wyatt Dr.)
W2 . . . . .4C **58**
(off Alfred Rd.)
Aston Ho. SW8 . . . . . .4F **89**
W11 . . . . .1B **72**
(off Westbourne Gro.)
Aston M. W10 . . . . . . .2F **57**
Aston St. E14 . . . . . . .4A **66**
Aston Ter. SW12 . . . .4D **103**
Astonville St. SW18 . .1C **114**
Aston Webb Ho. SE1 . .2D **77**
Astor Ct. E16 . . . . . . .5E **69**
(off Ripley Rd.)
SW6 . . . . .3E **87**
(off Maynard Cl.)
Astoria Ct. E8 . . . . . .4B **50**
(off Queensbridge Rd.)
Astoria Mans.
SW16 . . . . .3A **118**
Astoria Wlk. SW9 . . .1C **104**
Astra Ho. E3 . . . . .2B **66**
(off Alfred St.)
SE14 . . . . .2B **94**
(off Arklow Rd.)
Astral Ho. E1 . . . . . . .1E **19**
(off Middlesex St.)
Astrop M. W6 . . . . . . .4E **71**
Astrop Ter. W6 . . . . . .3E **71**
Astwood M. SW7 . . . . .5E **73**
Asylum Rd. SE15 . . . .3D **93**
Atalanta St. SW6 . . . .3F **85**
Atelier Ct. Central
E14 . . . . .4E **67**
(off Leven Rd.)
Atelier Ct. Nth. E14 . .4E **67**
(off Leven Rd.)
Atelier Ct. Sth. E14 . .4E **67**
(off Leven Rd.)
Atheldene Rd.
SW18 . . . . .1D **115**
Athelney St. SE6 . . . .3C **122**
Athelstane Gro. E3 . . .1B **66**
Athelstane M. N4 . . . .3C **34**
Athelstan Gdns. NW6 . .4A **44**
Athelstan Ho. E9 . . . . .2B **52**
(off Homerton Rd.)
Athena Bldgs. E15 . . .5B **53**
Athena Ct. SE1 . . . . . .5D **27**
(off City Wlk.)

Athenaeum Ct.
N5 . . . . .1E **49**
Athene Pl. EC4 . . . . . .2C **16**
(off Thavie's Inn)
Athenia Ho. E14 . . . . .5F **67**
(off Blair St.)
Athenlay Rd.
SE15 . . . . .3F **107**
Athens Gdns. W9 . . . . .3C **58**
(off Harrow Rd.)
Atherden Rd. E5 . . . . .1E **51**
Atherfold Rd. SW9 . . .1A **104**
Atherstone Ct. W2 . . . .4D **59**
(off Delamere Ter.)
Atherstone M. SW7 . . .5E **73**
Atherton Dr. SW19 . . .4F **113**
Atherton Leisure Cen.
. . . . .3B **54**
Atherton M. E7 . . . . . .3B **54**
Atherton Rd. E7 . . . . . .3B **54**
SW13 . . . . .3C **84**
Atherton St. SW11 . . . .5A **88**
Athlone Cl. E5 . . . . . . .2D **51**
Athlone Ho. E1 . . . . . .5E **65**
(off Sidney St.)
Athlone Rd. SW2 . . . .5B **104**
Athlone St. NW5 . . . . .3C **46**
Atholl Ho. W9 . . . . . . .2E **59**
(off Maida Va.)
Athol Sq. E14 . . . . . . .5E **67**
Atkin Bldg. WC1 . . . . .5A **8**
(off Raymond Bldgs.)
Atkins Ct. E3 . . . . .5B **52**
(off Willow Tree Cl.)
Atkins Lodge W8 . . . . .3C **72**
(off Thornwood Gdns.)
Atkinson Ct. E10 . . . . .2D **39**
(off Kings Cl.)
Atkinson Ho. E2 . . . . .1C **64**
(off Pritchards St.)
E13 . . . . .3B **68**
(off Sutton Rd.)
SE17 . . . . .5F **77**
(off Catesby St.)
SW11 . . . . .4C **88**
(off Austin Rd.)
Atkinson Morley Av.
SW17 . . . . .3F **115**
Atkinson Rd. E16 . . . . .4E **69**
Atkins Rd. E10 . . . . . .1D **39**
SW12 . . . . .5E **103**
Atlanta Bldg. SE10 . . . .4D **95**
(off Deal's Gateway)
Atlanta Ho. SE16 . . . . .4A **80**
(off Brunswick Quay)
Atlantic Apartments
E16 . . . . .1C **82**
(off Seagull La.)
Atlantic Ct. E14 . . . . . .1F **81**
(off Jamestown Way)
Atlantic Rd. SW9 . . . .2C **104**
Atlantic Wharf E1 . . . .1F **79**
Atlas Bus. Cen. NW2 . .3D **29**
Atlas Gdns. SE7 . . . . . .5E **83**
Atlas M. E8 . . . . .3B **50**
N7 . . . . .3B **48**
Atlas Rd. E13 . . . . .1C **68**
NW10 . . . . .2A **56**
Atlas Wharf E9 . . . . . .3C **52**
Atney Rd. SW15 . . . . .2A **100**

Atrium Apartments
N1 . . . . .5F **49**
(off Felton St.)
Atrium Ho. SE8 . . . . . .3B **94**
Atterbury Rd. N4 . . . . .1C **34**
Atterbury St. SW1 . . . .5A **76**
Attewood Av. NW10 . . .5A **28**
Attilburgh Ho. SE1 . . . .5F **27**
(off St Saviour's Est.)
Attleborough Ct.
SE23 . . . . .2C **120**
Attneave St.
WC1 . . . . . .2B **8** (2C **62**)
(off Farrier St.)
Atunbi Ct. NW1 . . . . . .4E **47**
(off Farrier St.)
Atwater Cl. SW2 . . . .1C **118**
Atwell Cl. E10 . . . . . . .1D **39**
Atwell Rd. SE15 . . . . . .5C **92**
Atwood Ho. W14 . . . . .5B **72**
(off Beckford Cl.)
Atwood Rd. W6 . . . . . . .5D **71**
Aubert Ct. N5 . . . . .1D **49**
Aubert Pk. N5 . . . . . . .1D **49**
Aubert Rd. N5 . . . . . . .1D **49**
Aubrey Beardsley Ho.
SW1 . . . . .5E **75**
(off Vauxhall Bri. Rd.)
Aubrey Mans. NW1 . . . .4A **60**
(off Lisson St.)
Aubrey Moore Point
E15 . . . . .1E **67**
(off Abbey La.)
Aubrey Pl. NW8 . . . . . .1E **59**
Aubrey Rd. N8 . . . . . . .1A **34**
W8 . . . . .2B **72**
Aubrey Wlk. W8 . . . . . .2B **72**
Auburn Cl. SE14 . . . . . .3A **94**
Aubyn Hill SE27 . . . . .4E **119**
Aubyn Sq. SW15 . . . . .3C **98**
Auckland Hill SE27 . . .4E **119**
Auckland Ho. W12 . . . .1D **71**
(off White City Est.)
Auckland Rd. E10 . . . . .5D **39**
SW11 . . . . .2A **102**
Auckland St. SE11 . . . .1B **90**
Auden Pl. NW1 . . . . . . .5C **46**
Audley Cl. SW11 . . . . .1C **102**
Audley Dr. E16 . . . . . . .2D **83**
Audley Rd. NW4 . . . . . .1C **28**
Audley Sq.
W1 . . . . . .1C **20** (2C **74**)
Audrey St. E2 . . . . .1C **64**
Augurs La. E13 . . . . . . .2D **69**
Augusta St. N1 . . . . . . .4C **48**
Augusta St. E14 . . . . . .5D **67**
Augustine Bell Twr.
E3 . . . . .1C **66**
(off Pancras Way)
Augustine Rd. W14 . . . .4F **71**
Augustus Bldg. E1 . . . .5D **65**
(off Tarling St.)
Augustus Cl. W12 . . . .3D **71**
Augustus Ct. SE1 . . . . .5A **78**
(off Old Kent Rd.)
SW16 . . . . .2F **117**
Augustus Ho. NW1 . . . . .1F **5**
(off Augustus St.)
Augustus Rd. SW19 . .1A **114**
Augustus St.
NW1 . . . . . .1E **5** (1D **61**)

Aulay Ho. SE16 . . . . .4B 78
Aulton Pl. SE11 . . . . . . .1C 90
Aura Ct. SE15 . . . . .2D 107
Auriga M. N1 . . . . .2F 49
Auriol Ho. W12 . . . . .2D 71
(off Ellerslie Rd.)
Auriol Mans. W14 . . . . . . .5A 72
(off Edith Rd.)
Auriol Rd. W14 . . . . .5A 72
Aurora Bldg. E14 . . . . . . .2E 81
(off Blackwall Way)
Aurora Ho. E14 . . . . . . .5D 67
(off Kerbey St.)
Austen Ho. NW6 . . . . . . .2C 58
(off Cambridge Rd.)
SW17 . . . . .3F 115
(off St George's Gro.)
Austin Cl. SE23 . . . . . .5A 108
Austin Ct. E6 . . . . .5E 55
SE15 . . . . .1C 106
(off Peckham Rye)
Austin Friars
EC2 . . . . . .2C 18 (5F 63)
Austin Friars Pas.
EC2 . . . . .2C 18
Austin Friars Sq. EC2 . . .2C 18
(off Austin Friars)
Austin Ho. SE14 . . . . . . .3B 94
(off Achilles St.)
Austin Rd. SW11 . . . . . . .4C 88
Austin St. E2 . .2F 11 (2B 64)
Austin Ter. SE1 . . . . . . .5C 24
(off Morley St.)
Australian War Memorial
. . . . .3C 20
(off Duke of Wellington Pl.)
Australia Rd. W12 . . . . . .1D 71
Austral St. SE11 . . . . . . .5D 77
Autumn Cl. SW19 . . . . . .5E 115
Autumn Gro.
BR1: Brom 5D 125
Autumn St. E3 . . . . .5C 52
Avalon Rd. SW6 . . . . . . .4D 87
Avarn Rd. SW17 . . . . . . .5B 116
Avebury Ct. N1 . . . . .5F 49
(off Imber St.)
Avebury Rd. E11 . . . . . . .3F 39
Avebury St. N1 . . . . .5F 49
Aveline St. SE11 . . . . . . .1C 90
Ave Maria La.
EC4 . . . . . .3E 17 (5D 63)
Avenell Mans. N5 . . . . . .1D 49
Avenell Rd. N5 . . . . .5D 35
Avenfield Ho. W1 . . . . . . .4A 12
(off Park La.)
Avening Rd. SW18 . . . . . .5C 100
Avening Ter. SW18 . . . . . .5C 100
Avenons Rd. E13 . . . . . . .3C 68
Avenue, The E11 . . . . . . .1D 41
EC2 . . . . .2E 19 (5A 64)
NW6 . . . . .5F 43
SE10 . . . . .3F 95
SW4 . . . . .2C 102
SW18 . . . . .5A 102
W4 . . . . .4A 70
Avenue Cl. NW8 . . . . . . .5A 46
(not continuous)
Avenue Cl. NW2 . . . . . . .5B 30
SW3 . . . . .5B 74
(off Draycott Av.)

Avenue Gdns. SW14 . . .1A 98
Avenue Ho. NW6 . . . . . . .4A 44
(off The Avenue)
NW8 . . . . .1A 60
(off Allitsen Rd.)
NW10 . . . . .1D 57
(off All Souls Av.)
Avenue Lodge NW8 . . . . .4F 45
(off Avenue Rd.)
Avenue Mans. NW3 . . . . .2D 45
(off Finchley Rd.)
Avenue Pk. Rd.
SE27 . . . . .2D 119
Avenue Rd. E7 . . . . .1D 55
N6 . . . . .2E 33
N15 . . . . .1F 35
NW3 . . . . .4F 45
NW8 . . . . .4F 45
NW10 . . . . .1B 56
Avenue Studios SW3 . . . .5F 73
(off Sydney Cl.)
Averill St. W6 . . . . .2F 85
Avershaw Ho. SW15 . . . . .3F 99
Avery Farm Row
SW1 . . . . .5C 74
Avery Row
W1 . . . . . . .4D 13 (1D 75)
Aviary Cl. E16 . . . . .4B 68
Avigdor M. N16 . . . . .4F 35
Avignon Rd. SE4 . . . . . . .1F 107
Avington Ct. SE1 . . . . . . .5A 78
(off Old Kent Rd.)
Avis Sq. E1 . . . . .5F 65
Avoca Rd. SW17 . . . . . . .4C 116
Avocet Cl. SE1 . . . . .1C 92
Avon Ct. SW15 . . . . .3A 100
W9 . . . . .3F 58
(off Elmfield Way)
Avondale Av. NW2 . . . . . .5A 28
Avondale Ct. E11 . . . . . . .3A 40
E16 . . . . .4A 68
Avondale Cres.
IG4: IIf 1F 41
Avondale Ho. SE1 . . . . . .1C 92
(off Avondale Sq.)
Avondale Mans.
SW6 . . . . .4B 86
(off Rostrevor Rd.)
Avondale Pk. Gdns.
W11 . . . . .1A 72
Avondale Pk. Rd.
W11 . . . . .1A 72
Avondale Pavement
SE1 . . . . .1C 92
Avondale Ri. SE15 . . . . . .1B 106
Avondale Rd.
BR1: Brom 5B 124
E16 . . . . .4A 68
E17 . . . . .2C 38
N15 . . . . .1D 35
SE9 . . . . .2F 125
SW14 . . . . .1A 98
SW19 . . . . .5D 115
Avondale Sq. SE1 . . . . . .1C 92
Avon Ho. W8 . . . . .4C 72
(off Allen St.)
W14 . . . . .5B 72
(off Kensington Village)
Avonhurst Ho. NW2 . . . . .4A 44
Avonley Rd. SE14 . . . . . . .3E 93

Avonmore Gdns.
W14 . . . . .5B 72
Avonmore Mans.
W14 . . . . .5A 72
(off Avonmore Rd.)
Avonmore Pl. W14 . . . . . .5A 72
Avonmore Rd.
W14 . . . . .5A 72
Avonmouth St.
SE1 . . . . . . .5F 25 (4E 77)
Avon Pl. SE1 . . . . .4A 26 (3E 77)
Avon Rd. SE4 . . . . .1C 108
Avro Ct. E9 . . . . .2A 52
(off Mabley St.)
Avro Ho. SW8 . . . . .3D 89
(off Havelock Ter.)
Axis Ct. SE10 . . . . .2A 96
(off Woodland Cres.)
SE16 . . . . .3C 78
(off East La.)
Axis Ho. SE13 . . . . .2E 109
(off Lewisham High St.)
Axminster Rd. N7 . . . . . . .5A 34
Aybrook St.
W1 . . . . . . .1B 12 (4C 60)
Aycliffe Ho. SE17 . . . . . . .2F 91
(off Portland St.)
Aycliffe Rd. W12 . . . . . . .2C 70
Ayerst Ct. E10 . . . . .2E 39
Aylesbury Cl. E7 . . . . . . .3B 54
Aylesbury Ho. SE15 . . . . .2C 92
(off Friary Est.)
Aylesbury Rd. SE17 . . . . .1F 91
Aylesbury St.
EC1 . . . . . . .4D 9 (3A 63)
NW10 . . . . .5A 28
Aylesford Ho. SE1 . . . . . .4C 26
(off Long La.)
Aylesford St. SW1 . . . . . .1F 89
Aylesham Cen. SE15 . . . . .4C 92
Aylestone Av. NW6 . . . . . .4F 43
Aylmer Ct. N2 . . . . .1B 32
Aylmer Ho. SE10 . . . . . . .1F 95
Aylmer Pde. N2 . . . . .1B 32
Aylmer Rd. E11 . . . . .3B 40
N2 . . . . .1A 32
W12 . . . . .3B 70
Aylton Est. SE16 . . . . . . .3E 79
Aylward Rd. SE23 . . . . . .2F 121
Aylward St. E1 . . . . .5E 65
(Jamaica St.)
E1 . . . . .5E 65
(Jubilee St.)
Aylwin Est.
SE1 . . . . . . .5E 27 (4A 78)
Aynhoe Mans. W14 . . . . . .5F 71
(off Aynhoe Rd.)
Aynhoe Rd. W14 . . . . . . .5F 71
Ayres Cl. E13 . . . . .2C 68
Ayres St.
SE1 . . . . .3A 26 (3E 77)
Ayrsome Rd. N16 . . . . . . .5A 36
Ayrton Gould Ho. E2 . . . . .2F 65
(off Roman Rd.)
Ayrton Rd. SW7 . . . . .4F 73
Aysgarth Rd. SE21 . . . . . .5A 106
Ayston Ho. SE16 . . . . . . .5F 79
(off Plough Way)
Aytoun Pl. SW9 . . . . .5B 90
Aytoun Rd. SW9 . . . . . . .5B 90

Azalea Ho. *SE14* 3B **94**
(off Achilles St.)
Azania M. NW5 . . . . .3D **47**
Azenby Rd. SE15 . . . . . .5B **92**
Azof St. SE10 . . . . .5A **82**
Azov Ho. *E1* 3A **66**
(off Commodore St.)
Azura Ct. *E15* 5E **53**
(off Warton Rd.)
Azure *W2* 4F **59**
(off Harbet Rd.)
Azure Ho. *E2* 2C **64**
(off Buckfast St.)

B

Baalbec Rd. N5 . . . . .2D **49**
Babington Ct. WC1 . . . . . .5F **7**
Babington Ho. *SE1* 3A **26**
(off Disney St.)
Babington Rd.
SW16 . . . . .5F **117**
Babmaes St.
SW1 . . . . . . .5B **14** (1F **75**)
Bacchus Wlk. *N1* 1A **64**
(off Regan Way)
Bache's St.
N1 . . . . . . .1C **10** (2F **63**)
Back All. EC3 . . . . .3E **19**
Bk. Church La. E1 . . . . . .5C **64**
Back Hill EC1 . . . .4C **8** (3C **62**)
Backhouse Pl. SE17 . . . . .5A **78**
Back La. N8 . . . . .1A **34**
NW3 . . . . .1E **45**
Back Pas. *EC1* 5E **9**
(off Long La.)
Bacon Gro. SE1 . . . . .4B **78**
Bacon's College Sports Cen.
. . . . .2A **80**
Bacons La. N6 . . . . .3C **32**
Bacon St. E1 . .3F **11** (3B **64**)
E2 . . . . .3B **64**
Bacton NW5 . . . . .2C **46**
Bacton St. E2 . . . . .2E **65**
Baddesley Ho. *SE11* 1B **90**
(off Jonathan St.)
Baddow Wlk. *N1* 5E **49**
(off New North Rd.)
Baden Pl.
SE1 . . . . . . .3B **26** (3F **77**)
Baden Powell Ho.
SW7 . . . . .5E **73**
(off Queen's Ga.)
Bader Way SW15 . . . . . . .4C **98**
Badger Ct. NW2 . . . . .5E **29**
Badminton M. E16 . . . . . .2C **82**
Badminton Rd.
SW12 . . . . .4C **102**
Badric Ct. SW11 . . . . .5F **87**
Badsworth Rd. SE5 . . . . . .4E **91**
Baffin Way E14 . . . . .2E **81**
Bagley's La. SW6 . . . . . . .4D **87**
Bagnigge Ho. *WC1* 2B **8**
(off Margery St.)
Bagshot Ho. NW1 . . . . . . .1E **5**
Bagshot St. SE17 . . . . . . .1A **92**
Baildon *E2* 1E **65**
(off Cyprus St.)
Baildon St. SE8 . . . . .3B **94**

Bailey Cotts. *E14* 4A **66**
(off Maroon St.)
Bailey Ho. *E3* 2D **67**
(off Talwin St.)
SW10 . . . . .3D **87**
(off Coleridge Gdns.)
Bailey M. SW2 . . . . .3C **104**
Bailey Pl. N16 . . . . .2A **50**
SE26 . . . . .5F **121**
Bainbridge St.
WC1 . . . . . . .2C **14** (5F **61**)
Baird Cl. E10 . . . . .3C **38**
Baird Gdns. SE19 . . . . . .4A **120**
Baird Ho. *W12* 1D **71**
(off White City Est.)
Baird St.
EC1 . . . . . . .3A **10** (3E **63**)
Baizdon Rd. SE3 . . . . .5A **96**
Baker Ho. *E3* 2D **67**
(off Bromley High St.)
WC1 . . . . .4E **7**
(off Colonnade)
Baker Pas. NW10 . . . . . . .5A **42**
Baker Rd. NW10 . . . . .5A **42**
Bakers Av. E17 . . . . .1D **39**
Baker's Fld. N7 . . . . .1A **48**
Bakers Hall Ct. EC3 . . . . . .5D **19**
Bakers Hill E5 . . . . .3E **37**
Bakers La. N6 . . . . .1B **32**
Baker's M.
W1 . . . . . . .2B **12** (5C **60**)
Bakers Pas. *NW3* 1E **45**
(off Heath St.)
Baker's Rents
. . . . . . .2F **11** (2B **64**)
Baker's Row E15 . . . . .1A **68**
EC1 . . . . . . .4B **8** (3C **62**)
BAKER STREET 4B **60**
Baker St. NW1 . . .4A **4** (3B **60**)
W1 . . . . . . .4A **4** (3B **60**)
Baker's Yd. EC1 . . . . .4B **8**
Bakery Cl. SW9 . . . . .3B **90**
Bakery Pl. SW11 . . . . . . .2B **102**
Balaam Leisure Cen.
. . . . .3C **68**
Balaam St. E13 . . . . .3C **68**
Balaclava Rd. SE1 . . . . . . .5B **78**
Bala Grn. NW9 . . . . .1A **28**
(off Ruthin Cl.)
Balchen Rd. SE3 . . . . .5F **97**
Balchier Rd. SE22 . . . . . . .4D **107**
Balcombe Ho. NW1 . . . . . .3A **60**
(off Taunton Pl.)
Balcombe St.
NW1 . . . . . . .5A **4** (3B **60**)
Balcorne St. E9 . . . . .4E **51**
Balder Ri. SE12 . . . . .2D **125**
Balderton Flats *W1* 3C **12**
(off Balderton St.)
Balderton St.
W1 . . . . . . .3C **12** (5C **60**)
Baldock St. E3 . . . . .1D **67**
Baldrey Ho. *SE10* 1B **96**
(off Blackwall La.)
Baldry Gdns. SW16 . . . . . .5B **118**
Baldwin Cres. SE5 . . . . . . .4E **91**
Baldwin Ho. SW2 . . . . . . .1C **118**
Baldwin Rd. SW11 . . . . . .4C **102**
Baldwins Gdns.
EC1 . . . . . . .5B **8** (4C **62**)

Baldwin St.
EC1 . . . . . . .2B **10** (2F **63**)
Baldwin Ter. N1 . . . . .1E **63**
Balearic Apartments
E16 . . . . .1C **82**
(off Western Gateway)
Bale Rd. E1 . . . . .4A **66**
Balfern Gro. W4 . . . . .1A **84**
Balfern St. SW11 . . . . .5A **88**
Balfe St. N1 . . . . .1A **62**
Balfour Ho. *SW11* 4C **88**
(off Forfar Rd.)
W10 . . . . .4F **57**
(off St Charles Sq.)
Balfour M.
W1 . . . . . . .1C **20** (2D **74**)
Balfour Pl. SW15 . . . . .2D **99**
W1 . . . . . . .5C **12** (1C **74**)
Balfour Rd. N5 . . . . .1E **49**
Balfour St. SE17 . . . . .5F **77**
Balfron Twr. E14 . . . . .5E **67**
Balgove Ct. NW10 . . . . . . .3D **43**
(off Eden Gro.)
BALHAM 1C **116**
Balham Continental Mkt.
. . . . .1D **117**
(off Shipka Rd.)
Balham Gro. SW12 . . . . . .5C **102**
Balham High Rd.
SW12 . . . . .3C **116**
SW17 . . . . .3C **116**
Balham Hill SW12 . . . . . . .5D **103**
Balham Leisure Cen.
. . . . .2D **117**
Balham New Rd.
SW12 . . . . .5D **103**
Balham Pk. Rd.
SW12 . . . . .1B **116**
Balham Sta. Rd.
SW12 . . . . .1D **117**
Balin Ho. *SE1* 3B **26**
(off Long La.)
Balkan Wlk. E1 . . . . .1D **79**
Balladier Wlk. E14 . . . . . . .4D **67**
Ballamore Rd.
BR1: Brom 3C **124**
Ballance Rd. E9 . . . . .3F **51**
Ballantine St. SW18 . . . . . .2E **101**
Ballantrae Ho. NW2 . . . . . .1B **44**
Ballard Ho. *SE10* 2D **95**
(off Thames St.)
Ballards Rd. NW2 . . . . .4C **28**
Ballast Quay SE10 . . . . . . .1F **95**
Ballater Rd. SW2 . . . . .2A **104**
Ball Ct. *EC3* 3C **18**
(off Cornhill)
Balletica Apartments
WC2 . . . . .3E **15**
(off Long Acre)
Ballina St. SE23 . . . . .5F **107**
Ballin Ct. *E14* 3E **81**
(off Stewart St.)
Ballingdon Rd.
SW11 . . . . .4C **102**
Ballinger Point *E3* 2D **67**
(off Bromley High St.)
Balliol Rd. W10 . . . . .5E **57**
Balloch Rd. SE6 . . . . .1F **123**
Ballogie Av. NW10 . . . . . . .1A **42**
Ballow Cl. SE5 . . . . .3A **92**

Balls Pond Pl. N1 . . . . . .3F **49**
Balls Pond Pl. N1 . . . . . .3F **49**
Balman Ho. SE16 . . . . . .5F **79**
   (off Rotherhithe New Rd.)
Balmer Rd. E3 . . . . .1B **66**
Balmes Rd. N1 . . . . .5F **49**
Balmoral Apartments
   W2 . . . . .4A **60**
             (off Praed St.)
Balmoral Cl. SW15 . . . . .4F **99**
Balmoral Cl. NW8 . . . . . .1F **59**
        (off Queen's Ter.)
   SE12 . . . . .4D **125**
   SE16 . . . . .2F **79**
   (off King & Queen Wharf)
   SE17 . . . . .1F **91**
         (off Merrow St.)
   SE27 . . . . .4E **119**
Balmoral Gro. N7 . . . . . .3B **48**
Balmoral Ho. E14 . . . . . .4D **81**
        (off Lanark Sq.)
   E16 . . . . .2D **83**
         (off Keats Av.)
   W14 . . . . .5A **72**
      (off Windsor Way)
Balmoral M. W12 . . . . . .4B **70**
Balmoral Rd. E7 . . . . . . .1E **55**
   E10 . . . . .4D **39**
   NW2 . . . . .3D **43**
Balmore Cl. E14 . . . . . . .5E **67**
Balmore St. N19 . . . . . . .4D **33**
Balmuir Gdns. SW15 . . . .2E **99**
Balnacraig Av. NW10 . . .1A **42**
Balniel Ga. SW1 . . . . . . .1F **89**
Balsam Ho. E14 . . . . .1D **81**
   (off E. India Dock Rd.)
Baltic Apartments
   E16 . . . . .1C **82**
      (off Western Gateway)
Baltic Ct. E1 . . . . .2E **79**
         (off Clave St.)
   SE16 . . . . .3F **79**
Baltic Ho. SE5 . . . . .5E **91**
Baltic Pl. N1 . . . . .5A **50**
Baltic St. E.
   EC1 . . . . .4F **9** (3E **63**)
Baltic St. W.
   EC1 . . . . .4F **9** (3E **63**)
Baltimore Ct. SW1 . . . . .5F **75**
   (off Vauxhall Bri. Rd.)
Baltimore Ho. SE11 . . . .5C **76**
       (off Hotspur St.)
   SW18 . . . . .1E **101**
Baltimore Wharf E14 . . .4D **81**
Balvaird Pl. SW1 . . . . . . .1F **89**
Balvernie Gro.
   SW18 . . . . .5B **100**
Balvernie M. SW18 . . . .5C **100**
Bamber Rd. SE15 . . . . . .4B **92**
Bamborough Gdns.
   W12 . . . . .3E **71**
Bamford Rd.
   BR1: Brom 5E **123**
Bampton Rd. SE23 . . . . .3F **121**
Banbury Ct. WC2 . . . . . .4D **15**
Banbury Ho. E9 . . . . .4F **51**
Banbury Rd. E9 . . . . .4F **51**
Banbury St. SW11 . . . . . .5A **88**
Banchory Rd. SE3 . . . . . .3D **97**
Bancroft Av. N2 . . . . . . .1A **32**

Bancroft Ct. SW8 . . . . . .3A **90**
   (off Allen Edwards Dr.)
Bancroft Ho. E1 . . . . .3E **65**
        (off Cephas St.)
Bancroft Rd. E1 . . . . .2E **65**
Banfield Rd. SE15 . . . . .1D **107**
Bangalore St. SW15 . . . .1E **99**
Bangla Ho. E8 . . . . .5B **50**
       (off Clarissa St.)
Banim St. W6 . . . . .5D **71**
Banister Ho. E9 . . . . .2F **51**
   SW8 . . . . .4E **89**
       (off Wadhurst Rd.)
   W10 . . . . .2A **58**
       (off Bruckner St.)
Banister M. NW6 . . . . . . .4D **45**
Banister Rd. W10 . . . . . .2F **57**
Bank, The N6 . . . . .3D **33**
Bank End SE1 . . . .1A **26** (2E **77**)
Bankfoot Rd.
   BR1: Brom 4A **124**
Bankhurst Rd. SE6 . . . . .5B **108**
Bank La. SW15 . . . . .3A **98**
Bank of England
   . . . . .3B **18** (5F **63**)
Bank of England Mus.
   . . . . .3C **18**
Bank of England Sports Cen.
   . . . . .3A **98**
Banks Ho. SE1 . . . . .5F **25**
   (off Rockingham St.)
Bankside SE1 . . . .5F **17** (1E **77**)
       (not continuous)
Bankside Av. SE13 . . . . .1E **109**
Bankside Gallery
   . . . . .5E **17** (1D **77**)
Bankside Lofts SE1 . . . . .1E **25**
Bankside Mix
   SE1 . . . . . . .1F **25** (2E **77**)
Bankside Pl. N4 . . . . . . .1E **35**
Bankside Way SE19 . . . .5A **120**
Bank St. E14 . . . . .2D **81**
Bankton Rd. SW2 . . . . . .2C **104**
Bankwell Rd. SE13 . . . . .2A **110**
Bannatyne's Health Club
   Grove Park 2D **125**
Banner Ct. SE16 . . . . . . .5E **79**
   (off Rotherhithe New Rd.)
Banner Ho. EC1 . . . . .4A **10**
        (off Roscoe St.)
Bannerman Ho. SW8 . . . .2B **90**
Banner St.
   EC1 . . . . . . .4A **10** (3E **63**)
Banning St. SE10 . . . . . .1A **96**
Bannister Cl. SW2 . . . . .1C **118**
Bannister Ho. SE14 . . . . .2F **93**
   (off John Williams Cl.)
Bannon Ct. SW6 . . . . . . .4D **87**
      (off Michael Rd.)
Banqueting House
   . . . . .2D **23** (2A **76**)
Banstead Ct. W12 . . . . . .1B **70**
Banstead St. SE15 . . . . .1E **107**
Bantock Ho. W10 . . . . . . .2A **58**
        (off Third Av.)
Bantry Ho. E1 . . . . .3F **65**
       (off Ernest St.)
Bantry St. SE5 . . . . .3F **91**
Banyard Rd. SE16 . . . . . .4D **79**

Baptist Gdns. NW5 . . . . .3C **46**
Baquba SE13 . . . . .1D **95**
Barandon Rd. W11 . . . . . .1F **71**
      (off Grenfell Rd.)
Barandon Wlk.
   W11 . . . . .1F **71**
Barbanel Ho. E1 . . . . .3E **65**
        (off Cephas St.)
Barbara Brosnan Ct.
   NW8 . . . . .1F **59**
Barbara Castle Cl.
   SW6 . . . . .2B **86**
Barbauld Rd. N16 . . . . . .5A **36**
Barber Beaumont Ho.
   E1 . . . . .2F **65**
        (off Bancroft Rd.)
Barberry Ct. E15 . . . . . . .3A **54**
Barbers All. E13 . . . . .2D **69**
Barbers Rd. E15 . . . . . . .1D **67**
Barbican EC2 . . . . .5A **10**
Barbican Arts Cen.
   . . . . .5A **10** (4E **63**)
Barbican Cinema 5A **10**
   (in Barbican Arts Cen.)
Barbican Theatre 5A **10**
   (in Barbican Arts Cen.)
Barbican Trade Cen.
   EC1 . . . . .5A **10**
        (off Beech St.)
Barb M. W6 . . . . .4E **71**
Barbon All. EC2 . . . . .2E **19**
      (off Devonshire Sq.)
Barbon Cl.
   WC1 . . . . .5E **7** (4B **62**)
Barchard St. SW18 . . . . .3D **101**
Barchester St. E14 . . . . . .4D **67**
Barclay Cl. SW6 . . . . . . .3C **86**
Barclay Ho. E9 . . . . .4E **51**
         (off Well St.)
Barclay Path E17 . . . . . . .1E **39**
Barclay Rd. E11 . . . . .3B **40**
   E13 . . . . .3E **69**
   E17 . . . . .1E **39**
   SW6 . . . . .3C **86**
Barcombe Av. SW2 . . . .2A **118**
Bardell Ho. SE1 . . . . .3C **78**
      (off Parkers Row)
Bardolph Rd. N7 . . . . . . .1A **48**
Bard Rd. W10 . . . . .1F **71**
Bardsey Pl. E1 . . . . .3E **65**
Bardsey Wlk. N1 . . . . . . .3E **49**
   (off Douglas Rd. Nth.)
Bardsley Ho. SE10 . . . . . .2E **95**
      (off Bardsley La.)
Bardsley La. SE10 . . . . . .2E **95**
Barents Ho. E1 . . . . .3F **65**
   (off White Horse La.)
Barfett St. W10 . . . . .3B **58**
Barfield Rd. E11 . . . . .3B **40**
Barfleur La. SE8 . . . . .5B **80**
Barford Ho. E3 . . . . .1B **66**
       (off Tredegar Rd.)
Barford St. N1 . . . . .5C **48**
Barforth Rd. SE15 . . . . .1D **107**
Barge Ho. St.
   SE1 . . . . . .1C **24** (2C **76**)
Barge La. E3 . . . . .5A **52**
Bargery Rd. SE6 . . . . . . .1D **123**
Barge Wlk. SE10 . . . . . . .4B **82**
Bargrove Cres. SE6 . . . .2B **122**

Barham Ho. *SE17* *1A 92*
   (off Kinglake Est.)
Baring Cl. SE12 . . . .*2C 124*
Baring Ct. *N1* *5F 49*
   (off Baring St.)
Baring Ho. *E14* *5C 66*
   (off Canton St.)
Baring Rd. SE12 . . . . . .*5C 110*
Baring St. N1 . . . .*5F 49*
Baritone Ct. *E15* *5B 54*
   (off Church St.)
Barker Dr. NW1 . . . .*4E 47*
Barker Ho. *SE17* *5A 78*
   (off Congreve St.)
Barker M. SW4 . . . .*2D 103*
Barkers Arc. W8 . . . .*3D 73*
Barker St. SW10 . . . .*2E 87*
Barker Wlk.
   SW16 . . . .*3F 117*
Barkham Ter. SE1 . . . .*5C 24*
Barking Rd. E6 . . . .*1E 69*
   E13 . . . .*1E 69*
   E16 . . . .*4A 68*
Bark Pl. W2 . . . .*1D 73*
Barkston Gdns. SW5 . . . . .*5D 73*
Barkway Ct. N4 . . . .*4E 35*
Barkwith Ho. *SE14* *2F 93*
   (off Cold Blow La.)
Barkworth Rd. SE16 . . . . .*1D 93*
Barlborough St. SE14 . . . . .*3F 93*
Barlby Gdns. W10 . . . .*3F 57*
Barlby Rd. W10 . . . .*4E 57*
Barleycorn Way E14 . . . . .*1B 80*
   (not continuous)
Barley Mow Pas. EC1 . . . . .*5E 9*
   W4 . . . .*1A 84*
Barley Shotts Bus. Pk.
   W10 . . . .*4B 58*
Barling NW1 . . . .*3D 47*
   (off Castlehaven Rd.)
Barlow Dr. SE18 . . . .*4F 97*
Barlow Ho. *N1* *1B 10*
   (off Provost Est.)
   SE16 . . . .*5D 79*
   (off Rennie Est.)
   W11 . . . .*1A 72*
   (off Walmer Rd.)
Barlow Pl.
   W1 . . . .*5E 13 (1D 75)*
Barlow Rd. NW6 . . . .*3B 44*
Barlow St. SE17 . . . .*5F 77*
Barmeston Rd. SE6 . . . . . .*2D 123*
Barmouth Rd. SW18 . . . . .*4E 101*
Barnabas Ho. EC1 . . . .*2F 9*
Barnabas Lodge *SW8* *4A 90*
   (off Guildford Rd.)
Barnabas Rd. E9 . . . .*2F 51*
Barnaby Ct. *SE16* *3C 78*
   (off Scott Lidgett Cres.)
Barnaby Pl. *SW7* *5F 73*
   (off Old Brompton Rd.)
Barnard Gro. E15 . . . .*4B 54*
Barnard Ho. *E2* *2D 65*
   (off Ellsworth St.)
Barnard Lodge *W9* *4C 58*
   (off Admiral Wlk.)
Barnard M. SW11 . . . .*2A 102*
Barnardo Gdns. E1 . . . . . .*1F 79*
Barnardo St. E1 . . . .*5F 65*
Barnard Rd. SW11 . . . . . .*2A 102*

Barnards Ho. *SE16* *3B 80*
   (off Wyatt Cl.)
Barnard's Inn EC1 . . . .*1B 16*
Barnborough NW1 . . . .*5E 47*
   (off Camden St.)
Barnby Sq. E15 . . . .*5A 54*
Barnby St. E15 . . . .*5A 54*
   NW1 . . . .*1A 6 (1E 61)*
Barn Cl. *NW5* *2F 47*
   (off Torriano Av.)
Barn Elms Athletics Track
   . . . .*5D 85*
Barn Elms Pk. SW15 . . . . . .*1E 99*
BARNES *5B 84*
Barnes Av. SW13 . . . .*3C 84*
Barnes Bri W4 . . . .*5A 84*
Barnes Cl. E12 . . . .*1F 55*
Barnes Common
   Nature Reserve *1C 98*
Barnes Ct. E16 . . . .*4E 69*
   N1 . . . .*4C 48*
Barnes High St.
   SW13 . . . .*5B 84*
Barnes Ho. *E2* *1E 65*
   (off Wadeson St.)
   SE14 . . . .*2F 93*
   (off John Williams Cl.)
Barnes St. E14 . . . .*5A 66*
Barnes Ter. SE8 . . . .*1B 94*
Barnet Gro. E2 . . . .*2C 64*
Barnett St. E1 . . . .*5D 65*
Barney Cl. SE7 . . . .*1E 97*
Barn Fld. NW3 . . . .*2B 46*
Barnfield Cl. N4 . . . .*2A 34*
   SW17 . . . .*3F 115*
Barnfield Pl. E14 . . . .*5C 80*
Barnham St.
   SE1 . . . .*3E 27 (3A 78)*
BARNSBURY *4B 48*
Barnsbury Est. N1 . . . .*5B 48*
   (not continuous)
Barnsbury Gro. N7 . . . .*4B 48*
Barnsbury Ho. SW4 . . . . . .*4F 103*
Barnsbury Pk. N1 . . . .*4C 48*
Barnsbury Rd. N1 . . . .*1C 62*
Barnsbury Sq. N1 . . . .*4C 48*
Barnsbury St. N1 . . . .*4C 48*
Barnsbury Ter. N1 . . . .*4B 48*
Barnsdale Av. E14 . . . .*5D 81*
Barnsdale Rd. W9 . . . .*3B 58*
Barnsley St. E1 . . . .*3D 65*
Barnstable La.
   SE13 . . . .*2E 109*
Barnstaple Ho. *SE10* *3D 95*
   (off Devonshire Dr.)
   SE12 . . . .*3B 110*
   (off Taunton Dr.)
Barnston Wlk. *N1* *5E 49*
   (off Popham St.)
Barn St. N16 . . . .*4A 36*
Barnwell Ho. *SE5* *4A 92*
   (off St Giles Rd.)
Barnwell Rd. SW2 . . . .*3C 104*
Barnwood Cl. W9 . . . .*3D 59*
Baron Cl. N1 . . . .*1C 62*
Baroness Rd.
   E2 . . . .*1F 11 (2B 64)*
Baronsclere Ct. N6 . . . .*2E 33*
BARONS COURT *1A 86*
Baron's Ct. Rd. W14 . . . . . .*1A 86*

Barons Court Theatre . . .*1A 86*
   (off Comeragh Rd.)
Barons Keep W14 . . . .*1A 86*
Barons Lodge *E14* *5F 81*
   (off Manchester Rd.)
Baronsmead Rd.
   SW13 . . . .*4C 84*
Baron's Pl.
   SE1 . . . .*4C 24 (3C 76)*
Baron Wlk. E16 . . . .*4B 68*
Barque M. SE8 . . . .*2C 94*
Barratt Ho. *N1* *4D 49*
   (off Sable St.)
Barratt Ind. Pk. E3 . . . .*3E 67*
Barret Ho. NW6 . . . .*5C 44*
   SW9 . . . .*1B 104*
   (off Benedict Rd.)
Barrett Ho. *SE17* *1E 91*
   (off Browning St.)
Barrett's Gro. N16 . . . .*2A 50*
Barrett St.
   W1 . . . .*3C 12 (5C 60)*
Barrhill Rd. SW2 . . . .*2A 118*
Barriedale SE14 . . . .*5A 94*
Barrie Est. W2 . . . .*1F 73*
Barrie Ho. *NW8* *5A 46*
   (off St Edmund's Ter.)
   W2 . . . .*1E 73*
   (off Lancaster Ga.)
Barrier App. SE7 . . . .*4F 83*
Barrier Point Rd. E16 . . . . . .*2E 83*
Barringer Sq. SW17 . . . . . .*4C 116*
Barrington Cl. NW5 . . . .*2C 46*
Barrington Ct. SW4 . . . .*5A 90*
Barrington Rd. SW9 . . . . . .*1D 105*
Barrow Ct. *SE6* *1B 124*
   (off Cumberland Pl.)
Barrowgate Rd. W4 . . . .*1A 84*
Barrow Hill Est. NW8 . . . . . .*1A 60*
   (off Barrow Hill Rd.)
Barrow Hill Rd. NW8 . . . . . .*1A 60*
Barrow Rd. SW16 . . . .*5F 117*
Barrow Store Ct. *SE1* *5D 27*
   (off Decima St.)
Barry Av. N15 . . . .*1B 36*
Barry Ho. *SE16* *5D 79*
   (off Rennie Est.)
Barry Pde. SE22 . . . .*2C 106*
Barry Rd. SE22 . . . .*4C 106*
Barset Rd. SE15 . . . .*1E 107*
   (not continuous)
Barston Rd. SE27 . . . .*3E 119*
Barstow Cres. SW2 . . . . . .*1B 118*
Barter St.
   WC1 . . . .*1E 15 (4A 62)*
Bartholomew Cl.
   EC1 . . . .*1E 17 (4E 63)*
   (not continuous)
   SW18 . . . .*2E 101*
Bartholomew Ct. *E14* *1F 81*
   (off Newport Av.)
   EC1 . . . .*3A 10*
   (off Old St.)
Bartholomew Ho.
   W10 . . . .*3A 58*
   (off Appleford Rd.)
Bartholomew La.
   EC2 . . . .*3C 18 (5F 63)*
Bartholomew Pl. EC1 . . .*1F 17*

Bartholomew Rd.
NW5 . . . . .3E 47
Bartholomew Sq. E1 . . .3D 65
EC1 . . . . .3A 10 (3E 63)
Bartholomew St. SE1 . . .4F 77
Bartholomew Vs.
NW5 . . . . .3E 47
Bartle Rd. W11 . . . . . .5A 58
Bartlett Cl. E14 . . . . . .5C 66
Bartlett Ct.
EC4 . . . . .2C 16 (5C 62)
Bartlett M. E14 . . . . . .1D 95
Bartletts Pas. EC4 . . . .2C 16
(off Fetter La.)
Barton Cl. E9 . . . . .2E 51
SE15 . . . . .1D 107
Barton Ct. W14 . . . . . .1A 86
(off Baron's La.)
Barton Ho. E3 . . . . . . .2D 67
(off Bow Rd.)
N1 . . . . .4D 49
(off Sable St.)
SW6 . . . . .1D 101
(off Wandsworth Bri. Rd.)
Barton Rd. W14 . . . . . .1A 86
Barton St.
SW1 . . . . .5D 23 (4A 76)
Bartonway NW8 . . . . . .5F 45
(off Queen's Ter.)
Bartram Rd. SE4 . . . . .3A 108
Bartrip St. E9 . . . . .3B 52
Barville Cl. SE4 . . . . . .2A 108
Barwell Ho. E2 . . . . . . .3C 64
(off Menotti St.)
Barwick Rd. E7 . . . . . .1D 55
Bascombe St. SW2 . . . .4C 104
Baseline Bus. Studios
W11 . . . . .1F 71
(off Barandon Wlk.)
Basevi Way SE8 . . . . . .2D 95
Bashley Ho. NW10 . . . . .3A 56
Basildon Ct. W1 . . . . . .5C 4
(off Devonshire St.)
Basil Gdns. SE27 . . . . .5E 119
Basil Ho. E1 . . . . .5C 64
(off Henriques St.)
SW8 . . . . .3A 90
(off Wyvil Rd.)
Basil Mans. SW3 . . . . . .4A 20
(off Basil St.)
Basil St.
SW3 . . . . .5A 20 (4B 74)
Basin App. E14 . . . . . . .5A 66
Basing Ct. SE15 . . . . . .4B 92
Basingdon Way SE5 . . .2F 105
Basinghall Av.
EC2 . . . . .2B 18 (5F 63)
Basinghall St.
EC2 . . . . .2B 18 (5F 63)
Basing Hill NW11 . . . . . .3B 30
Basing Ho. Yd. E2 . . . . .1E 11
Basing Pl. E2 . . .1E 11 (2A 64)
Basing St. W11 . . . . . . .5B 58
Basire St. N1 . . . . .5E 49
Baskerville Gdns.
NW10 . . . . .1A 42
Baskerville Rd.
SW18 . . . . .5A 102

Basketball Arena, Olympic Pk.
. . . . .2D 53
Basket Gdns. SE9 . . . . .3F 111
Baslow Wlk. E5 . . . . . . .1F 51
Basnett Rd. SW11 . . . . .1C 102
Basque Ct. SE16 . . . . . .3F 79
(off Garter Way)
Bassano St. SE22 . . . . .3B 106
Bass Ct. E15 . . . . .5B 54
(off Plaistow Rd.)
Bassein Pk. Rd. W12 . . .3B 70
Bassett Ho. SW19 . . . . .5D 115
Bassett Rd. W10 . . . . . .5F 57
Bassett St. NW5 . . . . . .3C 46
Bassingbourn Ho. N1 . . .4C 48
(off The Sutton Est.)
Bassingham Rd.
SW18 . . . . .5E 101
Bassishaw Highwalk
EC2 . . . . .1B 18
Bass M. SE22 . . . . .2C 106
Basswood Cl. SE15 . . . .1D 107
Basterfield Ho. EC1 . . . .4F 9
(off Golden La. Est.)
Bastion Highwalk
EC2 . . . . .1F 17
Bastion Ho. EC2 . . . . . .1A 18
(off London Wall)
Bastwick St.
EC1 . . . . .3F 9 (3E 63)
Basuto Rd. SW6 . . . . . . .4C 86
Batavia Ho. SE14 . . . . . .3A 94
(off Batavia Rd.)
Batavia M. SE14 . . . . . . .3A 94
Batavia Rd. SE14 . . . . . .3A 94
Batchelor St. N1 . . . . . . .5C 48
Bateman Ho. SE17 . . . . .2D 91
(off Otto St.)
Bateman M. SW4 . . . . . .4F 103
Bateman's Bldgs.
W1 . . . . .3B 14
Bateman's Row
EC2 . . . . .3E 11 (3A 64)
Bateman St.
W1 . . . . .3B 14 (5F 61)
Bates Point E13 . . . . . . .5C 54
(off Pelly Rd.)
Bate St. E14 . . . . .1B 80
Bath Cl. SE15 . . . . .3D 93
Bath Ct. EC1 . . . . .2B 10
(St Luke's Est.)
EC1 . . . . .4B 8
(Warner St.)
SE26 . . . . .3C 120
(off Droitwich Cl.)
Bathgate Ho. SW9 . . . . .4D 91
(off Lothian Rd.)
Bathgate Rd. SW19 . . . .3F 113
Bath Gro. E2 . . . . .1C 64
(off Horatio St.)
Bath Ho. E2 . . . . .3C 64
(off Ramsey St.)
SE1 . . . . .3C 26
(off Bath Ter.)
Bath Pl. EC2 . . .2D 11 (2A 64)
W6 . . . . .1E 85
(off Peabody Est.)
Bath Rd. E7 . . . . .3F 55
W4 . . . . .5A 70
Baths Ct. W12 . . . . .3D 71

Bath St. EC1 . . .2A 10 (2E 63)
Bath Ter. SE1 . . .5F 25 (4E 77)
Bathurst Gdns.
NW10 . . . . .1D 57
Bathurst Ho. W12 . . . . . .1D 71
(off White City Est.)
Bathurst M. W2 . . . . .5F 59
Bathurst St. W2 . . . . . . .1F 73
Batley Pl. N16 . . . . .5B 36
Batley Rd. N16 . . . . .5B 36
Batman Cl. W12 . . . . . . .2D 71
Batoum Gdns. W6 . . . . .4E 71
Batsford Ho. SW19 . . . .4D 115
(off Durnsford Rd.)
Batson Ho. E1 . . . . .5C 64
(off Fairclough St.)
Batson St. W12 . . . . .3C 70
Battenberg Wlk.
SE19 . . . . .5A 120
Batten Cotts. E14 . . . . . .4A 66
(off Maroon St.)
Batten Ho. SW4 . . . . . . .3E 103
W10 . . . . .2A 58
(off Third Av.)
Batten St. SW11 . . . . . .1A 102
Battersby Rd. SE6 . . . . .2F 123
BATTERSEA 4C 88
Battersea Arts Cen. 1B 102
Battersea Bri. SW3 . . . . .3F 87
Battersea Bri. Rd.
SW11 . . . . .3A 88
Battersea Bus. Cen.
SW11 . . . . .1C 102
Battersea Church Rd.
SW11 . . . . .4F 87
Battersea High St.
SW11 . . . . .4F 87
(not continuous)
BATTERSEA PARK 3D 89
Battersea Pk. 3B 88
Battersea Pk. Children's Zoo
. . . . .3C 88
Battersea Pk. Equestrian Cen.
. . . . .5A 88
Battersea Pk. Rd.
SW8 . . . . .4C 88
SW11 . . . . .5A 88
Battersea Ri. SW11 . . . .3A 102
Battersea Sports Cen.
. . . . .1F 101
Battersea Sq. SW11 . . . .4F 87
Battishill St. N1 . . . . . . .4D 49
Battlebridge Ct. N1 . . . .1A 62
(off Wharfdale Rd.)
Battle Bri. La.
SE1 . . . . .2D 27 (2A 78)
Battle Cl. SW19 . . . . . . .5E 115
Battledean Rd. N5 . . . . .2D 49
Battle Ho. SE15 . . . . . . .2C 92
(off Haymerle Rd.)
Batty St. E1 . . . . .5C 64
Batwa Ho. SE16 . . . . . . .1D 93
Baudwin Rd. SE6 . . . . .2A 124
Baulk, The SW18 . . . . . .5C 100
Bavaria Rd. N19 . . . . . . .4A 34
Bavent Rd. SE5 . . . . . . .5E 91
Bawdale Rd. SE22 . . . . .3B 106
Bawley Ter. E15 . . . . . . .5F 53
(off Rick Roberts Way)
Bawtree Rd. SE14 . . . . .3A 94

Baxendale St. E2 ......2C 64
Baxter Ho. E3 ....2D 67
(off Bromley High St.)
Baxter Rd. E16 ....5E 69
N1 ....3F 49
Baxter Wlk. SW16 .....2F 117
Bay Ct. E1 ....3F 65
(off Frimley Way)
Bayer Ho. EC1 ....4F 9
(off Golden La. Est.)
Bayes Cl. SE26 ....5E 121
Bayes Ct. NW3 ....4B 46
(off Primrose Hill Rd.)
Bayes Ho. N1 ....4C 48
(off Augustas La.)
Bayfield Ho. SE4 ......2F 107
(off Coston Wlk.)
Bayfield Rd. SE9 ......2F 111
Bayford M. E8 ....4D 51
(off Bayford St.)
Bayford Rd. NW10 .....2F 57
Bayford St. E8 ....4D 51
Bayford St. Bus. Cen.
E8 ....4D 51
(off Sidworth St.)
Bayham Pl. NW1 ....5E 47
Bayham Rd. W4 ....4A 70
Bayham St. NW1 ....5E 47
Bayley St.
WC1 ....1B 14 (4F 61)
Baylis Rd.
SE1 ....4B 24 (3C 76)
Baynes M. NW3 ....3F 45
Baynes St. NW1 ....4E 47
Bayonne Rd. W6 ....2A 86
Bayston Rd. N16 ....5B 36
BAYSWATER 1E 73
Bayswater Rd. W2 ......1D 73
Baythorne Ho. E16 ....5B 68
(off Turner St.)
Baythorne St. E3 ....4B 66
Bayton Ct. E8 ....4C 50
(off Lansdowne Dr.)
Baytree Ct. SW2 ......2B 104
Baytree M. SE17 ......5F 77
Baytree Rd. SW2 ......2B 104
Bazalgette Ho. NW8 ....3F 59
(off Orchardson St.)
Bazeley Ho. SE1 ......4D 25
(off Library St.)
Bazely St. E14 ....1E 81
BBC Broadcasting House
.............1E 13 (4D 61)
BBC Maida Vale Studios
.....................3D 59
(off Delaware Rd.)
BBC Television Cen. ...1E 71
Beacham Cl. SE7 ......1F 97
Beachborough Rd.
BR1: Brom 4E 123
Beachcroft Rd. E11 ....5A 40
Beachcroft Way N19 ...3F 33
Beach Ho. SW5 ....1C 86
(off Philbeach Gdns.)
Beachy Rd. E3 ....4C 52
Beacon Bingo
Cricklewood 1F 43
Streatham 1A 118
Beacon Ga. SE14 .....1F 107
Beacon Hill N7 ....2A 48

Beacon Ho. E14 ....1D 95
(off Burrells Wharf Sq.)
SE5 ....3A 92
(off Southampton Way)
Beacon Rd. SE13 .....4F 109
Beaconsfield WC1 .....1F 15
(off Red Lion St.)
Beaconsfield Cl. SE3 ..2C 96
Beaconsfield Rd. E10 ..4E 39
E16 ....3B 68
E17 ....1B 38
NW10 ....3B 42
SE3 ....3B 96
SE9 ....2F 125
SE17 ....1F 91
Beaconsfield Ter. Rd.
W14 ....4A 72
Beaconsfield Wlk.
SW6 ....4B 86
Beacontree Rd. E11 ...3B 40
Beadman Pl. SE27 .....4D 119
Beadman St. SE27 ....4D 119
Beadnell Rd. SE23 ....1F 121
Beadon Rd. W6 ....5E 71
Beak St. W1 ....4A 14 (1E 75)
Beale Pl. E3 ....1B 66
Beale Rd. E3 ....5B 52
Beames Rd. NW10 .....5A 42
Beaminster Ho. SW8 ...3B 90
(off Dorset Rd.)
Beamish Ho. SE16 .....5D 79
(off Rennie Est.)
Beanacre Cl. E9 ....3B 52
Bear All.
EC4 ....2D 17 (5D 63)
Beardell St. SE19 .....5B 120
Beardsfield E13 ......1C 68
Bear Gdns.
SE1 ....1F 25 (2E 77)
Bear La. SE1 ...1E 25 (2D 77)
Bear Pit Apartments
SE1 ....1F 25
(off New Globe Wlk.)
Bearstead Ri. SE4 ....3B 108
Bear St. WC2 ...4C 14 (1F 75)
Beaton Cl. SE15 ....4B 92
Beatrice Cl. E13 ......3C 68
Beatrice Ho. W6 ......1E 85
(off Queen Caroline St.)
Beatrice Pl. W8 ....4D 73
Beatrice Rd. E17 ......1C 38
N4 ....2C 34
SE1 ....5C 78
Beatrice Webb Ho.
E3 ....1A 66
(off Chisenhale Rd.)
Beatrix Ho. SW5 ......1D 87
(off Old Brompton Rd.)
Beatson Wlk. SE16 ....2A 80
(not continuous)
Beattie Ho. SW8 ......4E 89
Beatty Ho. E14 ....3C 80
(off Admirals Way)
.....................1E 89
(off Dolphin Sq.)
Beatty Rd. N16 ....1A 50
Beatty St. NW1 ....1E 61
Beauchamp Pl. SW3 ...4A 74
Beauchamp Rd. E7 ....4D 55
SW11 ....2A 102

Beauchamp St.
EC1 ....1B 16 (4C 62)
Beauchamp Ter.
SW15 ....1D 99
Beauclerc Rd. W6 .....4D 71
Beauclerk Ho.
SW16 ....3A 118
Beaufort Cl. SW15 ....5D 99
Beaufort Ct. E14 ......3C 80
(off Admirals Way)
SW6 ....2C 86
Beaufort Gdns. NW4 ..1E 29
SW3 ....4A 74
Beaufort Ho. E16 .....2D 83
(off Fairfax M.)
SW1 ....1F 89
(off Aylesford St.)
SW3 ....2F 87
(off Beaufort St.)
Beaufort Mans. SW3 ..2F 87
Beaufort M. SW6 .....2B 86
Beaufort St. SW3 .....2F 87
Beaufort Ter. E14 ....1E 95
(off Ferry St.)
Beaufoy Ho. SE27 ....3D 119
SW8 ....3B 90
(off Rita Rd.)
Beaufoy Wlk. SE11 ....5B 76
Beaulieu Av. E16 .....2D 83
SE26 ....4D 121
Beaulieu Cl. SE5 .....1F 105
Beaulieu Lodge E14 ...4F 81
(off Schooner Cl.)
Beaumanor Mans.
W2 ....1D 73
(off Queensway)
Beaumaris Grn. NW9 ..1A 28
Beaumont W14 ....5B 72
(off Kensington Village)
Beaumont Av. W14 ....1B 86
Beaumont Bldgs.
WC2 ....3E 15
(off Martlett Ct.)
Beaumont Ct. E1 ......2F 65
E5 ....5D 37
NW1 ....5F 47
W1 ....5C 4
(off Beaumont St.)
Beaumont Cres. W14 ..1B 86
Beaumont Gdns.
NW3 ....5C 30
Beaumont Gro. E1 ....3F 65
Beaumont Ho. E10 ....2D 39
(off Skelton's La.)
W9 ....2B 58
(off Fernhead Rd.)
Beaumont Lodge E8 ...3C 50
(off Greenwood Rd.)
Beaumont M.
W1 ....5C 4 (4C 60)
Beaumont Pl.
W1 ....3A 6 (3E 61)
Beaumont Ri. N19 .....3F 33
Beaumont Rd. E10 ....2D 39
(not continuous)
E13 ....2D 69
SW19 ....5A 100
Beaumont Sq. E1 .....4F 65
Beaumont St.
W1 ....5C 4 (4C 60)

Beaumont Ter. *SE13* 5A **110**
  (off Wellmeadow Rd.)
Beaumont Wlk. NW3 . . . .4B **46**
Beauvale *NW1* 4C **46**
  (off Ferdinand St.)
Beauval Rd. SE22 . . . . .4B **106**
Beaux Arts Building, The
  N7 . . . . .5A **34**
  (off Beavor La.)
Beavor Gro. *W6* 1C **84**
  (off Beavor La.)
Beavor La. W6 . . . . .1C **84**
Beccles St. E14 . . . . .6B **68**
Bechervaise Ct. E10 . . . . .3D **39**
  (off Leyton Grange Est.)
Bechtel Ho. *W6* 5F **71**
  (off Hammersmith Rd.)
Beck Cl. SE13 . . . . .4D **95**
Beckenham Bus. Cen.
  BR3: Beck 5A **122**
Beckenham Hill Est.
  BR3: Beck 5D **123**
Beckenham Hill Rd.
  BR3: Beck 5D **123**
  SE6 . . . . .5D **123**
Beckenham Place Pk.
  Golf Course 5D **123**
Beckenham Place Pk.
  Nature Reserve
  . . . . .5E **123**
Beckers, The N16 . . . . . .5C **36**
Becket Ho. *E16* 2D **83**
  (off Constable Av.)
  SE1 . . . . .4B **26**
Becket St.
  SE1 . . . . . .5B **26** (4F **77**)
Beckett Cl. NW10 . . . . . . .3A **42**
  SW16 . . . . .2F **117**
Beckett Ho. *E1* 4E **65**
  (off Jubilee St.)
  SW9 . . . . .5A **90**
Beckfoot *NW1* 1A **6**
  (off Ampthill Est.)
Beckford Cl. W14 . . . . . . .5B **72**
Beckford Ho. N16 . . . . . . .2A **50**
Beckford Pl. SE17 . . . . . . .1E **91**
Beckham Ho. SE11 . . . . . .5B **76**
Beckhaven Ho. *SE11* 5C **76**
  (off Gilbert Rd.)
Beckley Ho. *E3* 3B **66**
  (off Hamlets Way)
Becklow Gdns. *W12* 3C **70**
  (off Becklow Rd.)
Becklow M. *W12* 3C **70**
  (off Becklow Rd.)
Becklow Rd. W12 . . . . . . .3B **70**
  (not continuous)
Beck Rd. E8 . . . . .5D **51**
Beckton Rd. E16 . . . . .4B **68**
Beckway St. SE17 . . . . . . .5A **78**
  (not continuous)
Beckwith Ho. *E2* 1D **65**
  (off Wadeson St.)
Beckwith Rd. SE24 . . . . .3F **105**
Beclands Rd. SW17 . . . .5C **116**
Becmead Av. SW16 . . . . .4F **117**
Becondale Rd.
  SE19 . . . . .5A **120**
Becquerel Ct. *SE10* 4B **82**
  (off West Parkside)
Bective Pl. SW15 . . . . .2B **100**

Bective Rd. E7 . . . . .1C **54**
  SW15 . . . . .2B **100**
Bedale St.
  SE1 . . . . . .2B **26** (2F **77**)
Beddalls Farm Ct. E6 . . . .4F **69**
Bedefield
  WC1 . . . . .2E **7** (2A **62**)
Bede Ho. SE14 . . . . .4A **94**
  (off Clare Rd.)
Bedford Av.
  WC1 . . . . .1C **14** (4F **61**)
Bedfordbury
  WC2 . . . . . .4D **15** (1A **76**)
  (not continuous)
Bedford Cl. W4 . . . . .2A **84**
Bedford Cnr. *W4* 5A **70**
  (off South Pde.)
Bedford Ct.
  WC2 . . . . . .5D **15** (1A **76**)
Bedford Ct. Mans.
  WC1 . . . . .1C **14**
Bedford Gdns. W8 . . . . . .2C **72**
Bedford Gdns. Ho.
  W8 . . . . .2C **72**
  (off Bedford Gdns.)
Bedford Hill SW12 . . . .1D **117**
  SW16 . . . . .1D **117**
Bedford Ho. *SW4* 2A **104**
  (off Solon New Rd. Est.)
Bedford M. SE6 . . . . .2D **123**
BEDFORD PARK 4A **70**
Bedford Pk. Cnr. W4 . . . . .5A **70**
Bedford Pk. Mans.
  W4 . . . . .5A **70**
Bedford Pas. *SW6* 3A **86**
  (off Dawes Rd.)
  W1 . . . . .5A **6** (4E **61**)
Bedford Pl.
  WC1 . . . . .5D **7** (4A **62**)
Bedford Rd. N8 . . . . .1F **33**
  SW4 . . . . .2A **104**
  W4 . . . . .4A **70**
Bedford Row
  WC1 . . . . .5A **8** (4B **62**)
Bedford Sq.
  WC1 . . . . .1C **14** (4F **61**)
Bedford St.
  WC2 . . . . . .4D **15** (1A **76**)
Bedford Ter. SW2 . . . . . .3A **104**
Bedford Way
  WC1 . . . . .4C **6** (3F **61**)
Bedgebury Gdns.
  SW19 . . . . .2A **114**
Bedgebury Rd. SE9 . . . . .2F **111**
Bedivere Rd.
  BR1: Brom 3C **124**
Bedlam M. *SE11* 5C **76**
  (off Walnut Tree Wlk.)
Bedmond Ho. *SW3* 1A **88**
  (off Cale St.)
Bedser Cl. SE11 . . . . .2B **90**
Bedwell Ho. SW9 . . . . . . .5C **90**
Beeby Rd. E16 . . . . .4D **69**
Beech Av. W3 . . . . .2A **70**
Beech Cl. SE8 . . . . .2C **94**
  SW15 . . . . .5C **98**
  SW19 . . . . .5E **113**
Beech Ct. *W9* 4C **58**
  (off Elmfield Way)
Beech Cres. Ct. N5 . . . . . .1D **49**

Beechcroft Av. NW11 . . . .2B **30**
Beechcroft Cl.
  SW16 . . . . .5B **118**
Beechcroft Ct. NW11 . . . .2B **30**
  (off Beechcroft Av.)
Beechcroft Rd.
  SW17 . . . . .2A **116**
Beechdale Rd. SW2 . . . .4B **104**
Beechdene SE15 . . . . . . .4D **93**
  (off Carlton Gro.)
Beechen Pl. SE23 . . . . . . .2F **121**
Beeches Rd. SW17 . . . . .3A **116**
Beechey Ho. *E1* 2D **79**
  (off Watts St.)
Beechfield Rd. N4 . . . . . . .1E **35**
  SE6 . . . . .1B **122**
Beech Gdns. EC2 . . . . .5F **9**
  (off Beech St.)
Beech Ho. SE16 . . . . .3E **79**
  (off Ainsty Est.)
Beechmont Cl.
  BR1: Brom 5A **124**
Beechmore Rd. SW11 . . . .4B **88**
Beecholme Est. E5 . . . . . . .5D **37**
Beech St. EC2 . . . . .5F **9** (4E **63**)
Beech Tree Cl. N1 . . . . . . .4C **48**
Beechwood Gro. W3 . . . . .1A **70**
Beechwood Ho. *E2* 1C **64**
  (off Teale St.)
Beechwood Rd. E8 . . . . . . .3B **50**
Beechwoods Ct.
  SE19 . . . . .5B **120**
Beechworth NW6 . . . . .4A **44**
Beechworth Cl. NW3 . . . . .4B **30**
Beecroft La. SE4 . . . . . . .3A **108**
Beecroft M. SE4 . . . . .3A **108**
Beecroft Rd. SE4 . . . . . .3A **108**
Beehive Cl. E8 . . . . .4B **50**
Beehive Pas. *EC3* 3D **19**
  (off Lime St.)
Beehive Pl. SW9 . . . . . . .1C **104**
Beemans Row
  SW18 . . . . .2E **115**
Beeston Cl. E8 . . . . .2C **50**
Beeston Ho. *SE1* 5B **26**
  (off Burbage Cl.)
Beeston Pl.
  SW1 . . . . .5E **21** (4D **75**)
Beethoven St. W10 . . . . . .2A **58**
Beeton Way SE27 . . . . . .4F **119**
Begbie Rd. SE3 . . . . .4E **97**
Begonia Wlk. W12 . . . . . .5B **56**
Beira St. SW12 . . . . .5D **103**
Bekesbourne St. E14 . . . .5A **66**
Beldanes Lodge
  NW10 . . . . .4C **42**
Belfast Rd. N16 . . . . .4B **36**
Belfont Wlk. N7 . . . . .1A **48**
  (not continuous)
Belford Ho. E8 . . . . .5B **50**
Belfort Rd. SE15 . . . . .5E **93**
Belfry Cl. SE16 . . . . .1D **93**
Belgrade Rd. N16 . . . . . . .1A **50**
Belgrave Ct. *E2* 1D **65**
  (off Temple St.)
  E13 . . . . .3E **69**
  E14 . . . . .1B **80**
  (off Westferry Cir.)
  SW8 . . . . .3E **89**
  (off Ascalon St.)

Belgrave Gdns. NW8 . . .5D **45**
Belgrave Hgts. E11 . . . .3C **40**
Belgrave Ho. SW9 . . . . .3C **90**
Belgrave Mans.
  NW8 . . . .*5D 45*
    (off Belgrave Gdns.)
Belgrave M. Nth.
  SW1 . . . . . . .4B **20** (3C **74**)
Belgrave M. Sth.
  SW1 . . . . . . .5C **20** (4C **74**)
Belgrave M. W. SW1 . . .5B **20**
Belgrave Pl.
  SW1 . . . . . . .5C **20** (4C **74**)
Belgrave Rd. E10 . . . . . .3E **39**
  E11 . . . . .4C **40**
  E13 . . . . .3E **69**
  E17 . . . . .1C **38**
  SW1 . . . . .5D **75**
  SW13 . . . . .3B **84**
Belgrave Sq.
  SW1 . . . . . . .5B **20** (4C **74**)
Belgrave St. E1 . . . . . . .4F **65**
Belgrave Yd. SW1 . . . . .5D **21**
BELGRAVIA 4C **74**
Belgravia Ct. *SW1* *4D 75*
    (off Ebury St.)
Belgravia Ho. *SW1* *5B 20*
    (off Halkin Pl.)
Belgravia Ho. *SW1* *5B 20*
  SW4 . . . . .4F **103**
Belgravia Workshops
  N19 . . . .*4A 34*
    (off Marlborough Rd.)
Belgrove St.
  WC1 . . . . . . .1E **7** (2A **62**)
Belham Wlk. SE5 . . . . . .4F **91**
Belinda Rd. SW9 . . . . . .1D **105**
Belitha Vs. N1 . . . . .4B **48**
Bella Best Ho. *SW1* *1D 89*
    (off Westmoreland Ter.)
Bellamy Cl. E14 . . . . . . .3C **80**
  W14 . . . . .1B **86**
Bellamy Ho. SW17 . . . . .4F **115**
Bellamy's Ct. *SE16* *2F 79*
    (off Abbotshade Rd.)
Bellamy St. SW12 . . . . .5D **103**
Bellasis Av. SW2 . . . . . .2A **118**
Bell Dr. SW18 . . . . .5A **100**
Bellefields Rd. SW9 . . . .1B **104**
Bellenden Rd. SE15 . . . .4B **92**
Bellenden Rd. Retail Pk.
  SE15 . . . . .4C **92**
Belleville Rd. SW11 . . . .3A **102**
Bellevue Pde. SW17 . . . .1B **116**
Bellevue Pl. E1 . . . . .3E **65**
Bellevue Rd. SW13 . . . . .5C **84**
  SW17 . . . . .1A **116**
Bellew St. SW17 . . . . . . .3E **115**
Bellfield Cl. SE3 . . . . . . .3D **97**
Bellflower Cl. E6 . . . . . . .4F **69**
Bell Gdns. E10 . . . . .3C **38**
    (off Church Rd.)
Bellgate M. NW5 . . . . . . .1D **47**
BELL GREEN 4B **122**
Bell Grn. SE26 . . . . .4B **122**
Bell Grn. La. SE26 . . . . .5B **122**
Bellhaven E15 . . . . .3F **53**
Bell Ho. *SE10* *2E 95*
    (off Haddo St.)

Bellina M. NW5 . . . . .1D **47**
BELLINGHAM 3D **123**
Bellingham Grn.
  SE6 . . . . .3C **122**
Bellingham Leisure &
  Lifestyle Cen. 3D **123**
Bellingham Rd.
  SE6 . . . . .3D **123**
Bellingham Trad. Est.
  SE6 . . . . .3D **123**
Bell Inn Yd.
  EC3 . . . . . . .3C **18** (5F **63**)
Bell La. E1 . . . . . .1F **19** (4B **64**)
  E16 . . . . .2B **82**
Bellmaker Ct. E3 . . . . . .4C **66**
Bell Mdw. SE19 . . . . . . .5A **120**
Bell Moor NW3 . . . . .5E **31**
Bello Cl. SE24 . . . . .5D **105**
Bellot Gdns. SE10 . . . . .1A **96**
    (off Bellot St.)
Bellot St. SE10 . . . . .1A **96**
Bells All. SW6 . . . . .5C **86**
Bellsize Ct. SW3 . . . . . .2F **45**
Bell St. NW1 . . . . .4A **60**
Belltrees Gro.
  SW16 . . . . .5B **118**
Bell Wharf La.
  EC4 . . . . . . .5A **18** (1E **77**)
Bellwood Rd. SE15 . . . . .2F **107**
Bell Yd. WC2 . . .3B **16** (5C **62**)
Bell Yd. M.
  SE1 . . . . . . .4E **27** (3A **78**)
Belmont Cl. SW4 . . . . . .1E **103**
Belmont Ct. N5 . . . . .1E **49**
  NW11 . . . . .1B **30**
Belmont Gro. SE13 . . . . .1F **109**
  W4 . . . . .5A **70**
Belmont Hall Ct.
  SE13 . . . . .1F **109**
Belmont Hill SE13 . . . . .1F **109**
Belmont M. SW19 . . . . .2F **113**
Belmont Pde. NW11 . . . .1B **30**
Belmont Pk. SE13 . . . . . .2F **109**
Belmont Pk. Cl.
  SE13 . . . . .2A **110**
Belmont Pk. Rd. E10 . . .1D **39**
Belmont Rd. SW4 . . . . . .1E **103**
Belmont St. NW1 . . . . . .4C **46**
Belmore Ho. N7 . . . . . . .2F **47**
Belmore La. N7 . . . . .2F **47**
Belmore St. SW8 . . . . . .4F **89**
Beloe Cl. SW15 . . . . . . .2C **98**
Belsham St. E9 . . . . .3E **51**
Belsize Av. NW3 . . . . . . .3F **45**
Belsize Ct. Garages
  NW3 . . . .*2F 45*
    (off Belsize La.)
Belsize Cres. NW3 . . . . .3F **45**
Belsize Gro. NW3 . . . . . .3A **46**
Belsize La. NW3 . . . . . . .3F **45**
Belsize M. NW3 . . . . . . .3F **45**
Belsize Pk. NW3 . . . . . . .3F **45**
Belsize Pk. Gdns.
  NW3 . . . . .3F **45**
Belsize Pk. M. NW3 . . . .3F **45**
Belsize Pl. NW3 . . . . . . .2F **45**
Belsize Rd. NW6 . . . . . .5D **45**
Belsize Sq. NW3 . . . . . .3F **45**
Belsize Ter. NW3 . . . . . .3F **45**

Beltane Dr. SW19 . . . . . .3F **113**
Belthorn Cres.
  SW12 . . . . .5E **103**
Belton Rd. E7 . . . . .4D **55**
  E11 . . . . .1A **54**
  NW2 . . . . .3C **42**
Belton Way E3 . . . . .4C **66**
Beltran Rd. SW6 . . . . . . .5D **87**
Belvedere, The
  SW10 . . . .*4E 87*
    (off Chelsea Harbour)
Belvedere Av.
  SW19 . . . . .5A **114**
Belvedere Bldgs.
  SE1 . . . . . . .4E **25** (3D **77**)
Belvedere Ct. *N1* *5A 50*
    (off De Beauvoir Cres.)
  NW2 . . . .*3F 43*
    (off Willesden La.)
  SW15 . . . . .2E **99**
Belvedere Dr.
  SW19 . . . . .5A **114**
Belvedere Gro.
  SW19 . . . . .5A **114**
Belvedere M. SE3 . . . . . .3D **97**
  SE15 . . . . .1E **107**
Belvedere Pl.
  SE1 . . . . . . .4E **25** (3D **77**)
  SW2 . . . . .2B **104**
Belvedere Rd. E10 . . . . .3A **38**
  SE1 . . . . . . .4F **23** (3B **76**)
Belvedere Sq.
  SW19 . . . . .5A **114**
Belvoir Ho. SW1 . . . . . . .5E **75**
Belvoir Rd. SE22 . . . . . .5C **106**
Bembridge Cl. NW6 . . . .4A **44**
Bembridge Ho. *SE8* *5B 80*
    (off Longshore)
  SW18 . . . .*4D 101*
    (off Iron Mill Rd.)
Bemersyde Point
  E13 . . . .*2D 69*
    (off Dongola Rd. W.)
Bemerton Est. N1 . . . . . .4A **48**
Bemerton St. N1 . . . . . . .5B **48**
Bemish Rd. SW15 . . . . . .1F **99**
Benbow Ct. *W6* *4E 71*
    (off Benbow Rd.)
Benbow Ho. *SE8* *2C 94*
    (off Benbow St.)
Benbow Rd. W6 . . . . . . .4D **71**
Benbow St. SE8 . . . . . . .2C **94**
Benbury Cl.
  BR1: Brom 5E **123**
Bence Ho. *SE8* *5A 80*
    (off Rainsborough Av.)
Bendall Ho. *NW1* *4A 60*
    (off Penfold St.)
Bendall M. *NW1* *4A 60*
    (off Bell St.)
Bendemeer Rd.
  SW15 . . . . .1F **99**
Benden Ho. *SE13* *3E 109*
    (off Monument Gdns.)
Bendish Rd. E6 . . . . .4F **55**
Bendon Valley
  SW18 . . . . .5D **101**
Benedict Rd. SW9 . . . . .1B **104**
Benenden Ho. *SE17* *1A 92*
    (off Mina Rd.)

Ben Ezra Ct. SE17 . . . . . .5E 77
   (off Asolando Dr.)
Benfleet Ct. E8 . . . . .5B 50
Bengal Ct. EC3 . . . . .3C 18
   (off Birchin La.)
Bengeworth Rd.
   SE5 . . . . .1E 105
Benham Cl.
   SW11 . . . . .1F 101
Benham Ho. SW10 . . . . .3D 87
   (off Coleridge Gdns.)
Benham's Pl. NW3 . . . . .1E 45
Benhill Rd. SE5 . . . . .3F 91
Benhurst Ct. SW16 . . . . .5C 118
Benhurst La.
   SW16 . . . . .5C 118
Benin Ho. WC1 . . . . .1F 15
   (off Procter St.)
Benin St. SE13 . . . . .5F 109
Benjamin Cl. E8 . . . . .5C 50
Benjamin Franklin House
   . . . . .1D 23
   (off Craven St.)
Benjamin M. SW12 . . . .5E 103
Benjamin St.
   EC1 . . . . .5D 9 (4D 63)
Ben Jonson Ct. N1 . . . . .1A 64
Ben Jonson Ho. EC2 . . . .5A 10
Ben Jonson Pl. EC2 . . . . .5A 10
Benworth St. E3 . . . . .4F 65
Benledi Rd. E14 . . . . .5F 67
Bennelong Cl. W12 . . . . . .1D 71
Bennerley Rd.
   SW11 . . . . .3A 102
Bennet M. N19 . . . . .5F 33
   (off Wedmore St.)
Bennet's Hill
   EC4 . . . . . .4E 17 (1E 77)
Bennet St.
   SW1 . . . . .1F 21 (2E 75)
Bennett Cl. N7 . . . . .5B 34
Bennett Gro. SE13 . . . . . .4D 95
Bennett Ho. SW1 . . . . . . .5F 75
   (off Page St.)
Bennett Pk. SE3 . . . . .1B 110
Bennett Rd. E13 . . . . .3E 69
   N16 . . . . .1A 50
   SW9 . . . . .5C 90
Bennett St. W4 . . . . .2A 84
Bennett's Yd. SW1 . . . . . .4F 75
Benn St. E9 . . . . .3A 52
Bensbury Cl. SW15 . . . . .5D 99
Ben Smith Way SE16 . . . .4C 78
Benson Av. E6 . . . . .1E 69
Benson Ct. SW8 . . . . .4A 90
   (off Hartington Rd.)
Benson Ho. E2 . . . . .3F 11
   (off Ligonier St.)
   SE1 . . . . .2C 24
   (off Hatfields)
Benson Quay E1 . . . . . . .1E 79
Benson Rd. SE23 . . . . . .1E 121
Bentfield Gdns.
   SE9 . . . . .3F 125
Bentham Ct. N1 . . . . .4E 49
   (off Ecclesbourne Rd.)
Bentham Ho. SE1 . . . . . . .5B 26
Bentham Rd. E9 . . . . .3F 51
Bentinck Cl. NW8 . . . . . .1A 60

Bentinck Ho. SW1 . . . . . .5C 22
   (off Monck St.)
   W12 . . . . .1D 71
   (off White City Est.)
Bentinck Mans. W1 . . . .2C 12
   (off Bentinck St.)
Bentinck M.
   W1 . . . . . .2C 12 (5C 60)
Bentinck St.
   W1 . . . . . .2C 12 (5C 60)
Bentley Cl. SW19 . . . . . .3C 114
Bentley Ct. SE13 . . . . . . .2E 109
   (off Whitburn Rd.)
Bentley Dr. NW2 . . . . . . .5B 30
Bentley Ho. E3 . . . . .3C 66
   (off Wellington Way)
   SE5 . . . . .4A 92
   (off Peckham Rd.)
Bentley Rd. N1 . . . . .3A 50
Bentons La. SE27 . . . . . .4E 119
Benton's Ri. SE27 . . . . . .5F 119
Bentworth Ct. E2 . . . . . . .3C 64
   (off Granby St.)
Bentworth Rd. W12 . . . . .5D 57
Ben Uri Gallery 5D 45
Benville Ho. SW8 . . . . . . .3B 90
   (off Dorset Rd.)
Benwell Rd. N7 . . . . .1C 48
Benwick Cl. SE16 . . . . . . .5D 79
Benworth St. E3 . . . . .2B 66
Benyon Cl. N1 . . . . .5A 50
   (off De Beauvoir Est.)
Benyon Ho. EC1 . . . . .2C 8
   (off Myddelton Pas.)
Benyon Rd. N1 . . . . .5F 49
Benyon Wharf N1 . . . . . .5A 50
   (off Kingsland Rd.)
Berberis Ho. E3 . . . . .4C 66
   (off Gale St.)
Berber Pde. SE18 . . . . . . .4F 97
Berber Pl. E14 . . . . .1C 80
Berber Rd. SW11 . . . . . . .3B 102
Berebinder Ho. E3 . . . . . .1B 66
   (off Tredegar Rd.)
Beregaria Ct. SE11 . . . . .2C 90
   (off Kennington Pk. Rd.)
Berenger Twr.
   SW10 . . . . .3F 87
   (off Worlds End Est.)
Berenger Wlk. SW10 . . . .3F 87
   (off Worlds End Est.)
Berens Rd. NW10 . . . . . . .2F 57
Beresford Ct. E9 . . . . .2A 52
   (off Mabley St.)
Beresford Rd. N5 . . . . . . .2F 49
Beresford Ter. N5 . . . . . . .2E 49
Berestede Rd. W6 . . . . . . .1B 84
Bere St. E1 . . . . .1F 79
Bergen Ho. SE5 . . . . .5E 91
   (off Carew St.)
Bergen Sq. SE16 . . . . . . .4A 80
Berger Rd. E9 . . . . .3F 51
Berghem M. W14 . . . . . . .4F 71
Bergholt Cres. N16 . . . . . .2A 36
Bergholt M. NW1 . . . . . . .4F 47
Berglen Ct. E14 . . . . .5A 66
Bering Sq. E14 . . . . .1C 94
Bering Wlk. E16 . . . . .5F 69
Berisford M.
   SW18 . . . . .4E 101

Berkeley Ct. NW1 . . . . . . .4A 4
   NW10 . . . . .1A 42
   NW11 . . . . .2B 30
   (off Ravenscroft Av.)
Berkeley Gdns.
   W8 . . . . .2C 72
Berkeley Ho. E3 . . . . .2C 66
   (off Wellington Way)
   SE8 . . . . .1B 94
   (off Grove St.)
Berkeley M.
   W1 . . . . . .3A 12 (5B 60)
Berkeley Rd. E12 . . . . . . .2F 55
   N8 . . . . .1F 33
   N15 . . . . .1F 35
   SW13 . . . . .4C 84
Berkeley Sq.
   W1 . . . . . .5E 13 (1D 75)
Berkeley St.
   W1 . . . . . .5E 13 (1D 75)
Berkeley Twr. E14 . . . . . .2B 80
   (off Westferry Cir.)
Berkeley Wlk. N7 . . . . . . .4B 34
   (off Durham Rd.)
Berkley Gro. NW1 . . . . . . .4C 46
Berkley Rd. NW1 . . . . . . .4B 46
Berkshire Ho. SE6 . . . . . .4C 122
Berkshire Rd. E9 . . . . .3B 52
Bermans Way NW10 . . . . .1A 42
BERMONDSEY 3C 78
Bermondsey Exchange
   SE1 . . . . .5E 27
   (off Bermondsey St.)
Bermondsey Sq.
   SE1 . . . . . .5E 27 (4A 78)
Bermondsey St.
   SE1 . . . . . .2D 27 (2A 78)
Bermondsey Trad. Est.
   SE16 . . . . .1E 93
Bermondsey Wall E.
   SE16 . . . . .3C 78
Bermondsey Wall W.
   SE16 . . . . .3C 78
Bernard Angell Ho.
   SE10 . . . . .2F 95
   (off Trafalgar Rd.)
Bernard Ashley Dr.
   SE7 . . . . .1D 97
Bernard Cassidy St.
   E16 . . . . .4B 68
Bernard Gdns.
   SW19 . . . . .5B 114
Bernard Hegarty Lodge
   E8 . . . . .4C 50
   (off Lansdowne Dr.)
Bernard Ho. E1 . . . . .1F 19
Bernard Mans. WC1 . . . . .4D 7
   (off Bernard St.)
Bernard Myers Ho.
   SE5 . . . . .3A 92
   (off Harris St.)
Bernard Rd. N15 . . . . . . .1B 36
Bernard Shaw Ct.
   NW1 . . . . .4E 47
   (off St Pancras Way)
Bernard Shaw Ho.
   NW10 . . . . .5A 42
   (off Knatchbull Rd.)
Bernard St.
   WC1 . . . . . .4D 7 (3A 62)

Bernard Sunley Ho.
SW9 . . . .*3C* **90**
(off Sth. Island Pl.)
Bernays Gro.
SW9 . . . . .2B **104**
Berners Ho. *N1* *1C* **62**
(off Barnsbury Est.)
Berners M.
W1 . . . . . . .1A **14** (4E **61**)
Berners Pl.
W1 . . . . . . .2A **14** (5E **61**)
Berners Rd. *N1* 5D **49**
Berners St.
W1 . . . . . . .1A **14** (4E **61**)
Berner Ter. *E1* *5C* **64**
(off Fairclough St.)
Bernhard Baron Ho.
E1 . . . .*5C* **64**
(off Henriques St.)
Bernhardt Cres. NW8 . .3A **60**
Berridge M. NW6 . . . . .2C **44**
Berridge Rd. SE19 . . .5F **119**
Berriman Rd. N7 . . . . .5B **34**
Berrington Ho. *W2* *1C* **72**
(off Herrington Rd.)
Berry Cotts. *E14* *5A* **66**
(off Maroon St.)
Berryfield Rd. SE17 . . .1D **91**
Berry Ho. *E1* *3D* **65**
(off Headlam St.)
SW11 . . . .*5B* **88**
(off Culvert Rd.)
Berry La. SE21 . . . .4F **119**
Berryman's La.
SE26 . . . . .4F **121**
Berry Pl. EC1 . . .2E **9** (2D **63**)
Berry St. EC1 . . .3E **9** (3D **63**)
Bertal Rd. SW17 . . . . .4F **115**
Berthon St. SE8 . . . . . .3C **94**
Bertie Rd. NW10 . . . . .3C **42**
SE26 . . . . .5F **121**
Bertram Rd. NW4 . . . . .1C **28**
Bertram St. N19 . . . . . .4D **33**
Bertrand Ho. *E16* *5D* **69**
(off Russell Rd.)
SW16 . . . .*3A* **118**
(off Leigham Av.)
Bertrand St. SE13 . . .1D **109**
Berwick Ct. SE1 . . . . . .4A **26**
Berwick Rd. E16 . . . . . .5D **69**
Berwick St.
W1 . . . . . . .2A **14** (5E **61**)
Berwyn Rd. SE24 . . . .1D **119**
Beryl Rd. W6 . . . . .1F **85**
Besant Cl. NW2 . . . . . .5A **30**
Besant Ct. N1 . . . . .2F **49**
Besant Ho. *NW8* *5E* **45**
(off Boundary Rd.)
Besant Pl. SE22 . . . . .2B **106**
Besant Rd. NW2 . . . . . .1A **44**
Besant Wlk. N7 . . . . . .4B **34**
Besford Ho. *E2* *1C* **64**
(off Pritchard's Rd.)
Besley St. SW16 . . . .5E **117**
Bessborough Gdns.
SW1 . . . . .1F **89**
Bessborough Pl. SW1 . .1F **89**
Bessborough Rd.
SW15 . . . . .1C **112**
Bessborough St. SW1 . .1F **89**

Bessemer Ct. *NW1* *4E* **47**
(off Rochester Sq.)
Bessemer Pk. Ind. Est.
SE24 . . . . .2D **105**
Bessemer Pl.
SE10 . . . . .4B **82**
Bessemer Rd. SE5 . . . .5E **91**
Bessingham Wlk.
SE4 . . . .*2F* **107**
(off Aldersford Cl.)
Besson St. SE14 . . . . . .4E **93**
Bessy St. E2 . . . . .2E **65**
Bestwood St. SE8 . . . . .5F **79**
Beswick M. NW6 . . . . . .3D **45**
Beta Pl. SW4 . . . . .2B **104**
Bethel Cl. NW4 . . . . . . .1F **29**
Bethell Av. E16 . . . . . . .3B **68**
Bethersden Ho. *SE17* . . .*1A* **92**
(off Kinglake Est.)
Bethlehem Ho.
E14 . . . .*1B* **80**
(off Limehouse C'way.)
BETHNAL GREEN 2D **65**
Bethnal Green Cen. for
Sports & Performing Arts
. . . . .2B **64**
Bethnal Grn. Rd.
E1 . . . . .3F **11** (3B **64**)
E2 . . . . .3F **11** (3B **64**)
Bethune Cl. N16 . . . . . .3A **36**
Bethune Rd. N16 . . . . . .2F **35**
NW10 . . . . .3A **56**
Bethwin Rd. SE5 . . . . . .3D **91**
Betsham Ho. *SE1* *3B* **26**
(off Newcomen St.)
Betterton Ho. *WC2* *3E* **15**
(off Betterton St.)
Betterton St.
WC2 . . . . .3D **15** (5A **62**)
Bettons Pk. E15 . . . . . .5A **54**
Bettridge Rd. SW6 . . . . .5B **86**
Betts Ho. *E1* *1D* **79**
(off Betts St.)
Betts M. E17 . . . . .1B **38**
Betts Rd. E16 . . . . .1D **83**
Betts St. E1 . . . . .1D **79**
Betty Brooks Ho. E11 . . .5F **39**
Betty May Gray Ho.
E14 . . . .*5E* **81**
(off Pier St.)
Beulah Hill SE19 . . . .5D **119**
Beulah Rd. E17 . . . . . .1D **39**
Bevan Ct. *E3* *1C* **66**
(off Tredegar Rd.)
Bevan Ho. *N1* *5A* **50**
(off New Era Est.)
WC1 . . . .*5E* **7**
(off Boswell St.)
Bevan M. W12 . . . . . . .3C **70**
Bevan St. N1 . . . . .5E **49**
Bev Callender Cl.
SW8 . . . . .1D **103**
Bevenden St.
N1 . . . . .1C **10** (2F **63**)
Beveridge Rd.
NW10 . . . . .4A **42**
Beverley Cl. SW11 . . . .2F **101**
SW13 . . . . .5C **84**
Beverley Cotts.
SW15 . . . . .3A **112**

Beverley Ct. NW6 . . . . . .*4E* **45**
(off Fairfax Rd.)
SE4 . . . . .1B **108**
(not continuous)
Beverley Gdns.
NW11 . . . . .2A **30**
SW13 . . . . .1B **98**
Beverley Ho.
BR1: Brom *5F* **123**
(off Brangbourne Rd.)
Beverley La. SW15 . . . .3B **112**
Beverley Meads &
Fishpond Valleys
Nature Reserve
. . . . .5B **112**
Beverley Path SW13 . . .5B **84**
Beverley Rd. E6 . . . . . . .2F **69**
SW13 . . . . .1B **98**
W4 . . . . .1B **84**
Beversbrook Rd. N19 . . .5F **33**
Beverstone Rd.
SW2 . . . . .3B **104**
Beverston M. W1 . . . . . .1A **12**
Bevill Allen Cl.
SW17 . . . . .5B **116**
Bevin Cl. SE16 . . . . . . .2A **80**
Bevin Ct. WC1 . . .1A **8** (2B **62**)
Bevington Path SE1 . . . .4F **27**
Bevington Rd. W10 . . . . .4A **58**
Bevington St. SE16 . . . . .3C **78**
Bevin Ho. *E2* *2E* **65**
(off Butler St.)
E3 . . . .*2C* **66**
(off Alfred St.)
Bevin Sq. SW17 . . . . . .3B **116**
Bevin Way
WC1 . . . . .1B **8** (1C **62**)
Bevis Marks
EC3 . . . . .2E **19** (5A **64**)
Bew Ct. SE22 . . . . . . .5C **106**
Bewdley St. N1 . . . . . . .4C **48**
Bewick M. SE15 . . . . . .3D **93**
Bewick St. SW8 . . . . . . .5D **89**
Bewley Ho. *E1* *1D* **79**
(off Bewley St.)
Bewley St. E1 . . . . .1E **79**
Bewlys Rd. SE27 . . . . .5D **119**
Bexhill Rd. SE4 . . . . . . .4B **108**
Bexhill Wlk. E15 . . . . . .5A **54**
Bexley Ho. SE4 . . . . . . .2A **108**
Bezier Apartments
EC2 . . . . .3C **10** (3F **63**)
BFI Southbank 1A **24**
Bianca Ho. *N1* *1D* **11**
(off Crondall St.)
Bianca Rd. SE15 . . . . . .2C **92**
Bibury Cl. SE15 . . . . . . .2A **92**
(not continuous)
Bickels Yd. SE1 . . . . . .3A **78**
Bickenhall Mans. W1 . . .*5A* **4**
(not continuous)
Bickenhall St.
W1 . . . . . . .5A **4** (4B **60**)
Bickersteth Rd.
SW17 . . . . .5B **116**
Bickerton Rd. N19 . . . . .4E **33**
Bickley Rd. E10 . . . . . . .2D **39**
Bickley St. SW17 . . . . .5A **116**
Bicknell Ho. *E1* *5C* **64**
(off Ellen St.)

Bicknell Rd. SE5 . . . . . . .1E 105
Bicycle M. SW4 . . . . .1F 103
Bidborough St.
  WC1 . . . . .2D 7 (2A 62)
Biddenham Ho. SE16 . . . . .5F 79
  (off Plough Way)
Bidder St. E16 . . . . .4A 68
  (not continuous)
Biddesden Ho. SW3 . . . . .5B 74
  (off Cadogan St.)
Biddestone Rd. N7 . . . . . . .1B 48
Biddulph Mans. W9 . . . . .2D 59
  (off Elgin Av.)
Biddulph Rd. W9 . . . . . . .2D 59
Bideford Rd.
  BR1: Brom 3B 124
Bidwell St. SE15 . . . . . . .4D 93
Big Ben 4E 23 (3A 76)
Biggerstaff Rd. E15 . . . . .5E 53
Biggerstaff St. N4 . . . . . . .4C 34
Biggs Row SW13 . . . . . . .1F 99
Biggs Sq. E9 . . . . .3B 52
Big Hill E5 . . . . .3D 37
Bigland St. E1 . . . . .5D 65
Bignold Rd. E7 . . . . .1C 54
Bigwood Ct. NW11 . . . . . .1D 31
Bigwood Rd. NW11 . . . . . .1D 31
Bilberry Ho. E3 . . . . .4C 66
  (off Watts Gro.)
Billingford Cl. SE4 . . .2F 107
Billing Ho. E1 . . . . .5F 65
  (off Bower St.)
Billingley NW1 . . . . .5E 47
  (off Pratt St.)
Billing Pl. SW10 . . . . .3D 87
Billing Rd. SW10 . . . . . . .3D 87
Billingsgate Market . . .2D 81
Billing St. SW10 . . . . .3D 87
Billington Rd. SE14 . . . . . .3F 93
Billiter Sq. EC3 . . . . .3E 19
Billiter St.
  EC3 . . . . .3E 19 (5A 64)
Billson St. E14 . . . . .5E 81
Bilsby Gro. SE9 . . . . .4F 125
Bilton Towers W1 . . . . . .3A 12
  (off Gt. Cumberland Pl.)
Bina Gdns. SW5 . . . . .5E 73
Binbrook Ho. W10 . . . . . . .4E 57
  (off Sutton Way)
Binden Rd. W12 . . . . .4B 70
Binfield Rd. SW4 . . . . .4A 90
Bingfield St. N1 . . . . .5A 48
  (not continuous)
Bingham Ct. N1 . . . . .4D 49
  (off Halton Rd.)
Bingham Pl.
  W1 . . . . .5B 4 (4C 60)
Bingham St. N1 . . . . .3F 49
Bingley Rd. E16 . . . . .5E 69
Binley Ho. SW15 . . . . .4B 98
Binney St.
  W1 . . . . .3C 12 (5C 60)
Binnie Ct. SE10 . . . . .3D 95
  (off Greenwich High Rd.)
Binnie Ho. SE1 . . . . .5F 25
  (off Bath Ter.)
Binns Rd. W4 . . . . .1A 84
Binns Ter. W4 . . . . .1A 84
Bircham Path SE4 . . . .2F 107
  (off Aldersford Cl.)

Birch Cl. E16 . . . . .4A 68
  N19 . . . . .4E 33
  SE15 . . . . .5C 92
Birchdale Rd. E7 . . . . .2E 55
Birchdown Ho. E3 . . . . . .2D 67
  (off Rainhill Way)
Birchen Cl. NW9 . . . . .4A 28
Birchen Gro. NW9 . . . . . . .4A 28
Birches, The E12 . . . . . . .1F 55
  SE5 . . . . .5A 92
  SE7 . . . . .2D 97
Birchfield Ho. E14 . . . . . .1C 80
  (off Birchfield St.)
Birchfield St. E14 . . . . . . .1C 80
Birch Gro. E11 . . . . .1A 54
  SE12 . . . . .5B 110
Birch Ho. SE14 . . . . .4B 94
  SW2 . . . . .4C 104
  W10 . . . . .3A 58
  (off Droop St.)
Birchington Ct. NW6 . . . .5D 45
  (off West End La.)
Birchington Ho. E5 . . . . . .2D 51
Birchington Rd. N8 . . . . . .1F 33
  NW6 . . . . .5C 44
Birchin La.
  EC3 . . . . .3C 18 (5F 63)
Birchlands Av.
  SW12 . . . . .5B 102
Birchmere Lodge
  SE16 . . . . .1D 93
  (off Sherwood Gdns.)
Birchmere Row SE3 . . . . .5B 96
Birchmore Hall N5 . . . . . .5E 35
Birchmore Wlk. N5 . . . . . .5E 35
  (not continuous)
Birch Va. Ct. NW8 . . . . . . .3F 59
  (off Pollitt Dr.)
Birchwood Dr. NW3 . . . . .5D 31
Birchwood Rd.
  SW17 . . . . .5D 117
Birdbrook Ho. N1 . . . . . . .4E 49
  (off Popham Rd.)
Birdbrook Rd. SE3 . . . . . .2E 111
Birdcage Wlk.
  SW1 . . . . .4F 21 (3E 75)
Birdhurst Rd. SW18 . . . . . .3E 101
Bird in Bush BMX Track
  . . . . .3D 93
  (off Bird in Bush Rd.)
Bird in Bush Rd.
  SE15 . . . . .3C 92
Bird-in-Hand M.
  SE23 . . . . .2E 121
  (off Bird-in-Hand Pas.)
Bird-in-Hand Pas.
  SE23 . . . . .2E 121
Bird in Hand Yd.
  NW3 . . . . .1E 45
Birdsall Ho. SE5 . . . . .1A 106
Birdsfield La. E3 . . . . .5B 52
Bird St. W1 . . . .3C 12 (5C 60)
Birdwood Av. SE13 . . . . . .4F 109
Birkbeck Hill SE21 . . . . . .1D 119
Birkbeck M. E8 . . . . .2B 50
Birkbeck Pl. SE21 . . . . . . .2E 119
Birkbeck Rd. E8 . . . . .2B 50
  SW19 . . . . .5D 115
Birkbeck St. E2 . . . . .2D 65
Birkdale Cl. SE16 . . . . . . .1D 93

Birkenhead St.
  WC1 . . . . .1E 7 (2A 62)
Birkhall Rd. SE6 . . . . .1F 123
Birkwood Cl. SW12 . . . . . .5F 103
Birley Lodge NW8 . . . . . . .1F 59
  (off Acacia Rd.)
Birley St. SW11 . . . . .5C 88
Birnam Rd. N4 . . . . .4B 34
Birrell Ho. SW9 . . . . .5B 90
  (off Stockwell Rd.)
Birse Cres. NW10 . . . . .5A 28
Birstall Rd. N15 . . . . .1A 36
Birtwhistle Ho. E3 . . . . . .5B 52
  (off Parnell Rd.)
Biscay Ho. E1 . . . . .3F 65
  (off Mile End Rd.)
Biscayne Av. E14 . . . . .2F 81
Biscay Rd. W6 . . . . .1F 85
Biscoe Way SE13 . . . . .1F 109
Biscott Ho. E3 . . . . .3D 67
Bisham Gdns. N6 . . . . .3C 32
Bishop King's Rd.
  W14 . . . . .5A 72
Bishop's Av. E13 . . . . .5D 55
  SW6 . . . . .5F 85
Bishops Avenue, The
  N2 . . . . .2F 31
Bishop's Bri. Rd. W2 . . . .5D 59
Bishop's Cl. N19 . . . . .5E 33
Bishops Ct. EC4 . . . . .2D 17
  W2 . . . . .5D 59
  (off Bishop's Bri. Rd.)
  WC2 . . . . .2B 16
Bishopsdale Ho.
  NW6 . . . . .5C 44
  (off Kilburn Vale)
Bishopsgate
  EC2 . . . . .3D 19 (5A 64)
Bishopsgate Arc. EC2 . . .1E 19
Bishopsgate Churchyard
  EC2 . . . . .2D 19 (4A 64)
Bishopsgate
Institute & Libraries
  . . . . .1E 19
  (off Bishopsgate)
Bishopsgate Twr.
  EC3 . . . . .3D 19
Bishops Gro. N2 . . . . .1A 32
Bishops Ho. SW8 . . . . .3A 90
  (off Sth. Lambeth Rd.)
Bishop's Mans. SW6 . . . . .5F 85
Bishop's Mead SE5 . . . . . .3E 91
  (off Camberwell Rd.)
Bishop's Pk. Rd. SW6 . . . .5F 85
Bishops Rd. N6 . . . . .1C 32
  SW6 . . . . .4A 86
  SW11 . . . . .3A 88
Bishops Sq.
  E1 . . . . .5E 11 (4A 64)
Bishop's Ter. SE11 . . . . . . .5C 76
Bishopsthorpe Rd.
  SE26 . . . . .4F 121
Bishop St. N1 . . . . .5E 49
Bishop's Way E2 . . . . .1D 65
Bishops Wharf Ho.
  SW11 . . . . .3A 88
  (off Parkgate Rd.)
Bishops Wood Almshouses
  E5 . . . . .1D 51
  (off Lwr. Clapton Rd.)

Bishopswood Rd. N6 ...2B **32**
Bishop Wilfred Wood Cl.
 SE15 ....5C **92**
Bishop Wilfred Wood Ct.
 E13 ....*1E* **69**
 (off Pragel St.)
Bissextile Ho. SE13 ...5D **95**
Bisson Rd. E15 ......1E **67**
Bittern Ct. SE8 ......2C **94**
Bittern Ho. *SE1* *4F* **25**
 (off Gt. Suffolk St.)
Bittern St.
 SE1 ....4F **25** (3E **77**)
Blackall St.
 EC2 ....3D **11** (3A **64**)
Blackbird Yd. E2 .....2B **64**
Black Boy La. N15 ....1E **35**
Black Bull Yd. EC1 ....*5C* **8**
 (off Hatton Wall)
Blackburne's M.
 W1 ....4B **12** (1C **74**)
Blackburn Rd. NW6 ...3D **45**
Blackett St. SW15 ....1F **99**
Blackford's Path
 SW15 ....5C **98**
Blackfriars Bri.
 EC4 ....4D **17** (1D **77**)
Blackfriars Ct. EC4 ....4D **17**
Black Friars La.
 EC4 ....4D **17** (5D **63**)
 (not continuous)
Blackfriars Pas.
 EC4 ....4D **17** (1D **77**)
Blackfriars Rd.
 SE1 ....1D **25** (3D **77**)
Blackfriars Underpass
 EC4 ....4D **17** (1C **76**)
BLACKHEATH 5B **96**
Blackheath Av. SE10 ...3F **95**
 SE10 ....*4E* **95**
 (off Blackheath Hill)
Blackheath Concert Halls
 ....1B **110**
Blackheath Gro. SE3 ..5B **96**
Blackheath Hill SE10 ..4E **95**
BLACKHEATH PARK ...1C **110**
Blackheath Pk. SE3 ...1B **110**
Blackheath Ri. SE13 ...5E **95**
 (not continuous)
Blackheath Rd. SE10 ..4D **95**
Blackheath RUFC 3D **97**
BLACKHEATH VALE 5B **96**
Blackheath Va. SE3 ...5A **96**
Blackheath Village
 SE3 ....5B **96**
Black Horse Ct.
 SE1 ....5C **26** (4F **77**)
Blackhorse Rd. SE8 ...2A **94**
Blacklands Est. SE6 ...4E **123**
Blacklands Ter. SW3 ..5B **74**
Black Lion La. W6 ....5C **70**
Black Lion M. W6 .....5C **70**
Blackmans St. E2 .....3C **64**
Blackmore Gdns.
 SW13 ....2D **85**
Blackmore Ho. *N1* *5B* **48**
 (off Barnsbury Est.)
Black Path E10 ....2A **38**
Blackpool Rd. SE15 ...5D **93**

Black Prince Rd. SE1 ..5B **76**
 SE11 ....5B **76**
Blackshaw Rd.
 SW17 ....4E **115**
Blacks Rd. W6 ....1E **85**
Blackstock M. N4 .....4D **35**
Blackstock Rd. N4 ....4D **35**
 N5 ....4D **35**
Blackstone Est. E8 ....4C **50**
Blackstone Ho. *SW1* ...*1E* **89**
 (off Churchill Gdns.)
Blackstone Rd. NW2 ..2E **43**
Black Swan Yd.
 SE1 ....3E **27** (3A **78**)
Blackthorn Av. N7 ....3C **48**
Blackthorn Ct. *E15* ...*1F* **53**
 (off Hall Rd.)
Blackthorne Ct. SE15 ..3B **92**
 (off Cator St.)
Blackthorn St. E3 .....3C **66**
Blacktree M. SW9 ....1C **104**
BLACKWALL 2E **81**
Blackwall La. SE10 ...1A **96**
Blackwall Trad. Est.
 E14 ....4F **67**
Blackwall Tunnel E14 ..2F **81**
 (not continuous)
Blackwall Tunnel App.
 E14 ....1E **81**
Blackwall Tunnel
 Northern App.
 E3 ....1C **66**
 E14 ....3E **67**
Blackwall Tunnel
 Southern App.
 SE10 ....4A **82**
Blackwall Way E14 ....2E **81**
Blackwater Cl. E7 ....1B **54**
Blackwater Ho. *NW8* ..*4F* **59**
 (off Church St.)
Blackwater St.
 SE22 ....3B **106**
Blackwell Cl. E5 ......1F **51**
Blackwell Ho. SW4 ...4F **103**
Blackwood Ho. *E1* *3D* **65**
 (off Collingwood St.)
Blackwood St. SE17 ...1F **91**
Blade, The *W2* *4F* **59**
 (off Nth. Wharf Rd.)
Blade M. SW15 ......2B **100**
Bladen Ho. *E1* *5F* **65**
 (off Dunelm St.)
Blades Ct. SW15 .....2B **100**
 W6 ....*1D* **85**
 (off Lower Mall)
Blades Ho. *SE11* *2C* **90**
 (off Kennington Oval)
Bladon Cl. SW16 .....5A **118**
Blagdon Rd. SE13 ....4D **109**
Blagrove Rd. W10 ....4A **58**
Blair Av. NW9 ....2A **28**
Blair Cl. N1 ....3E **49**
 SE6 ....1B **124**
Blairderry Rd. SW2 ...2A **118**
Blairgowrie Ct. *E14* ...*5F* **67**
 (off Blair St.)
Blair Ho. SW9 ....5B **90**
Blair St. E14 ....5E **67**

Blake Cl. W10 ....4E **57**
Blake Ct. *NW6* *2C* **58**
 (off Malvern Rd.)
 SE16 ....*1D* **93**
 (off Stubbs Dr.)
Blake Gdns. SW6 .....4D **87**
Blake Hall Cres. E11 ..3C **40**
Blake Hall Rd. E11 ....2C **40**
Blake Ho. *E14* *3C* **80**
 (off Admirals Way)
 SE1 ......5B **24** (4C **76**)
 SE8 ....*2C* **94**
 (off New King St.)
Blakemore Rd.
 SW16 ....3A **118**
Blakeney Cl. E8 ......2C **50**
 NW1 ....4F **47**
Blakenham Rd.
 SW17 ....4B **116**
Blaker Ct. SE7 ....3E **97**
 (not continuous)
Blaker Rd. E16 ....3B **68**
Blake St. SE8 ....2C **94**
Blake's Rd. SE15 .....3A **92**
Blanch Cl. SE15 ......3E **93**
Blanchedowne SE5 ...2F **105**
Blanche St. E16 ......3B **68**
Blandfield Rd.
 SW12 ....5C **102**
Blandford Ct. *N1* *4A* **50**
 (off St Peter's Way)
 NW6 ....4F **43**
Blandford Ho. *SW8* ...*3B* **90**
 (off Richborne Ter.)
Blandford Rd. W4 ....4A **70**
Blandford Sq. NW1 ...3A **60**
Blandford St.
 W1 ......2A **12** (5B **60**)
Bland Ho. *SE11* *1B* **90**
 (off Vauxhall St.)
Bland St. SE9 ....2F **111**
Blann Cl. SE9 ....4F **111**
Blantyre St. SW10 ....3F **87**
Blantyre Twr. *SW10* ...*3F* **87**
 (off Blantyre St.)
Blantyre Wlk. *SW10* ...*3F* **87**
 (off Worlds End Est.)
Blashford *NW3* *4B* **46**
 (off Adelaide Rd.)
Blashford St. SE13 ...5F **109**
Blasker Wlk. E14 .....1D **95**
Blaxland Ho. *W12* *1D* **71**
 (off White City Est.)
Blazer Ct. *NW8* *2F* **59**
 (off St John's Wood Ct.)
Blechynden Ho. *W10* ..*5F* **57**
 (off Kingsdown Cl.)
Blechynden St. W10 ..1F **71**
Bledlow Cl. NW8 .....3F **59**
Bleeding Heart Yd.
 EC1 ....1C **16**
Blegborough Rd.
 SW16 ....5E **117**
Blemundsbury *WC1* ...*5F* **7**
 (off Dombey St.)
Blendon Row *SE17* ...*5F* **77**
 (off Orb St.)
Blendworth Point
 SW15 ....1D **113**

Blenheim Cl. SE12 . . . . .1D 125
Blenheim Cl. N7 . . . . . . .3A 48
N19 . . . . .4A 34
SE10 . . . . .1C 96
(off Denham St.)
SE16 . . . . .2F 79
(off King & Queen Wharf)
Blenheim Cres. W11 . . . .1A 72
Blenheim Gdns. NW2 . . . .3E 43
SW2 . . . . .4B 104
Blenheim Gro. SE15 . . . . .5C 92
Blenheim Ho. E16 . . . . . .2D 83
(off Constable Av.)
SW3 . . . . .1A 88
(off Kings Rd.)
Blenheim Pas. NW8 . . . . .1E 59
Blenheim Rd. E6 . . . . . . .2F 69
E15 . . . . .1A 54
NW8 . . . . .1E 59
W4 . . . . .4A 70
Blenheim St.
W1 . . . . . .3D 13 (5D 61)
Blenheim Ter. NW8 . . . . .1E 59
Blenkarne Rd.
SW11 . . . . .4B 102
Blessington Cl.
SE13 . . . . .1F 109
Blessington Rd.
SE13 . . . . .1F 109
Bletchley Ct. N1 . . . . . . .1B 10
Bletchley St.
N1 . . . . .1A 10 (1F 63)
Bletsoe Wlk. N1 . . . . . . .1E 63
Blick Ho. SE16 . . . . .4E 79
(off Neptune St.)
Blincoe Cl. SW19 . . . . . .2F 113
Bliss Cres. SE13 . . . . . . .5D 95
Blissett St. SE10 . . . . . . .4E 95
Bliss M. W10 . . . . .2A 58
Blisworth Ho. E2 . . . . . . .5C 50
(off Whiston Rd.)
Blithehale Ct. E2 . . . . . . .2D 65
(off Withan St.)
Blithfield St. W8 . . . . . . .4D 73
Block Wharf E14 . . . . . . .3C 80
(off Cuba St.)
Bloemfontein Av.
W12 . . . . .2D 71
Bloemfontein Rd.
W12 . . . . .1D 71
Bloemfontein Way
W12 . . . . .2D 71
Blomfield Ct. W9 . . . . . . .3E 59
(off Maida Va.)
Blomfield Mans. W12 . . . .2E 71
(off Stanlake Rd.)
Blomfield Rd. W9 . . . . . . .4D 59
Blomfield St.
EC2 . . . . . .1C 18 (4F 63)
Blomfield Vs. W2 . . . . . . .4D 59
Blondel St. SW11 . . . . . . .5C 88
Blondin St. E3 . . . . .1C 66
Bloomberg Ct. SW1 . . . . .5F 75
(off Vauxhall Bri. Rd.)
Bloomburg St. SW1 . . . . .5F 75
Bloomfield Ct. E10 . . . . . .5D 39
(off Brisbane Rd.)
N6 . . . . .1C 32
Bloomfield Ho. E1 . . . . . .4C 64
(off Old Montague St.)

Bloomfield Pl. W1 . . . . .4E 13
Bloomfield Rd. N6 . . . . .1C 32
Bloomfield Ter. SW1 . . .1C 88
Boom Gro. SE27 . . . . . .3D 119
Bloomhall Rd. SE19 . . . .5F 119
Bloom Pk. Rd. SW6 . . . .3B 86
BLOOMSBURY
. . . . .5D 7 (4A 62)
Bloomsbury Ct. WC1 . . .1E 15
Bloomsbury Ho.
SW4 . . . . .4F 103
Bloomsbury Pl.
SW18 . . . . .3E 101
WC1 . . . . .5E 7 (4A 62)
Bloomsbury Sq.
WC1 . . . . .1E 15 (4A 62)
Bloomsbury St.
WC1 . . . . .1C 14 (4F 61)
Bloomsbury Theatre 3B 6
Bloomsbury Way
WC1 . . . . .1D 15 (4A 62)
Blore Cl. SW8 . . . . .4F 89
Blore Ct. W1 . . . . .3B 14
Blore Ho. SW10 . . . . . . .3D 87
(off Coleridge Gdns.)
Blossom St.
E1 . . . . .4E 11 (3A 64)
Blount St. E14 . . . . .5A 66
Bloxam Gdns. SE9 . . . . .3F 111
Bloxhall Rd. E10 . . . . . . .3B 38
Bloxhall Rd. SE5 . . . . . . .3E 91
Blue Anchor La.
SE16 . . . . .5C 78
Blue Anchor Yd. E1 . . . .1C 78
Blue Ball Yd.
SW1 . . . . . . .2F 21 (2E 75)
Bluebell Av. E12 . . . . . . .2F 55
Bluebell Cl. E9 . . . . .5E 51
SE26 . . . . .4B 120
Blue Bldg. SE10 . . . . . . .1B 96
(off Glenforth St.)
Blue Ct. N1 . . . . .5F 49
(off Sherborne St.)
Blue Elephant Theatre
. . . . .3E 91
(off Bethwin Rd.)
Blue Fin Bldg. SE1 . . . . .1E 25
Bluegate M. E1 . . . . . . .1D 79
Blue Lion Pl.
SE1 . . . . . . .5D 27 (4A 78)
Blueprint Apartments
SW12 . . . . .5D 103
(off Balham Gro.)
Blues St. E8 . . . . .3B 50
Blue Water SW18 . . . . . .2D 101
Blundell Cl. E8 . . . . .2C 50
Blundell St. N7 . . . . .4A 48
Blunden Ct. SW6 . . . . . .3C 86
(off Farm La.)
Blurton Rd. E5 . . . . .1E 51
Blyth Cl. E14 . . . . .5F 81
Blythe Cl. SE6 . . . . .5B 108
Blythe Hill SE6 . . . . .5B 108
Blythe Hill La. SE6 . . . . .5B 108
Blythe Hill Pl. SE23 . . . .5A 108
Blythe Ho. SE11 . . . . . . .2C 90
Blythe M. W14 . . . . .4F 71
Blythendale Ho. E2 . . . . .1C 64
(off Mansford St.)

Blythe Rd. W14 . . . . . . .4F 71
Blythe St. E2 . . . . .2D 65
Blytheswood Pl.
SW16 . . . . .4B 118
Blythe Va. SE6 . . . . .1B 122
Blyth Hill Pl. SE23 . . . . .5A 108
(off Brockley Pk.)
Blyth Rd. E17 . . . . .2B 38
Blyth's Wharf E14 . . . . . .1A 80
Blythwood Rd. N4 . . . . . .2A 34
BMX Track, Olympic Pk.
. . . . .2D 53
Boades M. NW3 . . . . . . .1F 45
Boadicea St. N1 . . . . . . .5B 48
Boardwalk Pl. E14 . . . . . .2E 81
Boarley Ho. SE17 . . . . . .5A 78
(off Massinger St.)
Boatemah Wlk. SW9 . . . .5C 90
(off Peckford Pl.)
Boathouse Centre, The
W10 . . . . .3F 57
(off Canal Cl.)
Boathouse Wlk.
SE15 . . . . .3B 92
(not continuous)
Boat Lifter Way SE16 . . .5A 80
Boat Quay E16 . . . . .1E 83
Boatyard Apartments
E14 . . . . .1D 95
Bob Anker Cl. E13 . . . . . .2C 68
Bobbin Cl. SW4 . . . . . . .1E 103
Bob Marley Way
SE24 . . . . .2C 104
Bocking St. E8 . . . . .5D 51
Boddicott Cl. SW19 . . . . .2A 114
Boddington Ho. SE14 . . . .4E 93
(off Pomeroy St.)
SW13 . . . . .2D 85
(off Wyatt Dr.)
Bodeney Ho. SE5 . . . . . .4A 92
(off Peckham Rd.)
Boden Ho. E1 . . . . .4C 64
(off Woodseer St.)
Bodington Ct. W12 . . . . .3F 71
Bodley Mnr. Way
SW2 . . . . .5C 104
Bodmin St. SW18 . . . . . .1C 114
Bodney Rd. E8 . . . . .2D 51
Bogart Ct. E14 . . . . .1C 80
(off Premiere Pl.)
Bohemia Pl. E8 . . . . .3E 51
Bohn Rd. E1 . . . . .4A 66
Boileau Rd. SW13 . . . . . .3C 84
Boisseau Ho. E1 . . . . . . .4E 65
(off Stepney Way)
Bolanachi Bldg.
SE16 . . . . .4B 78
Bolden St. SE8 . . . . .5D 95
Boldero Pl. NW8 . . . . . . .3A 60
(off Gateforth St.)
Boleyn Ground / Upton Pk.
. . . . .1E 69
Boleyn Ho. E16 . . . . .2C 82
(off Southey M.)
Boleyn Rd. E6 . . . . .1F 69
E7 . . . . .4C 54
N16 . . . . .2A 50
Bolina Rd. SE16 . . . . . . .1E 93
Bolingbroke Gro.
SW11 . . . . .2A 102

Bolingbroke Rd. W14 ...4F **71**
Bolingbroke Wlk.
  SW11 ....4F **87**
Bolney Ga. SW7 ......3A **74**
Bolney St. SW8 ....3B **90**
Bolsover St.
  W1 ....4E **5** (3D **61**)
Bolt Cl. EC4 ....5C **62**
Bolt Ho. N1 ....5A **50**
  (off Phillipp St.)
Bolton Cres. SE5 ......3D **91**
Bolton Gdns. NW10 ...1F **57**
  SW5 ....1D **87**
Bolton Gdns. M.
  SW10 ....1E **87**
Bolton Ho. SE10 ......1A **96**
  (off Trafalgar Rd.)
  SE11 ....5D **77**
  (off George Mathers Rd.)
Bolton Pl. NW8 ....5D **45**
  (off Bolton Rd.)
Bolton Rd. E15 ....3B **54**
  NW8 ....5D **45**
  NW10 ....5A **42**
Boltons, The
  SW10 ....1E **87**
Boltons Ct. SW5 .....1D **87**
  (off Old Brompton Rd.)
Boltons Pl. SW5 ......1E **87**
Bolton St.
  W1 ....1E **21** (2D **75**)
Bolton Studios SW10 .1E **87**
Bolton Wlk. N7 ....4B **34**
  (off Durham Rd.)
Bombay Ct. SE16 .....3E **79**
  (off St Marychurch St.)
Bombay St. SE16 .....5D **79**
Bomore Rd. W11 .....1A **72**
Bonar Rd. SE15 ....3C **92**
Bonchurch Rd. W10 ..4A **58**
Bond Cl. EC4 ..4B **18** (1F **77**)
Bond Ho. NW6 ....1B **58**
  (off Rupert Rd.)
  SE14 ....3A **94**
  (off Goodwood Rd.)
Bonding Yd. Wlk.
  SE16 ....4A **80**
Bond St. E15 ....2A **54**
  W4 ....5A **70**
Bondway SW8 ....2A **90**
Bonfield Rd. SE13 ....2E **109**
Bonham Ho. W11 .....2B **72**
  (off Boyne Ter. M.)
Bonham Rd. SW2 .....3B **104**
Bonheur Rd. W4 ......3A **70**
Bonhill St.
  EC2 ....4C **10** (3F **63**)
Bonita M. SE4 ....1F **107**
Bon Marche Ter. M.
  SE27 ....4A **120**
  (off Gypsy Rd.)
Bonner Rd. E2 ....1E **65**
Bonner St. E2 ....1E **65**
Bonneville Gdns.
  SW4 ....4E **103**
Bonnington Ho. N1 ...1B **62**
Bonnington Sq. SW8 .2B **90**
Bonny St. NW1 ....4E **47**
Bonsor Ho. SW8 .....4E **89**
Bonsor St. SE5 ....3A **92**

Bonville Rd.
  BR1: Brom 5B **124**
Bookbinders Ct. E1 ...3D **65**
  (off Cudworth St.)
Booker Cl. E14 ....4B **66**
Boones Rd. SE13 ....2A **110**
Boone St. SE13 ......2A **110**
Boord St. SE10 ......4A **82**
Boothby Rd. N19 .....4F **33**
Booth Cl. E9 ....5D **51**
Booth La. EC4 ....4F **17**
Booth Rd. E16 ....3E **83**
Booth's Pl.
  W1 ....1A **14** (4E **61**)
Boot St. N1 ...2D **11** (2A **64**)
Bordeaux Ho. E15 ....2A **54**
  (off Luxembourg M.)
Border Cres.
  SE26 ....5D **121**
Border Rd. SE26 .....5D **121**
Bordon Wlk. SW15 ...5C **98**
Boreas Wlk. N1 ......1E **9**
Boreham Av. E16 .....5C **68**
Boreham Cl. E11 .....3E **39**
Boreman Ho. SE10 ...2E **95**
  (off Thames St.)
Borland Rd. SE15 ....2E **107**
Borneo St. SW15 ....1E **99**
BOROUGH, THE
  ....4A **26** (3F **77**)
Borough High St.
  SE1 ....4A **26** (3E **77**)
Borough Mkt. SE1 ...2B **26**
Borough Rd.
  SE1 ....5E **25** (4D **77**)
Borough Sq. SE1 .....4F **25**
Borrett Cl. SE17 .....1E **91**
Borrodaile Rd.
  SW18 ....4D **101**
Borrowdale NW1 .....2F **5**
  (off Robert St.)
Borthwick M. E15 ....1A **54**
Borthwick Rd. E15 ...1A **54**
  NW9 ....1B **28**
Borthwick St. SE8 ...1C **94**
Bosbury Rd. SE6 .....3E **123**
Boscastle Rd. NW5 ..5D **33**
Boscobel Ho. E8 .....3D **51**
Boscobel Pl. SW1 ....5C **74**
Boscobel St. NW8 ....3F **59**
Boscombe Av. E10 ...2F **39**
Boscombe Cl. E5 .....2A **52**
Boscombe Rd.
  SW17 ....5C **116**
  W12 ....2C **70**
Boss Ho. SE1 ....3F **27**
  (off Boss St.)
Boss St. SE1 ..3F **27** (3B **78**)
Boston Gdns. W4 ....2A **84**
Boston Ho. SW5 .....5D **73**
  (off Collingham Rd.)
Boston Pl. NW1 ......3B **60**
Boston Rd. E6 ....2F **69**
  E17 ....1C **38**
Bosun Cl. E14 ....3C **80**
Boswell St. W14 .....4F **71**
  (off Blythe Rd.)
  WC1 ......5E **7** (4A **62**)
Boswell Ho. WC1 ....5E **7**
  (off Boswell St.)

Boswell St.
  WC1 ......5E **7** (4A **62**)
Bosworth Ho. W10 ...3A **58**
  (off Bosworth Rd.)
Bosworth Rd. W10 ...3A **58**
Botha Rd. E13 ....4D **69**
Bothwell Cl. E16 .....4B **68**
Bothwell St. W6 .....2F **85**
Botolph All. EC3 .....4D **19**
Botolph La.
  EC3 ....5D **19** (1A **78**)
Botts M. W2 ....5C **58**
Boughton Ho. SE1 ...3B **26**
  (off Tennis St.)
Boulcott St. E1 ......5F **65**
Boulevard, The SW6 .4E **87**
  SW17 ....2C **116**
  SW18 ....2D **101**
Boulogne Ho. SE1 ...5F **27**
  (off St Saviour's Est.)
Boulter Ho. SE14 ....4E **93**
  (off Kender St.)
Boundaries Rd.
  SW12 ....2B **116**
Boundary Av. E17 ....2B **38**
Boundary Ho. SE5 ...3E **91**
  W11 ....2F **71**
  (off Queensdale Cres.)
Boundary La. E13 ....2F **69**
  SE17 ....2E **91**
Boundary Pas.
  E2 ....3F **11** (3B **64**)
Boundary Rd. E13 ....1E **69**
  E17 ....2B **38**
  NW8 ....5D **45**
  SW19 ....5F **115**
Boundary Row
  SE1 ....3D **25** (3D **77**)
Boundary St.
  E2 ....2F **11** (2B **64**)
Boundfield Rd. SE6 ..3A **124**
Bourbon Ho. SE6 ....5E **123**
Bourbon La. W12 ....2F **71**
Bourchier St.
  W1 ....4B **14** (1F **75**)
Bourdon Pl. W1 ......4E **13**
Bourdon St.
  W1 ....5D **13** (1D **75**)
Bourke Cl. NW10 ....3A **42**
  SW4 ....4A **104**
Bourlet Cl.
  W1 ....1F **13** (4E **61**)
Bournbrook Rd. SE3 .1F **111**
Bourne Est.
  EC1 ....5B **8** (4C **62**)
Bourne Rd.
  W1 ....3C **12** (5C **60**)
Bournemouth Cl.
  SE15 ....5C **92**
Bournemouth Rd.
  SE15 ....5C **92**
Bourne Pl. W4 ....1A **84**
Bourne Rd. E7 ....5B **40**
  N8 ....1A **34**
Bournes Ho. N15 ....1A **36**
  (off Chisley Rd.)
Bourneside Gdns.
  SE6 ....5E **123**
Bourne St. SW1 .....5C **74**
Bourne Ter. W2 .....4D **59**

Bournevale Rd.
SW16 . . . . . .4A 108
Bourneville Rd. SE6 . . .5C 108
Bousfield Rd. SE14 . . .5F 93
Boutflower Rd.
SW11 . . . . . .2A 102
Boutique Hall SE13 . . .2E 109
Bouton Pl. N1 . . . . . . .4D 49
(off Waterloo Ter.)
Bouverie M. N16 . . . . .4A 36
Bouverie Pl. W2 . . . . .5F 59
Bouverie Rd. N16 . . . . .4A 36
Bouverie St.
EC4 . . . .3C 16 (5C 62)
Boveney Rd. SE23 . . . .5F 107
Bovill Rd. SE23 . . . . . .5F 107
Bovingdon Cl. N19 . . . .4E 33
Bovingdon Rd. SW6 . . .4D 87
Bovril Cl. SW6 . . . . . .3D 87
(off Fulham Rd.)

BOW 2B 66
Bowater Cl. SW2 . . . . .4A 104
Bowater Ho. EC1 . . . . . .4F 9
(off Golden La.)
Bowater Pl. SE3 . . . . . .3D 97
Bowater Rd. SE18 . . . . .4F 83
Bow Bell Twr. E3 . . . . .5C 52
(off Pancras Way)
Bow Bri. Est. E3 . . . . . .2D 67
Bow Brook, The E2 . . . .1F 65
(off Mace St.)
Bow Central Sports Cen.
. . . . .2B 66
(off Harley Gro.)
Bow Chyd. EC4 . . . . . .3A 18
BOW COMMON 4C 66
Bow Comn. La. E3 . . . .3B 66
Bow Creek Ecology Pk.
. . . . .5A 68
Bowden Ho. E3 . . . . . .2D 67
(off Rainhill Way)
Bowden St. SE11 . . . . .1C 90
Bowditch SE8 . . . . . . .5B 80
Bowdon Rd. E17 . . . . . .2C 38
Bowen Dr. SE21 . . . . . .3A 120
Bowen St. E14 . . . . . . .5D 67
Bower Av. SE10 . . . . . .4A 96
Bowerdean St. SW6 . . . .4D 87
Bowerden Ct. NW10 . . .1D 57
Bowerman Av. SE14 . . .2A 94
Bowerman Ct. N19 . . . .4F 33
(off St John's Way)
Bower St. E1 . . . . .5F 65
Bowes-Lyon Hall E16 . . .2C 82
(off Wesley Av.)
Bowes Rd. W3 . . . . . . .1A 70
Bow Exchange E3 . . . . .4D 67
(off Yeo St.)
Bow Fair E3 . . . . .1C 66
(off Fairfield Rd.)
Bowfell Rd. W6 . . . . . . .2E 85
Bowhill Cl. SW9 . . . . . .3C 90
Bow Ho. E3 . . . . .2C 66
(off Bow Rd.)
N1 . . . . .5A 50
(off Whitmore Est.)
Bowie Cl. SW4 . . . . . . .5F 103
BOW INTERCHANGE . . .1D 67
Bowland Rd. SW4 . . . . .2F 103
Bowland Yd. SW1 . . . . .4A 20

Bow La. EC4 . . .3A 18 (5E 63)
Bowlby Ho. SE4 . . . . . .2F 107
(off Frendsbury Rd.)
Bowl Ct. EC2 . . .4E 11 (3A 64)
Bowles Rd. SE1 . . . . . .2C 92
Bowley Cl. SE19 . . . . . .5B 120
Bowley Ho. SE16 . . . . .4C 78
Bowley La. SE19 . . . . . .5B 120
Bowling Grn. Cl.
SW15 . . . . .5D 99
Bowling Grn. Ho.
SW10 . . . . .3F 87
(off Riley St.)
Bowling Grn. La.
EC1 . . . .3C 8 (3C 62)
Bowling Grn. Pl.
SE1 . . . .3B 26 (3F 77)
Bowling Grn. St.
SE11 . . . . .2C 90
Bowling Grn. Wlk.
N1 . . . . .1D 11 (2A 64)
Bow Locks E3 . . . . . . .3E 67
Bowman Av. E16 . . . . . .1B 82
Bowman Ho. N1 . . . . . .5A 50
(off Colville Est.)
Bowman M. SW18 . . . . .1B 114
Bowman's Bldgs.
NW1 . . . . .4A 60
(off Penfold Pl.)
Bowmans Lea SE23 . . .5E 107
Bowman's M. E1 . . . . . .5C 64
N7 . . . . .5A 34
Bowman's Pl. N7 . . . . . .5A 34
Bowmore Wlk. NW1 . . .4F 47
Bowness Cl. E8 . . . . . . .3B 50
(off Beechwood Rd.)
Bowness Cres.
SW15 . . . . .5A 112
Bowness Ho. SE15 . . . . .3E 93
(off Hillbeck Cl.)
Bowness Rd. SE6 . . . . .5D 109
Bowood Rd. SW11 . . . .3C 102
Bow Rd. E3 . . . . .2B 66
Bowry Ho. E14 . . . . . . .4B 66
(off Wallwood St.)
Bow St. E15 . . . . .2A 54
WC2 . . . .3E 15 (5A 62)
Bow Triangle Bus. Cen.
E3 . . . . .3C 66
(not continuous)
Bowyer Ho. N1 . . . . . . .5A 50
(off Mill Row)
Bowyer Pl. SE5 . . . . . . .3E 91
Bowyer St. SE5 . . . . . . .3E 91
Boxall Rd. SE21 . . . . . .4A 106
Boxley St. E16 . . . . . . .2D 83
Boxmoor Ho. E2 . . . . . .5C 50
(off Whiston Rd.)
W11 . . . . .2F 71
(off Queensdale Cres.)
Box Tree Ho. SE8 . . . . .2A 94
Boxworth Gro. N1 . . . . .5B 48
Boyce Ho. SW16 . . . . . .5E 117
W10 . . . . .2B 58
(off Bruckner St.)
Boyce Way E13 . . . . . . .3C 68
Boydell Ct. NW8 . . . . . .4F 45
(not continuous)

Boyd Rd. SW19 . . . . . .5F 115
Boyd St. E1 . . . . .5C 64
Boyfield St.
SE1 . . . .4E 25 (3D 77)
Boyland Rd.
BR1: Brom 5B 124
Boyle St. W1 . . .4F 13 (1E 75)
Boyne Rd. SE13 . . . . . .1E 109
Boyne Ter. M. W11 . . . .2B 72
Boyson Rd. SE17 . . . . . .2E 91
(not continuous)
Boyson Wlk. SE17 . . . . .2F 91
Boyton Cl. E1 . . . . .3E 65
Boyton Ho. NW8 . . . . . .1F 59
(off Wellington Rd.)
Brabant Ct. EC3 . . . . . .4D 19
Brabazon Ct. SW1 . . . . .1F 89
(off Moreton St.)
Brabazon St. E14 . . . . . .5D 67
Brabner Ho. E2 . . . . . . .2C 64
(off Wellington Row)
Brabourne Cl. SE19 . . .5A 120
Braburn Gro. SE15 . . . .5E 93
Bracer Ho. N1 . . . . .1A 64
(off Whitmore Est.)
Bracewell Rd. W10 . . . .4E 57
Bracey M. N4 . . . . .4A 34
Bracey St. N4 . . . . .4A 34
Bracken Av. SW12 . . . .4C 102
Brackenbury N4 . . . . . .3C 34
(off Osborne Rd.)
Brackenbury Gdns.
W6 . . . . .4D 71
Brackenbury Rd. W6 . . .4D 71
Brackenfield Cl. E5 . . . .5D 37
Bracken Gdns. SW13 . . .5C 84
Bracken Ho. E3 . . . . . . .4C 66
(off Devons Rd.)
Brackley Av. SE15 . . . . .1E 107
Brackley Cl. NW8 . . . . . .3F 59
(off Pollitt Dr.)
Brackley Rd. W4 . . . . . .1A 84
Brackley St.
EC1 . . . . .5A 10 (3E 63)
Brackley Ter. W4 . . . . . .1A 84
Bracklyn Cl. N1 . . . . . . .1F 63
(not continuous)
Bracklyn St. N1 . . . . . . .1F 63
Bracknell Gdns.
NW3 . . . . .1D 45
Bracknell Ga. NW3 . . . .2D 45
Bracknell Way NW3 . . .1D 45
Bradbeer Ho. E2 . . . . . .2E 65
(off Cornwall Av.)
Bradbourne St. SW6 . . .5C 86
Bradbury M. N16 . . . . . .2A 50
Bradbury St. N16 . . . . . .2A 50
Bradby Ho. NW8 . . . . . .1D 59
(off Hamilton Ter.)
Braddyll St. SE10 . . . . .1A 96
Bradenham SE17 . . . . . .2F 91
(off Bradenham Cl.)
Bradenham Cl. SE17 . . .2F 91
Braden St. W9 . . . . . . .3D 59
Bradfield Ct. NW1 . . . . .4D 47
(off Hawley Rd.)
Bradfield Rd. E16 . . . . .3C 82
Bradford Cl. SE26 . . . . .4D 121
Bradford Ho. W14 . . . . .4F 71
(off Spring Va. Ter.)

Bradford Rd. W3 . . . . . . .3A 70
Bradgate Rd. SE6 . . . .4D 109
Brading Cres. E11 . . . . . .4D 41
Brading Rd. SW2 . . . . .5B 104
Brading Ter. W12 . . . . . .4C 70
Bradiston Rd. W9 . . . . . .2B 58
Bradley Cl. N7 . . . . .3A 48
Bradley Ho. E3 . . . . .2D 67
 (off Bromley High St.)
SE16 . . . . .5E 79
 (off Raymouth Rd.)
Bradley M. SW17 . . . . .1B 116
Bradley Rd. SE19 . . . . .5E 119
Bradley's Cl. N1 . . . . . . .1C 62
Bradman Ho. NW8 . . . . .2E 59
 (off Abercorn Pl.)
Bradmead SW8 . . . . . . .3D 89
Bradmore Pk. Rd.
 W6 . . . . .5D 71
Bradshaw Cl. SW19 . . . .5C 114
Bradshaw Cotts.
 E14 . . . . .5A 66
 (off Repton St.)
Bradstock Ho. E9 . . . . . .4F 51
Bradstock Rd. E9 . . . . . .3F 51
Brad St. SE1 . . . .2C 24 (2C 76)
Bradwell Ho. NW6 . . . . .5D 45
 (off Mortimer Cres.)
Brady Ho. SW8 . . . . . . .4E 89
 (off Corunna Rd.)
Brady St. E1 . . . . .3D 65
Braemar SW15 . . . . . . .4F 99
Braemar Av. NW10 . . . .5A 28
 SW19 . . . . .2C 114
Braemar Cl. SE16 . . . . . .1D 93
 (off Masters Dr.)
Braemar Ct. SE6 . . . . . .1B 124
 (off Cumberland Pl.)
Braemar Ho. W9 . . . . . .2E 59
 (off Maida Va.)
Braemar Mans. SW7 . . .4D 73
 (off Cornwall Gdns.)
Braemar Rd. E13 . . . . . .3B 68
Braeside BR3: Beck . . .5C 122
Braes St. N1 . . . . .4D 49
Braganza St. SE17 . . . . .1D 91
Braham Ho. SE11 . . . . . .1B 90
Braham St. E1 . . . . .5B 64
Braid Av. W3 . . . . .5A 56
Braid Ho. SE10 . . . . . . .4E 95
 (off Blackheath Hill)
Braidwood Pas. EC1 . . . .5F 9
 (off Aldersgate St.)
Braidwood Rd. SE6 . . . .1F 123
Braidwood St.
 SE1 . . . . .2D 27 (2A 78)
Brailsford Rd. SW2 . . . .3C 104
Braintree Ho. E1 . . . . . .3E 65
 (off Malcolm Rd.)
Braintree St. E2 . . . . . . .2E 65
Braithwaite Ho. EC1 . . . .3B 10
 (off Bunhill Row)
Braithwaite St.
 E1 . . . . .4F 11 (3B 64)
Braithwaite Twr. W2 . . . .4F 59
 (off Hall Pl.)
Bramah Grn. SW9 . . . . .4C 90
Bramah Ho. SW1 . . . . . .1D 89
Bramalea Cl. N6 . . . . . . .1C 32
Bramall Cl. E15 . . . . . . .2B 54

Bramall Ct. N7 . . . . .2B 48
 (off George's Rd.)
Bramber WC1 . . . . .2D 7
Bramber Ct. W14 . . . . . .2B 86
 (off Bramber Rd.)
Bramber Rd. W14 . . . . .2B 86
Bramble Gdns.
 W12 . . . . .1B 70
Bramble Ho. E3 . . . . . . .4C 66
 (off Devons Rd.)
Brambles, The
 SW19 . . . . .5A 114
 (off Woodside)
Brambling Ct. SE8 . . . . .2B 94
 (off Abinger Gro.)
Bramcote Gro. SE16 . . . .1E 93
Bramcote Rd. SW15 . . .2D 99
Bramdean Cres.
 SE12 . . . . .1C 124
Bramdean Gdns.
 SE12 . . . . .1C 124
Bramerton M. NW6 . . . .4F 43
 (off Willesden La.)
Bramerton St. SW3 . . . .2A 88
Bramfield Cl. N4 . . . . . . .4E 35
 (off Queens Dr.)
Bramfield Rd.
 SW11 . . . . .4A 102
Bramford Rd. SW18 . . .2E 101
Bramham Gdns.
 SW5 . . . . .1D 87
Bramhope La. SE7 . . . . .2D 97
Bramlands Cl.
 SW11 . . . . .1A 102
Bramley Cres. SW8 . . . .3F 89
Bramley Ho. SW15 . . . . .4B 98
 (off Tunworth Cres.)
 W10 . . . . .5F 57
Bramley Rd. W10 . . . . . .5F 57
Brampton WC1 . . . . .1F 15
 (off Red Lion Sq.)
Brampton Cl. E5 . . . . . . .4D 37
Brampton Gdns. N15 . . .1E 35
Brampton Rd. E6 . . . . . .2F 69
 N15 . . . . .1E 35
Bramshaw Rd. E9 . . . . . .3F 51
Bramshill Gdns.
 NW5 . . . . .5D 33
Bramshill Rd. NW10 . . .1A 56
Bramshot Av. SE7 . . . . .2C 96
Bramshurst NW8 . . . . . .5D 45
 (off Abbey Rd.)
Bramston Rd. NW10 . . . .1C 56
 SW17 . . . . .3E 115
Bramwell Ho.
 SE1 . . . . .5A 26 (4E 77)
 SW1 . . . . .1E 89
 (off Churchill Gdns.)
Bramwell M. N1 . . . . . . .5B 48
Bramwell Way E16 . . . . .2E 83
Brancaster Ho. E1 . . . . .2F 65
 (off Moody St.)

Brandlehow Rd.
 SW15 . . . . .2B 100
Brandon Est. SE17 . . . . .2D 91
Brandon Ho.
 BR3: Beck 5D 123
 (off Beckenham Hill Rd.)
Brandon Mans. W14 . . . .2A 86
 (off Queen's Club Gdns.)
Brandon M. EC2 . . . . . .1B 18
 SE17 . . . . .5E 77
 (off Brandon St.)
Brandon Rd. N7 . . . . . . .4A 48
Brandon St. SE17 . . . . . .5E 77
 (not continuous)
Brandram M. SE13 . . . .2A 110
 (off Brandram Rd.)
Brandram Rd. SE13 . . . .1A 110
Brandrams Wharf
 SE16 . . . . .3E 79
Brandreth Rd.
 SW17 . . . . .2D 117
Brands Ho. NW6 . . . . . .5B 44
 (off Lincoln M.)
Brand St. SE10 . . . . . . .3E 95
Brangbourne Rd.
 BR1: Brom 5E 123
Brangton Rd. SE11 . . . . .1B 90
Brangwyn Ct. W14 . . . . .4A 72
 (off Blythe Rd.)
Branksea St. SW6 . . . . .3A 86
Branksome Ho. SW8 . . .3B 90
 (off Meadow Rd.)
Branksome Rd.
 SW2 . . . . .3A 104
Branscombe NW1 . . . . .5E 47
 (off Plender St.)
Branscombe St.
 SE13 . . . . .1D 109
Bransdale Cl. NW6 . . . . .5C 44
Brantwood Ho. SE5 . . . .3E 91
 (off Wyndam Est.)
Brantwood Rd.
 SE24 . . . . .3E 105
Brasenose Dr. SW13 . . . .2E 85
Brassett Point E15 . . . . .5A 54
 (off Abbey Rd.)
Brassey Ho. E14 . . . . . .5D 81
 (off Cahir St.)
Brassey Rd. NW6 . . . . . .3B 44
Brassey Sq. SW11 . . . .1C 102
Brassie Av. W3 . . . . . . .5A 56
Brass Talley All.
 SE16 . . . . .3F 79
Brasted Cl. SE26 . . . . . .4E 121
Brathay NW1 . . . . .1A 6
 (off Ampthill Est.)
Brathway Rd. SW18 . . . .5C 100
Bratley St. E1 . . . . .3C 64
Bravington Pl. W9 . . . . . .3B 58
Bravington Rd. W9 . . . . .1B 58
Bravingtons Wlk.
 N1 . . . . .1E 7
 (off York Way)
Brawne Ho. SE17 . . . . . .2D 91
 (off Brandon St.)
Braxfield Rd. SE4 . . . . .2A 108
Braxted Pk.
 SW16 . . . . .5B 118
Bray NW3 . . . . .4A 46
Brayards Rd. SE15 . . . . .5D 93

Brayards Rd. Est.
  SE15 . . . . .5D *93*
  (off Caulfield Rd.)
Braybrook St. W12 . . . .4B 56
Brayburne Av.
  SW4 . . . . .5E 89
Bray Ct. *E2* 2F *65*
  (off Meath Cres.)
  SW16 . . . . .5A 118
Bray Cres. SE16 . . . . .3F 79
Braydon Rd. N16 . . . . .3C 36
Bray Dr. E16 . . . . .1B 82
Brayfield Ter. N1 . . . . .4C 48
Brayford Sq. E1 . . . . . .5E 65
Bray Pas. E16 . . . . . . .1C 82
Bray Pl. SW3 . . . . .5B 74
Bread St. EC4 . . .3A 18 (5E 63)
  (not continuous)
Breakspears M. SE4 . . .5B 94
Breakspears Rd.
  SE4 . . . . .2B 108
  (not continuous)
Breakwell Ct. *W10* 3A *58*
  (off Wornington Rd.)
Breamore Cl. SW15 . . .1C 112
Breamore Ho. *SE15* . . .3C *92*
  (off Friary Est.)
Bream's Bldgs.
  EC4 . . . . . . .2B 16 (5C 62)
Bream St. E3 . . . . .4C 52
Breasley Cl. SW15 . . . .2D 99
Brechin Pl. SW7 . . . . . .5E 73
Brecknock Rd. N7 . . . . .2F 47
  N19 . . . . .1E 47
Brecknock Rd. Est.
  N19 . . . . .1E 47
Brecon Grn. NW9 . . . . .1A 28
Brecon Ho. *E3* 1B *66*
  (off Ordell Rd.)
  W2 . . . . .5E *59*
  (off Hallfield Est.)
Brecon M. N7 . . . . .2F 47
Brecon Rd. W6 . . . . . . .2A 86
Bredel Ho. *E14* 4C *66*
  (off St Paul's Way)
Bredgar SE13 . . . . . . .3D 109
Bredgar Rd. N19 . . . . . .4E 33
Bredhurst Cl. SE20 . . . .5E 121
Bredinghurst SE22 . . . .5C 106
Bredin Ho. *SW10* 3D *87*
  (off Coleridge Gdns.)
Breer St. SW6 . . . . . . .1D 101
Breezers Ct. *E1* 1C *78*
  (off The Highway)
Breezer's Hill E1 . . . . . .1C 78
Bremner Rd. SW7 . . . . .4E 73
Brenchley Gdns.
  SE23 . . . . .4E 107
Brenda Rd. SW17 . . . . .2B 116
Brendon Av. NW10 . . . .1A 42
Brendon St. W1 . . . . . .5A 60
Brenley Gdns. SE9 . . . .2F 111
Brenley Ho. *SE1* 3B *26*
  (off Tennis St.)
Brennand Ct. N19 . . . . .5E 33
Brent Cl. NW11 . . . . . . .2F 29
BRENT CROSS 2E 29
Brent Cross Fly-Over
  NW2 . . . . .2F 29
  NW4 . . . . .2F 29

Brent Cross Gdns.
  NW4 . . . . .1F 29
BRENT CROSS INTERCHANGE
  . . . . .1E 29
Brent Cross Shop. Cen.
  NW4 . . . . .2E 29
Brentfield Gdns. NW2 . .2F 29
Brentfield Ho. NW10 . . .4A 42
Brentfield Rd. NW10 . . .3A 42
Brent Grn. NW4 . . . . . .1E 29
Brent Ho. *E9* 3E *51*
  (off Brenthouse Rd.)
Brenthouse Rd. E9 . . . .4E 51
Brenthurst Rd. NW10 . .3B 42
Brentmead Pl. NW11 . . .1F 29
Brent Mus. 3D 43
  (off High Rd.)
Brent New Ent. Cen.
  NW10 . . . . .3B 42
Brenton Ct. *E9* 2A *52*
  (off Mabley St.)
Brenton St. E14 . . . . . .5A 66
Brent Pk. Rd. NW4 . . . .2D 29
  NW9 . . . . .2D 29
Brent Rd. E16 . . . . .5C 68
Brent St. NW4 . . . . .1F 29
Brent Ter. NW2 . . . . . . .2E 29
  (not continuous)
Brent Trad. Cen.
  NW10 . . . . .2A 42
Brent Vw. Rd. NW9 . . . .1C 28
Brentwood Ho. *SE18* . . .3F *97*
  (off Portway Gdns.)
Brentwood Lodge
  NW4 . . . . .1F *29*
  (off Holmdale Gdns.)
Bressenden Pl.
  SW1 . . . . . .5E 21 (4D 75)
Breton Highwalk *EC2* . .5A *10*
  (off Golden La.)
Breton Ho. EC2 . . . . . .5A 10
  SE1 . . . . .5F *27*
  (off St Saviour's Est.)
Brett Cl. N16 . . . . .4A 36
Brettell St. SE17 . . . . . .1F 91
Brett Ho. Cl. SW15 . . . .5F 99
Brettinghurst *SE1* 1C *92*
  (off Avondale Sq.)
Brett Pas. E8 . . . . .2D 51
Brett Rd. E8 . . . . .2D 51
Brewers Bldgs. *EC1* 1D *9*
  (off Rawstorne St.)
Brewers Ct. W2 . . . . . . .4E 59
Brewer's Grn. SW1 . . . .5B 22
Brewer's Hall Gdn.
  EC2 . . . . .1A *18*
  (off Aldermanbury Sq.)
Brewer St.
  W1 . . . . . . .4A 14 (1E 75)
Brewery, The
  EC2 . . . . . .5B 10 (4E 63)
Brewery Ind. Estate, The
  N1 . . . . .1A *10*
  (off Wenlock Rd.)
Brewery Rd. N7 . . . . . . .4A 48
Brewery Sq.
  EC1 . . . . . . .3E 9 (3D 63)
  SE1 . . . . .2F 27
Brewhouse La. E1 . . . . .2D 79
  SW15 . . . . .1A 100

Brewhouse Wlk.
  SE16 . . . . .2A 80
Brewhouse Yd.
  EC1 . . . . . . .3D 9 (3D 63)
Brewster Gdns. W10 . . .4E 57
Brewster Ho. *E14* 1B *80*
  (off Three Colt St.)
  SE1 . . . . .5B *78*
  (off Dunton Rd.)
Brewster Rd. E10 . . . . .3D 39
Briant Ho. SE1 . . . . . . .5B 24
Briant St. SE14 . . . . . . .4F 93
Briar Ct. *E3* 1C *66*
  (off Morville St.)
  SW15 . . . . .2D 99
Briardale Gdns. NW3 . . .5C 30
Briar Rd. NW2 . . . . . . .1E 43
Briar Wlk. SW15 . . . . . .2D 99
  W10 . . . . .3A 58
Briarwood Rd. SW4 . . . .3F 103
Briary Cl. NW3 . . . . . . .4A 46
Briary Ct. E16 . . . . .5B 68
Briary Gdns.
  BR1: Brom 5D 125
Brickbarn Cl. *SW10* 3E *87*
  (off King's Barn)
Brick Ct. EC4 . . .3B 16 (5C 62)
Brickfield Cl. E9 . . . . . . .3E 51
Brickfield Rd.
  SW19 . . . . .4D 115
Brick La. E1 . . . . .3B 64
  E2 . . . . .2B 64
Brick Lane Music Hall
  . . . . .2F 83
BRICKLAYER'S ARMS . .5F 77
Bricklayers Arms
  Distribution Cen.
  SE1 . . . . .5A 78
  (not continuous)
Brick St. W1 . . .2D 21 (2D 75)
Brickwood Cl. SE26 . . . .3D 121
Brideale Cl. SE15 . . . . .2B 92
Bride St. EC4 . . . . .3D 17
Bride La.
  EC4 . . . . . . .3D 17 (5D 63)
Bridel M. *N1* 5D *49*
  (off Colebrook Row)
Brides M. N7 . . . . .3B 48
Brides Pl. N1 . . . . .4A 50
Bride St. N7 . . . . .3B 48
Bridewain St.
  SE1 . . . . . . .5F 27 (4B 78)
Bridewell Pl. E1 . . . . . . .2D 79
  EC4 . . . . . . .3D 17 (5D 63)
Bridford M.
  W1 . . . . .5E 5 (4D 61)
Bridge, The SW8 . . . . . .3D 89
Bridge Academy 5B 50
  (off Laburnum St.)
Bridge App. NW1 . . . . . .4C 46
Bridge Av. W6 . . . . .5E 71
Bridge Av. Mans. *W6* . . .1E *85*
  (off Bridge Av.)
Bridge Cl. W10 . . . . . . .5F 57
Bridge Ct. E10 . . . . .3B 38
  E14 . . . . .1F *81*
  (off Newport Av.)
Bridgefield Ho. *W2* 5D *59*
  (off Queensway)

Bridgefoot SE1 . . . . . . .1A 90
Bridge Gdns. N16 . . . . . .1F 49
Bridge Ho. E9 . . . . .3F 51
  (off Shepherds La.)
NW3 . . . . .4C 46
  (off Adelaide Rd.)
NW10 . . . . .1F 57
  (off Chamberlayne Rd.)
SE4 . . . . .2B 108
SW1 . . . . .1D 89
  (off Ebury Bri.)
W2 . . . . .4F 59
  (off Nth. Wharf Rd.)
Bridgehouse Ct. SE1 . . .4D 25
  (off Blackfriars Rd.)
Bridge Ho. Quay E14 . . .2E 81
Bridgeland Rd. E16 . . . .1C 82
Bridge La. NW11 . . . . . .1B 30
SW11 . . . . .4A 88
Bridge Leisure Centre, The
  . . . . .4B 122
Bridgeman Ho. E9 . . . . .4E 51
  (off Frampton Pk. Rd.)
Bridgeman Rd. N1 . . . . .4B 48
Bridgeman St. NW8 . . . .1A 60
Bridge Mdws. SE14 . . . .2F 93
Bridgend Rd. SW18 . . . .2E 101
Bridgen Ho. E1 . . . . .5D 65
  (off Nelson St.)
Bridgepark SW18 . . . . . .3C 100
Bridge Pl. SW1 . . . . .5D 75
Bridgepoint Lofts E7 . . . .4E 55
Bridgepoint Pl. N6 . . . . .3E 33
  (off Hornsey La.)
Bridgeport Pl. E1 . . . . . .2C 78
Bridge Rd. E11 . . . . .1F 39
E15 . . . . .4F 53
E17 . . . . .2B 38
NW10 . . . . .3A 42
Bridge Rd. Depot
E15 . . . . .5A 54
Bridges Ct. SW11 . . . . .1F 101
  (not continuous)
Bridges Ho. SE5 . . . . . . .3F 91
  (off Elmington Est.)
Bridgeside Lodge N1 . . .1E 63
  (off Wharf Rd.)
Bridges Pl. SW6 . . . . . . .4B 86
Bridge St.
SW1 . . . . .4D 23 (3A 76)
Bridges Wharf
SW11 . . . . .1F 101
Bridge Ter. E15 . . . . .4F 53
Bridgetown Cl.
SE19 . . . . .5A 120
Bridge Vw. W6 . . . . .1E 85
Bridge Vw. Ct. SE1 . . . . .5E 27
  (off Grange Rd.)
Bridge Wlk. SE8 . . . . . . .2D 95
  (off Copperas St.)
Bridgewalk Hgts.
SE1 . . . . .3C 26
  (off Weston St.)
Bridgewater Highwalk
EC2 . . . . .5F 9
Bridgewater Sq.
EC2 . . . . .5F 9 (4E 63)
Bridgewater St.
EC2 . . . . .5F 9 (4E 63)
Bridge Way NW11 . . . . . .1B 30

Bridgeway St. NW1 . . . .1E 61
Bridge Wharf E2 . . . . . .1F 65
  (off Calshot St.)
N1 . . . . .1B 62
  (off Calshot St.)
Bridge Yd.
SE1 . . . . .1C 26 (2F 77)
Bridgford St. SW18 . . . .3E 115
Bridgnorth Ho. SE15 . . .2C 92
  (off Friary Est.)
Bridgwater Ho. W2 . . . .5E 59
  (off Hallfield Est.)
Bridle La.
W1 . . . . .4A 14 (1E 75)
Bridport SE17 . . . . .1F 91
  (off Cadiz St.)
Bridport Ho. N1 . . . . . . .5F 49
  (off Bridport Pl.)
Bridport Pl. N1 . . . . .5F 49
  (not continuous)
Bridstow Pl. W2 . . . . . . .5C 58
Brief St. SE5 . . . . .5D 91
Brierfield NW1 . . . . .5E 47
  (off Arlington Rd.)
Brierley Rd. E11 . . . . . . .1F 53
SW12 . . . . .2E 117
Brigade St. SE3 . . . . . . .5B 96
  (off Tranquil Va.)
Briggeford Cl. E5 . . . . . .4C 36
  (off Chambord St.)
Briggs Ho. E2 . . . . .1F 11
  (off Chambord St.)
Brightfield Rd.
SE12 . . . . .3A 110
Brightling Rd. SE4 . . . . .4B 108
Brightlingsea Pl. E14 . . .1B 80
Brightman Rd.
SW18 . . . . .1F 115
Brighton Av. E17 . . . . . .1B 38
Brighton Bldgs. SE1 . . .5D 27
  (off Tower Bri. Rd.)
Brighton Gro. SE14 . . . .4A 94
Brighton Ho. SE5 . . . . . .4F 91
  (off Camberwell Grn.)
Brighton Rd. N16 . . . . . .1A 50
Brighton Ter. SW9 . . . . .2B 104
Brightside Rd. SE13 . . . .4F 109
Bright St. E14 . . . . .4D 67
  (off Mackenzie Rd.)
Brightwell Cres.
SW17 . . . . .5B 116
Brig M. SE8 . . . . .2C 94
Brigstock Ho. SE5 . . . . .5E 91
Brill Pl. NW1 . . . . . . .1C 6 (1F 61)
Brimsdown Ho. E3 . . . . .3D 67
Brimstone Ho. E15 . . . . .4A 54
  (off Victoria St.)
Brindley Ho. W2 . . . . . . .4C 58
  (off Alfred Rd.)
Brindley St. SE14 . . . . . .4B 94
Brindley Way
BR1: Brom 5C 124
Brine Ho. E3 . . . . .1A 66
  (off St Stephen's Rd.)
Brinklow Ho. W2 . . . . . .4D 59
  (off Torquay St.)
Brinkworth Way E9 . . . .3B 52
Brinsley Ho. E1 . . . . .5E 65
  (off Tarling St.)
Brinton Wlk. SE1 . . . . . .2D 25

Brion Pl. E14 . . . . .4E 67
Brisbane Ho. W12 . . . . .1D 71
  (off White City Est.)
Brisbane Rd. E10 . . . . . .4D 39
Brisbane Road Stadium
  . . . . .5D 39
Brisbane St. SE5 . . . . . .3F 91
Briscoe Cl. E11 . . . . . . .4B 40
Briscoe Rd. SW19 . . . . .5F 115
Briset Rd. SE9 . . . . .1F 111
Briset St. EC1 . . . .5D 9 (4D 63)
Briset Way N7 . . . . .4B 34
Bristol Gdns. SW15 . . . .5E 99
W9 . . . . .3D 59
Bristol Ho. SE11 . . . . . . .4C 76
  (off Lambeth Wlk.)
SW1 . . . . .1C 88
  (off Lwr. Sloane St.)
WC1 . . . . .5E 7
  (off Southampton Row)
Bristol M. W9 . . . . .3D 59
Bristol Rd. E7 . . . . .3E 55
Briston Gro. N8 . . . . . . .1A 34
Bristow Ct. E8 . . . . .5D 51
  (off Triangle Rd.)
Bristowe Cl. SW2 . . . . .4C 104
Bristow Rd. SE19 . . . . . .5A 120
Britannia Bldg. N1 . . . . .1B 10
  (off Ebenezer St.)
Britannia Bus. Cen.
NW2 . . . . .1F 43
Britannia Cl. SW4 . . . . .2F 103
Britannia Ga. E16 . . . . . .2C 82
BRITANNIA JUNC. 5D 47
Britannia Leisure Cen.
  . . . . .5F 49
Britannia Rd. E14 . . . . . .5C 80
SW6 . . . . .3D 87
Britannia Row N1 . . . . . .5D 49
Britannia St.
WC1 . . . . .1F 7 (2B 62)
Britannia Wlk.
N1 . . . . .1B 10 (1F 63)
  (not continuous)
Britannia Way SW6 . . . .3D 87
  (off Britannia Rd.)
Britannic Highwalk
EC2 . . . . .1B 18
  (off Moor La.)
British Genius Site 3C 88
British Gro. W4 . . . . .1B 84
British Gro. Pas. W4 . . . .1B 84
British Gro. Sth. W4 . . . .1B 84
British Library 1C 6 (2F 61)
British Mus. 5D 7 (4A 62)
British Music Experience
  . . . . .2A 82
British Postal Mus. and
  Archive, The
  . . . . .3B 8 (3C 62)
British St. E3 . . . . .2B 66
British Telecom Cen.
  EC1 . . . . .2F 17
British Wharf Ind. Est.
  SE14 . . . . .1F 93
Britley Ho. E14 . . . . .5B 66
  (off Copenhagen Pl.)
Brittain Ct. SE9 . . . . .1F 125
Brittany Point SE11 . . . .5C 76
Britten Cl. NW11 . . . . . . .3D 31

Britten Ct. E15 . . . . .1F 67
Britten Ho. SW3 . . . . .1A 88
(off Britten St.)
Britten St. SW3 . . . . .1A 88
Brittidge Rd. NW10 . . . . . .4A 42
Britton Cl. SE6 . . . . .5F 109
Britton St.
EC1 . . . . .4D 9 (3D 63)
BRIXTON 2B 104
Brixton Hill SW2 . . . . .5A 104
Brixton Hill SW. SW2 . . . . .3B 104
Brixton Hill Pl. SW2 . . . . .5A 104
Brixton Oval SW2 . . . . . . .2C 104
Brixton Recreation Cen.
. . . . .1C 104
(off Brixton Sta. Rd.)
Brixton Rd. SE11 . . . . .2C 90
SW9 . . . . .2C 104
Brixton Sta. Rd.
SW9 . . . . .1C 104
Brixton Water La.
SW2 . . . . .3B 104
Broadbent Cl. N6 . . . . .3D 33
Broadbent St.
W1 . . . . .4D 13 (1D 75)
Broadbridge Cl. SE3 . . . . . .3C 96
Broad Comn. Est.
N16 . . . . .3C 36
(off Osbaldeston Rd.)
Broad Ct.
WC2 . . . . . . .3E 15 (5A 62)
Broadfield NW6 . . . . .3D 45
Broadfield Cl. NW2 . . . . . . .5E 28
Broadfield La. NW1 . . . . . . .4A 48
Broadfield Rd. SE6 . . . . . .5A 110
Broadfields Way
NW10 . . . . .2B 42
Broadford Ho. E1 . . . . .3A 66
(off Commodore St.)
Broadgate EC2 . . . . .1C 18
Broadgate Arena
. . . . .1D 19 (4A 64)
Broadgate Circ.
EC2 . . . . .5D 11 (4A 64)
Broadgate Ice Rink 1D 19
(off Broadgate Circ.)
Broadgate Plaza EC2 . . . .4A 64
Broadgate Rd. E16 . . . . . . .5F 69
Broadgates Ct. SE11 . . . .1C 90
(off Cleaver St.)
Broadgates Rd.
SW18 . . . . .1F 115
Broadgate Twr.
EC2 . . . . .4E 11 (3A 64)
Broadhinton Rd.
SW4 . . . . .1D 103
Broadhurst Cl. NW6 . . . . . .3E 45
Broadhurst Gdns.
NW6 . . . . .3D 45
Broadlands Av.
SW16 . . . . .2A 118
Broadlands Cl. N6 . . . . . . .2C 32
SW16 . . . . .2A 118
Broadlands Lodge N6 . . . .2B 32
Broadlands Rd.
BR1: Brom 4D 125
N6 . . . . .2B 32
Broad La.
EC2 . . . . .5D 11 (4A 64)
N8 . . . . .1B 34

Broadley St. NW8 . . . . .4F 59
Broadley Ter. NW1 . . . . . . .3A 60
Broadmayne SE17 . . . . . . .1F 91
(off Portland St.)
Broadmead SE6 . . . . .3C 122
W14 . . . . .5A 72
Broadoak Ct. SW9 . . . . . .1C 104
(off Gresham Rd.)
Broadoak Ho. NW6 . . . . . . .5D 45
(off Mortimer Cres.)
Broad Sanctuary
SW1 . . . . .4C 22 (3F 75)
Broadstone NW1 . . . . .4F 47
(off Agar Gro.)
Broadstone Ho. SW8 . . . . .3B 90
(off Dorset Rd.)
Broadstone Pl.
W1 . . . . .1B 12 (4C 60)
Broad St. Av.
EC2 . . . . .1D 19 (4A 64)
Broad St. Pl. EC2 . . . . .1C 18
Broad Wlk.
NW1 . . . . .1C 4 (5C 46)
SE3 . . . . .5E 97
W1 . . . . .5A 12 (1B 74)
Broad Walk, The W8 . . . . . .2D 73
Broadwalk Cl. N1 . . . . .2C 72
(off Palace Gdns. Ter.)
Broadwalk Ho. EC2 . . . . . . .5D 11
SW7 . . . . .3E 73
(off Hyde Pk. Ga.)
Broad Wlk. La.
NW11 . . . . .2B 30
Broadwall
SE1 . . . . .1C 24 (2C 76)
Broadwater Rd.
SW17 . . . . .4A 116
Broadway E13 . . . . .1D 69
E15 . . . . .4F 53
SW1 . . . . .4B 22 (4F 75)
Broadway, The N8 . . . . . . .1A 34
SW13 . . . . .5A 84
Broadway Arc. W6 . . . . .5E 71
(off Hammersmith B'way.)
Broadway Centre, The
W6 . . . . .5E 71
Broadway Chambers
W6 . . . . .5E 71
(off Hammersmith B'way.)
Broadway Ho.
BR1: Brom 5F 123
(off Bromley Rd.)
E8 . . . . .5D 51
(off Ada St.)
Broadway Mans.
SW6 . . . . .3C 86
(off Fulham Rd.)
Broadway Mkt. E8 . . . . . . .5D 51
(not continuous)
Broadway Mkt. M. E8 . . . . .5C 50
Broadway M. E5 . . . . .2B 36
Broadway Pde. N8 . . . . . . .1A 34
Broadway Retail Pk.
NW2 . . . . .1F 43
Broadway Shop. Mall
SW1 . . . . .5B 22 (4F 75)
Broadway Theatre, The
Catford 5D 109
Broadway Wlk. E14 . . . . . . .3C 80

Broadwell Pde. NW6 . . . .3D 45
(off Broadhurst Gdns.)
Broadwick St.
W1 . . . . .4A 14 (1E 75)
Broadwood Ter. W8 . . . . . .5B 72
Broad Yd.
EC1 . . . . .4D 9 (3D 63)
Brocas Cl. NW3 . . . . .4A 46
Brockbridge Ho.
SW15 . . . . .4B 98
Brocket Ho. SW8 . . . . .5F 89
Brockham Cl. SW19 . . . . . .5B 114
Brockham Dr. SW2 . . . . . . .5B 104
Brockham Ho. NW1 . . . . . . .5E 47
(off Bayham Pl.)
SW2 . . . . .5B 104
(off Brockham Dr.)
Brockham St.
SE1 . . . . .5A 26 (4E 77)
Brockill Cres. SE4 . . . . . . .2A 108
Brocklebank Ind. Est.
SE7 . . . . .5C 82
Brocklebank Rd. SE7 . . . . .5D 83
SW18 . . . . .5E 101
Brocklehurst St.
SE14 . . . . .3F 93
BROCKLEY 2F 107
Brockley Cross SE4 . . . . . .1A 108
Brockley Cross Bus. Cen.
SE4 . . . . .1A 108
Brockley Footpath
SE4 . . . . .3A 108
(not continuous)
SE15 . . . . .1E 107
Brockley Gdns. SE4 . . . . . .5B 94
Brockley Gro. SE4 . . . . . . .3B 108
Brockley Hall Rd.
SE4 . . . . .3A 108
Brockley Jack Theatre
. . . . .3A 108
Brockley M. SE4 . . . . .3A 108
Brockley Pk. SE23 . . . . . . .5A 108
Brockley Ri. SE23 . . . . . . .1A 122
Brockley Rd. SE4 . . . . .1B 108
Brockley Vw. SE23 . . . . . . .5A 108
Brockley Way SE4 . . . . . . .3F 107
Brockman Ri.
BR1: Brom 4F 123
Brockmer Ho. E1 . . . . .1D 79
(off Crowder St.)
Brock Pl. E3 . . . . .3D 67
Brock Rd. E13 . . . . .4D 69
Brock St. SE15 . . . . .1E 107
Brockway Cl. E11 . . . . .4A 40
Brockweir E2 . . . . .1E 65
(off Cyprus St.)
Brockwell Ct. SW2 . . . . . . .3C 104
Brockwell Ho. SE11 . . . . . .2B 90
(off Vauxhall St.)
Brockwell Pk. 4D 105
Brockwell Pk. Gdns.
SE24 . . . . .5C 104
Brockwell Pk. Lido 4D 105
Brockwell Pk. Row
SW2 . . . . .5C 104
Brockwell Pas.
SE24 . . . . .4D 105
Brodia Rd. N16 . . . . .5A 36
Brodick Ho. E3 . . . . .1B 66
(off Saxon Rd.)

Brodie Ho. *SE1* 1B **92**
  (off Cooper's Rd.)
Brodie St. SE1 . . . . .1B **92**
Brodlove La. E1 . . . . . . .1F **79**
Brodrick Rd. SW17 . . . . .2A **116**
Brody Ho. E1 . . . . .1F **19**
  (off Strype St.)
Broken Wharf
  EC4 . . . . .4F **17** (1E **77**)
Brokesley St. E3 . . . . . .2B **66**
Broke Wlk. E8 . . . . .5B **50**
Bromar Rd. SE5 . . . . . .1A **106**
Bromehead St. E1 . . . . . .5E **65**
Bromell's Rd. SW4 . . . . .2E **103**
Bromfelde Rd. SW4 . . . . .1F **103**
Bromfelde Wlk. SW4 . . . .5F **89**
Bromfield Ct. SE16 . . . . .4C **78**
  (off Ben Smith Way)
Bromfield St. N1 . . . . . . .5C **48**
Bromhead Rd. E1 . . . . . .5E **65**
  (off Jubilee St.)
Bromleigh Ct. SE23 . . . .2C **120**
Bromleigh Ho. SE1 . . . . .5F **27**
  (off St Saviour's Est.)
BROMLEY 2D **67**
Bromley Hall Rd.
  E14 . . . . .4E **67**
Bromley High St. E3 . . . .2D **67**
Bromley Hill
  BR1: Brom 5A **124**
Bromley Pl.
  W1 . . . . . . .5F **5** (4E **61**)
Bromley Rd.
  BR1: Brom 1D **123**
  E10 . . . . .1D **39**
  SE6 . . . . .1D **123**
Bromley St. E1 . . . . .4F **65**
BROMPTON 4A **74**
Brompton Arc. SW3 . . . . .4A **20**
Brompton Cotts.
  SW10 . . . . .2E **87**
  (off Hollywood Rd.)
Brompton Oratory 4A **74**
Brompton Pk. Cres.
  SW6 . . . . .2D **87**
Brompton Pl. SW3 . . . . . .4A **74**
Brompton Rd.
  SW1 . . . . .4A **20** (5A **74**)
  SW3 . . . . .4A **20** (5A **74**)
Brompton Sq. SW3 . . . . . .4A **74**
Brompton Vs. SW6 . . . . . .2C **86**
  (off Lillie Rd.)
Bromwich Av. N6 . . . . . . .4C **32**
Bromyard Av. W3 . . . . . . .1A **70**
Bromyard Ho. SE15 . . . . .3D **93**
  (off Commercial Way)
Bron Ct. NW6 . . . . .5C **44**
BRONDESBURY 4B **44**
Brondesbury Ct. NW2 . . .3F **43**
Brondesbury M. NW6 . . . .4C **44**
BRONDESBURY PARK
  . . . . .5E **43**
Brondesbury Pk.
  NW2 . . . . .3E **43**
  NW6 . . . . .3E **43**
Brondesbury Pk. Mans.
  NW6 . . . . .5A **44**
  (off Salusbury Rd.)
Brondesbury Rd.
  NW6 . . . . .1B **58**

Brondesbury Vs.
  NW6 . . . . .1B **58**
Bronsart Rd. SW6 . . . . . .3A **86**
Bronte Cl. E7 . . . . .1C **54**
Bronte Ct. W14 . . . . .4F **71**
  (off Girdler's Rd.)
Bronte Ho. N16 . . . . .2A **50**
  NW6 . . . . .2C **58**
  SW4 . . . . .5E **103**
  SW17 . . . . .3F **115**
  (off Grosvenor Way)
Bronti Cl. SE17 . . . . .1E **91**
Bronwen Ct. NW8 . . . . . .2F **59**
  (off Grove End Rd.)
Bronze St. SE8 . . . . .3C **94**
Brookbank Rd.
  SE13 . . . . .1C **108**
Brook Cl. SW17 . . . . . . .2C **116**
Brook Ct. E11 . . . . .5A **40**
  SE12 . . . . .3E **125**
Brookdale Rd.
  SE6 . . . . .5D **109**
  (Catford B'way.)
  SE6 . . . . .4D **109**
  (Medusa Rd.)
Brook Dr. SE11 . . . . .4C **76**
Brooke Cl. W10 . . . . .1A **58**
  (off Kilburn La.)
Brooke Ho. SE14 . . . . . . .4A **94**
  (off Goodwood Rd.)
Brookehowse Rd.
  SE6 . . . . .2C **122**
Brooke Rd. E5 . . . . .5C **36**
  N16 . . . . .5B **36**
Brooke's Ct.
  EC1 . . . . . .1B **16** (4C **62**)
Brooke's Mkt. EC1 . . . . . .5C **8**
Brooke St.
  EC1 . . . . . .1B **16** (4C **62**)
Brookfield N6 . . . . .5C **32**
Brookfield Pk. NW5 . . . . .5D **33**
Brookfield Rd. E9 . . . . . . .3A **52**
  W4 . . . . .3A **70**
Brook Gdns. SW13 . . . . . .1B **98**
Brook Ga.
  W1 . . . . . .5A **12** (1B **74**)
BROOK GREEN 5F **71**
Brook Grn. W6 . . . . .4F **71**
Brook Grn. Flats W14 . . .4F **71**
  (off Dunsany Rd.)
Brook Ho. E1 . . . . .1C **78**
  (off Fletcher St.)
  W6 . . . . .5E **71**
  (off Shepherd's Bush Rd.)
Brook Ho's. NW1 . . . . . . .1E **61**
  (off Cranleigh St.)
Brooking Rd. E7 . . . . .2C **54**
Brooklands Av.
  SW19 . . . . .2D **115**
Brooklands Ct. NW6 . . . .4B **44**
Brooklands Pk. SE3 . . . .1C **110**
Brooklands Pas. SW8 . . .4F **89**
Brook La.
  BR1: Brom 5C **124**
  SE3 . . . . .5D **97**
Brook Lodge NW11 . . . . .1F **29**
  (off Nth. Circular Rd.)
Brooklyn Ct. W12 . . . . . .2E **71**
  (off Frithville Gdns.)
Brooklyn Pas. W12 . . . . .3E **71**
  (off Lime Gro.)

Brookman Ho. E3 . . . . . .1B **66**
  (off Mostyn Gro.)
Brookmarsh Ind. Est.
  SE10 . . . . .3D **95**
Brook M. Nth. W2 . . . . . .1E **73**
Brook M. WC2 . . . . .3C **14**
  (off Denmark St.)
Brookmill Rd. SE8 . . . . . .4C **94**
Brook Rd. NW2 . . . . .4A **28**
Brooksbank Ho. E9 . . . . .3E **51**
  (off Retreat Pl.)
Brooksbank St. E9 . . . . . .3E **51**
Brooksby Ho. N1 . . . . . . .4C **48**
  (off Liverpool Rd.)
Brooksby M. N1 . . . . .4C **48**
Brooksby St. N1 . . . . .4C **48**
Brooksby's Wlk. E9 . . . . .2F **51**
Brooks Ct. SW8 . . . . .3E **89**
Brooks Farm 2D **39**
Brookside Rd. N19 . . . . . .4E **33**
  NW11 . . . . .1A **30**
Brooks Lodge N1 . . . . . . .1A **64**
  (off Hoxton St.)
Brook's M.
  W1 . . . . .4D **13** (1D **75**)
Brook Sq. SE18 . . . . .4F **97**
Brooks Rd. E13 . . . . .5C **54**
Brook St. W1 . . . .4C **12** (1D **75**)
  W2 . . . . .1F **73**
Brooksville Av. NW6 . . . . .5A **44**
Brookview Rd.
  SW16 . . . . .5E **117**
Brookville Rd. SW6 . . . . .3B **86**
Brookway SE3 . . . . .1C **110**
Brookwood Av. SW13 . . . .5B **84**
Brookwood Ho. SE1 . . . . .4E **25**
  (off Webber St.)
Brookwood Rd.
  SW18 . . . . .1B **114**
Broome Way SE5 . . . . . . .3F **91**
Broomfield E17 . . . . .2B **38**
  NW1 . . . . .4C **46**
  (off Ferdinand St.)
Broomfield Ho. SE17 . . . .5A **78**
  (off Massinger St.)
Broomfield St. E14 . . . . . .4C **66**
Broomgrove Rd.
  SW9 . . . . .5B **90**
Broomhill Rd.
  SW18 . . . . .3C **100**
Broomhouse La.
  SW6 . . . . .5C **86**
Broomhouse Rd.
  SW6 . . . . .5C **86**
Broomsleigh Bus. Pk.
  SE26 . . . . .5B **122**
Broomsleigh St.
  NW6 . . . . .2B **44**
Broomwood Rd.
  SW11 . . . . .4B **102**
Broseley Gro. SE26 . . . . .5A **122**
Brougham Rd. E8 . . . . . . .5C **50**
Brougham St. SW11 . . . . .5B **88**
Brough Cl. SW8 . . . . .3A **90**
Broughton Dr. SW9 . . . . .2C **104**
Broughton Gdns. N6 . . . .1E **33**
Broughton Rd. SW6 . . . . .5D **87**
Broughton Rd. App.
  SW6 . . . . .5D **87**
Broughton St. SW8 . . . . .5C **88**

Broughton St. Ind. Est.
  SW11 . . . . .5C **88**
Browne Ho. SE8 . . . . . .3C **94**
  (off Deptford Chu. St.)
Brownfield Area
  E14 . . . . .5D **67**
Brownfield St. E14 . . .5D **67**
Brown Hart Gdns.
  W1 . . . . .4C **12** (1C **74**)
Brownhill Rd. SE6 . . . .5D **109**
Browning Cl. W9 . . . . . .3E **59**
Browning Ct. W14 . . . .2B **86**
  (off Turneville Rd.)
Browning Ho. N16 . . . .1A **50**
  (off Shakspeare Wlk.)
  SE14 . . . . .4A **94**
  (off Loring Rd.)
  W12 . . . . .5E **57**
  (off Wood La.)
Browning M.
  W1 . . . . .1C **12** (4D **61**)
Browning Rd. E11 . . . . .2B **40**
Browning St. SE17 . . . . .1E **91**
Brownlow Ho. SE16 . . . .3C **78**
  (off George Row)
Brownlow M.
  WC1 . . . . .4A **8** (3B **62**)
Brownlow Rd. E7 . . . . . .1C **54**
  E8 . . . . .5B **50**
  NW10 . . . . .4A **42**
Brownlow St.
  WC1 . . . . . .1A **16** (4B **62**)
Brown's Bldgs.
  EC3 . . . . .3E **19** (5A **64**)
Browns La. NW5 . . . . . .2D **47**
Brown St. W1 . . . . .5B **60**
BROWNSWOOD PARK
  . . . . .4D **35**
Brownswood Rd. N4 . . .5D **35**
Broxash Rd. SW11 . . . .4C **102**
Broxbourne Ho. E3 . . . . .3D **67**
  (off Empson St.)
Broxbourne Rd. E7 . . . . .5C **40**
Broxholme Ho. SW6 . . . .4D **87**
  (off Harwood Rd.)
Broxholm Rd. SE27 . . . .3C **118**
Broxted Rd. SE6 . . . . .2B **122**
Broxwood Way NW8 . . . .5A **46**
Bruce Cl. W10 . . . . .4F **57**
Bruce Hall M.
  SW17 . . . . .4C **116**
Bruce Ho. W10 . . . . . . .4F **57**
Bruce Rd. E3 . . . . .2D **67**
  NW10 . . . . .4A **42**
Bruckner St. W10 . . . . .2A **58**
Brudenell Rd.
  SW17 . . . . .3B **116**
Bruford Ct. SE8 . . . . . . .2C **94**
Bruges Pl. NW1 . . . . . . .4E **47**
  (off Randolph St.)
Brune Ho. E1 . . . . .1F **19**
Brunei Gallery
  . . . . .5C **6** (4F **61**)
Brunel Cl. SE16 . . . . . . .3E **79**
  (off Canon Beck Rd.)
  SW13 . . . . .5B **84**
  (off Westfields Av.)
Brunel Est. W2 . . . . . . .4C **58**
Brunel Ho. E14 . . . . . . .1D **95**
  (off Ship Yd.)

Brunel M. W10 . . . . . . .2F **57**
  (off Kilburn La.)
Brunel Mus. 3E **79**
Brunel Rd. E17 . . . . . . .1A **38**
  SE16 . . . . .3E **79**
  W3 . . . . .4A **56**
Brunel St. E16 . . . . .5B **68**
Brunel Wlk. SW10 . . . . .3F **87**
  (off Cheyne Rd.)
Brune St.
  E1 . . . . .1F **19** (4B **64**)
Brunlees Ho. SE1 . . . . . .5F **25**
  (off Bath Ter.)
Brunner Cl. NW11 . . . . .1D **31**
Brunner Ho. SE6 . . . . . .4E **123**
Brunner Rd. E17 . . . . . .1A **38**
Brunswick Cen.
  WC1 . . . . .3D **7** (3A **62**)
Brunswick Cl. Est.
  EC1 . . . . .2D **9** (2D **63**)
Brunswick Ct. EC1 . . . . .2D **9**
  (off Tompion St.)
  SE1 . . . . .4E **27** (3A **78**)
  SW1 . . . . .5F **75**
  (off Regency St.)
Brunswick Flats W11 . . .5C **58**
  (off Westbourne Gro.)
Brunswick Gdns. W8 . . .2C **72**
Brunswick Ho. E2 . . . . . .1B **64**
  (off Thurtle Rd.)
  SE16 . . . . .4A **80**
  (off Brunswick Quay)
Brunswick Mans. WC1 . . .3E **7**
  (off Handel St.)
  W1 . . . . .2A **12** (5B **60**)
Brunswick Pk. SE5 . . . . .4A **92**
Brunswick Pl.
  N1 . . . . .2C **10** (2F **63**)
  NW1 . . . . .4C **4** (3C **60**)
  (not continuous)
Brunswick Quay SE16 . . .4F **79**
Brunswick Rd. E10 . . . . .3E **39**
  E14 . . . . .5E **67**
Brunswick Sq.
  WC1 . . . . .3E **7** (3A **62**)
Brunswick Vs. SE5 . . . . .4A **92**
Brunton Pl. E14 . . . . . . .5A **66**
Brushfield St.
  E1 . . . . .5E **11** (4A **64**)
Brushwood Cl. E14 . . . . .4D **67**
Brussels Rd. SW11 . . . . .2F **101**
Bruton La.
  W1 . . . . .5E **13** (1D **75**)
Bruton Pl.
  W1 . . . . .5E **13** (1D **75**)
Bruton St.
  W1 . . . . .5E **13** (1D **75**)
Brutus Ct. SE11 . . . . . . .5D **77**
  (off Kennington La.)
Bryan Av. NW10 . . . . . . .4D **43**
Bryan Ho. NW10 . . . . . . .4D **43**
  SE16 . . . . .3B **80**
Bryan Rd. SE16 . . . . . . .3B **80**
Bryan's All. SW6 . . . . . .5D **87**
Bryanston Ct. W1 . . . . . .2A **12**
  (not continuous)
Bryanstone Rd. N8 . . . . .1A **33**
Bryanston Mans. W1 . . . .5A **4**
  (off York La.)

Bryanston M. E.
  W1 . . . . .1A **12** (4B **60**)
Bryanston M. W.
  W1 . . . . .2A **12** (4B **60**)
Bryanston Pl. W1 . . . . . .4B **60**
Bryanston Sq.
  W1 . . . . .2A **12** (5B **60**)
Bryanston St.
  W1 . . . . .3A **12** (5B **60**)
Bryant Cl. E2 . . . . .1B **64**
  (off Whiston Rd.,
      not continuous)
Bryant Ho. E3 . . . . .1C **66**
  (off Thomas Fyre Dr.)
Bryant St. E15 . . . . .4F **53**
Bryantwood Rd. N7 . . . . .2C **48**
Bryce Ho. SE14 . . . . . . .2F **93**
  (off John Williams Cl.)
Brydale Ho. SE16 . . . . . .5F **79**
  (off Rotherhithe New Rd.)
Bryden Cl. SE26 . . . . . .5A **122**
Brydges Pl.
  WC2 . . . . . . .5D **15** (1A **76**)
Brydges Rd. E15 . . . . . . .2F **53**
Brydon Wlk. N1 . . . . .5A **48**
Bryer Cl. EC2 . . . . .5F **9**
Bryett Rd. N7 . . . . .5A **34**
Bryher Ct. SE11 . . . . . . .1C **90**
  (off Sancroft St.)
Brymay Cl. E3 . . . . .1C **66**
Brynmaer Rd. SW11 . . . .4B **88**
Bryony Rd. W12 . . . . . . .1C **70**
Buccleugh Ho. E5 . . . . . .2C **36**
Buchanan Ct. SE16 . . . . .5F **79**
  (off Worgan St.)
Buchanan Gdns.
  NW10 . . . . .1D **57**
Buchan Rd. SE15 . . . . .1E **107**
Bucharest Rd.
  SW18 . . . . .5E **101**
Buckden Cl. SE12 . . . . .4C **110**
Buckfast St. E2 . . . . .2C **64**
Buck Hill Wlk. W2 . . . . . .1F **73**
Buckhold Rd.
  SW18 . . . . .4C **100**
Buckhurst Ho. N7 . . . . . .2F **47**
Buckhurst St. E1 . . . . . . .3D **65**
Buckingham Arc.
  WC2 . . . . .5D **15**
Buckingham Chambers
  SW1 . . . . .5E **75**
  (off Greencoat Pl.)
Buckingham Cl. W11 . . . .1C **72**
  (off Kensington Pk. Rd.)
Buckingham Ga.
  SW1 . . . . . . .5F **21** (4E **75**)
Buckingham La.
  SE23 . . . . .5A **108**
Buckingham Mans.
  NW6 . . . . .2D **45**
  (off West End La.)
Buckingham M. N1 . . . . .3A **50**
  NW10 . . . . .1B **56**
  SW1 . . . . .5F **21**
Buckingham Palace
  . . . . .4E **21** (3D **75**)
Buckingham Pal. Rd.
  SW1 . . . . . . .5E **21** (5D **75**)
Buckingham Pl.
  SW1 . . . . . . .5F **21** (4E **75**)

Buckingham Rd. E10 . . . .5D **39**
  E11 . . . . .1E **41**
  E15 . . . . .2B **54**
  N1 . . . . .3A **50**
  NW10 . . . . .1B **56**
Buckingham St.
  WC2 . . . . . .1E **23** (1A **76**)
Buckland Ct. N1 . . . . . . .1A **64**
  (off St John's Est.)
Buckland Cres. NW3 . . . .4F **45**
Buckland Ho. SW1 . . . . .1D **89**
  (part of Abbots Mnr.)
Buckland Rd. E10 . . . . . .4E **39**
Buckland St. N1 . . . . . . .1F **63**
Bucklebury NW1 . . . . . . .3F **5**
  (off Stanhope St.)
Buckler Ct. N7 . . . . .2B **48**
Bucklers All. SW6 . . . . . .2B **86**
  (not continuous)
Bucklersbury
  EC4 . . . . . .3B **18** (5F **63**)
Bucklersbury Pas.
  EC4 . . . . .5F **63**
Buckle St. E1 . . . . .5B **64**
Buckley Cl. SE23 . . . . . .5D **107**
Buckley Ct. NW6 . . . . . . .4B **44**
Buckley Ho. NW14 . . . . . .3A **72**
  (off Holland Pk. Av.)
Buckley Rd. NW6 . . . . . . .4B **44**
Buckmaster Cl.
  SW9 . . . . .1C **104**
  (off Stockwell Pk. Rd.)
Buckmaster Ho. N7 . . . .1B **48**
Buckmaster Rd.
  SW11 . . . . .2A **102**
Bucknall St.
  WC2 . . . . . .2C **14** (5A **62**)
Bucknell Cl. SW2 . . . . . .2B **104**
Buckner Rd. SW2 . . . . . .2B **104**
Bucknill Ho. SW1 . . . . . .1D **89**
  (off Ebury Bri. Rd.)
Buckridge Ho. EC1 . . . . . .5B **8**
  (off Portpool La.)
Buckshead Ho. W2 . . . . . .4C **58**
  (off Gt. Western Rd.)
Buckstone Cl. SE23 . . . . .4E **107**
Buck St. NW1 . . . . .4D **47**
Buckters Rents SE16 . . . .2A **80**
Buckthorne Rd. SE4 . . . .3A **108**
Buckthorn Rd. E15 . . . . . .2A **68**
  (off Manor Rd.)
Budge Row
  EC4 . . . . . .4B **18** (1F **77**)
Budge's Wlk. W2 . . . . . . .2E **73**
  (off The Broad Wlk.)
Budleigh Ho. SE15 . . . . . .3C **92**
  (off Bird in Bush Rd.)
Buer Rd. SW6 . . . . .5A **86**
Bugsby's Way SE7 . . . . . .5B **82**
  SE10 . . . . .5B **82**
Buick Ho. E3 . . . . .3C **66**
  (off Wellington Way)
Building 1000 E16 . . . . . .1F **83**
  (off Abbey Rd.)
Bulbarrow NW8 . . . . .5D **45**
  (off John Islip St.)
Bulinga St. SW1 . . . . . . .5A **76**
  (off John Islip St.)
Bullace Row SE5 . . . . . . .4F **91**
Bullard's Pl. E2 . . . . .2F **65**

Bulleid Way SW1 . . . . . .5D **75**
Bullen Ho. E1 . . . . .3D **65**
  (off Collingwood St.)
Buller Cl. SE15 . . . . .5A **88**
Buller Cl. SW15 . . . . .3C **92**
Buller Rd. NW10 . . . . . . .2F **57**
Bullingham Mans.
  W8 . . . . .3C **72**
  (off Pitt St.)
Bull Inn Ct. WC2 . . . . . . .5E **15**
Bullivant St. E14 . . . . . . .1E **81**
Bull Rd. E15 . . . . .1B **68**
Bulls Gdns. SW3 . . . . . . .5A **74**
Bulls Head Pas.
  EC3 . . . . .3D **19**
Bull Yd. SE15 . . . . .4C **92**
Bulmer M. W11 . . . . .1C **72**
Bulmer Pl. W11 . . . . .2C **72**
Bulow Est. SW6 . . . . .4D **87**
  (off Pearscroft Rd.)
Bulrington Cnr. NW1 . . . .4E **47**
  (off Camden Rd.)
Bulstrode Pl.
  W1 . . . . . . .1C **12** (4C **60**)
Bulstrode St.
  W1 . . . . . . .2C **12** (5C **60**)
Bulwer Ct. Rd. E11 . . . . . .3F **39**
Bulwer Ct. Rd. E11 . . . . . .3F **39**
Bulwer Rd. E11 . . . . .2F **39**
Bulwer St. W12 . . . . .2E **71**
Bunbury Ho. SE15 . . . . . .3C **92**
  (off Fenham Rd.)
Bungalows, The E10 . . . .1E **39**
Bunhill Row
  EC1 . . . . . .3B **10** (3F **63**)
Bunhouse Pl. SW1 . . . . . .1C **88**
Bunkers Hill NW11 . . . . . .2E **31**
Bunning Way N7 . . . . . . .4A **48**
Bunsen Ho. E3 . . . . .1A **66**
  (off Grove Rd.)
Bunsen St. E3 . . . . .1A **66**
Bunwell Ho. E3 . . . . .3B **66**
Bunyan Ct. EC2 . . . . .5F **9**
Buonaparte M. SW1 . . . .1F **89**
Burbage Cl.
  SE1 . . . . . . .5B **26** (4F **77**)
Burbage Ho. N1 . . . . .5F **49**
  (off Poole St.)
  SE14 . . . . .2F **93**
  (off Samuel Cl.)
Burbage Rd. SE21 . . . . . .4E **105**
  SE24 . . . . .4E **105**
Burcham St. E14 . . . . . . .5D **67**
Burchell Ho. SE11 . . . . . .18 **90**
  (off Jonathan St.)
Burchell Rd. E10 . . . . . . .3D **39**
  SE15 . . . . .4D **93**
Burcher Gale Gro.
  SE15 . . . . .3B **92**
Burcote Rd. SW18 . . . . . .5F **101**
Burden Ho. SW8 . . . . .3A **90**
  (off Thorncroft St.)
Burden Way E11 . . . . . . .4D **41**
Burder Cl. N1 . . . . .3A **50**
Burder Rd. N1 . . . . .3A **50**
Burdett M. NW3 . . . . .3F **45**
  W2 . . . . .5D **59**
Burdett Rd. E3 . . . . .3A **66**
  E14 . . . . .3A **66**
Burfield Cl. SW17 . . . . . . .4F **115**

Burford Rd. E6 . . . . .2F **69**
  E15 . . . . .5F **53**
  SE6 . . . . .2B **122**
Burford Wlk. SW6 . . . . . .3E **87**
Burford Wharf Apartments
  E15 . . . . .5F **53**
  (off Cam Rd.)
Burges Gro. SW13 . . . . . .3D **85**
Burges Av. NW9 . . . . .1A **28**
Burges Bus. Pk. SE5 . . . .3F **91**
Burgess Hill NW2 . . . . . .1C **44**
Burgess Ho. SE5 . . . . . . .3E **91**
  (off Bethwin Rd.)
Burgess Lofts SE5 . . . . . .3E **91**
  (off Wyndham Est.)
Burgess Pk. 2F **91**
  (off Albany Rd.)
Burgess Pk. Kart Track
  . . . . .2F **91**
Burgess Rd. E15 . . . . . . .1A **54**
Burgess St. E14 . . . . .4C **66**
Burge St.
  SE1 . . . . . . .5C **26** (4F **77**)
Burgh House 1F **45**
Burghill Rd. SE26 . . . . . . .4A **122**
Burghley Hall Cl.
  SW19 . . . . .1A **114**
Burghley Ho. SW19 . . . . .3A **114**
Burghley Pas. E11 . . . . . .3A **40**
  (off Burghley Rd.)
Burghley Rd. E11 . . . . . . .3A **40**
  NW5 . . . . .1D **47**
  SW19 . . . . .4F **113**
Burghley Twr. W3 . . . . . . .1B **70**
Burgh St. N1 . . . . .1D **63**
Burgon St.
  EC4 . . . . . .3E **17** (5D **63**)
Burgos Gro. SE10 . . . . . . .4D **95**
Burgoyne Rd. N4 . . . . . . .1D **35**
  SW9 . . . . .1B **104**
Burgundy Pl. W12 . . . . . . .2F **71**
Burke Cl. SW15 . . . . .2A **98**
Burke Lodge E13 . . . . . . .2D **69**
Burke St. E16 . . . . .4B **68**
  (not continuous)
Burland Rd. SW11 . . . . . .3B **102**
Burleigh Ho. SW3 . . . . . . .2F **87**
  (off Beaufort St.)
  W10 . . . . .4A **58**
  (off St Charles Sq.)
Burleigh Pl. SW15 . . . . . .3F **99**
Burleigh St.
  WC2 . . . . . .4F **15** (1B **76**)
Burleigh Wlk. SE6 . . . . . .1E **123**
Burley Ho. E1 . . . . .5F **65**
  (off Chudleigh St.)
Burley Rd. E16 . . . . .5E **69**
Burlington Arc.
  W1 . . . . . . .5F **13** (1E **75**)
Burlington Cl. W9 . . . . . . .3C **58**
Burlington Gdns.
  SW6 . . . . .5A **86**
  W1 . . . . . . .5F **13** (1E **75**)
Burlington Ho. W15 . . . . .1F **35**
  (off Tewkesbury Rd.)
Burlington La. W4 . . . . . . .3A **84**
Burlington M. SW15 . . . . .3B **100**
Burlington Pl. SW6 . . . . . .5A **86**
Burlington Rd. SW6 . . . . .5A **86**
Burma M. N16 . . . . .1F **49**

Burma Rd. N16 . . . . .1F 49
Burmarsh NW5 . . . . .3C 46
Burma Ter. SE19 . . . . . .5A 120
Burmester Rd.
   SW17 . . . . .3E 115
Burnaby St. SW10 . . . . . .3E 87
Burnand Ho. W14 . . . . . .4F 71
   (off Redan St.)
Burnbury Rd. SW12 . . . .1E 117
Burne Jones Ho.
   W14 . . . . .5A 72
Burnelli Bldg. SW8 . . . . .3D 89
   (off Sopwith Way)
Burnell Wlk. SE1 . . . . . . .1B 92
   (off Cadet Dr.)
Burness Cl. N7 . . . . .3B 48
Burne St. NW1 . . . . .4A 60
Burnett Cl. E9 . . . . .2E 51
Burnett Ho. SE13 . . . . . .5E 95
   (off Lewisham Hill)
Burney St. SE10 . . . . . . .3E 95
Burnfoot Av. SW6 . . . . . .4A 86
Burnham NW3 . . . . .4A 46
Burnham Cl. SE1 . . . . . . .5B 78
Burnham Ct. NW6 . . . . . .4E 45
   (off Fairhazel Gdns.)
   W2 . . . . .1D 73
   (off Moscow Rd.)
Burnham Est. E2 . . . . . . .2E 65
   (off Burnham St.)
Burnham St. E2 . . . . .2E 65
Burnham Way SE26 . . . .5B 122
Burnhill Cl. SE15 . . . . . . .3D 93
Burnhill Ho. EC1 . . . . .2F 9
   (off Norman St.)
Burnley Rd. NW10 . . . . . .2B 42
   SW9 . . . . .5B 90
Burnsall St. SW3 . . . . . . .1A 88
Burns Cl. SW19 . . . . .5F 115
Burns Ho. E2 . . . . .2E 65
   (off Cornwall Av.)
   SE17 . . . . .1D 91
   (off Doddington Gro.)
Burnside Cl. SE16 . . . . . .2F 79
Burns Ho. NW10 . . . . . . .5B 42
   SW11 . . . . .5B 88
Burnt Ash Hgts.
   BR1: Brom 5D 125
Burnt Ash Hill SE12 . . . .4B 110
Burnt Ash La.
   BR1: Brom 5C 124
Burnt Ash Rd. SE12 . . . .3B 110
Burnthwaite Rd.
   SW6 . . . . .3B 86
Burnt Oak Apartments
   E16 . . . . .5C 68
   (off Pacific Rd.)
Burntwood Cl.
   SW18 . . . . .1A 116
Burntwood Grange Rd.
   SW18 . . . . .1F 115
Burntwood La.
   SW17 . . . . .3E 115
Burntwood Vw.
   SE19 . . . . .5B 120
Buross St. E1 . . . . .5D 65
Burrage Ct. SE16 . . . . . .5F 79
   (off Worgan St.)
Burrard Ho. E2 . . . . .1E 65
   (off Bishop's Way)

Burrard Rd. E16 . . . . . . .5D 69
NW6 . . . . .2C 44
Burr Cl. E1 . . . . .2C 78
Burrell St.
   SE1 . . . . . . .1D 25 (2D 77)
Burrells Wharf Sq.
   E14 . . . . .1D 95
Burrell Towers E10 . . . . .2C 38
Burrhill Ct. SE16 . . . . . . .4F 79
   (off Worgan St.)
Burroughs Cotts.
   E14 . . . . .4A 66
   (off Halley St.)
Burrow Ho. SW9 . . . . . . .5B 90
   (off Stockwell Pk. Rd.)
Burrow Rd. SE22 . . . . . .2A 106
Burrows M.
   SE1 . . . . . . .3D 25 (3D 77)
Burrows Rd. NW10 . . . . .2E 57
Burrow Wlk. SE21 . . . . . .5E 105
Burr Rd. SW18 . . . . .1C 114
Bursar St.
   SE1 . . . . . . .2D 27 (2A 78)
Burslem St. E1 . . . . .5C 64
Burstock Rd. SW15 . . . . .2A 100
Burston Rd. SW15 . . . . . .3F 99
Burston Vs. SW15 . . . . . .3F 99
   (off St John's Av.)
Burtley Cl. N4 . . . . .4E 35
Burton Bank N1 . . . . .4F 49
   (off Yeate St.)
Burton Ct. SW3 . . . . .1B 88
   (off Franklin's Row,
   not continuous)
Burton Gro. SE17 . . . . . .1F 91
Burton Ho. SE16 . . . . . . .3D 79
   (off Cherry Gdn. St.)
Burton La. SW9 . . . . .5C 90
   (not continuous)
Burton M. SW1 . . . . .5C 74
Burton Pl.
   WC1 . . . . . . .2C 6 (2F 61)
Burton Rd. NW6 . . . . . . .4B 44
   SW9 . . . . .5D 91
   (Akerman Rd.)
   SW9 . . . . .5C 90
   (Evesham Wlk.)
Burtons Ct. E15 . . . . .4F 53
Burton St.
   WC1 . . . . . . .2C 6 (2F 61)
Burtonwood Ho. N4 . . . . .2F 35
Burtop Rd. Est.
   SW17 . . . . .3E 115
Burt Rd. E16 . . . . .2E 83
Burtt Ho. N1 . . . . .1D 11
   (off Aske St.)
Burtwell La. SE27 . . . . . .4F 119
Burwash Ho. SE1 . . . . . . .4C 26
   (off Kipling Est.)
Burwell Cl. E1 . . . . .5D 65
Burwell Rd. E10 . . . . .3A 38
Burwell Rd. Ind. Est.
   E10 . . . . .3A 38
Burwell Wlk. E3 . . . . .3C 66
Burwood Ho. SW9 . . . . . .2D 105
Burwood Pl. W2 . . . . . . .5A 60
Bury Cl. SE16 . . . . .2F 79
Bury Ct. EC3 . . . . .2E 19 (5A 64)
Buryfield Ct. SE8 . . . . . . .1A 94
   (off Lower Rd.)

Bury Pl.
   WC1 . . . . . .1D 15 (4A 62)
Bury St. EC3 . . . .3E 19 (5A 64)
   SW1 . . . . . .1A 22 (2E 75)
Bury Wlk. SW3 . . . . .5A 74
Busbridge Ho. E14 . . . . . .4C 66
   (off Brabazon St.)
Busby Ho. SW16 . . . . . . .4E 117
Busby M. NW5 . . . . .3F 47
Busby Pl. NW5 . . . . .3F 47
Bushbaby Cl.
   SE1 . . . . .2D 27 (4A 78)
Bushberry Rd. E9 . . . . . . .3A 52
Bush Cotts.
   SW18 . . . . .3C 100
Bush Cl. W12 . . . . .3F 71
Bushell Cl. SW2 . . . . .2B 118
Bushell St. E1 . . . . .2C 78
Bushey Down SW12 . . . .2D 117
Bushey Hill Rd. SE5 . . . . .4A 92
Bushey Rd. E13 . . . . .1E 69
   N15 . . . . .1A 36
Bush Ind. Est. N19 . . . . . .5E 33
Bush La. EC4 . . . . .4B 18 (1F 77)
Bushnell Rd. SW17 . . . . .2D 117
Bush Rd. E8 . . . . .5D 51
   E11 . . . . .2B 40
   SE8 . . . . .5F 79
   (off Rotherhithe New Rd.)
Bush Theatre 3E 71
Bushwood E11 . . . . .2B 40
Bushwood Dr. SE1 . . . . . .5B 78
Business Design Cen.
   N1 . . . . .5C 48
   (off Upper St.)
Business Village, The
   SW18 . . . . .3C 100
Buspace Studios
   W10 . . . . .3A 58
   (off Conlan St.)
Butcher Row E14 . . . . . . .1F 79
Butchers Rd. E16 . . . . . . .5C 68
Bute Gdns. W6 . . . . .5F 71
Bute St. SW7 . . . . .5F 73
Bute Wlk. N1 . . . . .3F 49
Butfield Ho. E9 . . . . .3E 51
   (off Stevens Av.)
Butler Ho. E2 . . . . .2E 65
   (off Bacton St.)
   E3 . . . . .4B 66
   (off Geoffrey Chaucer Way)
   E14 . . . . .5B 66
   (off Burdett St.)
   SW9 . . . . .4D 91
   (off Lothian Rd.)
Butler Pl.
   SW1 . . . . . .5B 22 (4F 75)
Butler Rd. NW10 . . . . . . .4B 42
Butlers & Colonial Wharf
   SE1 . . . . .3F 27
   (off Shad Thames)
Butler St. E2 . . . . .2E 65
Butlers Wharf
   SE1 . . . . . . .2F 27 (2B 78)
Butlers Wharf W. SE1 . . . .2F 27
   (off Shad Thames)
Butley Ct. E3 . . . . .1A 66
   (off Ford St.)
Butterfield Cl. SE16 . . . . .3D 79
Butterfields E17 . . . . .1E 39

Butterfly Wlk. *SE5* 4F *91*
(off Denmark Hill)
Buttermere *NW1* 1E *5*
(off Augustus St.)
Buttermere Cl. E15 . . . . . .1F *53*
SE1 . . . . .5B *78*
Buttermere Ct. *NW8* 5F *45*
(off Boundary Rd.)
Buttermere Dr.
SW15 . . . . .3A *100*
Buttermere Ho. *E3* 2B *66*
(off Mile End Rd.)
Buttermere Wlk. E8 . . . . . .3B *50*
Butterwick W6 . . . . .5F *71*
Butterworth Ter.
SE17 . . . . .1E *91*
(off Sutherland Wlk.)
Buttesland St.
N1 . . . . .1C *10* (2F *63*)
Butts Rd.
BR1: Brom 5A *124*
Buxhall Cres. E9 . . . . .3B *52*
Buxted Rd. E8 . . . . .4B *50*
SE22 . . . . .2A *106*
Buxton Cl. E11 . . . . .2B *40*
N1 . . . . .1A *10*
(not continuous)
Buxton M. SW4 . . . . .5F *89*
Buxton Rd. E6 . . . . .2F *69*
E15 . . . . .2A *54*
N19 . . . . .3F *33*
NW2 . . . . .3D *43*
SW14 . . . . .1A *98*
Buxton St. E1 . . . . .3B *64*
Byam St. SW6 . . . . .5E *87*
Byards Ct. *SE16* 5F *79*
(off Worgan St.)
Byas Ho. *E3* 2B *66*
(off Benworth St.)
Bye, The W3 . . . . .5A *56*
Byelands Cl. SE16 . . . . . . .2F *79*
Byfeld Gdns. SW13 . . . . . . .4C *84*
Byfield Cl. SE16 . . . . .3B *80*
Byford Cl. E15 . . . . .4A *54*
Bygrove St. E14 . . . . .5D *67*
(not continuous)
Byne Rd. SE26 . . . . .5E *121*
Byng Pl. WC1 . . . . .4C *6* (3F *61*)
Byng St. E14 . . . . .3C *80*
Byrne Rd. SW12 . . . . .1D *117*
Byron Av. E12 . . . . .3F *55*
Byron Cl. E8 . . . . .5C *50*
SE26 . . . . .4A *122*
SW16 . . . . .5A *118*
Byron Ct. *NW6* 4E *45*
(off Fairfax Rd.)
SE22 . . . . .1C *120*
SW3 . . . . .5A *74*
(off Elystan Pl.)
W9 . . . . .3C *58*
(off Lanhill Rd.)
WC1 . . . . .3F *7*
(off Mecklenburgh Sq.)
Byron Dr. N2 . . . . .1F *31*
Byron M. NW3 . . . . .1A *46*
W9 . . . . .3C *58*
Byron Rd. E10 . . . . .3D *39*
NW2 . . . . .4D *29*
Byron St. E14 . . . . .5E *67*
Byron Ter. SE7 . . . . .3E *97*

Bythorn St. SW9 . . . . .1B *104*
Byton Rd. SW17 . . . . .5B *116*
Byward St.
EC3 . . . . . . .5E *19* (1A *78*)
Bywater Ho. SE18 . . . . . . .4F *83*
Bywater Pl. SE16 . . . . .2A *80*
Bywater St. SW3 . . . . .1B *88*
Byway E11 . . . . .1E *41*
Bywell Pl. W1 . . . . .1F *13*
Byworth Wlk. N19 . . . . . . .3A *34*

C

Cabbell St. NW1 . . . . .4A *60*
Cable Ct. *SE16* 5A *80*
(off Rope St.)
Cable Ho. *WC1* 1B *8*
(off Gt. Percy St.)
Cable Pl. SE10 . . . . .4E *95*
Cable St. E1 . . . . .1C *78*
Cabot Ct. *SE16* 5F *79*
(off Worgan St.)
Cabot Sq. E14 . . . . .2C *80*
Cabot Way E6 . . . . .5F *55*
Cab Rd. SE1 . . . . .2A *24*
Cabul Rd. SW11 . . . . .5A *88*
Caci Ho. *W14* 5B *72*
(off Kensington Village)
Cactus Cl. SE15 . . . . .5A *92*
Cactus Wlk. W12 . . . . .5B *56*
Cadbury Way SE16 . . . . . . .4B *78*
Caddington Rd. NW2 . . . . .5A *30*
Caddsdell Cl. E2 . . . . .1B *64*
Cade Rd. SE10 . . . . .4E *95*
Cader Rd. SW18 . . . . .4E *101*
Cadet Dr. SE1 . . . . .5B *78*
Cadet Pl. SE10 . . . . .1A *96*
Cadiz St. SE17 . . . . .1E *91*
Cadley Ter. SE23 . . . . .2E *121*
Cadman Cl. SW9 . . . . .3D *91*
Cadmore Ho. *N1* 4D *49*
(off The Sutton Est.)
Cadmus Cl. SW4 . . . . .1F *103*
Cadmus Ct. *SW9* 4C *90*
(off Southey Rd.)
Cadnam Lodge *E14* 4E *81*
(off Schooner Cl.)
Cadnam Point
SW15 . . . . .1D *113*
Cadogan Cl. E9 . . . . .4B *52*
Cadogan Ct. *E9* 4B *52*
(off Cadogan Ter.)
SW3 . . . . .5B *74*
(off Draycott Av.)
Cadogan Ct. Gdns.
SW1 . . . . .5C *74*
(off D'Oyley St.)
Cadogan Gdns. SW3 . . . . . .5B *74*
Cadogan Ga. SW1 . . . . . . .5B *74*
Cadogan Hall 5C *74*
(off Sloane Ter.)
Cadogan Ho. *SW3* 2F *87*
(off Beaufort St.)
Cadogan La.
SW1 . . . . . . .5B *20* (4C *74*)
Cadogan Mans. *SW3* 5B *74*
(off Cadogan Gdns.)

Cadogan Pl.
SW1 . . . . . . .5A *20* (4B *74*)
Cadogan Sq.
SW1 . . . . . . .5A *20* (4B *74*)
Cadogan St. SW3 . . . . .5B *74*
Cadogan Ter. E9 . . . . .3B *52*
Cadoxton Av. N15 . . . . .1B *36*
Caedmon Rd. N7 . . . . .1B *48*
Caernarvon Ho. *E16* 2D *83*
(off Audley Dr.)
W2 . . . . .5E *59*
(off Hallfield Est.)
Caesar Ct. *E2* 1F *65*
(off Palmer's Rd.)
Café Gallery 4E *79*
Cahill St.
EC1 . . . . . . .4A *10* (3E *63*)
Cahir St. E14 . . . . .5D *81*
Caird St. W10 . . . . .2A *58*
Cairncross M. *N8* 1A *34*
(off Felix Av.)
Cairnfield Av. NW2 . . . . . . .5A *28*
Cairns Rd. SW11 . . . . .3A *102*
Caister Ho. N7 . . . . .3B *48*
Caister Ho. E15 . . . . .5B *54*
(off Caistor Pk. Rd.)
Caistor M. SW12 . . . . .5D *103*
Caistor Pk. Rd. E15 . . . . . . .5B *54*
Caistor Rd. SW12 . . . . . . .5D *103*
Caithness Ho. *N1* 5B *48*
(off Twyford St.)
Caithness Rd. W14 . . . . . . .4F *71*
Calabria Rd. N5 . . . . .3D *49*
Calais Ga. SE5 . . . . .4D *91*
Calais St. SE5 . . . . .4D *91*
Calbourne Rd.
SW12 . . . . .5B *102*
Calcott Ct. *W14* 4A *72*
(off Blythe Rd.)
Calcott Wlk. SE9 . . . . .4F *125*
Calcraft Ho. *E2* 1E *65*
(off Bonner Rd.)
Caldecot Rd. SE5 . . . . .5E *91*
Caldecott Way E5 . . . . .5F *37*
Calder Ct. SE16 . . . . .2B *80*
Calderon Ho. *NW8* 1A *60*
(off Townshend Est.)
Calderon Pl. W10 . . . . .4E *57*
Calderon Rd. E11 . . . . .1E *53*
Caldervale Rd. SW4 . . . . . . .3F *103*
Caldew St. SE5 . . . . .3F *91*
Caldicote Grn. NW9 . . . . . . .1A *28*
Caldwell Ho. *SW13* 3E *85*
(off Trinity Chu. Rd.)
Caldwell St. SW9 . . . . .3B *90*
Caldy Wlk. N1 . . . . .4E *49*
Caleb St. SE1 . . . .3F *25* (3E *77*)
Caledonia Ho. *E14* 5A *66*
(off Salmon La.)
Caledonian Rd.
N1 . . . . .1E *7* (1A *62*)
N7 . . . . .1B *48*
Caledonian Sq.
NW1 . . . . .3F *47*
Caledonian Wharf
E14 . . . . .5F *81*
Caledonia St.
N1 . . . . .1E *7* (1A *62*)
Cale St. SW3 . . . . .1A *88*
Caletock Way SE10 . . . . . . .1B *96*

Calgarth NW1 . . . . .1A 6
  (off Ampthill Est.)
Calgary Ct. SE16 . . . . .3E 79
  (off Canada Est.)
Caliban Twr. N1 . . . . .1A 64
  (off Arden St.)
Calico Ho. EC4 . . . . .3A 18
  (off Well Ct.)
Calico Row SW11 . . . . . . .1E 101
Calidore Cl. SW2 . . . . . . .4B 104
California Bldg.
  SE10 . . . . .4D 95
  (off Deal's Gateway)
Callaby Ter. N1 . . . . .3F 49
Callaghan Cl.
  SE13 . . . . .2A 110
Callahan Cotts. E1 . . . . . .4E 65
  (off Lindley St.)
Callander Rd. SE6 . . . . .2D 123
Callcott Ct. NW6 . . . . .4B 44
Callcott Rd. NW6 . . . . .4B 44
Callcott St. W8 . . . . .2C 72
Callendar Rd. SW7 . . . . . .4F 73
Callingham Cl. E14 . . . . . .4B 66
Callisons Pl. SE10 . . . . . .1A 96
Callis Rd. E17 . . . . .1B 38
Calliston Ct. E16 . . . . .4C 68
  (off Hammersley Rd.)
Callow St. SW3 . . . . .2F 87
Cally Swimming Pool
  . . . . .5B 48
Calmington Rd. SE5 . . . . .2A 92
Calmont Rd.
  BR1: Brom 5F 123
Calonne Rd. SW19 . . . . .4F 113
Calshot Ho. N1 . . . . .1B 62
  (off Calshot St.)
Calshot St. N1 . . .1F 7 (1B 62)
Calstock NW1 . . . . .5E 47
  (off Royal Coll. St.)
Calstock Ho. SE11 . . . . .1C 90
  (off Kennings Way)
Calthorpe St.
  WC1 . . . . . . .3A 8 (3B 62)
Calton Av. SE21 . . . . .4A 106
Calverley Cl.
  BR3: Beck 5D 123
Calverley Gro. N19 . . . . . .3F 33
Calvert Av.
  E2 . . . . . . .2E 11 (2A 64)
Calvert Ho. W12 . . . . .1D 71
  (off White City Est.)
Calverton SE5 . . . . .2A 92
  (off Albany Rd.)
Calvert Rd. SE10 . . . . .1B 96
Calvert's Bldgs.
  SE1 . . . . . . .2B 26 (2F 77)
Calvert St. NW1 . . . . .5C 46
Calydon Rd. SE7 . . . . . . .1D 97
Calypso Cres. SE15 . . . . . .3B 92
Calypso Way SE16 . . . . . .4B 80
Camarthen Grn. NW9 . . . .1A 28
Cambalt Rd. SW15 . . . . . .3F 99
Cambay Ho. E1 . . . . .3A 66
  (off Harford St.)
Camber Ho. SE15 . . . . . . .2E 93
Camberley Ho. NW1 . . . . .1E 5
Cambert Way SE3 . . . . . .2D 111
CAMBERWELL 4F 91

Camberwell Bus. Cen.
  SE5 . . . . .3F 91
Camberwell Chu. St.
  SE5 . . . . .4F 91
Camberwell Glebe
  SE5 . . . . .4A 92
CAMBERWELL GREEN
  . . . . .4E 91
Camberwell Grn. SE5 . . . .4E 91
Camberwell Gro. SE5 . . . .4F 91
Camberwell Leisure Cen.
  . . . . .4F 91
Camberwell New Rd.
  SE5 . . . . .2C 90
Camberwell Pl. SE5 . . . . .4E 91
Camberwell Rd. SE5 . . . . .2E 91
Camberwell Sta. Rd.
  SE5 . . . . .4E 91
Camberwell Trad. Est.
  SE5 . . . . .4E 91
Camborne M. SW18 . . .5C 100
  W11 . . . . .5A 58
Camborne Rd.
  SW18 . . . . .5C 100
Cambray Rd. SW12 . . . .1E 117
Cambria Ho. E14 . . . . . . .5A 66
  (off Salmon La.)
  SE26 . . . . .4C 120
  (off High Level Dr.)
Cambrian Cl. SE27 . . . . .3D 119
Cambrian Grn. NW9 . . . .1A 28
  (off Snowden Dr.)
Cambrian Rd. E10 . . . . .2C 38
Cambria Rd. SE5 . . . . . .1E 105
Cambria St. SW6 . . . . . . .3D 87
Cambridge Arc. E9 . . . . .4E 51
  (off Elsdale St.)
Cambridge Av. NW6 . . . .1C 58
Cambridge Cir.
  WC2 . . . . . . .3C 14 (5F 61)
Cambridge Cl. E17 . . . . .1B 38
Cambridge Ct. E2 . . . . . .1D 65
  (off Cambridge Heath Rd.)
  N16 . . . . .2A 36
  (off Amhurst Pk.)
  NW6 . . . . .1C 58
  (not continuous)
  W2 . . . . .4A 60
  (off Edgware Rd.)
  W6 . . . . .5E 71
  (off Shepherd's Bush Rd.)
Cambridge Cres. E2 . . . .1D 65
Cambridge Dr. SE12 . . . .3C 110
Cambridge Gdns.
  NW6 . . . . .1C 58
  W10 . . . . .5F 57
Cambridge Ga.
  NW1 . . . . . . .3D 5 (3D 61)
Cambridge Ga. M.
  NW1 . . . . . .3E 5 (3D 61)
Cambridge Gro. W6 . . . .5D 71
Cambridge Heath Rd.
  E1 . . . . .4D 65
  E2 . . . . .3E 65
Cambridge Ho. W6 . . . .5D 71
  (off Cambridge Gro.)
Cambridge Pk. E11 . . . .2C 40
Cambridge Pk. Rd.
  E11 . . . . .2C 40
  (off Lonsdale Rd.)

Cambridge Pl. W8 . . . . . .3D 73
Cambridge Rd. E11 . . . .1B 40
  NW6 . . . . .1C 58
  (not continuous)
  SW11 . . . . .4B 88
  SW13 . . . . .5B 84
Cambridge Sq. W2 . . . . .5A 60
Cambridge St. SW1 . . . . .5D 75
Cambridge Ter.
  NW1 . . . . . . .2D 5 (2D 61)
Cambridge Ter. M.
  NW1 . . . . . . .2E 5 (2D 61)
Cambridge Theatre 3D 15
  (off Earlham St.)
Cambus Rd. E16 . . . . .4C 68
Cam Ct. SE15 . . . . .2B 92
Camden Arts Cen. 2D 45
Camden Ct. NW1 . . . . .4E 47
  (off Rousden St.)
Camden Gdns. NW1 . . . .4D 47
Camden High St.
  NW1 . . . . .4D 47
Camden Hill Rd.
  SE19 . . . . .5A 120
Camden Ho. SE8 . . . . . . .1B 94
Camdenhurst St. E14 . . .5A 66
Camden La. N7 . . . . .2F 47
  (not continuous)
Camden Lock Market
  . . . . .4D 47
  (off Camden Lock Pl.)
Camden Lock Pl.
  NW1 . . . . .4D 47
Camden Markets 4D 47
  (off Camden Lock Pl.)
Camden M. NW1 . . . . . . .4E 47
Camden Pk. Rd.
  NW1 . . . . .3F 47
Camden Pas. N1 . . . . . . .1D 63
Camden Peoples Theatre
  . . . . .3F 5
  (off Hampstead Rd.)
Camden Rd. E11 . . . . . . .1D 41
  E17 . . . . .1B 38
  N7 . . . . .1A 48
  NW1 . . . . .4E 47
Camden Row SE3 . . . . . .5A 96
Camden Sq. NW1 . . . . . .4F 47
  (not continuous)
  SE15 . . . . .4B 92
Camden St. NW1 . . . . . . .4E 47
Camden Studios
  NW1 . . . . .5E 47
  (off Camden St.)
Camden Ter. NW1 . . . . . .3F 47
CAMDEN TOWN 5D 47
Camden Wlk. N1 . . . . .5D 49
Cameford Ct. SW2 . . . . . .5A 104
Camelford NW1 . . . . .5E 47
  (off Royal Coll. St.)
Camelford Ct. W11 . . . . . .5A 58
Camelford Ho. SE1 . . . . .1A 90
Camelford Wlk. W11 . . . .5A 58
Camellia Cl. E10 . . . . .4C 38
Camellia Ho. SE8 . . . . . . .3B 94
  (off Idonia St.)
Camellia St. SW8 . . . . . . .3A 90
  (not continuous)
Camelot Cl. SW19 . . . .4B 114
Camelot Ho. NW1 . . . . . .3F 47
Camel Rd. E16 . . . . .2F 83

Camera Pl. SW10 . . . . .2F **87**
Camera Press Gallery, The
. . . . .3F **27**
(off Queen Elizabeth St.)
Cameret Ct. *W11* 3F **71**
(off Holland St.)
Cameron Ho. NW8 . . . . .1A **60**
(off St John's Wood Ter.)
SE5 . . . . .3E **91**
Cameron Pl. E1 . . . . . .5D **65**
SW16 . . . . .2C **118**
Cameron Rd. SE6 . . . . .2B **122**
Cameron Ter. SE12 . . . .3D **125**
Camerton Cl. E8 . . . . . .3B **50**
Camgate Mans. SE5 . . . .2E **91**
(off Camberwell Rd.)
Camilla Rd. SE16 . . . . .5D **79**
Camlan Rd.
BR1: Brom 4B **124**
Camlet St. E2 . . . .2F **11** (3B **64**)
Camley St. N1 . . . . .4F **47**
Camley Street Natural Pk.
Visitor Cen. 1F **61**
Camomile St.
EC3 . . . . . .2E **19** (5A **64**)
Campaign Ct. *W9* 3B **58**
(off Chantry Cl.)
Campana Rd. SW6 . . . . .4C **86**
Campania Bldg. *E1* 1F **79**
(off Jardine Rd.)
Campbell Cl. SW16 . . . .4F **117**
Campbell Ct. SE22 . . . .1C **120**
SW7 . . . . .4E **73**
(off Gloucester Rd.)
Campbell Gordon Way
NW2 . . . . .1D **43**
Campbell Ho. *SW1* 1E **89**
(off Churchill Gdns.)
W2 . . . . .4F **59**
(off Hall Pl.)
W12 . . . . .1D **71**
(off White City Est.)
Campbell Rd. E3 . . . . . .2C **66**
E15 . . . . .1B **54**
Campbell Wlk. *N1* 5A **48**
(off Outram Pl.)
Campdale Rd. N7 . . . . . .5F **33**
Campden Gro. W8 . . . . .3C **72**
Campden Hill W8 . . . . . .3C **72**
Campden Hill Ct. W8 . . .3C **72**
Campden Hill Gdns.
W8 . . . . .2C **72**
Campden Hill Ga.
W8 . . . . .3C **72**
Campden Hill Mans.
W8 . . . . .2C **72**
(off Edge St.)
Campden Hill Pl.
W11 . . . . .2B **72**
Campden Hill Rd.
W8 . . . . .2C **72**
Campden Hill Sq.
W8 . . . . .2B **72**
Campden Hill Towers
W11 . . . . .2C **72**
Campden Ho. NW6 . . . .4F **45**
(off Harben Rd.)
W8 . . . . .2C **72**
(off Sheffield Ter.)
Campden Ho. Cl. W8 . . .3C **72**

Campden Houses W8 . . .2C **72**
Campden Ho. Ter.
W8 . . . . .2C **72**
(off Kensington Chu. St.)
Campden Mans. W8 . . . .2C **72**
(off Kensington Mall)
Campden St. W8 . . . . . .2C **72**
Campen Cl. SW19 . . . . .2A **114**
Camperdown St. E1 . . . .5B **64**
Campfield Rd. SE9 . . . . .5F **111**
Campion Ho. *E14* 5B **66**
(off Frances Wharf)
Campion Rd. E10 . . . . . .2D **39**
SW15 . . . . .2E **99**
Campion Ter. NW2 . . . . .5F **29**
Camplin St. SE14 . . . . . .3F **93**
Camp Rd. SW19 . . . . . .5D **113**
(not continuous)
Campshill Pl. SE13 . . . . .3E **109**
Campshill Rd. SE13 . . . .3E **109**
Campus Rd. E17 . . . . . .1B **38**
Cam Vw. SW19 . . . . . . .5D **113**
Cam Rd. E15 . . . . .5F **53**
Canada Est. SE16 . . . . .4E **79**
Canada Gdns. SE13 . . . .3E **109**
Canada House 1C **22**
Canada Ho. E14 . . . . . .4A **80**
(off Brunswick Quay)
SW1 . . . . .1D **22**
(off Trafalgar Sq.)
Canada Memorial 3F **21**
(off Green Pk.)
Canada Pl. E14 . . . . . . .2D **81**
(off Up. Bank St.)
Canada Sq. E14 . . . . . . .2D **81**
Canada St. SE16 . . . . . .3F **79**
Canada Way W12 . . . . .1D **71**
Canada Wharf SE16 . . . .2B **80**
Canadian Av. SE6 . . . . .1D **123**
Canal Bldg. N1 . . . . . . .1E **63**
Canal Cl. E1 . . . . .3A **66**
W10 . . . . .3F **57**
Canal Cotts. *E3* 5B **52**
(off Parnell Rd.)
Canal Gro. SE15 . . . . . .2D **93**
Canal Market 4D **47**
(off Castlehaven Rd.)
Canal Path E2 . . . . .5B **50**
Canalside Activity Cen.
. . . . .3F **57**
Canal Side Studios
NW1 . . . . .5F **47**
(off St Pancras Way)
Canalside Studios N1 . . .5A **50**
(off Orsman Rd.)
Canal St. SE5 . . . . .2F **91**
Canal Wlk. N1 . . . . .5F **49**
SE26 . . . . .5E **121**
Canal Way W10 . . . . . . .3F **57**
Canberra Rd. SE7 . . . . .2E **97**
Canbury M. SE26 . . . . .3C **120**
Cancell Rd. SW9 . . . . . .4C **90**
Candahar Rd. SW11 . . . .5A **88**
Candida Ct. NW1 . . . . . .4D **47**
Candid Ho. NW10 . . . . .1D **57**
(off Trenmar Gdns.)
Candle Gro. SE15 . . . . .1D **107**

Candlelight Ct. E15 . . . .3B **54**
(off Romford Rd.)
Candler St. N15 . . . . . . .1F **35**
Candle St. E1 . . . . .4A **66**
Candover St.
W1 . . . . .1F **13** (4E **61**)
Candy St. E3 . . . . .5B **52**
Candy Wharf E3 . . . . . . .3A **66**
Caney M. NW2 . . . . . . .4F **29**
Canfield Gdns. NW6 . . . .4D **45**
Canfield Ho. N15 . . . . . .1A **36**
(off Albert Rd.)
Canfield Pl. NW6 . . . . . .3E **45**
Canford Rd. SW11 . . . . .3C **102**
Canham Rd. W3 . . . . . . .3A **70**
CANN HALL 1A **54**
Cann Hall Rd. E11 . . . . .1A **54**
Cann Ho. W14 . . . . .4A **72**
(off Russell Rd.)
Canning Cross SE5 . . . . .5A **92**
Canning Ho. W12 . . . . . .1D **71**
(off Australia Rd.)
Canning Pas. W8 . . . . . .4E **73**
Canning Pl. W8 . . . . . . .4E **73**
Canning Pl. M. W8 . . . . .4E **73**
(off Canning Pl.)
Canning Rd. E15 . . . . . .1A **68**
N5 . . . . .5D **35**
CANNING TOWN 5B **68**
CANNING TOWN 4A **68**
Cannizaro Rd.
SW19 . . . . .5E **113**
Cannock Ho. N4 . . . . . . .2E **35**
Cannon Ct. *EC1* 3E **9**
(off Brewhouse Yd.)
Cannon Dr. E14 . . . . . . .1C **80**
Cannon Hill NW6 . . . . . .2C **44**
Cannon Ho. SE11 . . . . . .5B **76**
(off Beaufoy Wlk.)
Cannon La. NW3 . . . . . .5F **31**
Cannon Pl. NW3 . . . . . .5F **31**
Cannon St.
EC4 . . . . .3F **17** (5E **63**)
Cannon St. Rd. E1 . . . . .5D **65**
Cannon Wharf Bus. Cen.
SE8 . . . . .5A **80**
Cannon Workshops
E14 . . . . .1C **80**
(off Cannon Dr.)
Canon All. EC4 . . . . . . .3F **17**
(off Queen's Head Pas.)
Canon Beck Rd.
SE16 . . . . .3E **79**
Canonbie Rd. SE23 . . . .5E **107**
CANONBURY 3E **49**
Canonbury Bus. Cen.
N1 . . . . .5E **49**
Canonbury Ct. *N1* 4D **49**
(off Hawes St.)
Canonbury Cres. N1 . . . .4E **49**
Canonbury Gro. N1 . . . .4E **49**
Canonbury Hgts. *N1* . . .3F **49**
(off Dove Rd.)
Canonbury La. N1 . . . . .4D **49**
Canonbury Pk. Nth.
N1 . . . . .3E **49**
Canonbury Pk. Sth.
N1 . . . . .3E **49**
Canonbury Pl. N1 . . . . . .3D **49**
(not continuous)

Canonbury Rd. N1 . . . . . .3D 49
Canonbury Sq. N1 . . . . . .4D 49
Canonbury St. N1 . . . . . .4E 49
Canonbury Vs. N1 . . . . . .4D 49
Canon Row
  SW1 . . . . .4D 23 (3A 76)
  (not continuous)
Canon's Cl. N2 . . . . .2F 31
Canons Ct. E15 . . . . .1A 54
Canon St. N1 . . . . .5E 49
Canrobert St. E2 . . . . . . .1D 65
Cantelowes Rd. NW1 . . . .3F 47
Canterbury Av.
  IG1: IIf 2F 41
Canterbury Ct. SE5 . . . .5E 91
  (off Lilford Rd.)
Canterbury Ct. NW6 . . . .1C 58
  (off Canterbury Rd.)
  SE5 . . . . .3C 90
  SE12 . . . . .3D 125
Canterbury Cres.
  SW9 . . . . .1C 104
Canterbury Gro.
  SE27 . . . . .4C 118
Canterbury Ho. E3 . . . . .2D 67
  (off Bow Rd.)
  SE1 . . . . .5A 24 (4B 76)
Canterbury Ind. Pk.
  SE15 . . . . .2E 93
Canterbury Pl. SE17 . . . .1D 91
Canterbury Rd. E10 . . . . .2E 39
  NW6 . . . . .1B 58
  (Carlton Va.)
  NW6 . . . . .1C 58
  (Princess Rd.)
Canterbury Ter. NW6 . . . .1C 58
Cantium Retail Pk.
  SE1 . . . . .2C 92
Canto Ct. EC1 . . . . .3A 10
  (off Old St.)
Canton St. E14 . . . . .5C 66
Cantrell Rd. E3 . . . . .3B 66
Canute Gdns. SE16 . . . . .5F 79
Canvey St.
  SE1 . . . . . .1F 25 (2E 77)
  (off Jamestown Way)
Cape Ho. E8 . . . . .3B 50
  (off Dalston La.)
Capel Ct. EC2 . . . . .3C 18
  (off Bartholomew La.)
Capel Ho. E9 . . . . .4E 51
  (off Loddiges Rd.)
Capel Rd. E7 . . . . .1D 55
  E12 . . . . .1D 55
Capener's Cl. SW1 . . . . . .4A 20
Capern Rd. SW18 . . . . . .1E 115
Cape Yd. E1 . . . . .2C 78
Capital E. Apartments
  E16 . . . . .1C 82
  (off Western Gateway)
Capital Wharf E1 . . . . . . .2C 78
Capland Ho. NW8 . . . . . .3F 59
  (off Capland St.)
Capland St. NW8 . . . . . .3F 59
Caple Ho. SW10 . . . . . . .3E 87
  (off King's Rd.)
Caple Rd. NW10 . . . . . . .1B 56
Capper St.
  WC1 . . . . . .4A 6 (3E 61)

Capstan Ct. E1 . . . . .1E 79
  (off Wapping Wall)
Capstan Ho. E14 . . . . . . .1F 81
  (off Clove Cres.)
  E14 . . . . .5E 81
  (off Stebondale St.)
Capstan Rd. SE8 . . . . . . .5B 80
Capstan Sq. E14 . . . . . . .3E 81
Capstan Way SE16 . . . . .2A 80
Capstone Rd.
  BR1: Brom 4B 124
Capulet M. E16 . . . . .2C 82
Capulet Sq. E3 . . . . .2D 67
  (off Talwin St.)
Capworth St. E10 . . . . . . .3C 38
Caradoc Cl. W2 . . . . .5C 58
Caradoc St. SE10 . . . . . .1A 96
Caradon Cl. E11 . . . . . . .3A 40
Cara Ho. N1 . . . . .4C 48
  (off Liverpool Rd.)
Caramel Ct. E3 . . . . .1D 67
  (off Taylor Pl.)
Caranday Vs. W11 . . . . . .2F 71
  (off Norland Rd.)
Carat Ho. E14 . . . . .4C 66
  (off Ursula Gould Way)
Caravel Cl. E14 . . . . .4C 80
Caravel M. SE8 . . . . .2C 94
Caraway Apartments
  SE1 . . . . .3F 27
  (off Cayenne Ct.)
Caraway Cl. E13 . . . . . . .4D 69
Caraway Hgts. E14 . . . . .1E 81
  (off Poplar High St.)
Carbis Rd. E14 . . . . .5B 66
Carbrooke Ho. E9 . . . . . .5E 51
  (off Templecombe Rd.)
Carburton St.
  W1 . . . . . .5E 5 (4D 61)
Cardale St. E14 . . . . .3E 81
Cardamon Bldg. SE1 . . . .2F 27
  (off Shad Thames)
Carden Rd. SE15 . . . . . .1D 107
Cardiff Ho. SE15 . . . . . . .2C 92
  (off Friary Est.)
Cardigan Pl. SE3 . . . . . . .5F 95
Cardigan Rd. E3 . . . . . . .1B 66
  SW13 . . . . .5C 84
Cardigan St. SE11 . . . . . .1C 90
Cardigan Wlk. N1 . . . . . .4E 49
  (off Ashby Gro.)
Cardinal Bourne St.
  SE1 . . . . .5C 26 (4F 77)
Cardinal Cap All. SE1: . .2E 77
Cardinal Ct. E1 . . . . .1C 78
  (off Thomas More St.)
Cardinal Hinsley Cl.
  NW10 . . . . .1C 56
Cardinal Mans. SW1 . . . .5E 75
  (off Carlisle Pl.)
Cardinal Pl.
  SW1 . . . . .5F 21 (4E 75)
  (not continuous)
  SW15 . . . . .2F 99
Cardinals Way N19 . . . . .3F 33
Cardinal Wlk. SW1 . . . . . .5F 21
Cardine M. SE15 . . . . . . .3D 93
Cardington St.
  NW1 . . . . . .1A 6 (2E 61)
Cardozo Rd. N7 . . . . .2A 48

Cardross Ho. W6 . . . . . . .4D 71
  (off Cardross St.)
Cardross St. W6 . . . . . . .4D 71
Cardwell Rd. N7 . . . . .1A 48
Cardwell Ter. N7 . . . . . . .1A 48
  (off Cardwell Rd.)
Career Ct. SE16 . . . . .3F 79
  (off Christopher Cl.)
Carew Cl. N7 . . . . .4B 34
Carew Ct. SE14 . . . . .2F 93
  (off Samuel Cl.)
Carew St. SE5 . . . . .5E 91
Carey Ct. SE5 . . . . .3E 91
Carey Gdns. SW8 . . . . . .4E 89
Carey La.
  EC2 . . . . . .2F 17 (5E 63)
Carey Mans. SW1 . . . . . .5F 75
  (off Rutherford St.)
Carey Pl. SW1 . . . . .5F 75
Carey St.
  WC2 . . . . . .3A 16 (5B 62)
Carfax Pl. SW4 . . . . .2F 103
Carfree Cl. N1 . . . . .4C 48
Cargill Rd. SW18 . . . . . .1D 115
Carholme Rd. SE23 . . . . .1B 122
Carillon Ct. E1 . . . . .4C 64
  (off Greatorex St.)
Carinthia Ct. SE16 . . . . . .5A 80
  (off Plough Way)
Carisbrooke Ct. W1 . . . . .1C 12
  (off Weymouth St.)
Carisbrooke Gdns.
  SE15 . . . . .3B 92
Carker's La. NW5 . . . . . . .2D 47
Carleton Gdns. N19 . . . . .2E 47
Carleton Rd. N7 . . . . .2E 47
Carleton Vs. NW5 . . . . . .2E 47
Carlile Cl. E3 . . . . .1B 66
Carlile Ho. SE1 . . . . .5C 26
  (off Tabard St.)
Carlingford Rd. NW3 . . . . .1F 45
Carlisle Av.
  EC3 . . . . . .3F 19 (5B 64)
  W3 . . . . .5A 56
Carlisle Gdns. IG1: IIf . . .1F 41
Carlisle Ho. IG1: IIf 1F 41
Carlisle La.
  SE1 . . . . .5A 24 (4B 76)
Carlisle Mans. SW1 . . . . .5E 75
  (off Carlisle Pl.)
Carlisle Pl.
  SW1 . . . . .5F 21 (4E 75)
Carlisle Rd. E10 . . . . .3C 38
  N4 . . . . .2C 34
  NW6 . . . . .5A 44
Carlisle St.
  W1 . . . . . .3B 14 (5F 61)
Carlisle Wlk. E8 . . . . .3B 50
Carlisle Way SW17 . . . . .5C 116
Carlos Pl.
  W1 . . . . . .5C 12 (1C 74)
Carlow St. NW1 . . . . .1E 61
Carlson Ct. SW15 . . . . . .2B 100
Carlton Cl. NW3 . . . . .4C 30
Carlton Ct. SW9 . . . . .4A 91
  W9 . . . . .1D 59
  (off Maida Va.)
Carlton Dr. SW15 . . . . . . .3F 99
Carlton Gdns.
  SW1 . . . . .2B 22 (2F 75)

Carlton Gro. SE15 . . . . . .4D 93
Carlton Hill NW8 . . . . . . .1D 59
Carlton Ho. NW6 . . . . . . .1C 58
   (off Canterbury Ter.,
   not continuous)
SE16 . . . . .3F 79
   (off Wolfe Cres.)
Carlton Ho. Ter.
SW1 . . . . . . .2B 22 (2F 75)
Carlton Lodge N4 . . . . . .2C 34
   (off Carlton Rd.)
Carlton Mans. N16 . . . . . .3B 36
NW6 . . . . .4C 44
   (off West End La.)
W9 . . . . .2D 59
W14 . . . . .3A 72
   (off Holland Pk. Gdns.)
Carlton M. NW6 . . . . . . .2C 44
   (off West Cotts.)
Carlton Rd. E11 . . . . . . .3B 40
E12 . . . . .1F 55
N4 . . . . .2C 34
Carlton Sq. E1 . . . . .3F 65
   (not continuous)
Carlton St.
SW1 . . . . .5B 14 (1F 75)
Carlton Ter. E7 . . . . .4E 55
SE26 . . . . .3E 121
Carlton Twr. Pl.
SW1 . . . . .5A 20 (4B 74)
Carlton Vale NW6 . . . . . .1B 58
Carlton Vs.
SW15 . . . . .3A 100
Carlton Works, The
SE15 . . . . .3D 93
   (off Asylum Rd.)
Carlwell St. SW17 . . . . . .5A 116
Carlyle Cl. N2 . . . . .1E 31
Carlyle Ct. SW6 . . . . . . .4D 87
   (off Imperial Rd.)
SW10 . . . . .4E 87
   (off Chelsea Harbour Dr.)
Carlyle Ho. N16 . . . . . . .3A 36
SE5 . . . . .3E 91
   (off Bethwin Rd.)
SW3 . . . . .2F 87
   (off Old Church St.)
Carlyle Mans. SW3 . . . . . .2A 88
   (off Cheyne Wlk.)
W8 . . . . .2C 72
   (off Kensington Mall)
Carlyle M. E1 . . . . .3F 65
Carlyle Pl. SW15 . . . . . . .2F 99
Carlyle Rd. E12 . . . . .1F 55
NW10 . . . . .5A 42
Carlyle's House 2A 88
   (off Cheyne Row)
Carlyle Sq. SW3 . . . . .1F 87
Carly M. E2 . . . . .2C 64
   (off Barnet Gro.)
Carmalt Gdns. SW15 . . . . .2E 99
Carmarthen Pl.
SE1 . . . . . .3D 27 (3A 78)
Carmel Ct. W8 . . . . .3D 73
   (off Holland St.)
Carmelite St.
EC4 . . . . . .4C 16 (1C 76)
Carmel Lodge SW6 . . . . . .2C 86
   (off Lillie Rd.)
Carmen St. E14 . . . . .5D 67

Carmichael Cl.
SW11 . . . . .1F 101
Carmichael Ct. SW13 . . . .5B 84
   (off Grove Rd.)
Carmichael Ho. E14 . . . . . .1E 81
   (off Poplar High St.)
Carmichael M.
SW18 . . . . .5F 101
Carmine Wharf E14 . . . . . .5B 66
Carmoor Rd. SW17 . . . .2D 117
Carnaby St.
W1 . . . . . . .3F 13 (5E 61)
Carnac St. SE27 . . . . .4F 119
Carnarvon Rd. E10 . . . . . .1E 39
E15 . . . . .3B 54
Carnbrook M. SE3 . . . . . . .1F 111
Carnbrook Rd. SE3 . . . . . .1F 111
Carnegie Pl. SW19 . . . . . .3F 113
Carnegie St. N1 . . . . .5B 48
Carnell Apartments
E14 . . . . .5B 66
   (off St Anne's Row)
Carnie Lodge SW17 . . . .3D 117
Carnival Ho. SE1 . . . . .3F 27
   (off Gainsford St.)
Carnoustie Dr. N1 . . . . . . .4B 48
   (not continuous)
Carnwath Rd. SW6 . . . . . .1C 100
Carole Ho. SW11 . . . . . . .5B 46
   (off Regent's Pk. Rd.)
Caroline Cl. E15 . . . . .2A 54
Caroline Cl. SW16 . . . . . . .3B 118
W2 . . . . .1D 73
Caroline Ct. SE6 . . . . .4F 123
Caroline Gdns.
E2 . . . . .1E 11 (2A 64)
SE15 . . . . .3D 93
   (not continuous)
Caroline Ho. W2 . . . . .1D 73
   (off Bayswater Rd.)
W6 . . . . .1E 85
   (off Queen Caroline St.)
Caroline Pl. SW11 . . . . . . .5C 88
W2 . . . . .1D 73
Caroline Pl. M. W2 . . . . . .1D 73
Caroline St. E1 . . . . .5F 65
Caroline Ter. SW1 . . . . . . .5C 74
Caroline Wlk. W6 . . . . .2A 86
   (off Lillie Rd.)
Carol St. NW1 . . . . .5E 47
Caronia Ct. SE16 . . . . .5A 80
   (off Plough Way)
Carpenter Ho. E14 . . . . . . .4C 66
   (off Burgess St.)
NW11 . . . . .1E 31
Carpenters Ct. NW1 . . . . . .5E 47
   (off Pratt St.)
Carpenters M. N7 . . . . .2A 48
Carpenters Pl. SW4 . . . .2F 103
Carpenter's Rd. E15 . . . . . .4E 53
Carpenter St.
W1 . . . . . .5D 13 (1D 75)
Carp Ho. E3 . . . . .5B 52
   (off Old Ford Rd.)
Carradale Ho. E14 . . . . . . .5E 67
   (off St Leonard's Rd.)
Carrara Cl. SE24 . . . . .2C 104
SW9 . . . . .2D 105
Carrara M. E8 . . . . .3C 50
   (off Dalston La.)

Carrara Wharf SW6 . . . . . .1A 100
Carre M. SE5 . . . . .4D 91
   (off Calais St.)
Carriage Dr. E.
SW11 . . . . .3C 88
Carriage Dr. Nth.
SW11 . . . . .2C 88
   (Carriage Dr. E.)
SW11 . . . . .3B 88
   (The Parade)
Carriage Dr. Sth.
SW11 . . . . .4B 88
   (not continuous)
Carriage Dr. W.
SW11 . . . . .3B 88
Carriage Pl. N16 . . . . .5F 35
SW16 . . . . .5E 117
Carrick Ho. N7 . . . . .3B 48
   (off Caledonian Rd.)
SE11 . . . . .1C 90
Carrick Ho. SE8 . . . . .2C 94
Carrington Ct.
SW11 . . . . .2A 102
   (off Barnard Rd.)
Carrington Gdns. E7 . . . . .1C 54
Carrington Ho. W1 . . . . . .2D 21
   (off Carrington St.)
Carrington St.
W1 . . . . . . .2D 21 (2D 75)
Carrol Cl. NW5 . . . . .1D 47
Carroll Ct. E15 . . . . .2B 54
Carroll Ho. W2 . . . . .1F 73
   (off Craven Ter.)
Carronade Ct. N7 . . . . . . .2B 48
Carron Cl. E14 . . . . .5D 67
Carroun Rd. SW8 . . . . . . .3B 90
Carr St. E14 . . . . .4A 66
Carslake Rd. SW15 . . . . . .4E 99
Carson Rd. E16 . . . . .3C 68
SE21 . . . . .2F 119
Carson Ter. W11 . . . . .2A 72
   (off Princes Pl.)
Carstairs Rd. SE6 . . . . . . .3E 123
Carston Cl. SE12 . . . . .3B 110
Carswell Rd. SE6 . . . . .5E 109
Carter Cl. NW9 . . . . .1A 28
Carter Ct. EC4 . . . . .3D 17
Carteret Ho. W12 . . . . . . .1D 71
   (off White City Est.)
Carteret St.
SW1 . . . . . .4B 22 (3F 75)
Carteret Way SE8 . . . . .5A 80
Carter Ho. E1 . . . . .1F 19
Carter La.
EC4 . . . . . . .3E 17 (5D 63)
Carter Pl. SE17 . . . . .1E 91
Carter Rd. E13 . . . . .5D 55
SW19 . . . . .5F 115
Carters Cl. NW5 . . . . .2F 47
   (off Torriano Av.)
Carters Hill Cl.
SE9 . . . . .1E 125
Carters La. SE23 . . . . .2A 122
Carter St. SE17 . . . . .2E 91
Carter's Yd. SW18 . . . . . . .3C 100
Carthew Rd. W6 . . . . .4D 71
Carthew Vs. W6 . . . . .4D 71
Carthusian St.
EC1 . . . . . . .5F 9 (4E 63)
Cartier Circ. E14 . . . . .2D 81

Carting La.
  WC2 . . . . .5E **15** (1A **76**)
Cartmel NW1 . . . . .1F **5**
  (off Hampstead Rd.)
Carton Ho. W11 . . . . . . .1F **71**
  (off St Ann's Rd.)
Cartoon Mus. 1D **15**
  (off Lit. Russell St.)
Cartwright Gdns.
  WC1 . . . . . .2D **7** (2A **62**)
Cartwright Ho. SE1 . . . . .4E **77**
  (off County St.)
Cartwright St. E1 . . . . . .1B **78**
Cartwright Way
  SW13 . . . . .3D **85**
Carvel Ho. E14 . . . . .1E **95**
  (off Manchester Rd.)
Carver Rd. SE24 . . . . . .4E **105**
Carville St. N4 . . . . .4C **34**
Cary Rd. E11 . . . . .1A **54**
Carysfort Rd.
  N16 . . . . .5F **35**
Casby Ho. SE16 . . . . . . .4C **78**
  (off Marine St.)
Cascades Twr. E14 . . . . . .2B **80**
Casella Rd. SE14 . . . . . . .3F **93**
Casewick Rd. SE27 . . . .5C **118**
Casey Cl. NW8 . . . . .2A **60**
Casey Ct. SE14 . . . . .4F **93**
  (off Besson St.)
Casimir Rd. E5 . . . . .4E **37**
Casino Av. SE24 . . . . . . .3E **105**
Caspian St. SE5 . . . . . . .3F **91**
Caspian Wlk. E16 . . . . . .5F **69**
Caspian Wharf E3 . . . . . .4D **67**
  (off Violet Rd.)
Casselden Ho. NW10 . . . .4A **42**
Cassell Ho. SW9 . . . . . . .5B **90**
  (off Stockwell Gdns. Est.)
Cass Ho. E9 . . . . .3F **51**
  (off Harrowgate Rd.)
Cassidy Rd. SW6 . . . . . . .3C **86**
  (not continuous)
Cassilis Rd. E14 . . . . . . .3C **80**
Cassini Apartments
  E16 . . . . .5C **68**
Cassiobury Rd. E17 . . . . .1A **38**
Cassland Rd. E9 . . . . . . .4F **51**
Casslee Rd. SE6 . . . . . .5B **108**
Casson Ho. E1 . . . . .4C **64**
  (off Hanbury St.)
Casson St. E1 . . . . .4C **64**
Castalia Sq. E14 . . . . . . .3E **81**
Castellain Mans.
  W9 . . . . .3D **59**
  (off Castellain Rd.,
  not continuous)
Castellain Rd. W9 . . . . . .3D **59**
Castell Ho. SE8 . . . . .3C **94**
Castello Av. SW15 . . . . . .3E **99**
CASTELNAU 2D **85**
Castelnau SW13 . . . . . . .4C **84**
Castelnau Gdns.
  SW13 . . . . .2D **85**
Castelnau Mans.
  SW13 . . . . .2D **85**
  (off Castelnau, not continuous)
Castelnau Row SW13 . . . .2D **85**
Casterbridge NW6 . . . . . .5D **45**
  (off Abbey Rd.)

Casterbridge W11 . . . . .5B **58**
  (off Dartmouth Cl.)
Casterbridge Rd.
  SE3 . . . . .1C **110**
Casterton St. E8 . . . . . . .3D **51**
Castillon Rd. SE6 . . . . . .2A **124**
Castlands Rd. SE6 . . . . . .2B **122**
Castleacre W2 . . . . .5A **60**
  (off Hyde Pk. Cres.)
Castle Baynard St.
  EC4 . . . . . .4E **17** (1D **77**)
Castlebrook Cl. SE11 . . . .5D **77**
Castle Climbing Centre, The
. . . . .4E **35**
Castle Cl. E9 . . . . .2A **52**
  SW19 . . . . .3F **113**
Castlecombe Dr.
  SW19 . . . . .5F **99**
Castlecombe Rd.
  SE9 . . . . .4F **125**
Castle Ct. EC3 . . . . .3C **18**
  (off Birchin La.)
  SE26 . . . . .4A **122**
Castleden Ho. NW3 . . . . .4F **45**
  (off Hilgrove Rd.)
Castle Dr. IG4: Ilf 1F **41**
Castleford Ct. NW8 . . . . .3F **59**
  (off Henderson Dr.)
Castlehaven Rd.
  NW1 . . . . .4D **47**
Castle Ho. SE1 . . . . .5E **77**
  (off Newington Butts)
  SW8 . . . . .3A **90**
  (off Sth. Lambeth Rd.)
Castle Ind. Est. SE17 . . . .5E **77**
Castle La.
  SW1 . . . . . .5A **22** (4E **75**)
Castlemain St. E1 . . . . . .4D **65**
Castle Mead SE5 . . . . . . .3E **91**
Castle M. NW1 . . . . .3D **47**
  SW17 . . . . .4A **116**
Castle Pl. NW1 . . . . .3D **47**
  W4 . . . . .5A **70**
Castle Point E13 . . . . . . .1E **69**
  (off Boundary Rd.)
Castlereagh St. W1 . . . . . .5B **60**
Castle Rd. NW1 . . . . .3D **47**
Castle St. E6 . . . . .1E **69**
Castleton Ho. E14 . . . . . .5E **81**
  (off Pier St.)
Castleton Rd. SE9 . . . . . .4F **125**
Castletown Rd. W14 . . . . .1A **86**
Castleview Cl. N4 . . . . . . .4E **35**
Castle Way SW19 . . . . . .3F **113**
Castle Wharf E14 . . . . . . .1A **82**
  (off Orchard Pl.)
Castlewood Rd. N15 . . . . .1C **36**
  N16 . . . . .1C **36**
Castle Yd. N6 . . . . .2C **32**
  SE1 . . . . . . .1E **25** (2D **77**)
Castor La. E14 . . . . .1D **81**
Catalpa Ct. SE13 . . . . . . .4F **109**
Caterham Rd. SE13 . . . . .1F **109**
Catesby Ho. E9 . . . . .4E **51**
  (off Frampton Pk. Rd.)
Catesby St. SE17 . . . . . . .5F **77**
CATFORD 5D **109**
Catford B'way. SE6 . . . . .5D **109**
CATFORD GYRATORY
. . . . .5D **109**

Catford Hill SE6 . . . . . . .1B **122**
Catford Island SE6 . . . . .5D **109**
Catford M. SE6 . . . . .5D **109**
Catford Rd. SE6 . . . . .5C **108**
Catford Trad. Est.
  SE6 . . . . .2D **123**
Cathall Leisure Cen. 4A **40**
Cathall Rd. E11 . . . . .4F **39**
Cathay Ho. SE16 . . . . . . .3D **79**
Cathay St. SE16 . . . . .3D **79**
Cathcart Hill N19 . . . . . . .5E **33**
Cathcart Ho. SW10 . . . . . .1E **87**
  (off Cathcart Rd.)
Cathcart Rd. SW10 . . . . . .2D **87**
Cathcart St. NW5 . . . . . . .3D **47**
Cathedral Lodge EC1 . . . .5F **9**
  (off Aldersgate St.)
Cathedral Mans.
  SW1 . . . . .5E **75**
  (off Vauxhall Bri. Rd.)
Cathedral Piazza
  SW1 . . . . . .5F **21** (4E **75**)
Cathedral St.
  SE1 . . . . . . .1B **26** (2F **77**)
Cathedral Wlk. SW1 . . . . .5F **21**
Catherall Rd. N5 . . . . . . .5E **35**
Catherine St. SW3 . . . . . .2F **87**
  (off Callow St.)
  SW19 . . . . .5B **114**
Catherine Griffiths Ct.
  EC1 . . . . .3C **8**
  (off Northampton Rd.)
Catherine Gro. SE10 . . . .4D **95**
Catherine Ho. E3 . . . . . . .1C **66**
  (off Thomas Fyre Dr.)
  N1 . . . . .5A **50**
  (off Whitmore Est.)
Catherine Pl.
  SW1 . . . . . .5F **21** (4E **75**)
Catherine St.
  WC2 . . . . . .4F **15** (1B **76**)
Catherine Wheel All.
  E1 . . . . . . .1E **19** (4A **64**)
Catherine Wheel Yd.
  SW1 . . . . .2F **21**
Catherwood Ct. N1 . . . . . .1B **10**
Cathles Rd. SW12 . . . . . .4D **103**
Cathnor Rd. W12 . . . . . . .3D **71**
Catling Cl. SE23 . . . . . . .3E **121**
Catlin St. SE16 . . . . .1C **92**
Cato Rd. SW4 . . . . .1F **103**
Cator Rd. SE26 . . . . .5F **121**
Cator St. SE15 . . . . .3B **92**
  (Commercial Way)
  SE15 . . . . .2B **92**
  (Ebley Cl.)
Cato St. W1 . . . . .4A **60**
Catton St.
  WC1 . . . . . .1F **15** (4B **62**)
Caudwell Ter. SW18 . . . . .4F **101**
Caughley Ho. SE11 . . . . . .4C **76**
  (off Lambeth Wlk.)
Caulfield Ct. NW1 . . . . . . .4E **47**
  (off Baynes St.)
Caulfield Rd. SE15 . . . . . .5D **93**
Causeway, The
  SW18 . . . . .3D **101**
  SW19 . . . . .5E **113**
Causton Cotts. E14 . . . . . .5A **66**
  (off Galsworthy Av.)

Causton Ho. SE5 . . . . . . .2E **91**
SW9 . . . . .4B **90**
Causton Rd. N6 . . . . . . .2D **33**
Causton St. SW1 . . . . . . .5F **75**
Cautley Av. SW4 . . . . . .3E **103**
Cavalry Gdns.
SW15 . . . . .3B **100**
Cavalry Sq. SW3 . . . . . . .1B **88**
Cavatina Point SE8 . . . . .2D **95**
(off Copperas St.)
Cavaye Ho. SW10 . . . . . .2E **87**
(off Cavaye Pl.)
Cavaye Pl. SW10 . . . . . . .1E **87**
Cavell St. E1 . . . . .4D **65**
Cavendish Av. NW8 . . . .1F **59**
Cavendish Cl. NW6 . . . . .3B **44**
NW8 . . . . .2F **59**
Cavendish Ct. EC3 . . . . . .2E **19**
SE6 . . . . .1D **123**
(off Bromley Rd.)
Cavendish Dr. E11 . . . . . .3F **39**
Cavendish Gdns.
SW4 . . . . .4E **103**
Cavendish Ho. NW8 . . . .1F **59**
(off Wellington Rd.)
SW1 . . . . .4F **75**
(off Monck St.)
W1 . . . . .1F **13**
(off Mortimer St.)
Cavendish Mans. EC1 . . .4B **8**
(off Rosebery Av.)
NW6 . . . . .2C **44**
Cavendish M. Nth.
W1 . . . . .5E **5** (4D **61**)
Cavendish M. Sth.
W1 . . . . .1E **13** (4D **61**)
Cavendish Pde.
SW4 . . . . .4D **103**
(off Clapham Comn. Sth. Side)
Cavendish Pl. NW2 . . . . .3F **43**
SW4 . . . . .3F **103**
W1 . . . . .2E **13** (5D **61**)
Cavendish Rd. N4 . . . . . .1D **35**
NW6 . . . . .4A **44**
SW12 . . . . .4D **103**
Cavendish Sq.
W1 . . . . .2E **13** (5D **61**)
Cavendish St. N1 . . . . . . .1F **63**
Cavendish Ter. E3 . . . . . .2B **66**
Cave Rd. E13 . . . . .2D **69**
Caversham Ho. SE15 . . .2C **92**
(off Haymerle Rd.)
Caversham M. SW3 . . . .2B **88**
(off Caversham St.)
Caversham Rd. NW5 . . . .3E **47**
Caversham St. SW3 . . . .2B **88**
Caverswall St. W12 . . . . .5E **57**
Cavour Ho. SE17 . . . . . . .1D **91**
(off Alberta Est.)
Cawnpore St. SE19 . . . . .5A **120**
Caxton Ct. SW11 . . . . . . .5A **88**
Caxton Gro. E3 . . . . .2C **66**
Caxton Hall SW1 . . . . . . .4F **75**
(off Caxton St.)
Caxton Rd. SW19 . . . . . .5E **115**
W12 . . . . .3F **71**
Caxtons, The SW9 . . . . . .3D **91**
(off Langton Rd.)

Caxton St.
SW1 . . . . . . .5B **22** (4E **75**)
Caxton St. Nth. E16 . . . .5B **68**
Caxton Wlk.
WC2 . . . . .3C **14** (5F **61**)
Cayenne Ct.
SE1 . . . . .2F **27** (3B **78**)
Cayton Pl. EC1 . . . . .2B **10**
Cayton St.
EC1 . . . . .2B **10** (2F **63**)
Cazenove Rd. N16 . . . . . .4B **36**
Cearns Ho. E6 . . . . .5F **55**
Cecil Ct. NW6 . . . . .4D **45**
SW10 . . . . .2E **87**
(off Fawcett St.)
WC2 . . . . .5D **15** (1A **76**)
Cecile Pk. N8 . . . . .1A **34**
Cecilia Rd. E8 . . . . .2B **50**
Cecil Mans. SW17 . . . . . .2C **116**
Cecil Rhodes Ho.
NW1 . . . . .1F **61**
(off Goldington St.)
Cecil Rd. E11 . . . . .5B **40**
E13 . . . . .5C **54**
NW10 . . . . .5A **42**
Cecil Sharp House 5C **46**
(off Gloucester Av.)
Cedar Cl. E3 . . . . .5B **52**
SE21 . . . . .1E **119**
Cedar Ct. N1 . . . . .4E **49**
SE1 . . . . .4D **27**
(off Royal Oak Yd.)
SE7 . . . . .2E **97**
SE13 . . . . .2F **109**
SW19 . . . . .3F **113**
Cedar Ho. E2 . . . . .1D **65**
(off Mowlem St.)
E14 . . . . .3E **81**
(off Manchester Rd.)
SE14 . . . . .4F **93**
SE16 . . . . .3F **79**
(off Woodland Cres.)
SW6 . . . . .5E **87**
(off Lensbury Av.)
W8 . . . . .4D **73**
(off Marloes Rd.)
Cedarhurst Dr. SE9 . . . . .3E **111**
Cedar M. SW15 . . . . .3F **99**
Cedar Mt. SE9 . . . . .1F **125**
Cedarne Rd. SW6 . . . . . . .3D **87**
Cedar Pk. Gdns.
SW19 . . . . .5D **113**
Cedar Pl. SE7 . . . . .1E **97**
Cedar Rd. NW2 . . . . .1E **43**
Cedars, The E9 . . . . .4F **51**
(off Banbury Rd.)
E15 . . . . .4B **54**
Cedars Av. E17 . . . . .1C **38**
Cedars Cl. SE13 . . . . .1F **109**
Cedars M. SW4 . . . . .2D **103**
(not continuous)
Cedars Rd. E15 . . . . .3A **54**
SW4 . . . . .1D **103**
SW13 . . . . .5C **84**
Cedar Tree Gro.
SE27 . . . . .5D **119**
Cedar Way NW1 . . . . .4E **47**
Cedar Way Ind. Est.
N1 . . . . .4F **47**

Caxton St. Nth. E16 . . . .5B **68**

Cedra Ct. N16 . . . . .3C **36**
Cedric Chambers
NW8 . . . . .3F **59**
(off Northwick Cl.)
Celandine Cl. E14 . . . . . . .4C **66**
Celandine Dr. E8 . . . . . . .4B **50**
Celandine Way E15 . . . . .2A **68**
Celbridge M. W2 . . . . . . .4D **59**
Celestial Gdns.
SE13 . . . . .2F **109**
Celia Ho. N1 . . . . .1A **64**
(off Arden Est.)
Celia Rd. N19 . . . . .1E **47**
Celtic St. E14 . . . . .4D **67**
Cemetery La. SE7 . . . . . . .2F **97**
Cemetery Rd. E7 . . . . . . .2B **54**
Cenacle Cl. NW3 . . . . . . .5C **30**
Cenotaph 3D **23** (3A **76**)
Centaur St.
SE1 . . . . .5A **24** (4B **76**)
Central Av. E11 . . . . .4F **39**
SW11 . . . . .3B **88**
Central Bus. Cen.
NW10 . . . . .2A **42**
Central Cir. NW4 . . . . . . .1D **29**
Central Courtyard
EC2 . . . . .2E **19**
(off Cutlers Gdns.)
Central Criminal Court
Old Bailey
. . . . .2E **17** (5D **63**)
Central Hill SE19 . . . . . . .5F **119**
Central Ho. E15 . . . . .1D **67**
Central London
Civil Justice Cen. 4D **5**
Central London Golf Course
. . . . .2F **115**
Central Mall SE18 . . . . . .4D **101**
(off Southside Shop. Cen.)
Central Mans. NW4 . . . . .1D **29**
(off Watford Way)
Central Markets (Smithfield)
. . . . .1D **17**
Central Pk. Rd. E6 . . . . . .1F **69**
Central St Martins
College of Art & Design
Back Hill Campus
. . . . .4C **8** (3C **62**)
Byam Shaw Campus
. . . . .4F **33**
King's Cross Campus
. . . . .5A **48**
Central Sq. NW11 . . . . . .1D **31**
Central St. EC1 . . .1F **9** (2E **63**)
Central Walkway N19 . . .1F **47**
(off Pleshey Rd.)
Central Wharf E14 . . . . . .5C **66**
(off Thomas Rd.)
Centre Av. W3 . . . . .2A **70**
Centre Ct. Shop. Cen.
SW19 . . . . .5B **114**
Centre for the Magic Arts, The
. . . . .3A **6**
(off Stephenson Way)
Centre for
Wildlife Gardening
Visitor Cen. 1B **106**
Centre Hgts. NW3 . . . . . .4F **45**
(off Finchley Rd.)

Centre of Cell 4D 65
   (off Newark St.)
Centre Point SE1 . . . . . .1C 92
Centrepoint WC2 . . . . . .2C 14
Centre Point Ho.
   WC2 . . . . .2C 14
   (off St Giles High St.)
Centre Rd. E7 . . . . .4C 40
   E11 . . . . .4C 40
Centre Sq. SW18 . . . . . .3C 100
   (off Buckhold Rd.)
Centre St. E2 . . . . .1D 65
Centric Cl. NW1 . . . . .5C 46
Centurion Bldg.
   SW8 . . . . .2D 89
Centurion Cl. N7 . . . . .4B 48
Centurion La. E3 . . . . .5B 52
Centurion Sq. SE18 . . . . . .4F 97
Century Cl. NW4 . . . . .1F 29
Century Ct. NW8 . . . . .2F 59
   (off Grove End Rd.)
Century Ho. SW15 . . . . . . .2F 99
Century M. E5 . . . . .1E 51
   N5 . . . . .5D 35
   (off Conewood St.)
Century Yd. SE23 . . . . . . .2E 121
   (not continuous)
Cephas Av. E1 . . . . .3E 65
Cephas Ho. E1 . . . . .3E 65
   (off Doveton St.)
Cephas St. E1 . . . . .3E 65
Cerise Rd. SE15 . . . . .4C 92
Cerney M. W2 . . . . .1F 73
Cervantes Ct. W2 . . . . .5D 59
Cester St. E2 . . . . .5C 50
Ceylon Rd. W14 . . . . .4F 71
Ceylon Wharf Apartments
   SE16 . . . . .3E 79
   (off St Marychurch St.)
Chabot Dr. SE15 . . . . . . .1D 107
Chadacre Ct. E15 . . . . . . .5C 54
   (off Vicars Cl.)
Chadacre Ho. SW9 . . . .2D 105
   (off Loughborough Pk.)
Chadbourn St. E14 . . . . . .4D 67
   (not continuous)
Chadd Grn. E13 . . . . .5C 54
Chadston Ho. N1 . . . . . . .4D 49
   (off Halton Rd.)
Chadswell WC1 . . . . .2E 7
   (off Cromer St.)
Chadwell Ho. SE17 . . . . .1F 91
   (off Inville Rd.)
Chadwell St.
   EC1 . . . . .1C 8 (2C 62)
Chadwick Av. SW19 . . .5C 114
Chadwick Cl. SW15 . . . .5B 98
Chadwick Rd. E11 . . . . . .1A 40
   NW10 . . . . .5B 42
   SE15 . . . . .5B 92
Chadwick St.
   SW1 . . . . . .5B 22 (4F 75)
Chadwin Rd. E13 . . . . .4D 69
Chadworth Ho. EC1 . . . . . .2F 9
   (off Lever St.)
   N4 . . . . .3E 35
Chagford Ho. E3 . . . . .2D 67
   (off Talwin St.)
Chagford St.
   NW1 . . . . .4A 4 (3B 60)

Chailey St. E5 . . . . .5E 37
Chalbury Wlk. N1 . . . . . . .1B 62
Chalcot Cres. NW1 . . . . . .5B 46
Chalcot Gdns. NW3 . . . . . .3B 46
Chalcot M. SW16 . . . . . . .3A 118
Chalcot Rd. NW1 . . . . .4C 46
Chalcot Sq. NW1 . . . . .4C 46
   (not continuous)
Chalcroft Rd. SE13 . . . . . .3A 110
Chaldon Rd. SW6 . . . . .3A 86
Chale Rd. SW2 . . . . .4A 104
Chalfont Ct. NW1 . . . . .4A 4
   (off Baker St.)
Chalfont Ho. SE16 . . . . . . .4D 79
   (off Keetons Rd.)
Chalford NW6 . . . . .3E 45
   (off Finchley Rd.)
Chalford Rd. SE21 . . . . . .4F 119
CHALK FARM 4C 46
Chalk Farm Pde.
   NW3 . . . . .4C 46
   (off Adelaide Rd.)
Chalk Farm Rd. NW1 . . . .4C 46
Chalk Hill Rd. W6 . . . . .5F 71
Chalk Rd. E13 . . . . .4D 69
Chalkwell Ho. E1 . . . . .5F 65
   (off Pitsea St.)
Challenge Cl. NW10 . . . . . .5A 42
Challenger Ho. E14 . . . . .1A 80
   (off Victory Pl.)
Challice Way SW2 . . . . . .1B 118
Challoner Ct. W14 . . . . . .1B 86
   (off Challoner St.)
Challoner Cres. W14 . . . .1B 86
Challoner Mans.
   W14 . . . . .1B 86
   (off Challoner St.)
Challoner St. W14 . . . . . . .1B 86
Chalmers Wlk. SE17 . . . .2D 91
   (off Hillingdon St.)
Chaloner Ct. SE1 . . . . .3B 26
Chalsey Rd. SE4 . . . . .2B 108
Chalton Dr. N2 . . . . .1F 31
Chalton Ho. NW1 . . . . .1B 6
   (off Chalton St.)
Chalton St.
   NW1 . . . . . . .1B 6 (1E 61)
   (not continuous)
Chamberlain Cotts.
   SE5 . . . . .4F 91
Chamberlain Ho. E1 . . . .1E 79
   (off Cable St.)
   NW1 . . . . .1C 6
   SE1 . . . . .4B 24
   (off Westminster Bri. Rd.)
Chamberlain St.
   NW1 . . . . .4B 46
Chamberlayne Mans.
   NW10 . . . . .2F 57
   (off Chamberlayne Rd.)
Chamberlayne Rd.
   NW10 . . . . .5E 43
Chamberlens Garages
   W6 . . . . .5D 71
   (off Dalling Rd.)
Chambers, The
   SW10 . . . . .4E 87
   (off Chelsea Harbour Dr.)
Chambers La.
   NW10 . . . . .4D 43

Chambers Rd. N7 . . . . .1A 48
Chambers St. SE16 . . . . . .3C 78
Chamber St. E1 . . . . .1B 78
Chambers Wharf
   SE16 . . . . .3C 78
Chambon Pl. W6 . . . . .5C 70
Chambord Ho. E2 . . . . .2F 11
   (off Chambord St.)
Chambord St.
   E2 . . . . .2F 11 (2B 64)
Chamomile Ct. E17 . . . . .1C 38
   (off Yunus Khan Cl.)
Champion Cres.
   SE26 . . . . .4A 122
Champion Gro. SE5 . . . . .1F 105
Champion Hill SE5 . . . . . .1F 105
Champion Hill Est.
   SE5 . . . . .1A 106
Champion Ho. SE7 . . . . .2E 97
   (off Charlton Rd.)
Champion Pk. SE5 . . . . . . .5F 91
Champion Rd. SE26 . . . . . .4A 122
Champlain Ho. W12 . . . .1D 71
   (off White City Est.)
Champness Cl.
   SE27 . . . . .4F 119
Chancel Ct. W1 . . . . .1F 75
   (off Old Compton St.)
Chancel Ind. Est.
   . . . . .2B 42
Chancellor Gro.
   SE21 . . . . .2E 119
Chancellor Ho. E1 . . . . .2D 79
   (off Green Bank)
   SW7 . . . . .4E 73
   (off Hyde Pk. Ga.)
Chancellor Pas. E14 . . . .2C 80
Chancellors Ct. WC1 . . . . .5F 7
Chancellor's Rd.
   W6 . . . . .1E 85
Chancellor's St. W6 . . . . . .1E 85
Chancellors Wharf
   W6 . . . . .1E 85
Chancel St.
   SE1 . . . . . . .2D 25 (2D 77)
Chancery Bldgs. E1 . . . .1D 79
   (off Lowood St.)
Chancery La.
   WC2 . . . . . . .1A 16 (5C 62)
Chancery M.
   SW17 . . . . .2A 116
Chance St.
   E1 . . . . .3F 11 (3B 64)
   E2 . . . . .3F 11 (3B 64)
Chandler Av. E16 . . . . .4C 68
Chandler Ho. NW6 . . . . .58 44
   (off Willesden La.)
   WC1 . . . . .4E 7
   (off Colonnade)
Chandlers Av. SE10 . . . . . .4B 82
Chandlers Ct. SE12 . . . .1D 125
Chandlers M. E14 . . . . .3C 80
Chandler St. E1 . . . . .2D 79
Chandlers Way
   SW2 . . . . .5C 104
Chandler Way SE15 . . . . . .2A 92
Chandlery, The SE1 . . . .5C 24
   (off Gerridge St.)
Chandlery Ho. E1 . . . . .5C 64
   (off Gower's Wlk.)

Chandos Pl.
WC2 . . . . .5D **15** (1A **76**)
Chandos Rd. E15 . . . . . .2F **53**
NW2 . . . . .2E **43**
NW10 . . . . .3A **56**
Chandos St.
W1 . . . . . .1E **13** (4D **61**)
Chandos Way NW11 . . . .3D **31**
Change All.
EC3 . . . . .3C **18** (5F **63**)
Chanin M. NW2 . . . . . .2E **43**
Channel 4 TV 4F **75**
(off Horseferry Rd.)
Channel Ga. Rd.
NW10 . . . . .2A **56**
Channel Ho. E14 . . . . . .4A **66**
(off Aston St.)
SE16 . . . . .3F **79**
(off Water Gdns. Sq.)
Channel Islands Est.
N1 . . . . .3E **49**
Channelsea Bus. Cen.
E15 . . . . .1F **67**
Channelsea Path E15 . . .5F **53**
Channelsea Rd. E15 . . . .5F **53**
Chantrey Ho. SW1 . . . . .5D **75**
(off Eccleston St.)
Chantrey Rd. SW9 . . . . .1B **104**
Chantry Cl. W9 . . . . . . .3C **58**
Chantry Cres. NW10 . . . .3B **42**
Chantry Sq. W8 . . . . . . .4D **73**
Chantry St. N1 . . . . . . .5D **49**
Chant Sq. E15 . . . . . . .4F **53**
Chant St. E15 . . . . .4F **53**
(not continuous)
Chapel, The SW15 . . . . .4A **100**
Chapel Cl. NW10 . . . . . .2B **42**
Chapel Ct. E10 . . . . . . .4D **39**
(off Rosedene Ter.)
SE1 . . . . . . .3B **26** (3F **77**)
Chapel Ho. St. E14 . . . . .1D **95**
Chapelier Ho. SW18 . . . .2C **100**
Chapel Mkt. N1 . . . . . . .1C **62**
Chapel of
St John the Evangelist
. . . . .5F **19**
(in The Tower of London)
Chapel of St Peter & St Paul
. . . . .2F **95**
Chapel Path E11 . . . . . .1D **41**
(off Woodbine Pl.)
Chapel Pl.
EC2 . . . . .2D **11** (2A **64**)
N1 . . . . .1C **62**
W1 . . . . .3D **13** (5D **61**)
Chapel Rd. SE27 . . . . . .4D **119**
Chapel Side W2 . . . . . . .1D **73**
Chapel St. NW1 . . . . . . .4A **60**
SW1 . . . . .5C **20** (4C **74**)
Chapel Way N7 . . . . . . .5B **34**
Chapel Yd. SW18 . . . . . .3D **101**
(off Wandsworth High St.)
Chaplin Cl.
SE1 . . . . . .3C **24** (3C **76**)
Chaplin Ho. N1 . . . . . . .5F **49**
Chaplin Rd. E15 . . . . . . .1B **68**
NW2 . . . . .3C **42**
Chapman Ho. E1 . . . . . . .5D **65**
(off Bigland St.)
Chapman Pl. N4 . . . . . . .4D **35**

Chapman Rd. E9 . . . . . .3B **52**
Chapmans Pk. Ind. Est.
NW10 . . . . .3B **42**
Chapman Sq. SW19 . . . .2F **113**
Chapman St. E1 . . . . . . .1D **79**
Chapone Pl.
W1 . . . . . . .3B **14** (5F **61**)
Chapter Chambers
SW1 . . . . .5F **75**
(off Chapter St.)
Chapter House 3F **17**
(off Dunbridge St.)
Chapter Ho. E2 . . . . . . .3C **64**
(off Dunbridge St.)
Chapter Ho. NW2 . . . . . .2C **42**
SE17 . . . . .1D **91**
Chapter St. SW1 . . . . . .5F **75**
Charcot Ho. SW15 . . . . .4B **98**
Charcroft Ct. W14 . . . . . .3F **71**
(off Minford Gdns.)
Chardin Ho. SW9 . . . . . .4C **90**
(off Gosling Way)
Chardin Rd. W4 . . . . . . .5A **70**
Chardmore Rd. N16 . . . .3C **36**
Charecroft Way
W12 . . . . .3F **71**
W14 . . . . .3F **71**
Charfield Ct. W9 . . . . . . .3D **59**
(off Shirland Rd.)
Charford Rd. E16 . . . . . .4C **68**
Chargeable La. E13 . . . . .3B **68**
Chargeable St. E16 . . . . .3B **68**
Chargrove Cl. SE16 . . . . .3F **79**
Charing Cross SW1 . . . . .1D **23**
Charing Cross Rd.
WC2 . . . . . .3C **14** (5F **61**)
Charing Cross Sports Club
. . . . .2F **85**
Charing Cross
Underground Shop. Cen.
WC2 . . . . .5D **15**
Charing Cross Ho. SE1 . . . .3C **24**
(off Windmill Wlk.)
Chariot Cl. E3 . . . . .5C **52**
Charis Ho. E3 . . . . .2D **67**
(off Grace St.)
Charlbert Ct. NW8 . . . . .1A **60**
(off Charlbert St.)
Charlbert St. NW8 . . . . .1A **60**
Charlecote Gro.
SE26 . . . . .3D **121**
Charles II Pl. SW3 . . . . . .1B **88**
Charles II St.
SW1 . . . . . . .1B **22** (2F **75**)
Charles Auffray Ho.
E1 . . . . .4E **65**
(off Smithy St.)
Charles Barry Cl.
SW4 . . . . .1E **103**
Charles Burton Ct. E5 . . .2A **52**
(off Homerton Rd.)
Charles Coveney Rd.
SE15 . . . . .4B **92**
Charles Darwin Ho.
E2 . . . . .2D **65**
(off Canrobert St.)
Charles Dickens Ho.
E2 . . . . .2C **64**
(off Mansford St.)
Charles Dickens Museum, The
. . . . .4F **7**

Charlesfield SE9 . . . . . . .3E **125**
Charles Flemwell M.
E16 . . . . .2C **82**
Charles Gardner Ct.
N1 . . . . .1C **10**
(off Haberdasher St.)
Charles Haller St.
SW2 . . . . .5C **104**
Charles Harrod Ct.
SW13 . . . . .2E **85**
(off Somerville Av.)
Charles House 5B **72**
(off Kensington High St.)
Charles Lamb Ct.
N1 . . . . .1D **63**
(off Gerrard Rd.)
Charles La. NW8 . . . . . .1A **60**
Charles Mackenzie Ho.
SE16 . . . . .5C **78**
(off Linsey St.)
Charles Nex M.
SE21 . . . . .2E **119**
Charles Pl.
NW1 . . . . .2A **6** (2E **61**)
Charles Rd. E7 . . . . .4E **55**
Charles Rowan Ho.
WC1 . . . . .2B **8**
(off Margery St.)
Charles Simmons Ho.
WC1 . . . . .2B **8**
(off Margery St.)
Charles Sq.
N1 . . . . . . .2C **10** (2F **63**)
Charles Sq. Est. N1 . . . .2C **10**
Charles St. E16 . . . . . . .2E **83**
SW13 . . . . .5A **84**
W1 . . . . . .1D **21** (2D **75**)
Charleston St. SE17 . . . . .5E **77**
Charles Townsend Ho.
EC1 . . . . .3D **9**
(off Skinner St.)
Charles Uton Ct. E8 . . . .1C **50**
Charles Whincup Rd.
E16 . . . . .2D **83**
Charlesworth Ho.
E14 . . . . .5C **66**
(off Dod St.)
Charlesworth Pl.
SW13 . . . . .1A **98**
Charleville Cir.
SE26 . . . . .5C **120**
Charleville Ct. W14 . . . . .1B **86**
(off Charleville Rd.)
Charleville Mans.
W14 . . . . .1A **86**
(off Charleville Rd.,
not continuous)
Charleville Rd.
W14 . . . . .1A **86**
Charlie Chaplin Wlk.
SE1 . . . . . .1A **24** (2B **76**)
Charlmont Rd.
SW17 . . . . .5A **116**
Charlotte Ct. N8 . . . . . . .1F **33**
SE1 . . . . .5A **78**
(off Old Kent Rd.)
W6 . . . . .5C **70**
(off Invermead Cl.)
Charlotte Despard Av.
SW11 . . . . .4C **88**

Charlotte Ho. *E16* 2D **83**
(off Fairfax M.)
W6 . . . . .1E **85**
(off Queen Caroline St.)
Charlotte M.
W1 . . . . . . .5A **6** (4E **61**)
W10 . . . . .5F **57**
W14 . . . . .5A **72**
W1 . . . . .1A **14** (4E **61**)
Charlotte Pl. *SW1* . . .5E **75**
Charlotte Rd.
EC2 . . . . . .2D **11** (2A **64**)
SW13 . . . . .4B **84**
Charlotte Row
SW4 . . . . .1E **103**
Charlotte St.
W1 . . . . . . .5A **6** (4E **61**)
Charlotte Ter. *N1* 5B **48**
Charlow Cl. *SW6* 5E **87**
CHARLTON 3F **97**
Charlton Athletic FC . .1E **97**
Charlton Chu. La.
SE7 . . . . .1E **97**
Charlton Ct. *E2* 5B **50**
NW5 . . . . .2F **47**
Charlton Dene *SE7* . . .3E **97**
Charlton Ga. Bus. Pk.
SE7 . . . . .5E **83**
Charlton King's Rd.
NW5 . . . . .2F **47**
Charlton La. *SE7* 5F **83**
Charlton Lido 3F **97**
Charlton Pk. La. *SE7* . .3F **97**
Charlton Pk. Rd. *SE7* . .2F **97**
Charlton Pl. *N1* 1D **63**
Charlton Rd. *NW10* . . .5A **42**
SE3 . . . . .3C **96**
SE7 . . . . .3D **97**
Charlton Way *SE3* 4A **96**
Charlwood Ho. *SW1* . . .5F **75**
(off Vauxhall Bri. Rd.)
Charlwood Ho's. *WC1* . .2E **7**
(off Midhope St.)
Charlwood Pl. *SW1* . . .5E **75**
Charlwood Rd. *SW15* . .2F **99**
Charlwood St. *SW1* . . .1E **89**
(not continuous)
Charlwood Ter. *SW15* . .2F **99**
Charmans Ho. *SW8* . . .3A **90**
(off Wandsworth Rd.)
Charmeuse Ct. *E2* 1D **65**
(off Silk Weaver Way)
Charmian Ho. *N1* 1D **11**
(off Crondall St.)
Charminster Rd.
SE9 . . . . .4F **125**
Charmouth Ho. *SW8* . . .3B **90**
Charnock Ho. *W12* 1D **71**
(off White City Est.)
Charnock Rd. *E5* 5D **37**
Charnwood Gdns.
E14 . . . . .5C **80**
Charnwood St. *E5* 4D **37**
(not continuous)
Charrington St. *NW1* . .1F **61**
Charsley Rd. *SE6* 2D **123**
Charter Bldgs. 4D **95**
(off Catherine Gro.)
Charter Ct. *N4* 3C **34**
Charterhouse 4E **9**

Charter Ho. *WC2* 3E **15**
(off Crown Ct.)
Charterhouse Apartments
SW18 . . . . .2E **101**
Charterhouse Bldgs.
EC1 . . . . . .4E **9** (3E **63**)
Charterhouse M.
EC1 . . . . . .5E **9** (4D **63**)
Charterhouse Rd. *E8* . .1C **50**
Charterhouse Sq.
EC1 . . . . . .5E **9** (4D **63**)
Charterhouse St.
EC1 . . . . . .1C **16** (4C **62**)
**Charteris Community
Sports Cen.** 5C **44**
Charteris Rd. *N4* 3C **34**
NW6 . . . . .5B **44**
Charters Cl. *SE19* 5A **120**
Chartes Ho. *SE1* 5E **27**
(off Stevens St.)
Chartfield Av. *SW15* . . .3D **99**
Chartfield Sq. *SW15* . . .3F **99**
Chartham Ct. *SW9* 1C **104**
(off Canterbury Cres.)
Chartham Gro.
SE27 . . . . .3D **119**
Chartham Ho. *SE1* 5C **26**
(off Weston St.)
Chart Ho. *E14* 1D **95**
(off Burrells Wharf Sq.)
Chartley Av. *NW2* 5A **28**
Chartridge *SE17* 2F **91**
(off Westmoreland St.)
Chart St. *N1* . . .1C **10** (2F **63**)
Chartwell Ho. *W11* 2B **72**
(off Ladbroke Rd.)
Charville Ct. *SE10* 2F **95**
(off Trafalgar Gro.)
Charwood *SW16* 4C **118**
Chase, The *E12* 1F **55**
SW4 . . . . .1D **103**
Chase Centre, The
NW10 . . . . .2A **56**
Chase Ct. *SW3* 4B **74**
(off Beaufort Gdns.)
Chasefield Ho.
SW17 . . . . .4B **116**
Chaseley St. *E14* 5A **66**
Chasemore Ho. *SW6* . . .3A **86**
(off Williams Cl.)
Chase Rd. *NW10* 3A **56**
Chase Rd. Trad. Est.
NW10 . . . . .3A **56**
Chaseway Lodge *E16* . .5C **68**
(off Butchers Rd.)
Chaston Pl. *NW5* 2C **46**
(off Grafton Ter.)
Chater Ho. *E2* 2F **65**
(off Roman Rd.)
Chatfield Rd. *SW11* . . .1E **101**
Chatham Cl. *NW11* 1C **30**
Chatham Pl. *E9* 3E **51**
Chatham Rd. *SW11* . . .4B **102**
Chatham St. *SE17* 5F **77**
Chats Palace Arts Cen.
. . . . .2F **51**
Chatsworth Av.
BR1: Brom 4D **125**
Chatsworth Ct. *W8* 5C **72**
(off Pembroke Rd.)

Chatsworth Est. *E5* 1F **51**
Chatsworth Ho. *E16* . . .2D **83**
(off Wesley Av.)
Chatsworth Lodge
W4 . . . . .1A **84**
(off Bourne Pl.)
Chatsworth Rd. *E5* 5E **37**
E15 . . . . .2B **54**
NW2 . . . . .3E **43**
Chatsworth Way
SE27 . . . . .3D **119**
Chatterton M. *N4* 5D **35**
(off Chatterton Rd.)
Chatterton Rd. *N4* 5D **35**
Chatto Rd. *SW11* 3B **102**
Chaucer Ct. *N16* 1A **50**
SW17 . . . . .3F **115**
(off Lanesborough Way)
Chaucer Dr. *SE1* 5B **78**
Chaucer Ho. *SW1* 1E **89**
(off Churchill Gdns.)
Chaucer Mans. *W14* . . .2A **86**
(off Queen's Club Gdns.)
Chaucer Rd. *E7* 3C **54**
E11 . . . . .1C **40**
SE24 . . . . .3C **104**
Chaucer Way *SW19* . . .5F **115**
Chaulden Ho. *EC1* 2C **10**
(off Cranwood St.)
Chauntler Cl. *E16* 5D **69**
Cheadle Ct. *NW8* 3F **59**
(off Henderson Dr.)
Cheadle Ho. *E14* 5B **66**
(off Copenhagen Pl.)
Cheam St. *SE15* 1E **107**
Cheapside
EC2 . . . . . .3F **17** (5E **63**)
Cheapside Pas. *EC2* . . .3F **17**
(off One New Change)
Chearsley *SE17* 5E **77**
(off Deacon Way)
Cheddington Ho. *E2* . . .5C **50**
(off Whiston Rd.)
Chedworth Cl. *E16* 5B **68**
(off Wouldham Rd.)
Cheesemans Ter.
W14 . . . . .1B **86**
(not continuous)
Chelford Rd.
BR1: Brom 5F **123**
Chelmer Rd. *E9* 2F **51**
Chelmsford Cl. *W6* 2F **85**
Chelmsford Ho. *N7* 1B **48**
(off Holloway Rd.)
Chelmsford Rd. *E11* . . .3F **39**
E17 . . . . .1C **38**
Chelmsford Sq.
NW10 . . . . .5E **43**
CHELSEA 1A **88**
Chelsea Bri. *SW1* 2D **89**
Chelsea Bri. Rd.
SW1 . . . . .1C **88**
Chelsea Bri. Wharf
SW8 . . . . .2D **89**
Chelsea Cinema 1A **88**
Chelsea Cloisters
SW3 . . . . .5A **74**
Chelsea Cl. *NW10* 5A **42**
Chelsea Ct. *SW3* 2B **88**
(off Embankment Gdns.)

Chelsea Cres. NW2 . . . . .3B 44
SW10 . . . . .4E 87
Chelsea Emb. SW3 . . . . .2A 88
Chelsea Farm Ho. Studios
  SW10 . . . . .2F 87
  (off Cremorne Est.)
Chelsea FC 3D 87
Chelsea Gdns. SW1 . . .1C 88
Chelsea Ga. SW1 . . . . .1C 88
  (off Ebury Bri. Rd.)
Chelsea Harbour
  SW10 . . . . .4E 87
Chelsea Harbour Design Cen.
  SW10 . . . . .4E 87
  (off Chelsea Harbour Dr.)
Chelsea Harbour Dr.
  SW10 . . . . .4E 87
Chelsea Lodge SW3 . . . .2B 88
  (off Tite St.)
Chelsea Mnr. Ct.
  SW3 . . . . .2A 88
Chelsea Mnr. Gdns.
  SW3 . . . . .1A 88
Chelsea Mnr. St.
  SW3 . . . . .1A 88
Chelsea Mnr. Studios
  SW3 . . . . .1A 88
  (off Flood St.)
Chelsea Pk. Gdns.
  SW3 . . . . .2F 87
Chelsea Physic Garden
  . . . . .2B 88
Chelsea Reach Twr.
  SW10 . . . . .3F 87
  (off Worlds End Est.)
Chelsea Sports Cen. . . .1A 88
Chelsea Sq. SW3 . . . . .1F 87
Chelsea Studios
  SW6 . . . . .3D 87
  (off Fulham Rd.)
Chelsea Theatre, The
  . . . . .3E 87
Chelsea Towers SW3 . . .2A 88
  (off Chelsea Mnr. Gdns.)
Chelsea Village SW6 . . .3D 87
  (off Fulham Rd.)
Chelsea Vista SW6 . . . .4E 87
Chelsea Wharf SW10 . . .3F 87
  (off Lots Rd.)
Chelsfield Gdns.
  SE26 . . . . .3E 121
Chelsfield Ho. SE17 . . . .5A 78
  (off Massinger St.)
Chelsfield Point E9 . . . . .4F 51
  (off Penshurst Rd.)
Chelsham Rd. SW4 . . . .1F 103
Cheltenham Gdns. E6 . . .1F 69
Cheltenham Rd. E10 . . . .1E 39
  SE15 . . . . .2E 107
Cheltenham Ter.
  SW3 . . . . .1B 88
Chelverton Rd. SW15 . . .2F 99
Chelwood Cl. SW11 . . . .4F 87
  (off Westbridge Rd.)
Chelwood Ho. W2 . . . . .5F 59
  (off Gloucester Sq.)
Chelwood Wlk. SE4 . . . .2A 108
Chenappa Cl. E13 . . . . .2C 68
Cheney Ct. SE23 . . . . . .1F 121
Cheneys Rd. E11 . . . . . .5A 40

Chenies, The NW1 . . . . .1F 61
  (off Pancras Rd.)
Chenies Ho. W2 . . . . . .1D 73
  (off Moscow Rd.)
  W4 . . . . .3B 84
  (off Corney Reach Way)
Chenies M.
  WC1 . . . . .4B 6 (3F 61)
Chenies Pl. NW1 . . . . . .1F 61
Chenies St.
  WC1 . . . . .5B 6 (4F 61)
Cheniston Gdns. W8 . . .4D 73
Chenla SE13 . . . . .5D 95
Chepstow Cl. SW15 . . . .3A 100
Chepstow Cnr. W2 . . . . .5C 58
  (off Chepstow Pl.)
Chepstow Ct. W11 . . . . .1C 72
  (off Chepstow Vs.)
Chepstow Cres. W11 . . .1C 72
Chepstow Pl. W2 . . . . . .5C 58
Chepstow Rd. W2 . . . . . .5C 58
Chepstow Vs. W11 . . . . .1B 72
Chequers Ct. EC1 . . . . .4A 10
  (off Chequer St.)
Chequers Ho. NW8 . . . . .3A 60
  (off Jerome Cres.)
Chequer St.
  EC1 . . . . .4A 10 (3E 63)
  (not continuous)
Cherbury Ct. N1 . . . . . . .1F 63
  (off St John's Est.)
Cherbury St. N1 . . . . . . .1F 63
Cheriton Ct. SE12 . . . . .5C 110
Cheriton Sq. SW17 . . . . .2C 116
Cherry Cl. SW2 . . . . . . .5C 104
Cherry Ct. W3 . . . . .2A 70
Cherry Gdn. Ho.
  SE16 . . . . .3D 79
  (off Cherry Gdn. St.)
Cherry Gdn. St. SE16 . . .3D 79
Cherry Laurel Wlk.
  SW2 . . . . .4B 104
Cherry Orchard SE7 . . . .2E 97
Cherry Tree Cl. E9 . . . . .5E 51
Cherry Tree Ct. NW1 . . . .4E 47
  (off Camden St.)
  SE7 . . . . .2E 97
Cherry Tree Dr.
  SW16 . . . . .3A 118
Cherry Tree Rd. E15 . . . .2A 54
Cherry Tree Ter. SE1 . . . .4E 27
  (off Whites Grounds)
Cherry Tree Wlk.
  EC1 . . . . .4A 10 (3E 63)
Cherry Tree Way E13 . . . .3F 69
Cherrywood Cl. E3 . . . . .2A 66
Cherrywood Dr.
  SW15 . . . . .3F 99
Cherrywood Lodge
  SE13 . . . . .4F 109
  (off Birdwood Av.)
Chertsey Ho. E2 . . . . . . .2F 11
  (off Arnold Cir.)
Chertsey Rd. E11 . . . . . .4F 39
Chertsey St. SW17 . . . . .5C 116
Cherwell Ho. NW8 . . . . .3F 59
  (off Church St. Est.)
Cheryls Cl. SW6 . . . . . . .4D 87
Cheseman St. SE26 . . . .3D 121
Chesham Cl. SW1 . . . . . .5B 20

Chesham Flats W1 . . . . .4C 12
  (off Brown Hart Gdns.)
Chesham Ho. SE8 . . . . . .4C 94
  (off Brookmill Rd.)
Chesham M. SW1 . . . . . .5B 20
Chesham Pl.
  SW1 . . . . . .5B 20 (4C 74)
  (not continuous)
Chesham Rd. SW19 . . .5F 115
  SW1 . . . . . .5B 20 (4C 74)
Cheshire Cl. SE4 . . . . . .5B 94
Cheshire Ct. EC4 . . . . . . .3C 16
  (off Fleet St.)
Cheshire St. E2 . . . . .3B 64
Chesholm Rd. N16 . . . . .5A 36
Cheshunt Ho. NW6 . . . . .5D 45
  (off Mortimer Cres.)
Cheshunt Rd. E7 . . . . . . .3D 55
Chesil Ct. E2 . . . . .1E 65
  SW3 . . . . .2A 88
Chesilton Rd. SW6 . . . . .4B 86
Chesley Gdns. E6 . . . . . .1F 69
Chesney Ct. W9 . . . . . . .3C 58
  (off Shirland Rd.)
Chesney Ho. SE13 . . . . .2F 109
  (off Mercator Rd.)
Chesney St. SW11 . . . . .4C 88
Chessington Ho.
  SW8 . . . . .5F 89
Chessington Mans.
  E10 . . . . .2C 38
  E11 . . . . .2A 40
Chesson Rd. W14 . . . . . .2B 86
Chester Cl.
  SW1 . . . . . .4D 21 (3D 75)
  SW13 . . . . .1D 99
Chester Cl. Nth.
  NW1 . . . . . .1E 5 (2D 61)
Chester Cl. Sth.
  NW1 . . . . . .2E 5 (2D 61)
Chester Cotts. SW1 . . . . .5C 74
  (off Bourne St.)
Chester Ct.
  NW1 . . . . . .1E 5 (2D 61)
  (not continuous)
  SE5 . . . . .3F 91
  (off Lomond Gro.)
  SE8 . . . . .1F 93
  W6 . . . . .5F 71
  (off Wolverton Gdns.)
Chester Cres. E8 . . . . . . .2B 50
Chesterfield Cl. SE13 . . .5F 95
Chesterfield Gdns.
  N4 . . . . .1D 35
  SE10 . . . . .4F 95
  W1 . . . . . .1D 21 (2D 75)
Chesterfield Gro.
  SE22 . . . . .3B 106
Chesterfield Hill
  W1 . . . . . .1D 21 (2D 75)
Chesterfield Ho. W1 . . . .1C 20
  (off Chesterfield Gdns.)
Chesterfield M. N4 . . . . .1D 35
Chesterfield Rd.
  E10 . . . . .1E 39
Chesterfield St.
  W1 . . . . . .1D 21 (2D 75)
Chesterfield Wlk.
  SE10 . . . . .4F 95

Chesterfield Way
SE15 . . . . .3E **93**
Chesterfield Gdns.
NW3 . . . . .1D **45**
Chesterfield Ho. SE18 . . .4F **97**
(off Tellson Av.)
Chester Ga.
NW1 . . . . .2D **5** (2D **61**)
Chester Ho. SE8 . . . . . . .2B **94**
SW1 . . . . .5D **75**
(off Eccleston Pl.)
SW9 . . . . .3C **90**
(off Cranmer Rd.)
Chesterman Cl. W4 . . . .3A **84**
(off Corney Reach Way)
Chester M.
SW1 . . . . .5D **21** (4D **75**)
Chester Pl.
NW1 . . . . .1D **5** (2D **61**)
Chester Rd. E7 . . . . .4F **55**
E11 . . . . .1D **41**
E16 . . . . .3A **68**
E17 . . . . .1F **37**
N19 . . . . .4D **33**
NW1 . . . . .2C **4** (2C **60**)
SW19 . . . . .5E **113**
Chester Row SW1 . . . . .5C **74**
Chester Sq. SW1 . . . . . .5C **74**
Chester Sq. M. SW1 . . .5D **21**
Chester St. E2 . . . . .3C **64**
SW1 . . . . .5C **20** (4C **74**)
Chester Ter.
NW1 . . . . .1D **5** (2D **61**)
(not continuous)
Chesterton Cl.
SW18 . . . . .3C **100**
Chesterton Ho.
SW11 . . . . .1F **101**
(off Ingrave St.)
W10 . . . . .4A **58**
(off Portobello Rd.)
Chesterton Rd. E13 . . . .2C **68**
W10 . . . . .4A **58**
Chesterton Sq. W8 . . . .5C **72**
Chesterton Ter. E13 . . . .2C **68**
Chester Way SE11 . . . . .5C **76**
Chestnut All. SW6 . . . . .2B **86**
Chestnut Av. E7 . . . . . . .1D **55**
Chestnut Ct. N16 . . . . . .4F **35**
SE6 . . . . .5E **123**
SE14 . . . . .4B **94**
SW16 . . . . .4C **118**
Chestnut Ct. SW6 . . . . .2B **86**
W8 . . . . .4D **73**
(off Abbots Wlk.)
Chestnut Dr. E11 . . . . . .1C **40**
Chestnut Gro. SW12 . . .5C **102**
Chestnut Ho. E3 . . . . . . .5B **52**
(off Sycamore Av.)
SW15 . . . . .2D **98**
W4 . . . . .5A **70**
(off The Orchard)
Chestnut Pl. SE26 . . . . .4B **120**
Chestnut Plaza E20 . . . .3E **53**
(within Westfield Stratford
City Shopping Cen.)
Chestnut Rd. SE27 . . . .3D **119**
Chestnuts, The N5 . . . . .1E **49**
(off Highbury Grange)
Chettle Cl. SE1 . . . . . . .5B **26**

Chettle Ct. N8 . . . . .1C **34**
Chetwode Ho. NW8 . . . .3A **60**
(off Grendon St.)
Chetwode Rd.
SW17 . . . . .3B **116**
Chetwynd Wlk. E6 . . . . .4F **69**
(off Greenwich Cres.)
Chetwynd Rd. NW5 . . . .1D **47**
Chetwynd Vs. NW5 . . . .1D **47**
(off Chetwynd Rd.)
Cheval Pl. SW7 . . . . . . .4A **74**
Cheval St. E14 . . . . .4C **80**
Chevening Rd. NW6 . . . .1F **57**
SE10 . . . . .1B **96**
Cheverell Ho. E2 . . . . . .1C **64**
(off Pritchard's Rd.)
Cheverton Rd. N19 . . . .3F **33**
Chevet St. E9 . . . . .2A **52**
Chevington NW2 . . . . . .3B **44**
Cheviot Cl. SE14 . . . . . .2E **93**
(off Avonley Rd.)
Cheviot Gdns. NW2 . . . .4F **29**
SE27 . . . . .4D **119**
Cheviot Ga. NW2 . . . . . .4A **30**
Cheviot Ho. E1 . . . . .5D **65**
(off Commercial Rd.)
Cheviot Rd. SE27 . . . . .5C **118**
Chevron Cl. E16 . . . . . . .5C **68**
Cheylesmore Ho.
SW1 . . . . .1D **89**
(off Ebury Bri. Rd.)
Cheyne Cl. NW4 . . . . . . .1E **29**
Cheyne Ct. SW3 . . . . . . .2B **88**
Cheyne Gdns. SW3 . . . .2A **88**
Cheyne Ho. SW3 . . . . . .2B **88**
(off Chelsea Emb.)
Cheyne M. SW3 . . . . . . .2A **88**
Cheyne Pl. SW3 . . . . . . .2B **88**
Cheyne Row SW3 . . . . .2A **88**
Cheyne Wlk. NW4 . . . . . .1E **29**
SW3 . . . . .2F **87**
(not continuous)
SW10 . . . . .3F **87**
Chichele Rd. NW2 . . . . .2F **43**
Chicheley St.
SE1 . . . . .3A **24** (3B **76**)
Chichester Cl. SE3 . . . . .3E **97**
Chichester Ct. NW1 . . . .4E **47**
(off Royal Coll. St.)
Chichester Ho. NW6 . . . .1C **58**
SW9 . . . . .3C **90**
(off Cranmer Rd.)
Chichester M. SE27 . . . .4C **118**
Chichester Rents
WC2 . . . . .2B **16**
Chichester Rd. E11 . . . . .5A **40**
NW6 . . . . .1C **58**
W2 . . . . .4D **59**
Chichester St. SW1 . . . .1E **89**
Chichester Way E14 . . . .5F **81**
Chicksand Ho. E1 . . . . . .4C **64**
(off Chicksand St.)
Chicksand St. E1 . . . . . .4B **64**
(not continuous)
Chiddingstone SE13 . . . .3E **109**
Chiddingstone St.
SW6 . . . . .5C **86**
Chigwell Ct. E9 . . . . .3A **52**
(off Ballance Rd.)
Chigwell Hill E1 . . . . . . .1D **79**

Chilcombe Ho. SW15 . . .5C **98**
(off Fontley Way)
Chilcot Cl. E14 . . . . .5D **67**
Childebert Rd.
SW17 . . . . .2D **117**
Childeric Rd. SE14 . . . . .3A **94**
Childerley St.
SW6 . . . . .4A **86**
Childers St. SE8 . . . . . . .2A **94**
Child La. SE10 . . . . .4B **82**
CHILD'S HILL 5B **30**
Childs Hill Wks. NW2 . . .5B **30**
(off Cricklewood La.)
Child's M. SW5 . . . . .5C **72**
(off Child's Pl.)
Child's Pl. SW5 . . . . .5C **72**
Child's St. SW5 . . . . .5C **72**
Child's Wlk. SW5 . . . . . .5C **72**
(off Child's St.)
Chilham Ho.
SE1 . . . . .5C **26** (4F **77**)
SE15 . . . . .2E **93**
Chilham Rd. SE9 . . . . . .4F **125**
Chilianwalla Memorial
. . . . .2C **88**
Chillerton Rd.
SW17 . . . . .5C **116**
Chillingford Ho.
SW17 . . . . .4E **115**
Chillington Dr.
SW11 . . . . .2F **101**
Chillingworth Rd. N7 . . .2C **48**
Chiltern Ct. NW1 . . . . . . .4A **4**
(off Baker St.)
SE14 . . . . .3E **93**
(off Avonley Rd.)
Chiltern Gdns. NW2 . . . .5F **29**
Chiltern Ho. SE17 . . . . . .2F **91**
(off Portland St.)
W10 . . . . .4A **58**
(off Telford Rd.)
Chiltern Rd. E3 . . . . .3C **66**
Chiltern St.
W1 . . . . .5B **4** (4C **60**)
Chilthorne Cl. SE6 . . . . .5B **108**
Chilton Gro. SE8 . . . . . . .5F **79**
Chiltonian Ind. Est.
SE12 . . . . .4B **110**
Chilton St. E2 . . . . .3B **64**
Chilver St. SE10 . . . . . . .1B **96**
Chilworth Ct. SW19 . . . .1F **113**
Chilworth M. W2 . . . . . . .5F **59**
Chilworth St. W2 . . . . . . .5E **59**
Chimney Ct. E1 . . . . .2D **79**
(off Brewhouse La.)
China Ct. E1 . . . . .2D **79**
(off Asher Way)
China Hall M. SE16 . . . . .4E **79**
China M. SW2 . . . . .5B **104**
China Town 4C **14**
(off Gerrard St.)
China Wlk. SE11 . . . . . . .5B **76**
China Wharf SE1 . . . . . . .3C **78**
Chinbrook Cres.
SE12 . . . . .3D **125**
Chinbrook Rd. SE12 . . .3D **125**
Ching Ct. WC2 . . . . .3D **15**
(off Monmouth St.)
Chingley Cl.
BR1: Brom 5A **124**

Chinnock's Wharf
E14 . . . . .1A *80*
(off Narrow St.)
Chipka St. E14 . . . . . . .3E *81*
(not continuous)
Chipley St. SW14 . . . . .2A *94*
Chippendale Ho.
SW1 . . . . .1D *89*
(off Churchill Gdns.)
Chippendale St. E5 . . .5F *37*
Chippenham Gdns.
NW6 . . . . .2C *58*
Chippenham M. W9 . . .3C *58*
Chippenham Rd. W9 . . .3C *58*
Chipperfield Ho.
SW3 . . . . .1A *88*
(off Cale St.)
Chipstead Gdns.
NW2 . . . . .4D *29*
Chipstead St. SW6 . . . .4C *86*
Chip St. SW4 . . . . .1F *103*
Chisenhale Rd. E3 . . . .1A *66*
Chisholm Ct. W6 . . . . . .1C *84*
Chiseldon Wlk. E9 . . . .3B *52*
(off Osborne Rd.)
Chisley Ho. N15 . . . . . .1A *36*
Chiswell Sq. SE3 . . . . .5D *97*
Chiswell St.
EC1 . . . . .5B *10* (4E *63*)
SE5 . . . . .3F *91*
(off Edmund St.)
CHISWICK 1A *84*
Chiswick Comn. Rd.
W4 . . . . .5A *70*
**Chiswick Community
Sports Hall** 3A *84*
Chiswick High Rd.
W4 . . . . .1A *84*
Chiswick House & Gardens
. . . . .2A *84*
Chiswick La. W4 . . . . . .1A *84*
Chiswick La. Sth.
W4 . . . . .2B *84*
Chiswick Mall W4 . . . .2B *84*
W6 . . . . .2B *84*
Chiswick Sq. W4 . . . . .2A *84*
Chiswick Wharf W4 . . .2B *84*
Chitty St. W1 . . .5A *6* (4E *61*)
Chivalry Rd. SW11 . . . .3A *102*
Chivelston SW19 . . . . .1F *113*
Chobham Gdns.
SW19 . . . . .2F *113*
Chobham Rd. E15 . . . .2F *53*
Chocolate Studios
N1 . . . . .1B *10*
(off Shepherdess Pl.)
Cholmeley Cl. N6 . . . . .2D *33*
Cholmeley Cres. N6 . . .2D *33*
Cholmeley Lodge N6 . . .3D *33*
Cholmeley Pk. N6 . . . . .3D *33*
Cholmley Gdns. NW6 . . .2C *44*
Cholmondeley Av.
NW10 . . . . .1C *56*
Choppin's Ct. E1 . . . . .2D *79*
Chopwell Cl. E15 . . . . .4F *53*
Choudhury Mans. N1 . . .4A *48*
(off Pembroke St.)
Choumert Gro. SE15 . . .5C *92*
Choumert M. SE15 . . . .5C *92*
Choumert Rd. SE15 . . .1B *106*

Choumert Sq. SE15 . . . .5C *92*
Chow Sq. E8 . . . . .2B *50*
Chrisp Ho. SE10 . . . . . .2A *96*
(off Maze Hill)
Chrisp St. E14 . . . . . . .4D *67*
(not continuous)
Christabel Pankhurst Ct.
SE5 . . . . .3F *91*
(off Brisbane St.)
Christchurch Av. NW6 . .5F *43*
Christ Church Ct.
NW10 . . . . .5A *42*
Christchurch Ct. EC4 . . .2E *17*
(off Warwick La.)
NW6 . . . . .4A *44*
(off Willesden La.)
Christchurch Hill
NW3 . . . . .5F *31*
Christchurch Ho.
SW2 . . . . .1B *118*
(off Christchurch Rd.)
Christchurch Pas.
NW3 . . . . .5E *31*
Christchurch Pl. SW8 . .5F *89*
Christchurch Rd. N8 . . .1A *34*
SW2 . . . . .1B *118*
Christchurch Sq. E9 . . .5E *51*
Christchurch St. SW3 . .2B *88*
Christchurch Ter.
SW3 . . . . .2B *88*
(off Christchurch St.)
Christchurch Way
SE10 . . . . .1A *96*
Christian Ct. SE16 . . . .2B *80*
Christian Pl. E1 . . . . . .5C *64*
(off Burslem St.)
Christian St. E1 . . . . . .5C *64*
Christie Ct. N19 . . . . . .4A *34*
Christie Ho. SE10 . . . . .1B *96*
(off Blackwall La.)
W12 . . . . .5D *57*
(off Du Cane Rd.)
Christie Rd. E9 . . . . . . .3A *52*
Christina Sq. N4 . . . . . .3D *35*
Christina St.
EC2 . . . . .3D *11* (3A *64*)
Christopher Bell Twr.
E3 . . . . .1C *66*
(off Pancras Way)
Christopher Cl. SE16 . . .3F *79*
Christopher Ct. E1 . . . . .5C *64*
(off Leman St.)
Christopher Pl.
NW1 . . . . . .1C *6* (2F *61*)
Christophers M. W11 . . .2A *72*
Christopher St.
EC2 . . . . .4C *10* (3F *63*)
Chryssell Rd. SW9 . . . .3C *90*
Chubworthy St. SE14 . . .2A *94*
Chudleigh Rd. NW6 . . . .4F *43*
SE4 . . . . .3B *108*
Chudleigh St. E1 . . . . . .5F *65*
Chulsa Rd. SE26 . . . . . .5D *121*
Chumleigh Gdns.
SE5 . . . . .2A *92*
(off Chumleigh St.)
Chumleigh St. SE5 . . . .2A *92*
Church App. SE21 . . . . .3F *119*
Church Av. NW1 . . . . . .3D *47*
Churchbury Rd. SE9 . . .5F *111*

Church Cloisters EC3 . . .5D *19*
Church Cl. W8 . . . . .3D *73*
Church Ct. EC4 . . . . . . .5C *62*
SE16 . . . . .3B *80*
(off Rotherhithe St.)
Church Cres. E9 . . . . . .4F *51*
Churchcroft Cl.
SW12 . . . . .5C *102*
Churchdown
BR1: Brom 4A *124*
CHURCH END 4A *42*
Church Entry EC4 . . . . .3E *17*
Churchfield Ho. W2 . . . .3F *59*
(off Hall Pl.)
Churchfield Mans.
SW6 . . . . .5B *86*
(off New Kings Rd.)
Churchfields SE10 . . . . .2E *95*
Church Gth. N19 . . . . . .4F *33*
(off St John's Gro.)
Church Ga. SW6 . . . . . .1A *100*
Church Grn. SW9 . . . . . .4C *90*
Church Gro. SE13 . . . . .3D *109*
Church Hill SW19 . . . . .5B *114*
Church Ho. EC1 . . . . . . .3E *9*
(off Compton St.)
SW1 . . . . .5C *22*
(off Gt. Smith St.)
Churchill Ct. N4 . . . . . .2C *34*
Churchill Gdns. SW1 . . .1E *89*
(off Churchill Gdns. Rd.,
not continuous)
Churchill Gdns. Rd.
SW1 . . . . .1D *89*
Churchill Pl. E14 . . . . . .2D *81*
Churchill Rd. E16 . . . . .5E *69*
NW2 . . . . .3D *43*
NW5 . . . . .1D *47*
Churchill Wlk. E9 . . . . .3E *51*
Churchill War Rooms
. . . . .3C *22* (3F *75*)
Church La. E11 . . . . .3A *40*
SW17 . . . . .5B *116*
Churchley Rd.
SE26 . . . . .4D *121*
Church Mead SE5 . . . . .3E *91*
(off Camberwell Rd.)
Churchmead Rd.
NW10 . . . . .3C *42*
Church Mt. N2 . . . . .1F *31*
Church Pas. EC2 . . . . . .2A *18*
(off Gresham St.)
Church Path E11 . . . . . .1C *40*
N5 . . . . .2D *49*
NW10 . . . . .4A *42*
SW14 . . . . .1A *98*
(not continuous)
Church Pl.
SW1 . . . . . .5A *14* (1E *75*)
Church Ri. SE23 . . . . . .2F *121*
Church Rd. E10 . . . . . . .3C *38*
E12 . . . . .2F *55*
N1 . . . . .3E *49*
N6 . . . . .1C *32*
NW10 . . . . .4A *42*
SW13 . . . . .5B *84*
SW19 . . . . .5A *114*
Church Rd. Almshouses
E10 . . . . .4D *39*
(off Church Rd.)

Church Rd. Ind. Est.
E10 . . . . .3C **38**
Church Row NW3 . . . . .1E **45**
SW6 . . . . .3D **87**
(off Park Rd.)
Church St. E15 . . . . . .5A **54**
NW8 . . . . .4F **59**
(not continuous)
W2 . . . . .4F **59**
(not continuous)
W4 . . . . .2B **84**
Church St. Est.
NW8 . . . . .3F **59**
Church St. Nth. E15 . . .5A **54**
Church St. Pas. E15 . . .5A **54**
(off Church St.)
Church Ter. SE13 . . . . .1A **110**
Church Va. SE23 . . . . .2F **121**
Church Vw. Gro.
SE26 . . . . .5F **121**
Church Wlk. N6 . . . . . .5C **32**
N16 . . . . .5F **35**
(not continuous)
NW2 . . . . .5B **30**
SW13 . . . . .4C **84**
SW15 . . . . .3D **99**
Churchward Ho.
SE17 . . . . .2D **91**
(off Lorrimore Sq.)
W14 . . . . .1B **86**
(off Ivatt Pl.)
Churchway
NW1 . . . . .1C **6** (2F **61**)
(not continuous)
Churchwell Path E9 . . . .2E **51**
Churchyard Pas. SE5 . . .5F **91**
Churchyard Row
SE11 . . . . .5D **77**
Church Yd. Wlk. W2 . . . .4F **59**
(off St Mary's Sq.)
Churston Av. E13 . . . . .5D **55**
Churston Cl. SW2 . . . . .1C **118**
Churston Mans. WC1 . . . .4A **8**
(off Gray's Inn Rd.)
Churton Pl. SW1 . . . . . .5E **75**
Churton St. SW1 . . . . . .5E **75**
Chusan Pl. E14 . . . . . .5B **66**
Chute Ho. SW9 . . . . . . .5C **90**
(off Stockwell Pk. Rd.)
Chuter Ede Ho. SW6 . . . .2B **86**
(off Clem Attlee Ct.)
Cibber Rd. SE23 . . . . . .2F **121**
Cicada Rd. SW18 . . . . .4E **101**
Cicely Ho. NW8 . . . . . .1F **59**
(off Cochrane St.)
Cicely Rd. SE15 . . . . . .4C **92**
Cinderella Path
NW11 . . . . .3D **31**
Cinderford Way
BR1: Brom 4A **124**
Cine Lumiere 5F **73**
(off Queensberry Pl.)
Cineworld Cinema
Chelsea, Fulham Rd.
. . . . .1E **87**
Chelsea, King's Rd.
. . . . .2F **87**
Hammersmith 5D **71**
Haymarket 5B **14**
(off Haymarket)

Cineworld Cinema
Shaftesbury Av. . . .5B **14**
(off Shaftesbury Av.)
Staples Corner 3D **29**
Wandsworth 3D **101**
West India Quay
. . . . .1C **80**
Cinnabar Wharf Central
E1 . . . . .2C **78**
(off Wapping High St.)
Cinnabar Wharf E. E1 . . .2C **78**
(off Wapping High St.)
Cinnabar Wharf W.
E1 . . . . .2C **78**
(off Wapping High St.)
Cinnamon Cl. SE15 . . . .3B **92**
Cinnamon Row
SW11 . . . . .1E **101**
Cinnamon St. E1 . . . . . .2D **79**
Cinnamon Wharf SE1 . . .3B **78**
(off Shad Thames)
Circa Apartments
NW1 . . . . .4C **46**
Circle, The NW2 . . . . . .5A **30**
SE1 . . . . .3F **27**
(off Queen Elizabeth St.)
Circus Lodge NW8 . . . . .2F **59**
(off Circus Rd.)
Circus M. W1 . . . . .4B **60**
(off Enford St.)
Circus Pl.
EC2 . . . . . . .1C **18** (4F **63**)
Circus Rd. NW8 . . . . . .2F **59**
Circus St. SE10 . . . . . . .3E **95**
Cirencester St. W2 . . . . .4D **59**
Cissbury Ho. SE26 . . . .3C **120**
Cissbury Rd. N15 . . . . . .1F **35**
Citadel Pl. SE11 . . . . . .1B **90**
Citius Apartments E3 . . .1C **66**
(off Tredegar La.)
Citizen Ho. N7 . . . . . . .1C **48**
Citizen Rd. N7 . . . . . . .1C **48**
Citrus Ho. SE8 . . . . . . .1B **94**
(off Alverton St.)
City Apartments E1 . . . .5C **64**
(off White Church La.)
City Bus. Cen. SE16 . . . .4E **79**
City Cross Bus. Pk.
SE10 . . . . .5A **82**
(off Cable St.)
City E. Bldg. E1 . . . . . .5D **82**
(off Cable St.)
City Forum
EC1 . . . . . . .1F **9** (2E **63**)
City Gdn. Row
N1 . . . . .1E **9** (1D **63**)
City Hall 2E **27** (2A **78**)
City Harbour E14 . . . . . .4D **81**
(off Selsdon Way)
City Hgts. E8 . . . . .5B **50**
(off Kingsland Rd.)
City Lights Ct. SE11 . . . .1C **90**
(off Bowden St.)
City Mill River Path
E15 . . . . .5E **53**
CITY OF LONDON
. . . . .3B **18** (5F **63**)
City of London Almshouses
SW9 . . . . .2B **104**
City of London Crematorium
E12 . . . . .5F **41**

City of London Point
N7 . . . . .3F **47**
(off York Way)
City of Westminster College
Paddington Green Campus
NW8 . . . . .4F **59**
(off Paddington Grn.)
City Pav. EC1 . . . . .5D **9**
(off Britton St.)
City Pl. Ho. EC2 . . . . . .1A **18**
(off Basinghall St.)
Citypoint EC2 . . . . .5B **10**
City Rd.
EC1 . . . . . . .1D **9** (1D **63**)
City Tower EC2 . . . . . . .1B **18**
(off Basinghall St.)
City University London
Goswell Pl. 2D **63**
Northampton Square
Campus 2D **9** (2D **63**)
Whitechapel 4D **65**
City University Saddlers
Sports Centre, The
. . . . .3E **9** (3D **63**)
Cityview SE7 . . . . .2E **97**
City Vw. Apartments
N1 . . . . .4E **49**
(off Essex Rd.)
City Vw. Ct. SE22 . . . . .5C **106**
City Wlk.
SE1 . . . . . . .4D **27** (3A **78**)
City Wlk. Apartments
EC1 . . . . .2F **9**
(off Seward St.)
Clabon M. SW1 . . . . . . .4B **74**
Clack St. SE16 . . . . .3E **79**
Clacton Rd. E6 . . . . .2F **69**
E17 . . . . .1A **38**
Claire Ct. NW2 . . . . . . .3A **44**
Claire Pl. E14 . . . . .4C **80**
Clairview Rd.
SW16 . . . . .5D **117**
Clairville Point
SE23 . . . . .3F **121**
(off Dacres Rd.)
Clancarty Rd. SW6 . . . . .5C **86**
Clandon Ho. SE1 . . . . . .4E **25**
(off Webber St.)
Clandon St. SE8 . . . . . . .5C **94**
Clanricarde Gdns.
W2 . . . . .1C **72**
CLAPHAM 2E **103**
CLAPHAM COMMON
. . . . .2F **103**
Clapham Comn. Nth. Side
SW4 . . . . .2B **102**
Clapham Comn. Sth. Side
SW4 . . . . .4D **103**
Clapham Comn. W. Side
SW4 . . . . .2B **102**
(not continuous)
Clapham Cres. SW4 . . . .2F **103**
Clapham High St.
SW4 . . . . .2F **103**
CLAPHAM JUNCTION
. . . . .1A **102**
Clapham Junc. App.
SW11 . . . . .1A **102**
Clapham Leisure Cen.
. . . . .1F **103**

Clapham Mnr. Ct.
 SW4 . . . . .1E 103
Clapham Mnr. St.
 SW4 . . . . .1E 103
CLAPHAM PARK 5F 103
Clapham Pk. Est.
 SW4 . . . . .4F 103
Clapham Pk. Rd.
 SW4 . . . . .2E 103
Clapham Pk. Ter.
 SW2 . . . . .3A 104
 (off Lyham Rd.)
Clapham Picturehouse
 . . . . .2E 103
Clapham Rd. SW9 . . .1A 104
Clapham Rd. Est.
 SW4 . . . . .1A 104
Clapton Comn. E5 . . . .2B 36
 (not continuous)
CLAPTON PARK 1F 51
Clapton Pk. Est.
 E5 . . . . .1F 51
Clapton Pas. E5 . . . . . .2E 51
Clapton Sq. E5 . . . . . . .2E 51
Clapton Ter. E5 . . . . . . .3C 36
Clapton Way E5 . . . . . .1C 50
Clara Grant Ho. E14 . . .4C 80
 (off Mellish St.)
Clara Nehab Ho.
 NW11 . . . . .1B 30
 (off Leeside Cres.)
Clare Ct. W11 . . . . . . .1A 72
 (off Clarendon Rd.)
 WC1 . . . . .2E 7
 (off Judd St.)
Claredale Ho. E2 . . . . .1D 65
 (off Claredale St.)
Claredale St. E2 . . . . . .1C 64
Clare Gdns. E7 . . . . . . .1C 64
 W11 . . . . .5A 58
Clare Ho. E3 . . . . .5B 52
 SE1 . . . . .1B 92
 (off Cooper's Rd.)
Clare La. N1 . . . . .4E 49
Clare Lawn Av.
 SW14 . . . . .3A 98
Clare Mkt.
 WC2 . . . . . .3A 16 (5B 62)
Clare M. SW6 . . . . . . .3D 87
Claremont Cl.
 N1 . . . . . . .1C 8 (1C 62)
 SW2 . . . . .1A 118
Claremont Ct. E2 . . . . .1D 65
 (off Cambridge Heath Rd.)
 E2 . . . . .1C 64
 (off Claredale St.)
 W2 . . . . .5D 59
 (off Queensway)
 W9 . . . . .1B 58
 (off Claremont Rd.)
Claremont Gro. W4 . . . .3A 84
Claremont Road 4F 29
Claremont Rd. E7 . . . . .2D 55
 E11 . . . . .5F 39
 N6 . . . . .2E 33
 NW2 . . . . .2F 29
 W9 . . . . .1A 58
Claremont Sq.
 N1 . . . . . . .1B 8 (1C 62)
Claremont St. SE10 . . . .2D 95

Claremont Vs. SE5 . . . .3F 91
 (off Southampton Way)
Claremont Way NW2 . . .3E 29
 (not continuous)
Claremont Way Ind. Est.
 NW2 . . . . .3E 29
Clarence Av. SW4 . . . . .5F 103
Clarence Ct. W6 . . . . . .5D 71
 (off Cambridge Gro.)
Clarence Cres. SW4 . . . .4F 103
Clarence Gdns.
 NW1 . . . . . . .2E 5 (2D 61)
Clarence Ga. Gdns.
 NW1 . . . . .4A 4
 (off Glentworth St.)
Clarence House 3A 22
Clarence Ho. SE17 . . . . .2F 91
 (off Merrow St.)
Clarence La. SW15 . . . . .4A 98
Clarence M. E5 . . . . . . .2D 51
 SE16 . . . . .2F 79
 SW12 . . . . .5D 103
Clarence Pl. E5 . . . . . . .2D 51
Clarence Rd. E5 . . . . . . .1D 51
 E12 . . . . .1E 55
 E16 . . . . .3A 68
 NW6 . . . . .4B 44
 SE8 . . . . .2D 95
 SE9 . . . . .2F 125
 SW19 . . . . .5D 115
Clarence Ter.
 NW1 . . . . . . .3A 4 (3B 60)
Clarence Wlk. SW4 . . . . .5A 90
Clarence Way NW1 . . . . .4D 47
Clarendon Cl. E9 . . . . . . .4E 51
 W2 . . . . .1A 74
Clarendon Ct. NW2 . . . . .4E 43
 W9 . . . . .3E 59
 (off Maida Va.)
Clarendon Cross
 W11 . . . . .1B 6 (2F 61)
Clarendon Dr. SW15 . . . . .2E 99
Clarendon Flats W1 . . . . .3C 12
 (off Balderton St.)
Clarendon Gdns. W9 . . . .3E 59
Clarendon Gro.
 NW1 . . . . . . .1B 6 (2F 61)
Clarendon Ho. NW1 . . . . .1A 6
 (off Werrington St.)
 W2 . . . . .1A 74
 (off Strathearn Pl.)
Clarendon Lodge
 W11 . . . . .1A 72
 (off Clarendon Rd.)
Clarendon M. W2 . . . . . .1A 74
Clarendon Pl. W2 . . . . . .1A 74
Clarendon Ri. SE13 . . . . .2E 109
Clarendon Rd. E11 . . . . .3F 39
 E17 . . . . .1D 39
 W11 . . . . .1A 72
Clarendon St. SW1 . . . . .1D 89
Clarendon Ter. W9 . . . . .3E 59
Clarendon Wlk. W11 . . . .5A 58
Clarens St. SE6 . . . . . . .2B 122
Clare Pl. SW15 . . . . . . .5B 98
Clare Point NW2 . . . . . . .3F 29
 (off Whitefield Av.)
Clare Rd. E11 . . . . .1F 39
 NW10 . . . . .4C 42
 SE14 . . . . .4B 94

Clare St. E2 . . . . .1D 65
Clareville Ct. SW7 . . . . .5E 73
 (off Clareville St.)
Clareville Gro. SW7 . . . .5E 73
Clareville Gro. M.
 SW7 . . . . .5E 73
Clareville St. SW7 . . . . .5E 73
Clarewood Ct. W1 . . . . .4B 60
 (off Seymour Pl.)
Clarewood Wlk.
 SW9 . . . . .2C 104
Clarges M.
 W1 . . . . . . .1D 21 (2D 75)
Clarges St.
 W1 . . . . . . .1E 21 (2D 75)
Claribel Rd. SW9 . . . . . .5D 91
Claridge Ct. SW6 . . . . . .5B 86
Clarion Ho. E3 . . . . . . .1A 66
 (off Roman Rd.)
 SW1 . . . . .1E 89
 (off Moreton Pl.)
 W1 . . . . .3B 14
 (off St Anne's Ct.)
Clarissa Ho. E14 . . . . . .5D 67
 (off Cordela St.)
Clarissa St. E8 . . . . . . .5B 50
Clarke Path N16 . . . . . .3C 36
Clarke's M.
 W1 . . . . .5C 4 (4C 60)
Clark Ho. SW10 . . . . . . .3E 87
 (off Coleridge Gdns.)
Clarkson Rd. E16 . . . . . .5B 68
Clarkson Row NW1 . . . . .1E 61
 (off Mornington Ter.)
Clarkson St. E2 . . . . . . .2D 65
Clark St. E1 . . . . .4D 65
 (not continuous)
Classic Mans. E9 . . . . . .4D 51
 (off Wells St.)
Claude Rd. E10 . . . . . . .4E 39
 E13 . . . . .5D 55
 SE15 . . . . .5D 93
Claude St. E14 . . . . . . .5C 80
Claudia Jones Way
 SW2 . . . . .4A 104
Claudia Pl. SW19 . . . . . .1A 114
Claughton Rd. E13 . . . . .1E 69
Clavell St. SE10 . . . . . . .2E 95
Claverdale Rd.
 SW2 . . . . .5B 104
Clavering Av. SW13 . . . . .2D 85
Clavering Ho. SE13 . . . . .2F 109
 (off Blessington Rd.)
Clavering Pl. SW12 . . . . .4C 102
Claverley Gro. E12 . . . . .3F 41
Claverton St. SW1 . . . . . .1E 89
Clave St. E1 . . . . .2E 79
Claxton Gro. W6 . . . . . . .1F 85
Claxton Path SE4 . . . . . .2F 107
 (off Coston Wlk.)
Claybank Gro. SE13 . . . .1D 109
Claybridge Rd.
 SE12 . . . . .4E 125
Claybrook Rd. W6 . . . . . .2F 85
Clay Ct. SE1 . . . . .5D 27
 (off Long La.)
Claydon SE17 . . . . .5C 77
 (off Deacon Way)
Clayhall Ct. E3 . . . . .1B 66
 (off St Stephen's Rd.)

Clayhill Cres. SE9 . . . . .4F 125
Claylands Pl. SW8 . . . . . .3C 90
Claylands Rd. SW8 . . . . . .2B 90
Claypole Ct. E17 . . . . .1C 38
   (off Yunus Khan Cl.)
Claypole Rd. E15 . . . . .1E 67
Clay St. W1 . . . . . .1A 12 (4B 60)
Clayton Cres. N1 . . . . .5A 48
Clayton Dr. SE8 . . . . .1A 94
Clayton Ho. E9 . . . . .4E 51
   (off Frampton Pk. Rd.)
SW13 . . . . .3E 85
   (off Trinity Church Rd.)
Clayton M. SE10 . . . . .4F 95
Clayton Rd. SE15 . . . . . . .4C 92
Clayton St. SE11 . . . . .2C 90
Clearbrook Way E1 . . . . . .5E 65
Clearwater Ter. W11 . . . . .3F 71
Clearwater Yd. NW1 . . . . .5D 47
   (off Inverness St.)
Clearwell Dr. W9 . . . . .3D 59
Cleaver Ho. NW3 . . . . .4A 46
   (off Adelaide Rd.)
Cleaver Sq. SE11 . . . . .1C 90
Cleaver St. SE11 . . . . .1C 90
Cleeve Hill SE23 . . . . .1D 121
Cleeve Ho. E2 . . . . .2E 11
   (off Calvert Av.)
Cleeve Way SW15 . . . . . . .5B 98
Cleeve Workshops
   E2 . . . . .2E 11
   (off Boundary Rd.)
Clegg Ho. SE3 . . . . .2D 111
SE16 . . . . .4E 79
   (off Moodkee St.)
Clegg St. E1 . . . . .2D 79
E13 . . . . .1C 68
Cleland Ho. E2 . . . . .1E 65
   (off Sewardstone Rd.)
Clematis Apartments
   E3 . . . . .2B 66
   (off Merchant St.)
Clematis St. W12 . . . . .1C 70
Clem Attlee Ct. SW6 . . . . . .2B 86
Clem Attlee Pde.
   SW6 . . . . .2B 86
   (off North End Rd.)
Clemence St. E14 . . . . . . .4B 66
Clement Av. SW4 . . . . .2F 103
Clement Ct. NW6 . . . . .4E 43
   W12 . . . . .5D 57
Clement Danes Ho.
   W12 . . . . .5D 57
Clement Ho. SE8 . . . . .5A 80
   W10 . . . . .4E 57
   (off Dalgarno Gdns.)
Clementina Ct. E3 . . . . . . .3A 66
   (off Copperfield Rd.)
Clementina Rd. E10 . . . . . .3B 38
Clement Rd. SW19 . . . . . .5A 114
Clement's Av. E16 . . . . . . .1C 82
Clement's Inn
   WC2 . . . . .3A 16 (5B 62)
Clement's Inn Pas.
   WC2 . . . . .3A 16
Clements La.
   EC4 . . . . .4C 18 (1F 77)
Clement's Rd. SE16 . . . . . .4E 78
Clemson Ho. E8 . . . . .5B 50
Clennam St.
   SE1 . . . . . .3A 26 (3E 77)

Cleopatra's Needle
   . . . . .1F 23 (2A 76)
Clephane Rd. N1 . . . . .3E 49
Clephane Rd. Nth.
   N1 . . . . .3E 49
Clephane Rd. Sth.
   N1 . . . . .3F 49
Clere Pl. EC2 . . .3C 10 (3F 63)
Clere St. EC2 . . .3C 10 (3F 63)
CLERKENWELL 3B 8 (3C 62)
Clerkenwell Cl.
   EC1 . . . . .3C 8 (3C 62)
   (not continuous)
Clerkenwell Grn.
   EC1 . . . . .4C 8 (3C 62)
Clerkenwell Rd.
   EC1 . . . . .4B 8 (3C 62)
Clerk's Pl.
   EC2 . . . . . .2D 19 (5A 64)
Clermont Rd. E9 . . . . .5E 51
Clevedon Ho. N16 . . . . . . .5B 36
Clevedon Ct. SW11 . . . . . .4A 88
   (off Bolingbroke Wlk.)
Clevedon Mans.
   NW5 . . . . .1C 46
Clevedon Pas. N16 . . . . . .4B 36
Cleve Ho. NW6 . . . . .4D 45
Cleveland Av. W4 . . . . .5B 70
Cleveland Gdns. N4 . . . . . .1E 35
   NW2 . . . . .4F 29
   SW13 . . . . .5B 84
   W2 . . . . .5E 59
Cleveland Gro. E1 . . . . .3E 65
Cleveland Mans.
   NW6 . . . . .4B 44
   (off Willesden La.)
   SW9 . . . . .3C 90
   (off Mowll St.)
   W9 . . . . .3C 58
Cleveland M.
   W1 . . . . .5F 5 (4E 61)
Cleveland Pl.
   SW1 . . . . . .1A 22 (2E 75)
Cleveland Rd. N1 . . . . .4F 49
   SW13 . . . . .5B 84
Cleveland Row
   SW1 . . . . . .2F 21 (2E 75)
Cleveland Sq. W2 . . . . .5E 59
Cleveland St.
   W1 . . . . .4E 5 (3D 61)
Cleveland Ter. W2 . . . . . . .5E 59
Cleveland Way E1 . . . . .3E 65
Cleveley Cl. SE7 . . . . .5F 83
Cleveleys Rd. E5 . . . . .5D 37
Cleverly Est. W12 . . . . .2C 70
Cleve Rd. NW6 . . . . .4C 44
Cleves Ho. E16 . . . . .2C 82
   (off Southey M.)
Cleves Rd. E6 . . . . .5F 55
Clewer Ct. E10 . . . . .3C 38
   (off Leyton Grange Est.)
Cley Ho. SE4 . . . . .2F 107
Clichy Est. E1 . . . . .4E 65
Clichy Ho. E1 . . . . .4E 65
   (off Stepney Way)
Clifden M. E5 . . . . .1F 51
Clifden Rd. E5 . . . . .2E 51
Cliffe Ho. SE10 . . . . .1B 96
   (off Blackwall La.)

Clifford Ct. W2 . . . . .4D 59
   (off Westbourne Pk. Vs.)
Clifford Dr. SW9 . . . . .2D 105
Clifford Gdns. NW10 . . . . .1E 57
   SW6 . . . . .3F 85
Clifford Haigh Ho.
   SW6 . . . . .3F 85
Clifford Ho.
   BR3: Beck. 5D 123
   (off Calverley Cl.)
   W14 . . . . .5B 72
   (off Edith Vs.)
Clifford Rd. E16 . . . . .3B 68
   N1 . . . . .5A 50
Clifford's Inn Pas.
   EC4 . . . . .3B 16 (5C 62)
Clifford St.
   W1 . . . . .5F 13 (1E 75)
Clifford Way NW10 . . . . . .1B 42
Cliff Rd. NW1 . . . . .3F 47
Cliffsend Ho. SW9 . . . . . . .4C 90
   (off Cowley Rd.)
Cliff Ter. SE8 . . . . .5C 94
Cliffview Rd. SE13 . . . . . . .1C 108
Cliff Vs. NW1 . . . . .3F 47
Cliff Wlk. E16 . . . . .4B 68
Clifton Av. W12 . . . . .2B 70
Clifton Ct. N4 . . . . .4C 34
   NW8 . . . . .3F 59
   (off Maida Va.)
   SE15 . . . . .3D 93
Clifton Cres. SE15 . . . . . . .3D 93
Clifton Est. SE15 . . . . .4D 93
Clifton Gdns. N15 . . . . . . .1B 36
   NW11 . . . . .1B 30
   W4 . . . . .5A 70
   (not continuous)
   W9 . . . . .3E 59
Clifton Ga. SW10 . . . . .2E 87
Clifton Gro. E8 . . . . .3C 50
Clifton Hill NW8 . . . . .1D 59
Clifton Hill Studios
   NW8 . . . . .1E 59
Clifton Ho. E2 . . . . .3F 11
   (off Club Row)
   E11 . . . . .4A 40
Clifton Pl. SE16 . . . . .3E 79
   SW10 . . . . .2E 87
   (off Hollywood Rd.)
   W2 . . . . .5F 59
Clifton Ri. SE14 . . . . .3A 94
   (not continuous)
Clifton Rd. E7 . . . . .3F 55
   E16 . . . . .4A 68
   N1 . . . . .3E 49
   N8 . . . . .1F 33
   NW10 . . . . .1C 56
   SW19 . . . . .5F 113
   W9 . . . . .3E 59
Clifton St.
   EC2 . . . . .4D 11 (3A 64)
Clifton Ter. N4 . . . . .4C 34
Clifton Vs. W9 . . . . .4E 59
Cliftonville Ct. SE12 . . . . . .1C 124
Clifton Wlk. W6 . . . . .5D 71
   (off King St.)
Clifton Way SE15 . . . . .3D 93
Climsland Ho.
   SE1 . . . . . .1C 24 (2C 76)
Clinger Ct. N1 . . . . .5A 50
   (off Hobbs Pl. Est.)

Clink Prison Mus. 1B 26
Clink St. SE1 . . . .1A 26 (2F 77)
Clink Wharf SE1 . . . . . . .1B 26
　　　　(off Clink St.)
Clinton Rd. E3 . . . . .2A 66
　E7 . . . . .1C 54
Clinton Ter. SE8 . . . . . . .2C 94
　　　　(off Watergate St.)
Clipper Apartments
　SE10 . . . . .2E 95
　　　　(off Welland St.)
Clipper Cl. SE16 . . . . . . .3F 79
Clipper Ho. E14 . . . . . . .1E 95
　　　　(off Manchester Rd.)
Clipper Way SE13 . . . . .2E 109
Clipstone M.
　W1 . . . . . .5F 5 (4E 61)
Clipstone St.
　W1 . . . . . .5E 5 (4D 61)
Clissold Ct. N4 . . . . .4E 35
Clissold Cres. N16 . . . . .5F 35
Clissold Leisure Cen.
　　　　　　. . . . . .5F 35
Clissold Rd. N16 . . . . . . .5F 35
Clitheroe Rd. SW9 . . . . .5A 90
Clitherhouse Cres.
　NW2 . . . . .3E 29
Clitterhouse Rd.
　NW2 . . . . .3E 29
Clive Ct. W9 . . . . .3E 59
Cliveden Ho. E16 . . . . . .2C 82
　　　　(off Fitzwilliam Rd.)
　SW1 . . . . .5C 74
　　　　(off Cliveden Pl.)
Cliveden Pl. SW1 . . . . . .5C 74
Clive Ho. SE10 . . . . .2E 95
　　　　(off Haddo St.)
Clive Lloyd Ho. N15 . . . .1E 35
　　　　(off Woodlands Pk. Rd.)
Clive Lodge NW4 . . . . . .1F 29
Clive Pas. SE21 . . . . . . .3F 119
Clive Rd. SE21 . . . . .3F 119
　SW19 . . . . .5A 116
Cloak La.
　EC4 . . . .4A 18 (1E 77)
Clochar Ct. NW10 . . . . . .5B 42
Clock Ho. E3 . . . . .2E 67
Clockhouse, The
　SW19 . . . . .3E 113
Clockhouse Cl.
　SW19 . . . . .2E 113
Clock Ho. Pde. E11 . . . . .1D 41
Clockhouse Pl.
　SW15 . . . . .4A 100
Clock Museum, The . . .2A 18
Clock Pl. SE1 . . . . .5D 77
　　　　(off Newington Butts)
Clock Twr. M. N1 . . . . . . .5E 49
Clock Twr. Pl. N7 . . . . . . .3A 48
　　　　(off Market Est.)
Clock Vw. Cres. N7 . . . . .3A 48
Cloister Rd. NW2 . . . . . . .5B 30
Cloisters, The 5D 23
Cloisters, The E1 . . . . . . .4F 11
　SW9 . . . . .4C 90
Cloisters Bus. Cen.
　SW8 . . . . .3D 89
　　　　(off Battersea Pk. Rd.)
Clonbrock Rd. N16 . . . . .1A 50
Cloncurry St. SW6 . . . . .5F 85

Clonmel Rd. SW6 . . . . . .3B 86
Clonmore St. SW18 . . . .1B 114
Clorane Gdns. NW3 . . . . .5C 30
Close, The SE3 . . . . .5F 95
Cloth Ct. EC1 . . . . .1E 17
Cloth Fair
　EC1 . . . . .1E 17 (4D 63)
Clothier St.
　E1 . . . . . . .2E 19 (5A 64)
Cloth St. EC1 . . . .5F 9 (4E 63)
Cloudesdale Rd.
　SW17 . . . . .2D 117
Cloudesley Mans. N1 . . . .5C 48
　　　　(off Cloudesley Rd.)
Cloudesley Pl. N1 . . . . . .5C 48
Cloudesley Rd. N1 . . . . . .5C 48
　　　　(not continuous)
Cloudesley Sq. N1 . . . . . .5C 48
Cloudesley St. N1 . . . . . .5C 48
Clova Rd. E7 . . . . .3B 54
Clove Cres. E14 . . . . . . .1E 81
Clove Hitch Quay
　SW11 . . . . .1E 101
Clovelly Cl. NW2 . . . . . . .2E 43
Clovelly Ho. W2 . . . . .5E 59
　　　　(off Hallfield Est.)
Clovelly Way E1 . . . . . . .5E 65
Clover Cl. E11 . . . . .4F 39
Clover M. SW3 . . . . .2B 88
Clove St. E13 . . . . .3C 68
Clowders Rd. SE6 . . . . . .3B 122
Cloysters Grn. E1 . . . . . .2C 78
Club Row E1 . . .3F 11 (3B 64)
　E2 . . . . .3F 11 (3B 64)
Clunbury St. N1 . . . . .1F 63
Clunie Ho. SW1 . . . . .5A 20
　　　　(off Hans Pl.)
Cluny Est.
　SE1 . . . . . .5D 27 (4A 78)
Cluny M. SW5 . . . . .5C 72
Cluny Pl. SE1 . . .5D 27 (4A 78)
Cluse Ct. N1 . . . . .1E 63
　　　　(off St Peters St.,
　　　　　not continuous)
Clutton St. E14 . . . . .4D 67
Clyde Ct. NW1 . . . . .1F 61
　　　　(off Hampden Cl.)
Clyde Flats SW6 . . . . . . .3B 86
　　　　(off Rhylston Rd.)
Clyde Pl. E10 . . . . .2D 39
Clydesdale Ho. W11 . . . . .5B 58
　　　　(off Clydesdale Rd.)
Clydesdale Rd. W11 . . . . .5B 58
Clyde St. SE8 . . . . .2B 94
Clyde Ter. SE23 . . . . . . .2E 121
Clyde Va. SE23 . . . . .2E 121
Clyde Wharf E16 . . . . . . .2C 82
Clynes Ho. E2 . . . . .2F 65
　　　　(off Knottisford St.)
Clyston St. SW8 . . . . .5E 89
Coach & Horses Yd.
　W1 . . . . .4E 13 (1E 75)
Coach Ho. La. N5 . . . . . . .1D 49
　SW19 . . . . .4F 113
Coach Ho. M. SE1 . . . . . .5D 27
　　　　(off Long La.)
　SE23 . . . . .4F 107
Coach Ho. Yd. NW3 . . . . .1E 45
　SW18 . . . . .2D 101

Coachmaker M.
　SW4 . . . . .1A 104
　　　　(off Bedford Rd.)
Coach Yd. M. N19 . . . . . .3A 34
Coaldale Wlk. SE21 . . . . .5E 105
Coalecroft Rd. SW15 . . . . .2E 99
Coalport Ho. SE11 . . . . . .5C 76
　　　　(off Walnut Tree Wlk.)
Coalstore Ct. E1 . . . . .4A 66
Coatbridge Ho. N1 . . . . . .4B 48
　　　　(off Carnoustie Dr.)
Coates Av. SW18 . . . . . . .4A 102
Coate St. E2 . . . . .1C 64
Cobalt Building, The
　EC2 . . . . .5F 9
　　　　(off Bridgewater Sq.)
Cobalt Sq. SW8 . . . . .2B 90
　　　　(off Sth. Lambeth Rd.)
Cobbetts Av. IG4: Ilf 1F 41
Cobbett St. SW8 . . . . .3B 90
Cobble La. N1 . . . . .4D 49
Cobble M. N5 . . . . .5E 35
　N6 . . . . .3C 32
　　　　(off Highgate West Hill)
Cobbold Ct. SW1 . . . . . . .5F 75
　　　　(off Elverton St.)
Cobbold Ind. Est.
　NW10 . . . . .3B 42
Cobbold M. W12 . . . . .3B 70
Cobbold Rd. E11 . . . . .5B 40
　NW10 . . . . .3B 42
　W12 . . . . .3A 70
Cobb's Ct. EC4 . . . . .3E 17
Cobb's Hall SW6 . . . . . . .2F 85
　　　　(off Fulham Pal. Rd.)
Cobbsthorpe Vs.
　SE26 . . . . .4F 121
Cobb St. E1 . . . .1F 19 (4B 64)
Cobden Bldgs. WC1 . . . . .1F 7
　　　　(off King's Cross Rd.)
Cobden Ho. E2 . . . . .2C 64
　　　　(off Nelson Gdns.)
　NW1 . . . . .1E 61
　　　　(off Arlington Rd.)
Cobden M. SE26 . . . . . . .5D 121
Cobden Rd. E11 . . . . .5A 40
Cobham Cl. SW11 . . . . . .4A 102
Cobham M. NW1 . . . . .4F 47
Cobland Rd. SE12 . . . . . .4E 125
Coborn M. E3 . . . . .2B 66
　　　　(off Coborn St.)
Coborn Rd. E3 . . . . .1B 66
Coborn St. E3 . . . . .2B 66
Cobourg Rd. SE5 . . . . . . .2B 92
Cobourg St.
　NW1 . . . . . . .2A 6 (2E 61)
Coburg Cl. SW1 . . . . .5E 75
Coburg Cres. SW2 . . . . .1B 118
Coburg Dwellings E1 . . . .1E 65
　　　　(off Hardinge St.)
Cochrane Cl. NW8 . . . . . .1F 59
　　　　(off Cochrane St.)
Cochrane Ct. E10 . . . . . . .3C 38
　　　　(off Leyton Grange Est.)
Cochrane Ho. E14 . . . . . .3C 80
　　　　(off Admirals Way)
Cochrane M. NW8 . . . . . .1F 59
Cochrane St. NW8 . . . . . .1F 59
Cochrane Theatre 1E 15
　　　　(off Southampton Row)

Cockburn Ho. *SW1* 1F **89**
  (off Aylesford St.)
Cockerell Rd. E17 . . . . . . .2A **38**
Cock Hill E1 . . . .1E **19** (4A **64**)
Cock La.
  EC1 . . . . . . .1D **17** (4D **63**)
Cockpit Steps SW1 . . . . . .4B **22**
Cockpit Theatre *3A 60*
  (off Gateforth St.)
Cockpit Yd.
  WC1 . . . . . . .5A **8** (4B **62**)
Cockspur Ct.
  SW1 . . . . . .1C **22** (2F **75**)
Cockspur St.
  SW1 . . . . . .1C **22** (2F **75**)
Coda Centre, The
  SW6 . . . . .3A **86**
Code St. E1 . . . . .3B **64**
Codicote Ho. *SE8* *5F 79*
  (off Chilton Gro.)
Codicote Ter. N4 . . . . .4E **35**
Codling Cl. E1 . . . . .2C **78**
Codrington Ct. E1 . . . . . . .3D **65**
  SE16 . . . . .1A **80**
Codrington Hill
  SE23 . . . . .5A **108**
Codrington M. W11 . . . . . .5A **58**
Cody Rd. E16 . . . . .3F **67**
Coffey St. SE8 . . . . .3C **94**
Coin St. SE1 . . .1B **24** (2C **76**)
  (not continuous)
Coity Rd. NW5 . . . . .3C **46**
Cokers La. SE21 . . . . .1F **119**
Coke St. E1 . . . . .5C **64**
Colas M. NW6 . . . . .5C **44**
Colbeck M. SW7 . . . . .5D **73**
Colberg Pl. N16 . . . . .2B **36**
Colbert *SE5* *4A 92*
  (off Sceaux Gdns.)
Colborne Ho. *E14* *1C 80*
  (off E. India Dock Rd.)
Colby M. SE19 . . . . .5A **120**
Colby Rd. SE19 . . . . .5A **120**
Colchester Rd. E10 . . . . . .2E **39**
  E17 . . . . .1C **38**
Coldbath Sq.
  EC1 . . . . . . .3B **8** (3C **62**)
Coldbath St. SE13 . . . . . . .4D **95**
Cold Blow La. SE14 . . . . . .3F **93**
  (not continuous)
Coldharbour E14 . . . . .3E **81**
Coldharbour Ind. Est.
  SE5 . . . . .5E **91**
Coldharbour La.
  SE5 . . . . .5E **91**
  SW9 . . . . .2C **104**
Coldharbour Pl. SE5 . . . . .5E **91**
Coldstream Gdns.
  SW18 . . . . .4B **100**
Colebeck M. N1 . . . . .3D **49**
Colebert Av. E1 . . . . .3E **65**
Colebert Ho. *E1* *3E 65*
  (off Colebert Av.)
Colebrook Cl. SW15 . . . . . .5F **99**
Colebrook Ct. *SW3* *5A 74*
  (off Makins St.)
Colebrooke Dr. E11 . . . . . .2E **41**
Colebrooke Pl. N1 . . . . . . .5D **49**

Colebrooke Row N1 . . . . . .1D **63**
Colebrook Ho. E14 . . . . . .*5D 67*
  (off Ellesmere St.)
Coleby Path SE5 . . . . .3F **92**
Colechurch Ho. *SE1* *1C 92*
  (off Avondale Sq.)
Coleford Rd. SW18 . . . . . .3E **101**
Colegrave Rd. E15 . . . . . . .2F **53**
Colegrove Rd. SE15 . . . . . .2B **92**
Coleherne Ct. SW5 . . . . . .1D **87**
Coleherne Mans.
  SW5 . . . .*1D 87*
  (off Old Brompton Rd.)
Coleherne M. SW10 . . . . . .1D **87**
Coleherne Rd. SW10 . . . . .1D **87**
Colehill Gdns. SW6 . . . . . .5A **86**
Colehill La. SW6 . . . . .4A **86**
Cole Ho. *SE1* *4C 24*
  (off Baylis Rd.)
Coleman Cl. SE18 . . . . . . .5C **100**
Coleman Flds. N1 . . . . .5E **49**
Coleman Mans. N8 . . . . . . .2A **34**
Coleman Rd. SE5 . . . . .3A **92**
Coleman St.
  EC2 . . . . . . .2B **18** (5F **63**)
Coleman St. Bldgs.
  EC2 . . . . .2B **18**
Colenso Rd. E5 . . . . .1E **51**
Coleraine Rd. SE3 . . . . . . .2B **96**
Coleridge Av. E12 . . . . .3F **55**
Coleridge Cl. SW8 . . . . . . .5D **89**
Coleridge Ct. *N1* *5E 49*
  (off Popham Rd.)
  SW1 . . . .*5F 75*
  (off Regency St.)
  W14 . . . .*4F 71*
  (off Blythe Rd.)
Coleridge Gdns. NW6 . . . . .4E **45**
  SW10 . . . . .3D **87**
Coleridge Ho. *SE17* *1E 91*
  (off Browning St.)
  SW1 . . . .*1E 89*
  (off Churchill Gdns.)
Coleridge La. N8 . . . . .1A **34**
Coleridge Rd. N4 . . . . .4C **34**
  N8 . . . . .1F **33**
Coleridge Sq. *SW10* *3E 87*
  (off Coleridge Gdns.)
Coles Grn. Ct. NW2 . . . . . .4C **28**
Coles Grn. Rd. NW2 . . . . . .4C **28**
Coleshill Flats *SW1* *5C 74*
  (off Pimlico Rd.)
Colestown St. SW11 . . . . . .5A **88**
Cole St. SE1 . . . . .4A **26** (3E **77**)
Colet Ct. *W6* *5F 71*
  (off Hammersmith Rd.)
Colet Flats *E1* *5A 66*
  (off Troon St.)
Colet Gdns. W14 . . . . .5F **71**
Colet Ho. *SE17* *1D 91*
  (off Doddington Gro.)
Colette Ct. *SE16* *3F 79*
  (off Eleanor Cl.)
Coley St. WC1 . . . .4A **8** (3B **62**)
Colfe & Hatcliffe Glebe
  SE13 . . . .*3D 109*
  (off Lewisham High St.)
Colfe Rd. SE23 . . . . .1A **122**
Colfes Leisure Cen. 4C **110**
Colin Ct. SE6 . . . . .5B **108**

Colin Dr. NW9 . . . . .1B **28**
Colinette Rd. SW15 . . . . . .2E **99**
Colin Rd. NW10 . . . . .3C **42**
Colinsdale *N1* *5D 49*
  (off Camden Wlk.)
Colin Winter Ho. *E1* *3E 65*
  (off Nicholas Rd.)
Coliseum Theatre *5D 15*
  (off St Martin's La.)
Coliston Pas.
  SW18 . . . . .5C **100**
  (off Coliston Rd.)
Coliston Rd. SW18 . . . . . . .5C **100**
Collamore Av.
  SW18 . . . . .1A **116**
Collard Pl. NW1 . . . . .4D **47**
Collards Almshouses
  E17 . . . .*1E 39*
  (off Maynard Rd.)
Collection Pl. NW8 . . . . . . .5D **45**
  (off Bolton Pl.)
College App. SE10 . . . . . . .2E **95**
College Cl. E9 . . . . .2E **51**
College Ct. *NW3* *3F 45*
  (off College Cres.)
  SW3 . . . .*1B 88*
  (off West Rd.)
  W6 . . . .*1E 85*
  (off Queen Caroline St.)
College Cres. NW3 . . . . . . .3E **45**
College Cross N1 . . . . .4C **48**
College East
  E1 . . . . .1F **19** (4B **64**)
College Gdns. IG4: Ilf . . .1F **41**
  SE21 . . . . .1A **120**
  SW17 . . . . .2A **116**
  (not continuous)
College Gro. NW1 . . . . .5E **47**
College Hill
  EC4 . . . . . . .4A **18** (1E **77**)
College Ho. SW15 . . . . .3F **99**
College La. NW5 . . . . .1D **47**
College Mans. *NW6* *5A 44*
  (off Salusbury Rd.)
College M. N1 . . . .*4C 48*
  *(off College Cross,
  not continuous)*
  SW1 . . . . .5D **23**
  SW18 . . . . .3D **101**
College of Arms 4F **17**
College Pde. NW6 . . . .*5A 44*
  (off Salusbury Rd.)
COLLEGE PARK 2D **57**
College Pk. Cl.
  SE13 . . . . .2F **109**
College Pl. NW1 . . . . .5E **47**
  SW10 . . . . .3E **87**
College Point E15 . . . . .3B **54**
College Rd. E17 . . . . .1E **39**
  NW10 . . . . .1E **57**
  SE19 . . . . .5A **106**
  SE21 . . . . .5A **106**
College Row E9 . . . . .2F **51**
College St.
  EC4 . . . . . . .4A **18** (1E **77**)
College Ter. E3 . . . . .2B **66**
College Vw. SE9 . . . . .1F **125**
College Yd. NW5 . . . . .1D **47**
  NW6 . . . . .5A **44**
Collent St. E9 . . . . .3E **51**

Collerston Ho. *SE10* 1B **96**
(off Armitage Rd.)
Colless Rd. N15 . . . . .1B **36**
Collett Rd. SE16 . . . . .4C **78**
Collier St. N1 . . . . .1B **62**
Collingbourne Rd.
W12 . . . . .2D **71**
Collingham Gdns.
SW5 . . . . .5D **73**
Collingham Pl. SW5 . . .5D **73**
Collingham Rd. SW5 . . .5D **73**
Collington St. SE10 . . .1F **95**
Collingtree Rd. SE26 . . .4E **121**
Collingwood Ho. E1 . . . .3D **65**
(off Darling Row)
SE16 . . . . .3D **79**
(off Cherry Gdn. St.)
SW1 . . . . .1F **89**
(off Dolphin Sq.)
W1 . . . . .5F **5**
(off Clipstone St.)
Collingwood Rd. E17 . . .1C **38**
Collingwood St. E1 . . . .3D **65**
Collins Ct. E8 . . . . .3C **50**
Collins Ho. E14 . . . . .1E **81**
(off Newby Pl.)
SE10 . . . . .1B **96**
(off Armitage Rd.)
Collinson Ct. SE1 . . . . . .4F **25**
(off Gt. Suffolk St.)
Collinson Ho. SE15 . . . .3C **92**
(off Peckham Pk. Rd.)
Collinson St.
SE1 . . . . .4F **25** (3E **77**)
Collinson Wlk.
SE1 . . . . .4F **25** (3E **77**)
Collins Rd. N5 . . . . .1E **49**
Collins Sq. SE3 . . . . .5B **96**
Collins St. SE3 . . . . .5A **96**
(not continuous)
Collin's Yd. N1 . . . . .5D **49**
Collison Pl. N16 . . . . .3A **36**
Coll's Rd. SE15 . . . . .4E **93**
Collyer Pl. SE15 . . . . . . .4C **92**
Colman Rd. E16 . . . . . . .5E **69**
Colmans Wharf E14 . . . .4D **67**
(off Morris Rd.)
Colmar Cl. E1 . . . . .3F **65**
Colmore M. SE15 . . . . . .4D **93**
Colnbrook St.
SE1 . . . . .5D **25** (4D **77**)
(off Penfold St.)
Colne Ho. NW8 . . . . .3F **59**
(off Penfold St.)
Colne Rd. E5 . . . . .1A **52**
Colne St. E13 . . . . .2C **68**
Colnmore Ct. E2 . . . . . . .2F **65**
(off Meath Cres.)
Cologne Rd. SW11 . . . . .2F **101**
Colombo St.
SE1 . . . . .2D **25** (2D **77**)
Colombo Street
Sports & Community Cen.
. . . . .2D **25**
Colomb St. SE10 . . . . . .1A **96**
Colonial Ct. N7 . . . . .5B **34**
Colonnade
WC1 . . . . .4E **7** (3A **62**)
Colonnade, The SE8 . . .5B **80**
Colonnades, The W2 . . .5D **59**
Colonnade Wlk. SW1 . . .5D **75**

Colony Mans. SW5 . . . .1D **87**
(off Earl's Ct.)
Colony M. N1 . . . . .2F **49**
(off Mildmay Gro. Nth.)
Colorado Bldg. SE10 . . .4D **95**
(off Deal's Gateway)
Colosseum Apartments
E2 . . . . .1F **65**
(off Palmers Rd.)
Colosseum Ter. NW1 . . .2E **5**
Colour Ct. SW1 . . . . .2A **22**
Colour Ho. SE1 . . . . .4E **27**
(off Bell Yd M.)
Colson Way SW16 . . . . .4E **117**
Colstead Ho. E1 . . . . .5D **65**
(off Watney Mkt.)
Colston Rd. E7 . . . . .3F **55**
Coltash Ct. EC1 . . . . .3A **10**
(off Whitecross St.)
Colthurst Cres. N4 . . . . .4D **35**
Coltman Ho. SE10 . . . . .2E **95**
(off Welland St.)
Coltman St. E14 . . . . .4A **66**
Columbas Dr. NW3 . . . . .3F **31**
Columbia Ho. E3 . . . . . . .3B **66**
(off Hamlets Way)
Columbia Point SE16 . . .4E **79**
(off Canada Est.)
Columbia Rd.
E2 . . . . .1F **11** (2B **64**)
E13 . . . . .1B **68**
Columbia Road Flower Market
. . . . .1F **11**
(off Columbia Rd.)
Columbine Av. E6 . . . . . .4F **69**
Columbine Way SE13 . . .5E **95**
Columbus Ct. SE16 . . . . .2E **79**
(off Rotherhithe St.)
Columbus Courtyard
E14 . . . . .2C **80**
Colva Wlk. N19 . . . . .4D **33**
Colverson Ho. E1 . . . . . . .4E **65**
(off Lindley St.)
Colvestone Cres. E8 . . . .2B **50**
Colview Ct. SE9 . . . . . . .1F **125**
Colville Est. N1 . . . . .5A **50**
Colville Est. W. E2 . . . . . .2B **64**
(off Turin St.)
Colville Gdns. W11 . . . . .5B **58**
(not continuous)
Colville Ho. E2 . . . . .1E **65**
(off Waterloo Gdns.)
Colville Ho's. W11 . . . . .5B **58**
Colville M. W11 . . . . .5B **58**
Colville Pl.
W1 . . . . .1A **14** (4E **61**)
Colville Rd. E11 . . . . .5E **39**
W11 . . . . .5B **58**
Colville Sq. W11 . . . . . . .5B **58**
Colville Ter. W11 . . . . . . .5B **58**
Colvin Cl. SE26 . . . . .5E **121**
Colvin Ho. W10 . . . . .5F **57**
(off Kingsdown Cl.)
Colvin Rd. E6 . . . . .4F **55**
Colwall Rd. SE22 . . . . . .3B **106**
Colwick Cl. N6 . . . . .2F **33**
Colwith Rd. W6 . . . . .2E **85**
Colworth Gro. SE17 . . . .5E **77**
Colworth Rd. E11 . . . . . .1A **40**
Colwyn Cl. SW16 . . . . . . .5E **117**

Colwyn Grn. NW9 . . . . . .1A **28**
(off Snowdon Dr.)
Colwyn Ho.
SE1 . . . . .5B **24** (4C **76**)
Colwyn Rd. NW2 . . . . . . .5D **29**
Colyton La. SW16 . . . . . .5C **118**
Colyton Rd. SE22 . . . . . .3D **107**
Combe, The
NW1 . . . . .2E **5** (2D **61**)
Combe Av. SE3 . . . . .3B **96**
Combedale Rd. SE10 . . .1C **96**
Combe Ho. W2 . . . . .4C **58**
(off Gt. Western Rd.)
Combemartin Rd.
SW18 . . . . .5A **100**
Combe M. SE3 . . . . .3B **96**
Comber Cl. NW2 . . . . . . .5D **29**
Comber Gro. SE5 . . . . . .3E **91**
Comber Ho. SE5 . . . . . . .3E **91**
Combermere Rd.
SW9 . . . . .1B **104**
Comberton Rd. E5 . . . . .4D **37**
Comedy Store 5B **14**
(off Oxendon St.)
Comedy Theatre 5B **14**
(off Panton St.)
Comeragh M. W14 . . . . .1A **86**
Comeragh Rd. W14 . . . . .1A **86**
Comerell Pl. SE10 . . . . . .1B **96**
Comerford Rd. SE4 . . . . .2A **108**
Comet Cl. E12 . . . . .1F **55**
Comet Pl. SE8 . . . . .3C **94**
(not continuous)
Comet St. SE8 . . . . .3C **94**
Comfort St. SE15 . . . . . . .2A **92**
Commercial Dock Path
SE16 . . . . .4B **80**
(off Gulliver St.)
Commercial Rd. E1 . . . . .5C **64**
E14 . . . . .5F **65**
Commercial St.
E1 . . . . .4F **11** (3B **64**)
Commercial Way
SE10 . . . . .5B **82**
SE15 . . . . .3B **92**
Commerell St. SE10 . . . .1A **96**
Commodity Quay E1 . . . .1B **78**
Commodore Ct. SE8 . . . .4C **94**
(off Albyn Rd.)
Commodore Ho. E14 . . . .1E **81**
(off Poplar High St.)
SW18 . . . . .1E **101**
Commodore Sq.
SW10 . . . . .4E **87**
Commodore St. E1 . . . . .3A **66**
Common, The E15 . . . . . .3A **54**
Commonedale SW15 . . . .5E **85**
Commonfield La.
SW17 . . . . .5A **116**
Common Mile Cl.
SW4 . . . . .3F **103**
Common Rd. SW13 . . . . .1D **99**
Commonwealth Av.
W12 . . . . .1D **71**
(not continuous)
Commonwealth
Conference Cen.
. . . . .2A **22**
Community La. N7 . . . . . .2F **47**
Community Rd. E15 . . . . .2F **53**

Como Rd. SE23 . . . . . .2A **122**
Compass Ct. SE1 . . . . . .2F **27**
   (off Shad Thames)
Compass Ho. SW18 . . .2D **101**
Compass Point E14 . . . .18 **80**
   (off Grenade St.)
Compayne Gdns.
  NW6 . . . . .4D **45**
Compayne Mans.
  NW6 . . . . .3D **45**
   (off Fairhazel Gdns.)
Compter Pas. EC2 . . . .3A **18**
Compton Av. E6 . . . . . .1F **69**
  N1 . . . . .3D **49**
  N6 . . . . .2A **32**
Compton Cl. E3 . . . . . .4C **66**
  NW1 . . . . .2E **5**
  NW11 . . . . .5F **29**
  SE15 . . . . .3C **92**
Compton Ct. SE19 . . . .5A **120**
Compton Ho. SW11 . . . .4A **88**
Compton Pas.
  EC1 . . . . .3E **9** (3D **63**)
Compton Pl.
  WC1 . . . . . . .3D **7** (3A **62**)
Compton Rd. N1 . . . . . .3D **49**
  NW10 . . . . .2F **57**
  SW19 . . . . .5B **114**
Compton St.
  EC1 . . . . .3D **9** (3D **63**)
Compton Ter. N1 . . . . .3D **49**
Comus Ho. SE17 . . . . .5A **78**
   (off Comus Pl.)
Comus Pl. SE17 . . . . . .5A **78**
Comyn Rd. SW11 . . . . .2A **102**
Comyns Cl. E16 . . . . . .4B **68**
Conant Ho. SE11 . . . . .2D **91**
   (off St Agnes Pl.)
Conant M. E1 . . . . .1C **78**
Concanon Rd. SW2 . . . .2B **104**
Concert Hall App.
  SE1 . . . . . . .2A **24** (2B **76**)
Concorde Way SE16 . . .5F **79**
Concordia Wharf E14 . . .2E **81**
   (off Coldharbour)
Condell Rd. SW8 . . . . .4E **89**
Conder St. E14 . . . . . . .5A **66**
Condray Pl. SW11 . . . . .3A **88**
Conduit Av. SE10 . . . . .4F **95**
Conduit M. W2 . . . . . . .5F **59**
Conduit Pas. W2 . . . . . .5F **59**
   (off Conduit Pl.)
Conduit Pl. W2 . . . . . . .5F **59**
Conduit St.
  W1 . . . . .4E **13** (1D **75**)
Conewood St. N5 . . . . .5D **35**
Coney Acre SE21 . . . . .1E **119**
Coney Way SW8 . . . . . .2B **90**
Congers Ho. SE8 . . . . .3C **94**
Congreve Ho. N16 . . . . .2A **50**
Congreve St. SE17 . . . .5A **78**
Congreve Wlk. E16 . . . .4F **69**
   (off Fulmer Rd.)
Conifer Gdns. SW16 . . .3B **118**
Conifer Ho. SE4 . . . . . .2B **108**
   (off Brockley Rd.)
Coniger Rd. SW6 . . . . .5C **86**
Coningham Ct. SW10 . . .3E **87**

Coningham M. W12 . . . .2C **70**
Coningham Rd.
  W12 . . . . .3D **71**
Coningsby Rd. N4 . . . . .2D **35**
Conington Rd. SE13 . . .5D **95**
Conisborough Cres.
  SE6 . . . . .3E **123**
Conisbrough NW1 . . . . .5E **47**
   (off Bayham St.)
Coniston NW1 . . . . . . .1F **5**
   (off Harrington St.)
Coniston Cl. SW13 . . . .3B **84**
Coniston Ct. SE16 . . . .3F **79**
   (off Eleanor Cl.)
  W2 . . . . .5A **60**
   (off Kendal St.)
Conistone Way N7 . . . . .4A **48**
Coniston Gdns. NW9 . . .1A **28**
Coniston Ho. E3 . . . . . .3B **66**
   (off Southern Gro.)
  SE5 . . . . .3E **91**
   (off Wyndham Rd.)
Coniston Rd.
  BR1: Brom 5A **124**
Coniston Wlk. E9 . . . . .2E **51**
Conlan St. W10 . . . . . . .3A **58**
Conley Rd. NW10 . . . . .3A **42**
Conley St. SE10 . . . . . .1A **96**
Connaught Bri. E16 . . . .2F **83**
Connaught Bus. Cen.
  NW9 . . . . .1B **28**
Connaught Cl. E10 . . . .4A **38**
  W2 . . . . .5A **60**
Connaught Ct. W2 . . . . .5B **60**
   (off Connaught St.)
Connaught Hgts. E16 . . .2F **83**
   (off Agnes George Wlk.)
Connaught Ho.
  NW10 . . . . .2D **57**
   (off Trenmar Gdns.)
  W1 . . . . .5D **13**
   (off Davies St.)
Connaught Lodge N4 . . .2C **34**
   (off Connaught Rd.)
Connaught M. NW3 . . . .1A **46**
  SW6 . . . . .4A **86**
Connaught Pl. W2 . . . . .1B **74**
Connaught Rd. E11 . . . .3F **39**
  E16 . . . . .2F **83**
  E17 . . . . .1C **38**
  N4 . . . . .2C **34**
  NW10 . . . . .5A **42**
Connaught Rdbt. E16 . . .1F **83**
   (off Victoria Dock Rd.)
Connaught Sq. W2 . . . . .5B **60**
Connaught St. W2 . . . . .5A **60**
Connaught Works E3 . . .5A **52**
   (off Old Ford Rd.)
Connell Ct. SE14 . . . . . .2F **93**
   (off Myers La.)
Connor Cl. E11 . . . . . . .2A **40**
Connor Cl. SW11 . . . . .4D **89**
Connor St. E9 . . . . .5F **51**
Conrad Ho. E8 . . . . . . .3C **50**
  E14 . . . . .1A **80**
   (off Victory Pl.)
  E16 . . . . .2D **83**
   (off Wesley Av.)
  N16 . . . . .2A **50**
   (off Matthias Rd.)

Conrad Ho. SW8 . . . . . .3A **90**
   (off Wyvil Rd.)
Consort Ct. W8 . . . . . . .4D **73**
   (off Wright's La.)
Consort Ho. E14 . . . . . .1D **95**
   (off St Davids Sq.)
  SW6 . . . . .5E **87**
   (off Lensbury Av.)
  W2 . . . . .1D **73**
   (off Queensway)
Consort Lodge NW8 . . .5B **46**
   (off Prince Albert Rd.)
Consort Rd. SE15 . . . . .4D **93**
Cons St. SE1 . . .3C **24** (3C **76**)
Constable Av. E16 . . . .2D **83**
Constable Cl. NW11 . . .1D **31**
Constable Ct. SE16 . . . .1D **93**
   (off Stubbs Dr.)
Constable Ho. NW3 . . . .4B **46**
Constable Ho's. E14 . . . .3C **80**
   (off Cassilis Rd.)
Constable Wlk.
  SE21 . . . . .3A **120**
Constance Allen Ho.
  W10 . . . . .5F **57**
   (off Bridge Cl.)
Constance St. E16 . . . . .2F **83**
Constant Ho. E14 . . . . .1D **81**
   (off Harrow La.)
Constantine Ct. E1 . . . . .5C **64**
   (off Fairclough St.)
Constantine Rd.
  NW3 . . . . .1A **46**
Constitution Hill
  SW1 . . . . . . .3D **21** (3D **75**)
Consul Ho. E3 . . . . . . .3C **66**
   (off Wellington Way)
Content St. SE17 . . . . . .5F **77**
Convent Gdns. W11 . . . .5A **58**
Convent Hill SE19 . . . . .5E **119**
Conway Gro. W3 . . . . . .4A **56**
Conway Ho. E14 . . . . . .5C **80**
   (off Cahir St.)
  SW3 . . . . .1B **88**
   (off Ormonde Ga.)
Conway M. W1 . . . . . . .4F **5**
Conway Rd. NW2 . . . . . .4E **29**
Conway St. W1 . . .4F **5** (3E **61**)
   (not continuous)
Conybeare NW3 . . . . . .4A **46**
Conyer's Rd. SW16 . . . .5F **117**
Conyer St. E3 . . . . .1A **66**
Cook Ct. SE8 . . . . .1A **94**
   (off Evelyn St.)
  SE16 . . . . .2E **79**
   (off Rotherhithe St.)
Cookes Cl. E11 . . . . . . .4B **40**
Cookham Cres. SE16 . . .3F **79**
Cookham Ho. E2 . . . . . .3F **11**
   (off Montclare St.)
Cooks Cl. E14 . . . . .2C **80**
   (off Cabot Sq.)
Cooks Rd. E15 . . . . . . .1D **67**
  SE17 . . . . .2D **91**
Coolfin Rd. E16 . . . . . . .5C **68**
Coolhurst Rd. N8 . . . . .1F **33**
Coolhurst
  Tennis & Squash Club
  . . . . .1F **33**
Cool Oak La. NW9 . . . . .2A **28**

Coomassie Rd. W9 . . . . .3B 58
Coombe Hill Golf Course
. . . . .5A 112
Coombe Ho. N7 . . . . . .2F 47
Coombe Lodge SE7 . . . .2E 97
Coombe Pk.
KT2: King T 5A 112
Coomber Ho. SW6 . . .1D 101
(off Wandsworth Bri. Rd.)
Coombe Rd. NW10 . . . .5A 28
SE26 . . . . .4D 121
W4 . . . . .1A 84
Coombrook Ct. SE16 . . . .3A 80
(off Elgar St.)
Coombs St.
N1 . . . . . . .1E 9 (1D 63)
Coomer M. SW6 . . . . . .2B 86
Coomer Pl. SW6 . . . . . .2B 86
Coomer Rd. SW6 . . . . . .2B 86
Cooperage, The SE1 . . . .3F 27
(off Gainsford St.)
SW8 . . . . .3B 90
(off Regent's Bri. Gdns.)
Co-operative Ho.
SE15 . . . . .1C 106
Cooper Cl.
SE1 . . . . . .4C 24 (3C 76)
Cooper Ho. NW8 . . . . . .3F 59
(off Lyons Pl.)
SE4 . . . . .3F 107
(off St Norbert Rd.)
Cooper Rd. NW4 . . . . . .1F 29
NW10 . . . . .2C 42
Coopersale Rd. E9 . . . . .2F 51
Coopers Cl. E1 . . . . . . .3E 65
Coopers Ct. E3 . . . . . . .3B 66
(off Eric St.)
Coopers La. E10 . . . . . .3D 39
NW1 . . . . .1F 61
(not continuous)
SE12 . . . . .2D 125
Coopers Lodge SE1 . . . . .3F 27
(off Tooley St.)
Cooper's Rd. SE1 . . . . . .1B 92
Coopers Row
EC3 . . . . . .4F 19 (1B 78)
Cooper St. E16 . . . . . . .4B 68
Coopers Wlk. E15 . . . . .2A 54
Coopers Yd. N1 . . . . . . .4D 49
(off Upper St.)
SE19 . . . . .5A 120
Cope Ho. EC1 . . . . .2A 10
Copeland Dr. E14 . . . . . .5C 80
Copeland Ho. SE11 . . . . .4C 76
(off Lambeth Wlk.)
SW17 . . . . .4F 115
Copeland Rd. E17 . . . . .1D 39
SE15 . . . . .5C 92
Copeman Cl. SE26 . . . . .5E 121
Copenhagen Ho. N1 . . . . .5B 48
(off Barnsbury Est.)
Copenhagen Pl. E14 . . . .5B 66
(not continuous)
Copenhagen St. N1 . . . . .5A 48
Cope Pl. W8 . . . . .4C 72
Copers Cope Rd.
BR3: Beck 5B 122
Cope St. SE16 . . . . . . .5F 79
Copford Wlk. N1 . . . . . .5E 49
(off Popham St.)

Copgate Path SW16 . . .5B 118
Copleston Ho. SE15 . . . .5B 92
Copleston Pas. SE5 . . . .5B 92
Copleston Rd. SE15 . . .1B 106
Copley Cl. SE17 . . . . . .2E 91
Copley Pk. SW16 . . . . .5B 118
Copley St. E1 . . . . . . .4F 65
Coppelia Rd. SE3 . . . . .2B 110
Copperas St. SE8 . . . . .2D 95
Copperbeech Cl.
NW3 . . . . .2F 45
Copper Box, Olympic Pk.
. . . . .3C 52
Copperfield Ho. SE1 . . . .3C 78
(off Wolseley St.)
W1 . . . . .5C 4
(off Marylebone High St.)
W11 . . . . .2F 71
(off St Ann's Rd.)
Copperfield M. E2 . . . . .1C 64
(off Claredale St.)
Copperfield Rd. E3 . . . . .3A 66
Copperfield St.
SE1 . . . . . .3E 25 (3D 77)
Coppermead Cl. NW2 . . . .5E 29
Copper Mill La.
SW17 . . . . .4E 115
Coppermill La. E17 . . . .1E 37
Copper Row SE1 . . . . . .2F 27
Copperworks, The N1 . . . .1A 62
(off Railway St.)
Coppice Dr. SW15 . . . . .4D 99
Coppock Cl. SW11 . . . . .5A 88
Copse Cl. SE7 . . . . . . .2D 97
Captain Ho. SW18 . . . .2C 100
Copthall Av.
EC2 . . . . . .2C 18 (5F 63)
(not continuous)
Copthall Bldgs. EC2 . . . .2C 18
Copthall Cl.
EC2 . . . . . .2B 18 (5F 63)
Copthorne Av. SW12 . . . .5F 103
Coptic St.
WC1 . . . . . .1D 15 (4A 62)
Coral Apartments
E16 . . . . .1C 82
(off Western Gateway)
Coral Ho. E1 . . . . .3A 66
(off Harford St.)
Coral Mans. NW6 . . . . . .5C 44
(off Kilburn High Rd.)
Coral Row SW11 . . . . .1E 101
Coral St. SE1 . . . .4C 24 (3C 76)
Coram Ho. W4 . . . . . . .1A 84
(off Wood St.)
WC1 . . . . .3D 7
Coram Mans. WC1 . . . . .4F 7
(off Millman St.)
Coram St.
WC1 . . . . . .4D 7 (3A 62)
Corbden Cl. SE15 . . . . .4B 92
Corben M. SW8 . . . . . .5E 89
Corbet Cl.
EC3 . . . . . .2C 18 (5F 63)
Corbet Ho. N1 . . . . . . .1C 62
(off Barnsbury Est.)
SE5 . . . . .3E 91
(off Wyndham Rd.)
Corbet Pl. E1 . . . .5F 11 (4B 64)

Corbett Ho. SW10 . . . . . .2E 87
(off Cathcart Rd.)
Corbett Rd. E11 . . . . . .1E 41
Corbetts La. SE16 . . . . . .5E 79
(not continuous)
Corbetts Pas. SE16 . . . . .5E 79
(off Corbetts La.)
Corbetts Wharf SE16 . . . .3D 79
(off Bermondsey Wall E.)
Corbicum E11 . . . . .2A 40
Corbidge Ct. SE8 . . . . . .2D 95
Corbiere Ho. N1 . . . . . . .5F 49
(off De Beauvoir Est.)
Corbin Ho. E3 . . . . .2D 67
(off Bromley High St.)
Corbridge Cres. E2 . . . . .1D 65
Corbyn St. N4 . . . . . . .3A 34
Corby Way E3 . . . . .3C 66
Cordelia Cl. SE24 . . . . .2D 105
Cordelia Ho. N1 . . . . . . .1A 64
(off Arden Est.)
Cordelia St. E14 . . . . . . .5D 67
Cording St. E14 . . . . . . .4D 67
Cordwainers Ct. E9 . . . . .4E 51
(off St Thomas's Sq.)
Cordwainers Wlk.
E13 . . . . .1C 68
Cord Way E14 . . . . . . .4C 80
Cordwell Rd. SE13 . . . .3A 110
Corelli Ct. SE1 . . . . . . .5D 79
SW5 . . . . .5C 72
(off W. Cromwell Rd.)
Corelli Rd. SE3 . . . . . . .5F 97
Corfe Ho. SW8 . . . . . . .3B 90
(off Dorset Rd.)
Corfield St. E2 . . . . . . .2D 65
Coriander Av. E14 . . . . . .5F 67
Coriander Ct. SE1 . . . . . .3B 78
(off Gainsford St.)
Corinne Rd. N19 . . . . . .1E 47
Corker Wlk. N7 . . . . . . .4B 34
Cork Ho. SW19 . . . . . .4D 115
Cork Sq. E1 . . . . .2D 79
Cork St. W1 . . . . .5F 13 (1E 75)
Cork St. M. W1 . . . . . . .5F 13
Cork Tree Ho. SE27 . . . . .5D 119
(off Lakeview Rd.)
Corlett St. NW1 . . . . . . .4A 60
Cormont Rd. SE5 . . . . . .4D 91
Cormorant Ct. SE8 . . . . .2B 94
(off Pilot Cl.)
Cormorant Lodge E1 . . . .2C 78
(off Thomas More St.)
Cormorant Rd. E7 . . . . . .2B 54
Cornbury Ho. SE8 . . . . . .2B 94
(off Evelyn St.)
Cornelia St. N7 . . . . . . .3B 48
Cornell Bldg. E1 . . . . . . .5C 64
(off Coke St.)
Cornell Sq. SW8 . . . . . .4F 89
Corner Ct. E2 . . . . .3D 65
(off Three Colts La.)
Corner Fielde SW2 . . . . .1B 118
Corner Grn. SE3 . . . . . .5C 96
Corner Ho. St. WC2 . . . .1D 23
Corney Reach Way
W4 . . . . .3A 84
Corney Rd. W4 . . . . . . .2A 84
Cornflower Ter.
SE22 . . . . .4D 107

Cornford Gro.
SW12 . . . . 2D **117**
Cornhill EC3 . . . 3C **18** (5F **63**)
Cornick Ho. SE16 . . . . . .4D **79**
(off Slippers Pl.)
Cornish Ho. SE17 . . . . . .2D **91**
(off Brandon Est.)
Cornmill La. SE13 . . . .1E **109**
Cornmow Dr. NW10 . . . .2B **42**
Cornthwaite Rd. E5 . . . . .5E **37**
Cornwall Av. E2 . . . . . . .2E **65**
Cornwall Cres. W11 . . . .5A **58**
Cornwall Gdns.
NW10 . . . . .3D **43**
SW7 . . . . .4D **73**
Cornwall Gdns. Wlk.
SW7 . . . . .4D **73**
Cornwall Gro. W4 . . . . .1A **84**
Cornwall Ho. SW7 . . . . .4D **73**
(off Cornwall Gdns.)
Cornwallis Ct. SW8 . . . .4A **90**
(off Lansdowne Grn.)
Cornwallis Ho. SE16 . . . .3D **79**
(off Cherry Gdn. St.)
W12 . . . . .1D **71**
(off India Way)
Cornwallis Rd. N19 . . . .4A **34**
Cornwallis Sq. N19 . . . .4A **34**
Cornwall Mans.
SW10 . . . . .3E **87**
(off Cremorne Rd.)
W8 . . . . .3D **73**
(off Kensington Ct.)
W14 . . . . .4F **71**
(off Blythe Rd.)
Cornwall M. Sth.
SW7 . . . . .4E **73**
Cornwall M. W. SW7 . .4D **73**
Cornwall Rd. N4 . . . . . .2C **34**
N15 . . . . .1F **35**
SE1 . . . . .1B **24** (2C **76**)
Cornwall Sq. SE11 . . . . .1D **91**
(off Seaton Cl.)
Cornwall St. E1 . . . . . . .1D **79**
Cornwall Ter.
NW1 . . . . . .4A **4** (3B **60**)
Cornwall Ter. M. NW1 . . .4A **4**
Corn Way E11 . . . . . . .5F **39**
Cornwood Dr. E1 . . . . . .5E **65**
Corona Bldg. E14 . . . . .2E **81**
(off Blackwall Way)
Corona Rd. SE12 . . . . .5C **110**
Coronation Av. N16 . . . .1B **50**
Coronation Ct. E15 . . . .3B **54**
W10 . . . . .4E **57**
(off Brewster Gdns.)
Coronation Rd. E13 . . . .2E **69**
Coroners Court
City of London
. . . . .4B **18** (1F **77**)
Poplar 1D **81**
(off Poplar High St.)
St Pancras 5F **47**
Southwark 3F **77**
West London 4E **87**
Westminster 5C **23**
Coronet Cinema 2C **72**
(off Notting Hill Ga.)
Coronet St.
N1 . . . . . .2D **11** (2A **64**)

Coronet Theatre 4E **77**
(off New Kent Rd.)
Corporation Row
EC1 . . . . . . .3C **8** (3C **62**)
Corporation St. E15 . . . .1A **68**
N7 . . . . .2A **48**
Corrance Rd. SW2 . . . .2A **104**
Corringham Ct.
NW11 . . . . .2C **30**
Corringham Ho. E1 . . . .5F **65**
(off Pitsea St.)
Corringham Rd.
NW11 . . . . .2C **30**
Corringway NW11 . . . .2D **31**
Corris Grn. NW9 . . . . . .1A **28**
Corry Dr. SW9 . . . . . . .2D **105**
Corry Ho. E14 . . . . .1D **81**
(off Wade's Pl.)
Corsehill St. SW16 . . . .5E **117**
Corsham St.
N1 . . . . . .2C **10** (2F **63**)
Corsica St. N5 . . . . .3D **49**
Corsley Way E9 . . . . . . .3B **52**
Cortayne Rd. SW6 . . . . .5B **86**
Cortis Rd. SW15 . . . . . .4D **99**
Cortis Ter. SW15 . . . . . .4D **99**
Corunna Rd. SW8 . . . . .4E **89**
Corunna Ter. SW8 . . . . .4E **89**
Corvette Sq. SE10 . . . . .2F **95**
Coryton Path W9 . . . . . .3B **58**
(off Ashmore Rd.)
Cosbycote Av. SE24 . . .3E **105**
Cosgrove Ho. E2 . . . . . .5C **50**
(off Whiston Rd.)
Cosmo Pl.
WC1 . . . . . . .5E **7** (4A **62**)
Cosmur Cl. W12 . . . . . .4B **70**
Cossall Wlk. SE15 . . . . .5D **93**
Cossar M. SW2 . . . . . .3C **104**
Cosser St.
SE1 . . . . .5B **24** (4C **76**)
Costa St. SE15 . . . . . . .5C **92**
Coston Wlk. SE4 . . . . . .2F **107**
Cosway Mans. NW1 . . . .4A **60**
(off Shroton St.)
Cosway St. NW1 . . . . . .4A **60**
Cotall St. E14 . . . . .4C **66**
Coteford St. SW17 . . . .4B **116**
Cotesbach Rd. E5 . . . . .5E **37**
Cotes Ho. NW8 . . . . . . .3A **60**
(off Broadley St.)
Cotham St. SE17 . . . . . .5E **77**
Cotherstone Rd.
SW2 . . . . .1B **118**
Cotleigh Rd. NW6 . . . . .4C **44**
Cotman Cl. NW11 . . . . . .1E **31**
SW15 . . . . .4F **99**
Cotman Ho. NW8 . . . . . .1A **60**
(off Townshend Est.)
Cotswold Ct. EC1 . . . . . .3F **9**
Cotswold Gdns. E6 . . . .2F **69**
NW2 . . . . .4F **29**
Cotswold Ga. NW2 . . . . .3A **30**
Cotswold M. SW11 . . . . .4F **87**
Cotswold St. SE27 . . . .4D **119**
Cottage Cl. E1 . . . . .3E **65**
(off Mile End Rd.)
Cottage Grn. SE5 . . . . . .3F **91**
Cottage Pl. SW9 . . . . . .1A **104**
Cottage Pl. SW3 . . . . . .4A **74**

Cottage Rd. N7 . . . . . . .2B **48**
(not continuous)
Cottage St. E14 . . . . . . .1D **81**
Cottage Wlk. N16 . . . . . .5B **36**
Cottesbrook St.
SE14 . . . . .3A **94**
Cottesloe Ho. NW8 . . . . .3A **60**
(off Jerome Cres.)
Cottesloe M. SE1 . . . . . .5C **24**
(off Emery St.)
Cottesloe Theatre 1A **24**
(in National Theatre)
Cottesmore Ct. W8 . . . . .4D **73**
(off Stanford Rd.)
Cottesmore Gdns.
W8 . . . . .4D **73**
Cottingham Rd. SW8 . . . .3B **90**
Cottington St. SE11 . . . . .1C **90**
Cottle Way SE16 . . . . . .3D **79**
(off Paradise St.)
Cotton Av. W3 . . . . .5A **56**
Cotton Cl. E11 . . . . .4A **40**
Cotton Hill
BR1: Brom 4E **123**
Cotton Ho. SW2 . . . . . .5A **104**
Cotton Row SW11 . . . . .1E **101**
Cottons Cen.
SE1 . . . . .1D **27** (2A **78**)
Cotton's Gdns.
E2 . . . . . . .1E **11** (2A **64**)
Cottons La.
SE1 . . . . .1C **26** (2F **77**)
Cotton St. E14 . . . . .1E **81**
Cottrell Ct. SE10 . . . . . .5B **82**
(off Hop St.)
Cottrill Gdns. E8 . . . . . . .3D **51**
Coulgate St. SE4 . . . . . .1A **108**
Coulson St. SW3 . . . . . .1B **88**
Coulter Rd. W6 . . . . . . .4D **71**
Councillor St. SE5 . . . . . .3E **91**
Counter Ct. SE1 . . . . . . .2B **26**
(off Borough High St.)
Counters Ct. W14 . . . . . .4A **72**
(off Holland Rd.)
Counter St.
SE1 . . . . .2D **27** (2A **78**)
Countess Rd. NW5 . . . . .2E **47**
County Court
Bow 3B **54**
(off Romford Rd.)
Central London 4D **5**
Clerkenwell and
Shoreditch
. . . . .3F **9** (3E **63**)
Lambeth 1C **90**
Wandsworth 3A **100**
West London 1F **85**
(off Talgarth Rd.)
Willesden 1B **56**
County Gro. SE5 . . . . . .4E **91**
County Hall Apartments
SE1 . . . . .3F **23**
County Hall (Former)
SE1 . . . . .3F **23** (3B **76**)
County Ho. SW9 . . . . . . .4C **90**
(off Brixton Rd.)
County St. SE1 . . . . .4E **77**
Courland Gro. SW8 . . . . .4F **89**
Courland St. SW8 . . . . . .4F **89**
Court Annexe 4A **26** (3E **77**)

Courtauld Ho. *E2* 5C **50**
(off Goldsmiths Row)
Courtauld Institute of Art
. . . . .4F **15**
Courtauld Rd. N19 . . . . .3A **34**
Court Cl. *NW8* 4F **45**
(off Boydell Ct., not continuous)
Courtenay Av. N6 . . . . . .2A **32**
Courtenay M. E17 . . . . . .1A **38**
Courtenay Pl. E17 . . . . . .1A **38**
Courtenay Rd. E11 . . . . . .5B **40**
Courtenay Sq. SE11 . . . . .1C **90**
Courtenay St. SE11 . . . . .1C **90**
Court Farm Rd.
SE9 . . . . .2F **125**
Courtfield Gdns.
SW5 . . . . .5D **73**
Courtfield Ho. *EC1* 5B **8**
(off Baldwins Gdns.)
Courtfield M. SW5 . . . . . .5E **73**
Courtfield Rd. SW7 . . . . .5E **73**
Court Gdns. N1 . . . . .3C **48**
N7 . . . . .3C **48**
Courthill Rd. SE13 . . . . . .2E **109**
Courthope Ho. *SE16* 4E **79**
(off Lower Rd.)
SW8 . . . . .3A **90**
(off Hartington Rd.)
Courthope Rd. NW3 . . . . .1B **46**
SW19 . . . . .5A **114**
Courthouse La.
N16 . . . . .1B **50**
Courtland Rd. E6 . . . . . . .5F **55**
Courtlands Av. SE12 . . . .3D **111**
Court La. SE21 . . . . . . .4A **106**
Court La. Gdns.
SE21 . . . . .5A **106**
Courtleigh NW11 . . . . . . .1B **30**
Court Lodge *SW1* 5C **74**
(off Sloane Sq.)
Courtmead Cl. SE24 . . . .4E **105**
Courtnell St. W2 . . . . . . .5C **58**
Courtney Cl. N7 . . . . .2C **48**
Courtney Ho. *W14* 4A **72**
(off Russell Rd.)
Courtney Rd. N7 . . . . . . .2C **48**
Courtrai Rd. SE23 . . . . . .4A **108**
Court Royal SW15 . . . . . .3A **100**
Courtside N8 . . . . .1F **33**
SE26 . . . . .3D **121**
Court St. E1 . . . . .4D **65**
Courtville Ho. *W10* 2A **58**
(off Third Av.)
Courtyard *SW3* 1B **88**
(off Smith St.)
Courtyard, The *E2* 2B **64**
(off Ezra St.)
EC3 . . . . .3C **18**
(in Royal Exchange)
N1 . . . . .4B **48**
NW1 . . . . .4C **46**
SE14 . . . . .4F **93**
(off Besson St.)
SW3 . . . . .2F **87**
(off Trident Pl.)
Courtyard Ho. SW6 . . . . .5E **87**
(off Lensbury Av.)
Courtyard Theatre
Shoreditch
. . . . .2D **11** (2A **64**)

Cousin La.
EC4 . . . . . . .5B **18** (1F **77**)
Couthurst Rd. SE3 . . . . . .2D **97**
Coutt's Cres. NW5 . . . . . .5C **32**
Couzens Ho. *E3* 4B **66**
(off Weatherley Cl.)
Covell Ct. SE8 . . . . .3C **94**
COVENT GARDEN
. . . . .4E **15** (1A **76**)
Covent Garden
. . . . .4E **15** (1A **76**)
Covent Gdn.
WC2 . . . . . . .4E **15** (1A **76**)
Coventry Cl. NW6 . . . . . . .1C **58**
Coventry Hall SW16 . . . . .5A **118**
Coventry Rd. E1 . . . . .3D **65**
E2 . . . . .3D **65**
Coventry St.
W1 . . . . .5B **14** (1F **75**)
Coverdale Rd. NW2 . . . . .4F **43**
W12 . . . . .3D **71**
Coverham Ho. SE4 . . . . .2F **107**
(off Billingford Cl.)
Coverley Cl. E1 . . . . .4C **64**
Coverley Point SE11 . . . . .5B **76**
(off Tyers St.)
Coverton Rd. SW17 . . . . .5A **116**
Covington Way
SW16 . . . . .5B **118**
(not continuous)
Cowcross St.
EC1 . . . . .5D **9** (4D **63**)
Cowdenbeath Path
N1 . . . . .5B **48**
Cowden St. SE6 . . . . .4C **122**
Cowdrey Rd. SW19 . . . . .5D **115**
Cowick Rd. SW17 . . . . . .4B **116**
Cowley La. E11 . . . . .5A **40**
Cowley Rd. E11 . . . . .1D **41**
SW9 . . . . .4C **90**
(not continuous)
SW14 . . . . .1A **98**
W3 . . . . .2B **70**
Cowley St.
SW1 . . . . . . .5D **23** (4A **76**)
Cowling Cl. W11 . . . . .2A **72**
Cowper Av. E6 . . . . .4F **55**
Cowper Ho. *SE17* 1E **91**
(off Browning St.)
SW1 . . . . .1F **89**
(off Aylesford St.)
Cowper Rd. N16 . . . . .2A **50**
SW19 . . . . .5E **115**
Cowper's Ct. *EC3* 3C **18**
(off Birchin La.)
Cowper St.
EC2 . . . . .3C **10** (3F **63**)
Cowper Ter. W10 . . . . . . .4F **57**
Cowthorpe Rd. SW8 . . . . .4F **89**
Cox Ho. *W6* 2A **86**
(off Field Rd.)
Coxmount Rd. SE7 . . . . . .1F **97**
Coxson Way
SE1 . . . . . . .4F **27** (3B **78**)
Cox's Wlk. SE21 . . . . . . .1C **120**
Crabtree Cl. E2 . . . . .1B **64**
Crabtree Hall *SW6* 3E **85**
(off Crabtree La.)
Crabtree La. SW6 . . . . . . .3E **85**
(not continuous)

Crace St. NW1 . . . .1B **6** (2F **61**)
Craddock St. NW5 . . . . . .3C **46**
Crafts Council & Gallery
. . . . .1C **62**
Cragie Ho. *SE1* 5B **78**
(off Balaclava Rd.)
Craigerne Rd. SE3 . . . . . .3D **97**
Craignair Rd. SW2 . . . . . .5C **104**
Craig's Ct.
SW1 . . . . . . .1D **23** (2A **76**)
Craik Ct. *NW6* 1B **58**
(off Carlton Vale)
Crail Row SE17 . . . . .5F **77**
Cramer St.
W1 . . . . .1C **12** (4C **60**)
Crammond Cl. W6 . . . . . . .2A **86**
Crampton Ho. SW8 . . . . . .4E **89**
Crampton Rd. SE20 . . . . .5E **121**
Crampton St. SE17 . . . . . .5E **77**
Cranberry Cl. E16 . . . . . . .3A **68**
Cranberry La. E16 . . . . . . .3A **68**
Cranbourn All. *WC2* 4C **14**
(off Cranbourn St.)
Cranbourne NW1 . . . . . . .4F **47**
(off Agar Gro.)
Cranbourne Ct.
SW11 . . . . .3A **88**
(off Albert Bri. Rd.)
Cranbourne Gdns.
NW11 . . . . .1A **30**
Cranbourne Pas.
SE16 . . . . .3D **79**
Cranbourne Rd. E12 . . . . .2F **55**
E15 . . . . .1E **53**
Cranbourn Ho. *SE16* 3D **79**
(off Marigold St.)
Cranbourn St.
WC2 . . . . . . .4C **14** (1F **75**)
Cranbrook *NW1* 5E **47**
(off Camden St.)
Cranbrook Est. E2 . . . . . . .1F **65**
Cranbrook Rd. SE8 . . . . . .4C **94**
W4 . . . . .1A **84**
Cranbrook St. E2 . . . . .1F **65**
Cranbury Rd. SW6 . . . . . .5D **87**
Crandley Ct. SE8 . . . . .5A **80**
(not continuous)
Crane Ct. EC4 . . . . .5C **62**
Crane Gro. N7 . . . . .3C **48**
Crane Ho. *E3* 1A **66**
(off Roman Rd.)
SE15 . . . . .4B **92**
Crane Mead SE16 . . . . . . .1E **93**
Crane St. SE10 . . . . .1F **95**
SE15 . . . . .4B **92**
Cranfield Cl. SE27 . . . . . .3E **119**
Cranfield Ct. *W1* 4A **60**
(off Homer St.)
Cranfield Ho. WC1 . . . . . . .5D **7**
Cranfield Rd. SE4 . . . . . . .1B **108**
Cranfield Row SE1 . . . . . .5C **24**
Cranford Cotts. *E1* 1F **79**
(off Cranford St.)
Cranford St. E1 . . . . .1F **79**
Cranford Way N8 . . . . . . .1B **34**
Cranhurst Rd. NW2 . . . . . .2E **43**
Cranleigh W11 . . . . .2B **72**
(off Ladbroke Rd.)
Cranleigh Ho's. *NW1* 1E **61**
(off Cranleigh St.)
Cranleigh M. SW11 . . . . . .5A **88**

Cranleigh St. NW1 . . . . .1E 61
CRANLEY GARDENS 1D 33
Cranley Gdns. SW7 . . . . .1E 87
Cranley M. SW7 . . . . . . .1E 87
Cranley Pl. SW7 . . . . . . .5F 73
Cranley Rd. E13 . . . . . . .4D 69
Cranmer Ct. SW3 . . . . . .5A 74
SW4 . . . . .1F 103
Cranmer Ho. SW9 . . . . . .3C 90
(off Cranmer Rd.)
SW11 . . . . .4A 88
(off Surrey La. Est.)
Cranmer Rd. E7 . . . . . . .1D 55
SW9 . . . . .3C 90
Cranmer Ter. SW17 . . . . .5F 115
Cranmore Rd.
BR1: Brom 3B 124
Cranston Est. N1 . . . . . .1F 63
Cranston Rd. SE23 . . . . .1A 122
Cranswick Rd. SE16 . . . .1D 93
Crantock Rd. SE6 . . . . . .2D 123
Cranwell Cl. E3 . . . . .3D 67
Cranwich Rd. N16 . . . . . .2F 35
Cranwood St.
EC1 . . . . . . .2B 10 (2F 63)
Cranworth Gdns.
SW9 . . . . .4C 90
Craster Rd. SW2 . . . . . .5B 104
Crathie Rd. SE12 . . . . . .4D 111
Craven Cl. N16 . . . . .2C 36
Craven Cottage 5F 85
Craven Ct. NW10 . . . . . .5A 42
Craven Gdns. SW19 . . . .5C 114
Craven Hill W2 . . . . .1E 73
Craven Hill Gdns.
W2 . . . . .1E 73
(not continuous)
Craven Hill M. W2 . . . . . .1E 73
Craven Lodge SW6 . . . . .4F 85
(off Harbord St.)
W2 . . . . .1E 73
(off Craven Hill)
Craven M. SW11 . . . . . .1C 102
Craven Pk. NW10 . . . . . .5A 42
Craven Pk. M. NW10 . . . .4A 42
Craven Pk. Rd. N15 . . . .1B 36
NW10 . . . . .5A 42
Craven Pas. WC2 . . . . . .1D 23
(off Craven St.)
Craven Rd. NW10 . . . . . .5A 42
W2 . . . . .1E 73
Craven St.
WC2 . . . . . .1D 23 (2A 76)
Craven Ter. W2 . . . . .1E 73
Craven Wlk. N16 . . . . . . .2C 36
Crawford Bldgs. W1 . . . .4A 60
(off Homer St.)
Crawford Est. SE5 . . . . . .5E 91
Crawford Mans. W1 . . . .4A 60
(off Crawford St.)
Crawford M.
W1 . . . . . .1A 12 (4B 60)
Crawford Pas.
EC1 . . . . . .4C 8 (3C 62)
Crawford Pl. W1 . . . . . . .5A 60
Crawford Rd. SE5 . . . . . .4E 91
Crawford St.
W1 . . . . . .1A 12 (4A 60)
Crawley Rd. E10 . . . . . . .3D 39

Crawshay Ct. SW9 . . . . .4C 90
Crawthew Gro.
SE22 . . . . .2B 106
Crayford Cl. E6 . . . . .5F 69
Crayford Ho. SE1 . . . . . .4C 26
(off Long La.)
Crayford Rd. N7 . . . . . . .1F 47
Cray Ho. NW8 . . . . .4F 59
(off Penfold St.)
Crayle Ho. EC1 . . . . .3E 9
(off Malta St.)
Crealock St. SW18 . . . . .4D 101
Creasy Est. SE1 . . . . . . .4A 78
Creative Ho. SW8 . . . . . .3D 89
(off Prince of Wales Dr.)
Crebor St. SE22 . . . . . . .4C 106
Crecy Ct. SE11 . . . . .1C 90
(off Hotspur St.)
Credenhill Ho. SE15 . . . .3D 93
Credenhill St.
SW16 . . . . .5E 117
Crediton Hgts. NW10 . . . .5F 43
(off Okehampton Rd.)
Crediton Hill NW6 . . . . . .2D 45
Crediton Rd. E16 . . . . . .5C 68
NW10 . . . . .5F 43
Credon Rd. E13 . . . . . . .1E 69
SE16 . . . . .1D 93
Creechurch La.
EC3 . . . . . .3E 19 (5A 64)
(not continuous)
Creechurch Pl. EC3 . . . .3E 19
Creed Ct. E1 . . . . .2A 66
EC4 . . . . .3E 17
Creed La.
EC4 . . . . . .3E 17 (5D 63)
Creek Ho. W14 . . . . .4A 72
(off Russell Rd.)
Creek Rd. SE8 . . . . .2C 94
SE10 . . . . .2C 94
Creekside SE8 . . . . .3D 95
Creekside Foyer SE8 . . . .2D 95
(off Stowage)
Creeland Gro. SE6 . . . . .1B 122
Crefeld Cl. W6 . . . . .2A 86
Creighton Av. E6 . . . . . . .1F 69
Creighton Cl. W12 . . . . . .1C 70
Creighton Rd. NW6 . . . . .1F 57
Cremer Bus. Cen. E2 . . . .1F 11
(off Cremer St.)
Cremer Ho. SE8 . . . . . . .3C 94
(off Deptford Chu. St.)
Cremer St. E2 . . .1F 11 (1B 64)
Cremorne Est. SW10 . . . .2F 87
(not continuous)
Cremorne Riverside Cen.
. . . . .3F 87
Cremorne Rd. SW10 . . . .3E 87
Creon Ct. SW9 . . . . .3C 90
(off Caldwell St.)
Crescent EC3 . . .4F 19 (1B 78)
Crescent, The E17 . . . . . .1A 38
NW2 . . . . .5D 29
SW13 . . . . .5B 84
SW19 . . . . .3C 114
W3 . . . . .5A 56
Crescent Arc. SE10 . . . . .2E 95
(off Creek Rd.)
Crescent Ct. SW4 . . . . . .3F 103
(off Park Hill)

Crescent Ct. Bus. Cen.
E16 . . . . .3F 67
Crescent Gdns.
SW19 . . . . .3C 114
Crescent Gro. SW4 . . . . .2E 103
Crescent Ho. EC1 . . . . . .4F 9
(off Golden La. Est.)
SE13 . . . . .5D 95
Crescent La. SW4 . . . . . .2E 103
Crescent Mans.
W11 . . . . .1A 72
(off Elgin Cres.)
Crescent Pl. SW3 . . . . . .5A 74
Crescent Rd. E6 . . . . . . .5E 55
E10 . . . . .4D 39
E13 . . . . .5C 54
N8 . . . . .1F 33
Crescent Row
EC1 . . . . .4F 9 (3E 63)
Crescent Stables
SW15 . . . . .3A 100
Crescent St. N1 . . . . .4B 48
Crescent Way SE4 . . . . .1C 108
Crescent Wharf E16 . . . .3D 83
(not continuous)
Crescent Wood Rd.
SE26 . . . . .3C 120
Cresford Rd. SW6 . . . . . .4D 87
Crespigny Rd. NW4 . . . . .1D 29
Cressal Ho. E14 . . . . .4C 80
(off Tiller Rd.)
Cresset Ho. E9 . . . . .3E 51
Cresset Rd. E9 . . . . .3E 51
Cresset St. SW4 . . . . . . .1F 103
Cressfield Cl. NW5 . . . . . .2C 46
Cressida Rd. N19 . . . . . . .3E 33
Cressingham Rd.
SE13 . . . . .1E 109
Cressington Cl. N16 . . . . .2A 50
Cress M. BR1: Brom 5F 123
Cresswell Gdns.
SW5 . . . . .1E 87
Cresswell Pk. SE3 . . . . .1B 110
Cresswell Pl. SW10 . . . . .1E 87
Cressy Ct. E1 . . . . .4E 65
W6 . . . . .4D 71
Cressy Ho. SW15 . . . . . .1D 99
Cressy Ho's. E1 . . . . .4E 65
(off Hannibal Rd.)
Cressy Pl. E1 . . . . .4E 65
Cressy Rd. NW3 . . . . . . .2B 46
Cresta Ho. E3 . . . . .3C 66
(off Dimson Cres.)
NW3 . . . . .4F 45
(off Finchley Rd.)
Crestfield St.
WC1 . . . . . .1E 7 (2A 62)
Crest Rd. NW2 . . . . .4B 28
Crestway SW15 . . . . .4C 98
Creswick Wlk. E3 . . . . . . .2C 66
Creukhorne Rd.
NW10 . . . . .4A 42
Crewdson Rd. SW9 . . . . .3C 90
Crewe Pl. NW10 . . . . . . .2B 56
Crewkerne Ct. SW11 . . . .4F 87
(off Bolingbroke Wlk.)
Crews St. E14 . . . . .5C 80
Crewys Rd. NW2 . . . . . . .4B 30
SE15 . . . . .5D 93
Crichton St. SW8 . . . . . . .5E 89

Cricketers Ct. SE11 ....5D **77**
    (off Kennington La.)
Cricketers M. SW18 ...3D **101**
Cricketers Wlk.
    SE26 ....5E **121**
Cricketfield Rd. E5 ....1D **51**
Cricket La.
    BR3: Beck 5A **122**
Cricklade Av. SW2 ...2A **118**
CRICKLEWOOD 1F **43**
Cricklewood B'way.
    NW2 ....5E **29**
Cricklewood La. NW2 ..1F **43**
Cridland St. E15 ......5B **54**
Crieff Rd. SW18 ......4E **101**
Criffel Av. SW2 ......2F **117**
Crimscott St.
    SE1 ....5E **27** (4A **78**)
Crimsworth Rd. SW8 ..4F **89**
Crinan St. N1 ....1A **62**
Cringle St. SW8 ......3E **89**
Cripplegate St.
    EC2 .....5A **10** (4E **63**)
Crispe Ho. N1 ....5B **48**
    (off Barnsbury Est.)
Crispian Cl. NW10 ....1A **42**
Crispin Ct. SE17 .....5A **78**
    (off Freemantle St.)
Crispin Pl.
    E1 ....5F **11** (4B **64**)
Crispin St.
    E1 ....1F **19** (4B **64**)
Crisp Rd. W6 ....1E **85**
Cristowe Rd. SW6 .....5B **86**
Criterion Ct. E8 ......4B **50**
    (off Middleton Rd.)
Criterion M. N19 .....4F **33**
    SE24 ....3D **105**
    (off Shakespeare Rd.)
Criterion Theatre 5B **14**
    (off Piccadilly Cir.)
Crockerton Rd.
    SW17 ....2B **116**
Croft, The NW10 ....1B **56**
Croft Ct. SE13 ......4E **109**
Croftdown Rd. NW5 ..5C **32**
Crofters Ct. SE8 .....5A **80**
    (off Croft St.)
Crofters Way NW1 ....5F **47**
Croft Ho. W10 ....2A **58**
    (off Third Av.)
Croftongate Way
    SE4 ....3A **108**
Crofton Ho. SW3 .....2A **88**
    (off Old Church St.)
CROFTON PARK 3B **108**
Crofton Pk. Rd. SE4 ..4B **108**
Crofton Rd. E13 .....3D **69**
    SE5 ....4A **92**
Crofton Ter. E5 ......2A **52**
Crofts Ho. E2 ....1C **64**
    (off Teale St.)
Crofts St. E1 ....1C **78**
Croft St. SE8 ....5A **80**
Croftway NW3 ......1C **44**
Crogsland Rd. NW1 ..4C **46**
Cromartie Rd. N19 ...2F **33**
Cromarty Ct. SW2 ...3B **104**
Cromarty Ho. E1 .....4A **66**
    (off Ben Jonson Rd.)

Crombie M. SW11 ....5A **88**
Crome Rd. NW10 .....3A **42**
Cromer Rd. E10 .....2F **39**
    SW17 ....5C **116**
Cromer St.
    WC1 ......2D **7** (2A **62**)
Cromer Ter. E8 ......2C **50**
Cromer Vs. Rd.
    SW18 ....4B **100**
Cromford Path E5 ....1F **51**
Cromford Rd.
    SW18 ....3C **100**
Crompton Ct. SW3 ...5A **74**
Crompton Ho. SE1 ...4B **78**
    (off County St.)
    W2 ....3F **59**
    (off Hall Pl.)
Crompton St. W2 ....3F **59**
Cromwell Av. N6 .....3D **33**
    W6 ....1D **85**
Cromwell Cl. E1 .....2C **78**
Cromwell Cres. SW5 ..5C **72**
Cromwell Gdns. SW7 ..4F **73**
Cromwell Gro. W6 ....4E **71**
Cromwell Highwalk
    EC2 ....5A **10**
Cromwell Ho. SW11 ..4C **88**
    (off Charlotte Despard Av.)
Cromwell Ind. Est.
    E10 ....3A **38**
Cromwell Lodge E1 ..3E **65**
    (off Cleveland Gro.)
Cromwell Mans.
    SW5 ....5C **72**
    (off Cromwell Rd.)
Cromwell M. SW7 ....5F **73**
Cromwell Pl. EC2 ....5A **10**
    (off Silk St.)
    N6 ....3D **33**
    SW7 ....5F **73**
Cromwell Rd. E7 .....4E **55**
    E17 ....1E **39**
    SW5 ....5C **72**
    SW7 ....5C **72**
    SW9 ....4D **91**
    SW19 ....5C **114**
Cromwell Twr. EC2 ...5A **10**
Crondace Rd. SW6 ...4C **86**
Crondall Ct. N1 ......1C **10**
Crondall Ho. SW15 ...5C **98**
Crondall St.
    N1 ....1C **10** (1F **63**)
Crone Ct. NW6 ....1B **58**
    (off Denmark Rd.)
Cronin St. SE15 .....3B **92**
Crooked Billet Yd.
    E2 ....1E **11**
Crooke Rd. SE8 ......1A **94**
Crookham Rd. SW6 ...4B **86**
Croombs Rd. E16 ....4E **69**
Croom's Hill SE10 ...3E **95**
Croom's Hill Gro.
    SE10 ....3E **95**
Cropley Ct. N1 ....1F **63**
    (off Cropley St., not continuous)
Cropley St.
    N1 ....1B **10** (1F **63**)
Cropthorne Ct. W9 ...2E **59**
Crosby Ct.
    SE1 ......3B **26** (3F **77**)

Crosby Ho. E7 ....3C **54**
    E14 ....4E **81**
    (off Manchester Rd.)
Crosby Rd. E7 ....3C **54**
Crosby Row
    SE1 ......4B **26** (3F **77**)
Crosby Sq.
    EC3 ......3D **19** (5A **64**)
Crosby Wlk. E8 ......3B **50**
    SW2 ....5C **104**
Crosby Way SW2 ....5C **104**
Crosier Cl. SE3 ......4F **97**
Crosland Pl. SW11 ...1C **102**
Cross Av. SE10 ......2F **95**
Crossbow Ho. N1 ....5A **50**
    (off Whitmore Est.)
Crossbrook Rd. SE3 ..5F **97**
Cross Cl. SE15 ......5D **93**
Crossfield Cl. W10 ...5F **57**
    (off Cambridge Gdns.)
Crossfield Ho. W11 ..1A **72**
    (off Mary Pl.)
Crossfield Rd. NW3 ..3F **45**
Crossfield St. SE8 ...3C **94**
    (not continuous)
Crossford St. SW9 ...5B **90**
Cross Keys Cl.
    W1 ....1C **12** (4C **60**)
Cross Keys Sq. EC1 ..1F **17**
    (off Little Britain)
Cross La.
    EC3 ......5D **19** (1A **78**)
Crossleigh Ct. SE14 ..3B **94**
    (off New Cross Rd.)
Crosslet St. SE17 ....5F **77**
Crosslet Va. SE10 ....4D **95**
Crossley St. N7 ......3C **48**
Crossmount Ho. SE5 ..3E **91**
    (off Bowyer St.)
Cross Rd. SE5 ....5A **92**
Cross St. N1 ....5D **49**
    SE5 ....1F **105**
    SW13 ....5A **84**
Crossthwaite Av.
    SE5 ....2F **105**
Crosstrees Ho. E14 ..4C **80**
    (off Cassilis Rd.)
Crosswall
    EC3 ......4F **19** (1B **78**)
Cross Way NW10 ....4C **42**
Crossway N16 ....2A **50**
Crossway, The SE9 ..2F **125**
Crossway Ct. SE4 ....5A **94**
Crossways Ter. E5 ...1E **51**
Croston St. E8 ....5C **50**
Crouch End Hill N8 ..2F **33**
Crouch Hall Ct. N19 ..3A **34**
Crouch Hall Rd. N8 ..1F **33**
Crouch Hill N4 ....1A **34**
    N8 ....1A **34**
Crouchman's Cl.
    SE26 ....3B **120**
Crowborough Rd.
    SW17 ....5C **116**
Crowder St. E1 ......1D **79**
Crowfield Ho. N5 ....1E **49**
Crowfoot Cl. E9 .....2B **52**
Crowhurst Cl. SW9 ..5C **90**

Crowhurst Ho. SW9 ....5B **90**
    (off Aytoun Rd.)
Crowland Ho. NW4 ....5E **45**
    (off Springfield Rd.)
Crowland Rd. N15 .....1B **36**
Crowland Ter. N1 ....4F **49**
Crowline Wlk. N1 ......3E **49**
Crowmarsh Gdns.
   SE23 ....5E **107**
Crown Cl. E3 ....5C **52**
  NW6 ....3D **45**
Crown Cl. Bus. Cen.
   E3 ....5C **52**
    (off Crown Cl.)
Crown Court
  Blackfriars
    ....3E **25** (3D **77**)
  Inner London
    ....5F **25** (4E **77**)
  Snaresbrook ...1B **40**
  Southwark
    ....1D **27** (2A **78**)
Crown Ct. EC2 ....3A **18**
  NW8 ....2A **60**
    (off Park Rd.)
  SE12 ....4D **111**
  WC2 ....3E **15** (5A **62**)
Crown Dale SE19 .....5D **119**
    (not continuous)
Crowndale Ct. NW1 ....1F **61**
    (off Crowndale Rd.)
Crowndale Rd. NW1 ....1E **61**
Crownfield Rd. E15 ....1F **53**
Crowngate Ho. E3 .....1B **66**
    (off Hereford Rd.)
Crownhill Rd. NW10 ....5B **42**
Crown La. SW16 ......5C **118**
Crown La. Gdns.
   SW16 ....5C **118**
Crown Lodge SW3 .....5A **74**
    (off Elystan St.)
Crown M. E1 ....4F **65**
    (off White Horse La.)
  E13 ....5E **55**
  W6 ....5C **70**
Crown Office Row
  EC4 ....4B **16** (1C **76**)
Crown Pas.
  SW1 ......2A **22** (2E **75**)
Crown Pl.
  EC2 .....5D **11** (4A **64**)
  NW5 ....3D **47**
  SE19 ....1D **93**
Crown Point SE19 .....5D **119**
Crown Point Pde.
   SE19 ....5D **119**
    (off Crown Dale)
Crown Reach SW1 ....1F **89**
Crownstone Ct.
  SW2 ....3C **104**
Crownstone Rd.
  SW2 ....3C **104**
Crown St. SE5 ....3E **91**
Crown Wharf E14 ......2E **81**
    (off Coldharbour)
  SE8 ....1B **94**
    (off Grove St.)
Crown Yd. SW6 ....5C **86**
Crows Rd. E3 ....2F **67**
  E15 ....2F **67**

Crowther Cl. SW6 ......2B **86**
    (off Bucklers All.)
Crowthorne Cl.
  SW18 ....5B **100**
Crowthorne Rd. W10 ...5F **57**
Croxley Rd. W9 ....2B **58**
Croxted Cl. SE21 ......5E **105**
Croxted M. SE24 ......4E **105**
Croxted Rd. SE21 .....5E **105**
  SE24 ....5E **105**
Croxteth Ho. SW8 .....5F **89**
Croydon Ho. SE1 ......3C **24**
    (off Wootton St.)
Croydon Rd. E13 ......3B **68**
Crozier Ho. SE3 ....1D **111**
  SW8 ....3B **90**
    (off Wilkinson St.)
Crozier Ter. E9 ....2F **51**
    (not continuous)
Crucifix La.
  SE1 ....3E **27** (3A **78**)
Cruden Ho. E3 ....1B **66**
    (off Vernon Rd.)
  SE17 ....2D **91**
    (off Brandon Est.)
Cruden St. N1 ....5D **49**
Cruikshank Ho. NW8 ...1A **60**
    (off Townshend Rd.)
Cruikshank Rd. E15 ....1A **54**
Cruikshank St. WC1 ....1B **8**
Crummock Gdns.
   NW9 ....1A **28**
Crusader Ind. Est. N4 ...1E **35**
Crusoe M. N16 ....4F **35**
Crutched Friars
  EC3 ....4E **19** (1A **78**)
Crutchley Rd. SE6 .....2A **124**
Crystal Ct. SE19 ......5B **120**
    (off College Rd.)
CRYSTAL PALACE 5B **120**
Crystal Palace
  Athletics Stadium
    ....5C **120**
Crystal Palace Mus.
    ....5B **120**
Crystal Palace National
  Sports Cen. 5C **120**
Crystal Pal. Pde.
   SE19 ....5B **120**
Crystal Palace Pk. ...5C **120**
Crystal Pal. Pk. Rd.
   SE26 ....5C **120**
Crystal Pal. Rd.
   SE22 ....4B **106**
Crystal Ter. SE19 .....5F **119**
Crystal Vw. Ct.
  BR1: Brom 4F **123**
Crystal Wharf N1 ......1D **63**
Cuba St. E14 ....3C **80**
Cube Ho.
  SE16 ......5F **27** (4B **78**)
Cubitt Bldg. SW1 ......1D **89**
Cubitt Ct. NW1 ....1F **5**
    (off Park Village E.)
Cubitt Ho. SW4 ....4E **103**
Cubitt Steps E14 ......2C **80**
Cubitt St. WC1 ...2A **8** (2B **62**)
Cubitt Ter. SW4 ....1E **103**
CUBITT TOWN 5E **81**

Cuddington SE17 ......5E **77**
    (off Deacon Way)
Cudham St. SE6 ......5E **109**
Cudworth Ho. SW8 ....4E **89**
Cudworth St. E1 ......3D **65**
Cuff Cres. SE9 ....4F **111**
Cuffley Ho. W10 ......4E **57**
    (off Sutton Way)
Cuff Point E2 ....1F **11**
    (off Columbia Rd.)
Culand Ho. SE17 ......5A **78**
    (off Congreve St.)
Culford Gdns. SW3 ....5B **74**
Culford Gro. N1 ....3A **50**
Culford Mans. SW3 ....5B **74**
    (off Culford Gdns.)
Culford M. N1 ....3A **50**
Culford Rd. N1 ....4A **50**
Culford Ter. N1 ....3A **50**
    (off Balls Pond Rd.)
Culham Ho. E2 ....2F **11**
    (off Palissy St.)
  W2 ....4C **58**
    (off Gt. Western Rd.)
Culling Rd. SE16 ......4E **79**
Cullingworth Rd.
  NW10 ....2C **42**
Culloden Cl. SE7 ......2D **97**
  SE16 ....1C **92**
Cullum St.
  EC3 ....4D **19** (1A **78**)
Cullum Welch Ct. N1 ...1C **10**
    (off Haberdasher St.)
Cullum Welch Ho. EC1 ..4F **9**
    (off Golden La. Est.)
Culmore Rd. SE15 .....3D **93**
Culmstock Rd.
  SW11 ....3C **102**
Culpepper Ct. SE11 ...5C **76**
    (off Kennington Rd.)
Culross Ho. W10 ......5F **57**
    (off Bridge Cl.)
Culross St.
  W1 ......5B **12** (1C **74**)
Culverden Rd.
  SW12 ....2E **117**
Culverhouse WC1 .....1F **15**
    (off Red Lion Sq.)
Culverhouse Gdns.
   SW16 ....3B **118**
Culverley Rd. SE6 .....1D **123**
Culvert Pl. SW11 ......5C **88**
Culvert Rd. N15 ......1A **36**
    (not continuous)
  SW11 ....5B **88**
Culworth Ho. NW8 .....1A **60**
    (off Allitsen Rd.)
Culworth St. NW8 .....1A **60**
Culzean Cl. SE27 .....3D **119**
Cumberland Cl. E8 ....3B **50**
Cumberland Ct. SW1 ...1D **89**
    (off Cumberland St.)
  W1 ....3A **12**
    (off Gt. Cumberland Pl.)
Cumberland Cres.
  W14 ....5A **72**
    (not continuous)
Cumberland Gate
  (Park & Ride)
    ....4A **12** (1B **74**)

Cumberland Gdns.
WC1 . . . . . . .1B 8 (2C 62)
Cumberland Ga.
W1 . . . . . .4A 12 (1B 74)
Cumberland Ho. E16 . . . .2C 82
(off Wesley Av.)
W8 . . . . .3D 73
(off Kensington Ct.)
Cumberland Mans.
W1 . . . . .5B 60
(off George St.)
Cumberland Mkt.
NW1 . . . . .1E 5 (2D 61)
Cumberland M. SE11 . . .1C 90
Cumberland Mills Sq.
E14 . . . . .1F 95
Cumberland Pk. Ind. Est.
NW10 . . . . .2C 56
Cumberland Pl.
NW1 . . . . .1D 5 (2D 61)
SE6 . . . . .1B 124
Cumberland Rd. E12 . . . .1F 55
E13 . . . . .4D 69
SW13 . . . . .4B 84
Cumberland St. SW1 . . .1D 89
Cumberland Ter.
NW1 . . . . .1D 5 (1D 61)
Cumberland Ter. M.
NW1 . . . . .1D 5
(not continuous)
Cumberland Wharf
SE16 . . . . .3E 79
(off Rotherhithe St.)
Cumbrian Gdns. NW2 . . .4F 29
Cuming Mus. 5E 77
(off Walworth Rd.)
Cumming St.
N1 . . . . . . .1A 8 (1B 62)
Cumnor Cl. SW9 . . . . . .5B 90
(off Robsart St.)
Cunard Pl.
EC3 . . . . . . .3E 19 (5A 64)
Cunard Rd. NW10 . . . . .2A 56
Cunard Wlk. SE16 . . . . .5F 79
Cundy Rd. E16 . . . . . . .5E 69
Cundy St. SW1 . . . . . . .5C 74
Cunliffe St. SW16 . . . . .5E 117
Cunningham Ct. E10 . . . .5D 39
(off Oliver Rd.)
W9 . . . . .3E 59
(off Maida Va.)
Cunningham Ho. SE5 . . . .3F 91
(off Elmington Est.)
Cunningham Pl. NW8 . . .3F 59
Cupar Rd. SW11 . . . . . .4C 88
Cupola Cl.
BR1: Brom 5D 125
Cureton St. SW1 . . . . . .5F 75
Curlew Ho. SE4 . . . . . .2A 108
(off St Norbert Rd.)
SE15 . . . . .4B 92
Curlew St.
SE1 . . . . . . .3F 27 (3B 78)
Curness St. SE13 . . . . . .2E 109
Curnick's La. SE27 . . . . .4E 119
Curran Ho. SW3 . . . . . .5A 74
(off Lucan Pl.)
Curricle St. W3 . . . . . . .2A 70
Currie Hill Cl.
SW19 . . . . .4B 114

Cursitor St.
EC4 . . . . . .2B 16 (5C 62)
Curtain Pl.
EC2 . . . . . .3E 11 (2A 64)
Curtain Rd.
EC2 . . . . . .2E 11 (3A 64)
Curtis Dr. W3 . . . . .5A 56
Curtis Fld. Rd.
SW16 . . . . .4B 118
Curtis Ho. SE17 . . . . . . .1F 91
(off Morecambe St.)
Curtis St. SE1 . . . . .5B 78
Curtis Way SE1 . . . . . . .5B 78
Curve, The W12 . . . . . . .1C 70
Curwen Av. E7 . . . . . . .1D 55
Curwen Rd. W12 . . . . . .3C 70
Curzon Cinema
Mayfair 2D 21
(off Curzon St.)
Soho 4C 14
(off Shaftesbury Av.)
Curzon Ct. SW6 . . . . . . .4E 87
(off Imperial Rd.)
Curzon Cres. NW10 . . . . .4A 42
Curzon Ga.
W1 . . . . . . .2C 20 (2C 74)
Curzon Sq.
W1 . . . . . . .2C 20 (2C 74)
Curzon St.
W1 . . . . . . .2C 20 (2C 74)
Custance Ho. N1 . . . . . .1B 10
(off Provost Est.)
Custance St.
N1 . . . . . . .1B 10 (2F 63)
CUSTOM HOUSE 5E 69
Custom Ho.
EC3 . . . . . .5D 19 (1A 78)
Custom Ho. Reach
SE16 . . . . .3B 80
Custom Ho. Wlk.
EC3 . . . . . .5D 19 (1A 78)
Cut, The SE1 . . . .3C 24 (3C 76)
Cutbush Ho. N7 . . . . . . .2F 47
Cutcombe Rd. SE5 . . . . .5E 91
Cuthbert Bell Twr. E3 . . .1C 66
(off Pancras Way)
Cuthbert Harrowing Ho.
EC1 . . . . .4F 9
(off Golden La. Est.)
Cuthbert Ho. W2 . . . . . .4F 59
(off Hall Pl.)
Cuthbert St. W2 . . . . . . .4F 59
Cuthill Wlk. SE5 . . . . . .4F 91
Cutlers Gdns.
EC2 . . . . . .1E 19 (4A 64)
Cutlers Gdns. Arc.
EC2 . . . . .2E 19
(off Devonshire Sq.)
Cutlers Sq. E14 . . . . . . .5C 80
Cutlers Ter. N1 . . . . .3A 50
(off Balls Pond Rd.)
Cutler St. E1 . . . .2E 19 (5A 64)
Cutter La. SE10 . . . . . . .3A 82
Cutty Sark E14 . . . . . . .2E 95
Cutty Sark Gdns.
SE10 . . . . .2E 95
(off King William Wlk.)
Cuxton Ho. SE17 . . . . . .1A 92
(off Mina Rd.)
Cyclops M. E14 . . . . . . .5C 80

Cygnet Cl. NW10 . . . . . .2A 42
Cygnet Ho. SW3 . . . . . .1A 88
(off King's Rd.)
Cygnet Ho. Nth. E14 . . . .5D 67
(off Chrisp St.)
Cygnet Ho. Sth. E14 . . . .5D 67
(off Chrisp St.)
Cygnet St. E1 . . .3F 11 (3B 64)
Cygnus Bus. Cen.
NW10 . . . . .2B 42
Cynthia St. N1 . . . .1A 8 (1B 62)
Cyntra Pl. E8 . . . . .4D 51
Cypress Cl. E5 . . . . .4C 36
Cypress Cl. E15 . . . . . . .1F 53
(off Langthorne Rd.)
Cypress Gdns. SE4 . . . . .3A 108
Cypress Ho. SE14 . . . . . .4F 93
(off Woodland Cres.)
Cypress Pl.
W1 . . . . . . .4A 6 (3E 61)
Cyprus Cl. N4 . . . . .1D 35
Cyprus Pl. E2 . . . . .1E 65
Cyprus St. E2 . . . . .1E 65
(not continuous)
Cyrena Rd. SE22 . . . . . .4B 106
Cyril Mans. SW11 . . . . . .4B 88
Cyrus Ho. EC1 . . . . .3E 9
Cyrus St. EC1 . . . . .3E 9
Czar St. SE8 . . . . .2C 94

D

Dabbs La. EC1 . . . . .4C 8
(off Farringdon Rd.)
Dabin Cres. SE10 . . . . . .4E 95
Dacca St. SE8 . . . . .2B 94
Dace Rd. E3 . . . . .5C 52
Dacre Gdns. SE13 . . . . . .2A 110
Dacre Ho. SW3 . . . . . . .2F 87
(off Beaufort St.)
Dacre Pk. SE13 . . . . . . .1A 110
Dacre Pl. SE13 . . . . . . .1A 110
Dacre Rd. E11 . . . . .3B 40
E13 . . . . .5D 55
Dacres Est. SE23 . . . . . .3F 121
Dacres Ho. SW4 . . . . . . .1D 103
Dacres Rd. SE23 . . . . . .2F 121
Dacre St.
SW1 . . . . . .5B 22 (4F 75)
Daffodil St. W12 . . . . . . .1B 70
Dafforne Rd. SW17 . . . . .3C 116
Da Gama Pl. E14 . . . . . .1C 94
Dagenham Rd. E10 . . . . .3B 38
Dagmar Ct. E14 . . . . . . .4E 81
Dagmar Gdns. NW10 . . . .1F 57
Dagmar Pas. N1 . . . . . . .5D 49
(off Cross St.)
Dagmar Rd. N4 . . . . . . .2C 34
SE5 . . . . .4A 92
Dagmar Ter. N1 . . . . . . .5D 49
Dagnall St. SW11 . . . . . .5B 88
Dagnan Rd. SW12 . . . . . .5D 103
Dagobert Ho. E1 . . . . . . .4E 65
(off Smithy St.)
Dagonet Gdns.
BR1: Brom 3C 124
Dagonet Rd.
BR1: Brom 3C 124

Dahomey Rd. SW16 . . . . .5E 117
Daimler Ho. E3 . . . . .3C 66
   (off Wellington Way)
Dain Ct. W8 . . . . .5C 72
   (off Lexham Gdns.)
Dainford Cl.
  BR1: Brom 5E 123
Dainton Ho. W2 . . . . . . .4C 58
   (off Gt. Western Rd.)
Daintry Way E9 . . . . .3B 52
Dairy Cl. NW10 . . . . .5C 42
  SW6 . . . . .4C 86
Dairyman Cl. NW2 . . . . . .5F 29
Dairy M. SW9 . . . . . . .1A 104
Dairy Rd. E16 . . . . .3A 68
Dairy Wlk. SW19 . . . . . .4A 114
Daisy Dobbings Wlk.
  N19 . . . . .2A 34
   (off Jessie Blythe La.)
Daisy La. SW6 . . . . .1C 100
Daisy Rd. E16 . . . . .3A 68
Dakin Pl. E1 . . . . .4A 66
Dakota Bldg. SE10 . . . . .4D 95
   (off Deal's Gateway)
Dakota Gdns. E6 . . . . . . .3F 69
Dalberg Rd. SW2 . . . . . .2C 104
   (not continuous)
Dalby Rd. SW18 . . . . . . .2E 101
Dalby St. NW5 . . . . .3D 47
Dalebury Rd. SW17 . . . . .2B 116
Dale Cl. SE3 . . . . .1C 110
Daleham Gdns. NW3 . . . .2F 45
Daleham M. NW3 . . . . . .3F 45
Dalehead NW1 . . . . .1F 5
   (off Hampstead Rd.)
Dale Ho. N1 . . . . .5A 50
   (off New Era Est.)
  NW8 . . . . .5E 45
   (off Boundary Rd.)
  SE4 . . . . .2A 108
Dale Rd. N6 . . . . .1E 33
Dalemain M. E16 . . . . . .2C 82
Dale Rd. NW5 . . . . .2C 46
  SE17 . . . . .2D 91
Dale Row W11 . . . . .5A 58
Daleside Rd. SW16 . . .5D 117
Dale St. W4 . . . . .1A 84
Daleview Rd. N15 . . . . .1A 36
Daley Ho. W12 . . . . .5D 57
Daley St. E9 . . . . .3F 51
Daley Thompson Way
  SW8 . . . . .5D 89
Dalgarno Gdns. W10 . . . .4E 57
Dalgarno Way W10 . . . . .3E 57
Dalgleish St. E14 . . . . . .5A 66
Daling Way E3 . . . . .5A 52
Dalkeith Cl. SW1 . . . . . .5F 75
   (off Vincent St.)
Dalkeith Ho. SW9 . . . . . .4D 91
   (off Lothian Rd.)
Dalkeith Rd. SE21 . . . . .1E 119
Dallas Rd. NW4 . . . . . . .2C 28
  SE26 . . . . .3D 121
Dallinger Rd. SE12 . . . .4B 110
Dalling Rd. W6 . . . . .5D 71
Dallington Sq. EC1 . . . . .3E 9
   (off Dallington St.)
Dallington St.
  EC1 . . . . .3E 9 (3D 63)
Dalmain Rd. SE23 . . . . .1F 121
Dalmeny Av. N7 . . . . . . .1F 47

Dalmeny Rd. N7 . . . . . . .5F 33
   (not continuous)
Dalmeyer Rd. NW10 . . . .3B 42
Dalmore Rd. SE21 . . . . .2E 119
Dalo Lodge E3 . . . . .4C 66
   (off Gale St.)
Dalrymple Rd. SE4 . . . . .2A 108
DALSTON 3B 50
Dalston La. E8 . . . . .3B 50
Dalston Sq. E8 . . . . .3B 50
   (not continuous)
Dalton Ho. E3 . . . . .1A 66
   (off Ford St.)
  SE14 . . . . .2F 93
   (off John Williams Cl.)
  SW1 . . . . .1D 89
   (off Ebury Bri. Rd.)
Dalton St. SE27 . . . . . . .3D 119
Dalwood St. SE5 . . . . . . .4A 92
Dalyell Rd. SW9 . . . . . . .1B 104
Damascene Wlk.
  SE21 . . . . .1E 119
Damask Cres. E16 . . . . . .3A 68
Damer Ter. SW10 . . . . . .3E 87
Dames Rd. E7 . . . . .5C 40
Dame St. N1 . . . . .1E 63
Damien Ct. E1 . . . . .5D 65
   (off Damien St.)
Damien St. E1 . . . . .5D 65
Damory Ho. SE16 . . . . . .5D 79
   (off Abbeyfield Rd.)
Danbury St. N1 . . . . .1D 63
Danby Ho. E9 . . . . .4E 51
   (off Frampton Pk. Rd.)
  W10 . . . . .2A 58
   (off Bruckner St.)
Danby St. SE15 . . . . . . .1B 106
Dance Ho. SE4 . . . . .3F 107
   (off St Norbert Rd.)
Dancer Rd. SW6 . . . . . . .4B 86
Dance Sq. EC1 . . .2F 9 (2E 63)
Dando Cres. SE3 . . . . . .1D 111
Dandridge Cl. SE10 . . . . .1B 96
Dandridge Ho. E1 . . . . . .5F 11
   (off Lamb St.)
Danebury Av. SW15 . . . .4A 98
Daneby Rd. SE6 . . . . . . .3D 123
Danecroft Rd. SE24 . . . .3E 105
Danehurst St. SW6 . . . . .4A 86
Danemere St. SW15 . . . .1E 99
Dane Pl. E3 . . . . .1A 66
Danescombe SE12 . . . . .1C 124
Danes Ct. NW8 . . . . .5B 46
   (off St Edmund's Ter.)
Danescroft NW4 . . . . . . .1F 29
Danescroft Av. NW4 . . . .1F 29
Danescroft Gdns.
  NW4 . . . . .1F 29
Danesdale Rd. E9 . . . . . .3A 52
Danesfield SE5 . . . . .2A 92
   (off Albany Rd.)
Danes Ho. W10 . . . . .4E 57
   (off Sutton Way)
Dane St.
  WC1 . . . . . .1F 15 (4B 62)
Daneswood Av. SE6 . . . .3E 123
Daneville Rd. SE5 . . . . . .4F 91
Dangan Rd. E11 . . . . . . .1C 40
Daniel Bolt Cl. E14 . . . . .4D 67
Daniel Cl. SW17 . . . . . . .5A 116

Daniel Gdns. SE15 . . . . . .3B 92
Daniell Ho. N1 . . . . .1F 63
   (off Cranston Est.)
Daniel Pl. NW4 . . . . .2D 29
Daniels Rd. SE15 . . . . . .1E 107
Dan Leno Wlk. SW6 . . . . .3D 87
Dan Mason Dr. W4 . . . . .5A 84
Danny Fiszman Bri.
  N5 . . . . .1C 48
  N7 . . . . .1C 48
Dansey Pl. W1 . . . . .4B 14
Danson Rd. SE17 . . . . . .1D 91
Dante Pl. SE11 . . . . .5D 77
Dante Rd. SE11 . . . . .5D 77
Danube Ct. SE15 . . . . . . .3B 92
   (off Daniel Gdns.)
Danube St. SW3 . . . . . . .1A 88
Danvers Ho. E1 . . . . .5C 64
   (off Christian St.)
Danvers St. SW3 . . . . . . .2F 87
Dao Ct. E13 . . . . .5D 55
Da Palma Ct. SW6 . . . . . .2C 86
   (off Anselm Rd.)
Daphne St. SW18 . . . . . .4E 101
Daplyn St. E1 . . . . .4C 64
D'Arblay St.
  W1 . . . . .3A 14 (5E 61)
Darcy Ho. E8 . . . . .5D 51
   (off London Flds. E. Side)
Darent Ho.
  BR1: Brom 5F 123
  NW8 . . . . .4F 59
   (off Church St. Est.)
Darenth Rd. N16 . . . . . . .2B 36
Darfield NW1 . . . . .5E 47
   (off Bayham St.)
Darfield Rd. SE4 . . . . . . .3B 108
Darfield Way W10 . . . . . .5F 57
Darfur St. SW15 . . . . . . .1F 99
Darien Rd. SW11 . . . . . . .1F 101
Daring Ho. E3 . . . . .1A 66
   (off Roman Rd.)
Dark Ho. Wlk.
  EC3 . . . . . .5C 18 (1F 77)
Darlan Rd. SW6 . . . . . . .3B 86
Darley Ho. SE11 . . . . .1B 90
   (off Laud St.)
Darley Rd. SW11 . . . . . . .4B 102
Darling Rd. SE4 . . . . . . .1C 108
Darling Row E1 . . . . .3D 65
Darlington Ct. SE6 . . . . . .1B 124
Darlington Ho. SW8 . . . . .3F 89
   (off Hemans St.)
Darlington Rd. SE27 . . . .5D 119
Darnall Ho. SE10 . . . . . . .4E 95
   (off Royal Hill)
Darnaway Pl. E14 . . . . . .4E 67
   (off Aberfeldy St.)
Darnay Apartments
  E15 . . . . .3F 53
Darnley Ho. E14 . . . . . . .5A 66
   (off Camdenhurst St.)
Darnley Rd. E9 . . . . .3E 51
Darnley St. SW8 . . . . . . .4B 90
Darnley Ter. W11 . . . . . . .2F 71
Darrell Rd. SE22 . . . . . . .3C 106
Darren Cl. N4 . . . . .2B 34
Darren St. N7 . . . . .1A 48
Darsley Dr. SW8 . . . . . . .4F 89
Dartford Ho. SE1 . . . . . . .5B 78
   (off Longfield Est.)

Dartford St. SE17 . . . . . .2E 91
Dartington NW1 . . . . . . .5E 47
(off Plender St.)
Dartington Ho. SW8 . . . .5F 89
(off Union Gro.)
W2 . . . . .4D 59
(off Senior St.)
Dartle Ct. SE16 . . . . .3C 78
(off Scott Lidgett Cres.)
Dartmoor Wlk. E14 . . . .5C 80
(off Severnake Cl.)
Dartmoor Cl. W11 . . . .5B 58
Dartmouth Cl. SE10 . . .4E 95
Dartmouth Gro. SE10 . .4E 95
Dartmouth Hill SE10 . . .4E 95
Dartmouth Ho. SE10 . . .4D 95
(off Catherine Gro.)
DARTMOUTH PARK 5D 33
Dartmouth Pk. Av.
NW5 . . . . .5D 33
Dartmouth Pk. Hill
N19 . . . . .3D 33
NW5 . . . . .3D 33
Dartmouth Pk. Rd.
NW5 . . . . .1D 47
Dartmouth Pl. SE23 . . .2E 121
W4 . . . . .2A 84
Dartmouth Rd. NW2 . . .3F 43
NW4 . . . . .1C 28
SE23 . . . . .3D 121
SE26 . . . . .3D 121
Dartmouth Row SE10 . .5E 95
Dartmouth St.
SW1 . . . . .4C 22 (3F 75)
Dartmouth Ter. SE10 . . .4F 95
Dartrey Twr. SW10 . . . . .3E 87
(off Worlds End Est.)
Dartrey Wlk. SW10 . . . . .3E 87
Dart St. W10 . . . . .2A 58
Darvell Ho. SE17 . . . . . .1F 91
(off Inville Rd.)
Darville Rd. N16 . . . . . . .5B 36
Darwen Pl. E2 . . . . .1D 65
Darwin Ct. E13 . . . . .2D 69
NW1 . . . . .5D 47
SE17 . . . . .5F 77
(off Barlow Rd.)
Darwin Ho. SW1 . . . . . .2E 89
(off Grosvenor Rd.)
Darwin St. SE17 . . . . . .5F 77
(not continuous)
Darwood Ct. NW6 . . . . .4E 45
(off Belsize Rd.)
Daryngton Ho. SE1 . . . .4C 26
(off Hankey Pl.)
SW8 . . . . .3A 90
(off Hartington Rd.)
Dashwood Ho. N8 . . . . .1B 34
Dassett Rd. SE27 . . . . .5D 119
Data Point Bus. Cen.
E16 . . . . .3F 67
Datchelor Pl. SE5 . . . . . .4F 91
Datchet Ho. E2 . . . . .2B 64
(off Virginia Rd.)
NW1 . . . . .1E 5
(off Augustus St.)
Datchet Rd. SE6 . . . . . .2B 122
Datchworth Ho. N1 . . . .4D 49
(off The Sutton Est.)

Date St. SE17 . . . . .1F 91
Daubeney Rd. E5 . . . . . .1A 52
Daubeney Twr. SE8 . . . .1B 94
(off Bowditch)
Dault Rd. SW18 . . . . . . .4E 101
Dauncey Ho. SE1 . . . . . .4E 25
Dave Adams Ho. E3 . . . .1B 66
(off Norman Gro.)
Davenant Ho. E1 . . . . . .4C 64
(off Old Montague St.)
Davenant Rd. N19 . . . . .4F 33
Davenant St. E1 . . . . . . .4C 64
Davenport Ho. SE11 . . . .5C 76
(off Walnut Tree Wlk.)
Davenport Rd. SE6 . . . .4D 109
Daventry Av. E17 . . . . . .1C 38
Daventry St. NW1 . . . . . .4A 60
Daver Cl. SW3 . . . . .1A 88
Davern Cl. SE10 . . . . . . .5B 82
Davey Cl. N7 . . . . .3B 48
Davey Rd. E9 . . . . .4C 52
Davey's Ct. WC2 . . . . . .4D 15
Davey St. SE15 . . . . .2B 92
Davidge Ho.
SE1 . . . . .4D 25 (3D 77)
David Hewitt Ho. E3 . . . .4D 67
(off Watts Gro.)
David Ho. SW8 . . . . .3A 90
(off Wyvil Rd.)
David Lee Point E15 . . . .5A 54
(off Leather Gdns.)
David Lloyd Leisure
Fulham 3C 86
(within Fulham Broadway
Shopping Cen.)
Kidbrooke 2D 111
South Kensington
. . . . .5D 73
(off Point West)
David M. W1 . . . .5A 4 (4B 60)
Davidson Gdns. SW8 . . .3A 90
Davidson Terraces E7 . . .2D 55
(off Claremont Rd.)
David's Rd. SE23 . . . . . .1E 121
David St. E15 . . . . .3F 53
Davies La. E11 . . . . .4A 40
Davies M.
W1 . . . . . .4D 13 (1D 75)
Davies St.
W1 . . . . . .3D 13 (5D 61)
Da Vinci Ct. SE16 . . . . . .1D 93
(off Rossetti Rd.)
Da Vinci Lodge SE10 . . .4B 82
(off West Parkside)
Davis Ho. W12 . . . . .1D 71
(off White City Est.)
Davis Rd. W3 . . . . .2B 70
Davis St. E13 . . . . .1D 69
Davisville Rd. W12 . . . . .3C 70
Dawes Ho. SE17 . . . . . . .5F 77
(off Orb St.)
Dawes Rd. SW6 . . . . . . .3A 86
Dawes St. SE17 . . . . .1F 91
Dawlish Av. SW18 . . . . .2D 115
Dawlish Rd. E10 . . . . .3E 39
NW2 . . . . .3F 43
Dawnay Gdns.
SW18 . . . . .2F 115

Dawnay Rd. SW18 . . . . .2E 115
Dawn Cres. E15 . . . . . . .5F 53
Dawpool Rd. NW2 . . . . .4B 28
Dawson Ho. E2 . . . . .2E 65
(off Sceptre Rd.)
Dawson Pl. W2 . . . . .1C 72
Dawson Rd. NW2 . . . . . .2E 43
Dawson St.
E2 . . . . .1F 11 (1B 64)
Day Ho. SE5 . . . . .3E 91
(off Bethwin Rd.)
Daylesford Av. SW15 . . .2C 98
Daynor Ho. NW6 . . . . . . .5C 44
(off Quex Ho.)
Daysbrook Rd. SW2 . . . .1B 118
Dayton Gro. SE15 . . . . . .4E 93
Deacon Ho. SE11 . . . . . .5B 76
(off Black Prince Rd.)
Deacon M. N1 . . . . .4F 49
Deacon Rd. NW2 . . . . . .2C 42
Deacon's Ri. N2 . . . . .1F 31
Deacons Ter. N1 . . . . . . .3E 49
(off Harecourt Rd.)
Deacon Way SE17 . . . . . .5E 77
Deal Ho. SE15 . . . . .2F 93
(off Lovelinch La.)
SE17 . . . . .1A 92
(off Mina Rd.)
Deal Porters Wlk.
SE16 . . . . .3F 79
Deal Porters Way
SE16 . . . . .4E 79
Deal Rd. SW17 . . . . .5C 116
Deal's Gateway SE10 . . .4C 94
Deal St. E1 . . . . .4C 64
Dealtry Rd. SW15 . . . . . .2E 99
Deal Wlk. SW9 . . . . .3C 90
Dean Abbott Ho.
SW1 . . . . .5F 75
(off Vincent St.)
Dean Bradley St.
SW1 . . . . .4A 76
Dean Cl. E9 . . . . .2E 51
SE16 . . . . .2F 79
Dean Ct. SW8 . . . . .3A 90
(off Thorncroft St.)
Deancross St. E1 . . . . . . .5E 65
Deanery M. W1 . . . . .1C 20
Deanery Rd. E15 . . . . . . .3A 54
Deanery St.
W1 . . . . . . .1C 20 (2C 74)
Dean Farrar St.
SW1 . . . . . .5C 22 (4F 75)
Dean Ho. E1 . . . . .5E 65
(off Tarling St.)
SE14 . . . . .3A 94
(off New Cross Rd.)
Dean Rd. NW2 . . . . .3E 43
Dean Ryle St. SW1 . . . . .5A 76
Dean's Bldgs. SE17 . . . . .5F 77
Dean's Ct.
EC4 . . . . . . .3E 17 (5D 63)
Deans Ga. Cl. SE23 . . . .3F 121
Deanshanger Ho.
SE8 . . . . .5F 79
(off Chilton Gro.)
Dean's M.
W1 . . . . . . .2E 13 (5D 61)
Dean Stanley St.
SW1 . . . . . .5D 23 (4A 76)

Deanston Wharf E16 . . .3D 83
   (not continuous)
Dean St. E7 . . . . .2C 54
   W1 . . . . .2B 14 (5F 61)
Dean's Yd.
   SW1 . . . . . . .5C 22 (4F 75)
Dean Trench St.
   SW1 . . . . . .5D 23 (4A 76)
Death Trap, London's
   . . . . .4F 23
Deauville Ct. SE16 . . . . .3F 79
   (off Eleanor Cl.)
   SW4 . . . . .4E 103
De Barowe M. N5 . . . . . .1D 49
Debdale Ho. E2 . . . . .5C 50
   (off Whiston Rd.)
De Beauvoir Ct. N1 . . . . .4F 49
   (off Northchurch Rd.)
De Beauvoir Cres.
   N1 . . . . .5A 50
De Beauvoir Est. N1 . . . .5A 50
De Beauvoir Pl. N1 . . . . .3A 50
De Beauvoir Rd. N1 . . . . .5A 50
De Beauvoir Sq. N1 . . . . .4A 50
DE BEAUVOIR TOWN 5A 50
Debenham Ct. E8 . . . . . .5C 50
   (off Pownall Rd.)
Debham Ct. NW2 . . . . . . .5E 29
Debnams Rd. SE16 . . . . .5E 79
De Bruin Ct. E14 . . . . . . .1E 95
   (off Ferry St.)
Decima St.
   SE1 . . . . . .5D 27 (4A 78)
Decima Studios
   SE1 . . . . .5A 24
   (off Decima St.)
Deck Cl. SE16 . . . . .2F 79
De Crespigny Pk.
   SE5 . . . . .5F 91
Deeley Rd. SW8 . . . . .4F 89
Deepdale SW19 . . . . . . .4F 113
Deepdene Gdns.
   SW2 . . . . .5B 104
Deepdene Mans.
   SW6 . . . . .4B 86
   (off Rostrevor Rd.)
Deepdene Point
   SE23 . . . . .3F 121
Deepdene Rd.
   SE5 . . . . .2F 105
Deerbrook Rd.
   SE24 . . . . .1D 119
Deerdale Rd. SE24 . . . . .2E 105
Deerfield Cotts.
   NW9 . . . . .1B 28
Deerhurst Ho. SE15 . . . . .2C 92
   (off Haymerle Rd.)
Deerhurst Rd. NW2 . . . . .3F 43
   SW16 . . . . .5B 118
Deeside Rd. SW17 . . . . . .3F 115
Dee St. E14 . . . . .5E 67
Defoe Cl. SE16 . . . . .3B 80
   SW17 . . . . .5A 116
Defoe Ho. EC2 . . . . .5A 10
Defoe Pl. EC2 . . . . .5A 10
   (off Beech St.)
   SW17 . . . . .4B 116
Defoe Rd. N16 . . . . .4A 36
De Frene Rd. SE26 . . . . .4F 121
Dehar Cres. NW9 . . . . . . .2B 28

Dehavilland Studios
   E5 . . . . .4E 37
   (off Theydon Rd.)
Dekker Ho. SE5 . . . . .3F 91
   (off Elmington Est.)
Dekker Rd. SE21 . . . . . . .4A 106
Delacourt Rd. SE3 . . . . . .3D 97
Delafield Ho. E1 . . . . .5C 64
   (off Christian St.)
Delafield Rd. SE7 . . . . . . .1D 97
Delaford Rd. SE16 . . . . . .1D 93
Delaford St. SW6 . . . . . . .3A 86
Delahay Ho. SW3 . . . . . . .2B 88
   (off Chelsea Emb.)
Delamare Ct. SE6 . . . . . .3D 123
Delamere M. W2 . . . . . . .4D 59
Delamere St. W2 . . . . . . .4D 59
Delamere Ter. W2 . . . . . . .4D 59
Delancey Pas. NW1 . . . . .5D 47
   (off Delancey St.)
Delancey St. NW1 . . . . . .5D 47
Delancey Studios
   NW1 . . . . .5D 47
Delany Ho. SE10 . . . . . . .2E 95
   (off Thames St.)
Delarch Ho. SE1 . . . . . . .4D 25
De Laune St. SE17 . . . . . .1D 91
Delaware Mans. W9 . . . . .3D 59
   (off Delaware Rd.)
Delaware Rd. W9 . . . . . . .3D 59
Delawyk Cres. SE24 . . . . .4E 105
Delft Way SE22 . . . . .3A 106
Delhi St. N1 . . . . .5A 48
Delia St. SW18 . . . . .5D 101
Delius Gro. E15 . . . . .1F 67
Della Path E5 . . . . .5C 36
Dell Cl. E15 . . . . .5F 53
Dellow Ho. E1 . . . . .1D 79
   (off Dellow St.)
Dellow St. E1 . . . . .1D 79
Dell's M. SW1 . . . . .5E 75
   (off Churton Pl.)
Delmare Cl. SW9 . . . . . . .2B 104
Delme Cres. SE3 . . . . .5D 97
Delmerend Ho. SW3 . . . . .1A 88
   (off Cale St.)
Deloraine Ho. SE8 . . . . . . .4C 94
Delorme St. W6 . . . . .2F 85
Delta Bldg. E14 . . . . .5E 67
   (off Ashton St.)
Delta Ct. NW2 . . . . .4C 28
   SE8 . . . . .2A 94
   (off Trundleys Rd.)
Delta Ho. N1 . . . . .1B 10
   (off Nile St.)
Delta Pk. SW18 . . . . .2D 101
Delta Point E2 . . . . .2C 64
   (off Delta St.)
Delta St. E2 . . . . .2C 64
Delverton Ho. SE17 . . . . . .1D 91
   (off Delverton Rd.)
Delverton Rd. SE17 . . . . . .1D 91
Delvino Rd. SW6 . . . . .4C 86
De Montfort Pde.
   SW16 . . . . .3A 118
De Montfort Rd.
   SW16 . . . . .3A 118
De Morgan Rd.
   SW6 . . . . .1D 101
Dempster Rd. SW18 . . . . .3E 101
Den, The 1E 93

Denbigh Cl. W11 . . . . . . .1B 72
Denbigh Ct. E6 . . . . .2F 69
Denbigh Ho. SW1 . . . . . . .5A 20
   (off Hans Pl.)
   W11 . . . . .1B 72
   (off Westbourne Gro.)
Denbigh M. SW1 . . . . .5E 75
   (off Denbigh St.)
Denbigh Pl. SW1 . . . . .1E 89
Denbigh Rd. E6 . . . . .2F 69
   W11 . . . . .1B 72
Denbigh St. SW1 . . . . .5E 75
   (not continuous)
Denbigh Ter. W11 . . . . . . .1B 72
Denbury Ho. E3 . . . . .2D 67
   (off Talwin St.)
Denby Ct. SE11 . . . . .5B 76
   (off Lambeth Wlk.)
Dence Ho. E2 . . . . .2C 64
   (off Turin St.)
Denchworth Ho. SW9 . . . .5C 90
Dene Cl. E10 . . . . .4D 39
   SE4 . . . . .1A 108
Denehurst Gdns.
   NW4 . . . . .1E 29
Denesmead SE24 . . . . . . .3E 105
Denewood Rd. N6 . . . . . . .1B 32
Denford St. SE10 . . . . .1B 96
   (off Glenforth St.)
Dengie Wlk. N1 . . . . .5E 49
   (off Basire St.)
Denham Ct. NW6 . . . . . . .4E 45
   (off Fairfax Rd.)
   SE26 . . . . .3D 121
   (off Kirkdale)
Denham Ho. W12 . . . . . . .1D 71
   (off White City Est.)
Denham St. SE10 . . . . . . .1C 96
Denholme Rd. W9 . . . . . . .2B 58
Denison Ho. E14 . . . . .4D 81
Denison Rd. SW19 . . . . . .5F 115
Denland Ho. SW8 . . . . . . .3B 90
   (off Dorset Rd.)
Denman Ho. N16 . . . . .4A 36
Denman Pl. W1 . . . . .4B 14
Denman Rd. SE15 . . . . . . .4B 92
Denman St.
   W1 . . . . .5B 14 (1F 75)
Denmark Gro. N1 . . . . .1C 62
DENMARK HILL 1E 105
Denmark Hill SE5 . . . . . . .4F 91
Denmark Hill Est.
   SE5 . . . . .2F 105
Denmark Ho. SE7 . . . . . . .5E 83
Denmark Mans. SE5 . . . . .5E 91
   (off Coldharbour La.)
Denmark Pl. E3 . . . . .2C 66
   WC2 . . . . . . .2C 14 (5F 61)
Denmark Rd. NW6 . . . . . . .1B 58
   SE5 . . . . .4E 91
Denmark St. E11 . . . . .5A 40
   E13 . . . . .4D 69
   WC2 . . . . . . .2C 14 (5F 61)
Denmark Wlk. SE27 . . . . . .4E 119
Denmead Ho. SW15 . . . . .4B 98
   (off Highcliffe Dr.)
Denne Ter. E8 . . . . .5B 50
Dennett's Gro. SE14 . . . . .5F 93
Dennett's Rd. SE14 . . . . . .4E 93

Denning Cl. NW8 . . . . . .2E 59
Denning M. SW12 . . . . .4C 102
Denning Point E1 . . . . . . .2F 19
(off Commercial St.)
Denning Rd. NW3 . . . . . .1F 45
Dennington Cl. E5 . . . . . .4E 37
Dennington Pk. Rd.
NW6 . . . . .3C 44
Dennis Ho. E3 . . . . .1B 66
(off Roman Rd.)
Dennison Point E15 . . . . .4E 53
Dennis Way SW4 . . . . . .1F 103
Denny Cl. E6 . . . . .4F 69
Denny Cres. SE11 . . . . . .1C 90
Denny St. SE11 . . . . .1C 90
Densham Ho. NW8 . . . . . .1F 59
(off Cochrane St.)
Densham Rd. E15 . . . . . .5A 54
Denstone Ho. SE15 . . . . .2C 92
(off Haymerle Rd.)
Dent Ho. SE17 . . . . .5A 78
(off Peacock St.)
Denton NW1 . . . . .3C 46
Denton Ho. N1 . . . . .4D 49
(off Halton Rd.)
Denton Rd. N8 . . . . .1B 34
Denton St. SW18 . . . . . .4D 101
Denton Way E5 . . . . .5E 37
Dents Rd. SW11 . . . . . . .4B 102
Denver Rd. N16 . . . . .2A 36
Denwood SE23 . . . . .3F 121
Denyer St. SW3 . . . . .5A 74
Denys Ho. EC1 . . . . .5B 8
(off Bourne Est.)
Denzil Rd. NW10 . . . . . . .2B 42
Deodar Rd. SW15 . . . . . .2A 100
Department for Communities
. . . . .5F 21
Depot App. NW2 . . . . . . .1F 43
Depot Rd. W12 . . . . .1E 71
Depot St. SE5 . . . . .2F 91
DEPTFORD 3C 94
Deptford Bri. SE8 . . . . . .4C 94
Deptford B'way.
SE8 . . . . .4C 94
Deptford Bus. Pk.
SE15 . . . . .2E 93
Deptford Chu. St.
SE8 . . . . .2C 94
Deptford Creek Bri.
SE8 . . . . .2D 95
(off Creek Rd.)
Deptford Ferry Rd.
E14 . . . . .5C 80
Deptford Grn. SE8 . . . . . .2C 94
Deptford High St.
SE8 . . . . .2C 94
Deptford Pk. Bus. Cen.
SE8 . . . . .1A 94
Deptford Strand SE8 . . . .5B 80
Deptford Trad. Est.
SE8 . . . . .1A 94
Deptford Wharf SE8 . . . . .5B 80
De Quincey Ho. SW1 . . . .1E 89
(off Lupus St.)
De Quincey M. E16 . . . . .2C 82
Derby Ga.
SW1 . . . . .3D 23 (3A 76)
(not continuous)
Derby Hill SE23 . . . . .2E 121

Derby Hill Cres.
SE23 . . . . .2E 121
Derby Ho. SE11 . . . . .5C 76
(off Walnut Tree Wlk.)
Derby Lodge WC1 . . . . . . .1F 7
(off Britannia St.)
Derby Rd. E7 . . . . .4F 55
E9 . . . . .5F 51
Derbyshire St. E2 . . . . . .2C 64
(not continuous)
Derby St. W1 . . . .2C 20 (2C 74)
Dereham Ho. SE4 . . . . . .2F 107
(off Frendsbury Rd.)
Dereham Pl.
EC2 . . . . . .2E 11 (2A 64)
Derek Walcott Cl.
SE24 . . . . .3D 105
Dericote St. E8 . . . . .5D 51
Dering St.
W1 . . . . . . .3E 13 (5D 61)
Dering Yd.
W1 . . . . . . .3E 13 (5D 61)
Derinton Rd. SW17 . . . . .4B 116
Dermody Gdns.
SE13 . . . . .3F 109
Dermody Rd. SE13 . . . . .3F 109
Deronda Rd. SE24 . . . . .1D 119
Derrick Gdns. SE7 . . . . . .4E 83
Derrycombe Ho. W2 . . . . .4C 58
(off Gt. Western Rd.)
Derry Ho. NW8 . . . . .3F 59
(off Church St. Est.)
Derry M. N19 . . . . .4A 34
Derry St. W8 . . . . .3D 73
Dersingham Rd.
NW2 . . . . .5A 30
Derwent NW1 . . . . .2F 5
(off Robert St.)
Derwent Av. NW9 . . . . . .1A 28
SW15 . . . . .4A 112
Derwent Ct. SE16 . . . . . .3F 79
(off Eleanor Cl.)
Derwent Gro. SE22 . . . . .2B 106
Derwent Ho. E3 . . . . .3B 66
(off Southern Gro.)
SW7 . . . . .5E 73
(off Cromwell Rd.)
Derwent Point EC1 . . . . . .1D 9
(off Goswell Rd.)
Derwent Ri. NW9 . . . . . . .1A 28
Derwent St. SE10 . . . . . .1A 96
Desborough Cl. W2 . . . . .4D 59
Desborough Ho. W14 . . . .2B 86
(off North End Rd.)
Desborough St. W2 . . . . .4D 59
(off Cirencester St.)
Desenfans Rd.
SE21 . . . . .4A 106
Desford Rd. E16 . . . . .3A 68
Design Mus. 3B 78
Desmond St. SE14 . . . . . .2A 94
Desmond Tutu Dr.
SE23 . . . . .1B 122
Despard Rd. N19 . . . . . . .3E 33
Desvignes Dr. SE13 . . . . .4F 109
Dethick Ct. E3 . . . . .5A 52
Detling Ho. SE17 . . . . . . .5A 78
(off Congreve St.)
Detling Rd.
BR1: Brom 5C 124

Detmold Rd. E5 . . . . .4E 37
Devane Way SE27 . . . . . .3D 119
Devas St. E3 . . . . .3D 67
Devenay Rd. E15 . . . . . . .4B 54
Deventer Cres.
SE22 . . . . .3A 106
De Vere Cotts. W8 . . . . . .4E 73
(off Canning Pl.)
De Vere Gdns. W8 . . . . . .3E 73
Deverell St.
SE1 . . . . . . .5B 26 (4F 77)
Devereux Ct. W8 . . . . . . .4E 73
(off Canning Pl.)
Devereux Ct. WC2 . . . . . .3B 16
Devereux La. SW13 . . . . .3D 85
Devereux Rd. SW11 . . . . .4B 102
Devitt Ho. E14 . . . . .1D 81
(off Wade's Pl.)
Devizes St. N1 . . . . .5F 49
Devon Gdns. N4 . . . . .1D 35
Devon Ho. N1 . . . . .1D 63
(off Upper St.)
Devonia Rd. N1 . . . . .1D 63
Devon Mans. SE1 . . . . . . .3F 27
(off Tooley St.)
Devonport W2 . . . . .5A 60
Devonport Ho. W2 . . . . . .4C 58
(off Gt. Western Rd.)
Devonport M. W12 . . . . . .3D 71
Devonport Rd. W12 . . . . .2D 71
(not continuous)
Devonport St. E1 . . . . . . .5E 65
Devons Est. E3 . . . . .2D 67
Devonshire Cl. E15 . . . . . .1A 54
W1 . . . . .5D 5 (4D 61)
Devonshire Ct. E1 . . . . . . .2E 65
(off Bancroft Rd.)
WC1 . . . . .5E 7
(off Boswell St.)
Devonshire Dr. SE10 . . . .3D 95
Devonshire Gro.
SE15 . . . . .2D 93
Devonshire Hall E9 . . . . . .3E 51
(off Frampton Pk. Rd.)
Devonshire Ho. E14 . . . . .5C 80
(off Westferry Rd.)
NW6 . . . . .3B 44
(off Kilburn High Rd.)
SE1 . . . . .5F 25
(off Bath Ter.)
SW1 . . . . .1F 89
(off Lindsay Sq.)
SW15 . . . . .3F 99
W2 . . . . .4F 59
(off Adpar St.)
Devonshire M. SW10 . . . . .2F 87
(off Park Wlk.)
W4 . . . . .1A 84
Devonshire M. Nth.
W1 . . . . .5D 5 (4D 61)
Devonshire M. Sth.
W1 . . . . .5D 5 (4D 61)
Devonshire M. W.
W1 . . . . .4C 4 (3C 60)
Devonshire Pas. W4 . . . . .1A 84
Devonshire Pl. NW2 . . . . .5C 30
W1 . . . . .4C 4 (3C 60)
W8 . . . . .4D 73
Devonshire Pl. M.
W1 . . . . .4C 4 (4C 60)

Devonshire Rd. E16 . . . . .5D **69**
  E17 . . . . .1C **38**
  SE9 . . . . .2F **125**
  SE23 . . . . .1E **121**
  W4 . . . . .1A **84**
Devonshire Road
  Nature Reserve . .5F **107**
Devonshire Road
  Nature Reserve Vis. Cen.
   . . . . .5F **107**
Devonshire Row
  EC2 . . . . . .1E **19** (4A **64**)
Devonshire Row M.
  W1 . . . . .4E **5**
Devonshire Sq.
  EC2 . . . . . .1E **19** (5A **64**)
Devonshire St.
  W1 . . . . . . .5C **4** (4C **60**)
  W4 . . . . .1A **84**
Devonshire Ter. W2 . . .5E **59**
Devon St. SE15 . . . . . . .2D **93**
Devon Wharf E14 . . . . . .4F **67**
De Walden Ho. NW8 . . . .1A **60**
  (off Allitsen Rd.)
De Walden St.
  W1 . . . . . . .1C **12** (4C **60**)
Dewar St. SE15 . . . . . . .1C **106**
Dewberry Gdns. E6 . . . . .4F **69**
Dewberry St. E14 . . . . . .4E **67**
Dewey La. SW2 . . . . . . .4C **104**
  (off Tulse Hill)
Dewey Rd. N1 . . . . .1C **62**
Dewey St. SW17 . . . . . .5B **116**
Dewhurst Rd. W14 . . . . .4F **71**
Dewsbury Rd. NW10 . . . .2C **42**
Dewsbury Ter. NW1 . . . . .5D **47**
Dexter Apartments
  SE16 . . . . .4D **93**
  (off Eleanor Cl.)
D'Eynsford Rd. SE5 . . . .4F **91**
Dhonau Ho. SE1 . . . . . . .5B **78**
  (off Longfield Est.)
Diadem Ct. W1 . . . . .2B **14**
Dial Walk, The W8 . . . .3D **73**
Diamond Est. SW17 . . . .3A **116**
Diamond Ho. E3 . . . . . . .1A **66**
  (off Roman Rd.)
Diamond St. SE15 . . . . .3A **92**
Diamond Ter. SE10 . . . . .4E **95**
Diamond Way SE8 . . . . .2C **94**
Diana Cl. SE8 . . . . .2B **94**
Diana Ho. SW13 . . . . . . .4B **84**
Diana, Princess of Wales
  Memorial Playground
   . . . . .2D **73**
Diana, Princess of Wales
  Memorial Walk . . .2E **73**
  (in Kensington Gdns.)
Dianne Ct. SE12 . . . . . .1C **124**
Dibden Ho. SE5 . . . . . . .3A **92**
Dibden St. N1 . . . . .5E **49**
Dibdin Ho. W9 . . . . .1D **59**
Dibdin Row
  SE1 . . . . . . .5C **24** (4C **76**)
Dicey Av. NW2 . . . . .1E **43**
Dickens Est. SE1 . . . . . .3C **78**
  SE16 . . . . .4C **78**

Dickens Ho. NW6 . . . . . .2C **58**
  (off Malvern Rd.)
  NW8 . . . . .3F **59**
  (off Fisherton St.)
  SE17 . . . . .1D **91**
  (off Doddington Gro.)
  WC1 . . . . .3D **7**
Dickens M. EC1 . . . . . . .5D **9**
  (off Turnmill St.)
Dickenson Rd. N8 . . . . .2A **34**
Dickens Rd. E6 . . . . .1F **69**
Dickens Sq.
  SE1 . . . . . . .5A **26** (4E **77**)
Dickens St. SW8 . . . . . .5D **89**
Dickinson Ct. EC1 . . . . . .3E **9**
  (off Brewhouse Yd.)
Dicksee Ho. NW8 . . . . . .3F **59**
  (off Lyons Pl.)
Dickson Ho. E1 . . . . . . .5D **65**
  (off Philpot St.)
  N1 . . . . .4C **48**
  (off Drummond Way)
Dickson Rd. SE9 . . . . . .1F **111**
Dieppe Cl. W14 . . . . . . .1B **86**
Digby Bus. Cen. E9 . . . . .3F **51**
  (off Digby Rd.)
Digby Cres. N4 . . . . .4E **35**
Digby Mans. W6 . . . . . . .1D **85**
  (off Hammersmith Bri. Rd.)
Digby Rd. E9 . . . . .3F **51**
Digby St. E2 . . . . .2E **65**
Diggon St. E1 . . . . .4F **65**
Dighton Ct. SE5 . . . . . . .2E **91**
Dighton Rd. SW18 . . . . .3E **101**
Dignum St. N1 . . . . .1C **62**
Digswell St. N7 . . . . .3C **48**
Dilhorne Cl. SE12 . . . . . .3D **125**
Dilke St. SW3 . . . . .2B **88**
Dillwyn Cl. SE26 . . . . . . .4A **122**
Dilston Gro. SE16 . . . . . .5E **79**
Dilton Gdns. SW15 . . . . .1C **112**
Dimes Pl. W6 . . . . .5D **71**
Dimond Cl. E7 . . . . .1C **54**
Dimsdale Hgts. E1 . . . . .5D **65**
  (off Spencer Way)
Dimsdale Wlk. E13 . . . . .1C **68**
Dimson Cres. E3 . . . . . . .2C **66**
Dinerman Ct. NW8 . . . . .5E **45**
Dingle Gdns. E14 . . . . . .1C **80**
Dingley La. SW16 . . . . . .2F **117**
Dingley Pl.
  EC1 . . . . . . .1A **10** (2E **63**)
Dingley Rd.
  EC1 . . . . . . .2F **9** (2E **63**)
Dingwall Gdns.
  NW11 . . . . .1C **30**
Dingwall Rd. SW18 . . . .5E **101**
Dinmont Est. E2 . . . . . . .1C **64**
Dinmont Ho. E2 . . . . . . .1C **64**
  (off Pritchard's Rd.)
Dinmont St. E2 . . . . .1D **65**
Dinmore Ho. E9 . . . . . . .5E **51**
  (off Templecombe Rd.)
Dinnington Ho. E1 . . . . .3D **65**
  (off Coventry Rd.)
Dinsdale Rd. SE3 . . . . . .2B **96**
Dinsmore Rd.
  SW12 . . . . .5D **103**
Dinton Ho. NW8 . . . . . . .3A **60**
  (off Lilestone St.)

Dinton Rd. SW19 . . . . . .5F **115**
Diprose Lodge
  SW17 . . . . .4F **115**
Dirleton Rd. E15 . . . . . . .5B **54**
Disbrowe Rd. W6 . . . . . .2A **86**
Discover 4F **53**
Discover Greenwich Vis. Cen.
   . . . . .2E **95**
Discovery Bus. Pk.
  SE16 . . . . .4C **78**
  (off St James's Rd.)
Discovery Dock Apartments E.
  E14 . . . . .3D **81**
  (off Sth. Quay Sq.)
Discovery Dock
  Apartments W.
  E14 . . . . .3D **81**
  (off Sth. Quay Sq.)
Discovery Ho. E14 . . . . .1E **81**
  (off Newby Pl.)
Discovery Wlk. E1 . . . . .2D **79**
Disney Pl.
  SE1 . . . . . . .3A **26** (3E **77**)
Disney St.
  SE1 . . . . . . .3A **26** (3E **77**)
Disraeli Gdns.
  SW15 . . . . .2B **100**
Disraeli Rd. E7 . . . . .3C **54**
  SW15 . . . . .2A **100**
Diss St. E2 . . . . .1F **11** (2B **64**)
Distaff La.
  EC4 . . . . . . .4F **17** (1E **77**)
Distillery, The SE8 . . . . .4C **94**
Distillery La. W6 . . . . . . .1E **85**
Distillery Rd. W6 . . . . . . .1E **85**
Distin St. SE11 . . . . .5C **76**
Ditch All. SE13 . . . . .4D **95**
Ditchburn St. E14 . . . . . .1E **81**
Dittisham Rd. SE9 . . . . .4F **125**
Divis Way SW15 . . . . . . .4D **99**
  (off Dover Pk. Dr.)
Dixon Clark Ct. N1 . . . . .3D **49**
Dixon Ho. W10 . . . . .5F **57**
  (off Darfield Way)
Dixon Rd. SE14 . . . . . . .4A **94**
Dixon's All. SE16 . . . . . .3D **79**
Dixon Way NW10 . . . . . .4A **42**
Dobree Av. NW10 . . . . . .4D **43**
Dobson Cl. NW6 . . . . . . .4F **45**
Dobson Ho. SE14 . . . . . .2F **93**
  (off John Williams Cl.)
Doby Ct. EC4 . . . . .4A **18**
Dock Cotts. E1 . . . . .1E **79**
  (off The Highway)
Dockers Tanner Rd.
  E14 . . . . .4C **80**
Dockhead SE1 . . . . .3B **78**
Dockhead Wharf SE1 . . .4F **27**
  (off Shad Thames)
Dock Hill Av. SE16 . . . . .2F **79**
Docklands Ct. E14 . . . . .5B **66**
  (off Wharf La.)
Docklands Sailing Cen.
   . . . . .4C **80**
Dockley Rd. SE16 . . . . . .4C **78**
Dockley Rd. Ind. Est.
  SE16 . . . . .4C **78**
  (off Dockley Rd.)
Dock Offices SE16 . . . . .4E **79**
  (off Surrey Quays Rd.)

Dock Rd. E16 . . . . .1B 82
Dockside Ct. E5 . . . . . . .4E 37
Dockside Rd. E16 . . . . .1F 83
Dock St. E1 . . . . .1C 78
Doctor Johnson Av.
 SW17 . . . . .3D 117
Dr Johnson's House . . .3C 16
 (off Pemberton Row)
Doctors Cl. SE26 . . . . .5E 121
Docura Ho. N7 . . . . . . .4B 34
Docwra's Bldgs. N1 . . . .3A 50
Dodbrooke Rd.
 SE27 . . . . .3C 118
Dodd Ho. SE16 . . . . . . .5D 79
 (off Rennie Est.)
Doddington Gro.
 SE17 . . . . .2D 91
Doddington Pl. SE17 . . .2D 91
Dodson St.
 SE1 . . . . . .4C 24 (3C 76)
Dod St. E14 . . . . .5B 66
Dog & Duck Yd. WC1 . . .5A 8
Doggett Rd. SE6 . . . . . .5C 108
Dog Kennel Hill
 SE22 . . . . .1A 106
Dog Kennel Hill Est.
 SE22 . . . . .1A 106
 (off Albrighton Rd.)
Dog La. NW10 . . . . . . .1A 42
Doherty Rd. E13 . . . . . .3C 68
Dolben Ct. SW1 . . . . . . .5F 75
 (off Montaigne Cl.)
Dolben St.
 SE1 . . . . .2D 25 (2D 77)
 (not continuous)
Dolby Rd. SW6 . . . . . . .5B 86
Dolland Ho. SE11 . . . . . .1B 90
 (off Newburn St.)
Dolland St. SE11 . . . . . .1B 90
Dollar Bay Ct. E14 . . . . .3E 81
 (off Lawn Ho. Cl.)
DOLLIS HILL 4D 29
Dollis Hill Av. NW2 . . . .5D 29
Dollis Hill La. NW2 . . . .1B 42
Dolman Rd. W4 . . . . . . .5A 70
Dolman St. SW4 . . . . . .2B 104
Dolphin Cl. SE16 . . . . . .3F 79
Dolphin Ct. NW11 . . . . .1A 30
Dolphin Ho. SW6 . . . . . .5E 87
 (off Lensbury Av.)
 SW18 . . . . .2D 101
Dolphin La. E14 . . . . . .1D 81
Dolphin Sq. SW1 . . . . . .1E 89
 W4 . . . . .3A 84
Dolphin Twr. SE8 . . . . . .2B 94
 (off Abinger Gro.)
Dombey Ho. SE1 . . . . . .3C 78
 (off Wolseley St.)
 W11 . . . . .2F 71
 (off St Ann's Rd.)
Dombey St.
 WC1 . . . . . .5F 7 (4B 62)
 (not continuous)
Domecq Ho. EC1 . . . . . .3E 9
 (off Dallington St.)
Dome Hill Pk. SE26 . . .4B 120
Domelton Ho.
 SW18 . . . . .4D 101
 (off Iron Mill Rd.)
Domett Cl. SE5 . . . . . . .2F 105

Domino Pl. E5 . . . . .1E 51
Domingo St.
 EC1 . . . . . . .3F 9 (3E 63)
Dominica Cl. E13 . . . . . .1F 69
Dominion Cl. E8 . . . . . .4B 50
 (off Middleton Rd.)
Dominion Ho. E14 . . . . .1D 95
 (off St Davids Sq.)
Dominion St.
 EC2 . . . . .5C 10 (4F 63)
Dominion Theatre 2C 14
 (off Tottenham Ct. Rd.)
Domville Ct. SE17 . . . . .1A 92
 (off Bagshott St.)
Donald Hunter Ho.
 E7 . . . . .2D 55
 (off Woodgrange Rd.)
Donald Rd. E13 . . . . . .5D 55
Donaldson Rd. NW6 . . . .5B 44
Donato Dr. SE15 . . . . . .2A 92
Doncaster Gdns. N4 . . . .1E 35
Donegal Ho. E1 . . . . . . .3D 65
 (off Cambridge Heath Rd.)
Donegal St. N1 . . . . . . .1B 62
Doneraile Ho. SW1 . . . .1D 89
 (off Ebury Bri. Rd.)
Doneraile St. SW6 . . . . .5F 85
Dongola Rd. E1 . . . . . . .4A 66
 E13 . . . . .2D 69
Dongola Rd. W. E13 . . .2D 69
Don Gratton Ho. E1 . . . .4C 64
 (off Old Montague St.)
Donkey All. SE22 . . . . . .5C 106
Donkin Ho. SE16 . . . . . .5D 79
 (off Rennie Est.)
Donmar Warehouse Theatre
 . . . . .3D 15
 (off Earlham St.)
Donnatt's Rd. SE14 . . . .4B 94
Donne Ct. SE24 . . . . . . .4E 105
Donne Ho. E14 . . . . . . .5C 66
 (off Dod St.)
 SE14 . . . . .2F 93
 (off Samuel Cl.)
Donnelly Ct. SW6 . . . . . .3A 86
 (off Dawes Rd.)
Donnelly Ho. SE1 . . . . . .4C 76
 (off Cosser St.)
Donne Pl. SW3 . . . . . . .5A 74
Donnington Ct. NW1 . . .4D 47
 (off Castlehaven Rd.)
 NW10 . . . . .4D 43
 (off Donnington Rd.)
Donnington Mans.
 NW10 . . . . .5E 43
 (off Donnington Rd.)
Donnington Rd.
 NW10 . . . . .4D 43
Donnybrook Ct. E3 . . . .5B 52
 (off Old Ford Rd.)
Donoghue Bus. Pk.
 NW2 . . . . .5F 29
Donoghue Cotts. E14 . . .4B 66
 (off Galsworthy Av.)
Donovan Ct. SW10 . . . .1F 87
 (off Drayton Gdns.)
Donovan Ho. E1 . . . . . .1E 79
 (off Cable St.)
Don Phelan Cl. SE5 . . . .4F 91
Doon St. SE1 . . .2B 24 (2C 76)

Dora Ho. E14 . . . . .5B 66
 (off Rhodeswell Rd.)
 W11 . . . . .1F 71
 (off St Ann's Rd.)
Dorando Cl. W12 . . . . . .1D 71
Doran Mnr. N2 . . . . . . .1B 32
 (off Great Nth. Rd.)
Doran Wlk. E15 . . . . . . .4E 53
Dora Rd. SW19 . . . . . . .5C 114
Dora St. E14 . . . . .5B 66
Dora Way SW9 . . . . . . .5C 90
Dorchester Ct. N1 . . . . .4A 50
 (off Englefield Rd.)
 NW2 . . . . .5F 29
 SE24 . . . . .3E 105
 SW1 . . . . .5A 20
 (off Sloane St.)
Dorchester Dr. SE24 . . .3E 105
Dorchester Gro. W4 . . .1A 84
Dorchester Ter. NW2 . . .5F 29
 (off Needham Ter.)
Dordrecht Rd. W3 . . . . .2A 70
Doreen Av. NW9 . . . . . .3A 28
Doreen Capstan Ho.
 E11 . . . . .5A 40
 (off Apollo Pl.)
Doria Rd. SW6 . . . . .5B 86
Doric Ho. E2 . . . . .1F 65
 (off Mace St.)
Doric Way
 NW1 . . . . . . .1B 6 (2F 61)
Doris Emmerton Ct.
 SW11 . . . . .2E 101
Doris Rd. E7 . . . . .4C 54
Dorking Cl. SE8 . . . . . . .2B 94
Dorking Ho.
 SE1 . . . . .5C 26 (4F 77)
Dorlcote Rd. SW18 . . . .5A 102
Dorman Way NW8 . . . . .5F 45
Dorma Trad. Pk. E10 . . .3F 37
Dormay St. SW18 . . . . .3D 101
Dormer Cl. E15 . . . . . . .3B 54
Dormstone Ho.
 SE17 . . . . .5A 78
 (off Congreve St.)
Dornberg Cl. SE3 . . . . . .3C 96
Dornberg Rd. SE3 . . . . .3D 97
Dorncliffe Rd. SW6 . . . .5A 86
Dorney NW3 . . . . .4A 46
Dornfell St. NW6 . . . . . .2B 44
Dornoch Ho. E3 . . . . . . .1B 66
 (off Anglo Rd.)
Dornton Rd. SW12 . . . .2D 117
Dorothy Rd. SW11 . . . .1B 102
Dorrell Pl. SW9 . . . . . . .1C 104
Dorrien Wlk. SW16 . . . .2F 117
Dorrington Point E3 . . . .2D 67
 (off Bromley High St.)
Dorrington St.
 EC1 . . . . . . .5B 8 (4C 62)
Dorrit Ho. W11 . . . . .2F 71
 (off St Ann's Rd.)
Dorrit St.
 SE1 . . . . . . .3A 26 (3E 77)
Dorryn Ct. SE26 . . . . . . .5F 121
Dors Cl. NW9 . . . . .3A 28
Dorset Bldgs.
 EC4 . . . . . . .3D 17 (5D 63)
Dorset Cl.
 NW1 . . . . . . .5A 4 (4B 60)

Dorset Ct. *N1* 4A **50**
   (off Hertford Rd.)
Dorset Ho. *NW1* 5A **4**
   (off Gloucester Pl.)
Dorset Mans. *SW6* 2F **85**
   (off Lillie Rd.)
Dorset M.
   SW1 . . . . .5D **21** (4D **75**)
Dorset Ri.
   EC4 . . . . .3D **17** (5D **63**)
Dorset Rd. E7 . . . . .4E **55**
   SE9 . . . . .2F **125**
   SW8 . . . . .3A **90**
Dorset Sq.
   NW1 . . . . . . .4A **4** (3B **60**)
Dorset St.
   W1 . . . . .1A **12** (4B **60**)
Dorset Wharf *W6* 3E **85**
   (off Rainville Rd.)
Dorton Cl. SE15 . . . . . . .3A **92**
Dorville Cres. W6 . . . . . .4D **71**
Dorville Rd. SE12 . . . . . .3B **110**
Doughty Ct. *E1* 2D **79**
   (off Prusom St.)
Doughty Ho. *SW10* 2E **87**
   (off Netherton Gro.)
Doughty M.
   WC1 . . . . . . .4F **7** (3B **62**)
Doughty St.
   WC1 . . . . . . .3F **7** (3B **62**)
Douglas Ct. *NW6* 4C **44**
   (off Quex Rd.)
Douglas Est. *N1* 3E **49**
   (off Oransay Rd.)
Douglas Eyre Sports Cen.
   . . . . .1F **37**
Douglas Johnstone Ho.
   SW6 . . . . .2B **86**
   (off Clem Attlee Ct.)
Douglas M. NW2 . . . . . . .5A **30**
Douglas Path *E14* 1E **95**
   (off Manchester Rd.)
Douglas Rd. E16 . . . . . . .4C **68**
   N1 . . . . .4E **49**
   NW6 . . . . .5B **44**
Douglas Rd. Nth.
   N1 . . . . .3E **49**
Douglas Rd. Sth. N1 . . . . .3E **49**
Douglas St. SW1 . . . . . . .5F **75**
Douglas Waite Ho.
   NW6 . . . . .4C **44**
Douglas Way SE8 . . . . . . .3B **94**
   (Stanley St.)
   SE8 . . . . .3C **94**
   (Watsons St.)
Doulton Ho. *SE11* 4B **76**
   (off Lambeth Wlk.)
Doulton M. NW6 . . . . . . .3D **45**
Dounesforth Gdns.
   SW18 . . . . .1D **115**
Douro Pl. W8 . . . . .4D **73**
Douro St. E3 . . . . .1C **66**
Douthwaite Sq. E1 . . . . . .2C **78**
Dove App. E6 . . . . .4F **69**
Dove Commercial Cen.
   NW5 . . . . .2E **47**
Dovecote Gdns.
   SW14 . . . . .1A **98**
Dovecote Ho. *SE16* 3F **79**
   (off Water Gdns. Sq.)

Dovedale Bus. Est.
   SE15 . . . . .5C **92**
   (off Blenheim Gro.)
Dovedale Rd. SE22 . . .3D **107**
Dovehouse St.
   SW3 . . . . .1F **87**
Dove M. SW5 . . . . .5E **73**
Dover Cl. NW2 . . . . .4F **29**
Dover Ct. EC1 . . . . .3D **9**
   (off St John St.)
   N1 . . . . .4F **49**
   (off Southgate Rd.)
Dovercourt Est. N1 . . . . . .3F **49**
Dovercourt Rd.
   SE22 . . . . .4A **106**
Doverfield Rd. SW2 . . . . .5A **104**
Dover Flats SE1 . . . . .5A **78**
Dover Ho. SE15 . . . . .2E **93**
Dover Ho. Rd. SW15 . . . . .2C **98**
Dove Rd. N1 . . . . .3F **49**
Dove Row E2 . . . . .5C **50**
Dover Pk. Dr. SW15 . . . . .4D **99**
Dover Patrol SE3 . . . . . . .5D **97**
Dover Rd. E12 . . . . .4E **41**
   SE19 . . . . .5F **119**
Dover St. W1 . . . .5E **13** (1D **75**)
Doves Yd. N1 . . . . .5C **48**
Dover Yd. W1 . . . . .1F **21**
Dovet Ct. SW9 . . . . .4B **90**
Doveton Ho. *E1* 3E **65**
   (off Doveton St.)
Doveton St. E1 . . . . .3E **65**
Dove Wlk. SW1 . . . . .1C **88**
Dovey Lodge *N1* 4C **48**
   (off Bewdley St.)
Dovoll Ct. *SE16* 4C **78**
   (off Marine St.)
Dowanhill Rd. SE6 . . . . .1F **123**
Dowdeswell Cl.
   SW15 . . . . .2A **98**
Dowding Dr. SE9 . . . . . .3E **111**
Dowding Ho. *N6* 2C **32**
   (off Hillcrest)
Dowdney Cl. NW5 . . . . . .2E **47**
Dowe Ho. SE3 . . . . .1A **110**
Dowes Ho. SW16 . . . . . .3A **118**
Dowgate Hill
   EC4 . . . . .4B **18** (1F **77**)
Dowland St. W10 . . . . . .2A **58**
Dowlas St. SE5 . . . . .3A **92**
Dowler Ho. *E1* 5C **64**
   (off Burslem St.)
Downbarton Ho. *SW9* . .4C **90**
   (off Gosling Way)
Downbury M. SW18 . . .3C **100**
Downderry Rd.
   BR1: Brom 3F **123**
Downend Ct. *SE15* 2A **92**
   (off Bibury Cl.)
Downer's Cott. SW4 . . .2E **103**
Downesbury *NW3* 3B **46**
   (off Steele's Rd.)
Downey Ho. *E1* 3F **65**
   (off Globe Rd.)
Downfield Cl. W9 . . . . . . .3D **59**
DOWNHAM 5F **123**
Downham Ct. *N1* 4F **49**
   (off Downham Rd.)
Downham Ent. Cen.
   SE6 . . . . .2B **124**

Downham Health &
   Leisure Cen. 4B **124**
Downham La.
   BR1: Brom 5F **123**
Downham Rd. N1 . . . . . .4F **49**
Downham Way
   BR1: Brom 5F **123**
Downing Cl. *WC1* 4E **7**
   (off Grenville St.)
Downing Ho. *SW5* 5F **57**
   (off Cambridge Gdns.)
Downing St.
   SW1 . . . . . .3D **23** (3A **76**)
Downland Cl. E11 . . . . . . .4A **40**
Down Pl. W6 . . . . .5D **71**
Downs Ct. Pde. E8 . . . . . .2D **51**
   (off Amhurst Rd.)
Downsell Rd. E15 . . . . . . .1E **53**
Downsfield Rd. E17 . . . . .1A **38**
Downshire Hill NW3 . . . . .1F **45**
Downside Cres. NW3 . . . .2A **46**
Downs La. E5 . . . . .1D **51**
Downs Pk. Rd. E5 . . . . . . .2B **50**
   E8 . . . . .2B **50**
Downs Rd. E5 . . . . .1C **50**
Down St. W1 . . . .2D **21** (2D **75**)
Down St. M.
   W1 . . . . .2D **21** (2D **75**)
Downton Av. SW2 . . . . . .2A **118**
Downtown Rd. SE16 . . . . .3A **80**
Dowrey St. N1 . . . . .5C **48**
Dowson Cl. SE5 . . . . . . .2F **105**
Dowson Ho. *E1* 5F **65**
   (off Bower St.)
Doyce St.
   SE1 . . . . . . .3F **25** (3E **77**)
Doyle Gdns. NW10 . . . . . .5C **42**
Doyle Ho. *SW13* 3E **85**
   (off Trinity Chu. Rd.)
D'Oyley St. SW1 . . . . .5C **74**
Doynton St. N19 . . . . .4D **33**
Draco Ga. SW15 . . . . .1E **99**
Draco St. SE17 . . . . .2E **91**
Dragmore St. SW4 . . . . .4F **103**
Dragonfly Cl. E13 . . . . . . .2D **69**
Dragon Rd. SE15 . . . . . . .2A **92**
Dragon Yd.
   WC1 . . . . . .2E **15** (5A **62**)
Dragoon Rd. SE8 . . . . . . .1B **94**
Drake Cl. SE16 . . . . .3F **79**
Drake Ct. *SE1* 4A **26**
   (off Swan St.)
   SE19 . . . . .5B **120**
   W12 . . . . .3E **71**
   (off Scott's Rd.)
Drakefell Rd. SE4 . . . . . . .5F **93**
   SE14 . . . . .5F **93**
Drakefield Rd.
   SW17 . . . . .3C **116**
Drake Hall *E16* 2D **83**
   (off Wesley Av.)
Drake Ho. *E1* 4E **65**
   (off Stepney Way)
   E14 . . . . .1A **80**
   (off Victory Pl.)
   SW1 . . . . .2F **89**
   (off Dolphin Sq.)
Drakeland Ho. W9 . . . . . .3B **58**
   (off Fernhead Rd.)
Drakeley Ct. N5 . . . . .1D **49**

Drake Rd. SE4 . . . . . . .1C **108**
Drakes, The SE8 . . . . . .2C **94**
Drakes Ct. SE23 . . . . . .1E **121**
Drakes Courtyard
  NW6 . . . . .4B **44**
Drake St.
  WC1 . . . . . .1F **15** (4B **62**)
Draper Ho. SE1 . . . . . . .5D **77**
  (off Newington Butts)
Draper Pl. N1 . . . . .5D **49**
  (off Dagmar Ter.)
Drapers Almshouses
  E3 . . . . .2D **67**
  (off Rainhill Way)
Draper's Ct. SW11 . . . . .4C **88**
  (off Battersea Pk. Rd.)
Drapers Gdns.
  EC2 . . . . . .2C **18** (5F **63**)
Drapers Rd. E15 . . . . . . .1F **53**
Drappers Way SE16 . . . .5C **78**
Drawdock Rd. SE10 . . . .3F **81**
Draxmont SW19 . . . . . .5A **114**
Draycot Rd. E11 . . . . . . .1D **41**
Draycott Av. SW3 . . . . . .5A **74**
Draycott Cl. NW2 . . . . . .5F **29**
  SE5 . . . . .3F **91**
  (not continuous)
Draycott Ct. SW11 . . . . .4A **88**
  (off Westbridge Rd.)
Draycott M. SW6 . . . . . .5B **86**
  (off Laurel Bank Gdns.)
Draycott Pl. SW3 . . . . . .5B **74**
Draycott Ter. SW3 . . . . . .5B **74**
Drayford Cl. W9 . . . . . . .3B **58**
Dray Gdns. SW2 . . . . . . .3B **104**
Drayson M. W8 . . . . . . .3C **72**
Drayton Gdns.
  SW10 . . . . .1E **87**
Drayton Ho. E11 . . . . . . .3F **39**
  SE5 . . . . .3F **91**
  (off Elmington Rd.)
Drayton Pk. N5 . . . . .1C **48**
Drayton Pk. M. N5 . . . . .2C **48**
Drayton Rd. E11 . . . . . . .3F **39**
  NW10 . . . . .5B **42**
Dray Wlk. E1 . . . .4F **11** (3B **64**)
Dreadnought St.
  SE10 . . . . .4A **82**
Dresden Cl. NW6 . . . . . .3D **45**
Dresden Ho. SE11 . . . . .5B **76**
  (off Lambeth Wlk.)
  SW11 . . . . .5C **88**
  (off Dagnall St.)
Dresden Rd. N19 . . . . . .3E **33**
Dressington Av.
  SE4 . . . . .4C **108**
Drewery Ct. SE3 . . . . . .1A **110**
Drewett Ho. E1 . . . . .5C **64**
  (off Christian St.)
Drew Ho. SW16 . . . . . . .3A **118**
Drew Rd. E16 . . . . .2F **83**
  (not continuous)
Drewstead La.
  SW16 . . . . .2F **117**
Drewstead Rd.
  SW16 . . . . .2F **117**
Driffield Rd. E3 . . . . .1A **66**
Driftway Ho. E3 . . . . .1B **66**
  (off Stafford Rd.)

Drill Hall Arts 5B **91**
  (off Chenies St.)
Drinkwater Ho. SE5 . . . . .3F **91**
  (off Picton St.)
Drive, The N7 . . . . .3B **48**
  (not continuous)
  NW10 . . . . .5B **42**
  NW11 . . . . .2A **30**
  SW6 . . . . .5A **86**
Drive Mans. SW6 . . . . . .5A **86**
  (off Fulham Rd.)
Driveway, The E17 . . . . .1D **39**
  (off Hoe St.)
Droitwich Cl. SE26 . . . . .3C **120**
Dromore Rd. SW15 . . . . .4A **100**
Dron Ho. E1 . . . . .4E **65**
  (off Adelina Gro.)
Droop St. W10 . . . . .2F **57**
Drovers Pl. SE15 . . . . . .3E **93**
Drovers Way N7 . . . . . . .3A **48**
Druce Rd. SE21 . . . . . . .4A **106**
Druid St. SE1 . . .3E **27** (3A **78**)
  (not continuous)
Drummond Cres.
  NW1 . . . . .1B **6** (2F **61**)
Drummond Ga. SW1 . . . .1F **89**
Drummond Ho. E2 . . . . .1C **64**
  (off Goldsmiths Row)
Drummond Rd. E11 . . . . .1E **41**
  SE16 . . . . .4D **79**
Drummond St.
  NW1 . . . . .3F **5** (3E **61**)
Drummond Way
  N1 . . . . .4C **48**
Drury Ho. SW8 . . . . .4E **89**
Drury La.
  WC2 . . . . .2E **15** (5A **62**)
Drury Lane Theatre Royal
  . . . . .3E **15**
  (off Drury La.)
Drury Way NW10 . . . . . .2A **42**
Dryad St. SW15 . . . . . . .1F **99**
Dryburgh Rd. SW1 . . . . .1D **89**
  (part of Abbots Mnr.)
Dryburgh Rd. SW15 . . . .1D **99**
Dryden Bldg. E1 . . . . . . .5C **64**
  (off Commercial Rd.)
Dryden Cl. SW4 . . . . . . .3F **103**
Dryden Ct. SE11 . . . . . . .5D **77**
Dryden Mans. W14 . . . . .2A **86**
  (off Queen's Club Gdns.)
Dryden Rd. SW19 . . . . .5E **115**
Dryden St.
  WC2 . . . . .3E **15** (5A **62**)
Dryfield Wlk. SE8 . . . . . .2C **94**
Dryfield Rd. N8 . . . . .1A **34**
Drysdale Dwellings
  E8 . . . . .2B **50**
  (off Dunn St.)
Drysdale Pl.
  N1 . . . . .1E **11** (2A **64**)
Drysdale St.
  N1 . . . . .1E **11** (2A **64**)
Dublin Av. E8 . . . . .5C **50**
Ducaine Apartments
  E3 . . . . .2B **66**
  (off Merchant St.)
Ducal St. E2 . . . . .2B **64**
Du Cane Cl. W12 . . . . . .5E **57**
Du Cane Ct. SW17 . . . . .1C **116**

Du Cane Rd. W12 . . . . . .5B **56**
Ducavel Ho. SW2 . . . . . .1B **118**
Duchess M.
  W1 . . . . .1E **13** (4D **61**)
Duchess of Bedford Ho.
  W8 . . . . .3C **72**
  (off Duchess of Bedford's Wlk.)
Duchess of Bedford's Wlk.
  W8 . . . . .3C **72**
Duchess St.
  W1 . . . . .1E **13** (4D **61**)
Duchess Theatre 4F **15**
  (off Catherine St.)
Duchy St.
  SE1 . . . . . .1C **24** (2C **76**)
  (not continuous)
Ducie St. SW4 . . . . .2B **104**
Duckett M. N4 . . . . .1D **35**
Duckett Rd. N4 . . . . .1D **35**
Duckett's Apartments
  E3 . . . . .4B **52**
  (off Wick La.)
Duckett St. E1 . . . . .3F **65**
Duck La. W1 . . . . .3B **14**
Du Cros Rd. W3 . . . . . . .2A **70**
DUDDEN HILL 2D **43**
Dudden Hill La. 1B **42**
Dudden Hill Pde.
  NW10 . . . . .1B **42**
Duddington Cl. SE9 . . . . .4F **125**
Dudley Ct. W1 . . . . .5B **60**
  (off Up. Berkeley St.)
  WC2 . . . . . .2D **15** (5A **62**)
Dudley Ho. W2 . . . . .4F **59**
  (off Nth. Wharf Rd.)
Dudley M. SW2 . . . . .4C **104**
Dudley Rd. NW6 . . . . . . .1A **58**
  SW19 . . . . .5C **114**
Dudley St. W2 . . . . .4F **59**
Dudlington Rd. E5 . . . . . .4E **37**
Dudmaston M.
  SW3 . . . . .1F **87**
  (off Fulham Rd.)
Dudrich M. SE22 . . . . . .3B **106**
Duffell Ho. SE11 . . . . . . .1B **90**
  (off Loughborough St.)
Dufferin Av. EC1 . . . . . . .4B **10**
Dufferin Ct. EC1 . . . . . . .4B **10**
  (off Dufferin St.)
Dufferin St.
  EC1 . . . . . .4A **10** (3E **63**)
Duff St. E14 . . . . .5D **67**
Dufour's Pl.
  W1 . . . . .3A **14** (5E **61**)
Dufton Dwellings
  E15 . . . . .1A **54**
  (off High Rd. Leyton)
Dugard Way SE11 . . . . . .5D **77**
Dugdale Ct. NW10 . . . . .2D **57**
  (off Harrow Rd.)
Duggan Dr.
  BR7: Chst 5F **125**
Duke Humphrey Rd.
  SE3 . . . . .4A **96**
Duke of Clarence Ct.
  SE17 . . . . .1E **91**
  (off Manor Pl.)
Duke of Wellington Pl.
  SW1 . . . . . .3C **20** (3C **74**)

Duke of York Column
(Memorial) 2B 22
Duke of York Sq.
SW3 . . . . .1B 88
Duke of York's Theatre
. . . . .5D 15
(off St Martin's La.)
Duke of York St.
SW1 . . . . . .1A 22 (2E 75)
Duke Rd. W4 . . . . .1A 84
Duke's Av. W4 . . . . . . .1A 84
Dukes Ct. SE13 . . . . . .5E 95
SW14 . . . . .5A 84
W2 . . . . .1D 73
(off Moscow Rd.)
Duke's Head Yd. N6 . . .3D 33
Duke Shore Wharf
E14 . . . . .1B 80
Duke's Ho. SW1 . . . . . .5F 75
(off Vincent St.)
Dukes La. W8 . . . . .3D 73
Duke's La. Chambers
W8 . . . . .3D 73
(off Dukes La.)
Duke's La. Mans.
W8 . . . . .3D 73
(off Dukes La.)
Dukes Lodge W8 . . . . . .2B 72
(off Holland Wlk.)
Duke's M. W1 . . . . .2C 12
Dukes Pl.
EC3 . . . . . .3E 19 (5A 64)
Dukes Point N6 . . . . . . .3D 33
(off Dukes Head Yd.)
Duke's Rd.
WC1 . . . . . . .2C 6 (2F 61)
Dukesthorpe Rd.
SE26 . . . . .4F 121
Duke St.
W1 . . . . . .2C 12 (5C 60)
Duke St. Hill
SE1 . . . . . .1C 26 (2F 77)
Duke St. Mans. W1 . . . .3C 12
(off Duke St.)
Duke St. St James's
SW1 . . . . . .1A 22 (2E 75)
Duke's Yd.
W1 . . . . . .4C 12 (1C 74)
Dulas St. N4 . . . . .3B 34
Dulford St. W11 . . . . . .1A 72
Dulka Rd. SW11 . . . . . .3B 102
Dulverton NW1 . . . . . . .5E 47
(off Royal College St.)
Dulverton Mans. WC1 . . .4A 8
DULWICH 2A 120
Dulwich & Sydenham Hill
Golf Course 2B 120
Dulwich Bus. Cen.
SE23 . . . . .1F 121
Dulwich Comn.
SE21 . . . . .1A 120
SE22 . . . . .1A 120
Dulwich Lawn Cl.
SE22 . . . . .3B 106
Dulwich Leisure Cen.
. . . . .2C 106
Dulwich Oaks, The
SE21 . . . . .3B 120
Dulwich Picture Gallery
. . . . .5F 105

Dulwich Ri. Gdns.
SE22 . . . . .3B 106
Dulwich Rd. SE24 . . . .3C 104
Dulwich Upper Wood
Nature Pk. 5B 120
DULWICH VILLAGE . . .5A 106
Dulwich Village
SE21 . . . . .4F 105
Dulwich Wood Av.
SE19 . . . . .4A 120
Dulwich Wood Pk.
SE19 . . . . .4A 120
Dumain Ct. SE11 . . . . . .5D 77
(off Opal St.)
Dumbarton Ct. SW2 . . .4A 104
Dumbarton Rd.
SW2 . . . . .4A 104
Dumont Rd. N16 . . . . . .5A 36
Dumpton Pl. NW1 . . . . . .4C 46
Dunbar Rd. E7 . . . . .3C 54
Dunbar St. SE27 . . . . . .3E 119
Dunbar Twr. E8 . . . . . . .3B 50
(off Dalston Sq.)
Dunbar Wharf E14 . . . . .1B 80
(off Narrow St.)
Dunboyne Rd. NW3 . . . .2B 46
Dunbridge Ho. SW15 . . .4B 98
(off Highcliffe Dr.)
Dunbridge St. E2 . . . . . .3C 64
Duncan Ct. E14 . . . . . . .4E 67
(off Teviot St.)
Duncan Gro. W3 . . . . . .5A 56
Duncan Ho. NW3 . . . . . .4B 46
(off Fellows Rd.)
SW1 . . . . .1E 89
(off Dolphin Sq.)
Duncannon Ho. SW1 . . .1F 89
(off Lindsay Sq.)
Duncannon St.
WC2 . . . . . .5D 15 (1A 76)
Duncan Rd. E8 . . . . . . .5D 51
Duncan St. N1 . . . . .1D 63
Duncan Ter. N1 . . . . . . .1D 63
(not continuous)
Dunch St. E1 . . . . .5D 65
Duncombe Hill
SE23 . . . . .5A 108
Duncombe Rd. N19 . . . .3F 33
Duncrievie Rd.
SE13 . . . . .4F 109
Dundalk Ho. E1 . . . . . . .5E 65
(off Clark St.)
Dundalk Rd. SE4 . . . . . .1A 108
Dundas Ho. E2 . . . . .1E 65
(off Bishop's Way)
Dundas Rd. SE15 . . . . . .5E 93
Dundee Ct. E1 . . . . .2D 79
(off Wapping High St.)
SE1 . . . . .5D 27
(off Long La.)
Dundee Ho. W9 . . . . . . .2E 59
(off Maida Va.)
Dundee Rd. E13 . . . . . . .1D 69
Dundee St. E1 . . . . .2D 79
Dundee Wharf E14 . . . . .1B 80
Dundonald Rd. NW10 . . .5F 43
Dundry Ho. SE26 . . . . . .3C 120
Dunedin M. SW2 . . . . . .1A 118
Dunedin Rd. E10 . . . . . .5D 39
Dunelm Gro. SE27 . . . . .3E 119

Dunelm St. E1 . . . . .5F 65
Dunfield Gdns. SE6 . . . .5D 123
Dunfield Rd. SE6 . . . . . .5D 123
(not continuous)
Dunford Rd. N7 . . . . .1B 48
Dungarvan Av. SW15 . . .2C 98
Dunhill Point SW15 . . . .1C 112
Dunkery Rd. SE9 . . . . . .4F 125
Dunkirk Ho. SE1 . . . . . . .4C 26
(off Long La.)
Dunkirk St. SE27 . . . . . .4E 119
Dunlace Rd. E5 . . . . .1E 51
Dunlin Ho. SE16 . . . . . . .5F 79
(off Tawny Way)
Dunloe Ct. E2 . . . . .1B 64
Dunloe Pas. E2 . . . . .1B 64
(off Dunloe St.)
Dunloe St. E2 . . . . .1B 64
Dunlop Pl. SE16 . . . . . . .4B 78
Dunmore Point E2 . . . . . .2F 11
(off Gascoigne Pl.)
Dunmow Rd. NW6 . . . . . .5A 44
Dunmow St. SE11 . . . . . .1B 90
(off Newburn St.)
Dunmow Rd. E15 . . . . . .1F 53
Dunmow Wlk. N1 . . . . . . .5E 49
(off Popham St.)
Dunnage Cres. SE16 . . .5A 80
(not continuous)
Dunnett Ho. E3 . . . . .1B 66
(off Vernon Rd.)
Dunnico Ho. SE17 . . . . .1A 92
(off East St.)
Dunn's Pas. WC1 . . . . . .2E 15
Dunn St. E8 . . . . .2B 50
Dunollie Pl. NW5 . . . . . .2E 47
Dunollie Rd. NW5 . . . . . .2E 47
Dunoon Gdns. SE23 . . . .5F 107
Dunoon Ho. N1 . . . . .5B 48
(off Bemerton Est.)
Dunoon Rd. SE23 . . . . . .5E 107
Dunraven Rd. W12 . . . . .2C 70
Dunraven St.
W1 . . . . . .4A 12 (1B 74)
Dunsany Rd. W14 . . . . . .4F 71
Dunsford Way SW15 . . . .4D 99
Dunsmure Rd. N16 . . . . .3A 36
Dunstable M.
W1 . . . . .5C 4 (4C 60)
Dunstan Ho's. E1 . . . . . .4E 65
(off Stepney Grn.)
Dunstan Rd. NW11 . . . . .3B 30
Dunstan's Gro.
SE22 . . . . .4D 107
Dunstan's Rd. SE22 . . . .5C 106
Dunster Ct.
EC3 . . . . . .4E 19 (1A 78)
Dunster Gdns. NW6 . . . .4B 44
Dunster Ho. SE6 . . . . . . .3E 123
Dunsterville Way
SE1 . . . . . .4C 26 (3F 77)
Dunston Rd. E8 . . . . .5B 50
(not continuous)
SW11 . . . . .5C 88
Dunston St. E8 . . . . .5B 50
Dunton Ct. SE23 . . . . . . .2D 121
Dunton Rd. E10 . . . . . . .2D 39
SE1 . . . . .1B 92
Duntshill Rd. SW18 . . . .1D 115
Dunworth M. W11 . . . . . .5B 58

Duplex Ride
SW1 . . . . . .4A **20** (3B **74**)
Dupree Rd. SE7 . . . . . . .1D **97**
Durand Gdns. SW9 . . . . .4B **90**
Durands Wlk. SE16 . . . . .3B **80**
Durant St. E2 . . . . .1C **64**
Durban Ho. W12 . . . . . .1D **71**
(off White City Est.)
Durban Rd. E15 . . . . . . .4E **53**
SE27 . . . . .4E **119**
Durdans Ho. NW1 . . . . .4D **47**
(off Farrier St.)
Durell Ho. SE16 . . . . . . .3F **79**
(off Wolfe Cres.)
Durfey Pl. SE5 . . . . .3F **91**
Durford Cres. SW15 . . .1D **113**
Durham Ct. NW6 . . . . . .1C **58**
(off Kilburn Pk. Rd.)
Durham Hill
BR1: Brom 4B **124**
Durham Ho. NW8 . . . . . .2A **60**
(off Lorne Cl.)
Durham Ho. St. WC2 . . .5E **15**
Durham Pl. SW3 . . . . . . .1B **88**
Durham Rd. E12 . . . . . . .1F **55**
E16 . . . . .3A **68**
N7 . . . . .4B **34**
Durham Row E1 . . . . . . .4A **66**
Durham St. SE11 . . . . . . .1B **90**
Durham Ter. W2 . . . . . . .5D **59**
Durham Yd. E2 . . . . .2D **65**
Durley Ho. N16 . . . . .2A **36**
Durlston Rd. E5 . . . . .4C **36**
Durnford Ho. SE6 . . . . . .3E **123**
Durnford St. N15 . . . . . . .1A **36**
SE10 . . . . .2E **95**
Durning Rd. SE19 . . . . . .5F **119**
Durnsford Av. SW19 . . . .2C **114**
Durnsford Rd.
SW19 . . . . .2C **114**
Durrant Ho. EC1 . . . . . . .5B **10**
(off Chiswell St.)
Durrell Rd. SW6 . . . . . . .4B **86**
Durrels Ho. W14 . . . . . . .5B **72**
(off Warwick Gdns.)
Durrington Rd. E5 . . . . . .1A **52**
Durrington Twr. SW8 . . . .5E **89**
Durrisdeer Ho. NW2 . . . .1B **44**
(off Lyndale)
Dursley Cl. SE3 . . . . .5E **97**
Dursley Gdns. SE3 . . . . .4F **97**
Dursley Rd. SE3 . . . . .5E **97**
Durward Ho. W8 . . . . . . .3D **73**
(off Kensington Ct.)
Durward St. E1 . . . . .4D **65**
Durweston M. W1 . . . . . .5A **4**
Durweston St.
W1 . . . . . .1A **12** (4B **60**)
Dutch Yd. SW18 . . . . . . .3C **100**
Dutton St. SE10 . . . . .4E **95**
Duval Ho. N19 . . . . .4F **33**
(off Ashbrook Rd.)
Dye Ho. La. E3 . . . . .5C **52**
Dyer's Bldgs.
EC1 . . . . .1B **16** (4C **62**)
Dyers Hall Rd. E11 . . . . . .3A **40**
Dyers Hill Rd. E11 . . . . . .4F **39**
Dyers La. SW15 . . . . . . .2D **99**
Dylan Rd. SE24 . . . . . . .2D **105**

Dylways SE5 . . . . .2F **105**
Dymes Path SW19 . . . . .2F **113**
Dymock St. SW6 . . . . . .1D **101**
Dyneley Rd. SE12 . . . . .3E **125**
Dyne Rd. NW6 . . . . .4A **44**
Dynevor Rd. N16 . . . . . . .5A **36**
Dynham Rd. NW6 . . . . . .4C **44**
Dyott St. WC1 . . .2C **14** (5F **61**)
Dysart St.
EC2 . . . . . .4D **11** (3F **63**)
Dyson Ct. NW2 . . . . .3E **29**
Dyson Ho. SE10 . . . . .1B **96**
(off Blackwall La.)
Dyson Rd. E11 . . . . .1A **40**
E15 . . . . .3B **54**

E

Eade Rd. N4 . . . . .2E **35**
Eagle Cl. SE16 . . . . .1E **93**
Eagle Ct. EC1 . . . .5D **9** (4D **63**)
Eagle Dwellings EC1 . . .1A **10**
(off City Rd.)
Eagle Hgts. SW11 . . . . .1A **102**
Eagle Hill SE19 . . . . . . .5F **119**
Eagle Ho. E1 . . . . .3D **65**
(off Headlam St.)
N1 . . . . .1F **63**
(off Eagle Wharf Rd.)
Eagle Ho. M. SW4 . . . . .3E **103**
Eagle Lodge NW11 . . . . .2B **30**
Eagle Mans. N16 . . . . . . .2B **50**
(off Salcombe Rd.)
Eagle M. N1 . . . . .3A **50**
Eagle Pl. SW1 . . . . .5A **14**
SW7 . . . . .1E **87**
Eagle St.
WC1 . . . . . .1F **15** (4B **62**)
Eagle Wharf Ct. SE1 . . . .2F **27**
(off Lafone St.)
Eagle Wharf E. E14 . . . . .1A **80**
(off Narrow St.)
Eagle Wharf Rd. N1 . . . . .1E **63**
Eagle Wharf W. E14 . . . .1A **80**
(off Narrow St.)
Eagle Works E. E1 . . . . . .4F **11**
Eagle Works W. E1 . . . . .4F **11**
Eagling Cl. E3 . . . . .2C **66**
Ealdham Sq. SE9 . . . . . .2E **111**
Eamont Ct. NW8 . . . . . . .1A **60**
(off Eamont St.)
Eamont St. NW8 . . . . . . .1A **60**
Eardley Cres. SW5 . . . . . .1C **86**
Eardley Rd. SW16 . . . . . .5E **117**
Earldom Rd. SW15 . . . . .2E **99**
Earle Ho. SW1 . . . . .5F **75**
(off Montaigne Cl.)
Earlham St. E11 . . . . .2B **40**
Earlham Gro. E7 . . . . .2B **54**
Earlham St.
WC2 . . . . . .3C **14** (5A **62**)
Earl Ho. NW1 . . . . .3A **60**
(off Lisson Gro.)
Earlom Ho. WC1 . . . . . . .2B **8**
(off Margery St.)
EARL'S COURT 5D **73**
Earls Court 1C **86**
Earls Court Exhibition Building
. . . . .1C **86**

Earl's Ct. Gdns. SW5 . . .5D **73**
Earls Ct. Rd. SW5 . . . . . .4C **72**
W8 . . . . .4C **72**
Earl's Ct. Sq. SW5 . . . . .1D **87**
Earlsferry Way N1 . . . . . .4A **48**
(not continuous)
EARLSFIELD 1E **115**
Earlsfield Rd. SW18 . . .1E **115**
Earlsmead Rd. NW10 . . . .2E **57**
Earls Ter. W8 . . . . .4B **72**
Earlsthorpe M.
SW12 . . . . .4C **102**
Earlsthorpe Rd.
SE26 . . . . .4F **121**
Earlstoke St.
EC1 . . . . . . .1D **9** (2D **63**)
Earlston Gro. E9 . . . . .5D **51**
Earl St. EC2 . . . .5D **11** (4F **63**)
Earls Wlk. W8 . . . . .4C **72**
Earlswood Cl. SE10 . . . . .2A **96**
Earlswood St. SE10 . . . . .1A **96**
Earl M. NW1 . . . . .5D **47**
Earnshaw Ho. EC1 . . . . . .2E **9**
(off Percival St.)
Earnshaw St.
WC2 . . . . . .2C **14** (5F **61**)
Earsby St. W14 . . . . .5A **72**
(not continuous)
Eashing Point
SW15 . . . . .1D **113**
(off Wanborough Dr.)
Easleys M.
W1 . . . . . . .2C **12** (5C **60**)
EAST ACTON 1B **70**
E. Acton Arc. W3 . . . . . . .5A **56**
E. Acton Ct. W3 . . . . .1A **70**
E. Acton La. W3 . . . . .2A **70**
E. Arbour St. E1 . . . . .5F **65**
East Bank N16 . . . . .2A **36**
E. Bank Cl. E17 . . . . .1D **39**
East Block SE1 . . . . .3A **24**
(off York Rd.)
Eastbourne M. W2 . . . . . .5E **59**
Eastbourne Rd. E15 . . . . .5A **54**
N15 . . . . .1A **36**
SW17 . . . . .5C **116**
Eastbourne Ter. W2 . . . . .5E **59**
Eastbrook Rd. SE3 . . . . . .4D **97**
Eastbury Gro. W4 . . . . . . .1A **84**
Eastbury Ter. E1 . . . . .3F **65**
Eastcastle St.
W1 . . . . . . .2F **13** (5E **61**)
Eastcheap
EC3 . . . . . .4D **19** (1A **78**)
E. Churchfield Rd.
W3 . . . . .2A **70**
Eastcombe Av. SE7 . . . . .2D **97**
Eastcote St. SW9 . . . . . . .5B **90**
E. Cross Route E3 . . . . . .4B **52**
E9 . . . . .2B **52**
(Crowfoot Cl.)
E9 . . . . .4B **52**
(Wansbeck Rd.)
E10 . . . . .2B **52**
Eastdown Ct. SE13 . . . . .2F **109**
Eastdown Ho. E8 . . . . . . .1C **50**
Eastdown Pk.
SE13 . . . . .2F **109**
EAST DULWICH 2B **106**

E. Dulwich Gro.
 SE22 . . . .3A **106**
E. Dulwich Rd.
 SE15 . . . . . .2B **106**
 SE22 . . . . . .2B **106**
 (not continuous)
Eastern Av. E11 . . . .1D **41**
 IG4: Ilf 1F **41**
Eastern Ct. E15 . . . .3A **54**
 (off Gt. Eastern Rd.)
Eastern Gateway E16 . .1E **83**
Eastern Ho. E2 . . . .2D **65**
 (off Bethnal Grn. Rd.)
Eastern Quay Apartments
 E16 . . . . .2D **83**
 (off Portsmouth M.)
Eastern Rd. E13 . . . .1D **69**
 E17 . . . . .1E **39**
 SE4 . . . . .2C **108**
E. Ferry Rd. E14 . . . .5D **81**
Eastfields Av. SW18 . .2C **100**
Eastfield St. E14 . . . .4A **66**
East Gdns. SW17 . . . .5A **116**
Eastgate Bus. Pk.
 E10 . . . . .3A **38**
EAST HAM 2F **69**
E. Ham Ind. Est. E6 . .3F **69**
E. Harding St.
 EC4 . . . .2C **16** (5C **62**)
E. Heath Rd. NW3 . . .5E **31**
East Hill SW18 . . . . .3D **101**
E. India Bldgs. E14 . .1C **80**
 (off Saltwell St.)
E. India Ct. SE16 . . .3E **79**
 (off St Marychurch St.)
East India Dock Basin
 Nature Reserve . . .1A **82**
E. India Dock Ho.
 E14 . . . . .5E **67**
E. India Dock Rd.
 E14 . . . . .5C **66**
Eastlake Ho. NW8 . . .3F **59**
 (off Frampton St.)
Eastlake Rd. SE5 . . . .5E **91**
Eastlands Cres.
 SE21 . . . . . . .4B **106**
East La. SE16 . . . . . .3C **78**
 (Chambers St.)
 SE16 . . . . . . .3C **78**
 (Scott Lidgett Cres.)
Eastlea M. E16 . . . . .3A **68**
Eastleigh Cl. NW2 . . .5A **28**
Eastleigh Wlk. SW15 . .5C **98**
East Lodge E16 . . . . .2C **82**
 (off Wesley Av.)
E. London Crematorium
 E13 . . . . .2B **68**
Eastman Ho. SW4 . . . .4E **103**
Eastman Rd. W3 . . . .3A **70**
Eastmearn Rd. SE21 . .2E **119**
Eastmoor Pl. SE7 . . . .4F **83**
Eastmoor St. SE7 . . . .4F **83**
East Mt. St. E1 . . . . .4D **65**
 (not continuous)
Eastney St. SE10 . . . .1F **95**
Eastone Apartments
 E1 . . . . .1F **19**
 (off Lolesworth Cl.)
Easton St.
 WC1 . . . . .3B **8** (3C **62**)

East Parkside SE10 . . .3A **82**
East Pas. EC1 . . . . . .5F **9**
East Pl. SE27 . . . . . .4E **119**
East Point SE1 . . . . .1C **92**
E. Poultry Av.
 EC1 . . . .1D **17** (4D **63**)
East Rd. E15 . . . . . . .5C **54**
 N1 . . . . .2B **10** (2E **63**)
 SW3 . . . . .1C **88**
East Row E11 . . . . . .1C **40**
 W10 . . . . .3A **58**
Eastry Ho. SW8 . . . . .3A **90**
 (off Hartington Rd.)
EAST SHEEN 2A **98**
E. Sheen Av. SW14 . . .3A **98**
East Side W12 . . . . . .3E **71**
 (off Shepherd's Bush Mkt.)
Eastside Halls SW7 . . .4F **73**
 (off Prince's Gdns.)
Eastside M. E3 . . . . .1C **66**
 (off Morville St.)
East Smithfield
 E1 . . . . .5F **19** (1B **78**)
East Sq. E10 . . . . . . .2D **39**
East Stand N5 . . . . . .5D **35**
East St. SE17 . . . . . .1E **91**
 (not continuous)
E. Surrey Gro. SE15 . . .3B **92**
E. Tenter St. E1 . . . . .5B **64**
East Twr. E14 . . . . . .3D **81**
 (off Pan Peninsula Sq.)
East Va. W3 . . . . . . .2B **70**
Eastville Av. NW11 . . .1B **30**
Eastway E9 . . . . .3B **52**
 (not continuous)
Eastwell Ho. SE1 . . . .5C **26**
East Wintergarden . . .2D **81**
 (off Bank St.)
Eastwood Cl. N7 . . . . .2C **48**
Eatington Rd. E10 . . . .1F **39**
Eaton Cl. SW1 . . . . . .5C **74**
Eaton Dr. SW9 . . . . . .2D **105**
Eaton Ga. SW1 . . . . . .5C **74**
Eaton Ho. E14 . . . . . .1B **80**
 (off Westferry Cir.)
 SW11 . . . . . . .4F **87**
Eaton La.
 SW1 . . . . .5E **21** (4D **75**)
Eaton Mans. SW1 . . . .5C **74**
 (off Bourne St.)
Eaton M. Nth.
 SW1 . . . . .5C **20** (5C **74**)
Eaton M. Sth. SW1 . . .5C **74**
Eaton M. W. SW1 . . . .5C **74**
Eaton Pl.
 SW1 . . . . .5C **20** (5C **74**)
Eaton Row SW1 . . . . .4D **75**
Eaton Sq.
 SW1 . . . . .5C **20** (5C **74**)
Eaton Ter. E3 . . . . . . .2A **66**
 SW1 . . . . .5C **74**
Eaton Ter. M. SW1 . . . .5C **74**
 (off Eaton Ter.)
Eatonville Rd.
 SW17 . . . . . . .2B **116**
Eatonville Vs.
 SW17 . . . . . . .2B **116**
Ebbett Ct. W3 . . . . . .4A **56**
Ebbisham Dr. SW8 . . . .2B **90**
Ebbsfleet Rd. NW2 . . .2A **44**

Ebdon Way SE3 . . . . .1D **111**
Ebenezer Ho. SE11 . . .5D **77**
Ebenezer Mussel Ho.
 E2 . . . . .1E **65**
 (off Patriot Sq.)
Ebenezer St.
 N1 . . . . .1B **10** (2F **63**)
Ebley Cl. SE15 . . . . . .2B **92**
Ebner St. SW18 . . . . .3D **101**
Ebony Ho. E2 . . . . . . .2C **64**
 (off Buckfast St.)
Ebor Cotts. SW15 . . . .3A **112**
Ebor St. E1 . . .3F **11** (3B **64**)
Ebsworth St.
 SE23 . . . . . . .5F **107**
Eburne Rd. N7 . . . . . .5A **34**
Ebury Bri. SW1 . . . . . .1D **89**
Ebury Bri. Est. SW1 . . .1D **89**
Ebury Bri. Rd. SW1 . . .1C **88**
Ebury M. SW1 . . . . . . .5E **35**
 SE27 . . . . . . .3D **119**
Ebury M. E. SW1 . . . .4D **75**
Ebury Sq. SW1 . . . . . .5C **74**
Ebury St. SW1 . . . . . .5C **74**
Ecclesbourne Apartments
 N1 . . . . .4F **49**
 (off Ecclesbourne Rd.)
Ecclesbourne Rd. N1 . .4E **49**
Eccles Rd. SW11 . . . .2B **102**
Eccleston Bri. SW1 . . .5D **75**
Eccleston Ho. SW2 . . .4C **104**
Eccleston M.
 SW1 . . . . .5C **20** (4C **74**)
Eccleston Pl. SW1 . . . .5D **75**
Eccleston Sq. SW1 . . .5D **75**
 (not continuous)
Eccleston Sq. M.
 SW1 . . . . .5D **75**
Eccleston St. SW1 . . . .4D **75**
Eckford St. N1 . . . . . .1C **62**
Eckington Ho. N15 . . .1F **35**
 (off Fladbury Rd.)
Eckstein Rd. SW11 . . .2A **102**
Eclipse Bldg. N1 . . . . .3C **48**
 (off Laycock St.)
Eclipse Rd. E13 . . . . .4D **69**
Ecology Centre and
 Arts Pavilion 2A **66**
Ector Rd. SE6 . . . . . . .2A **124**
Edans Ct. W12 . . . . . .3B **70**
Edbrooke Rd. W9 . . . .3C **58**
Eddisbury Ho. SE26 . . .3C **120**
Eddiscombe Rd.
 SW6 . . . . .5B **86**
Eddystone Rd. SE4 . . .3A **108**
Eddystone Twr. SE8 . . .1A **94**
Edenbridge Cl. SE16 . .1D **93**
 (off Masters Dr.)
Edenbridge Rd. E9 . . . .4F **51**
Eden Cl. NW3 . . . . . . .4C **30**
 W8 . . . . .4C **72**
Edencourt Rd.
 SW16 . . . . . . .5D **117**
Eden Gro. E17 . . . . . .1D **39**
 N7 . . . . .2B **48**
 N10 . . . . .3D **43**
Edenham Way W10 . . .3B **58**
Eden Ho. NW8 . . . . . .3A **60**
 (off Church St.)

Eden Ho. *SE8* 3C **94**
   (off Deptford High St.)
  SE16 . . . . .3F **79**
   (off Water Gdns. Sq.)
Edenhurst Av. SW6 . . . .1B **100**
Eden Lodge NW6 . . . . . .4F **43**
Eden M. SW17 . . . . .3E **115**
Eden Rd. E17 . . . . .1D **39**
  SE27 . . . . .4D **119**
Edensor Gdns. W4 . . . . .3A **84**
Edensor Rd. W4 . . . . . . .3A **84**
Edenvale St. SW6 . . . . . .5E **87**
Eden Way E3 . . . . .5B **52**
Edgar Ho. *E9* 2A **52**
   (off Homerton Rd.)
  E11 . . . . .2C **40**
  SW8 . . . . .3A **90**
   (off Wyvil Rd.)
Edgar Kail Way
  SE22 . . . . .2A **106**
Edgarley Ter. SW6 . . . . . .4A **86**
Edgar Myles Ho. *E16* . . .4B **68**
   (off Ordnance Rd.)
Edgar Rd. E3 . . . . .2D **67**
Edgar Wallace Cl.
  SE15 . . . . .3A **92**
Edgar Wright Ct.
  SW6 . . . . .3B **86**
   (off Dawes Rd.)
Edgcott Ho. *W10* 4E **57**
   (off Sutton Way)
Edge, The *SE8* 3B **94**
   (off Glenville Gro.)
Edge Apartments E15 . . .4F **53**
Edge Bus. Centre, The
  NW2 . . . . .4D **29**
Edgecombe Ho. SE5 . . . .5A **92**
  SW19 . . . . .1A **114**
Edgecot Gro. N15 . . . . . .1A **36**
Edgehill Ho. SW9 . . . . . .5D **91**
Edgeley La. SW4 . . . . . . .1F **103**
Edgeley Rd. SW4 . . . . . .1F **103**
Edgel St. SW18 . . . . .2D **101**
Edge Point Cl. SE27 . . . .5D **119**
Edge St. W8 . . . . .2C **72**
Edgeworth Ho. *NW8* 5E **45**
   (off Boundary Rd.)
Edgeworth Rd. SE9 . . . . .2E **111**
Edgson Ho. *SW1* 1D **89**
   (off Ebury Bri. Rd.)
Edgware Rd. NW2 . . . . . .3D **29**
  W2 . . . . .3A **12** (3F **59**)
Edinburgh Cl. E2 . . . . . . .1E **65**
Edinburgh Ct. *SE16* 2F **79**
   (off Rotherhithe St.)
Edinburgh Ga. SW1 . . . . .3B **74**
Edinburgh Ho. *W9* 2D **59**
   (off Maida Va.)
Edinburgh Rd. E13 . . . . .1D **69**
  E17 . . . . .1C **38**
   (not continuous)
Edington NW5 . . . . .3C **46**
Edison Bldg. E14 . . . . . . .3C **80**
Edison Ct. *SE10* 4B **82**
   (off Schoolbank Rd.)
  W3 . . . . .3A **70**
Edison Ho. *SE1* 5F **77**
   (off New Kent Rd.)
Edison Rd. N8 . . . . .1F **33**
Edis St. NW1 . . . . .5C **46**

Editha Mans. *SW10* 2E **87**
   (off Edith Gro.)
Edith Brinson Ho.
  E14 . . . . .5F **67**
   (off Oban St.)
Edith Cavell Cl. N19 . . . .2A **34**
Edith Cavell Ho. *E14* . . .5D **67**
   (off Sturry St.)
Edith Gro. SW10 . . . . . . .2E **87**
Edith Ho. *W6* 1E **85**
   (off Queen Caroline St.)
Edithna St. SW9 . . . . . .1A **104**
Edith Neville Cotts.
  NW1 . . . . .1B **6**
   (off Drummond Cres.)
Edith Ramsay Ho. *E1* . . .4A **66**
   (off Duckett St.)
Edith Rd. E6 . . . . .4F **55**
  E15 . . . . .2F **53**
  SW19 . . . . .5D **115**
  W14 . . . . .5A **72**
Edith Row SW6 . . . . .4D **87**
Edith St. E2 . . . . .1C **64**
Edith Summerskill Ho.
  SW6 . . . . .3B **86**
   (off Clem Attlee Ct.)
Edith Ter. SW10 . . . . . . .3E **87**
Edith Vs. W14 . . . . .5B **72**
Edith Yd. SW10 . . . . .3E **87**
Edmeston Cl. E9 . . . . . . .3A **52**
Edmond Ct. SE14 . . . . . . .4E **93**
Edmonton Ct. *SE16* 4E **79**
   (off Canada Est.)
Edmund Halley Way
  SE10 . . . . .3A **82**
Edmund Ho. *SE17* 2D **91**
Edmundsbury Ct. Est.
  SW9 . . . . .2B **104**
Edmund St. SE5 . . . . . . .3F **91**
Ednam Ho. *SE15* 2C **92**
   (off Haymerle Rd.)
Edna St. SW11 . . . . .4A **88**
Edred Ho. *E9* 1A **52**
   (off Lindisfarne Way)
Edrich Ho. SW4 . . . . .4A **90**
Edric Ho. *SW1* 5F **75**
   (off Page St.)
Edric Rd. SE14 . . . . .3F **93**
Edward VII Mans.
  NW10 . . . . .2F **57**
   (off Chamberlayne Rd.)
Edward Bond Ho. *WC1* . . .2E **7**
   (off Cromer St.)
Edward Clifford Ho.
  SE17 . . . . .5F **77**
   (off Elsted St.)
Edward Cl. NW2 . . . . . . .1F **43**
Edward Ct. E16 . . . . .4C **68**
Edward Dodd Ct. *N1* 1C **10**
   (off Chart St.)
Edward Edward's Ho.
  SE1 . . . . .2D **25**
Edward Edwardes Pl. W8 . . . .4B **72**
Edwardes Sq. W8 . . . . . .4B **72**
Edward Heylin Ct.
  E15 . . . . .1D **67**
   (off High St.)
Edward Heylyn Ho.
  E3 . . . . .1C **66**
   (off Thomas Fyre Dr.)

Edward Ho. *SE11* 1B **90**
   (off Newburn St.)
  W2 . . . . .3F **59**
   (off Hall Pl.)
Edward Kennedy Ho.
  W10 . . . . .3A **58**
   (off Wornington Rd.)
Edward Mann Cl. E1 . . . . .5F **65**
   (off Pitsea St.)
Edward M.
  NW1 . . . . . . .1E **5** (2D **61**)
Edward Pl. SE8 . . . . .2B **94**
Edward Rd. E17 . . . . .1F **37**
Edward's Cotts. N1 . . . . .3D **49**
Edward's La. N16 . . . . . . .4A **36**
Edwards M. N1 . . . . .4D **49**
  W1 . . . . .3B **12** (5C **60**)
Edward Sq. N1 . . . . .5B **48**
  SE16 . . . . .2A **80**
Edward St. E16 . . . . .3C **68**
   (not continuous)
  SE8 . . . . .2B **94**
  SE14 . . . . .3A **94**
Edward Temme Av.
  E15 . . . . .4B **54**
Edward Tyler Rd.
  SE12 . . . . .2E **125**
Edwina Gdns. IG4: IIf . . .1F **41**
Edwin Hall Pl. SE13 . . . .4F **109**
Edwin Ho. SE15 . . . . .3C **92**
Edwin's Mead E9 . . . . . . .1A **52**
Edwin St. E1 . . . . .3E **65**
  E16 . . . . .4C **68**
Edwy Ho. *E9* 1B **52**
   (off Homerton Rd.)
Edwyn Ho. *SW18* 4D **101**
   (off Neville Gill Cl.)
Eel Brook Cl. SW6 . . . . . .4D **87**
Effie Pl. SW6 . . . . .3C **86**
Effie Rd. SW6 . . . . .3C **86**
Effingham Rd. SE12 . . . .3A **110**
Effort St. SW17 . . . . .5A **116**
Effra Ct. *SW2* 3B **104**
   (off Brixton Hill)
Effra Pde. SW2 . . . . .3C **104**
Effra Rd. SW2 . . . . .2C **104**
  SW19 . . . . .5D **115**
Effra Rd. Retail Pk.
  SW2 . . . . .3C **104**
Egbert Ho. *E9* 2A **52**
   (off Homerton Rd.)
Egbert St. NW1 . . . . .5C **46**
Egbury Ho. *SW15* 4B **98**
   (off Tangley Gro.)
Egeremont Rd. SE13 . . . .5D **95**
Egerton Ct. E11 . . . . .2F **39**
Egerton Cres. SW3 . . . . .5A **74**
Egerton Dr. SE10 . . . . . . .4D **95**
Egerton Gdns. NW10 . . . .5E **43**
  SW3 . . . . .5A **74**
Egerton Gdns. M.
  SW3 . . . . .4A **74**
Egerton Pl. SW3 . . . . . . .4A **74**
Egerton Rd. N16 . . . . . . .2B **36**
Egerton Ter. SW3 . . . . . .4A **74**
Egham Cl. SW19 . . . . . .2A **114**
Egham Rd. E13 . . . . .4D **69**
Eglantine Rd. SW18 . . . .3E **101**
Eglington Ct. SE17 . . . . .2E **91**
Egliston M. SW15 . . . . . .1E **99**

Egliston Rd. SW15 . . . . .1E 99
Eglon M. NW1 . . . . .4B 46
Egmont St. SE14 . . . . . . .3F 93
Egremont Ho. SE13 . . . . .5D 95
  (off Russett Way)
Egremont Rd.
  SE27 . . . . .3C 118
Egret Ho. SE16 . . . . .5F 79
  (off Tawny Way)
Eider Cl. E7 . . . . .2B 54
Eider Ct. SE8 . . . . .2B 94
  (off Pilot Cl.)
Ekarro Ho. SW8 . . . . . . .4A 90
  (off Guildford Rd.)
Elaine Gro. NW5 . . . . . . .2C 46
Elam Cl. SE5 . . . . .5D 91
Elam St. SE5 . . . . .5D 91
Elan Cl. E1 . . . . .4D 65
Eland Rd. SW11 . . . . . . .1B 102
Elba Pl. SE17 . . . . .5E 77
Elbe St. SW6 . . . . .5E 87
Elborough St. SW18 . . . .1C 114
Elbourne Ct. SE16 . . . . . .4F 79
  (off Worgan St.)
Elbourn Ho. SW3 . . . . . .1A 88
  (off Cale St.)
Elbury Dr. E16 . . . . .5C 68
Elcho St. SW11 . . . . .3A 88
Elcot Av. SE15 . . . . .3D 93
Elden Ho. SW3 . . . . .5A 74
  (off Sloane Av.)
Elder Av. N8 . . . . .1A 34
Elderberry Gro.
  SE27 . . . . .4E 119
Elderfield Ho. E14 . . . . . .1C 80
  (off Pennyfields)
Elderfield Pl. SW17 . . . . .4D 117
Elderfield Rd. E5 . . . . . . .1F 51
Elderflower Way E15 . . . .4A 54
Elder Gdns. SE27 . . . . . .5E 119
Elder Ho. E15 . . . . .2A 68
  (off Manor Rd.)
Elder Rd. SE27 . . . . .5E 119
Elder St. E1 . . . . . .5F 11 (3B 64)
  (not continuous)
Elderton Rd. SE26 . . . . . .4A 122
Elder Wlk. N1 . . . . .5D 49
  (off Popham St.)
  SE13 . . . . .1E 109
Elderwood Pl. SE27 . . . . .5E 119
Eldon Ct. NW6 . . . . .5C 44
Eldon Gro. NW3 . . . . . . .2F 45
Eldon Rd. W8 . . . . .4D 73
Eldon St. EC2 . . .1C 18 (4F 63)
Eldridge Ct. SE16 . . . . . .4C 78
Eleanor Cl. SE16 . . . . . . .3F 79
Eleanor Ct. E2 . . . . .5C 50
  (off Whiston Rd.)
Eleanor Gro. SW13 . . . . .1A 98
Eleanor Ho. W6 . . . . .1E 85
  (off Queen Caroline St.)
Eleanor Rathbone Ho.
  N6 . . . . .2F 33
  (off Avenue Rd.)
Eleanor Rd. E8 . . . . .3D 51
  E15 . . . . .3B 54
Eleanor St. E3 . . . . .2C 66
Electra Bus. Pk. E16 . . . .4F 67
Electric Av. SW9 . . . . . . .2C 104
Electric Cinema 5B 58

Electric Empire, The
  SE14 . . . . .4F 93
  (off New Cross Rd.)
Electric Ho. E3 . . . . .2C 66
  (off Bow Rd.)
Electric La. SW9 . . . . . . .2C 104
  (not continuous)
Elektron Twr. E14 . . . . . . .1F 81
ELEPHANT & CASTLE
  . . . . .4D 77
Elephant & Castle
  SE1 . . . . .5D 77
Elephant & Castle
  Leisure Cen. 5D 77
Elephant & Castle Shop. Cen.
  SE1 . . . . .5E 77
Elephant La. SE16 . . . . . .3E 79
Elephant Rd. SE17 . . . . . .5E 77
Elfindale Rd. SE24 . . . . . .3E 105
Elford Cl. SE3 . . . . .2D 111
Elford M. SW4 . . . . .3E 103
Elfort Rd. N5 . . . . .1C 48
Elfrida Cres. SE6 . . . . . . .4C 122
Elf Row E1 . . . . .1E 79
Elgar Av. NW10 . . . . .3A 42
  (not continuous)
Elgar Cl. E13 . . . . .1E 69
  SE8 . . . . .3C 94
Elgar Ct. NW6 . . . . .2B 58
  W14 . . . . .4A 72
  (off Blythe Rd.)
Elgar Ho. NW6 . . . . .4E 45
  (off Fairfax Rd.)
  SW1 . . . . .1D 89
  (off Churchill Gdns.)
Elgar St. SE16 . . . . .4A 80
Elgin Av. W9 . . . . .3B 58
  W12 . . . . .3C 70
Elgin Cl. W12 . . . . .3D 71
Elgin Ct. W9 . . . . .3D 59
Elgin Cres. W11 . . . . .1A 72
Elgin Est. W9 . . . . .3C 58
  (off Elgin Av.)
Elgin Ho. E14 . . . . .5D 67
  (off Ricardo St.)
Elgin Mans. W9 . . . . .2D 59
Elgin M. W11 . . . . .5A 58
Elgin M. Nth. W9 . . . . . . .2D 59
Elgin M. Sth. W9 . . . . . . .2D 59
Elgood Cl. W11 . . . . .1A 72
Elgood Ho. NW8 . . . . . . .1F 59
  (off Wellington Rd.)
  SE1 . . . . .4B 26
  (off Tabard St.)
Elham Ho. E5 . . . . .2D 51
Elia M. N1 . . . . . . .1D 9 (1D 63)
Elias Pl. SW8 . . . . .2C 90
Elia St. N1 . . . . . . .1E 9 (1D 63)
Elim Est.
  SE1 . . . . .5D 27 (4A 78)
Elim St. SE1 . . . .5C 26 (4F 77)
  (not continuous)
Elim Way E13 . . . . .2B 68
Eliot Bank SE23 . . . . .2D 121
Eliot Cotts. SE3 . . . . .5A 96
Eliot Ct. SW18 . . . . .4D 101
Eliot Gdns. SW15 . . . . . . .2C 98
Eliot Hill SE13 . . . . .5E 95
Eliot M. NW8 . . . . .1E 59
Eliot Pk. SE13 . . . . .5E 95

Eliot Pl. SE3 . . . . .5A 96
Eliot Va. SE3 . . . . .5F 95
Elizabeth Av. N1 . . . . .5E 49
Elizabeth Barnes Ct.
  SW6 . . . . .5D 87
  (off Marinefield Rd.)
Elizabeth Blount Ct.
  E14 . . . . .5A 66
  (off Carr St.)
Elizabeth Bri. SW1 . . . . . .5D 75
Elizabeth Cl. E14 . . . . . . .5D 67
  W9 . . . . .3E 59
Elizabeth Ct. E10 . . . . . . .2D 39
  NW1 . . . . .3A 60
  (off Palgrave Gdns.)
  SW1 . . . . .5C 22
  SW10 . . . . .2F 87
  (off Milman's St.)
Elizabeth Croll Ho.
  WC1 . . . . .1A 8
  (off Penton Ri.)
Elizabeth Fry M. E8 . . . . . .4D 51
Elizabeth Gdns. W3 . . . . . .2B 70
Elizabeth Ho. E3 . . . . . . .2D 67
  (off St Leonard's St.)
  SE11 . . . . .5C 76
  (off Reedworth St.)
  W6 . . . . .1E 85
  (off Queen Caroline Rd.)
Elizabeth Ind. Est.
  SE14 . . . . .2F 93
Elizabeth M. E2 . . . . .1C 64
  (off Kay St.)
  NW3 . . . . .3A 46
Elizabeth Newcomen Ho.
  SE1 . . . . .3B 26
  (off Newcomen St.)
Elizabeth Rd. E6 . . . . .5F 55
  N15 . . . . .1A 36
Elizabeth Sq. SE16 . . . . . .1A 80
  (off Sovereign Cres.)
Elizabeth St. SW1 . . . . . . .5C 74
Elkington Point SE11 . . . . .5C 76
  (off Lollard St.)
Elkington Rd. E13 . . . . . . .3D 69
Elkstone Rd. W10 . . . . . . .4B 58
Ellacott M. SW16 . . . . . . .2F 117
Ellaline Rd. W6 . . . . .2F 85
Ella M. NW3 . . . . .1B 46
Elland Ho. E14 . . . . .5B 66
  (off Copenhagen Pl.)
Elland Rd. SE15 . . . . .2E 107
Ella Rd. N8 . . . . .2A 34
Ellenborough Ho.
  W12 . . . . .1D 71
  (off White City Est.)
Ellenborough Pl.
  SW15 . . . . .2C 98
Ellen Julia Ct. E1 . . . . .5E 65
  (off James Voller Way)
Ellen St. E1 . . . . .5C 64
Ellen Terry Ct. NW1 . . . . . .4D 47
  (off Farrier St.)
Ellen Wilkinson Ho.
  E2 . . . . .2F 65
  (off Usk St.)
  SW6 . . . . .2B 86
  (off Clem Attlee Ct.)
Ellerby St. SW6 . . . . .4F 85
Ellerdale Cl. NW3 . . . . . . .1E 45

Ellerdale Rd. NW3 . . . . .2E 45
Ellerdale St. SE13 . . . .2D 109
Ellerslie Gdns.
   NW10 . . . . .5C 42
Ellerslie Rd. W12 . . . . . .2D 71
Ellerslie Sq. Ind. Est.
   SW2 . . . . .3A 104
Ellerton Rd. SW13 . . . . .4C 84
   SW18 . . . . .1F 115
Ellery Ho. SE17 . . . . . . .5F 77
Ellery St. SE15 . . . . . . .5D 93
Ellesmere Ct. E11 . . . . .1B 40
Ellesmere Ct. SE12 . . .1C 124
   W4 . . . . .1A 84
Ellesmere Ho. SW10 . . . .2E 87
   (off Fulham Rd.)
Ellesmere Mans.
   NW6 . . . . .3E 45
   (off Canfield Gdns.)
Ellesmere Rd. E3 . . . . . .1A 66
   NW10 . . . . .2C 42
   W4 . . . . .2A 84
Ellesmere St. E14 . . . . . .5D 67
Ellingfort Rd. E8 . . . . . .4D 51
Ellingham Rd. E15 . . . . .1F 53
   W12 . . . . .3C 70
Ellington Ho.
   SE1 . . . . .5A 26 (4E 77)
Ellington St. N7 . . . . . . .3C 48
Elliot Cl. E15 . . . . .4A 54
Elliot Ho. SW17 . . . . . . .3F 115
   (off Grosvenor Way)
   W1 . . . . .4A 60
   (off Cato St.)
Elliot Rd. NW4 . . . . .1D 29
Elliott Rd. SW9 . . . . .4D 91
   W4 . . . . .5A 70
Elliott's Pl. N1 . . . . .5D 49
Elliott Sq. NW3 . . . . .4A 46
Elliotts Row SE11 . . . . . .5D 77
Ellis Cl. NW10 . . . . .3D 43
Elliscombe Mt. SE7 . . . . .2E 97
Elliscombe Rd. SE7 . . . . .2E 97
Ellis Ct. E1 . . . . .5E 65
   (off James Voller Way)
Ellisfield Dr. SW15 . . . . .5C 98
Ellis Franklin Ct.
   NW8 . . . . .1E 59
   (off Abbey Rd.)
Ellis Ho. SE17 . . . . .1F 91
   (off Brandon St.)
Ellison Apartments
   E3 . . . . .2C 66
   (off Merchant St.)
Ellison Ho. SE13 . . . . . .5D 95
   (off Lewisham Rd.)
Ellison Rd. SW13 . . . . . .5B 84
Ellis St. SW1 . . . . .5C 74
Ellora Rd. SW16 . . . . . . .5F 117
Ellsworth St. E2 . . . . . . .2D 65
Ellwood Ct. W9 . . . . .3D 59
   (off Clearwell Dr.)
Elm Bank Gdns.
   SW13 . . . . .5A 84
Elmbourne Rd.
   SW17 . . . . .3D 117
Elmbridge Wlk. E8 . . . . .4C 50
Elm Cl. E11 . . . . .1D 41
   N19 . . . . .4E 33
   NW4 . . . . .1F 29

Elm Ct. EC4 . . . . .3B 16
   SE1 . . . . .4D 27
   (off Royal Oak Yd.)
   SE13 . . . . .1F 109
   SW9 . . . . .4C 90
   (off Cranworth Gdns.)
   W9 . . . . .4C 58
   (off Admiral Wlk.)
Elmcourt Rd. SE27 . . . .2D 119
Elmcroft N6 . . . . .2E 33
Elmcroft Av. NW11 . . . . .2B 30
Elmcroft Cres. NW11 . . .2A 30
Elmcroft St. E5 . . . . .1E 51
Elmer Ho. NW8 . . . . .4A 60
   (off Penfold St.)
Elmer Rd. SE6 . . . . .5E 109
Elmfield Av. N8 . . . . .1A 34
Elmfield Ho. NW8 . . . . . .3F 59
   (off Carlton Hill)
   W9 . . . . .3C 58
   (off Goldney Rd.)
Elmfield Rd. E17 . . . . . . .1F 37
   SW17 . . . . .2C 116
Elmfield Way W9 . . . . . .4C 58
Elm Friars Wlk. NW1 . . . .4F 47
Elm Grn. W3 . . . . .5A 56
Elmgreen Cl. E15 . . . . . .5A 54
Elm Gro. N8 . . . . .1A 34
   NW2 . . . . .1F 43
   SE15 . . . . .5B 92
Elm Gro. Rd. SW13 . . . . .4C 84
Elm Hall Gdns. E11 . . . .1D 41
   (not continuous)
Elm Ho. E3 . . . . .5B 52
   (off Sycamore Av.)
   E14 . . . . .3E 81
   (off E. Ferry Rd.)
   W10 . . . . .3A 58
   (off Briar Wlk.)
Elmhurst Mans.
   SW4 . . . . .1F 103
Elmhurst Rd. E7 . . . . . . .4D 55
   SE9 . . . . .2F 125
Elmhurst St. SW4 . . . . . .1F 103
Elmington Est. SE5 . . . . .3F 91
Elmington Rd. SE5 . . . . .3F 91
Elmira St. SE13 . . . . . . .1D 109
Elm La. SE6 . . . . .2B 122
Elm Lodge SW6 . . . . . . .4E 85
   (off Elmore St.)
   SW9 . . . . .5D 91
Elmore Ho. N1 . . . . .4F 49
Elmore St. N1 . . . . .4E 49
Elm Pk. SW2 . . . . .4B 104
Elm Pk. Av. N15 . . . . . . .1B 36
Elm Pk. Chambers
   SW10 . . . . .1F 87
   (off Fulham Rd.)
Elm Pk. Gdns.
   NW4 . . . . .1F 29
   SW10 . . . . .1F 87
Elm Pk. Ho. SW10 . . . . .1F 87
Elm Pk. La. SW3 . . . . . . .1F 87
Elm Pk. Mans. SW10 . . .2F 87
   (off Park Wlk.)
Elm Pk. Rd. E10 . . . . . . .3A 38
   SW3 . . . . .2F 87
Elm Pl. SW7 . . . . .1F 87
Elm Quay Ct. SW8 . . . . .2F 89

Elm Rd. E7 . . . . .3B 54
   E11 . . . . .4F 39
   E17 . . . . .1E 39
Elm Row NW3 . . . . .5E 31
Elms, The E12 . . . . .3F 55
   SW13 . . . . .1B 98
Elms Av. NW4 . . . . .1F 29
Elmscott Rd.
   BR1: Brom 5A 124
Elms Cres. SW4 . . . . . . .4E 103
Elmshaw Rd. SW15 . . . . .3C 98
Elmslie Point E3 . . . . . . .4B 66
   (off Leopold St.)
Elms M. W2 . . . . .1F 73
Elms Rd. SW4 . . . . .3E 103
ELMSTEAD 5F 125
Elmstead Rd. SW6 . . . . .4C 86
Elm St. WC1 . . . . .4A 8 (3B 62)
Elm Ter. NW2 . . . . .5C 30
   NW3 . . . . .1A 46
Elmton Ct. NW8 . . . . .3F 59
   (off Cunningham Pl.)
Elm Tree Cl. NW8 . . . . . .2F 59
Elm Tree Ct. NW8 . . . . . .2F 59
   (off Elm Tree Rd.)
   SE7 . . . . .2E 97
Elm Tree Rd. NW8 . . . . . .2F 59
Elm Wlk. NW3 . . . . .4C 30
Elm Way NW10 . . . . .1A 42
Elmwood Ct. E10 . . . . . . .3C 38
   (off Goldsmith Rd.)
   SW11 . . . . .4D 89
Elmwood Ho. NW10 . . . . .1D 57
   (off All Souls Av.)
Elmwood Rd. SE24 . . . . .3F 105
Elmworth Gro. SE21 . . . .2F 119
Elnathan M. W9 . . . . .3D 59
Elphinstone Ct.
   SW16 . . . . .5A 118
Elphinstone St. N5 . . . . .1D 49
Elrington Rd. E8 . . . . . . .3C 50
Elsa Cotts. E14 . . . . .4A 66
   (off Halley St.)
Elsa St. E1 . . . . .4A 66
Elsdale St. E9 . . . . .3E 51
Elsden M. E2 . . . . .1E 65
Elsenham St. SW18 . . . .1B 114
Elsham Rd. E11 . . . . .5A 40
   W14 . . . . .3A 72
Elsham Ter. W14 . . . . . . .4A 72
   (off Elsham Rd.)
Elsie La. Ct. W2 . . . . . . .4C 58
   (off Westbourne Pk. Vs.)
Elsiemaud Rd. SE4 . . . . .3B 108
Elsinore Ho. SE22 . . . . .2B 106
Elsinore Gdns. NW2 . . . .5A 30
Elsinore Ho. N1 . . . . . . .5C 48
   (off Denmark Gro.)
   SE5 . . . . .5E 91
   (off Denmark Rd.)
   SE7 . . . . .5F 83
   W6 . . . . .1F 85
   (off Fulham Pal. Rd.)
Elsinore Rd. SE23 . . . . . .1A 122
Elsley Rd. SW11 . . . . . . .1B 102
Elspeth Rd. SW11 . . . . . .2B 102
Elstead Ho. SW2 . . . . . . .5B 104
   (off Redlands Way)
Elsted St. SE17 . . . . .5F 77
Elstow Grange NW6 . . . . .4F 43

Elswick Rd. SE13 . . . . . . .5D 95
Elswick St. SW6 . . . . . . .5E 87
Elsworthy Ct. NW3 . . . . . .4B 46
  (off Primrose Hill Rd.)
Elsworthy Ri. NW3 . . . . . .4A 46
Elsworthy Rd. NW3 . . . . . .4A 46
Elsworthy Ter. NW3 . . . . .5A 46
Elsynge Rd. SW18 . . . . . .3F 101
Eltham Grn. SE9 . . . . . . .3F 111
Eltham Grn. Rd.
  SE9 . . . . .2E 111
Eltham Hill SE9 . . . . . . .3F 111
Eltham Pal. Rd.
  SE9 . . . . .4E 111
Eltham Rd. SE9 . . . . .3B 110
  SE12 . . . . .3B 110
Elthiron Rd. SW6 . . . . . . .4C 86
Elthorne Rd. N19 . . . . . . .4F 33
  NW9 . . . . .2A 28
Elthorne Way NW9 . . . . . .1A 28
Elthruda Rd. SE13 . . . . . .4F 109
Elton Ho. E3 . . . . .5B 52
  (off Candy St.)
Elton Pl. N16 . . . . .2A 50
Eltringham St.
  SW18 . . . . .2E 101
Eluna Apartments E1 . . . .1D 79
  (off Wapping La.)
Elvaston M. SW7 . . . . . . .4E 73
Elvaston Pl. SW7 . . . . . . .4E 73
Elveden Ho. SE24 . . . . . .3D 105
Elven M. SE15 . . . . .4E 93
Elver Gdns. E2 . . . . .2C 64
Elverson Rd. SE8 . . . . . . .5D 95
Elverton St. SW1 . . . . . . .5F 75
Elvino Rd. SE26 . . . . .5A 122
Elvis Rd. NW2 . . . . .3E 43
Elwin St. E2 . . . . .2C 64
Elwood St. N5 . . . . .5D 35
Elworth Ho. SW8 . . . . . . .3B 90
  (off Oval Pl.)
Elwyn Gdns. SE12 . . . . . .5C 110
Ely Cotts. SW8 . . . . .3B 90
Ely Ct. EC1 . . . . .1C 16
  NW6 . . . . .1C 58
  (off Chichester Rd.)
Ely Ho. SE15 . . . . .3C 92
  (off Friary Est.)
Elyne Rd. N4 . . . . .1C 34
Ely Pl. EC1 . . . . . . .1C 16 (4C 62)
Ely Rd. E10 . . . . .1E 39
Elysium Pl. SW6 . . . . .5B 86
  (off Elysium St.)
Elysium St. SW6 . . . . .5B 86
Elystan Pl. SW3 . . . . .1A 88
Elystan St. SW3 . . . . .5A 74
Elystan Wlk. N1 . . . . .5C 48
Ely's Yd. E1 . . . . . .5F 11 (4B 64)
Emanuel Ho. SW1 . . . . . .4F 75
Embankment SW15 . . . . . .5F 85
Embankment Galleries
  . . . . .4A 16
  (within Somerset House)
Embankment Gdns.
  SW3 . . . . .2B 88
Embankment Pl.
  WC2 . . . . .1E 23 (2A 76)
Embassy Apartments
  SE5 . . . . .5E 91
  (off Coldharbour La.)

Embassy Ct. E2 . . . . .3D 65
  (off Brady St.)
  NW8 . . . . .1F 59
  (off Wellington Rd.)
Embassy Ho. NW6 . . . . . .4D 45
Embassy Theatre
  Central School of
  Speech & Drama
  . . . . .4F 45
  (off College Cres.)
Emba St. SE16 . . . . .3C 78
Emberton SE5 . . . . .2A 92
  (off Albany Rd.)
Emberton Ct. EC1 . . . . . . .2D 9
  (off Tompion St.)
Embleton Rd. SE13 . . . . . .2D 109
Embry Rd. SE9 . . . . .3E 111
Emden St. SW6 . . . . .4D 87
Emerald Cl. E16 . . . . .5F 69
Emerald Rd. NW10 . . . . . .5A 42
  (not continuous)
Emerald St.
  WC1 . . . . .5F 7 (4B 62)
Emerson St.
  SE1 . . . . .1F 25 (2E 77)
Emery Hill St. SW1 . . . . . .4E 75
Emery St.
  SE1 . . . . .5C 24 (4C 76)
Emery Theatre 5D 67
  (off Annabel Cl.)
Emery Walker Trust 1C 84
Emily Ct. SE1 . . . . .4F 25
  (off Sudrey St.)
Emily Duncan Pl. E7 . . . . .1D 55
Emily Ho. W10 . . . . .3A 58
  (off Kensal Rd.)
Emily St. E16 . . . . .5B 68
  (off Jude St.)
Emirates Air Line 3B 82
Emirates Stadium 1C 48
Emlyn Gdns. W12 . . . . . . .3A 70
Emlyn Rd. W12 . . . . .3A 70
Emmanuel Ct. E10 . . . . . .2D 39
Emmanuel Ho. SE11 . . . . .5C 76
Emmanuel Rd.
  SW12 . . . . .1E 117
Emma Rd. E13 . . . . .1B 68
Emma St. E2 . . . . .1D 65
Emminster NW6 . . . . .5D 45
  (off Abbey Rd.)
Emmott Cl. E1 . . . . .3A 66
  NW11 . . . . .1E 31
Emperor's Ga. SW7 . . . . . .4E 73
Empingham St. SE8 . . . . . .5F 79
  (off Chilton Gro.)
Empire Cinema
  Leicester Sq. 4C 14
  (off Leicester Sq.)
Empire Cl. SE7 . . . . .2D 97
Empire Ho. SW7 . . . . .4A 74
  (off Thurloe Pl.)
Empire M. SW16 . . . . .5A 118
Empire Sq. N7 . . . . .5A 34
  SE1 . . . . .4B 26
  (off Long La.)
Empire Sq. E. SE1 . . . . . . .4B 26
Empire Sq. Sth. SE1 . . . . .4B 26
Empire Sq. W. SE1 . . . . . .4B 26
Empire Wharf E3 . . . . .5A 52
  (off Old Ford Rd.)

Empire Wharf Rd.
  E14 . . . . .5F 81
Empress App. NW6 . . . . . .1C 86
Empress Av. E12 . . . . .4E 41
Empress M. SE5 . . . . .5E 91
Empress Pl. SW6 . . . . . . .1C 86
Empress State Bldg.
  SW6 . . . . .1C 86
Empress St. SE17 . . . . . . .2E 91
Empson St. E3 . . . . .3D 67
Emsworth Ct.
  SW16 . . . . .3A 118
Emsworth St. SW2 . . . . . .2B 118
Emu Rd. SW8 . . . . .5D 89
Enard Ho. E3 . . . . .1B 66
  (off Cardigan Rd.)
Enbrook St. W10 . . . . .2A 58
Enclave, The SW13 . . . . . .5B 84
Enclave Ct. EC1 . . . . .3E 9
  (off Dallington St.)
Endeavour Ho. E14 . . . . . .3C 80
  (off Cuba St.)
Endeavour Way
  SW19 . . . . .4D 115
Endell St.
  WC2 . . . . .2D 15 (5A 62)
Enderby St. SE10 . . . . . . .1F 95
Endlesham Rd.
  SW12 . . . . .5C 102
Endsleigh Ct. WC1 . . . . . . .3C 6
Endsleigh Gdns.
  WC1 . . . . .3B 6 (3F 61)
Endsleigh Pl.
  WC1 . . . . .3C 6 (3F 61)
Endsleigh St.
  WC1 . . . . .3C 6 (3F 61)
Endwell Rd. SE4 . . . . .5A 94
Endymion Rd. N4 . . . . . . .2C 34
  SW2 . . . . .4B 104
Energen Cl. NW10 . . . . . .3A 42
Energize Fitness Club
  . . . . .1A 86
  (in Hammersmith &
  West London College)
Energy Centre, The
  N1 . . . . .1D 11
  (off Bowling Grn. Wlk.)
Enfield Cloisters N1 . . . .1D 11
  (off Fanshaw St.)
Enfield Ho. SW9 . . . . .5A 90
  (off Stockwell Rd.)
Enfield Rd. N1 . . . . .4A 50
Enford St. W1 . . . . .4B 60
Engadine St. SW18 . . . . . .1B 114
Engate St. SE13 . . . . .2E 109
Engine Cl. SW1 . . . . .2A 22
  (off Ambassador's Ct.)
England's La. NW3 . . . . . .3B 46
Englefield NW1 . . . . .2F 5
  (off Clarence Gdns.)
Englefield Rd. N1 . . . . . . .4F 49
Engleheart Rd. SE6 . . . . . .5D 109
Englewood Rd.
  SW12 . . . . .4D 103
English Grounds
  SE1 . . . . .2D 27 (2A 78)
English St. E3 . . . . .3B 66
Enid St. SE16 . . . . . .5F 27 (4B 78)
Enmore Gdns. SW14 . . . . .3A 98
Enmore Rd. SW15 . . . . . . .2E 99

Ennerdale NW1 . . . . .1F **5**
(off Varndell St.)
Ennerdale Ct. E11 . . . . .2C **40**
(off Cambridge Rd.)
Ennerdale Dr. NW9 . . . . . .1A **28**
Ennerdale Ho. E3 . . . . . .3B **66**
Ennersdale Rd.
SE13 . . . . .3F **109**
(off Vesey Path)
Ennis Ho. E14 . . . . .5D **67**
(off Vesey Path)
Ennismore Av. W4 . . . . . . .5B **70**
Ennismore Gdns.
SW7 . . . . .3A **74**
Ennismore Gdns. M.
SW7 . . . . .4A **74**
Ennismore M. SW7 . . . .4A **74**
Ennismore St. SW7 . . . .4A **74**
Ennis Rd. N4 . . . . .3C **34**
Ensbury Ho. SW8 . . . . . . .3B **90**
(off Carroun Rd.)
Ensign Ho. E14 . . . . .3C **80**
(off Admirals Way)
SW18 . . . . .1E **101**
Ensign Ind. Cen. E1 . . . .1C **78**
(off Ensign St.)
Ensign St. E1 . . . . .1C **78**
Ensor M. SW7 . . . . .1F **87**
Enterprise Bus. Pk.
E14 . . . . .3D **81**
Enterprise Centre, The
BR3: Beck 5A **122**
(off Cricket La.)
Enterprise Ho. E9 . . . . . . .4E **51**
(off Tudor Gro.)
E14 . . . . .1D **95**
(off St Davids Sq.)
Enterprise Ind. Est.
SE16 . . . . .1E **93**
Enterprise Row N15 . . . .1B **36**
Enterprise Way
NW10 . . . . .2B **56**
SW18 . . . . .2C **100**
Enterprize Way SE8 . . . .5B **80**
Entertainment Av.
SE10 . . . . .2A **82**
Epcot M. NW10 . . . . .2F **57**
Epirus M. SW6 . . . . .3C **86**
Epirus Rd. SW6 . . . . .3B **86**
Epping Cl. E14 . . . . .5C **80**
Epping Pl. N1 . . . . .3C **48**
Epple Rd. SW6 . . . . .4B **86**
Epsom Rd. E10 . . . . .1E **39**
Epworth St.
EC2 . . . . . .4C **10** (3F **63**)
Equana Apartments
SE8 . . . . .1A **94**
(off Evelyn St.)
Equiano Ho. SW9 . . . . . . .4B **90**
(off Lett Rd.)
Equity Sq. E2 . . . . .2B **64**
(off Shacklewell St.)
Erasmus St. SW1 . . . . . .5F **75**
Erconwald St. W12 . . . . .5B **56**
Eresby Ho. SW7 . . . . . . .3A **74**
(off Rutland Ga.)
Eresby Pl. NW6 . . . . .4C **44**
Erica Ho. SE4 . . . . .1B **108**
Erica St. W12 . . . . .1C **70**
Eric Cl. E7 . . . . .1C **54**
Ericcson Cl. SW18 . . . . .3C **100**

Eric Fletcher Ct. N1 . . . . .4E **49**
(off Essex Rd.)
Eric Liddell Sports Cen.
. . . . .2F **125**
Eric Rd. E7 . . . . .1C **54**
NW10 . . . . .3B **42**
Eric Shipman Ter.
E13 . . . . .3C **68**
(off Balaam St.)
Ericson Ho. SE13 . . . . . . .2F **109**
(off Blessington Rd.)
Eric St. E3 . . . . .3B **66**
(not continuous)
Eric Wilkins Ho.
SE1 . . . . .1C **92**
(off Old Kent Rd.)
Eridge Rd. W4 . . . . .4A **70**
Erin Cl. SW6 . . . . .2C **86**
Erlanger Rd. SE14 . . . . .4F **93**
Erlich Cotts. E1 . . . . .4E **65**
(off Sidney St.)
Ermine Ho. E3 . . . . .5B **52**
(off Parnell Rd.)
Ermine M. E2 . . . . .5B **50**
Ermine Rd. N15 . . . . .1B **36**
SE13 . . . . .2D **109**
Ernest Av. SE27 . . . . . . .4D **119**
Ernest Harriss Ho.
W9 . . . . .3C **58**
(off Elgin Av.)
Ernest Shackleton Lodge
SE10 . . . . .5A **82**
(off Christchurch Way)
Ernest St. E1 . . . . .3F **65**
Ernshaw Pl. SW15 . . . . .3A **100**
Eros 5B **14** (1F **75**)
Eros Ho. Shops SE6 . . . .5D **109**
(off Brownhill Rd.)
Erpingham Rd. SW15 . . . .1E **99**
Errington Rd. W9 . . . . . . .3B **58**
Errol St. EC1 . . . .4A **10** (3E **63**)
Erskine Ho. SW1 . . . . . . .1E **89**
(off Churchill Gdns.)
Erskine M. NW3 . . . . .4B **46**
(off Erskine Rd.)
Erskine Rd. NW3 . . . . . . .4B **46**
Esam Way SW16 . . . . . . .5C **118**
Escott Gdns. SE9 . . . . . .4F **125**
Esher Gdns. SW19 . . . . .2F **113**
Eskdale NW1 . . . . .1F **5**
(off Stanhope St.)
Esk Ho. E3 . . . . .3B **66**
(off British St.)
Esk Rd. E13 . . . . .3C **68**
Esmar Cres. NW9 . . . . . .2C **28**
Esmeralda Rd.
SE1 . . . . .5C **78**
Esmond Ct. W8 . . . . .4D **73**
(off Thackeray St.)
Esmond Gdns. W4 . . . . . .5A **70**
Esmond Rd. NW6 . . . . . . .5B **44**
W4 . . . . .5A **70**
Esmond St. SW15 . . . . . .2A **100**
Esparto St. SW18 . . . . . .5D **101**
Esprit Ct. E1 . . . . .1F **19**
(off Brune St.)
Essendine Mans.
W9 . . . . .2C **58**
Essendine Rd. W9 . . . . . .2C **58**

Essex Ct. EC4 . . . . .3B **16**
SW13 . . . . .5B **84**
W6 . . . . .4E **71**
(off Hammersmith Gro.)
Essex Gdns. N4 . . . . .1D **35**
Essex Gro. SE19 . . . . . . .5F **119**
Essex Ho. E14 . . . . .5D **67**
(off Girauld St.)
Essex Mans. E11 . . . . . . .2F **39**
Essex Pk. M. W3 . . . . . . .2A **70**
Essex Rd. E10 . . . . .1E **39**
E17 . . . . .1A **38**
N1 . . . . .5D **49**
NW10 . . . . .4A **42**
Essex Rd. Sth. E11 . . . . . .2F **39**
Essex St. E7 . . . . .2C **54**
WC2 . . . . . .3B **16** (5C **62**)
Essex Vs. W8 . . . . .3C **72**
Essex Wharf E5 . . . . .4F **37**
Essian St. E1 . . . . .4A **66**
Estate Way E10 . . . . .3B **38**
Estcourt Rd. SW6 . . . . . .3B **86**
Estella Apartments
E15 . . . . .3F **53**
(off Grove Cres. Rd.)
Estella Ho. W11 . . . . .1F **71**
(off St Ann's Rd.)
Estelle Rd. NW3 . . . . .1B **46**
Esterbrooke St. SW1 . . . .5F **75**
Este Rd. SW11 . . . . .1A **102**
Esther Randall Ct.
NW1 . . . . .3E **5**
(off Lit. Albany St.)
Esther Rd. E11 . . . . .2A **40**
Estoria Cl. SW2 . . . . . . .5C **104**
Estorick Collection of
Modern Italian Art
. . . . .3D **49**
Estreham Rd. SW16 . . . .5F **117**
Estuary Ho. E16 . . . . .2F **83**
(off Agnes George Wlk.)
Eswyn Rd. SW17 . . . . . . .4B **116**
Etal Ho. N1 . . . . .4D **49**
(off The Sutton Est.)
Etcetera Theatre 4D **47**
(off Camden High St.)
Etchingham Rd. E15 . . . . .1E **53**
Eternit Wlk. SW6 . . . . . . .4E **85**
Ethelbert Ho. E9 . . . . .1A **52**
(off Homerton Rd.)
Ethelbert St. SW12 . . . .1D **117**
Ethelburga St. SW11 . . . .4A **88**
Ethelburga Twr.
SW11 . . . . .4A **88**
(off Maskelyne Cl.)
Ethelden Rd. W12 . . . . . .2D **71**
Ethel Rd. E16 . . . . .5D **69**
Ethel St. SE17 . . . . .5E **77**
Etheridge Rd. NW4 . . . . .2E **29**
(not continuous)
Etherow St. SE22 . . . . . .5C **106**
Etherstone Grn.
SW16 . . . . .4C **118**
Etherstone Rd.
SW16 . . . . .4C **118**
Ethnard Rd. SE15 . . . . . .2D **93**
Ethos Sport Imperial 3F **73**
Etloe Ho. E10 . . . . .3C **38**
Etloe Rd. E10 . . . . .4C **38**
Eton Av. NW3 . . . . .4F **45**

Eton Cl. SW18 . . . . . . .5D **101**
Eton Coll. Rd. NW3 . . . .3B **46**
Eton Ct. NW3 . . . . .4F **45**
Eton Garages NW3 . . . . .3A **46**
Eton Gro. SE13 . . . . . . .1A **110**
Eton Hall NW3 . . . . .3B **46**
Eton Ho. N5 . . . . .1D **49**
   (off Leigh Rd.)
Eton Mnr. Ct. E10 . . . . . .4C **38**
   (off Leyton Grange Est.)
Eton Manor, Olympic Pk.
   . . . . .1D **53**
Eton Pl. NW3 . . . . .4C **46**
Eton Ri. NW3 . . . . .3B **46**
Eton Rd. NW3 . . . . .4B **46**
Eton Vs. NW3 . . . . .3B **46**
Etta St. SE8 . . . . .2A **94**
Ettrick St. E14 . . . . .5E **67**
   (not continuous)
Eucalyptus M. SW16 . . . .5F **117**
Eugene Cotter Ho.
   SE17 . . . . .5F **77**
   (off Tatum St.)
Eugenia Rd. SE16 . . . . . .5E **79**
Euro Cl. NW10 . . . . .3C **42**
Eurolink Bus. Cen.
   SW2 . . . . .3C **104**
Europa Ho. E16 . . . . . . .5B **68**
   (off Shirley St.)
Europa Pl. EC1 . . .2F **9** (2E **63**)
Europa Trade Pk.
   E16 . . . . .3A **68**
Eustace Bldg. SW8 . . . . .2D **89**
Eustace Ho. SE11 . . . . . .5B **76**
   (off Old Paradise St.)
Eustace Rd. E6 . . . . .2F **69**
   SW6 . . . . .3C **86**
Euston Gro. NW1 . . . . . . .2B **6**
Euston Rd.
   NW1 . . . . .4F **5** (3D **61**)
Euston Sq.
   NW1 . . . . . .2B **6** (2F **61**)
   (not continuous)
Euston Sta. Colonnade
   NW1 . . . . . .2B **6** (2F **61**)
Euston St.
   NW1 . . . . . .2A **6** (2E **61**)
Euston Twr.
   NW1 . . . . . .3F **5** (3E **61**)
EUSTON UNDERPASS
   . . . . .3E **61**
Evan Cook Cl. SE15 . . . . .4E **93**
Evandale Rd. SW9 . . . . . .5C **90**
Evangelist Ho. EC4 . . . . .3D **17**
   (off Black Friars La.)
Evangelist Rd. NW5 . . . . .1D **47**
Evans Bus. Cen.
   NW2 . . . . .5C **28**
Evans Cl. E8 . . . . .3B **50**
Evans Ho. SW8 . . . . .3F **89**
   (off Wandsworth Rd.)
   W12 . . . . .1D **71**
   (off White City Est.)
Evans Rd. SE6 . . . . .2A **124**
Evanston Gdns.
   IG4: Ilf 1F **41**
Evedon Ho. N1 . . . . .5A **50**
   (off New Era Est.)
Evelina Mans. SE5 . . . . . .3F **91**
Evelina Rd. SE15 . . . . . .1E **107**

Eveline Lowe Est.
   SE16 . . . . .4C **78**
Evelyn Ct. E8 . . . . .1C **50**
   N1 . . . . .1B **10**
   (off Evelyn Wlk.)
Evelyn Denington Ct.
   N1 . . . . .4D **49**
   (off The Sutton Est.)
Evelyn Fox Ct. W10 . . . . .4E **57**
Evelyn Gdns. SW7 . . . . . .1E **87**
Evelyn Ho. SE14 . . . . . . .4A **94**
   (off Loring Rd.)
   W8 . . . . .3D **73**
   (off Hornton St.)
   W12 . . . . .3B **70**
   (off Cobbold Rd.)
Evelyn Mans. SW1 . . . . . .5F **21**
   (off Carlisle Pl.)
   W14 . . . . .2A **86**
   (off Queen's Club Gdns.)
Evelyn Rd. E16 . . . . .2C **82**
   SW19 . . . . .5D **115**
Evelyn St. SE8 . . . . .5A **80**
Evelyn Wlk.
   N1 . . . . . . .1B **10** (1F **63**)
Evelyn Yd.
   W1 . . . . . . .2B **14** (5F **61**)
Evenwood Cl. SW15 . . . . .3A **100**
Everard Ho. E1 . . . . .5C **64**
   (off Boyd St.)
Everatt Cl. SW18 . . . . . . .4B **100**
Everdon Rd. SW13 . . . . . .2C **84**
Everest Pl. E14 . . . . .4E **67**
Everett Ho. SE17 . . . . . . .1F **91**
   (off East St.)
Evergreen Sq. E8 . . . . . . .4B **50**
Everilda St. N1 . . . . .5B **48**
Evering Rd. E5 . . . . .5B **36**
   N16 . . . . .5B **36**
Everington Rd. W6 . . . . . .2F **85**
   (not continuous)
Everitt Rd. NW10 . . . . . . .2A **56**
Everleigh St. N4 . . . . .3B **34**
Eve Rd. E11 . . . . .1A **54**
   E15 . . . . .1A **68**
Evershed Ho. E1 . . . . .2F **19**
   (off Old Castle St.)
Eversholt St.
   NW1 . . . . . . .1A **6** (1E **61**)
Evershot Rd. N4 . . . . .3B **34**
Eversleigh Rd. E6 . . . . . . .5F **55**
   SW11 . . . . .1B **102**
Eversley Ho. E2 . . . . .2C **64**
   (off Gosset St.)
Eversley Pk. SW19 . . . . . .5D **113**
Eversley Rd. SE7 . . . . . . .2D **97**
Everthorpe Rd.
   SE15 . . . . .1B **106**
Everton Bldgs.
   NW1 . . . . . . .2F **5** (2E **61**)
Evesham Ho. E2 . . . . .1E **65**
   (off Old Ford Rd.)
   NW8 . . . . .5E **45**
   (off Abbey Rd.)
   SW1 . . . . .1D **89**
   (part of Abbots Mnr.)
Evesham Rd. E15 . . . . . . .4B **54**
Evesham St. W11 . . . . . . .1F **71**
Evesham Wlk. SE5 . . . . . .5F **91**
   SW9 . . . . .5C **90**

Evesham Way
   SW11 . . . . .1C **102**
Ewald Rd. SW6 . . . . .5B **86**
Ewart Pl. E3 . . . . .1B **66**
Ewart Rd. SE23 . . . . .5F **107**
Ewe Cl. N7 . . . . .3A **48**
Ewelme Rd. SE23 . . . . . .1E **121**
Ewen Cres. SW2 . . . . . . .5C **104**
Ewen Henderson Ct.
   SE14 . . . . .3A **94**
   (off Goodwood Rd.)
Ewen Ho. N1 . . . . .5B **48**
   (off Barnsbury Est.)
Ewer St.
   SE1 . . . . . . .2F **25** (2E **77**)
Ewhurst Cl. E1 . . . . .4E **65**
Ewhurst Rd. SE4 . . . . . . .4B **108**
Exbury Ho. E9 . . . . .4E **51**
   SW1 . . . . .1F **89**
   (off Rampayne St.)
Exbury Rd. SE6 . . . . .2C **122**
ExCeL 1D **83**
Excel Ct. WC2 . . . . .5C **14**
Excel Marina E16 . . . . . . .1C **82**
Excelsior Gdns. SE13 . . . .5E **95**
Excelsior Ind. Est.
   SE15 . . . . .2E **93**
Excel Waterfront E16 . .1D **83**
Exchange Arc.
   EC2 . . . . . . .5E **11** (4A **64**)
Exchange Bldg. E1 . . . . . .4F **11**
   (off Commercial St.)
Exchange Ct.
   WC2 . . . . . . .5E **15** (1A **76**)
Exchange Ho. EC2 . . . . . .5E **11**
   NW10 . . . . .4D **43**
   SW1 . . . . .5F **75**
   (off Vauxhall Bri. Rd.)
Exchange Mans.
   NW11 . . . . .2B **30**
Exchange Pl.
   EC2 . . . . . . .5D **11** (4A **64**)
Exchange Sq.
   EC2 . . . . . . .5D **11** (4A **64**)
Exchange St.
   EC1 . . . . . . .2F **9** (2E **63**)
Exeter Ct. NW6 . . . . .1C **58**
   (off Cambridge Rd.)
Exeter Ho. N1 . . . . .5A **50**
   (off New Era Est.)
   SE15 . . . . .2C **92**
   (off Friary Est.)
   SW15 . . . . .4E **99**
   W2 . . . . .5E **59**
   (off Hallfield Est.)
Exeter Mans. NW2 . . . . . .3A **44**
Exeter M. NW6 . . . . .3D **45**
   SW6 . . . . .3C **86**
Exeter Rd. E16 . . . . .4C **68**
   E17 . . . . .1C **38**
   NW2 . . . . .2A **44**
Exeter St.
   WC2 . . . . . . .4E **15** (1A **76**)
Exeter Way SE14 . . . . . . .3B **94**
Exford Ct. SW11 . . . . .4F **87**
   (off Bolingbroke Wlk.)
Exford Gdns. SE12 . . . . . .1D **125**
Exford Rd. SE12 . . . . .2D **125**
Exhibition Cl. W12 . . . . . . .1E **71**
Exhibition Rd. SW7 . . . . . .3F **73**

Exmoor Ho. *E3* 1A *66*
    (off Gernon Rd.)
Exmoor St. *W10* 3F *57*
Exmouth Ho. *E14* 5D *81*
    (off Cahir St.)
EC1 . . . . .3B *8*
    (off Pine St.)
Exmouth Mkt.
  EC1 . . . . .3B **8** (3C *62*)
Exmouth M.
  NW1 . . . . . . .2A **6** (2E *61*)
Exmouth Pl. *E8* 4D *51*
Exmouth Rd. *E17* 1B *38*
Exmouth St. *E1* 5E *65*
Exning Rd. *E16* 3A *68*
Exonbury *NW8* 5D *45*
    (off Abbey Rd.)
Exon St. *SE17* 1A *92*
Explorers Ct. *E14* 1F *81*
    (off Newport Av.)
Export Ho. *SE1* 4E *27*
    (off Tower Bri. Rd.)
Express Newspapers
  SE1 . . . . .1D *25*
    (off Blackfriars Rd.)
Express Wharf *E14* 3C *80*
    (off Hutchings St.)
Exton St.
  SE1 . . . . . . .2B **24** (2C *76*)
Eyhurst Cl. *NW2* 4C *28*
Eylewood Rd.
  SE27 . . . . .5E *119*
Eynella Rd. *SE22* 5B *106*
Eynham Rd. *W12* 5E *57*
Eynsford Ho. *SE1* 4B *26*
    (off Crosby Row)
  SE15 . . . . .2E *93*
  SE17 . . . . .5A *78*
    (off East St.)
Eyot Gdns. *W6* 1B *84*
Eyot Grn. *W4* 1B *84*
Eyot Ho. *SE16* 4C *78*
    (off Frean St.)
Eyre Ct. *NW8* 1F *59*
Eyre St. Hill
  EC1 . . . . .4B **8** (3C *62*)
Eythorne Rd. *SW9* 4C *90*
Ezra St. *E2* 2B *64*

F

Faber Gdns. *NW4* 1C *28*
Fabian Bell Twr. *E3* 1C *66*
    (off Pancras Way)
Fabian Rd. *SW6* 3B *86*
Facade, The *SE23* 2E *121*
Factory Rd. *E16* 2F *83*
Fairacres *SW15* 2B *98*
Fairbairn Grn. *SW9* 4D *91*
Fairbank Est.
  N1 . . . . .1B **10** (1F *63*)
Fairbourne Rd. *SW4* 4F *103*
Fairbriar Residence
  SW7 . . . . .5E *73*
    (off Cromwell Rd.)
Fairbridge Rd. *N19* 4F *33*
Fairburn Ct. *SW15* 3A *100*
Fairburn Ho. *W14* 1B *86*
    (off Ivatt Pl.)

Fairby Ho. *SE1* 5B *78*
    (off Longfield Est.)
Fairby Rd. *SE12* 3D *111*
Faircharm Trad. Est.
  SE8 . . . . .3D *95*
Fairchild Cl. *SW11* 5F *87*
Fairchild Ho. *E2* 1D *65*
    (off Cambridge Cres.)
  E9 . . . . .4E *51*
    (off Frampton Pk. Rd.)
  N1 . . . . .1D *11*
    (off Fanshaw St.)
Fairchild Pl. *EC2* 4E *11*
Fairchild St.
  EC2 . . . . . . .3E **11** (3A *64*)
Fairclough St. *E1* 5C *64*
Fairdale Gdns.
  SW15 . . . . .2D *99*
Fairfax Cl. *NW6* 4E *45*
    (off Fairfax Rd.)
Fairfax Gdns. *SE3* 4E *97*
Fairfax Mans. *NW6* 4E *45*
    (off Finchley Rd.)
Fairfax M. *E16* 2D *83*
  SW15 . . . . .2E *99*
Fairfax Pl. *NW6* 4E *45*
  W14 . . . . .4A *72*
Fairfax Rd. *NW6* 4E *45*
  W4 . . . . .4A *70*
Fairfield *E1* 4E *65*
    (off Redman's Rd.)
  NW1 . . . . .5E *47*
    (off Arlington Rd.)
Fairfield Av. *NW4* 1D *29*
Fairfield Ct. *NW10* 5C *42*
Fairfield Dr. *SW18* 3D *101*
Fairfield Gdns. *N8* 1A *34*
Fairfield Gro. *SE7* 2F *97*
Fairfield Rd. *E3* 1C *66*
  N8 . . . . .1A *34*
Fairfield St. *SW18* 3D *101*
Fairfoot Rd. *E3* 3C *66*
Fairford *SE6* 1C *122*
Fairford Ho. *SE11* 5C *76*
Fairhazel Gdns. *NW6* 3D *45*
Fairhazel Mans. *NW6* 4E *45*
    (off Fairhazel Gdns.)
Fairholme Rd. *W14* 1A *86*
Fairholt Cl. *N16* 3A *36*
Fairholt Rd. *N16* 3F *35*
Fairholt St. *SW7* 4A *74*
Fairland Rd. *E15* 3B *54*
Fairlawn *SE7* 3E *97*
Fairlawn Ct. *SE7* 3E *97*
    (not continuous)
Fairlawn Mans. *SE14* 4F *93*
Fairlawn Pk. *SE26* 5A *122*
Fairlead Ho. *E14* 4C *80*
    (off Alpha Gro.)
Fairlie Ct. *E3* 2D *67*
    (off Stroudley Wlk.)
Fairlie Gdns. *SE23* 5E *107*
Fairlight Av. *NW10* 1A *56*
Fairlight Ct. *NW10* 1A *56*
Fairlight Rd. *SW17* 4F *115*
Fairlop Ct. *E11* 2F *39*
Fairlop Rd. *E11* 2F *39*
Fairmead Gdns.
  IG4: Ilf 1F *41*
Fairmead Ho. *E9* 1A *52*

Fairmead Rd. *N19* 5F *33*
Fairmile Av. *SW16* 5F *117*
Fairmont Av. *E14* 2F *81*
Fairmont Ho. *E3* 3C *66*
    (off Wellington Way)
Fairmount Rd. *SW2* 4B *104*
Fairsted Wlk. *N1* 5E *49*
    (off Popham St.)
Fair St. *SE1* 3E **27** (3A *78*)
Fairthorne Vs. *SE7* 1C *96*
    (off Felltram Way)
Fairthorn Rd. *SE7* 1C *96*
Fairview Cl. *SE26* 5A *122*
Fairview Ho. *SW2* 5B *104*
Fairview Pl. *SW2* 5B *104*
Fairview Rd. *N15* 1B *36*
Fairwall Ho. *SE5* 4A *92*
Fairway, The *W3* 5A *56*
Fairway Cl. *NW11* 2E *31*
Fairway Ct. *SE16* 3F *79*
    (off Christopher Cl.)
Fairways Bus. Pk.
  E10 . . . . .4A *38*
Fairweather Ho. *N7* 1A *48*
Fairweather Rd. *N16* 1C *36*
Fairwyn Rd. *SE26* 4A *122*
Faith Ct. *E3* 1C *66*
    (off Lefevre Wlk.)
  SE1 . . . . .1B *92*
    (off Cooper's Rd.)
Fakruddin St. *E1* 3C *64*
Falcon *WC1* 5E *7*
    (off Old Gloucester St.)
Falconberg M.
  W1 . . . . . . .2C **14** (5F *61*)
Falcon Ct.
  EC4 . . . . . . .3C **16** (5C *62*)
  N1 . . . . .1E *9*
    (off Gtn. Row)
Falconer Wlk. *N7* 4B *34*
Falconet Ct. *E1* 2D *79*
    (off Wapping High St.)
Falcon Gro. *SW11* 1A *102*
Falcon Highwalk *EC2* 1F *17*
Falcon Ho. *E14* 1D *95*
    (off St Davids Sq.)
  NW6 . . . . .5D *45*
    (off Springfield Wlk.)
  SW5 . . . . .1D *87*
    (off Old Brompton Rd.)
Falcon La. *SW11* 1A *102*
Falcon Lodge *W9* 4C *58*
    (off Admiral Wlk.)
Falcon Pk. Ind. Est.
  NW10 . . . . .1A *42*
Falcon Point
  SE1 . . . . . .5E **17** (1D *77*)
Falcon Rd. *SW11* 1A *102*
Falcon St. *E13* 3C *68*
Falcon Ter. *SW11* 1A *102*
Falcon Way *E14* 5D *81*
Falcon Wharf *SW11* 5F *87*
Falconwood Ct.
  SE3 . . . . .5B *96*
    (off Montpelier Row)
Falkirk Ct. *SE16* 2F *79*
    (off Rotherhithe St.)
Falkirk Ho. *W9* 1D *59*
    (off Maida Va.)
Falkirk St. *N1* 1E **11** (1A *64*)

Falkland Ho. SE6 . . . . .4E 123
  W8 . . . . .4D 73
  W14 . . . . .1B 86
    (off Edith Vs.)
Falkland Pl. NW5 . . . . . .2E 47
Falkland Rd. NW5 . . . . . .2E 47
Fallodon Ho. W11 . . . . . .4B 58
    (off Tavistock Cres.)
Fallow Ct. SE16 . . . . . . .1C 92
    (off Argyle Way)
Fallsbrook Rd.
  SW16 . . . . .5E 117
Falmouth Cl. SE12 . . . . .3B 110
Falmouth Gdns.
  IG4: Ilf 1F 41
Falmouth Ho. SE11 . . . . .1C 90
    (off Seaton Cl.)
  W2 . . . . .1A 74
    (off Clarendon Pl.)
Falmouth Rd.
  SE1 . . . . . . .5A 26 (4E 77)
Falmouth St. E15 . . . . . .2F 53
Falmouth Wlk. SW15 . . . .4C 98
Falmouth Way E17 . . . . .1B 38
Falstaff Bldg. E1 . . . . . . .1D 79
    (off Cannon St. Rd.)
Falstaff Ct. SE11 . . . . . . .5D 77
    (off Opal St.)
Falstaff Ho. N1 . . . . .1D 11
    (off Regan Way)
Fambridge Cl. SE26 . . . .4B 122
Fane St. W14 . . . . .2B 86
Fan Museum, The 3E 95
Fann St. EC1 . . . .4F 9 (3E 63)
  EC2 . . . . .4F 9 (3E 63)
    (not continuous)
Fanshaw St.
  N1 . . . . . . .1D 11 (2A 64)
Fanthorpe St. SW15 . . . . .1E 99
Faraday Ho. E14 . . . . . . .1B 80
    (off Brightlingsea Pl.)
  SE1 . . . . .4B 26
    (off Cole St.)
  W10 . . . . .4A 58
    (off Wornington Rd.)
Faraday Lodge SE10 . . . .4B 82
Faraday Mans. W14 . . . . .2A 86
    (off Queen's Club Gdns.)
Faraday Rd. E15 . . . . . . .3B 54
  SW19 . . . . .5C 114
  W10 . . . . .4A 58
Faraday Way SE18 . . . . . .4F 83
Faringford Rd. E15 . . . . . .4A 54
Farjeon Ho. NW6 . . . . . .4F 45
    (off Hilgrove Rd.)
Farjeon Rd. SE3 . . . . . . .4F 97
Farleigh Ho. N1 . . . . .4D 49
    (off Halton Rd.)
Farleigh Pl. N16 . . . . . . .1B 50
Farleigh Rd. N16 . . . . . . .1B 50
Farley Ct. NW1 . . . . .4B 4
    (off Allsop Pl.)
  W14 . . . . .4B 72
Farley Ho. SE26 . . . . . . .3D 121
Farley M. SE6 . . . . .5E 109
Farley Rd. SE6 . . . . .5D 109
Farlington Pl. SW15 . . . . .5D 99
Farlow Rd. SW15 . . . . . . .1F 99
Farlton Rd. SW18 . . . . . .1D 115

Farm Av. NW2 . . . . .5A 30
  SW16 . . . . .4A 118
Farm Cl. SW6 . . . . .3C 86
Farmcote Rd. SE12 . . . . .1C 124
Farmdale Rd. SE10 . . . . .1C 96
Farmer Rd. E10 . . . . .3D 39
Farmer's Rd. SE5 . . . . . . .3D 91
Farmer St. W8 . . . . .2C 72
Farmfield Rd.
  BR1: Brom 5A 124
Farmilo Rd. E17 . . . . .2B 38
Farm La. SW6 . . . . .2C 86
Farm La. Trad. Est.
  SW6 . . . . .2C 86
Farmleigh Ho. SW9 . . . . .3D 105
Farm Pl. W8 . . . . .2C 72
Farm Rd. NW10 . . . . .5A 42
Farm St. W1 . . . .5D 13 (1D 75)
Farm Wlk. NW11 . . . . . . .1B 30
Farnaby Ho. W10 . . . . . . .2B 58
    (off Bruckner St.)
Farnaby Rd. SE9 . . . . . . .2E 111
Farnan Lodge
  SW16 . . . . .5A 118
Farnan Rd. SW16 . . . . . .5A 118
Farnborough Ho.
  SW15 . . . . .1C 112
Farncombe St. SE16 . . . . .3C 78
Farndale Cl. SE18 . . . . . . .3F 97
Farndale Ho. NW6 . . . . . .5D 45
    (off Kilburn Vale)
Farnell M. SW5 . . . . .1D 87
Farnham Ho. NW1 . . . . . .3A 60
    (off Harewood Av.)
  SE1 . . . . .2F 25
    (off Union St.)
Farnham Pl.
  SE1 . . . . . . .2E 25 (2D 77)
Farnham Royal SE11 . . . .1B 90
Farningham Ho. N4 . . . . . .2F 35
Farnley Ho. SW8 . . . . . . .5F 89
Farnsworth Ct. SE10 . . . . .4B 82
    (off West Parkside)
Farnworth Ho. E14 . . . . . .5F 81
    (off Manchester Rd.)
Faroe Rd. W14 . . . . .4F 71
Farquhar Rd. SE19 . . . . . .5B 120
  SW19 . . . . .3C 114
Farrance St. E14 . . . . . . .5C 66
Farrell Ho. E1 . . . . .5E 65
    (off Ronald St.)
Farren Rd. SE23 . . . . . . .2A 122
Farrer Ho. SE8 . . . . .3C 94
Farriers Ho. EC1 . . . . .4A 10
    (off Errol St.)
Farriers M. SE15 . . . . . . .1E 107
Farrier St. NW1 . . . . .4D 47
Farrier Wlk. SW10 . . . . . .2E 87
Farringdon La.
  EC1 . . . . . . .4C 8 (3C 62)
Farringdon Rd.
  EC1 . . . . . . .3B 8 (3C 62)
Farringdon St.
  EC4 . . . . . .1D 17 (4D 63)
Farrins Rents EC1 . . . . . .2A 80
Farrow La. SE14 . . . . .3E 93
Farrow Pl. SE16 . . . . .4A 80
Farthingale Wlk. E15 . . . . .4F 53
Farthing All. SE1 . . . . .3C 78

Farthing Flds. E1 . . . . . . .2D 79
Fashion & Textile Mus.
  . . . . .3E 27 (3A 78)
Fashion St.
  E1 . . . . .1F 19 (4B 64)
Fassett Rd. E8 . . . . .3C 50
Fassett Sq. E8 . . . . .3C 50
Faulkners All.
  EC1 . . . . .5D 9 (4D 63)
Faulkner St. SE14 . . . . . . .4E 93
Faunce Ho. SE17 . . . . . . .2D 91
    (off Doddington Gro.)
Faunce St. SE17 . . . . . . .1D 91
Favart Rd. SW6 . . . . .4C 86
Faversham Ho. NW1 . . . . .5E 47
    (off Bayham Pl.)
  SE17 . . . . .1A 92
    (off Kinglake St.)
Faversham Rd. SE6 . . . . .5B 108
Fawcett Cl. SW11 . . . . . . .5F 87
  SW16 . . . . .5C 118
Fawcett Cl. SW10 . . . . . . .2E 87
    (off Fawcett St.)
Fawcett Est. E5 . . . . .3C 36
Fawcett Rd. NW10 . . . . . .4B 42
Fawcett St. SW10 . . . . . . .2E 87
Fawe Pk. M. SW15 . . . . .2B 100
Fawe Pk. Rd. SW15 . . . . .2B 100
Fawe St. E14 . . . . .4D 67
Fawkham Ho. SE1 . . . . . . .5B 78
    (off Longfield Est.)
Fawley Lodge E14 . . . . . . .5F 81
    (off Millennium Dr.)
Fawley Rd. NW6 . . . . .2D 45
Fawnbrake Av.
  SE24 . . . . .3D 105
Fawn Rd. E13 . . . . .1E 69
Fawood Av. NW10 . . . . . . .4A 42
Faygate Rd. SW2 . . . . . .2B 118
Fayland Av. SW16 . . . . . . .5E 117
Fazeley Ct. W9 . . . . .4C 58
    (off Elmfield Way)
Fearnley Ho. SE5 . . . . . . .5A 92
Fearon St. SE10 . . . . .1C 96
Feathers Pl. SE10 . . . . . . .2F 95
Featherstone Av.
  SE23 . . . . .2D 121
Featherstone St.
  EC1 . . . . . . .3B 10 (3F 63)
Featley Rd. SW9 . . . . . . .1D 105
Feeny Cl. NW10 . . . . .1B 42
Felbridge Cl. SW16 . . . . . .4C 118
Felbridge Ho. SE22 . . . . .1A 106
Felday Rd. SE13 . . . . . . .4D 109
Felden St. SW6 . . . . .4B 86
Feldman Cl. N16 . . . . .3C 36
Felgate M. W6 . . . . .5D 71
Felix Av. N8 . . . . .1A 34
Felix Pl. SW2 . . . . .3C 104
    (off Talma Rd.)
Felixstowe Rd.
  NW10 . . . . .2D 57
Felix St. E2 . . . . .1D 65
Fellbrigg Rd. SE22 . . . . . .3B 106
Fellbrigg St. E1 . . . . .3D 65
Fellmongers Path
  SE1 . . . . .4F 27
Fellows Ct.
  E2 . . . . . . .1F 11 (1B 64)
    (not continuous)

Fellows Rd. NW3 ......4F 45
Felltram M. SE7 ......1C 96
Felltram Way SE7 ....1C 96
Felmersham Cl.
   SW4 ....2A 104
Felsberg Rd. SW2 ....4A 104
Felsham M. SW15 ....1F 99
   (off Felsham Rd.)
Felsham Rd. SW15 ....1E 99
Felstead Gdns.
   E14 ....1E 95
Felstead Rd. E9 ......3B 52
   E11 ....2C 40
Felstead St. E9 ......3B 52
Felstead Wharf E14 ...1E 95
Felsted Rd. E16 ......5F 69
Felton Ho. N1 ....5F 49
   (off Branch Pl.)
   SE3 ....2D 111
Felton St. N1 ....5F 49
Fenchurch Av.
   EC3 ......3D 19 (5A 64)
Fenchurch Bldgs.
   EC3 ......3E 19 (5A 64)
Fenchurch Ho. EC3 ...3F 19
   (off Minories)
Fenchurch Pl.
   EC3 ......4E 19 (5A 64)
Fenchurch St.
   EC3 ......4D 19 (1A 78)
Fen Ct. EC3 ..4D 19 (5A 64)
Fendall St.
   SE1 ......5E 27 (4A 78)
   (not continuous)
Fendt Cl. E16 ....5B 68
Fenelon Pl. W14 ......5B 72
Fenham Rd. SE15 .....3C 92
Fenland Ho. E5 ....4E 37
Fen La. SW13 ....4D 85
Fennel Apartments
   SE1 ....2F 27
   (off Cayenne Ct.)
Fennel Cl. E16 ....3A 68
Fenner Cl. SE16 ......5D 79
Fenner Ho. E1 ....2D 79
   (off Watts St.)
Fenner Sq. SW11 .....1F 101
Fennings Rd. SW4 ....4F 103
Fenning St.
   SE1 ......3D 27 (3A 78)
Fenn St. E9 ....2F 51
Fenstanton N4 ....3B 34
   (off Marquis St.)
Fen St. E16 ....1B 82
Fentiman Rd. SW8 ....2A 90
Fenton Cl. SE16 ......3B 50
   SW9 ....5B 90
Fenton House 1E 45
   (off Windmill Hill)
Fenton Ho. SE14 .....3A 94
Fentons Av. E13 .....2D 69
Fenton St. E1 ....5D 65
Fenwick Gro. SE15 ...1C 106
Fenwick Pl. SW9 .....1A 104
Fenwick Rd. SE15 ....1C 106
Ferdinand Dr. SE15 ..3A 92
Ferdinand Ho. NW1 ..4C 46
   (off Ferdinand Pl.)
Ferdinand Pl. NW1 ...4C 46
Ferdinand St. NW1 ...4C 46

Ferguson Centre, The
   E17 ....1A 38
Ferguson Cl. E14 .....5C 80
Ferguson Dr. W3 .....3A 56
Ferguson Ho. SE10 ...4E 95
   (off Sparta St.)
Fergus Rd. N5 ....2D 49
Ferial Ct. SE15 ......3C 92
   (off Fenham Rd.)
Fermain Ct. E. N1 ....5A 50
   (off De Beauvoir Est.)
Fermain Ct. Nth. N1 ..5A 50
   (off De Beauvoir Est.)
Fermain Ct. W. N1 ...5A 50
   (off De Beauvoir Est.)
Ferme Pk. Rd. N4 ....1A 34
   N8 ....1A 34
Fermor Rd. SE23 .....1A 122
Fermoy Ho. W9 ....3B 58
   (off Fermoy Rd.)
Fermoy Rd. W9 ......3B 58
   (not continuous)
Fernbank M. SW12 ...4E 103
Fernbrook Cres.
   SE13 ....4A 110
   (off Leahurst Rd.)
Fernbrook Rd. SE13 ..3A 110
Ferncliff Rd. E8 ......2C 50
Fern Cl. N1 ....1A 64
Fern Ct. SE14 ....5F 93
Ferncroft Av. NW3 ...5C 30
Ferndale Community
   Sports Cen. 1B 104
Ferndale Rd. E7 ......4D 55
   E11 ....4A 40
   N15 ....1B 36
   SW4 ....2A 104
   SW9 ....2A 104
Ferndene Rd. SE24 ...2E 105
Ferndown NW1 ....4F 47
   (off Camley St.)
Ferndown Lodge E14 ..4E 81
   (off Manchester Rd.)
Ferndown Rd. SE9 ....5F 111
Fernhall Dr. IG4: Ilf ..1F 41
Fernhead Rd. W9 ....2B 58
Fernholme Rd.
   SE15 ....3F 107
Fernhurst Rd. SW6 ...4A 86
Fernlea Rd. SW12 ....1D 117
Fernleigh Cl. W9 .....2B 58
Fernsbury St.
   WC1 ......2B 8 (2C 62)
Fernshaw Cl. SW10 ...2E 87
Fernshaw Mans.
   SW10 ....2E 87
   (off Fernshaw Rd.)
Fernshaw Rd. SW10 ..2E 87
Fernside NW11 ....4C 30
Fernside Rd. SW12 ...1B 116
Ferns Rd. E15 ....3B 54
Fern St. E3 ....3C 66
Fernthorpe Rd.
   SW16 ....5E 117
Ferntower Rd. N5 ....2F 49
Fern Wlk. SE16 ......1C 92
Fernwood SW19 .....1B 114
Fernwood Av. SW16 ..4F 117
Ferranti Cl. SE18 ....4F 83
Ferrers Rd. SW16 ....5F 117

Ferrey M. SW9 ......5C 90
Ferriby Cl. N1 ....4C 48
Ferrier Ind. Est.
   SW18 ....2D 101
   (off Ferrier St.)
Ferrier Point E16 ....4C 68
   (off Forty Acre La.)
Ferrier St. SW18 .....2D 101
Ferrings SE21 ....3A 120
Ferris Rd. SE22 ......2C 106
Ferron Rd. E5 ....5D 37
Ferrybridge Ho. SE11 .4C 76
   (off Lambeth Wlk.)
Ferry Ho. E5 ....3D 37
   (off Harrington Hill)
Ferry La. SW13 ......2B 84
Ferryman's Quay
   SW6 ....5E 87
Ferry Rd. SW13 ......3C 84
Ferry St. E14 ....1E 95
Festing Rd. SW15 ....1F 99
Festival Ct. E8 ......4B 50
   (off Holly St.)
Festoon Way E16 ....1F 83
Fetter La.
   EC4 ......3C 16 (5C 62)
   (not continuous)
Fettes Ho. NW8 .....1F 59
   (off Wellington Rd.)
Ffinch St. SE8 ....3C 94
Fidelis Ho. E1 ....1F 19
   (off Gun St.)
Field Cl. NW2 ....4C 28
Field Ct. SW19 ......3C 114
   WC1 ......1A 16 (4B 62)
Fieldgate Mans. E1 ...4C 64
   (off Fieldgate St.,
   not continuous)
Fieldgate St. E1 .....4C 64
Field Ho. NW6 ......2F 57
   (off Harvist Rd.)
Fieldhouse Rd.
   SW12 ....1E 117
Fielding Ct. WC2 .....3D 15
   (off Earlham St.)
Fielding Ho. NW6 ....2C 58
   NW8 ....5E 45
   (off Ainsworth Way)
   W4 ....2A 84
   (off Devonshire St.)
Fielding M. SW13 ....2D 85
Fielding Rd. W4 .....4A 70
   W14 ....4F 71
Fieldings, The SE23 ..1E 121
Fielding St. SE17 ....2E 91
Field Point E7 ....1C 54
Field Rd. E7 ....1B 54
   W6 ....1A 86
Fields Est. E8 ....4C 50
Fieldside Rd.
   BR1: Brom 5F 123
Field St. WC1 ....1F 7 (2B 62)
Fieldsway Ho. N5 ....2C 48
Fieldview SW18 .....1F 115
Fieldway Cres. N5 ...2C 48
Fife Rd. E16 ....4C 68
Fife Ter. N1 ....1B 62
Fifield Path SE23 ....3F 121
Fifth Av. W10 ....2A 58
Fig Tree Cl. NW10 ...5A 42

Figure Ct. *SW3* 1B **88**
   (off West Rd.)
Filey Av. N16 . . . . .3C **36**
Filigree Ct. SE16 . . . . .2B **80**
Fillebrook Rd. E11 . . . . . .3F **39**
Filmer Chambers
  SW6 . . . . .4A **86**
   (off Filmer Rd.)
Filmer Ho. *SW6* 4B **86**
   (off Filmer Rd.)
Filmer M. SW6 . . . . .4B **86**
Filmer Rd. SW6 . . . . .4A **86**
Filton Ct. *SE14* 3E **93**
   (off Farrow La.)
Finborough Ho.
  SW10 . . . . .2E **87**
   (off Finborough Rd.)
Finborough Rd.
  SW10 . . . . .1D **87**
Finborough Theatre, The
  . . . . .2D **87**
   (off Finborough Rd.)
Finch Av. SE27 . . . . .4F **119**
Finchdean Ho. SW15 . . . .5B **98**
Finch Ho. *E3* 5B **52**
   (off Jasmine Sq.)
  SE8 . . . . .3D **95**
   (off Bronze St.)
Finch La. EC3 . . .3C **18** (5F **63**)
Finchley Pl. NW8 . . . . . . .1F **59**
Finchley Rd. NW2 . . . . . . .5C **30**
  NW3 . . . . .1C **44**
  NW8 . . . . .5F **45**
  NW11 . . . . .1B **30**
Finch Lodge *W9* 4C **58**
   (off Admiral Wlk.)
Finch M. SE15 . . . . .4B **92**
Finch's Ct. E14 . . . . .1D **81**
Finden Rd. E7 . . . . .2E **55**
Findhorn St. E14 . . . . . . .5E **67**
Findon Cl. SW18 . . . . . . .4C **100**
Findon Rd. W12 . . . . .3C **70**
Fingal St. SE10 . . . . .1B **96**
Fingest Ho. *NW8* 3A **60**
   (off Lilestone St.)
Finland Rd. SE4 . . . . . . .1A **108**
Finland St. SE16 . . . . . . .4A **80**
Finlay St. SW6 . . . . .4B **85**
Finley Ct. *SE5* 3E **91**
   (off Redcar St.)
Finmere Ho. N4 . . . . .2E **35**
Finnemore Ho. *N1* 5E **49**
   (off Britannia Row)
Finn Ho. *N1* 1C **10**
   (off Bevenden St.)
Finnis St. E2 . . . . .2D **65**
FINSBURY 3F **9** (2C **62**)
Finsbury Av.
  EC2 . . . . .1C **18** (4F **63**)
Finsbury Av. Sq.
  EC2 . . . . .5D **11** (4A **64**)
Finsbury Cir.
  EC2 . . . . .1C **18** (4F **63**)
Finsbury Est.
  EC1 . . . .2C **8** (2C **62**)
Finsbury Leisure Cen.
  . . . . .3F **9** (2E **63**)
Finsbury Mkt.
  EC2 . . . . .5E **11** (3A **64**)
   (not continuous)

FINSBURY PARK 3C **34**
Finsbury Pk. Av. N4 . . . . .1E **35**
Finsbury Pk. Rd. N4 . . . . .4D **35**
Finsbury Pavement
  EC2 . . . . .5C **10** (4F **63**)
Finsbury Sq.
  EC2 . . . . .4C **10** (3F **63**)
Finsbury St.
  EC2 . . . . .5B **10** (4F **63**)
Finsen Rd. SE5 . . . . .2E **105**
Finstock Rd. W10 . . . . . . .5F **57**
Finwhale Ho. *E14* 4D **81**
   (off Glengall Gro.)
Fiona Ct. NW6 . . . . .1C **58**
Firbank Cl. E16 . . . . .4F **69**
Firbank Rd. SE15 . . . . . . .5D **93**
Fircroft Rd. SW17 . . . . . .2B **116**
Firecrest Dr. NW3 . . . . . . .5D **31**
Firefly Gdns. E6 . . . . .3F **69**
Firehorn Ho. *E15* 2A **68**
   (off Teasel Way)
Firewatch Ct. *E1* 4A **66**
   (off Candle St.)
Fir Gro. Rd. SW9 . . . . . . .5C **90**
Firhill Rd. SE6 . . . . .4C **122**
Fir Ho. *W10* 3A **58**
   (off Droop St.)
Firle Ho. *W10* 4E **57**
   (off Sutton Way)
Firs, The E6 . . . . .4F **55**
  SE26 . . . . .5D **121**
   (Border Rd.)
  SE26 . . . . .5E **121**
   (Waverley Ct.)
Firsby Rd. N16 . . . . .3C **36**
Firs Cl. SE23 . . . . .5A **108**
First Av. E13 . . . . .2C **68**
  SW14 . . . . .1A **98**
  W3 . . . . .2B **70**
  W10 . . . . .3B **58**
First St. SW3 . . . . .5A **74**
Firth Gdns. SW6 . . . . . . .4A **86**
Firth Ho. *E2* 2C **64**
   (off Turin St.)
Fir Tree Cl. SW16 . . . . . . .5E **117**
Firtree Ho. *SE13* 5F **109**
   (off Birdwood Av.)
Fir Trees Cl. SE16 . . . . . . .2A **80**
Fisher Cl. E9 . . . . .2F **51**
Fisher Ho. *E1* 1E **79**
   (off Cable St.)
  N1 . . . . .5C **48**
   (off Barnsbury Est.)
Fishermans Dr. SE16 . . . .3F **79**
Fisherman's Pl. W4 . . . . .2B **84**
Fisherman's Wlk.
  E14 . . . . .2C **80**
Fisher's Cl. SW16 . . . . . .3F **117**
Fishers Ct. SE14 . . . . . . .4F **93**
Fisher's La. W4 . . . . .5A **70**
Fisher St. E16 . . . . .4C **68**
  WC1 . . . .1F **15** (4B **62**)
Fisherton St. NW8 . . . . . .3F **59**
Fishmongers Hall Wharf
  EC4 . . . . .5B **18**
Fishponds Rd. SW17 . . . .4A **116**
Fish St. Hill
  EC3 . . . . .5C **18** (1F **77**)
Fish Wharf
  EC3 . . . . .5C **18** (1F **77**)

Fitness First
  America Square . . .4F **19**
  Baker Street 4B **60**
  Beckenham 5B **122**
  Bloomsbury 4D **7**
  Bow Wharf 1F **65**
  Brixton 1C **104**
  Camden 5D **47**
  Chancery Lane . . .1C **16**
  Clapham Junction
  . . . . .1A **102**
   (off Lavender Hill)
  Covent Garden . . .5E **15**
   (off Bedford St.)
  Crouch End 1A **34**
  Embankment 1E **23**
   (off Embankment Pl.)
  Fetter Lane 3C **16**
   (off Fetter La.)
  Gracechurch Street
  . . . . .4D **19**
   (off Gracechurch St.)
  Great Marlborough Street
  . . . . .3F **13**
  Hammersmith 5E **71**
  High Holborn 1F **15**
   (off High Holborn)
  Holloway 5B **34**
  Islington 1D **9** (1D **63**)
  Kilburn 5B **44**
  Kingly Street 4F **13**
  Lewisham 1E **109**
  Leyton Mills 5E **39**
  London Bridge . . .2C **26**
   (off London Bri. St.)
  London Victoria . . .5E **21**
  Old Street 3B **10**
   (off Bunhill Row)
  Paternoster Square
  . . . . .2E **17**
  Queen Victoria Street
  . . . . .4F **17**
   (off Queen Victoria St.)
  South Kensington
  . . . . .5F **73**
   (off Harrington Rd.)
  Streatham 2A **118**
  Thomas More Square
  . . . . .1C **78**
   (off Thomas More Sq.)
  Tooting Bec 3C **116**
  Walworth Road . . .1E **91**
Fitness First for Women
  Chalk Farm 4C **46**
   (off Chalk Farm Rd.)
Fitrooms 2B **86**
Fitzalan St. SE11 . . . . . . .5C **76**
Fitzclarence Ho. W11 . . . .3A **72**
   (off Holland Park Av.)
Fitzgeorge Av. W14 . . . . .5A **72**
Fitzgerald Av. SW14 . . . . .1A **98**
Fitzgerald Ct. E10 . . . . . . .3D **39**
   (off Leyton Grange Est.)
Fitzgerald Ho. E14 . . . . . .5D **67**
   (off E. India Dock Rd.)
  SW9 . . . . .5C **90**
Fitzgerald Rd. E11 . . . . . .1C **40**
  SW14 . . . . .1A **98**
Fitzhardinge Ho. *W1* 2B **12**
   (off Portman Sq.)

Fitzhardinge St.
W1 . . . . . . .2B **12** (5C **60**)
Fitzhugh Gro.
SW18 . . . . .4F **101**
Fitzjames Av. W14 . . . . .5A **72**
Fitzjohn's Av. NW3 . . . . .1E **45**
Fitzmaurice Ho.
SE16 . . . . .5D **79**
(off Rennie St.)
Fitzmaurice Pl.
W1 . . . . . . .1E **21** (2D **75**)
Fitzneal St. W12 . . . . . .5B **56**
FITZROVIA 5E **5**
Fitzrovia Apartments
W1 . . . . .4E **5**
(off Bolsover St.)
Fitzroy Bri. NW1 . . . . . .5C **46**
Fitzroy Cl. N6 . . . . .3B **32**
Fitzroy Ct. N6 . . . . .1E **33**
W1 . . . . .4A **6**
Fitzroy Ho. E14 . . . . .4B **66**
(off Wallwood St.)
SE1 . . . . .1B **92**
(off Cooper's Rd.)
Fitzroy House Mus.
. . . . .4F **5** (3E **61**)
Fitzroy M. W1 . . . . .4F **5**
Fitzroy Pk. N6 . . . . .3B **32**
Fitzroy Rd. NW1 . . . . . . .5C **46**
Fitzroy Sq. W1 . .4F **5** (3E **61**)
Fitzroy St. W1 . . .4F **5** (3E **61**)
(not continuous)
Fitzroy Yd. NW1 . . . . . . .5C **46**
Fitzwarren Gdns.
N19 . . . . .3E **33**
Fitzwilliam Hgts.
SE23 . . . . .2E **121**
Fitzwilliam M. E16 . . . . .2C **82**
Fitzwilliam Rd.
SW4 . . . . .1E **103**
Five Bell All. E14 . . . . . . .5B **66**
(off Three Colt St.)
Five Oaks M.
BR1: Brom 3C **124**
Fives Ct. SE11 . . . . .4D **77**
Fiveways Rd. SW9 . . . . . .5C **90**
Flack Cl. E10 . . . . .2D **39**
Fladbury Rd. N15 . . . . . . .1F **35**
Fladgate Rd. E11 . . . . . . .1A **40**
Flamborough Ho.
SE15 . . . . .4C **92**
(off Clayton Rd.)
Flamborough St. E14 . . .5A **66**
Flamborough Wlk.
E14 . . . . .5A **66**
(off Flamborough St.)
Flamingo Ct. SE8 . . . . . . .3C **94**
(off Hamilton St.)
SE17 . . . . .1E **91**
(off Crampton St.)
Flamstead Ho. SW3 . . . .1A **88**
(off Cale St.)
Flamsteed Rd. SE7 . . . . .1F **97**
Flanchford Rd. W12 . . . . .4B **70**
Flanders Cl. E17 . . . . . . .2A **38**
Flanders Mans. W4 . . . . .5B **70**
Flanders Rd. W4 . . . . . . .5A **70**
Flanders Way E9 . . . . . . .3F **51**
Flank St. E1 . . . . .1C **78**
Flannery Ct. SE16 . . . . . .4D **79**

Flansham Ho. E14 . . . . . . .5B **66**
(off Clemence St.)
Flask Wlk. NW3 . . . . .1E **45**
Flatford Ho. SE6 . . . . . . .4E **123**
Flather Cl. SW16 . . . . . . .5E **117**
Flat Iron Sq. SE1 . . . . . . .2A **26**
(off Union St.)
Flatiron Yd. SE1 . . . . .2A **26**
(off Union St.)
Flavell M. SE10 . . . . .1A **96**
Flaxley Ho. SW1 . . . . .1D **89**
(part of Abbots Mnr.)
Flaxman Ct.
W1 . . . . . . .3B **14** (5F **61**)
WC1 . . . . .2C **6**
(off Flaxman Ter.)
Flaxman Ho. SE1 . . . . .5D **25**
(off London Rd.)
W4 . . . . .1A **84**
(off Devonshire St.)
Flaxman Rd. SE5 . . . . . .1D **105**
Flaxman Sports Cen. 5B **6**
Flaxman Ter.
WC1 . . . . . . .2C **6** (2F **61**)
Flecker Ho. SE5 . . . . .3F **91**
(off Lomond Gro.)
Fleece Wlk. N7 . . . . .3A **48**
Fleetbank Ho. EC4 . . . . . . .3C **16**
(off Salisbury Sq.)
Fleet Bldg. EC4 . . . . .2D **17**
Fleetfield WC1 . . . . .1E **7**
(off Birkenhead St.)
Fleet Ho. E14 . . . . .1A **80**
(off Victory Pl.)
Fleet Pl. EC4 . . .2D **17** (5D **63**)
(not continuous)
Fleet Rd. NW3 . . . . .2A **46**
Fleet Sq.
WC1 . . . . . . .2A **8** (2B **62**)
Fleet St. EC4 . . .3B **16** (5C **62**)
Fleetway WC1 . . . . .1E **7**
(off Birkenhead St.)
Fleetwood Cl. E16 . . . . . .4F **69**
Fleetwood Rd.
NW10 . . . . .2C **42**
Fleetwood St. N16 . . . . . . .4A **36**
Fleming Cl. SW10 . . . . . . .2E **87**
(off Winterton Pl.)
W9 . . . . .3C **58**
Fleming Ct. W2 . . . . .4F **59**
(off St Mary's Sq.)
Fleming Ho. N4 . . . . .3E **35**
SE16 . . . . .3C **78**
(off George Row)
SW17 . . . . .3F **115**
Fleming Lodge W9 . . . . . . .4C **58**
(off Admiral Wlk.)
Fleming Rd. SE17 . . . . . .2D **91**
Flempton Rd. E10 . . . . . . .3A **38**
Fletcher Bldgs. WC2 . . . . .3E **15**
(off Martlett Ct.)
Fletcher Ho. N1 . . . . .5A **50**
(off Nuttall St.)
SE15 . . . . .3E **93**
(off Clifton Way)
Fletcher La. E10 . . . . .2E **39**
Fletcher Path SE8 . . . . . . .3C **94**
Fletcher St. E1 . . . . .1C **78**
Fletching Rd. E5 . . . . .5E **37**
SE7 . . . . .2E **97**

Fleur de Lis St.
E1 . . . . . . .4E **11** (3B **64**)
Fleur Gates SW19 . . . . . . .5F **99**
Flight Ho. N1 . . . . .5A **50**
(off Whitmore Est.)
Flimwell Cl.
BR1: Brom 5A **124**
Flinders Ho. E1 . . . . .2D **79**
(off Green Bank)
Flint Cl. E15 . . . . .4B **54**
Flintmill Cres. SE3 . . . . . . .5F **97**
Flinton St. SE17 . . . . .1A **92**
Flint St. SE17 . . . . .5F **77**
Flitcroft St.
WC2 . . . . . . .3C **14** (5F **61**)
Flitton Ho. N1 . . . . .4D **49**
(off The Sutton Est.)
Flock Mill Pl. SW18 . . . .1D **115**
Flockton St. SE16 . . . . . . .3C **78**
Flodden Rd. SE5 . . . . .4E **91**
Flood St. SW3 . . . . .1A **88**
Flood Wlk. SW3 . . . . .2A **88**
Flora Cl. E14 . . . . .5D **67**
Flora Gdns. W6 . . . . .5D **71**
(off Albion Gdns.)
Flora Ho. E3 . . . . .5C **52**
(off Garrison Rd.)
Floral Pl. N1 . . . . .2F **49**
Floral St.
WC2 . . . . .4D **15** (1A **76**)
Florence Cantwell Wlk.
N19 . . . . .2A **34**
(off Jessie Blythe La.)
Florence Ct. N1 . . . . .4D **49**
(off Florence St.)
SW19 . . . . .5A **114**
W9 . . . . .2E **59**
(off Maida Va.)
Florence Ho. SE16 . . . . . . .1D **93**
(off Rotherhithe New Rd.)
W11 . . . . .1F **71**
(off St Ann's Rd.)
Florence Mans.
NW4 . . . . .1D **29**
(off Vivian Av.)
SW6 . . . . .3B **86**
(off Rostrevor Rd.)
Florence Nightingale Mus.
. . . . .4F **23** (3B **76**)
Florence Rd. E6 . . . . .5C **55**
E13 . . . . .1C **68**
N4 . . . . .2B **34**
(not continuous)
SE14 . . . . .4B **94**
SW19 . . . . .5D **115**
Florence Sq. E3 . . . . .3D **67**
Florence St. E16 . . . . .3B **68**
N1 . . . . .4D **49**
Florence Ter. SE14 . . . . . .4B **94**
SW15 . . . . .3A **112**
Florence Way
SW12 . . . . .1B **116**
Florey Lodge W9 . . . . .4C **58**
(off Admiral Wlk.)
Florfield Pas. E8 . . . . .3D **51**
(off Reading La.)
Florfield Rd. E8 . . . . .3D **51**
Florian SE5 . . . . .4A **92**
Florian Rd. SW15 . . . . . .2A **100**
Florida St. E2 . . . . .2C **64**

Florin Ct. EC1 . . . . .5F **9**
SE1 . . . . .4F **27**
(off Tanner St.)
Floris Pl. SW4 . . . . .1E **103**
Florys Ct. SW19 . . . . . . .1A **114**
Floss St. SW15 . . . . .5E **85**
Flower & Dean Wlk.
E1 . . . . .1F **19** (4B **64**)
Flower M. NW11 . . . . . . .1A **30**
Flower Pot Cl. N15 . . . . .1B **36**
Flowers Cl. NW2 . . . . . . .5C **28**
Flowersmead
SW17 . . . . .2C **116**
Flowers M. N19 . . . . .4E **33**
Flower Walk, The
SW7 . . . . .3E **73**
Floyd Rd. SE7 . . . . .1E **97**
Fludyer St. SE13 . . . . . .2A **110**
Flying Angel Ho. E16 . . . .1D **83**
(off Victoria Dock Rd.)
Flynn Ct. E14 . . . . .1C **80**
(off Garford St.)
Foley Ho. E1 . . . . .5E **65**
(off Tarling St.)
Foley St. W1 . . .1F **13** (4E **61**)
Folgate St.
E1 . . . . . . .5E **11** (4A **64**)
(not continuous)
Foliot Ho. N1 . . . . .1B **62**
(off Priory Grn. Est.)
Foliot St. W12 . . . . .5B **56**
Folkestone Ho. SE17 . . .1A **92**
(off Upnor Way)
Follett Ho. SW10 . . . . . . .3F **87**
(off Worlds End Est.)
Follett St. E14 . . . . .5E **67**
Follingham Ct. N1 . . . . . .1E **11**
(off Drysdale St.)
Folly M. W11 . . . . .5B **58**
Folly Wall E14 . . . . .3E **81**
Fonda Ct. E14 . . . . .1C **80**
(off Premiere Pl.)
Fondant Ct. E3 . . . . .1D **67**
(off Taylor Pl.)
Fontarabia Rd.
SW11 . . . . .2C **102**
Fontenelle SE5 . . . . .4A **92**
Fontenoy Ho. SE11 . . . . .5D **77**
(off Kennington La.)
Fontenoy Rd. SW12 . . . .2D **117**
Fonthill Ho. SW1 . . . . . . .1D **89**
(part of Abbots Mnr.)
W14 . . . . .4A **72**
(off Russell Rd.)
Fonthill M. N4 . . . . .4B **34**
Fonthill Rd. N4 . . . . .3B **34**
Fontley Way SW15 . . . . .5C **98**
Footpath, The SW15 . . . .4C **98**
Forber Ho. E2 . . . . .2E **65**
(off Cornwall Av.)
Forbes Cl. NW2 . . . . .5C **28**
Forbes Ho. E7 . . . . .2E **55**
(off Romford Rd.)
Forbes St. E1 . . . . .5C **64**
Forburg Rd. N16 . . . . . . .3C **36**
Ford Cl. E3 . . . . .1A **66**
Fordel Rd. SE6 . . . . .1E **123**
Fordham Ho. SE14 . . . . .3A **94**
(off Angus St.)
Fordham St. E1 . . . . .5C **64**

Fordie Ho. SW1 . . . . .4B **74**
(off Sloane St.)
Fordingley Rd. W9 . . . . . .2B **58**
Fordington Ho.
SE26 . . . . .3C **120**
Fordmill Rd. SE6 . . . . . .2C **122**
Ford Rd. E3 . . . . .1B **66**
Fords Pk. Rd. E16 . . . . . .4C **68**
Ford Sq. E1 . . . . .4D **65**
Ford St. E3 . . . . .5A **52**
E16 . . . . .5B **68**
Fordwych Rd. NW2 . . . . .1A **44**
Fordyce Rd. SE13 . . . . . .4E **109**
Foreign St. SE5 . . . . .5D **91**
Foreland Ho. W11 . . . . . .1A **72**
(off Walmer Rd.)
Foreman Ho. SE4 . . . . . .2F **107**
(off Billingford Cl.)
Foreshore SE8 . . . . .5B **80**
Forest Bus. Pk.
E10 . . . . .2F **37**
Forest Cl. E11 . . . . .1C **40**
NW6 . . . . .4A **44**
Forest Cft. SE23 . . . . . . .2D **121**
Forest Dr. E12 . . . . .5F **41**
Forest Dr. E. E11 . . . . . . .2F **39**
Forest Dr. W. E11 . . . . . . .2F **39**
Forester Ho. E14 . . . . . . .1A **80**
(off Victory Pl.)
Forester Rd. SE15 . . . . . .1D **107**
FOREST GATE 2C **54**
Forest Ga. Retreat
E7 . . . . .2C **54**
(off Odessa Rd.)
Forest Glade E11 . . . . . . .1A **40**
Forest Gro. E8 . . . . .3B **50**
FOREST HILL 2E **121**
Forest Hill Bus. Cen.
SE23 . . . . .2E **121**
(off Clyde Va.)
Forest Hill Ind. Est.
SE23 . . . . .2E **121**
Forest Hill Pool 2E **121**
Forest Hill Rd.
SE22 . . . . .3D **107**
SE23 . . . . .3D **107**
Forestholme Cl.
SE23 . . . . .2E **121**
Forest La. E7 . . . . .2A **54**
E15 . . . . .2A **54**
Forest Lodge SE23 . . . . .3E **121**
(off Dartmouth Rd.)
Forest Point E7 . . . . .2D **55**
(off Windsor Rd.)
Fore St. EC2 . . . .1A **18** (4E **63**)
Fore St. Av.
EC2 . . . . .1B **18** (4F **63**)
Forest Rd. E7 . . . . .1C **54**
E8 . . . . .3B **50**
E11 . . . . .2F **39**
Forest Side E7 . . . . .1D **55**
Forest St. E7 . . . . .2C **54**
Forest Vw. E11 . . . . .2B **40**
Forest Vw. Av. E10 . . . . . .1F **39**
Forest Vw. Rd. E12 . . . . .1F **55**
Forest Way N19 . . . . .4E **33**
Forfar Rd. SW11 . . . . . . .4C **88**
Forge Pl. NW1 . . . . .3C **46**
Forge Sq. E14 . . . . .5D **81**
Forman Pl. N16 . . . . .1B **50**

Formby Ct. N7 . . . . .2C **48**
(off Morgan Rd.)
Formosa Ho. E1 . . . . .3A **66**
(off Ernest St.)
Formosa St. W9 . . . . .3D **59**
Formunt Cl. E16 . . . . .4B **68**
Forres Gdns. NW11 . . . . .1C **30**
Forrester Path
SE26 . . . . .4E **121**
Forset Ct. W2 . . . . .5A **60**
(off Edgware Rd.)
Forset St. W1 . . . . .5A **60**
(not continuous)
Forster Ho.
BR1: Brom 4F **123**
SW17 . . . . .3F **115**
(off Grosvenor Way)
Forster Rd. E17 . . . . .1A **38**
SW2 . . . . .5A **104**
Forston St. N1 . . . . .1E **63**
Forsyte Ho. SW3 . . . . . . .1A **88**
(off Chelsea Mnr. St.)
Forsyth Gdns. SE17 . . . . .2D **91**
Forsyth Ho. E9 . . . . .4E **51**
(off Frampton Pk. Rd.)
SW1 . . . . .1E **89**
(off Tachbrook St.)
Fortescue Av. E8 . . . . . . .4D **51**
Fortess Gro. NW5 . . . . . .2E **47**
Fortess Rd. NW5 . . . . . . .2D **47**
Fortess Wlk. NW5 . . . . . .2D **47**
Fortess Yd. NW5 . . . . . . .1D **47**
Forthbridge Rd.
SW11 . . . . .2C **102**
Forth Ho. E3 . . . . .1B **66**
(off Tredegar Rd.)
Fortis Cl. E16 . . . . .5E **69**
Fortius Apartments
E3 . . . . .1C **66**
(off Tredegar La.)
Fortnam Rd. N19 . . . . . . .4F **33**
Fort Rd. SE1 . . . . .5B **78**
Fortrose Cl. E14 . . . . .5F **67**
Fortrose Gdns. SW2 . . . .1A **118**
(not continuous)
Fort St. E1 . . . . . .1E **19** (4A **64**)
E16 . . . . .2D **83**
Fortuna Cl. N7 . . . . .3B **48**
Fortune Ct. E8 . . . . .4B **50**
(off Queensbridge Rd.)
Fortunegate Rd.
NW10 . . . . .5A **42**
FORTUNE GREEN 2C **44**
Fortune Grn. Rd.
NW6 . . . . .1C **44**
Fortune Ho. EC1 . . . . .4A **10**
(off Fortune St.)
SE11 . . . . .5C **76**
(off Marylee Way)
Fortune Pl. SE1 . . . . .1B **92**
Fortune St.
EC1 . . . . .4A **10** (3E **63**)
Fortune Theatre 3E **15**
(off Russell St.)
Fortune Way NW10 . . . . .2C **56**
Forty Acre La. E16 . . . . . .4C **68**
Forum Cl. E3 . . . . .5C **52**
Forum Magnum Sq.
SE1 . . . . .3A **24**
(off York Rd.)

Forward Bus. Centre, The
E16 . . . . .3F 67
Fosbrooke Ho. SW8 . . . .3A 90
(off Davidson Gdns.)
Fosbury M. W2 . . . . . . .1D 73
Foscote Ct. W9 . . . . . . .3C 58
(off Amberley Rd.)
Foscote M. W9 . . . . . .3C 58
Foscote Rd. NW4 . . . .1D 29
Foskett M. E8 . . . . .2B 50
Foskett Rd. SW6 . . . . . .5B 86
Fossdene Rd. SE7 . . . .1D 97
Foss Ho. NW8 . . . . .1D 59
(off Carlton Hill)
Fossil Ct. SE1 . . . . .5D 27
(off Long La.)
Fossil Rd. SE13 . . . . . .1C 108
Foss Rd. SW17 . . . . . .4F 115
Foster Ct. E16 . . . . . . .1B 82
(off Tarling Rd.)
NW1 . . . . .4E 47
(off Royal College St.)
Foster Ho. SE14 . . . . . .4B 94
Foster La.
EC2 . . . . . . .2F 17 (5E 63)
Foster Rd. E13 . . . . . . .3C 68
W3 . . . . .1A 70
W4 . . . . .1A 84
Foster's Way
SW18 . . . . .1D 115
Fothergill Cl. E13 . . . .1C 68
Foubert's Pl.
W1 . . . . . .3F 13 (5E 61)
Foulden Rd. N16 . . . . .1B 50
Foulden Ter. N16 . . . . .1B 50
Foulis Ter. SW7 . . . . . .1F 87
Foulser Rd.
SW17 . . . . .3B 116
Founders Ct. EC2 . . . . .2B 18
Founders Ho. SW1 . . . .1F 89
(off Aylesford St.)
Foundling Ct. WC1 . . . .3D 7
(off Brunswick Cen.)
Foundling Museum, The
. . . . .3E 7
Foundry, The EC2 . . . . .2E 11
(off Dereham Pl.)
Foundry Cl. SE16 . . . . .2A 80
Foundry Ho. E14 . . . . .4D 67
(off Morris Rd.)
Foundry M.
NW1 . . . . .3A 6 (3E 61)
Foundry Pl. E1 . . . . . . .4E 65
(off Jubilee St.)
SW18 . . . . .5D 101
Fountain Ct.
EC4 . . . . .4B 16 (1C 76)
SE23 . . . . .2F 121
SW1 . . . . .5D 75
(off Buckingham Pal. Rd.)
W11 . . . . .3F 71
(off Clearwater Ter.)
Fountain Dr. SE19 . . . .4B 120
Fountain Grn. Sq.
SE16 . . . . .3C 78
Fountain Ho. E2 . . . . . .3F 11
(off Redchurch St.)
NW6 . . . . .4A 44
SE16 . . . . .3C 78
(off Bermondsey Wall E.)

Fountain Ho. SW6 . . . . .5E 87
W1 . . . . .1B 20
(off Park St.)
Fountain M. N5 . . . . . . .1E 49
(off Highbury Grange)
NW3 . . . . .3B 46
Fountain Pl. SW9 . . . . .4C 90
Fountain Rd. SW17 . . . .5F 115
Fountain Sq. SW1 . . . . .5D 75
Fount St. SW8 . . . . .3F 89
Four Dials E20 . . . . . . .3E 53
(within Westfield Stratford
City Shopping Cen.)
Fournier St.
E1 . . . . . . .5F 11 (4B 64)
Fourscore Mans. E8 . . . .4C 50
(off Shrubland Rd.)
Four Seasons Cl. E3 . . . .1C 66
Fourth Av. W10 . . . . . . .3A 58
Fovant Ct. SW8 . . . . . .5E 89
Fowey Cl. E1 . . . . .2D 79
Fowey Ho. SE11 . . . . . .1C 90
(off Kennings Way)
Fowler Cl. SW11 . . . . . .1F 101
Fowler Ho. N15 . . . . . . .1F 35
(off South Gro.)
Fowler Rd. E7 . . . . .1C 54
N1 . . . . .5D 49
Fowlers M. N19 . . . . . .4E 33
(off Holloway Rd.)
Fownes St. SW11 . . . . .1A 102
Fox & Knot St. EC1 . . . . .5E 9
Foxberry Rd. SE4 . . . . .1A 108
Foxborough Gdns.
SE4 . . . . .3C 108
Foxbourne Rd.
SW17 . . . . .2C 116
Fox Cl. E1 . . . . .3E 65
E16 . . . . .4C 68
Foxcombe Cl. E6 . . . . . .1F 69
Foxcombe Rd.
SW15 . . . . .1C 112
Foxcote SE5 . . . . .1A 92
Foxcroft WC1 . . . . .1A 8
(off Penton Ri.)
Foxes Dale SE3 . . . . . .1C 110
Foxfield NW1 . . . . .5D 47
(off Arlington Rd.)
Foxglove Ct. E3 . . . . . . .1C 66
(off Four Seasons Cl.)
Foxglove St. W12 . . . . . .1B 70
Foxham Rd. N19 . . . . . .5F 33
Foxhole Rd. SE9 . . . . . .3F 111
Foxley Cl. E8 . . . . .2C 50
Foxley Ho. E3 . . . . .2D 67
(off Bow Rd.)
Foxley Rd. SW9 . . . . . .3C 90
Foxley Sq. SW9 . . . . . .4D 91
Foxmore St. SW11 . . . . .4B 88
Fox Rd. E16 . . . . .4B 68
Fox's Yd. E2 . . . . .3F 11
Foxwell M. SE4 . . . . . .1A 108
Foxwell St. SE4 . . . . . .1A 108
Foxwood Rd. SE3 . . . . .2B 110
Foyle Rd. SE3 . . . . .2B 96
Framfield Rd. N5 . . . . . .2D 49
Framlingham Cl. E5 . . . .4E 37
Frampton NW1 . . . . . . .4F 47
(off Wrotham Rd.)

Frampton Ho. NW8 . . . .3F 59
(off Frampton St.)
Frampton Pk. Est. E9 . . .4E 51
Frampton Pk. Rd. E9 . . .3E 51
Frampton St. NW8 . . . . .3F 59
Francemary Rd.
SE4 . . . . .3C 108
Frances Ct. E17 . . . . . .1C 38
Frances Wharf E14 . . . .5B 66
Franche Cl. Rd.
SW17 . . . . .3E 115
Francis Bacon Ct.
SE16 . . . . .5D 79
(off Galleywall Rd.)
Francis Barber Cl.
SW16 . . . . .5B 118
Francis Bentley M.
SW4 . . . . .1E 103
Franciscan Rd.
SW17 . . . . .5B 116
Francis Chichester Way
SW11 . . . . .4C 88
Francis Cl. E14 . . . . . . .5F 81
Francis Ct. EC1 . . . . . . .5D 9
SE14 . . . . .2F 93
(off Myers La.)
Francis Ho. E17 . . . . . . .1B 38
N1 . . . . .5A 50
(off Colville Est.)
SW10 . . . . .3D 87
(off Coleridge Gdns.)
Francis M. SE12 . . . . . .5C 110
Francis Pl. N6 . . . . .2D 33
(off Shepherd's Cl.)
Francis Rd. E10 . . . . . . .3E 39
Francis St. E15 . . . . . . .2A 54
SW1 . . . . .5A 22 (5E 75)
Francis Ter. N19 . . . . . .5E 33
Francis Ter. M. N19 . . . .5E 33
Francis Wlk. N1 . . . . . . .5B 48
Franconia Rd. SW4 . . . .3F 103
Frank Beswick Ho.
SW6 . . . . .2B 86
(off Clem Attlee Ct.)
Frank Burton Cl. SE7 . . .1D 97
Frank Dixon Cl.
SE21 . . . . .5A 106
Frank Dixon Way
SE21 . . . . .1A 120
Frankfurt Rd. SE24 . . . .3E 105
Frankham Ho. SE8 . . . .3C 94
(off Frankham St.)
Frankham St. SE8 . . . . .3C 94
Frank Ho. SW8 . . . . . . .3A 90
(off Wyvil Rd.)
Frankland Cl. SE16 . . . .4D 79
Frankland Rd. SW7 . . . .4F 73
Franklin Bldg. E14 . . . . .3C 80
Franklin Cl. SE13 . . . . .4D 95
SE27 . . . . .3D 119
Franklin Ho. E1 . . . . . . .2D 79
(off Watts St.)
E14 . . . . .5F 67
(off E. India Dock Rd.)
NW9 . . . . .1B 28
Franklin Pl. SE13 . . . . .4D 95
Franklin Sq. W14 . . . . . .1B 86
Franklin's Row SW3 . . . .1B 88
Franklin St. E3 . . . . .2D 67
N15 . . . . .1A 36

Franklyn Rd. NW10 . . . .3B 42
Frank M. SE1 . . . . .5D 79
Frank Soskice Ho.
    SW6 . . . . .2B 86
    (off Clem Attlee Ct.)
Frank St. E13 . . . . .3C 68
Frank Whymark Ho.
    SE16 . . . . .3E 79
    (off Rupack St.)
Fransfield Gro.
    SE26 . . . . .3D 121
Frans Hals Ct. E14 . . . .4F 81
Franthorne Way
    SE6 . . . . .2D 123
Fraserburgh Ho. E3 . . .1B 66
    (off Vernon Rd.)
Fraser Cl. E6 . . . . .5F 69
Fraser Ct. E14 . . . . . . .1E 95
    (off Ferry St.)
    SE1 . . . . .5A 26
    SW11 . . . . .4A 88
    (off Surrey La. Est.)
Fraser Rd. E17 . . . . . . .1D 39
Fraser St. W4 . . . . .1A 84
Frazier St.
    SE1 . . . . .4B 24 (3C 76)
Frean St. SE16 . . . . . . .4C 78
Frearson Ho. WC1 . . . . .1A 8
    (off Penton Ri.)
Freda Corbett Cl.
    SE15 . . . . .3C 92
Frederica Ct. SW2 . . . .1D 119
Frederica St. N7 . . . . . .4B 48
Frederick Charrington Ho.
    E1 . . . . .3E 65
    (off Wickford St.)
Frederick Cl. W2 . . . . . .1B 74
Frederick Ct. SW3 . . . . .5B 74
    (off Duke of York Sq.)
Frederick Crcs. SW9 . . .3D 91
Frederick Dobson Ho.
    W11 . . . . .1A 72
    (off Cowling Cl.)
Frederick Ho. SE18 . . . .5F 83
    (off Pett St.)
Frederick Pl. N8 . . . . . .1F 33
    (off Crouch Hall Rd.)
Frederick Rd. SE17 . . . .2D 91
Frederick's Pl.
    EC2 . . . . .3B 18 (5F 63)
Frederick Sq. SE16 . . . .1A 80
    (off Sovereign Cres.)
Frederick's Row
    EC1 . . . . .1D 9 (2D 63)
Frederick St.
    WC1 . . . . .2F 7 (2B 62)
Frederick Ter. E8 . . . . .4B 50
Frederic M. SW1 . . . . . .4A 20
Frederic St. E17 . . . . . .1A 38
Fred Styles Ho. SE7 . . .2E 97
Fred White Wlk. N7 . . . .3A 48
Freedom St. SW11 . . . . .5B 88
Freegrove Rd. N7 . . . . .2A 48
    (not continuous)
Freeling Ho. NW8 . . . . .5F 45
    (off Dorman Way)
Freeling St. N1 . . . . . . .4B 48
    (Carnoustie Dr.)
    N1 . . . . .4A 48
    (Pembroke St.)

Freeman Ho. SE11 . . . . .5D 77
    (off George Mathers Rd.)
Freemantle St. SE17 . . .1A 92
Freeman Wlk. SE9 . . . . .3E 111
Freemasons' Hall 2E 15
Free Trade Wharf E1 . . .1F 79
Freight La. N1 . . . . .4F 47
Freightliners City Farm
    . . . . .3C 48
Freke Rd. SW11 . . . . . .1C 102
Fremantle Ho. E1 . . . . .3D 65
    (off Somerford St.)
Fremont St. E9 . . . . . . .5D 51
    (not continuous)
French Horn Yd. WC1 . . .1F 15
French Ordinary Ct.
    EC3 . . . . .4E 19
French Pl. E1 . . .2E 11 (2A 64)
Frendsbury Rd. SE4 . . . .2A 108
Frensham Dr. SW15 . . . .3B 112
Frensham St. SE15 . . . .2C 92
Frere St. SW11 . . . . . . .5A 88
Freshfield Av. E8 . . . . . .4B 50
Freshfield Cl. SE13 . . . .2F 109
Freshford St. SW18 . . . .3E 115
Freshwater Cl.
    SW17 . . . . .5C 116
Freshwater Ct. W1 . . . . .4A 60
    (off Crawford St.)
Freshwater Rd.
    SW17 . . . . .5C 116
Freston Rd. W10 . . . . . .1F 71
    W11 . . . . .1F 71
Freswick Ho. SE8 . . . . .5A 80
    (off Chilton Gro.)
Freud Mus. 3E 45
Frewell Ho. EC1 . . . . . . .5B 8
    (off Bourne Est.)
Frewin Rd. SW18 . . . . . .1F 115
Friar M. SE27 . . . . .3D 119
Friars Av. SW15 . . . . . .3B 112
Friars Cl. SE1 . . . . .2E 25
Friars Gdns. W3 . . . . . .5A 56
Friars Mead E14 . . . . . .4E 81
Friars Pl. La. W3 . . . . . .1A 70
Friars Rd. E6 . . . . .5F 55
Friar St. EC4 . .3E 17 (5D 63)
Friars Way W3 . . . . .5A 56
Friary Ct. SW1 . . . . .2A 22
Friary Est. SE15 . . . . . .2C 92
    (not continuous)
Friary Rd. SE15 . . . . . . .3C 92
    W3 . . . . .5A 56
Friday St.
    EC4 . . . . .4F 17 (1E 77)
Frideswide Pl. NW5 . . . .2E 47
Friendly Pl. SE13 . . . . . .4D 95
Friendly St. SE8 . . . . . .5C 94
Friendly St. M. SE8 . . . .5C 94
Friendship Ho. SE1 . . . . .4E 25
    (off Belvedere Pl.)
Friendship Way E15 . . . .5E 53
Friern Barnet Rd. EC1 . .1D 9 (2D 63)
Friern Rd. SE22 . . . . . . .5C 106
    (not continuous)
Frigate Ho. E14 . . . . . . .5E 81
    (off Stebondale St.)
Frigate M. SE8 . . . . . . .2C 94

Frimley Cl. SW19 . . . .2A 114
Frimley Ct. E1 . . . . . . .3F 65
    (off Frimley Way)
Frimley Way E1 . . . . . .3F 65
Frinstead Ho. W10 . . . .1F 71
    (off Freston Rd.)
Frinton Rd. E6 . . . . . . .2F 69
    N15 . . . . .1A 36
Friston St. SW6 . . . . . .5D 87
Frith Ho. NW8 . . . . . . .3F 59
    (off Frampton St.)
Frith Rd. E11 . . . . .1E 53
Frith St. W1 . . .3B 14 (5F 61)
Frithville Ct. W12 . . . . .2F 71
    (off Frithville Gdns.)
Frithville Gdns. W12 . . .2F 71
Frobisher Ct. SE8 . . . . .1A 94
    (off Evelyn St.)
    SE10 . . . . .2F 95
    (off Old Woolwich Rd.)
    SE23 . . . . .2D 121
    W12 . . . . .3E 71
    (off Lime Gro.)
Frobisher Cres. EC2 . . .5A 10
    (off Silk St.)
Frobisher Gdns. E10 . . .2D 39
Frobisher Ho. E1 . . . . . .2D 79
    (off Watts St.)
    SW1 . . . . .2F 89
    (off Dolphin Sq.)
Frobisher Pas. E14 . . . .2C 80
Frobisher Pl. SE15 . . . .4E 93
Frobisher St. SE10 . . . .2A 96
Frogley Rd. SE22 . . . . .2B 106
Frogmore SW18 . . . . . .3C 100
Frogmore Ind. Est.
    N5 . . . . .2E 49
Frognal NW3 . . . . .1E 45
Frognal Cl. NW3 . . . . . .2E 45
Frognal Ct. NW3 . . . . . .3E 45
Frognal Gdns. NW3 . . . .1E 45
Frognal La. NW3 . . . . . .2D 45
Frognal Pde. NW3 . . . . .3E 45
Frognal Ri. NW3 . . . . . .5E 31
Frognal Way NW3 . . . . .1E 45
Frogwell Pl. N15 . . . . . .1F 35
Froissart Rd. SE9 . . . . .3F 111
Frome Ho. SE15 . . . . . .2D 107
Frome St. N1 . . . . .1E 63
Frontenac NW10 . . . . . .4D 43
Frostic Wlk. E1 . . . . . . .4C 64
Froude St. SW8 . . . . . . .5D 89
Fruiterers Pas. EC4 . . . .5A 18
    (off Queen St. Pl.)
Fryday Gro. M.
    SW12 . . . . .5E 103
    (off Weir Rd.)
Frye Ct. E3 . . . . .2B 66
    (off Benworth St.)
Fryent Cres. NW9 . . . . .1A 28
Fryent Flds. NW9 . . . . . .1A 28
Fryent Gro. NW9 . . . . . .1A 28
Fryers Vw. SE4 . . . . . . .2F 107
    (off Frendsbury Rd.)
Fry Ho. E6 . . . . .4E 55
Frying Pan Alley E1 . . . .1F 19
Fry Rd. E6 . . . . .4F 55
    NW10 . . . . .5B 42
Fulbeck Ho. N7 . . . . . . .3B 48
    (off Sutterton St.)

Fulbeck Rd. N19 . . . . . . .1E 47
Fulbourne St. E1 . . . . .4D 65
Fulbrook M. N19 . . . . .1E 47
Fulcher Ho. N1 . . . . .5A 50
   (off Colville Est.)
SE8 . . . . .1B 94
Fulford St. SE16 . . . . . . .3D 79
FULHAM 5A 86
FULHAM
  BROADWAY
  . . . . .3C 86
Fulham B'way. SW6 . . .3C 86
Fulham Broadway Shop. Cen.
SW6 . . . . .3C 86
Fulham Bus. Exchange
SW6 . . . . .4E 87
   (off The Boulevard)
Fulham Ct. SW6 . . . . . . .4C 86
Fulham FC 4F 85
Fulham High St.
SW6 . . . . .5A 86
Fulham Island SW6 . . . .3C 86
   (off Fulham Rd.)
Fulham Palace 5A 86
Fulham Pal. Rd.
SW6 . . . . .1E 85
W6 . . . . .1E 85
Fulham Pk. Gdns.
SW6 . . . . .5B 86
Fulham Pk. Rd. SW6 . . .5B 86
Fulham Pools
  Virgin Active 2A 86
Fulham Rd. SW3 . . . . . . .3D 87
SW6 . . . . .3D 87
   (Fulham B'way.)
SW6 . . . . .5A 86
   (Fulham High St.)
SW10 . . . . .3D 87
Fuller Cl. E2 . . . . .3C 64
   (off Cheshire St.)
Fuller's Griffin Brewery &
  Visitors Cen. 2B 84
Fullerton Rd. SW18 . . .3D 101
Fullwood's M.
N1 . . . . . . .1C 10 (2F 63)
Fulmar Ho. SE16 . . . . . . .5F 79
   (off Tawny Way)
Fulmead St. SW6 . . . . . . .4D 87
Fulmer Ho. NW8 . . . . .3A 60
   (off Mallory St.)
Fulmer Rd. E16 . . . . .4F 69
Fulneck E1 . . . . .4E 65
   (off Mile End Rd.)
Fulready Rd. E10 . . . . . . .1F 39
Fulthorp Rd. SE3 . . . . . . .5B 96
Fulton M. W2 . . . . .1E 73
Fulwood Pl.
WC1 . . . . . . .1A 16 (4B 62)
Fulwood Wlk.
SW19 . . . . .1A 114
Funland 5B 14
   (in Trocadero Cen.)
Furber St. W6 . . . . .4D 71
Furley Ho. SE15 . . . . .3C 92
   (off Peckham Pk. Rd.)
Furley Rd. SE15 . . . . .3C 92
Furlong Rd. N7 . . . . .3C 48
Furmage St. SW18 . . . . .5D 101
Furneaux Av. SE27 . . . . .5D 119
Furness Ho. SW1 . . . . . . .1D 89
   (part of Abbots Mnr.)

Furness Rd. NW10 . . . . . .1C 56
SW6 . . . . .5D 87
Furnival Cl. E3 . . . . .1C 66
   (off Four Seasons Cl.)
Furnival Mans. W1 . . . . . .1F 13
   (off Wells St.)
Furnival St.
EC4 . . . . . .2B 16 (5C 62)
Furrow La. E9 . . . . .2E 51
Fursecroft W1 . . . . .5B 60
   (off George St.)
Further Grn. Rd.
SE6 . . . . .5A 110
FURZEDOWN 5D 117
Furzedown Dr.
SW17 . . . . .5D 117
Furzedown Rd.
SW17 . . . . .5D 117
Furzefield Rd. SE3 . . . . . .2D 97
Furze St. E3 . . . . .4C 66
Fye Foot La. EC4 . . . . . . .4F 17
   (off Queen Victoria St.)
Fyfield N4 . . . . .4C 34
   (off Six Acres Est.)
Fyfield Ct. E7 . . . . .3C 54
Fyfield Rd. SW9 . . . . .1C 104
Fynes St. SW1 . . . . .5F 75

G

Gable St. SE26 . . . . .4D 121
Gables Cl. SE5 . . . . .4A 92
SE12 . . . . .1C 124
Gabriel Ho. N1 . . . . .5D 49
   (off Islington Grn.)
SE11 . . . . .5B 76
SE16 . . . . .4B 80
   (off Odessa St.)
Gabrielle Ct. NW3 . . . . . . .3F 45
Gabriel M. NW2 . . . . .4B 30
Gabriel St. SE23 . . . . .5F 107
Gabriels Wharf
SE1 . . . . . . .1B 24 (2C 76)
Gad Cl. E13 . . . . .2D 69
Gaddesden Ho. EC1 . . . . .2C 10
   (off Cranwood St.)
Gadebridge Ho.
SW3 . . . . .1A 88
   (off Cale St.)
Gadsbury Cl. NW9 . . . . . .1B 28
Gadsden Ho. W10 . . . . . . .3A 58
   (off Hazlewood Cres.)
Gadwall Cl. E16 . . . . .5D 69
Gage Brown Ho.
W10 . . . . .5F 57
   (off Bridge Cl.)
Gage Rd. E16 . . . . .4A 68
Gage St. WC1 . . . . .5E 7 (4A 62)
Gainford St. N1 . . . . .5C 48
Gainsborough Ct.
SE16 . . . . .1D 93
   (off Stubbs Dr.)
SE21 . . . . .2A 120
W12 . . . . .3E 71
Gainsborough Gdns.
NW3 . . . . .5F 31
NW11 . . . . .2B 30

Gainsborough Ho.
E14 . . . . .3C 80
   (off Cassilis Rd.)
E14 . . . . .1A 80
   (off Victory Pl.)
SW1 . . . . .5F 75
   (off Erasmus St.)
Gainsborough Mans.
W14 . . . . .2A 86
   (off Queen's Club Gdns.)
Gainsborough Rd.
SE26 . . . . .3D 121
E11 . . . . .2A 40
E15 . . . . .2A 68
W4 . . . . .5B 70
Gainsborough St. E9 . . . .3B 52
Gainsborough Studios E.
N1 . . . . .5F 49
   (off Poole St.)
Gainsborough Studios Nth.
N1 . . . . .5F 49
   (off Poole St.)
Gainsborough Studios Sth.
N1 . . . . .5F 49
   (off Poole St.)
Gainsborough Studios W.
N1 . . . . .5F 49
   (off Poole St.)
Gainsfield Ct. E11 . . . . . . .5A 40
Gainsford St.
SE1 . . . . . . .3F 27 (3B 78)
Gairloch Ho. NW1 . . . . . . .4F 47
   (off Stratford Vs.)
Gairloch Rd. SE5 . . . . . . .5A 92
Gaisford St. NW5 . . . . . . .3E 47
Gaitskell Ct. SW11 . . . . . .5A 88
Gaitskell Ho. E6 . . . . .5F 55
SE17 . . . . .2A 92
   (off Villa St.)
Gaitskell Way SE1 . . . . . .3F 25
   (off Weller St.)
Gala Bingo
  Camberwell 3E 91
  Leyton 3B 38
  Stratford 5F 53
  Surrey Quays 4F 79
  Tooting 5A 116
Galahad Rd.
BR1: Brom 4C 124
Galata Rd. SW13 . . . . . . .3C 84
Galatea Sq. SE15 . . . . . .1D 107
Galaxy Bldg. E14 . . . . . . .5C 80
   (off Crews St.)
Galaxy Ho. EC2 . . . . .3C 10
   (off Leonard St.)
Galbraith St. E14 . . . . . . .4E 81
Galena Arches W6 . . . . . .5D 71
   (off Galena Rd.)
Galena Rd. W6 . . . . .5D 71
Galen Pl.
WC1 . . . . . .1E 15 (4A 62)
Galesbury Rd.
SW18 . . . . .4E 101
Gales Gdns. E2 . . . . .2D 65
Gale St. E3 . . . . .4C 66
Galgate Cl. SW19 . . . . . . .1F 113
Galleon Cl. SE16 . . . . . . .3F 79
Galleon Ho. E14 . . . . .5E 81
   (off Glengarnock Av.)

Galleons Vw. E14 . . . . . .3E 81
Galleria Ct. SE15 . . . . . .2B 92
Galleries, The NW8 . . . .1E 59
(off Abbey Rd.)
Gallery, The E20 . . . . . .3E 53
(within Westfield Stratford City Shopping Cen.)
Gallery Apartments
E1 . . . . .5E 65
(off Commercial Rd.)
Gallery Ct. SE1 . . . . . . .4B 26
(off Pilgrimage St.)
SW10 . . . . .2E 87
(off Gunter Gro.)
Gallery Rd. SE21 . . . . . .1F 119
Galleywall Rd. SE16 . . . .5D 79
Galleywall Rd. Trad. Est.
SE16 . . . . .5D 79
Galleywood Ho. W10 . . . .4E 57
(off Sutton Way)
Gallia Rd. N5 . . . . .2D 49
Gallions Rd. E7 . . . . .5D 83
(not continuous)
Gallon Cl. SE7 . . . . .5E 83
Galloway Rd. W12 . . . . . .2C 70
Gallus Sq. SE3 . . . . .1D 111
Galsworthy Av. E14 . . . . .5A 66
Galsworthy Cl. NW2 . . . .1A 44
Galsworthy Cres.
SE3 . . . . .3E 97
Galsworthy Ho. W11 . . . .5A 58
(off Elgin Cres.)
Galsworthy Rd. NW2 . . . .1A 44
Galsworthy Ter. N16 . . . .5A 36
Galton St. W10 . . . . .2A 58
Galveston Ho. E1 . . . . . .3A 66
(off Harford St.)
Galveston Rd.
SW15 . . . . .3B 100
Galway Cl. SE16 . . . . . .1D 93
(off Masters Dr.)
Galway Ho. E1 . . . . .4F 65
(off White Horse La.)
EC1 . . . . .2A 10
Galway St.
EC1 . . . . .2A 10 (2E 63)
Gambado
Beckenham 5C 122
Chelsea 4E 87
(off Station Cl.)
Gambetta St. SW8 . . . . . .5D 89
Gambia St.
SE1 . . . . .2E 25 (2D 77)
Gambier Ho. EC1 . . . . . .2A 10
(off Mora St.)
Gambole Rd. SW17 . . . . .4A 116
Gamlen Rd. SW15 . . . . . .2F 99
Gamuel Cl. E17 . . . . .1C 38
Gandhi Cl. E17 . . . . .1C 38
Gandolfi St. SE15 . . . . . .2A 92
Ganley Ct. SW11 . . . . . .1F 101
(off Winstanley Est.)
Ganton St.
W1 . . . . .4F 13 (1E 75)
Gap Rd. SW19 . . . . .5C 114
Garand Ct. N7 . . . . .2B 48
Garbett Ho. SE17 . . . . . .2D 91
(off Doddington Gro.)
Garbutt Pl.
W1 . . . . .5C 4 (4C 60)

Garden Cl. SE12 . . . . . . .3D 125
SW15 . . . . .5E 99
Garden Cl. EC4 . . . . .4B 16
NW8 . . . . .2F 59
(off Garden Rd.)
W11 . . . . .1A 72
(off Clarendon Rd.)
Garden Ho. SW7 . . . . . . .4D 73
(off Cornwall Gdns.)
Garden Houses, The
W6 . . . . .2F 85
(off Bothwell St.)
Garden La.
BR1: Brom 5D 125
SW2 . . . . .1B 118
Garden M. W2 . . . . .1C 72
Garden Museum, The
. . . . .4B 76
Garden Pl. E8 . . . . .5B 50
Garden Rd. NW8 . . . . . . .2E 59
Garden Row
SE1 . . . . .5D 25 (4D 77)
Garden Royal
SW15 . . . . .4F 99
Gardens, The E5 . . . . . . .2B 36
SE22 . . . . .2C 106
Garden St. E1 . . . . .4F 65
Garden Ter. SW1 . . . . . . .1F 89
SW7 . . . . .3A 74
(off Trevor Pl.)
Garden Wlk.
EC2 . . . . .2D 11 (2A 64)
Gardiner Av. NW2 . . . . . .2E 43
Gardiner Cl. SW11 . . . . . .4A 88
Gardiner Cl. E11 . . . . . . .1D 41
Gardner Ct. EC1 . . . . . . .3D 9
(off Brewery Sq.)
N5 . . . . .1E 49
Gardner Ind. Est.
BR3: Beck 5B 122
Gardner Rd. E13 . . . . . . .3D 69
Gardners La.
EC4 . . . . .4F 17 (1E 77)
Gardnor Rd. NW3 . . . . . .1F 45
Gard St. EC1 . . . .1E 9 (2D 63)
Gareth Ct. SW16 . . . . . . .3F 117
Gareth Gro.
BR1: Brom 4C 124
Garfield Ct. NW6 . . . . . . .4A 44
(off Willesden La.)
Garfield M. SW11 . . . . . . .1C 102
Garfield Rd. E13 . . . . . . .3B 68
SW11 . . . . .1C 102
SW19 . . . . .5E 115
Garford St. E14 . . . . .1C 80
Garganey Ct. NW10 . . . . .3A 42
(off Elgar Av.)
Garland Ct. E14 . . . . .1C 80
(off Premiere Pl.)
SE17 . . . . .5E 77
(off Wansey St.)
Garlands Ho. NW8 . . . . . .1E 59
(off Carlton Hill)
Garlick Hill
EC4 . . . . .4A 18 (1E 77)
Garlies Rd. SE23 . . . . . . .3A 122
Garlinge Ho. SW9 . . . . . .4C 90
(off Gosling Way)
Garlinge Rd. NW2 . . . . . .3B 44
Garnault M. EC1 . . . . . . .2C 8

Garnault Pl.
EC1 . . . . . . .2C 8 (2C 62)
Garner St. E2 . . . . .1C 64
Garnet Ho. E1 . . . . .2E 79
(off Garnet St.)
Garnet Rd. NW10 . . . . . .3A 42
Garnet St. E1 . . . . .1E 79
Garnett Rd. NW3 . . . . . . .2B 46
Garnham Cl. N16 . . . . . . .4B 36
Garnham St. N16 . . . . . . .4B 36
Garnies Cl. SE15 . . . . . . .3B 92
Garrad's Rd. SW16 . . . . .3F 117
Garrard Wlk. NW10 . . . . .3A 42
Garratt Ct. SW18 . . . . . . .5D 101
Garratt La. SW17 . . . . . . .3E 115
SW18 . . . . .4D 101
Garratt Ter. SW17 . . . . . .4A 116
Garraway Ct. SW13 . . . . .3E 85
(off Wyatt Dr.)
Garrett Cl. W3 . . . . .4A 56
Garrett Ho. SE1 . . . . .3D 25
(off Burrows M.)
Garrett St.
EC1 . . . . . . .3A 10 (3E 63)
Garrick Av. NW11 . . . . . .1A 30
Garrick Cl. SW18 . . . . . . .2E 101
Garrick Ct. E8 . . . . .4B 50
(off Jacaranda Gro.)
Garrick Ho. W1 . . . . .2D 21
W4 . . . . .2A 84
Garrick Ind. Cen.
NW9 . . . . .1B 28
Garrick Rd. NW9 . . . . . . .1B 28
Garrick St.
WC2 . . . . .4D 15 (1A 76)
Garrick Theatre 5D 15
(off Charing Cross Rd.)
Garrick Yd. WC2 . . . . . . .4D 15
Garrison Rd. E3 . . . . .5C 52
Garsdale Ter. W14 . . . . . .1B 86
(off Aisgill Av.)
Garsington M. SE4 . . . . . .1B 108
Garson Ho. W2 . . . . .1F 73
(off Gloucester Ter.)
Garston Ho. N1 . . . . .4D 49
(off The Sutton Est.)
Garter Way SE16 . . . . . . .3F 79
Garth Ho. NW2 . . . . .4B 30
Garthorne Rd. SE23 . . . . .5F 107
Garthorne Road
Nature Reserve
. . . . .5F 107
Garth Rd. NW2 . . . . .4B 30
Gartmoor Gdns.
SW19 . . . . .1B 114
Garton Pl. SW18 . . . . . . .4E 101
Gartons Way SW11 . . . . .1E 101
Garvary Rd. E16 . . . . . . .5D 69
Garway Ct. E3 . . . . .1C 66
(off Matilda Gdns.)
Garway Rd. W2 . . . . .5D 58
Gascoigne Pl.
E2 . . . . .1F 11 (2B 64)
(not continuous)
Gascony Av. NW6 . . . . . .4C 44
Gascony Pl. W12 . . . . . . .2F 71
Gascoyne Ho. E9 . . . . . . .4A 52
Gascoyne Rd. E9 . . . . . . .4F 51
Gaselee St. E14 . . . . .2E 81
(off Baffin Way)

Gaskarth Rd. SW12 ...4D 103
Gaskell Rd. N6 ....1B 32
Gaskell St. SW4 ......5A 90
Gaskin St. N1 ....5D 49
Gaspar Cl. SW5 ....5D 73
Gaspar M. SW5 ....5D 73
Gassiot Rd. SW17 ....4B 116
Gasson Ho. SE14 ......2F 93
  (off John Williams Cl.)
Gastein Rd. W6 ....2F 85
Gastigny Ho. EC1 ......2A 10
Gataker Ho. SE16 .....4D 79
  (off Slippers Pl.)
Gataker St. SE16 .....4D 79
Gatcombe Ho. SE22 ...1A 106
Gatcombe Rd. E16 .....2C 82
  N19 ....5F 33
Gate Cinema 2C 72
  (off Notting Hill Ga.)
Gateforth St. NW8 .....3A 60
Gate Hill Ct. W11 ......2B 72
  (off Ladbroke Rd.)
Gate Ho. E3 ....5A 52
  (off Gunmakers La.)
  N1 ....4F 49
  (off Ufton Rd.)
Gatehouse Sq. SE1 ....1A 26
Gatehouse Theatre 3C 32
Gateley Ho. SE4 ......2F 107
  (off Coston Wlk.)
Gateley Rd. SW9 ......1B 104
Gate Lodge W9 ....4C 58
  (off Admiral Wlk.)
Gately Ct. SE15 ....3B 92
Gate M. SW7 ....3A 74
  (off Rutland Ga.)
Gatesborough St.
  EC2 ....3D 11 (3A 84)
Gates Ct. SE17 ....1E 91
Gatesden WC1 ...2F 7 (2A 62)
Gateside Rd. SW17 ....3B 116
Gate St. WC2 ...1F 15 (5B 62)
Gate Theatre, The 2C 72
  (off Pembridge Rd.)
Gateway SE17 ....2E 91
Gateway Arc. N1 ....1D 63
  (off Upper St.)
Gateway Bus. Cen.
  BR3: Beck 5A 122
Gateway Ind. Est.
  NW10 ....2B 56
Gateway M. E8 ....2B 50
Gateway Rd. E10 .....5D 39
Gateways, The
  SW3 ....5A 74
Gathorne St. E2 ....1F 65
Gatliff Cl. SW1 ....1D 89
  (off Ebury Bri. Rd.)
Gatliff Rd. SW1 ....1D 89
Gatonby St. SE15 .....4B 92
Gattis Wharf N1 ....1A 62
  (off New Wharf Rd.)
Gatton Rd. SW17 .....4A 116
Gatwick Ho. E14 ......5B 66
  (off Clemence St.)
Gatwick Rd. SW18 ....5B 100
Gauden Cl. SW4 ......1F 103
Gauden Rd. SW4 .....5F 89
Gaugin Ct. SE16 ......1D 93
  (off Stubbs Dr.)

Gaumont Ter. W12 .....3E 71
  (off Lime Gro.)
Gaumont Twr. E8 ......3B 50
  (off Dalston Sq.)
Gaunt St. SE1 ...5F 25 (4E 77)
Gautrey Rd. SE15 .....5E 93
Gawber St. E2 ....2E 65
Gaverick M. E14 ......5C 80

Gavestone Cres.
  SE12 ....5E 111
Gavestone Rd.
  SE12 ....5D 111
Gaviller Pl. E5 ....1D 51
Gawber St. E2 ....2E 65
Gawsworth Cl. E15 ....2B 54
Gawthorne Ct. E3 .....1C 66
Gay Cl. NW2 ....2D 43
Gaydon Ho. W2 ....4D 59
  (off Bourne Ter.)
Gayfere St.
  SW1 ....5D 23 (4A 76)
Gayford Rd. W12 ......3B 70
Gay Ho. N16 ....2A 50
Gayhurst SE17 ....2F 91
  (off Hopwood Rd.)
Gayhurst Ho. NW8 .....3A 60
  (off Mallory St.)
Gayhurst Rd. E8 ......4C 50
Gaymead NW8 ....5D 45
  (off Abbey Rd.)
Gaynesford Rd.
  SE23 ....2F 121
Gaysley Ho. SE11 .....5C 76
  (off Hotspur St.)
Gay St. SW15 ....1F 99
Gayton Cres. NW3 .....1F 45
Gayton Ho. E3 ....3C 66
  (off Chiltern Rd.)
Gayton Rd. NW3 ......1F 45
Gayville Rd. SW11 ....4B 102
Gaywood Cl. SW2 .....1B 118
Gaywood St.
  SE1 ....5E 25 (4D 77)
Gaza St. SE17 ....1D 91
Gaze Ho. E14 ....5F 67
  (off Blair St.)
Gazelle Ho. E15 ......3A 54
Gean Ct. E11 ....1F 53
Gearing Cl. SW17 .....4C 116
Geary Rd. NW10 ......2C 42
Geary St. N7 ....2B 48
Gedling Ct. SE1 ....3B 78
  (off Jamaica Rd.)
Gedling Pl.
  SE1 ....5F 27 (4B 78)
Geere Rd. E15 ....5B 54
Gees Ct.
  W1 ....3C 12 (5C 60)
Gee St. EC1 ....3F 9 (3E 63)
Geffrye Ct. N1 ....1A 64
Geffrye Est. N1 ....1A 64
Geffrye Mus. 1F 11
Geffrye St.
  E2 ....1F 11 (1B 64)
Geldart Rd. SE15 .....3D 93
Geldeston Rd. E5 .....4C 36
Gellatly Rd. SE14 .....5E 93
Gem Ct. SE10 ....3D 95
  (off Merryweather Pl.)

Gemini Bus. Cen.
  E16 ....3F 67
Gemini Bus. Est.
  SE14 ....1F 93
Gemini Ct. E1 ....1C 78
  (off Vaughan Way)
Gemini Ho. E3 ....5C 52
  (off Garrison Rd.)
General Wolfe Rd.
  SE10 ....4F 95
Geneva Ct. NW9 ......1A 28
Geneva Dr. SW9 .....2C 104
Genoa Av. SW15 ......3E 99
Genoa Ho. E1 ....3F 65
  (off Ernest St.)
Gentry Gdns. E13 .....3C 68
Geoffrey Chaucer Way
  E3 ....4B 66
Geoffrey Cl. SE5 ......5E 91
Geoffrey Ct. SE4 ......5B 94
Geoffrey Gdns. E6 ....1F 69
Geoffrey Ho. SE1 .....5C 26
  (off Pardoner St.)
Geoffrey Jones Ct.
  NW10 ....5C 42
Geoffrey Rd. SE4 ....1B 108
George Beard Rd.
  SE8 ....5B 80
George Belt Ho.
  E2 ....2F 65
  (off Smart St.)
George Ct. WC2 ......5E 15
George Downing Est.
  N16 ....4B 36
George Eliot Ho.
  SW1 ....5E 75
  (off Vauxhall Bri. Rd.)
George Elliot Ho.
  SE17 ....1E 91
  (off Thursh St.)
George Elliston Ho.
  SE1 ....1C 92
  (off Old Kent Rd.)
George Eyre Ho.
  NW8 ....1F 59
  (off Cochrane St.)
George Furness Ho.
  NW10 ....3D 43
  (off Grange Rd.)
George Gillett Ct.
  EC1 ....3A 10
George Hudson Twr.
  E15 ....1D 67
  (off High St.)
George Inn Yd.
  SE1 ....2B 26 (2F 77)
George La. SE13 .....4D 109
George Lansbury Ho.
  E3 ....2B 66
  (off Bow Rd.)
  NW10 ....4A 42
George Leybourne Ho.
  E1 ....1C 78
  (off Fletcher St.)
George Lindgren Ho.
  SW6 ....3B 86
  (off Clem Attlee Ct.)
George Loveless Ho.
  E2 ....1F 11
  (off Diss St.)

George Lowe Ct. W2 . . . .4D 59
  (off Bourne Ter.)
George Mathers Rd.
  SE11 . . . . .5D 77
George M. NW1 . . . . . .2A 6
  SW9 . . . . .5C 90
George Padmore Ho.
  E8 . . . . .5C 50
  (off Brougham Rd.)
George Peabody Ct.
  NW1 . . . . .4A 60
  (off Burne St.)
George Potter Ho.
  SW11 . . . . .5F 87
  (off George Potter Way)
George Potter Way
  SW11 . . . . .5F 87
George Row SE16 . . . .3C 78
George Scott Ho. E1 . .5F 65
  (off W. Arbour St.)
George's Rd. N7 . . . . .2B 48
George's Sq. SW6 . . . .2B 86
  (off North End Rd.)
George St. E16 . . . . . .5B 68
  W1 . . . . . .2A 12 (5B 60)
George Tingle Ho.
  SE1 . . . . .5F 27
Georgetown Cl.
  SE19 . . . . .5A 120
Georgette Pl. SE10 . . . .3E 95
George Vale Ho. E2 . . .1C 64
  (off Mansford St.)
George Walter Ct.
  SE16 . . . . .5E 79
  (off Millender Wlk.)
George Wyver Cl.
  SW18 . . . . .5A 100
George Yd.
  EC3 . . . . .3C 18 (5F 63)
  W1 . . . . . .4C 12 (1C 74)
Georgia Ct. SE16 . . . . .4C 78
  (off Priter Rd.)
Georgiana St. NW1 . . . .5E 47
Georgian Ct. E9 . . . . . .5E 51
  NW4 . . . . .1D 29
  SW16 . . . . .4A 118
Georgian Ho. E16 . . . . .2C 82
  (off Capulet M.)
Georgina Gdns. E2 . . . .2B 64
Geraint Rd.
  BR1: Brom 4C 124
Geraldine Rd.
  SW18 . . . . .3E 101
Geraldine St.
  SE11 . . . . .5D 25 (4D 77)
Gerald M. SW1 . . . . . .5C 74
  (off Gerald Rd.)
Gerald Rd. E16 . . . . . .3B 68
  SW1 . . . . .5C 74
Gerard Pl. E9 . . . . . . .4F 51
Gerard Rd. SW13 . . . . .4B 84
Gerards Cl. SE16 . . . . .1E 93
Germander Way E15 . . .2A 68
Gernigan Ho. SW18 . . .4F 101
Gernon Rd. E3 . . . . . . .1A 66
Geron Way NW2 . . . . .3D 29
Gerrard Ho. SE14 . . . . .3E 93
  (off Briant St.)
Gerrard Pl.
  W1 . . . . . .4C 14 (1F 75)

Gerrard Rd. N1 . . . . . .1D 63
Gerrards Pl. SW4 . . . . .2F 103
Gerrard St.
  W1 . . . . . .4C 14 (1F 75)
Gerridge Ct. SE1 . . . . .5C 24
  (off Gerridge St.)
Gerridge St.
  SE1 . . . . .5C 24 (4C 76)
Gerry Raffles Sq. E15 . .3F 53
Gertrude St. SW10 . . . .2E 87
Gervase St. SE15 . . . . .3D 93
Ghent St. SE6 . . . . . . .2C 122
Ghent Way E8 . . . . . . .3B 50
Gherkin, The 3E 19
Giant Arches Rd.
  SE24 . . . . .5E 105
Gibbings Ho. SE1 . . . . .4E 25
  (off King James St.)
Gibbins Rd. E15 . . . . . .4E 53
Gibbon Ho. NW8 . . . . .3F 59
  (off Fisherton St.)
Gibbon Rd. SE15 . . . . .5E 93
  W3 . . . . .1A 70
Gibbon's Rents SE1 . . .2D 27
Gibbons Rd. NW10 . . . .3A 42
Gibbon Wlk. SW15 . . . .2C 98
Gibbs Av. SE19 . . . . . .5F 119
Gibbs Cl. SE19 . . . . . .5F 119
Gibbs Grn. W14 . . . . . .1B 86
  (not continuous)
Gibbs Sq. SE19 . . . . . .5F 119
Gibney Ter.
  BR1: Brom 4B 124
Gibraltar Wlk. E2 . . . . .2B 64
  (off Shackwell St.)
Gibson Cl. E1 . . . . . . .3E 65
Gibson Gdns. N16 . . . .4B 36
Gibson Rd. SE11 . . . . .5B 76
Gibsons Hill SW16 . . . .5D 119
  (not continuous)
Gibson Sq. N1 . . . . . . .5C 48
Gibson Sq. Gdns. N1 . .5C 48
  (off Gibson Sq.)
Gibson St. SE10 . . . . . .1A 96
Gideon Rd. SW11 . . . . .1C 102
Gielgud Theatre 4B 14
  (off Shaftesbury Av.)
Giesbach Rd. N19 . . . . .4F 33
Giffin Sq. Mkt. SE8 . . . .3C 94
  (off Giffin St.)
Giffin St. SE8 . . . . . . .3C 94
Gifford Ho. SE10 . . . . .1F 95
  (off Eastney St.)
  SW1 . . . . .1E 89
  (off Churchill Gdns.)
Gifford Rd. NW10 . . . . .4A 42
Gifford St. N1 . . . . . . .4A 48
Gift La. E15 . . . . .5A 54
Gilbert Bri. EC2 . . . . . .5A 10
  (off Wood St.)
Gilbert Ho. E2 . . . . . . .2F 65
  (off Usk St.)
  EC2 . . . . .5A 10
  SE8 . . . . .2C 94
  SW1 . . . . .1D 89
  (off Churchill Gdns.)
  SW8 . . . . .3A 90
  (off Wyvil Rd.)
  SW13 . . . . .3D 85
  (off Trinity Chu. Rd.)

Gilbert Pl.
  WC1 . . . . .1D 15 (4A 62)
Gilbert Rd. SE11 . . . . .5C 76
Gilbert Scott Bldg.
  SW15 . . . . .4A 100
Gilbert Sheldon Ho.
  W2 . . . . .4F 59
  (off Edgware Rd.)
Gilbertson Ho. E14 . . . .4C 80
  (off Mellish St.)
Gilbert St. E15 . . . . . . .1A 54
  W1 . . . . . .3C 12 (5C 60)
Gilbey Ho. NW1 . . . . . .4D 47
Gilbey Rd. SW17 . . . . .4A 116
Gilbeys Yd. NW1 . . . . .4C 46
Gilby Ho. E9 . . . . .3F 51
Gilda Cres. N16 . . . . . .3C 36
Gildea St.
  W1 . . . . . .1E 13 (4D 61)
Gilden Cres. NW5 . . . . .2C 46
Giles Coppice SE19 . . .4B 120
Giles Ho. W11 . . . . . . .5C 58
  (off Westbourne Gro.)
Gilesmead SE5 . . . . . .4F 91
Gilkes Cres. SE21 . . . . .4A 106
Gilkes Pl. SE21 . . . . . .4A 106
Gillam Ho. SE16 . . . . .5E 79
  (off Silwood St.)
Gillan Ct. SE12 . . . . . .3D 125
Gill Av. E16 . . . . .5C 68
Gillender St. E3 . . . . . .3E 67
  E14 . . . . .3E 67
Gillespie Pk. Nature Reserve
  . . . . .5C 34
Gillespie Rd. N5 . . . . . .5C 34
Gillett Av. E6 . . . . .1F 69
Gillett Pl. N16 . . . . . . .2A 50
Gillett Sq. N16 . . . . . . .2A 50
  (off Gillett St.)
Gillett St. N16 . . . . . . .2A 50
Gillfoot NW1 . . . . .1F 5
  (off Hampstead Rd.)
Gillian St. SE13 . . . . . .3D 109
Gillies Ho. NW6 . . . . . .4F 45
  (off Hilgrove Rd.)
Gillies St. NW5 . . . . . .2C 46
Gilling Ct. NW3 . . . . . .3A 46
Gillingham M. SW1 . . . .5E 75
Gillingham Rd. NW2 . . .5A 30
Gillingham Row SW1 . . .5E 75
Gillingham St. SW1 . . . .5E 75
Gillison Wlk. SE16 . . . . .4D 79
Gillis Sq. SW15 . . . . . .4C 98
Gillman Dr. E15 . . . . . .5B 54
Gilman Ho. E2 . . . . . . .1C 64
  (off Pritchard's Rd.)
Gillray Ho. SW10 . . . . .2F 87
  (off Ann La.)
Gill St. E14 . . . . .5B 66
Gilman Ho. N1 . . . . . . .4C 48
  (off Drummond Way)
Gilmore Rd. SE13 . . . . .2F 109
Gilpin Av. SW14 . . . . . .2A 98
Gilpin Cl. W2 . . . . .4E 59
  (off Porteus Rd.)
Gilpin Rd. E5 . . . . .1A 52
Gilray Ho. W2 . . . . . . .1F 73
  (off Gloucester Ter.)
Gilstead Rd. SW6 . . . . .5D 87
Gilston Rd. SW10 . . . . .1E 87

Gilton Rd. SE6 . . . . . . .3A 124
Giltspur St.
  EC1 . . . . . .2E 17 (5D 63)
Ginger Apartments
  SE1 . . . . .3F 27
    (off Cayenne Ct.)
Ginsburg Yd. NW3 . . . . .1E 45
Gipsy Hill SE19 . . . . . .4A 120
Gipsy La. SW15 . . . . . .1D 99
Gipsy Rd. SE27 . . . . . .4E 119
Gipsy Rd. Gdns.
  SE27 . . . . .4E 119
Giralda Cl. E16 . . . . . . .4F 69
Giraud St. E14 . . . . . . .5D 67
Girdler's Rd. W14 . . . . .5F 71
Girdlestone Wlk.
  N19 . . . . .4E 33
Girdwood Rd.
  SW18 . . . . .5A 100
Girling Ho. N1 . . . . .5A 50
    (off Colville Est.)
Gironde Rd. SW6 . . . . . .3B 86
Girton Rd. SE26 . . . . . .5F 121
Girton Vs. W10 . . . . . . .5F 57
Gisburn Ho. SE15 . . . . .2C 92
    (off Friary Est.)
Gissing Wlk. N1 . . . . . . .4C 48
Gittens Cl.
  BR1: Brom 4B 124
Given Wilson Wlk.
  E13 . . . . .1B 68
Giverny Ho. SE16 . . . . .3F 79
    (off Water Gdns. Sq.)
Gladding Rd. E12 . . . . .1F 55
Glade, The E8 . . . . .3C 50
  SE7 . . . . .3E 97
  W12 . . . . .3D 71
    (off Coningham Rd.)
Gladesmore
  Community School &
    Sports Cen. 1C 36
Gladesmore Rd. N15 . . .1B 36
Gladiator St. SE23 . . . .5A 108
Glading Ter. N16 . . . . . .5B 36
Gladsmuir Rd. N19 . . . . .3E 33
Gladstone Ct. NW6 . . . . .4E 45
    (off Fairfax Rd.)
  SW1 . . . . .5F 75
    (off Regency St.)
Gladstone Ct. Bus. Cen.
  SW8 . . . . .4D 89
    (off Pagden St.)
Gladstone Ho. E14 . . . .5C 66
    (off E. India Dock Rd.)
Gladstone M. NW6 . . . . .4B 44
Gladstone Pde. NW2 . . . .4E 29
Gladstone Pk. Gdns.
  NW2 . . . . .1D 43
Gladstone Pl. E3 . . . . . .1B 66
Gladstone St.
  SE1 . . . . . .5D 25 (4D 77)
Gladstone Ter. SE27 . . .5E 119
    (off Bentons La.)
  SW8 . . . . .4D 89
Gladwell Rd.
  BR1: Brom 5C 124
  N8 . . . . .1B 34
Gladwin Ho. NW1 . . . . .1A 6
    (off Werrington St.)
Gladwyn Rd. SW15 . . . . .1F 99

Gladys Dimson Ho.
  E7 . . . . .2B 54
Gladys Rd. NW6 . . . . . . .4C 44
Glaisher St. SE8 . . . . . .2C 94
Glamis Pl. E1 . . . . .1E 79
Glamis Rd. E1 . . . . .1E 79
Glanville Rd. SW2 . . . . .3A 104
Glasbrook Rd.
  SE9 . . . . .5F 111
Glaserton Rd. N16 . . . . .2A 36
Glasford St. SW17 . . . . .5B 116
Glasgow Ho. W9 . . . . . . .1D 59
    (off Maida Va.)
Glasgow Rd. E13 . . . . . .1D 69
Glasgow Ter. SW1 . . . . . .1E 89
Glasier Ct. E15 . . . . . . .4A 54
Glaskin M. E9 . . . . .3A 52
Glass Art Gallery, The
  . . . . .3D 27
Glass Building, The
  NW1 . . . . .5D 47
    (off Jamestown Rd.)
Glass Foundry Rd.
  E13 . . . . .4D 69
    (off Denmark St.)
Glasshill St.
  SE1 . . . . . .3E 25 (3D 77)
Glass Ho. WC2 . . . . .3D 15
    (off Shaftesbury Av.)
Glass House, The
  SE1 . . . . .4D 27
    (off Royal Oak Yd.)
Glasshouse Flds. E1 . . .1F 79
    (not continuous)
Glasshouse St.
  W1 . . . . . . .5A 14 (1E 75)
Glasshouse Wlk.
  SE11 . . . . .1A 90
Glasshouse Yd.
  EC1 . . . . . . .4F 9 (3E 63)
Glasslyn Rd. N8 . . . . . . .1F 33
Glass St. E2 . . . . .3D 65
Glassworks Studios
  E2 . . . . .1E 11
    (off Basing Pl.)
Glastonbury Ct. SE14 . . .3E 93
    (off Farrow La.)
Glastonbury Ho.
  SE12 . . . . .3B 110
    (off Wantage Rd.)
  SW1 . . . . .1D 89
    (part of Abbots Mnr.)
Glastonbury Pl. E1 . . . . .5E 65
Glastonbury St. NW6 . . .2B 44
Glaucus St. E3 . . . . .4D 67
Glazbury Rd. W14 . . . . . .5A 72
Glazebrook Cl. SE21 . . .2F 119
Glebe, The SE3 . . . . . . .1A 110
  SW16 . . . . .4F 117
Glebe Cl. W4 . . . . .1A 84
Glebe Ct. E3 . . . . .2D 67
    (off Rainhill Way)
  SE3 . . . . .1A 110
Glebe Ho. SE16 . . . . . . .4D 79
    (off Slippers Pl.)
Glebe Hyrst SE19 . . . . .4A 120
Glebelands E10 . . . . . . .4D 39
Glebelands Cl.
  SE5 . . . . .1A 106
Glebe Pl. SW3 . . . . .2A 88

Glebe Rd. E8 . . . . .4B 50
  NW10 . . . . .3C 42
  SW13 . . . . .5C 84
Glebe St. W4 . . . . .1A 84
Glebe Ter. W4 . . . . .1A 84
Gledhow Gdns. SW5 . . . .5E 73
Gledstanes Rd. W14 . . . .1A 86
Glegg Pl. SW15 . . . . . . .2F 99
Glen Albyn Rd.
  SW19 . . . . .2F 113
Glenallan Ho. W14 . . . . .5B 72
    (off North End Cres.)
Glenalvon Way SE18 . . . .5F 83
Glenarm Rd. E5 . . . . . . .1E 51
Glenavon Rd. E15 . . . . . .4A 54
Glenbow Rd.
  BR1: Brom 5A 124
Glenbrook Rd. NW6 . . . .2C 44
Glenburnie Rd.
  SW17 . . . . .3B 116
Glencairne Cl. E16 . . . . .4F 69
Glencoe Mans. SW9 . . . .3C 90
    (off Mowll St.)
Glendale Dr. SW19 . . . . .5B 114
Glendall St. SW9 . . . . . .2B 104
Glendarvon St. SW15 . . .1F 99
Glendower Gdns.
  SW14 . . . . .1A 98
Glendower Pl. SW7 . . . . .5F 73
Glendower Rd. SW14 . . .1A 98
Glendown Ho. E8 . . . . . .2C 50
Glendun Ct. W3 . . . . . . .1A 70
Glendun Rd. W3 . . . . . . .1A 70
Gleneagle M. SW16 . . . .5F 117
Gleneagle Rd.
  SW16 . . . . .5F 117
Gleneagles Cl. SE16 . . . .1D 93
Gleneldon M. SW16 . . . .4A 118
Gleneldon Rd.
  SW16 . . . . .4A 118
Glenelg Rd. SW2 . . . . . .3A 104
Glenfarg Rd. SE6 . . . . . .1E 123
Glenfield Rd. SW12 . . . .1E 117
Glenfinlas Way SE5 . . . .3D 91
Glenforth St. SE10 . . . . .1B 96
Glengall Bus. Cen.
  SE15 . . . . .2B 92
Glengall Gro. E14 . . . . . .4D 81
Glengall Pas. NW6 . . . . .5C 44
    (off Priory Pk. Rd.)
Glengall Rd. NW6 . . . . . .5B 44
  SE15 . . . . .1B 92
Glengall Ter. SE15 . . . . .2B 92
Glengariff Mans.
  SW9 . . . . .3C 90
    (off Sth. Island Pl.)
Glengarnock Av. E14 . . . .5E 81
Glengarry Rd. SE22 . . . .3A 106
Glenhurst Av. NW5 . . . . .1C 46
Glenhurst Ct. SE19 . . . .5B 120
Glenilla Rd. NW3 . . . . . .3A 46
Glenister Rd. SE10 . . . . .1B 96
Glenkerry Ho. E14 . . . . .5E 67
    (off Burcham St.)
Glenloch Rd. NW3 . . . . .3A 46
Glenluce Rd. SE3 . . . . . .2C 96
Glenmere Row
  SE12 . . . . .4C 110
Glen M. E17 . . . . .1B 38

Glennie Rd. NW3 . . . . . .3A 46
Glennie Ct. SE22 . . . . . .1C 120
Glennie Ho. SE10 . . . . . .4E 95
   (off Blackheath Hill)
Glennie Rd. SE27 . . . . . .3C 118
Glenparke Rd. E7 . . . . . .3D 55
Glenridding NW1 . . . . . .1A 6
   (off Ampthill Est.)
Glen Rd. E13 . . . . .3E 69
   E17 . . . . .1B 38
Glenrosa St. SW6 . . . . . .5E 87
Glenrose Ct. SE1 . . . . . .5D 27
   (off Long La.)
Glenroy St. W12 . . . . . . .5E 57
Glensdale Rd. SE4 . . . . .1B 108
Glenshaw Mans.
   SW9 . . . . .3C 90
   (off Brixton Rd.)
Glenston M.
   W1 . . . . . .2A 12 (5B 60)
Glentanner Way
   SW17 . . . . .3F 115
Glen Ter. E14 . . . . .3E 81
   (off Manchester Rd.)
Glentham Gdns.
   SW13 . . . . .2D 85
Glentham Rd. SW13 . . . .2C 84
Glenthorne M. W6 . . . . .5D 71
Glenthorne Rd. W6 . . . . .5D 71
Glenthorpe Av. SW15 . . .2C 98
Glenton Rd. SE13 . . . . .2A 110
Glentworth St.
   NW1 . . . . . .4A 4 (3B 60)
Glenville Gro. SE8 . . . . .3B 94
Glenville M. SW18 . . . . .5D 101
Glenville M. Ind. Est.
   SW18 . . . . .5C 100
Glenwood Av. NW9 . . . . .3A 28
Glenwood Rd. N15 . . . . .1D 35
   SE6 . . . . .1B 122
Glenworth Av. E14 . . . . .5F 81
Gliddon Dr. E5 . . . . .1D 51
Gliddon Rd. W14 . . . . . . .5A 72
Global App. E3 . . . . .1E 67
Globe Pond Rd.
   SE16 . . . . .2A 80
Globe Rd. E1 . . . . .2E 65
   E2 . . . . .2E 65
   E15 . . . . .2B 54
Globe Rope Wlk.
   E14 . . . . .5D 81
   (off E. Ferry Rd.)
Globe St.
   SE1 . . . . . .5B 26 (4F 77)
Globe Ter. E2 . . . . .2E 65
Globe Town Mkt. E2 . . . .2F 65
Globe Vw. EC4 . . . . .4F 17
   (off High Timber St.)
Globe Wharf SE16 . . . . .1F 79
Globe Yd. W1 . . . . .3D 13
Gloster Ridley Ct.
   E14 . . . . .5B 66
   (off St Anne's Row)
Gloucester W14 . . . . . . .5B 72
   (off Kensington Village)
Gloucester Arc. SW7 . . . .5E 73
Gloucester Av. NW1 . . . .4C 46
Gloucester Cir. SE10 . . . .3E 95
Gloucester Cl. NW10 . . . .4A 42

Gloucester Ct.
   EC3 . . . . . . .5E 19 (1A 78)
   NW11 . . . . .2B 30
   (off Golders Grn. Rd.)
   SE1 . . . . .1B 92
   (off Rolls Rd.)
   SE1 . . . . .5A 26
   (off Swan St.)
   SE22 . . . . .1C 120
Gloucester Cres.
   NW1 . . . . .5D 47
Gloucester Dr. N4 . . . . . .4D 35
Gloucester Gdns.
   NW11 . . . . .2B 30
   W2 . . . . .5E 59
Gloucester Gate
   NW1 . . . . .1D 61
   (not continuous)
Gloucester Gate Bri.
   NW1 . . . . .5D 47
   (off Gloucester Gate)
Gloucester Gate M.
   NW1 . . . . .1D 61
Gloucester Ho. E16 . . . . .2C 82
   (off Gatcombe Rd.)
   NW6 . . . . .1C 58
   (off Cambridge Rd.)
   SW9 . . . . .3C 90
Gloucester M. E10 . . . . . .2C 38
   W2 . . . . .5E 59
Gloucester M. W. W2 . . . .5E 59
Gloucester Pk. Apartments
   SW7 . . . . .5E 73
   (off Ashburn Pl.)
Gloucester Pl.
   NW1 . . . . . .4A 4 (3B 60)
   W1 . . . . . . .5A 4 (3B 60)
Gloucester Pl. M.
   W1 . . . . . .1A 12 (4B 60)
Gloucester Rd. E10 . . . . .2C 38
   E11 . . . . .1D 41
   SW7 . . . . .4E 73
Gloucester Sq. E2 . . . . . .5C 50
   W2 . . . . .5F 59
   (not continuous)
Gloucester St. SW1 . . . . .1E 89
Gloucester Ter. W2 . . . . .5D 59
Gloucester Wlk. W8 . . . . .3C 72
Gloucester Way
   EC1 . . . . . . .2C 8 (2C 62)
Glover Ho. NW6 . . . . .4E 45
   (off Harben Rd.)
   SE15 . . . . .2D 107
Glycena Rd. SW11 . . . . .1B 102
Glyn Ct. SW16 . . . . .3C 118
Glynde M. SW3 . . . . .4A 74
   (off Walton St.)
Glynde Reach WC1 . . . . .2E 7
Glynde St. SE4 . . . . .4B 108
Glynfield Rd. NW10 . . . . .4A 42
Glyn Mans. W14 . . . . . . .5A 72
   (off Hammersmith Rd.)
Glyn Rd. E5 . . . . .5F 37
Glyn St. SE11 . . . . .1B 90
Glynwood Ct. SE23 . . . . .2E 121
Goals Soccer Cen.
   Eltham 4E 111
Goater's All. SW6 . . . . . .3B 86
   (off Dawes Rd.)
Godalming Rd. E14 . . . . .4D 67

Godbold Rd. E15 . . . . . . .3A 68
Goddard Ho. SE11 . . . . . .5D 77
   (off George Mathers Rd.)
Goddard Pl. N19 . . . . .5E 33
Godfree Ct. SE1 . . . . .3B 26
   (off Long La.)
Godfrey Ho. EC1 . . . . . . .2B 10
Godfrey Pl. E2 . . . . .2F 11
   (off Austin St.)
Godfrey St. E15 . . . . .1E 67
   SW3 . . . . .1A 88
Goding St. SE11 . . . . .1A 90
Godley Cl. SE14 . . . . .4E 93
Godley Rd. SW18 . . . . . .1F 115
Godliman St.
   EC4 . . . . . . .3E 17 (5D 63)
Godman Rd. SE15 . . . . . .5D 93
Godolphin Ho. NW3 . . . . .4A 46
   (off Fellows Rd.)
Godolphin Pl. W3 . . . . . . .1A 70
Godolphin Rd. W12 . . . . .2D 71
   (not continuous)
Godson St. N1 . . . . .1C 62
Godson Yd. W9 . . . . .2C 58
   (off Kilburn Pk. Rd.)
Godstone Ho. SE1 . . . . . .5C 26
   (off Pardoner St.)
Godwin Cl. N1 . . . . .1E 63
Godwin Ct. NW1 . . . . . . .1E 61
   (off Chalton St.)
Godwin Ho. E2 . . . . .1B 64
   (off Thurtle Rd.)
   NW6 . . . . .1D 59
   (off Tollgate Gdns.
   not continuous)
Godwin Rd. E7 . . . . .1D 55
Goffers Rd. SE3 . . . . .4A 96
Golborne Gdns. W10 . . . .3A 58
   (not continuous)
Golborne M. W10 . . . . . . .4A 58
Golborne Rd. W10 . . . . . .4A 58
Goldbeaters Ho. W1 . . . . .3C 14
   (off Manette St.)
Goldcrest Cl. E16 . . . . . . .4F 69
Golden Bus. Pk. E10 . . . .3A 38
Golden Cross M.
   W11 . . . . .5B 58
   (off Portobello Rd.)
Golden Hinde
   . . . . .1B 26 (2F 77)
Golden Hind Pl. SE8 . . . . .5B 80
   (off Grove St.)
Golden Jubilee Bridges
   . . . . .2F 23
Golden La.
   EC1 . . . . . . .3F 9 (3E 63)
Golden La. Campus
   EC1 . . . . .4A 10
Golden La. Est.
   EC1 . . . . . . .4F 9 (3E 63)
Golden Lane Leisure Cen.
   . . . . .4F 9
Golden Plover Cl.
   E16 . . . . .5C 68
Golden Sq.
   W1 . . . . . .4A 14 (1E 75)
Golden Yd. NW3 . . . . .1E 45
   (off Holly Mt.)
Golders Ct. NW11 . . . . . .2B 30
Golders Gdns. NW11 . . . .2A 30

GOLDERS GREEN 1A 30
Golders Grn. Crematorium
　NW11 . . . . .2C 30
Golders Grn. Cres.
　NW11 . . . . .2B 30
Golders Grn. Rd.
　NW11 . . . . .1A 30
Golderslea NW11 . . . . .3C 30
Golders Mnr. Dr.
　NW11 . . . . .1F 29
Golders Pk. Cl.
　NW11 . . . . .3C 30
Golders Way NW11 . . . .2B 30
Goldfinch Ct. E3 . . . . . .1C 66
　(off Four Seasons Cl.)
Goldhawk Ind. Est.
　W6 . . . . .4D 71
Goldhawk M. W12 . . . . .3D 71
Goldhawk Rd. W6 . . . . .5B 70
　W12 . . . . .4C 70
Goldhurst Mans.
　NW6 . . . . .3E 45
　(off Goldhurst Ter.)
Goldhurst Ter. NW6 . . . .4D 45
Goldie H. N19 . . . . .2F 33
Golding St. E1 . . . . .5C 64
Golding Ter. E1 . . . . . . .5C 64
　(off Rope Wlk. Gdns.)
　SW11 . . . . .5C 88
Goldington Bldgs.
　NW1 . . . . .5F 47
　(off Royal College St.)
Goldington Cres.
　NW1 . . . . .1F 61
Goldington St. NW1 . . . .1F 61
Goldman Cl. E2 . . . . . . .3C 64
Goldmark Ho. SE3 . . . .1D 111
Goldney Rd. W9 . . . . . . .3C 58
Goldsboro' Rd. SW8 . . .4F 89
Goldsborough Ho.
　E14 . . . . .1D 95
　(off St Davids Sq.)
Goldsmith Av. E12 . . . . .3F 55
　NW9 . . . . .1A 28
Goldsmith Ct. WC2 . . . . .2E 15
　(off Stukeley St.)
Goldsmith Est. SE15 . . . .4C 92
Goldsmith Rd. E10 . . . . .3C 38
　SE15 . . . . .4C 92
Goldsmith's Bldgs.
　W3 . . . . .2A 70
Goldsmiths Cl. W3 . . . . .2A 70
Goldsmiths College 4A 94
Goldsmith's Pl. NW6 . . . .5D 45
　(off Springfield La.)
Goldsmith's Row E2 . . . .1C 64
Goldsmith's Sq. E2 . . . . .1C 64
Goldsmith St.
　EC2 . . . . . . .2A 18 (5E 63)
Goldsworthy Gdns.
　SE16 . . . . .1E 93
Goldthorpe NW1 . . . . . . .5E 47
　(off Camden St.)
Goldwell Ho. SE22 . . . . .1A 106
　(off Quorn Rd.)
Goldwin Cl. SE14 . . . . . .4E 93
Goldwing Cl. E16 . . . . . .5C 68
Gollogly Ter. SE7 . . . . . .1E 97
Gomm Rd. SE16 . . . . . .4E 79
Gondar Gdns. NW6 . . . .2B 44

Gonson St. SE8 . . . . . . .2D 95
Gonston Cl. SW19 . . . . .2A 114
Gonville St. SW6 . . . . . .1A 100
Gooch Ho. E5 . . . . .5D 37
　EC1 . . . . .5B 8
　(off Portpool La.)
Goodall Ho. SE4 . . . . . .2F 107
Goodall Rd. E11 . . . . . . .5E 39
Goodfaith Ho. E14 . . . . .1D 81
　(off Simpson's Rd.)
Goodge Pl.
　W1 . . . . . . .1A 14 (4E 61)
Goodge St.
　W1 . . . . . . .1A 14 (4E 61)
Goodhall St. NW10 . . . .2B 56
　(not continuous)
Goodhart Pl. E14 . . . . . .1A 80
Goodhope Ho.
　E14 . . . . .1D 81
　(off Poplar High St.)
Gooding Cl. N7 . . . . .3A 48
Gooding Ho. SE7 . . . . . .1E 97
Goodman Cres.
　SW2 . . . . .2A 118
Goodman Rd. E10 . . . . .2E 39
Goodman's Ct. E1 . . . . .4F 19
Goodman's Stile E1 . . . .5C 64
Goodmans Yd.
　E1 . . . . . . .4F 19 (1B 78)
Goodrich Ct. W10 . . . . .5F 57
Goodrich Ho. E2 . . . . . .1E 65
　(off Sewardstone Rd.)
Goodrich Rd. SE22 . . . . .4B 106
Goodson Rd. NW10 . . . .4A 42
Goodspeed Ho. E14 . . . .1D 81
　(off Simpson's Rd.)
Goods Way NW1 . . . . . .1A 62
Goodway Gdns. E14 . . . .5F 67
Goodwill Ho. E14 . . . . . .1D 81
　(off Simpson's Rd.)
Goodwin Cl. SE16 . . . . .4B 78
Goodwin Ho. W12 . . . . .3C 70
Goodwins Ct.
　WC2 . . . . . . .4D 15 (1A 76)
Goodwin St. N4 . . . . . . .4C 34
Goodwood Ct. W1 . . . . . .5E 5
　(off Devonshire St.)
Goodwood Ho. SE14 . . . .3A 94
　(off Goodwood Rd.)
Goodwood Rd. SE14 . . . .3A 94
Goodyear Pl. SE5 . . . . . .2E 91
Goodyer Ho. SW1 . . . . . .1F 89
　(off Tachbrook St.)
Goodyers Gdns.
　NW4 . . . . .1F 29
Goose Grn. Trad. Est.
　SE22 . . . . .2B 106
Gophir La.
　EC4 . . . . . .4B 18 (1F 77)
Gopsall St. N1 . . . . .5F 49
Gordon Av. SW14 . . . . . .2A 98
Gordonbrock Rd.
　SE4 . . . . .3C 108
Gordon Cl. E17 . . . . . . .1C 38
　N19 . . . . .3E 33
Gordon Cotts. W8 . . . . . .3D 73
　(off Dukes La.)
Gordondale Rd.
　SW19 . . . . .2C 114
Gordon Gro. SE5 . . . . . .5D 91

Gordon Ho. E1 . . . . .1E 79
　(off Glamis Rd.)
　SW1 . . . . .4E 75
　(off Greencoat Pl.)
Gordon Ho. Rd. NW5 . . .1C 46
Gordon Mans. W14 . . . . .4F 71
　(off Addison Gdns.)
　WC1 . . . . .4B 6
　(off Torrington Pl.)
Gordon Pl. W8 . . . . .3C 72
Gordon Rd. E11 . . . . . . .1C 40
　E15 . . . . .1E 53
　SE15 . . . . .5D 93
Gordon Sq.
　WC1 . . . . . . .3B 6 (3F 61)
Gordon St. E13 . . . . . . .2C 68
　WC1 . . . . . . .3B 6 (3F 61)
Gorefield Ho. NW6 . . . . .1C 58
　(off Gorefield Pl.)
Gorefield Pl. NW6 . . . . . .1C 58
Gore Ho. N1 . . . . .4C 48
　(off Drummond Way)
Gore Rd. E9 . . . . .5E 51
Gore St. SW7 . . . . .4E 73
Gorham Ho. SE16 . . . . . .3F 79
　(off Wolfe Cres.)
Gorham Pl. W11 . . . . . . .1A 72
Goring Cl. EC3 . . . . .2E 19
Gorleston St. W14 . . . . . .5A 72
　(not continuous)
Gorse Cl. E16 . . . . .5C 68
Gorsefield Ho. E14 . . . . .1C 80
　(off E. India Dock Rd.)
Gorse Ri. SW17 . . . . . . .5C 116
Gorst Rd. NW10 . . . . . . .3A 56
　SW11 . . . . .4B 102
Gorsuch Pl.
　E2 . . . . .1F 11 (2B 64)
Gorsuch St.
　E2 . . . . .1F 11 (1B 64)
Gosberton Rd.
　SW12 . . . . .1B 116
Gosfield St.
　W1 . . . . .1F 13 (4E 61)
Gosford Ho. E3 . . . . .1B 66
　(off Tredegar Rd.)
Goslett Yd.
　WC2 . . . . . . .3C 14 (5F 61)
Gosling Ho. E1 . . . . .1E 79
　(off Sutton St.)
Gosling Way SW9 . . . . . .4C 90
GOSPEL OAK 1C 46
Gosport Rd. E17 . . . . . . .1B 38
Gosset St. E2 . . . . .2B 64
Gosterwood St. SE8 . . . .2A 94
Goston Ga. SW8 . . . . . . .4B 90
　(off Hampson Way)
Goswell Pl. EC1 . . . . .2E 9
Goswell Rd.
　EC1 . . . . .1D 9 (1D 63)
Gothic Ct. SE5 . . . . .3E 91
　(off Wyndham Rd.)
Gottfried M. NW5 . . . . . .1E 47
Goudhurst Rd.
　BR1: Brom 5A 124
Gough Ho. N1 . . . . .5D 49
　(off Windsor St.)
Gough Rd. E15 . . . . .1B 54
Gough Sq.
　EC4 . . . . . . .3C 16 (5C 62)

Gough St.
　WC1 . . . . . . .3A 8 (3B 62)
Gough Wlk. E14 . . . . .5C 66
Goulden Ho. SW11 . . .5A 88
Goulden Ho. App.
　SW11 . . . . . . .5A 88
Gouldman Ho. E1 . . . . .3E 65
　(off Wyllen Cl.)
Gould Ter. E8 . . . . .2D 51
Goulston St.
　E1 . . . . . .2F 19 (5B 64)
Goulton Rd. E5 . . . . . .1D 51
Gourley Pl. N15 . . . . . .1A 36
Gourley St. N15 . . . . . .1A 36
Govan St. E2 . . . . .5C 50
Gover Cl. SW4 . . . . . .5A 90
Govier Cl. E15 . . . . . . .4A 54
Gowan Av. SW6 . . . . . .4A 86
Gowan Ho. E2 . . . . . . .2F 11
　(off Chambord St.)
Gowan Rd. NW10 . . . . .3D 43
Gower Cl. SW4 . . . . . .4E 103
Gower Ct. WC1 . .3B 6 (3F 61)
Gower Ho. SE17 . . . . . .1E 91
　(off Morecambe St.)
Gower M.
　WC1 . . . . .1C 14 (4F 61)
Gower M. Mans. WC1 . . .5C 6
　(off Gower M.)
Gower Pl.
　WC1 . . . . . . .3A 6 (3F 61)
Gower Rd. E7 . . . . . . .3C 54
Gower St.
　WC1 . . . . . . .3A 6 (3E 61)
Gower's Wlk. E1 . . . . . .5C 64
Gowlett Rd. SE15 . . . . .1C 106
Gowrie Rd. SW11 . . . . .1C 102
Gracechurch St.
　EC3 . . . . .4C 18 (1F 77)
Grace Cl. SE9 . . . . . . .3F 125
Gracedale Rd.
　SW16 . . . . .5D 117
Gracefield Gdns.
　SW16 . . . . .3A 118
Gracehill E1 . . . . .4E 65
　(off Hannibal Rd.)
Grace Ho. SE11 . . . . . .2B 90
　(off Vauxhall St.)
Grace Jones Cl. E8 . . . .3C 50
Grace M. BR3: Beck . . .5C 122
Grace Path SE26 . . . . .4E 121
Grace Pl. E3 . . . . .2D 67
Graces All. E1 . . . . . . .1C 78
Graces M. NW8 . . . . . .1E 59
　SE5 . . . . .5F 91
Grace's Rd. SE5 . . . . . .5A 92
Grace St. E3 . . . . .2D 67
Gradient, The SE26 . . .4C 120
Graduate Pl. SE1 . . . . .5D 27
Grafton Chambers
　NW1 . . . . .2C 6
　(off Grafton Pl.)
Grafton Cres. NW1 . . .3D 47
Grafton Gdns. N4 . . . . .1E 35
Grafton Ho. E3 . . . . . . .2C 66
　(off Wellington Way)
Grafton M. W1 . . .4F 5 (3E 61)
Grafton Pl.
　NW1 . . . . . . .2C 6 (2F 61)

Grafton Rd. NW5 . . . . .2C 46
Graftons, The NW2 . . .5C 30
Grafton Sq. SW4 . . . . .1E 103
Grafton St.
　W1 . . . . . . .5E 13 (1D 75)
Grafton Ter. NW5 . . . . .2B 46
Grafton Way
　W1 . . . . .4F 5 (3E 61)
　(not continuous)
　WC1 . . . . . . .4F 5 (3E 61)
Grafton Yd. NW5 . . . . .3D 47
Graham Ct. SE14 . . . . .2F 93
　(off Myers La.)
Graham Lodge
　NW4 . . . . .1D 29
Graham Rd. E8 . . . . . .3C 50
　E13 . . . . .3C 68
Graham St. N1 . . .1F 9 (1D 63)
Graham Ter. SW1 . . . . .5C 74
Grainger Ct. SE5 . . . . .3E 91
Grainstore, The E16 . . .1C 82
Gramer Cl. E11 . . . . . . .4F 39
Grampian Gdns.
　NW2 . . . . .3A 30
Grampians, The W6 . . .3F 71
　(off Shepherd's Bush Rd.)
Gramsci Way SE6 . . . . .3D 123
Granada St. SW17 . . .5B 116
Granard Av. SW15 . . .3D 99
Granard Ho. E9 . . . . . . .3F 51
Granard Rd. SW12 . . .5B 102
Granary Ct. E15 . . . . . . .3F 53
　(off Millstone Cl.)
Granary Rd. E1 . . . . . . .3D 65
Granary Sq. N1 . . . . . . .5A 48
Granary St. NW1 . . . . .5F 47
Granby Pl. SE1 . . . . . . .4B 24
　(off Lower Marsh)
Granby St. E2 . . . . .3C 64
Granby Ter.
　NW1 . . . . .1F 5 (1E 61)
　(not continuous)
Grand Av. EC1 . . .5E 9 (4D 63)
Grand Pde. N4 . . . . . . .1D 35
Grand Pde. M.
　SW15 . . . . .3A 100
Grand Union Canal Wlk.
　W10 . . . . .3E 57
　(off Canal Way)
Grand Union Cen.
　W10 . . . . .3F 57
　(off West Row)
Grand Union Cl. W9 . . .4C 58
Grand Union Cres.
　E8 . . . . .5C 50
Grand Union Wlk.
　NW1 . . . . .4D 47
　(off Kentish Town Rd.)
Grand Vitesse Ind. Cen.
　SE1 . . . . .2E 25
　(off Gt. Suffolk St.)
Grand Wlk. E1 . . . . . . .3A 66
Granfield St. SW11 . . .4F 87

Grange, The E17 . . . . . . .1A 38
　(off Lynmouth Rd.)
　SE1 . . . . .5F 27 (4B 78)
　SW19 . . . . .5F 113
　W14 . . . . .5B 72
Grange Ct. NW10 . . . . .5A 28
　(off Neasden La.)
　WC2 . . . . .3A 16 (5B 62)
Grangecourt Rd.
　N16 . . . . .3A 36
Grangefield NW1 . . . . .4F 47
　(off Marquis Rd.)
Grange Gdns. NW3 . . .5D 31
Grange Gro. N1 . . . . . .3E 49
Grange Ho. NW10 . . .4D 43
　SE1 . . . . .5F 27 (4B 78)
Grange La. SE21 . . . . .2B 120
Grange Lodge SW19 . . .5F 113
Grangemill Rd. SE6 . . .3C 122
Grangemill Way
　SE6 . . . . .2C 122
Grange Pk. Rd. E10 . . .3D 39
Grange Pl. NW6 . . . . . .4C 44
Grange Rd. E10 . . . . . .3C 38
　E13 . . . . .2B 68
　E17 . . . . .1A 38
　(not continuous)
　N6 . . . . .1C 32
　NW10 . . . . .3D 43
　SE1 . . . . .5E 27 (4A 78)
　SW13 . . . . .4C 84
Grange St. N1 . . . . . . .5F 49
Grange Wlk.
　SE1 . . . . .5E 27 (4B 78)
Grange Wlk. M. SE1 . . .5E 27
Grange Way NW6 . . . . .4C 44
Grangewood St. E6 . . .5F 55
Grange Yd.
　SE1 . . . . .5F 27 (4B 78)
Granite Apartments
　E15 . . . . .3A 54
Granleigh Rd. E11 . . . . .4A 40
Gransden Av. E8 . . . . . .4D 51
Gransden Ho. SE8 . . . . .1B 94
Gransden Rd. W12 . . .3B 70
Grantbridge St. N1 . . .1D 63
Grantham Ct. SE16 . . .3F 79
　(off Eleanor Cl.)
Grantham Ho. SE15 . . .2C 92
　(off Friary Est.)
Grantham Pl.
　W1 . . . . . . .2D 21 (2D 75)
Grantham Rd. SW9 . . .5A 90
　W4 . . . . .3A 84
Grant Ho. SW9 . . . . . . .4B 90
　(off Liberty St.)
Grantley Ho. SE14 . . .2F 93
　(off Myers La.)
Grantley St. E1 . . . . . . .2F 65
Grant Mus. of Zoology
　. . . . . .4B 6
Grant Rd. SW11 . . . . . . .2F 101
Grants Quay Wharf
　EC3 . . . . .5C 18 (1F 77)
Grant St. E13 . . . . .2C 68
　N1 . . . . .1C 62
Grant Ter. N16 . . . . . . .2C 36
　(off Castlewood Rd.)
Grantully Rd. W9 . . . . .2D 59
Granville Arc. SW9 . . .2C 104

Granville Ct. N1 . . . . . .5A 50
   N4 . . . . .1B 34
   SE14 . . . . .3A 94
   (off Nynehead La.)
Granville Gro. SE13 . . .1E 109
Granville Ho. E14 . . . .5C 66
   (off E. India Dock Rd.)
Granville Mans. W12 . . .3E 71
   (off Shepherd's Bush Grn.)
Granville Pk. SE13 . . . .1E 109
Granville Pl. SW6 . . . . .3D 87
   W1 . . . . . . .3B 12 (5C 60)
Granville Point NW2 . . . .4B 30
Granville Rd. E17 . . . . .1D 39
   N4 . . . . .1B 34
   NW2 . . . . .4B 30
   NW6 . . . . .1C 58
   (not continuous)
   SW18 . . . . .5B 100
Granville Sq. SE15 . . . . .3A 92
   WC1 . . . . . . .2A 8 (2B 62)
Granville St.
   WC1 . . . . . . .2A 8 (2B 62)
Grape St.
   WC2 . . . . .2D 15 (5A 62)
Graphite Apartments, The
   N1 . . . . .1B 10
   (off Provost St.)
Graphite Sq. SE11 . . . .1B 90
Grasmere NW1 . . . . . . .2E 5
   (off Osnaburgh St.)
Grasmere Av. SW15 . . . .4A 112
Grasmere Ct. SE26 . . . .5C 120
   SW13 . . . . .2C 84
   (off Verdun Rd.)
Grasmere Point SE15 . . .3E 93
   (off Old Kent Rd.)
Grasmere Rd. E13 . . . . .1C 68
   SW16 . . . . .5A 118
Grassmount SE23 . . . .2D 121
Gratton Rd. W14 . . . . . .4A 72
Gratton Ter. NW2 . . . . . .5F 29
Gravel La. E1 . . . .2F 19 (5B 64)
Gravely Ho. SE8 . . . . . . .5A 80
   (off Chilton Gro.)
Gravenel Gdns.
   SW17 . . . . .5A 116
   (off Nutwell St.)
Graveney Rd. SW17 . . . .4A 116
Gravesend Rd. W12 . . . .1C 70
Gray Ct. E1 . . . . .4A 66
Gray Ho. SE17 . . . . . . .1E 91
   (off King & Queen St.)
Grayling Cl. E16 . . . . . .3A 68
Grayling Rd. N16 . . . . . .4F 35
Grayling Sq. E2 . . . . . . .2C 64
   (off Nelson Gdns.)
Grayshott Rd. SW11 . . . .5C 88
Gray's Inn 5A 8 (4B 62)
Gray's Inn Bldgs. EC1 . . . .4B 8
   (off Rosebery Av.)
Gray's Inn Pl.
   WC1 . . . . . .1A 16 (4B 62)
Gray's Inn Rd.
   WC1 . . . . . .1E 7 (2A 62)
Gray's Inn Sq.
   WC1 . . . . . . .5B 8 (4B 62)
Grayson Ho. EC1 . . . . . .2A 10
Grays Ter. E7 . . . . .3E 55
Gray St. SE1 . . .4C 24 (3C 76)

Grayswood Point
   SW15 . . . . .1C 112
Gray's Yd. W1 . . . . .3C 12
Grazebrook Rd. N16 . . . .4F 35
Grazeley Ct. SE19 . . . . .5A 120
Gt. Acre Ct. SW4 . . . . . .2F 103
Gt. Arthur Ho. EC1 . . . . .4F 9
   (off Golden La. Est.)
Gt. Bell All.
   EC2 . . . . . .2B 18 (5F 63)
Great Brownings
   SE21 . . . . .4B 120
Gt. Castle St.
   W1 . . . . . .2E 13 (5D 61)
Gt. Central St. NW1 . . . .4B 60
Gt. Central Way
   NW10 . . . . .1A 42
Gt. Chapel St.
   W1 . . . . . .2B 14 (5F 61)
Gt. Chart St. SW11 . . . . .2F 101
Gt. Chertsey Rd. W4 . . . .4A 84
   (not continuous)
Gt. Church La. W6 . . . . .5F 71
Gt. College St.
   SW1 . . . . .5D 23 (4A 76)
Great Cft. WC1 . . . . . . .2E 7
   (off Cromer St.)
Gt. Cross Av. SE10 . . . . .3F 95
Gt. Cumberland M.
   W1 . . . . . . .3A 12 (5B 60)
Gt. Cumberland Pl.
   W1 . . . . . .2A 12 (5B 60)
Gt. Dover St.
   SE1 . . . . . .4A 26 (3E 77)
Gt. Eastern Ent. Cen.
   E14 . . . . .3D 81
Gt. Eastern Rd. E15 . . . .4F 53
Gt. Eastern St.
   EC2 . . . . . .2D 11 (2A 64)
Gt. Eastern Wlk. EC2 . . .1E 19
Gt. Eastern Wharf
   SW11 . . . . .3A 88
Greater London Ho.
   NW1 . . . . .1E 61
   (off Hampstead Rd.)
Greatfield NW5 . . . . . . .2E 47
Greatfield Cl. N19 . . . . . .1E 47
   SE4 . . . . .2C 108
Gt. George St.
   SW1 . . . . . .4C 22 (3F 75)
Gt. Guildford Bus. Sq.
   SE1 . . . . . .2F 25 (2E 77)
Gt. Guildford St.
   SE1 . . . . . .1F 25 (2E 77)
Great Hall 1B 88
Great Hall SW11 . . . . . . .4C 88
   (off Battersea Pk. Rd.)
Greatham Wlk.
   SW15 . . . . .1C 112
Gt. James St.
   WC1 . . . . . .5F 7 (4B 62)
Gt. Marlborough St.
   W1 . . . . . .3F 13 (5E 61)
Gt. Maze Pond
   SE1 . . . . . .3C 26 (3F 77)
Gt. Newport St.
   WC2 . . . . .4D 15 (1A 76)
Gt. New St. EC4 . . . . . . .2C 16
   (off Bartlett Ct.)

Great Nth. Rd. N2 . . . . . .1B 32
   N6 . . . . .1B 32
Greatorex Ho. E1 . . . . . .4C 64
   (off Greatorex St.)
Greatorex St. E1 . . . . . .4C 64
Gt. Ormond St.
   WC1 . . . . . . .5E 7 (4A 62)
Gt. Percy St.
   WC1 . . . . . .1A 8 (2B 62)
Gt. Peter St.
   SW1 . . . . . .5B 22 (4F 75)
Gt. Portland St.
   W1 . . . . .4E 5 (3D 61)
Gt. Pulteney St.
   W1 . . . . . . .4A 14 (1E 75)
Gt. Queen St.
   WC2 . . . . .3E 15 (5A 62)
Gt. Russell Mans.
   WC1 . . . . .1D 15
   (off Gt. Russell St.)
Gt. Russell St.
   WC1 . . . . . .2C 14 (5F 61)
Gt. St Helen's
   EC3 . . . . . .2D 19 (5A 64)
Gt St Thomas Apostle
   EC4 . . . . . .4A 18 (1E 77)
Gt. Scotland Yd.
   SW1 . . . . . .2D 23 (2A 76)
Gt. Smith St.
   SW1 . . . . . .5C 22 (4F 75)
Great Spilmans
   SE22 . . . . .3A 106
Gt. Suffolk St.
   SE1 . . . . . .2E 25 (2D 77)
Gt. Sutton St.
   EC1 . . . . . . .4E 9 (3D 63)
Gt. Swan All.
   EC2 . . . . . .2B 18 (5F 63)
Gt. Titchfield St.
   W1 . . . . .4E 5 (3D 61)
Gt. Tower St.
   EC3 . . . . . .4D 19 (1A 78)
Gt. Trinity La.
   EC4 . . . . . .4A 18 (1E 77)
Great Turnstile 1A 16 (4B 62)
Gt. Turnstile Ho. WC1 . . .1A 16
   (off Great Turnstile)
Gt. Western Rd. W9 . . . . .4B 58
   W11 . . . . .4B 58
Gt. West Rd. W4 . . . . . . .1B 84
   W6 . . . . .1B 84
Gt. Winchester St.
   EC2 . . . . . .2C 18 (5F 63)
Gt. Windmill St.
   W1 . . . . . . .4B 14 (1F 75)
Great Yd. SE1 . . . . .3E 27
Greaves Cotts. E14 . . . . .4A 66
   (off Maroon St.)
Greaves Pl. SW17 . . . . .4A 116
Greaves Twr. SW10 . . . . .3E 87
   (off Worlds End Est.)
Grebe Cl. E17 . . . . .2B 54
Grebe Cl. E14 . . . . .3E 81
   (off River Barge Cl.)
   SE8 . . . . .2B 94
   (off Dorking Cl.)
Grecian Cres. SE19 . . . .5D 119
Greek Ct. W1 . . .3C 14 (5F 61)
Greek St. W1 . . .3C 14 (5F 61)

Green, The
BR1: Brom 3C **124**
(not continuous)
E11 . . . . .1D **41**
E15 . . . . .3A **54**
SW19 . . . . .5F **113**
W3 . . . . .5A **56**
Greenacre Sq. SE16 . . .3F **79**
Greenan Ct. E2 . . . . .2F **65**
(off Meath Cres.)
Green Arbour Ct.
EC1 . . . . .2D **17**
Greenaway Gdns.
NW3 . . . . .1D **45**
Greenaway Ho. NW8 . . .5E **45**
(off Boundary Rd.)
WC1 . . . . .2B **8**
(off Fernsbury St.)
Green Bank E1 . . . . . . .2D **79**
Greenbay Rd. SE7 . . . .3F **97**
Greenberry St. NW8 . . .1A **60**
Green Cl. NW11 . . . . . .2E **31**
Greencoat Mans.
SW1 . . . . .3A **66**
(off Greencoat Row)
Greencoat Pl.
SW1 . . . . .5A **22** (5E **75**)
Greencoat Row SW1 . . .4E **75**
Greencourt Ho. E1 . . . . .3F **65**
(off Mile End Rd.)
Greencrest Pl. NW2 . . .5C **28**
Greencroft Cl. E6 . . . . .4F **69**
Greencroft Gdns.
NW6 . . . . .4D **45**
Green Dale SE5 . . . . . .2F **105**
Green Dale Cl.
SE22 . . . . .3A **106**
Green Dragon Ct.
SE1 . . . . .1B **26**
Green Dragon Ho.
WC2 . . . . .2E **15**
(off Stukeley St.)
Green Dragon Yd. E1 . .4C **64**
Greene Ct. SE14 . . . . . .2F **93**
(off Samuel Cl.)
Greene Ho. SE1 . . . . . .5B **26**
(off Burbage Cl.)
Greenend Rd. W4 . . . . .3A **70**
Greener Ho. SW4 . . . . .1F **103**
Greenfell Mans. SE8 . . .2D **95**
Greenfield Gdns.
NW2 . . . . .4A **30**
Greenfield Ho.
SW19 . . . . .1F **113**
Greenfield Rd. E1 . . . . .4C **64**
N15 . . . . .1A **36**
Greengate Lodge
E13 . . . . .1D **69**
(off Hollybush St.)
Greengate St. E13 . . . . .1D **69**
Greenham Cl.
SE1 . . . . . .4B **24** (3C **76**)
Greenham Ho. E9 . . . . . .5E **51**
(off Templecombe Rd.)
Greenheath Bus. Cen.
E2 . . . . .3D **65**
(off Three Colts La.)
Greenhill NW3 . . . . .1F **45**
Greenhill Gro. E12 . . . . .1F **55**

Greenhill Pk. NW10 . . . . .5A **42**
Greenhill Rd. NW10 . . . .5A **42**
Greenhill's Rents
EC1 . . . . . .5D **9** (4D **63**)
Greenhills Ter. N1 . . . . .3F **49**
Green Hundred Rd.
SE15 . . . . .2C **92**
Greenhurst Rd.
SE27 . . . . .5C **118**
Greenland Ho. E1 . . . . . .3A **66**
(off Ernest St.)
Greenland M. SE8 . . . . .1F **93**
Greenland Pl. NW1 . . . . .5D **47**
Greenland Quay
SE16 . . . . .5F **79**
Greenland Rd. NW1 . . . .5E **47**
Green La. NW4 . . . . . . .1F **29**
Green Lanes N4 . . . . . . .2D **35**
N8 . . . . .1D **35**
N16 . . . . .2D **35**
Greenleaf Cl. SW2 . . . . .5C **104**
Greenleaf Rd. E6 . . . . . .5E **55**
GREEN MAN RDBT. . . .2B **40**
Greenman St. N1 . . . . . .4E **49**
Greenoak Way
SW19 . . . . .4F **113**
Green Pk. 2E **21** (3D **75**)
Green Pl. SE10 . . . . . . .3A **82**
Green Point E15 . . . . . .3A **54**
Greenroof Way SE10 . . .4B **82**
Green's Ct. W1 . . . . . . .4B **14**
W11 . . . . .2B **72**
(off Lansdowne M.)
Greenshields Ind. Est.
E16 . . . . .3C **82**
Greenside Cl. SE6 . . . . .2F **123**
Greenside Rd. W12 . . . .4C **70**
Greenstead Gdns.
SW15 . . . . .3D **99**
Greenstone Ho. E11 . . . .1C **40**
Green St. E7 . . . . .3D **55**
E13 . . . . .3D **55**
W1 . . . . .4B **12** (1C **74**)
Greenstreet Hill SE14 . . .5F **93**
Green Ter.
EC1 . . . . . .2C **8** (2C **62**)
Greenview Cl. W3 . . . . . .2A **70**
Green Wlk.
SE1 . . . . . .5D **27** (4A **78**)
Green Way SE9 . . . . . . .3F **111**
Greenway E15 . . . . .1F **67**
E20 . . . . .5D **53**
Greenway Cl. N4 . . . . . .4E **35**
Greenwell St.
W1 . . . . .4E **5** (3D **61**)
GREENWICH 3E **95**
Greenwich Bus. Pk.
SE10 . . . . .3D **95**
Greenwich Chu. St.
SE10 . . . . .2E **95**
Greenwich Ct. E1 . . . . . .5D **65**
(off Cavell St.)
Greenwich Cres. E6 . . . .4F **69**
Greenwich Foot Tunnel
SE10 . . . . .1E **95**
Greenwich Hgts.
SE18 . . . . .3F **97**
Greenwich High Rd.
SE10 . . . . .4D **95**

Greenwich Ho.
SE13 . . . . .4F **109**
Greenwich Mkt. SE10 . . .2E **95**
GREENWICH
MILLENNIUM VILLAGE
. . . . .4B **82**
Greenwich Pk. 3F **95**
Greenwich Pk. Ho.
SE10 . . . . .2F **95**
Greenwich Peninsula
Ecology Pk. 4C **82**
Greenwich Picturehouse
. . . . .3E **95**
Greenwich Quay SE8 . . .2D **95**
Greenwich Shop. Pk.
SE7 . . . . .5D **83**
Greenwich Sth. St.
SE10 . . . . .4D **95**
Greenwich Theatre 3E **95**
Greenwich Vw. Pl.
E14 . . . . .4D **81**
Greenwich Yacht Club
. . . . .4C **82**
Greenwood NW5 . . . . . .2E **47**
(off Osney Cres.)
Greenwood Ho. EC1 . . . .2B **8**
(off Rosebery Av.)
SE4 . . . . .2F **107**
Greenwood Pl. NW5 . . . .2D **47**
Greenwood Rd. E8 . . . . .3C **50**
E13 . . . . .1B **68**
Greenwood Ter.
NW10 . . . . .5A **42**
Greenwood Theatre 3F **77**
Green Yd.
WC1 . . . . .3A **8** (3B **62**)
Green Yard, The EC3 . . .3D **19**
Greet Ho. SE1 . . . . .4C **24**
Greet St. SE1 . . . .2C **24** (2C **76**)
Greg Cl. E10 . . . . .1E **39**
Gregor M. SE3 . . . . .3C **96**
Gregory Cres. SE9 . . . . .5F **111**
Gregory Pl. W8 . . . . . . .3D **73**
Greig Ter. SE17 . . . . . . .2D **91**
Grenada Ho. E14 . . . . . .1B **80**
(off Limehouse C'way.)
Grenada Rd. SE7 . . . . . .3F **97**
Grenade St. E14 . . . . . . .1B **80**
Grenard Cl. SE15 . . . . . .3C **92**
Grendon Ho. E9 . . . . .4E **51**
(off Shore Pl.)
N1 . . . . .1B **62**
(off Calshot St.)
Grendon St. NW8 . . . . . .3A **60**
Grenfell Ho. SE5 . . . . . . .3E **91**
Grenfell Rd. W11 . . . . . .1F **71**
Grenfell Twr. W11 . . . . . .1F **71**
Grenfell Wlk. W11 . . . . . .1F **71**
Grenier Apartments
SE15 . . . . .3D **93**
Grenville Ho. E3 . . . . . . .1A **66**
(off Arbery Rd.)
SE8 . . . . .2C **94**
(off New King St.)
SW1 . . . . .2F **89**
(off Dolphin Sq.)
Grenville M. N19 . . . . . . .3A **34**
SW7 . . . . .5E **73**
Grenville Pl. SW7 . . . . . .4E **73**
Grenville Rd. N19 . . . . . .3A **34**

Grenville St.
WC1 . . . . .4E **7** (3A **62**)
Gresham Gdns.
NW11 . . . . .3A **30**
Gresham Lodge E17 . . . .1D **39**
Gresham Pl. N19 . . . . . . .4F **33**
Gresham Rd. E16 . . . . . .5D **69**
NW10 . . . . .2A **42**
SW9 . . . . .1C **104**
Gresham St.
EC2 . . . . . . .2F **17** (5E **63**)
Gresham Way
SW19 . . . . .3D **115**
Gresham Way Ind. Est.
SW19 . . . .*3D 115*
(off Gresham Way)
Gresley Cl. E17 . . . . .1A **38**
Gresley Rd. N19 . . . . . . .3E **33**
Gressenhall Rd.
SW18 . . . . .4B **100**
Gresse St.
W1 . . . . . . .1B **14** (5F **61**)
Greswell St. SW6 . . . . . .4F **85**
Gretton Ho. *E2* *2E 65*
(off Globe Rd.)
Greville Ct. *E5* *5D 37*
(off Napoleon Rd.)
Greville Hall NW6 . . . . . .1D **59**
Greville Ho. *SW1* *5B 20*
(off Kinnerton St.)
Greville Lodge E13 . . . . .5D **55**
Greville M. *NW6* *5D 45*
(off Greville Rd.)
Greville Pl. NW6 . . . . . . .1D **59**
Greville Rd. NW6 . . . . . . .1D **59**
Greville St.
EC1 . . . . . .1B **16** (4C **62**)
(not continuous)
Grey Cl. NW11 . . . . .1E **31**
Greycoat Gdns. *SW1* *4F 75*
(off Greycoat St.)
Greycoat Pl.
SW1 . . . . . . .5B **22** (4F **75**)
Greycoat St. SW1 . . . . . .4F **75**
Greycot Rd.
BR3: Beck 5C **122**
Grey Eagle St.
E1 . . . . . . .4F **11** (3B **64**)
Greyfriars *SE26* *3C 120*
(off Wells Pk. Rd.)
Greyfriars Pas.
EC1 . . . . . .2E **17** (5D **63**)
Greyhound Ct.
WC2 . . . . . .4A **16** (1B **76**)
Greyhound La.
SW16 . . . . .5A **118**
Greyhound Mans.
W6 . . . .*2A 86*
(off Greyhound Rd.)
Greyhound Rd.
NW10 . . . . .2D **57**
W6 . . . . .2F **85**
W14 . . . . .2F **85**
Grey Ho. *W12* *1D 71*
(off White City Est.)
Greyladies Gdns.
SE10 . . . . .5E **95**
Greystead Rd. SE23 . . . .5E **107**
Greystoke Ho. *SE15* *2C 92*
(off Peckham Pk. Rd.)

Greystoke Pl.
EC4 . . . . . . .2B **16** (5C **62**)
Greyswood St.
SW16 . . . . .5D **117**
Grey Turner Ho. W12 . . . .5C **56**
Grierson Ho. SW16 . . . . .4E **117**
Grierson Rd. SE23 . . . . . .5F **107**
Griffin Cl. NW10 . . . . . . .2D **43**
Griffin Ct. W4 . . . . .1B **84**
Griffin Ho. *E14* *5D 67*
(off Ricardo St.)
N1 . . . .*5A 50*
(off New Era Est.)
W6 . . . .*5F 71*
(off Hammersmith Rd.)
Griggs Ct. *SE1* *5E 27*
(off Grigg's Pl.)
Grigg's Pl. SE1 . . . . .5E **27**
Griggs Rd. E10 . . . . .1E **39**
Grimaldi Ho. *N1* *1B 62*
(off Calshot St.)
Grimsby St. E2 . . . . .3B **64**
Grimsel Path SE5 . . . . . . .3D **91**
Grimshaw Cl. N6 . . . . . . .2C **32**
Grimston Rd. SW6 . . . . . .5B **86**
Grimthorpe Ho. EC1 . . . . .3D **9**
Grimwade Cl. SE15 . . . . . .1E **107**
Grindall Ho. *E1* *3D 65*
(off Darling Row)
Grindal St.
SE1 . . . . . . .4B **24** (3C **76**)
Grindley Ho. *E3* *4B 66*
(off Leopold St.)
Grinling Pl. SE8 . . . . .2C **94**
Grinstead Rd. SE8 . . . . . .1A **94**
Grisedale *NW1* *1F 5*
(off Cumberland Mkt.)
Grittleton Rd. W9 . . . . . . .3C **58**
Grizedale Ter. SE23 . . . . .2D **121**
Grocer's Hall Ct.
EC2 . . . . . . .3B **18** (5F **63**)
Grocer's Hall Gdns.
EC2 . . . . .3B **18**
Groombridge Ho.
SE17 . . . .*1A 92*
(off Upnor Way)
Groombridge Rd. E9 . . . . .4F **51**
Groom Cres. SW18 . . . . . .5F **101**
Groome Ho. SE11 . . . . . . .5B **76**
Groomfield Cl.
SW17 . . . . .4C **116**
Groom Pl.
SW1 . . . . . . .5C **20** (4C **74**)
Grosse Way SW15 . . . . . .4D **99**
Grosvenor Av. N5 . . . . . . .2E **49**
SW14 . . . . .1A **98**
Grosvenor Cotts.
SW1 . . . . .5C **74**
Grosvenor Ct. E10 . . . . . .3D **39**
E14 . . . .*5B 66*
(off Wharf La.)
NW6 . . . . .5F **43**
SE5 . . . . .2E **91**
W14 . . . .*4F 71*
(off Irving Rd.)
Grosvenor Ct. Mans.
W2 . . . .*5B 60*
(off Edgware Rd.)
Grosvenor Cres.
SW1 . . . . . .4C **20** (3C **74**)

Grosvenor Cres. M.
SW1 . . . . . .4B **20** (3C **74**)
Grosvenor Est. SW1 . . . . .5F **75**
Grosvenor Gdns. E6 . . . . .2F **69**
NW2 . . . . .3E **43**
NW11 . . . . .1B **30**
SW1 . . . . . .5D **21** (4D **75**)
SW14 . . . . .1A **98**
Grosvenor Gdns. M. E.
SW1 . . . . .5E **21**
Grosvenor Gdns. M. Nth.
SW1 . . . . .5D **21**
Grosvenor Gdns. M. Sth.
SW1 . . . . .5E **21**
Grosvenor Ga.
W1 . . . . . . .5B **12** (1C **74**)
Grosvenor Hill
SW19 . . . . .5A **114**
W1 . . . . . . .4D **13** (1D **75**)
Grosvenor Hill Ct.
W1 . . . .*4D 13*
(off Bourdon St.)
Grosvenor Pk. SE5 . . . . . .3E **91**
Grosvenor Pk. Rd.
E17 . . . . .1C **38**
Grosvenor Pl.
SW1 . . . . . .4C **20** (3C **74**)
Grosvenor Ri. E. E17 . . . .1D **39**
Grosvenor Rd. E6 . . . . . . .5F **55**
E7 . . . . .3D **55**
E10 . . . . .3E **39**
E11 . . . . .1D **41**
SW1 . . . . .2D **89**
Grosvenor Sq.
W1 . . . . . . .4C **12** (1C **74**)
Grosvenor St.
W1 . . . . . . .4D **13** (1D **75**)
Grosvenor Studios
SW1 . . . .*5C 74*
(off Eaton Ter.)
Grosvenor Ter. SE5 . . . . . .3E **91**
Grosvenor Way E5 . . . . . .4E **37**
SW17 . . . . .3F **115**
Grosvenor Wharf Rd.
E14 . . . . .5F **81**
Grotes Bldgs. SE3 . . . . . .5A **96**
Grote's Pl. SE3 . . . . .5A **96**
Groton Rd. SW18 . . . . . . .2D **115**
Grotto Cl.
SE1 . . . . . . .3E **25** (3D **77**)
Grotto Pas.
W1 . . . . . . .5C **4** (4C **60**)
GROVE, THE **1C 120**
Grove, The E15 . . . . .3A **54**
N4 . . . . .2B **34**
N6 . . . . .3C **32**
N8 . . . . .1F **33**
NW11 . . . . .2A **30**
Grove Cl. SE23 . . . . .1A **122**
Grove Cotts. *SW3* *2A 88*
(off Chelsea Mnr. St.)
W4 . . . . .2A **84**
Grove Ct. *NW8* *2F 59*
(off Grove End Rd.)
SE15 . . . .*3A 92*
(off Blake's Rd.)
SW10 . . . .*1E 87*
(off Drayton Gdns.)
Grove Cres. Rd. E15 . . . . .3F **53**
Grovedale Rd. N19 . . . . . .4F **33**

Grove Dwellings. E1 . . . . . .4E **65**
Grove End. NW5 . . . . . . .1D **47**
Grove End Gdns.
  NW8 . . . . .1F **59**
Grove End Ho. NW8 . . . . .2F **59**
  (off Grove End Rd.)
Grove End Rd. NW8 . . . . .1F **59**
Grove Gdns. NW8 . . . . . .2A **60**
Grove Grn. Rd. E11 . . . . .5E **39**
Grove Hall Ct. E3 . . . . . .1C **66**
  (off Jebb St.)
  NW8 . . . . .2E **59**
Grovehill Ct.
  BR1: Brom 5B **124**
Grove Hill Rd. SE5 . . . . .1A **106**
Grove Ho. SW3 . . . . .2A **88**
  (off Chelsea Mnr. St.)
Groveland Ct. EC4 . . . . . .3A **18**
Grovelands Cl. SE5 . . . . . .5A **92**
Grovelands Rd. N15 . . . . .1C **36**
Grove La. SE5 . . . . .4F **91**
Grove La. Ter. SE5 . . . . . .5F **91**
Grove Mans. W6 . . . . . . .3E **71**
  (off Hammersmith Gro.)
Grove M. W6 . . . . .4E **71**
GROVE PARK 3D **125**
Grove Pk. E11 . . . . .1D **41**
  SE5 . . . . .5A **92**
Grove Pk. Nature Reserve
  . . . . .1B **124**
Grove Pk. Rd. SE9 . . . . . .3E **125**
Grove Pas. E2 . . . . .1D **65**
Grove Pl. NW3 . . . . .5F **31**
  SW12 . . . . .5D **103**
Grover Ct. SE13 . . . . .5D **95**
Grover Ho. SE11 . . . . . . .1B **90**
Grove Rd. E3 . . . . .5F **51**
  E11 . . . . .2B **40**
  E17 . . . . .1D **39**
  N15 . . . . .1A **36**
  NW2 . . . . .3E **43**
  SW13 . . . . .5B **84**
Groveside Ct. SW11 . . . . .5F **87**
Grove St. SE8 . . . . .5B **80**
Grove Ter. NW5 . . . . .5D **33**
Grove Ter. M. NW5 . . . . . .5D **33**
Grove Va. SE22 . . . . .2B **106**
Groveway SW9 . . . . .4B **90**
Grummant Rd. SE15 . . . . .4B **92**
Grundy St. E14 . . . . .5D **67**
Gtec Ho. E15 . . . . .1F **67**
  (off Canning Rd.)
Guardian Ct. SE12 . . . . . .3A **110**
Guards Memorial
  . . . . .2C **22** (2F **75**)
  (off Horse Guards Rd.)
Guards' Mus.
  . . . . .4A **22** (3E **75**)
Gubyon Av. SE24 . . . . . .3D **105**
Guerin Sq. E3 . . . . .2B **66**
Guernsey Gro. SE24 . . . . .5E **105**
Guernsey Ho. N1 . . . . . . .3E **49**
  (off Douglas Rd. Nth.)
Guernsey Rd. E11 . . . . . .3F **39**
Guibal Rd. SE12 . . . . . . .5D **111**
Guildford Ct. SW8 . . . . . .3A **90**
  (off Guildford Rd.)
Guildford Gro. SE10 . . . . .4D **95**
Guildford Rd. SW8 . . . . . .4A **90**

Guildhall
  City 2B **18**
  Westminster 4D **23**
Guildhall Art Gallery 2B **18**
  (off Aldermanbury)
Guildhall Bldgs. EC2 . . . . .2B **18**
Guildhall Library 2A **18**
Guildhall Offices EC2 . . . .2A **18**
Guildhall Yd.
  EC2 . . . . . . .2A **18** (5E **63**)
Guild Rd. SE7 . . . . .2F **97**
Guildhouse St. SW1 . . . . .5E **75**
Guild St. SE7 . . . . .2F **97**
Guilford Pl.
  WC1 . . . . . . .4F **7** (3B **62**)
Guilford St.
  WC1 . . . . . . .4D **7** (3A **62**)
Guillemot Ct. SE8 . . . . . . .2B **94**
  (off Alexandra Cl.)
Guinea Ct. E1 . . . . .1C **78**
  (off Royal Mint St.)
Guinea Point E14 . . . . . . .5A **66**
  (off Repton St.)
Guinness Cl. E9 . . . . .4A **52**
Guinness Ct. E1 . . . . .3F **19**
  EC1 . . . . .2A **10**
  NW8 . . . . .5A **46**
  SE1 . . . . .3D **27**
  SW3 . . . . .5B **74**
Guinness Sq. SE1 . . . . . . .5A **78**
Guinness Trust SW3 . . . . .5B **74**
  (off Cadogan St.)
Guinness Trust Bldgs.
  SE11 . . . . .1D **91**
  W6 . . . . .1F **85**
  (off Fulham Pal. Rd.)
Guinness Trust Estate, The
  N16 . . . . .3A **36**
Guion Rd. SW6 . . . . .5B **86**
Gulland Wlk. N1 . . . . .3E **49**
  (off Church Rd.)
Gullane Ho. E3 . . . . .1B **66**
  (off Shetland Rd.)
Gulliver's Ho. EC1 . . . . . . .4F **9**
Gulliver St. SE16 . . . . . . .4A **80**
Gulston Wlk. SW3 . . . . . . .5B **74**
  (off Blackland Ter.)
Gun Ho. E1 . . . . .2D **79**
  (off Wapping High St.)
Gunmakers La. E3 . . . . . .5A **52**
Gunnell Cl. SE26 . . . . . . .4C **120**
Gunners Rd. SW18 . . . . .2F **115**
Gunpowder Sq. EC4 . . . . .2C **16**
  (off E. Harding St.,
  not continuous)
Gunstor Rd. N16 . . . . . . .1A **50**
Gun St. E1 . . . . . .1F **19** (4B **64**)
Gunter Gro. SW10 . . . . . .2E **87**
Gunter Hall Studios
  SW10 . . . . .2E **87**
  (off Gunter Gro.)
Gunterstone Rd. W14 . . . .5A **72**
Gunthorpe St. E1 . . . . . . .4B **64**
Gunton M. SE13 . . . . . . .3F **109**
Gunton Rd. E5 . . . . .5D **37**
Gunwhale Cl. SE16 . . . . . .2F **79**
Gun Wharf E1 . . . . .2E **79**
  (off Wapping High St.)
Gun Wharf Bus. Cen.
  E3 . . . . .5A **52**
  (off Old Ford Rd.)

Gunyard M. SE18 . . . . . . .3F **97**
Gurdon Ho. E14 . . . . .5C **66**
  (off Dod St.)
Gurdon Rd. SE7 . . . . .1C **96**
Gurney Cl. E15 . . . . .2A **54**
Gurney Ho. E2 . . . . .1C **64**
  (off Goldsmiths Row)
Gurney Rd. E15 . . . . .2A **54**
  SW6 . . . . .1E **101**
Guthrie Ct. SE1 . . . . .4C **24**
Guthrie St. SW3 . . . . .1F **87**
Gutter La.
  EC2 . . . . . . .2F **17** (5E **63**)
Guy Barnett Gro.
  SE3 . . . . .1C **110**
Guyscliff Rd. SE13 . . . . . .3E **109**
Guy St. SE1 . . . . . .3C **26** (3F **77**)
Gwalior Rd. SW15 . . . . . .2F **99**
Gwendolen Av. SW15 . . . .2F **99**
Gwendolen Cl. SW15 . . . .3F **99**
Gwendoline Av. E13 . . . . .5D **55**
Gwendwr Rd. W14 . . . . . .1A **86**
Gwen Morris Ho. SE5 . . . .3E **91**
Gwent Ct. SE16 . . . . .2F **79**
  (off Rotherhithe St.)
Gwilym Maries Ho.
  E2 . . . . .2D **65**
  (off Blythe St.)
Gwyn Cl. SW6 . . . . .3E **87**
Gwynne Cl. W4 . . . . .2B **84**
Gwynne Ho. E1 . . . . .4D **65**
  (off Turner St.)
  SW1 . . . . .1C **88**
  (off Lwr. Sloane St.)
  WC1 . . . . .2B **8**
  (off Lloyd Baker St.)
Gwynne Pl.
  WC1 . . . . . .2A **8** (2B **62**)
Gwynne Rd. SW11 . . . . . .5F **87**
Gylcote Cl. SE5 . . . . .2F **105**

H

Haarlem Rd. W14 . . . . . . .4F **71**
Haberdasher Est.
  N1 . . . . .1C **10** (2F **63**)
Haberdasher Pl.
  N1 . . . . .1C **10** (2F **63**)
Haberdashers Ct.
  SE14 . . . . .1F **107**
Haberdasher St.
  N1 . . . . .1C **10** (2F **63**)
Habitat Cl. SE15 . . . . .5D **93**
Habitat Sq. SE10 . . . . . . .4B **82**
  (off Teal St.)
Hackford Rd. SW9 . . . . . .4B **90**
Hackford Wlk. SW9 . . . . .4B **90**
Hackington Cres.
  BR3: Beck 5C **122**
HACKNEY 3D **51**
Hackney City Farm 1C **64**
Hackney Empire Theatre
  . . . . .3D **51**
Hackney Gro. E8 . . . . .3D **51**
Hackney Mus. 3D **51**
Hackney Rd.
  E2 . . . . .2F **11** (2B **64**)
HACKNEY WICK 3B **52**
HACKNEY WICK 3A **52**

Hackworth Point E3 . . . .2D **67**
  (off Rainhill Way)
Hacon Sq. E8 . . . . .4D **51**
  (off Mare St.)
Haddington Rd.
  BR1: Brom 3F **123**
Haddo Ho. SE10 . . . . . . .2D **95**
  (off Haddo St.)
Haddonfield SE8 . . . . . .5F **79**
Haddon Ct. W3 . . . . .1B **70**
Haddonfield SE8 . . . . . .5F **79**
Haddon Hall St. SE1 . . . .4F **77**
  (off Rephidim St.)
Haddo St. SE10 . . . . .2D **95**
Haden Cl. N4 . . . . .4C **34**
Hadfield Ho. E1 . . . . .5C **64**
  (off Ellen St.)
Hadleigh Cl. E1 . . . . .3E **65**
Hadleigh Ct. NW2 . . . . . .3E **43**
Hadleigh Ho. E1 . . . . . . .3E **65**
  (off Hadleigh Cl.)
Hadleigh St. E2 . . . . .2E **65**
Hadley Cl. N16 . . . . .3C **36**
Hadley Gdns. W4 . . . . . .1A **84**
Hadley St. NW1 . . . . .3D **47**
  (not continuous)
Hadlow Ho. SE17 . . . . . .1A **92**
  (off Kinglake Est.)
Hadrian Cl. E3 . . . . .5C **52**
  (off Garrison Rd.)
Hadrian Est. E2 . . . . .1C **64**
Hadrian M. N7 . . . . .4B **48**
Hadrian St. SE10 . . . . . .1A **96**
Hadstock Ho. NW1 . . . . . .1C **6**
  (off Ossulston St.)
Hadyn Pk. Ct. W12 . . . . .3C **70**
  (off Curwen Rd.)
Hadyn Pk. Rd. W12 . . . . .3C **70**
Hafer Rd. SW11 . . . . . . .2B **102**
Hafton Rd. SE6 . . . . .1A **124**
HAGGERSTON 4B **50**
Haggerston Rd. E8 . . . . .4B **50**
Haggerston Studios
  E8 . . . . .5B **50**
  (off Kingsland Rd.)
Hague St. E2 . . . . .2C **64**
Haig Ho. E2 . . . . .1C **64**
  (off Shipton St.)
Haig Rd. E. E13 . . . . .2E **69**
Haig Rd. W. E13 . . . . .2E **69**
Hailes St. SW19 . . . . . . .5E **115**
Hailsham Av. SW2 . . . . .2B **118**
Hailsham Ho.
  NW8 . . . . .3A **60**
  (off Salisbury Rd.)
Haimo Rd. SE9 . . . . .3F **111**
Hainault Rd. E11 . . . . . . .3E **39**
Haines Cl. N1 . . . . .4A **50**
Haines St. SW8 . . . . .3E **89**
Hainford Cl. SE4 . . . . . . .2F **107**
Hainthorpe Rd.
  SE27 . . . . .3D **119**
Hainton Cl. E1 . . . . .5D **65**
Halberd M. E5 . . . . .4D **37**
Halcomb St. N1 . . . . .5A **50**
Halcrow St. E1 . . . . .4D **65**
Halcyon Wharf E1 . . . . . .2C **78**
  (off Hermitage Wall)
Haldane Pl. SW18 . . . . .1D **115**
Haldane Rd. E6 . . . . .2F **69**
  SW6 . . . . .3B **86**
Haldon Rd. SW18 . . . . .4B **100**

Hale Ho. SW1 . . . . .1F **89**
  (off Lindsay Sq.)
Hale Path SE27 . . . . . . .4D **119**
Hale Rd. E6 . . . . .3F **69**
Hales Prior N1 . . . . .1F **7**
  (off Calshot St.)
Hales St. SE8 . . . . .3C **94**
Hale St. E14 . . . . .1D **81**
Halesworth Cl. E5 . . . . . .4E **37**
Halesworth Rd.
  SE13 . . . . .1D **109**
Haley Rd. NW4 . . . . .1E **29**
Half Moon Ct. EC1 . . . . .1F **17**
Half Moon Cres. N1 . . . .1B **62**
  (not continuous)
Half Moon La. SE24 . . . .4E **105**
Half Moon Pas. E1 . . . . .5B **64**
Half Moon St.
  W1 . . . . .1E **21** (2D **75**)
Halford Rd. E10 . . . . .1F **39**
  SW6 . . . . .2C **86**
Haliday Ho. N1 . . . . .3F **49**
  (off Mildmay St.)
Haliday Wlk. N1 . . . . .3F **49**
Halidon Cl. E9 . . . . .2E **51**
Halifax St. SE26 . . . . . . .3D **121**
Haliwell Ho. NW6 . . . . . .5D **45**
  (off Mortimer Cres.)
Halkett Ho. E2 . . . . .5E **51**
  (off Waterloo Gdns.)
Halkin Arc.
  SW1 . . . . .5A **20** (4B **74**)
Halkin M.
  SW1 . . . . .5B **20** (4C **74**)
Halkin Pl.
  SW1 . . . . .5B **20** (4C **74**)
Halkin St.
  SW1 . . . . .4C **20** (3C **74**)
Hall, The SE3 . . . . .1C **110**
Hallam Ct. W1 . . . . .5E **5**
  (off Hallam St.)
Hallam Ho. SW1 . . . . .1E **89**
  (off Churchill Gdns.)
Hallam M. W1 . . .5E **5** (4D **61**)
Hallam Rd. SW13 . . . . . .1D **99**
Hallam St.
  W1 . . . . .4E **5** (3D **61**)
Hallane Ho. SE27 . . . . . .5E **119**
Hall Dr. SE26 . . . . .5E **121**
Halley Gdns. SE13 . . . . .2F **109**
Halley Ho. E2 . . . . .1C **64**
  (off Pritchards Rd.)
  SE10 . . . . .1B **96**
  (off Armitage Rd.)
Halley Rd. E7 . . . . .3E **55**
  E12 . . . . .3E **55**
Halley St. E14 . . . . .4A **66**
Hallfield Est. W2 . . . . . . .5E **59**
  (not continuous)
Hall Ga. NW8 . . . . .2F **59**
Halliday Ho. E1 . . . . .5C **64**
  (off Christian St.)
Halliford St. N1 . . . . .4E **49**
Halling Ho. SE1 . . . . .4C **26**
  (off Long La.)
Hallings Wharf Studios
  E15 . . . . .5F **53**
Halliwell St. SE22 . . . . .3C **106**
Halliwell Rd. SW2 . . . . .4B **104**

Hallmark Ho. E14 . . . . . .4C **66**
  (off Ursula Gould Way)
Hall Oak Wlk. NW6 . . . . .3B **44**
Hall Pl. W2 . . . . .3F **59**
  (not continuous)
Hall Rd. E15 . . . . .1F **53**
  NW8 . . . . .2E **59**
Hall St. EC1 . . . . . .1E **9** (2D **63**)
Hallsville Rd. E16 . . . . . .5B **68**
Hallswelle Rd. NW11 . . . .1B **30**
Hall Twr. W2 . . . . .4F **59**
  (off Hall Pl.)
Hall Vw. SE9 . . . . .2F **125**
Halo E15 . . . . .5E **53**
Halpin Pl. SE17 . . . . .5F **77**
Halsbrook Rd. SE3 . . . . .1E **111**
Halsbury Ho. N7 . . . . .1B **48**
  (off Biddestone Rd.)
Halsbury Rd. W12 . . . . . .2D **71**
Halsey Ho. WC1 . . . . .1F **15**
  (off Red Lion Sq.)
Halsey M. SW3 . . . . .5B **74**
Halsey St. SW3 . . . . .5B **74**
Halsmere Rd. SE5 . . . . . .4D **91**
Halstead Ct. E17 . . . . . . .2B **38**
  N1 . . . . .1C **10**
  (off Murray Gro.)
Halstead Rd. E11 . . . . . . .1C **40**
Halston Cl. SW11 . . . . . .4B **102**
Halstow Rd. NW10 . . . . .2F **57**
  SE10 . . . . .1C **96**
Halton Cross St. N1 . . . . .5D **49**
Halton Ho. N1 . . . . .4D **49**
  (off Halton Rd.)
Halton Mans. N1 . . . . . . .4D **49**
Halton Pl. N1 . . . . .5E **49**
Halton Rd. N1 . . . . .4D **49**
Halyard Ho. E14 . . . . .4E **81**
  (off Manchester Rd.)
Hamara Ghar E13 . . . . . .5E **55**
Hambalt Rd. SW4 . . . . . .3E **103**
Hambledon SE17 . . . . . . .2F **91**
  (off Villa St.)
Hambledon Ct.
  SE22 . . . . .2A **106**
Hambledon Pl.
  SE21 . . . . .1A **120**
Hambledon Rd.
  SW18 . . . . .5B **100**
Hamble St. SW6 . . . . . . .1D **101**
Hambley Ho. SE16 . . . . . .5D **79**
  (off Camilla Rd.)
Hambridge Way
  SW2 . . . . .5C **104**
Hambro Rd. SW16 . . . . . .5F **117**
Hamfrith Rd. E15 . . . . . . .3B **54**
Hamilton Cl. NW8 . . . . . . .2F **59**
  SE16 . . . . .3A **80**
Hamilton Ct. SE6 . . . . . .1B **124**
  SW15 . . . . .1A **100**
  W9 . . . . .2E **59**
  (off Maida Va.)
Hamilton Gdns.
  NW8 . . . . .2E **59**
Hamilton Hall NW8 . . . . .1E **59**
  (off Hamilton Ter.)
Hamilton Ho. E3 . . . . . . .2B **66**
  (off British St.)
  E14 . . . . .1D **95**
  (off St Davids Sq.)

Hamilton Ho. E14 . . . . . . .1B **80**
   (off Victory Pl.)
NW8 . . . . .2F **59**
   (off Hall Rd.)
W4 . . . . .2A **84**
W8 . . . . .3D **73**
   (off Vicarage Ga.)
Hamilton La. N5 . . . . .1D **49**
Hamilton Lodge E1 . . . . .3E **65**
   (off Cleveland Gro.)
Hamilton M. SW18 . . . . . .1C **114**
W1 . . . . . . .3D **21** (3D **75**)
Hamilton Pk. N5 . . . . .1D **49**
Hamilton Pk. W.
N5 . . . . .1D **49**
Hamilton Pl. N19 . . . . . .5F **33**
W1 . . . . . . .2C **20** (2C **74**)
Hamilton Rd. E15 . . . . . .2A **68**
NW10 . . . . .2C **42**
NW11 . . . . .2F **29**
SE27 . . . . .4F **119**
W4 . . . . .3A **70**
Hamilton Rd. Ind. Est.
SE27 . . . . .4F **119**
Hamilton Sq.
SE1 . . . . . .3C **26** (3F **77**)
Hamilton St. SE8 . . . . . .2C **94**
Hamilton Ter. NW8 . . . . .1D **59**
Hamlea Cl. SE12 . . . . . .3C **110**
Hamlet, The SE5 . . . . . .1F **105**
Hamlet Cl. SE13 . . . . . .2A **110**
Hamlet Ct. E3 . . . . .2C **66**
   (off Tomlin's Gro.)
SE11 . . . . .1D **91**
   (off Opal St.)
W6 . . . . .5C **70**
Hamlet Gdns. W6 . . . . . .5C **70**
Hamlet Ind. Est. E9 . . . .4C **52**
Hamlet Sq. NW2 . . . . . . .5A **30**
Hamlet M. SE21 . . . . . . .1F **119**
Hamlets Way E3 . . . . . . .3B **66**
Hamlet Way
SE1 . . . . . .3C **26** (3F **77**)
Hammelton Grn.
SW9 . . . . .4D **91**
Hammerfield Ho.
SW3 . . . . .1A **88**
   (off Cale St.)
Hammersley Ho.
SE14 . . . . .3E **93**
   (off Pomeroy St.)
Hammersley Rd. E16 . . . .4C **68**
HAMMERSMITH 5E **71**
Hammersmith Apollo . .1E **85**
Hammersmith Bri.
SW13 . . . . .2D **85**
Hammersmith Bri. Rd.
W6 . . . . .2D **85**
HAMMERSMITH BROADWAY
. . . . .5E **71**
Hammersmith B'way.
W6 . . . . .5E **71**
Hammersmith Emb.
W6 . . . . .2E **85**
Hammersmith
Fitness & Squash Cen.
. . . . .5F **71**
   (off Chalk Hill Rd.)
HAMMERSMITH FLYOVER
. . . . .1E **85**

Hammersmith Flyover
W6 . . . . .1E **85**
Hammersmith Gro.
W6 . . . . .3E **71**
Hammersmith Rd.
W6 . . . . .5F **71**
W14 . . . . .5F **71**
Hammersmith Ter.
W6 . . . . .1C **84**
Hammett St.
EC3 . . . . . .4F **19** (1B **78**)
Hammond Ct. E10 . . . . . .4D **39**
   (off Leyton Grange Est.)
SE11 . . . . .5F **77**
   (off Hotspur St.)
Hammond Ho. E14 . . . . . .4C **80**
   (off Tiller Rd.)
SE14 . . . . .3E **93**
   (off Lubbock St.)
Hammond Lodge W9 . . . .4C **58**
   (off Admiral Wlk.)
Hammond St. NW5 . . . . .3E **47**
Hamond Sq. N1 . . . . .1A **64**
Ham Pk. Rd. E7 . . . . .4B **54**
E15 . . . . .4B **54**
Hampden Cl. NW1 . . . . . .1F **61**
Hampden Gurney St.
W1 . . . . . . .3A **12** (5B **60**)
Hampden Ho. SW9 . . . . . .5C **90**
   (off Overton Rd.)
Hampden Rd. N19 . . . . . .4F **33**
Hampshire Hog La.
W6 . . . . .1D **85**
Hampshire St. NW5 . . . . .3F **47**
Hampson Way SW8 . . . . .4B **90**
HAMPSTEAD 1F **45**
Hampstead Gdns.
NW11 . . . . .1C **30**
HAMPSTEAD GARDEN SUBURB
. . . . .1E **31**
Hampstead Ga. NW3 . . . .2E **45**
Hampstead Golf Course
. . . . .2F **31**
Hampstead Grn.
NW3 . . . . .2A **46**
Hampstead Gro.
NW3 . . . . .5E **31**
Hampstead Heath 4F **31**
Hampstead High St.
NW3 . . . . .1F **45**
Hampstead Hill Gdns.
NW3 . . . . .1F **45**
Hampstead Ho. NW1 . . . .2F **5**
   (off William Rd.)
Hampstead La. N6 . . . . . .3F **31**
NW3 . . . . .3F **31**
Hampstead Lodge
NW1 . . . . .4A **60**
   (off Bell St.)
Hampstead Mus. 1F **45**
   (off New End Sq.)
Hampstead Rd.
NW1 . . . . . .1F **5** (1E **61**)
Hampstead Sq. NW3 . . . .5E **31**
Hampstead Theatre 4F **45**
Hampstead Wlk. E3 . . . . .5B **52**
Hampstead Way
NW11 . . . . .1B **30**
Hampstead W. NW6 . . . .3C **44**
Hampton Cl. NW6 . . . . . .2C **58**

Hampton Ct. N1 . . . . .3D **49**
SE16 . . . . .1F **79**
   (off King & Queen Wharf)
Hampton Ho. SW8 . . . . . .3E **89**
   (off Ascalon St.)
Hampton Rd. E7 . . . . . . .2D **55**
E11 . . . . .3F **39**
Hampton St. SE1 . . . . . . .5E **77**
SE17 . . . . .5D **77**
Hamston Ho. W8 . . . . . . .4D **73**
   (off Kensington Ct. Pl.)
Ham Yd. W1 . . . .4B **14** (1F **75**)
Hanameel St. E16 . . . . . .2C **82**
Hana M. E5 . . . . .1D **51**
Hanbury Dr. E11 . . . . .2B **40**
Hanbury Ho. E1 . . . . .4C **64**
   (off Hanbury St.)
SW8 . . . . .3A **90**
   (off Regent's Bri. Gdns.)
Hanbury M. N1 . . . . .5E **49**
Hanbury St.
E1 . . . . .5F **11** (4B **64**)
Hancock Nunn Ho.
NW3 . . . . .3B **46**
   (off Fellows Rd.)
Hancock Rd. E3 . . . . .2E **67**
Handa Wlk. N1 . . . . .3F **49**
Hand Ct.
WC1 . . . . . .1A **16** (4B **62**)
Handel Bus. Cen.
SW8 . . . . .2A **90**
Handel House Mus. 4D **13**
   (off Brook St.)
Handel Mans. SW13 . . . .3E **85**
WC1 . . . . .3E **7**
   (off Handel St.)
Handel Pl. NW10 . . . . . . .3A **42**
Handel St.
WC1 . . . . . .3D **7** (3A **62**)
Handen Rd. SE12 . . . . . .3A **110**
Handforth Rd. SW9 . . . . .3C **90**
Handley Gro. NW2 . . . . . .5F **29**
Handley Rd. E9 . . . . .4E **51**
Hands Wlk. E16 . . . . .5C **68**
Handyside St. N1 . . . . . . .5A **48**
Hanford Cl. SW18 . . . . . .1C **114**
Hanford Row SW15 . . . . .5E **113**
Hanging Sword All.
EC4 . . . . .3C **16**
Hankey Ho. SE1 . . . . .4C **26**
   (off Hankey Pl.)
Hankey Pl.
SE1 . . . . . .4C **26** (3F **77**)
Hanley Gdns. N4 . . . . . . .3B **34**
Hanley Rd. N4 . . . . .3A **34**
Hanmer Wlk. N7 . . . . .4B **34**
Hannaford Wlk. E3 . . . . . .3D **67**
Hannah Barlow Ho.
SW8 . . . . .4B **90**
Hannah Bldg. E1 . . . . . . .5D **65**
   (off Watney St.)
Hannah Ct. E15 . . . . .1B **68**
Hannah Mary Way
SE1 . . . . .5C **78**
Hannay Ho. SW15 . . . . . .4A **100**
Hannay La. N8 . . . . .2F **33**
Hannay Wlk. SW16 . . . . . .2F **117**
Hannell Rd. SW6 . . . . . . .3A **86**
Hannen Rd. SE27 . . . . . . .3D **119**
Hannibal Rd. E1 . . . . .4E **65**

Hannington Rd.
SW4 . . . . .1D **103**
Hanover Av. E16 . . . . . . .2C **82**
Hanover Ct. SW15 . . . . .2B **98**
W12 . . . .*2C 70*
(off Uxbridge Rd.)
Hanover Flats *W1* *4C 12*
(off Binney St.)
Hanover Gdns.
SE11 . . . . .2C **90**
Hanover Ga. NW1 . . . . .2A **60**
Hanover Ga. Mans.
NW1 . . . . .3A **60**
Hanover Ho. *E14* *2B 80*
(off Westferry Cir.)
NW8 . . . .*1A 58*
(off St John's Wood High St.)
SW9 . . . .*1C 104*
Hanover Mans.
SW2 . . . .*3C 104*
(off Barnwell Rd.)
Hanover Mead NW11 . . .1A **30**
Hanover Pk. SE15 . . . . .4C **92**
Hanover Pl. E3 . . . . .2B **66**
WC2 . . . . .3E **15** (5A **62**)
Hanover Rd. NW10 . . . . .4E **43**
Hanover Sq.
W1 . . . . .3E **13** (5D **61**)
Hanover Steps *W2* *5A 60*
(off St George's Flds.)
Hanover St.
W1 . . . . .3E **13** (5D **61**)
Hanover Ter. NW1 . . . . .2A **60**
Hanover Ter. M.
NW1 . . . . .2A **60**
Hanover Trad. Est.
N7 . . . . .2A **48**
Hanover Yd. *N1* *1E 63*
(off Noel Rd.)
Hansard M. W14 . . . . . . .3F **71**
Hanscomb M. SW4 . . . .2E **103**
Hans Ct. *SW3* *4B 74*
(off Hans Rd.)
Hans Cres.
SW1 . . . . . . .5A **20** (4B **74**)
Hanseatic Wlk. EC4 . . . . .5B **18**
Hansler Ct. *SW19* *1A 114*
(off Princes Way)
Hansler Rd. SE22 . . . . . .3B **106**
Hanson Cl. SW12 . . . . . .5D **103**
Hanson Ct. E17 . . . . . . .1D **39**
Hanson Ho. *E1* *1C 78*
(off Pinchin St.)
Hanson St. W1 . . . .5F **5** (4E **61**)
Hans Pl.
SW1 . . . . . . .5A **20** (4B **74**)
Hans Rd.
SW3 . . . . . . .5A **20** (4B **74**)
Hans St.
SW1 . . . . . . .5A **20** (4B **74**)
Hanway Pl.
W1 . . . . .2B **14** (5F **61**)
Hanway St.
W1 . . . . .2B **14** (5F **61**)
Hanwell Ho. *W2* *4C 58*
(off Gt. Western Rd.)
Harad's Pl. E1 . . . . .1C **78**
Harben Pde. *NW3* *4E 45*
(off Finchley Rd.)
Harben Rd. NW6 . . . . . .4E **45**

Harberson Rd. E15 . . . . .5B **54**
SW12 . . . . .1D **117**
Harberton Rd. N19 . . . . .3E **33**
Harbet Rd. W2 . . . . .4F **59**
Harbinger Rd. E14 . . . . .5D **81**
Harbledown Ho. *SE1* *4B 26*
(off Manciple St.)
Harbledown Rd. SW6 . . .4C **86**
Harbord Cl. SE5 . . . . . . .5F **91**
Harbord Ho. *SE16* *5F 79*
(off Cope St.)
Harbord St. SW6 . . . . . .4F **85**
Harborough Rd.
SW16 . . . . .4B **118**
Harbour Av. SW10 . . . . .4E **87**
Harbour Club
Leisure Centre, The
. . . . .5E **87**
Harbour Club Notting Hill
. . . . .4C **58**
Harbour Exchange Sq.
E14 . . . . .3D **81**
Harbour Quay E14 . . . . .2E **81**
Harbour Reach SW6 . . . .4E **87**
Harbour Rd. SE5 . . . . . .1E **105**
Harbour Ter. SW10 . . . . .4E **87**
Harbridge Av. SW15 . . . .5B **98**
Harbut Rd. SW11 . . . . . .2F **101**
Harcombe Rd. N16 . . . . .5A **36**
Harcourt Bldgs. EC4 . . . . .4B **16**
Harcourt Ho. w1 . . . . . . .2D **13**
Harcourt Rd. E15 . . . . . .1B **68**
SE4 . . . . .1B **108**
Harcourt St. W1 . . . . . . .4A **60**
Harcourt Ter. SW10 . . . . .1D **87**
Hardcastle Ho. *SE14* *4A 94*
(off Loring Rd.)
Hardel Ri. SW2 . . . . . . .1D **119**
Hardel Wlk. SW2 . . . . . .5C **104**
Harden Cl. SE7 . . . . .5F **83**
Harden Ho. SE5 . . . . . . .5A **92**
Harden's Manorway
SE7 . . . . .4F **83**
(not continuous)
Harders Rd. SE15 . . . . . .5D **93**
Hardess St. SE24 . . . . . .1E **105**
Harding Cl. SE17 . . . . . .2E **91**
Harding La. E1 . . . . .5E **65**
(not continuous)
Harding Rd. NW10 . . . . .5D **43**
Hardinge St. E1 . . . . . . .1E **79**
(Johnson St.)
E1 . . . . .5E **65**
(Steel's La.)
Harding Ho. *SW13* *2D 85*
(off Wyatt Dr.)
Hardington *NW1* *4C 46*
(off Belmont St.)
Hardman Rd. SE7 . . . . . .1D **97**
Hardwicke M. WC1 . . . . .2A **8**
Hardwick Ho. *NW8* *3A 60*
(off Lilestone St.)
Hardwick St.
EC1 . . . . .2C **8** (2C **62**)
Hardwicks Way
SW18 . . . . .3C **100**
Hardwidge St.
SE1 . . . . . . .3D **27** (3A **78**)
Hardy Av. E16 . . . . .2C **82**
Hardy Cl. SE16 . . . . .3F **79**

Hardy Cotts. SE10 . . . . .2F **95**
Hardy Ct. *SW17* *3F 115*
(off Grosvenor Way)
Hardy Ho. SW4 . . . . . . .5E **103**
SW18 . . . . .5D **101**
Hardy Rd. SE3 . . . . .3B **96**
Hare & Billet Rd. SE3 . . .4F **95**
Hare Ct. EC4 . . . . .3B **16**
Harecourt Rd. N1 . . . . . .3E **49**
Haredale Ho. *SE16* *3C 78*
(off East La.)
Haredale Rd. SE24 . . . . .2E **105**
Haredon Cl. SE23 . . . . . .5F **107**
Harefield M. SE4 . . . . . . .1B **108**
Harefield Rd. SE4 . . . . . .1B **108**
Hare Marsh E2 . . . . .3C **64**
Hare Pl. *EC4* *3C 16*
(off Fleet St.)
Hare Row E2 . . . . .1D **65**
Hare Wlk. N1 . . . . .1A **64**
(not continuous)
Harewood Av. NW1 . . . . .3A **60**
Harewood Pl.
W1 . . . . .3E **13** (5D **61**)
Harewood Row NW1 . . . .4A **60**
Harfield Gdns. SE5 . . . . .1A **106**
Harfleur Ct. *SE11* *5D 77*
(off Opal St.)
Harford Ho. *SE5* *2E 91*
(off Bethwin Rd.)
W11 . . . .*4B 58*
Harford M. N19 . . . . .5F **33**
Harford St. E1 . . . . .3A **66**
Hargood Rd. SE3 . . . . . .4E **97**
Hargrave Mans. N19 . . . .4F **33**
Hargrave Pk. N19 . . . . . .4E **33**
Hargrave Pl. N7 . . . . . . .2F **47**
Hargrave Rd. N19 . . . . . .4E **33**
Hargraves Ho. *W12* *1D 71*
(off White City Est.)
Hargwyne St. SW9 . . . . .1B **104**
Haringey Pk. N8 . . . . . . .1A **34**
Harkness Ho. *E1* *5C 64*
(off Christian St.)
Harland Rd. SE12 . . . . . .1C **124**
Harlequin Ct. *E1* *1C 78*
(off Thomas More St.)
NW10 . . . .*3A 42*
(off Mitchellbrook Way)
Harlescott Rd. SE15 . . . .2F **107**
HARLESDEN 1B **56**
Harlesden Gdns.
NW10 . . . . .5B **42**
Harlesden La. NW10 . . . .5C **42**
Harlesden Plaza
NW10 . . . . .1B **56**
Harlesden Rd. NW10 . . . .5C **42**
Harleston Cl. E5 . . . . . . .4E **37**
Harley Ct. E11 . . . . .2C **40**
Harleyford Ct. *SE11* *2B 90*
(off Harleyford Rd.)
Harleyford Rd.
SE11 . . . . .2B **90**
Harleyford St. SE11 . . . . .2C **90**
Harley Gdns. SW10 . . . . .1E **87**
Harley Gro. E3 . . . . .2B **66**
Harley Ho. E11 . . . . .2F **39**
E14 . . . .*5B 66*
(off Frances Wharf)
NW1 . . . . .4C **4**

Harley Pl.
  W1 . . . . . .1D **13** (4D **61**)
Harley Rd. NW3 . . . . . . .4F **45**
  NW10 . . . . .1A **56**
Harley St. W1 . . .4D **5** (3D **61**)
Harley Vs. NW10 . . . . . . .1A **56**
Harling Ct. SW11 . . . . . . .5B **88**
Harlinger St. SE18 . . . . . .4F **83**
Harlynwood SE5 . . . . . . .3E **91**
  (off Wyndham Rd.)
Harman Cl. NW2 . . . . .5A **30**
  SE1 . . . . .1C **92**
Harman Dr. NW2 . . . . .5A **30**
Harmon Ho. SE8 . . . . .5B **80**
Harmont Ho. W1 . . . . .1D **13**
  (off Harley St.)
Harmony Cl. NW11 . . . . . . .1A **30**
Harmony Pl. SE1 . . . . .1B **92**
Harmood Gro. NW1 . . . . . . .4D **47**
Harmood Ho. NW1 . . . . . . .4D **47**
  (off Harmood St.)
Harmood Pl. NW1 . . . . .4D **47**
Harmood St. NW1 . . . . .3D **47**
Harmsworth M. SE11 . . . . . .4C **76**
Harmsworth St.
  SE17 . . . . .1D **91**
Harold Ct. SE16 . . . . .3F **79**
  (off Christopher Cl.)
Harold Est. SE1 . . . . .4A **78**
Harold Gibbons Ct.
  SE7 . . . . .2E **97**
Harold Ho. E2 . . . . .1F **65**
  (off Mace St.)
Harold Laski Ho. EC1 . . . . . .2E **9**
  (off Percival St.)
Harold Maddison Ho.
  SE17 . . . . .1D **91**
  (off Penton Pl.)
Harold Pl. SE11 . . . . .1C **90**
Harold Rd. E11 . . . . .3A **40**
  E13 . . . . .5D **55**
  NW10 . . . . .2A **56**
Haroldstone Rd. E17 . . . . . .1F **37**
Harold Wilson Ho.
  SW6 . . . . .2B **86**
  (off Clem Attlee Ct.)
Harp All.
  EC4 . . . . . .2D **17** (5D **63**)
Harp Bus. Centre, The
  NW2 . . . . .4C **28**
Harpenden Rd. E12 . . . . . . .4E **41**
  SE27 . . . . .3D **119**
Harpenmead Point
  NW2 . . . . .4B **30**
Harper Ho. SW9 . . . . .1D **105**
Harper M. SW17 . . . . .3E **115**
Harper Rd.
  SE1 . . . . . . .5F **25** (4E **77**)
Harp Island Cl.
  NW10 . . . . .4A **28**
Harp La. EC3 . . . .5D **19** (1A **78**)
Harpley Sq. E1 . . . . .3F **65**
Harpsden St. SW11 . . . . . . .4C **88**
Harpur M.
  WC1 . . . . . . .5F **7** (4B **62**)
Harpur St.
  WC1 . . . . . . .5F **7** (4B **62**)
Harraden Rd. SE3 . . . . . . .4E **97**
Harrier Av. E11 . . . . .1D **41**
Harriet Cl. E8 . . . . .5C **50**

Harriet Ho. SW6 . . . . .3D **87**
  (off Wandon Rd.)
Harriet St.
  SW1 . . . . . . .4A **20** (3B **74**)
Harriet Tubman Cl.
  SW2 . . . . .5B **104**
Harriet Wlk.
  SW1 . . . . . . .4A **20** (3B **74**)
HARRINGAY 1D **35**
Harrington Ct. SW7 . . . . . . .5F **73**
  (off Harrington Rd.)
  W10 . . . . .2B **58**
Harrington Gdns.
  SW7 . . . . .5D **73**
Harrington Hill E5 . . . . . . .3D **37**
Harrington Ho. NW1 . . . . . . .1F **5**
  (off Harrington St.)
Harrington Rd. E11 . . . . . . .3A **40**
  SW7 . . . . .5F **73**
Harrington Sq. NW1 . . . . . .1E **61**
Harrington St.
  NW1 . . . . . . .1F **5** (1E **61**)
  (not continuous)
Harrington Way SE18 . . . . . .4F **83**
Harriott Cl. SE10 . . . . .5B **82**
Harriott Ho. E1 . . . . .4E **65**
  (off Jamaica St.)
Harris Bldgs. E1 . . . . .5C **64**
  (off Burslem St.)
Harris Ho. E3 . . . . .2C **66**
  (off Alfred St.)
  SW9 . . . . .1C **104**
  (off St James's Cres.)
Harris Lodge SE6 . . . . . . .1E **123**
Harrison Ho. SE17 . . . . .1F **91**
  (off Brandon St.)
Harrison Rd. NW10 . . . . . . .5A **42**
Harrisons Ct. SE14 . . . . . . .2F **93**
  (off Myers La.)
Harrison St.
  WC1 . . . . . . .2E **7** (2A **62**)
Harris Sports Cen. 3E **107**
Harris St. E17 . . . . .2B **38**
  SE5 . . . . .3F **91**
Harrods 5A **20** (4B **74**)
Harrogate Ct. SE12 . . . . . . .5C **110**
  SE26 . . . . .3C **120**
  (off Droitwich Cl.)
Harrold Ho. NW3 . . . . .4F **45**
Harroway Rd. SW11 . . . . . . .5F **87**
Harrowby Ho. W1 . . . . .5B **60**
  (off Harrowby St.)
Harrowby St. W1 . . . . .5A **60**
Harrow Club Sports Cen.
   . . . . .1F **71**
Harrowgate Ho. E9 . . . . . . .3F **51**
Harrowgate Rd. E9 . . . . . . .3A **52**
Harrow Grn. E11 . . . . .5A **40**
Harrow La. E14 . . . . .1D **81**
Harrow Lodge NW8 . . . . . . .3F **59**
  (off Northwick Ter.)
Harrow Pl.
  E1 . . . . . . .2E **19** (1A **64**)
Harrow Rd. E6 . . . . .5F **55**
  E11 . . . . .5A **40**
  NW10 . . . . .2D **57**
  W2 . . . . .4E **59**
  (not continuous)
  W9 . . . . .3A **58**
  W10 . . . . .3A **58**

Harrow Rd. Bri. W2 . . . . . . .4E **59**
Harrow St. NW1 . . . . .4A **60**
  (off Daventry St.)
Harry Day M. SE27 . . . . . .3E **119**
Harry Hinkins Ho.
  SE17 . . . . .1E **91**
  (off Bronti Cl.)
Harry Lambourn Ho.
  SE15 . . . . .3D **93**
  (off Gervase St.)
Harry Zeital Way
  E5 . . . . .4E **37**
Hartfield Ter. E3 . . . . .1C **66**
Hartham Cl. N7 . . . . .2A **48**
Hartham Rd. N7 . . . . .2A **48**
Harting Rd. SE9 . . . . .3F **125**
Hartington Ct. SW8 . . . . . . .4A **90**
Hartington Ho. SW1 . . . . . . .1F **89**
  (off Drummond Ga.)
Hartington Rd. E16 . . . . . . .5D **69**
  E17 . . . . .1A **38**
  SW8 . . . . .4A **90**
Hartismere Rd. SW6 . . . . . .3B **86**
Hartlake Rd. E9 . . . . .3F **51**
Hartland NW1 . . . . .5E **47**
  (off Royal College St.)
Hartland Rd. E15 . . . . .4B **54**
  NW1 . . . . .4D **47**
  NW6 . . . . .1B **58**
Hartley Av. E6 . . . . .5F **55**
Hartley Ho. SE1 . . . . .5B **78**
  (off Longfield Est.)
Hartley Rd. E11 . . . . .3B **40**
Hartley St. E2 . . . . .2E **65**
  (not continuous)
Hartmann Rd. E16 . . . . .2F **83**
Hartnoll St. N7 . . . . .2B **48**
Harton Lodge SE8 . . . . .4C **94**
  (off Harton St.)
Harton St. SE8 . . . . .4C **94**
Hartop Point SW6 . . . . .3A **86**
  (off Pellant Rd.)
Hartshorn All. EC3 . . . . . . .3E **19**
Hart's La. SE14 . . . . .4A **94**
Hart St. EC3 . . . .4E **19** (1A **78**)
Hartswood Gdns.
  W12 . . . . .4B **70**
Hartswood Rd. W12 . . . . . . .3B **70**
Hartsworth Cl. E13 . . . . . . .1B **68**
Hartwell Cl. SW2 . . . . .1B **118**
Hartwell Ho. SE7 . . . . .1D **97**
  (off Troughton Rd.)
Hartwell St. E8 . . . . .3B **50**
Harvard Ct. NW6 . . . . .2D **45**
Harvard Ho. SE17 . . . . .2D **91**
  (off Doddington Gro.)
Harvard Rd. SE13 . . . . . . .3E **109**
Harvey Gdns. E11 . . . . .3B **40**
  SE7 . . . . .1E **97**
Harvey Ho. E1 . . . . .3D **65**
  (off Brady St.)
  N1 . . . . .5F **49**
  (off Colville St.)
  SW1 . . . . .1F **89**
  (off Aylesford St.)
Harvey Lodge W9 . . . . .4C **58**
  (off Admiral Wlk.)
Harvey Rd. E11 . . . . .3A **40**
  SE5 . . . . .4F **91**
  (not continuous)

Harvey's Bldgs.
WC2 . . . . .5E **15** (1A 76)
Harvey St. N1 . . . . .5F 49
Harvington Wlk.
E8 . . . . .4C 50
Harvist Est. N7 . . . . . . .1C 48
Harvist Rd. NW6 . . . . . .1F 57
Harwicke Ho. E3 . . . . . .2D 67
(off Bromley High St.)
Harwood Ct. N1 . . . . . . .5F 49
(off Colville Est.)
SW15 . . . . .2E 99
Harwood M. SW6 . . . . . .3C 86
Harwood Point SE16 . . .3B 80
Harwood Rd. SW6 . . . . .3C 86
Harwood Ter. SW6 . . . . .4D 87
Haseley End SE23 . . . . .5E 107
Haselrigge Rd. SW4 . . . .2F 103
Haseltine Rd. SE26 . . . .4B 122
Hasker St. SW3 . . . . . . .5A 74
Haslam Cl. N1 . . . . .4C 48
Haslam Ho. N1 . . . . . . .4E 49
(off Canonbury Rd.)
Haslam St. SE15 . . . . . .3B 92
Haslemere Av. NW4 . . . .1F 29
SW18 . . . . .2D 115
Haslemere Ind. Est.
SW18 . . . . .2D 115
Haslemere Rd. N8 . . . . .2F 33
Haslers Wharf E3 . . . . .5A 52
(off Old Ford Rd.)
Hassard St. E2 . . . . .1B 64
Hassendean Rd. SE3 . . . .3D 97
Hassett Rd. E9 . . . . .3F 51
Hassocks Cl. SE26 . . . . .3D 121
Hassop Rd. NW2 . . . . . .1F 43
Hassop Wlk. SE9 . . . . . .4F 125
Hasted Rd. SE7 . . . . . . .1F 97
Hastings Cl. SE15 . . . . .3C 92
Hastings Ho. W12 . . . . .1D 71
(off White City Est.)
WC1 . . . . .2D 7
(off Hastings St.)
Hastings Rd. E16 . . . . . .4C 68
Hastings St.
WC1 . . . . .2D 7 (2A 62)
Hat & Mitre Ct. EC1 . . . .4E 9
Hatcham Mews Bus. Cen.
SE14 . . . . .4F 93
(off Hatcham Pk. Rd.)
Hatcham Pk. M.
SE14 . . . . .4F 93
Hatcham Pk. Rd.
SE14 . . . . .4F 93
Hatcham Rd. SE15 . . . . .2E 93
Hatchard Rd. N19 . . . . . .4F 33
Hatchers M. SE1 . . . . . .4E 27
Hatchfield Ho. N15 . . . . .1A 36
(off Albert Rd.)
Hatcliffe Almshouses
SE10 . . . . .1A 96
(off Tuskar St.)
Hatcliffe Cl. SE3 . . . . . .1B 110
Hatcliffe St. SE10 . . . . .1B 96
Hatfield Cl. SE14 . . . . . .3F 93
Hatfield Ct. SE3 . . . . . . .3C 96
Hatfield Ho. EC1 . . . . . .4F 9
SE10 . . . . .3D 95
Hatfield Rd. E15 . . . . . . .2A 54
W4 . . . . .3A 70

Hatfields
SE1 . . . . .1C **24** (2C 76)
Hathaway Ho.
N1 . . . . . . .1D **11** (1A 64)
Hatherley Ct. W2 . . . . . .5D 59
(off Hatherley Gro.)
Hatherley Gdns. E6 . . . . .2F 69
N8 . . . . .1A 34
Hatherley Gro. W2 . . . . .5D 59
Hatherley St. SW1 . . . . .5E 75
Hathersage Ct. N1 . . . . .2F 49
Hathorne Cl. SE15 . . . . .5D 93
Hathway St. SE14 . . . . . .5F 93
Hathway Ter. SE14 . . . . .5F 93
(off Hathway St.)
Hatley Rd. N4 . . . . .4B 34
Hatteraick St. SE16 . . . . .3E 79
Hatton Gdn.
EC1 . . . . . .5C **8** (4C 62)
Hatton Ho. E1 . . . . .1C 78
(off Hindmarsh Cl.)
Hatton Pl. EC1 . . . .5C **8** (4C 62)
Hatton Row NW8 . . . . . .3F 59
(off Hatton St.)
Hatton St. NW8 . . . . .3F 59
Hatton Wall
EC1 . . . . . .5C **8** (4C 62)
Haunch of Venison Yd.
W1 . . . . . . .3D **13** (5D 61)
Hauteville Ct. Gdns.
W6 . . . . .4B 70
(off South Side)
Havana Rd. SW19 . . . . .2C 114
Havannah St. E14 . . . . . .3C 80
Havelock Cl. W12 . . . . . .1D 71
Havelock Ho. SE1 . . . . . .5B 78
(off Fort Rd.)
SE23 . . . . .1E 121
Havelock Rd. SW19 . . . .5E 115
Havelock St. N1 . . . . . . .5A 48
Havelock Ter. SW8 . . . . .4D 89
Havelock Ter. Arches
SW8 . . . . .4D 89
(off Havelock Ter.)
Havelock Wlk. SE23 . . . .1E 121
Haven Cl. SW19 . . . . . . .3F 113
Haven M. E3 . . . . .4B 66
N1 . . . . .4C 48
Havenpool NW8 . . . . . . .5D 45
(off Abbey Rd.)
Haven St. NW1 . . . . .4D 47
Haverfield Rd. E3 . . . . . .2A 66
Haverhill Rd. SW12 . . . .1E 117
Havering NW1 . . . . .4D 47
(off Castlehaven Rd.)
Havering St. E1 . . . . .5F 65
Haversham Pl. N6 . . . . . .4B 32
Haverstock Hill NW3 . . . .2A 46
Haverstock Pl. N1 . . . . . .1E 9
(off Haverstock St.)
Haverstock Rd. NW5 . . . .2C 46
Haverstock St.
N1 . . . . . .1E **9** (1D 63)
Havil St. SE5 . . . . .3A 92
Havisham Apartments
E15 . . . . .3F 53
(off Grove Cres. Rd.)
Havisham Ho. SE16 . . . .3C 78
Hawarden Gro.
SE24 . . . . .5E 105

Hawarden Hill NW2 . . . .5C 28
Hawbridge Rd. E11 . . . . .3F 39
Hawes St. N1 . . . . .4D 49
Hawgood St. E3 . . . . . . .4C 66
Hawke Ho. E1 . . . . .3F 65
(off Ernest St.)
Hawke Pl. SE16 . . . . . . .3F 79
Hawke Rd. SE19 . . . . . . .5F 119
Hawkesbury Rd.
SW15 . . . . .3D 99
Hawkesfield Rd.
SE23 . . . . .2A 122
Hawke Twr. SE14 . . . . . .2A 94
Hawkins Ho. SE8 . . . . . .2C 94
(off New King St.)
SW1 . . . . .2E 89
(off Dolphin Sq.)
Hawkins Rd. NW10 . . . . .4A 42
Hawkins Way SE6 . . . . . .5C 122
Hawkley Gdns.
SE27 . . . . .2D 119
Hawkshaw Cl. SW2 . . . . .5A 104
Hawkshead NW1 . . . . . .1F 5
Hawkshead Rd.
NW10 . . . . .4B 42
W4 . . . . .3A 70
Hawkslade Rd.
SE15 . . . . .3F 107
Hawksley Rd. N16 . . . . . .5A 36
Hawks M. SE10 . . . . . . .3E 95
Hawksmoor Cl. E6 . . . . .5F 69
Hawksmoor M. E1 . . . . . .1D 79
Hawksmoor Pl. E2 . . . . . .3C 64
(off Cheshire St.)
Hawksmoor St. W6 . . . . .2F 85
Hawkstone Rd. SE16 . . . .5E 79
Hawkwell Wlk. N1 . . . . . .5E 49
(off Maldon Cl.)
Hawkwood Mt. E5 . . . . . .3D 37
Hawley Cres. NW1 . . . . .4D 47
Hawley M. NW1 . . . . . . .4D 47
Hawley Rd. NW1 . . . . . . .4D 47
(not continuous)
Hawley St. NW1 . . . . . . .4D 47
Hawstead Rd. SE6 . . . . . .4D 109
Hawthorn Av. E3 . . . . . . .5B 52
Hawthorn Cres.
SW17 . . . . .5C 116
Hawthorne Cl. N1 . . . . . .3A 50
Hawthorne Ho. N15 . . . .1C 36
SW1 . . . . .1E 89
(off Churchill Gdns.)
Hawthorn Rd. NW10 . . . .4C 42
Hawthorn Ter. N19 . . . . .3F 33
(off Calverley Gro.)
Hawthorn Wlk. W10 . . . . .3A 58
Hawtrey Rd. NW3 . . . . . .4A 46
Hay Cl. E15 . . . . .4A 54
Haycroft Gdns. NW10 . . .5C 42
Haycroft Rd. SW2 . . . . . .3A 104
Hay Currie St. E14 . . . . . .5D 67
Hayday Rd. E16 . . . . .4C 68
(not continuous)
Hayden Piper Ho.
SW3 . . . . .2B 88
(off Caversham St.)
Hayden's Pl. W11 . . . . . .5B 58
Haydon Pk. Rd.
SW19 . . . . .5C 114
Haydons Rd. SW19 . . . . .5D 115

Haydon St. E1 . . . . 5B **64**
  EC3 . . . . .4F **19** (1B **78**)
Haydon Wlk.
  E1 . . . . .3F **19** (5B **64**)
Haydon Way SW11 . . . .2F **101**
Hayes Ct. SE5 . . . . .3E **91**
  (off Camberwell New Rd.)
  SW2 . . . . .1A **118**
Hayes Cres. NW11 . . . . . . .1B **30**
Hayesens Ho.
  SW17 . . . . .4E **115**
Hayes Gro. SE22 . . . . . .1B **106**
Hayes Pl. NW1 . . . . .3A **60**
Hayfield Pas. E1 . . . . .3E **65**
Hayfield Yd. E1 . . . . .3E **65**
Haygarth Pl. SW19 . . . . . .5F **113**
Hay Hill W1 . . . . .5E **13** (1D **75**)
Hayhurst Ct. N1 . . . . .5D **49**
  (off Dibden St.)
Hayles Bldgs. SE11 . . . . .5D **77**
  (off Elliotts Row)
Hayles St. SE11 . . . . .5D **77**
Hayling Cl. N16 . . . . .2A **50**
Haymans Point SE11 . . . .5B **76**
Hayman St. N1 . . . . .4D **49**
Haymarket
  SW1 . . . . . .5B **14** (1F **75**)
Haymarket Arc. SW1 . . . .5B **14**
Haymarket Ct. E8 . . . . . . .4B **50**
  (off Jacaranda Gro.)
Haymarket Theatre Royal
  .5C **14**
  (off Haymarket)
Haymerle Ho. SE15 . . . . .2C **92**
  (off Haymerle Rd.)
Haymerle Rd. SE15 . . . . .2C **92**
Hay M. NW3 . . . . .3B **46**
Hayne Ho. W11 . . . . .2A **72**
  (off Penzance Pl.)
Haynes Cl. SE3 . . . . .1A **110**
Hayne St. EC1 . . . .5E **9** (4D **63**)
Hay's Ct. SE16 . . . . .3E **79**
  (off Rotherhithe St.)
Hay's Galleria
  SE1 . . . . . . .1D **27** (2A **78**)
Hays La.
  SE1 . . . . . . .1D **27** (2A **78**)
Hay's M. W1 . . . .1D **21** (2D **75**)
Hay St. E2 . . . . .5C **50**
Hayter Ct. E11 . . . . .4D **41**
Hayter Rd. SW2 . . . . .3A **104**
Hayton Cl. E8 . . . . .3B **50**
Hayward Cl. SW9 . . . . . . .5A **90**
  (off Studley Rd.)
Hayward Gallery
  . . . . .2A **24** (2B **76**)
Hayward Gdns.
  SW15 . . . . .4E **99**
Hayward Ho. N1 . . . . .1C **62**
  (off Penton St.)
Hayward's Pl.
  EC1 . . . . .3D **9** (3D **63**)
Haywards Yd. SE4 . . . . . .3B **108**
  (off Lindal Rd.)
Hazelbank Rd. SE6 . . . . .2F **123**
Hazelbourne Rd.
  SW12 . . . . .4D **103**
Hazel Cl. N19 . . . . .4E **33**
  SE15 . . . . .5C **92**
  (off Bournemouth Cl.)

Hazeldean Rd. NW10 . . . .4A **42**
Hazeldon Rd. SE4 . . . . . .3A **108**
Hazel Gro. SE26 . . . . . . .4F **121**
Hazel Ho. E3 . . . . .5B **52**
  (off Barge La.)
Hazelhurst Ct. SE6 . . . . .5E **123**
  (off Beckenham Hill Rd.)
Hazelhurst Rd.
  SW17 . . . . .4E **115**
Hazellville Rd. N19 . . . . . .2F **33**
Hazelmere Ct. SW2 . . . . .1B **118**
Hazelmere Rd. NW6 . . . . .5B **44**
Hazel Rd. E15 . . . . .2A **54**
  NW10 . . . . .2D **57**
  (not continuous)
Hazel Way SE1 . . . . .5B **78**
Hazelwood Cl. NW10 . . . .5A **28**
Hazelwood Ho. SE8 . . . . .5A **80**
Hazelwood Rd. E17 . . . . .1A **38**
Hazlebury Rd. SW6 . . . . .5D **87**
Hazlewell Rd. SW15 . . . . .3E **99**
Hazlewood Cl. E5 . . . . . . .5A **38**
Hazlewood Cres.
  W10 . . . . .3A **58**
Hazlewood M. SW9 . . . . .1A **104**
Hazlewood Twr. W10 . . . .3A **58**
  (off Golborne Gdns.)
Hazlitt M. W14 . . . . .4A **72**
Hazlitt Rd. W14 . . . . .4A **72**
Headbourne Ho.
  SE1 . . . . . . .5C **26** (4F **77**)
Headcorn Rd.
  BR1: Brom 5B **124**
Headfort Pl.
  SW1 . . . . . .4C **20** (3C **74**)
Headington Rd.
  SW18 . . . . .2E **115**
Headlam Rd. SW4 . . . . . .4F **103**
  (not continuous)
Headlam St. E1 . . . . .3D **65**
Headley Ct. SE26 . . . . . . .5E **121**
Head's M. W11 . . . . .5C **58**
Head's M.
  .1F **65**
  (not continuous)
Heald St. SE14 . . . . .4C **94**
Healey Ho. E3 . . . . .3C **66**
  (off Wellington Way)
  SW9 . . . . .3C **90**
Healey St. NW1 . . . . .3D **47**
Hearn's Bldgs. SE17 . . . .5F **77**
Hearnshaw St. E14 . . . . . .5A **66**
Hearn St.
  EC2 . . . . . .4E **11** (3A **64**)
Hearnville Rd.
  SW12 . . . . .1C **116**
Heath Brow NW3 . . . . . . .5E **31**
Heath Cl. NW11 . . . . .2D **31**
Heathcock Ct. WC2 . . . . .5E **15**
  (off Exchange Ct.)
Heathcote St.
  WC1 . . . . . . .3F **7** (3B **62**)
Heath Ct. NW11 . . . . .3D **31**
Heath Dr. NW3 . . . . .1D **45**
Heathedge SE26 . . . . . . .2D **121**
Heather Cl. N7 . . . . .5B **34**
  SE13 . . . . .5F **109**
  SW8 . . . . .1D **103**
Heather Gdns. NW11 . . . .1A **30**
Heather Ho. E14 . . . . .5E **67**
  (off Dee St.)

Heatherley Ct. E5 . . . . . . .5C **36**
Heather Rd. NW2 . . . . . . .4B **28**
  SE12 . . . . .2C **124**
Heather Wlk. W10 . . . . . . .3A **58**
Heatherwood Cl. E12 . . . .4E **41**
Heathfield Av. SW18 . . . . .5F **101**
Heathfield Cl. E16 . . . . . . .4F **69**
Heathfield Ct. E3 . . . . . . .1C **66**
  (off Tredegar Rd.)
  SE14 . . . . .3E **93**
Heathfield Gdns.
  NW11 . . . . .1F **29**
  SE3 . . . . .5A **96**
  (off Baizdon Rd.)
  SW18 . . . . .4F **101**
Heathfield Ho. SE3 . . . . . .5A **96**
Heathfield Pk. NW2 . . . . . .3E **43**
Heathfield Rd.
  SW18 . . . . .4E **101**
Heathfield Sq.
  SW18 . . . . .5F **101**
Heathgate NW11 . . . . .1D **31**
Heathgate Pl. NW3 . . . . . .2B **46**
Heath Hurst Rd. NW3 . . . .1A **46**
Heathland Rd. N16 . . . . . .3A **36**
Heath La. SE3 . . . . .5F **95**
  (not continuous)
Heathlee Rd. SE3 . . . . . . .2B **110**
Heathmans Rd. SW6 . . . . .4B **86**
Heath Mead SW19 . . . . . .3F **113**
Heath Pas. NW3 . . . . .4D **31**
Heathpool Ct. E1 . . . . .3D **65**
Heath Ri. SW15 . . . . .4F **99**
Heath Rd. SW8 . . . . .5D **89**
Heath Royal SW15 . . . . . .4F **99**
Heath Side NW3 . . . . .1F **45**
Heathside NW11 . . . . .3C **30**
  SE13 . . . . .5E **95**
Heathstan Rd. W12 . . . . . .5C **56**
Heath St. NW3 . . . . .5E **31**
Heathview NW5 . . . . .1C **46**
Heathview Gdns.
  SW15 . . . . .5E **99**
Heath Vs. NW3 . . . . .5F **31**
Heathville Rd. N19 . . . . . .2A **34**
Heathwall St. SW11 . . . . .1B **102**
Heathway SE3 . . . . .3C **96**
Heathway Ct. NW3 . . . . . .4C **30**
Heathwood Gdns.
  SE7 . . . . .5F **83**
Heathwood Point
  SE23 . . . . .3F **121**
Heaton Ho. SW10 . . . . . . .2E **87**
  (off Fulham Rd.)
Heaton Rd. SE15 . . . . . . .5D **93**
Heaven Tree Cl. N1 . . . . . .3E **49**
Heaver Rd. SW11 . . . . . . .1F **101**
Hebden Ct. E2 . . . . .5B **50**
Hebden Rd. SW17 . . . . . .3A **116**
Heber Mans. W14 . . . . . . .2A **86**
  (off Queen's Club Gdns.)
Heber Rd. NW2 . . . . .2F **43**
  SE22 . . . . .4B **106**
Hebron Rd. W6 . . . . .4E **71**
Heckfield Pl. SW6 . . . . . . .3C **86**
Heckford Ho. E14 . . . . . . .5D **67**
  (off Grundy St.)
Heckford St. E1 . . . . .1F **79**
Hector Ct. SW9 . . . . .3C **90**
  (off Caldwell St.)

Hector Ho. E2 . . . . .1D 65
(off Old Bethnal Grn. Rd.)
Heddington Gro. N7 . . . .2B 48
Heddon St.
  W1 . . . . . . .4F 13 (1E 75)
Hedgegate Ct. W11 . . . .5B 58
(off Powis Ter.)
Hedgers Gro. E9 . . . . . .3A 52
Hedger St. SE11 . . . . . .5D 77
Hedge Wlk. SE6 . . . . . .5D 123
Hedgley M. SE12 . . . . . .3B 110
Hedgley St.
  SE12 . . . . .3B 110
Hedingham Cl. N1 . . . . . .4E 49
Hedley Ho. E14 . . . . .4E 81
(off Stewart St.)
Hedley Row N5 . . . . .2F 49
Hedsor Ho. E2 . . . . .3F 11
(off Ligonier St.)
Hega Ho. E14 . . . . .4E 67
(off Ullin St.)
Heidegger Cres.
  SW13 . . . . .3D 85
Heigham Rd. E6 . . . . . . .4F 55
Heights, The SE7 . . . . . . .1E 97
Heiron St. SE17 . . . . .2D 91
Helby Rd. SW4 . . . . .4F 103
Heldar Ct.
  SE1 . . . . .4C 26 (3F 77)
Helder Gro. SE12 . . . . . .5B 110
Helena Pl. E9 . . . . .5D 51
Helena Rd. E13 . . . . .1B 68
  E17 . . . . .1C 38
  NW10 . . . . .2D 43
Helena Sq. SE16 . . . . . . .1A 80
(off Sovereign Cres.)
Helen Gladstone Ho.
  SE1 . . . . .3D 25
(off Surrey Row)
Helen Ho. E2 . . . . .1D 65
(off Old Bethnal Grn. Rd.)
Helen Mackay Ho.
  E14 . . . . .5F 67
(off Blair St.)
Helen Peele Cotts.
  SE16 . . . . .4E 79
(off Lower Rd.)
Helenslea Av. NW11 . . . .3C 30
Helen's Pl. E2 . . . . .2E 65
Helen Taylor Ho.
  SE16 . . . . .4C 78
(off Evelyn Lowe Est.)
Heligan Ho. SE16 . . . . . . .3F 79
(off Water Gdns. Sq.)
Heliport Ind. Est.
  SW11 . . . . .5F 87
Helix Ct. W11 . . . . .2F 71
(off Swanscombe Rd.)
Helix Gdns. SW2 . . . . . .4B 104
Helix Rd. SW2 . . . . .4B 104
Helix Ter. SW19 . . . . .2F 113
Hellings St. E1 . . . . .2C 78
Helme Cl. SW19 . . . . . . .5B 114
Helmet Row
  EC1 . . . . .2A 10 (3E 63)
(off Carlton Vale)
Helmsdale Ho. NW6 . . . . .1D 59
(off Carlton Vale)
Helmsley Pl. E8 . . . . .4D 51
Helmsley St. E8 . . . . .4D 51
Helperby Rd. NW10 . . . . .4A 42

Helsby Ct. NW8 . . . . .3F 59
(off Pollitt Dr.)
Helsinki Sq. SE16 . . . . . . .4F 79
Helston Ho. NW1 . . . . .1E 61
(off Camden St.)
Helston Ct. N15 . . . . .1A 36
(off Culvert Rd.)
Helston Ho. SE11 . . . . . . .1C 90
(off Kennings Way)
Helvetia St. SE6 . . . . . . .2B 122
Hemans St. SW8 . . . . . . .3F 89
Hemans St. Est.
  SW8 . . . . .3F 89
Hemberton Rd.
  SW9 . . . . .1A 104
Hemingford Rd. N1 . . . . . .5B 48
Hemingway Cl. NW5 . . . .1C 46
Hemlock Rd. W12 . . . . . . .1B 70
(not continuous)
Hemming St. E1 . . . . .3C 64
Hemp Wlk. SE17 . . . . .5F 77
Hemstal Rd. NW6 . . . . . . .4C 44
Hemsworth Ct. N1 . . . . . .1A 64
Hemsworth St. N1 . . . . . .1A 64
Hemus Pl. SW3 . . . . .1A 88
Hen & Chicken Ct.
  EC4 . . . . .3B 16
(off Fleet St.)
Hen & Chickens Theatre
  .3D 49
(off St Paul's Rd.)
Henchman St. W12 . . . . . .5B 56
Henderson Ct. NW3 . . . . . .2F 45
(off Fitzjohn's Av.)
  SE14 . . . . .2F 93
(off Myers La.)
Henderson Dr. NW8 . . . . .3F 59
Henderson Rd. E7 . . . . . . .3E 55
  SW18 . . . . .5A 102
Hendham Rd.
  SW17 . . . . .2A 116
HENDON 1D 29
Hendon FC 3F 29
Hendon Ho. NW4 . . . . . . .1F 29
Hendon Leisure Cen.
  .2F 29
Hendon Pk. Mans.
  NW4 . . . . .1E 29
Hendon Pk. Row
  NW11 . . . . .1B 30
Hendon Way NW2 . . . . . .2F 29
  NW4 . . . . .1D 29
Hendre Ho. SE1 . . . . .5A 78
(off Hendre Rd.)
Hendre Rd. SE1 . . . . .5A 78
Hendrick Av. SW12 . . . . .5B 102
Heneage La.
  EC3 . . . . . . .3E 19 (5A 64)
Heneage Pl.
  EC3 . . . . . . .3E 19 (5A 64)
Heneage St. E1 . . . . .4B 64
Henfield Cl. N19 . . . . .3E 33
Hengist Rd. SE12 . . . . . .5D 111
Hengrave Rd. SE23 . . . . .4E 107
Henley Cl. SE16 . . . . .3E 79
(off St Marychurch St.)
Henley Dr. SE1 . . . . .5B 78
Henley Dr. SE1 . . . . .5B 78
Henley Ho. E2 . . . . .3F 11
(off Swanfield St.)

Henley Prior N1 . . . . .1F 7
(off Affleck St.)
Henley Rd. NW10 . . . . . . .5E 43
Henley St. SW11 . . . . .5C 88
Hennel Cl. SE23 . . . . .3E 121
Henniker Gdns. E6 . . . . . .2F 69
Henniker M. SW3 . . . . . . .2F 87
Henniker Point E15 . . . . . .2A 54
(off Leytonstone Rd.)
Henniker Rd. E15 . . . . .2F 53
Henning St. SW11 . . . . . . .4A 88
Henrietta Barnet Wlk.
  NW11 . . . . .1C 30
Henrietta Cl. SE8 . . . . . . .2C 94
Henrietta Ho. N15 . . . . . . .1A 36
(off St Ann's Rd.)
  W6 . . . . .1E 85
(off Queen Caroline St.)
Henrietta M.
  WC1 . . . . . . .3E 7 (3A 62)
Henrietta Pl.
  W1 . . . . . . .3D 13 (5D 61)
Henrietta St.
  WC2 . . . . . .4E 15 (1A 76)
Henriques St. E1 . . . . .5C 64
Henry Cooper Way
  SE9 . . . . .3F 125
Henry Dent Cl. SE5 . . . . .1F 105
Henry Dickens Ct.
  W11 . . . . .1F 71
Henry Doulton Dr.
  SW17 . . . . .4C 116
Henry Ho.
  SE1 . . . . . . .2B 24 (2C 76)
  SW8 . . . . .3A 90
(off Wyvil Rd.)
Henry Jackson Rd.
  SW15 . . . . .1F 99
Henry Moore Ct.
  SW3 . . . . .1A 88
Henry Purcell Ho.
  E16 . . . . .2D 83
(off Evelyn Rd.)
Henry Rd. N4 . . . . .3C 35
Henryson Rd. SE4 . . . . . .3D 108
Henry Tate M.
  SW16 . . . . .5B 118
Henry Wise Ho. SW1 . . . . .5E 75
(off Vauxhall Bri. Rd.)
Hensford Gdns.
  SE26 . . . . .4D 121
Henshall Point E3 . . . . . . .2D 67
(off Bromley High St.)
Henshall St. N1 . . . . .3F 49
Henshaw St. SE17 . . . . . . .5F 77
Henshawe Rd. SE22 . . . .3C 106
Henslow Ho. SE15 . . . . . . .3C 92
(off Peckham Pk. Rd.)
Henson Av. NW2 . . . . .2E 43
Henstridge Pl. NW8 . . . . .5A 46
Henty Cl. SW11 . . . . .3A 88
Henty Wlk. SW15 . . . . .3D 99
Henwick Rd. SE9 . . . . .1F 111
Hepburn M. SW11 . . . . . .3B 102
Hepplestone Cl.
  SW15 . . . . .4D 99
Hepscott Rd. E9 . . . . .3C 52
Hepworth Ct. N1 . . . . .5D 49
(off Gaskin St.)

Hepworth Ct. NW3 . . . . .2A 46
  SW1 . . . . .1D 89
Hera Ct. E14 . . . . .5C 80
  (off Homer Dr.)
Herald's Pl. SE11 . . . . . .5D 77
Herald St. E2 . . . . .3D 65

Herbal Hill
  EC1 . . . . . .4C 8 (3C 62)
Herbal Hill Gdns. EC1 . . . .4C 8
  (off Herbal Hill)
Herbal Pl. EC1 . . . . .4C 8
Herbert Cres.
  SW1 . . . . . .5A 20 (4B 74)
Herbert Gdns. NW10 . . . .1D 57
Herbert Ho. E1 . . . . .2F 19
  (off Old Castle St.)
Herbert M. SW2 . . . . . . .4C 104
Herbert Morrison Ho.
  SW6 . . . . .2B 86
  (off Clem Attlee Ct.)
Herbert Rd. E12 . . . . .1F 55
  E17 . . . . .2B 38
  NW9 . . . . .1C 28
Herbert St. E13 . . . . .1C 68
  NW5 . . . . .3C 46
Herbrand Est.
  WC1 . . . . . . .3D 7 (3A 62)
Herbrand St.
  WC1 . . . . . . .3D 7 (3A 62)
Hercules Ct. SE14 . . . . . .2A 94
Hercules Pl. N7 . . . . .5A 34
  (not continuous)
Hercules Rd.
  SE1 . . . . . .5A 24 (4B 76)
Hercules St. N7 . . . . .5A 34
Hercules Wharf E14 . . . . .1A 82
  (off Orchard Pl.)
Hercules Yd. N7 . . . . .5A 34
Hereford Bldgs. SW3 . . . .2F 87
  (off Old Church St.)
Hereford Gdns.
  SE13 . . . . .3A 110
Hereford Ho. NW6 . . . . . .1C 58
  (off Carlton Vale)
  SW3 . . . . .4A 74
  (off Ovington Gdns.)
  SW10 . . . . .3D 87
  (off Fulham Rd.)
Hereford Mans. W2 . . . . .5C 58
  (off Hereford Rd.)
Hereford M. W2 . . . . . . .5C 58
Hereford Pl. SE14 . . . . . .3B 94
Hereford Retreat
  SE15 . . . . .3C 92
Hereford Rd. E3 . . . . .1B 66
  E11 . . . . .1D 41
  W2 . . . . .5C 58
Hereford Sq. SW7 . . . . . .5E 73
Hereford St. E2 . . . . .3C 64
Hereward Rd.
  SW17 . . . . .4B 116
Heritage Cl. SW9 . . . . . .1D 105
Heritage Ct. SE8 . . . . . . .1F 93
Heritage Pl. SW18 . . . . .1E 115
Herlwyn Gdns.
  SW17 . . . . .4B 116
Her Majesty's Theatre
  . . . . .1B 22
  (off Haymarket)
Hermes Cl. W9 . . . . .3C 58

Hermes Ct. SW2 . . . . . . .4B 104
  SW9 . . . . .4C 90
  (off Southey Rd.)
Hermes St.
  N1 . . . . .1B 8 (1C 62)
Herm Ho. N1 . . . . .3E 49
  (off Clifton Rd.)
Hermiston Av. N8 . . . . . . .1A 34
Hermitage, The SE13 . . . .5E 95
  SE23 . . . . .1E 121
  SW13 . . . . .4B 84
Hermitage Ct. E1 . . . . . . .2C 78
  (off Knighten St.)
  NW2 . . . . .5C 30
Hermitage Gdns.
  NW2 . . . . .5C 30
Hermitage Ho. N1 . . . . . .1D 63
  (off Gerrard Rd.)
Hermitage La. NW2 . . . . .5C 30
Hermitage Moorings
  E1 . . . . .2C 78
Hermitage Rd. N4 . . . . . .2D 35
  N15 . . . . .2D 35
  SE19 . . . . .5F 119
Hermitage Row E8 . . . . . .2C 50
Hermitage St. W2 . . . . . . .4F 59
Hermitage Vs. SW6 . . . . .2C 86
  (off Lillie Rd.)
Hermitage Wall E1 . . . . . .2C 78
Hermitage Waterside
  E1 . . . . .2C 78
  (off Thomas More St.)
Hermit Pl. NW6 . . . . .5D 45
Hermit Rd. E16 . . . . .4B 68
Hermit St.
  EC1 . . . . . . .1D 9 (2D 63)
Hermon Hill E11 . . . . .1C 40
Herndon Rd. SW18 . . . . .3E 101
Herne Cl. NW10 . . . . .2A 42
HERNE HILL 3E 105
Herne Hill SE24 . . . . . . .4E 105
Herne Hill Ho.
  SE24 . . . . .4D 105
  (off Railton Rd.)
Herne Hill Rd. SE24 . . . .1E 105
Herne Hill Stadium 4F 105
Herne Pl. SE24 . . . . .3D 105
Heron Cl. NW10 . . . . .3A 42
Heron Ct. E14 . . . . .4F 81
  (off New Union Cl.)
Herondale Av.
  SW18 . . . . .1F 115
Heron Dr. N4 . . . . .4E 35
Herongate N1 . . . . .5E 49
  (off Ridgewell Cl.)
Herongate Rd. E12 . . . . . .4E 41
Heron Ho. E3 . . . . .5B 52
  (off Sycamore Av.)
  E6 . . . . .4F 55
  NW8 . . . . .1A 60
  (off Newcourt St.)
  SW11 . . . . .3A 88
  (off Searles Cl.)
Heron Pl. E16 . . . . .2E 83
  (off Bramwell Way)
  SE16 . . . . .2A 80
  W1 . . . . .2C 12
  (off Thayer St.)
Heron Quay E14 . . . . .2C 80
Heron Rd. SE24 . . . . .2E 105

Herons, The E11 . . . . .1B 40
Heron's Lea N6 . . . . .1B 32
Heron Tower 2D 19
Herrick Ho. N16 . . . . .1F 49
  (off Howard Rd.)
  SE5 . . . . .3F 91
  (off Elmington Est.)
Herrick Rd. N5 . . . . .5E 35
Herrick St. SW1 . . . . .5F 75
Herries St. W10 . . . . .1A 58
Herringham Rd. SE7 . . . . .4E 83
Hersant Cl. NW10 . . . . . .5C 42
Herschell M. SE5 . . . . . . .1E 105
Herschell Rd. SE23 . . . . .5A 108
Hersham Cl. SW15 . . . . . .5C 98
Hertford Av. SW14 . . . . . .3A 98
Hertford Lock Ho. E3 . . . .5B 52
  (off Parnell Rd.)
Hertford Pl.
  W1 . . . . .4A 6 (3E 61)
Hertford Rd. N1 . . . . .5A 50
  (not continuous)
Hertford St.
  W1 . . . . . . .2D 21 (2D 75)
Hertslet Rd. N7 . . . . .5B 34
Hertsmere Ho. E14 . . . . . .1C 80
  (off Hertsmere Rd.)
Hertsmere Rd. E14 . . . . . .2C 80
Hervey Rd. SE3 . . . . .4D 97
Hesewall Cl. SW4 . . . . . . .5E 89
Hesketh Pl. W11 . . . . .1A 72
Hesketh Rd. E7 . . . . .5C 40
Heslop Rd. SW12 . . . . . .1B 116
Hesper M. SW5 . . . . .5D 73
Hesperus Cres. E14 . . . . .5D 81
Hessel St. E1 . . . . .5D 65
Hestercombe Av.
  SW6 . . . . .5A 86
Hester Rd. SW11 . . . . . . .3A 88
Hestia Ho. SE1 . . . . .4D 27
Heston Ho. SE8 . . . . .4C 94
Heston St. SE14 . . . . .4C 94
Hetherington Rd.
  SW4 . . . . .2A 104
Hethpool Ho. W2 . . . . . . .3F 59
  (off Hall Pl.)
Hetley Rd. W12 . . . . .2D 71
Hevelius Cl. SE10 . . . . . . .1B 96
Hever Ho. SE15 . . . . .2F 93
  (off Lovelinch Cl.)
Heversham Ho. SE15 . . . .2E 93
Hewer St. W10 . . . . .4F 57
Hewett St.
  EC2 . . . . . . .4E 11 (3A 64)
Hewison St. E3 . . . . .1B 66
Hewitt Rd. N8 . . . . .1C 34
Hewlett Ho. SW8 . . . . . . .3D 89
  (off Havelock Ter.)
Hewlett Rd. E3 . . . . .1A 66
Hexagon, The N6 . . . . . . .3B 32
Hexal Rd. SE6 . . . . .3A 124
Hexham Rd. SE27 . . . . . .2E 119
Heybridge NW1 . . . . .3D 47
  (off Lewis St.)
Heybridge Av.
  SW16 . . . . .5B 118
Heybridge Way E10 . . . . . .2A 38
Heydon Ho. SE14 . . . . . . .4E 93
  (off Kender St.)
Heyford Av. SW8 . . . . . . .3A 90

Heyford Ter. SW8 . . . . .3A **90**
Heygate St. SE17 . . . . . .5E **77**
Heylyn Sq. E3 . . . . .2B **66**
Heysham La. NW3 . . . . .5D **31**
Heysham Rd. N15 . . . . .1F **35**
Heythorp St. SW18 . . . .1B **114**
Heywood Ho. SE14 . . . . .2F **93**
    (off Myers La.)
Heyworth Rd. E5 . . . . . .1D **51**
  E15 . . . . .2B **54**
Hibbert Ho. E14 . . . . . .4C **80**
    (off Tiller Rd.)
Hibbert Rd. E17 . . . . . . .2B **38**
Hibbert St. SW11 . . . . .1F **101**
Hibiscus Lodge E15 . . . .4A **54**
    (off Gleavon Rd.)
Hichisson Rd. SE15 . . . .3E **107**
Hicken Rd. SW2 . . . . . .3B **104**
Hickes Ho. NW6 . . . . . .4F **45**
Hickin Cl. SE7 . . . . .5F **83**
Hickin St. E14 . . . . .4E **81**
Hickleton NW1 . . . . . . .5E **47**
    (off Camden St.)
Hickling Ho. SE16 . . . . .4D **79**
    (off Slippers Pl.)
Hickman Cl. E16 . . . . . .4A **68**
Hickmore Wlk. SW4 . . .1F **103**
Hicks Bolton Ho.
  NW6 . . . . .1B **58**
    (off Denmark Ho.)
Hicks Cl. SW11 . . . . . . .1A **102**
Hicks Gallery 5C **114**
Hicks Ho. SE16 . . . . . . .4C **78**
    (off Spa Rd.)
Hicks St. SE8 . . . . .1A **94**
Hide Pl. SW1 . . . . .5F **75**
Hider Ct. SE3 . . . . .3E **97**
Hides St. N7 . . . . .3B **48**
Hide Twr. SW1 . . . . . . .5F **75**
    (off Regency St.)
Higgins Ho. N1 . . . . . . .5A **50**
    (off Colville Est.)
Higginson Ho. NW3 . . . .4B **46**
    (off Fellows Rd.)
Higgs Ind. Est.
  SE24 . . . . .1D **105**
Highbank Way N8 . . . . .1C **34**
High Bri. SE10 . . . . .1F **95**
Highbridge Ct. SE14 . . . .3E **93**
    (off Farrow La.)
High Bri. Wharf SE10 . . .1F **95**
    (off High Bri.)
Highbrook Rd. SE3 . . . .1F **111**
HIGHBURY 1D **49**
HIGHBURY CORNER . . .3D **49**
Highbury Cres. N5 . . . . .2D **49**
Highbury Est. N5 . . . . . .2E **49**
Highbury Grange N5 . . .1E **49**
Highbury Gro. N5 . . . . . .2D **49**
Highbury Gro. Ct. N5 . . .3E **49**
Highbury Hill N5 . . . . . .5C **34**
Highbury Mans. N1 . . . .4D **49**
    (off Upper St.)
Highbury New Pk. N5 . . .2E **49**
Highbury Pk. N5 . . . . . .5D **35**
Highbury Pk. M. N5 . . . .1E **49**
Highbury Pl. N5 . . . . . . .3D **49**
Highbury Pool 3D **49**
Highbury Quad. N5 . . . .5E **35**
Highbury Rd. SW19 . . . .5A **114**

Highbury Sta. Rd. N1 . . .3C **48**
Highbury Ter. N5 . . . . . .2D **49**
Highbury Ter. M. N5 . . . .2D **49**
Highclere St. SE26 . . . .4A **122**
Highcliffe Dr. SW15 . . . .4B **98**
Highcliffe Gdns.
  IG4: Ilf 1F **41**
Highcombe SE7 . . . . . . .2D **97**
Highcombe Cl. SE9 . . . .1F **125**
Highcroft Est. N19 . . . . .2A **34**
Highcroft Gdns.
  NW11 . . . . .1B **30**
Highcroft Rd. N19 . . . . .2A **34**
Highcross Way
  SW15 . . . . .1C **112**
Highdown Rd. SW15 . . .4D **99**
Highfield Av. NW11 . . . .2F **29**
Highfield Cl. SE13 . . . . .4F **109**
Highfield Ct. NW11 . . . .1A **30**
Highfield Gdns.
  NW11 . . . . .1A **30**
Highfield M. NW6 . . . . .4D **45**
    (off Compayne Gdns.)
Highfield Rd. NW11 . . . .1A **30**
Highfields Gro. N6 . . . . .3B **32**
HIGHGATE 1C **32**
Highgate Av. N6 . . . . . .2D **33**
Highgate Cemetery
  N6 . . . . .3C **32**
Highgate Cl. N6 . . . . . . .2C **32**
Highgate Edge N2 . . . . .1A **32**
Highgate Golf Course
  . . . . .1A **32**
Highgate Hgts. 1E **33**
Highgate High St. N6 . . .3C **32**
Highgate Hill N6 . . . . . .3D **33**
  N19 . . . . .3D **33**
Highgate Ho. SE26 . . . .3C **120**
Highgate Rd. NW5 . . . . .5C **32**
Highgate Spinney N8 . . .1F **33**
Highgate Wlk. SE23 . . . .2E **121**
Highgate West Hill
  N6 . . . . .3C **32**
Highgate Wood School
  Sports Cen. 1E **33**
High Hill Est. E5 . . . . . .3D **37**
High Hill Ferry E5 . . . . .3D **37**
High Holborn
  WC1 . . . . .2D **15** (5A **62**)
Highland Cft.
  BR3: Beck 5D **123**
Highland Rd. SE19 . . . .5A **120**
Highlands Cl. N4 . . . . . .2A **34**
Highlands Heath
  SW15 . . . . .5E **99**
Highland Ter. SE13 . . . .1D **109**
    (off Algernon Rd.)
High Level Dr. SE26 . . . .4C **120**
Highlever Rd. W10 . . . . .4E **57**
High Meads Rd. E16 . . .5F **69**
Highmore Rd. SE3 . . . . .3A **96**
High Mt. NW4 . . . . .1C **28**
High Parade, The
  SW16 . . . . .3A **118**
High Point N6 . . . . .2C **32**
High Rd. N15 . . . . .1B **36**
  NW10 . . . . .3A **42**
High Rd. Leyton
  E10 . . . . .1D **39**
  E15 . . . . .4E **39**

High Rd. Leytonstone
  E11 . . . . .1A **54**
  E15 . . . . .1A **54**
High Sheldon N6 . . . . . .1B **32**
Highshore Rd. SE15 . . . .5B **92**
    (not continuous)
Highstone Av. E11 . . . . .1C **40**
Highstone Ct. E11 . . . . .1B **40**
    (off New Wanstead)
Highstone Mans.
  NW1 . . . . .4E **47**
    (off Camden Rd.)
High St. E11 . . . . .1C **40**
  E13 . . . . .1C **68**
  E15 . . . . .1E **67**
  SW19 . . . . .5F **113**
High St. Colliers Wood
  SW19 . . . . .5F **115**
High St. Harlesden
  NW10 . . . . .1B **56**
High St. Mews
  SW19 . . . . .5A **114**
High St. Nth. E12 . . . . . .2F **55**
High Timber St.
  EC4 . . . . . . .4F **17** (1E **77**)
High Trees SW2 . . . . . .1C **118**
Hightrees Ho.
  SW12 . . . . .4C **102**
Highview N6 . . . . .1E **33**
Highway, The E1 . . . . . .1C **78**
Highway Bus. Park, The
  E1 . . . . .1F **79**
    (off Heckford St.)
Highway Trad. Centre, The
  E1 . . . . .1F **79**
    (off Heckford St.)
Highwood Cl. SE22 . . . .1C **120**
Highwood Rd. N19 . . . . .5A **34**
Highworth St. NW1 . . . .4A **60**
    (off Daventry St.)
Hi-Gloss Cen. SE8 . . . . .1A **94**
Hilary Cl. SW6 . . . . .3D **87**
Hilary Rd. W12 . . . . . . .5B **56**
    (not continuous)
Hilborough Ct. E8 . . . . . .4B **50**
Hilda Lockert Wlk.
  SW9 . . . . .5D **91**
    (off Loughborough Rd.)
Hilda Rd. E6 . . . . .4F **55**
  E16 . . . . .3A **68**
Hilda Ter. SW9 . . . . .5C **90**
Hildenborough Gdns.
  BR1: Brom 5A **124**
Hildreth St. SW12 . . . . .1D **117**
Hildreth St. M.
  SW12 . . . . .1D **117**
Hildyard Rd. SW6 . . . . .2C **86**
Hiley Rd. NW10 . . . . . . .2E **57**
Hilgrove Rd. NW6 . . . . .4E **45**
Hillary Ct. W12 . . . . . . .3E **71**
    (off Titmuss St.)
Hillbeck Cl. SE15 . . . . . .3E **93**
    (not continuous)
Hillboro Ct. E11 . . . . . . .2F **39**
Hillbrook Rd. SW17 . . . .3B **116**
Hillbury Rd. SW17 . . . . .3D **117**
Hill Cl. NW2 . . . . .5D **29**
  NW11 . . . . .1C **30**
Hillcourt Est. N16 . . . . .3F **35**
Hillcourt Rd. SE22 . . . . .4D **107**

Hillcrest N6 . . . . .2C 32
  SE24 . . . . .2F 105
  W11 . . . . .1B 72
  (off St John's Gdns.)
Hillcrest Cl. SE26 . . . . .4C 120
Hillcrest Gdns. NW2 . . . .5C 28
Hillcrest Rd.
  BR1: Brom 5C 124
Hilldrop Cres. N7 . . . . . .2F 47
Hilldrop Est. N7 . . . . . . .2F 47
  (not continuous)
Hilldrop La. N7 . . . . .2F 47
Hilldrop Rd.
  BR1: Brom 5D 125
  N7 . . . . .2F 47
Hillersden Ho. SW1 . . . . .1D 89
  (off Ebury Bri. Rd.)
Hillersdon Av. SW13 . . . .5C 84
Hillery Cl. SE17 . . . . . . .5F 77
Hill Farm Rd. W10 . . . . .4E 57
Hillfield Ct. NW3 . . . . . . .2A 46
Hillfield Ho. N5 . . . . .2E 49
Hillfield Rd. NW6 . . . . . .2B 44
Hillgate Pl. SW12 . . . . .5D 103
  W8 . . . . .2C 72
Hillgate St. W8 . . . . .2C 72
Hill Ga. Wlk. N6 . . . . . . .1E 33
Hill Ho. E5 . . . . .3D 37
  (off Harrington Hill)
Hill Ho. Apartments
  N1 . . . . .1A 8
  (off Pentonville Rd.)
Hill Ho. Rd. SW16 . . . . .5B 118
Hilliard Ho. E1 . . . . .2D 79
  (off Prusom St.)
Hilliards Ct. E1 . . . . .2E 79
Hillier Ho. NW1 . . . . . . .4F 47
  (off Camden Sq.)
Hillier Rd. SW11 . . . . . .4B 102
Hillingdon St. SE17 . . . .2D 91
Hillman Dr. W10 . . . . . . .3E 57
Hillman St. E8 . . . . .3D 51
Hillmarton Rd. N7 . . . . . .2A 48
Hillmarton Ter. N7 . . . . . .2A 48
  (off Hillmarton Rd.)
Hillmead Dr. SW9 . . . . . .2D 105
Hillmore Cl. SE13 . . . . . .1F 109
  (off Belmont Hill)
Hillmore Gro. SE26 . . . . .5A 122
Hill Path SW16 . . . . .5B 118
Hill Ri. SE23 . . . . .1D 121
Hillrise Mans. N19 . . . . . .2A 34
  (off Warltersville Rd.)
Hillrise Rd. N19 . . . . .2A 34
Hill Rd. NW8 . . . . .1E 59
Hillsboro' Rd. SE22 . . . . .3A 106
Hillsborough Ct.
  NW6 . . . . .5D 45
  (off Mortimer Cres.)
Hillside N8 . . . . .1F 33
  NW5 . . . . .5C 32
  NW10 . . . . .5A 42
  SE10 . . . . .4F 95
  (off Croom's Hill)
Hillside Cl. NW8 . . . . . . .1D 59
Hillside Gdns. N6 . . . . . .1D 33
  SW2 . . . . .2C 118
Hillside Pas. SW16 . . . . .2B 118
Hillside Rd. N15 . . . . .2A 36
  SW2 . . . . .2B 118

Hillsleigh Rd. W8 . . . . . .2B 72
Hills Pl. W1 . . . . . .3F 13 (5E 61)
Hillstone Ct. E3 . . . . .3D 67
  (off Empson St.)
Hillstowe St. E5 . . . . .5E 37
Hill St. W1 . . . . .1C 20 (2C 74)
Hilltop Ct. NW8 . . . . .4E 45
  (off Alexandra Rd.)
Hilltop Ho. N6 . . . . .2F 33
Hilltop Rd. NW6 . . . . . . .4C 44
Hill Vw. NW3 . . . . .5B 46
  (off Ainger Rd.)
Hill Vw. Gdns. NW9 . . . . .1A 28
Hillway N6 . . . . .4C 32
  NW9 . . . . .3A 28
Hill-Wood Ho. NW1 . . . . . .1A 6
  (off Polygon Rd.)
Hillworth Rd. SW2 . . . . . .5C 104
Hillyard Ho. SW9 . . . . . . .4C 90
Hillyard St. SW9 . . . . . . .4C 90
Hillyfield Cl. E9 . . . . .2A 52
Hilly Flds. Cres.
  SE4 . . . . .1C 108
  SE13 . . . . .1C 108
Hilsea Point SW15 . . . . . .1D 113
Hilsea St. E5 . . . . .1E 51
Hilton Ho. SE4 . . . . .2F 107
Hilton's Wharf SE10 . . . . .2D 95
  (off Norman Rd.)
Hilversum Cres.
  SE22 . . . . .3A 106
Himley Rd. SW17 . . . . . .5A 116
Hinchinbrook Ho.
  NW6 . . . . .5D 45
  (off Mortimer Cres.)
Hinckley Rd. SE15 . . . . . .2C 106
Hind Ct. EC4 . . . .3C 16 (5C 62)
Hinde Ho. W1 . . . . .2C 12
  (off Hinde St.)
Hinde M. W1 . . . . .2C 12
Hinde St. W1 . . . .2C 12 (5C 60)
Hind Gro. E14 . . . . .5C 66
Hindhead Cl. N16 . . . . . . .3A 36
Hindhead Point
  SW15 . . . . .1D 113
Hind Ho. N7 . . . . .1C 48
  SE14 . . . . .2F 93
  (off Myers La.)
Hindle Ho. E8 . . . . .2B 50
Hindlip Ho. SW8 . . . . . . .4F 89
Hindmans Rd. SE22 . . . . .3C 106
Hindmarsh Cl. E1 . . . . . . .1C 78
Hindon Ct. SW1 . . . . .5E 75
  (off Guildhouse St.)
Hindrey Rd. E5 . . . . .2D 51
Hindsley's Pl. SE23 . . . . . .2E 121
Hinstock NW6 . . . . .5D 45
  (off Belsize Rd.)
Hinton Ct. E10 . . . . .4D 39
  (off Leyton Grange Est.)
Hinton Rd. SE24 . . . . . . .1D 105
  SW9 . . . . .1D 105
Hippodrome M. W11 . . . . .1A 72
Hippodrome Pl. W11 . . . . .1A 72
Hiroshima Prom.
  SE7 . . . . .4E 83
Hirst Ct. SW1 . . . . .2D 89
Hitcham Rd. E17 . . . . .2B 38
Hitchcock La. E20 . . . . . . .3E 53
Hitchin Sq. E3 . . . . .1A 66

Hithe Gro. SE16 . . . . .4E 79
Hither Farm Rd.
  SE3 . . . . .1E 111
Hitherfield Rd.
  SW16 . . . . .2B 118
HITHER GREEN 4F 109
Hither Green Crematorium
  SE6 . . . . .2B 124
Hither Grn. La.
  SE13 . . . . .3E 109
Hitherwood Dr.
  SE19 . . . . .4B 120
HMP Brixton SW2 . . . .4A 104
HMP Holloway N7 . . . . .1A 48
HMP Pentonville N7 . . .3B 48
HMP Wandsworth
  SW18 . . . . .5F 101
HMP Wormwood Scrubs
  W12 . . . . .5C 56
HMS Belfast 1E 27 (2A 78)
Hoadly Ho. SE1 . . . . .2F 25
  (off Union St.)
Hoadly Rd. SW16 . . . . . . .3F 117
Hobart Pl.
  SW1 . . . . .5D 21 (4D 75)
Hobbes Wlk. SW15 . . . . . .3D 99
Hobbs Ct. SE1 . . . . .3B 78
  (off Mill St.)
Hobbs Pl. N1 . . . . .5A 50
Hobbs Pl. Est. N1 . . . . . .1A 64
  (off Hobbs Pl.)
Hobbs Rd. SE27 . . . . .4E 119
Hobby Ho. SE1 . . . . .5D 79
Hobday St. E14 . . . . .5D 67
Hobhouse Ct. WC2 . . . . . .5C 14
  (off Whitcomb St.)
Hobson's Pl. E1 . . . . .4C 64
Hobury St. SW10 . . . . . . .2E 87
Hocker St.
  E2 . . . . .2F 11 (2B 64)
Hockett Cl. SE8 . . . . .5A 80
Hockley Av. E6 . . . . .1F 69
Hockliffe Ho. W10 . . . . . . .4E 57
  (off Sutton Way)
Hockney Ct. SE16 . . . . . . .1D 93
  (off Rossetti Rd.)
Hocroft Av. NW2 . . . . .5B 30
Hocroft Ct. NW2 . . . . .5B 30
Hocroft Rd. NW2 . . . . .1B 44
Hocroft Wlk. NW2 . . . . . . .5B 30
Hodes Row NW3 . . . . .1C 46
Hodford Rd. NW11 . . . . . . .3B 30
Hodister Cl. SE5 . . . . .3E 91
Hodnet Gro. SE16 . . . . . . .5F 79
Hoe St. E17 . . . . .1C 38
Hoever Ho. SE6 . . . . .4E 123
Hoffman Sq. N1 . . . . .1C 10
Hofland Rd. W14 . . . . .4A 72
Hogan M. W2 . . . . .4E 59
Hogan Way E5 . . . . .4C 36
Hogarth Bus. Pk. W4 . . . .2A 84
Hogarth Cl. E16 . . . . .4F 69
Hogarth Ct. E1 . . . . .5C 64
  (off Batty St.)
  EC3 . . . . .4E 19 (5A 64)
  NW1 . . . . .4E 47
  (off St Pancras Way)
  SE19 . . . . .4B 120
Hogarth Health Club, The
  . . . . .5B 70

Hogarth Ho. *SW1* 5F **75**
 (off Erasmus St.)
Hogarth Ind. Est.
 NW10 . . . . .3C **56**
Hogarth La. W4 . . . . . . .2A **84**
Hogarth Pl. *SW5* 5D **73**
 (off Hogarth Rd.)
Hogarth Rd. SW5 . . . . .5D **73**
HOGARTH RDBT. 2A **84**
Hogarth's House *2A 84*
 (off Hogarth La.)
Hogarth Ter. W4 . . . . . .2A **84**
Hogshead Pas. *E1* 1D **79**
 (off Tobacco Dock)
Holbeach M.
 SW12 . . . . .1D **117**
Holbeach Rd. SE6 . . . . .5C **108**
Holbeck Row SE15 . . . .3C **92**
Holbein Ho. *SW1* 1C **88**
 (off Holbein M.)
Holbein M. SW1 . . . . . .1C **88**
Holbein Pl. SW1 . . . . . .5C **74**
Holberton Gdns.
 NW10 . . . . .2D **57**
HOLBORN 1F **15** (4B **62**)
Holborn EC1 . . . . .4C **62**
Holborn Bars *EC1* 1B **16**
 (off Holborn)
Holborn Cir.
 EC1 . . . . . .1C **16** (4C **62**)
Holborn Ho. W12 . . . . .5D **57**
Holborn Pl.
 WC1 . . . . . .1F **15** (4B **62**)
Holborn Rd. E13 . . . . . .3D **69**
Holborn Viaduct
 EC1 . . . . . .1C **16** (4D **62**)
Holbrook Cl. N19 . . . . . .3D **33**
Holbrooke Ct. N7 . . . . . .1A **48**
Holbrook Rd. E15 . . . . .1B **68**
Holburne Cl. SE3 . . . . . .4E **97**
Holburne Gdns. SE3 . . .4F **97**
Holburne Rd. SE3 . . . . .4E **97**
Holcombe Ho. *SW9* . . .1A **104**
 (off Landor Rd.)
Holcombe Pl. *SE4* 1A **108**
 (off St Asaph Rd.)
Holcombe St. W6 . . . . .5D **71**
Holcroft Ct. W1 . . . . . . .5F **5**
Holcroft Ho. SW11 . . . .1F **101**
Holcroft Rd. E9 . . . . . . .4E **51**
Holdenby SE4 . . . . . . .3A **108**
Holden Ho. *N1* 5E **49**
 (off Prebend St.)
 SE8 . . . . .3C **94**
Holden Point E15 . . . . . .3F **53**
 (off Waddington St.)
Holden St. SW11 . . . . . .5C **88**
Holdernesse Rd.
 SW17 . . . . .3B **116**
Holderness Ho. SE5 . . .1A **106**
Holderness Way
 SE27 . . . . .5D **119**
Holford Ho. *SE16* 5D **79**
 (off Camilla Rd.)
 WC1 . . . . .1A **8**
 (off Gt. Percy St.)
Holford M. WC1 . . . . . .1B **8**
Holford Pl.
 WC1 . . . . . . .1A **8** (2B **62**)
Holford Rd. NW3 . . . . . .5E **31**

Holford St.
 WC1 . . . . . .1B **8** (2B **62**)
Holford Way SW15 . . . .4C **98**
Holford Yd. *WC1* 1B **8**
 (off Cruikshank St.)
Holgate Av. SW11 . . . .1F **101**
Holgate St. SE7 . . . . . .4F **83**
Holland Dr. SE23 . . . . .3A **122**
Holland Dwellings
 WC2 . . . . .2E **15**
 (off Newton St.)
Holland Gdns. W14 . . . .4A **72**
Holland Gro. SW9 . . . . .3C **90**
Holland Ho. *NW10* 1D **57**
 (off Holland Rd.)
HOLLAND PARK 2B **72**
Holland Pk. 3B **72**
Holland Pk. W11 . . . . . .2A **72**
Holland Pk. Av. W11 . . .2A **72**
Holland Pk. Ct. *W14* . . .3A **72**
 (off Holland Pk. Gdns.)
Holland Pk. Gdns.
 W14 . . . . .3A **72**
Holland Pk. Mans.
 W14 . . . . .2A **72**
 (off Holland Pk. Gdns.)
Holland Pk. M. W11 . . . .2A **72**
Holland Pk. Rd. W14 . . .4B **72**
HOLLAND PARK RDBT.
 . . . . .3F **71**
Holland Pk. Ter. *W11* . .2A **72**
 (off Portland Rd.)
Holland Pk. Theatre
 (Open Air) 3B **72**
Holland Pas. *N1* 5E **49**
 (off Basire St.)
Holland Pl. *W8* 3D **73**
 (off Kensington Chu. St.)
Holland Pl. Chambers
 W8 . . . . .3D **73**
 (off Holland Pl.)
Holland Ri. Ho. *SW9* . . .3B **90**
 (off Clapham Rd.)
Holland Rd. E15 . . . . . .2A **68**
 NW10 . . . . .5C **42**
 W14 . . . . .3F **71**
Holland St.
 SE1 . . . . . .1E **25** (2D **77**)
 W8 . . . . .3C **72**
Holland Vs. Rd. W14 . . .3A **72**
Holland Wlk. N19 . . . . . .3F **33**
 W8 . . . . .2B **72**
Hollar Rd. N16 . . . . .5B **36**
Hollen St.
 W1 . . . . . . .2B **14** (5D **61**)
Holles Ho. SW9 . . . . . .5C **90**
Holles St.
 W1 . . . . . . .2E **13** (5D **61**)
Holley Rd. W3 . . . . .3A **70**
Holliday Sq. *SW11* 1F **101**
 (off Fowler Cl.)
Hollies, The *E11* 1C **40**
 (off New Wanstead)
Hollies Way SW12 . . . .5C **102**
Hollingbourne Rd.
 SE24 . . . . .3E **105**
Hollins Ho. N7 . . . . .1A **48**
Hollisfield *WC1* 2E **7**
 (off Cromer St.)
HOLLOWAY 5A **34**

Holloway Ho. *NW2* 5E **29**
 (off Stoll Cl.)
Holloway Rd. E11 . . . . . .5F **39**
 N7 . . . . .1B **48**
 N19 . . . . .4F **33**
Hollyberry La. NW3 . . . .1E **45**
Hollybush Cl. E11 . . . . . .1C **40**
Hollybush Gdns. E2 . . . .2D **65**
Holly Bush Hill NW3 . . . .1E **45**
Hollybush Hill E11 . . . . .1B **40**
Hollybush Ho. E2 . . . . . .2D **65**
Hollybush Pl. E2 . . . . . . .2D **65**
Holly Bush Steps
 NW3 . . . . .1E **45**
 (off Holly Mt.)
Hollybush St. E13 . . . . . .2D **69**
Holly Bush Va. NW3 . . . .1E **45**
Hollybush Wlk.
 SW9 . . . . .2D **105**
Holly Ct. SE10 . . . . .4B **82**
Hollycroft Av. NW3 . . . . .5C **30**
Hollydale Rd. SE15 . . . .4E **93**
Hollydene SE13 . . . . . . .4F **109**
 SE15 . . . . .5D **93**
Hollydown Way E11 . . . .5F **39**
Holly Gro. SE15 . . . . . . .5B **92**
Holly Hedge Ter.
 SE13 . . . . .3F **109**
Holly Hill NW3 . . . . .1E **45**
Holly Ho. *W10* 3A **58**
 (off Hawthorn Wlk.)
Holly Lodge *W8* 3C **72**
 (off Thornwood Gdns.)
Holly Lodge Gdns.
 N6 . . . . .4C **32**
Holly Lodge Mans.
 N6 . . . . .4C **32**
Holly M. SW10 . . . . .1E **87**
Holly Mt. NW3 . . . . .1E **45**
Hollymount Cl. SE10 . . . .4E **95**
Holly Pk. N4 . . . . .2A **34**
 (not continuous)
Holly Pk. Est. N4 . . . . . .2B **34**
Holly Pl. *NW3* 1E **45**
 (off Holly Berry La.)
Holly Rd. E11 . . . . .2B **40**
 W4 . . . . .5A **70**
Holly St. E8 . . . . .4B **50**
Holly Ter. N6 . . . . .3C **32**
Holly Tree Cl. SW19 . . . .1F **113**
Holly Tree Ho. *SE4* 1B **108**
 (off Brockley Rd.)
Hollyview Cl. NW4 . . . . .1C **28**
Holly Village N6 . . . . . . .4D **33**
Holly Vs. *W6* 4D **71**
 (off Wellesley Av.)
Holly Wlk. NW3 . . . . . . .1E **45**
Hollywood Bowl
 Surrey Quays 4F **79**
Hollywood Ct. *SW10* . . .2E **87**
 (off Hollywood Rd.)
Hollywood M. SW10 . . . .2E **87**
Hollywood Rd. SW10 . . .2E **87**
Holman Ho. *E2* 2F **65**
 (off Roman Rd.)
Holman Hunt Ho. *W6* . .1A **86**
 (off Field Rd.)
Holman Rd. SW11 . . . . .5F **87**
Holmbrook *NW1* 1E **61**
 (off Eversholt St.)

Holmbury Ct. SW17 . . . .3B 116
Holmbury Ho. SE24 . . . .3D 105
Holmbury Vw. E5 . . . . . .3D 37
Holmbush Rd.
   SW15 . . . . .4A 100
Holmcote Gdns. N5 . . . . .2E 49
Holm Ct. SE12 . . . . .3D 125
Holmdale Gdns. NW4 . . .1F 29
Holmdale Rd. NW6 . . . . .2C 44
Holmdale Ter. N15 . . . . .2A 36
Holmdene Av. SE24 . . . . .3E 105
Holmead Rd. SW6 . . . . . .3D 87
Holmefield Ho. W10 . . . . .3A 58
   (off Hazlewood Cres.)
Holme Ho. SE15 . . . . . . .3D 93
   (off Studholme St.)
Holme Lacey Rd.
   SE12 . . . . .4B 110
Holmes Cl. SE22 . . . . . . .2C 106
Holmesdale Ho.
   NW6 . . . . .5C 44
   (off Kilburn Vale)
Holmesdale Rd. N6 . . . . .2D 33
Holmesley Rd.
   SE23 . . . . .4A 108
Holmes Pl. SW10 . . . . . .2E 87
Holmes Rd. NW5 . . . . . . .2D 47
Holmes Ter. SE1 . . . . . . .3B 24
Holmewood Gdns.
   SW2 . . . . .5B 104
Holmewood Rd.
   SW2 . . . . .5B 104
Holmfield Ct. NW3 . . . . .2A 46
Holmhurst SE13 . . . . . . .4F 109
Holmleigh Rd. N16 . . . . .3A 36
Holmleigh Rd. Est.
   N16 . . . . .3A 36
Holm Oak Cl. SW15 . . . .4B 100
Holm Oak M. SW4 . . . . .3A 104
Holmsdale Ho. E14 . . . . .1D 81
   (off Poplar High St.)
Holmshaw Cl. SE26 . . . . .4A 122
Holmside Rd.
   SW12 . . . . .4C 102
Holmsley Ho. SW15 . . . . .5B 98
   (off Tangley Gro.)
Holm Wlk. SE3 . . . . .5C 96
   (off Tangley Gro.)
Holmwood Vs. SE7 . . . . .1C 96
Holne Chase N2 . . . . . . .1E 31
Holness Rd. E15 . . . . . . .3B 54
Holocaust Memorial
   Garden, The 3A 20
Holroyd Rd. SW15 . . . . . .2E 99
Holst Ct. SE1 . . . . .5B 24
   (off Kennington Rd.)
Holst Ho. W12 . . . . .5D 57
   (off Du Cane Rd.)
Holst Mans. SW13 . . . . . .2E 85
Holsworthy Ho. E3 . . . . . .2D 67
   (off Talwin St.)
Holsworthy Sq. WC1 . . . .4A 8
Holt Ct. SE10 . . . . .2E 95
   (off Horseferry St.)
Holt Ho. SW2 . . . . .4C 104
Holton St. E1 . . . . .3F 65
Holwood Pl. SW4 . . . . . . .2F 103
Holybourne Av.
   SW15 . . . . .5C 98
Holyhead Cl. E3 . . . . .2C 66
Holyoake Cl. SE16 . . . . . .3B 80

Holyoak Rd. SE11 . . . . . .5D 77
Holyport Rd. SW6 . . . . . .3F 85
Holyrood Ct. NW1 . . . . . .5D 47
   (off Gloucester Av.)
Holyrood M. E16 . . . . . . .2C 82
Holyrood St.
   SE1 . . . . .2D 27 (2A 78)
   (off Phipp St.)
Holywell Cen. EC2 . . . . . .3D 11
   (off Phipp St.)
Holywell Cl. SE3 . . . . .2C 96
   SE16 . . . . .1D 93
Holywell La.
   EC2 . . . . .3E 11 (3A 64)
Holywell Row
   EC2 . . . . .4D 11 (3A 64)
Homecroft Rd.
   SE26 . . . . .5E 121
Homefield Ho. SE23 . . . . .3F 121
Homefield Rd.
   SW19 . . . . .5F 113
   W4 . . . . .1B 84
Homefield St.
   N1 . . . . .1D 11 (1A 64)
Homeleigh Ct.
   SW16 . . . . .3A 118
Homeleigh Rd.
   SE15 . . . . .3F 107
Home Mdw. M.
   SE22 . . . . .3C 106
Home Pk. Rd.
   SW19 . . . . .4B 114
Homer Dr. E14 . . . . .5C 80
Home Rd. SW11 . . . . . . .5A 88
Homer Rd. E9 . . . . .3A 52
Homer Row W1 . . . . .4A 60
Homer St. W1 . . . . .4A 60
HOMERTON 2F 51
Homerton Gro. E9 . . . . . .2F 51
Homerton High St.
   E9 . . . . .2F 51
Homerton Rd. E9 . . . . . . .2A 52
Homerton Row E9 . . . . . .2E 51
Homerton Ter. E9 . . . . . . .3E 51
   (not continuous)
Homesdale Cl. E11 . . . . . .1C 40
Homestall Rd. SE22 . . . . .3E 107
Homestead Pk. NW2 . . . . .5B 28
Homestead Rd. SW6 . . . . .3B 86
Homewalk Ho.
   SE26 . . . . .4D 121
Homewoods SW12 . . . . . .5E 103
Homildon Ho. SE26 . . . . .3D 120
Honduras St.
   EC1 . . . . .3F 9 (3E 63)
Honeybourne Rd.
   NW6 . . . . .2D 45
Honeybrook Rd.
   SW12 . . . . .5E 103
Honeyfield SE23 . . . . . . .3F 121
Honey La. EC2 . . . . .3A 18
Honey La. Ho. SW10 . . . . .2D 87
   (off Finborough Rd.)
Honeyman Cl. NW6 . . . . .4F 43
Honey M. SE27 . . . . .4E 119
   (off Norwood High St.)
Honeywell Rd.
   SW11 . . . . .4B 102
Honeywood Ho.
   SE15 . . . . .4C 92
   (off Goldsmith Rd.)

Honeywood Rd.
   NW10 . . . . .1B 56
Honiton Gdns. SE15 . . . .5E 93
   (off Gibbon Rd.)
Honiton Rd. NW6 . . . . . . .1B 58
Honley Rd. SE6 . . . . .5D 109
HONOR OAK 4E 107
Honor Oak Crematorium
   SE23 . . . . .3F 107
HONOR OAK PARK . . .5A 108
Honor Oak Pk. SE23 . . . .4E 107
Honor Oak Ri. SE23 . . . . .4E 107
Honor Oak Rd. SE23 . . . .1E 121
Hood Ct. EC4 . . . . .3C 16
Hood Ho. SE5 . . . . .3F 91
   (off Elmington Est.)
   SW1 . . . . .1F 89
   (off Dolphin Sq.)
Hood Point SE16 . . . . . . .3B 80
   (off Rotherhithe St.)
Hooke Ct. SE10 . . . . .4E 95
   (off Winforton St.)
Hooke Ho. E3 . . . . .1A 66
   (off Gernon Rd.)
Hookham Ct. SW8 . . . . . .4F 89
Hooks Cl. SE15 . . . . .4D 93
Hooper Rd. E16 . . . . .5C 68
Hooper's Ct. SW3 . . . . . .3B 74
Hooper Sq. E1 . . . . .5C 64
   (off Hooper St.)
Hooper St. E1 . . . . .5C 64
Hoopers Yd. E1 . . . . .5C 64
   (off Hooper St.)
   NW6 . . . . .5B 44
   (off Kimberley Rd.)
Hoop La. NW11 . . . . .2B 30
Hope Cl. N1 . . . . .3E 49
   SE12 . . . . .3D 125
Hope Ct. NW10 . . . . .2F 57
   (off Chamberlayne Rd.)
   SE1 . . . . .1C 92
   (off Avocet Cl.)
Hopedale Rd. SE7 . . . . . .2D 97
Hopefield Av. NW6 . . . . . .1A 58
Hope Sq. EC2 . . . . .1D 19
Hope St. SW11 . . . . .1F 101
Hopetown St. E1 . . . . . . .4B 64
Hopewell St. SE5 . . . . . . .3F 91
Hopewell Yd. SE5 . . . . . . .3F 91
   (off Hopewell St.)
Hope Wharf SE16 . . . . . . .3E 79
Hop Gdns.
   WC2 . . . . .5D 15 (1A 76)
Hopgood St. W12 . . . . . . .2E 71
Hopkins Ho. E14 . . . . .5C 66
   (off Canton St.)
Hopkins M. E15 . . . . .5B 54
Hopkinsons Pl. NW1 . . . .5C 46
Hopkins Rd. E10 . . . . .2D 39
Hopkins St.
   W1 . . . . .3A 14 (5E 61)
Hopping La. N1 . . . . .3D 49
Hop St. SE10 . . . . .5B 82
Hopton Rd. SW16 . . . . . .5A 118
Hopton's Gdns. SE1 . . . . .1E 25
Hopton St.
   SE1 . . . . .5D 17 (1D 77)
Hopwood Cl. SW17 . . . . .3E 115
Hopwood Rd. SE17 . . . . .2F 91
Hopwood Wlk. E8 . . . . . . .4C 50

Horace Bldg. SW8 . . . . .3D 89
Horace Rd. E7 . . . . .1D 55
Horatio Ct. SE16 . . . . . .2E 79
   (off Rotherhithe St.)
Horatio Ho. E2 . . . . .1B 64
   (off Horatio St.)
W6 . . . . .1F 85
   (off Fulham Pal. Rd.)
Horatio Pl. E14 . . . . . . .2E 81
   (off Managers St.)
Horatio St. E2 . . . . .1B 64
Horbury Cres. W11 . . . .1C 72
Horbury M. W11 . . . . . .1B 72
Horder Rd. SW6 . . . . . .4A 86
Hordle Prom. E.
   SE15 . . . . .3B 92
Hordle Prom. Sth.
   SE15 . . . . .3B 92
   (off Quarley Way)
Horizon Bldg. E14 . . . .1C 80
   (off Hertsmere Rd.)
Horizon Ind. Est.
   SE15 . . . . .2C 92
Horizon Way SE7 . . . . .5D 83
Horle Wlk. SE5 . . . . . . .5D 91
Horley Rd. SE9 . . . . . .4F 125
Hormead Rd. W9 . . . . . .3B 58
Hornbeam Cl. SE11 . . . .5C 76
Hornbeam Sq. E3 . . . . .5B 52
Hornbean Ho. E15 . . . . .2A 68
   (off Manor Rd.)
Hornblower Cl. SE16 . . .4A 80
Hornby Cl. NW3 . . . . . . .4F 45
Hornby Ho. SE11 . . . . . .2C 90
   (off Clayton St.)
Horncastle Cl. SE12 . . .5C 110
Horncastle Rd.
   SE12 . . . . .5C 110
Horndean Cl. SW15 . . .1C 112
Horner Ho. N1 . . . . .5A 50
   (off Whitmore Est.)
Horner Sq. E1 . . . . .5F 11
   (within Old Spitalfields Market)
Horne Way SW15 . . . . .5E 85
Hornfair Rd. SE7 . . . . . .2E 97
Horniman Dr. SE23 . . . .1D 121
Horniman Mus. 1D 121
Horn La. SE10 . . . . .1C 96
   (not continuous)
Horn Link Way SE10 . . .5C 82
HORN PARK 3D 111
Horn Pk. Cl. SE12 . . . .3D 111
Horn Pk. La. SE12 . . . .3D 111
Hornsey Club, The 1F 33
Hornsey La. N6 . . . . . . .3D 33
Hornsey La. Est. N19 . . .2F 33
Hornsey La. Gdns.
   N6 . . . . .2E 33
Hornsey Ri. N19 . . . . . . .2F 33
Hornsey Ri. Gdns.
   N19 . . . . .2F 33
Hornsey Rd. N7 . . . . . . .3A 34
   N19 . . . . .3A 34
Hornsey St. N7 . . . . . . .2B 48
HORNSEY VALE 1B 34
Hornshay St. SE15 . . . . .2E 93
Hornton Ct. W8 . . . . . . .3C 72
   (off Kensington High St.)
Hornton Pl. W8 . . . . . . .3D 73
Hornton St. W8 . . . . . . .3C 72

Horsa Rd. SE12 . . . . . .5E 111
Horse & Dolphin Yd.
   W1 . . . . .4C 14
Horseferry Pl. SE10 . . . .2E 95
Horseferry Rd. E14 . . . .1A 80
   SW1 . . . . .4F 75
Horseferry Rd. Est.
   SW1 . . . . .5B 22
Horse Guards Av.
   SW1 . . . . . .2D 23 (2A 76)
Horse Guards Parade
   . . . . .2C 22 (2F 75)
Horse Guards Rd.
   SW1 . . . . . .2C 22 (2F 75)
Horseley Ct. E1 . . . . . . .4A 66
Horsell Rd. N5 . . . . .2C 48
   (not continuous)
Horselydown La.
   SE1 . . . . . . .3F 27 (3B 78)
Horselydown Mans.
   SE1 . . . . .3F 27
   (off Lafone St.)
Horsemongers M.
   SE1 . . . . .4A 26
Horse Ride
   SW1 . . . . . .2B 22 (2E 75)
Horseshoe Cl. E14 . . . . .1E 95
   NW2 . . . . .4D 29
Horseshoe Ct. EC1 . . . . .3E 9
   (off Brewhouse Yd.)
Horseshoe M. SW2 . . . .2A 104
Horseshoe Wharf
   SE1 . . . . .1B 26
   (off Clink St.)
Horse Yd. N1 . . . . .5D 49
   (off Essex Rd.)
Horsfeld Gdns. SE9 . . . .3F 111
Horsfeld Rd. SE9 . . . . . .3F 111
Horsfield Ho. N1 . . . . . . .4E 49
   (off Northampton St.)
Horsford Rd. SW2 . . . . .3B 104
Horsley Cl. SW1 . . . . . . .5F 75
   (off Vincent St.)
Horsley St. SE17 . . . . . . .2F 91
Horsman Ho. SE5 . . . . . .2E 91
   (off Bethwin Rd.)
Horsman St. SE5 . . . . . .2E 91
Horsmonden Rd.
   SE4 . . . . .3B 108
Hortensia Ho. SW10 . . . .3E 87
   (off Gunter Gro.)
Hortensia Rd. SW10 . . . .3E 87
Horton Av. NW2 . . . . . . .1A 44
Horton Halls SW17 . . . .3F 115
Horton Ho. SE15 . . . . . . .2E 93
   SW8 . . . . .3B 90
   W6 . . . . .1A 86
   (off Field Rd.)
Horton Rd. E8 . . . . .3D 51
Horton St. SE13 . . . . . . .1D 109
Horwood Ho. E2 . . . . . . .2D 65
   (off Pott St.)
   NW8 . . . . .3A 60
   (off Paveley St.)
Hosack Rd. SW17 . . . . . .2C 116
Hoser Av. SE12 . . . . . . .2C 124
Hosier La.
   EC1 . . . . . . .1D 17 (4D 63)
Hoskins Cl. E16 . . . . . . .5E 69
Hoskins St. SE10 . . . . . .1F 95

Hospital Rd. E9 . . . . . . .2F 51
   E11 . . . . .1F 39
Hospital Way SE13 . . . .5F 109
Hotel (Gallery) 4C 64
   (off Greenfield Rd.)
Hotham Rd. SW15 . . . . .1E 99
Hotham St. E15 . . . . . . .5A 54
Hothfield Pl. SE16 . . . . . .4E 79
Hotspur St. SE11 . . . . . .5C 76
Houghton Cl. E8 . . . . . . .3B 50
Houghton Sq. SW9 . . . . .5A 90
   (off Clapham Rd.)
Houghton St.
   WC2 . . . . . . .3A 16 (5B 62)
   (not continuous)
Houlton Ho. SW3 . . . . . .1B 88
   (off Walpole St.)
Houndsditch
   EC3 . . . . . . .2E 19 (5A 64)
Household Cavalry
   Museum, The
   Whitehall
   . . . . .2C 22 (2F 75)
Houseman Way SE5 . . . .3F 91
House Mill, The 2E 67
Houses of Parliament
   . . . . .5E 23 (4A 76)
Houston Rd. SE23 . . . . .2A 122
Hove Av. E17 . . . . .1B 38
Hoveden Rd. NW2 . . . . .2A 44
Hove St. SE15 . . . . .3E 93
   (off Culmore Rd.)
Howard Bldg. SW8 . . . . .2D 89
Howard Cl. NW2 . . . . . . .1A 44
Howard Ho. E16 . . . . . . .2D 83
   (off Wesley Av.)
   SE8 . . . . .2B 94
   (off Evelyn St.)
   SW1 . . . . .1E 89
   (off Dolphin Sq.)
   SW9 . . . . .1D 105
   (off Barrington Rd.)
   W1 . . . . .4E 5
   (off Cleveland St.)
Howard M. N5 . . . . .1D 49
Howard Rd. E11 . . . . . . .5A 40
   N15 . . . . .1A 36
   N16 . . . . .1F 49
   NW2 . . . . .1F 43
Howard's La. SW15 . . . .2D 99
Howards Rd. E13 . . . . . .2C 68
Howbury Rd. SE15 . . . . .1E 107
Howcroft Ho. E3 . . . . . . .2B 66
   (off Benworth St.)
Howden St. SE15 . . . . . .1C 106
Howell Ct. E10 . . . . .2D 39
Howell Wlk. SE1 . . . . . . .5D 77
Howick Pl.
   SW1 . . . . . .5A 22 (4E 75)
Howie St. SW11 . . . . . . .3A 88
Howitt Cl. N16 . . . . .1A 50
   NW3 . . . . .3A 46
Howitt Rd. NW3 . . . . . . .3A 46
Howland Est.
   SE16 . . . . .4E 79
Howland Ho. SW16 . . . .3A 118
Howland Mews E.
   W1 . . . . .5A 6 (4E 61)

Howland St.
  W1 . . . . .5F **5** (4E **61**)
Howland Way SE16 . . . . .3A **80**
Howlett's Rd. SE24 . . . .4E **105**
Howley Pl. W2 . . . . .4E **59**
Howsman Rd. SW13 . . . .2C **84**
Howson Rd. SE4 . . . . . .2A **108**
How's St. E2 . . . . .1B **64**
HOXTON 1A **64**
Hoxton Hall Theatre . .1A **64**
  (off Hoxton St.)
Hoxton Mkt. N1 . . . . .2D **11**
Hoxton Sq.
  N1 . . . . .2D **11** (2A **64**)
Hoxton St. N1 . .2E **11** (5A **50**)
Hoylake Rd. W3 . . . . . . .5A **56**
Hoyland Cl. SE15 . . . . . .3D **93**
Hoyle Rd. SW17 . . . . . .5A **116**
Hoy St. E16 . . . . .5B **68**
HQS Wellington 5B **16**
Hub, The
  Westminster
  . . . . .1A **4** (1B **60**)
Hubbard Ho. SW10 . . . . .3F **87**
  (off Worlds End Pas.)
Hubbard Rd. SE27 . . . . .4E **119**
Hubbard St. E15 . . . . . . .5A **54**
Huberd Ho. SE1 . . . . . . .5C **26**
  (off Manciple St.)
Hubert Gro. SW9 . . . . .1A **104**
Hubert Ho. NW8 . . . . .3A **60**
  (off Ashbridge St.)
Hubert Rd. E6 . . . . .2F **69**
Hucknall Ct. NW8 . . . . . . .3F **59**
  (off Cunningham Pl.)
Huddart St. E3 . . . . .4B **66**
  (not continuous)
Huddleston Cl. E2 . . . . . .1E **65**
Huddlestone Rd.
  E7 . . . . .1B **54**
  NW2 . . . . .3D **43**
Huddleston Rd. N7 . . . . .5E **33**
Hudson Bldg. E1 . . . . . . .4C **64**
  (off Chicksand St.)
Hudson Cl. E15 . . . . .5C **54**
  W12 . . . . .1D **71**
Hudson Ct. E14 . . . . .1C **94**
  (off Maritime Quay)
Hudson Ho. SW10 . . . . . .3E **87**
  (off Hortensia Rd.)
  W11 . . . . .2B **72**
  (off Ladbroke Gro.)
Hudson's Pl. SW1 . . . . . .5D **75**
Hudson Way NW2 . . . . . .5F **29**
Huggin Ct. EC4 . . . . .4A **18**
Huggin Hill
  EC4 . . . . . . .4F **17** (1E **77**)
Huggins Ho. E3 . . . . .2C **66**
  (off Alfred St.)
Huggins Pl. SW2 . . . . . .1B **118**
Hughan Rd. E15 . . . . . . .2F **53**
Hugh Astor Ct. SE1 . . . . .5E **25**
  (off Keyworth St.)
Hugh Cubitt Ho. N1 . . . . .1B **62**
  (off Collier St.)
Hugh Dalton Av. SW6 . . .2B **86**
Hughenden Ho. NW8 . . . . .3A **60**
  (off Jerome Cres.)
Hughendon Ter. E15 . . . .1E **53**
Hughes Ct. N7 . . . . .2F **47**

Hughes Ho. E2 . . . . .2E **65**
  (off Sceptre Rd.)
  SE5 . . . . .4E **91**
  (off Flodden Rd.)
  SE8 . . . . .2C **94**
  (off Benbow St.)
  SE17 . . . . .5D **77**
  (off Peacock St.)
Hughes Mans. E1 . . . . . .3C **64**
Hughes Ter. SW9 . . . . . .1D **105**
  (off Styles Gdns.)
Hugh Gaitskell Cl.
  SW6 . . . . .2B **86**
Hugh Gaitskell Ho.
  N16 . . . . .4B **36**
Hugh M. SW1 . . . . .5D **75**
Hugh Platt Ho. E2 . . . . . .1D **65**
  (off Patriot Sq.)
Hugh St. SW1 . . . . .5D **75**
Hugo Ho. SW1 . . . . .5A **20**
  (off Sloane St.)
Hugon Rd. SW6 . . . . . . .1D **101**
Hugo Rd. N19 . . . . .1E **47**
Huguenot Pl. E1 . . . . . . .4B **64**
  SW18 . . . . .3E **101**
Huguenot Sq. SE15 . . . .1D **107**
Hullbridge M. N1 . . . . . . .5F **49**
Hull Cl. SE16 . . . . .3F **79**
Hull St. EC1 . . . .2F **9** (2E **63**)
Hulme Pl.
  SE1 . . . . .4A **26** (3E **77**)
Humber Dr. W10 . . . . . . .3F **57**
Humber Rd. NW2 . . . . . .4D **29**
  SE3 . . . . .2B **96**
Humberstone Rd. E13 . . .2E **69**
Humberton Cl. E9 . . . . . .2A **52**
Humber Trad. Est.
  NW2 . . . . .4D **29**
Humbolt Rd. W6 . . . . . . .2A **86**
Hume Ct. N1 . . . . .4D **49**
  (off Hawes St.)
Hume Ho. W11 . . . . .2F **71**
  (off Queensdale Cres.)
Hume Ter. E16 . . . . .4D **69**
Humphrey St. SE1 . . . . . .1B **92**
Hungerford Ho. SW1 . . . .2E **89**
  (off Churchill Gdns.)
Hungerford La. WC2 . . . .1E **23**
  (not continuous)
Hungerford Rd. N7 . . . . .3F **47**
Hunsdon Rd. SE14 . . . . .2F **93**
Hunslett St. E2 . . . . .2E **65**
Hunstanton Ho. NW1 . . . .4A **60**
  (off Cosway St.)
Hunt Cl. W11 . . . . .2F **71**
Hunter Cl.
  SE1 . . . . .5C **26** (4F **77**)
  SW12 . . . . .1C **116**
Hunter Ho. SE1 . . . . .4E **25**
  (off King James St.)
  SW5 . . . . .1C **86**
  (off Old Brompton Rd.)
  SW8 . . . . .3F **89**
  (off Fount St.)
  WC1 . . . . .3E **7**
  (off Hunter St.)
Hunterian Museum, The
  . . . . .2A **16**
  (off Portugal St.)

Hunter Lodge W9 . . . . . .4C **58**
  (off Admiral Wlk.)
Hunters Mdw. SE19 . . . .4A **120**
Hunter St.
  WC1 . . . . .3E **7** (3A **62**)
Hunter Wlk. E13 . . . . .1C **68**
Huntingdon Ct.
  E16 . . . . .5B **68**
  N1 . . . . .4B **48**
Huntingfield Rd.
  SW15 . . . . .2C **98**
Huntley St.
  WC1 . . . . .4A **6** (3E **61**)
Huntloe SE14 . . . . .4E **93**
  (off Kender St.)
Hunton St. E1 . . . . .4C **64**
Hunt's Cl. SE3 . . . . .5C **96**
Hunt's Ct.
  WC2 . . . . .5C **14** (1F **75**)
Huntshaw Ho. E3 . . . . . . .2D **67**
  (off Devons Rd.)
Hunts La. E15 . . . . .1E **67**
Huntsman St. SE17 . . . . .5A **78**
Huntspill St. SW17 . . . . .3E **115**
Hunts Slip Rd. SE21 . . . .3A **120**
Huntsworth M.
  NW1 . . . . .3A **4** (3B **60**)
Hurdwick Ho. NW1 . . . . . .1E **61**
  (off Harrington Sq.)
Hurdwick Pl. NW1 . . . . . .1E **61**
  (off Hampstead Rd.)
Hurleston Ho. SE8 . . . . . .1B **94**
Hurley Ct. SW17 . . . . . . .5C **116**
  (off Mitcham Rd.)
Hurley Cres. SE16 . . . . . .3F **79**
Hurley Ho. SE11 . . . . . . .5D **77**
HURLINGHAM 1D **101**
Hurlingham Bus. Pk.
  SW6 . . . . .1C **100**
Hurlingham Club, The
  . . . . .1C **100**
Hurlingham Ct.
  SW6 . . . . .1B **100**
Hurlingham Gdns.
  SW6 . . . . .1B **100**
Hurlingham Pk. 5B **86**
Hurlingham Retail Pk.
  SW6 . . . . .1D **101**
Hurlingham Rd. SW6 . . . .5B **86**
Hurlingham Sq.
  SW6 . . . . .1C **100**
Hurlock St. N5 . . . . .5D **35**
Huron Rd. SW17 . . . . . . .2C **116**
Hurren Cl. SE3 . . . . .1A **110**
Hurry Cl. E15 . . . . .4A **54**
Hurst Av. N6 . . . . .1E **33**
Hurstbourne Ho.
  SW15 . . . . .4B **98**
  (off Tangley Gro.)
Hurstbourne Rd.
  SE23 . . . . .1A **122**
Hurst Cl. NW11 . . . . .1D **31**
Hurst Ct. E6 . . . . .4F **69**
  (off Tollgate Rd.)
Hurstdene Gdns. N15 . . .2A **36**
Hurst Ho. WC1 . . . . .1A **8**
  (off Penton Ri.)
Hurst St. SE24 . . . . .4D **105**
Hurstway Rd. W11 . . . . . .1F **71**
Hurstway Wlk. W11 . . . . .1F **71**

Husborne Ho. *SE8* 5A **80**
(off Chilton Gro.)
Huson Cl. NW3 . . . . .4A **46**
Hutchings St. E14 . . . . . .3C **80**
Hutchings Wharf *E14* . . .3C **80**
(off Hutchings St.)
Hutchins Cl. E15 . . . . . . .4E **53**
Hutchinson Ho. NW3 . . . .4B **46**
SE14 . . . . .3E **93**
Hutton Cl. *N4* 3B **34**
(off Victoria Rd.)
Hutton M. SW15 . . . . . . .3D **99**
Hutton St.
EC4 . . . . . . .4C **16** (5D **63**)
Huxbear St. SE4 . . . . . .3B **108**
Huxley Ho. *NW8* 3F **59**
(off Fisherton St.)
Huxley Rd. E10 . . . . .4E **39**
Huxley St. W10 . . . . .2A **58**
Hyacinth Rd. SW15 . . .1C **112**
HYDE, THE 1B **28**
Hyde, The NW9 . . . . .1B **28**
(not continuous)
Hyde Cl. E13 . . . . .1C **68**
Hyde Cres. NW9 . . . . . . .1A **28**
Hyde Est. Rd. NW9 . . . . .1B **28**
Hyde Farm M. SW12 . . .1F **117**
Hyde Ind. Estate, The
NW9 . . . . .1B **28**
Hyde La. SW11 . . . . .4A **88**
Hyde Pk. 1A **20** (2B **74**)
Hyde Pk. Barracks 3A **74**
(off Knightsbridge)
HYDE PARK CORNER
. . . . .3D **75**
Hyde Pk. Cnr.
W1 . . . . . . .3C **20** (3C **74**)
Hyde Pk. Cres. W2 . . . . .5A **60**
Hyde Pk. Gdns. W2 . . . . .1F **73**
(not continuous)
Hyde Pk. Gdns. M.
W2 . . . . .1F **73**
Hyde Pk. Ga. SW7 . . . . . .3E **73**
Hyde Pk. Ga. M.
SW7 . . . . .3E **73**
Hyde Pk. Mans. NW1 . . . .4A **60**
(off Cabbell St., not continuous)
Hyde Pk. Pl. W2 . . . . .1A **74**
Hyde Pk. Sq. W2 . . . . . . .5A **60**
Hyde Pk. Sq. M. W2 . . . .5A **60**
(off Southwick St.)
Hyde Pk. St. W2 . . . . .5A **60**
Hyde Pk. Towers W2 . . .1E **73**
Hyderabad Way E15 . . . . .4A **54**
Hyde Rd. N1 . . . . .5A **50**
Hyde's Pl. N1 . . . . .4D **49**
Hyde St. SE8 . . . . .2C **94**
Hydethorpe Rd.
SW12 . . . . .1E **117**
Hyde Va. SE10 . . . . .3E **95**
Hydra Building, The
EC1 . . . . .2C **8**
Hyndewood SE23 . . . . .3F **121**
Hyndman St. SE15 . . . . . .2D **93**
Hyperion Ct. *E16* 4C **68**
(off Robertson Rd.)
Hyperion Ho. *E3* 1A **66**
(off Arbery Rd.)
SW2 . . . . .4B **104**

Hyson Rd. SE16 . . . . . . .1D **93**
Hythe Ho. *SE16* 3E **79**
(off Swan Rd.)
W6 . . . . .5E **71**
(off Shepherd's Bush Rd.)
Hythe Rd. NW10 . . . . . . .2B **56**
Hythe Rd. Ind. Est.
NW10 . . . . .2C **56**

I

Ian Bowater Ct. *N1* 1C **10**
(off East Rd.)
Ian Ct. SE23 . . . . .2E **121**
Ibberton Ho. *SW8* 3B **90**
(off Meadow Rd.)
W14 . . . . .4A **72**
(off Russell Rd.)
Ibbotson Av. E16 . . . . . . .5B **68**
Ibbott St. E1 . . . . .3E **65**
Iberia Ho. N19 . . . . .2F **33**
Ibex Ho. *E15* 2A **54**
(off Forest La.)
Ibis Ct. *SE8* 2B **94**
(off Edward Pl.)
Ibsley Gdns. SW15 . . . . .1C **112**
ICA Cinema 1C **22**
(off Carlton Ho. Ter.)
Icarus Ho. *E3* 2B **66**
(off British St.)
ICA Theatre 1C **22**
(off Carlton Ho. Ter.)
Iceland Rd. E3 . . . . .5C **52**
Iceland Wharf
SE16 . . . . .5A **80**
Iceni Ct. *E3* 5B **52**
(off Parnell Rd.)
Ice Wharf N1 . . . . .1A **62**
Ice Wharf Marina *N1* . . .1A **62**
(off New Wharf Rd.)
Ice Works, The NW1 . . . .4D **47**
(off Jamestown Rd.)
Ickburgh Est. E5 . . . . . . .4D **37**
Ickburgh Rd. E5 . . . . . . .5D **37**
Icknield Ho. *SW3* 1A **88**
(off Cale St.)
Icon Apartments *SE1* . . .5D **27**
(off Cluny Pl.)
Icona Point *E15* 5E **53**
(off Warton Rd.)
Idaho Bldg. *SE10* 4D **95**
(off Deal's Gateway)
Ida St. E14 . . . . .5E **67**
(not continuous)
Ide Mans. *E1* 1F **79**
(off Cable St.)
Idlecombe Rd.
SW17 . . . . .5C **116**
Idmiston Rd. E15 . . . . . . .1B **54**
SE27 . . . . .3E **119**
Idol La. EC3 . . .5D **19** (1A **78**)
Idonia St. SE8 . . . . .3C **94**
Iffley Rd. W6 . . . . .4D **71**
Ifield Ho. *SE17* 1A **92**
(off Madron St.)
Ifield Rd. SW10 . . . . .2D **87**
Ifor Evans Pl. E1 . . . . . . .3F **65**
Ightham Ho. *SE17* 5A **78**
(off Beckway St.)

Ikon Ho. *E1* 1E **79**
(off Devonport St.)
Ilbert St. W10 . . . . .2F **57**
Ilchester Gdns. W2 . . . . .1D **73**
Ilchester Mans. *W8* 4C **72**
(off Abingdon Rd.)
Ilchester Pl. W14 . . . . . . .4B **72**
Ildersly Gro. SE21 . . . . .2F **119**
Ilderton Rd. SE15 . . . . . .1E **93**
SE16 . . . . .1E **93**
Ilderton Wharf *SE15* . . .2E **93**
(off Rollins St.)
Ilex Rd. NW10 . . . . .3B **42**
Ilex Way SW16 . . . . . . .5C **118**
Ilford Ho. *N1* 3F **49**
(off Dove Rd.)
Ilfracombe Flats
SE1 . . . . .3A **26**
(off Marshalsea Rd.)
Ilfracombe Rd.
BR1: Brom 3B **124**
Iliffe St. SE17 . . . . .1D **91**
Iliffe Yd. *SE17* 1D **91**
(off Crampton St.)
Ilkeston Ct. *E5* 1F **51**
(off Overbury St.)
Ilkley Rd. E16 . . . . .4E **69**
Ilminster Gdns.
SW11 . . . . .2A **102**
Ilsley Ct. SW8 . . . . .5E **89**
Imani Mans. SW11 . . . . .5F **87**
IMAX National Film Theatre
. . . . .2B **24** (2C **76**)
Imber St. N1 . . . . .5F **49**
Imperial Av. N16 . . . . . . .1A **50**
Imperial Cl. NW2 . . . . . . .2D **43**
Imperial College London
Chelsea &
Westminster Campus
. . . . .2E **87**
(within Chelsea &
Westminster Hospital)
Royal Brompton Campus
. . . . .1A **88**
(off Manresa Rd.)
Sth. Kensington Campus
. . . . .4F **73**
Imperial Coll. Rd.
SW7 . . . . .4F **73**
Imperial Ct. N6 . . . . .1E **33**
NW8 . . . . .1A **60**
(off Prince Albert Rd.)
SE11 . . . . .1C **90**
Imperial Cres. SW6 . . . . .5E **87**
Imperial Ho. *E3* 2A **66**
(off Grove Rd.)
E14 . . . . .1B **80**
(off Victory Pl.)
Imperial M. E6 . . . . .1F **69**
Imperial Rd. SW6 . . . . . .4D **87**
Imperial Sq. SW6 . . . . . .4D **87**
Imperial St. E3 . . . . .2E **67**
Imperial War Mus.
Lambeth Rd.
. . . . .5C **24** (4C **76**)
Imperial Wharf *E2* 1D **65**
(off Darwen Pl.)
SW6 . . . . .5E **87**
Imperium Ho. *E1* 5D **65**
(off Cannon St. Rd.)

Imre Cl. W12 . . . . .2D **71**
Inchmery Rd. SE6 . . . .2D **123**
Independent Pl. E8 . . . .2B **50**
Independents Rd.
   SE3 . . . . .1B **110**
Inderwick Rd. N8 . . . . .1B **34**
Indescon Ct. E14 . . . . .3D **81**
Indescon Sq. E14 . . . . .3C **80**
India Ho. WC2 . . . . . . .1B **76**
   (off Aldwych)
Indiana Bldg. SE10 . . . .4C **94**
   (off Deal's Gateway)
India Pl. WC2 . . . . .4F **15**
India St. EC3 . . .3F **19** (5B **64**)
India Way SW15 . . . . . .4C **98**
   W12 . . . . .1D **71**
Indigo2 . . . . .2A **82**
Indigo M. E14 . . . . .1E **81**
   N16 . . . . .5F **35**
Indus Cl. SE15 . . . . . . .3B **92**
   (off Amstel Ct.)
Indus Rd. SE7 . . . . .3E **97**
Infirmary Ct. SW3 . . . . .2B **88**
   (off West Rd.)
Inforum M. SE15 . . . . . .3C **92**
Ingal Rd. E13 . . . . .3C **68**
Ingate Pl. SW8 . . . . . . .4D **89**
Ingatestone Rd. E12 . . . .3E **41**
Ingelow Ho. W8 . . . . . . .3D **73**
   (off Holland St.)
Ingelow Rd. SW8 . . . . . .5D **89**
Ingersoll Rd. W12 . . . . .2D **71**
Ingestre Pl.
   W1 . . . . . . .3A **14** (5E **61**)
Ingestre Rd. E7 . . . . . . .1C **54**
   NW5 . . . . .1D **47**
Ingham Rd. NW6 . . . . . .1C **44**
Inglebert St.
   EC1 . . . . . .1B **8** (2C **62**)
Ingleborough St.
   SW9 . . . . .5C **90**
Ingleby Rd. N7 . . . . . . .5A **34**
Inglefield Sq. E1 . . . . . .2D **79**
   (off Prusom St.)
Inglemere Rd. SE23 . . . .3F **121**
Ingle M. EC1 . . . .1B **8** (2C **62**)
Inglesham Wlk. E9 . . . . .3B **52**
Ingleside Gro. SE3 . . . . .2B **96**
Inglethorpe St. SW6 . . . .4F **85**
Ingleton St. SW9 . . . . . .5C **90**
Inglewood Cl. E14 . . . . .5C **80**
Inglewood M. SE27 . . . .5E **119**
   (off Elder Rd.)
Inglewood Rd. NW6 . . . .2C **44**
Inglis St. SE5 . . . . .4D **91**
Ingoldisthorpe Gro.
   SE15 . . . . .2B **92**
Ingot Twr. E14 . . . . .4C **66**
   (off Ursula Gould Way)
Ingram Av. NW11 . . . . . .2E **31**
Ingram Cl. SE11 . . . . . .5B **76**
Ingram Ho. E3 . . . . .5A **52**
Ingrave St. SW11 . . . . . .1F **101**
Ingrebourne Ho.
   BR1: Brom 5F **123**
   (off Brangbourne Rd.)
   NW8 . . . . .3F **59**
   (off Broadley St.)
Ingress St. W4 . . . . .1A **84**
Inigo Jones Rd. SE7 . . . .3F **97**

Inigo Pl. WC2 . . . . .4D **15**
Ink Bldg. W10 . . . . .4F **57**
Inkerman Rd. NW5 . . . . .3D **47**
Inkerman Ter. W8 . . . . . .4C **72**
   (off Allen St.)
Inkster Ho. SW11 . . . . . .1A **102**
Ink Works Ct. SE1 . . . . .3A **78**
   (off Bell Yd. M.)
Inman Rd. NW10 . . . . . .5A **42**
   SW18 . . . . .5E **101**
Inner Circ.
   NW1 . . . . . .2B **4** (2C **60**)
Inner Pk. Rd. SW19 . . . .1F **113**
Inner Temple La. EC4 . . .3B **16**
Innes Gdns. SW15 . . . . .4D **99**
Innes St. SE15 . . . . .3A **92**
Innis Ho. SE17 . . . . . . .1A **92**
   (off East St.)
Inniskilling Rd. E13 . . . .1E **69**
Innovation Centre, The
    . . . . .3E **81**
   (off Marsh Wall)
Inns of Court &
   City Yeomanry Mus.
    . . . . . . .1A **16** (4B **62**)
Inskip Cl. E10 . . . . .4D **39**
Insley Ho. E3 . . . . .2D **67**
   (off Bow Rd.)
Institute of
   Archaeology Collections
    . . . . .3F **61**
Institute of Contemporary Arts
    . . . . .1C **22**
Institute Pl. E8 . . . . .2D **51**
Integer Gdns. E11 . . . . . .2F **39**
Interchange, The
   NW1 . . . . .4D **47**
   (off Camden Lock Pl.)
International Bus. Pk.
   E15 . . . . .5F **53**
International Ho. E1 . . . . .5F **19**
   (off St Katharine's Way)
International Sq. E20 . . . .3E **53**
   (within Westfield Stratford
   City Shopping Cen.)
International Way
   E20 . . . . .3E **53**
Inver Cl. E5 . . . . .4E **37**
Inver Ct. W2 . . . . .5D **59**
   W6 . . . . .4C **70**
Inverforth Cl. NW3 . . . . .4E **31**
Invergarry Ho. NW6 . . . .1D **59**
   (off Carlton Vale)
Inverine Rd. SE7 . . . . . .1D **97**
Invermead Cl. W6 . . . . . .4C **70**
Inverness Ct. SE6 . . . . . .1B **124**
Inverness Gdns. W8 . . . .2D **73**
Inverness M. W2 . . . . . . .1D **73**
Inverness Pl. W2 . . . . . . .1D **73**
Inverness St. NW1 . . . . . .5D **47**
Inverness Ter. W2 . . . . . .5D **59**
Inverton Rd. SE15 . . . . . .2F **107**
Invicta Cl. E3 . . . . .4C **66**
Invicta Plaza
   SE1 . . . . . . .1D **25** (2D **77**)

Invicta Rd. SE3 . . . . . . .3C **96**
Inville Rd. SE17 . . . . . . .1F **91**
   (not continuous)
Inville Wlk. SE17 . . . . . .1F **91**
Inwen Ct. SE8 . . . . .1A **94**
   (not continuous)
Inwood Ct. NW1 . . . . . . .4E **47**
   (off Rochester Sq.)
Inworth St. SW11 . . . . . .5A **88**
Inworth Wlk. N1 . . . . . . .5E **49**
   (off Popham St.)
Iona Cl. SE6 . . . . .5C **108**
Ion Ct. E2 . . . . .1C **64**
Ionian Bldg. E14 . . . . . .1A **80**
   (off Narrow St.)
Ionian Ho. E1 . . . . .3F **65**
   (off Duckett St.)
Ion Sq. E2 . . . . .1C **64**
Ipsden Bldgs. SE1 . . . . .2C **24**
Ira Ct. SE27 . . . . .2D **119**
Ireland Yd.
   EC4 . . . . . .3E **17** (5D **63**)
Irene Rd. SW6 . . . . .4C **86**
Ireton St. E3 . . . . .3C **66**
Iris Ct. SE14 . . . . .4E **93**
   (off Briant St.)
Iron Bri. Cl. NW10 . . . . .2A **42**
Iron Bri. Ho. NW1 . . . . . .4B **46**
Iron Mill Pl. SW18 . . . . .4D **101**
Iron Mill Rd. SW18 . . . . .4D **101**
Ironmonger La.
   EC2 . . . . . .3A **18** (5E **63**)
Ironmonger Pas. EC1 . . .2A **10**
   (off Ironmonger Row)
Ironmonger Row
   EC1 . . . . . .2A **10** (2E **63**)
Ironmonger Row Baths
    . . . . .2F **9**
Ironmongers Pl. E14 . . . .5C **80**
Ironside Cl. SE16 . . . . . .3F **79**
Ironside Ho. E9 . . . . .1A **52**
Iron Works E3 . . . . .5C **52**
Ironworks, The N1 . . . . . .1A **62**
   (off Albion Wlk.)
Irvine Cl. E14 . . . . .4D **67**
Irvine Ct. W1 . . . . .4A **6**
   (off Whitfield St.)
Irvine Ho. N7 . . . . .3B **48**
   (off Caledonian Rd.)
Irving Gro. SW9 . . . . . . .5B **90**
Irving Ho. SE17 . . . . . . .1D **91**
   (off Doddington Gro.)
Irving Mans. W14 . . . . . .2A **86**
   (off Queen's Club Gdns.)
Irving M. N1 . . . . .3E **49**
Irving Rd. W14 . . . . .4F **71**
Irving St.
   WC2 . . . . . .5C **14** (1F **75**)
Irving Way NW9 . . . . . . .1C **28**
Irwell Est. SE16 . . . . . . .4E **79**
Irwin Gdns. NW10 . . . . .5D **43**
Isaac Way SE1 . . . . .3A **26**
   (off Lant St.)
Isabella Ho. SE11 . . . . . .1D **91**
   (off Othello Cl.)
   W6 . . . . .1E **85**
   (off Queen Caroline St.)
Isabella M. N1 . . . . .2E **51**
Isabella St.
   SE1 . . . . . . .2D **25** (2D **77**)

Isabel St. SW9 . . . . .4B **90**
Isambard M. E14 . . . . . . .4E **81**
Isambard Pl. SE16 . . . . . .2E **79**
Isel Way SE22 . . . . . .3A **106**
Isis Cl. SW15 . . . . .2E **99**
Isis Ho. NW8 . . . . .3F **59**
 (off Church St. Est.)
Isis St. SW18 . . . . . . .2E **115**
Island Apartments
 N1 . . . . .5E **49**
Island Ho. E3 . . . . .2E **67**
Island Rd. SE16 . . . . . . .5F **79**
Island Row E14 . . . . . . .5B **66**
Islay Wlk. N1 . . . . .3E **49**
 (off Douglas Rd. Sth.)
Isleden Ho. N1 . . . . .5E **49**
 (off Prebend St.)
Isledon Rd. N7 . . . . .5C **34**
ISLEDON VILLAGE 5C **34**
ISLE OF DOGS 3D **81**
Isley Ct. SW8 . . . . .5E **89**
ISLINGTON 4D **49**
Islington Bus. Cen.
 N1 . . . . .5E **49**
 (off Coleman Flds.)
Islington Ecology Centre, The
 . . . . .5C **34**
Islington Grn. N1 . . . . . .5D **49**
 (not continuous)
Islington High St. N1 . . .1C **62**
 (not continuous)
Islington Mus.
 . . . . .2D **9** (2D **63**)
Islington Pk. M. N1 . . . . .4D **49**
Islington Pk. St. N1 . . . . .4C **48**
Islington Pl. N1 . . . . .5C **48**
Islington Tennis Cen. . . .3A **48**
Islip St. NW5 . . . . .2E **47**
Ismailia Rd. E7 . . . . . . .4D **55**
Isola Ct. N1 . . . . .5E **49**
 (off Popham Rd.)
Isom Cl. E13 . . . . .2D **69**
Issigonis Ho. W3 . . . . . .2B **70**
 (off Cowley Rd.)
Italia Conti Academy of
 Theatre Arts
 Avondale 1A **104**
 (off Landor Rd.)
Ivanhoe Ho. E3 . . . . . . .1A **66**
 (off Grove Rd.)
Ivanhoe Rd. SE5 . . . . .1B **106**
Ivatt Pl. W14 . . . . .1B **86**
Iveagh Cl. E9 . . . . .5F **51**
Iveagh Ct. E1 . . . . .3F **19**
Iveagh Ho. SW9 . . . . . .5D **91**
 SW10 . . . . .3E **87**
 (off King's Rd.)
Ive Farm Cl. E10 . . . . . .4C **38**
Ive Farm La. E10 . . . . . .4C **38**
Iveley Rd. SW4 . . . . . . .5E **89**
Iver Ho. N1 . . . . .5A **50**
 (off New Era Est.)
Iverna Ct. W8 . . . . .4C **72**
Iverna Gdns. W8 . . . . . .4C **72**
Iverson Rd. NW6 . . . . . .3B **44**
Ives Rd. E16 . . . . .4A **68**
Ives St. SW3 . . . . .5A **74**
Ivestor Ter. SE23 . . . . .5E **107**
Ivimey St. E2 . . . . .2C **64**
Ivinghoe Ho. N7 . . . . . . .2F **47**

Ivor Ct. N8 . . . . .1A **34**
 NW1 . . . . .3B **60**
 (off Gloucester Pl.)
Ivories, The N1 . . . . .4E **49**
 (off Northampton St.)
Ivor Pl. NW1 . . . .4A **4** (3B **60**)
Ivor St. NW1 . . . . .4E **47**
Ivorydown
 BR1: Brom 4C **124**
Ivory Ho. E1 . . . . .2B **78**
Ivory Pl. W11 . . . . .1A **72**
 (off Treadgold St.)
Ivory Sq. SW11 . . . . . . .1E **101**
Ivybridge Ct. NW1 . . . . .4D **47**
 (off Lewis St.)
Ivybridge La.
 WC2 . . . . .5E **15** (1A **76**)
Ivychurch La. SE17 . . . .1B **92**
Ivy Cotts. E14 . . . . .1E **81**
Ivy Ct. SE16 . . . . .1C **92**
 (off Argyle Way)
Ivydale Rd. SE15 . . . . .1F **107**
Ivyday Gro. SW16 . . . . .3B **118**
Ivy Gdns. N8 . . . . .1A **34**
Ivy Lodge W11 . . . . .2C **72**
 (off Notting Hill Ga.)
Ivymount Rd. SE27 . . . .3C **118**
Ivy Rd. E16 . . . . .5C **68**
 E17 . . . . .1C **38**
 NW2 . . . . .1E **43**
 SE4 . . . . .2B **108**
 SW17 . . . . .5A **116**
Ivy St. N1 . . . . .1A **64**
Ixworth Pl. SW3 . . . . . . .1A **88**

J

Jacana Ct. E1 . . . . .1B **78**
 (off Star Pl.)
Jacaranda Gro. E8 . . . . .4B **50**
Jack Clow Rd. E15 . . . . .1A **68**
Jack Dash Way E6 . . . . .3F **69**
Jackman Ho. E1 . . . . . . .2D **79**
 (off Watts St.)
Jackman M. NW2 . . . . . .5A **28**
Jackman St. E8 . . . . . . .5D **51**
Jackson & Joseph Bldg.
 E1 . . . . .5F **11**
 (off Princelet St.)
Jackson Cl. E9 . . . . .4E **51**
Jackson Ct. E7 . . . . .3D **55**
Jackson Rd. N7 . . . . . . .1B **48**
Jacksons La. N6 . . . . . . .2C **32**
Jacksons Lane Theatre
 . . . . .1D **33**
 (off Archway Rd.)
Jacks Pl. E1 . . . . .5F **11**
 (off Corbet Pl.)
Jack Walker Ct. N5 . . . . .1D **49**
Jacobin Lodge N7 . . . . .2A **48**
Jacob Mans. E1 . . . . . . .5D **65**
 (off Commercial Rd.)
Jacobs Ct. E1 . . . . .5C **64**
 (off Plumber's Row)
Jacobs Ho. E13 . . . . . . .2E **69**
 (off New City Rd.)
Jacobs Island Ho.
 SE16 . . . . .4B **78**
 (off Dunlop Pl.)

Jacobs Island Pier
 SE16 . . . . .3C **78**
 (off Bermondsey Wall W.)
Jacob St. SE1 . . . . .3C **78**
Jacob's Well M.
 W1 . . . . .1C **12** (4C **60**)
 (off Sutton Way)
Jacqueline Creft Ter.
 N6 . . . . .1C **32**
 (off Grange Rd.)
Jacqueline Ho. NW1 . . . .5B **46**
 (off Regent's Pk. Rd.)
Jade Cl. E16 . . . . .5F **69**
 NW2 . . . . .2F **29**
Jade Ter. NW6 . . . . .4E **45**
Jaffray Pl. SE27 . . . . . .4D **119**
Jaggard Way SW12 . . . .5B **102**
Jagger Ho. SW11 . . . . . .4B **88**
 (off Rosenau Rd.)
Jago Wlk. SE5 . . . . .3F **91**
Jake Russell Wlk.
 E16 . . . . .1E **83**
Jamaica Rd.
 SE1 . . . . .4F **27** (3B **78**)
 SE16 . . . . .3B **78**
Jamaica St. E1 . . . . .5E **65**
James Allens School
 Swimming Pool
 . . . . .3A **106**
James Anderson Ct.
 E2 . . . . .1A **64**
 (off Kingsland Rd.)
James Av. NW2 . . . . . . .2E **43**
James Boswell Cl.
 SW16 . . . . .4B **118**
James Brine Ho. E2 . . . .1F **11**
 (off Ravenscroft St.)
James Campbell Ho.
 E2 . . . . .1E **65**
 (off Old Ford Rd.)
James Cl. E13 . . . . .1C **68**
 NW11 . . . . .1A **30**
James Collins Cl. W9 . . .3B **58**
James Ct. N1 . . . . .5E **49**
 (off Raynor Pl.)
James Docherty Ho.
 E2 . . . . .1D **65**
 (off Patriot Sq.)
James Hammett Ho.
 E2 . . . . .1F **11**
 (off Ravenscroft St.)
James Hill Ho. W10 . . . .3A **58**
 (off Kensal Rd.)
James Ho. E1 . . . . .3A **66**
 (off Solebay St.)
 SE16 . . . . .3F **79**
 (off Wolfe Cres.)
 SW8 . . . . .3A **90**
 (off Wyvil Rd.)
 W10 . . . . .3A **58**
James Joyce Wlk.
 SE24 . . . . .2D **105**
James La. E10 . . . . .2E **39**
 E11 . . . . .2F **39**
James Lighthill Ho.
 WC1 . . . . .1A **8**
 (off Penton Ri.)
James Lind Ho. SE8 . . . .5B **80**
 (off Grove St.)

James Middleton Ho.
E2 . . . . .2D 65
(off Middleton St.)
Jameson Ct. *E2* 1E 65
(off Russia La.)
Jameson Ho. *SE11* 1B 90
(off Glasshouse Wlk.)
Jameson Lodge N6 . . . . .1E 33
Jameson St. W8 . . . . . . .2C 72
James Riley Point
E15 . . . . .5E 53
(off Carpenters St.)
James Stewart Ho.
NW6 . . . . .4B 44
James St.
W1 . . . . . .3C 12 (5C 60)
WC2 . . . . .3E 15 (1A 76)
James Stroud Ho.
SE17 . . . . .1E 91
(off Walworth Pl.)
James Ter. *SW14* 1A 98
(off Church Path)
Jamestown Rd. NW1 . . .5D 47
Jamestown Way E14 . . .1F 81
James Voller Way E1 . . .5E 65
Jam Factory, The
SE1 . . . . .5D 27
Jamuna Cl. E14 . . . . . . .4A 66
Jane Austen Hall
E16 . . . . .2D 83
(off Wesley Av.)
Jane Austen Ho.
SW1 . . . . .1E 89
(off Churchill Gdns.)
Jane St. E1 . . . . .5D 65
Janet Adegoke
Swimming Pool 1C 70
Janet St. E14 . . . . .4C 80
Janeway Pl. SE16 . . . . . .3D 79
Janeway St. SE16 . . . . . .3C 78
Jansen Wlk. SW11 . . . . .1F 101
Janson Cl. E15 . . . . .2A 54
NW10 . . . . .5A 28
Janson Rd. E15 . . . . .2A 54
Japan Cres. N4 . . . . .2B 34
Jaquard Ct. *E2* 1E 65
(off Bishop's Way)
Jardine Rd. E1 . . . . .1F 79
Jarman Ho. *E1* 4E 65
(off Jubilee St.)
SE16 . . . . .5F 79
(off Hawkstone Rd.)
Jarret Ho. *E3* 2C 66
(off Bow Rd.)
Jarrett Cl. SW2 . . . . . . .1D 119
Jarrow Rd. SE16 . . . . . . .5E 79
Jarrow Way E9 . . . . .1B 52
Jarvis Ho. *SE15* 4C 92
(off Goldsmith Rd.)
Jarvis Rd. SE22 . . . . . . .2A 106
Jasmin Ct. SE12 . . . . . . .4C 110
Jasmine Ct. SW19 . . . . . .5C 114
Jasmine Sq. *E3* 5B 52
(off Hawthorn Av.)
Jasmin Lodge SE16 . . . .1D 93
(off Sherwood Gdns.)
Jason Ct. SW9 . . . . .4C 90
(off Southey Rd.)
W1 . . . . .2C 12
Jasper Pas. SE19 . . . . . .5B 120

Jasper Rd. E16 . . . . .5F 69
SE19 . . . . .5B 120
Jasper Wlk. N1 . . . . .2F 63
Java Wharf *SE1* 3B 78
(off Shad Thames)
Jay Ho. *E3* 5B 52
(off Hawthorn Av.)
Jay M. SW7 . . . . .3E 73
Jean Darling Ho.
SW10 . . . . .2F 87
(off Milman's St.)
Jean Ho. SW17 . . . . . . .5A 116
Jean Pardies Ho. *E1* 4E 65
(off Jubilee St.)
Jebb Av. SW2 . . . . .4A 104
(not continuous)
Jebb St. E3 . . . . .1C 66
Jedburgh Rd. E13 . . . . . .2E 69
Jedburgh St. SW11 . . . . .2C 102
Jeddo M. W12 . . . . .3B 70
Jeddo Rd. W12 . . . . .3B 70
Jefferson Bldg. E14 . . . . .3C 80
Jeffrey Row SE12 . . . . . .3D 111
Jeffrey's Pl. NW1 . . . . . . .4E 47
Jeffreys Rd. SW4 . . . . . . .5A 90
Jeffrey's St. NW1 . . . . . . .4E 47
Jeffreys Wlk. SW4 . . . . . .5A 90
Jeger Av. E2 . . . . .5B 50
Jeken Rd. SE9 . . . . .2E 111
Jelf Rd. SW2 . . . . .3C 104
Jelico Point *SE16* 3B 80
(off Rotherhithe St.)
Jellicoe Ho. *E2* 1C 64
(off Ropley St.)
Jellicoe Rd. E13 . . . . .3C 68
Jemma Knowles Cl.
SW2 . . . . .1C 118
(off Tulse Hill)
Jemotts Ct. *SE14* 2F 93
(off Myers La.)
Jenkinson Ho. *E2* 2F 65
(off Usk St.)
Jenkins Rd. E13 . . . . .3D 69
Jenner Av. W3 . . . . .4A 56
Jenner Ho. *WC1* 3E 7
(off Hunter St.)
Jenner Pl. SW13 . . . . . . .2D 85
Jenner Rd. N16 . . . . .5B 36
Jennifer Ho. *SE11* 5C 76
(off Reedworth St.)
Jennifer Rd.
BR1: Brom 3B 124
Jenningsbury Ho.
SW3 . . . . .1A 88
(off Cale St.)
Jennings Ho. *SE10* 1F 95
(off Old Woolwich Rd.)
Jennings Rd. SE22 . . . . .4B 106
Jenny Hammond Cl.
E11 . . . . .5B 40
Jensen Ho. *E3* 3C 66
(off Wellington Way)
Jephson Ct. SW4 . . . . . . .5A 90
Jephson Ho. *SE17* 2D 91
(off Doddington Gro.)
Jephson Rd. E7 . . . . .4E 55
Jephson St. SE5 . . . . .4F 91
Jephtha Rd. SW18 . . . . . .4C 100
Jepson Ho. *SW6* 4D 87
(off Pearscroft Rd.)

Jerdan Ho. *SW6* 3C 86
(off North End Rd.)
Jerdan Pl. SW6 . . . . .3C 86
Jeremiah St. E14 . . . . . . .5D 67
Jeremy Bentham Ho.
E2 . . . . .2C 64
(off Mansford St.)
Jermyn St.
SW1 . . . . .1F 21 (2E 75)
Jermyn Street Theatre
. . . . .5B 14
Jerningham Ct. SE14 . . . .4A 94
Jerningham Rd.
SE14 . . . . .5A 94
Jerome Cres. NW8 . . . . . .3A 60
Jerome Ho. *NW1* 4A 60
(off Lisson Gro.)
SW7 . . . . .5F 73
(off Glendower Pl.)
Jerome St.
E1 . . . . . . .5F 11 (3B 64)
Jerrard St. SE13 . . . . .1D 109
Jerrold St.
N1 . . . . . . .1E 11 (1A 64)
Jersey Ho. *N1* 3E 49
(off Jersey Rd.)
Jersey Rd. E11 . . . . .3F 39
E16 . . . . .5E 69
N1 . . . . .3E 49
Jersey St. E2 . . . . .2D 65
Jerusalem Pas.
EC1 . . . . . .4D 9 (3D 63)
Jervis Bay Ho. *E14* 5F 67
(off Blair St.)
Jervis Ct. *SE10* 4E 95
(off Blissett St.)
W1 . . . . .3E 13
Jervis Rd. SW6 . . . . .2B 86
Jerviston Gdns.
SW16 . . . . .5C 118
Jerwood Space Art Gallery
. . . . .3F 25
Jessam Av. E5 . . . . .3D 37
Jessel Ho. *SW1* 5F 75
(off Page St.)
WC1 . . . . .2D 7
(off Judd St.)
Jessel Mans. *W14* 2A 86
(off Queen's Club Gdns.)
Jesse Rd. E10 . . . . .3E 39
Jessica Ho. SW18 . . . . . .4E 101
Jessie Blythe La.
N19 . . . . .2A 34
Jessie Duffett Ho.
SE5 . . . . .3E 91
(off Pitman St.)
Jessie Wood Ct. *SW9* . . .3C 90
(off Caldwell St.)
Jesson Ho. *SE17* 5F 77
(off Orb St.)
Jessop Ct. N1 . . . . .1D 63
Jessop Ho. W4 . . . . .5A 70
(off Kirton Cl.)
Jessop Rd. SE24 . . . . . . .2D 105
Jessop Sq. E14 . . . . .2C 80
Jevington Way
SE12 . . . . .1D 125
Jevons Ho. *NW8* 4F 45
(off Hilgrove Rd.)

Jewel Tower 5D 23
(off College M.)
Jewish Mus.
Camden Town 5D 47
Jewry St.
EC3 . . . .3F **19** (5B 64)
Jew's Row SW18 . . . . .2D **101**
Jews' Wlk. SE26 . . . . .4D **121**
Jeymer Av. NW2 . . . . .2D **43**
Jeypore Pas. SW18 . . . .5E **101**
Jeypore Rd. SW18 . . . .5E **101**
Jim Griffiths Ho.
SW6 . . . . .2B **86**
(off Clem Attlee Ct.)
Jim Veal Dr. N7 . . . . . .3A **48**
Joan Cres. SE9 . . . . . .5F **111**
Joanna Ho. W6 . . . . . .1E **85**
(off Queen Caroline St.)
Joan St. SE1 . . .2D **25** (2D 77)
Jocelin Ho. N1 . . . . .5B **48**
(off Barnsbury Est.)
Jocelyn St. SE15 . . . . . .4C **92**
Jockey's Flds.
WC1 . . . . . . .5A **8** (4B 62)
Jodane St. SE8 . . . . . . .5B **80**
Jodrell Rd. E3 . . . . .5B **52**
Joe Hunte Ct. SE27 . . .5D **119**
Johanna St.
SE1 . . . . . .4B **24** (3C 76)
John Adam St.
WC2 . . . . . .5E **15** (1A 76)
John Aird Ct. W2 . . . . . .4E **59**
(off Howley Pl., not continuous)
John Archer Way
SW18 . . . . .4F **101**
John Ashby Cl.
SW2 . . . . .4A **104**
John Baird Ct. SE26 . . .4E **121**
John Barker Ct.
NW6 . . . . .4A **44**
John Barnes Wlk.
E15 . . . . .3B **54**
John Bell Twr. E. E3 . . .1C **66**
(off Pancras Way)
John Bell Twr. W. E3 . . .1C **66**
(off Pancras Way)
John Betts' Ho. W12 . . .4B **70**
John Bond Ho. E3 . . . . .1B **66**
(off Wright's Rd.)
John Bowles Ct. E1 . . . .1F **79**
(off Schoolhouse La.)
John Brent Ho. SE8 . . . .5F **79**
(off Haddonfield)
John Buck Ho. NW10 . .5B **42**
John Campbell Rd.
N16 . . . . .2A **50**
John Carpenter St.
EC4 . . . . .4D **17** (1D 77)
John Cartwright Ho.
E2 . . . . .2D **65**
(off Old Bethnal Grn. Rd.)
John Drinkwater Cl.
E11 . . . . .2B **40**
John Fearon Wlk.
W10 . . . . .2A **58**
(off Dart St.)
John Felton Rd.
SE16 . . . . .3C **78**
John Fielden Ho. E2 . . .2D **65**
(off Canrobert St.)

John Fisher St. E1 . . . . .1C **78**
John Harrison Way
SE10 . . . . .4B **82**
John Horner M. N1 . . . .1E **63**
John Islip St. SW1 . . . . .5F **75**
John Kennedy Ct. N1 . . .3F **49**
(off Newington Grn. Rd.)
John Kennedy Ho.
SE16 . . . . .5F **79**
(off Rotherhithe Old Rd.)
John Knight Lodge
SW6 . . . . .3C **86**
John McDonald Ho.
E14 . . . . .4E **81**
(off Glengall Gro.)
John McKenna Wlk.
SE16 . . . . .4C **78**
John Masefield Ho.
N15 . . . . .1F **35**
(off Fladbury Rd.)
John Maurice Cl.
SE17 . . . . .5E **77**
John Milton Pas. EC4 . . .5E **63**
Johnny Andrews Ho.
E1 . . . . .5F **65**
(off Boulcott St.)
John Orwell Sports Cen.
. . . . .2D **79**
John Parker Sq.
SW11 . . . . .1F **101**
John Parry St. N1 . . . . .1A **64**
(off Hare Wlk.)
John Penn Ho. SE14 . . .3B **94**
(off Amersham Va.)
John Penn St. SE13 . . . .4D **95**
John Penry Ho. SE1 . . . .1C **92**
(off Marlborough Gro.)
John Prince's St.
W1 . . . . . . .2E **13** (5D 61)
John Pritchard Ho.
E1 . . . . .3C **64**
(off Buxton St.)
John Ratcliffe Ho.
NW6 . . . . .2C **58**
(off Chippenham Gdns.)
John Rennie Wlk. E1 . . .1D **79**
John Riley Ho. E3 . . . . .3D **67**
(off Geoffrey Chaucer Way)
John Roll Way SE16 . . . .4C **78**
John Ruskin St. SE5 . . . .3D **91**
John Scurr Ho. E14 . . . .5A **66**
(off Ratcliffe La.)
John Silkin La. SE8 . . . .1F **93**
John's M.
WC1 . . . . . .4A **8** (3B 62)
John Smith Av. SW6 . . . .3B **86**
John Smith M. E14 . . . .1F **81**
Johnson Cl. E8 . . . . . . .5C **50**
Johnson Ho. E2 . . . . . . .2C **64**
(off Roberta St.)
NW1 . . . . .1E **61**
(off Cranleigh St.)
NW3 . . . . .4B **46**
(off Adelaide Rd.)
SW1 . . . . .5C **74**
(off Cundy St.)
SW8 . . . . .3F **89**
(off Wandsworth Rd.)
W8 . . . . .3C **72**
(off Campden Hill)

Johnson Lock Ct. E1 . . .4A **66**
Johnson Lodge W9 . . . .4C **58**
(off Admiral Wlk.)
Johnson Mans. W14 . . .2A **86**
(off Queen's Club Gdns.)
Johnson's Ct. EC4 . . . . .5C **62**
Johnson's Pl. SW1 . . . . .1E **89**
Johnson St. E1 . . . . . . .1E **79**
John Spencer Sq. N1 . . .3D **49**
John's Pl. E1 . . . . .5D **65**
Johnston Cl. SW9 . . . . .4B **90**
Johnston Ct. E10 . . . . . .5D **39**
Johnstone Ho. SE13 . . .1F **109**
(off Belmont Hill)
Johnston Ter. NW2 . . . .5F **29**
John Strachey Ho.
SW6 . . . . .2B **86**
(off Clem Attlee Ct.)
John St. E15 . . . . .5B **54**
WC1 . . . . . .4A **8** (3B 62)
John Strype Ct. E10 . . . .3D **39**
John Trundle Ct. EC2 . . .5F **9**
John Trundle Highwalk
EC2 . . . . .5F **9**
(off Aldersgate St.)
John Tucker Ho. E14 . . .4C **80**
(off Mellish St.)
John Wesley Highwalk
EC2 . . . . .1F **17**
(off Aldersgate St.)
John Wetherby Ct.
E15 . . . . .1D **67**
(off High St.)
John Wetherby Ct. E.
E15 . . . . .1D **67**
(off High St.)
John Wetherby Ct. W.
E15 . . . . .1D **67**
(off High St.)
John Wheatley Ho.
SW6 . . . . .2B **86**
(off Clem Attlee Ct.)
John Williams Cl.
SE14 . . . . .2F **93**
John Woolley Cl.
SE13 . . . . .2A **110**
Joiners Arms Yd. SE5 . . .4F **91**
Joiners Pl. N5 . . . . .1F **49**
Joiner St.
SE1 . . . . . .2C **26** (2F 77)
Joiners Yd. N1 . . . . .1E **7**
(off Caledonia St.)
Jolles Ho. E3 . . . . .2D **67**
(off Bromley High St.)
Jonathan St. SE11 . . . . .1B **90**
Jones Ho. E14 . . . . .5F **67**
(off Blair St.)
Jones M. SW15 . . . . . . .2A **100**
Jones Rd. E13 . . . . .3D **69**
Jones St.
W1 . . . . . .5D **13** (1D 75)
Jonson Ho. SE1 . . . . . . .5C **26**
(off Burbage Cl.)
Jordan Ct. SW15 . . . . . .2F **99**
Jordan Ho. N1 . . . . .5F **49**
(off Colville Est.)
SE4 . . . . .2F **107**
(off St Norbert Rd.)
Jordans Ho. NW8 . . . . .3F **59**
(off Capland St.)

Joscoyne Ho. *E1* 5D **65**
    (off Philpot St.)
Joseph Conrad Ho.
    SW1 . . . . .5E **75**
    (off Tachbrook St.)
Joseph Ct. *N16* 1A **36**
    (off Amhurst Pk.)
Joseph Hardcastle Cl.
    SE14 . . . . .3F **93**
Josephine Av. *SW2* 3B **104**
Joseph Irwin Ho.
    E14 . . . . .1B **80**
    (off Gill St.)
Joseph Lister Ct. *E7* 4C **54**
Joseph M. *SE15* 3F **107**
Joseph Powell Cl.
    SW12 . . . . .4E **103**
Joseph Priestley Ho.
    E2 . . . . .2D **65**
    (off Canrobert St.)
Joseph Ray Rd.
    E11 . . . . .4A **40**
Joseph St. *E3* 3B **66**
Joseph Trotter Cl.
    EC1 . . . . .2C **8**
Joshua St. *E14* 5E **67**
Joslings Cl. *W12* 1C **70**
Jossiline Ct. *E3* 1A **66**
    (off Ford Cl.)
Joubert Mans. *SW3* 1A **88**
    (off Jubilee Pl.)
Joubert St. *SW11* 5B **88**
Jowett St. *SE15* 3B **92**
Jowitt Ho. *E2* 2F **65**
    (off Morpeth St.)
Joyce Page Cl. *SE7* 2F **97**
Joyce Wlk. *SW2* 4C **104**
Joy of Life Fountain 2B **74**
Jubb Powell Ho.
    N15 . . . . .1A **36**
Jubilee, The *SE10* 3D **95**
Jubilee Bldgs. *NW8* 5F **45**
Jubilee Cl. *NW9* 1A **28**
    NW10 . . . . .1A **56**
Jubilee Cres. *E14* 4E **81**
Jubilee Hall Sports Cen.
    . . . . .4E **15**
    (off The Piazza)
Jubilee Ho. *SE11* 5C **76**
    (off Reedworth St.)
    WC1 . . . . .3F **7**
    (off Jubilee St.)
Jubilee Mans. *E1* 5E **65**
    (off Jubilee St.)
Jubilee Mkt. *WC2* 4E **15**
Jubilee Pl. *SW3* 1A **88**
Jubilee Pl. Shop. Mall
    E14 . . . . .2D **81**
    (off Bank St.)
Jubilee Sports Centre & Baths
    . . . . .2B **58**
Jubilee St. *E1* 5E **65**
Jubilee Walkway
    SE1 . . . . . .5E **17** (1D **77**)
Jubilee Yd. *SE1* 3F **27**
Judd St.
    WC1 . . . . .2D **7** (2A **62**)
Jude St. *E16* 5B **68**
Judges Wlk. *NW3* 5E **31**
Juer St. *SW11* 3A **88**
Julia Ct. *E17* 1D **39**

Julia Garfield M.
    E16 . . . . .2D **83**
    (not continuous)
Julian Ct. *NW1* 4E **47**
    (off Rochester Sq.)
Julian Ho. *SE21* 4A **120**
Julian Pl. *E14* 1D **95**
Julian Taylor Path
    SE23 . . . . .2D **121**
Julia St. *NW5* 1C **46**
Juliet Ho. *N1* 1A **64**
    (off Arden Est.)
Juliette Rd. *E13* 1C **68**
Julius Ho. *E14* 5F **67**
    (off E. India Dock Rd.)
Julius Nyerere Cl.
    N1 . . . . .5B **48**
    (off Copenhagen St.)
Junction App.
    SE13 . . . . .1E **109**
    SW11 . . . . .1A **102**
Junction M. *W2* 5A **60**
Junction Pl. *W2* 5F **59**
    (off Praed St.)
Junction Rd. *E13* 1D **69**
    N19 . . . . .1E **47**
Juniper Ct. *W8* 4D **73**
    (off St Mary's Pl.)
Juniper Cres.
    NW1 . . . . .4C **46**
Juniper Dr. *SW18* 2E **101**
Juniper Ho. *E16* 5B **68**
    (off Turner St.)
    SE14 . . . . .3E **93**
    W10 . . . . .3A **58**
    (off Fourth Av.)
Juniper St. *E1* 1E **79**
Juno Ct. *SW9* 3C **90**
    (off Caldwell St.)
Juno Enterprise Cen.
    SE14 . . . . .2F **93**
Juno Ho. *E3* 5C **52**
    (off Garrison Rd.)
Juno Way *SE14* 2F **93**
Juno Way Ind. Est.
    SE14 . . . . .2F **93**
Jupiter Ct. *E3* 1C **66**
    (off Four Seasons Cl.)
    SW9 . . . . .3C **90**
    (off Caldwell St.)
Jupiter Ho. *E14* 1D **95**
    (off St Davids Sq.)
Jupiter Way *N7* 3B **48**
Jupp Rd. *E15* 4F **53**
Jupp Rd. W. *E15* 5F **53**
Jura Rd. *SE16* 5F **79**
    (off Plough Way)
Jurston Ct. *SE1* 4C **24**
Justice Apartments
    E1 . . . . .5F **65**
    (off Aylward St.)
Justice Wlk. *SW3* 2A **88**
Justines Pl.
    E2 . . . . .2F **65**
Jutland Cl. *N19* 3A **34**
Jutland Ho. *SE5* 5E **91**
Jutland Rd. *E13* 3C **68**
    SE6 . . . . .5E **109**
Juxon Ho. *EC4* 3E **17**
    (off Ave Maria La.)

Juxon St. *SE11* 5B **76**
JVC Bus. Pk. *NW2* 3C **28**

K

Kambala Rd.
    SW11 . . . . .1F **101**
Kamen Ho. *SE1* 2D **27**
    (off Magdalen St.)
Kangley Bri. Rd.
    SE26 . . . . .5B **122**
Kangley Bus. Cen.
    SE26 . . . . .5B **122**
Kapuvar Cl. *SE15* 5C **92**
Karachi Ho. *E15* 3A **54**
    (off Well St.)
Karanjia Ct. *NW2* 3E **43**
Kara Way *NW2* 1F **43**
Karen Ter. *E11* 4B **40**
Kashmir Rd. *SE7* 3F **97**
Kassala Rd. *SW11* 4B **88**
Katherine Bell Twr.
    E3 . . . . .1C **66**
    (off Pancras Way)
Katherine Cl. *SE16* 2F **79**
Katherine Ct.
    SE23 . . . . .1D **121**
Katherine Gdns.
    SE9 . . . . .2F **111**
Katherine Ho. *W10* 3A **58**
    (off Portobello Rd.)
Katherine Rd. *E6* 2E **55**
    E7 . . . . .2E **55**
Katherine Sq. *W11* 2A **72**
Kathleen Godfree Ct.
    SW19 . . . . .5C **114**
Kathleen Rd. *SW11* 1B **102**
Kayani Ho. *E16* 5D **69**
    (off Burrard Rd.)
Kay Rd. *SW9* 5A **90**
Kay St. *E2* 1C **64**
    E15 . . . . .4F **53**
    (off New Mount St.)
Kean Ho. *SE17* 2D **91**
Kean St.
    WC2 . . . . . .3F **15** (5B **62**)
Keats Av. *E16* 2D **83**
Keats Cl. *E11* 1D **41**
    NW3 . . . . .1A **46**
    SE1 . . . . .5B **78**
    SE7 . . . . .3E **97**
    SW19 . . . . .5F **115**
Keats Est. *N16* 4B **36**
    (off Kyverdale Rd.)
Keats Gro. *NW3* 1A **46**
Keats House 1A **46**
Keats Ho. *E2* 2E **65**
    (off Roman Rd.)
    SE5 . . . . .3E **91**
    (off Elmington Est.)
    SW1 . . . . .2E **89**
    (off Churchill Gdns.)
Keats Pl. *EC2* 1B **18**
    (off Moorfields)
Keats Rd. *E10* 2D **39**
Kebbell Ter. *E7* 2D **55**
    (off Claremont Rd.)
Keble Pl. *SW13* 2D **85**
Keble St. *SW17* 4E **115**

Kedge Ho. *E14* 4C **80**
(off Tiller Rd.)
Kedleston Wlk. E2 . . . . .2D **65**
Keedonwood Rd.
BR1: Brom 5A **124**
Keel Cl. SE16 . . . . .2F **79**
Keel Ct. *E14* 1F **81**
(off Newport Av.)
Keeley St.
WC2 . . . . . .3F **15** (5B **62**)
Keeling Ho. *E2* 1D **65**
(off Claredale St.)
Keeling Rd. SE9 . . . . .3F **111**
Keelson Ho. *E14* 4C **80**
(off Mellish St.)
Keens Cl. SW16 . . . . .5F **117**
Keen's Yd. N1 . . . . .3D **49**
Keep, The SE3 . . . . .5C **96**
Keepier Wharf *E14* 1F **79**
(off Narrow St.)
Keeton's Rd. SE16 . . . . . .4D **79**
(not continuous)
Keevil Dr. SW19 . . . . .5F **99**
Keighley Cl. N7 . . . . .2A **48**
Keildon Rd. SW11 . . . . . .2B **102**
Keir, The SW19 . . . . .5E **113**
Keir Hardie Est. E5 . . . . . .3D **37**
Keir Hardie Ho. N19 . . . . .2F **33**
NW10 . . . . .4B **42**
W6 . . . . .2F **85**
(off Fulham Pal. Rd.)
Keith Connor Cl.
SW8 . . . . .1D **103**
Keith Gro. W12 . . . . .3C **70**
Keith Ho. *NW6* 1D **59**
(off Carlton Vale)
SW8 . . . . .3A **90**
(off Wheatsheaf La.)
Kelbrook Rd. SE3 . . . . . . .5F **97**
Kelby Ho. *N7* 3B **48**
(off Sutterton St.)
Kelceda Cl. NW2 . . . . . . .4C **28**
Kelday Hgts. *E1* 5D **65**
(off Spencer Way)
Kelfield Ct. W10 . . . . .5F **57**
Kelfield Gdns. W10 . . . . . .5F **57**
Kelfield M. W10 . . . . .5F **57**
Kelland Rd. E13 . . . . .3C **68**
Kellaway Rd. SE3 . . . . . . .1F **55**
Keller Cres. E12 . . . . .1F **55**
Kellerton Rd. SE13 . . . . . .3A **110**
Kellet Ho's. *WC1* 2E **7**
(off Tankerton St.)
Kellett Ho. *N1* 5A **50**
(off Colville Est.)
Kellett Rd. SW2 . . . . .2C **104**
Kellino St. SW17 . . . . .4B **116**
Kellow Ho. *SE1* 3B **26**
(off Tennis St.)
Kell St. SE1 . . . . .5E **25** (4D **77**)
Kelly Av. SE15 . . . . .3B **92**
Kelly Cl. NW10 . . . . .5A **28**
Kelly Ct. *E14* 1C **80**
(off Garford St.)
Kelly M. W9 . . . . .3B **58**
Kelly St. NW1 . . . . .3D **47**
Kelman Cl. SW4 . . . . .5F **89**
Kelmore Gro. SE22 . . . . .2C **106**
Kelmscott Gdns.
W12 . . . . .4C **70**

Kelmscott House 1C **84**
(off Upper Mall)
Kelmscott Leisure Cen.
. . . . .1B **38**
Kelmscott Rd.
SW11 . . . . .3A **102**
Kelross Pas. N5 . . . . .1E **49**
Kelross Rd. N5 . . . . .1E **49**
Kelsall Cl. SE3 . . . . .5D **97**
Kelsey St. E2 . . . . .3C **64**
Kelson Ho. E14 . . . . .4E **81**
Kelso Pl. W8 . . . . .4D **73**
Kelvedon Ho. SW8 . . . . . .4A **90**
Kelvedon Rd.
SW6 . . . . .3B **86**
Kelvin Ct. *W11* 1C **72**
(off Kensington Pk. Rd.)
Kelvin Gro. SE26 . . . . . . .3D **121**
Kelvington Rd.
SE15 . . . . .3F **107**
Kelvin Rd. N5 . . . . .1E **49**
Kelway Ho. W14 . . . . .1B **86**
Kember St. N1 . . . . .4B **48**
Kemble Ho. *SW9* 1D **105**
(off Barrington Rd.)
Kemble Rd. SE23 . . . . . . .1F **121**
Kemble St.
WC2 . . . . . .3F **15** (5B **62**)
Kemerton Rd. SE5 . . . . . .1E **105**
Kemeys St. E9 . . . . .2A **52**
Kemp Ct. *SW8* 3A **90**
(off Hartington Rd.)
Kempe Ho. *SE1* 4F **77**
(off Burbage Cl.)
Kempe Rd. NW6 . . . . .1F **57**
Kemp Ho. *E2* 1F **65**
(off Sewardstone Rd.)
W1 . . . . .4B **14**
(off Berwick St.)
Kempis Way SE22 . . . . . .3A **106**
Kemplay Rd. NW3 . . . . . . .1F **45**
Kemps Ct. *W1* 3A **14**
(off Hopkins St.)
Kempsford Gdns.
SW5 . . . . .1C **86**
Kempsford Rd. SE11 . . . . .5C **76**
(not continuous)
Kemps Gdns. SE13 . . . . . .3E **109**
Kempson Rd. SW6 . . . . . .4C **86**
Kempthorne Rd. SE8 . . . . .5B **80**
Kempton Ct. E1 . . . . .4D **65**
Kempton Ho. *N1* 5A **50**
(off Hoxton St.)
Kemsing Ho. *SE1* 4C **26**
(off Long La.)
Kemsing Rd. SE10 . . . . . .1C **96**
Kemsley SE13 . . . . .3D **109**
Kenbrook Ho. NW5 . . . . . .2E **47**
W14 . . . . .4B **72**
Kenbury Gdns. SE5 . . . . . .5E **91**
Kenbury Mans. *SE5* 5E **91**
(off Kenbury St.)
Kenbury St. SE5 . . . . .5E **91**
Kenchester Cl. SW8 . . . . .3A **90**
Kendal *NW1* 1E **5**
(off Augustus St.)
Kendal Cl. SW9 . . . . .3D **91**
Kendale Rd.
BR1: Brom 5A **124**

Kendal Ho. E9 . . . . .5E **51**
N1 . . . . .1B **62**
(off Priory Grn. Est.)
Kendall Pl.
W1 . . . . . .1B **12** (4C **60**)
Kendal Pl. SW15 . . . . .3B **100**
Kendal Rd. NW10 . . . . . . .1C **42**
Kendal Steps *W2* 5A **60**
(off St George's Flds.)
Kendal St. W2 . . . . .5A **60**
Kender Est. *SE14* 4E **93**
(off Queen's Rd.)
Kender St. SE14 . . . . .3E **93**
Kendoa Rd. SW4 . . . . . . .2F **103**
Kendon Cl. E11 . . . . .1D **41**
Kendon Ho. *E15* 4F **53**
(off Bryant St.)
Kendrick Ct. *SE15* 4D **93**
(off Woods Rd.)
Kendrick M. SW7 . . . . .5F **73**
Kendrick Pl. SW7 . . . . .5F **73**
Ken Friar Bri. N7 . . . . .1C **48**
Kenilford Rd. SW12 . . . . . .5D **103**
Kenilworth Av.
SW19 . . . . .5C **114**
Kenilworth Ct.
SW15 . . . . .1A **100**
(off Lwr. Richmond Rd.)
Kenilworth Rd. E3 . . . . . . .1A **66**
NW6 . . . . .5B **44**
Kenley Wlk. W11 . . . . .1A **72**
Kenlor Rd. SW17 . . . . . . .5F **115**
Kenmont Gdns.
NW10 . . . . .2D **57**
Kenmore Ct. *NW6* 4D **45**
(off Acol Rd.)
Kenmure Rd. E8 . . . . .2D **51**
Kenmure Yd. E8 . . . . .2D **51**
Kennacraig Cl. E16 . . . . . .2C **82**
Kennard Ho. SW11 . . . . . .5C **88**
Kennard Rd. E15 . . . . .4F **53**
Kennard St. SW11 . . . . . . .4C **88**
Kennedy Cl. E13 . . . . .1C **68**
Kennedy Cox Ho. *E16* 4B **68**
(off Burke St.)
Kennedy Ho. *SE11* 1B **90**
(off Vauxhall Wlk.)
Kennedy Wlk. *SE17* 5F **77**
(off Elsted St.)
Kennet Cl. SW11 . . . . .2F **101**
Kennet Ct. *W9* 4C **58**
(off Elmfield Way)
Kenneth Campbell Ho.
NW8 . . . . .3F **59**
(off Orchardson St.)
Kenneth Ct. SE11 . . . . . . .5C **76**
Kenneth Cres. NW2 . . . . . .2D **43**
Kennet Ho. *NW8* 3F **59**
(off Church St. Est.)
Kenneth Younger Ho.
SW6 . . . . .2B **86**
(off Clem Attlee Ct.)
Kennet Rd. W9 . . . . .3B **58**
Kennet St. E1 . . . . .2C **78**
Kennett Wharf La.
EC4 . . . . . . .5A **18** (1E **77**)
Kenninghall Rd. E5 . . . . . .5C **36**
Kenning Ho. *N1* 5A **50**
(off Colville Est.)
Kenning St. SE16 . . . . .3E **79**

Kennings Way SE11 . . . .1C 90
KENNINGTON 2C 90
Kennington Grn.
  SE11 . . . . .1C 90
Kennington La. SE11 . . .1B 90
KENNINGTON OVAL 2C 90
Kennington Oval
  SE11 . . . . .2B 90
Kennington Pal. Ct.
  SE11 . . . . .1C 90
  (off Sancroft St.)
Kennington Pk. Gdns.
  SE11 . . . . .2D 91
Kennington Pk. Ho.
  SE11 . . . . .1C 90
  (off Kennington Pk. Pl.)
Kennington Pk. Pl.
  SE11 . . . . .2C 90
Kennington Pk. Rd.
  SE11 . . . . .2C 90
Kennington Rd.
  SE1 . . . . . .5B 24 (4C 76)
  SE11 . . . . . .5B 24 (4C 76)
Kennistoun Ho. NW5 . . .2E 47
Kennoldes SE21 . . . . . . .2F 119
Kennyland Ct. NW4 . . . .1D 29
  (off Hendon Way)
Kenrick Pl.
  W1 . . . . . .1B 12 (4C 60)
KENSAL GREEN 2E 57
Kensal Ho. *W10 . . . . . . .3F 57*
  (off Ladbroke Gro.)
KENSAL RISE 1F 57
Kensal Rd. W10 . . . . . . .3A 58
KENSAL TOWN 3A 58
Kensal Wharf W10 . . . . .3F 57
KENSINGTON 4C 72
Kensington Arc. *W8 . . . .3D 73*
  (off Kensington High St.)
Kensington Cen.
  W14 . . . . .5A 72
  (not continuous)
Kensington Chu. Ct.
  W8 . . . . .3D 73
Kensington Chu. St.
  W8 . . . . .2C 72
Kensington Chu. Wlk.
  W8 . . . . .3D 73
  (not continuous)
Kensington Ct. *SE16 . . .2F 79*
  (off King & Queen Wharf)
  W8 . . . . .3D 73
Kensington Ct. Gdns.
  W8 . . . . .4D 73
  (off Kensington Ct. Pl.)
Kensington Ct. Mans.
  W8 . . . . .3D 73
  (off Kensington Ct.)
Kensington Ct. M.
  W8 . . . . .4D 73
  (off Kensington Ct. Pl.)
Kensington Ct. Pl.
  W8 . . . . .4D 73
Kensington Gdns. 2E 73
Kensington Gdns. Sq.
  W2 . . . . .5D 59
Kensington Ga. W8 . . . .4E 73
Kensington Gore
  SW7 . . . . .3E 73

Kensington Hall Gdns.
  W14 . . . . .1B 86
Kensington Hgts. *W8 . .2C 72*
Kensington High St.
  W8 . . . . .4B 72
  W14 . . . . .4B 72
Kensington Ho. *W8 . . . .3D 73*
  (off Kensington Ct.)
  W14 . . . . .3F 71
Kensington Mall W8 . . . .2C 72
Kensington Mans.
  SW5 . . . . .1C 86
  (off Trebovir Rd.,
  not continuous)
Kensington Palace 2D 73
Kensington Pal. Gdns.
  W8 . . . . .2D 73
Kensington Pk. Gdns.
  W11 . . . . .1B 72
Kensington Pk. M.
  W11 . . . . .5B 58
Kensington Pk. Rd.
  W11 . . . . .5B 58
Kensington Path *E10 . . .4D 39*
  (off Osborne Rd.)
Kensington Pl. W8 . . . . .2C 72
Kensington Rd. W8 . . . . .3D 73
Kensington Sports Cen.
  . . . . .1A 72
Kensington Sq. W8 . . . . .4D 73
Kensington Village
  W14 . . . . .5B 72
Kensington W. W14 . . . .5A 72
Kensworth Ho. *EC1 . . . .2C 10*
  (off Cranwood St.)
Kent Ct. E2 . . . . .1B 64
Kent Ho. SE1 . . . . .1B 92
  SW1 . . . . .1F 89
  (off Aylesford St.)
  W4 . . . . .1A 84
  (off Devonshire St.)
  W8 . . . . .3D 73
  (off Kensington Ct.)
  W11 . . . . .5B 58
  (off Boyne Ter. M.)
Kent Ho. La.
  BR3: Beck 5A 122
Kent Ho. Rd. SE26 . . . . .5A 122
Kentish Bldgs.
  SE1 . . . . . .2B 26 (3F 77)
KENTISH TOWN 2D 47
Kentish Town Forum . . .2D 47
Kentish Town Ind. Est.
  NW5 . . . . .2D 47
Kentish Town Rd.
  NW1 . . . . .4D 47
  NW5 . . . . .4D 47
Kentish Town Sports Cen.
  . . . . .3D 47
Kentmere Ho. SE15 . . . .2E 93
Kenton Ct. *SE26 . . . . . .4A 122*
  (off Adamsrill Rd.)
  W14 . . . . .4B 72
Kenton Ho. *E1 . . . . .3E 65*
  (off Mantus Cl.)
Kenton Rd. E9 . . . . .3F 51
Kenton St.
  WC1 . . . . . . .3D 7 (3A 62)
Kent Pk. Ind. Est.
  SE15 . . . . .2D 93

Kent Pas. NW1 . . . . .3B 60
Kent St. E2 . . . . .1B 64
  E13 . . . . .2E 69
Kent Ter. NW1 . . . . .2A 60
Kent Wlk. SW9 . . . . .2D 105
Kentwell Cl. SE4 . . . . . . .2A 108
Kent Wharf *SE8 . . . . . . .3D 95*
  (off Creekside)
Kentwode Grn. SW13 . . .3C 84
Kent Yd. SW7 . . . . .3A 74
Kenward Rd. SE9 . . . . . .3E 111
Kenward Way SW11 . . . .5C 88
Kenway Rd. SW5 . . . . . . .5D 73
Ken Wilson Ho. *E2 . . . . .1C 64*
  (off Pritchards Rd.)
Kenwood Cl. NW3 . . . . . .3F 31
Kenwood House 3A 32
Kenwood Ho. SW9 . . . . .2D 105
Kenwood Pl. N6 . . . . .3B 32
Kenwood Rd. N6 . . . . . . .1B 32
Kenworthy Rd. E9 . . . . . .2A 52
Kenwrick Ho. *N1 . . . . . .5B 48*
  (off Barnsbury Est.)
Kenwyn Dr. NW2 . . . . . . .4A 28
Kenwyn Rd. SW4 . . . . . . .2F 103
Kenya Rd. SE7 . . . . .3F 97
Kenyon Ho. *SE5 . . . . . . .3E 91*
  (off Camberwell Rd.)
Kenyon Mans. *W14 . . . .2A 86*
  (off Queen's Club Gdns.)
Kenyon St. SW6 . . . . .4F 85
Keogh Rd. E15 . . . . .3A 54
Kepler Ho. *SE10 . . . . . . .1B 96*
  (off Armitage Rd.)
Kepler Rd. SW4 . . . . .2A 104
Keppel Ho. SE8 . . . . .1B 94
  SW3 . . . . .5A 74
  (off Elystan St.)
Keppel Row
  SE1 . . . . . . .2F 25 (2E 77)
Keppel St.
  WC1 . . . . . . .5C 6 (4F 61)
Kerbela St. E2 . . . . .3C 64
Kerbey St. E14 . . . . .5D 67
Kerfield Cres. SE5 . . . . . .4F 91
Kerfield Pl. SE5 . . . . .4F 91
Kerridge Ct. *N1 . . . . .3A 50*
  (off Balls Pond Rd.)
Kerrier Ho. *SW10 . . . . . .3E 87*
  (off Stadium St.)
Kerrington Ct. *W10 . . . . .3A 58*
  (off Wornington Rd.)
  W12 . . . . .3E 71
  (off Uxbridge Rd.)
Kerris Ho. *SE11 . . . . .1C 90*
  (off Tavy Cl.)
Kerrison Rd. E15 . . . . . . .5F 53
  SW11 . . . . .1A 102
Kerry Cl. E16 . . . . .5D 69
Kerry Ho. *E1 . . . . .5E 65*
  (off Sidney St.)
Kerry Path SE14 . . . . . . .2B 94
Kerry Rd. SE14 . . . . .2B 94
Kerscott Ho. *E3 . . . . . . .2D 67*
  (off Rainhill Way)
Kersey Gdns. SE9 . . . . . .4F 125
Kersfield Ho. SW15 . . . . .4F 99
Kersfield Rd. SW15 . . . . .4F 99
Kershaw Cl. SW18 . . . . . .4F 101
Kersley M. SW11 . . . . . . .4B 88

Kersley Rd. N16 . . . . . . .4A **36**
Kersley St. SW11 . . . . . .5B **88**
Kerswell Cl. N15 . . . . . . .1A **36**
Kerwick Cl. N7 . . . . .4A **48**
Keslake Mans. *NW10* . .1F **57**
    (off Station Ter.)
Keslake Rd. NW6 . . . . . .1F **57**
Keston Ho. *SE17* 1A **92**
    (off Kinglake Est.)
Keston Rd. SE15 . . . . . .1C **106**
Kestrel Av. E6 . . . . .4F **69**
  SE24 . . . . .3D **105**
Kestrel Cl. NW10 . . . . . .2A **42**
Kestrel Ct. *E3* 1C **66**
    (off Four Seasons Cl.)
Kestrel Ho. *EC1* 1F **9**
    (off Pickard St.)
Kestrel Pl. SE14 . . . . . . .2A **94**
Keswick Av. SW15 . . . . .5A **112**
Keswick B'way.
  SW15 . . . . .3B **100**
    (off Up. Richmond Rd.)
Keswick Ct. SW15 . . . . .1B **124**
  SE13 . . . . .3D **109**
Keswick Ho. SE5 . . . . . . .5E **91**
Keswick Rd. SW15 . . . . .3A **100**
Kett Gdns. SW2 . . . . . . .3B **104**
Kettlebaston Rd. E10 . . .3B **38**
Kettleby Ho. *SW9* 1D **105**
    (off Barrington Rd.)
Ketton Ho. *W10* 3E **57**
    (off Sutton Way)
Kevan Ho. SE5 . . . . .3E **91**
Keybridge Ho. *SW8* 2A **90**
    (off Miles St.)
Key Cl. E1 . . . . .3E **65**
Keyes Ho. *SW1* 1F **89**
    (off Dolphin Sq.)
Keyes Rd. NW2 . . . . .2F **43**
Keyham Ho. *W2* 4C **58**
    (off Westbourne Pk. Rd.)
Key Ho. SE11 . . . . .2C **90**
Keymer Rd. SW2 . . . . . .2B **118**
Keynsham Gdns.
  SE9 . . . . .3F **111**
Keynsham Rd. SE9 . . . . .3F **111**
Keyse Rd. SE1 . . . . .4B **78**
Keystone Cres.
  N1 . . . . .1E **7** (1A **62**)
Keyworth Cl. E5 . . . . . . .1A **52**
Keyworth Pl. SE1 . . . . . .5E **25**
Keyworth
  St. SE1 . . . . .5E **25** (4D **77**)
Kezia M. SE8 . . . . .1A **94**
Kezia St. SE8 . . . . .1A **94**
Khama Rd. SW17 . . . . . .4A **116**
Khartoum Rd. E13 . . . . .2D **69**
  SW17 . . . . .4F **115**
Khyber Rd. SW11 . . . . . .5A **88**
Kia Oval 2B **90**
Kibworth St. SW8 . . . . . .3B **90**
KIDBROOKE 5D **97**
Kidbrooke Est. SE3 . . . .1E **111**
Kidbrooke Gdns. SE3 . . .5C **96**
Kidbrooke Green
  Nature Reserve
  . . . . .1E **111**
Kidbrooke Gro. SE3 . . . .4C **96**
Kidbrooke La. SE9 . . . . .2F **111**
Kidbrooke Pk. Cl. SE3 . .4D **97**

Kidbrooke Pk. Rd.
  SE3 . . . . .4D **97**
Kidbrooke Way SE3 . . . .5D **97**
Kidderpore Av. NW3 . . . .1C **44**
Kidderpore Gdns.
  NW3 . . . . .1C **44**
Kierbeck Bus. Complex
  E16 . . . . .3D **83**
    (not continuous)
Kiffen St.
  EC2 . . . . . . .3C **10** (3F **63**)
Kilbrennan Ho. *E14* 5E **67**
    (off Findhorn St.)
KILBURN 1B **58**
Kilburn Bri. NW6 . . . . . .5C **44**
Kilburn Ga. NW6 . . . . . .1D **58**
Kilburn High Rd.
  NW6 . . . . .4B **44**
Kilburn Ho. *NW6* 1B **58**
    (off Malvern Pl.)
Kilburn La. W9 . . . . .2F **57**
  W10 . . . . .2F **57**
Kilburn Pk. Rd. NW6 . . .2C **58**
Kilburn Pl. NW6 . . . . . . .5C **44**
Kilburn Priory NW6 . . . .5D **45**
Kilburn Sq. NW6 . . . . . . .5C **44**
Kilburn Vale NW6 . . . . . .5D **45**
Kilburn Vale Est.
  NW6 . . . . .5D **45**
    (off Kilburn Vale)
Kilby Ct. *SE10* 4B **82**
    (off Greenroof Way)
Kildare Ct. *W2* 5C **58**
    (off Kildare Ter.)
Kildare Gdns. W2 . . . . . .5C **58**
Kildare Rd. E16 . . . . .4C **68**
Kildare Ter. W2 . . . . .5C **58**
Kildare Wlk. E14 . . . . . . .5C **66**
Kildoran Rd. SW2 . . . . . .3A **104**
Kilgour Rd. SE23 . . . . . .4A **108**
Kilkie St. SW6 . . . . .5E **87**
Killarney Rd. SW18 . . . . .4E **101**
Killarn Rd. SE6 . . . . . . .1F **123**
Killick St. N1 . . . . .1F **7** (1B **62**)
Killieser Av. SW2 . . . . . .2A **118**
Killip Cl. E16 . . . . .5B **68**
Killoran Ho. *E14* 4E **81**
    (off Galbraith St.)
Killowen Rd. E9 . . . . . . .3F **51**
Killyon Rd. SW8 . . . . . . .5E **89**
Killyon Ter. SW8 . . . . . . .5E **89**
Kilmaine Rd. SW6 . . . . . .3A **86**
Kilmarsh Rd. W6 . . . . . . .5E **71**
Kilmington
  SW13 . . . . .2C **84**
Kilmore Ho. *E14* 5D **67**
    (off Vesey Path)
Kilmorie Rd. SE23 . . . . .1A **122**
Kilmuir Ho. *SW1* 5C **74**
    (off Bury St.)
Kiln Ct. *E14* 1B **80**
    (off Newell St.)
Kilner Ho. *E16* 4D **69**
    (off Freemasons Rd.)
  SE11 . . . . .2C **90**
    (off Clayton St.)
Kilner St. E14 . . . . .4C **66**
Kiln M. SW17 . . . . .5F **115**
Kiln Pl. NW5 . . . . .2C **46**
Kilravock St. W10 . . . . . .2A **58**

Kimball Gdns. SW6 . . . . .4A **86**
Kimball Pl. SE3 . . . . . . .2E **111**
Kimber Ct. *SE1* 5D **27**
    (off Long La.)
Kimberley Av. E6 . . . . . . .1F **69**
  SE15 . . . . .5D **93**
Kimberley Ct. *NW6* 5A **44**
    (off Kimberley Rd.)
Kimberley Gdns. N4 . . . .1D **35**
Kimberley Ho. *E14* 4E **81**
    (off Galbraith St.)
Kimberley Rd. E11 . . . . .4F **39**
  E16 . . . . .3B **68**
  NW6 . . . . .5A **44**
  SW9 . . . . .5A **90**
Kimber Rd. SW18 . . . . . .5C **100**
Kimble Ho. *NW8* 3A **60**
    (off Lilestone St.)
Kimble Rd. SW19 . . . . . .5F **115**
Kimbolton Cl. SE12 . . . .4B **110**
Kimbolton Row *SW3* . . .5A **74**
    (off Fulham Rd.)
Kimbolton Row *SW3* . . .5A **74**
    (off Fulham Rd.)
Kimmeridge Rd.
  SE9 . . . . .4F **125**
Kimpton Ho. SW15 . . . . .5C **98**
Kimpton Rd. SE5 . . . . . . .4F **91**
Kinburn St. SE16 . . . . . .3F **79**
Kincaid Rd. SE15 . . . . . .3D **93**
Kincardine Gdns. *W9* . . .3C **58**
    (off Harrow Rd.)
Kinder Ho. *N1* 1F **63**
    (off Cranston Est.)
Kindersley Ho. *E1* 5C **64**
    (off Pinchin St.)
Kinder St. E1 . . . . .5D **65**
    (not continuous)
Kinefold Ho. *N7* 3A **48**
    (off York Way Est.)
Kinfauns Rd. SW2 . . . . .2C **118**
King Alfred Av. SE6 . . . .4C **122**
    (not continuous)
King & Queen St.
  SE17 . . . . .1E **91**
King & Queen Wharf
  SE16 . . . . .1F **79**
King Arthur Cl. SE15 . . .3E **93**
King Charles I Island
  SW1 . . . . .1D **23**
King Charles Ct.
  SE17 . . . . .2D **91**
    (off Royal Rd.)
King Charles Ho.
  SW6 . . . . .3D **87**
    (off Wandon Rd.)
King Charles's Ct.
  SE10 . . . . .2E **95**
    (off Park Row)
King Charles St.
  SW1 . . . . . . .3C **22** (3F **75**)
King Charles Ter. *E1* . . .1D **79**
    (off Sovereign Cl.)
King Charles Wlk.
  SW19 . . . . .1A **114**
King Ct. E10 . . . . .2D **39**
King David La. E1 . . . . . .1E **79**
Kingdom St. W2 . . . . . . .4E **59**
Kingdon Ho. *E14* 4E **81**
    (off Galbraith St.)

Kingdon Rd. NW6 . . . . . . .3C **44**
King Edward III M.
   SE16 . . . . .3D **79**
King Edward Bldg.
   EC1 . . . . .2E **17**
    (off Newgate St.)
King Edward Mans.
   E8 . . . . .5D **51**
    (off Mare St.)
King Edward M.
   SW13 . . . . .4C **84**
King Edward Rd.
   E10 . . . . .3E **39**
King Edwards Mans.
   SW6 . . . . .3C **86**
    (off Fulham Rd.)
King Edward's Rd.
   E9 . . . . .5D **51**
King Edward St.
   EC1 . . . . .2F **17** (5E **63**)
King Edward Wlk.
   SE1 . . . . .5C **24** (4C **76**)
Kingfield St. E14 . . . . . . .5E **81**
Kingfisher Av. E11 . . . . . .1D **41**
Kingfisher Ct. E14 . . . . . .3E **81**
    (off River Barge Cl.)
   SE1 . . . . .4A **26**
    (off Swan St.)
   SW19 . . . . .2F **113**
Kingfisher Hgts. E16 . . . .2E **83**
    (off Bramwell Way)
Kingfisher Ho.
   SW18 . . . . .1E **101**
   W14 . . . . .4B **72**
    (off Melbury Rd.)
Kingfisher M. SE13 . . . .2C **108**
Kingfisher Sq. SE8 . . . . . .2B **94**
    (off Clyde St.)
Kingfisher Way
   NW10 . . . . .3A **42**
King Frederick IX Twr.
   SE16 . . . . .4B **80**
King George IV Ct.
   SE17 . . . . .1F **91**
    (off Dawes St.)
King George VI Memorial
   . . . . .2B **22**
King George Av. E16 . . . .5E **69**
King George M.
   SW17 . . . . .5B **116**
King George St.
   SE10 . . . . .3E **95**
Kingham Cl. SW18 . . . .5E **101**
   W11 . . . . .3A **72**
King Henry's Reach
   W6 . . . . .2E **85**
King Henry's Rd.
   NW3 . . . . .4A **46**
King Henry's Stairs
   E1 . . . . .2D **79**
King Henry St. N16 . . . . .2A **50**
King Henry's Wlk. N1 . . . .3A **50**
King Henry Ter. E1 . . . . .1D **79**
    (off Sovereign Cl.)
Kinghorn St.
   EC1 . . . . . . .1F **17** (4E **63**)
King Ho. W12 . . . . .5D **57**
Kingsholt Ct. NW10 . . . . .2F **57**
    (off Wellington Rd.)
King James Est. SE1 . . . .4E **25**

King James St.
   SE1 . . . . . .4E **25** (3D **77**)
King John Ct.
   EC2 . . . . . . .3E **11** (3A **64**)
King John St. E1 . . . . . . .4F **65**
King John's Wlk.
   SE9 . . . . .5F **111**
Kinglake Est. SE17 . . . . .1A **92**
Kinglake St. SE17 . . . . . .1A **92**
    (not continuous)
Kinglet Cl. E7 . . . . .3C **54**
Kingly Ct. W1 . . . . .4A **14**
Kingly St. W1 . . .3F **13** (5E **61**)
Kingsand Rd. SE12 . . . .2C **124**
Kings Arms Ct. E1 . . . . . .4C **64**
Kings Arms Yd.
   EC2 . . . . . . .2B **18** (5F **63**)
Kings Av. BR1: Brom . . .5B **124**
   SW4 . . . . .1F **117**
   SW12 . . . . .1F **117**
King's Bench St.
   SE1 . . . . . . .3E **25** (3D **77**)
King's Bench Wlk.
   EC4 . . . . . . .3C **16** (5C **62**)
King's Blvd. N1 . . . . .1A **62**
Kingsbridge Ct. E14 . . . .4C **80**
    (off Dockers Tanner Rd.)
   NW1 . . . . .4D **47**
    (off Castlehaven Rd.)
Kingsbridge Rd. W10 . . .5E **57**
KINGSBURY GREEN 1A **28**
Kingsbury Rd. N1 . . . . . .3A **50**
   NW9 . . . . .1A **28**
Kingsbury Ter. N1 . . . . . .3A **50**
Kingsbury Trad. Est.
   NW9 . . . . .1A **28**
Kingsclere Cl. SW15 . . . .5C **98**
Kingscliffe Gdns.
   SW19 . . . . .1B **114**
Kings Cl. E10 . . . . .2D **39**
Kings Coll. Ct. NW3 . . . . .4A **46**
King's College London
  Denmark Hill Campus
   . . . . .5F **91**
  Guy's Campus 2B **26**
    (within Guy's Hospital)
  St Thomas' Campus -
  Lambeth Pal. Rd.
   . . . . .5E **23**
  St Thomas' House
   . . . . .5F **23**
  Strand Campus
   . . . . .4A **16** (1B **76**)
  Waterloo Campus
   . . . . .2B **24** (2C **76**)
King's Coll. Rd. NW3 . . . .4A **46**
King's College School of
  Medicine & Dentistry
   . . . . .5E **91**
Kingscote St.
   EC4 . . . . . . .4D **17** (1D **77**)
Kings Ct. E13 . . . . .5D **55**
   N7 . . . . .4B **48**
    (off Caledonian Rd.)
   NW8 . . . . .5B **46**
    (off Prince Albert Rd.)
   SE1 . . . . . . .3E **25** (3D **77**)
   W6 . . . . .5C **70**
Kings Ct. Mans. SW6 . . .4B **86**
    (off Fulham Rd.)

Kings Ct. Nth. SW3 . . . . .1A **88**
Kingscourt Rd.
   SW16 . . . . .3F **117**
Kings Ct. Sth. SW3 . . . . .1A **88**
    (off Chelsea Mnr. Gdns.)
King's Cres. N4 . . . . .5E **35**
Kings Cres. Est. N4 . . . . .4E **35**
Kingscroft SW4 . . . . .4A **104**
Kingscroft Rd. NW2 . . . . .3B **44**
KING'S CROSS 1A **62**
King's Cross Bri. N1 . . . . .1E **7**
King's Cross Rd.
   WC1 . . . . . . .1F **7** (2B **62**)
Kingsdale Gdns. W11 . . . .2F **71**
Kingsdown Av. W3 . . . . . .1A **70**
Kingsdown Cl. SE16 . . . . .1D **93**
    (off Masters Dr.)
   W10 . . . . .5F **57**
Kingsdown Ho. E8 . . . . . .2C **50**
Kingsdown Point
   SW2 . . . . .2C **118**
Kingsdown Rd. E11 . . . . .5A **40**
   N19 . . . . .4A **34**
Kingsfield Ho. SE9 . . . . .3F **125**
Kingsford St. NW5 . . . . . .2B **46**
King's Gdns. NW6 . . . . . .4C **44**
Kings Gth. M. SE23 . . . .2E **121**
Kingsgate Est. N1 . . . . . .3A **50**
Kingsgate Ho. SW9 . . . . .4C **90**
Kingsgate Mans.
   WC1 . . . . .1F **15**
    (off Red Lion Sq.)
Kingsgate Pde. SW1 . . . .5A **22**
Kingsgate Pl. NW6 . . . . . .4C **44**
Kingsgate Rd. NW6 . . . . .4C **44**
Kingsground SE9 . . . . . .5F **111**
    (not continuous)
King's Gro. SE15 . . . . . . .3D **93**
    . . . . .2E **51**
Kingshall M. SE13 . . . .1E **109**
Kings Hall Rd.
   BR3: Beck 5A **122**
Kings Head Pas.
   SW4 . . . . .2F **103**
    (off Clapham Pk. Rd.)
Kings Head Theatre 5D **49**
    (off Upper St.)
King's Head Yd.
   SE1 . . . . . . .2B **26** (2F **77**)
Kingshill SE17 . . . . .5E **77**
    (off Brandon St.)
Kingshold Rd. E9 . . . . . . .4E **51**
Kingsholm Gdns.
   SE9 . . . . .2F **111**
Kings Ho. SW8 . . . . .3A **90**
    (off Sth. Lambeth Rd.)
   SW10 . . . . .2F **87**
    (off King's Rd.)
King's Ho. Studios
   SW10 . . . . .2F **87**
    (off Lamont Rd. Pas.)
Kingshurst Rd.
   SE12 . . . . .5C **110**
Kings Keep SW15 . . . . . .3F **99**
KINGSLAND 3A **50**
Kingsland NW8 . . . . .5A **46**
Kingsland Grn. E8 . . . . . .3A **50**

Kingsland High St.
E8 . . . . .3B **50**
Kingsland Pas. E8 . . . .3A **50**
Kingsland Rd.
E2 . . . . . .2E **11** (2A **64**)
E8 . . . . .2A **64**
E13 . . . . .2E **69**
Kingsland Shop. Cen.
E8 . . . . .3B **50**
Kingslaw Cl.
SW15 . . . . .3D **99**
Kingsley Ct. NW2 . . . .3D **43**
Kingsley Flats SE1 . . .5A **78**
(off Old Kent Rd.)
Kingsley Ho. SW3 . . .2F **87**
(off Beaufort St.)
W14 . . . . .5A **72**
(off Avonmore Rd.)
Kingsley Mans. W14 . .2A **86**
(off Greyhound Rd.)
Kingsley M. E1 . . . . . .1D **79**
W8 . . . . .4D **73**
Kingsley Pl. N6 . . . . .2C **32**
Kingsley Rd. E7 . . . . .4C **54**
NW6 . . . . .5B **44**
SW19 . . . . .5D **115**
Kingsley St. SW11 . . .1B **102**
Kingsley Way N2 . . . .1E **31**
Kings Mall W6 . . . . . .5E **71**
(not continuous)
Kings Mans. SW3 . . . .2A **88**
(off Lawrence St.)
Kingsmead Av. NW9 . . .2A **28**
Kingsmead Ct. N6 . . . .2F **33**
Kingsmead Ho. E9 . . . .1A **52**
Kingsmead Rd.
SW2 . . . . .2C **118**
Kingsmead Way E9 . . .1A **52**
Kingsmere Cl. SW15 . . .1F **99**
Kingsmere Pl. N16 . . . .3F **35**
Kingsmere Rd.
SW19 . . . . .2F **113**
King's M. SW4 . . . . . .3A **104**
WC1 . . . . . .4A **8** (3B **62**)
Kingsmill NW8 . . . . . .1F **59**
(off Kingsmill Ter.)
Kingsmill Ho. SW3 . . . .1A **88**
(off Cale St.)
Kingsmill Ter. NW8 . . . .1F **59**
Kingsnorth Ho. W10 . . .5F **57**
Kings Pde. NW10 . . . . .5E **43**
W12 . . . . .4C **70**
Kings Pas. E11 . . . . . . .2A **40**
Kings Place 1A **62**
King's Pl.
SE1 . . . . . .4F **25** (3E **77**)
King Sq. EC1 . . . . .2F **9** (2B **63**)
Kings Quarter Apartments
N1 . . . . .5B **48**
(off Copenhagen St.)
King's Quay SW10 . . . .4E **87**
(off Chelsea Harbour Dr.)
Kings Reach Tower.
SE1 . . . . .1D **25**
Kingsridge SW19 . . . . .2A **114**
Kings Rd. E6 . . . . .5E **55**
E11 . . . . .2A **40**
NW10 . . . . .4D **43**
SW3 . . . . .2F **87**
SW6 . . . . .3D **87**

Kings Rd. SW10 . . . . . .3D **87**
SW14 . . . . .1A **98**
SW19 . . . . .5C **114**
King's Scholars' Pas.
SW1 . . . . .4E **75**
(off Carlisle Pl.)
King Stairs Cl.
SE16 . . . . .3D **79**
King's Ter. NW1 . . . . . .5E **47**
Kingsthorpe Rd.
SE26 . . . . .4F **121**
Kingston By-Pass
SW15 . . . . .5A **112**
SW20 . . . . .5A **112**
Kingston Ho. NW1 . . . . .5E **47**
(off Camden St.)
NW6 . . . . .4A **44**
Kingston Ho. E. SW7 . . .3A **74**
(off Prince's Ga.)
Kingston Ho. Nth.
SW7 . . . . .3A **74**
(off Prince's Ga.)
Kingston Ho. Sth.
SW7 . . . . .3A **74**
(off Ennismore Gdns.)
Kingston Mans. SW9 . . .4B **90**
(off Clapham Rd.)
Kingston Rd. SW15 . . . .2C **112**
SW19 . . . . .2C **112**
Kingston Sq. SE19 . . . . .5F **119**
Kingston University
Kingston Hill Campus
. . . . .5A **112**
Roehampton Vale Cen.
. . . . .3B **112**
KINGSTON VALE 4A **112**
Kingston Va. SW15 . . . . .4A **112**
Kingstown St. NW1 . . . . .5C **46**
(not continuous)
King St. E13 . . . . .3C **68**
EC2 . . . . . . .3A **18** (5E **63**)
SW1 . . . . . .2A **22** (2E **75**)
W6 . . . . .5C **70**
WC2 . . . . .4D **15** (1A **76**)
King St. Cloisters
W6 . . . . .5D **71**
(off King St.)
Kings Wlk. Shop. Cen.
SW3 . . . . .1B **88**
Kingswater Pl. SW11 . . .3A **88**
Kingsway
WC2 . . . . . .2F **15** (5B **62**)
Kingsway Mans. WC1 . . .5F **7**
(off Red Lion Sq.)
Kingsway Pde. N16 . . . . .5F **35**
(off Albion Rd.)
Kingsway Pl. EC1 . . . . . .3C **8**
(off Sans Wlk.)
Kingswear Rd. NW5 . . . .5D **33**
Kings Wharf E8 . . . . . . .5A **50**
(off Kingsland Rd.)
Kingswood E2 . . . . .1E **65**
(off Cyprus St.)
Kingswood Av. NW6 . . . .5A **44**
Kingswood Cl. SW8 . . . .3A **90**
Kingswood Ct. NW6 . . . .4C **44**
(off West End La.)
SE13 . . . . .4F **109**
Kingswood Dr.
SE26 . . . . .4A **120**

Kingswood Est.
SE21 . . . . .4A **120**
Kingswood Pl. SE13 . . . .2A **110**
Kingswood Rd. E11 . . . .2A **40**
SW2 . . . . .5E **121**
SW19 . . . . .4A **104**
Kings Yd. SW15 . . . . . .1E **99**
(off Lwr. Richmond Rd.)
Kingthorpe Ter.
NW10 . . . . .3A **42**
Kington Ho. NW6 . . . . . .5D **45**
(off Mortimer Cres.)
Kingward Ho. E1 . . . . . .4C **64**
(off Hanbury St.)
King Wardrobe Apartments
EC4 . . . . .3E **17**
(off Carter La.)
Kingweston Cl. NW2 . . . .5A **30**
King William La.
SE10 . . . . .1A **96**
King William's Ct.
SE10 . . . . .2F **95**
(off Park Row)
King William St.
EC4 . . . . . .3C **18** (5F **63**)
King William Wlk.
SE10 . . . . .2E **95**
(not continuous)
Kingwood Rd. SW6 . . . .4A **86**
Kinloch Dr. NW9 . . . . . .2A **28**
Kinloch St. N7 . . . . . . .5B **34**
Kinnaird Av.
BR1: Brom 5B **124**
Kinnear Rd. W12 . . . . . .3B **70**
Kinnerton Pl. Nth.
SW1 . . . . .4A **20**
Kinnerton Pl. Sth.
SW1 . . . . .4A **20**
Kinnerton St.
SW1 . . . . . .4B **20** (3C **74**)
Kinnerton Yd. SW1 . . . .4B **20**
Kinnoul Rd. W6 . . . . . . .2A **86**
Kinross Ct. SE6 . . . . . .1B **124**
Kinross Ho. N1 . . . . . . .5B **48**
(off Bemerton St.)
Kinsale Rd. SE15 . . . . . .1C **106**
Kinsella Gdns.
SW19 . . . . .5D **113**
Kinsham Ho. E2 . . . . . .3C **64**
(off Ramsey St.)
Kintore Way SE1 . . . . . .5B **78**
Kintyre Ct. SW2 . . . . . .5A **104**
Kintyre Ho. E14 . . . . . . .2E **81**
(off Coldharbour)
Kinveachy Gdns.
SE7 . . . . .1F **97**
Kinver Ho. N19 . . . . . . .4F **33**
Kinver Rd. SE26 . . . . . .4E **121**
Kipling Dr. SW19 . . . . . .5F **115**
Kipling Est.
SE1 . . . . . .4C **26** (3F **77**)
Kipling Ho. SE5 . . . . . . .3F **91**
(off Elmington Est.)
Kipling St.
SE1 . . . . . .4C **26** (3F **77**)
Kippington Dr. SE9 . . . . .1F **125**
Kira Bldg. E3 . . . . .2B **66**
Kiran Apartments E1 . . . .4B **64**
(off Chicksand St.)
Kirby Est. SE16 . . . . . . .4D **79**

Kirby Gro.
SE1 . . . . . .3D 27 (3A 78)
Kirby St. EC1 . . . . .5C 8 (4C 62)
Kirkdale SE26 . . . . . .2D 121
Kirkdale Cnr.
SE26 . . . . .4E 121
Kirkdale Rd. E11 . . . . .3A 40
Kirkeby Rd. EC1 . . . . . .5B 8
(off Leather La.)
Kirkland Ho. E14 . . . . .1D 95
(off St Davids Sq.)
E14 . . . . .1D 95
(off Westferry Rd.)
Kirkland Ter.
BR3: Beck 5C 122
Kirkland Wlk. E8 . . . . .3B 50
Kirkmichael Rd. E14 . . .5E 67
Kirk Rd. E17 . . . . .1B 38
Kirkside Rd. SE3 . . . . .2C 96
Kirk's Place 4B 66
Kirkstall Gdns. SW2 . .1A 118
Kirkstall Ho. SW1 . . . . .1D 89
(part of Abbots Mnr.)
Kirkstall Rd. SW2 . . . .1F 117
Kirkstead Ct. E5 . . . . . .1F 51
Kirkstone NW1 . . . . . . .1F 5
(off Harrington St.)
Kirk St. WC1 . . . . .4F 7
Kirkwall Pl. E2 . . . . . . .2E 65
Kirkwood Pl. NW1 . . . . .4C 46
Kirkwood Rd. SE15 . . . .5D 93
Kirtley Ho. SW8 . . . . . .4E 89
Kirtley Rd. SE26 . . . . .4A 122
Kirtling St. SW8 . . . . . .3E 89
Kirton Cl. W4 . . . . .5A 70
Kirton Gdns.
E2 . . . . . . .2F 11 (2B 64)
(not continuous)
Kirton Lodge SW18 . . .4D 101
Kirton Rd. E13 . . . . . . .1E 69
Kirwyn Way SE5 . . . . . .3D 91
Kitcat Ter. E3 . . . . .2C 66
Kitchen Ct. E10 . . . . . .4D 39
Kitchener Rd. E7 . . . . . .3D 55
Kite Ho. SE1 . . . . .5D 79
Kite Pl. E2 . . . . .2C 64
(off Warner Pl.)
Kite Yd. SW11 . . . . . . .4B 88
(off Cambridge Rd.)
Kitson Rd. SE5 . . . . . . .3F 91
SW13 . . . . .4C 84
Kittiwake Ct. SE1 . . . . .4A 26
(off Gt. Dover St.)
SE8 . . . . .2B 94
(off Abinger Gro.)
Kitto Rd. SE14 . . . . . . .5F 93
Kiver Rd. N19 . . . . .4F 33
Klea Av. SW4 . . . . . . .4E 103
Kleine Wharf N1 . . . . . .5A 50
Klein's Wharf E14 . . . . .4C 80
(off Westferry Rd.)
Knapdale Cl. SE23 . . . .2D 121
Knapmill Rd. SE6 . . . . .2C 122
Knapmill Way SE6 . . . .2D 123
Knapp Cl. NW10 . . . . . .3A 42
Knapp Rd. E3 . . . . .3C 66
Knapton M. SW17 . . . . .5C 116
Knaresborough Dr.
SW18 . . . . .1D 115

Knaresborough Pl.
SW5 . . . . .5D 73
Knatchbull Rd.
NW10 . . . . .5A 42
SE5 . . . . .5D 91
Knebworth Ho.
SW8 . . . . .5F 89
Knebworth Rd. N16 . . .1A 50
Kneller Rd. SE4 . . . . . .2A 108
Knighten St. E1 . . . . . .2D 79
Knighthead Point
E14 . . . . .3C 80
(off Tatum St.)
Knightland Rd. E5 . . . . .4D 37
Knightleas Ct. NW2 . . . .3E 43
Knightleys Ct. E10 . . . . .3A 38
(off Wellington Rd.)
Knighton Pk. Rd.
SE26 . . . . .5F 121
Knighton Rd. E7 . . . . . .5C 40
Knightrider Ct. EC4 . . . .4E 17
Knightrider St.
EC4 . . . . . .4E 17 (5D 63)
Knights Arc. SW1 . . . . .4A 20
KNIGHTSBRIDGE 3A 74
Knightsbridge
SW1 . . . . .4A 20 (3B 74)
SW7 . . . . .3B 74
Knightsbridge
Apartments, The
SW7 . . . . .3B 74
(off Knightsbridge)
Knightsbridge Ct.
SW1 . . . . .4A 20
Knightsbridge Grn.
SW1 . . . . .3B 74
(not continuous)
Knights Cl. E9 . . . . .2E 51
Knights Ct.
BR1: Brom 3B 124
Knights Hill SE27 . . . . .5D 119
Knight's Hill Sq.
SE27 . . . . .4D 119
Knights Ho. SW8 . . . . .3A 90
(off Sth. Lambeth Rd.)
SW10 . . . . .3E 87
(off Hortensia Rd.)
W14 . . . . .1B 86
(off Baron's Ct. Rd.)
Knight's Rd. E16 . . . . . .3C 82
Knight's Wlk. SE11 . . . .5D 77
(not continuous)
Knightswood Ct. N6 . . .2F 33
Knivet Rd. SW6 . . . . . .2C 86
Knockholt Rd. SE9 . . . .3F 111
Knoll Ct. SE19 . . . . . . .5B 120
(off Farquhar Rd.)
Knoll Rd. SW18 . . . . . .3E 101
Knolls Cl. SW16 . . . . . .3C 118
Knolly's Ho. WC1 . . . . . .3D 7
(off Tavistock Pl.)
Knollys Rd. SW16 . . . . .3B 118
Knot Ho. SE1 . . . . .2F 27
(off Brewery Sq.)
Knottisford St. E2 . . . . .2E 65
Knotts Grn. M. E10 . . . .1D 39
Knotts Grn. Rd. E10 . . .1D 39

Knowlden Ho. E1 . . . . . .1E 79
(off Cable St.)
Knowle Cl. SW9 . . . . . .1C 104
Knowles Hill Cres.
SE13 . . . . .3F 109
Knowles Ho. SW18 . . . .4D 101
(off Neville Gill Cl.)
Knowles Wlk.
SW4 . . . . .1E 103
Knowles Wharf NW1 . . .5E 47
(off St Pancras Way)
Knowlton Ho. SW9 . . . . .4C 90
(off Cowley Rd.)
Knowsley Rd. SW11 . . . .5B 88
Knox Ct. SW4 . . . . .5A 90
Knox Rd. E7 . . . . .3B 54
Knox St. W1 . . . . .5A 4 (4B 60)
Knoyle Ho. W14 . . . . . . .4A 72
(off Russell Rd.)
Knoyle St. SE14 . . . . . . .2A 94
Kohat Rd. SW19 . . . . . .5D 115
Kossuth St. SE10 . . . . .1A 96
Kotree Way SE1 . . . . . .5C 78
Kramer M. SW5 . . . . . .1C 86
Kreedman Wlk. E8 . . . . .2C 50
Krupnik Pl. EC2 . . . . . . .3E 11
(shown as Curtail Pl.)
Kubrick Bus. Est. E7 . . .1D 55
(off Station App.)
Kuhn Way E7 . . . . .2C 54
Kurdish Mus. 5C 70
Kwesi M. SE27 . . . . . . .5C 118
Kyle Ho. NW6 . . . . .5C 44
Kylemore Cl. E6 . . . . . . .1F 69
Kylemore Rd. NW6 . . . . .4C 44
Kylestrome Ho. SW1 . . . .5C 74
(off Cundy St.)
Kynance M. SW7 . . . . . .4D 73
Kynance Pl. SW7 . . . . . .4E 73
Kynaston Av. N16 . . . . . .5B 36
Kynaston Rd.
BR1: Brom 5C 124
N16 . . . . .5A 36
Kyrle Rd. SW11 . . . . . .4C 102
Kyverdale Rd. N16 . . . . .2B 36

L

Laban Cen. 2D 95
(off Creekside)
Laban Wlk. SE8 . . . . . . .2D 95
(off Copperas St.)
Laburnum Cl. SE15 . . . .3E 93
Laburnum Ct. E2 . . . . . .5B 50
SE16 . . . . .3E 79
(off Albion St.)
Laburnum St. E2 . . . . . .5B 50
Labyrinth Twr. E8 . . . . . .3B 50
(off Dalston Sq.)
Lacewing Cl. E13 . . . . . .2C 68
Lacey M. E3 . . . . .1C 66
Lacine Ct. SE16 . . . . . . .3F 79
(off Christopher Cl.)
Lackington St.
EC2 . . . . . .5C 10 (4F 63)
Lackland Ho. SE1 . . . . . .1B 92
(off Rowcross St.)
Lacland Ho. SW10 . . . . .3F 87
(off Worlds End Est.)

Lacon Ho. WC1 . . . . .5F 7
(off Theobald's Rd.)
Lacon Rd. SE22 . . . . . . .2C **106**
Lacy Rd. SW15 . . . . .2F **99**
Ladas Rd. SE27 . . . . . . .4E **119**
Ladbroke Cres. W11 . . . .5A **58**
Ladbroke Gdns. W11 . . . .1B **72**
Ladbroke Gro. W10 . . . . .3F **57**
    W11 . . . . .3F **57**
Ladbroke Gro. Ho.
    W11 . . . . .1B **72**
    (off Ladbroke Gro.)
Ladbroke Grove Memorial
    . . . . .3F **57**
    (off Canal Way)
Ladbroke M. W11 . . . . . .2A **72**
Ladbroke Rd. W11 . . . . . .2B **72**
Ladbroke Sq. W11 . . . . . .1B **72**
Ladbroke Ter. W11 . . . . . .2B **72**
Ladbroke Wlk. W11 . . . . .2B **72**
Ladbroke Cl.
    BR1: Brom 5A **124**
Ladlands SE22 . . . . .5C **106**
Ladycroft Rd. SE13 . . . . .1D **109**
Lady Dock Path SE16 . . . .3A **80**
Ladyfern Ho. E3 . . . . .4C **66**
    (off Gail St.)
Lady Florence Courtyard
    SE8 . . . . .3C **94**
    (off Reginald Sq.)
Lady Margaret Ho.
    SE17 . . . . .2F **91**
    (off Queen's Row)
Lady Margaret Rd.
    N19 . . . . .2E **47**
    NW5 . . . . .2E **47**
Lady May Ho. SE5 . . . . . .3E **91**
    (off Pitman St.)
Lady Micos Almshouses
    E1 . . . . .5E **65**
    (off Aylward St.)
Ladyship Ter. SE22 . . . .5C **106**
Ladysmith Av. E6 . . . . . . .1F **69**
Ladysmith Rd. E16 . . . . . .2B **68**
Lady Somerset Rd.
    NW5 . . . . .1D **47**
LADYWELL 3D **109**
Ladywell Arena
    (Running Track)
    . . . . .4D **109**
Ladywell Cl. SE4 . . . . . .3C **108**
Ladywell Hgts. SE4 . . .4B **108**
Ladywell Leisure Cen.
    . . . . .3E **109**
Ladywell Rd. SE13 . . . .3C **108**
Ladywell St. E15 . . . . . .5B **54**
LA Fitness
    Aldgate 4F **19**
    (off Mansell St.)
    Bayswater 1D **73**
    (off Moscow Rd.)
    Bloomsbury 5F 7
    (off Theobald's Rd.)
    Golders Green . . .2B **30**
    Gospel Oak 1D **47**
    Leadenhall 3E **19**
    (off Leadenhall St.)
    London Wall 1B **18**
    Marylebone
    . . . . .5A 4 (4B **60**)

LA Fitness
    Novello 4F **15**
    Piccadilly 5B **14**
    (off Regent St.)
    St Pauls 1F **17**
    (off Little Britain)
    South Kensington
    . . . . .5A **74**
    Sydenham 4E **121**
    Victoria 5F **21**
    (off Bressenden Pl.)
    West India Quay
    . . . . .1C **80**
Lafone St.
    SE1 . . . . . . .3F **27** (3B **78**)
Lagado M. SE16 . . . . . .2F **79**
Lagare Apartments
    SE1 . . . . .3E **25**
    (off Surrey Row)
Lagonda Ho. E3 . . . . . . .3C **66**
    (off Tidworth Rd.)
Lagonier Ho. EC1 . . . . .2A **10**
    (off Ironmonger Row)
Laing Ho. SE5 . . . . .3E **91**
Lainson St. SW18 . . . . .5C **100**
Lairdale Cl. SE21 . . . . .1E **119**
Laird Ho. SE5 . . . . .3E **91**
    (off Redcar St.)
Lairs Cl. N7 . . . . .2A **48**
Laitwood Rd. SW12 . . . .1D **117**
Lakanal SE5 . . . . .4A **92**
    (off Sceaux Gdns.)
Lake Av. BR1: Brom . . .5C **124**
Lake Cl. SW19 . . . . .5B **114**
Lake Ho. SE1 . . . . .4F **25**
    (off Southwark Bri. Rd.)
Lake Ho. Rd. E11 . . . . . .5C **40**
Laker Ct. SW4 . . . . .4A **90**
Laker Ind. Est.
    BR3: Beck 5A **122**
Lake Rd. E10 . . . . .2D **39**
    SW19 . . . . .5B **114**
Laker Pl. SW15 . . . . . . .4A **100**
Lakeside Cl. N4 . . . . .4E **35**
Lakeside Rd. W14 . . . . . .4F **71**
Lakeside Ter. EC2 . . . . .5A **10**
Lake Vw. Cl. SW1 . . . . . .5E **21**
    (off Bressenden Pl.)
Lake Vw. Est. E3 . . . . . .1A **66**
Lakeview Rd. SE27 . . . .5C **118**
Lakis Cl. NW3 . . . . .1E **45**
Laleham Ho. E2 . . . . .3F **11**
    (off Camlet St.)
Laleham Rd. SE6 . . . . . .5E **109**
Lalor St. SW6 . . . . .5A **86**
Lambard Ho. SE10 . . . . .3E **95**
    (off Langdale Rd.)
Lamb Ct. E14 . . . . .1A **80**
    (off Narrow St.)
Lamberhurst Ho.
    SE15 . . . . .2E **93**
Lamberhurst Rd.
    SE27 . . . . .4C **118**
Lambert Jones M.
    EC2 . . . . .5F **9**
Lambert Rd. E16 . . . . . . .5D **69**
    SW2 . . . . .3A **104**
Lambert St. N1 . . . . .4C **48**
LAMBETH 5F **23** (4B **76**)
Lambeth Bri. SW1 . . . . . .5A **76**

Lambeth Crematorium
    SW17 . . . . .4E **115**
Lambeth High St.
    SE1 . . . . .5B **76**
Lambeth Hill
    EC4 . . . . . . .4F **17** (1E **77**)
Lambeth Palace
    . . . . .5F **23** (4B **76**)
Lambeth Pal. Rd.
    SE1 . . . . . . .5F **23** (4B **76**)
Lambeth Rd.
    SE1 . . . . . . .5B **24** (5B **76**)
    SE11 . . . . . .5A **24** (5B **76**)
Lambeth Towers
    SE11 . . . . .5B **24**
Lambeth Wlk. SE11 . . . . .5B **76**
    (not continuous)
Lambfold Ho. N7 . . . . . . .3A **48**
    (off North Rd.)
Lamb Ho. SE10 . . . . .3E **91**
    (off Elmington Est.)
    SE10 . . . . .2E **95**
    (off Haddo St.)
Lamb La. E8 . . . . .4D **51**
Lamble St. NW5 . . . . . . .2C **46**
Lambolle Pl. NW3 . . . . . .3A **46**
Lambolle Rd. NW3 . . . . . .3A **46**
Lambourn Cl. NW5 . . . . . .1E **47**
Lambourne Av.
    SW19 . . . . .4B **114**
Lambourne Gro. SE16 . . .1F **93**
Lambourne Ho. NW8 . . . .4F **59**
    (off Broadley St.)
Lambourne Pl. SE3 . . . . . .4D **97**
Lambourne Rd. E11 . . . . .2E **39**
Lamburn Rd. SW4 . . . . .1D **103**
Lambrook Ho. SE15 . . . . .4C **92**
Lambrook Ter. SW6 . . . . .4A **86**
Lamb's Bldgs.
    EC1 . . . . .4B **10** (3F **63**)
Lamb's Conduit Pas.
    WC1 . . . . .5F 7 (4B **62**)
Lamb's Conduit St.
    WC1 . . . . . . .4F 7 (3B **62**)
    (not continuous)
Lambscroft Av. SE9 . . . .3E **125**
Lamb's M. N1 . . . . .5D **49**
Lamb's Pas.
    EC1 . . . . .5B **10** (3F **63**)
Lamb St. E1 . . . . . .5F **11** (4B **64**)
Lambton M. N19 . . . . .3A **34**
    (off Lambton Rd.)
Lambton Pl. W11 . . . . . . .1B **72**
Lambton Rd. N19 . . . . . . .3A **34**
Lamb Wlk.
    SE1 . . . . . . .4D **27** (3A **78**)
LAMDA 1F **85**
    (off Talgarth Rd.)
LAMDA Theatre 5C **72**
    (off Logan Pl.)
Lamerock Rd.
    BR1: Brom 4B **124**
Lamerton St. SE8 . . . . . .2C **94**
Lamington St. W6 . . . . . .5D **71**
Lamlash St. SE11 . . . . . .5D **77**
Lamley Ho. SE10 . . . . . . .3D **95**
    (off Ashburnham Pl.)
Lammas Grn. SE26 . . . .3D **121**
Lammas Rd. E9 . . . . .4F **51**
    E10 . . . . .4A **38**

Lammermoor Rd.
SW12 . . . . 5D 103
Lamont Rd. SW10 . . . . . 2F 87
Lamont Rd. Pas.
SW10 . . . . 2F 87
(off Lamont Rd.)
Lampard Gro. N16 . . . . . 3B 36
Lampern Sq. E2 . . . . . . 2C 64
Lampeter Cl. NW9 . . . . 1A 28
Lampeter Sq. W6 . . . . . 2A 86
Lamplighter Cl. E1 . . . . 3E 65
Lampmead Rd.
SE12 . . . . 3B 110
Lamp Office Ct. WC1 . . . 4F 7
Lampton Ho. Cl.
SW19 . . . . 4F 113
Lanain Ct. SE12 . . . . . 5B 110
Lanark Ho. SE1 . . . . . . 1C 92
(off Old Kent Rd.)
Lanark Mans. W9 . . . . . 3E 59
(off Lanark Rd.)
W12 . . . . 3E 71
(off Pennard Rd.)
Lanark M. W9 . . . . 2E 59
Lanark Pl. W9 . . . . 3E 59
Lanark Rd. W9 . . . . . . 1D 59
Lanark Sq. E14 . . . . . . 4D 81
Lanbury Rd. SE15 . . . . 2F 107
Lancashire Ct. W1 . . . . 4E 13
Lancaster Av. SE27 . . . 2D 119
SW19 . . . . 5F 113
Lancaster Cl. N1 . . . . . 4A 50
W2 . . . . 1D 73
(off St Petersburgh Pl.)
Lancaster Ct. SE27 . . . 2D 119
SW6 . . . . 3B 86
W2 . . . . 1E 73
(off Lancaster Ga.)
Lancaster Dr. E14 . . . . 2E 81
NW3 . . . . 3A 46
Lancaster Gdns.
SW19 . . . . 5A 114
Lancaster Ga. W2 . . . . 1E 73
Lancaster Gro. NW3 . . . 3F 45
Lancaster Hall E16 . . . . 2C 82
(off Wesley Av.)
Lancaster House 3F 21
Lancaster Ho. E11 . . . . 4B 40
Lancaster Lodge
W11 . . . . 5A 58
(off Lancaster Rd.)
Lancaster M. SW18 . . . 3D 101
W2 . . . . 1E 73
Lancaster Pl. SW19 . . . 5F 113
WC2 . . . . . . 4F 15 (1B 76)
Lancaster Rd. E7 . . . . . 4C 54
E11 . . . . 4A 40
N4 . . . . 2B 34
NW10 . . . . 2C 42
SW19 . . . . 5F 113
W11 . . . . 5A 58
Lancaster Stables
NW3 . . . . 3A 46
Lancaster St.
SE1 . . . . . . 4D 25 (3D 77)
Lancaster Ter. W2 . . . . 1F 73
Lancaster Wlk. W2 . . . . 2E 73
Lancefield Ho.
SE15 . . . . 2D 107
Lancefield St. W10 . . . . 2B 58

Lancell St. N16 . . . . . . 4B 36
Lancelot Pl. SW7 . . . . . 3B 74
Lancer Sq. W8 . . . . . . 3D 73
(off Kensington Chu. St.)
Lancey Cl. SE7 . . . . . . 5F 83
Lanchester Ct. W2 . . . . 5B 60
(off Seymour St.)
Lanchester Rd. N6 . . . . 1B 32
Lanchester Way
SE14 . . . . 4E 93
Lancing St.
NW1 . . . . . . 2B 6 (2F 61)
Lancresse Ct. N1 . . . . . 5A 50
(off De Beauvoir Est.)
Landale Ho. SE16 . . . . . 4E 79
(off Lower Rd.)
Landcroft Rd. SE22 . . . 3B 106
Landells Rd. SE22 . . . . 4B 106
Landford Rd. SW15 . . . . 1E 99
Landgrove Rd.
SW19 . . . . 5C 114
Landin Ho. E14 . . . . . . 5C 66
(off Thomas Rd.)
Landleys Fld. N7 . . . . . 2F 47
(off Long Mdw.)
Landmann Ho. SE16 . . . 5D 79
(off Rennie Est.)
Landmann Way SE14 . . 1F 93
Landmark East Twr.
E14 . . . . 3C 80
(off Marsh Wall)
Landmark Hgts. E5 . . . . 1A 52
Landmark Ho. W6 . . . . . 1E 85
(off Hammersmith Bri. Rd.)
Landmark Sq. E14 . . . . 3C 80
Landmark West Twr.
E14 . . . . 3C 80
(off Marsh Wall)
Landon Pl.
SW1 . . . . . . 5A 20 (4B 74)
Landon's Cl. E14 . . . . . 2E 81
Landon Wlk. E14 . . . . . 1D 81
Landor Ho. SE5 . . . . . . 3F 91
(off Elmington Est.)
W2 . . . . 4C 58
(off Westbourne Pk. Rd.)
Landor Rd. SW9 . . . . . 1A 104
Landor Theatre 1A 104
Landor Wlk. W12 . . . . . 3C 70
(off Plender St.)
Landrake NW1 . . . . . . 5E 47
Landridge Rd. SW6 . . . . 5B 86
Landrock Rd. N8 . . . . . 1A 34
Landseer Ho. NW8 . . . . 3F 59
(off Frampton St.)
SW1 . . . . 5F 75
(off Herrick St.)
SW11 . . . . 4C 88
Landseer Rd. N19 . . . . 5A 34
(not continuous)
Landulph Ho. SE11 . . . . 1C 90
(off Kennings Way)
Landward Ct. W1 . . . . . 5A 60
(off Harrowby St.)
Lane, The NW8 . . . . . . 1E 59
SE3 . . . . 1C 110
Lane End SW15 . . . . . . 4F 99
Lanercost Cl. SW2 . . . . 2C 118
Lanercost Rd. SW2 . . . 2C 118

Lanesborough Ct. N1 . . 1D 11
(off Fanshaw St.)
Lanesborough Pl.
SW1 . . . . 3C 20
Lanesborough Way
SW17 . . . . 3F 115
Laneway SW15 . . . . . . 3D 99
Laney Ho. EC1 . . . . . . 5B 8
(off Leather La.)
Lanfranc Rd. E3 . . . . . 1A 66
Lanfrey Pl. W14 . . . . . . 1B 86
Langbourne Av. N6 . . . . 4C 32
Langbourne La.
E17 . . . . 1A 38
Langbourne Mans.
N6 . . . . 4C 32
Langbourne Pl. E14 . . . 1D 95
Langbrook Rd. SE3 . . . 1F 111
Langdale NW1 . . . . 1F 5
(off Stanhope St.)
Langdale Cl. SE17 . . . . 2E 91
Langdale Ho. SW1 . . . . 1E 89
(off Churchill Gdns.)
Langdale Rd. SE10 . . . 3E 95
Langdale St. E1 . . . . . . 5D 65
Langdon Ct. EC1 . . . . . 1E 9
(off City Rd.)
NW10 . . . . 5A 42
Langdon Ho. E14 . . . . . 5E 67
(off Ida St.)
Langdon Pk. Leisure Cen.
. . . . 5E 67
Langdon Pk. Rd. N6 . . . 2E 33
Langdon Way SE1 . . . . 5C 78
Langford Cl. E8 . . . . . . 2C 50
NW8 . . . . 1E 59
Langford Ct. NW8 . . . . 1E 59
(off Abbey Rd.)
Langford Grn. SE5 . . . . 1A 106
Langford Ho. SE8 . . . . . 2C 94
Langford M. N1 . . . . . . 4C 48
SW11 . . . . 2F 101
(off St John's Hill)
Langford Pl. NW8 . . . . 1E 59
Langford Rd. SW6 . . . . 5D 87
Langham Mans.
SW5 . . . . 1D 87
(off Earl's Ct. Sq.)
Langham Pl.
W1 . . . . 1E 13 (4D 61)
W4 . . . . 2A 84
Langham St.
W1 . . . . 1E 13 (4D 61)
(not continuous)
Langholm Cl. SW12 . . . 5F 103
Langhorne Ct. NW8 . . . 4F 45
(off Dorman Way)
Lang Ho. SW8 . . . . 3A 90
(off Hartington Rd.)
Langland Gdns. NW3 . . 2D 45
Langland Ho. SE5 . . . . . 3F 91
(off Edmund St.)
Langler Rd. NW10 . . . . 1E 57
Langley Ct.
WC2 . . . . . . 4D 15 (1A 76)
Langley Cres. E11 . . . . 2E 41
Langley Dr. E11 . . . . . . 2D 41
Langley Ho. W2 . . . . . . 4C 58
(off Alfred Rd.)
Langley La. SW8 . . . . . 2B 90

Langley Mans. *SW8* 2B **90**
Langley St.
  WC2 . . . . .3D **15** (5A **62**)
  (off Langley La.)
Langmead Ho. *E3* 2D **67**
  (off Bruce Rd.)
Langmead St.
  SE27 . . . . .4D **119**
Langmore Ho. *E1* 5C **64**
  (off Stutfield St.)
Langport Ho. SW9 . . . . . .5D **91**
Langroyd Rd. SW17 . . . . .2B **116**
Langside Av. SW15 . . . . .2C **98**
Langston Hughes Cl.
  SE24 . . . . .2D **105**
Lang St. E1 . . . . .3E **65**
Langthorn Ct.
  EC2 . . . . .2B **18** (5F **63**)
Langthorne Ct.
  BR1: Brom 4E **123**
Langthorne Ho. *E3* 2B **66**
  (off Merchant St.)
Langthorne Rd. E11 . . . . .5E **39**
  (not continuous)
Langthorne St. SW6 . . . . .3F **85**
Langton Cl.
  WC1 . . . . . .3A **8** (3B **62**)
Langton Ho. *SE11* 5B **76**
  (off Lambeth Wlk.)
Langton Pl. SW18 . . . . . .1C **114**
Langton Ri. SE23 . . . . . .5D **107**
Langton Rd. NW2 . . . . . .5E **29**
  SW9 . . . . .3D **91**
Langton St. SW10 . . . . . .2E **87**
Langton Way SE3 . . . . . .4B **96**
Langtry Pl. SW6 . . . . . . .2C **86**
Langtry Rd. NW8 . . . . . . .5D **45**
Langtry Wlk. NW8 . . . . . .5D **45**
Lanhill Rd. W9 . . . . .3C **58**
Lanier Rd. SE13 . . . . . . .4F **109**
Lannoy Point *SW6* 3A **86**
  (off Pellant Rd.)
Lanrick Rd. E14 . . . . . . .5F **67**
Lansbury Est. E14 . . . . . .5D **67**
Lansbury Gdns. E14 . . . . .5F **67**
Lanscombe Wlk.
  SW8 . . . . .4A **90**
Lansdell Ho. SW2 . . . . . .4C **104**
Lansdowne Ct. *W11* 1A **72**
  (off Lansdowne Ri.)
Lansdowne Cres.
  W11 . . . . .1A **72**
Lansdowne Dr. E8 . . . . . .3C **50**
Lansdowne Gdns.
  SW8 . . . . .4A **90**
Lansdowne Grn.
  SW8 . . . . .4A **90**
Lansdowne Gro.
  NW10 . . . . .1A **42**
Lansdowne Hill
  SE27 . . . . .3D **119**
Lansdowne Ho.
  W11 . . . . .2B **72**
  (off Ladbroke Rd.)
Lansdowne La. SE7 . . . . .2F **97**
Lansdowne M. SE7 . . . . .1F **97**
  W11 . . . . .2B **72**
Lansdowne Pl.
  SE1 . . . . . .5C **26** (4F **77**)
Lansdowne Ri. W11 . . . . .1A **72**

Lansdowne Rd. E11 . . . . .4B **40**
  E17 . . . . .1C **38**
  W11 . . . . .1A **72**
Lansdowne Row
  W1 . . . . .1E **21** (2D **75**)
Lansdowne Ter.
  WC1 . . . . . . .4E **7** (3A **62**)
Lansdowne Wlk.
  W11 . . . . .2B **72**
Lansdowne Way SW8 . . . .4F **89**
Lansdowne Wood Cl.
  SE27 . . . . .3D **119**
Lansdowne Workshops
  SE7 . . . . .1E **97**
Lansdown Rd. E7 . . . . . . .4E **55**
Lanson Apartments
  SW8 . . . . .3D **89**
Lantern *SE1* 3D **78**
  (off Lant St.)
Lantern Cl. SW15 . . . . . .2C **98**
Lanterns Way E14 . . . . . .4C **80**
Lant Ho. *SE1* 4F **25**
  (off Toulmin St.)
Lant St. SE1 . . . .3F **25** (3E **77**)
Lanvanor Rd. SE15 . . . . .5E **93**
Lanyard Ho. SE8 . . . . . . .5B **80**
Lapford Cl. W9 . . . . .3B **58**
Lapis M. E15 . . . . .1E **53**
Lapse Wood Wlk.
  SE23 . . . . .1D **121**
Lapwing Cl. *SE1* 4A **26**
  (off Swan St.)
Lapwing Ter. E7 . . . . . . .2F **55**
Lapwing Twr. *SE8* 2B **94**
  (off Taylor Cl.)
Lapworth Ct. *W2* 4D **59**
  (off Delamere Ter.)
Lara Cl. SE13 . . . . .4E **109**
Larch Av. W3 . . . . .2A **70**
Larch Cl. E13 . . . . .3D **69**
  N19 . . . . .4E **33**
  SE8 . . . . .2B **94**
  SW12 . . . . .2D **117**
Larch Ct. *SE1* 4D **27**
  (off Royal Oak Yd.)
  W9 . . . . .4C **58**
  (off Admiral Wlk.)
Larch Ho. *SE16* 3E **79**
  (off Ainsty Est.)
  W10 . . . . .3A **58**
  (off Rowan Wlk.)
Larch Rd. E10 . . . . .4C **38**
  NW2 . . . . .1E **43**
Larcom St. SE17 . . . . . . .5E **77**
Larden Rd. W3 . . . . .2A **70**
Larissa St. SE17 . . . . . . .1F **91**
Larkbere Rd. SE26 . . . . . .4A **122**
Larkhall La. SW4 . . . . . . .5F **89**
Larkhall Ri. SW4 . . . . . . .1E **103**
  (not continuous)
Lark Row E2 . . . . .5E **51**
Larkspur Cl. E6 . . . . .4F **69**
Larnaca Ho. *SE1* 5F **27**
  (off Grange Wlk.)
Larnach Rd. W6 . . . . .2F **85**
Larpent Av. SW15 . . . . . .3E **99**
Lascar Wharf Bldg.
  E14 . . . . .5A **66**
  (off Parnham St.)
Lascelles Cl. E11 . . . . . . .4F **39**

Lascelles Ho. NW1 . . . .3A **60**
  (off Harewood Av.)
Lassell St. SE10 . . . . . . .1F **95**
Lasseter Pl. SE3 . . . . . . .3B **96**
Latchmere Leisure Cen.
  . . . . .5B **88**
Latchmere Pas.
  SW11 . . . . .5A **88**
Latchmere Rd. SW11 . . . .5B **88**
Latchmere St. SW11 . . . .5B **88**
Latham Ct. *SW5* 5C **72**
  (off W. Cromwell Rd.)
Latham Ho. *E1* 5F **65**
  (off Chudleigh St.)
Latimer Ho. E9 . . . . .3F **51**
  W11 . . . . .1B **72**
  (off Kensington Pk. Rd.)
Latimer Ind. Est.
  W10 . . . . .5E **57**
Latimer Pl. W10 . . . . . . .5E **57**
Latimer Rd. E7 . . . . .1D **55**
  N15 . . . . .1A **36**
  W10 . . . . .4E **57**
  (not continuous)
Latitude Ho. *NW1* 5D **47**
  (off Oval Rd.)
Latona Ct. SW9 . . . . . . .3C **90**
  (off Caldwell St.)
Latona Rd. SE15 . . . . . . .2C **92**
Lattimer Pl. W4 . . . . .3A **84**
Latvia Ct. *SE17* 1E **91**
  (off Macleod St.)
Latymer Ct. W6 . . . . .5F **71**
Lauderdale Community
  Arts Cen. 3D **33**
  (within Lauderdale House)
Lauderdale House 3D **33**
Lauderdale Ho. SW9 . . . .4C **90**
  (off Gosling Way)
Lauderdale Mans.
  W9 . . . . .2D **59**
  (off Lauderdale Rd.)
Lauderdale Pde.
  W9 . . . . .3D **59**
Lauderdale Pl. *EC2* 5F **9**
  (off Beech St.)
Lauderdale Rd. W9 . . . . .2D **59**
Lauderdale Twr. EC2 . . . . .5F **9**
Laud St. SE11 . . . . .1B **90**
Laugan Wlk. SE17 . . . . . .1E **91**
Launcelot Rd.
  BR1: Brom 4C **124**
Launcelot St.
  SE1 . . . . . .4B **24** (3C **76**)
Launceston Pl. W8 . . . . . .4E **73**
Launch St. E14 . . . . .4E **81**
Laundress La. N16 . . . . . .5C **36**
Laundry La. N1 . . . . .5E **49**
Laundry M. SE23 . . . . . . .5A **108**
Laundry Rd. W6 . . . . .2A **86**
Laura Pl. E5 . . . . .1E **51**
Laura Ter. N4 . . . . .4D **35**
Laurel Apartments
  SE17 . . . . .5A **78**
  (off Townsend St.)
Laurel Bank Gdns.
  SW6 . . . . .5B **86**
Laurel Cl. N19 . . . . .4E **33**
  SW17 . . . . .5A **116**
Laurel Gro. SE26 . . . . . . .4F **121**

Laurel Ho. *E3* 5B *52*
(off Hornbeam St.)
SE8 . . . . .2B *94*
Laurel Rd. SW13 . . . . .5C *84*
Laurels, The NW10 . . . .5D *43*
SW9 . . . . .3D *91*
(off Langton St.)
Laurel St. E8 . . . . .3B *50*
Laurence Ct. E10 . . . . .2D *39*
W11 . . . . .1A *72*
(off Lansdowne Rd.)
Laurence M. W12 . . . . .3C *70*
Laurence Pountney Hill
EC4 . . . . .4B *18* (1F *77*)
Laurence Pountney La.
EC4 . . . . .4B *18* (1F *77*)
Laurie Gro. SE14 . . . . .4A *94*
Laurie Ho. *SE1* 5E *25*
(off St George's Rd.)
W8 . . . . .2C *72*
(off Airlie Gdns.)
Laurier Rd. NW5 . . . . . .5D *33*
Lauriston Ho. E9 . . . . . .4E *51*
(off Lauriston Rd.)
Lauriston Rd. E9 . . . . . .4E *51*
SW19 . . . . .5F *113*
Lausanne Rd.
SE15 . . . . .4E *93*
Lavell St. N16 . . . . .1F *49*
Lavender Cl. SW3 . . . . .2F *87*
Lavender Gdns.
SW11 . . . . .2B *102*
Lavender Gro. E8 . . . . .4C *50*
Lavender Hill SW11 . . . .2A *102*
Lavender Ho. *SE16* 2F *79*
(off Rotherhithe St.)
Lavender Pond Nature Pk.
. . . . .2A *80*
Lavender Rd. SE16 . . . .2A *80*
SW11 . . . . .1F *101*
Lavender St. E15 . . . . .3A *54*
Lavender Sweep
SW11 . . . . .2B *102*
Lavender Ter. SW11 . . .1A *102*
Lavender Wlk.
SW11 . . . . .2B *102*
Lavendon Ho. *NW8* 3A *60*
(off Paveley St.)
Lavengro Rd. SE27 . . . .2E *119*
Lavenham Rd.
SW18 . . . . .2B *114*
Lavers Rd. N16 . . . . . . .5A *36*
Laverstoke Gdns.
SW15 . . . . .5B *98*
Laverton M. SW5 . . . . .5D *73*
Laverton Pl. SW5 . . . . .5D *73*
Lavette Ho. E3 . . . . . . .2C *66*
(off Rainhill Way)
Lavina Gro. N1 . . . . . . .1B *62*
Lavington Cl. E9 . . . . . .3B *52*
Lavington St.
SE1 . . . . . .2E *25* (2D *77*)
Lavisham Ho.
BR1: Brom 5D *125*
Lawes Ho. *W10* 2B *58*
(off Lancefield St.)
Lawford Rd. N1 . . . . . . .4A *50*
NW5 . . . . .3E *47*
Lawfords Wharf NW1 . . .4E *47*
(off Lyme St.)

Lawless Ho. *E14* 1E *81*
(off Bazely St.)
Lawless St. E14 . . . . . . .1D *81*
Lawley St. E5 . . . . .1E *51*
Lawnfield Ct. NW6 . . . . .4F *43*
(off Coverdale Rd.)
Lawn Ho. Cl. E14 . . . . . .3E *81*
Lawn La. SW8 . . . . .2B *90*
Lawn Rd. NW3 . . . . .2B *46*
Lawns, The SE3 . . . . . .1B *110*
SW19 . . . . .5B *114*
Lawnside SE3 . . . . . . .2B *110*
Lawn Ter. SE3 . . . . . . .1A *110*
Lawrence Av. NW10 . . . .5A *42*
Lawrence Bldgs. N16 . . .5B *36*
Lawrence Cl. E3 . . . . . .2C *66*
W12 . . . . .1D *71*
Lawrence Ct. N16 . . . . .5B *36*
(off Smalley Rd. Est.)
Lawrence Ho. NW1 . . . .4D *47*
(off Hawley Cres.)
SW1 . . . . .5F *75*
(off Cureton St.)
Lawrence La.
EC2 . . . . .2A *18* (5E *63*)
Lawrence Mans.
SW3 . . . . .2A *88*
(off Lordship Pl.)
Lawrence Pl. *N1* 5A *48*
(off Brydon Wlk.)
Lawrence Rd. E6 . . . . . .5F *55*
E13 . . . . .5D *55*
Lawrence St. E16 . . . . .4B *68*
SW3 . . . . .2A *88*
Lawrence Trad. Est.
SE10 . . . . .5A *82*
Lawrie Ho. *SW19* 5D *115*
(off Dunsford Rd.)
Lawrie Pk. Av.
SE26 . . . . .5D *121*
Lawrie Pk. Cres.
SE26 . . . . .5D *121*
Lawrie Pk. Gdns.
SE26 . . . . .4D *121*
Lawrie Pk. Rd.
SE26 . . . . .5D *121*
Lawson Ho. E16 . . . . . . .4E *69*
SW19 . . . . .3F *113*
Lawson Ct. N4 . . . . .3B *34*
(off Lorne Rd.)
Lawson Ho. W12 . . . . . .1D *71*
(off White City Est.)
Law St. SE1 . . . .5C *26* (4F *77*)
Lawton Rd. E3 . . . . .2A *66*
(not continuous)
E10 . . . . .3E *39*
Laxfield Ct. E8 . . . . .5C *50*
(off Pownall Rd.)
Laxford Ho. *SW1* 5C *74*
(off Cundy St.)
Laxley Cl. SE5 . . . . .3D *91*
Laxton Pl.
NW1 . . . . . .3E *5* (3D *61*)
Layard Rd. SE16 . . . . . .5D *79*
Layard Sq. SE16 . . . . . .5D *79*
Laybourne Ho. *E14* 3C *80*
(off Admirals Way)
Laycock St. N1 . . . . .3C *48*
Layfield Cl. NW4 . . . . . . .2D *29*
Layfield Cres. NW4 . . . .2D *29*

Layfield Ho. *SE10* 1C *96*
(off Kemsing Rd.)
Layfield Rd. NW4 . . . . . .2D *29*
Laystall Ct. WC1 . . . . . . .4B *8*
(off Mt. Pleasant)
Laystall St.
EC1 . . . . . . .4B *8* (3C *62*)
Layzell Wlk. SE9 . . . . . .1F *125*
Lazar Wlk. N7 . . . . .4B *34*
Lazenby Ct. WC2 . . . . . .4D *15*
Leabank Sq. E9 . . . . . . .3C *52*
Leabank Vw. N15 . . . . . .1C *36*
Lea Bon Ct. *E15* 5B *54*
(off Plaistow Gro.)
Leabourne Rd. N16 . . . . .2C *36*
LEA BRIDGE 5F *37*
Lea Bri. Ind. Cen.
E10 . . . . .3A *38*
Lea Bri. Rd. E5 . . . . .5E *37*
E10 . . . . .5E *37*
E17 . . . . .2C *38*
Lea Ct. E13 . . . . .2C *68*
Leacroft Av. SW12 . . . . .5B *102*
Leadale Rd. N15 . . . . . .1C *36*
N16 . . . . .1C *36*
Leadenhall Mkt.
EC3 . . . . . .3D *19* (5A *64*)
Leadenhall Pl.
EC3 . . . . . .3D *19* (5A *64*)
Leadenhall St.
EC3 . . . . . .3D *19* (5A *64*)
Leadenham Ct. E3 . . . . .3C *66*
Leaf Gro. SE27 . . . . . . .5C *118*
Leafy Oak Rd. SE12 . . . .4E *125*
Leagrave St. E5 . . . . . . .5E *37*
Lea Hall Gdns. E10 . . . . .3C *38*
Lea Hall Rd. E10 . . . . . .3C *38*
Lea Ho. NW8 . . . . .3A *60*
(off Salisbury St.)
Leahurst Rd. SE13 . . . . .3F *109*
LEA INTERCHANGE 2C *52*
Leake Ct.
SE1 . . . . . .4A *24* (3B *76*)
Leake St.
SE1 . . . . . .3A *24* (3B *76*)
(not continuous)
Lealand Rd. N15 . . . . . .1B *36*
Leamington Av.
BR1: Brom 5E *125*
E17 . . . . .1C *38*
Leamington Cl.
BR1: Brom 4E *125*
Leamington Ct. SE3 . . . .2A *96*
Leamington Ho. W11 . . . .4B *58*
(off Tavistock Rd.)
Leamington Rd. Vs.
W11 . . . . .4B *58*
Leamore Ct. E2 . . . . . . .2F *65*
Leamore St. W6 . . . . . . .5E *71*
LEAMOUTH 1A *82*
Leamouth Rd. E6 . . . . . .4F *69*
E14 . . . . .5F *67*
Leander Ct. *E9* 4F *51*
(off Lauriston Rd.)
SE8 . . . . .4C *94*
Leander Rd. SW2 . . . . . .4B *104*
Lea Pk. Trad. Est.
E10 . . . . .2B *38*
Leary Ho. SE11 . . . . . . .1B *90*
Leaside Rd. E5 . . . . .3E *37*

Leasowes Rd. E10 . . . . .3C **38**
Lea Sq. E3 . . . . .5B **52**
Leatherdale St. E1 . . . .3E **65**
(Harpley Sq.)
E1 . . . . .2F **65**
(Portelet Rd.)
Leather Gdns. E15 . . . . .5A **54**
Leatherhead Cl. N16 . . .3B **36**
Leather La.
EC1 . . . . . .5B **8** (4C **62**)
(not continuous)
Leathermarket, The
SE1 . . . . .4D **27**
Leathermarket Ct.
SE1 . . . . . .4D **27** (3A **78**)
Leathermarket St.
SE1 . . . . . .4D **27** (3A **78**)
Leather Rd. SE16 . . . . .5F **79**
Leather St. E1 . . . . . . .1F **79**
Leathwaite Rd.
SW11 . . . . .2B **102**
Leathwell Rd. SE8 . . . .5D **95**
Lea Valley Bus. Pk.
E10 . . . . .4A **38**
Lea Vw. Ho. E5 . . . . . . .3D **37**
Leaway E10 . . . . .3F **37**
Lebanon Gdns.
SW18 . . . . .4C **100**
Lebanon Rd. SW18 . . .3C **100**
Lebrun Sq. SE3 . . . . . .2D **111**
Lebus Ho. NW8 . . . . . .1A **60**
(off Cochrane St.)
Lechmere Rd. NW2 . . . .3D **43**
Leckford Rd. SW18 . . . .2E **115**
Leckhampton Pl.
SW2 . . . . .5C **104**
Lecky St. SW7 . . . . . . .1F **87**
Leclair Ho. SE3 . . . . . .1D **111**
Leconfield Av. SW13 . .1B **98**
Leconfield Ho. SE5 . . .2A **106**
Leconfield Rd. N5 . . . .1F **49**
Le Cordon Bleu London
Culinary Arts Institute
. . . . .1C **12**
(off Marylebone La.)
Leda Ct. SW9 . . . . .3C **90**
(off Caldwell St.)
Ledam Ho. EC1 . . . . . . .5B **8**
(off Bourne Est.)
Ledbury Ho. SE22 . . . .1A **106**
W11 . . . . .5B **58**
(off Colville Rd.)
Ledbury M. Nth.
W11 . . . . .1C **72**
Ledbury M. W. W11 . . .1C **72**
Ledbury Rd. W11 . . . . .5B **58**
Ledbury St. SE15 . . . . .3C **92**
LEE 4C **110**
Lee Bri. SE13 . . . . .1E **109**
Lee Chu. St. SE13 . . . .2A **110**
Lee Conservancy Rd.
E9 . . . . .2B **52**
Lee Ct. SE13 . . . . .2F **109**
(off Lee High Rd.)
Leeds Ct. EC1 . . . . .3D **9**
(off St John St.)
Leeds Pl. N4 . . . . .3B **34**
Leefern Rd. W12 . . . . . .3C **70**
Leegate SE12 . . . . .3B **110**
LEE GREEN 3B **110**

Lee High Rd. SE12 . . . .1E **109**
SE13 . . . . .1E **109**
Leeke St. WC1 . . .1F **7** (2B **62**)
Leeland Way NW10 . . .1B **42**
Lee Pk. SE3 . . . . .2B **110**
Leerdam Dr. E14 . . . . . .4E **81**
Lee Rd. SE3 . . . . .1B **110**
Lees Ct. W1 . . . . .4B **12**
(off Lees Pl.)
Lees Ho. SE17 . . . . .1F **91**
(off Inville Rd.)
Leeside SE16 . . . . .2F **79**
(off Rotherhithe St.)
Leeside Cres. NW11 . . .1A **30**
Leeson Rd. SE24 . . . . .2C **104**
Lees Pl. W1 . . . .4B **12** (1C **74**)
Lee St. E8 . . . . .5B **50**
Lee Ter. SE3 . . . . .1A **110**
SE13 . . . . .1A **110**
Lee Valley Ice Cen. . . .4F **37**
Leeve Ho. W10 . . . . . . .2B **58**
(off Lancefield St.)
Leeward Ct. E1 . . . . . . .1C **78**
Leeward Gdns.
SW19 . . . . .5A **114**
Leeward Ho. N1 . . . . . .5A **50**
(off New Era Est.)
Leeway SE8 . . . . .1B **94**
Leewood Cl. SE12 . . . .4C **110**
Lefevre Wlk. E3 . . . . . .1C **66**
Leff Ho. NW6 . . . . .5A **44**
Lefroy Ho. SE1 . . . . . . .4F **25**
(off Southwark Bri. Rd.)
Lefroy Rd. W12 . . . . . . .3B **70**
Legard Rd. N5 . . . . .5D **35**
Legatt Rd. SE9 . . . . . . .3F **111**
Leggatt Rd. E15 . . . . . .1E **67**
Legge St. SE13 . . . . . . .3E **109**
Leghorn Rd. NW10 . . . .1B **56**
Legion Cl. N1 . . . . .4C **48**
Legion Ter. E3 . . . . .5B **52**
Leicester Ct. W9 . . . . . .4C **58**
(off Elmfield Way)
WC2 . . . . .4C **14**
Leicester Flds. WC2 . . .5C **14**
Leicester Ho. SW9 . . . .1D **105**
(off Loughborough Rd.)
Leicester Pl.
WC2 . . . . . .4C **14** (1F **75**)
Leicester Rd. E11 . . . . .1D **41**
NW10 . . . . .4A **42**
Leicester Sq.
WC2 . . . . . .5C **14** (1F **75**)
Leicester Square Theatre
. . . . .1F **75**
(off Leicester Pl.)
Leicester St.
WC2 . . . . . .4C **14** (1F **75**)
Leigham Av. SW16 . . . .3A **118**
Leigham Cl. SW16 . . . .3B **118**
Leigham Ct. Rd.
SW16 . . . . .2A **118**
Leigham Hall Pde.
SW16 . . . . .3A **118**
(off Streatham High Rd.)
Leigham Va. SW2 . . . . .3B **118**
SW16 . . . . .3B **118**
Leigh Ct. W14 . . . . .5B **72**
(off Avonmore Pl.)
Leigh Gdns. NW10 . . . .1E **57**

Leigh Orchard Cl.
SW16 . . . . .3B **118**
Leigh Pl. EC1 . . . . .5B **8** (4C **62**)
Leigh Rd. E10 . . . . .2E **39**
N5 . . . . .1D **49**
Leigh St. WC1 . . .2D **7** (2A **62**)
Leighton Cres. NW5 . . .2E **47**
Leighton Gdns.
NW10 . . . . .1D **57**
Leighton Gro. NW5 . . . .2E **47**
Leighton Ho. SW1 . . . . .5F **75**
(off Herrick St.)
Leighton House Mus.
. . . . .4B **72**
Leighton Mans. W14 . . .2A **86**
(off Greyhound Rd.)
Leighton Pl. NW5 . . . . .2E **47**
Leighton Rd. NW5 . . . . .2E **47**
Leila Parnell Pl. SE7 . . .2E **97**
Leinster Gdns. W2 . . . .5E **59**
Leinster M. W2 . . . . . . .1E **73**
Leinster Pl. W2 . . . . . . .5E **59**
Leinster Sq. W2 . . . . . .5C **58**
(not continuous)
Leinster Ter. W2 . . . . . .1E **73**
Leitch Ho. NW8 . . . . . . .4F **45**
(off Hilgrove Rd.)
Leithcote Gdns.
SW16 . . . . .4B **118**
Leithcote Path
SW16 . . . . .3B **118**
Leith Mans. W9 . . . . . . .2D **59**
(off Grantully Rd.)
Leith Yd. NW6 . . . . .5C **44**
(off Quex Rd.)
Lelitia Cl. E8 . . . . .5C **50**
Leman Pas. E1 . . . . . . .5C **64**
(off Leman St.)
Leman St. E1 . . . . .5B **64**
Le May Av. SE12 . . . . .3D **125**
Lemmon Rd. SE10 . . . . .2A **96**
Lemna Rd. E11 . . . . . . .2B **40**
Le Moal Ho. E1 . . . . . . .4E **65**
(off Stepney Way)
Lemon Tree Ho. E3 . . . .2B **66**
(off Bow Rd.)
Lemsford Cl. N15 . . . . .1C **36**
Lemsford Ct. N4 . . . . . .4E **35**
Lemuel St. SW18 . . . . .4E **101**
Lena Gdns. W6 . . . . . . .4E **71**
Lenanton Steps E14 . . .3C **80**
(off Manilla St.)
Len Bishop Ct. E1 . . . . .1F **79**
(off Schoolhouse La.)
Lendal Ter. SW4 . . . . . .1F **103**
Len Freeman Pl.
SW6 . . . . .2B **86**
W6 . . . . .5B **70**
(off Goldhawk Rd.)
Lenham Ho. SE1 . . . . . .4C **26**
(off Staple St.)
Lenham Rd. SE12 . . . . .2B **110**
Lennard Rd. SE20 . . . . .5F **121**
Lennon Rd. NW2 . . . . . .2E **43**
Lennox Gdns. NW10 . . .1B **42**
SW1 . . . . .4B **74**
Lennox Gdns. M.
SW1 . . . . .4B **74**
Lennox Rd. E17 . . . . . . .1B **38**
N4 . . . . .4B **34**

Lensbury Av. SW6 . . . . .5E **87**
Lens Rd. E7 . . . . .4E **55**
Lenthall Ho. *SW1* 1E **89**
  (off Churchill Gdns.)
Lenthall Rd. E8 . . . . .4C **50**
Lenthorp Rd. SE10 . . . . . .5B **82**
Lentmead Rd.
  BR1: Brom 3B **124**
Lenton Ter. N4 . . . . .4C **34**
Len Williams Ct.
  NW6 . . . . .1C **58**
Leof Cres. SE6 . . . . .5D **123**
Leonard Ct. W8 . . . . .4C **72**
  WC1 . . . . .3C **6** (3F **61**)
Leonard Pl. N16 . . . . .1A **50**
Leonard Rd. E7 . . . . .1C **54**
Leonard St.
  EC2 . . . . .3C **10** (3F **63**)
Leonora Ho. *W9* 3E **59**
  (off Lanark Rd.)
Leonora Tyson M.
  SE21 . . . . .2F **119**
Leontine Cl. SE15 . . . . . . .3C **92**
Leopards Ct. EC1 . . . . .5B **8**
Leopold Av. SW19 . . . . . . .5B **114**
Leopold Bldgs. *E2* 1F **11**
  (off Columbia Rd.)
Leopold M. E9 . . . . .5E **51**
Leopold Rd. E17 . . . . .1C **38**
  NW10 . . . . .4A **42**
  SW19 . . . . .4B **114**
Leopold St. E3 . . . . .4B **66**
Leopold Ter. SW19 . . . . . .5B **114**
Leopold Wlk. *SE11* 1B **90**
  (off Tyers St.)
Leo St. SE15 . . . . .3D **93**
Leo Yd. EC1 . . . . .4E **9**
Leppoc Rd. SW4 . . . . .3F **103**
Leroy St. SE1 . . . . .5A **78**
Lerry Cl. W14 . . . . .2B **86**
Lescombe Cl. SE23 . . . . .3A **122**
Lescombe Rd. SE23 . . . . .3A **122**
Lesley Ct. *SW1* 5B **22**
  (off Strutton Ground)
Leslie Ho. *SW8* 3A **90**
  (off Wheatsheaf La.)
Leslie Prince Ct. SE5 . . . .3F **91**
Leslie Rd. E11 . . . . .1E **53**
  E16 . . . . .5D **69**
Lessar Av. SW4 . . . . .4E **103**
Lessingham Av.
  SW17 . . . . .4B **116**
Lessing St. SE23 . . . . . . .5A **108**
Lester Av. E15 . . . . .3A **68**
Lester Ct. *E3* 2D **67**
  (off Bruce Rd.)
Leswin Pl. N16 . . . . .5B **36**
Leswin Rd. N16 . . . . .5B **36**
Letchford Gdns.
  NW10 . . . . .2C **56**
Letchford Ho. *E3* 1C **66**
  (off Thomas Fyre Dr.)
Letchford M. NW10 . . . . . .2C **56**
Letchmore Ho. *W10* 3E **57**
  (off Sutton Way)
Letchworth St.
  SW17 . . . . .4B **116**
Lethbridge Cl. SE13 . . . . .4E **95**
Letterstone Rd. SW6 . . . . .3B **86**
Lettice St. SW6 . . . . .4B **86**

Lett Rd. E15 . . . . .4F **53**
  SW9 . . . . .5A **90**
Lettsom St. SE5 . . . . .5A **92**
Lettsom Wlk. E13 . . . . .1C **68**
Leucha Rd. E17 . . . . .1A **38**
Levana Cl. SW19 . . . . . . .1A **114**
Levant Ho. *E1* 3F **65**
  (off Ernest St.)
Levehurst Ho. SE27 . . . . .5E **119**
Levendale Rd.
  SE23 . . . . .2A **122**
Levenhurst Way SW4 . . . . .5A **90**
Leven Rd. E14 . . . . .4E **67**
Leverett St. SW3 . . . . .5A **74**
Leverington Pl.
  N1 . . . . .2C **10** (2F **63**)
Leverson St. SW16 . . . . . .5E **117**
Leverstock Ho. *SW3* 1A **88**
  (off Cale St.)
Lever St. EC1 . . . . .2E **9** (2D **63**)
Leverton Pl. NW5 . . . . .2E **47**
Leverton St. NW5 . . . . .2E **47**
Levison Way N19 . . . . .3F **33**
Levita Ho. NW1 . . . . .1C **6**
  (not continuous)
Levyne Ct. *EC1* 3B **8**
  (off Pine St.)
Lewesdon Cl. SW19 . . . . .1F **113**
Lewes Ho. *SE1* 3E **27**
  (off Druid St.)
  SE15 . . . . .2C **92**
  (off Friary Est.)
Leweston Pl. N16 . . . . . . .2B **36**
Lew Evans Ho.
  SE22 . . . . .3C **106**
Lewey Ho. *E3* 3B **66**
  (off Joseph St.)
Lewington Apartments
  SE16 . . . . .5E **79**
  (off Alpine Rd.)
Lewington Cen. *SE16* . . .5E **79**
  (off Alpine Rd.)
Lewin Rd. SW14 . . . . .1A **98**
  SW16 . . . . .5F **117**
Lewis Ct. *SE16* 1D **93**
  (off Stubbs Dr.)
Lewis Gdns. N16 . . . . .1B **36**
Lewis Gro. SE13 . . . . .2E **109**
LEWISHAM 1E **109**
Lewisham Cen.
  SE13 . . . . .2E **109**
Lewisham Hgts.
  SE23 . . . . .1E **121**
Lewisham High St.
  SE13 . . . . .4D **109**
  (not continuous)
Lewisham Hill SE13 . . . . .5E **95**
Lewisham Indoor Bowls Cen.
  . . . . .5B **122**
Lewisham Lions Cen.
  . . . . .1E **93**
Lewisham Model Mkt.
  SE13 . . . . .2E **109**
  (off Lewisham High St.)
Lewisham Pk. SE13 . . . . .3E **109**
Lewisham Rd. SE13 . . . . .4D **95**
Lewisham St.
  SW1 . . . . . . .4C **22** (3F **75**)
Lewisham Way SE4 . . . . . .4B **94**
  SE14 . . . . .4B **94**

Lewis Ho. *E14* 2E **81**
  (off Coldharbour)
Lewis Pl. E8 . . . . .2C **50**
Lewis Silkin Ho.
  SE15 . . . . .2E **93**
  (off Lovelinch Cl.)
Lewis St. NW1 . . . . .3D **47**
  (not continuous)
Lexham Gdns. W8 . . . . . . .5C **72**
Lexham Gdns. M.
  W8 . . . . .4D **73**
Lexham Ho. *W8* 5D **73**
  (off Lexham Gdns.)
Lexham M. W8 . . . . .5C **72**
Lexham Wlk. W8 . . . . .4D **73**
Lexington Apartments
  EC1 . . . . .3C **10** (3F **63**)
Lexington Bldg. E3 . . . . . .1C **66**
Lexington St.
  W1 . . . . .4A **14** (1E **75**)
Lexton Gdns. SW12 . . . . .1F **117**
Leybourne Ho. *E14* 5B **66**
  (off Dod St.)
  SE15 . . . . .2E **93**
Leybourne Rd. E11 . . . . . .3B **40**
  NW1 . . . . .4D **47**
Leybourne St. NW1 . . . . . .4D **47**
Leybridge Ct. SE12 . . . . . .3C **110**
Leyden Mans. N19 . . . . . .2A **34**
Leyden St.
  E1 . . . . .1F **19** (4B **64**)
Leydon Cl. SE16 . . . . .2F **79**
Ley Ho. *SE1* 4F **25**
  (off Scovell Rd.)
Leyland Ho. *E14* 1D **81**
  (off Hale St.)
Leyland Rd. SE12 . . . . . . .3C **110**
Leylands SW18 . . . . .4B **100**
Leylang Rd. SE14 . . . . . . .3F **93**
Leys Ct. SW9 . . . . .5C **90**
Leysdown Ho. *SE17* 1A **92**
  (off Madron St.)
Leysfield Rd. W12 . . . . . . .4C **70**
Leyspring Rd. E11 . . . . . . .3B **40**
LEYTON 4E **39**
Leyton Bus. Cen.
  E10 . . . . .4C **38**
Leyton Ct. SE23 . . . . .1E **121**
Leyton Grange Est.
  E10 . . . . .3C **38**
Leyton Grn. Rd. E10 . . . . .1E **39**
Leyton Grn. Twr. *E10* 1E **39**
  (off Leyton Grn. Rd.)
Leyton Ho. *E2* 2F **11**
  (off Calvert Av.)
Leyton Ind. Village
  E10 . . . . .2F **37**
Leyton Leisure Lagoon
  . . . . .2D **39**
Leyton Link Est. E10 . . . . .2A **38**
Leyton Mills E10 . . . . .1E **53**
Leyton Orient FC 5D **39**
Leyton Pk. Rd. E10 . . . . . .5E **39**
Leyton Rd. E15 . . . . .2E **53**
LEYTONSTONE 3A **40**
Leytonstone Ho. *E11* 2B **40**
  (off Hanbury Dr.)
Leytonstone Rd. E15 . . . . .3A **54**
Leyton Way E11 . . . . .2A **40**

Leywick St. E15 . . . . . . .1A 68
Lianne Gro. SE9 . . . . . .3E 125
Liardet St. SE14 . . . . . . .2A 94
Liberia Rd. N5 . . . . .3D 49
Liberty Ho. E1 . . . . .1C 78
(off Ensign St.)
E13 . . . . .1C 68
Liberty M. SW12 . . . . . .4D 103
Liberty St. SW9 . . . . . . .4B 90
Libra Mans. E3 . . . . . . .1B 66
(off Libra Rd.)
Libra Rd. E3 . . . . .5B 52
E13 . . . . .1C 68
Library Mans. W12 . . . . .3E 71
(off Pennard Rd.)
Library Pde. NW10 . . . . .5A 42
(off Craven Pk. Rd.)
Library Pl. E1 . . . . .1D 79
Library St.
SE1 . . . . . . .5D 25 (3D 77)
Lichfield Rd. E3 . . . . .2A 66
E6 . . . . .2F 69
NW2 . . . . .1A 44
Lickey Ho. W14 . . . . . . .2B 86
(off North End Rd.)
Lidcote Gdns. SW9 . . . . .5B 90
Liddell Gdns. NW10 . . . . .1E 57
Liddell Rd. NW6 . . . . . . .3C 44
Liddiard Ho. W11 . . . . . .1A 72
(off Lansdowne Rd.)
Liddington Rd. E15 . . . . .5B 54
Liddon Rd. E13 . . . . .2D 69
Liden Cl. E17 . . . . .2B 38
Lidfield Rd. N16 . . . . . . .1F 49
Lidgate Rd. SE15 . . . . . .3B 92
Lidiard Rd. SW18 . . . . . .2E 115
Lidlington Pl.
NW1 . . . . .1E 61
Lidyard Rd. N19 . . . . . . .3E 33
Liffords Pl. SW13 . . . . . .5B 84
Lifford St. SW15 . . . . . . .2F 99
Lighter Cl. SE16 . . . . . . .5A 80
Lighterman Ho. E14 . . . . .1E 81
Lighterman M. E1 . . . . . .5F 65
Lightermans Rd.
E14 . . . . .3C 80
Lightermans Wlk.
SW18 . . . . .2C 100
Lightfoot Vs. N1 . . . . . . .4C 48
(off Augustas La.)
Light Horse Ct. SW3 . . . .1C 88
(off Royal Hospital Rd.)
Lighthouse Apartments
E1 . . . . .5E 65
(off Commercial Rd.)
Ligonier St.
E2 . . . . . . .3F 11 (3B 64)
Lilac Ct. E13 . . . . .5E 55
Lilac Ho. SE4 . . . . .1C 108
Lilac Pl. SE11 . . . . .5B 76
Lilac St. W12 . . . . .1C 70
Lilburne Rd. SE9 . . . . . . .3F 111
Lilestone Ho. NW8 . . . . . .3F 59
(off Frampton St.)
Lilestone St. NW8 . . . . . .3A 60
Lilford Ho. SE5 . . . . .5E 91
Lilford Rd. SE5 . . . . .5D 91
Lilian Barker Cl.
SE12 . . . . .3C 110
Lilian Cl. N16 . . . . .5A 36

Lilian Knowles Ho.
E1 . . . . .1F 19
(off Crispin St.)
Lilley Cl. E1 . . . . .2C 78
Lillian Rd. SW13 . . . . . . .2C 84
Lillie Bri. Dpt. W14 . . . . .1B 86
Lillie Mans. SW6 . . . . . .2A 86
(off Lillie Rd.)
Lillie Rd. SW6 . . . . .2F 85
Lillie Road Fitness Cen.
. . . . .3F 85
Lillieshall Rd. SW4 . . .1D 103
Lillie Yd. SW6 . . . . .2C 86
Lillington Ho. N7 . . . . . . .1C 48
Lillington Gdns. Est.
SW1 . . . . .5E 75
(off Vauxhall Bri. Rd.)
Lilliput Ct. SE12 . . . . . . .3D 111
Lily Cl. W14 . . . . .5F 71
Lily Nichols Ho. E16 . . . .2F 83
(off Connaught Rd.)
Lily Pl. EC1 . . . . .5C 8 (4C 62)
Lily Rd. E17 . . . . .1C 38
Lilyville Rd. SW6 . . . . . . .4B 86
Limborough Ho. E14 . . . .4C 66
(off Thomas Rd.)
Limburg Rd. SW11 . . . . .2A 102
Limeburner La.
EC4 . . . . . . .3D 17 (5D 63)
Lime Cl. E1 . . . . .2C 78
Lime Ct. E11 . . . . .4A 40
(off Trinity Cl.)
E17 . . . . .1E 39
Lime Gro. W12 . . . . .3E 71
Limeharbour E14 . . . . . . .4D 81
LIMEHOUSE 5B 66
Limehouse C'way.
E14 . . . . .1B 80
Lime Ho. Ct. E14 . . . . . .5B 66
(off Wharf La.)
Limehouse Ct. E14 . . . . .5C 66
Limehouse Cut E14 . . . .4D 67
(off Morris Rd.)
Limehouse Flds. Est.
E14 . . . . .4A 66
Limehouse Link E14 . . . .5A 66
Lime Kiln Dr. SE7 . . . . . .2D 97
Limekiln Wharf E14 . . . . .1B 80
Limelight Ho. SE11 . . . . .5D 77
(off George Mathers Rd.)
Limerick Cl. SW12 . . . . .5E 103
Limerston St. SW10 . . . . .2E 87
Limes, The SW18 . . . . . .4C 100
W2 . . . . .1C 72
Limes Av. NW11 . . . . . . .2A 30
SW13 . . . . .5B 84
Limes Ct. NW6 . . . . .4A 44
(off Brondesbury Pk.)
Limes Fld. Rd.
SW14 . . . . .1A 98
Limesford Rd. SE15 . . . . .2F 107
Limes Gdns. SW18 . . . . .4C 100
Limes Gro. SE13 . . . . . . .2E 109
Lime St. EC3 . . .4D 19 (1A 78)
Lime St. Pas.
EC3 . . . . . . .3D 19 (5A 64)
Limes Wlk. SE15 . . . . . . .2E 107
Limetree Cl. SW2 . . . . . .1B 118
Lime Tree Ct. E3 . . . . . . .4C 66
(off Whitehorn St.)

Limetree Ter. SE6 . . . . . .1B 122
Limetree Wlk.
SW17 . . . . .5C 116
Lime Wlk. E15 . . . . .5A 54
Limpsfield Av.
SW19 . . . . .2F 113
Limscott Ho. E3 . . . . . . .2D 67
(off Bruce Rd.)
Linacre Cl. SE15 . . . . . . .1D 107
Linacre Ct. W6 . . . . .1F 85
Linacre Rd. NW2 . . . . . . .3D 43
Linale Ho. N1 . . . . .1B 10
Linberry Wlk. SE8 . . . . . .5B 80
Linchmere Rd.
SE12 . . . . .5B 110
Lincoln Av. SW19 . . . . . .3F 113
Lincoln Ct. N16 . . . . .2F 35
SE12 . . . . .3D 125
Lincoln Ho. SE5 . . . . .3C 90
SW3 . . . . .3B 74
Lincoln M. NW6 . . . . .5B 44
SE21 . . . . .2F 119
Lincoln Rd. E7 . . . . .3F 55
E13 . . . . .3D 69
Lincolns Inn Flds.
WC2 . . . . . . .2F 15 (5B 62)
Lincoln's Inn Hall
. . . . .2A 16 (5B 62)
Lincoln St. E11 . . . . .4A 40
SW3 . . . . .5B 74
Lincombe Rd.
BR1: Brom 3B 124
Lindal Rd. SE4 . . . . .3B 108
Linden Av. NW10 . . . . . . .1F 57
Linden Ct. W12 . . . . .2E 71
Linden Gdns. W2 . . . . . . .1C 72
W4 . . . . .1A 84
Linden Gro. SE15 . . . . . .1D 107
Linden Ho. SE8 . . . . .2B 94
(off Abinger Gro.)
Linden Lea N2 . . . . .1E 31
Linden Mans. N6 . . . . . . .3D 33
(off Hornsey La.)
Linden M. N1 . . . . .2F 49
W2 . . . . .1C 72
Linden Wlk. N19 . . . . . . .4E 33
Lindfield Gdns. NW3 . . . .2D 45
Lindfield St. E14 . . . . . . .5C 66
Lindisfarne Way E9 . . . . .1A 52
Lindley Est. SE15 . . . . . . .3C 92
Lindley Ho. E1 . . . . .4E 65
(off Lindley St.)
SE15 . . . . .3C 92
(off Peckham Pk. Rd.)
Lindley Rd. E10 . . . . .4E 39
Lindley St. E1 . . . . .4E 65
Lindop Ho. E1 . . . . .3A 66
(off Mile End Rd.)
Lindore Rd. SW11 . . . . . .2B 102
Lindo St. SE15 . . . . .5E 93
Lindrop St. SW6 . . . . . . .5E 87
Lindsay Ct. SW11 . . . . . .4F 87
(off Battersea High St.)
Lindsay Ho. SW7 . . . . . .4E 73
(off Gloucester Rd.)
Lindsay Sq. SW1 . . . . . . .1F 89
Lindsell St. SE10 . . . . . . .4E 95
Lindsey M. N1 . . . . .4E 49
Lindsey St.
EC1 . . . . . . .5E 9 (4D 63)

Lind St. SE8 . . . . .5C 94
Lindway SE27 . . . . .5D 119
Linen House, The
W10 . . . . .1A 58
Linfield WC1 . . . . .2F 7
(off Sidmouth St.)
Linford Christie Stadium
. . . . .4C 56
Linford Ho. E2 . . . . .5C 50
(off Whiston Rd.)
Linford St. SW8 . . . . .4E 89
Linford St. Bus. Est.
SW8 . . . . .4E 89
(off Linford St.)
Lingard Ho. E14 . . . . .4E 81
(off Marshfield St.)
Lingards Rd. SE13 . . . . . .2E 109
Lingfield Ho. SE1 . . . . . . .4E 26
Lingfield Rd. SW19 . . . . . .5F 113
Lingham Ct. SW9 . . . . .5A 90
Lingham St. SW9 . . . . .5A 90
Ling Rd. E16 . . . . .4C 68
Lings Coppice SE21 . . . . . .2F 119
Lingwell Rd. SW17 . . . . . .3A 116
Lingwood Rd. E5 . . . . .2C 36
Linhope St. NW1 . . . . .3B 60
Link, The NW2 . . . . .3C 28
Linkenholt Mans. W6 . . . . .5B 70
(off Stamford Brook Av.)
Link Ho. E3 . . . . .1D 67
W10 . . . . .5F 57
(off Kingsdown Cl.)
Link Rd. E1 . . . . .1C 78
Links Rd. NW2 . . . . .4B 28
Link St. E9 . . . . .3E 51
Linksview N2 . . . . .1B 32
(off Great Nth. Rd.)
Links Yd. E1 . . . . .4C 64
(off Spelman St.)
Linkway N4 . . . . .2E 35
Linkwood Wlk. NW1 . . . . . .4E 47
Linley Sambourne House
. . . . .4C 72
(off Stafford Ter.)
Linnell Cl. NW11 . . . . .1D 31
Linnell Dr. NW11 . . . . .1D 31
Linnell Ho. E1 . . . . .5F 11
(off Folgate St.)
NW8 . . . . .5E 45
(off Ainsworth Way)
Linnell Rd. SE5 . . . . .5A 92
Linnet M. SW12 . . . . .5C 102
Linom Rd. SW4 . . . . .2A 104
Linscott Rd. E5 . . . . .1E 51
Linsey Ct. E10 . . . . .3C 38
(off Grange Rd.)
Linsey St. SE16 . . . . .5C 78
(not continuous)
Linslade Ho. E2 . . . . .5C 50
NW8 . . . . .3A 60
(off Paveley St.)
Linstead St. NW6 . . . . .4C 44
Linstead Way SW18 . . . . . .5A 100
Lintaine Cl. W6 . . . . .2A 86
Linthorpe Rd. N16 . . . . . . .2A 36
Linton Cl. SE7 . . . . .1E 97
Linton Ct. NW1 . . . . .4E 47
(off Agar Gro.)
Linton Gdns. E6 . . . . .5F 69
Linton Gro. SE27 . . . . . . .5D 119

Linton Ho. E3 . . . . .4C 66
(off St Paul's Way)
Linton St. N1 . . . . .5E 49
(not continuous)
Linwood Cl. SE5 . . . . .5B 92
Lion Apartments
SE16 . . . . .1D 93
(off Rotherhithe New Rd.)
Lion Cl. SE4 . . . . .4C 108
Lion Ct. E1 . . . . .1F 79
(off The Highway)
N1 . . . . .5B 48
(off Copenhagen St.)
SE1 . . . . .2D 27
(off Magdalen St.)
Lionel Gdns. SE9 . . . . . . .3F 111
Lionel Ho. W10 . . . . .4A 58
(off Portobello Rd.)
Lionel Mans. W14 . . . . . . .4F 71
(off Haarlem Rd.)
Lionel M. W10 . . . . .4A 58
Lionel Rd. SE9 . . . . .3F 111
Lion Ga. M. SW18 . . . . . . .5C 100
Lion Mills E2 . . . . .1C 64
Lions Cl. SE9 . . . . .3E 125
Lion Yd. SW4 . . . . .2F 103
Liphook Cres. SE23 . . . . . .5E 107
Lipton Rd. E1 . . . . .5F 65
Lisburne Rd. NW3 . . . . . . .1B 46
Lisford St. SE15 . . . . .4B 92
Lisgar Ter. W14 . . . . .5B 72
Liskeard Gdns. SE3 . . . . . .4C 96
Liskeard Ho. SE11 . . . . . . .1C 90
(off Kennings Way)
Lisle Cl. SW17 . . . . .4D 117
Lisle Ct. NW2 . . . . .5A 30
Lisle St. WC2 . . . .4C 14 (1F 75)
Lismore SW19 . . . . .5B 114
(off Woodside)
Lismore Cir. NW5 . . . . .2C 46
Lismore Wlk. N1 . . . . .3E 49
(off Clephane Rd. Nth.)
Lissenden Gdns.
NW5 . . . . .1C 46
(not continuous)
Lissenden Mans.
NW5 . . . . .1C 46
Lisson Grn. Est.
NW8 . . . . .3A 60
(off Tresham Cres.)
LISSON GROVE 4A 60
Lisson Gro. NW1 . . . . .3F 59
NW8 . . . . .3F 59
Lisson Ho. NW1 . . . . .4A 60
(off Lisson St.)
Lisson St. NW1 . . . . .4A 60
Lister Cl. W3 . . . . .4A 56
Lister Ct. N16 . . . . .4A 36
Listergate Ct. SW15 . . . . . .2E 99
Lister Ho. E1 . . . . .4C 64
(off Lomas St.)
Lister Lodge W9 . . . . .4C 58
(off Admiral Wlk.)
Liston Rd. SW4 . . . . .1E 103
Listowel Cl. SW9 . . . . .3C 90
Listria Pk. N16 . . . . .4A 36
Litcham Ho. E1 . . . . .2F 65
(off Longnor Rd.)

Litchfield Av. E15 . . . . .3A 54
Litchfield Ct. E17 . . . . .1C 38
Litchfield Gdns.
NW10 . . . . .3C 42
Litchfield St.
WC2 . . . . . .4C 14 (1F 75)
Litchfield Way NW11 . . . . . .1E 31
Lithos Rd. NW3 . . . . .3D 45
Lit. Albany St. NW1 . . . . . . .3E 5
Little Angel Theatre 5D 49
(off Dagmar Pl.)
Lit. Argyll St.
W1 . . . . .3F 13 (5E 61)
Little Boltons, The
SW5 . . . . .1D 87
SW10 . . . . .1D 87
Little Bornes SE21 . . . . . . .4A 120
Littlebourne SE13 . . . . . . .5A 110
Littlebourne Ho.
SE17 . . . . .1A 92
(off Upnor Way)
Little Britain
EC1 . . . . . . .1E 17 (4D 63)
Little Brownings
SE23 . . . . .2D 121
Littlebury Rd. SW4 . . . . . . .1F 103
Lit. Chelsea Ho.
SW10 . . . . .2E 87
(off Edith Gro.)
Lit. Chester St.
SW1 . . . . .5D 21 (4D 75)
Little Cloisters
SW1 . . . . .5D 23 (4A 76)
Lit. College La. EC4 . . . . . .4B 18
(off College St.)
Lit. College St.
SW1 . . . . .5D 23 (4A 76)
Littlecombe SE7 . . . . .2D 97
Littlecombe Cl.
SW15 . . . . .4F 99
Littlecote Cl. SW19 . . . . . .5A 100
Lit. Cottage Pl. SE10 . . . . . .3D 95
Lit. Dean's Yd. SW1 . . . . . .5D 23
Little Dimocks
SW12 . . . . .2D 117
Lit. Dorrit Ct.
SE1 . . . . .3A 26 (3E 77)
Lit. Edward St.
NW1 . . . . .1E 5 (2D 61)
Lit. Essex St. WC2 . . . . . . .4B 16
Littlefield Cl. N19 . . . . .1E 47
Lit. George St.
SW1 . . . . .4D 23 (3A 76)
Lit. Green St. NW5 . . . . . . .1D 47
Little Heath SE7 . . . . .2F 97
Little Holt E11 . . . . .1C 40
Lit. London Ct. SE1 . . . . . . .3B 78
(off Wolseley St.)
Lit. Marlborough St.
W1 . . . . .3F 13
Lit. Newport St.
WC2 . . . . . .4C 14 (1F 75)
Lit. Portland St.
W1 . . . . .2E 13 (5E 61)
Lit. Russell St.
WC1 . . . . .1D 15 (4A 62)
Lit. St James's St.
SW1 . . . . . .2F 21 (2E 75)

Little Sanctuary
SW1 . . . . . .4C 22 (3F 75)
Lit. Smith St.
SW1 . . . . . .5C 22 (4F 75)
Lit. Somerset St.
E1 . . . . .3F 19 (5B 64)
Lit. South St. SE5 . . . . . .4A 92
Lit. Titchfield St.
W1 . . . . .1F 13 (4E 61)
Littleton Ho. SW1 . . . . . .1E 89
(off Lupus St.)
Littleton St. SW18 . . . . .2E 115
Lit. Trinity La.
EC4 . . . . . .4A 18 (1E 77)
Little Turnstile
WC1 . . . . . .1F 15 (4B 62)
Little Venice Sports Cen.
. . . . .4E 59
Littlewood SE13 . . . . . .4E 109
Livermere Ct. E8 . . . . . . .5B 50
(off Queensbridge Rd.)
Livermere Rd. E8 . . . . . .5B 50
Liverpool Gro. SE17 . . . .1E 91
Liverpool Rd. E10 . . . . . .1E 39
E16 . . . . .4A 68
N1 . . . . .4C 48
N7 . . . . .2C 48
Liverpool St.
EC2 . . . . . .1D 19 (4A 64)
Livesey Pl. SE15 . . . . . . .2C 92
Livingstone Ct. E10 . . . . .1E 39
Livingstone Ho. SE5 . . . . .3E 91
(off Wyndham Rd.)
Livingstone Lodge
W9 . . . . .4C 58
(off Admiral Wlk.)
Livingstone Mans.
W14 . . . . .2A 86
(off Queen's Club Gdns.)
Livingstone Pl. E14 . . . . .1E 95
Livingstone Rd. E17 . . . . .1D 39
SW11 . . . . .1F 101
LivingWell Health Club
Regents Plaza 1D 59
(off Greville Rd.)
Livonia St.
W1 . . . . . . .3A 14 (5E 61)
Lizard St.
EC1 . . . . . .2A 10 (2E 63)
Lizban St. SE3 . . . . .3D 97
Lizmans Ter. W8 . . . . . . .4C 72
(off Earl's Ct. Rd.)
Llandovery Ho. E14 . . . . .3E 81
(off Chipka St.)
Llanelly Rd. NW2 . . . . . .4B 30
Llanvanor Rd. NW2 . . . . .4B 30
Llewellyn Mans.
W14 . . . . .5A 72
(off Hammersmith Rd.)
Llewellyn St. SE16 . . . . . .3C 78
Lloyd Baker St.
WC1 . . . . . .2A 8 (2B 62)
(not continuous)
Lloyd's Av.
EC3 . . . . . .3E 19 (5A 64)
Lloyd's Building
. . . . .3D 19 (5A 64)
Lloyd's Pl. SE3 . . . . .5A 96
Lloyd Sq.
WC1 . . . . . . .1B 8 (2C 62)

Lloyd's Row
EC1 . . . . . . .2C 8 (2C 62)
Lloyd St. WC1 . . .1B 8 (2C 62)
Lloyds Wharf SE1 . . . . . .3B 78
(off Mill St.)
Lloyd Vs. SE4 . . . . .5C 94
Loampit Hill SE13 . . . . . .5C 94
LOAMPIT VALE 1E 109
Loampit Va. SE13 . . . . . .1D 109
Loanda Ct. E8 . . . . .5B 50
Loats Rd. SW2 . . . . .4A 104
Lobelia Ct. E6 . . . . .4F 69
Locarno Ct. SW16 . . . . . .5E 117
Lochaber Rd. SE13 . . . . .2A 110
Lochaline St. W6 . . . . . . .2E 85
Lochinvar St. SW12 . . . . .5D 103
Lochmore Ho. SW1 . . . . . .5C 74
(off Cundy St.)
Lochnagar St. E14 . . . . . .4E 67
Lockbridge Ct. W9 . . . . . .4C 58
(off Woodfield Rd.)
Lock Building, The
E15 . . . . .1E 67
Lock Chase SE3 . . . . . . .1A 110
Locke Ho. SW8 . . . . .4E 89
(off Wadhurst Rd.)
Lockesfield Pl. E14 . . . . .1D 95
Lockgate Cl. E9 . . . . .2B 52
Lockhart Cl. N7 . . . . .3B 48
Lockhart St. E3 . . . . .3B 66
Lockhouse, The NW1 . . . .5C 46
Lockhurst St. E5 . . . . .1F 51
Lockington Rd. SW8 . . . . .4D 89
Lock Keepers Hgts.
SE16 . . . . .4F 79
(off Brunswick Quay)
Lockmead Rd. N15 . . . . .1C 36
SE13 . . . . .1E 109
Lock M. NW1 . . . . .3F 47
(off Northpoint Sq.)
Locksfields SE17 . . . . . . .5F 77
(off Catesby St.)
Lockside E14 . . . . .1A 80
(off Narrow St.)
Locksley Est. E14 . . . . . . .5B 66
Locksley St. E14 . . . . .4B 66
Locksons Cl. E14 . . . . . . .4D 67
Lockton St. W10 . . . . .1F 71
(off Bramley Rd.)
Lock Vw. Ct. E14 . . . . . . .1A 80
(off Narrow St.)
Lockwood Cl. SE26 . . . . .4F 121
Lockwood Ho. E5 . . . . . . .4E 37
SE11 . . . . .2C 90
Lockwood Sq. SE16 . . . . .4D 79
Lockyer Est. SE1 . . . . .4C 26
(not continuous)
Lockyer Ho. SE10 . . . . . . .1B 96
(off Armitage Rd.)
SW8 . . . . .3F 89
(off Wandsworth Rd.)
SW15 . . . . .1F 99
Lockyer St.
SE1 . . . . . .4C 26 (3F 77)
Locton Grn. E3 . . . . .5B 52
Loddiges Ho. E9 . . . . .4E 51
Loddiges Rd. E9 . . . . .4E 51
Loddon Ho. NW8 . . . . . . .3F 59
(off Church St. Est.)
Loder St. SE15 . . . . .3E 93

Lodge, The W12 . . . . . . .3F 71
(off Richmond Way)
Lodge Av. SW14 . . . . . . .1A 98
Lodge Rd. NW8 . . . . .2F 59
Lodore Gdns. NW9 . . . . .1A 28
Lodore St. E14 . . . . .5E 67
Loftie St. SE16 . . . . .3C 78
Lofting Ho. N1 . . . . .4C 48
(off Liverpool Rd.)
Lofting Rd. N1 . . . . .4B 48
Lofts on the Pk. E9 . . . . . .3F 51
(off Cassland Rd.)
Loftus Road 2D 71
Loftus Rd. W12 . . . . .2D 71
Loftus Vs. W12 . . . . .2D 71
(off Loftus Rd.)
Logan M. W8 . . . . .5C 72
Logan Pl. W8 . . . . .5C 72
Loggetts SE21 . . . . .2A 120
Lohmann Ho. SE11 . . . . . .2C 90
(off Kennington Oval)
Lolesworth Cl.
E1 . . . . . . .1F 19 (4B 64)
Lollard St. SE11 . . . . .5B 76
(not continuous)
Loman St.
SE1 . . . . . .3E 25 (3D 77)
Lomas Dr. E8 . . . . .4B 50
Lomas St. E1 . . . . .4C 64
Lombard Ct.
EC3 . . . . . .4C 18 (1F 77)
Lombard La.
EC4 . . . . . .3C 16 (5C 62)
Lombard Rd. SW11 . . . . . .5F 87
Lombard St.
EC3 . . . . . .3C 18 (5F 63)
Lombard Trad. Est.
SE7 . . . . .5D 83
Lombard Wall SE7 . . . . . .4D 83
Lombardy Pl. W2 . . . . . . .1D 73
Lomond Gro. SE5 . . . . . . .3F 91
Lomond Ho. SE5 . . . . .3F 91
Loncroft Rd. SE5 . . . . . . .2A 92
Londesborough Rd.
N16 . . . . .1A 50
Londinium Twr. E1 . . . . . .4F 19
(off W. Tenter St.)
London Bombing Memorial
. . . . .2B 20 (2C 74)
London Bri.
SE1 . . . . . .1C 26 (2F 77)
London Bridge Experience
. . . . .1C 26
(off Tooley St.)
London Bri. St.
SE1 . . . . . .2C 26 (2F 77)
London Bri. Wlk. SE1 . . . .1C 26
(off Duke St. Hill)
London Business School
. . . . .3A 4 (3B 60)
London Canal Mus. 1A 62
LONDON CITY AIRPORT
. . . . .2F 83
London City College 2B 24
(off Waterloo Rd.)
London Coliseum 5D 15
(off St Martin's La.)
London College of
Fashion, The
Hackney 4D 51

London Dungeon 2C 26
London Eye 3F 23 (3B 76)
London Flds. E. Side
. . . . .4D 51
London Fields Lido 4D 51
London Flds. W. Side
. . . . .4C 50
London Film Mus.
. . . . . 3F 23 (3B 76)
London Fire Brigade Mus.
. . . . .3E 77
London Fruit Exchange
. . . . .1F 19
(off Brushfield St.)
London Group Bus. Pk.
NW2 . . . . .3B 28
London Heliport, The . .5E 87
London Ho. EC1 . . . . . .1F 17
(off Aldersgate St.)
NW8 . . . . .1A 60
(off Avenue Rd.)
WC1 . . . . . .3F 7 (3B 62)
London International
Gallery of Children's Art
. . . . .3D 33
(off Dartmouth Pk. Hill)
London La. E8 . . . . . . .4D 51
London Master
Bakers Almshouses
E10 . . . . .1D 39
London Metropolitan Archives
. . . . .3C 8 (3C 62)
London Metropolitan
University
London City Campus -
Central House 5C 64
(off Whitechapel High St.)
Commercial Rd. . .5C 64
Jewry St. 3F 19
(off Jewry St.)
Moorgate 1B 18
Tower Hill 4F 19
North London Campus -
Eden Grove 2B 48
Stapleton House
. . . . .2B 48
Tower Building &
Graduate Cen. . . .2C 48
Old Castle St.
. . . . .2F 19 (5B 64)
London M. W2 . . . . . . .5F 59
London Palladium 3F 13
(off Argyll St.)
London Pavilion 5B 14
(off Shaftesbury Av.)
London Plane Ho.
E15 . . . . .2A 68
(off Teasel Way)
London Regatta Cen. . . .1F 83
London Rd.
E13 . . . . .1C 68
SE1 . . . . .5D 25 (4D 77)
SE23 . . . . .1D 121
London School of
Economics &
Political Science, The
. . . . .3F 15 (5B 62)
London Scottish Golf Course
. . . . .3D 113
London's Death Trap . . .4F 23

London South Bank University
Keyworth St.
. . . . .5E 25 (4D 77)
London Rd. 5D 25
Perry Library 5E 25
Southwark Campus
. . . . .5E 25 (4D 77)
London South Bank
University Sports Cen.
. . . . .5E 25
(in London
South Bank University)
London South Bank
University Technopark
. . . . .5E 25
London's Pleasure Gdns.
. . . . .2E 83
London Stock Exchange
. . . . .2F 17
London St.
EC3 . . . . . . .4E 19 (1A 78)
W2 . . . . .5F 59
London Telecom Tower, The
. . . . .5F 5
London Television Centre, The
. . . . .1B 24 (1C 76)
London Ter. E2 . . . . . .1C 64
London Transport Mus.
. . . . .4E 15 (1A 76)
London Trocadero
. . . . .4B 14 (1F 75)
London Underwriting Cen.
. . . . .4E 19
London Wall
EC2 . . . . .1F 17 (4E 63)
London Wall Bldgs.
EC2 . . . . .1C 18
London Wetland Cen.
. . . . .4D 85
London Wetland Cen.
Visitor Cen. 4D 85
London Wharf E2 . . . . .5D 51
(off Wharf Pl.)
London Zoo 1C 60
Long Acre
WC2 . . . . .4D 15 (1A 76)
Longbeach Rd.
SW11 . . . . .1B 102
Longberrys NW2 . . . . . .5B 30
Longbow Ho. EC1 . . . . .5B 10
(off Chiswell St.)
Longbridge Way
SE13 . . . . .3E 109
Longdown Rd. SE6 . . . .4C 122
Long Dr. W3 . . . . .5A 56
Longfellow Rd. E17 . . . .1B 38
Longfellow Way SE1 . . . .5B 78
Longfield Cres.
SE26 . . . . .3E 121
Longfield Est. SE1 . . . . .5B 78
Longfield St. SW18 . . . .5C 100
Longford Ct. E5 . . . . . . .1F 51
(off Pedro St.)
Longford Ho.
BR1: Brom 5F 123
(off Brangbourne Rd.)
E1 . . . . .6E 65
(off Jubilee St.)
Longford St.
NW1 . . . . . .3E 5 (3D 61)

Longford Wlk. SW2 . . .5C 104
Longhedge Ho.
SE26 . . . . .4C 120
(off High Level Dr.)
Longhedge St.
SW11 . . . . .5C 88
Longhill Rd. SE6 . . . . . .2F 123
Longhope Cl. SE15 . . . .2A 92
Longhurst Ho. W10 . . . .2B 58
(off Lancefield St.)
Longhurst Rd. SE13 . . .3F 109
Longland Ct. E9 . . . . . . .2A 52
(off Mabley St.)
SE1 . . . . .1C 92
Longlands Ct. W11 . . . . .1B 72
Long La. EC1 . . .1E 17 (4D 63)
SE1 . . . . . .4B 26 (3F 77)
Longleat Ho. SW1 . . . . .1F 89
(off Rampayne St.)
Longleigh Ho. SE5 . . . . .4A 92
(off Peckham Rd.)
Long Lents Ho.
NW10 . . . . .5A 42
(off Shrewsbury Cres.)
Longley Ct. SW8 . . . . . .4A 90
Longley Rd. SW17 . . . .5A 116
Longley St. SE1 . . . . . . .5C 78
Longley Way NW2 . . . . .5E 29
Longman Ho. E2 . . . . . .1F 65
(off Mace St.)
E8 . . . . .3B 50
(off Haggerston Rd.)
Long Mark Rd. E16 . . . .4F 69
Longmead Ho. SE27 . . .5E 119
Long Meadow NW5 . . . .2F 47
Longmead Rd.
SW17 . . . . .5B 116
Long Mill SE10 . . . . .4D 95
(off Greenwich High Rd.)
Longmoore St. SW1 . . . .5E 75
Longmoor Point
SW15 . . . . .1D 113
(off Norley Va.)
Longmore Gdns. Est.
SW1 . . . . .5E 75
(off Vauxhall Bri. Rd.)
Longnor Est. E1 . . . . . . .2F 65
Longnor Rd. E1 . . . . . . .2F 65
Long Pond Rd. SE3 . . . .4A 96
Longridge Ho.
SE1 . . . . . .5A 26 (4E 77)
Longridge Rd. SW5 . . . .5C 72
Long Rd. SW4 . . . . . . .2D 103
Long's Ct. WC2 . . . . .5C 14
Longshore SE8 . . . . .5B 80
Longshott Ct. SW5 . . . . .5C 72
(off W. Cromwell Rd.)
Longstaff Cres.
SW18 . . . . .4C 100
Longstaff Rd. SW18 . . .4C 100
Longstone Av. NW10 . . .4B 42
Longstone Ct. SE1 . . . . .4B 26
(off Gt. Dover St.)
Longstone Rd.
SW17 . . . . .5D 117
Long St. E2 . . .1F 11 (2B 64)
Longthorpe Ct. W6 . . . . .5C 70
Longton Av. SE26 . . . . .4C 120
Longton Gro. SE26 . . . .4D 121
Longville Rd. SE11 . . . . .5D 77

Long Wlk. SE1 . . . . .5E 27
   SW13 . . . . .5A 84
Long Wall E15 . . . . .2F 67
Longwood Dr. SW15 . . . .4C 98
Long Yd. WC1 . . .4F 7 (3B 62)
Lonsdale Av. E6 . . . . . . .2F 69
Lonsdale Cl. E6 . . . . . . .3F 69
   SE9 . . . . .3F 125
Lonsdale Ho. W11 . . . . . .5B 58
   (off Lonsdale Rd.)
Lonsdale M. W11 . . . . . .5B 58
   (off Colville M.)
Lonsdale Pl. N1 . . . . . . .4C 48
Lonsdale Rd. E11 . . . . . .1B 40
   NW6 . . . . .1B 58
   SW13 . . . . .4B 84
   W4 . . . . .5B 70
   W11 . . . . .5B 58
Lonsdale Road Reservoir
   Local Nature Reserve
   . . . . .3B 84
Lonsdale Sq. N1 . . . . . . .4C 48
Lonsdale Yd. W11 . . . . . .1C 72
Lookout Education Centre, The
   . . . . . . .1A 20 (2B 74)
Lopez Ho. W9 . . . . .1A 104
Loraine Cotts. N7 . . . . . .1B 48
Loraine Rd. N7 . . . . .1B 48
Lord Amory Way E14 . . . .3E 81
Lordell Pl. SW19 . . . . . .5E 113
Lorden Wlk. E2 . . . . .2C 64
Lord Hills Bri. W2 . . . . . .4D 59
Lord Hills Rd. W2 . . . . . .4D 59
Lord Holland La.
   SW9 . . . . .5C 90
Lord Napier Pl. W6 . . . . .1C 84
Lord Nth. St.
   SW1 . . . . . .5D 23 (4A 76)
Lord Roberts M. SW6 . . . .3D 87
Lord's Cricket Ground
   . . . . .2F 59
Lords Cl. SE21 . . . . .2E 119
Lordship Gro. N16 . . . . . .4F 35
Lordship La. SE22 . . . . .2B 106
Lordship La. Est.
   SE21 . . . . .5C 106
Lordship Pk. N16 . . . . . .4E 35
Lordship Pk. M. N16 . . . .4E 35
Lordship Pl. SW3 . . . . . .2A 88
Lordship Rd. N16 . . . . . .3F 35
Lordship Ter. N16 . . . . . .4F 35
Lords Vw. NW8 . . . . .2F 59
   (not continuous)
Loreburn Ho. N7 . . . . . . .1B 48
Lorenzo St.
   WC1 . . . . . .1F 7 (2B 62)
Loring Rd. SE14 . . . . . . .4A 94
Loris Rd. W6 . . . . .4E 71
Lorn Ct. SW9 . . . . .5C 90
Lorne Cl. NW8 . . . . .2A 60
Lorne Gdns. W11 . . . . . .3F 71
Lorne Ho. E1 . . . . .4A 66
   (off Ben Jonson Rd.)
Lorne Rd. E7 . . . . .1D 55
   E17 . . . . .1C 38
   N4 . . . . .3B 34
Lorn Rd. SW9 . . . . .5B 90
Lorraine Ct. NW1 . . . . . .4D 47
Lorrimore Rd. SE17 . . . . .2D 91
Lorrimore Sq. SE17 . . . . .2D 91

Lorton Ho. NW6 . . . . . . .5C 44
   (off Kilburn Vale)
Lost Theatre 4F 89
Lothair Rd. Nth. N4 . . . . .1D 35
Lothair Rd. Sth. N4 . . . . .2C 34
Lothair St. SW11 . . . . . .1A 102
Lothbury
   EC2 . . . . . .2B 18 (5F 63)
Lothian Rd. SW9 . . . . . . .4D 91
Lothrop St. W10 . . . . . . .2A 58
Lots Rd. SW10 . . . . .3E 87
Lotus Cl. SE21 . . . . . . .3F 119
Loubet St. SW17 . . . . . .5B 116
Loudoun Rd. NW8 . . . . . .5E 45
Loughborough Est.
   SW9 . . . . .1D 105
Loughborough Pk.
   SW9 . . . . .2D 105
Loughborough Rd.
   SW9 . . . . .5C 90
Loughborough St.
   SE11 . . . . .1B 90
Lough Rd. N7 . . . . .2B 48
Louisa Cl. E9 . . . . .5F 51
Louisa Gdns. E1 . . . . . . .3F 65
Louisa St. E1 . . . . .3F 65
Louise Aumonier Wlk.
   N19 . . . . .2A 34
   (off Jessie Blythe La.)
Louise Bennett Cl.
   SE24 . . . . .2D 105
Louise De Marillac Ho.
   E1 . . . . .4E 65
   (off Smithy St.)
Louise Rd. E15 . . . . .3A 54
Louise White Ho.
   N19 . . . . .3F 33
Louisville Rd.
   SW17 . . . . .3C 116
Louvaine Rd. SW11 . . . . .2F 101
Lovat Cl. NW2 . . . . .5B 28
Lovat La.
   EC3 . . . . . .4D 19 (1A 78)
   (not continuous)
Lovatt Ct. SW12 . . . . . .1D 117
Lovegrove St. SE1 . . . . . .1C 92
Lovegrove Wlk. E14 . . . . .2E 81
Lovelace Rd. SE21 . . . . .2E 119
Love La. EC2 . . . .2A 18 (5E 63)
Lovelinch Cl. SE15 . . . . .2E 93
Lovell Ho. E8 . . . . .5C 50
   (off Shrubland Rd.)
Lovell Pl. SE16 . . . . .4A 80
Loveridge M. NW6 . . . . . .3B 44
Loveridge Rd. NW6 . . . . .3B 44
Lovers Wlk. SE10 . . . . . .2F 95
Lovett's Pl. SW18 . . . . . .2D 101
Love Wlk. SE5 . . . . .5F 91
Low Cross Wood La.
   SE21 . . . . .3B 120
Lowden Rd. SE24 . . . . . .2D 105
Lowder Ho. E1 . . . . .2D 79
   (off Wapping La.)
Lowe Av. E16 . . . . .4C 68
Lowell Ho. SE5 . . . . .3E 91
   (off Wyndham Est.)
Lowell St. E14 . . . . .5A 66
Lwr. Addison Gdns.
   W14 . . . . .3A 72

Lwr. Belgrave St.
   SW1 . . . . . .5D 21 (4D 75)
LOWER CLAPTON 1D 51
Lwr. Clapton Rd. E5 . . . . .5D 37
Lwr. Clarendon Wlk.
   W11 . . . . .5A 58
   (off Clarendon Rd.)
Lwr. Common St.
   SW15 . . . . .1D 99
Lwr. Grosvenor Pl.
   SW1 . . . . . .5E 21 (4D 75)
LOWER HOLLOWAY 2B 48
Lwr. James St.
   W1 . . . . . . .4A 14 (1E 75)
Lwr. John St.
   W1 . . . . . . .4A 14 (1E 75)
Lwr. Lea Crossing
   E14 . . . . .1A 82
   E16 . . . . .1A 82
Lower Mall W6 . . . . .1D 85
Lower Marsh
   SE1 . . . . . .4B 24 (3C 76)
Lwr. Merton Ri. NW3 . . . .4A 46
Lwr. New Change Pas.
   EC4 . . . . .3A 18
   (off One New Change)
Lwr. Richmond Rd.
   SW15 . . . . .1D 99
Lower Rd.
   SE1 . . . . . .3B 24 (3C 76)
   SE8 . . . . .5F 79
   SE16 . . . . .3E 79
   (not continuous)
Lwr. Robert St. WC2 . . . .5E 15
   (off Robert St.)
Lwr. Sloane St. SW1 . . . .5C 74
LOWER SYDENHAM 4F 121
Lwr. Sydenham Ind. Est.
   SE26 . . . . .5B 122
Lower Ter. NW3 . . . . .5E 31
   SE27 . . . . .5D 119
   (off Woodcote Rd.)
Lwr. Thames St.
   EC3 . . . . . .5C 18 (1F 77)
Lowerwood Ct. W11 . . . . .5A 58
   (off Westbourne Pk. Rd.)
Lowestoft Cl. E5 . . . . . . .4E 37
   (off Theydon Rd.)
Loweswater Ho. E3 . . . . . .3B 66
Lowfield Rd. NW6 . . . . . .4C 44
Low Hall La. E17 . . . . . . .1A 38
Low Hall Mnr. Bus. Cen.
   E17 . . . . .1A 38
Lowman Rd. N7 . . . . .1B 48
Lownde M. SW16 . . . . . .2A 118
Lowndes Cl. SW1 . . . . . .4C 74
Lowndes Ct.
   SW1 . . . . . .5A 20 (4B 74)
   W1 . . . . .3F 13
   (off Carnaby St.)
Lowndes Lodge SW1 . . . .5A 20
   (off Cadogan Pl.)
Lowndes M. SW16 . . . . .2A 118
Lowndes Pl. SW1 . . . . . .4C 74
Lowndes Sq.
   SW1 . . . . . .4A 20 (3B 74)
Lowndes St.
   SW1 . . . . . .5A 20 (4C 74)
Lowood Ct. SE19 . . . . . .5B 120
   (off Farquhar Rd.)

Lowood Ho. *E1* *1E 79*
  (off Bewley St.)
Lowood St. E1 . . . . .1D **79**
Lowry Ct. *SE16* *1D 93*
  (off Stubbs Dr.)
Lowry Ho. *E14* *3C 80*
  (off Cassilis Rd.)
Lowther Hill
  SE23 . . . . .5A **108**
Lowther Ho. *SW1* *1E 89*
  (off Churchill Gdns.)
Lowther Rd. N7 . . . . .2C **48**
  SW13 . . . . .4B **84**
Lowth Rd. SE5 . . . . .4E **91**
Loxford Av. E6 . . . . .1F **69**
Loxham St.
  WC1 . . . . .2E **7** (2A **62**)
Loxley Cl. SE26 . . . . .5F **121**
Loxley Rd. SW18 . . . . .1F **115**
Loxton Rd. SE23 . . . . .1F **121**
LSO St Lukes *3A 10*
  (off Odl St.)
Lubbock Ho. *E14* *1D 81*
  (off Poplar High St.)
Lubbock St. SE14 . . . . .3E **93**
Lucan Ho. *N1* *5F 49*
  (off Colville Est.)
Lucan Pl. SW3 . . . . .5A **74**
Lucas Av. E13 . . . . .5D **55**
Lucas Cl. NW10 . . . . .4C **42**
Lucas Ct. SE26 . . . . .5A **122**
  SW11 . . . . .4C **88**
Lucas Ho. *SW10* *3D 87*
  (off Coleridge Gdns.)
  WC1 . . . .*2A 62*
  (off Argyle Wlk.)
Lucas Sq. NW11 . . . . .1C **30**
Lucas St. SE8 . . . . .4C **94**
Lucerne M. W8 . . . . .2C **72**
Lucerne Rd. N5 . . . . .1D **49**
Lucey Rd. SE16 . . . . .4C **78**
Lucey Way SE16 . . . . .4C **78**
Lucien Rd. SW17 . . . . .4C **116**
  SW19 . . . . .2D **115**
Lucorn Cl. SE12 . . . . .4B **110**
Lucy Brown Ho. SE1 . . . . .2A **26**
Ludgate B'way.
  EC4 . . . . . .3D **17** (5D **63**)
Ludgate Cir.
  EC4 . . . . . .3D **17** (5D **63**)
Ludgate Hill
  EC4 . . . . . .3D **17** (5D **63**)
Ludgate Sq.
  EC4 . . . . . .3E **17** (5D **63**)
Ludham NW5 . . . . .2B **46**
Ludlow St.
  EC1 . . . . .3F **9** (3E **63**)
Ludovick Wlk. SW15 . . . . . .2A **98**
Ludwell Ho. *W14* *4A 72*
  (off Russell Rd.)
Ludwick M. SE14 . . . . .3A **94**
Luffman Ho. SE12 . . . . . . .3D **125**
Lugard Ho. *W12* *2D 71*
Lugard Rd. SE15 . . . . .5D **93**
Luke Ho. *E1* *5D 65*
  (off Tillman St.)
Luke St. EC2 . . .3D **11** (3A **64**)
Lukin St. E1 . . . . .5E **65**
Luli Ct. SE14 . . . . .2B **94**

Lullingstone Ho.
  SE15 . . . . .2E **93**
  (off Lovelinch Cl.)
Lullingstone La.
  SE13 . . . . .4F **109**
Lulot Gdns. N19 . . . . .4D **33**
Lulworth NW1 . . . .*4F 47*
  (off Wrotham Rd.)
  SE17 . . . .*1F 91*
  (off Portland St.)
Lulworth Ct. *N1* *4A 50*
  (off St Peter's Way)
Lulworth Ho. SW8 . . . . .3B **90**
Lulworth Rd. SE9 . . . . .2F **125**
  SE15 . . . . .5D **93**
Lumiere Apartments
  SW11 . . . . .2F **101**
Lumiere Building, The
  E7 . . . .*2F 55*
  (off Romford Rd.)
Lumiere Ct. SW17 . . . . . . .2C **116**
Lumina Bldgs. *E14* *2E 81*
  (off Prestons Rd.)
Lumina Loft Apartments
  SE1 . . . .*4E 27*
  (off Tower Bri. Rd.)
Lumley Ct.
  WC2 . . . . . . .5E **15** (1A **76**)
Lumley Flats *SW1* *1C 88*
  (off Holbein Pl.)
Lumley St.
  W1 . . . . .3C **12** (5C **60**)
Lumsdon NW8 . . . .*5D 45*
  (off Abbey Rd.)
Luna Ho. SE16 . . . . .3C **78**
Lunan Ho. *E3* *1B 66*
  (off Shetland Rd.)
Lund Point E15 . . . . .5E **53**
Lundy Wlk. N1 . . . . .3E **49**
Lunham Rd. SE19 . . . . .5A **120**
Luntley Pl. *E1* *4C 64*
  (off Chicksand St.)
Lupin Cl. SW2 . . . . .2D **119**
Lupino Ct. SE11 . . . . .5B **76**
Lupin Point *SE1* *3B 78*
  (off Abbey St.)
Lupton Cl. SE12 . . . . .3D **125**
Lupton St. NW5 . . . . .1E **47**
  (not continuous)
Lupus St. SW1 . . . . .1D **89**
Luralda Wharf E14 . . . . . . .1F **95**
Lurgan Av. W6 . . . . .2F **85**
Lurline Gdns. SW11 . . . . . .4C **88**
Luscombe Way SW8 . . . . . .3A **90**
Lushington Rd.
  NW10 . . . . .1D **57**
  SE6 . . . . .4D **123**
Lushington Ter. E8 . . . . . . .2C **50**
Luther King Cl. E17 . . . . . . .1B **38**
Luton Ho. *E13* *3C 68*
  (off Luton Rd.)
Luton Pl. SE10 . . . . .3E **95**
Luton Rd. E13 . . . . .3C **68**
Luton St. NW8 . . . . .3F **59**
Luton Ter. *NW3* *1E 45*
  (off Lakis Cl.)
Luttrell Av. SW15 . . . . .3D **99**
Lutwyche Rd. SE6 . . . . .2B **122**
Lutyens Ho. *SW1* *1E 89*
  (off Churchill Gdns.)

Luxborough Ho. *W1* *5B 4*
  (off Luxborough St.)
Luxborough St.
  W1 . . . . .5B **4** (4C **60**)
Luxborough Twr. W1 . . . . . .5B **4**
Luxemburg M. E15 . . . . . . .2A **54**
Luxemburg Gdns. W6 . . . . .5F **71**
Luxfield Rd. SE9 . . . . .1F **125**
Luxford St. SE16 . . . . .5F **79**
Luxmore St. SE4 . . . . .4B **94**
Luxor St. SE5 . . . . .1E **105**
Lyall Av. SE21 . . . . .4A **120**
Lyall M.
  SW1 . . . . .5B **20** (4C **74**)
Lyall M. W. SW1 . . . . .4C **74**
Lyall St.
  SW1 . . . . .5B **20** (4C **74**)
Lyal Rd. E3 . . . . .1A **66**
Lycett Pl. W12 . . . . .3C **70**
Lyceum Theatre
  Covent Garden . .4F **15**
Lydden Gro. SW18 . . . . . . .5D **101**
Lydden Rd. SW18 . . . . .5D **101**
Lydford *NW1* *5E 47*
  (off Royal College St.)
Lydford Cl. *N16* *2A 50*
  (off Pellerin Rd.)
Lydford Rd. N15 . . . . .1F **35**
  NW2 . . . . .3E **43**
  W9 . . . . .3B **58**
Lydhurst Av. SW2 . . . . .2B **118**
Lydney Cl. SW19 . . . . .2A **114**
Lydon Rd. SW4 . . . . .1E **103**
Lyford Rd. SW18 . . . . .5F **101**
Lygon Ho. *E2* *2B 64*
  (off Gosset St.)
  SW6 . . . .*4A 86*
  (off Fulham Pal. Rd.)
Lygon Pl.
  SW1 . . . . .5D **21** (4D **75**)
Lyham Cl. SW2 . . . . .4A **104**
Lyham Rd. SW2 . . . . .3A **104**
Lyly House *SE1* *5C 26*
  (off Burbage Cl.)
Lyme Farm Rd.
  SE12 . . . . .2C **110**
Lyme Gro. E9 . . . . .4E **51**
Lyme Gro. Ho. *E9* *4E 51*
  (off Lyme Gro.)
Lymer Av. SE19 . . . . .5B **120**
Lyme St. NW1 . . . . .4E **47**
Lyme Ter. NW1 . . . . .4E **47**
Lyminge Gdns.
  SW18 . . . . .1A **116**
Lymington Lodge *E14* *4F 81*
  (off Schooner Cl.)
Lymington Rd. NW6 . . . . . .3D **45**
Lympstone Gdns.
  SE15 . . . . .3C **92**
Lynbrook Gro. SE15 . . . . . .3A **92**
Lynch Cl. SE3 . . . . .5B **96**
Lynch Wlk. *SE8* *2B 94*
  (off Prince St.)
Lyncott Cres. SW4 . . . . . . .2D **103**
Lyncourt SE3 . . . . .5F **95**
Lyncroft Gdns. NW6 . . . . . .2C **44**
Lyncroft Mans. NW6 . . . . . .2C **44**
Lyndale NW2 . . . . .1B **44**
Lyndale Av. NW2 . . . . .5B **30**
Lyndale Cl. SE3 . . . . .2B **96**

Lynde Ho. SW4 . . . . . . .1F 103
Lynden Ho. E1 . . . . .2F 65
　(off Westfield Way)
Lyndhurst Cl. NW10 . . . .5A 28
Lyndhurst Ct. NW8 . . . . . .5F 45
　(off Finchley Rd.)
Lyndhurst Dr. E10 . . . . . .2E 39
Lyndhurst Gdns. NW3 . . .2F 45
Lyndhurst Gro. SE15 . . . .5A 92
Lyndhurst Lodge E14 . . .5F 81
　(off Millennium Dr.)
Lyndhurst Rd. NW3 . . . . .2F 45
Lyndhurst Sq. SE15 . . . .4B 92
Lyndhurst Ter. NW3 . . . . .2F 45
Lyndhurst Way SE15 . . . .4B 92
Lyndon Yd. SW17 . . . .4E 115
Lyneham Wlk. E5 . . . . . .2A 52
Lynette Av. SW4 . . . . .4D 103
Lynford French Ho.
　SE17 . . . . .1E 91
　(off Thrush St.)
Lyn M. E3 . . . . .2B 66
　N16 . . . . .1A 50
Lynmouth Rd. E17 . . . . .1A 38
　N16 . . . . .3B 36
Lynne Cl. SE23 . . . . . . .5B 108
Lynne Ct. NW6 . . . . .4D 45
　(off Priory Rd.)
Lynnett Ct. E9 . . . . .3A 52
　(off Annis Rd.)
Lynn Ho. SE15 . . . . .2D 93
　(off Friary Est.)
Lynn M. E11 . . . . .4A 40
Lynn Rd. E11 . . . . .4A 40
　SW12 . . . . .5D 103
Lynsted Gdns. SE9 . . . .2F 111
Lynton Cl. NW10 . . . . . . .2A 42
Lynton Est. SE1 . . . . .5C 78
Lynton Ho. W2 . . . . .5C 59
　(off Hallfield Est.)
Lynton Mans. SE1 . . . . .5B 24
　(off Westminster Bri. Rd.)
Lynton Rd. N8 . . . . .1F 33
　(not continuous)
　NW6 . . . . .1B 58
　SE1 . . . . .5B 78
Lynwood Rd. SW17 . . .3B 116
Lynx Way E16 . . . . .1F 83
Lyon Ho. NW8 . . . . .3A 60
　(off Broadley St.)
Lyon Ind. Est. NW2 . . . .4D 29
Lyons Pl. NW8 . . . . .3F 59
Lyon St. N1 . . . . .4B 48
Lyons Wlk. W14 . . . . . . .5A 72
Lyric Ct. E8 . . . . .4B 50
　(off Holly St.)
Lyric M. SE26 . . . . .4E 121
Lyric Rd. SW13 . . . . . . .4B 84
Lyric Sq. W6 . . . . .5D 71
　(off King St.)
Lyric Theatre
　Hammersmith 5E 71
　Westminster 4B 14
　(off Shaftesbury Av.)
Lysander Gro. N19 . . . . .3F 33
Lysander Ho. E2 . . . . . . .1D 65
　(off Temple St.)
Lysander M. N19 . . . . . .3E 33
Lysia Ct. SW6 . . . . .3F 85
　(off Lysia St.)

Lysias Rd. SW12 . . . . . .4D 103
Lysia St. SW6 . . . . .3F 85
Lysons Wlk. SW15 . . . .2C 98
Lytcott Gro. SE22 . . . . .3A 106
Lytham St. SE17 . . . . . .1F 91
Lyttelton Cl. NW3 . . . . . .4A 46
Lyttelton Ho. E9 . . . . .4E 51
　(off Well St.)
Lyttelton Rd. E10 . . . . . .5D 39
Lyttelton Theatre 1A 24
　(in National Theatre)
Lytton Cl. N2 . . . . .1F 31
Lytton Ct. WC1 . . . . .1E 15
　(off Barter St.)
Lytton Gro. SW15 . . . . . .3F 99
Lytton Rd. E11 . . . . .2A 40
Lyveden Rd. SE3 . . . . . .3D 97

M

Mableden Pl.
　WC1 . . . . .2C 6 (2F 61)
Mablethorpe Rd.
　SW6 . . . . .3A 86
Mabley St. E9 . . . . .2A 52
Macarthur Cl. E7 . . . . . .3C 54
Macarthur Ter. SE7 . . . . .2F 97
Macartney Ho. SE10 . . . .3F 95
　(off Chesterfield Wlk.)
　SW9 . . . . .4C 90
　(off Gosling Way)
Macaulay Cl. SW4 . . . . .1D 103
Macaulay Rd. E6 . . . . . .1F 69
　SW4 . . . . .1D 103
Macaulay Sq. SW4 . . . . .2D 103
McAuley Cl. SE1 . . . . . . .5B 24
Macaulay Ho. W10 . . . . .4A 58
　(off Portobello Rd.)
Macaulay M. SE13 . . . . . .5E 95
McAusland Ho. E3 . . . . .1B 66
　(off Wright's Rd.)
Macbeth Ho. N1 . . . . . . .1A 64
Macbeth St. W6 . . . . . . .1D 85
McBride Ho. E3 . . . . . . .1B 66
　(off Libra Rd.)
McCabe Ct. E16 . . . . . . .4B 68
　(off Barking Rd.)
McCall Cl. SW4 . . . . .5A 90
McCall Cres. SE7 . . . . . . .1F 97
McCall Ho. N7 . . . . .1A 48
Macclesfield Rd. EC1 . . .2F 9
　(off Central St.)
Macclesfield Rd.
　EC1 . . . . .1F 9 (2E 63)
Macclesfield St.
　W1 . . . . .4C 14 (1F 75)
McCoid Way
　SE1 . . . . .4F 25 (3E 77)
McCrone M. NW3 . . . . . .3F 45
McCullum Rd. E3 . . . . . .5B 52
McDermott Cl.
　SW11 . . . . .1A 102
McDermott Rd.
　SE15 . . . . .1C 106
Macdonald Ho.
　SW11 . . . . .5C 88
　(off Dagnall St.)
Macdonald Rd. E7 . . . . .1C 54
　N19 . . . . .4E 33

McDowall Cl. E16 . . . . . .4B 68
McDowall Rd. SE5 . . . . .4E 91
Macduff Rd. SW11 . . . . .4C 88
Mace Cl. E1 . . . . .2D 79
Mace St. E2 . . . . .1F 65
McEwan Ho. E3 . . . . . . .1B 66
　(off Roman Rd.)
McEwen Way E15 . . . . . .5F 53
　(off Rokeby St.)
Macey Ho. SW11 . . . . . .4A 88
Macey St. SE10 . . . . .2E 95
　(off Thames St.)
McFadden Ct. E10 . . . . .5D 39
　(off Buckingham Rd.)
Macfarland Gro.
　SE15 . . . . .3A 92
Macfarlane Rd. W12 . . . .2E 71
Macfarren Pl.
　NW1 . . . . .4C 4 (3C 60)
Macfarron Ho. W10 . . . .2A 58
　(off Parry Rd.)
McGlashon Ho. E1 . . . . .3C 64
　(off Hunton St.)
McGrath Rd. E15 . . . . . .2B 54
McGregor Ct. N1 . . . . . . .1E 11
Macgregor Rd. E16 . . . . .4E 69
McGregor Rd. W11 . . . . .5B 58
Machell Rd. SE15 . . . . . .1E 107
McIndoe Ct. N1 . . . . .5F 49
　(off Sherborne St.)
Macintosh Ho. W1 . . . . . .5C 4
　(off Beaumont St.)
McIntosh Ho. SE16 . . . . .5E 79
　(off Millender Wlk.)
Mackay Ho. W12 . . . . . .1D 71
　(off White City Est.)
Mackay Rd. SW4 . . . . .1D 103
McKenna Ho. E3 . . . . . .1B 66
　(off Wright's Rd.)
Mackennal St. NW8 . . . .1A 60
Mackenzie Cl. W12 . . . .1D 71
Mackenzie Ho. NW2 . . .5C 28
Mackenzie Rd. N7 . . . . .3B 48
Mackenzie Wlk. E14 . . . .2C 80
McKerrell Rd. SE15 . . . .4C 92
Mackeson Rd. NW3 . . . .1B 46
Mackie Rd. SW2 . . . . . . .5C 104
Mackintosh La. E9 . . . . .2F 51
Macklin St.
　WC2 . . . . .2E 15 (5A 62)
Mackonochie Ho. EC1 . . .5B 8
　(off Baldwins Gdns.)
Mackrow Wlk. E14 . . . . .1E 81
Mack's Rd. SE16 . . . . . .5C 78
Mackworth Ho. NW1 . . . .1F 5
　(off Augustus St.)
Mackworth St.
　NW1 . . . . .1F 5 (2E 61)
McLaren Ho. SE1 . . . . . .4D 25
　(off St Georges Cir.)
Maclaren M. SW15 . . . . .2E 99
Maclean Rd. SE23 . . . . .4A 108
McLeod Ct. SE22 . . . . . .1C 120
McLeod's M. SW7 . . . . .5D 73
Macleod St. SE17 . . . . . .1E 91
Maclise Ho. SW1 . . . . . . .5A 76
　(off Marsham St.)
Maclise Rd. W14 . . . . . . .4A 72
Macmillan Ho. NW8 . . . .2A 60
　(off Lorne Cl.)

McMillan Ho. *SE4* 1A **108**
   (off Arica Rd.)
  SE14 ....4A **94**
McMillan St. SE8 .....2C **94**
McMillan Student Village
  SE8 ....2C **94**
Macmillan Way
  SW17 ....4D **117**
Macnamara Ho.
  SW10 ....3F **87**
   (off Worlds End Est.)
McNeil Rd. SE5 .....5A **92**
Maconochies Rd. E14 ..1D **95**
Macquarie Way E14 ..5D **81**
Macready Ho. *W1* 4A **60**
   (off Crawford St.)
Macready Pl. N7 .....1A **48**
   (not continuous)
Macrea Ho. *E3* 2B **66**
   (off Bow Rd.)
Macroom Ho. *W9* 2B **58**
   (off Macroom Rd.)
Macroom Rd. W9 .....2B **58**
Mac's Pl. EC4 ....2B **16**
Madame Tussaud's
  ....4B **4** (3C **60**)
Maddams St. E3 ....3D **67**
Maddocks Ho. *E1* 1D **79**
   (off Cornwall St.)
Maddock Way SE17 ...2D **91**
Maddox St.
  W1 .....4E **13** (1D **75**)
Madeira Rd. E11 .....3F **39**
  SW16 ....5A **118**
Madinah Rd. E8 ....3C **50**
Madison, The *SE1* 3B **26**
   (off Long La.)
Madison Bldg. *SE10* ..4D **95**
   (off Blackheath Rd.)
Madison Ho. *E14* 1B **80**
   (off Victory Pl.)
Madoc Cl. NW2 ....4C **30**
Madras Pl. N7 ....3C **48**
Madras Rd. SW13 .....4C **84**
Madrigal La. SE5 .....3D **91**
Madron St. SE17 .....1A **92**
Mafeking Av. E6 .....1F **69**
Mafeking Rd. E16 .....3B **68**
Magazine Ga. W2 .....2A **74**
Magdala Av. N19 .....4E **33**
Magdalene Cl. SE15 ..5D **93**
Magdalen Ho. *E16* 2D **83**
   (off Keats Av.)
Magdalen M. NW3 .....3E **45**
   (off Frognal)
Magdalen Pas. E1 .....1B **78**
Magdalen Rd.
  SW18 ....1E **115**
Magdalen St.
  SE1 .....2D **27** (2A **78**)
Magee St. SE11 ....2C **90**
Magellan Cl. NW10 ....4A **42**
   (off Brentfield Rd.)
Magellan Ho. *E1* 3F **65**
   (off Ernest St.)
Magellan Pl. E14 .....5C **80**
Magistrates' Court
  Camberwell Green
  ....4F **91**
  City of London ..3B **18**

Magistrates' Court
  City of Westminster
  ....5A **76**
  Clerkenwell 1A **8**
  Greenwich 4D **95**
  Hendon 1B **28**
  Highbury Corner
  ....3C **48**
  Inner London
  Family Proceedings Court
  ....2F **13** (4E **61**)
  South Western ..1B **102**
  Stratford 4F **53**
  Thames 2C **84**
  West London ...1F **85**
  Wimbledon 5C **114**
Magnin Cl. E8 ....5C **50**
Magnolia Cl. E10 .....4C **38**
Magnolia Gdns. E10 ..4C **38**
Magnolia Ho. *SE8* 2B **94**
   (off Evelyn St.)
Magnolia Lodge *W8* ...4D **73**
   (off St Mary's Ga.)
Magnolia Pl. SW4 .....3A **104**
Magpie All.
  EC4 .....3C **16** (5C **62**)
Magpie Cl. E7 ....2B **54**
Magpie Ho. *E3* 5B **52**
   (off Sycamore Av.)
Magpie Pl. SE14 .....2A **94**
Magri Wlk. E1 ....4E **65**
Maguire St. SE1 .....3B **78**
Maha Bldg. *E3* 2C **66**
   (off Merchant St.)
Mahatma Gandhi Ind. Est.
  SE24 ....2D **105**
Mahogany Cl. SE16 ...2A **80**
Mahoney Ho. SE14 ....4B **94**
   (off Heald St.)
Maida Av. W2 ....4E **59**
MAIDA HILL 3B **58**
MAIDA VALE 3D **59**
Maida Vale W9 ....1D **59**
Maiden La. NW1 .....4F **47**
  SE1 .....2A **26** (2E **77**)
  WC2 .....5E **15** (1A **76**)
Maiden Pl. NW5 .....5E **33**
Maiden Rd. E15 .....4A **54**
Maidenstone Hill
  SE10 ....4E **95**
Maidstone Bldgs. M.
  SE1 .....2A **26** (2E **77**)
Mail Coach Yd. E2 ....1E **11**
Main Mill *SE10* 3D **95**
   (off Greenwich High St.)
Mais Ho. SE26 ....2D **121**
Maismore St. SE15 ...2C **92**
Maitland Cl. SE10 ....3D **95**
Maitland Ct. *W2* 1F **73**
   (off Lancaster Ter.)
Maitland Ho. E2 ....1E **65**
   (off Waterloo Gdns.)
  SW1 ....2E **89**
   (off Churchill Gdns.)
Maitland Pk. Est.
  NW3 ....3B **46**
Maitland Pk. Rd.
  NW3 ....3B **46**

Maitland Pk. Vs.
  NW3 ....3B **46**
Maitland Pl. E5 ....1D **51**
Maitland Rd. E15 .....3B **54**
  SE26 ....5F **121**
Maize Row E14 ....1B **80**
Major Cl. SW9 ....1D **105**
Major Rd. E15 ....2F **53**
  SE16 ....4C **78**
Makepeace Av. N6 ....4C **32**
Makepeace Mans.
  N6 ....4C **32**
Makins St. SW3 .....5A **74**
Malabar Cl. *W12* 1D **71**
   (off India Way)
Malabar St. E14 .....3C **80**
Malam Ct. SE11 .....5C **76**
Malam Gdns. E14 ....1D **81**
Malbrook Rd.
  SW15 ....2D **99**
Malcolm Cl. E7 ....3B **54**
  NW4 ....1C **28**
Malcolm Cres. NW4 ..1C **28**
Malcolm Ho. *N1* 1A **64**
   (off Arden Est.)
Malcolm Pl. E2 ....3E **65**
Malcolm Rd. E1 ....3E **65**
Malcolm Sargent Ho.
  E16 ....2D **83**
   (off Evelyn Rd.)
Malcolmson Ho. *SW1* ..1F **89**
   (off Aylesford St.)
Malden Ct. N4 ....1E **35**
Malden Cres. NW1 ...3C **46**
Malden Pl. NW5 .....2C **46**
Malden Rd. NW5 .....2B **46**
Malden Ct. E15 .....2A **54**
  N1 ....5E **49**
  SE5 ....1A **106**
Malet Pl. WC1 ..4B **6** (3F **61**)
Malet St. WC1 ..4B **6** (3F **61**)
Maley Av. SE27 .....2D **119**
Malfort Rd. SE5 .....1A **106**
Malham Rd. SE23 ....1F **121**
Malham Rd. Ind. Est.
  SE23 ....1F **121**
Malibu Cl. SE26 .....3D **121**
Mall, The 3B **22** (3F **75**)
Mall, The E15 ....4F **53**
  SW1 ....3A **22** (3E **75**)
Mallams M. SW9 .....1D **105**
Mallard Cl. E9 ....3B **52**
  NW6 ....1C **58**
Mallard Ho. NW8 .....1A **60**
   (off Bridgeman St.)
  SW6 ....4E **87**
   (off Station Cl.)
Mallard Point *E3* 2D **67**
   (off Rainhill Way)
Mallards E11 ....2C **40**
   (off Blake Hall Rd.)
Mall Chambers *W8* ...2C **72**
   (off Kensington Mall)
Mallet Rd. SE13 .....4F **109**
Mall Galleries 1C **22**
Malling SE13 ....3D **109**
Mallinson Rd.
  SW11 ....3A **102**
Mallinson Sports Cen.
  ....2B **32**

Mallon Gdns. *E1* 2F **19**
(off Commercial St.)
Mallord St. *SW3* 2F **87**
Mallory Bldgs. *EC1* 4D **9**
(off St John St.)
Mallory Ct. *E14* 4D **67**
SE4 . . . . .2A **108**
Mallory Ct. *SE12* 5D **111**
Mallory St. *NW8* 3A **60**
Mallow St.
EC1 . . . . .3B **10** (3F **63**)
Mall Rd. *W6* 1D **85**
Mall Vs. *W6* 1D **85**
(off Mall Rd.)
Malmesbury *E2* 1E **65**
(off Cyprus St.)
Malmesbury Rd. *E3* 2B **66**
E16 . . . . .4A **68**
Malmesbury Ter. *E16* . . .4B **68**
Malmsey Ho. *SE11* 1B **90**
Malmsmead Ho. *E9* 2B **52**
(off King's Mead Way)
Malpas Rd. *E8* 2D **51**
SE4 . . . . .5B **94**
Malswick Ct. *SE15* 3A **92**
(off Tower Mill Rd.)
Malta Rd. *E10* 3C **38**
Malta St. *EC1* 3D **9** (3D **63**)
Maltby Ho. *SE1* 5F **27**
(off Maltby St.)
Maltby St.
SE1 . . . . .4F **27** (3B **78**)
Malthouse Dr. *W4* 2B **84**
Malthouse Pas.
SW13 . . . . .5B **84**
(off Clevelands Gdns.)
Malting Ho. *E14* 1B **80**
(off Oak La.)
Maltings Cl. *E3* 2E **67**
SW13 . . . . .5B **84**
Maltings Lodge *W4* 2A **84**
(off Corney Reach Way)
Maltings Pl. *SE1* 4E **27**
SW6 . . . . .4D **87**
Malton M. *W10* 5A **58**
Malton Rd. *W10* 5A **58**
Maltravers St.
WC2 . . . . . .4A **16** (1B **76**)
Malt St. *SE1* 2C **92**
Malva Cl. *SW18* 3D **101**
Malvern Cl. *W10* 4B **58**
Malvern Ct. *SW7* 5F **73**
(off Onslow Sq.)
W12 . . . . .3C **70**
(off Hadyn Pk. Rd.)
Malvern Gdns. *NW2* 4A **30**
Malvern Ho. *N16* 3B **36**
SE17 . . . . .1E **91**
(off Liverpool Gro.)
Malvern M. *NW6* 2C **58**
Malvern Pl. *NW6* 2B **58**
Malvern Rd. *E6* 5F **55**
E8 . . . . .4C **50**
E11 . . . . .4A **40**
NW6 . . . . .1B **58**
(not continuous)
Malvern Ter. *N1* 5C **48**
Malwood Rd. *SW12* 4D **103**
Malyons Rd. *SE13* 4D **109**
Malyons Ter. *SE13* 3D **109**

Managers St. *E14* 2E **81**
Manaton Cl. *SE15* 1D **107**
Manbey Gro. *E15* 3A **54**
Manbey Pk. Rd.
E15 . . . . .3A **54**
Manbey Rd. *E15* 3A **54**
Manbey St. *E15* 3A **54**
Manbre Rd. *W6* 2E **85**
Manchester Ct. *E16* 5D **69**
(off Garvary Rd.)
Manchester Dr. *W10* 3A **58**
Manchester Gro. *E14* . . .1E **95**
Manchester Ho.
SE17 . . . . .1E **91**
(off East St.)
Manchester M. *W1* 1B **12**
Manchester Rd. *E14* 1E **95**
N15 . . . . .1F **35**
Manchester Sq.
W1 . . . . . .2B **12** (5C **60**)
Manchester St.
W1 . . . . . .1B **12** (4C **60**)
Manchuria Rd.
SW11 . . . . .4C **102**
Manciple St.
SE1 . . . . . .4B **26** (3F **77**)
Mancroft Ct. *NW8* 5F **45**
(off St John's Wood Pk.)
Mandalay Rd. *SW4* 3E **103**
Mandarin Ct. *NW10* 3A **42**
(off Mitchellbrook Way)
SE8 . . . . .2B **94**
Mandarin St. *E14* 1C **80**
Mandarin Wharf *N1* 5A **50**
(off De Beauvoir Cres.)
Mandela Cl. *W12* 1D **71**
Mandela Ho. *E2* 2F **11**
(off Virginia Rd.)
SE5 . . . . .5D **91**
Mandela Rd. *E16* 5C **68**
Mandela St. *NW1* 5E **47**
SW9 . . . . .3C **90**
(not continuous)
Mandela Way *SE1* 5A **78**
Mandel Ho. *SW18* 2C **100**
Manderley *W14* 4B **72**
(off Oakwood La.)
Mandeville Cl. *SE3* 3B **96**
Mandeville Ho. *SE1* 1B **92**
(off Rolls Rd.)
SW4 . . . . .3E **103**
Mandeville M. *SW4* 2A **104**
Mandeville Pl.
W1 . . . . . .2C **12** (5C **60**)
Mandeville St. *E5* 5A **38**
Mandrake Rd.
SW17 . . . . .3B **116**
Mandrake Way *E15* 4A **54**
Mandrell Rd. *SW2* 3A **104**
Manette St.
W1 . . . . . . .3C **14** (5F **61**)
Manfred Rd. *SW15* 3B **100**
Manger Rd. *N7* 3A **48**
Manhattan Bldg. *E3* 1C **66**
Manilla St. *E14* 3C **80**
Manitoba Ct. *SE16* 3E **79**
(off Canada Est.)
Manley Ct. *N16* 5B **36**
Manley Ho. *SE11* 5C **76**
Manley St. *NW1* 5C **46**

Mannan Ho. *E3* 1B **66**
(off Roman Rd.)
Manneby Prior *N1* 1A **8**
(off Cumming St.)
Manningford Cl.
EC1 . . . . . .1D **9** (2D **63**)
Manning Ho. *W11* 5A **58**
(off Westbourne Pk. Rd.)
Manningtree Cl.
SW19 . . . . .1A **114**
Manningtree St. *E1* 5C **64**
Manny Shinwell Ho.
SW6 . . . . .2B **86**
(off Clem Attlee Ct.)
Manor Av. *SE4* 5B **94**
Manorbrook *SE3* 2C **110**
Manor Ct. *E10* 3D **39**
N2 . . . . .1B **32**
SW2 . . . . .3B **104**
SW3 . . . . .1A **88**
(off Hemus Pl.)
SW6 . . . . .4D **87**
SW16 . . . . .3A **118**
Manor Est. *SE16* 5D **79**
Manorfield Cl. *N19* 1E **47**
(off Fulbrook M.)
Manor Flds. *SW15* 4F **99**
Manor Gdns. *N7* 5A **34**
SW4 . . . . .5E **89**
(off Larkhall Ri.)
W4 . . . . .1A **84**
Manor Gro. *SE15* 2E **93**
Manorhall Gdns. *E10* . . .3C **38**
MANOR HOUSE 2F **35**
MANOR HOUSE 2E **35**
Manor Ho. *NW1* 4A **60**
(off Lisson Gro.)
Manor Ho. Ct. *W9* 3E **59**
(off Warrington Gdns.)
Manor Ho. Dr. *NW6* 4F **43**
Manor Ho. Gdn. *E11* 1D **41**
Manor La. *SE13* 3A **110**
SE13 . . . . .3A **110**
Manor La. Ter.
SE13 . . . . .2A **110**
Manor Lodge *NW6* 4F **43**
(off Willesden La.)
Manor M. *NW6* 1C **58**
(off Cambridge Av.)
SE4 . . . . .5B **94**
Manor Mt. *SE23* 1E **121**
Manor Pde. *N16* 4B **36**
NW10 . . . . .2C **56**
(off High St. Harlesden)
MANOR PARK 1F **55**
Manor Pk. *SE13* 2F **109**
Manor Pk. Crematorium
E7 . . . . .1E **55**
Manor Pk. Pde.
SE13 . . . . .2F **109**
(off Lee High Rd.)
Manor Pk. Rd.
E12 . . . . .1F **55**
(not continuous)
NW10 . . . . .5B **42**
Manor Pl. *SE17* 1D **91**
Manor Rd. *E10* 2C **38**
E15 . . . . .1A **68**
E16 . . . . .1A **68**
N16 . . . . .4F **35**

Manor Way SE3 . . . . . .2B **110**
  SE23 . . . . .5E **107**
Manorway SE7 . . . . . . .5F **83**
Manresa Rd. SW3 . . . . .1A **88**
Mansard Beeches
  SW17 . . . . .5C **116**
Mansell St.
  E1 . . . . . . .3F **19** (5B **64**)
  EC3 . . . . .1B **78**
Mansel Rd. SW19 . . . . .5A **114**
Manse Rd. N16 . . . . . . .5B **36**
Mansfield Ct. E2 . . . . . .5B **50**
  (off Whiston Rd.)
  SE15 . . . . .3B **92**
  (off Sumner Rd.)
Mansfield Hgts. N2 . . . .1A **32**
Mansfield Ho. N1 . . . . . .5A **50**
  (off New Era Est.)
Mansfield M.
  W1 . . . . . .1D **13** (4D **61**)
Mansfield Pl. NW3 . . . . .1E **45**
Mansfield Rd. E11 . . . . .1D **41**
  NW3 . . . . .2B **46**
Mansfield St.
  W1 . . . . . .1D **13** (4D **61**)
Mansford St. E2 . . . . . .1C **64**
Mansion Cl. SW9 . . . . . .4C **90**
  (not continuous)
Mansion Gdns. NW3 . . .5D **31**
Mansion House
  . . . . .3B **18** (5F **63**)
Mansion Ho. Pl.
  EC4 . . . . . .3B **18** (5F **63**)
Mansion Ho. St. EC4 . . .3B **18**
Mansions, The SW5 . . . .1D **87**
Manson Ho. N1 . . . . . . .4C **48**
  (off Drummond Way)
Manson M. SW7 . . . . . .5F **73**
Manson Pl. SW7 . . . . . .5F **73**
Manston NW1 . . . . .4E **47**
  (off Agar Gro.)
Manstone Rd. NW2 . . . .2A **44**
Manston Ho. W14 . . . . .4A **72**
  (off Russell Rd.)
Mantilla Rd. SW17 . . . . .4C **116**
Mantle Ct. SW18 . . . . . .4D **101**
  (off Mapleton Rd.)
Mantle Rd. SE4 . . . . . . .1A **108**
Mantle Way E15 . . . . . . .4A **54**
Mantua St. SW11 . . . . . .1F **101**
Mantus Cl. E1 . . . . .3E **65**
Mantus Rd. E1 . . . . .3E **65**
Manville Gdns.
  SW17 . . . . .3D **117**
Manville Rd. SW17 . . . .2C **116**
Manwood Rd. SE4 . . . . .3B **108**
Manygates SW12 . . . . .2D **117**
Mapesbury Ct. NW2 . . . .2A **44**
Mapesbury M. NW4 . . . .1C **28**
Mapesbury Rd. NW2 . . . .4A **44**
Mapeshill Pl. NW2 . . . . .3E **43**
Mapes Ho. NW6 . . . . . . .4A **44**
Mape St. E2 . . . . .3D **65**
  (not continuous)
Maple Av. W3 . . . . .2A **70**
Maple Cl. N16 . . . . .1C **36**
  SW4 . . . . .4F **103**
Maple Ct. E3 . . . . .1C **66**
  (off Four Seasons Cl.)
  SE6 . . . . .1D **123**

Maplecroft Cl. E6 . . . . . .5F **69**
Mapledene Est. E8 . . . . .4C **50**
Mapledene Rd. E8 . . . . .4B **50**
Maple Ho. N19 . . . . .3E **33**
  SE8 . . . . .3B **94**
  (off Idonia St.)
Maple Leaf Sq. SE16 . . .3F **79**
Maple Lodge W8 . . . . . .4D **73**
  (off Abbots Wlk.)
Maple M. NW6 . . . . .1D **59**
  SE16 . . . . .3F **79**
  SW16 . . . . .5B **118**
Maple Pl. W1 . . . . .5A **6** (3E **61**)
Maple Rd. E11 . . . . .1A **40**
Maples Pl. E1 . . . . .4D **65**
Maplestead Rd.
  SW2 . . . . .5B **104**
Maple St. E2 . . . . .1D **65**
  W1 . . . . . . .5F **5** (4E **61**)
Mapleton Cres.
  SW18 . . . . .4D **101**
Mapleton Rd. SW18 . . . .4C **100**
  (not continuous)
Maple Tree Pl. SE3 . . . . .4F **97**
Maplin Rd. E16 . . . . .5C **68**
Maplin St. E3 . . . . .2B **66**
Mapperley Cl. E11 . . . . .1B **40**
Marabou Ct. E12 . . . . . .2F **55**
Marathon Ho. NW1 . . . . .5A **4**
  (off Marylebone Rd.)
Maran Rd. W9 . . . . .2B **58**
Marble Arch 4A **12**
MARBLE ARCH 1B **74**
Marble Arch
  W1 . . . . . . .4A **12** (1B **74**)
Marble Arch Apartments
  W1 . . . . .5B **60**
  (off Harrowby St.)
Marble Dr. NW2 . . . . . . .3F **29**
Marble Ho. W9 . . . . .3B **58**
Marble Quay E1 . . . . . . .2C **78**
Marbles Ho. SE5 . . . . . .2E **91**
  (off Grosvenor Ter.)
Marbrook Ct. SE12 . . . . .3E **125**
Marcella Rd. SW9 . . . . .5C **90**
Marchant Ho. N1 . . . . . .5A **50**
  (off New Era Est.)
Marchant Rd. E11 . . . . .4F **39**
Marchant St. SE14 . . . . .2A **94**
Marchbank Rd. W14 . . . .2B **86**
Marchbank Rd. SW15 . . .2D **99**
Marchmont St.
  WC1 . . . . . .3D **7** (3A **62**)
Marchwood Cl. SE5 . . . .3A **92**
Marcia Ct. SE1 . . . . .5A **78**
  (off Marcia Rd.)
Marcia Rd. SE1 . . . . . . .5A **78**
Marcilly Rd. SW18 . . . . .3F **101**
Marcon Ct. E8 . . . . .2D **51**
  (off Amhurst Rd.)
Marconi Rd. E10 . . . . . .3C **38**
Marcon Pl. E8 . . . . .3D **51**
Marco Polo Ho. SW8 . . .3D **89**
Marco Rd. W6 . . . . .4E **71**
Marcus Ct. E15 . . . . . . .5A **54**
Marcus Garvey M.
  SE22 . . . . .4D **107**
Marcus Garvey Way
  SE24 . . . . .2C **104**

Marcus St. E15 . . . . . . .5B **54**
  SW18 . . . . .4D **101**
Marcus Ter. SW18 . . . . .4D **101**
Mardale Dr. NW9 . . . . . .1A **28**
Marden Ho. E8 . . . . .2D **51**
Marden Sq. SE16 . . . . . .4D **79**
Mardyke Ho. SE17 . . . . .5F **77**
  (off Mason St.)
Maresfield Gdns.
  NW3 . . . . .2E **45**
Mare St. E8 . . . . .2D **51**
Margaret Bondfield Ho.
  E3 . . . . .1A **66**
  (off Driffield Rd.)
Margaret Bldgs. N16 . . . .3B **36**
Margaret Cl. E11 . . . . . .1A **40**
Margaret Ct. W1 . . . . . . .2F **13**
Margaret Herbison Ho.
  SW6 . . . . .2B **86**
  (off Clem Attlee Ct.)
Margaret Ho. W6 . . . . . .1E **85**
  (off Queen Caroline St.)
Margaret Ingram Cl.
  SW6 . . . . .2B **86**
Margaret McMillan Ho.
  E16 . . . . .5E **69**
Margaret Rd. N16 . . . . . .3B **36**
Margaret Rutherford Pl.
  SW12 . . . . .1E **117**
Margaret St.
  W1 . . . . . . .2E **13** (5D **61**)
Margaretta Ter. SW3 . . . .2A **88**
Margaretting Rd. E12 . . . .3E **41**
Margaret Way IG4: Ilf . . .1F **41**
Margaret White Ho.
  NW1 . . . . .1C **6**
  (off Chalton St.)
Margate Rd. SW2 . . . . . .3A **104**
Margery Fry Ct. N7 . . . . .5A **34**
Margery Pk. Rd. E7 . . . . .3C **54**
Margery St.
  WC1 . . . . . .2B **8** (2C **62**)
Margery Ter. E7 . . . . .3C **54**
  (off Margery Pk. Rd.)
Margin Dr. SW19 . . . . . .5F **113**
Margravine Gdns.
  W6 . . . . .1F **85**
Margravine Rd. W6 . . . . .1F **85**
Marham Gdns.
  SW18 . . . . .1A **116**
Maria Cl. SE1 . . . . .5D **79**
Marian Ct. E9 . . . . .2E **51**
Marian Pl. E2 . . . . .1D **65**
Marian St. E2 . . . . .1D **65**
Maria Way NW10 . . . . . .4B **42**
Maria Ter. E11 . . . . .4F **65**
Maribor SE10 . . . . .3E **95**
  (off Burney St.)
Marie Curie SE5 . . . . . . .4A **92**
Marie Lloyd Gdns.
  N19 . . . . .2A **34**
Marie Lloyd Ho. N1 . . . . .1B **10**
  (off Murray Gro.)
Marie Lloyd Wlk. E8 . . . .3B **50**
Marigold All.
  SE1 . . . . . .5D **17** (1D **77**)
Marigold St. SE16 . . . . . .3D **79**
Marina Ct. E3 . . . . .2B **66**
  (off Alfred St.)
  SW6 . . . . .5E **87**

Marina One N1 . . . . .1A 62
(off New Wharf Rd.)
Marina Point E14 . . . . .4D 81
(off Goulston St.)
Marine Ct. E11 . . . . .4A 40
Marinefield Rd.
SW6 . . . . .5D 87
Marinel Ho. SE5 . . . . . .3E 91
Mariners M. E14 . . . . . .5F 81
Marine St. SE16 . . . . . .4C 78
Marine Twr. SE8 . . . . . .2B 94
(off Abinger Gro.)
Marion Ho. NW1 . . . . . .5B 46
(off Regent's Pk. Rd.)
Marion M. SE21 . . . . . .3F 119
Marischal Rd. SE13 . . .1F 109
Maritime Ind. Est.
SE7 . . . . .5D 83
Maritime Quay E14 . . .1C 94
Maritime St. E3 . . . . . .3B 66
Marius Mans.
SW17 . . . . .2C 116
Marius Rd. SW17 . . . . .2C 116
Marjorie Gro. SW11 . . .2B 102
Marjorie M. E1 . . . . . . .5F 65
Market App. W12 . . . . . .3E 71
Market Ct. W1 . . . . .2F 13
Market Dr. W4 . . . . .3A 84
Market Entrance SW8 . .3E 89
Market Est. N7 . . . . . . .3A 48
Market La. W12 . . . . . . .3E 71
Market M.
W1 . . . . . .2D 21 (2D 75)
Market Pde. E10 . . . . . .1E 39
(off High Rd. Leyton)
N16 . . . . .3C 36
(off Oldhill St.)
Market Pav. E10 . . . . . .5C 38
Market PI. SE16 . . . . . .5C 78
(not continuous)
W1 . . . . . .2F 13 (5E 61)
Market Rd. N7 . . . . .3A 48
Market Row SW9 . . . . .2C 104
Market Sq. E14 . . . . . . .5D 67
Market St. E1 . . .5F 11 (4B 64)
Market Way E14 . . . . . .5D 67
Market Yd. M.
SE1 . . . . . .5D 27 (3A 78)
Markfield Beam Engine &
Museum 1C 36
Markham PI. SW3 . . . . . .1B 88
Markham Sq. SW3 . . . . .1B 88
Markham St. SW3 . . . . . .1A 88
Mark Ho. E2 . . . . .1F 65
(off Sewardstone Rd.)
Markhouse Av. E17 . . . .1A 38
Markhouse Pas. E17 . . .1B 38
(off Downsfield Rd.)
Markhouse Rd. E17 . . . .1B 38
Markland Ho. W10 . . . . .1F 71
(off Darfield Way)
Mark La. EC3 . . .4E 19 (1A 78)
Markmanor Av. E17 . . . .2A 38
Mark Sq. EC2 . . .3D 11 (3A 64)
Markstone Ho. SE1 . . . .4D 25
(off Lancaster St.)
Mark St. E15 . . . . .4A 54
EC2 . . . . .3D 11 (3A 64)
Mark Wade Cl. E12 . . . . .3F 41
Markwell Cl. SE26 . . . . .4D 121

Markyate Ho. W10 . . . . .3E 57
(off Sutton Way)
Marland Ho. SW1 . . . . . .5A 20
(off Sloane St.)
Marlborough
SW19 . . . . .1F 113
(off Inner Pk. Rd.)
W9 . . . . .2E 59
(off Maida Va.)
Marlborough Av. E8 . . . .5C 50
(not continuous)
SE17 . . . . .5E 77
Marlborough Ct. W1 . . . .3A 14
(off Carnaby St.)
W8 . . . . .5C 72
(off Pembroke Rd.)
Marlborough Cres.
W4 . . . . .4A 70
Marlborough Flats
SW3 . . . . .5A 74
(off Walton St.)
Marlborough Ga. Ho.
W2 . . . . .1F 73
(off Elms M.)
Marlborough Gro.
SE1 . . . . .1C 92
Marlborough Hill
NW8 . . . . .1E 59
Marlborough House
. . . . .2A 22 (2E 75)
Marlborough Ho. E16 . . .2C 82
(off Hardy Av.)
Marlborough La. SE7 . . .2E 97
Marlborough Lodge
NW8 . . . . .1E 59
(off Hamilton Ter.)
Marlborough Mans.
NW6 . . . . .2D 45
(off Canon Hill)
Marlborough M.
SW2 . . . . .2B 104
Marlborough PI.
NW8 . . . . .1E 59
Marlborough Rd. E7 . . . .4E 55
E15 . . . . .1A 54
N19 . . . . .4F 33
SW1 . . . . .2A 22 (2E 75)
Marlborough St.
SW3 . . . . .5A 74
Marlborough Yd. N19 . . .4F 33
Marlbury NW8 . . . . .5D 45
(off Abbey Rd.)
Marler Rd. SE23 . . . . . .1A 122
Marley Ho. W11 . . . . . . .1F 71
(off St Ann's Rd.)
Marley St. SE16 . . . . . . .5F 79
Marley Wlk. NW2 . . . . . .2E 43
Marloes Rd. W8 . . . . . . .4D 73
Marlow Ct. NW6 . . . . . . .4F 43
Marlowe Bus. Cen.
SE14 . . . . .3A 94
(off Batavia Rd.)
Marlowe Ct. SE19 . . . . .5B 120
SW3 . . . . .5A 74
(off Petyward)
Marlowe Path SE8 . . . . .2C 94
Marlowes, The NW8 . . . .5F 45
Marlow Ho. E2 . . . . .2F 11
(off Calvert Av.)

Marlow Ho. SE1 . . . . . . .5F 27
(off Abbey St.)
W2 . . . . .5D 59
(off Hallfield Est.)
Marlow Way SE16 . . . . .3F 79
Marlow Workshops
E2 . . . . .2F 11
(off Virginia Rd.)
Marl Rd. SW18 . . . . . . .2E 101
Marlton St. SE10 . . . . . .1B 96
Marmara Apartments
E16 . . . . .1C 82
(off Western Gateway)
Marmion Ho. SW11 . . . .1C 102
Marmion M. SW11 . . . . .2C 102
Marmion Rd. SW11 . . . . .2C 102
Marmont Rd. SE15 . . . . .4C 92
Marmora Rd. SE22 . . . . .4E 107
Marne St. W10 . . . . .2A 58
Marney Rd. SW11 . . . . . .2C 102
Marnfield Cres.
SW2 . . . . .1C 118
Marnham Av. NW2 . . . . .1A 44
Marnock Ho. SE17 . . . . . .1F 91
(off Brandon St.)
Marnock Rd. SE4 . . . . . .3B 108
Maroon St. E14 . . . . . . .4A 66
Maroons Way SE6 . . . . .5C 122
Marqueen Ct. W8 . . . . . .3D 73
(off Kensington Chu. St.)
Marquess Rd. N1 . . . . . .3F 49
Marquis Ct. N4 . . . . .3B 34
(off Marquis Rd.)
Marquis Rd. N4 . . . . .3B 34
NW1 . . . . .3F 47
Marrick Cl. SW15 . . . . . .2C 98
Marrick Ho. NW6 . . . . . .5D 45
(off Mortimer Cres.)
Marriett Ho. SE6 . . . . . .4E 123
Marriott Rd. E15 . . . . . . .5A 54
N4 . . . . .3B 34
Marriotts Cl. NW9 . . . . . .1B 28
Marryat Ho. SW1 . . . . . . .1E 89
(off Churchill Gdns.)
Marryat PI. SW19 . . . . .4A 114
Marryat Rd. SW19 . . . . .5F 113
Marryat Sq. SW6 . . . . . .4A 86
Marsala Rd. SE13 . . . . . .2D 109
Marsalis Ho. E3 . . . . . . .2C 66
(off Rainhill Way)
Marsden Rd. SE15 . . . . .1B 106
Marsden St. NW5 . . . . . .3C 46
Marshall Bldg. W2 . . . . . .4F 59
(off Hermitage St.)
Marshall Cl.
SW18 . . . . .4E 101
Marshall Ct. NW6 . . . . . .4F 43
(off Coverdale Rd.)
Marshall Ho. N1 . . . . . . .1F 63
(off Cranston Est.)
NW6 . . . . .1B 58
(off Albert Rd.)
SE1 . . . . .5E 27
SE17 . . . . .1F 91
(off East St.)
Marshall Rd. E10 . . . . . .5D 39
(not continuous)
Marshall's PI.
SE16 . . . . .5F 27 (4B 78)
Marshall St.
W1 . . . . . .3A 14 (5E 61)

Marshall Street Leisure Cen.
. . . . . . .3A 14 (5E 61)
Marshalsea Rd.
SE1 . . . . . . .3A 26 (3E 77)
Marsham Ct. SW1 . . . . .5F 75
Marsham St.
SW1 . . . . . .5C 22 (4F 75)
Marshbrook Cl. SE3 . . . .1F 111
Marsh Centre, The E1 . . .2F 19
(off Whitechapel St.)
Marsh Ct. E8 . . . . .3C 50
Marsh Dr. NW9 . . . . .1B 28
Marshfield St. E14 . . . . .4E 81
Marshgate La. E15 . . . . .1E 67
Marsh Hill E9 . . . . .2A 52
Marsh Ho. SW1 . . . . . . .1F 89
(off Aylesford St.)
SW8 . . . . .4E 89
Marsh La. E10 . . . . .4B 38
Marsh St. E14 . . . . .5D 81
Marsh Wall E14 . . . . . . .2C 80
Marshwood Ho. NW6 . . . .5C 44
(off Kilburn Vale)
Marsland Cl. SE17 . . . . .1D 91
Marsom Ho. N1 . . . . . . .1B 10
(off Provost Est.)
Marston Cl. NW6 . . . . . .4E 45
Marston Ho. SW9 . . . . . .5C 90
Marsworth Ho. E2 . . . . . .5C 50
(off Whiston Rd.)
Martaban Rd. N16 . . . . . .4B 36
Martara M. SE17 . . . . . . .1E 91
Martello St. E8 . . . . .4D 51
Martello Ter. E8 . . . . . . .4D 51
Martell Rd. SE21 . . . . . .3F 119
Martel Pl. E8 . . . . .3B 50
Martha Rd. E15 . . . . .3A 54
Martha's Bldgs.
EC1 . . . . . . .3B 10 (3F 63)
Martha St. E1 . . . . .5E 65
Martin Ct. E14 . . . . .3E 81
(off River Barge Cl.)
Martindale Av. E16 . . . . .1C 82
Martindale Ho. E14 . . . . .1D 81
(off Poplar High St.)
Martindale Rd.
SW12 . . . . .5D 103
Martineau Est. E1 . . . . . .1E 79
Martineau Ho. SW1 . . . . .1E 89
(off Churchill Gdns.)
Martineau M. N5 . . . . . . .1D 49
Martineau Rd. N5 . . . . . .1D 49
Martin Ho. E3 . . . . .2B 52
(off Old Ford Rd.)
SE1 . . . . . .5A 26 (4E 77)
SW8 . . . . .3A 90
(off Wyvil Rd.)
Martin La.
EC4 . . . . . .4C 18 (1F 77)
(not continuous)
Martins, The SE26 . . . . .5D 121
Martlett Ct.
WC2 . . . . . .3E 15 (5A 62)
Marton Cl. SE6 . . . . .3C 122
Marton Rd. N16 . . . . .4A 36
Martys Yd. NW3 . . . . . . .1F 45
Marvell Ho. SE5 . . . . . . .3F 91
(off Camberwell Rd.)
Marvels Cl. SE12 . . . . . .2D 125
Marvels La. SE12 . . . . . .2D 125

Marville Rd. SW6 . . . . . .3B 86
Marvin St. E8 . . . . .3D 51
Mary Adelaide Cl.
SW15 . . . . .4A 112
Mary Ann Gdns. SE8 . . . .2C 94
Mary Bayly Ho. W11 . . . .2A 72
(off Wilsham St.)
Mary Boast Wlk. SE5 . . . .5F 91
Mary Datchelor Cl.
SE5 . . . . .4F 91
Mary Datchelor Ho.
SE5 . . . . .4F 91
(off Grove La.)
Mary Flux Ct. SW5 . . . . .1D 87
(off Bramham Gdns.)
Mary Grn. NW8 . . . . .5D 45
Mary Holben Ho.
SW16 . . . . .5E 117
Mary Ho. W6 . . . . .1E 85
(off Queen Caroline St.)
Mary Jones Ct. E14 . . . . .1C 80
(off Garford St.)
Maryland Ind. Est.
E15 . . . . .2A 54
Maryland Pk. E15 . . . . . .2A 54
(not continuous)
Maryland Point E15 . . . . .3A 54
(off The Grove)
Maryland Rd. E15 . . . . . .2F 53
Maryland Sq. E15 . . . . . .2A 54
Marylands Rd. W9 . . . . . .3C 58
(not continuous)
Maryland St. E15 . . . . . .2F 53
Maryland Wlk. N1 . . . . . .5E 49
(off Popham St.)
Mary Lawrenson Pl.
SE3 . . . . .3C 96
MARYLEBONE 5C 4 (4C 60)
Marylebone Cricket Club
. . . . .2F 59
(within Lord's Cricket Ground)
MARYLEBONE FLYOVER
. . . . .4A 60
Marylebone Fly-Over
NW1 . . . . .4F 59
W2 . . . . .4F 59
Marylebone High St.
W1 . . . . . . .5C 4 (4C 60)
Marylebone La.
W1 . . . . . . .1C 12 (4C 60)
Marylebone M.
W1 . . . . . . .1D 13 (4D 61)
Marylebone Pas.
W1 . . . . . . .2A 14 (5E 61)
Marylebone Rd.
NW1 . . . . . .5A 4 (4A 60)
Marylebone St.
W1 . . . . . . .1C 12 (4C 60)
Marylee Way SE11 . . . . .5B 76
Mary Macarthur Ho.
E2 . . . . .2F 65
(off Warley St.)
W6 . . . . .2A 86
Maryon Ho. NW6 . . . . . . .4F 45
(off Goldhurst Ter.)
Maryon M. NW3 . . . . . . .1A 46
Maryon Rd. SE7 . . . . . . .5F 83
SE18 . . . . .5F 83
Mary Pl. W11 . . . . .1A 72

Marys Ct. NW1 . . . . .3A 60
(off Palgrave Gdns.)
Mary Seacole Cl. E8 . . . .5B 50
Mary Seacole Ho.
W6 . . . . .4C 70
(off Invermead Cl.)
Mary Smith Ct. SW5 . . . .5C 72
(off Trebovir Rd.)
Marysmith Ho. SW1 . . . . .1F 89
(off Cureton St.)
Mary St. E16 . . . . .4B 68
N1 . . . . .5E 49
Mary Ter. NW1 . . . . .5D 47
Mary Wharrie Ho.
NW3 . . . . .4B 46
(off Fellows Rd.)
Marzell Ho. W14 . . . . . . .1B 86
(off North End Rd.)
Masbro' Rd. W14 . . . . . . .4F 71
Mascalls Ct. SE7 . . . . . . .2E 97
Mascalls Rd. SE7 . . . . . .2E 97
Mascotte Rd. SW15 . . . . .2F 99
Mascotts Cl. NW2 . . . . . .5D 29
Masefield Ho. NW6 . . . . .2C 58
(off Stafford Rd.)
Mashie Rd. W3 . . . . .5A 56
Maskall Cl. SW2 . . . . . . .1C 118
Maskell Rd. SW17 . . . . . .3E 115
Maskelyne Cl. SW11 . . . .4A 88
Mason Cl. E16 . . . . .1C 82
SE16 . . . . .1C 92
Mason Ho. E9 . . . . .4E 51
(off Frampton Pk. Rd.)
SE1 . . . . .5C 78
(off Simms Rd.)
Mason's Arms M.
W1 . . . . . . .3E 13 (5D 61)
Mason's Pl.
EC2 . . . . . .2B 18 (5F 63)
Masons Pl.
EC1 . . . . . . .1E 9 (2E 63)
Mason St. SE17 . . . . . . .5F 77
Masons Yd.
EC1 . . . . . . .1E 9 (2D 63)
SW1 . . . . . .1A 22 (2E 75)
SW19 . . . . .5F 113
Massey Ct. E6 . . . . .5E 55
(off Florence Rd.)
Massie Rd. E8 . . . . .3C 50
Massingberd Way
SW17 . . . . .4D 117
Massinger St. SE17 . . . . .5A 78
Massingham St. E1 . . . . .3F 65
Mast Cl. SE16 . . . . .5A 80
(off Boat Lifter Way)
Master Gunner Pl.
SE18 . . . . .3F 97
Masterman Ho. SE5 . . . . .3F 91
(off Elmington St.)
Masterman Rd. E6 . . . . . .2F 69
Masters Cl. SW16 . . . . . .5E 117
Masters Dr. SE16 . . . . . .1D 93
Masters Lodge E1 . . . . . .5E 65
(off Johnson St.)
Masters St. E1 . . . . .4F 65
Mast Ho. Ter. E14 . . . . . .5C 80
(not continuous)
Mastmaker Ct. E14 . . . . .3C 80
Mastmaker Rd. E14 . . . . .3C 80
Matcham Rd. E11 . . . . . .5A 40

Match Ct. *E3* *1C 66*
(off Blondin St.)
Matching Ct. *E3* *2B 66*
(off Merchant St.)
Matham Gro. SE22 . . . .2B 106
Matheson Lang Ho.
SE1 . . . . .4B 24
Matheson Rd. W14 . . . .5B 72
Mathews Pk. Av. E15 . .3B 54
Mathews Yd.
WC2 . . . . . .3D 15 (5A 62)
Mathieson Ct. SE1 . . . .4E 25
(off King James St.)
Mathison Ho. SW10 . . .3E 87
(off Coleridge Gdns.)
Matilda Gdns. E3 . . . . .1C 66
Matilda Ho. E1 . . . . . . .2C 78
(off St Katherine's Way)
Matilda St. N1 . . . . .5B 48
Matisse Ct. EC1 . . . . . .3B 10
Matlock Cl. SE24 . . . . .2E 105
Matlock Ct. NW8 . . . . . .1E 59
(off Abbey Rd.)
SE5 . . . . .2F 105
W11 . . . . .1C 72
(off Kensington Pk. Rd.)
Matlock Rd. E10 . . . . . .1E 39
Matlock St. E14 . . . . . .5A 66
Maton Ho. SW6 . . . . . . .3B 86
(off Estcourt Rd.)
Matrimony Pl. SW8 . . . .5E 89
Matson Ho. SE16 . . . . .4D 79
Matthew Cl. W10 . . . . .3F 57
Matthew Parker St.
SW1 . . . . .4C 22 (3F 75)
Matthews Ho. E14 . . . . .4C 66
(off Burgess St.)
Matthews St. SW11 . . . .5B 88
Matthias Apartments
N1 . . . . .4F 49
(off Northchurch Rd.)
Matthias Rd. N16 . . . . .2A 50
Mattison Rd. N4 . . . . . .1C 34
Maud Chadburn Pl.
SW4 . . . . .4D 103
Maude Ho. E2 . . . . .1C 64
(off Ropley St.)
Maude Rd. SE5 . . . . . . .4A 92
Maud Gdns. E13 . . . . . .5B 54
Maudlins Grn. E1 . . . . .2C 78
Maud Rd. E10 . . . . .5E 39
E13 . . . . .1B 68
Maud St. E16 . . . . .4B 68
Maud Wilkes Cl.
NW5 . . . . .2E 47
Mauleverer Rd.
SW2 . . . . .3A 104
Maundeby Wlk.
NW10 . . . . .3A 42
Maunsel St. SW1 . . . . .5F 75
Maurer Ct. SE10 . . . . . .4B 82
Mauretania Bldg. E1 . . .1F 79
(off Jardine Rd.)
Maurice Ct. E1 . . . . . . .2F 65
Maurice Drummond Ho.
SE10 . . . . .4D 95
(off Catherine Gro.)
Maurice St. W12 . . . . . .5D 57
Mauritius Rd. SE10 . . . .5A 82
Maury Rd. N16 . . . . . . .4C 36

Maverton Rd. E3 . . . . . .5C 52
Mavis Wlk. E6 . . . . .4F 69
(off Greenwich Cres.)
Mavor Ho. N1 . . . . .5B 48
(off Barnsbury Est.)
Mawbey Ho. SE1 . . . . .1C 92
Mawbey Pl. SE1 . . . . . .1B 92
Mawbey Rd. SE1 . . . . . .1B 92
Mawbey St. SW8 . . . . . .3A 90
Mawdley Ho. SE1 . . . . .4D 25
Mawson Ct. N1 . . . . . . .5F 49
(off Gopsall St.)
Mawson Ho. EC1 . . . . . .5B 8
(off Baldwins Gdns.)
Mawson La. W4 . . . . . . .2B 84
Maxden Ct. SE15 . . . . .1B 106
Maxilla Wlk. W10 . . . . . .5F 57
Maxted Rd. SE15 . . . . .1B 106
Maxwell Ct. SE22 . . . . .1C 120
SW4 . . . . .3F 103
Maxwell Rd. SW6 . . . . . .3D 87
Maya Cl. SE15 . . . . .5D 93
Mayall Rd. SE24 . . . . . .3D 105
Maybourne Cl.
SE26 . . . . .5D 121
Maybury Ct. W1 . . . . . . .1C 12
(off Marylebone St.)
Maybury Gdns.
NW10 . . . . .3D 43
Maybury M. N6 . . . . . . .2E 33
Maybury Rd. E13 . . . . . .3E 69
Maybury St. SW17 . . . .5A 116
Mayday Gdns. SE3 . . . . .5F 97
Maydew Ho. SE16 . . . . .5E 79
(off Abbeyfield Rd.)
Maydwell Ho. E14 . . . . .4C 66
(off Thomas Rd.)
Mayerne Rd. SE9 . . . . .3F 111
Mayeswood Rd.
SE12 . . . . .4E 125
MAYFAIR 5D 13 (1D 75)
Mayfair M. NW1 . . . . . . .4B 46
(off Regents Pk. Rd.)
Mayfair Pl.
W1 . . . . . . .1E 21 (2D 75)
Mayfield Av. W4 . . . . . . .5A 70
Mayfield Cl. E8 . . . . . . .3B 50
SW4 . . . . .3F 103
Mayfield Gdns. NW4 . . .1F 29
Mayfield Ho. E2 . . . . . . .1D 65
(off Cambridge Heath Rd.)
Mayfield Mans.
SW15 . . . . .3B 100
Mayfield Rd. E8 . . . . . . .4B 50
E13 . . . . .3B 68
N8 . . . . .1B 34
W12 . . . . .3A 70
Mayfield Rd. Flats
N8 . . . . .1B 34
Mayflower Cl. SE16 . . . .5F 79
Mayflower Ho. E14 . . . . .3C 80
(off Westferry Rd.)
Mayflower Rd. SW9 . . . .1A 104
Mayflower St. SE16 . . . .3E 79
Mayford NW1 . . . . .1E 61
(not continuous)
Mayford Cl. SW12 . . . . .5B 102
Mayford Rd. SW12 . . . .5B 102
Maygood Ho. N1 . . . . . .1B 62
(off Maygood St.)

Maygood St. N1 . . . . . . .1C 62
Maygrove Rd. NW6 . . . . .3B 44
Mayhew Ct. SE5 . . . . . .2F 105
Mayhill Ct. SE15 . . . . . . .3A 92
(off Newent Cl.)
Mayhill Rd. SE7 . . . . . . .2D 97
May Ho. E3 . . . . .1C 66
(off Thomas Fyre Dr.)
Maylands Ho. SW3 . . . . .5A 74
(off Cale St.)
Maylie Ho. SE16 . . . . . . .3D 79
(off Marigold St.)
Maynard Cl. SW6 . . . . . .3D 87
Maynard Rd. E17 . . . . . .1E 39
Maynards Quay E1 . . . . .1E 79
Mayne Ct. SE26 . . . . . .5D 121
Mayo Ho. E1 . . . . .4E 65
(off Lindley St.)
Mayola Rd. E5 . . . . .1E 51
Mayow Rd. NW10 . . . . . .3A 42
Mayor's and
City of London Court, The
. . . . .2B 18
Mayow Rd. SE23 . . . . . .4F 121
SE26 . . . . .4F 121
May Rd. E13 . . . . .1C 68
Mays Ct. SE10 . . . . .3E 95
SE10 . . . . .3E 95
Mays Ct. SE10 . . . . .3F 95
WC2 . . . . .5D 15 (1A 76)
Maysoule Rd. SW11 . . . .2F 101
Mayston M. SE10 . . . . . .1C 96
(off Ormiston Rd.)
May St. W14 . . . . .1B 86
(Kelway Ho.)
W14 . . . . .1B 86
(Orchard Sq.)
Maythorne Cotts.
SE13 . . . . .3F 109
Mayton St. N7 . . . . .5B 34
May Tree Ho. SE4 . . . . . .1B 108
(off Wickham Rd.)
Maytree Wlk. SW2 . . . . .2C 118
Mayville Est. N16 . . . . . .2A 50
Mayville Rd. E11 . . . . . . .4A 40
(not continuous)
May Wlk. E13 . . . . .1D 69
Mayward Ho. SE5 . . . . . .4A 92
(off Peckham Rd.)
May Wynne Ho.
E16 . . . . .1D 83
(off Murray Sq.)
Maze Hill SE3 . . . . .3B 96
SE10 . . . . .2A 96
Maze Hill Lodge
SE10 . . . . .2F 95
(off Park Vista)
Mazenod Av. NW6 . . . . . .4C 44
MCC Cricket Museum & Tours
. . . . .2F 59
Meadbank Studios
SW11 . . . . .3A 88
(off Parkgate Rd.)
Mead Cl. NW1 . . . . .3C 46
Meadcroft Rd. SE11 . . . .2D 91
(not continuous)
SE17 . . . . .2D 91
Meader Ct. SE14 . . . . . .3F 93
Mead Ho. W11 . . . . .2B 72
(off Ladbroke Gro.)

Meadowbank NW3 . . . . .4B 46
   SE3 . . . . .1B 110
Meadowbank Cl.
   SW6 . . . . .3E 85
Meadowbank Rd.
   NW9 . . . . .2A 28
Meadow Cl. E9 . . . . . . .3B 52
   SE6 . . . . .5C 122
Meadow Ct. E16 . . . . . . .2E 83
   (off Booth Rd.)
   N1 . . . . .1A 64
Meadowcourt Rd.
   SE3 . . . . .2B 110
Meadow La. E12 . . . . .3D 125
Meadow M. SW8 . . . . . .2B 90
Meadow Pl. SW8 . . . . . .3A 90
   W4 . . . . .3A 84
Meadow Rd. SW8 . . . . . .3B 90
Meadow Row SE1 . . . . . .4E 77
Meadows Cl. E10 . . . . . .4C 38
Meadowside SE9 . . . . . .2E 111
Meadowsweet Cl.
   E16 . . . . .4F 69
Meadowview Rd.
   SE6 . . . . .5B 122
Mead Path SW17 . . . . .4E 115
Mead Pl. E9 . . . . .3E 51
Mead Row
   SE1 . . . . . . .5B 24 (4C 76)
Meads Ct. E15 . . . . . . .3B 54
Meadway NW11 . . . . . . .1C 30
Meadway, The SE3 . . . . .5F 95
Meadway Cl. NW11 . . . . .1D 31
Meadway Ga.
   NW11 . . . . .1C 30
Meakin Est.
   SE1 . . . . . . .5D 27 (4A 78)
Meanley Rd. E12 . . . . . .1F 55
Meard St.
   W1 . . . . . . .3B 14 (5F 61)
   (not continuous)
Mears Cl. E1 . . . . .4C 64
   (off Settles St.)
Meath Cres. E2 . . . . . . .2F 65
Meath Ho. SE24 . . . . . .4D 105
   (off Dulwich Rd.)
Meath Rd. E15 . . . . . . .1B 68
Meath St. SW11 . . . . . .4D 89
Mecca Bingo
   Camden 5D 47
   (off Arlington Rd.)
   Catford 5D 109
   Hackney 1B 64
   (off Hackney Rd.)
   Wandsworth 1D 115
Mecklenburgh Pl.
   WC1 . . . . . .3F 7 (3B 62)
Mecklenburgh Sq.
   WC1 . . . . . .3F 7 (3B 62)
Mecklenburgh St.
   WC1 . . . . . .3F 7 (3B 62)
Medburn St. NW1 . . . . . .1F 61
Medebourne Cl.
   SE3 . . . . .1C 110
Mede Ho.
   BR1: Brom 5D 125
   (off Pike Cl.)
Medfield St. SW15 . . . . .5C 98
Medhurst Cl. E3 . . . . . .1A 66
   (not continuous)

Medhurst Dr.
   BR1: Brom 5A 124
Median Rd. E5 . . . . . . .2E 51
Medina Gro. N7 . . . . . . .5C 34
Medina Rd. N7 . . . . . . .5C 34
Medland Ho. E14 . . . . . .1A 80
Medlar St. SE5 . . . . . . .4E 91
Medley Rd. NW6 . . . . . .3C 44
Medora Rd. SW2 . . . . . .5B 104
Medusa Rd. SE6 . . . . . .4D 109
Medway Bldgs.
   E3 . . . . .1A 66
   (off Medway Rd.)
Medway Ct. NW11 . . . . .1D 31
   WC1 . . . . .2D 7
   (off Judd St.)
Medway Ho. NW8 . . . . . .3A 60
   (off Penfold St.)
   SE1 . . . . .4C 26
   (off Hankey Pl.)
Medway M. E3 . . . . . . .1A 66
Medway Rd. E3 . . . . . . .1A 66
Medway St. SW1 . . . . . .4F 75
Medwin St. SW4 . . . . . .2E 104
Meerbrook Rd. SE3 . . . .1E 111
Meeson Rd. E15 . . . . . .4B 54
Meeson St. E5 . . . . . . .1A 52
Meeson's Wharf E15 . . . .1E 67
Meeting Fld. Path E9 . . . .3E 51
Meeting Ho. All. E1 . . . . .2D 79
Meeting Ho. La.
   SE15 . . . . .4D 93
Mehetabel Rd. E9 . . . . . .2E 51
Melba Way SE13 . . . . . .4D 95
Melbourne Ct. E5 . . . . . .1A 52
   (off Daubeney Rd.)
   W9 . . . . .3E 59
   (off Randolph Av.)
Melbourne Gro.
   SE22 . . . . .2A 106
Melbourne Ho. W8 . . . . .2C 72
   (off Kensington Pl.)
Melbourne Mans.
   W14 . . . . .2A 86
   (off Musard Rd.)
Melbourne M. SE6 . . . .5E 109
   SW9 . . . . .4C 90
Melbourne Pl.
   WC2 . . . . . . .3A 16 (5B 62)
Melbourne Rd. E10 . . . . .2D 39
Melbourne Sq. SW9 . . . . .4C 90
Melbourne Ter. SW6 . . . . .3D 87
   (off Moore Pk. Rd.)
Melbray M. SW6 . . . . . .5B 86
Melbreak Ho. SE22 . . . .1A 106
Melbury Ct. W8 . . . . . . .4B 72
Melbury Dr. SE5 . . . . . .3A 92
Melbury Ho. SW8 . . . . . .3B 90
   (off Richborne Ter.)
Melbury Rd. W14 . . . . . .4B 72
Melchester W11 . . . . . . .5B 58
   (off Ledbury Rd.)
Melchester Ho.
   N19 . . . . .5F 33
   (off Wedmore St.)
Melcombe Ct. NW1 . . . . .5A 4
   (off Melcombe Pl.)
Melcombe Ho. SW8 . . . . .3B 90
   (off Dorset Rd.)
Melcombe Pl. NW1 . . . . .4B 60

Melcombe Regis Ct.
   W1 . . . . .1C 12
   (off Weymouth St.)
Melcombe St.
   NW1 . . . . . .4A 4 (3B 60)
Meldon Cl. SW6 . . . . . . .4D 87
Melfield Gdns. SE6 . . . . .4E 123
Melford Ct. SE1 . . . . . . .5E 27
   (off Fendall St.)
   SE22 . . . . .1C 120
   (not continuous)
Melford Pas. SE22 . . . . .5C 106
Melford Rd. E11 . . . . . . .4A 40
   SE22 . . . . .5C 106
Melgund Rd. N5 . . . . . . .2C 48
Melina Ct. NW8 . . . . . . .2F 59
   (off Grove End Rd.)
   SW15 . . . . .1C 98
Melina Pl. NW8 . . . . . . .2F 59
Melina Rd. W12 . . . . . . .3D 71
Melior Ct. N6 . . . . .1E 33
Melior Pl.
   SE1 . . . . . . .3D 27 (3A 78)
Melior St.
   SE1 . . . . . . .3D 27 (3A 78)
Meliot Rd. SE6 . . . . . . .2F 123
Mellish Flats E10 . . . . . .2C 38
Mellish Ho. E1 . . . . .5D 65
   (off Varden St.)
Mellish Ind. Est.
   SE18 . . . . .4F 83
Mellish St. E14 . . . . . . .4C 80
Mellison Rd. SW17 . . . . .5A 116
Mellitus St. W12 . . . . . . .4B 56
Mell St. SE10 . . . . .1A 96
Melody La. N5 . . . . .2E 49
Melody Rd. SW18 . . . . . .3E 101
Melon Pl. W8 . . . . .3C 72
Melon Rd. E11 . . . . .5A 40
   SE15 . . . . .4C 92
Melrose Av. NW2 . . . . . .2D 43
   SW19 . . . . .2B 114
Melrose Cl. SE12 . . . . . .1C 124
Melrose Gdns. W6 . . . . . .4E 71
Melrose Ho. NW6 . . . . . .2C 58
   (off Carlton Vale)
   SW1 . . . . .1D 89
   (part of Abbots Mnr.)
Melrose Rd. SW13 . . . . . .5B 84
   SW18 . . . . .4B 100
Melrose Ter. W6 . . . . . . .4E 71
Melthorpe Gdns. SE3 . . . .4F 97
Melton Cl. SW7 . . . . . . .5F 73
Melton St.
   NW1 . . . . . .2A 6 (2E 61)
Melville Ct. SE8 . . . . . . .5A 80
   W12 . . . . .4D 71
   (off Goldhawk Rd.)
Melville Ho. SE10 . . . . . .4E 95
   (off Sparta St.)
Melville Pl. N1 . . . . .4E 49
Melville Rd. SW13 . . . . . .4C 84
Melwood Ho. E1 . . . . . . .5D 65
   (off Watney Mkt.)
Melyn Cl. N7 . . . . .1E 47
Memel Ct. EC1 . . . . .4F 9
Memel St. EC1 . . .4F 9 (3E 63)
Memorial Av. E15 . . . . . .2A 68
Menai Pl. E3 . . . . .1C 66
   (off Blondin St.)

Menard Ct. *EC1* 2A **10**
(off Galway St.)
Mendez Way SW15 . . . . .4C **98**
Mendham Ho. *SE1* 5D **27**
(off Cluny Pl.)
Mendip Cl. SE26 . . . . .4E **121**
Mendip Ct. *SE14* 2E **93**
(off Avonley Rd.)
SW11 . . . . .1E **101**
Mendip Dr. NW2 . . . . . .4A **30**
Mendip Ho's. *E2* 2E **65**
(off Welwyn St.)
Mendip Rd. SW11 . . . . .1E **101**
Mendora Rd. SW6 . . . . .3A **86**
Menelik Rd. NW2 . . . . . .1A **44**
Menier Chocolate Factory
(Theatre and Art Gallery)
. . . . .2A **26**
(off Southwark St.)
Menotti St. E2 . . . . .3C **64**
Menteath Ho. *E14* 5C **66**
(off Dod St.)
Mentmore Ter. E8 . . . . .4D **51**
Mentone Mans.
SW10 . . . . .3D **87**
(off Fulham Rd.)
Mepham St.
SE1 . . . . .2A **24** (2C **76**)
Merbury Cl. SE13 . . . . .3E **109**
Mercator Pl. E14 . . . . . .1C **94**
Mercator Rd. SE13 . . . . .2F **109**
Mercer Bldg. *EC2* 3E **11**
(off New Inn Yd.)
Mercer Cl. E1 . . . . .4A **65**
Mercer Ho. *SW1* 1D **89**
(off Ebury Bri. Rd.)
Merceron Ho's. *E2* 2E **65**
(off Globe Rd.)
Merceron St. E1 . . . . . . .3D **65**
Mercers Cl. SE10 . . . . . .5B **82**
Mercer's Cotts. *E1* 5A **66**
(off White Horse Rd.)
Mercers M. N19 . . . . . . .5F **33**
Mercers Pl. W6 . . . . .5F **71**
Mercers Rd. N19 . . . . . . .5F **33**
(not continuous)
Mercer St.
WC2 . . . . .3D **15** (5A **62**)
Merchant Ct. *E1* 2E **79**
(off Wapping Wall)
Merchant Ho. *E14* 4D **81**
(off Goulston St.)
Merchants Ho. SE10 . . . .1F **95**
(off Collington St.)
Merchants Row SE10 . . . .1F **95**
(off Hoskins St.)
Merchant St. E3 . . . . . . .2B **66**
Merchiston Rd. SE6 . . . . .2F **123**
Mercia Gro. SE13 . . . . . .2E **109**
Mercia Ho. *SE5* 5E **91**
(off Denmark Rd.)
Mercier Rd. SW15 . . . . . .3A **100**
Mercury Ct. *E14* 5C **80**
(off Homer Dr.)
SW9 . . . . .4C **90**
(off Southey Rd.)
Mercury Ho. *E3* 5C **52**
(off Garrison Rd.)
E16 . . . . .5B **68**
(off Jude St.)

Mercury Way SE14 . . . . .2F **93**
Mercy Ter. SE13 . . . . . . .3E **109**
Mere Cl. SW15 . . . . .5F **99**
Meredith Av. NW2 . . . . . .2E **43**
Meredith Ho. N16 . . . . . .2A **50**
Meredith M. SE4 . . . . . . .2B **108**
Meredith St. E13 . . . . . . .2C **68**
EC1 . . . . .2D **9** (2D **63**)
Meredyth Rd. SW13 . . . . .5C **84**
Meretone Cl. SE4 . . . . . . .2A **108**
Mereton Mans.
SE8 . . . . .4C **94**
(off Brookmill Rd.)
Mereworth Ho. SE15 . . . .2E **93**
Merganser Ct. *E1* 1C **78**
(off Edward St.)
SE8 . . . . .2B **94**
(off Edward St.)
Meriden Ct. SW3 . . . . . . .1A **88**
(off Chelsea Mnr. St.)
Meriden Ho. *N1* 5A **50**
(off Wilmer Gdns.)
Meridia Ct. E15 . . . . .5E **53**
(off Biggerstaff Rd.)
Meridian Ct. SE15 . . . . . .3D **93**
(off Gervase St.)
SE16 . . . . .3C **78**
(off East La.)
Meridian Ga. E14 . . . . . . .3D **81**
Meridian Ho. *NW1* 4E **47**
(off Baynes St.)
SE10 . . . . .5A **82**
(off Azof St.)
SE10 . . . . .3E **95**
(off Royal Hill)
Meridian Pl. E14 . . . . . . .3D **81**
Meridian Point SE8 . . . . .2D **95**
Meridian Rd. SE7 . . . . . . .3F **97**
Meridian Sq. E15 . . . . . . .4F **53**
Meridian Trad. Est.
SE7 . . . . .5D **83**
Merifield Rd. SE9 . . . . . . .2E **111**
Merino Cl. *EC1* 2A **10**
(off Lever St.)
Merita Ho. *E1* 2C **78**
(off Nesham St.)
Merivale Rd. SW15 . . . . .2A **100**
Merlin Gdns.
BR1: Brom 3C **124**
Merlin Rd. E12 . . . . .4F **41**
Merlins St. *WC1* 2B **8**
(off Margery St.)
Merlin St.
WC1 . . . . . . .2B **8** (2C **62**)
Mermaid Ct. *E8* 4B **50**
(off Celandine Dr.)
SE1 . . . . .3B **26** (3F **77**)
SE16 . . . . .2B **80**
Mermaid Ho. *E14* 1E **81**
(off Bazely St.)
Mermaid Twr. *SE8* 2B **94**
(off Abinger Gro.)
Meroe Ct. N16 . . . . .4A **36**
Merredene St. SW2 . . . . .4B **104**
Merriam Av. E9 . . . . .3B **52**
Merrick Sq.
SE1 . . . . .5B **26** (4F **77**)
Merriman Rd. SE3 . . . . . .4E **97**
Merrington Rd. SW6 . . . . .2C **86**
Merritt Rd. SE4 . . . . .3B **108**

Merrivale NW1 . . . . .5E **47**
(off Camden St.)
Merrow Bldgs. *SE1* 3E **25**
(off Rushworth St.)
Merrow St. SE17 . . . . . . .1F **91**
Merrow Wlk. SE17 . . . . . .1F **91**
Merryfield SE3 . . . . .5B **96**
Merryfield Ho. SE9 . . . . . .3E **125**
(off Grove Pk. Rd.)
Merryfields Way
SE6 . . . . .5D **109**
Merryweather Ct.
N19 . . . . .5E **33**
Merryweather Pl.
SE10 . . . . .3D **95**
Merthyr Ter. SW13 . . . . . .2D **85**
Merton Av. W4 . . . . .5B **70**
Merton La. N6 . . . . .4B **32**
Merton Ri. NW3 . . . . .4A **46**
Merton Rd. E17 . . . . .1E **39**
SW18 . . . . .4C **100**
Mertoun Ter. *W1* 4B **60**
(off Seymour Pl.)
Mertins Rd. SE15 . . . . . . .3F **107**
Meru Cl. NW5 . . . . .1C **46**
Mervan Rd. SW2 . . . . . . .2C **104**
Messenger Ct. *SE16* 4C **78**
(off Spa Rd.)
Messent Rd. SE9 . . . . . . .3E **111**
Messina Av. NW6 . . . . . . .4C **44**
Messiter Ho. *N1* 5B **48**
(off Barnsbury Est.)
Metcalfe Ct. SE10 . . . . . .4B **82**
Meteor St. SW11 . . . . . . .2C **102**
Methley St. SE11 . . . . . . .1C **90**
Methwold Rd. W10 . . . . . .4F **57**
Metro Bus. Cen.
SE26 . . . . .5B **122**
Metro Central Hgts.
SE1 . . . . .5F **25**
Metropolis *SE11* 4D **77**
(off Oswin St.)
Metropolitan Bus. Cen.
N1 . . . . .4A **50**
(off Enfield Rd.)
Metropolitan Cl.
E14 . . . . .4C **66**
Metropolitan Sta. Bldgs.
W6 . . . . .5D **71**
(off Beadon Rd.)
Metropolitan Wharf
E1 . . . . .2E **79**
Mews, The IG4: Ilf 1F **41**
N1 . . . . .5E **49**
Mews St. E1 . . . . .2C **78**
Mexborough NW1 . . . . . . .5E **47**
Mexfield Rd. SW15 . . . . . .3B **100**
Meymott St.
SE1 . . . . .2D **25** (2D **77**)
Meynell Cres. E9 . . . . . . .4F **51**
Meynell Gdns. E9 . . . . . . .4F **51**
Meynell Rd. E9 . . . . .4F **51**
Meyrick Ho. *E14* 4C **66**
(off Burgess St.)
Meyrick Rd. NW10 . . . . . .3C **42**
SW11 . . . . .1F **101**
Miah Ter. E1 . . . . .2C **78**
Miall Wlk. SE26 . . . . .4A **122**
Micawber Ct. *N1* 1A **10**
(off Windsor Ter.)

Micawber Ho. *SE16* 3C 78
(off Llewellyn St.)
Micawber St.
N1 . . . . .1A 10 (2E 63)
Michael Cliffe Ho.
EC1 . . . . .2D 9
Michael Faraday Ho.
SE17 . . . . .1A 92
(off Beaconsfield Rd.)
Michael Haines Ho.
SW9 . . . . .3C 90
(off Sth. Island Pl.)
Michael Manley Ind. Est.
SW8 . . . . .4E 89
Michael Rd. E11 . . . . . . .3A 40
SW6 . . . . .4D 87
Michaels Cl. SE13 . . . . .2A 110
Michael Stewart Ho.
SW6 . . . . .2B 86
(off Clem Attlee Ct.)
Michelangelo Ct.
SE16 . . . . .1D 93
(off Stubbs Dr.)
Micheldever Rd.
SE12 . . . . .4A 110
Michelle Ct. W3 . . . . . . .1A 70
Michelson Ho. *SE11* 5B 76
(off Black Prince Rd.)
Michigan Bldg. E14 . . . .2F 81
(off Biscayne Av.)
Michigan Ho. E14 . . . . .4C 80
Mickledore NW1 . . . . .1A 6
(off Ampthill Est.)
Micklethwaite Rd.
SW6 . . . . .2C 86
Mickleton Ho. *W2* 4C 58
(off Westbourne Pk. Rd.)
Middle Dartrey Wlk.
SW10 . . . . .3E 87
(off Dartrey Wlk.)
Middlefield NW8 . . . . . . .5F 45
Middle La. N8 . . . . .1A 34
Middle La. M. N8 . . . . . .1A 34
Middle New St. EC4 . . . .2C 16
(off Pemberton Row)
Middlesex Building, The
E1 . . . . .1E 19
(off Artillery La.)
Middlesex CCC 2F 59
(within Lord's Cricket Ground)
Middlesex Ct. W4 . . . . . .5B 70
Middlesex Filter Beds
Nature Reserve 5F 37
Middlesex Pas. EC1 . . . .1E 17
Middlesex Rd. E9 . . . . . .3E 51
(off Elsdale St.)
Middlesex St.
E1 . . . . .1E 19 (4A 64)
Middlesex University
The Archway Campus
. . . . .3E 33
Middlesex Wharf E5 . . . .4E 37
Middle St. EC1 . . . .5F 9 (4E 63)
Middle Temple La.
EC4 . . . . . . .3B 16 (5C 62)
Middleton Dr. SE16 . . . . .3F 79
Middleton Gro. N7 . . . . .2A 48

Middleton Ho. E8 . . . . . .4C 50
SE1 . . . . .5B 26
(off Burbage Cl.)
SW1 . . . . .5F 75
(off Causton St.)
Middleton M. N7 . . . . . .2A 48
Middleton Pl. W1 . . . . . .1F 13
Middleton Rd. E8 . . . . . .4B 50
NW11 . . . . .2C 30
Middleton St. E2 . . . . . .2D 65
Middleton Way
SE13 . . . . .2F 109
Middleway NW11 . . . . . .1D 31
Middle Yd.
SE1 . . . . . .1D 27 (2A 78)
Midford Pl.
W1 . . . . .4A 6 (3E 61)
Midhope Ho. WC1 . . . . . . .2E 7
(off Midhope St.)
Midhope St.
WC1 . . . . . .2E 7 (2A 62)
Midhurst SE26 . . . . . . .5E 121
Midhurst Ho. E14 . . . . . .5B 66
(off Salmon La.)
Midhurst Way E5 . . . . . .1C 50
Midland Pde.
NW6 . . . . .3D 45
Midland Pl. E14 . . . . . . .1E 95
Midland Rd. E10 . . . . . .2E 39
NW1 . . . . .1C 6 (1F 61)
Midland Ter. NW2 . . . . . .5F 29
NW10 . . . . .3A 56
Midlothian Rd. E3 . . . . . .3B 66
(off Burdett Rd.)
Midmoor Rd. SW12 . . . .1E 117
Midnight Av. SE5 . . . . . .2D 91
Midship Cl. SE16 . . . . . .2F 79
Midship Point E14 . . . . .3C 80
(off The Quarterdeck)
Midstrath Rd. NW10 . . . .1A 42
Midway Ho. EC1 . . . . . . .1E 9
Midwood Cl. NW2 . . . . . .5D 29
Mighell Av. IG4: Ilf 1F 41
Mikardo Cl. E14 . . . . . . .1E 81
(off Poplar High St.)
Milborne Gro. SW10 . . . .1E 87
Milborne St. E9 . . . . .3E 51
Milborough Cres.
SE12 . . . . .4A 110
Milcote St.
SE1 . . . . . . .4D 25 (3D 77)
Mildenhall Rd. E5 . . . . . .1E 51
Mildmay Av. N1 . . . . . . .3F 49
Mildmay Gro. Nth.
N1 . . . . .2F 49
Mildmay Gro. Sth.
N1 . . . . .2F 49
Mildmay Pk. N1 . . . . . . .2F 49
Mildmay Pl. N16 . . . . . . .2A 50
Mildmay Rd. N1 . . . . . . .2F 49
Mildmay St. N1 . . . . . . .3F 49
Mildred Ct. NW6 . . . . . . .2C 58
(off Malvern M.)

MILE END 3B 66
Mile End Climbing Wall
. . . . .2A 66
Mile End Pk. 1A 66
Mile End Pk. Leisure Cen.
. . . . .4A 66
Mile End Pl. E1 . . . . .3F 65

Mile End Rd. E1 . . . . . . .4E 65
E3 . . . . .4E 65
Mile End Stadium 4B 66
Miles Bldg. NW1 . . . . . .4A 60
(off Penfold Pl.)
Miles Bldgs. NW1 . . . . . .4A 60
(off Penfold Pl.)
Miles Ct. E1 . . . . .5D 65
(off Tillman St.)
Miles Ho. SE10 . . . . .1A 96
(off Tuskar St.)
Miles Lodge E15 . . . . . . .2F 53
(off Colegrave Rd.)
Miles Pl. NW8 . . . . .4F 59
(off Broadley St.)
Miles St. SW8 . . . . .2A 90
(not continuous)
Milestone Cl. E10 . . . . . .2D 39
Milfoil St. W12 . . . . .1C 70
Milford La.
WC2 . . . . . .4A 16 (1C 76)
Milford M. SW16 . . . . . .3B 118
Milford Towers SE6 . . . .5D 109
Milk St. BR1: Brom 5D 125
EC2 . . . . . . .2A 18 (5E 63)
Milkwell Yd. SE5 . . . . . . .4E 91
Milkwood Rd. SE24 . . . . .3D 105
Milk Yd. E1 . . . . .1E 79
Millais Ho. SW1 . . . . . . .5A 76
(off Marsham St.)
Millais Rd. E11 . . . . .1E 53
Millard Cl. N16 . . . . .2A 50
Millard Rd. SE8 . . . . .1B 94
Millbank
SW1 . . . . . . .5D 23 (4A 76)
Millbank Ct. SW1 . . . . . .5A 76
(off John Islip St.)
Millbank Twr. SW1 . . . . .5A 76
Millbank Way SE12 . . . .3C 110
Millbrook Ho. SE15 . . . . .2C 92
(off Peckham Pk. Rd.)
Millbrook Pas. SW9 . . . .1D 105
Millbrook Pl. NW1 . . . . . .1E 61
(off Hampstead Rd.)
Millbrook Rd. SW9 . . . .1D 105
Mill Ct. E10 . . . . .5E 39
Millcroft Ho. SE6 . . . . . .4E 123
(off Melfield Gdns.)
Millender Wlk. SE16 . . . .5E 79
(off New Rotherhithe Rd.)
Millennium Arena 3C 88
Millennium Bridge
. . . . .5E 17 (1D 77)
Millennium Bri. Ho.
EC4 . . . . .4F 17
(off Up. Thames St.)
Millennium Bus. Cen.
NW2 . . . . .4D 29
Millennium Cl. E16 . . . . .5D 69
Millennium Dome
(The O2) 2A 82
Millennium Dr. E14 . . . . .5F 81
Millennium Pl. E2 . . . . . .1D 65
Millennium Sq. SE1 . . . . .3B 78
Millennium Way
SE10 . . . . .3A 82
Miller Cl.
BR1: Brom 5D 125
Miller Ho. W10 . . . . .3B 58
(off Harrow Rd.)

Miller Rd. SW19 . . . . . .5F **115**
Miller's Av. E8 . . . . .2B **50**
Millers Mdw. Cl.
SE3 . . . . .2B **110**
Miller's Ter. E8 . . . . . . .2B **50**
Miller St. NW1 . . . . .1E **61**
(not continuous)
Millers Way W6 . . . . . . .3E **71**
Millers Wharf Ho. E1 . . .2C **78**
(off St Katherine's Way)
Miller Wlk.
SE1 . . . . . .2C **24** (2C **76**)
Millfield N4 . . . . .4C **34**
Millfield La. N6 . . . . .3A **32**
Millfield Pl. N6 . . . . .4C **32**
Millfields Rd. E5 . . . . . . .1E **51**
Mill Gdns. SE26 . . . . . .3D **121**
Millgrove St. SW11 . . . . .4C **88**
Millharbour E14 . . . . . . .3D **81**
Mill Hill SW13 . . . . .5C **84**
Mill Hill Rd. SW13 . . . . . .5C **84**
Millhouse Pl. SE27 . . . . .4D **119**
Millicent Rd. E10 . . . . . .3B **38**
Milligan St. E14 . . . . . . .1B **80**
Milliner Ho. SW10 . . . . . .3E **87**
(off Hortensia Rd.)
Milliners Ho. SE1 . . . . . .4E **27**
(off Bermondsey St.)
SW18 . . . . .2C **100**
Millington Ho. N16 . . . . .5F **35**
Mill La. NW6 . . . . .2B **44**
Millman M.
WC1 . . . . . . .4F **7** (3B **62**)
Millman Pl. WC1 . . . . . . .4F **7**
(off Millman St.)
Millman St.
WC1 . . . . . . .4F **7** (3B **62**)
Millmark Gro. SE14 . . . . .5A **94**
MILL MEADS 1F **67**
Mill Pl. E14 . . . . .5A **66**
Mill Pond Cl. SW8 . . . . . .3F **89**
Millpond Est. SE16 . . . . .3D **79**
Mill Rd. E16 . . . . .2D **83**
Mill Row N1 . . . . .5A **50**
Mills Ct. EC2 . . . . .3D **11**
Mills Gro. E14 . . . . .5E **67**
Millshott Cl. SW6 . . . . . .4E **85**
Mills Ho. SW8 . . . . .4E **89**
(off Thessaly Rd.)
Millstone Cl. E15 . . . . . . .3F **53**
Millstone Ho. SE16 . . . . .3D **79**
(off Jamaica Rd.)
Millstream Rd.
SE1 . . . . . .4F **27** (3B **78**)
Mill St. SE1 . . . . .3B **78**
W1 . . . . . . .4F **13** (1D **75**)
Mills Yd. SW6 . . . . .1D **101**
MILLWALL 5D **81**
Millwall Dock Rd.
E14 . . . . .4C **80**
Millwall FC 1E **93**
Millwall Pk. 5E **81**
Millwood St. W10 . . . . . .4A **58**
Mill Yd. E1 . . . . .1C **78**
Milman Rd. NW6 . . . . . . .1F **57**
Milman's Ho. SW10 . . . . .2F **87**
(off Milman's St.)
Milman's St. SW10 . . . . .2F **87**

Milne Gdns. SE9 . . . . . . .3F **111**
Milner Ct. SE15 . . . . . . .3B **92**
(off Colegrove Rd.)
Milner Pl. N1 . . . . .5C **48**
Milner Rd. E15 . . . . .2A **68**
Milner Sq. N1 . . . . .4D **49**
Milner St. SW3 . . . . .5B **74**
Milo Gdns. SE22 . . . . . .4B **106**
Milo Rd. SE22 . . . . .4B **106**
Milrood Ho. E1 . . . . .4F **65**
(off Stepney Grn.)
Milroy Wlk.
SE1 . . . . . .1D **25** (2D **77**)
Milson Rd. W14 . . . . . . .4F **71**
Milstead Ho. E5 . . . . . . .2D **51**
Milton Av. E6 . . . . .4F **55**
N6 . . . . .2E **33**
Milton Cl. N2 . . . . .1E **31**
SE1 . . . . .5B **78**
Milton Ct.
EC2 . . . . . . .5B **10** (4F **63**)
SE14 . . . . .2B **94**
(not continuous)
SW18 . . . . .3C **100**
Milton Ct. Rd. SE14 . . . . .2A **94**
Milton Gdn. Est. N16 . . . .1F **49**
Milton Gro. N16 . . . . . . .1F **49**
Milton Ho. E2 . . . . .2E **65**
(off Roman Rd.)
SE5 . . . . .3F **91**
(off Elmington Est.)
Milton Mans. W14 . . . . . .2A **86**
(off Queen's Club Gdns.)
Milton Pk. N6 . . . . .2E **33**
Milton Pl. N7 . . . . .2C **48**
(off Eastwood Cl.)
Milton Rd. N6 . . . . .2E **33**
NW9 . . . . .2C **28**
SE24 . . . . .3D **105**
SW19 . . . . .5E **115**
Milton St.
EC2 . . . . . . .5B **10** (4F **63**)
Milverton Ho. SE6 . . . . .3A **122**
Milverton Rd. NW6 . . . . .4E **43**
Milverton St. SE11 . . . . .1C **90**
Milward St. E1 . . . . .4D **65**
Mimosa Lodge
NW10 . . . . .2B **42**
Mimosa St. SW6 . . . . . . .4B **86**
Minard Rd. SE6 . . . . . . .5A **110**
Mina Rd. SE17 . . . . .1A **92**
Minchin Ho. E14 . . . . . . .5C **66**
(off Dod St.)
Mincing La.
EC3 . . . . . .4D **19** (1A **78**)
Minehead Rd.
SW16 . . . . .5B **118**
Minera M. SW1 . . . . . . .5C **74**
Minerva Cl. SW9 . . . . . . .3C **90**
Minerva St. EC1 . . . . .4C **8**
(off Bowling Grn. La.)
Minerva Lodge N7 . . . . . .3B **48**
Minerva Rd. NW10 . . . . .2A **56**
Minerva St. E2 . . . . .1D **65**
Minerva Wlk.
EC1 . . . . . .2E **17** (5D **63**)
Minet Av. NW10 . . . . . . .1A **56**
Minet Gdns. NW10 . . . . . .1A **56**
Minet Rd. SW9 . . . . .5D **91**
Minford Gdns. W14 . . . . .3F **71**

Minford Ho. W14 . . . . . . .3F **71**
(off Minford Gdns.)
Mingard Wlk. N7 . . . . . . .4B **34**
Ming St. E14 . . . . .1C **80**
Miniver Pl. EC4 . . . . .4A **18**
Minnow St. SE17 . . . . . . .5A **78**
Minnow Wlk. SE17 . . . . . .5A **78**
Minories EC3 . . . .3F **19** (5B **64**)
Minshill St. SW8 . . . . . . .4F **89**
Minson Rd. E9 . . . . .5F **51**
Minstead Gdns.
SW15 . . . . .5B **98**
Minster Ct. EC3 . . . . .4E **19**
Minster Pavement
EC3 . . . . .4E **19**
(off Mincing La.)
Minster Rd. NW2 . . . . . . .2A **44**
Mint Bus. Pk. E16 . . . . . .4D **69**
Mintern St. N1 . . . . .1F **63**
Minton Ho. SE11 . . . . . . .5C **76**
(off Walnut Tree Wlk.)
Minton M. NW6 . . . . .3D **45**
Mint St. SE1 . . . . .3F **25** (3E **77**)
Mirabel Rd. SW6 . . . . . . .3B **86**
Miranda Cl. E1 . . . . .4E **65**
Miranda Ho. N1 . . . . .1D **11**
(off Crondall St.)
Miranda Rd. N19 . . . . . . .3E **33**
Mirfield St. SE7 . . . . .5F **83**
Mirror Path SE9 . . . . . . .3E **125**
Missenden SE17 . . . . . . .1F **91**
(off Roland Way)
Missenden Ho. NW8 . . . . .3A **60**
(off Jerome Cres.)
Mission, The E14 . . . . . . .5B **66**
(off Commercial Rd.)
Mission Pl. SE15 . . . . . . .4C **92**
Mistral SE5 . . . . .4A **92**
Mitali Pas. E1 . . . . .5C **64**
Mitcham Ho. SE5 . . . . . . .4E **91**
Mitcham La. SW16 . . . . .5E **117**
Mitcham Rd. SW17 . . . . .5B **116**
Mitchellbrook Way
NW10 . . . . .3A **42**
Mitchell Ho. N1 . . . . .4D **49**
(off College Cross)
W12 . . . . .1D **71**
(off White City Est.)
Mitchell's Pl. SE21 . . . . .4A **106**
(off Aysgarth Rd.)
Mitchell St.
EC1 . . . . .3F **9** (3E **63**)
(not continuous)
Mitchell Wlk. E6 . . . . .4F **69**
(off Allhallows Rd.)
Mitchison Rd. N1 . . . . . . .3F **49**
Mitford Bldgs. SW6 . . . . .3C **86**
(off Dawes Rd.)
Mitford Rd. N19 . . . . .4A **34**
Mitre, The E14 . . . . .1B **80**
Mitre Bri. Ind. Pk.
W10 . . . . .3D **57**
(not continuous)
Mitre Ho. SW3 . . . . .1B **88**
(off King's Rd.)
Mitre Pas. SE10 . . . . . . .3A **82**
Mitre Rd. E15 . . . . .1A **68**
SE1 . . . . . . .3C **24** (3C **76**)
Mitre Sq.
EC3 . . . . . . .3E **19** (5A **64**)

Mitre St. EC3 . . .3E **19** (5A **64**)
Mitre Way W10 . . . . .3D **57**
Mitre Yd. SW3 . . . . .5A **74**
Mizen Ct. E14 . . . . .3C **80**
(off Alpha Gro.)
Moat Dr. E13 . . . . .1E **69**
Moatfield NW6 . . . . .4A **44**
Moatlands Ho. WC1 . . . . . .2E **7**
(off Cromer St.)
Moat Pl. SW9 . . . . .1B **104**
Moberly Rd. SW4 . . . . . .5F **103**
Moberly
Sports & Education Cen.
. . . . .2F **57**
(off Chamberlayne Rd.)
Mobil Ct. WC2 . . . . .3A **16**
(off Clement's Inn)
Mocatta Ho. E1 . . . . .3D **65**
(off Brady St.)
Mocha Ct. E3 . . . . .1D **67**
(off Taylor Pl.)
Modbury Gdns. NW5 . . .3C **46**
Modder Pl. SW15 . . . . . .2F **99**
Model Farm Cl. SE9 . . .3F **125**
Modern Ct. EC4 . . . . . . .2D **17**
Modling Ho. E2 . . . . .1F **65**
(off Mace St.)
Moelwyn N7 . . . . .2F **47**
Moffat Ct. SW19 . . . . . .5C **114**
Moffat Ho. SE5 . . . . .3E **91**
Moffat Rd. SW17 . . . . . .4B **116**
Mohawk Ho. E3 . . . . .1A **66**
(off Gernon Rd.)
Mohmmad Khan Rd.
E11 . . . . .3B **40**
Moira Ho. SW9 . . . . .4C **90**
(off Gosling Way)
Molasses Ho. SW11 . . .1E **101**
(off Clove Hitch Quay)
Molasses Row
SW11 . . . . .1E **101**
Mole Ho. NW8 . . . . .3F **59**
(off Church St. Est.)
Molesford Rd. SW6 . . . .4C **86**
Molesworth Ho. SE17 . . .2D **91**
(off Brandon St.)
Molesworth St.
SE13 . . . . .2E **109**
Mollis Ho. E3 . . . . .4C **66**
(off Gale St.)
Molly Huggins Cl.
SW12 . . . . .5E **103**
Molton Ho. N1 . . . . .5B **48**
(off Barnsbury Est.)
Molyneux Dr. SW17 . . . .4D **117**
Molyneux St. W1 . . . . . . .4A **60**
Monarch Dr. E16 . . . . . . .4F **69**
Monarch Ho. W8 . . . . . . .4C **72**
(off Earl's Ct. Rd.)
Monarch M. E17 . . . . .1D **39**
SW16 . . . . .5C **118**
Monarch Point SW6 . . . .5E **87**
Mona Rd. SE15 . . . . .5E **93**
Mona St. E16 . . . . .4B **68**
Moncks Row SW18 . . . .4B **100**
Monck St.
SW1 . . . . . . .5C **22** (4F **75**)
Monckton Ct. W14 . . . . .4B **72**
(off Strangways Ter.)
Monclar Rd. SE5 . . . . . .2F **105**

Moncorvo Cl. SW7 . . . . . .3A **74**
Moncrieff Cl. E6 . . . . .5F **69**
Moncrieff Pl. SE15 . . . . . .5C **92**
Moncrieff St. SE15 . . . . . .5C **92**
Monday All. N16 . . . . .4B **36**
(off High St.)
Mondragon Ho. SW8 . . . .4A **90**
(off Guildford Rd.)
Monega Rd. E7 . . . . .3E **55**
E12 . . . . .3E **55**
Moneyer Ho. N1 . . . . .1B **10**
(off Provost Est.)
Mongers Almshouses
E9 . . . . .4F **51**
(off Church Cres.)
Monica Shaw Ct. NW1 . . .1C **6**
(off Purchese St.,
not continuous)
Monier Rd. E3 . . . . .4C **52**
Monk Cl. W12 . . . . .2C **70**
Monk Dr. E16 . . . . .1C **82**
Monk Pas. E16 . . . . .1C **82**
(off Monk Dr.)
Monkton Ho. E5 . . . . .2D **51**
SE16 . . . . .3F **79**
(off Wolfe Cres.)
Monkton St. SE11 . . . . . .5C **76**
Monkwell Sq.
EC2 . . . . . . .1A **18** (4E **63**)
Monmouth Pl. W2 . . . . .5D **59**
(off Monmouth Rd.)
Monmouth Rd. W2 . . . . .5C **58**
Monmouth St.
WC2 . . . . . . .3D **15** (5A **62**)
Monnery Rd. N19 . . . . . .5E **33**
Monnow Rd. SE1 . . . . . . .1C **92**
Monroe Ho. NW8 . . . . . . .2A **60**
(off Lorne Cl.)
Monro Way E5 . . . . .1C **50**
Monsell Ct. N4 . . . . .5D **35**
Monsell Rd. N4 . . . . .5C **34**
Monson Rd. NW10 . . . . . .1C **56**
SE14 . . . . .3F **93**
Montacute Rd. SE6 . . . . .5B **108**
Montagu Cl. W1 . . . . . . .1A **12**
(off Montagu Pl.)
Montague Av. SE4 . . . . . .2B **108**
Montague Cl.
SE1 . . . . .1B **26** (2F **77**)
Montague Ct. N7 . . . . .4C **48**
(off St Clements St.)
Montague Ho. E16 . . . . . .2D **83**
(off Wesley Av.)
N1 . . . . .5A **50**
(off New Era Est.)
Montague M. E3 . . . . .2B **66**
(off Tredegar Ter.)
Montague Pl.
WC1 . . . . .5C **6** (4F **61**)
Montague Rd. E8 . . . . . . .2C **50**
E11 . . . . .4B **40**
N8 . . . . .1B **34**
Montague Sq. SE15 . . . . .3E **93**
Montague St.
EC1 . . . . .1F **17** (4E **63**)
WC1 . . . . . . .5D **7** (4A **62**)
Montagu Mans.
W1 . . . . .5A **4** (4B **60**)

Montagu M. Nth.
W1 . . . . .1A **12** (4B **60**)
Montagu M. Sth.
W1 . . . . .2A **12** (5B **60**)
Montagu M. W.
W1 . . . . .2A **12** (5B **60**)
Montagu Pl.
W1 . . . . .1A **12** (4B **60**)
Montagu Rd. NW4 . . . . . .1C **28**
Montagu Row
W1 . . . . .1A **12** (4B **60**)
Montagu Sq.
W1 . . . . .1A **12** (4B **60**)
Montagu St.
W1 . . . . .2A **12** (5B **60**)
Montaigne Cl. SW1 . . . . .5F **75**
Montana Bldg. SE10 . . . .4D **95**
(off Deal's Gateway)
Montana Gdns.
SE26 . . . . .5B **122**
Montana Rd. SW17 . . . .3C **116**
Montcalm Ho. E14 . . . . . .5B **80**
Montcalm Rd. SE7 . . . . . .3F **97**
Montclare St.
E2 . . . . .3F **11** (3B **64**)
Monteagle Ct. N1 . . . . . . .1A **64**
Monteagle Way E5 . . . . .5C **36**
SE15 . . . . .1D **107**
Montefiore Ct. N16 . . . . . .3B **36**
Montefiore St. SW8 . . . . .5D **89**
Montego Cl. SE24 . . . . . .2C **104**
Montem Rd. SE23 . . . . . .5B **108**
Montem St. N4 . . . . .3B **34**
Montenotte Rd. N8 . . . . . .1E **33**
Monterey Studios
W10 . . . . .1A **58**
Montevetro SW11 . . . . . .4F **87**
Montfichet Rd. E20 . . . . . .4E **53**
Montford Pl. SE11 . . . . . .1C **90**
Montfort Ho. E2 . . . . .2E **65**
(off Victoria Pk. Sq.)
E14 . . . . .4E **81**
(off Galbraith St.)
Montfort Pl. SW19 . . . . . .1F **113**
Montgomerie M.
SE23 . . . . .5E **107**
Montgomery Ho. W2 . . . .4F **59**
(off Harrow Rd.)
Montgomery Lodge
E1 . . . . .3E **65**
(off Cleveland Gro.)
Montgomery St. E14 . . . .2D **81**
Montholme Rd.
SW11 . . . . .4B **102**
Monthope Rd. E1 . . . . . . .4C **64**
Montolieu Gdns.
SW15 . . . . .3D **99**
Montpelier Gdns. E6 . . . .2F **69**
Montpelier Gro. NW5 . . .2E **47**
Montpelier M. SW7 . . . . .4A **74**
Montpelier Pl. E1 . . . . . . .5E **65**
SW7 . . . . .4A **74**
Montpelier Ri. NW11 . . . .2A **30**
Montpelier Rd. SE15 . . . .4D **93**
Montpelier Row SE3 . . . .5B **96**
Montpelier Sq. SW7 . . . .3A **74**
Montpelier St. SW7 . . . . .4A **74**
Montpelier Ter. SW7 . . . .3A **74**
Montpelier Va. SE3 . . . . .5B **96**
Montpelier Wlk. SW7 . . . .4A **74**

Montpelier Way
NW11 . . . . .2A **30**
Montreal Ho. SE16 . . . .3F **79**
(off Maple M.)
Montreal Pl.
WC2 . . . . . .4F **15** (1B **76**)
Montrell Rd. SW2 . . . .1A **118**
Montrose Av. NW6 . . . .1A **58**
Montrose Ct. SE6 . . . .2B **124**
SW7 . . . . .3F **73**
Montrose Ho. E14 . . . .4C **80**
SW1 . . . . .4C **20**
(off Montrose Pl.)
Montrose Pl.
SW1 . . . .4C **20** (3C **74**)
Montrose Way SE23 . .1F **121**
Montserrat Cl. SE19 . .5F **119**
Montserrat Rd.
SW15 . . . . .2A **100**
Monument, The
. . . . .5C **18** (1F **77**)
Monument Gdns.
SE13 . . . . .3E **109**
Monument St.
EC3 . . . .4C **18** (1F **77**)
Monza St. E1 . . . . . .1E **79**
Moodkee St. SE16 . . . .4E **79**
Moody Rd. SE15 . . . .4B **92**
Moody St. E1 . . . . . .2F **65**
Moon Ct. SE12 . . . .2C **110**
Moon St. N1 . . . . . .5D **49**
Moorcroft Rd.
SW16 . . . . .3A **118**
Moore Ct. N1 . . . . . .5D **49**
(off Gaskin St.)
Moorehead Way
SE3 . . . . .1C **110**
Moore Ho. E1 . . . . . .1E **79**
(off Cable St.)
E2 . . . . .2E **65**
(off Roman Rd.)
E14 . . . . .3C **80**
SE10 . . . . .1B **96**
(off Armitage Rd.)
SW1 . . . . .1D **89**
(off Gatliff Rd.)
Moore Pk. Rd. SW6 . . .3C **86**
Moore Rd. SE19 . . . .5E **119**
Moore St. SW3 . . . . .5B **74**
Moore Wlk. E7 . . . . .1C **54**
Moorey Cl. E15 . . . . .5B **54**
Moorfields
EC2 . . . .1B **18** (4F **63**)
Moorfields Highwalk
EC2 . . . . .1B **18**
(off New Union St.,
not continuous)
Moorgate
EC2 . . . .2B **18** (5F **63**)
Moorgate Pl. EC2 . . . .2B **18**
Moorgreen Ho. EC1 . . .1D **9**
Moorhen Ho. E3 . . . . .5B **52**
Moorhouse Rd. W2 . . .5C **58**
Moorings, The E16 . . . .4E **69**
(off Prince Regent La.)
Moorland Rd. SW9 . . .2D **105**
Moor La. EC2 . . .1B **18** (4F **63**)
(not continuous)
Moor Pl. EC2 . . .1B **18** (4F **63**)

Moorside Rd.
BR1: Brom 3A **124**
Moor St. W1 . . .3C **14** (5F **61**)
Moran Ho. E1 . . . . . .2D **79**
(off Wapping La.)
Morant St. E14 . . . . .1C **80**
Mora Rd. NW2 . . . . .1E **43**
Mora St. EC1 . . .2A **10** (2E **63**)
Morat St. SW9 . . . . .4B **90**
Moravian Cl. SW10 . . .2F **87**
Moravian Pl.
SW10 . . . . .2F **87**
Moravian St. E2 . . . . .1E **65**
Moray Ho. E1 . . . . . .3A **66**
(off Harford St.)
Moray M. N7 . . . . . .4B **34**
Moray Rd. N4 . . . . . .4B **34**
Mordaunt Ho. NW10 . . .5A **42**
(off Stracey Rd.)
Mordaunt Rd. NW10 . . .5A **42**
Mordaunt St. SW9 . . .1B **104**
Morden Hill SE13 . . . .5E **95**
(not continuous)
Morden La. SE13 . . . .5E **95**
Morden Rd. SE3 . . . . .5C **96**
Morden Rd. M. SE3 . . .5C **96**
Morden St. SE13 . . . .4D **95**
Morden Wharf Rd. 4A **82**
(off Morden Wharf Rd.)
Morden Wharf Rd.
SE10 . . . . .4A **82**
Mordern Ho. NW1 . . . .3A **60**
(off Harewood Av.)
Mordred Rd. SE6 . . . .2A **124**
Morecambe Cl. E1 . . . .4F **65**
Morecambe St. SE17 . .5E **77**
More Cl. E16 . . . . . .5B **68**
W14 . . . . .5F **71**
More Copper Ho.
SE1 . . . . .2D **27**
(off Magdalen St.)
Moreland Cotts. E3 . . .1C **66**
(off Fairfield Rd.)
Moreland Ct. NW2 . . . .5C **30**
Moreland St.
EC1 . . . . . .1E **9** (2D **63**)
Morella Rd. SW12 . . .5B **102**
More London Pl.
SE1 . . . .2D **27** (2A **78**)
(not continuous)
More London Riverside
SE1 . . . .2E **27** (2A **78**)
(not continuous)
Moremead Rd. SE6 . . .4B **122**
Morena St. SE6 . . . .5D **109**
Moresby Rd. E5 . . . . .3D **37**
Moresby Wlk. SW8 . . .5E **89**
More's Gdn. SW3 . . . .2F **87**
(off Cheyne Wlk.)
Moreton Cl. E5 . . . . .4D **37**
N15 . . . . .1F **35**
SW1 . . . . .1E **89**
(off Moreton Ter.)
Moreton Ho. SE16 . . . .4D **79**
Moreton Pl. SW1 . . . .1E **89**
Moreton Rd. N15 . . . .1F **35**
Moreton St. SW1 . . . .1E **89**
Moreton Ter. SW1 . . . .1E **89**
Moreton Ter. M. Nth.
SW1 . . . . .1E **89**

Moreton Ter. M. Sth.
SW1 . . . . .1E **89**
Morgan Ho. SW1 . . . .5E **75**
(off Vauxhall Bri. Rd.)
SW8 . . . . .4E **89**
(off Wadhurst Rd.)
Morgan Mans. N7 . . . .2C **48**
(off Morgan Rd.)
Morgan Rd. N7 . . . . .2C **48**
W10 . . . . .4B **58**
Morgans La. SE1 . . . .2D **27**
(off Tooley St.)
Morgan St. E3 . . . . .2A **66**
(not continuous)
E16 . . . . .4B **68**
Moriatry Cl. N7 . . . . .1A **48**
Morie St. SW18 . . . . .3D **101**
Morieux Rd. E10 . . . .3B **38**
Moring Rd. SW17 . . . .4C **116**
Morkyns Wlk. SE21 . . .3A **120**
Morland Cl. NW11 . . . .3D **31**
Morland Ct. W12 . . . .3D **71**
(off Coningham Rd.)
Morland Est. E8 . . . . .4C **50**
Morland Gdns. NW10 . . .4A **42**
Morland Ho. NW1 . . . .1A **6**
(off Werrington St.)
NW6 . . . . .5C **44**
SW1 . . . . .5A **76**
(off Marsham St.)
W11 . . . . .5A **58**
(off Lancaster Rd.)
Morland M. N1 . . . . . .4C **48**
Morland Rd. E17 . . . .1F **37**
Morley Ho. SE15 . . . .3B **92**
(off Commercial Way)
Morley Rd. E10 . . . . .3E **39**
E15 . . . . .1B **68**
SE13 . . . . .2E **109**
Morley St.
SE1 . . . .5C **24** (4C **76**)
Morna Rd. SE5 . . . . .5E **91**
Morning La. E9 . . . . .3E **51**
Mornington Av. W14 . . .5B **72**
Mornington Av. Mans.
W14 . . . . .5B **72**
(off Mornington Av.)
Mornington Ct. NW1 . . .1E **61**
(off Mornington Cres.)
Mornington Cres.
NW1 . . . . .1E **61**
Mornington Gro. E3 . . .2C **66**
Mornington M. SE5 . . .4E **91**
Mornington Pl. NW1 . . .1E **61**
SE8 . . . . .3B **94**
(off Mornington Rd.)
Mornington Rd. E11 . . .2B **40**
(not continuous)
SE8 . . . . .3B **94**
**Mornington
Sports & Leisure Cen.**
. . . . .5D **47**
(off Arlington Rd.)
Mornington St. NW1 . . .1D **61**
Mornington Ter. NW1 . . .5D **47**
Morocco St.
SE1 . . . .4D **27** (3A **78**)
Morocco Wharf E1 . . . .2D **79**
(off Wapping High St.)
Morpeth Gro. E9 . . . . .5F **51**

Morpeth Mans. *SW1* *5E 75*
   (off Morpeth Ter.)
Morpeth Rd. E9 . . . . .5F 51
Morpeth St. SW1 . . . . . . .2E 65
Morpeth Ter. SW1 . . . . . .4E 75
Morrel Ct. *E2* *1C 64*
   (off Goldsmiths Row)
Morrells Yd. *SE11* *1C 90*
   (off Cleaver St.)
Morris Blitz Ct. N16 . . . .1B 50
Morris Gdns. SW18 . . . .5C 100
Morris Ho. *E2* *2E 65*
   (off Roman Rd.)
   NW8 . . . .*3A 60*
   (off Salisbury St.)
   W3 . . . . .3B 70
Morrish Rd. SW2 . . . . . .5A 104
Morrison Bldgs. Nth.
   E1 . . . .*5C 64*
   (off Commercial Rd.)
Morrison Ct. *SW1* *4F 75*
   (off Gt. Smith St.)
Morrison Ho. *SW2* *1C 118*
   (off High Trees)
Morrison Rd. SW9 . . . . . .5C 90
Morrison St. SW11 . . . . .1C 102
Morris Pl. N4 . . . . .4C 34
Morris Rd. E14 . . . . .4D 67
   E15 . . . . .1A 54
Morriss Ho. *SE16* *3D 79*
   (off Cherry Gdn.)
Morris St. E1 . . . . .5D 65
Morse Cl. E13 . . . . .2C 68
Morshead Mans. *W9* . . .*2C 58*
   (off Morshead Rd.)
Morshead Rd. W9 . . . . . .2C 58
Mortain Ho. *SE16* *5D 79*
   (off Roseberry St.)
Morten Cl. SW4 . . . . . . .4F 103
Mortham St. E15 . . . . . . .5A 54
Mortimer Cl. NW2 . . . . . .4B 30
   SW16 . . . . .2F 117
Mortimer Ct. *NW8* *1E 59*
   (off Abbey Rd.)
Mortimer Cres. NW6 . . . .5D 45
Mortimer Est. *NW6* *5D 45*
   (off Mortimer Pl.)
Mortimer Ho. W11 . . . . . .2F 71
   W14 . . . .*5A 72*
   (off North End Rd.)
Mortimer Mkt.
   WC1 . . . . .4A 6 (3E 61)
Mortimer Pl. NW6 . . . . . .5D 45
Mortimer Rd. N1 . . . . . . .4A 50
   (not continuous)
   NW10 . . . . .2E 57
Mortimer Sq. W11 . . . . . .1F 71
Mortimer St.
   W1 . . . . . . .2E 13 (5E 61)
Mortimer Ter. NW5 . . . . .1D 47
MORTLAKE 1A 98
Mortlake High St.
   SW14 . . . . .1A 98
Mortlake Rd. E16 . . . . . . .5D 69
Mortlock Cl. SE15 . . . . . .4D 93
Mortlock Ct. E7 . . . . .1F 55
Morton Cl. E1 . . . . .5E 65
Morton Ho. SE17 . . . . . . .2D 91
Morton M. SW5 . . . . .5D 73
Morton Pl. SE1 . . . . .4C 76

Morton Rd. E15 . . . . .4B 54
   N1 . . . . .4E 49
Morval Rd. SW2 . . . . . . .3C 104
Morven Rd. SW17 . . . . . .3B 116
Morville Ho. *SW18* *4F 101*
   (off Fitzhugh Gro.)
Morville St. E3 . . . . .1C 66
Morwell St.
   WC1 . . . . . . .1B 14 (4F 61)
Moscow Mans. *SW5* *5C 72*
   (off Cromwell Rd.)
Moscow Pl. W2 . . . . .1D 73
Moscow Rd. W2 . . . . . . .1C 72
Mosedale Ho. *E1* *2E 5*
   (off Cumberland Mkt.)
Moseley Row SE10 . . . . .5B 82
Mosque Ter. *E1* *4C 64*
   (off Whitechapel Rd.)
Mosque Twr. *E1* *4C 64*
   (off Fieldgate St.)
   E3 . . . .*1A 66*
   (off Ford St.)
Mossbury Rd.
   SW11 . . . . .1A 102
Moss Cl. E1 . . . . .4C 64
Mossford St. E3 . . . . .3B 66
Mossington Gdns.
   SE16 . . . . .5E 79
Mossop St. SW3 . . . . . . .5A 74
Mostyn Gdns. NW10 . . . .2F 57
Mostyn Gro. E3 . . . . .1C 66
Mostyn Rd. SW9 . . . . . . .4C 90
Motcomb St.
   SW1 . . . . . .5B 20 (4C 74)
Mothers Sq. E5 . . . . .1D 51
Motley Av. EC2 . . . . .4D 11
Motley St. SW8 . . . . .5E 89
MOTTINGHAM 2F 125
Mottingham Gdns.
   SE9 . . . . .1F 125
Mottingham La.
   SE9 . . . . .1E 125
   SE12 . . . . .1E 125
Mottingham Rd.
   SE9 . . . . .2F 125
Moules Ct. SE5 . . . . .3E 91
Moulins Rd. E9 . . . . .4E 51
Moulsford Ho. N7 . . . . . .2F 47
   W2 . . . .*4C 58*
   (off Westbourne Pk. Rd.)
Moundfield Rd. N16 . . . . .1C 36
Mounsey Ho. *W10* *2A 58*
   (off Third Av.)
Mount, The E5 . . . . .4D 37
   (not continuous)
   NW3 . . . . .5E 31
   W8 . . . .*2C 72*
   (off Bedford Gdns.)
Mountacre Cl. SE26 . . . .4B 120
Mt. Adon Pk. SE22 . . . . .5C 106
Mountague Pl. E14 . . . . . .1E 81
Mountain Ho. SE11 . . . . .5B 76
Mt. Angelus Rd.
   SW15 . . . . .5B 98
Mt. Ash Rd. SE26 . . . . . .3D 121
Mountbatten Cl.
   SE19 . . . . .5A 120
Mountbatten Ct.
   SE16 . . . .*2E 79*
   (off Rotherhithe St.)

Mountbatten Ho. *N6* *2C 32*
   (off Hillcrest)
Mountbatten M.
   SW18 . . . . .5E 101
Mt. Carmel Chambers
   W8 . . . .*3C 72*
   (off Dukes La.)
Mount Ct. SW15 . . . . . . .1A 100
Mountearl Gdns.
   SW16 . . . . .3B 118
Mt. Ephraim La.
   SW16 . . . . .3F 117
Mt. Ephraim Rd.
   SW16 . . . . .3F 117
Mountfield Cl. SE6 . . . . . .5F 109
Mountfield Ter. SE6 . . . . .5F 109
Mountford Mans.
   SW11 . . . .*4C 88*
   (off Battersea Pk. Rd.)
Mountford Rd. E8 . . . . . . .2C 50
Mountfort Cres. N1 . . . . . .4C 48
Mountfort Ter. N1 . . . . . . .4C 48
Mount Gdns. SE26 . . . . . .3D 121
Mountgrove Rd. N5 . . . . . .5D 35
Mountjoy Cl. *EC2* *1A 18*
   (off Monkwell Sq.)
Mountjoy Ho. EC2 . . . . . .1F 17
Mount Lodge N6 . . . . .1E 33
Mount Mills
   EC1 . . . . .2E 9 (2D 63)
Mt. Nod Rd. SW16 . . . . . .3B 118
Mt. Pleasant SE27 . . . . . .4E 119
   WC1 . . . . .4B 8 (3C 62)
Mt. Pleasant Cres.
   N4 . . . . .3B 34
Mt. Pleasant Hill E5 . . . . .4D 37
Mt. Pleasant La. E5 . . . . .3D 37
Mt. Pleasant M. *N4* *3B 34*
   (off Mt. Pleasant Cres.)
Mt. Pleasant Rd.
   NW10 . . . . .4E 43
   SE13 . . . . .4D 109
Mt. Pleasant Vs. N4 . . . . .2B 34
Mount Rd. NW2 . . . . .5D 29
   NW4 . . . . .1C 28
   SW19 . . . . .2C 114
Mount Row
   W1 . . . . .5D 13 (1D 75)
Mountsfield Ct.
   SE13 . . . . .4F 109
Mounts Pond Rd. SE3 . . .5F 95
   (not continuous)
Mount Square, The
   NW3 . . . . .5E 31
Mount St. W1 . . . .5B 12 (1C 74)
Mount St. M.
   W1 . . . . .5D 13 (1D 75)
Mount Ter. E1 . . . . .4D 65
Mount Vernon NW3 . . . . . .1E 45
Mountview Cl. NW11 . . . . .3D 31
Mount Vw. Rd. N4 . . . . . .2A 34
Mount Vs. SE27 . . . . .3D 119
Mowatt Cl. N19 . . . . .3F 33
Mowbray Rd. NW6 . . . . . .4A 44
Mowlem St. E2 . . . . .1D 65
Mowll St. SW9 . . . . .3C 90
Moxon Cl. E13 . . . . .1B 68
Moxon St.
   W1 . . . . .1B 12 (4C 60)
Moye Cl. E2 . . . . .1C 64

Moyers Rd. E10 . . . . . . .2E 39
Moylan Rd. W6 . . . . .2A 86
Moyle Ho. SW1 . . . . .1E **89**
(off Churchill Gdns.)
Moyne Ho. SW9 . . . . . . .3D **105**
Moyser Rd. SW16 . . . . .5D **117**
Mozart St. W10 . . . . .2B **58**
Mozart Ter. SW1 . . . . . . .5C **74**
MTV Europe 4D **47**
Mudchute Farm 5E **81**
Mudlarks Blvd.
SE10 . . . . .4B **82**
Mudlarks Way SE10 . . . .4C **82**
Muir Dr. SW18 . . . . .4A **102**
Muirfield W3 . . . . .5A **56**
Muirfield Cl. SE16 . . . . . .1D **93**
Muirfield Cres. E14 . . . . .4D **81**
Muirkirk Rd. SE6 . . . . . .1E **123**
Muir Rd. E5 . . . . .5C **36**
Mulberry Bus. Cen.
SE16 . . . . .3F **79**
Mulberry Cl. NW3 . . . . . .1F **45**
SE7 . . . . .2F **97**
SE22 . . . . .3C **106**
SW3 . . . . .2F **87**
(off Beaufort St.)
SW16 . . . . .4E **117**
Mulberry Ct. E11 . . . . . .1F **53**
(off Langthorne Rd.)
EC1 . . . . .2E **9**
(off Tompion St.)
SW3 . . . . .2F **87**
(not continuous)
W9 . . . . .2B **58**
(off Ashmore Rd.)
Mulberry Ho. E2 . . . . . . .2E **65**
(off Victoria Pk. Sq.)
SE8 . . . . .2B **94**
Mulberry Housing Co-operative
SE1 . . . . .1C **24**
Mulberry M. SE14 . . . . . .4B **94**
Mulberry Pl. E14 . . . . . . .1E **81**
(off Clove Cres.)
SE9 . . . . .2F **111**
W6 . . . . .1C **84**
Mulberry Rd. E8 . . . . . . .4B **50**
Mulberry St. E1 . . . . .5C **64**
Mulberry Wlk. SW3 . . . . .2F **87**
Mulgrave Rd. NW10 . . . .1B **42**
SW6 . . . . .2B **86**
Mulkern Rd. N19 . . . . . . .3F **33**
(not continuous)
Mullen Twr. WC1 . . . . . . .4B **8**
(off Mt. Pleasant)
Muller Rd. SW4 . . . . . . .4F **103**
Mullet Gdns. E2 . . . . . . .2C **64**
Mulletsfield WC1 . . . . . . .2E **7**
(off Cromer St.)
Mull Ho. E3 . . . . .1B **66**
(off Stafford Rd.)
Mulligans Apartments
NW6 . . . . .4C **44**
(off Kilburn High Rd.)
Mull Wlk. N1 . . . . .3E **49**
(off Clephane Rd.)
Mulready Ho. SW1 . . . . .5A **76**
(off Marsham St.)
Mulready St. NW8 . . . . . .3A **60**
Multon Ho. E9 . . . . .4E **51**
Multon Rd. SW18 . . . . . .5F **101**

Mulvaney Way
SE1 . . . . .4C **26** (3F **77**)
(not continuous)
Mumford Mills
SE10 . . . . .4D **95**
(off Greenwich High Rd.)
Mumford Rd. SE24 . . . . .3D **105**
Muncaster Rd.
SW11 . . . . .3B **102**
Muncies M. SE6 . . . . . . .2E **123**
Mundania Ct. SE22 . . . . .4D **107**
Mundania Rd. SE22 . . . .4D **107**
Munday Ho. SE1 . . . . . . .5B **26**
(off Burbage Cl.)
Munday Rd. E16 . . . . . . .1C **82**
Munden Ho. E3 . . . . .2D **67**
(off Bromley High St.)
Munden St. W14 . . . . . . .5A **72**
Mundford Rd. E5 . . . . . . .4E **37**
Mund St. W14 . . . . .1B **86**
Mundy Ho. W10 . . . . .2A **58**
(off Dart St.)
Mundy St.
N1 . . . . .1D **11** (2A **64**)
Munkenbeck Bldg.
W2 . . . . .4F **59**
(off Hermitage St.)
Munnings Ho. E16 . . . . . .2D **83**
(off Portsmouth M.)
Munro Ho.
SE1 . . . . .4B **24** (3C **76**)
Munro M. W10 . . . . .4A **58**
(not continuous)
Munro Ter. SW10 . . . . . . .3F **87**
Munster Ct. SW6 . . . . . . .5B **86**
Munster M. SW6 . . . . . . .3A **86**
Munster Rd. SW6 . . . . . .3A **86**
Munster Sq.
NW1 . . . . .2E **5** (2D **61**)
Munton Rd. SE17 . . . . . .5E **77**
Murchison Ho. W10 . . . . .4A **58**
(off Ladbroke Gro.)
Murchison Rd. E10 . . . . .4E **39**
Murdoch Ho. SE16 . . . . . .4E **79**
(off Moodkee St.)
Murdock Cl. E16 . . . . . . .5B **68**
Murdock St. SE15 . . . . . .2D **93**
Murfett Cl. SW19 . . . . . .2A **114**
Muriel St. N1 . . . . .1B **62**
(not continuous)
Murillo Rd. SE13 . . . . . . .2F **109**
Muro Ct. SE1 . . . . .4E **25**
(off Milcote St.)
Murphy Ho. SE1 . . . . . . .5E **25**
(off Borough Rd.)
Murphy St.
SE1 . . . . .4B **24** (3C **76**)
Murray Gro.
N1 . . . . .1A **10** (1E **63**)
Murray M. NW1 . . . . .4F **47**
Murray Rd. SW19 . . . . . .5F **113**
Murray Sq. E16 . . . . .5C **68**
Murray St. NW1 . . . . .4F **47**
Murray Ter. NW3 . . . . . . .1E **45**
Mursell Est. SW8 . . . . . . .4B **90**
Musard Rd. W6 . . . . .2A **86**
Musbury St. E1 . . . . .5E **65**
Muscal W6 . . . . .2A **86**
(off Field Rd.)
Muscatel Pl. SE5 . . . . . . .4A **92**

Muschamp Rd. SE15 . . . .1B **106**
Muscott Ho. E2 . . . . .5C **50**
(off Whiston Rd.)
Muscovy St.
EC3 . . . . .4E **19** (1A **78**)
Museum Chambers
WC1 . . . . .1D **15**
(off Bury Pl.)
Museum Ho. E2 . . . . .2E **65**
(off Burnham St.)
Museum La. SW7 . . . . . . .4F **73**
Museum Mans. WC1 . . . .1D **15**
(off Gt. Russell St.)
Mus. of Brands,
Packaging and Advertising
. . . . .5B **58**
(off Colville M.)
Mus. of Childhood 2E **65**
Mus. of Classical Archaeology
. . . . .3B **6**
(off Gower Pl.)
Mus. of Freemasonry 2E **15**
(within Freemasons' Hall)
Mus. of London
. . . . .1F **17** (4E **63**)
Mus. of
London Docklands, The
. . . . .1C **80**
Mus. of The Order of St John
. . . . .4D **9**
(off St John's La.)
Museum Pas. E2 . . . . . . .2E **65**
Museum St.
WC1 . . . . .1D **15** (4A **62**)
Musgrave Cl. SW11 . . . . .4A **88**
Musgrave Cres. SW6 . . . .3C **86**
Musgrove Rd. SE14 . . . . .4F **93**
Musjid Rd. SW11 . . . . . . .5F **87**
Muston Rd. E5 . . . . .4D **37**
Mustow Pl. SW6 . . . . .5B **86**
Muswell Hill Rd. N6 . . . . .1C **32**
N10 . . . . .1C **32**
Mutrix Rd. NW6 . . . . .5C **44**
Mutton Pl. NW1 . . . . .3C **46**
Myatt Rd. SW9 . . . . .4D **91**
Myatts Fld. Sth. SW9 . . . .5C **90**
Mycenae Rd. SE3 . . . . . . .3C **96**
Myddelton Pas.
EC1 . . . . .1C **8** (2C **62**)
Myddelton Sq.
EC1 . . . . .1C **8** (2C **62**)
Myddelton St.
EC1 . . . . .2C **8** (2C **62**)
Myddelton Av. N4 . . . . . . .4E **35**
Myddleton Ho. N1 . . . . . . .1B **8**
Myers Ho. SE5 . . . . .3E **91**
(off Bethwin Rd.)
Myers La. SE14 . . . . .2F **93**
Myles Cl. SE16 . . . . .4E **79**
(off Neptune St.)
Mylis Cl. SE26 . . . . .4D **121**
Mylius Cl. SE14 . . . . .3E **93**
Mylne Cl. W6 . . . . .1C **84**
Mylne St. EC1 . . . .1B **8** (2C **62**)
Myrdle Cl. E1 . . . . .5C **64**
(off Myrdle St.)
Myrdle St. E1 . . . . .4C **64**
Myron Pl. SE13 . . . . .1E **109**
Myrtleberry Cl. E8 . . . . . . .3B **50**
(off Beechwood Rd.)

Myrtle Rd. E17 . . . . .1A 38
Myrtle Wlk.
   N1 . . . . . . .1D 11 (1A 64)
Mysore Rd. SW11 . . . . . .1B 102
Myton Rd. SE21 . . . . . .1F 119
Mytton Ho. SW8 . . . . . . .3B 90
   (off St Stephens Ter.)

N

N1 Shop. Cen. N1 . . . . . .1C 62
N16 Fitness Cen. 1F 49
Nadine St. SE7 . . . . .1E 97
Nagasaki Wlk. SE7 . . . . .4D 83
NAG'S HEAD 5A 34
Nags Head Ct. EC1 . . . . .4A 10
Nags Head Shop. Cen.
   N7 . . . . .1B 48
Nainby Ho. SE11 . . . . . .5C 76
   (off Hotspur St.)
Nairne Gro. SE24 . . . . . .3F 105
Nairn St. E14 . . . . .4E 67
Naldera Gdns. SE3 . . . . .2C 96
Nalton Ho. NW6 . . . . . . .4E 45
   (off Belsize Rd.)
Namba Roy Cl.
   SW16 . . . . .4B 118
Nankin St. E14 . . . . .5C 66
Nansen Rd. SW11 . . . . . .1C 102
Nant Ct. NW2 . . . . .4B 30
Nantes Cl. SW18 . . . . . .2E 101
Nantes Pas.
   E1 . . . . .5F 11 (4B 64)
Nant Rd. NW2 . . . . .4B 30
Nant St. E2 . . . . .2D 65
Naoroji St.
   WC1 . . . . . . .2B 8 (2C 62)
Napier Av. E14 . . . . .1C 94
   SW6 . . . . .1B 100
Napier Cl. SE8 . . . . .3B 94
   W14 . . . . .4A 72
Napier Ct. N1 . . . . .1F 63
   (off Cropley St.)
   SE12 . . . . .3D 125
   SW6 . . . . .1B 100
   (off Ranelagh Gdns.)
Napier Gro. N1 . . . . .1E 63
Napier Ho. SE17 . . . . . . .2D 91
   (off Cooks Rd.)
Napier Pl. W14 . . . . .4B 72
Napier Rd. E11 . . . . .1A 54
   E15 . . . . .1A 68
   (not continuous)
   NW10 . . . . .2D 57
   W14 . . . . .4B 72
Napier St. SE8 . . . . .3B 94
   (off Napier Cl.)
Napier Ter. N1 . . . . .4D 49
Napoleon Rd. E5 . . . . . . .5D 37
Nara SE13 . . . . .5F 95
Narbonne Av. SW4 . . . . .3E 103
Narborough St. SW6 . . . .5D 87
Narcissus Rd. NW6 . . . . .2C 44
Narford Rd. E5 . . . . .5C 36
Narrow St. E14 . . . . .1A 80
Narvic Ho. SE5 . . . . .5E 91
Narwhal Inuit Art Gallery
   . . . . .1A 84
Nascot St. W12 . . . . .5E 57

Naseby Cl. NW6 . . . . . . .4E 45
Naseby Rd. SE19 . . . . . .5F 119
Nashe Ho. SE1 . . . . .5B 26
   (off Burbage Cl.)
Nash Ho. E14 . . . . .3C 80
   (off Alpha Gro.)
   NW1 . . . . .1D 61
   (off Park Village E.)
   SW1 . . . . .1D 89
   (off Lupus St.)
Nash Pl. E14 . . . . .2D 81
Nash Rd. SE4 . . . . .2A 108
Nash St. NW1 . . . . .1E 5 (2D 61)
Nasmyth St. W6 . . . . . . .4D 71
Nassau Rd. SW13 . . . . . .4B 84
Nassau St.
   W1 . . . . .1F 13 (4E 61)
Nassington Rd. NW3 . . . .1B 46
Natal Rd. SW16 . . . . . . .5F 117
Nathan Ho. SE11 . . . . . .5C 76
   (off Reedworth St.)
Nathaniel Cl.
   E1 . . . . .1F 19 (4B 64)
Nathaniel Ct. E17 . . . . . .2A 38
National Army Mus. 2B 88
National Gallery
   . . . . .5C 14 (1F 75)
National Maritime Mus.
   . . . . .2F 95
National Portrait Gallery
   . . . . .5C 14
National Tennis Cen. 3A 98
National Ter. SE16 . . . . .3D 79
   (off Bermondsey Wall E.)
National Theatre
   . . . . .1A 24 (2C 76)
Natural History Mus.
   Knightsbridge 4F 73
Nautilus Building, The
   EC1 . . . . .1E 9
   (off Myddelton Pas.)
Naval Ho. E14 . . . . .1F 81
   (off Quixley St.)
Naval Row E14 . . . . .1E 81
Navarino Gro. E8 . . . . . .3C 50
Navarino Mans. E8 . . . . .3C 50
Navarino Rd. E8 . . . . . . .3C 50
Navarre St.
   E2 . . . . .3F 11 (3B 64)
Navenby Wlk. E3 . . . . . . .3C 66
Navy St. SW4 . . . . .1F 103
Naxos Bldg. E14 . . . . . . .3B 80
Nayim Pl. E8 . . . . .2D 51
Nayland Ho. SE6 . . . . . . .4E 123
Naylor Bldg. E. E1 . . . . . .5C 64
   (off Assam St.)
Naylor Bldg. W. E1 . . . . .5C 64
   (off Adler St.)
Naylor Ho. SE17 . . . . . . .5F 77
   (off Flint St.)
   W10 . . . . .2A 58
   (off Dart St.)
Naylor Rd. SE15 . . . . . . .3D 93
Nazareth Gdns. SE15 . . .5D 93
Nazrul St. E2 . . . .1F 11 (2B 64)
NCR Bus. Cen.
   NW10 . . . . .2A 42
Neagle Ho. NW2 . . . . . . .5E 29
   (off Stoll Cl.)
Nealden St. SW9 . . . . . .1B 104

Neal St.
   WC2 . . . .3D 15 (5A 62)
Neal's Yd.
   WC2 . . . .3D 15 (5A 62)
NEASDEN 5A 28
Neasden Cl. NW10 . . . . .2A 42
NEASDEN JUNC. 1A 42
Neasden La. NW10 . . . . .5A 28
Neasden La. Nth.
   NW10 . . . . .5A 28
Neate Ho. SW1 . . . . .1E 89
   (off Lupus St.)
Neate St. SE5 . . . . .2A 92
Neathouse Pl. SW1 . . . . .5E 75
Neatscourt Rd. E6 . . . . . .4F 69
Nebraska Bldg. SE10 . . .4D 95
   (off Deal's Gateway)
Nebraska St.
   SE1 . . . . . . .4B 26 (3F 77)
Nebula SW11 . . . . .5B 88
Nebula E. E13 . . . . .1C 68
   (off Umbriel Pl.)
Neckinger
   SE16 . . . . . . .5F 27 (4B 78)
Neckinger Est.
   SE16 . . . . . . .5F 27 (4B 78)
Neckinger St. SE1 . . . . . .3B 78
Nectarine Way SE13 . . . .5D 95
Needham Ho. SE11 . . . . .1C 90
   (off Marylee Way)
Needham Rd. W11 . . . . . .5C 58
Needham Ter. NW2 . . . . .5F 29
Needleman St. SE16 . . . .3F 79
Needwood Ho. N4 . . . . . .3E 35
Neeld Cres. NW4 . . . . . . .1D 29
Neil Wates Cres.
   SW2 . . . . .1C 118
Nelgarde Rd. SE6 . . . . . .5C 108
Nella Rd. W6 . . . . .2F 85
Nelldale Rd. SE16 . . . . . .5E 79
Nell Gwynn Ho. SW3 . . . .5A 74
Nello James Gdns.
   SE27 . . . . .4F 119
Nelson Cl. NW6 . . . . .2C 58
Nelson Ct. SE16 . . . . . . .2E 79
   (off Brunel Rd.)
Nelson Gdns. E2 . . . . . . .2C 64
Nelson Ho. SW1 . . . . . . .2E 89
   (off Dolphin Sq.)
Nelson Mandela Ho.
   N16 . . . . .4C 36
Nelson Mandela Ho.
   SE3 . . . . .1E 111
Nelson Pas.
   EC1 . . . . . . .1A 10 (2E 63)
Nelson Pl. N1 . . . .1E 9 (1D 63)
Nelson Rd. N8 . . . . .1B 34
   SE10 . . . . .2E 95
Nelson's Column
   . . . . .1C 22 (2F 75)
Nelson Sq.
   SE1 . . . . . . .3D 25 (3D 77)
Nelson's Row SW4 . . . . .2F 103
Nelson St. E1 . . . . .5D 65
   E16 . . . . .5B 68
Nelsons Yd. NW1 . . . . . . .1E 61
   (off Mornington Cres.)
Nelson Ter. N1 . . . .1E 9 (1D 63)
Nelson Wlk. E3 . . . . .3D 67
   SE16 . . . . .2A 80

Nepaul Rd. SW11 . . . . .5A 88
Nepean St. SW15 . . . . .4C 98
Neptune Ct. E14 . . . . .5C 80
(off Homer Dr.)
E16 . . . . .4C 68
(off Hammersley Rd.)
Neptune Ho. E3 . . . . .5C 52
(off Garrison Rd.)
SE16 . . . . .4E 79
(off Moodkee St.)
Neptune St. SE16 . . . . .4E 79
Nesbit Rd. SE9 . . . . . .2F 111
Nesbitt Cl. SE3 . . . . . .1A 110
Nesham Ho. N1 . . . . .5A 50
(off Hoxton St.)
Nesham St. E1 . . . . . .1C 78
Ness St. SE16 . . . . . . .4C 78
Nestor Ho. E2 . . . . . . .1D 65
(off Old Bethnal Grn. Rd.)
Netheravon Rd. W4 . . . .5B 70
Netheravon Rd. Sth.
W4 . . . . .1B 84
Netherby Rd. SE23 . . . .5E 107
Nethercott Ho. E3 . . . . .2D 67
(off Bruce Rd.)
Netherfield Rd.
SW17 . . . . .3C 116
Netherford Rd. SW4 . . . .5E 89
Netherhall Gdns.
NW3 . . . . .3E 45
Netherhall Way NW3 . . .2E 45
Netherleigh Cl. N6 . . . .3D 33
Netherton Gro. SW10 . . .2E 87
Netherton Rd. N15 . . . .1F 35
Netherwood Pl. W14 . . .4F 71
(off Netherwood Rd.)
Netherwood Rd. W14 . . .4F 71
Netherwood St. NW6 . . .4B 44
Netley SE5 . . . . .4A 92
(off Redbridge Gdns.)
Netley Rd. E17 . . . . . . .1B 38
Netley St.
NW1 . . . . . . .2F 5 (2E 61)
Nettlecombe NW1 . . . . .4F 47
(off Agar Gro.)
Nettleden Ho. SW3 . . . .5A 74
(off Cale St.)
Nettlefold Pl. SE27 . . . .3D 119
Nettleton Ct. EC2 . . . . .1F 17
(off London Wall)
Nettleton Rd. SE14 . . . .4F 93
Neuchatel Rd. SE6 . . . .2B 122
Neutron Twr. E14 . . . . .1F 81
Nevada Bldg. SE10 . . . .4D 95
(off Blackheath Rd.)
Nevada St. SE10 . . . . .2E 95
Nevern Mans. SW5 . . . .1C 86
(off Warwick Rd.)
Nevern Pl. SW5 . . . . . .5C 72
Nevern Rd. SW5 . . . . . .5C 72
Nevern Sq. SW5 . . . . . .5C 72
Nevil Ho. SW9 . . . . . . .5D 91
(off Loughborough Est.)
Nevill Ct. SW10 . . . . . .3E 87
(off Edith Ter.)
Neville Cl. E11 . . . . . . .5B 40
NW1 . . . . .1F 61
(off Brill Pl.)
NW6 . . . . .1B 58
SE15 . . . . .4C 92

Neville Ct. NW8 . . . . . .1F 59
(off Abbey Rd.)
Neville Dr. N2 . . . . . . .1E 31
Neville Gill Cl.
SW18 . . . . .4C 100
Neville Ho. NW6 . . . . . .1B 58
(off Denmark Rd.)
Neville Rd. E7 . . . . . . .4C 54
NW6 . . . . .1B 58
Nevilles Ct. NW2 . . . . .5C 28
Neville St. SW7 . . . . . .1F 87
Neville Ter. SW7 . . . . . .1F 87
Nevill Rd. N16 . . . . . . .1A 50
Nevinson Cl. SW18 . . . .4F 101
Nevis Cl. E13 . . . . .1D 69
Nevis Rd. SW17 . . . . . .2C 116
Nevitt Ho. N1 . . . . .1F 63
(off Cranston Est.)
Newall Ho. SE1 . . . . . .5A 26
(off Bath Ter.)
Newark Ho. SW9 . . . . . .5D 91
Newark St. E1 . . . . . . .4D 65
(not continuous)
New Atlas Wharf E14 . . .4C 80
(off Arnhem Pl.)
New Baltic Wharf
SE8 . . . . .1A 94
(off Evelyn St.)
New Barn St. E13 . . . . .3C 68
New Bell Yd. EC4 . . . . .3E 17
(off Carter La.)
New Bentham Ct. N1 . . .4E 49
(off Ecclesbourne Rd.)
Newbery Ho. N1 . . . . . .4E 49
(off Northampton St.)
Newbold Cotts. E1 . . . . .5E 65
Newbolt Ho. SE17 . . . . .1F 91
(off Brandon St.)
New Bond St.
W1 . . . . . . .3D 13 (5D 61)
Newbridge Point
SE23 . . . . .3F 121
(off Windrush La.)
New Bridge St.
EC4 . . . . . . .3D 17 (5D 63)
New Broad St.
EC2 . . . . . . .1D 19 (4A 64)
Newburgh St.
W1 . . . . .3A 14 (5E 61)
New Burlington M.
W1 . . . . .4F 13 (1E 75)
New Burlington Pl.
W1 . . . . .4F 13 (1E 75)
New Burlington St.
W1 . . . . .4F 13 (1E 75)
Newburn Ho. SE11 . . . .1B 90
(off Newburn St.)
Newburn St. SE11 . . . . .1B 90
Newbury Ct. E5 . . . . . .2A 52
(off Daubeney Rd.)
Newbury Ho. SW9 . . . . .5D 91
W2 . . . . .5D 59
(off Hallfield Est.)
Newbury M. NW5 . . . . .3C 46
Newbury St.
EC1 . . . . . . .1F 17 (4E 63)
New Bus. Centre, The
NW10 . . . . .2B 56

New Butt La. SE8 . . . . .3C 94
New Butt La. Nth.
SE8 . . . . .3C 94
(off Hales St.)
Newby NW1 . . . . .2F 5
(off Robert St.)
Newby Ho. E14 . . . . . . .1E 81
(off Newby Pl.)
Newby Pl. E14 . . . . . . .1E 81
Newby St. SW8 . . . . . .1D 103
New Caledonian Mkt.
SE1 . . . . .5E 27
(off Bermondsey Sq.)
New Caledonian Wharf
SE16 . . . . .4B 80
Newcastle Cl.
EC4 . . . . . .2D 17 (5D 63)
Newcastle Ct. EC4 . . . . .4A 18
(off College Hill)
Newcastle Ho. W1 . . . . .5B 4
(off Luxborough St.)
Newcastle Pl. W2 . . . . .4F 59
Newcastle Row
EC1 . . . . . . .4C 8 (3C 62)
New Cavendish St.
W1 . . . . .1C 12 (4C 60)
New Century St. E16 . . . .5B 68
(off Jude St.)
New Change
EC4 . . . . . . .3F 17 (5E 63)
New Change Pas.
EC4 . . . . .3F 17
(off New Change)
New Charles St.
EC1 . . . . . . .1E 9 (2D 63)
NEW CHARLTON 5E 83
New Chiswick Pool 3A 84
New Church Rd. SE5 . . .3E 91
(not continuous)
New City Rd. E13 . . . . .2E 69
New Clocktower Pl.
N7 . . . . .3A 48
New College Ct.
NW3 . . . . .3E 45
(off College Cres.)
New College M. N1 . . . .4C 48
New College Pde.
NW3 . . . . .3F 45
(off Finchley Rd.)
Newcombe Gdns.
SW16 . . . . .4A 118
Newcombe Ho. E5 . . . . .5D 37
Newcombe St. W8 . . . . .2C 72
Newcomen Rd. E11 . . . .5B 40
SW11 . . . . .1F 101
Newcomen St.
SE1 . . . . . . .3B 26 (3F 77)
New Compton St.
WC2 . . . . . . .3C 14 (5F 61)
New Concordia Wharf
SE1 . . . . .3C 78
New Ct. EC4 . . . . .4B 16
Newcourt Ho. E2 . . . . . .2D 65
(off Pott St.)
Newcourt St. NW8 . . . . .1A 60
New Covent Garden Market
. . . . .3F 89
New Crane Pl. E1 . . . . .2E 79
New Crane Wharf E1 . . .2E 79
(off New Crane Pl.)

New Crescent Yd.
  NW10 . . . . .1B 56
NEW CROSS 3B 94
NEW CROSS 4B 94
NEW CROSS GATE 4F 93
NEW CROSS GATE 4F 93
New Cross Rd. SE14 . . .3E 93
Newdigate Ho. E14 . . . .5B 66
  (off Norbiton Rd.)
New Diorama Theatre
  . . . . .3D 61
Newell St. E14 . . . . . . .5B 66
New End NW3 . . . . . . .5E 31
New End Sq. NW3 . . . .1F 45
New End Theatre 5E 31
  (off New End)
Newent Cl. SE15 . . . . .3A 92
New Era Est. N1 . . . . . .5A 50
  (off Halcomb St.)
New Era Ho. N1 . . . . . .5A 50
  (off New Era Est.)
New Fetter La.
  EC4 . . . . .2C 16 (5C 62)
Newfield Ri. NW2 . . . . .5C 28
Newgate St.
  EC1 . . . . .2E 17 (5D 63)
New Globe Wlk.
  SE1 . . . . .1F 25 (2E 77)
New Goulston St.
  E1 . . . . . .2F 19 (5B 64)
New Grn. Pl. SE19 . . . .5A 120
Newhall Ct. N1 . . . . . . .5E 49
  (off Popham Rd.)
Newham City Farm 5F 69
Newham Leisure Cen.
  . . . . .3E 69
Newham's Row
  SE1 . . . . .4E 27 (4A 78)
Newham Way E6 . . . . . .4B 68
  E16 . . . . .4B 68
Newhaven Gdns.
  SE9 . . . . .2F 111
Newhaven La. E16 . . . .3B 68
New Hope Ct. NW10 . . .2D 57
Newick Rd. E5 . . . . . . .1D 51
NEWINGTON . . .5F 25 (4E 77)
Newington Barrow Way
  N7 . . . . .5B 34
Newington Butts SE1 . .5D 77
  SE11 . . . . .5D 77
Newington C'way.
  SE1 . . . . .5E 25 (4D 77)
Newington Ct. N16 . . . .1E 49
  (off Green Lanes)
Newington Ct. Bus. Cen.
  SE1 . . . . .5F 25
Newington Grn. N1 . . . .2F 49
  N16 . . . . .2F 49
Newington Grn.
    Community Gdns.
  N16 . . . . .2F 49
Newington Grn. Mans.
  N16 . . . . .2F 49
Newington Grn. Rd.
  N1 . . . . .3F 49
Newington Ind. Est.
  SE17 . . . . .5D 77
New Inn B'way.
  EC2 . . . . .3E 11 (3A 64)
New Inn Pas. WC2 . . . .3A 16

New Inn Sq. EC2 . . . . .3E 11
New Inn St.
  EC2 . . . . .3E 11 (3A 64)
New Inn Yd.
  EC2 . . . . .3E 11 (3A 64)
New Jubilee Wharf
  E1 . . . . .2E 79
  (off Wapping Wall)
New Kent Rd. SE1 . . . .4E 77
New Kings Rd. SW6 . . .5B 86
New King St. SE8 . . . . .2C 94
Newland Ct. EC1 . . . . .2B 10
Newland Ho. SE14 . . . .2F 93
  (off John Williams Cl.)
NEWLANDS 3F 107
Newlands NW1 . . . . .1F 5
  (off Harrington St.)
Newlands Pk. SE26 . . .5E 121
Newlands Quay E1 . . . .1E 79
New London St. EC3 . . .4E 19
New London Theatre . .2E 15
  (off Parker St.)
New Lydenburg
    Commercial Est.
  SE7 . . . . .4E 83
New Lydenburg St.
  SE7 . . . . .4E 83
Newlyn NW1 . . . . .5E 47
  (off Plender St.)
Newman Ho. SE1 . . . . .4D 77
Newman Pas.
  W1 . . . . . .1A 14 (4E 61)
Newman Rd. E13 . . . . .2D 69
Newman's Ct. EC3 . . . .3C 18
Newman's Row
  WC2 . . . . .1A 16 (4B 62)
Newman St.
  W1 . . . . . .1A 14 (4E 61)
Newman Yd.
  W1 . . . . . .2B 14 (5E 61)
Newmarket Grn.
  SE9 . . . . .5F 111
Newmill Ho. E3 . . . . . .3E 67
New Mount St.
  E15 . . . . .4F 53
Newnes Path SW15 . . .2D 99
Newnham Ter.
  SE1 . . . . .5B 24 (4C 76)
New North Pl.
  EC2 . . . . .3D 11 (3A 64)
New North Rd.
  N1 . . . . .1C 10 (4E 49)
New North St.
  WC1 . . . . .5F 7 (4B 62)
Newnton Cl. N4 . . . . . .2F 35
  (not continuous)
New Orleans Wlk.
  N19 . . . . .2F 33
New Oxford St.
  WC1 . . . . .2C 14 (5F 61)
New Pk. Pde. SW2 . . . .5A 104
  (off New Pk. Rd.)
New Pl. Sq. SE16 . . . . .4D 79
New Plaistow Rd.
  E15 . . . . .5A 54
New Players Theatre . .2A 76
  (off Villiers St.)
Newport Av. E13 . . . . .3D 69
  E14 . . . . .1F 81

Newport Ct.
  WC2 . . . . .4C 14 (1F 75)
Newport Ho. E3 . . . . . .2A 66
  (off Strahan Rd.)
Newport Pl.
  WC2 . . . . .4C 14 (1F 75)
Newport Rd. E10 . . . . .4E 39
  SW13 . . . . .4C 84
Newport St. SE11 . . . . .5B 76
New Priory Ct. NW6 . . .4C 44
  (off Mazenod Av.)
New Providence Wharf
  E14 . . . . .2F 81
Newquay Ho. SE11 . . . .1C 90
Newquay Rd. SE6 . . . . .2D 123
New Quebec St.
  W1 . . . . . .3A 12 (5B 60)
New Ride SW1 . . . . . . .3A 74
  SW7 . . . . . .3A 20 (3A 74)
New River Ct. N5 . . . . .1E 49
New River Head
  EC1 . . . . .1C 8 (2C 62)
New River Wlk. N1 . . . .3E 49
  (not continuous)
New River Way N4 . . . .2F 35
New Rd. E1 . . . . .4D 65
  N8 . . . . .1A 34
New Rochford St.
  NW5 . . . . .2B 46
New Row NW2 . . . . . . .5E 29
  WC2 . . . . .4D 15 (1A 76)
New Spitalfields Mkt.
  E10 . . . . .5C 38
New Spring Gdns. Wlk.
  SE11 . . . . .1A 90
New Sq. WC2 . . . .2B 16 (5C 62)
New Sq. Pas. WC2 . . . .2B 16
Newstead Ho. N1 . . . . .1C 62
  (off Tolpuddle St.)
Newstead Rd. SE12 . . .5B 110
Newstead Way
  SW19 . . . . .4F 113
New St. EC2 . . .1E 19 (4A 64)
New St. Hill
  BR1: Brom 5D 125
New St. Sq.
  EC4 . . . . .2C 16 (5C 62)
  (not continuous)
Newton Cl. E17 . . . . . .1A 38
Newton Ct. NW6 . . . . . .4E 45
  (off Fairfax Rd.)
  SW17 . . . . .3F 115
  (off Grosvenor Way)
  W8 . . . . .3C 72
  (off Kensington Chu. St.)
Newton Gro. W4 . . . . . .5A 70
Newton Ho. E1 . . . . . . .1D 79
  (off Cornwall St.)
  NW8 . . . . .5D 45
  (off Abbey Rd.)
Newton Lodge SE10 . . .4B 82
  (off Teal St.)
Newton Mans. W14 . . . .2A 86
  (off Queen's Club Gdns.)
Newton Pl. E14 . . . . . .5C 80
Newton Rd. E15 . . . . . .2F 53
  NW2 . . . . .1E 43
  W2 . . . . .5D 59
Newton St.
  WC2 . . . . .2E 15 (5A 62)

Newton's Yd. SW18 . . .3C 100
New Tower Bldgs.
  E1 . . . . .2D 79
Newtown St. SW11 . . .4D 89
New Turnstile WC1 . . . .1F 15
New Union Cl. E14 . . . .4E 81
New Union St.
  EC2 . . . .1B 18 (4F 63)
New Wanstead E11 . . . .1B 40
New Wharf Rd. N1 . . . .1A 62
New Zealand War Memorial
  . . . . .3C 74
  (off Hyde Pk. Cnr.)
New Zealand Way
  W12 . . . . .1D 71
Nexus Ct. E11 . . . . . . .3A 40
  NW6 . . . . .2C 58
Niagara Cl. N1 . . . . . . .1E 63
Niagra Ct. SE16 . . . . . .4E 79
  (off Canada Est.)
Nice Bus. Pk. SE15 . . . .2D 93
Nicholas Ct. E13 . . . . . .2D 69
  SE12 . . . . .1C 124
  W4 . . . . .2A 84
  (off Corney Reach Way)
Nicholas La.
  EC4 . . . . . .4C 18 (1F 77)
  (not continuous)
Nicholas M. W4 . . . . . .2A 84
Nicholas Pas. EC4 . . . .4C 18
Nicholas Rd. E1 . . . . . .3E 65
  W11 . . . . .1F 71
Nicholas Stacey Ho.
  SE7 . . . . .1D 97
  (off Frank Burton Cl.)
Nicholay Rd. N19 . . . . .3F 33
  (not continuous)
Nicholl Ho. N4 . . . . . . .3E 35
Nichollsfield Wlk. N7 . . .2B 48
Nicholls M. SW16 . . . .4A 118
Nicholls Point E15 . . . .5C 54
  (off Park Gro.)
Nicholl St. E2 . . . . .5C 50
Nichols Cl. N4 . . . . . . .3C 34
  (off Osborne Rd.)
Nichols Ct. E2 . . . . . . .1B 64
Nicholson Ho. SE17 . . . .1F 91
Nicholson St.
  SE1 . . . . .2D 25 (2D 77)
Nickelby Apartments
  E15 . . . . .3F 53
  (off Grove Cres. Rd.)
Nickleby Ho. SE16 . . . . .3C 78
  (off Parkers Row)
  W11 . . . . .2F 71
  (off St Ann's Rd.)
Nickols Wlk. SW18 . . . .2D 101
Nicoll Ct. NW10 . . . . . .5A 42
Nicoll Pl. NW4 . . . . . . .1D 29
Nicoll Rd. NW10 . . . . . .5A 42
Nicosia Rd. SW18 . . . .5A 102
Niederwald Rd.
  SE26 . . . . .4A 122
Nigel Ho. EC1 . . . . .5B 8
  (off Portpool La.)
Nigel Playfair Av.
  W6 . . . . .5D 71
Nigel Rd. E7 . . . . .2E 55
  SE15 . . . . .1C 106
Nigeria Rd. SE7 . . . . . .3E 97

Nightingale Ct. E14 . . . .3E 81
  (off Ovex Cl.)
  N4 . . . . .4B 34
  (off Tollington Pk.)
  SW6 . . . . .4D 87
  (off Maltings Pl.)
Nightingale Gro.
  SE13 . . . . .3F 109
Nightingale Ho. E1 . . . . .2C 78
  (off Thomas More St.)
  E2 . . . . .5A 50
  (off Kingsland Rd.)
  NW8 . . . . .3A 60
  (off Samford St.)
  W12 . . . . .5E 57
  (off Du Cane Rd.)
Nightingale La.
  SW4 . . . . .5B 102
  SW12 . . . . .5B 102
Nightingale Lodge
  W9 . . . . .4C 58
  (off Admiral Wlk.)
Nightingale M. E3 . . . . .1F 65
  E11 . . . . .1C 40
  SE11 . . . . .5D 77
Nightingale Pl.
  SW10 . . . . .2E 87
Nightingale Rd. E5 . . . . .5D 37
  N1 . . . . .3E 49
  NW10 . . . . .1B 56
Nightingale Sq.
  SW12 . . . . .5C 102
Nightingale Wlk. N1 . . . .3E 49
  SW4 . . . . .4D 103
Nile Cl. N16 . . . . .5B 36
Nile Ho. N1 . . . . .1B 10
  (off Nile St.)
Nile Rd. E13 . . . . .1E 69
Nile St. N1 . . . . .1A 10 (2E 63)
Nile Ter. SE15 . . . . .1B 92
Nimegen Way SE22 . .3A 106
Nimrod Ho. E16 . . . . . . .4D 69
  (off Vanguard Cl.)
Nimrod Pas. N1 . . . . . . .3A 50
Nimrod Rd. SW16 . . . . .5D 117
Nina Mackay Cl. E15 . . .5A 54
Nine Elms La. SW8 . . . .3E 89
NINE ELMS 3E 89
Nipponzan Myohoji
  Peace Pagoda 2B 88
Nisbet Ho. E9 . . . . .2F 51
Nita Ct. SE12 . . . . .1C 124
Niton St. SW6 . . . . .3F 85
Nobel Ho. SE5 . . . . .5E 91
Noble Ct. E1 . . . . .1D 79
Noblefield Hgts. N2 . . . .1A 32
Noble M. N16 . . . . .5F 35
  (off Albion Rd.)
Noble St.
  EC2 . . . . . .2F 17 (5E 63)
Noble Yd. N1 . . . . .5D 49
  (off Camden Pas.)
Nocavia Ho. SW6 . . . . .5E 87
  (off Townmead Rd.)
Noel Coward Ho.
  SW1 . . . . .5E 75
  (off Vauxhall Bri. Rd.)
Noel Coward Theatre
  . . . . .4D 15
  (off St Martin's La.)

Noel Ho. NW6 . . . . .4F 45
  (off Harben Rd.)
Noel Rd. E6 . . . . .3F 69
  N1 . . . . .1D 63
Noel St. W1 . . . .3A 14 (5E 61)
Noel Ter. SE23 . . . . . . .2E 121
Noko W10 . . . . .2F 57
Nolan Way E5 . . . . .1C 50
Noll Ho. N7 . . . . .4B 34
  (off Tomlins Wlk.)
Nora Leverton Ct.
  NW1 . . . . .4E 47
  (off Randolph St.)
Norbiton Ho. NW1 . . . . .5E 47
  (off Camden St.)
Norbiton Rd. E14 . . . . . .5B 66
Norbroke St. W12 . . . . .1B 70
Norburn St. W10 . . . . . .4A 58
Norcombe Ho. N19 . . . .5F 33
  (off Wedmore St.)
Norcott Rd. N16 . . . . . .4C 36
Norcroft Gdns.
  SE22 . . . . .5C 106
Norden Ho. E2 . . . . .2D 65
  (off Pott St.)
Norfolk Av. N15 . . . . . . .1B 36
Norfolk Cres. W2 . . . . . .5A 60
Norfolk Ho. EC4 . . . . . . .4F 17
  SW1 . . . . .5F 75
  (off Page St.)
Norfolk Ho. Rd.
  SW16 . . . . .3F 117
Norfolk Mans. SW11 . . .4B 88
  (off Prince of Wales Dr.)
Norfolk M. W10 . . . . . . .4A 58
  (off Blagrove Rd.)
Norfolk Pl. W2 . . . . .5F 59
  (not continuous)
Norfolk Rd. NW8 . . . . . .5F 45
  NW10 . . . . .4A 42
Norfolk Row SE1 . . . . . .5B 76
  (not continuous)
Norfolk Sq. W2 . . . . . . .5F 59
Norfolk Sq. M. W2 . . . . .5F 59
  (off London St.)
Norfolk St. E7 . . . . .2C 54
Norfolk Ter. W6 . . . . . . .1A 86
Norgrove St. SW12 . . . .5C 102
Norland Ho. W11 . . . . . .2F 71
  (off Queensdale Cres.)
Norland Pl. W11 . . . . . .2A 72
Norland Rd. W11 . . . . . .2F 71
Norland Sq. W11 . . . . . .2A 72
Norland Sq. Mans.
  W11 . . . . .2A 72
  (off Norland Sq.)
Norley Va. SW15 . . . . . .1C 112
Norlington Rd. E10 . . . . .3E 39
  E11 . . . . .3E 39
Norman Butler Ho.
  W10 . . . . .3A 58
  (off Ladbroke Gro.)
Normanby Cl. SW15 . . .3B 100
Normanby Rd. NW10 . . .1B 42
Norman Ct. N4 . . . . . . .2C 34
  NW10 . . . . .4C 42
Normand Gdns. W14 . . .2A 86
  (off Greyhound Rd.)
Normand Mans. W14 . . .2A 86
  (off Normand M.)

Normand M. W14 . . . . . .2A **86**
Normand Rd. W14 . . . . .2B **86**
Normandy Cl. SE26 . . . .3A **122**
Normandy Ho. E14 . . . . .3E **81**
   (off Plevna St.)
Normandy Pl. W12 . . . . .2F **71**
Normandy Rd.
  SW9 . . . . .4C **90**
Normandy Ter. E16 . . . . .5D **69**
Norman Gro. E3 . . . . . .1A **66**
Norman Ho. SE1 . . . . . .5E **27**
   (off Riley Rd.)
  SW8 . . . . .3A **90**
   (off Wyvil Rd.)
Normanhurst Rd.
  SW2 . . . . .2B **118**
Norman Rd. E11 . . . . . .4F **39**
  SE10 . . . . .3D **95**
Normanton Av.
  SW19 . . . . .2C **114**
Normanton St. SE23 . . .2F **121**
Normington Cl.
  SW16 . . . . .5C **118**
Norrice Lea N2 . . . . . . .1F **31**
Norris Ho. E9 . . . . .5E **51**
   (off Handley Rd.)
  N1 . . . . .5A **50**
   (off Colville Est.)
  SE8 . . . . .1B **94**
   (off Grove St.)
Norris St.
  SW1 . . . . . .5B **14** (1F **75**)
Norroy Rd. SW15 . . . . .2F **99**
Norstead Pl. SW15 . . . .2C **112**
Nth. Access Rd. E17 . . .1F **37**
NORTH ACTON 4A **56**
Nth. Acton Rd. NW10 . .1A **56**
Northampton Gro. N1 . . .2E **49**
Northampton Pk. N1 . . . .3E **49**
Northampton Rd.
  EC1 . . . . .3C **8** (3C **62**)
Northampton Row EC1 . .3C **8**
Northampton Sq.
  EC1 . . . . . . .2D **9** (2D **63**)
Northampton St. N1 . . . .4E **49**
Nth. Audley St.
  W1 . . . . .3B **12** (1C **74**)
Northaw Ho. W10 . . . . .3E **57**
   (off Sutton Way)
North Bank NW8 . . . . . .2A **60**
NORTH BECKTON 4F **69**
Nth. Birkbeck Rd.
  E11 . . . . .5F **39**
North Block SE1 . . . . . .3A **24**
   (off Chicheley St.)
Northbourne Rd.
  SW4 . . . . .3F **103**
Northbrook Rd.
  SE13 . . . . .3A **110**
Northburgh St.
  EC1 . . . . .4E **9** (3D **63**)
Nth. Carriage Dr. W2 . . .1A **74**
   (off Bayswater Rd.)
Northchurch SE17 . . . . .1F **91**
   (not continuous)
Northchurch Ho. E2 . . . .5C **50**
   (off Whiston Rd.)

Northchurch Rd. N1 . . . .4F **49**
   (not continuous)
Northchurch Ter. N1 . . . .4A **50**
Nth. Circular Rd.
  NW2 . . . . .5A **28**
  NW4 . . . . .2E **29**
  NW10 . . . . .2A **42**
  NW11 . . . . .2E **29**
   (not continuous)
Northcote M. SW11 . . . .2A **102**
Northcote Rd. NW10 . . .4A **42**
  SW11 . . . . .3A **102**
Northcroft Ct. W12 . . . . .3C **70**
North Crofts SE23 . . . . .1D **121**
Nth. Cross Rd.
  SE22 . . . . .3B **106**
Northdene Gdns.
  N15 . . . . .1B **36**
Northdown St.
  N1 . . . . .1F **7** (1A **62**)
North Dr. SW16 . . . . . . .4E **117**
NORTH END 4E **31**
North End NW3 . . . . . . .4E **31**
North End Av. NW3 . . . . .4E **31**
North End Cres. W14 . . . .5B **72**
North End Ho. W14 . . . . .5A **72**
North End Pde. W14 . . . .5A **72**
   (off North End Rd.)
North End Rd. NW11 . . . .3C **30**
  SW6 . . . . .5A **72**
  W14 . . . . .5A **72**
North End Way NW3 . . . .4E **31**
Northern Hgts. N8 . . . . . .2F **33**
   (off Crescent Rd.)
Northesk Ho. E13 . . . . . .1D **69**
Northesk Ho. E1 . . . . . . .3D **65**
   (off Tent St.)
Nth. Eyot Gdns. W6 . . . .1B **84**
Northey St. E14 . . . . . . .1A **80**
Northfield Ho. SE15 . . . .2C **92**
Northfield Rd. N16 . . . . .2A **36**
Northfields SW18 . . . . . .2C **100**
Northfields Prospect Bus. Cen.
  SW18 . . . . .2C **100**
Northfleet Ho. SE1 . . . . .3B **26**
   (off Tennis St.)
Northflock St. SE16 . . . .3C **78**
Nth. Flower Wlk. W2 . . . .1E **73**
   (off Lancaster Wlk.)
North Gdn. E14 . . . . . . .2B **80**
North Gate NW8 . . . . . . .1A **60**
   (off Prince Albert Rd.)
Northgate Ct. SW9 . . . . .1C **104**
Northgate Dr. NW9 . . . . .1A **28**
Northgate Ho. E14 . . . . .1C **80**
   (off E. India Dock Rd.)
Nth. Gower St.
  NW1 . . . . . . .2A **6** (2E **61**)
North Greenwich Arena
  (The O2) 2A **82**
North Gro. N6 . . . . .2C **32**
  N15 . . . . .1F **35**

North Hill N6 . . . . .1B **32**
North Hill Av. N6 . . . . . . .1C **32**
North Ho. SE8 . . . . .1B **94**
Northiam WC1 . . . . .2E **7**
   (off Cromer St.)
Northiam St. E9 . . . . . . .5D **51**
Northington St.
  WC1 . . . . . . .4A **8** (3B **62**)
NORTH KENSINGTON 4E **57**
Northlands St. SE5 . . . . .5E **91**
Northleigh Ho. E3 . . . . . .2D **67**
   (off Powis Rd.)
North Lodge E16 . . . . . .2D **83**
   (off Wesley Av.)
Nth. Lodge Cl.
  SW15 . . . . .3F **99**
North Mall SW18 . . . . . .3D **101**
   (off Southside Shop. Cen.)
North M. WC1 . . . . .4A **8** (3B **62**)
Northolme Rd. N5 . . . . . .1E **49**
Northover
  BR1: Brom 3B **124**
North Pas. SW18 . . . . . .3C **100**
Northpoint Ho. N1 . . . . . .3F **49**
   (off Essex Rd.)
Northpoint Sq. NW1 . . . .3F **47**
Nth. Pole Rd. W10 . . . . .4E **57**
Northport St. N1 . . . . . . .5F **49**
Nth. Quay Pl. E14 . . . . . .1D **81**
North Ride W2 . . . . .1A **74**
North Ri. W2 . . . . .5A **60**
North Rd. N6 . . . . .2C **32**
  N7 . . . . .3A **48**
  SW19 . . . . .5E **115**
North Row
  W1 . . . . .4A **12** (1B **74**)
Nth. Row Bldgs. W1 . . . .4B **12**
   (off North Row)
North Several SE3 . . . . . .5F **95**
Northside Studios E8 . . .5D **51**
   (off Andrew's Rd.)
Nth. Side Wandsworth Comn.
  SW18 . . . . .3F **101**
North Sq. NW11 . . . . . . .1C **30**
North Stand N5 . . . . .5D **35**
Northstead Rd.
  SW2 . . . . .2C **118**
North St. E13 . . . . .1D **69**
  SW4 . . . . .1E **103**
North St. Pas. E13 . . . . .1D **69**
Nth. Tenter St. E1 . . . . . .5B **64**
North Ter. SW3 . . . . .4A **74**
  WC2 . . . . .1D **23**
Northumberland All.
  EC3 . . . . .3E **19** (5A **64**)
   (not continuous)
Northumberland Av.
  E12 . . . . .3A **41**
  WC2 . . . . . . .1D **23** (2A **76**)
Northumberland Ho.
  SW1 . . . . .1D **23**
   (off Northumberland Av.)
Northumberland Pl.
  W2 . . . . .5C **58**
Northumberland Rd.
  E17 . . . . .2C **38**
Northumberland St.
  WC2 . . . . . . .1D **23** (2A **76**)
Northumbria St. E14 . . . .5C **66**

Nth. Verbena Gdns.
  W6 . . . . .1C **84**
North Vw. SW19 . . . . .5E **113**
Northview Cres.
  NW10 . . . . .1B **42**
Northview Pde. N7 . . . .5A **34**
North Vs. NW1 . . . . . . .3F **47**
North Wlk. W2 . . . . . . .1D **73**
  W8 . . . . .1D **73**
    (off The Broad Wlk.)
Northway NW11 . . . . . .1D **31**
Northway Rd. SE5 . . . .1E **105**
Northways NW3 . . . . . . .4F **45**
    (off College Cres.)
Northways Pde.
  NW3 . . . . .4F **45**
    (off College Cres.,
      not continuous)
Nth. Western Commercial Cen.
  NW1 . . . . .4A **48**
Northwest Pl. N1 . . . . .1C **62**
North Wharf E14 . . . . . .2E **81**
    (off Coldharbour)
Nth. Wharf Rd. W2 . . . .4F **59**
Northwick Cl. NW8 . . . .3F **59**
Northwick Ho. NW8 . . . .3E **59**
    (off St John's Wood Rd.)
Northwick Ter. NW8 . . .3F **59**
Northwold Rd. E5 . . . . .4B **36**
  N16 . . . . .4B **36**
Northwood Est. E5 . . . .4C **36**
Northwood Hall N6 . . . .2E **33**
Northwood Ho.
  SE27 . . . . .4F **119**
Northwood Rd. N6 . . . .2D **33**
  SE23 . . . . .1B **122**
Northwood Way
  SE19 . . . . .5F **119**
Nth. Woolwich Rd.
  E16 . . . . .2B **82**
Nth. Worple Way
  SW14 . . . . .1A **98**
Norton Folgate
  E1 . . . . . . .5E **11** (4A **64**)
Norton Folgate Ho.
  E1 . . . . .5F **11**
    (off Puma Ct.)
Norton Ho. E1 . . . . . . .5D **65**
    (off Bigland St.)
  E2 . . . . .1F **65**
    (off Mace St.)
  SW1 . . . . .4F **75**
    (off Arneway St.)
  SW9 . . . . .5B **90**
    (off Aytoun Rd.)
Norton Rd. E10 . . . . . .3B **38**
Norway Ga. SE16 . . . . .4A **80**
Norway Pl. E14 . . . . . .5B **66**
Norway St. SE10 . . . . . .2D **95**
Norway Wharf E14 . . . .5B **66**
Norwich Ho. E14 . . . . . .5D **67**
    (off Cordelia St.)
Norwich Rd. E7 . . . . . .2C **54**
Norwich St.
  EC4 . . . . . .2B **16** (5C **62**)
Norwood Cl. NW2 . . . . .5A **30**
Norwood High St.
  SE27 . . . . .3D **119**
Norwood Ho. E14 . . . . . .1D **81**
    (off Poplar High St.)

NORWOOD NEW TOWN
  . . . . .5E **119**
Norwood Pk. Rd.
  SE27 . . . . .5E **119**
Norwood Rd. SE24 . . . .1D **119**
  SE27 . . . . .2D **119**
Notley St. SE5 . . . . . . .3F **91**
Notting Barn Rd. W10 . .3F **57**
Nottingdale Sq. W11 . . .2A **72**
Nottingham Av. E16 . . . .4E **69**
Nottingham Ct.
  WC2 . . . . . .3D **15** (5A **62**)
Nottingham Ho. WC2 . . .3D **15**
    (off Shorts Gdns.)
Nottingham Pl.
  W1 . . . . . . .4B **4** (4C **60**)
Nottingham Rd. E10 . . . .1E **39**
  SW17 . . . . .1B **116**
Nottingham St.
  W1 . . . . . . .5B **4** (4C **60**)
Nottingham Ter. NW1 . . .4B **4**
NOTTING HILL 1C **72**
Notting Hill Ga. W11 . . .2C **72**
Nottingwood Ho.
  W11 . . . . .1A **72**
    (off Clarendon Rd.)
Nova Bldg. E14 . . . . . . .5C **80**
Nova Ct. E. E14 . . . . . . .2E **81**
    (off Yabsley St.)
Nova Ct. W. E14 . . . . . .2E **81**
    (off Yabsley St.)
Novello Ct. N1 . . . . .5E **49**
    (off Popham Rd.)
Novello St. SW6 . . . . . .4C **86**
Novello Theatre
  Covent Garden . . .1B **76**
    (off Aldwych)
Novem Ho. E1 . . . . .4C **64**
    (off Chicksand St.)
Nowell Rd. SW13 . . . . . .2C **84**
Noyna Rd. SW17 . . . . . .3B **116**
Nubia Way
  BR1: Brom 3A **124**
Nuding Cl. SE13 . . . . . .1C **108**
Nuffield Health Club
  Battersea 5B **88**
    (within Latchmere
      Leisure Cen.)
  Bloomsbury 3F **7**
    (off Mecklenburgh Pl.)
  Cannon Street 5B **18**
  Fulham 4F **85**
  Southfields 5D **101**
  Westminster 4E **59**
  Willesden Green
    . . . . .4E **43**
Nuffield Lodge N6 . . . .1E **33**
  W9 . . . . .4C **58**
    (off Admiral Wlk.)
Nugent Rd. N19 . . . . . .3A **34**
Nugent Ter. NW8 . . . . . .1E **59**
Number One
  EC1 . . . . . .4A **10** (3E **63**)
Nun Ct. EC2 . . . . .2B **18**
NUNHEAD 1D **107**
Nunhead Cemetery
  Nature Reserve
    . . . . .2E **107**
Nunhead Cres.
  SE15 . . . . .1D **107**

Nunhead Est. SE15 . . . .2D **107**
Nunhead Grn. SE15 . . . .1D **107**
Nunhead Gro. SE15 . . . .1D **107**
Nunhead La. SE15 . . . . .1D **107**
Nunhead Pas. SE15 . . . .1C **106**
Nursery Cl. SE4 . . . . . . .5B **94**
  SW15 . . . . .2F **99**
Nursery La. E2 . . . . . . .5B **50**
  E7 . . . . .3C **54**
  W10 . . . . .4E **57**
Nursery Rd. E9 . . . . . . .3E **51**
  SW9 . . . . .2B **104**
Nursery Row SE17 . . . . .5F **77**
Nutbourne St. W10 . . . .2A **58**
Nutbrook St. SE15 . . . . .1C **106**
Nutcroft Rd. SE15 . . . . .3D **93**
Nutfield Rd. E15 . . . . . . .1E **53**
  NW2 . . . . .5C **28**
  SE22 . . . . .2B **106**
Nutford Pl. W1 . . . . .5B **60**
Nuthurst Av. SW2 . . . . .2B **118**
Nutley Ter. NW3 . . . . . .3E **45**
Nutmeg Cl. E16 . . . . . . .3A **68**
Nutmeg La. E14 . . . . . . .5F **67**
Nuttall St. N1 . . . . .1A **64**
Nutter La. E11 . . . . .1E **41**
Nutt St. SE15 . . . . .3B **92**
Nutwell St. SW17 . . . . . .5A **116**
Nye Bevan Est. E5 . . . . .5F **37**
Nye Bevan Ho. SW6 . . . .3B **86**
    (off St Thomas's Way)
Nynehead St. SE14 . . . .3A **94**
Nyon Gro. SE6 . . . . . . .2B **122**
Nyton Cl. N19 . . . . .3A **34**

O

O2, The 2A **82**
O2 Brixton Academy
  . . . . .1C **104**
O2 Apple Ct. SE12 . . . .1C **124**
O2 Cen. NW3 . . . . .3E **45**
Oak Apple Ct. SE12 . . . .1C **124**
Oakbank Gro. SE24 . . . .2E **105**
Oakbrook Cl.
  BR1: Brom 4D **125**
Oakbury Rd. SW6 . . . . . .5D **87**
Oak Cott. Cl. SE6 . . . . . .1B **124**
Oak Ct. SE15 . . . . .3B **92**
    (off Sumner Rd.)
Oak Cres. E16 . . . . .4A **68**
Oakcroft Rd. SE13 . . . . .5F **95**
Oakdale Rd. E7 . . . . . . .4D **55**
  E11 . . . . .4F **39**
  N4 . . . . .1E **35**
  SE15 . . . . .1E **107**
  SW16 . . . . .5A **118**
Oakdene SE15 . . . . . . .4D **93**
Oakden St. SE11 . . . . . .5C **76**
Oake Ct. SW15 . . . . . . .3A **100**
Oakeford Ho. W14 . . . . .4A **72**
    (off Russell Rd.)
Oakend Ho. N4 . . . . . . .2F **35**
Oakeshott Av. N6 . . . . .4C **32**
Oakey La.
  SE1 . . . . . . .5B **24** (4C **76**)
Oakfield Ct. N8 . . . . . . .2A **34**
  NW2 . . . . .2F **29**
Oakfield Gdns. SE19 . . .5A **120**
    (not continuous)

Oakfield Ho. *E3* 4C *66*
    (off Gale St.)
Oakfield Rd. E6 . . . . .5F *55*
  N4 . . . . .1C *34*
  SW19 . . . . .3F *113*
Oakfields Rd.
  NW11 . . . . .1A *30*
Oakfield St. SW10 . . . . .2E *87*
Oakford Rd. NW5 . . . . . . .1E *47*
Oak Gro. NW2 . . . . .1A *44*
Oakhall Ct. E11 . . . . .1D *41*
Oak Hall Rd. E11 . . . . . .1D *41*
Oakham Cl. SE6 . . . . . . .2B *122*
Oakham Ho. W10 . . . . . .3E *57*
    (off Sutton Way)
Oakhill Av. NW3 . . . . .1D *45*
Oakhill Ct. SE23 . . . . . . .4E *107*
Oak Hill Pk. NW3 . . . . . . .1D *45*
Oak Hill Pk. M. NW3 . . . .1E *45*
Oakhill Pl. SW15 . . . . . . .3C *100*
Oakhill SW15 . . . . .3B *100*
Oak Hill Way NW3 . . . . . .1D *45*
    (not continuous)
Oak Ho. *W10* 3A *58*
    (off Sycamore Wlk.)
Oakhurst Gro. SE22 . . . .2C *106*
Oakington Rd. W9 . . . . . .3C *58*
Oakington Way N8 . . . . . .2A *34*
Oakland Quay E14 . . . . . .4D *81*
Oakland Rd. E15 . . . . . . .1F *53*
Oaklands Ct. *NW10* 5A *42*
    (off Nicoll Rd.)
Oaklands Est. SW4 . . . . .4E *103*
Oaklands Gro. W12 . . . . .2C *70*
Oaklands M. *NW2* 1F *43*
    (off Oaklands Rd.)
Oaklands Pas. *NW2* 1F *43*
    (off Oaklands Rd.)
Oaklands Pl. SW4 . . . . . .2E *103*
Oaklands Rd. NW2 . . . . . .1F *43*
Oak La. E14 . . . . .1B *80*
Oakleigh Ct. N1 . . . . .1B *10*
Oakley Cres. EC1 . . . . . .1D *63*
Oakley Dr. SE13 . . . . . . .4F *109*
Oakley Gdns. SW3 . . . . . .2A *88*
Oakley Ho. *SE11* 5C *76*
    (off Hotspur St.)
  SW1 . . . . .5B *74*
Oakley Pl. SE1 . . . . .1B *92*
Oakley Rd. N1 . . . . .4F *49*
Oakley Sq. NW1 . . . . .1E *61*
Oakley St. SW3 . . . . .2A *88*
Oakley Studios *SW3* 2A *88*
    (off Up. Cheyne Row)
Oakley Wlk. W6 . . . . .2F *85*
Oakley Yd. E2 . . . . .3B *64*
Oak Lock M. W4 . . . . . . .1A *84*
Oak Lodge E11 . . . . .1C *40*
  W8 . . . . .4D *73*
    (off Chantry Sq.)
Oakman Ho. SW19 . . . .1F *113*
Oakmead Rd. SW12 . .1C *116*
Oak Pk. Gdns.
  SW19 . . . . .1F *113*
Oak Pk. M. N16 . . . . .5B *36*
Oak Pavilion M.
  SE19 . . . . .5A *120*
Oak Pl. SW18 . . . . .3D *101*
Oakridge La.
  BR1: Brom 5F *123*

Oakridge Rd.
  BR1: Brom 4F *123*
Oaks, The *NW6* 4F *43*
    (off Brondesbury Pk.)
  NW10 . . . . .4D *43*
Oaks Av. SE19 . . . . . . .5A *120*
Oaksford Av.
  SE26 . . . . .3D *121*
Oakshade Rd.
  BR1: Brom 4F *123*
Oakshaw Rd. SW18 . . .5D *101*
Oakshott Ct.
  NW1 . . . . .1B **6** (1F **61**)
    (not continuous)
Oak Sq. SW9 . . . . .5B *90*
Oak St. *E14* 3E *81*
    (off Stewart St.)
Oak Tree Gdns.
  BR1: Brom 5D *125*
Oak Tree Ho. *W9* 3C *58*
    (off Shirland Rd.)
Oak Tree M. NW2 . . . . . .3C *42*
Oak Tree Rd. NW8 . . . . . .2A *60*
Oakview Lodge
  NW11 . . . . .2B *30*
    (off Beechcroft Av.)
Oakview Rd. SE6 . . . . . .5D *123*
Oak Village NW5 . . . . . .1C *46*
Oak Vs. *NW11* 1B *30*
    (off Hendon Pk. Row)
Oak Way W3 . . . . .2A *70*
Oakwood Bus. Pk.
  NW10 . . . . .3A *56*
Oakwood Cl. SE13 . . . . .4F *109*
Oakwood Ct. E6 . . . . . . .5F *55*
  W14 . . . . .4B *72*
Oakwood Dr. SE19 . . . .5F *119*
Oakwood Ho. *E9* 3E *51*
    (off Frampton Pk. Rd.)
Oakwood La. W14 . . . . . .4B *72*
Oakwood Mans. *W14* . . .4B *72*
    (off Oakwood Ct.)
Oakworth Rd. W10 . . . . .4E *57*

Oasis Sports Cen.
    . . . . . .2D **15** (5A **62**)
Oast Ct. *E14* 1B *80*
    (off Newell St.)
Oast Lodge *W4* 3A *84*
    (off Corney Reach Way)
Oatfield Ho. N15 . . . . . .1A *36*
    (off Perry Ct.)
Oat La. EC2 . . . .2F **17** (5E **63**)
Oatwell Ho. SW3 . . . . . .1A *88*
    (off Cale St.)
Oban Cl. E13 . . . . .3E *69*
Oban Ho. E14 . . . . .5F *67*
    (off Oban St.)
Oban Rd. E13 . . . . .2E *69*
Oban St. E14 . . . . .5F *67*
Oberon Ho. N1 . . . . .1A *64*
    (off Arden Est.)
Oberstein Rd. SW11 . . .2F *101*
Oborne Cl. SE24 . . . . . .3D *105*
O'Brien Ho. *E2* 2F *65*
    (off Roman Rd.)
Observatory Gdns.
  W8 . . . . .3C *72*
Observatory M. E14 . . . .5F *81*
Observatory Rd. SW7 . . .4F *73*
Occupation Rd. SE17 . . .1E *91*

Ocean Est. E1 . . . . .4A *66*
    (Ben Jonson Rd.)
  E1 . . . . .3F *65*
    (Ernest St.)
Oceanis Apartments
  E16 . . . . .1C *82*
    (off Seagull La.)
Ocean Music Venue . . .3D *51*
    (off Mare St.)
Ocean St. E1 . . . . .4F *65*
Ocean Wharf E14 . . . . . .3B *80*
Ockbrook *E1* 4E *65*
    (off Hannibal Rd.)
Ockendon M. N1 . . . . . . .3F *49*
Ockendon Rd. N1 . . . . . .3F *49*
Ockley Rd. SW16 . . . . .4A *118*
Octagon, The *SW10* 3D *87*
    (off Coleridge Gdns.)
Octagon Arc.
  EC2 . . . . .1D **19** (4A **64**)
Octagon Ct. *SE16* 2F *79*
    (off Rotherhithe St.)
Octavia Ho. SW1 . . . . . .4F *75*
    (off Medway St.)
  W10 . . . . .3A *58*
Octavia M. W9 . . . . .3B *58*
Octavia St. SW11 . . . . . .4A *88*
Octavius St. SE8 . . . . . . .3C *94*
Odelia Ct. E15 . . . . .5E *53*
    (off Biggerstaff Rd.)
Odell Wlk. SE13 . . . . . .1E *109*
Odeon Cinema
  Camden Town 5D *47*
    (off Parkway)
  Covent Garden 5F *61*
    (off Shaftesbury Av.)
  Greenwich 5B *82*
  Holloway 5A *34*
  Kensington 4C *72*
  Leicester Square
    . . . . .5C **14**
    (off Leicester Sq.)
  Marble Arch 5B *60*
    (off Marble Arch)
  Panton Street 5C *14*
    (off Panton St.)
  Putney 1A *100*
  Streatham 3A *118*
  Surrey Quays 4F *79*
  Swiss Cottage 4F *45*
  Tottenham Court Road
    . . . . .4F *61*
    (off Tottenham Ct. Rd.)
  West End 5C *14*
    (off Leicester Sq.)
  Whiteleys 5D *59*
Odeon Ct. E16 . . . . .4C *68*
  NW10 . . . . .5A *42*
    (off St Albans Rd.)
Odessa Rd. E7 . . . . .5B *40*
  NW10 . . . . .1C *56*
Odessa St. SE16 . . . . . . .3B *80*
Odessa Wharf *SE16* . . .4B *80*
    (off Odessa St.)
Odette Duval Ho. E1 . . .4E *65*
    (off Stepney Way)
Odger St. SW11 . . . . .5B *88*
Odhams Wlk.
  WC2 . . . . . . .3E **15** (5A **62**)
Odin Ho. SE5 . . . . .5E *91*

O'Donnell Ct.
 WC1 . . . . . . .3E **7** (3A **62**)
Odontological Museum, The
 . . . . .2A **16**
 *(within Royal College of
 Surgeons)*
O'Driscoll Ho. W12 . . . . .5D **57**
Offa's Mead E9 . . . . .1B **52**
Offenbach Ho. E2 . . . . . .1F **65**
 (off Mace St.)
Offerton Rd. SW4 . . . . . .1E **103**
Offham Ho. SE17 . . . . . . .5A **78**
 (off Beckway St.)
Offley Rd. SW9 . . . . .3C **90**
Offord Rd. N1 . . . . .4B **48**
Offord St. N1 . . . . .4B **48**
Ogilvie Ho. E1 . . . . .5F **65**
 (off Stepney C'way.)
Oglander Rd. SE15 . . . . . .2B **106**
Ogle St. W1 . . . . .5F **5** (4E **61**)
O'Gorman Ho. SW10 . . . .3E **87**
 (off King's Rd.)
Ohio Bldg. SE10 . . . . . . .4D **95**
 (off Deal's Gateway)
Ohio Rd. E13 . . . . .3B **68**
Oil Mill La. W6 . . . . .1C **84**
Okeburn Rd. SW17 . . . . .5C **116**
Okehampton Rd.
 NW10 . . . . .5E **43**
Olaf Ct. W8 . . . . .3C **72**
 (off Kensington Chu. St.)
Olaf St. W11 . . . . .1F **71**
Oldacre M. SW12 . . . . . .5C **102**
Old Aeroworks, The
 NW8 . . . . .3F **59**
 (off Hatton St.)
Old Bailey
 Central Criminal Court
 . . . . .2E **17** (5D **63**)
Old Bailey
 EC4 . . . . . . .3E **17** (5D **63**)
Old Barge Ho. All.
 SE1 . . . . .5C **16**
Old Barracks W8 . . . . . . .3D **73**
Old Barrack Yd.
 SW1 . . . . .4B **20** (3C **74**)
 (not continuous)
Old Barrowfield E15 . . . . .5A **54**
Old Bellgate Pl. E14 . . . .4C **80**
Old Bethnal Grn. Rd.
 E2 . . . . .2C **64**
Old Billingsgate Mkt.
 EC3 . . . . .5C **18**
Old Billingsgate Wlk.
 EC3 . . . . . .5D **19** (1A **78**)
Old Bond St.
 W1 . . . . .5F **13** (1E **75**)
Old Brewer's Yd.
 WC2 . . . . . . .3D **15** (5A **62**)
Old Brewery M. NW3 . . .1F **45**
Old Broad St.
 EC2 . . . . . . .2C **18** (5F **63**)
Old Bromley Rd.
 BR1: Brom 5F **123**
Old Brompton Rd.
 SW5 . . . . .1C **86**
 SW7 . . . . .1C **86**
Old Buildings WC2 . . . . .2B **16**
Old Burlington St.
 W1 . . . . .4F **13** (1E **75**)

Oldbury Ct. E9 . . . . .2A **52**
 (off Mabley St.)
Oldbury Ho. W2 . . . . .4D **59**
 (off Harrow Rd.)
Oldbury Pl.
 W1 . . . . .5C **4** (4C **60**)
Old Canal M. SE15 . . . . . .1B **92**
 (off Trafalgar Av.)
Old Castle St.
 E1 . . . . .2F **19** (5B **64**)
Old Cavendish St.
 W1 . . . . . . .2D **13** (5D **61**)
Old Change Ct. EC4 . . . . .3F **17**
Old Chapel Pl. SW9 . . . . .5C **90**
Old Chelsea M. SW3 . . . .2A **88**
Old Chiswick Yd. W4 . . . .2A **84**
 (off Pumping Sta. Rd.)
Old Church La. NW9 . . . . .4A **28**
Old Church Rd. E1 . . . . . .5F **65**
Old Church St. SW3 . . . . .1F **87**
Old Compton St.
 W1 . . . . .4B **14** (1F **75**)
Old Cople La. SE19 . . . . .5B **120**
Old Court Ho. W8 . . . . . . .3D **73**
 (off Old Court Pl.)
Old Court Pl. W8 . . . . . . .3D **73**
Old Curiosity Shop 2F **15**
 (off Portsmouth St.)
Old Dairy M. NW5 . . . . . .3D **47**
 SW12 . . . . .1C **116**
Old Dairy Pl. N15 . . . . . .1A **36**
Old Devonshire Rd.
 SW12 . . . . .5D **103**
Old Dover Rd. SE3 . . . . . .3C **96**
Oldegate Ho. E6 . . . . . . .4F **55**
Old Farm Cl. SW17 . . . . .2A **116**
Oldfield Gro. SE16 . . . . . .5F **79**
Oldfield Ho. W4 . . . . .1A **84**
 (off Devonshire St.)
Oldfield M. N6 . . . . .2E **33**
Oldfield Rd. N16 . . . . .5A **36**
 NW10 . . . . .4B **42**
 SW19 . . . . .5A **114**
 W3 . . . . .3B **70**
Old Fish St. Hill EC4 . . . . .4F **17**
 (off Queen Victoria St.)
Old Fleet La.
 EC4 . . . . . . .2D **17** (5D **63**)
OLD FORD 5B **52**
OLD FORD 5C **52**
Old Ford Rd. E2 . . . . .2E **65**
 E3 . . . . .1A **66**
Old Ford Trading Cen.
 E3 . . . . .5C **52**
 (off Maverton Rd.)
Old Forge M. W12 . . . . . .3D **71**
Old Forge Rd. N19 . . . . . .4F **33**
Old Gloucester St.
 WC1 . . . . . . .5E **7** (4A **62**)
Old Goods Yard, The
 W2 . . . . .4E **59**
Oldhill St. N16 . . . . .3C **36**
Old Hospital Cl.
 SW12 . . . . .1B **116**
Old House Cl.
 SW19 . . . . .5A **114**
Old Jamaica Bus. Est.
 SE16 . . . . .4B **78**
Old Jamaica Rd.
 SE16 . . . . .4C **78**

Old James St. SE15 . . . .1D **107**
Old Jewry
 EC2 . . . . . . .3B **18** (5F **63**)
Old Kent Rd. SE1 . . . . . . .5A **78**
 SE15 . . . . .5A **78**
Old Library Ho. E3 . . . . . .1A **66**
 (off Roman Rd.)
Old Manor Ct. NW8 . . . . .1E **59**
Old Manor Yd. SW5 . . . . .5D **73**
Old Market Sq.
 E2 . . . . .1F **11** (2B **64**)
Old Marylebone Rd.
 NW1 . . . . .4A **60**
Old Mitre Ct.
 EC4 . . . . . . .3C **16** (5C **62**)
Old Montague St. E1 . . . .4C **64**
Old Nichol St.
 E2 . . . . .3F **11** (3B **64**)
Old North St. WC1 . . . . . .5F **7**
Old Nursery Ct. E2 . . . . . .1B **64**
 (off Dawson St.)
OLD OAK COMMON 4A **56**
Old Oak Comn. La.
 NW10 . . . . .4A **56**
 W3 . . . . .4A **56**
Old Oak La. NW10 . . . . . .2A **56**
Old Oak Rd. W3 . . . . .1B **70**
Old Operating Theatre
 Museum & Herb Garret
 . . . . .2C **26**
Old Orchard, The
 NW3 . . . . .1B **46**
Old Palace Yd.
 SW1 . . . . . . .5D **23** (4A **76**)
Old Paradise St.
 SE11 . . . . .5B **76**
Old Park Av. SW12 . . . . .4C **102**
Old Park La.
 W1 . . . . .2D **21** (2D **75**)
Old Pearson St.
 SE10 . . . . .3D **95**
Old Police House, The
 . . . . .2B **74**
Old Post Office La.
 SE3 . . . . .1D **111**
Old Pye St.
 SW1 . . . . . . .5B **22** (4F **75**)
Old Pye St. Est. SW1 . . .5B **22**
 (off Old Pye St.)
Old Quebec St.
 W1 . . . . .3A **12** (5B **60**)
 (not continuous)
Old Queen St.
 SW1 . . . . . . .4C **22** (3F **75**)
Old Red Lion Theatre 1C **8**
 (off St John St.)
Oldridge Rd. SW12 . . . . .5C **102**
Old Rd. SE13 . . . . .2A **110**
Old Royal Free Pl.
 N1 . . . . .5C **48**
Old Royal Free Sq.
 N1 . . . . .5C **48**
Old Royal Naval College
 . . . . .1F **95**
Old School, The WC1 . . . .5A **8**
 (off Princeton St.)
Old School Cl. SE10 . . . . .4A **82**
Old School Cres. E7 . . . . .3D **54**
Old School Sq. E14 . . . . .5C **66**
 (off Pelling St.)

Old Seacoal La.
  EC4 . . . . . . .2D **17** (5D **63**)
Old Sth. Lambeth Rd.
  SW8 . . . . .3A **90**
Old Spitalfields Market
  . . . . .5F **11** (4B **64**)
Old Square
  WC2 . . . . .2B **16** (5B **62**)
Old Stable M. N5 . . . . .5E **35**
Old Stables Ct. SE5 . . . .4E **91**
  (off Camberwell New Rd.)
Old Station Ho. SE17 . . .1E **91**
Old Station Way
  SW4 . . . . .1F **103**
  (off Voltaire Rd.)
Oldstead Rd.
  BR1: Brom 4E **123**
OLD STREET 3F **9**
Old St. E13 . . . . .1D **69**
  EC1 . . . . . . .3F **9** (3E **63**)
Old Sun Wharf E14 . . . . .1A **80**
  (off Narrow St.)
Old Swan Wharf
  SW11 . . . . .4F **87**
Old Theatre Ct. SE1 . . .1A **26**
Old Town SW4 . . . . . .1E **103**
Old Vic Theatre, The . .3C **24**
Old Vic Tunnels, The . . .3C **76**
  (off Station App. Rd.)
Old Woolwich Rd.
  SE10 . . . . .2F **95**
Old York Rd. SW18 . . .3D **101**
O'Leary Sq. E1 . . . . . . .4E **65**
Olga St. E3 . . . . .1A **66**
Olinda Rd. N16 . . . . . .1B **36**
Oliphant St. W10 . . . . .2F **57**
Olive Blythe Ho. W10 . .3A **58**
  (off Ladbroke Gro.)
Olive Ct. E5 . . . . .4E **37**
  (off Woodmill Rd.)
  N1 . . . . .5C **48**
  (off Liverpool Rd.)
Olive Haines Lodge
  SW15 . . . . .3B **100**
Olive Ho. EC1 . . . . .3D **9**
  (off Bowling Grn. La.)
Oliver Goldsmith Est.
  SE5 . . . . .4C **92**
Oliver Ho. SE14 . . . . . .3B **94**
  (off New Cross Rd.)
  SE16 . . . . .3C **78**
  (off George Row)
  SW8 . . . . .3A **90**
  (off Wyvil Rd.)
Oliver M. SE15 . . . . . . .5C **92**
Oliver Rd. E13 . . . . . . .2E **69**
  NW2 . . . . .1D **43**
  E10 . . . . .4D **39**
Olivers Wharf E1 . . . . .2D **79**
  (off Wapping High St.)
Olivers Yd.
  EC1 . . . . . .3C **10** (3F **63**)
Olive Tree Ho. SE15 . . .2E **93**
  (off Sharratt St.)
Olivette St. SW15 . . . . .1F **99**
Olive Waite Ho. NW6 . . .4C **44**
Olivier Theatre 1A **24**
  (in National Theatre)
Ollerton Grn. E3 . . . . . .5B **52**
Ollgar Cl. W12 . . . . . . .2B **70**

Olliffe St. E14 . . . . . . .4E **81**
Olmar St. SE1 . . . . . . .2C **92**
Olney Ho. NW8 . . . . . . .3A **60**
  (off Tresham Cres.)
Olney Rd. SE17 . . . . . .2D **91**
  (not continuous)
Olympia 4A **72**
Olympia M. W2 . . . . . .1D **73**
Olympian Ct. E3 . . . . . .1C **66**
  (off Wick La.)
  E14 . . . . .5C **80**
  (off Homer Dr.)
Olympia Way W14 . . . . .4A **72**
Olympic Ho. N16 . . . . . .1B **50**
Olympic Park 4D **53**
Olympic Pk. Avenue
  E20 . . . . .3D **53**
Olympic Stadium, Olympic Pk.
  . . . . .4D **53**
Olympus Sq. E5 . . . . . .5C **36**
O'Mahoney Ct.
  SW17 . . . . .3E **115**
O'Meara St.
  SE1 . . . . . .2A **26** (2E **77**)
Omega Cl. E14 . . . . . . .4D **81**
Omega Ho. SW10 . . . . .3E **87**
  (off King's Rd.)
Omega Pl. N1 . . . . .1E **7**
Omega St. SE14 . . . . . .4C **94**
Omega Works E3 . . . . . .4C **52**
Ommaney Rd. SE14 . . . .4F **93**
Omnium Ct. WC1 . . . . . .5F **7**
  (off Princeton St.)
Ondine Rd. SE15 . . . . . .2B **106**
Onedin Ct. E1 . . . . .1C **78**
  (off Ensign St.)
Onega Ga. SE16 . . . . . .4A **80**
One Hyde Pk.
  SW1 . . . . . .4A **20** (3B **74**)
O'Neill Ho. NW8 . . . . . .1A **60**
  (off Cochrane St.)
One New Change
  EC4 . . . . . . .3F **17** (5E **63**)
One Owen St. EC1 . . . . .1D **9**
  (off Goswell St.)
One Tree Cl. SE23 . . . .4E **107**
One Tree Hill
  Local Nature Reserve
  . . . . .4E **107**
Ongar Rd. SW6 . . . . . . .2C **86**
Onra Rd. E17 . . . . .2C **38**
Onslow Cl. W10 . . . . . .2B **58**
Onslow Ct. SW10 . . . . . .1E **87**
  (off Drayton Gdns.)
Onslow Cres. SW7 . . . . .5F **73**
Onslow Gdns. SW7 . . . .5F **73**
Onslow M. E. SW7 . . . . .5F **73**
Onslow M. W. SW7 . . . .5F **73**
Onslow Sq. SW7 . . . . . .5F **73**
Onslow St.
  EC1 . . . . . . .4C **8** (3C **62**)
Ontario St.
  SE1 . . . . . .5E **25** (4D **77**)
Ontario Twr. E14 . . . . .1F **81**
Ontario Way E14 . . . . . .1C **80**
  (not continuous)
Onyx M. E15 . . . . .3B **54**
Opal Apartments W2 . . .5C **58**
  (off Hereford Rd.)

Opal Cl. E16 . . . . .5F **69**
Opal Ct. E15 . . . . .5E **53**
Opal M. NW6 . . . . .5B **44**
Opal St. SE11 . . . . . . .1D **91**
Open Air Stage 3A **32**
Openview SW18 . . . . . .1E **115**
Opera Ct. N19 . . . . .5F **33**
  (off Wedmore St.)
Ophelia Gdns. NW2 . . . .5A **30**
Ophelia Ho. W6 . . . . . .1F **85**
  (off Fulham Pal. Rd.)
Ophir Ter. SE15 . . . . . .4C **92**
Opie Ho. NW8 . . . . .1A **60**
  (off Townshend Est.)
Oppenheim Rd. SE13 . .5E **95**
Oppidan Apartments
  NW6 . . . . .4C **44**
  (off Netherwood St.)
Oppidans Rd. NW3 . . . .4B **46**
Orange Gro. E11 . . . . . .5A **40**
Orange Pl. SE16 . . . . . .4E **79**
Orangery Gallery, The
  . . . . .3B **72**
Orange St.
  WC2 . . . . . .5C **14** (1F **75**)
Orange Tree Ct. SE5 . . .3A **92**
  (off Havil St.)
Orange Yd. W1 . . . . . . .3C **14**
Oransay Rd. N1 . . . . . . .3E **49**
Oratory La. SW3 . . . . . .1F **87**
Orbain Rd. SW6 . . . . . .3A **86**
Orbel St. SW11 . . . . . . .4A **88**
Orbis Wharf SW11 . . . .1F **101**
Orb St. SE17 . . . . .5F **77**
Orchard, The NW11 . . . .1C **30**
  SE3 . . . . .5F **95**
  SW4 . . . . .5A **70**
Orchard Bus. Cen.
  SE26 . . . . .5B **122**
Orchard Cl. N1 . . . . .4E **49**
  NW2 . . . . .5C **28**
  SE23 . . . . .4E **107**
  W10 . . . . .4B **58**
Orchard Ct. E10 . . . . . . .3D **39**
  W1 . . . . .2B **12**
  (off Fitzhardinge St.)
Orchard Dr. SE3 . . . . . .5D **95**
Orchard Hill SE13 . . . . .5D **95**
Orchard Ho. SE5 . . . . . .4E **91**
  (off County Gro.)
  SE16 . . . . .4E **79**
  SW6 . . . . .3B **86**
  (off Varna Rd.)
  W12 . . . . .2C **70**
Orchard Mead Ho.
  NW2 . . . . .4C **30**
Orchard M. N1 . . . . .4F **49**
  N6 . . . . .2D **33**
  SW17 . . . . .3E **115**
Orchard Pl. E5 . . . . .2D **51**
  E14 . . . . .1A **82**
  (not continuous)
Orchard Rd. N6 . . . . . . .2D **33**
  SE3 . . . . .5A **96**
Orchardson Ho. NW8 . . .3F **59**
  (off Orchardson St.)
Orchardson St. NW8 . . .3F **59**
Orchard Sq. W14 . . . . . .1B **86**
Orchard St.
  W1 . . . . . . .3B **12** (5C **60**)

Orchard Studios *W6* 5F **71**
Orchard Ter. NW10 . . . .1B **42**
Orchard Wharf
 E14 . . . . .1A **82**
   (off Orchard Pl.)
Orchid Cl. E6 . . . . .4F **69**
 SE13 . . . . .3F **109**
Orchid St. W12 . . . . . . .1C **70**
Orde Hall St.
 WC1 . . . . . . .4F **7** (3B **62**)
Ordell Ct. *E3* 1B **66**
   (off Ordell Rd.)
Ordell Rd. E3 . . . . .1B **66**
Ordnance Cres. SE10 . .3A **82**
Ordnance Hill NW8 . . . .5F **45**
Ordnance M. NW8 . . . . .1F **59**
Ordnance Rd. E16 . . . . .4B **68**
Oregano Dr. E14 . . . . . .5F **67**
Oregon Bldg. *SE10* 4D **95**
   (off Deal's Gateway)
Orestes M. NW6 . . . . . .2C **44**
Orford Ct. SE27 . . . . .2D **119**
Orford St. E17 . . . . .1C **38**
 SE6 . . . . .3D **123**
Oriana Ho. *E14* 1B **80**
   (off Victory Pl.)
Oriel Ct. NW3 . . . . .1E **45**
Oriel Dr. SW13 . . . . . . .2E **85**
Oriel Ho. NW6 . . . . .5C **44**
   (off Priory Rd.)
Oriel Pl. *NW3* 1E **45**
   (off Heath St.)
Oriel Rd. E9 . . . . .3F **51**
Oriental Rd. E16 . . . . . .2F **83**
Oriental St. *E14* 1C **80**
   (off Pennyfields)
Orient Ho. *SW6* 4E **87**
   (off Station Ct.)
Orient Ind. Pk. E10 . . . .4C **38**
Orient St. SE11 . . . . . . .5D **77**
Orient Way E5 . . . . .5F **37**
 E10 . . . . .3A **38**
Orient Wharf *E1* 2D **79**
   (off Wapping High St.)
Orion *E14* 5C **80**
   (off Crews St.)
Orion Bus. Cen. SE14 . .1F **93**
Orion Ho. *E1* 3D **65**
   (off Coventry Rd.)
Orkney Ho. *N1* 5B **48**
   (off Bemerton Est.)
Orkney St. SW11 . . . . . .5C **88**
Orlando Rd. SW4 . . . . .1E **103**
Orleston M. N7 . . . . . . .3C **48**
Orleston Rd. N7 . . . . . . .3C **48**
Orlop St. SE10 . . . . .1A **96**
Ormanton Rd. SE26 . . .4C **120**
Orme Ct. W2 . . . . .1D **73**
Orme Ct. M. *W2* 1D **73**
   (off Orme La.)
Orme Ho. E8 . . . . .5B **50**
Orme La. W2 . . . . .1D **73**
Ormeley Rd.
 SW12 . . . . .1D **117**
Orme Sq. W2 . . . . .1D **73**
Ormiston Gro. W12 . . . .2D **71**
Ormiston Rd. SE10 . . . .1C **96**
Ormond Cl.
 WC1 . . . . . . .5E **7** (4A **62**)

Ormonde Ct. *NW8* 5B **46**
   (off St Edmund's Cl.)
 SW15 . . . . .2E **99**
Ormonde Ga. SW3 . . . .1B **88**
   (not continuous)
Ormonde Mans. *WC1* . . .5E **7**
   (off Southampton Row)
Ormonde Pl. SW1 . . . . .5C **74**
Ormonde Ter. NW8 . . . .5B **46**
Ormond Ho. N16 . . . . . .4F **35**
Ormond M.
 WC1 . . . . . . .4E **7** (3A **62**)
Ormond Rd. N19 . . . . . .3A **34**
Ormond Yd.
 SW1 . . . . . . .1A **22** (2E **75**)
Ormrod Ct. *W11* 5A **58**
   (off Westbourne Pk. Rd.)
Ormsby Lodge W4 . . . .4A **70**
Ormsby Pl. N16 . . . . . . .5B **36**
Ormsby St. E2 . . . . .1B **64**
Ormside St. SE15 . . . . .2E **93**
Ornan Rd. NW3 . . . . . . .2A **46**
Orpen Ho. *SW5* 5C **72**
   (off Trebovir Rd.)
Orpen Wlk. N16 . . . . . . .5A **36**
Orpheus Ho. *W10* 3B **58**
   (off Harrow Rd.)
Orpheus St. SE5 . . . . . .4F **91**
Orsett M. W2 . . . . .5D **59**
   (not continuous)
Orsett St. SE11 . . . . . . .1B **90**
Orsett Ter. W2 . . . . .5D **59**
Orsman Rd. N1 . . . . . . .5A **50**
Orton St. E1 . . . . .2C **78**
Orville Rd. SW11 . . . . . .5F **87**
Orwell Ct. *E8* 5C **50**
   (off Pownall Rd.)
 N5 . . . . .1E **49**
 SW17 . . . . .3F **115**
   (off Grosvenor Way)
Orwell Rd. E13 . . . . .1E **69**
Osbaldeston Rd. N16 . . .4C **36**
Osberton Rd. SE12 . . . .3C **110**
Osbert St. SW1 . . . . . . .5F **75**
Osborn Cl. E8 . . . . .5C **50**
Osborne Ct. E10 . . . . . .2D **39**
Osborne Gro. N4 . . . . . .3C **34**
Osborne Ho. *E16* 2C **82**
   (off Wesley Av.)
Osborne Rd. E7 . . . . . . .2D **55**
 E9 . . . . .3B **52**
 E10 . . . . .4D **39**
 N4 . . . . .3C **34**
 NW2 . . . . .3D **43**
Osborne Ter. *SW17* 5B **116**
   (off Church La.)
Osborn La. SE23 . . . . .5A **108**
Osborn St. E1 . . . . .4B **64**
Osborn Ter. SE3 . . . . .2B **110**
Oscar Faber Pl. N1 . . . .4A **50**
Oscar St. SE8 . . . . .5C **94**
   (not continuous)
Oseney Cres. NW5 . . . .2E **47**
Osier Ct. *E1* 3F **65**
   (off Osier St.)
Osier La. SE10 . . . . .4B **82**
Osier M. W4 . . . . .2A **84**
Osiers Estate, The
 SW18 . . . . .2C **100**
Osiers Rd. SW18 . . . . .2C **100**

Osier St. E1 . . . . .3E **65**
Osier Way E10 . . . . .5D **39**
Oslac Rd. SE6 . . . . . . .5D **123**
Oslo Ct. *NW8* 1A **60**
   (off Prince Albert Rd.)
Oslo Ho. *E9* 3B **52**
   (off Felstead St.)
 SE5 . . . . .5E **91**
   (off Carew St.)
Oslo Sq. SE16 . . . . .4A **80**
Osman Cl. N15 . . . . . . .1F **35**
Osmani School Sports Cen.
 . . . . .3C **64**
Osman Rd. W6 . . . . .4E **71**
Osmington Ho. *SW8* . . .3B **90**
   (off Dorset Rd.)
Osmund Ct. *E1* 5C **64**
   (off Myrdle St.)
Osmund St. W12 . . . . . .4B **56**
Osnaburgh St.
 NW1 . . . . . . .4E **5** (3D **61**)
   (Euston St.)
 NW1 . . . . .2E **5**
   (Robert St.)
Osnaburgh Ter.
 NW1 . . . . . . .3E **5** (3D **61**)
Osprey Cl. E6 . . . . .4F **69**
Osprey Ct. *E1* 1C **78**
   (off Star Pl.)
Osprey Est. SE16 . . . . .5F **79**
Osprey Ho. *E14* 1A **80**
   (off Victory Pl.)
 SE1 . . . . .1D **93**
   (off Lynton Rd.)
Ospringe Ho. *SE1* 3C **24**
   (off Wootton St.)
Ospringe Rd. NW5 . . . . .1E **47**
Osram Ct. W6 . . . . .4E **71**
Osric Path N1 . . . . .1A **64**
Ossian M. N4 . . . . .2B **34**
Ossian Rd. N4 . . . . .2B **34**
Ossington Bldgs.
 W1 . . . . .5B **4** (4C **60**)
Ossington Cl. W2 . . . . . .1C **72**
Ossington St. W2 . . . . . .1C **72**
Ossory Rd. SE1 . . . . . . .2C **92**
Ossulston St.
 NW1 . . . . . . .1C **6** (1F **61**)
Ostade Rd. SW2 . . . . . .5B **104**
Ostend Pl. SE1 . . . . . . .5E **77**
Osten M. SW7 . . . . .4D **73**
Osterley Ho. *E14* 5D **67**
   (off Giraud St.)
Osterley Rd. N16 . . . . . .1A **50**
Oswald Bldg. SW8 . . . . .2D **89**
Oswald's Mead E9 . . . . .1A **52**
Oswald St. E5 . . . . .5F **37**
Oswald Ter. NW2 . . . . . .5E **29**
Osward Rd. SW17 . . . .2B **116**
Oswell Ho. *E1* 2D **79**
   (off Farthing Flds.)
Oswin St. SE11 . . . . . . .5D **77**
Oswyth Rd. SE5 . . . . . . .5A **92**
Otford Cres. SE4 . . . . .4B **108**
Otford Ho. *SE1* 5C **26**
   (off Staple St.)
 SE15 . . . . .2E **93**
   (off Lovelinch Cl.)
Othello Cl. SE11 . . . . . .1D **91**
Otis St. E3 . . . . .2E **67**

Otley Ho. N5 . . . . .5C 34
Otley Rd. E16 . . . . .5E 69
Otley Ter. E5 . . . . .5F 37
Ottaway Ct. E5 . . . . . . .5C 36
Ottaway St. E5 . . . . . . .5C 36
Otterburn Ho. SE5 . . . . .3E 91
(off Sultan St.)
Otterburn St. SW17 . . .5B 116
Otter Cl. E15 . . . . .5E 53
Otterden St. SE6 . . . . .4C 122
Otterden Ter. SE1 . . . . .5B 78
(off Lynton Rd.)
Otto Cl. SE26 . . . . .3D 121
Otto St. SE17 . . . . .2D 91
Oulton Cl. E5 . . . . .4E 37
Oulton Rd. N15 . . . . . . .1F 35
Ouseley Rd. SW12 . . . .1B 116
Outer Circ.
NW1
. . . . .2A 4 (1A 60) & 1D 5
Outgate Rd. NW10 . . . . .4B 42
Outram Pl. N1 . . . . .5A 48
Outram Rd. E6 . . . . .5F 55
Outwich St. EC3 . . . . . .2E 19
Outwood Ho. SW2 . . . . .5B 104
(off Deepdene Gdns.)
Oval, The E2 . . . . .1D 65
Oval Cricket Ground, The
. . . . .2C 90
Oval House Theatre 2C 90
Oval Mans. SE11 . . . . . .2B 90
Oval Pl. SW8 . . . . .3B 90
Oval Rd. NW1 . . . . .5D 47
Oval Way SE11 . . . . . . .1B 90
Ovanna M. N1 . . . . .5A 50
Overbrae BR3: Beck . .5C 122
Overbury Rd. N15 . . . . .1F 35
Overbury St. E5 . . . . . . .1F 51
Overcliff Rd. SE13 . . . .1C 108
Overdown Rd. SE6 . . . .4C 122
Overhill Rd. SE22 . . . . .5C 106
Overlea Rd. E5 . . . . . . .2C 36
Oversley Ho. W2 . . . . . .4C 58
(off Alfred Rd.)
Overstone Ho. E14 . . . . .5C 66
(off E. India Dock Rd.)
Overstone Rd. W6 . . . . .4E 71
Overstrand Mans.
SW11 . . . . .4B 88
Overton Ct. E11 . . . . . . .2C 40
Overton Dr. E11 . . . . . . .2C 40
Overton Ho. SW15 . . . .5B 98
(off Tangley Gro.)
Overton Rd. E10 . . . . . . .3A 38
SW9 . . . . .5C 90
Overy Ho.
SE1 . . . . .4D 25 (3D 77)
Ovex Cl. E14 . . . . .3E 81
Ovington Ct. SW3 . . . . . .4A 74
(off Brompton Rd.)
Ovington Gdns. SW3 . . . .4A 74
Ovington M. SW3 . . . . . .4A 74
(off Ovington Gdns.)
Ovington Sq. SW3 . . . . . .4A 74
Ovington St. SW3 . . . . . .4A 74
Owen Mans. W14 . . . . . .2A 86
(off Queen's Club Gdns.)
Owens M. E11 . . . . .4A 40
Owen's Row
EC1 . . . . . . .1D 9 (2D 63)

Owen St. EC1 . . . .1D 9 (1D 63)
Owens Way SE23 . . . . .5A 108
Owgan Cl. SE5 . . . . .3F 91
Oxberry Av. SW6 . . . . . .5A 86
Oxendon St.
SW1 . . . . . .5B 14 (1F 75)
Oxenford St. SE15 . . . . .1B 106
Oxenham Ho. SE8 . . . . .2C 94
(off Benbow St.)
Oxenholme NW1 . . . . . . .1F 5
(off Hampstead Rd.)
Oxestall's Rd. SE8 . . . . .1A 94
Oxford & Cambridge Mans.
NW1 . . . . .4A 60
(off Old Marylebone Rd.)
Oxford Cir. W1 . . . . .3F 13
Oxford Cir. Av.
W1 . . . . . . .3F 13 (5E 61)
Oxford Ct. EC4 . . . . .4B 18
W9 . . . . .4C 58
(off Elmfield Way)
Oxford Dr.
SE1 . . . . . .2D 27 (2A 78)
Oxford Gdns. W10 . . . . .5E 57
Oxford Ga. W6 . . . . .5F 71
Oxford Ho. E3 . . . . .4B 66
(off William Whiffin Sq.)
Oxford Pl. NW10 . . . . . . .5A 28
(off Press Rd.)
Oxford Rd. E15 . . . . .3F 53
(not continuous)
N4 . . . . .3C 34
NW6 . . . . .1C 58
SE19 . . . . .5F 119
SW15 . . . . .2A 100
Oxford Sq. W2 . . . . .5A 60
Oxford St.
W1 . . . . . . .3B 12 (5C 60)
Oxgate Cen. NW2 . . . . . .4D 29
Oxgate Ct. NW2 . . . . . . .4C 28
Oxgate Ct. Pde. NW2 . . .4C 28
Oxgate Gdns. NW2 . . . . .5D 29
Oxgate La. NW2 . . . . . . .4C 28
Oxgate Pde. NW2 . . . . . .4C 28
Oxley Cl. SE1 . . . . .1B 92
Oxleys Rd. NW2 . . . . . . .5D 29
Oxonian St. SE22 . . . . . .2B 106
Oxo Tower Wharf
SE1 . . . . . .5C 16 (1C 76)
Oxygen, The E16 . . . . . .1C 82
Oystercatcher Cl.
E16 . . . . .5D 69
Oyster Ct. SE17 . . . . . . .5E 77
(off Crampton St.)
Oystergate Wlk. EC4 . . .5B 18
Oyster Row E1 . . . . .5E 65
Oyster Wharf SW11 . . . .5F 87
Ozolins Way E16 . . . . . .5C 68

P

Pablo Neruda Cl.
SE24 . . . . .2D 105
Pace Pl. E1 . . . . .5D 65
Pacific Cl. E1 . . . . .4E 65
Pacific Ho. E1 . . . . .3F 65
(off Ernest St.)
Pacific M. SW2 . . . . .2C 104
Pacific Rd. E16 . . . . .5C 68

Pacific Wharf SE16 . . . . .2F 79
Packenham Ho. E2 . . . . .2B 64
(off Wellington Row)
Packington Sq. N1 . . . . .5E 49
(not continuous)
Packington St. N1 . . . . . .5D 49
Padbury SE17 . . . . .1A 92
(off Bagshot St.)
Padbury Ct. E2 . . . . .2B 64
Padbury Ho. NW8 . . . . . .3A 60
(off Tresham Cres.)
Paddenswick Rd. W6 . . . .4C 70
PADDINGTON 5F 59
Paddington
Bowling & Sports Club
. . . . .3D 59
Paddington Grn. W2 . . . . .4F 59
Paddington St.
W1 . . . . . . .5B 4 (4C 60)
Paddock Cl. SE3 . . . . . . .5C 96
SE26 . . . . .4F 121
Paddock Rd. NW2 . . . . . .5C 28
Paddock Way SW15 . . . .5E 99
Padfield Rd. SE5 . . . . . . .1E 105
Padstone Ho. E3 . . . . . . .2D 67
(off Talwin St.)
Padstow Ho. E14 . . . . . . .1B 80
(off Three Colt St.)
Pagden St. SW8 . . . . . . .4D 89
Pageant Cres. SE16 . . . .2A 80
Pageantmaster Ct.
EC4 . . . . .3D 17
Page Grn. Rd. N15 . . . . .1C 36
Page Grn. Ter. N15 . . . . .1B 36
Page Ho. SE10 . . . . .2E 95
(off Welland St.)
Page St. SW1 . . . . .5F 75
Pages Wlk.
SE1 . . . . . .5E 27 (5A 78)
Pages Yd. W4 . . . . .2B 84
Paget Ho. E2 . . . . .1E 65
(off Bishop's Way)
Paget Rd. N16 . . . . .3F 35
Paget St. EC1 . . . . .1D 9 (2D 63)
Pagham Ho. W10 . . . . . . .3E 57
(off Sutton Way)
Pagnell St. SE14 . . . . . . .3B 94
Pagoda Gdns. SE3 . . . . . .5F 95
Pagoda Gro. SE27 . . . . . .2E 119
Paignton Rd. N15 . . . . . . .1A 36
Painsthorpe Rd. N16 . . . . .5A 36
Painted Hall
Greenwich 2E 95
Painters M. SE16 . . . . . . .5C 78
Pakeman Ho. SE1 . . . . . .3E 25
(off Surrey Row)
Pakeman St. N7 . . . . .5B 34
Pakenham Cl. SW12 . . . .1C 116
Pakenham St.
WC1 . . . . . .2A 8 (2B 62)
Pakington Ho. SW9 . . . . .5A 90
(off Stockwell Gdns. Est.)
Palace Av. W8 . . . . .3D 73
Palace Bingo Club 5E 77
(within Elephant & Castle
Shopping Cen.)
Palace Cl. E9 . . . . .3B 52
Palace Ct. NW3 . . . . .2D 45
W2 . . . . .1D 73
(not continuous)

Palace Gdns. M. W8 . . .2D 73
Palace Gdns. Ter.
  W8 . . . . .2C 72
Palace Ga. W8 . . . . .3E 73
Palace Grn. W8 . . . . . . .2D 73
Palace Mans. W14 . . .5A 72
  (off Hammersmith Rd.)
Palace M. SW1 . . . . . . .5C 74
  (off Eaton Ter.)
  SW6 . . . . .3B 86
Palace Pl.
  SW1 . . . . .5F 21 (4E 75)
Palace Pl. Mans. W8 . . .3D 73
  (off Kensington Ct.)
Palace Rd. N8 . . . . .1F 33
  (not continuous)
  SW2 . . . . .1B 118
Palace St.
  SW1 . . . . .5F 21 (4E 75)
Palace Superbowl 5E 77
  (within Elephant & Castle
  Shopping Cen.)
Palace Theatre
  Soho 3C 14
  (off Shaftesbury Av.)
Palace Vw. SE12 . . . . . .2C 124
Palace Wharf W6 . . . . . .3E 85
  (off Rainville Rd.)
Palamos Rd. E10 . . . . . .3C 38
Palatine Av. N16 . . . . . .1A 50
Palatine M. N16 . . . . . . .1A 50
Palazzo Apartments
  N1 . . . . .4A 50
  (off Ardleigh Rd.)
Palemead Cl. SW6 . . . . .4F 85
Palermo Rd. NW10 . . . . .1C 56
Palestra Ho. SE1 . . . . . .2D 25
  (off Blackfriars Rd.)
Palewell Comn. Dr.
  SW14 . . . . .3A 98
Palfrey Pl. SW8 . . . . . . .3B 90
Palgrave Gdns. NW1 . . .3A 60
Palgrave Ho. SE5 . . . . . .3E 91
  (off Wyndham Est.)
Palgrave Rd. W12 . . . . .4B 70
Palissy St.
  E2 . . . . .2F 11 (2B 64)
  (not continuous)
Palladino Ho. SW17 . . .5A 116
  (off Laurel Cl.)
Palladio Ct. SW18 . . . .4D 101
  (off Mapleton Cres.)
Palladium Ct. E8 . . . . . .4B 50
  (off Queensbridge Rd.)
Pallant Ho. SE1 . . . . . . .5C 26
Pallet Way SE18 . . . . . .4F 97
Palliser Ct. W14 . . . . . .1A 86
  (off Palliser Rd.)
Palliser Ho. E1 . . . . .3F 65
  (off Ernest St.)
  SE10 . . . . .2F 95
  (off Trafalgar Rd.)
Palliser Rd. W14 . . . . . .1A 86
Pallister Ter. SW15 . . .3B 112
Pall Mall
  SW1 . . . . . .2A 22 (2E 75)
Pall Mall E.
  SW1 . . . . .1C 22 (2F 75)
Pall Mall Pl. SW1 . . . . .2A 22
Palm Cl. E10 . . . . .5D 39

Palm Ct. SE15 . . . . .3B 92
  (off Garnies Cl.)
Palmer Ho. SE14 . . . . . .3F 93
  (off Lubbock St.)
Palmer Pl. N7 . . . . .2C 48
Palmer Rd. E13 . . . . . . .3D 69
Palmer's Rd. E2 . . . . . . .1F 65
Palmerston Ct. E3 . . . . . .1F 65
  (off Old Ford Rd.)
Palmerston Ho.
  SE1 . . . . .4B 24
  (off Westminster Bri. Rd.)
  W8 . . . . .2C 72
  (off Kensington Pl.)
Palmerston Mans.
  W14 . . . . .2A 86
  (off Queen's Club Gdns.)
Palmerston Rd. E7 . . . . .3D 55
  NW6 . . . . .4B 44
  (not continuous)
Palmerston Way
  SW8 . . . . .3D 89
Palmer St.
  SW1 . . . . . .5B 22 (4F 75)
  (not continuous)
Palyn Ho. EC1 . . . . .2A 10
  (off Radnor St.)
Pamela Wlk. E8 . . . . . . .5C 50
  (off Marlborough Av.)
Panama Ho. E1 . . . . . . .4F 65
  (off Beaumont Sq.)
Pancras La.
  EC4 . . . . . . .3B 18 (5E 63)
Pancras Rd.
  N1 . . . . .1D 7 (1A 62)
  NW1 . . . . .1F 61
Pancras Sq. N1 . . . . . . .1A 62
Pancras Way E3 . . . . . . .1C 66
Pandangle Ho. E8 . . . . . .5B 50
  (off Kingsland Rd.)
Pandian Way NW1 . . . . .3F 47
Pandora Ct. E16 . . . . . . .4C 68
  (off Robertson Rd.)
Pandora Rd. NW6 . . . . .3C 44
Pangbourne NW1 . . . . . .2F 5
  (off Stanhope St.)
Pangbourne Av.
  W10 . . . . .4E 57
Pankhurst Av. E16 . . . . .2D 83
Pankhurst Cl. SE14 . . . .3F 93
Pankhurst Ho. W12 . . . .5D 57
Panmure Cl. N5 . . . . . . .1D 49
Panmure Rd.
  SE26 . . . . .3D 121
Panorama Ct. N6 . . . . . .1E 33
Pan Peninsula Sq.
  E14 . . . . .3D 81
Pansy Gdns. W12 . . . . .1C 70
Panton St.
  SW1 . . . . . .5B 14 (1F 75)
Panyer All. EC1 . . . . .2F 17
  (off Newgate St.)
Paper Bldgs. EC4 . . . . . .4C 16
Paper Mill Wharf
  E14 . . . . .1A 80
Papillons Wlk. SE3 . . . . .5C 96
Papworth Gdns. N7 . . . .2B 48
Papworth Way SW2 . . . .5C 104
Papyrus Ho.
  N1 . . . . .1F 9 (2E 63)

Parade, The N4 . . . . . . .3C 34
  SE4 . . . . .5B 94
  (off Up. Brockley Rd.)
  SE26 . . . . .3D 121
  (off Wells Pk. Rd.)
  SW11 . . . . .3B 88
Parade Mans. NW4 . . . .1D 29
Parade M. SE27 . . . . . . .2D 119
Paradise Pk. E5 . . . . . . .5F 37
Paradise Pas. N7 . . . . . .2C 48
Paradise Rd. SW4 . . . . .5A 90
Paradise Row E2 . . . . . .2D 65
Paradise St. SE16 . . . . . .3D 79
Paradise Wlk. SW3 . . . . .2B 88
Paragon, The SE3 . . . . . .5B 96
Paragon Cl. E16 . . . . . . .5C 68
Paragon M. SE1 . . . . . . .5F 77
Paragon Pl. SE3 . . . . . . .5B 96
Paragon Rd. E9 . . . . . . .3E 51
Paramount Bldg. EC1 . .3D 9
  (off St John St.)
Paramount St. WC1 . . . .4A 6
Parbury Rd. SE23 . . . . .4A 108
Pardoe Rd. E10 . . . . . . .2D 39
Pardoner Ho. SE1 . . . . . .5C 26
  (off Pardoner St.)
Pardoner St.
  SE1 . . . . .5C 26 (4F 77)
  (not continuous)
Pardon St.
  EC1 . . . . . . .3E 9 (3D 63)
Parfett St. E1 . . . . .4C 64
  (not continuous)
Parfitt Cl. NW3 . . . . .3E 31
Parfrey St. W6 . . . . .2E 85
Paris Gdn.
  SE1 . . . . .1D 25 (2D 77)
Paris Ho. E2 . . . . .1D 65
  (off Old Bethnal Grn. Rd.)
Park & Ride
  Cumberland Gate
   . . . . .4A 12 (1B 74)
Park, The N6 . . . . .1C 32
  NW11 . . . . .3D 31
  SE23 . . . . .1E 121
Park App. SE16 . . . . . . .4D 79
Park Av. E15 . . . . .3A 54
  NW2 . . . . .2D 43
  NW10 . . . . .2D 43
  NW11 . . . . .3D 31
  SW14 . . . . .2A 98
Park Av. Nth. NW10 . . . .2D 43
Park Central Bldg.
   . . . . .1C 66
Park Cl. E9 . . . . .5E 51
  NW2 . . . . .5D 29
  SW1 . . . . .3B 74
  W4 . . . . .2A 84
  W14 . . . . .4B 72
Park Club, The 2A 70
Park Ct. E17 . . . . .1D 39
  SE21 . . . . .3E 119
  SE26 . . . . .5D 121
  SW11 . . . . .4D 89
  W6 . . . . .5C 70
Park Cres. W1 . .4D 5 (3D 61)
Park Cres. M. E.
  W1 . . . . . .4E 5 (3D 61)
Park Cres. M. W.
  W1 . . . . . .4D 5 (3D 61)

Parkcroft Rd. SE12 . . . . . .5B 110
Park Dr. NW11 . . . . .3D 31
    SE7 . . . . .2F 97
    SW14 . . . . .3A 98
Park Dwellings NW3 . . . . . .2B 46
Park E. Bldg. E3 . . . . .1C 66
    (off Fairfield Rd.)
Park End NW3 . . . . .1A 46
Parker Cl. E16 . . . . .2F 83
Parker Ct. N1 . . . . .5E 49
    (off Basire St.)
Parker Ho. E14 . . . . .3C 80
    (off Admirals Way)
Parker M.
    WC2 . . . . . .2E 15 (5A 62)
Parke Rd. SW13 . . . . .4C 84
Parkers Row SE1 . . . . .3C 78
Parker St. E16 . . . . .2F 83
    WC2 . . . . . .2E 15 (5A 62)
Parkfield Av.
    SW14 . . . . .2A 98
Parkfield Ct. SE14 . . . . . . .4B 94
    (off Parkfield Rd.)
Parkfield Ind. Est.
    SW11 . . . . .5C 88
Parkfield Rd. NW10 . . . . . .4D 43
    SE14 . . . . .4B 94
    SW4 . . . . .4F 103
Parkfields SW15 . . . . .2E 99
Parkfields Av. NW9 . . . . . . .3A 28
Parkfield St. N1 . . . . .1C 62
Park Gdns. E10 . . . . .3C 38
Parkgate N1 . . . . .5F 49
    (off Southgate Rd.)
    SE3 . . . . .1B 110
Parkgate M. N6 . . . . .2E 33
Parkgate Rd. SW11 . . . . . . .3A 88
Park Gro. E15 . . . . .5C 54
Park Gro. Rd. E11 . . . . .4A 40
Park Hall SE10 . . . . .3F 95
    (off Croom's Hill)
Park Hall Rd. SE21 . . . . . .3E 119
Park Hall Trad. Est.
    SE21 . . . . .3E 119
Parkham St. SW11 . . . . . . .4A 88
Park Hgts. Ct. E14 . . . . . . .5B 66
    (off Wharf La.)
Park Hill SE23 . . . . .2D 121
    SW4 . . . . .3F 103
Park Hill Ct. SW17 . . . . . . .3B 116
Parkhill Rd. NW3 . . . . .2B 46
Parkhill Wlk. NW3 . . . . .2B 46
Parkholme Rd. E8 . . . . .3B 50
Park Ho. E9 . . . . .4E 51
    (off Shore Rd.)
    SE5 . . . . .4F 91
    (off Camberwell Grn.)
    W1 . . . . .3B 12
Park Ho. Pas. N6 . . . . .2C 32
Parkhouse St. SE5 . . . . . . .3F 91
Parkhurst Ct. N7 . . . . .1A 48
Parkhurst Rd. N7 . . . . .1A 48
Parkinson Ct. N1 . . . . .2C 10
    (off Charles Sq. Est.)
Parkinson Ho. E9 . . . . .4E 51
    (off Frampton Pk. Rd.)
    SW1 . . . . .5E 75
    (off Tachbrook St.)
Parkland Ct. E15 . . . . .2A 54
    (off Maryland Pk.)

Parkland Ct. W14 . . . . . .3A 72
    (off Holland Pk. Av.)
Parkland Gdns.
    SW19 . . . . .1F 113
Parklands N6 . . . . .2D 33
Parklands Rd.
    SW16 . . . . .5D 117
Parkland Walk
    Local Nature Reserve
    . . . . .2A 34
    W1 . . . . .4A 12 (1B 74)
Park La. E15 . . . . .5F 53
Park Lee Ct. N16 . . . . .2A 36
Park Lodge NW8 . . . . .4F 45
    W14 . . . . .4B 72
    (off Melbury Rd.)
Park Lofts SW2 . . . . .3A 104
    (off Lyham Rd.)
Park Lorne NW8 . . . . .2A 60
    (off Park Rd.)
Park Mans. NW4 . . . . .1D 29
    NW8 . . . . .1A 60
    (off Allitsen Rd.)
    SW1 . . . . .4A 20
    (off Knightsbridge)
    SW8 . . . . .2A 90
    SW11 . . . . .4B 88
    (off Prince of Wales Dr.)
Parkmead SW15 . . . . .4D 99
Park M. N8 . . . . .1A 34
    SE10 . . . . .1B 96
    SE24 . . . . .5E 105
    W10 . . . . .1A 58
Park Pde. NW10 . . . . .1B 56
Park Piazza
    SE13 . . . . .4F 109
Park Pl. E14 . . . . .2C 80
    N1 . . . . .4F 49
    (off Downham Rd.)
    SW1 . . . . . . .2F 21 (2E 75)
Park Pl. Vs. W2 . . . . .4E 59
Park Ri. SE23 . . . . .1A 122
Park Ri. Rd.
    SE23 . . . . .1A 122
Park Rd. E6 . . . . .5E 55
    E10 . . . . .3C 38
    E12 . . . . .3D 41
    E15 . . . . .5C 54
    E17 . . . . .1B 38
    N8 . . . . .1F 33
    NW1 . . . . . . .3A 4 (2A 60)
    NW4 . . . . .2C 28
    NW8 . . . . .2A 60
    NW10 . . . . .5A 42
    SW19 . . . . .5A 116
    W4 . . . . .2A 84
Park Road Leisure Cen.
    . . . . .1F 33
Park Rd. Nth. W4 . . . . .1A 84
Park Row SE10 . . . . .2F 95
    SW2 . . . . .4C 104
Park St James
    NW8 . . . . .5B 46
    (off St James's Ter. M.)
Park Side NW2 . . . . .5C 28
Parkside SE3 . . . . .3B 96
    SW1 . . . . .3A 20
    SW19 . . . . .3F 113
    W3 . . . . .2A 70
Parkside Av. SW19 . . . . . . .5F 113

Parkside Bus. Est.
    SE8 . . . . .2A 94
    (Blackhorse Rd.)
    SE8 . . . . .2A 94
    (Rolt St.)
Parkside Ct. E11 . . . . .1C 40
    (off Wanstead Pl.)
    E16 . . . . .3E 83
    (off Booth Rd.)
Parkside Cres. N7 . . . . .5C 34
Parkside Est. E9 . . . . .5E 51
    (not continuous)
Parkside Gdns.
    SW19 . . . . .4F 113
Parkside Rd.
    SW11 . . . . .4C 88
Parks Info. Cen. 2A 74
Park Sth. SW11 . . . . .4C 88
    (off Austin Rd.)
Park Sq. E.
    NW1 . . . . . . .3D 5 (3D 61)
Park Sq. M.
    NW1 . . . . . . .4D 5 (3C 60)
Park Sq. W.
    NW1 . . . . . . .3D 5 (3D 61)
Parkstead Rd. SW15 . . . . . .3C 98
Park Steps W2 . . . . .1A 74
    (off St George's Flds.)
Parkstone Rd. SE15 . . . . . .5C 92
Park St. SE1 . . . . . .1F 25 (2E 77)
    W1 . . . . .4B 12 (1C 74)
Parkthorne Rd.
    SW12 . . . . .5F 103
Park Towers W1 . . . . .2D 21
    (off Brick St.)
Park Vw. N5 . . . . .1E 49
    SE8 . . . . .1F 93
    (off Trundleys Rd.)
Park Vw. Apartments
    SE16 . . . . .4D 79
    (off Banyard Rd.)
Parkview Apartments
    E14 . . . . .5D 67
    (off Chrisp St.)
Park Vw. Ct. E3 . . . . .4C 66
    SE12 . . . . .3E 125
Parkview Ct. SW6 . . . . .5A 86
    SW18 . . . . .4C 100
Park Vw. Est. E2 . . . . .1F 65
Park Vw. Gdns. NW4 . . . . . .1E 29
Park Vw. Ho. SE24 . . . . . . .4D 105
    (off Hurst St.)
Park Vw. Mans. N4 . . . . . . .1D 35
Park Vw. M. SW9 . . . . .5B 90
Park Vw. Rd. NW10 . . . . . . .1B 42
Park Village E.
    NW1 . . . . . . .1E 5 (1D 61)
Park Village W. NW1 . . . . . .1D 61
Parkville Rd. SW6 . . . . .3B 86
Park Vista SE10 . . . . .2F 95
Park Wlk. N6 . . . . .2C 32
    SE10 . . . . .3F 95
    SW10 . . . . .2E 87
Park Way NW11 . . . . .1A 30
Parkway NW1 . . . . .5D 47
Parkway Cres. E15 . . . . . . .2E 53
Park W. W2 . . . . .5A 60
    (off Park W. Pl.)
Park W. Bldg. E3 . . . . .1C 66
Park W. Pl. W2 . . . . .5A 60

Park Wharf *SE8* 1A **94**
(off Evelyn St.)
Parkwood *NW8* 5B **46**
(off St Edmund's Ter.)
Parkwood M. *N6* 1D **33**
Parkwood Rd.
SW19 . . . . .5B **114**
Parliament Ct. *E1* 1E **19**
Parliament Hill 5B **32**
Parliament Hill *NW3* . . .1A **46**
Parliament Hill Fields
. . . . .5C **32**
Parliament Hill Lido . .1C **46**
Parliament Hill Mans.
NW5 . . . . .1C **46**
Parliament Sq.
SW1 . . . . . . .4D **23** (3A **76**)
Parliament St.
SW1 . . . . . . .3D **23** (3A **76**)
Parliament Vw. *SE1* . . .5B **76**
Parma Cres. *SW11* . . .2B **102**
Parmiter St. *E2* 1D **65**
Parmoor Ct. *EC1* 3F **9**
Parnell St. *W12* 4D **71**
Parnell Ho.
WC1 . . . . .1C **14** (4F **61**)
Parnell Rd. *E3* 5B **52**
Parnham St. *E14* 5A **66**
(not continuous)
Parolles Rd. *N19* 3E **33**
Parr Ct. *N1* 1F **63**
(off New North Rd.)
Parr Ho. *E16* 2D **83**
(off Beaulieu Av.)
Parrington Ho. *SW4* . . .4F **103**
Parr Rd. *E6* 5F **55**
Parr St. *N1* 1F **63**
Parry Ho. *E1* 2D **79**
(off Green Bank)
Parry Rd. *W10* 2A **58**
Parry St. *SW8* 2A **90**
Parsifal Rd. *NW6* 2C **44**
Parsonage St. *E14* 5E **81**
PARSONS GREEN 5B **86**
Parson's Grn. *SW6* 4C **86**
Parson's Grn. La.
SW6 . . . . .4C **86**
Parsons Ho. *W2* 3F **59**
(off Hall Pl.)
Parsons Lodge *NW6* . . .4D **45**
(off Priory Rd.)
Parson's Rd. *E13* 1E **69**
Parthenia Rd. *SW6* 4C **86**
Partington Cl. *N19* 3F **33**
Partridge Cl. *E16* 4F **69**
Partridge Ct. *EC1* 3D **9**
Partridge Ho. *E3* 1B **66**
(off Stafford Rd.)
Pascall St. *SE17* 2E **91**
(off Draco St.)
Pascal St. *SW8* 3F **89**
Pascoe Rd. *SE13* 3F **109**
Pasley Cl. *SE17* 1D **91**
Passfield Dr. *E14* 4D **67**
Passfield Hall *WC1* 3C **6**
(off Endsleigh Pl.)
Passfields *SE6* 3D **123**
W14 . . . . .1B **86**
(off Star St.)
Passing All. *EC1* 4E **9**

Passmore Ho. *E2* 5B **50**
(off Kingsland Rd.)
Passmore St. *SW1* 1C **88**
Paston Cl. *E5* 5F **37**
Paston Cres. *SE12* 5D **111**
Pastor Cl. *N6* 1E **33**
Pastor St. *SE11* 5D **77**
Pasture Rd. *SE6* 1B **124**
Pastures Path *E11* 3B **40**
Patcham Ter. *SW8* 4D **89**
Patent Ho. *E14* 4D **67**
(off Morris Rd.)
Paternoster La.
EC4 . . . . . . .3E **17** (5D **63**)
Paternoster Row
EC4 . . . . . . .3F **17** (5E **63**)
Paternoster Sq.
EC4 . . . . . . .3E **17** (5D **63**)
Paterson Ct. *EC1* 2B **10**
Pater St. *W8* 4C **72**
Pathfield Rd. *SW16* 5F **117**
Patience Rd. *SW11* 5A **88**
Patio Cl. *SW4* 4F **103**
Patmore Est. *SW8* 4E **89**
Patmore Ho. *N16* 2A **50**
Patmore St. *SW8* 4E **89**
Patmos Lodge *SW9* 4D **91**
(off Elliott Rd.)
Patmos Rd. *SW9* 3D **91**
Paton Cl. *E3* 2C **66**
Paton Ho. *SW9* 5B **90**
(off Stockwell Rd.)
Paton St. *EC1* . .2F **9** (2E **63**)
Patrick Coman Ho.
EC1 . . . . .2D **9**
(off St John St.)
Patrick Connolly Gdns.
E3 . . . . .2D **67**
Patrick Ct. *SE1* 4E **25**
(off Webber St.)
Patrick Pas. *SW11* 5A **88**
Patrick Rd. *E13* 2E **69**
Patriot Sq. *E2* 1D **65**
Patrol Pl. *SE6* 4D **109**
Patroni Ct. *E15* 2A **68**
(off Durban Rd.)
Pat Shaw Ho. *E1* 3F **65**
(off Globe Rd.)
Patshull Pl. *NW5* 3E **47**
Patshull Rd. *NW5* 3E **47**
Pattenden Rd. *SE6* 1B **122**
Patten Ho. *N4* 4E **35**
Patten Rd. *SW18* 5A **102**
Patterdale *NW1* 2E **5**
(off Osnaburgh St.)
Patterdale Rd. *SE15* 3E **93**
Pattern Ho.
EC1 . . . . .3D **9** (3D **63**)
Pattina Wlk. *SE16* 2A **80**
(off Silver Wlk.)
Pattison Ho. *E1* 5F **65**
(off Wellesley St.)
SE1 . . . . .3A **26**
(off Redcross Way)
Pattison Rd. *NW2* 5C **30**
Paul Cl. *E15* 5A **54**
Paul Daisley Ct.
NW6 . . . . .4A **44**
(off Christchurch Av.)
Paulet Rd. *SE5* 5D **91**

Paulet Way *NW10* 4A **42**
Paul Ho. *W10* 3A **58**
(off Ladbroke Gro.)
Pauline Ho. *E1* 4C **64**
(off Old Montague St.)
Paul Julius Cl. *E14* 1F **81**
Paul Robeson Ho.
WC1 . . . . .1A **8**
(off Penton Ri.)
Paul St. *E15* 5A **54**
EC2 . . . . .4C **10** (3F **63**)
Paul's Wlk.
EC4 . . . . .4E **17** (1E **77**)
Paultons Ho. *SW3* 2F **87**
(off Paultons Sq.)
Paultons Sq. *SW3* 2F **87**
Paultons St. *SW3* 2F **87**
Pauntley St. *N19* 3E **33**
Pavan Ct. *E2* 2E **65**
(off Sceptre Rd.)
Paveley Dr. *SW11* 3A **88**
Paveley Ho. *N1* 1B **62**
(off Priory Grn. Est.)
Paveley St. *NW8* 2A **60**
Pavement, The *E11* 3E **39**
(off Hainault Rd.)
SW4 . . . . .2E **103**
Pavilion, The *SW8* 3F **89**
Pavilion Apartments
NW8 . . . . .2F **59**
Pavilion Ct. *NW6* 2C **58**
(off Stafford Rd.)
Pavilion Pde. *W12* 5E **57**
(off Wood La.)
Pavilion Rd.
SW1 . . . . . . .4A **20** (4B **74**)
Pavilion Sq. *SW17* 3B **116**
Pavilion St.
SW1 . . . . .5A **20** (4B **74**)
Pavilion Ter. *W12* 5E **57**
(off Wood La.)
Pavilion Way *SE10* 3A **82**
Pavillion Ho. *SE16* 3F **79**
(off Water Gdns. Sq.)
Pavillion M. *N4* 4B **34**
(off Tollington Pl.)
Pawsey Cl. *E13* 5D **55**
Paxton Ct. *N7* 3C **48**
(off Westbourne Rd.)
SE12 . . . . .3E **125**
SE26 . . . . .4A **122**
(off Adamsrill Rd.)
Paxton Ho. *SE17* 1F **91**
(off Morecambe St.)
Paxton Pl. *SE27* 4A **120**
Paxton Point *SE10* 3D **95**
Paxton Rd. *SE23* 3A **122**
W4 . . . . .2A **84**
Paxton Ter. *SW1* 2D **89**
Paymal Ho. *E1* 4E **65**
(off Stepney Grn.)
Payne Ho. *N1* 5B **48**
(off Barnsbury Est.)
Paynell Ct. *SE3* 1A **110**
Payne Rd. *E3* 1D **67**
Paynesfield Av.
SW14 . . . . .1A **98**
Payne St. *SE8* 3B **94**
Paynes Wlk. *W6* 2A **86**
Peabody Av. *SW1* 1D **89**

Peabody Bldgs. *E1* *1C 78*
  (off John Fisher St.)
EC1 . . . .*4A 10*
  (off Roscoe St.)
SW3 . . . .*2A 88*
  (off Cheyne Row)
Peabody Cl. SE10 . . . .*4D 95*
SW1 . . . .*1D 89*
Peabody Cl. *EC1* *4A 10*
  (off Roscoe St.)
SE5 . . . .*4F 91*
  (off Kimpton Rd.)
Peabody Est. *E1* *1F 79*
  (off Brodlove La.)
E2 . . . .*1D 65*
  (off Minerva St.)
EC1 . . . .*4A 10*
  (off Dufferin St.,
  not continuous)
EC1 . . . .*4C 8*
  (off Farringdon La.)
N1 . . . .*5E 49*
SE1 . . . .*2C 24 (2C 76)*
  (Duchy St.)
SE1 . . . .*3A 26*
  (Marshalsea Rd.)
SE1 . . . . .*2F 25 (2E 77)*
  (Southwark St.)
SE5 . . . .*4F 91*
  (off Camberwell Grn.)
SE24 . . . .*5D 105*
SW1 . . . .*5E 75*
  (off Vauxhall Bri. Rd.)
SW3 . . . .*2A 88*
SW6 . . . .*2C 86*
  (off Lillie Rd.)
SW11 . . . .*2A 102*
W6 . . . .*1E 85*
W10 . . . .*4E 57*
Peabody Hill
SE21 . . . .*1D 119*
Peabody Sq.
SE1 . . . . . .*4D 25 (3D 77)*
  (not continuous)
Peabody Ter. *EC1* *4C 8*
  (off Farringdon La.)
Peabody Twr. *EC1* *4A 10*
  (off Golden La.)
Peabody Trust SE17 . . . .*5F 77*
Peabody Yd. N1 . . . .*5E 49*
Peace Ct. *SE1* *1C 92*
  (off Harmony Pl.)
Peach Gro. E11 . . . .*5F 39*
Peach Rd. W10 . . . .*2F 57*
Peachum Rd. SE3 . . . .*2B 96*
Peachwalk M. E3 . . . .*1F 65*
Peacock Ho. *SE5* *4A 92*
  (off St Giles Rd.)
Peacock Pl. N1 . . . .*3C 48*
Peacock St. SE17 . . . .*5D 77*
Peacock Theatre *3F 15*
  (off Portugal St.)
Peacock Wlk. E16 . . . .*5D 69*
  (off Mortlake Rd.)
N6 . . . .*2D 33*
Peacock Yd. *SE17* *1D 91*
  (off Iliffe St.)
Peak, The SE26 . . . .*3E 121*
Peak Hill SE26 . . . .*4E 121*
Peak Hill Av. SE26 . . . . . .*4E 121*

Peak Hill Gdns.
SE26 . . . .*4E 121*
Peak Ho. *N4* *3E 35*
  (off Woodberry Down Est.)
Pearce Ho. *SW1* *5F 75*
  (off Causton St.)
Pear Cl. SE14 . . . .*3A 94*
Pear Ct. *SE15* *3B 92*
  (off Thruxton Way)
Pearcroft Rd. E11 . . . .*4F 39*
Peardon St. SW8 . . . .*5D 89*
Pearfield Rd. SE23 . . . . . .*3A 122*
Pearl Cl. NW2 . . . .*2F 29*
Pearl St. E1 . . . .*2D 79*
Pearman St.
SE1 . . . .*5C 24 (4C 76)*
Pear Pl. SE1 . . . .*3B 24 (3C 76)*
Pear Rd. E11 . . . .*5F 39*
Pearscroft Ct. SW6 . . . . . .*4D 87*
Pearscroft Rd. SW6 . . . . . .*4D 87*
Pearse St. SE15 . . . .*2A 92*
Pearson Cl. *SE5* *4E 91*
  (off Camberwell New Rd.)
Pearson M. *SW4* *1F 103*
  (off Edgeley Rd.)
Pearson St. E2 . . . .*1B 64*
Pearson's Av. SE14 . . . .*4C 94*
Peartree SE26 . . . .*5A 122*
Pear Tree Cl. E2 . . . .*5B 50*
Pear Tree Ct.
EC1 . . . .*4C 8 (3C 62)*
Pear Tree Ho. SE4 . . . . . .*1B 108*
Peartree La. E1 . . . .*1E 79*
Pear Tree St.
EC1 . . . .*3E 9 (3E 63)*
Peartree Way SE10 . . . .*5C 82*
Peary Ho. NW10 . . . .*4A 42*
Peary Pl. E2 . . . .*2E 65*
Peckarmans Wood
SE26 . . . .*3C 120*
Peckett Sq. N5 . . . .*1E 49*
Peckford Pl. SW9 . . . .*5C 90*
PECKHAM *4C 92*
Peckham Gro. SE15 . . . .*3A 92*
Peckham High St.
SE15 . . . .*4C 92*
Peckham Hill St.
SE15 . . . .*3C 92*
Peckham Pk. Rd.
SE15 . . . .*3C 92*
Peckham Pulse
  Health & Leisure Cen.
. . . .*4C 92*
Peckham Rd. SE5 . . . .*4A 92*
SE15 . . . .*4A 92*
Peckham Rye SE15 . . . .*1C 106*
SE22 . . . .*2C 106*
Peckham Sq. SE15 . . . .*4C 92*
Pecks Yd. *E1* *5F 11*
  (off Hanbury St.)
Peckwater St. NW5 . . . .*2E 47*
Pedlar's Wlk. N7 . . . .*2B 48*
Pedley St. E1 . . . .*3C 64*
Pedro St. E5 . . . .*5F 37*
Pedworth Gdns. SE16 . . . .*5E 79*
Peebles Ho. *NW6* *1D 59*
  (off Carlton Vale)
Peek Cres. SW19 . . . .*5F 113*

Peel Gro. E2 . . . .*1E 65*
Peel Pas. W8 . . . .*2C 72*
Peel Pct. NW6 . . . .*1C 58*
Peel St. W8 . . . .*2C 72*
Peerless St.
EC1 . . . .*2B 10 (2F 63)*
Pegasus Cl. N16 . . . .*1F 49*
Pegasus Cl. *NW10* *2D 57*
  (off Trenmar Gdns.)
Pegasus Ho. *E1* *3F 65*
  (off Beaumont Sq.)
E13 . . . .*2D 69*
Pegasus Pl. SE11 . . . .*2C 90*
SW6 . . . .*4C 86*
Pegley Gdns. SE12 . . . . . .*2C 124*
Pekin Cl. *E14* *5C 66*
  (off Pekin St.)
Pekin St. E14 . . . .*5C 66*
Peldon Wlk. *N1* *5D 49*
  (off Popham St.)
Pelham Cl. SE5 . . . .*1A 106*
Pelham Cl. *SW3* *5A 74*
  (off Fulham Rd.)
Pelham Cres. SW7 . . . .*5A 74*
Pelham Ho. *SW1* *5C 22*
  (off Gt. Peter St.)
W14 . . . .*5B 72*
  (off Mornington Av.)
Pelham Pl. SW7 . . . .*5A 74*
Pelham St. SW7 . . . .*5F 73*
Pelican Est. SE15 . . . .*4B 92*
Pelican Ho. SE5 . . . .*4B 92*
SE8 . . . .*5B 80*
Pelican Pas. E1 . . . .*3E 65*
Pelican Wlk. SW9 . . . .*2D 105*
Pelican Wharf *E1* *2E 79*
  (off Wapping Wall)
Pelier St. SE17 . . . .*2E 91*
Pelinore Rd. SE6 . . . .*2A 124*
Pella Ho. SE11 . . . .*1B 90*
Pellant Rd. SW6 . . . .*3A 86*
Pellatt Rd. SE22 . . . .*3B 106*
Pellerin Rd. N16 . . . .*2A 50*
Pellew Ho. *E1* *3D 65*
  (off Somerford St.)
Pelling St. E14 . . . .*5C 66*
Pelly Rd. E13 . . . .*5C 54*
  (not continuous)
Pelter St. E2 . . . .*1F 11 (2B 64)*
Pelton Rd. SE10 . . . .*1A 96*
Pember Rd. NW10 . . . .*2F 57*
Pemberton Ct. *E1* *2F 65*
  (off Portelet Rd.)
Pemberton Gdns.
N19 . . . .*5E 33*
Pemberton Ho.
SE26 . . . .*4C 120*
  (off High Level Dr.)
Pemberton Pl. E8 . . . .*4D 51*
Pemberton Rd. N4 . . . .*1C 34*
Pemberton Row
EC4 . . . .*2C 16 (5C 62)*
Pemberton Ter. N19 . . . . . .*5E 33*
Pembridge Cres.
W11 . . . .*1C 72*
Pembridge Gdns. W2 . . . .*1C 72*
Pembridge M. W11 . . . . . .*1C 72*
Pembridge Pl.
SW15 . . . .*3C 100*
W2 . . . .*1C 72*

Pembridge Rd.
W11 . . . . .1C 72
Pembridge Sq. W2 . . .1C 72
Pembridge Studios
W11 . . . . .1C *72*
(off Pembridge Vs.)
Pembridge Vs. W2 . . . .1C 72
W11 . . . . .1C 72
Pembroke W14 . . . . .5B 72
(off Kensington Village)
Pembroke Av. N1 . . . .5A 48
Pembroke Bldgs.
NW10 . . . . .2C 56
Pembroke Cl.
SW1 . . . . .4C 20 (3C 74)
Pembroke Cotts. *W8* . .*4C 72*
(off Pembroke Sq.)
Pembroke Ct. *W8* *4C 72*
(off Sth. Edwardes Sq.)
Pembroke Gdns. W8 . .5B 72
Pembroke Gdns. Cl.
W8 . . . . .4C 72
Pembroke Ho. *SW1* . . .*5B 20*
(off Chesham St.)
W2 . . . .*5D 59*
(off Hallfield Est.)
Pembroke Mans.
NW6 . . . .*3E 45*
(off Canfield Gdns.)
Pembroke M. E3 . . . . .2A 66
W8 . . . . .4C 72
Pembroke Pl. W8 . . . . .4C 72
Pembroke Rd. E17 . . .1D 39
N15 . . . . .1B 36
W8 . . . . .5B 72
Pembroke Sq. W8 . . . .4C 72
Pembroke St. N1 . . . . .4A 48
(not continuous)
Pembroke Studios
W8 . . . . .4B 72
Pembroke Ter. *NW8* . . .*5F 45*
(off Queen's Ter.)
Pembroke Vs. W8 . . . .5C 72
Pembroke Wlk. W8 . . .5C 72
Pembrook M. SW11 . . .2F 101
Pembry Cl. SW9 . . . . .4C 90
Pembury Cl. E5 . . . . . .2D 51
Pembury Pl. E5 . . . . . .2D 51
Pembury Rd. E5 . . . . .2D 51
Pemell Cl. E1 . . . . . . .3E 65
Pemell Ho. *E1* *3E 65*
(off Pemell Cl.)
Penally Pl. N1 . . . . . . .5F 49
Penang Ho. *E1* *2D 79*
(off Prusom St.)
Penang St. E1 . . . . . . .2D 79
Penarth Cen. SE15 . . . .2E 93
Penarth St. SE15 . . . . .2E 93
Penberth Rd. SE6 . . . .2E 123
Pencombe M. W11 . . . .1B 72
Pencraig Way SE15 . . .2D 93
Penda's Mead E9 . . . . .1A 52
Pendennis Ho. SE8 . . . .5A 80
Pendennis Rd.
SW16 . . . . .4A 118
Penderry Ri. SE6 . . . . .2F 123
Penderyn Way N7 . . . . .1F 47
Pendle Ho. SE26 . . . . .3C 120
Pendle Rd. SW16 . . . . .5D 117
Pendlestone Rd. E17 . . .1D 39

Pendley Ho. *E2* *5C 50*
(off Whiston Rd.)
Pendragon Rd.
BR1: Brom 3B 124
Pendragon Wlk.
NW9 . . . . .1A 28
Pendrell Ho. *WC2* *3C 14*
(off New Compton St.)
Pendrell Rd. SE4 . . . . .5A 94
Pendulum M. E8 . . . . .2B 50
Penerley Rd. SE6 . . . . .1D 123
Penfield Lodge *W9* *4C 58*
(off Admiral Wlk.)
Penfields Ho. *N7* *3A 48*
(off York Way Est.)
Penfold Pl. NW1 . . . . .4A 60
Penfold St. NW1 . . . . .3F 59
NW8 . . . . .3F 59
Penford Gdns. SE9 . . . .1F 111
Penford St. SE5 . . . . . .5D 91
Penge Ho. SW11 . . . . .1F 101
Pengelly Apartments
E14 . . . .*1D 95*
(off Bartlett M.)
Penge Rd. E13 . . . . . . .5D 55
Penhall Rd. SE7 . . . . . .5F 83
Penhurst Mans. *SW6* . .*4B 86*
(off Rostrevor Rd.)
Penhurst Pl. SE1 . . . . .5A 24
Peninsula Apartments
N1 . . . .*5E 49*
(off Basire St.)
W2 . . . .*4F 59*
(off Praed St.)
Peninsula Ct. *E14* *4D 81*
(off E. Ferry Rd.)
N1 . . . .*5E 49*
(off Basire St.)
Peninsula Hgts. SE1 . . .1A 90
Peninsular Pk. SE7 . . . .5C 82
Peninsular Pk. Rd.
SE7 . . . . .5C 82
Peninsula Sq. SE10 . . . .3A 82
Penley Ct.
WC2 . . . . .4A 16 (1B 76)
Penmayne Ho. *SE11* . . .*1C 90*
(off Kennings Way)
Pennack Rd. SE15 . . . . .2B 92
Penn Almshouses
SE10 . . . .*4E 95*
(off Greenwich Sth. St.)
Pennant M. W8 . . . . . .5D 73
Pennant Mans. *W12* . . .*3E 71*
(off Goldhawk Rd.)
Pennard Rd. W12 . . . . .3E 71
Penner Cl. SW19 . . . . .2A 114
Pennethorne Cl. E9 . . . .5E 51
Pennethorne Ho.
SW11 . . . . .1F 101
Pennethorne Rd.
SE15 . . . . .3D 93
Penn Ho. *NW8* *3A 60*
(off Mallory St.)
Pennine Dr. NW2 . . . . .4F 29
Pennine La. NW2 . . . . .4A 30
Pennine Pde. NW2 . . . .4A 30
Pennington Cl.
SE27 . . . . .4F 119
Pennington Ct. SE16 . . .2A 80
Pennington St. E1 . . . . .1D 79

Pennington Way
SE12 . . . . .2D 125
Penn Rd. N7 . . . . .2A 48
Penn St. N1 . . . . .5F 49
Pennyfields E14 . . . . . .1C 80
(not continuous)
Pennyford Ct. *NW8* *3F 59*
(off St John's Wood Rd.)
Penny M. SW12 . . . . . .5D 103
Pennymoor Wlk. W9 . . .3B 58
(off Fernhead Rd.)
Penpoll Rd. E8 . . . . . . .3D 51
Penrith Cl. SW15 . . . . .3A 100
Penrith Pl. SE27 . . . . . .2D 119
Penrith Rd. N15 . . . . . .1F 35
Penrith St. SW16 . . . . .5E 117
Penrose Gro. SE17 . . . .1E 91
Penrose Ho. SE17 . . . . .1E 91
Penrose St. SE17 . . . . .1E 91
Penrose Way SE10 . . . .2A 82
Penryn Ho. *SE11* *1D 91*
(off Seaton Cl.)
Penryn St. NW1 . . . . . .1F 61
Penry St. SE1 . . . . .5A 78
Pensbury Pl. SW8 . . . . .5E 89
Pensbury St. SW8 . . . . .5E 89
Penshurst NW5 . . . . . . .3C 46
Penshurst Ho. *SE15* . . .*2E 93*
(off Lovelinch Cl.)
Penshurst Rd. E9 . . . . .4F 51
Pentagram Yd. *W11* . . .*5C 58*
(off Needham Rd.)
Pentland Cl. NW11 . . . .4A 30
Pentland Gdns.
SW18 . . . . .4E 101
Pentland Rd. NW6 . . . .2C 58
Pentland St. SW18 . . . .4E 101
Pentlow St. SW15 . . . . .1E 99
Pentney Rd. SW12 . . . .1E 117
Penton Gro. N1 . . . . . . .1C 62
Penton Ho. *N1* *1B 8*
(off Pentonville Rd.)
Penton Pl. SE17 . . . . . .1D 91
Penton Ri.
WC1 . . . . . .1A 8 (2B 62)
Penton St. N1 . . . . .1C 62
PENTONVILLE 1B 62
Pentonville Rd.
N1 . . . . .1F 7 (1A 62)
Pentridge St. SE15 . . . .3B 92
Penwith Rd. SW18 . . . .2C 114
Penwood Ho. SW15 . . . .4B 98
Penworth Rd.
SW16 . . . . .5D 117
Penywern Rd. SW5 . . . .1C 86
Penzance Pl. W11 . . . . .2A 72
Penzance St. W11 . . . . .2A 72
Peony Ct. SW10 . . . . . .2E 87
Peony Gdns. W12 . . . . .1C 70
Peperfield *WC1* *2F 7*
(off Cromer St.)
Pepler Ho. *W10* *3A 58*
(off Wornington Rd.)
Pepler M. SE5 . . . . .1B 92
Peploe Rd. NW6 . . . . . .1F 57
Peppermead Sq.
SE13 . . . . .3C 108
Peppermint Pl. E11 . . . .5A 40
Pepper St. E14 . . . . . . .4D 81
SE1 . . . . .3F 25 (3E 77)

Peppie Cl. N16 . . . . . . .4A 36
Pepys Cres. E16 . . . . . .2C 82
Pepys Ho. E1 . . . . .2E 65
  (off Kirkwall Pl.)
Pepys St.
  EC3 . . . . . .4E 19 (1A 78)
Perceval Av. NW3 . . . . .2A 46
Perch St. E8 . . . . .1B 50
Percival St.
  EC1 . . . . . .3D 9 (3D 63)
Percy Cir.
  WC1 . . . . . .1A 8 (2B 62)
Percy Laurie Ho.
  SW15 . . . . .2F 99
  (off Nursery Cl.)
Percy M. W1 . . . . .1B 14
Percy Pas. W1 . . . . .1B 14
Percy Rd. E11 . . . . .2A 40
  E16 . . . . .4A 68
  W12 . . . . .3C 70
Percy St. W1 . . .1B 14 (4F 61)
Percy Yd.
  WC1 . . . . . .1A 8 (2B 62)
Peregrine Cl.
  NW10 . . . . .2A 42
Peregrine Ct. SE8 . . . . .2C 94
  (off Edward St.)
  SW16 . . . . .4B 118
Peregrine Ho. EC1 . . . . .1E 9
Perham Rd. W14 . . . . . .1A 86
Peridot Ct. E2 . . . . .2F 11
  (off Virginia Rd.)
Perifield SE21 . . . . .1E 119
Periton Rd. SE9 . . . . . . .2F 111
Perkins Ho. E14 . . . . . . .4B 66
  (off Wallwood St.)
Perkin's Rents
  SW1 . . . . . .5B 22 (4F 75)
Perkins Sq.
  SE1 . . . . . .1A 26 (2E 77)
Perks Cl. SE3 . . . . .1A 110
Perley Ho. E3 . . . . .4B 66
  (off Weatherley Cl.)
Perran Rd. SW2 . . . . . .1D 119
Perren St. NW5 . . . . . . .3D 47
Perrers Rd. W6 . . . . .5D 71
Perring Est. E3 . . . . .4C 66
  (off Gale St.)
Perrin Ho. NW6 . . . . . . .2C 58
Perrin's Ct. NW3 . . . . . .1E 45
Perrin's La. NW3 . . . . . .1E 45
Perrin's Wlk. NW3 . . . . .1E 45
Perronet Ho. SE1 . . . . . .5E 25
Perry Av. W3 . . . . .5A 56
Perry Ct. E14 . . . . .1C 94
  (off Maritime Quay)
  N15 . . . . .1A 36
Perryfield Way NW9 . . . .1B 28
Perry Hill SE6 . . . . .3B 122
Perry Lodge E12 . . . . . . .3F 41
Perrymead St. SW6 . . . .4C 86
Perryn Ho. W3 . . . . .1A 70
Perryn Rd. SE16 . . . . . .4D 79
  W3 . . . . .2A 70
Perry Ri. SE23 . . . . .3A 122
Perry's Pl.
  W1 . . . . . . .2B 14 (5F 61)
Perry Va. SE23 . . . . . . .2E 121
Persant Rd. SE6 . . . . . .2A 124

Perseverance Pl.
  SW9 . . . . .3C 90
Perseverance Works
  E2 . . . . .1E 11
  (off Kingsland Rd.)
Perth Av. NW9 . . . . .2A 28
Perth Cl. SE5 . . . . .2F 105
Perth Ho. N1 . . . . .4B 48
  (off Bemerton Est.)
Perth Rd. E10 . . . . .3A 38
  E13 . . . . .1D 69
  N4 . . . . .3C 34
Perystreete SE23 . . . . . .2E 121
Peter Av. NW10 . . . . . . .4D 43
Peter Best Ho. E1 . . . . .5D 65
  (off Nelson St.)
Peterboat Cl. SE10 . . . . .5A 82
Peterborough Ct.
  EC4 . . . . .3C 16 (5C 62)
Peterborough M.
  SW6 . . . . .5C 86
Peterborough Rd.
  E10 . . . . .1E 39
  SW6 . . . . .5C 86
Peterborough Vs.
  SW6 . . . . .4D 87
Peter Butler Ho. SE1 . . .3C 78
  (off Wolseley St.)
Peterchurch Ho.
  SE15 . . . . .2D 93
  (off Commercial Way)
Petergate SW11 . . . . . .2E 101
Peter Harrison Planetarium
  . . . . .3F 95
Peter Heathfield Ho.
  E15 . . . . .5F 53
  (off Wise Rd.)
Peter Hills Ho. SE16 . . . .5C 78
  (off Alexis St.)
Peter Ho. SW8 . . . . .3A 90
  (off Luscombe Way)
Peterley Bus. Cen.
  E2 . . . . .1D 65
Peter Pan Statue 2F 73
Peters Ct. W2 . . . . .5D 59
  (off Porchester St.)
Petersfield Ri.
  SW15 . . . . .1D 113
Petersham Ho. SW7 . . . .5F 73
  (off Kendrick M.)
Petersham La. SW7 . . . .4E 73
Petersham M. SW7 . . . . .4E 73
Petersham Rd. SW7 . . . .4E 73
Peter's Hill
  EC4 . . . . . .4F 17 (1E 77)
Peter Shore Ct. E1 . . . . .4F 65
  (off Beaumont Sq.)
Peter's La.
  EC1 . . . . . .5E 9 (4D 63)
  (not continuous)
Peter's Path SE26 . . . . .4D 121
Peterstow Cl. SW19 . . . .2A 114
Petherton Cl. NW10 . . . .5F 43
  (off Tiverton Rd.)
Petherton Ho. N4 . . . . . .3E 35
  (off Woodberry Down Est.)
Petherton Rd. N5 . . . . . .2E 49
Petiver Cl. E9 . . . . .4E 51
Petley Rd. W6 . . . . .2F 85

Peto Pl. NW1 . . .3E 5 (3D 61)
Peto St. Nth. E16 . . . . . .5B 68
Petrie Cl. NW2 . . . . .3A 44
Petrie Mus. of
  Egyptian Archaeology
  . . . . .4B 6 (3F 61)
Petros Gdns. NW3 . . . . .3E 45
Petticoat La.
  E1 . . . . .1F 19 (4A 64)
Petticoat Lane Market
  . . . . .2F 19
  (off Middlesex St.)
Petticoat Sq.
  E1 . . . . . . .2F 19 (5B 64)
Petticoat Twr. E1 . . . . . .2F 19
Pettiward Cl. SW15 . . . .2E 99
Pett St. SE18 . . . . .5F 83
Petty France
  SW1 . . . . . .5A 22 (4E 75)
Petty Wales
  EC3 . . . . . .5E 19 (1A 78)
Petworth St. SW11 . . . . .4A 88
Petyt Pl. SW3 . . . . .2A 88
Petyward SW3 . . . . .5A 74
Pevensey Ct. SW16 . . . .3C 118
Pevensey Ho. E1 . . . . . . .4F 65
  (off Ben Jonson Rd.)
Pevensey Rd. E7 . . . . . . .1B 54
  SW17 . . . . .4F 115
Peveril Ho. SE1 . . . . . . .5C 26
Peyton Pl. SE10 . . . . . . .3E 95
Pharamond NW2 . . . . . .3F 43
Pheasant Cl. E16 . . . . . .5D 69
Pheasantry Ho. SW3 . . .1A 88
  (off Jubilee Pl.)
Phelp St. SE17 . . . . .2F 91
Phene St. SW3 . . . . .2A 88
Philadelphia Ct.
  SW10 . . . . .3E 87
  (off Uverdale Rd.)
Philbeach Gdns.
  SW5 . . . . .1C 86
Phil Brown Pl. SW8 . . . .1D 103
  (off Daley Thompson Way)
Philchurch Pl. E1 . . . . . .5C 64
Philia Ho. NW1 . . . . .4E 47
  (off Farrier St.)
Philip Ct. W2 . . . . .4F 59
  (off Hall Pl.)
Philip Ho. NW6 . . . . .5D 45
  (off Mortimer Pl.)
Philip Jones Ct. N4 . . . . .3B 34
Philip Mole Ho. W9 . . . .3C 58
  (off Chippenham Rd.)
Philippa Gdns. SE9 . . . .3F 111
Philip Sq. SW8 . . . . .5D 89
Philip St. E13 . . . . .3C 68
Philip Wlk. SE15 . . . . . .1C 106
  (not continuous)
Phillimore Ct. W8 . . . . . .3C 72
  (off Kensington High St.)
Phillimore Gdns.
  NW10 . . . . .5E 43
  W8 . . . . .3C 72
Phillimore Gdns. Cl.
  W8 . . . . .4C 72
Phillimore Pl. W8 . . . . . .3C 72
Phillimore Ter. W8 . . . . .4C 72
  (off Allen St.)
Phillimore Wlk. W8 . . . .4C 72

Phillip Ho. E1 . . . . .4B 64
(off Heneage St.)
Phillips St. N1 . . . . .5A 50
Philpot La.
EC3 . . . .4D 19 (1A 78)
Philpot St. SW6 . . . .1D 101
Philpot Sq. SW1 . . . . . .5D 65
Phineas Pett Rd.
SE9 . . . . .1F 111
Phipps Ho. SE7 . . . . . . .1D 97
(off Woolwich Rd.)
W12 . . . . .1D 71
(off White City Est.)
Phipp's M. SW1 . . . . . . .4D 75
(off Buckingham Palace Rd.)
Phipp St.
EC2 . . . . .3D 11 (3A 64)
Phoebeth Rd.
SE4 . . . . .3C 108
Phoebe Wlk. E16 . . . . . .5D 69
Phoenix Av. SE10 . . . . . .3A 82
Phoenix Cl. E8 . . . . .5B 50
W12 . . . . .1D 71
Phoenix Ct. E1 . . . . .3D 65
(off Buckhurst St.)
E14 . . . . .5C 80
NW1 . . . . .1C 6
(off Purchese St.)
SE14 . . . . .2A 94
(off Chipley St.)
Phoenix Hgts. E. E14 . . .3C 80
(off Byng St.)
Phoenix Hgts. W.
E14 . . . . .3C 80
(off Mastmaker Ct.)
Phoenix Lodge Mans.
W6 . . . . .5F 71
(off Brook Grn.)
Phoenix Pk. NW2 . . . . . .4C 28
Phoenix Pl.
WC1 . . . . . .3A 8 (3B 62)
Phoenix Rd.
NW1 . . . . . .1B 6 (2F 61)
Phoenix Sports & Fitness Cen.
. . . . .1C 70
Phoenix St.
WC2 . . . .3C 14 (5F 61)
Phoenix Theatre 3C 14
(off Charing Cross Rd.)
Phoenix Way SW18 . . .3E 101
Phoenix Wharf E1 . . . . .2D 79
(off Wapping High St.)
Phoenix Wharf Rd.
SE1 . . . . .4F 27
Phoenix Yd. WC1 . . . . . .2A 8
Photographers Gallery
. . . . .3F 13
(off Ramillies St.)
Phyllis Hodges Ho.
NW1 . . . . .1B 6
(off Aldenham St.)
Physic Pl. SW3 . . . . . . .2B 88
Piano La. N16 . . . . .5F 35
Piazza, The WC2 . . . . . .4E 15
(not continuous)
Piccadilly
W1 . . . . . .2E 21 (2D 75)
Piccadilly Arc. SW1 . . . .1F 21
Piccadilly Circus
. . . . .5B 14 (1F 75)

Piccadilly Cir.
W1 . . . . . .5B 14 (1F 75)
Piccadilly Ct. N7 . . . . . . .3B 48
(off Caledonian Rd.)
Piccadilly Pl. W1 . . . . . . .5A 14
Piccadilly Theatre 4A 14
(off Denman St.)
Pickard Gdns. E3 . . . . . .4B 66
Pickard St.
EC1 . . . . . .1E 9 (2D 63)
Pickering Cl. E9 . . . . . . .4F 51
Pickering Ho. W2 . . . . . .5E 59
(off Hallfield Est.)
Pickering M. W2 . . . . . . .5D 59
Pickering Pl. SW1 . . . . . .2A 22
Pickering St. N1 . . . . . . .5D 49
Picketts SW12 . . . . . . .5D 103
Picketts Ter. SE22 . . . . .3C 106
Pickfords Wharf
N1 . . . . .1E 63
SE1 . . . . .1B 26 (2F 77)
Pickwick Ho. SE16 . . . .3C 78
(off George Row)
W11 . . . . .2F 71
(off St Ann's Rd.)
Pickwick Rd. SE21 . . . . .5F 105
Pickwick St.
SE1 . . . . .4F 25 (3E 77)
Pickworth Cl. SW8 . . . . .3A 90
Picton Pl.
W1 . . . . . .3C 12 (5C 60)
Picton St. SE5 . . . . .3F 91
Picture Ho. SW16 . . . . .2A 118
Pied Bull Ct. WC1 . . . . .1D 15
(off Bury Pl.)
Pied Bull Yd. N1 . . . . . . .5D 49
(off Theberton St.)
WC1 . . . . .1D 15
Pier Head E1 . . . . .2D 79
(not continuous)
Pier Ho. SW3 . . . . .2A 88
Piermont Grn. SE22 . . . .3D 107
Piermont Rd. SE22 . . . .3D 107
Pierpoint Bldg. E14 . . . . .3B 80
Pierrepont Arc. N1 . . . . .1D 63
(off Islington High St.)
Pierrepont Row N1 . . . . .1D 63
(off Camden Pas.)
Pier St. E14 . . . . .5E 81
(not continuous)
Pier Ter. SW18 . . . . . . .2D 101
Pier Wlk. SE10 . . . . . . .3A 82
Pietra Lara Bldg. EC1 . . .3F 9
(off Pear Tree St.)
Piggott Ho. E2 . . . . .1F 65
(off Sewardstone Rd.)
Pigott St. E14 . . . . .5C 66
Pike Cl. BR1: Brom 5D 125
Pikemans Ct. SW5 . . . . .5C 72
(off W. Cromwell Rd.)
Pikethorne SE23 . . . . . .2F 121
Pilgrimage St.
SE1 . . . . . .4B 26 (3F 77)
Pilgrim Hill SE27 . . . . . .4E 119
Pilgrim Ho. SE1 . . . . . . .5C 26
(off Tabard St.)
SE16 . . . . .3E 79
(off Brunel Rd.)

Pilgrims Cloisters
SE5 . . . . .3A 92
(off Sedgmoor Pl.)
Pilgrims Cnr. NW6 . . . . .1C 58
(off Chichester Rd.)
Pilgrim's La. NW3 . . . . . .1F 45
Pilgrims M. E14 . . . . . . .1A 82
Pilgrim's Pl. NW3 . . . . . .1F 45
Pilgrim St.
EC4 . . . . . .3D 17 (5D 63)
Pilgrims Way N19 . . . . . .3F 33
Pilkington Rd. SE15 . . . .5D 93
Pillfold Ho. SE11 . . . . . . .5B 76
(off Old Paradise St.)
Pilot Cl. SE8 . . . . .2B 94
Pilot Ind. Cen. NW10 . . .3A 56
Pilsdon Cl. SW19 . . . . .1F 113
Pilton Pl. SE17 . . . . .1E 91
PIMLICO 1E 89
Pimlico Ho. SW1 . . . . . .1D 89
(off Ebury Bri. Rd.)
Pimlico Rd. SW1 . . . . . .1C 88
Pimlico Wlk. N1 . . . . . . .1D 11
Pinchin & Johnsons Yd.
E1 . . . . .1C 78
(off Pinchin St.)
Pinchin St. E1 . . . . .1C 78
Pincombe Ho. SE17 . . . .1F 91
(off Orb St.)
Pincott Pl. SE4 . . . . .1F 107
Pindar St.
EC2 . . . . . .5D 11 (4A 64)
Pindock M. W9 . . . . .3D 59
Pineapple Ct. SW1 . . . . .5A 22
Pine Av. E15 . . . . .2F 53
Pine Cl. E10 . . . . .4D 39
N19 . . . . .4E 33
Pinedene SE15 . . . . .4D 93
Pinefield Cl. E14 . . . . . . .1C 80
Pine Gro. N4 . . . . .4A 34
SW19 . . . . .5B 114
Pine Ho. E3 . . . . .5A 52
(off Barge La.)
SE16 . . . . .3E 79
(off Ainsty Est.)
W10 . . . . .3A 58
(off Droop St.)
Pinehurst Ct. W11 . . . . . .5B 58
(off Colville Gdns.)
Pinemartin Cl. NW2 . . . .5E 29
Pine M. NW10 . . . . .1F 57
(off Clifford Gdns.)
Pine Rd. NW2 . . . . .1E 43
Pine St. EC1 . . . . .3C 8 (3C 62)
Pine Tree Way
SE13 . . . . .1D 109
Pinewood Cl. SW4 . . . . .4F 103
Pinfold Rd. SW16 . . . . .4A 118
Pinkerton Pl.
SW16 . . . . .4F 117
Pinnace Ho. E14 . . . . . . .4E 81
(off Manchester Rd.)
Pinnacle Way E14 . . . . .5A 66
(off Commercial Rd.)
Pinnell Rd. SE9 . . . . . . .2F 111
Pinner Ct. NW8 . . . . . . .3F 59
(off St John's Wood Rd.)
Pinners Pas. EC2 . . . . . .2C 18
(off Austin Friars)
Pintail Cl. E6 . . . . .4F 69

Pintail Ct. *SE8* 2B **94**
   (off Pilot Cl.)
Pinter Ho. *SW9* 5A **90**
   (off Grantham Rd.)
Pinto Way *SE3* 2D **111**
Pioneer Centre, The
   SE15 ....4E **93**
Pioneer Cl. *E14* 4D **67**
Pioneer Ho. *WC1* 1F **7**
   (off Britannia St.)
Pioneer St. *SE15* 4C **92**
Pioneer Way *W12* 5D **57**
Piper Building, The
   SW6 ....1D **101**
Piper Cl. *N7* 2B **48**
Pipers Ho. *SE10* 1F **95**
   (off Collington St.)
Pippin Cl. *NW2* 5C **28**
Pippin Ct. *SW8* 2B **90**
   (off Vauxhall St.)
Pippin Ho. *W10* 1F **71**
   (off Freston Rd.)
Pirbright Rd. *SW18* 1B **114**
Pirie Cl. *SE5* 1F **105**
Pirie St. *E16* 2D **83**
Pissaro Ho. *N1* 4C **48**
   (off Augustas La.)
Pitcairn Ho. *E9* 4E **51**
Pitchford St. *E15* 4F **53**
Pitfield Est.
   N1 ....1D **11** (2A **64**)
Pitfield St.
   N1 ....1D **11** (2A **64**)
Pitfold Cl. *SE12* 4D **111**
Pitfold Rd. *SE12* 4C **110**
Pitlochry Ho. *SE27* 2D **119**
   (off Elmcourt Rd.)
Pitman Ho. *SE8* 4C **94**
Pitman St. *SE5* 3E **91**
Pitmaston Ho. *SE13* 5E **95**
   (off Lewisham Rd.)
Pitsea Pl. *E1* 5F **65**
Pitsea St. *E1* 5F **65**
Pitt Cres. *SW19* 4D **115**
Pitt's Head M.
   W1 ....2C **20** (2C **74**)
Pitt St. *W8* 3C **72**
Pixley St. *E14* 5B **66**
Place, The *E2* 2F **61**
Plaisterers Highwalk
   EC2 ....1F **17**
   (off London Wall)
PLAISTOW 1C **68**
Plaistow Gro. *E15* 5B **54**
Plaistow Pk. Rd. *E13* ...1D **69**
   (not continuous)
Plaistow Rd. *E13* 5B **54**
   E15 ....5B **54**
Plaistow Wharf *E16* 3C **82**
Plane St. *SE26* 3D **121**
Planetarium
   Greenwich 3F **95**
Planetree Ct. *W6* 5F **71**
   (off Brook Grn.)
Plane Tree Ho. *SE8* 2A **94**
   (off Etta St.)
   W8 ....3B **72**
   (off Duchess of Bedford's Wlk.)
Plane Tree Wlk.
   SE19 ....5A **120**

Plantain Gdns. *E11* 5F **39**
   (off Hollydown Way)
Plantain Pl.
   SE1 ....3B **26** (3F **77**)
Plantation, The *SE3* 5C **96**
Plantation Cl. *SW4* 3A **104**
Plantation La. *EC3* 4D **19**
Plantation Pl. *EC3* 4D **19**
Plantation Wharf
   SW11 ....1E **101**
Plasel Ct. *E13* 5D **55**
   (off Pawsey Cl.)
PLASHET 3F **55**
Plashet Gro. *E6* 5E **55**
Plashet Rd. *E13* 5C **54**
Plassy Rd. *SE6* 5D **109**
Plate Ho. *E14* 1D **95**
   (off Burrells Wharf Sq.)
Platina St. *EC2* 3C **10**
Platinum Ct. *E1* 3E **65**
   (off Cephas Av.)
Platinum M. *N15* 1B **36**
Plato Rd. *SW2* 2A **104**
Platt, The *SW15* 1F **99**
Platt's La. *NW3* 1C **44**
Platt St. *NW1* 1F **61**
Plaxdale Ho. *SE17* 5A **78**
   (off Congreve St.)
Plaxton Ct. *E11* 5B **40**
Playfair Ho. *E14* 5C **66**
   (off Saracen St.)
Playfair Mans. *W14* 2A **86**
   (off Queen's Club Gdns.)
Playfair St. *W6* 1E **85**
Playfield Cres.
   SE22 ....3B **106**
Playford Rd. *N4* 4B **34**
   (not continuous)
Playgreen Way *SE6* 3C **122**
Playhouse Ct. *SE1* 3F **25**
   (off Southwark Bri. Rd.)
Playhouse Theatre 1E **23**
   (off Northumberland Av.)
Playhouse Yd.
   EC4 ....3D **17** (5D **63**)
Plaza Hgts. *E10* 5E **39**
Plaza Pde. *NW6* 1D **59**
Plaza Shop. Centre, The
   W1 ....2A **14** (5E **61**)
Pleasance, The
   SW15 ....2D **99**
Pleasance Rd. *SW15* 3D **99**
Pleasance Theatre 3A **48**
   (off Carpenters M.)
Pleasant Pl. *N1* 4D **49**
Pleasant Row *NW1* 5D **47**
Pleasaunce Mans.
   SE10 ....1C **96**
   (off Halstow Rd.)
Plender Ct. *NW1* 5E **47**
   (off College Pl.)
Plender St. *NW1* 5E **47**
Pleshey Rd. *N7* 1F **47**
Plessey Bldg. *E14* 5C **66**
   (off Dod St.)
Plevna Cres. *N15* 1A **36**
Plevna St. *E14* 4E **81**
Pleydell Av. *W6* 5B **70**
Pleydell Ct. *EC4* 3C **16**
   (off Pleydell St.)

Pleydell Est. *EC1* 2A **10**
Pleydell St. *EC4* 3C **16**
Plimley Pl. *W12* 3F **71**
   (off Shepherd's Bush Pl.)
Plimsoll Cl. *E14* 5D **67**
Plimsoll Rd. *N4* 5C **34**
Plough Cl. *NW10* 2D **57**
Plough Ct.
   EC3 ....4C **18** (1F **77**)
Plough La. *SE22* 4B **106**
   SW17 ....5D **115**
   SW19 ....5D **115**
Ploughmans Cl. *NW1* 5F **47**
Plough M. *SW11* 2F **101**
Plough Pl.
   EC4 ....2C **16** (5C **62**)
Plough Rd. *SW11* 1F **101**
Plough St. *E1* 5B **64**
   (off Buckle St.)
Plough Ter. *SW11* 2F **101**
Plough Way *SE16* 5F **79**
Plough Yd.
   EC2 ....4E **11** (3A **64**)
Plover Ho. *SW9* 3C **90**
   (off Brixton Rd.)
Plover Way *SE16* 4A **80**
Plowden Bldgs. *EC4* 4B **16**
Plumber's Row *E1* 4C **64**
Plumbridge St. *SE10* 4E **95**
Plume Ho. *SE10* 2D **95**
   (off Creek Rd.)
Plummer Rd. *SW4* 5F **103**
Plumtree Ct.
   EC4 ....2D **17** (5D **63**)
Plymouth Ho. *SE10* 4D **95**
   (off Devonshire Dr.)
Plymouth Rd. *E16* 4C **68**
Plymouth Ter. *NW2* 3E **43**
   (off Glengall Rd.)
Plymouth Wharf *E14* 5F **81**
Plympton Av. *NW6* 4B **44**
Plympton Pl. *NW8* 3A **60**
Plympton Rd. *NW6* 4B **44**
Plympton St. *NW8* 3A **60**
Pocklington Cl. *W12* 4C **70**
   (off Ashchurch Pk. Vs.)
Pocklington Ct.
   SW15 ....1C **112**
Pocklington Lodge
   W12 ....4C **70**
Pocock St.
   SE1 ....3D **25** (3D **77**)
Podmore Rd. *SW18* 2E **101**
Poet's Rd. *N5* 2F **49**
Point, The *W2* 5F **59**
   (off Nth. Wharf Rd.)
Point Cl. *SE10* 4E **95**
Pointers Cl. *E14* 1D **95**
Point Hill *SE10* 3E **95**
Point Pleasant
   SW18 ....2C **100**
Point Ter. *E7* 2D **55**
   (off Claremont Rd.)
Point West *SW7* 5D **73**
Poland Ho. *E15* 5F **53**
   (off High St.)
Poland St.
   W1 ....3A **14** (5E **61**)
Polebrook Rd. *SE3* 1E **111**
Polecroft La. *SE6* 2B **122**

Polesworth Ho. W2 . . . .4C **58**
   (off Alfred Rd.)
Pollard Cl. E16 . . . . .1C **82**
N7 . . . . .1B **48**
Pollard Ho. N1 . . . . .1F **7**
   (off Northdown St.)
SE16 . . . . .4B **78**
   (off Spa Rd.)
Pollard Row E2 . . . . . . .2C **64**
Pollard St. E2 . . . . .2C **64**
Pollen St.
   W1 . . . . .3F **13** (5E **61**)
Pollitt Dr. NW8 . . . . . . .3F **59**
Pollock Ho. W10 . . . . .3A **58**
   (off Kensal Rd.)
Pollock's Toy Mus.
   . . . . .5A **6** (4E **61**)
Polperro Ho. W2 . . . . . .4C **58**
   (off Westbourne Pk. Rd.)
Polperro M. SE11 . . . . . .5D **77**
Polsted Rd. SE6 . . . . . .5B **108**
Polworth Rd. SW16 . . . .5A **118**
Polychrome Ct. SE1 . . . .4D **25**
   (off Waterloo Rd.)
Polygon, The NW8 . . . .5F **45**
   (off Avenue Rd.)
SW4 . . . . .2E **103**
Polygon Rd.
   NW1 . . . . . .1B **6** (1F **61**)
   (not continuous)
Pomell Way
   E1 . . . . . . .2F **19** (5B **64**)
Pomeroy Ho. E2 . . . . . .1F **65**
   (off St James's Av.)
W11 . . . . .5A **58**
   (off Lancaster Rd.)
Pomeroy St. SE14 . . . . .3E **93**
Pomfret Rd. SE5 . . . . . .1D **105**
Pomoja La. N19 . . . . . .4A **34**
Pomona Ho. SE8 . . . . .5A **80**
   (off Evelyn St.)
Pond Cl. SE3 . . . . .5C **96**
Pond Cotts. SE21 . . . . .1A **120**
Ponder St. N7 . . . . .4B **48**
Pond Farm Est. E5 . . . . .5E **37**
Pondfield Ho. SE27 . . . .5E **119**
Pond Ho. SW3 . . . . . . .5A **74**
Pond Mead SE21 . . . . .4F **105**
Pond Pl. SW3 . . . . .5A **74**
Pond Rd. E15 . . . . .1A **68**
SE3 . . . . .5B **96**
Pond Sq. N6 . . . . .3C **32**
Pond St. NW3 . . . . .2A **46**
Ponler St. E1 . . . . .5D **65**
Ponsard Rd. NW10 . . . . .2D **57**
Ponsford St. E9 . . . . . . .3E **51**
Ponsonby Ho. E2 . . . . . .1E **65**
   (off Bishop's Way,
   not continuous)
Ponsonby Pl. SW1 . . . . .1F **89**
Ponsonby Rd. SW15 . . . .5D **99**
Ponsonby Ter. SW1 . . . .1F **89**
Pontefract Rd.
   BR1: Brom 5B **124**
Ponton Rd. SW8 . . . . . .3F **89**
Pont St. SW1 . . . .5A **20** (4B **74**)
Pont St. M.
   SW1 . . . .5A **20** (4B **74**)
Pontypool Pl.
   SE1 . . . . . .3D **25** (3D **77**)

Pooja Ct. NW1 . . . . .4E **47**
   (off Agar Gro.)
Pool Cl. BR3: Beck 5C **122**
Pool Ct. SE6 . . . . .2C **122**
Poole Cl. N1 . . . . .4A **50**
   (off St Peter's Way)
Poole Ho. SE11 . . . . . . .4C **76**
   (off Lambeth Wlk.)
Poole Rd. E9 . . . . .3F **51**
Pooles Bldgs. WC1 . . . . .4B **8**
Pooles La. SW10 . . . . . .3E **87**
Pooles Pk. N4 . . . . .4C **34**
Poole St. N1 . . . . .5F **49**
Pooley Ho. E1 . . . . .2F **65**
Pool Ho. NW8 . . . . .4F **59**
   (off Penfold St.)
Poolmans St. SE16 . . . . .3F **79**
Poonah St. E1 . . . . .5E **65**
Pope Ho. SE5 . . . . .3F **91**
   (off Elmington St.)
SE16 . . . . .5D **79**
   (off Manor Est.)
Pope's Head All.
   EC3 . . . . .3C **18** (5F **63**)
Pope's Rd. SW9 . . . . . .1C **104**
Pope St. SE1 . . . .4E **27** (3A **78**)
Popham Rd. N1 . . . . . . .5E **49**
Popham St. N1 . . . . .5D **49**
   (not continuous)
POPLAR 1D **81**
Poplar Bath St. E14 . . . . .5D **67**
Poplar Bus. Pk. E14 . . . . .1E **81**
Poplar Cl. E9 . . . . .2B **52**
Poplar Ct. SW19 . . . . . .5C **114**
Poplar Gro. W6 . . . . . . .3E **71**
Poplar High St. E14 . . . . .1D **81**
Poplar Ho. SE4 . . . . . . .2B **108**
   (off Wickham Rd.)
SE16 . . . . .3F **79**
   (off Woodland Cres.)
Poplar M. W12 . . . . .2E **71**
Poplar Pl. W2 . . . . .1D **73**
Poplar Rd. SE24 . . . . . .2E **105**
Poplars Av. NW2 . . . . . .3E **43**
Poplars Rd. E17 . . . . . . .1D **39**
Poplar Wlk. SE24 . . . . . .1E **105**
   (not continuous)
Poppins Ct.
   EC4 . . . . .3D **17** (5D **63**)
Poppleton Rd. E11 . . . . .1A **40**
Porchester Cl. SE5 . . . . .2E **105**
Porchester Ct. W2 . . . . . .1D **73**
   (off Porchester Gdns.)
Porchester Gdns. W2 . . . .1D **73**
Porchester Gdns. M.
   W2 . . . . .5D **59**
Porchester Ga. W2 . . . . . .1D **73**
   (off Bayswater Rd.,
   not continuous)
Porchester Ho. E1 . . . . . .5D **65**
   (off Philpot St.)
Porchester Leisure Cen.
   . . . . .5D **59**
Porchester Mead
   BR3: Beck 5D **123**
Porchester Pl. W2 . . . . . .5A **60**
Porchester Rd. W2 . . . . . .5D **59**
Porchester Sq. W2 . . . . . .5D **59**
Porchester Sq. M.
   W2 . . . . .5D **59**

Porchester Ter. W2 . . . . . .1E **73**
Porchester Ter. Nth.
   W2 . . . . .5D **59**
Porchester Wlk. W2 . . . .5D **59**
   (off Porchester Ter. Nth.)
Porden Rd. SW2 . . . . . .2B **104**
Porlock Ho. SE26 . . . . . .3C **120**
Porlock St.
   SE1 . . . . . .3C **26** (3F **77**)
Porson Ct. SE13 . . . . . . .1D **109**
Portal Cl. SE27 . . . . .3C **118**
Portal Way W3 . . . . .4A **56**
Portbury Cl. SE15 . . . . . .4C **92**
Port Cres. E13 . . . . .3D **69**
Portcullis Ho. SW1 . . . . .4D **23**
Port E. Apartments
   E14 . . . . .1C **80**
   (off Hertsmere Rd.)
Portelet Ct. N1 . . . . .5A **50**
   (off De Beauvoir Est.)
Portelet Rd. E1 . . . . .2F **65**
Porten Ho's. W14 . . . . . .4A **72**
   (off Porten Rd.)
Porten Rd. W14 . . . . . . .4A **72**
Porters Lodge, The
   SW10 . . . . .3E **87**
   (off Coleridge Gdns.)
Porter Sq. N19 . . . . .3A **34**
Porter St.
   SE1 . . . . . .1A **26** (2E **77**)
   W1 . . . . . .5A **4** (4B **60**)
Porters Wlk. E1 . . . . .1D **79**
   (off Tobacco Dock)
Porteus Rd. W2 . . . . . . .4E **59**
Portgate Cl. W9 . . . . .3B **58**
Porthcawe Rd. SE26 . . . .4A **122**
Port Ho. E14 . . . . .1D **95**
   (off Burrells Wharf Sq.)
Portia Ct. SE11 . . . . .1D **91**
   (off Opal St.)
Portia Way E3 . . . . .3B **66**
Porticos, The SW3 . . . . . .2F **87**
   (off King's Rd.)
Portinscale Rd.
   SW15 . . . . .3A **100**
Portishead Ho.
   W2 . . . . .4C **58**
   (off Westbourne Pk. Rd.)
Portland Av. N16 . . . . . . .2B **36**
Portland Ct. N1 . . . . .4A **50**
   (off St Peter's Way)
SE1 . . . . .5B **26**
   (off Gt. Dover St.)
SE14 . . . . .2A **94**
   (off Whitcher Cl.)
Portland Cres.
   SE9 . . . . .2F **125**
Portland Gdns. N4 . . . . . .1D **35**
Portland Gro. SW8 . . . . . .4B **90**
Portland Ho. SW1 . . . . . .5F **21**
   SW15 . . . . .3F **99**
Portland Mans.
   W14 . . . . .5B **72**
   (off Addison Bri. Pl.)
Portland M.
   W1 . . . . . .3A **14** (5E **61**)
Portland Pl.
   W1 . . . . . .4D **5** (4D **61**)
Portland Ri. N4 . . . . .3D **35**
   (not continuous)

Portland Rd.
  BR1: Brom 4E **125**
  SE9 ....2F **125**
  W11 ....1A **72**
Portland Sq. E1 ....2D **79**
Portland St. SE17 .....1F **91**
Portland Wlk.
  SE17 ....2F **91**
Portman Av. SW14 ...1A **98**
Portman Cl.
  W1 ......2A **12** (5B **60**)
Portman Ga. NW1 .....3A **60**
Portman Mans. W1 .....5A **4**
      (off Chiltern St.)
Portman M. Sth.
  W1 ......3B **12** (5C **60**)
Portman Pl. E2 ....2E **65**
Portman Sq.
  W1 ......2B **12** (5C **60**)
Portman St.
  W1 ......3B **12** (5C **60**)
Portman Towers
  W1 ......2A **12** (5B **60**)
Portmeers Cl. E17 ....1B **38**
Portnall Ho. W9 ......2B **58**
      (off Portnall Rd.)
Portnall Rd. W9 ......1B **58**
Portobello Ct. Est.
  W11 ....5B **58**
Portobello Grn. W10 ..4A **58**
      (off Portobello Rd.)
Portobello M. W11 ....1C **72**
Portobello Rd. W10 ...4A **58**
  W11 ....5B **58**
Portobello Road Market
  ....1B **72**
      (off Portobello Rd.)
Portpool La.
  EC1 ......5B **8** (4C **62**)
Portree St. E14 ......5F **67**
Portsdown Av. NW11 ..1B **30**
Portsdown M. NW11 ...1B **30**
Portsea Hall W2 ......5B **60**
      (off Portsea Pl.)
Portsea M. W2 ....5A **60**
      (off Portsea Pl.)
Portsea Pl. W2 ....5A **60**
Portslade Rd. SW8 ....5E **89**
Portsmouth M. E16 ...2D **83**
Portsmouth Rd.
  SW15 ....5D **99**
Portsmouth St.
  WC2 ......3F **15** (5B **62**)
Portsoken St.
  E1 ......4F **19** (1B **78**)
Portswood Pl. SW15 ..4B **98**
Portugal St.
  WC2 ......3F **15** (5B **62**)
Portway E15 ....5B **54**
Portway Gdns. SE18 ..3F **97**
Pory Ho. SE11 ....5A **76**
Poseidon Ct. E14 .....5C **80**
      (off Homer Dr.)
POSK 5C **70**
      (off King St.)
Postern, The EC2 .....1A **18**
Post Office App. E7 ...2D **55**
Post Office Ct. EC3 ...3C **18**
      (off King William St.)
Post Office Way SW8 ..3F **89**

Potier St.
  SE1 ......5C **26** (4F **77**)
Potter Cl. SE15 ......3A **92**
Potterne Cl. SW19 ....5F **99**
Potters Flds.
  SE1 ......2E **27** (2A **78**)
Potters Lodge E14 .....1E **95**
      (off Manchester Rd.)
Potters Rd. SW6 .....5E **87**
Pottery La. W11 ......2A **72**
Pottery St. SE16 .....3D **79**
Pott St. E2 ....2D **65**
Poulton Cl. E8 ....3D **51**
Poulton Ho. W3 ......4A **56**
      (off Victoria Rd.)
Poultry EC2 ......3B **18** (5F **63**)
Pound La. NW10 .....3C **42**
Pound Pk. Rd. SE7 ...5F **83**
Pountney Rd. SW11 ...1C **102**
Povey Ho. SE17 ......5A **78**
      (off Beckway St.)
Powell Ho. W2 ....1F **73**
      (off Gloucester Ter.)
Powell Rd. E5 ....5D **37**
Powell's Wlk. W4 .....2A **84**
Powergate Bus. Pk.
  NW10 ....2A **56**
Powerleague
  Catford 1C **122**
Powerscroft Rd. E5 ...1E **51**
Powis Ct. W11 ....5B **58**
      (off Powis Gdns.)
Powis Gdns. NW11 ...2B **30**
  W11 ....5B **58**
Powis Ho. WC2 ......2E **15**
      (off Macklin St.)
Powis M. W11 ....5B **58**
Powis Pl.
  WC1 ......4E **7** (3A **62**)
Powis Rd. E3 ....2D **67**
Powis Sq. W11 ....5B **58**
      (not continuous)
Powis Ter. W11 ......5B **58**
Powlesland Ct. E1 ....5A **66**
      (off White Horse Rd.)
Powlett Ho. NW1 .....3D **47**
      (off Powlett Pl.)
Powlett Pl. NW1 .....4C **46**
Pownall Rd. E8 ......5B **50**
Powster Rd.
  BR1: Brom 5C **124**
Poynders Ct. SW4 ....4E **103**
Poynders Gdns.
  SW4 ....5E **103**
Poynders Rd. SW4 ...4E **103**
Poynings Rd. N19 ....5E **33**
Poynter Ho. NW8 .....3F **59**
      (off Fisherton St.)
  W11 ....2F **71**
      (off Queensdale Cres.)
Poyntz Rd. SW11 .....5B **88**
Poyser St. E2 ....1D **65**
Praed M. W2 ....5F **59**
Praed St. E13 ....1E **69**
Pragnell Rd. SE12 ....2D **125**
Prague Pl. SW2 ......3A **104**
Prah Rd. N4 ....4C **34**
Prairie St. SW8 ......5C **88**

Praline Ct. E3 ....1D **67**
      (off Taylor Pl.)
Pratt M. NW1 ....5E **47**
Pratt St. NW1 ....5E **47**
Pratt Wlk. SE11 ......5B **76**
Prayle Gro. NW2 .....3F **29**
Preachers Ct. EC1 .....5E **9**
      (off Charterhouse Sq.)
Prebend Gdns. W4 ...5B **70**
  W6 ....5B **70**
      (not continuous)
Prebend Mans.
  W4 ....5B **70**
      (off Chiswick High Rd.)
Prebend St. N1 ......5E **49**
Precinct, The N1 .....5E **49**
      (not continuous)
Premier Cinema 5C **92**
Premier Cnr. W9 .....1B **58**
Premiere Pl. E14 .....1C **80**
Premier Ho. N1 ......4D **49**
      (off Waterloo Ter.)
Premier Pl. SW15 ....2A **100**
Prendergast Rd.
  SE3 ....1A **110**
Prentice Ct. SW19 ....5B **114**
Prentis Rd. SW16 ....4F **117**
Prentiss Ct. SE7 .....5F **83**
Presburg Rd. E3 .....5F **37**
Presburg St. E5 .....5F **37**
Prescot St. E1 ....1B **78**
Prescott Ho. SE17 ....2D **91**
      (off Hillingdon St.)
Prescott Pl. SW4 .....1F **103**
Presentation M.
  SW2 ....2B **118**
President Dr. E1 ......2D **79**
President Ho.
  EC1 ......2E **9** (2D **63**)
President Quay E1 ....2B **78**
      (off St Katherine's Way)
President St. EC1 .....1F **9**
Press Ct. SE1 ....1C **92**
Press Ho. NW10 .....5A **28**
Press Rd. NW10 .....5A **28**
Prestage Way E14 ....1E **81**
Prestbury Rd. E7 .....4E **55**
Prested Rd. SW11 ....2A **102**
Preston Cl. SE1 ......5A **78**
Preston Dr. E11 ......1E **41**
Preston Gdns. NW10 ..3B **42**
Preston Ho. SE1 .....5A **78**
      (off Preston Cl.)
  SE1 ....5F **27**
      (off St Saviour's Est.)
Preston Rd. NW2 .....3C **42**
Preston Rd. E11 ......1A **40**
  SE19 ....5D **119**
Preston's Rd. E14 ....1E **81**
Preston St. E2 ....1F **65**
Prestwich Ter. SW4 ...3E **103**
Prestwood Ho. SE16 ..4D **79**
      (off Drummond Rd.)
Prestwood St.
  N1 ....1A **10** (1E **63**)
Pretoria Rd. E11 .....3F **39**
  E16 ....3B **68**
  SW16 ....5D **117**
Priam Ho. E2 ....1D **65**
      (off Old Bethnal Grn. Rd.)
Price Cl. SW17 ......3B **116**

Price Ho. *N1* 5E **49**
(off Britannia Row)
Price's Ct. SW11 . . . . .1F **101**
Price's M. N1 . . . . .5B **48**
Price's St.
SE1 . . . . . .2E **25** (2D **77**)
Prichard Ct. N7 . . . . . . .3B **48**
Prichard Ho. SE11 . . . .5C **76**
(off Kennington Rd.)
Prideaux Ho. WC1 . . . . .1A **8**
(off Prideaux Pl.)
Prideaux Pl. W3 . . . . . .1A **70**
WC1 . . . . . .1A **8** (2B **62**)
Prideaux Rd. SW9 . . . .1A **104**
Priestfield Rd. SE23 . . .3A **122**
Priestley Cl. N16 . . . . . .2B **36**
Priestley Ho. EC1 . . . . . .3A **10**
(off Old St.)
Priestley Way NW2 . . . . .3C **28**
Priestman Point E3 . . . .2D **67**
(off Rainhill Way)
Priests Bri. SW14 . . . . .1A **98**
SW15 . . . . .1A **98**
Priest's Ct. EC2 . . . . . . .2F **17**
Prima Rd. SW9 . . . . .3C **90**
Prime Meridian Line . . .3F **95**
Prime Meridian Wlk.
E14 . . . . .1F **81**
Primezone M. N8 . . . . . .1A **34**
Primrose Cl. E3 . . . . . . .1C **66**
SE6 . . . . .5E **123**
Primrose Ct. *NW8* 1B **60**
(off Prince Albert Rd.)
SW12 . . . . .5F **103**
Primrose Gdns. NW3 . . . .3A **46**
PRIMROSE HILL 5C **46**
Primrose Hill
EC4 . . . . .3C **16** (5C **62**)
Primrose Hill Ct.
NW3 . . . . .4B **46**
Primrose Hill Rd.
NW3 . . . . .4B **46**
Primrose Hill Studios
NW1 . . . . .5C **46**
Primrose Ho. SE15 . . . .4C **92**
(off Peckham Hill St.)
Primrose Mans.
SW11 . . . . .4C **88**
Primrose M. NW1 . . . . . .4B **46**
(off Sharpleshall St.)
SE3 . . . . .3C **96**
Primrose Rd. E10 . . . . . .3D **39**
Primrose Sq. E9 . . . . . . .4E **51**
Primrose St.
EC2 . . . . .5D **11** (4A **64**)
Primrose Wlk. SE14 . . . .3A **94**
Primula St. W12 . . . . . . .5C **56**
Prince Albert Ct.
NW8 . . . . .5B **46**
(off Prince Albert Rd.)
Prince Albert Rd.
NW1 . . . . .2A **60**
NW8 . . . . .2A **60**
Prince Arthur M.
NW3 . . . . .1E **45**
Prince Arthur Rd.
NW3 . . . . .2E **45**
Prince Charles Cinema
. . . . .4C **14**
(off Leicester Pl.)

Prince Charles Dr.
NW4 . . . . .2E **29**
Prince Charles Rd.
SE3 . . . . .5B **96**
Prince Consort Rd.
SW7 . . . . .4E **73**
Princedale Rd. W11 . . . .2A **72**
Prince Edward Mans.
W2 . . . . .1C **72**
(off Moscow Rd.)
Prince Edward Rd.
E9 . . . . .3B **52**
Prince Edward Theatre
. . . . .3C **14**
(off Old Compton St.)
Prince George Rd.
N16 . . . . .1A **50**
Prince Henry Rd. SE7 . .3F **97**
Prince John Rd.
SE9 . . . . .3F **111**
Princelet St.
E1 . . . . . .5F **11** (4B **64**)
Prince of Orange Ct.
SE16 . . . . .4E **79**
(off Lower Rd.)
Prince of Orange La.
SE10 . . . . .3E **95**
Prince of Wales Dr.
SW8 . . . . .3D **89**
SW11 . . . . .4A **88**
Prince of Wales Mans.
SW11 . . . . .4C **88**
Prince of Wales Pas.
NW1 . . . . .2F **5**
Prince of Wales Rd.
E16 . . . . .5E **69**
NW5 . . . . .3C **46**
SE3 . . . . .5B **96**
Prince of Wales Ter.
W4 . . . . .1A **84**
W8 . . . . .3D **73**
Prince of Wales Theatre
. . . . .5B **14**
(off Coventry St.)
Prince Regent Ct.
NW8 . . . . .1A **60**
(off Avenue Rd.)
SE16 . . . . .1A **80**
(off Edward Sq.)
Prince Regent La.
E13 . . . . .2D **69**
E16 . . . . .2D **69**
Prince Regent M.
NW1 . . . . .2F **5**
Princes Arc. SW1 . . . . .1A **22**
Princes Cir.
WC2 . . . . .2D **15** (5A **62**)
Princes Cl. N4 . . . . .3D **35**
SW4 . . . . .1E **103**
Prince's Ct. SE16 . . . . . .4B **80**
SW3 . . . . .4B **74**
(off Brompton Sq.)
Princes Ct. Bus. Cen.
E1 . . . . .1D **79**
Prince's Gdns. SW7 . . . .4F **73**
Prince's Ga. SW7 . . . . . .3F **73**
(not continuous)
Prince's Ga. Ct. SW7 . . .3F **73**
Prince's Ga. M. SW7 . . .4F **73**
Princes Ho. W11 . . . . . .1B **72**

Princes M. W2 . . . . .1D **73**
W6 . . . . .1D **73**
(off Down Pl.)
Princes Pde. NW11 . . . .1A **30**
(off Golders Grn. Rd.)
Princes Pk. Av.
NW11 . . . . .1A **30**
Princes Pl. SW1 . . . . . . .1A **22**
W11 . . . . .2A **72**
Prince's Ri. SE13 . . . . . .5E **95**
Princes Riverside Rd.
SE16 . . . . .2F **79**
Princes Rd. SW14 . . . . .1A **98**
SW19 . . . . .5C **114**
Princess Alice Ho.
W10 . . . . .3E **57**
Princess Ct. N6 . . . . .2E **33**
NW6 . . . . .3D **45**
(off Compayne Gdns.)
W1 . . . . .4B **60**
(off Bryanston Pl.)
W2 . . . . .1D **73**
(off Queensway)
Princess Cres. N4 . . . . .4D **35**
Princess Louise Bldg.
SE8 . . . . .3C **94**
(off Hales St.)
Princess Louise Cl.
W2 . . . . .4F **59**
Princess Mary Ho.
SW1 . . . . .5F **75**
(off Vincent St.)
Princess May Rd.
N16 . . . . .1A **50**
Princess M. NW3 . . . . . .2F **45**
Princess of Wales
Memorial Fountain
. . . . .3F **73**
Princes Sq. W2 . . . . .1D **73**
(not continuous)
Princes Rd. NW1 . . . . . .5C **46**
NW6 . . . . .1C **58**
Princess St.
SE1 . . . . . .5E **25** (4D **77**)
Princes St.
EC2 . . . . . .3B **18** (5F **63**)
W1 . . . . . . .3E **13** (5D **61**)
Princes Ter. E13 . . . . . . .5D **55**
Prince's Twr. SE16 . . . . .2E **79**
(off Elephant La.)
Prince St. SE8 . . . . .2B **94**
Princes Way SW19 . . . . .5F **99**
Prince's Yd. W11 . . . . . .2A **72**
Princethorpe Ho. *W2* . .4D **59**
(off Woodchester Sq.)
Princethorpe Rd.
SE26 . . . . .4F **121**
Princeton Ct. SW15 . . . .1F **99**
Princeton St.
WC1 . . . . . .1F **15** (4B **62**)
Principal Sq. E9 . . . . . . .2F **51**
Pringle Gdns. SW16 . . . .4E **117**
(not continuous)
Printers Inn Ct. EC4 . . . .5C **62**
Printers M. E3 . . . . .5A **52**
Printers Rd. SW9 . . . . . .4B **90**
Printer St.
EC4 . . . . .2C **16** (5C **62**)
Printing Ho. Yd.
E2 . . . . .1E **11** (2A **64**)

Printon Ho. *E14* 4B **66**
  (off Wallwood St.)
Print Room, The 5C **58**
  (off Hereford Rd.)
Print Village *SE15* 5B **92**
Printwork Apartments
  SE1 . . . . .5D **27**
  (off Long La.)
  SE5 . . . . .5E **91**
  (off Coldharbour La.)
Priolo Rd. *SE7* 1E **97**
Prior Bolton St. *N1* 3D **49**
Prioress Ho. *E3* 2D **67**
  (off Bromley High St.)
Prioress Rd. *SE27* 3D **119**
Prioress St.
  SE1 . . . . .5C **26** (4A **78**)
Prior St. *SE10* 3E **95**
Priory, The *SE3* 2B **110**
Priory Apartments, The
  SE6 . . . . .1D **123**
Priory Av. *W4* 5A **70**
Priory Ct. *E6* 5E **55**
  E9 . . . . .2F **51**
  EC4 . . . . .3E **17**
  (off Pilgrim St.)
  SW8 . . . . .4F **89**
Priory Gdns. *N6* 1D **33**
  SW13 . . . . .1B **98**
  W4 . . . . .5A **70**
Priory Grn. *N1* 1B **62**
Priory Grn. Est. *N1* 1B **62**
Priory Gro. *SW8* 4A **90**
Priory Hgts. *N1* 1B **62**
  (off Wynford St.)
Priory Ho. *E1* 5F **11**
  (off Folgate St.)
  EC1 . . . . .3D **9**
  (off Sans Wlk.)
  SW1 . . . . .1F **89**
  (off Rampayne St.)
Priory La. *SW15* 4A **98**
Priory Mans. *SW10* 1E **87**
  (off Drayton Gdns.)
Priory M. *SW8* 4A **90**
Priory Pk. *SE3* 1B **110**
Priory Pk. Rd. *NW6* 5B **44**
Priory Rd. *E6* 5F **55**
  NW6 . . . . .5D **45**
Priory St. *E3* 2D **67**
Priory Ter. *NW6* 5D **45**
Priory Wlk. *SW10* 1E **87**
Pritchard Ho. *E2* 1D **65**
  (off Ada Pl.)
Pritchard's Rd. *E2* 5C **50**
Priter Rd. *SE16* 4C **78**
Priter Rd. Hostel
  SE16 . . . . .4C **78**
  (off Dockley Rd.)
Priter Way *SE16* 4C **78**
Probert Rd. *SW2* 3C **104**
Probyn Ho. *SW1* 5F **75**
  (off Page St.)
Probyn Rd. *SW2* 2D **119**
Procter Ho. *SE1* 1C **92**
  (off Avondale Sq.)
  SE5 . . . . .3F **91**
  (off Picton St.)
Procter St.
  WC1 . . . . . . .1F **15** (4B **62**)

Project Pk. *E16* 3F **67**
Prologis Ho. *E3* 3E **67**
Promenade, The *W4* 5A **84**
Promenade App. Rd.
  W4 . . . . .3A **84**
Prospect Cl. *SE26* 4D **121**
Prospect Cotts.
  SW18 . . . . .2C **100**
Prospect Ho. *N1* 1C **62**
  (off Donegal St.)
  SE1 . . . . .5D **25**
  SE16 . . . . .4C **78**
  (off Frean St.)
  W10 . . . . .3F **57**
  (off Bridge Cl.)
Prospect Pl. *E1* 2E **79**
  (not continuous)
  N7 . . . . .1A **48**
  NW2 . . . . .5B **30**
  NW3 . . . . .1E **45**
  SE8 . . . . .2B **94**
  (off Evelyn St.)
  W4 . . . . .1A **84**
Prospect Quay
  SW18 . . . . .2C **100**
  (off Lightermans Wlk.)
Prospect Rd. *NW2* 5B **30**
Prospect St. *SE16* 4D **79**
Prospect Wharf *E1* 1E **79**
Prospero Ho. *E1* 4F **19**
  (off Portsoken St.)
Prospero Rd. *N19* 3F **33**
Protea Cl. *E16* 3B **68**
Prothero Rd. *SW6* 3A **86**
Proton Twr. *E14* 1F **81**
Proud Ho. *E1* 5D **65**
  (off Amazon St.)
Prout Gro. *NW10* 1A **42**
Prout Rd. *E5* 5D **37**
Provence St. *N1* 1E **63**
Providence Cl. *E9* 5F **51**
Providence Ct.
  W1 . . . . .4C **12** (1C **74**)
Providence Ho. *E14* 5B **66**
  (off Three Colt St.)
Providence Pl. *N1* 5D **49**
Providence Row *N1* 1F **7**
Providence Row Cl.
  E2 . . . . .2D **65**
Providence Sq. *SE1* 3C **78**
Providence Twr.
  SE16 . . . . .3C **78**
  (off Bermondsey Wall W.)
Providence Yd. *E2* 2C **64**
  (off Ezra St.)
Provost Ct. *NW3* 3B **46**
  (off Eton Rd.)
Provost Est. *N1* 1B **10**
Provost Rd. *NW3* 4B **46**
Provost St.
  N1 . . . . .1B **10** (1F **63**)
Prowse Pl. *NW1* 4E **47**
Prudent Pas. *EC2* 2A **18**
Prusom's Island *E1* 2E **79**
  (off Wapping High St.)
Prusom St. *E1* 2D **79**
Pryors, The *NW3* 5F **31**
Pudding La.
  EC3 . . . . . . .5C **18** (1F **77**)
Pudding Mill La. *E15* 5D **53**

Puddle Dock
  EC4 . . . . .4D **17** (1D **77**)
  (not continuous)
Pugin Ct. *N1* 4E **48**
  (off Liverpool Rd.)
Pulborough Rd.
  SW18 . . . . .5B **100**
Pulford Rd. *N15* 1F **35**
Pulham Ho. *SW8* 3B **90**
  (off Dorset Rd.)
Pullen's Bldgs. *SE17* 1D **91**
  (off Iliffe St.)
Pullman Ct. *SW2* 1A **118**
Pullman Gdns. *SW15* 4E **99**
Pullman M. *SE12* 3D **125**
Pulross Rd. *SW9* 1B **104**
Pulse Apartments
  NW6 . . . . .2D **45**
  (off Lymington Rd.)
Pulteney Cl. *E3* 5B **52**
Pulteney Ter. *N1* 5B **48**
  (not continuous)
Pulton Ho. *SE4* 2A **108**
  (off Turnham Rd.)
Pulton Pl. *SW6* 3C **86**
Puma Ct. *E1* 5F **11** (4B **64**)
Pump Ct. *EC4* 3B **16** (5C **62**)
Pump Ho. Cl. *SE16* 3E **79**
Pumphouse
  Educational Museum, The
  . . . . .2A **80**
Pump House Gallery 3D **88**
Pump Ho. M. *E1* 1C **78**
  (off Hooper St.)
Pump House
  Steam & Transport Mus.
  . . . . .1A **38**
Pumping Ho. *E14* 1F **81**
  (off Naval Row)
Pumping Sta. Rd. *W4* . . .3A **84**
Pump La. *SE14* 3E **93**
Punderson's Gdns.
  E2 . . . . .2D **65**
Purbeck Dr. *NW2* 4F **29**
Purbeck Ho. *SW8* 3B **90**
  (off Bolney St.)
Purbrook Est.
  SE1 . . . . .4E **27** (3A **78**)
Purbrook St.
  SE1 . . . . .5E **27** (4A **78**)
Purcell Cres. *SW6* 3F **85**
Purcell Ho. *SW10* 2F **87**
  (off Milman's St.)
Purcell Mans. *W14* 2A **86**
  (off Queen's Club Gdns.)
Purcell Ho. *NW10* 4A **42**
Purcell Room 1A **24**
  (off Belvedere Rd.)
Purcell St. *N1* 1A **64**
Purchese St.
  NW1 . . . . .1C **6** (1F **61**)
Purday Ho. *W10* 2A **58**
  (off Bruckner St.)
Purdon Ho. *SE15* 4C **92**
  (off Oliver Goldsmith Est.)
Purdy St. *E3* 3D **67**
Purelake M. *SE13* 1F **109**
  (off Marischal Rd.)
Purley Av. *NW2* 4A **30**
Purley Pl. *N1* 4D **49**

Purneys Rd. SE9 . . . . . .2F **111**
Purser Ho. SW2 . . . . . . .4C **104**
Pursers Cross Rd.
　　SW6 . . . . .4B **86**
Purves Rd. NW10 . . . . . .2D **57**
Pusey Ho. E14 . . . . .5C **66**
　　(off Saracen St.)
Puteaux Ho. E2 . . . . .1F **65**
　　(off Mace St.)
PUTNEY 2F **99**
Putney Arts Theatre 2F **99**
Putney Bri. SW15 . . . . .1A **100**
Putney Bri. App.
　　SW6 . . . . .1A **100**
Putney Bri. Rd.
　　SW15 . . . . .2A **100**
　　SW18 . . . . .2A **100**
Putney Comn. SW15 . . . .1E **99**
Putney Exchange
　　(Shopping Centre)
　　SW15 . . . . .2F **99**
PUTNEY HEATH 4E **99**
Putney Heath SW15 . . . .5D **99**
Putney Heath La.
　　SW15 . . . . .4F **99**
Putney High St.
　　SW15 . . . . .2F **99**
Putney Hill SW15 . . . . . .5F **99**
　　(not continuous)
Putney Leisure Cen. 2E **99**
Putney Pk. Av. SW15 . . .2C **98**
Putney Pk. La. SW15 . . .2D **99**
　　(not continuous)
PUTNEY VALE 3C **112**
Putney Va. Crematorium
　　SW19 . . . . .2C **112**
Putney Wharf SW15 . . .1A **100**
Pymers Mead SE21 . . . .1E **119**
Pynfolds SE16 . . . . .3D **79**
Pynnersmead SE24 . . . .3E **105**
Pyrford Ho. SW9 . . . . . .2D **105**
Pyrland Rd. N5 . . . . .2F **49**
Pyrmont Gro. SE27 . . . .3D **119**
Pytchley Rd. SE22 . . . . .1A **106**

Q

Q Building, The E15 . . . .3A **54**
　　(off The Grove)
Quad Ct. SE1 . . . . .5E **27**
　　(off Grigg's Pl.)
Quadrangle, The
　　E15 . . . . .3A **54**
　　SE24 . . . . .3E **105**
　　SW6 . . . . .3A **86**
　　SW10 . . . . .4E **87**
　　W2 . . . . .5A **60**
Quadrangle Cl. SE1 . . . .5A **78**
Quadrant, The W10 . . . .2F **57**
Quadrant Arc. W1 . . . . . .5A **14**
Quadrant Bus. Cen.
　　NW6 . . . . .5A **44**
Quadrant Gro. NW5 . . . .2B **46**
Quadrant Ho. E15 . . . . . .2A **68**
　　(off Durban Rd.)
　　SE1 . . . . .1D **25**
Quaggy Wlk. SE3 . . . . .2C **110**
Quain Mans. W14 . . . . .2A **86**
　　(off Queen's Club Gdns.)

Quainton St. NW10 . . . .5A **28**
Quaker Ct. E1 . . . . .4F **11**
　　(off Quaker St.)
　　EC1 . . . . .3B **10**
Quakers Pl. E7 . . . . .2F **55**
Quaker St. E1 . . .4F **11** (3B **64**)
Quality Ct. WC2 . . . . . . .2B **16**
Quantock Gdns. NW2 . . .4F **29**
Quantock Ho. N16 . . . . .3B **36**
Quantock M. SE15 . . . . .5C **92**
Quarrendon St. SW6 . . .5C **86**
Quarry Rd. SW18 . . . . .4E **101**
Quarterdeck, The
　　E14 . . . . .3C **80**
Quastel Ho. SE1 . . . . . . .4B **26**
　　(off Long La.)
Quay Ho. E14 . . . . .3C **80**
　　(off Admirals Way)
Quayside Cotts. E1 . . . . .2C **78**
　　(off Mews St.)
Quayside Ct. SE16 . . . . .2F **79**
　　(off Abbotshade Rd.)
Quayside Ho. E14 . . . . .2B **80**
　　W10 . . . . .3A **58**
Quay Vw. Apartments
　　E14 . . . . .4C **80**
　　(off Arden Cres.)
Quebec M.
　　W1 . . . . . . .3A **12** (5B **60**)
Quebec Way SE16 . . . . .3F **79**
Quebec Way Ind. Est.
　　SE16 . . . . .3A **80**
　　(not continuous)
Quebec Wharf E8 . . . . .5A **50**
　　(off Kingsland Rd.)
　　E14 . . . . .5C **66**
Quedgeley Ct. SE15 . . . .2B **92**
　　(off Ebley Cl.)
Queen Alexandra Mans.
　　WC1 . . . . .2D **7**
　　(off Bidborough St.)
Queen Alexandra's Ct.
　　SW19 . . . . .5B **114**
　　(off Hardy Av.)
Queen Anne Ho. E16 . . .2C **82**
　　(off Hardy Av.)
Queen Anne M.
　　W1 . . . . . .1E **13** (4D **61**)
Queen Anne Rd. E9 . . . .3F **51**
Queen Anne's Ct.
　　SE10 . . . . .1F **95**
　　(off Park Row)
Queen Anne's Gdns.
　　W4 . . . . .4A **70**
Queen Anne's Ga.
　　SW1 . . . . . . .4B **22** (3F **75**)
Queen Anne's Gro.
　　W4 . . . . .4A **70**
Queen Annes Sq. SE1 . .5C **78**
　　(off Monnow Rd.)
Queen Anne St.
　　W1 . . . . . . .2D **13** (5D **61**)
Queen Anne's Wlk.
　　WC1 . . . . .4E **7**
Queen Anne Ter. E1 . . . .1D **79**
　　(off Sovereign Cl.)
Queen Caroline St.
　　W6 . . . . .1E **85**
Queen Catherine Ho.
　　SW6 . . . . .3D **87**
　　(off Wandon Rd.)

Queen Ct. WC1 . . . . .4E **7**
　　(off Queen Sq.)
Queen Elizabeth Bldgs.
　　EC4 . . . . .4B **16**
Queen Elizabeth Hall
　　. . . . . .1A **24** (2B **76**)
Queen Elizabeth Ho.
　　SW12 . . . . .5C **102**
Queen Elizabeth II
　　Conference Cen.
　　. . . . . .4C **22** (3F **75**)
Queen Elizabeth's Cl.
　　N16 . . . . .4F **35**
Queen Elizabeth's Coll.
　　SE10 . . . . .3E **95**
Queen Elizabeth St.
　　SE1 . . . . . . .3F **27** (3A **78**)
Queen Elizabeth's Wlk.
　　N16 . . . . .3F **35**
Queen Elizabeth Wlk.
　　SW13 . . . . .4C **84**
Queenhithe
　　EC4 . . . . . .4A **18** (1E **77**)
Queen Isabella Way
　　EC1 . . . . .2E **17**
Queen Margaret Flats
　　E2 . . . . .2D **65**
　　(off St Jude's Rd.)
Queen Margaret's Gro.
　　N1 . . . . .2A **50**
Queen Mary Ho.
　　E16 . . . . .2D **83**
　　(off Wesley Av.)
Queen Mary Rd.
　　SE19 . . . . .5D **119**
Queen Marys Bldgs.
　　SW1 . . . . .5E **75**
　　(off Stillington St.)
Queen Mary's Ct.
　　SE10 . . . . .2F **95**
　　(off Park Row)
Queen Mary's Ho.
　　SW15 . . . . .4C **98**
Queen Mary
　　University of London
　　Charterhouse Square
　　. . . . . .4E **9** (3D **63**)
　　Lincoln's
　　Inn Fields Campus
　　. . . . . .2F **15**
　　(off Remnant St.)
　　Mile End Campus
　　. . . . . .3A **66**
　　West Smithfield Campus
　　. . . . . .1E **17**
Queen Mother
　　Sports Centre, The
　　. . . . . .5E **75**
　　(off Vauxhall Bri. Rd.)
Queen of Denmark Ct.
　　SE16 . . . . .4B **80**
Queensberry Mews W.
　　SW7 . . . . .5F **73**
Queensberry Pl.
　　E12 . . . . .2F **55**
　　SW7 . . . . .5F **73**
Queensberry Way
　　SW7 . . . . .5F **73**
Queensborough M.
　　W2 . . . . .1E **73**

Queensborough Pas.
W2 . . . . .1E **73**
(off Queensborough M.)
Queensborough Studios
W2 . . . . .1E **73**
(off Queensborough M.)
Queensborough Ter.
W2 . . . . .1D **73**
Queensbridge Ct. E2 . . . .5B **50**
(off Queensbridge Rd.)
Queensbridge Rd. E2 . .3B **50**
E8 . . . . .3B **50**
**Queensbridge
Sports & Community Cen.**
. . . . .4B **50**
Queensbury St. N1 . . . . .4E **49**
**Queen's Chapel of the
Savoy, The** 5F **15**
(off Savoy Hill)
Queen's Cir. SW8 . . . . . .3D **89**
Queen's Club Gdns.
W14 . . . . .2A **86**
**Queen's Club, The
(Tennis Courts)** 1A **86**
Queens Club Ter.
W14 . . . . .2B **86**
(off Normand Rd.)
Queens Ct. E11 . . . . . . .2A **40**
NW6 . . . . .2D **45**
NW8 . . . . .1F **59**
(off Queen's Ter.)
NW11 . . . . .1B **30**
SE23 . . . . .2E **121**
W2 . . . . .1D **73**
(off Queensway)
Queen's Cres. NW5 . . . .3C **46**
Queenscroft Rd.
SE9 . . . . .3F **111**
Queensdale Cres.
W11 . . . . .2F **71**
(not continuous)
Queensdale Pl. W11 . . . .2A **72**
Queensdale Rd. W11 . . .2F **71**
Queensdale Wlk.
W11 . . . . .2A **72**
Queensdown Rd. E5 . . .1D **51**
Queens Dr. E10 . . . . . . .2C **38**
N4 . . . . .4D **35**
Queen's Elm Pde.
SW3 . . . . .1F **87**
(off Old Church St.)
Queen's Elm Sq.
SW3 . . . . .1F **87**
Queen's Gallery
. . . . .4E **21** (3D **75**)
W2 . . . . .1E **73**
Queen's Gdns. NW4 . . . .1E **29**
W2 . . . . .1D **73**
Queens Ga. SW7 . . . . . .3E **73**
Queens Gate Gdns.
SW7 . . . . .4E **73**
SW15 . . . . .2D **99**
Queensgate Ho. E3 . . . .1B **66**
(off Hereford Rd.)
Queen's Ga. M. SW7 . . .4E **73**
Queen's Ga. Pl. SW7 . . .4E **73**
Queensgate Pl. NW6 . . .4C **44**
Queen's Ga. Pl. M.
SW7 . . . . .4E **73**
Queen's Ga. Ter.
SW7 . . . . .4E **73**

Queens Gate Vs. E9 . . .4A **52**
Queen's Gro. NW8 . . . . .5F **45**
Queen's Gro. Studios
NW8 . . . . .5F **45**
Queen's Head Pas.
EC4 . . . . . . .2F **17** (5E **63**)
Queen's Head St. N1 . . .5D **49**
Queen's Head Yd.
SE1 . . . . .2B **26**
Queen's House, The . .2F **95**
*(within National
Maritime Mus.)*
Queens Ho. SE17 . . . . . .2F **91**
(off Merrow St.)
SW8 . . . . .3A **90**
(off Sth. Lambeth Rd.)
W2 . . . . .1D **73**
(off Queensway)
Queen's Ice Bowl 1D **73**
Queensland Rd. N7 . . . .1C **48**
Queen's Mans. W6 . . . . .5F **71**
(off Brook Grn.)
Queen's Mkt. E13 . . . . . .5E **55**
Queensmead NW8 . . . . .5F **45**
Queensmere Cl.
SW19 . . . . .2F **113**
Queensmere Ct.
SW13 . . . . .3B **84**
Queensmere Rd.
SW19 . . . . .2F **113**
Queen's M. W2 . . . . . . .1D **73**
Queensmill Rd. SW6 . . .3F **85**
Queens Pde. NW2 . . . . .3E **43**
(off Willesden La.)
NW4 . . . . .1E **29**
(off Queens Rd.)
Queens Pk. Ct. W10 . . . .2F **57**
Queen's Pk. Rangers FC
. . . . .2D **71**
Queen Sq.
WC1 . . . . . . .4E **7** (3A **62**)
Queen Sq. Pl. WC1 . . . . . .4E **7**
Queen's Quay EC4 . . . . .4F **17**
(off Up. Thames St.)
Queens Ride SW13 . . . .1C **98**
SW15 . . . . .1C **98**
Queens Rd. E11 . . . . . . .2F **39**
E13 . . . . .5D **55**
E17 . . . . .1B **38**
NW4 . . . . .1E **29**
SE14 . . . . .4D **93**
SE15 . . . . .4D **93**
SW14 . . . . .1A **98**
SW19 . . . . .5C **114**
Queens Rd. W. E13 . . . .1C **68**
Queens Row SE17 . . . . .2F **91**
Queens Ter. E1 . . . . .3E **65**
(off Cephas St.)
E13 . . . . .5D **55**
NW8 . . . . .5F **45**
**Queen's Theatre
Westminster** 4B **14**
(off Shaftesbury Av.)
Queensthorpe Ho.
SE26 . . . . .4F **121**
Queensthorpe Rd.
SE26 . . . . .4F **121**
Queens Tower 4F **73**
*(within Imperial
College London)*

Queenstown M. SW8 . . .5D **89**
Queenstown Rd.
SW8 . . . . .2D **89**
Queen St.
EC4 . . . . .4A **18** (1E **77**)
(not continuous)
W1 . . . . .1D **21** (2D **75**)
Queen St. Pl.
EC4 . . . . .4A **18** (1E **77**)
Queensville Rd.
SW12 . . . . .5F **103**
Queen's Wlk. N5 . . . . . .2D **49**
SW1 . . . . .2F **21** (2E **75**)
Queen's Walk, The
SE1 . . . . .5C **16** (1C **76**)
(Oxo Tower Wharf)
SE1 . . . . .1C **26** (2A **78**)
(Tooley St.)
SE1 . . . . .1A **24** (2B **76**)
(Waterloo Rd.)
Queen's Way NW4 . . . . .1E **29**
Queensway W2 . . . . . . .5D **59**
Queens Wharf W6 . . . . .1E **85**
Queenswood Ct.
SE27 . . . . .4F **119**
SW4 . . . . .3A **104**
Queenswood Gdns.
. . . . .3D **41**
Queens Wood Rd.
N10 . . . . .1D **33**
Queenswood Rd.
SE23 . . . . .3F **121**
Queens Yd. E9 . . . . .3C **52**
WC1 . . . . .4A **6** (4E **61**)
Queen Victoria Memorial
. . . . .4F **21** (3E **75**)
Queen Victoria Seaman's Rest
E14 . . . . .5D **67**
(off E. India Dock Rd.)
Queen Victoria St.
EC4 . . . . .4D **17** (1D **77**)
Queen Victoria Ter.
E1 . . . . .1D **79**
(off Sovereign Cl.)
Quemerford Rd. N7 . . . .2B **48**
Quendon Ho. W10 . . . . .3E **57**
(off Sutton Way)
Quenington Ct. SE15 . . .2B **92**
Quentin Ho. SE1 . . . . . . .3D **25**
(off Chaplin Cl., not continuous)
Quentin Pl. SE13 . . . . . .1A **110**
Quentin Rd. SE13 . . . . . .1A **110**
Quernmore Cl.
BR1: Brom 5C **124**
Quernmore Rd.
BR1: Brom 5C **124**
N4 . . . . .1C **34**
Querrin St. SW6 . . . . . . .5E **87**
Quest, The W11 . . . . . . .1A **72**
(off Clarendon Rd.)
Quested Ct. E8 . . . . .2D **51**
(off Brett Rd.)
Quex Ct. NW6 . . . . .5D **45**
(off West End La.)
Quex M. NW6 . . . . .5C **44**
Quex Rd. NW6 . . . . .5C **44**
Quick Rd. W4 . . . . .1A **84**
Quick St. N1 . . . . .1D **63**
Quick St. M. N1 . . . . .1D **63**
Quickswood NW3 . . . . . .4A **46**

Quill Ho. E2 . . . . .3C 64
(off Cheshire St.)
Quill La. SW15 . . . . .2F 99
Quill St. N4 . . . . .5C 34
Quilp St. SE1 . . .3F 25 (3E 77)
(not continuous)
Quilter St. E2 . . . . .2C 64
Quilting Ct. SE16 . . . . . . .3F 79
(off Garter Way)
Quince Ho. SE13 . . . . .5D 95
(off Quince Rd.)
Quince Rd. SE13 . . . . .5D 95
Quinton Ho. SW8 . . . . .3A 90
(off Wyvil Rd.)
Quinton St. SW18 . . . . . . .2E 115
Quixley St. E14 . . . . .1F 81
Quorn Rd. SE22 . . . . . .2A 106

R

Rabbit Row W8 . . . . .2C 72
Raby St. E14 . . . . .5A 66
Racine SE5 . . . . .4A 92
(off Sceaux Gdns.)
Rackham M. SW16 . . . . . .5E 117
Rackstraw Ho. NW3 . . . .4B 46
Racton Rd. SW6 . . . . .2C 86
RADA
   Chenies St. 5B 6
   Gower St. 4F 61
   (off Gower St.)
Radbourne Cl. E5 . . . . . . .1F 51
Radbourne Rd.
   SW12 . . . . .5E 103
Radcliffe Av. NW10 . . . . . .1C 56
Radcliffe Ho. SE16 . . . . . .5D 79
(off Anchor St.)
Radcliffe Path SW8 . . . . . .5D 89
Radcliffe Rd.
   SE1 . . . . . .5E 27 (4A 78)
Radcliffe Sq. SW15 . . . . . .4F 99
Radcot Point SE23 . . . . . .3F 121
Radcot St. SE11 . . . . .1C 90
Raddington Rd. W10 . . . .4A 58
Raddon Twr. E8 . . . . .3B 50
(off Dalston Sq.)
Radford Ct. SE15 . . . . . . .3D 93
(off Old Kent Rd.)
Radford Est. NW10 . . . . .2A 56
Radford Ho. E14 . . . . .4D 67
(off St Leonard's Rd.)
   N7 . . . . .2B 48
Radipole Rd. SW6 . . . . . .4B 86
Radisson Ct. SE1 . . . . . . .5D 27
(off Long La.)
Radius Apartments N1 . . .1F 7
(off Omega Pl.)
Radland Rd. E16 . . . . .5B 68
Radlet Av. SE26 . . . . .3D 121
Radlett Cl. E7 . . . . .3B 54
Radlett Pl. NW8 . . . . .5A 46
Radley Ct. SE16 . . . . .3F 79
(off Gloucester Pl.)
Radley Ho. NW1 . . . . .3A 4
(off Gloucester Pl.)
Radley M. W8 . . . . .4C 72
Radley Sq. E5 . . . . .4E 37
Radley Ter. E16 . . . . .4B 68
(off Hermit Rd.)

Radlix Rd. E10 . . . . . . .3C 38
Radnor Ho. EC1 . . . . . . .2A 10
(off Radnor Rd.)
Radnor Lodge W2 . . . . . .5F 59
(off Sussex Pl.)
Radnor M. W2 . . . . .5F 59
Radnor Pl. W2 . . . . .5A 60
Radnor Rd. NW6 . . . . . . .5A 44
   SE15 . . . . .3C 92
Radnor St.
   EC1 . . . . . . .2A 10 (2E 63)
Radnor Ter. W14 . . . . . . .5B 72
Radnor Wlk. E14 . . . . . . .5C 80
(off Barnsdale Av.)
   SW3 . . . . .1A 88
Radstock St. SW11 . . . . . .3A 88
(not continuous)
Radway Ho. W2 . . . . .4C 58
(off Alfred Rd.)
Raeburn Cl. NW11 . . . .1E 31
Raeburn St. SW2 . . . . .2A 104
Ragged School Mus. . . .4A 66
Raglan Ct. SE12 . . . . . . .3C 110
Raglan Rd. E17 . . . . .1E 39
Raglan St. NW5 . . . . .3D 47
Ragwort Ct. SE26 . . . . . .5D 121
Rahere Ct. E1 . . . . .3A 66
(off Toby La.)
Railey M. NW5 . . . . .2E 47
Railton Rd. SE24 . . . . . .2C 104
Railway App. N4 . . . . . . .1C 34
   SE1 . . . . . . .2C 26 (2F 77)
Railway Arches E1 . . . . . .5F 65
(off Barnardo St.)
   E1 . . . . .1D 79
(off Chapman St.)
   E2 . . . . .1F 11
(off Cremer St.)
   E2 . . . . .1B 64
(off Geffrye St.)
   E2 . . . . .5B 50
(off Laburnum St.)
   E3 . . . . .3B 66
(off Cantrell Rd.)
   E8 . . . . .4D 51
(off Mentmore Ter.)
   E16 . . . . .2C 82
   W6 . . . . .4E 71
   W12 . . . . .3E 71
(off Shepherd's Bush Mkt.)
Railway Av. SE16 . . . . . . .3E 79
(not continuous)
Railway Children Wlk.
   BR1: Brom 2C 124
   SE12 . . . . .2C 124
Railway Cotts. E15 . . . . . .1A 68
(off Baker's Row)
   SW19 . . . . .4D 115
   W6 . . . . .3E 71
(off Sulgrave Rd.)
Railway Fields
   Local Nature Reserve
      . . . . .1D 35
Railway Gro. SE8 . . . . . . .3B 94
Railway M. W10 . . . . .5A 58
Railway Ri. SE22 . . . . . .2A 106
Railway Side SW13 . . . . .1A 98
Railway St. N1 . . . . .1A 62
Railway Ter. SE13 . . . . . .3D 109
Rainbow Av. E14 . . . . . . .1D 95

Rainbow Ct. SE14 . . . . . . .2A 94
(off Chipley St.)
Rainbow Quay SE16 . . . . . .4A 80
(not continuous)
Rainbow St. SE5 . . . . .3A 92
Rainbow Theatre 4C 34
Raines Est. Ct. N16 . . . . .4B 36
Raine St. E1 . . . . .2D 79
Rainham Cl. SW11 . . . . . .4A 102
Rainham Ho. NW1 . . . . . .5E 47
(off Bayham St.)
Rainham Rd. NW10 . . . . .2E 57
Rainhill Way E3 . . . . .2C 66
(not continuous)
Rainsborough Av.
   SE8 . . . . .5A 80
Rainsford St. W2 . . . . . . .5A 60
Rainton Rd. SE7 . . . . .1C 96
Rainville Rd. W6 . . . . .2E 85
Rajsee Apartments
   E2 . . . . .2C 64
(off Bethnal Grn. Rd.)
Raleana Rd. E14 . . . . . . .2E 81
Raleigh Ct. SE8 . . . . .1A 94
(off Evelyn St.)
   SE16 . . . . .2F 79
(off Clarence M.)
   W12 . . . . .3E 71
(off Scott's Rd.)
Raleigh Gdns. SW2 . . . .4B 104
Raleigh Ho. E14 . . . . .3D 81
(off Admirals Way)
   SW1 . . . . .2F 89
(off Dolphin Sq.)
Raleigh M. N1 . . . . .5D 49
(off Packington St.)
Raleigh St. N1 . . . . .5D 49
Ralph Brook Ct. N1 . . . . . .1C 10
(off Chart St.)
Ralph Ct. W2 . . . . .5D 59
(off Queensway)
Ralston St. SW3 . . . . .1B 88
Ramac Ind. Est. SE7 . . . . .5D 83
Ramac Way SE7 . . . . .5D 83
Ramar Ho. E1 . . . . .4C 64
(off Hanbury St.)
Rambler Cl. SW16 . . . . . .4E 117
Rame Cl. SW17 . . . . .5C 116
Ramilles Cl. SW2 . . . . . .4A 104
Ramillies Pl.
   W1 . . . . . . .3F 13 (5E 61)
Ramillies Rd. W4 . . . . . . .5A 70
Ramillies St.
   W1 . . . . . . .3F 13 (5E 61)
Rampart St. E1 . . . . .5D 65
Rampayne St. SW1 . . . . . .1F 89
Ram Pl. E9 . . . . .3E 51
Ramsay Ho. NW8 . . . . . . .1A 60
(off Townshend Est.)
Ramsay M. SW3 . . . . .2A 88
Ramsay Rd. E7 . . . . .1A 54
Ramsdale Rd.
   SW17 . . . . .5C 116
Ramsden Rd. SW12 . . . .4C 102
Ramsey Cl. NW9 . . . . .1B 28
Ramsey Ho. SW9 . . . . . . .3C 90
Ramsey St. E2 . . . . .3C 64
Ramsey Wlk. N1 . . . . .3F 49
Ramsfort Ho. SE16 . . . . . .5D 79
(off Camilla Rd.)

Ramsgate Cl. E16 . . . . . .2D 83
Ramsgate St. E8 . . . . . .3B 50
Ram St. SW18 . . . . . .3D 101
Rancliffe Gdns.
 SE9 . . . . .2F 111
Randall Av. NW2 . . . . . .4A 28
Randall Cl. SW11 . . . . . .4A 88
Randall Pl. SE10 . . . . . .3E 95
Randall Rd. SE11 . . . . . .1B 90
Randall Row SE11 . . . . . .5B 76
Randalls Rents SE16 . . . .4B 80
 (off Gulliver St.)
Randell's Rd. N1 . . . . . .5A 48
Randisbourne Gdns.
 SE6 . . . . .3D 123
Randlesdown Rd.
 SE6 . . . . .4C 122
 (not continuous)
Randolph App. E16 . . . . .5E 69
Randolph Av. W9 . . . . . .1D 59
Randolph Cl. NW8 . . . . . .5E 45
Randolph Cres. W9 . . . . .3E 59
Randolph Gdns.
 NW6 . . . . .1D 59
Randolph M. W9 . . . . . . .3E 59
Randolph Rd. E17 . . . . . .1D 39
 W9 . . . . .3E 59
Randolph St. NW1 . . . . . .4E 47
Ranelagh Av. SW6 . . . .1B 100
 SW13 . . . . .5C 84
Ranelagh Bri. W2 . . . . . .4D 59
Ranelagh Cotts. SW1 . .1D 89
 (off Ebury Bri. Rd.)
Ranelagh Gdns.
 SW6 . . . . .1A 100
 (not continuous)
 W6 . . . . .5B 70
Ranelagh Gdns. Mans.
 SW6 . . . . .1A 100
 (off Ranelagh Gdns.)
Ranelagh Gro. SW1 . . . .1C 88
Ranelagh Rd. SW3 . . . . .1B 88
 (off Elystan Pl.)
Ranelagh Rd. E11 . . . . . .1A 54
 E15 . . . . .1A 68
 NW10 . . . . .1B 56
 SW1 . . . . .1E 89
Rangbourne Ho. N7 . . . . .2A 48
Rangefield Rd.
 BR1: Brom 5A 124
Rangemoor Rd. N15 . . . .1B 36
Ranger's House 4F 95
Rangers Sq. SE10 . . . . .4F 95
Rangoon St. EC3 . . . . . .3F 19
Rankine Ho. SE1 . . . . . .5F 25
 (off Bath Ter.)
Ranmere St. SW12 . . . .1D 117
Rannoch Rd. W6 . . . . . .2E 85
Rannock Av. NW9 . . . . . .2A 28
Ransome's Dock Bus. Cen.
 SW11 . . . . .3A 88
Ransom Rd. SE7 . . . . . .5E 83
Ranston St. NW1 . . . . . .4A 60
Ranulf Rd. NW2 . . . . . . .1B 44
Ranwell Cl. E3 . . . . .5B 52
Ranwell Ho. E3 . . . . . . .5B 52
 (off Ranwell Cl.)
Raphael Ct. SE16 . . . . . .1D 93
 (off Stubbs Dr.)
Raphael St. SW7 . . . . . .3B 74

Raphen Apartments
 E3 . . . . .1A 66
 (off Medway Rd.)
Rapley Ho. E2 . . . . .2C 64
 (off Turin St.)
Raquel Ct. SE1 . . . . . . .3D 27
 (off Snowfields)
Rashleigh Ct. SW8 . . . . .5D 89
Rashleigh Ho.
 WC1 . . . . .2D 7
 (off Thanet St.)
Rashleigh St. SW8 . . . . .5D 89
 (off Peardon St.)
Rastell Av. SW2 . . . . . .2F 117
Ratcliffe Cl. SE12 . . . . .5C 110
Ratcliffe Ct. SE1 . . . . . .4A 26
 (off Gt. Dover St.)
RATCLIFF 4A 66
Ratcliffe Cross St. E1 . . .5F 65
Ratcliffe Ho. E14 . . . . . .5A 66
 (off Barnes St.)
Ratcliffe La. E14 . . . . . . .5A 66
Ratcliffe Orchard E1 . . . .1F 79
Ratcliff Rd. E7 . . . . .2E 55
Rathbone Ho. E16 . . . . . .5B 68
 (off Rathbone St.)
 NW6 . . . . .5C 44
Rathbone Mkt. E16 . . . . .4B 68
Rathbone Pl.
 W1 . . . . .1B 14 (4F 61)
Rathbone St. E16 . . . . . .5B 68
 W1 . . . . .1A 14 (4E 61)
Rathcoole Gdns. N8 . . . .1B 34
Rathfern Rd. SE6 . . . . . .1B 122
Rathgar Rd. SW9 . . . . .1D 105
Rathmell Dr. SW4 . . . . .4F 103
Rathmore Rd. SE7 . . . . .1D 97
Rathnew Ct. E2 . . . . . . .2F 65
 (off Meath Cres.)
Rattray Ct. SE6 . . . . . .2B 124
Rattray Rd. SW2 . . . . . .2C 104
Raul Rd. SE15 . . . . .5C 92
Raveley St. NW5 . . . . . .1E 47
 (not continuous)
Ravenet St. SW11 . . . . . .4D 89
 (not continuous)
Ravenfield Rd.
 SW17 . . . . .3B 116
Ravenhill Rd. E13 . . . . . .1E 69
Raven Ho. SE16 . . . . . . .5F 79
 (off Tawny Way)
Ravenna Rd. SW15 . . . . .3F 99
Raven Row E1 . . . . .4D 65
Raven Row
 Contemporary Art Cen.
 . . . . .1F 19
 (off Artillery La.)
Ravensbourne Ct.
 SE6 . . . . .5C 108
Ravensbourne Ho.
 BR1: Brom 5F 123
 NW8 . . . . .4A 60
 (off Broadley St.)
Ravensbourne Mans.
 SE8 . . . . .2C 94
 (off Berthon St.)
Ravensbourne Pk.
 SE6 . . . . .5C 108
Ravensbourne Pk. Cres.
 SE6 . . . . .5B 108

Ravensbourne Pl.
 SE13 . . . . .5D 95
Ravensbourne Rd.
 SE6 . . . . .5B 108
Ravensbury Rd.
 SW18 . . . . .2D 115
Ravensbury Ter.
 SW18 . . . . .2D 115
Ravenscar NW1 . . . . . . .5E 47
 (off Bayham St.)
Ravenscar Rd.
 BR1: Brom 4A 124
Ravenscourt Av. W6 . . . .5C 70
Ravenscourt Gdns.
 W6 . . . . .5C 70
Ravenscourt Pk.
 W6 . . . . .4C 70
Ravenscourt Pk. Mans.
 W6 . . . . .4D 71
 (off Paddenswick Rd.)
Ravenscourt Pl. W6 . . . .5D 71
Ravenscourt Rd. W6 . . . .5D 71
Ravenscourt Sq. W6 . . . .4C 70
Ravenscroft Av.
 NW11 . . . . .2B 30
Ravenscroft Cl. E16 . . . .4C 68
Ravenscroft Pk. E2 . . . . .2B 64
 (off Baroness Rd.)
Ravenscroft Rd. E16 . . . .4C 68
Ravenscroft St. E2 . . . . .1B 64
Ravensdale Ind. Est.
 N16 . . . . .1C 36
Ravensdale Mans.
 N8 . . . . .1A 34
 (off Haringey Pk.)
Ravensdale Rd. N16 . . . .2B 36
Ravensdon St. SE11 . . . .1C 90
Ravenshaw St. NW6 . . . .2B 44
Ravenslea Rd.
 SW12 . . . . .5B 102
Ravensleigh Gdns.
 BR1: Brom 5D 125
Ravensmede Way
 W4 . . . . .5B 70
Ravens M. SE12 . . . . . .3C 110
Ravenstone SE17 . . . . . .1A 92
Ravenstone Rd. NW9 . . .1B 28
Ravenstone St.
 SW12 . . . . .1C 116
Ravens Way SE12 . . . . .3C 110
Ravenswood Rd.
 SW12 . . . . .5D 103
Ravensworth Ct.
 SW6 . . . . .3C 86
 (off Fulham Rd.)
Ravensworth Rd.
 NW10 . . . . .2D 57
Raven Wharf SE1 . . . . . .3F 27
 (off Lafone St.)
Ravey St.
 EC2 . . . . .3D 11 (3A 64)
Rav Pinter Cl. N16 . . . . .2A 36
Rawalpindi Ho. E16 . . . .3B 68
Rawchester Cl.
 SW18 . . . . .1B 114
Rawlings St. SW3 . . . . . .5B 74
Rawlinson Ct. NW2 . . . . .2E 29
Rawlinson Ho. SE13 . . . .2F 109
 (off Mercator Rd.)

Rawreth Wlk. *N1* 5E **49**
Rawson St. SW11 . . . . . . .4C **88**
  (not continuous)
Rawstone Wlk. E13 . . . . .1C **68**
Rawstone Pl.
  EC1 . . . . . .1D **9** (2D **63**)
Rawstone St.
  EC1 . . . . . .1D **9** (2D **63**)
Rayburne Ct. W14 . . . . . .4A **72**
Raydon St. N19 . . . . .4D **33**
Rayford Av. SE12 . . . . . .5B **110**
Ray Gunter Ho. *SE17* . . .1D **91**
  (off Marsland Cl.)
Ray Ho. *N1* 5A **50**
  (off Colville Est.)
  W10 . . . . .5F **57**
  (off Cambridge Gdns.)
Rayleigh Rd. E16 . . . . . . .2D **83**
Raymede Towers
  W10 . . . . .4F **57**
  (off Treverton St.)
Raymond Bldgs.
  WC1 . . . . . .5A **8** (4B **62**)
Raymond Chadburn Ho.
  E7 . . . . .1D **55**
Raymond Cl. SE26 . . . . . .5E **121**
Raymond Rd. E13 . . . . . .5E **55**
  SW19 . . . . .5A **114**
Raymouth Rd. SE16 . . . . .5D **79**
Raynald Ho. SW16 . . . . .3A **118**
Rayne Ho. SW12 . . . . . . .4C **102**
  W9 . . . . .3D **59**
  (off Delaware Rd.)
Rayner Ct. *W12* 3E **71**
  (off Bamborough Gdns.)
Rayners Rd. SW15 . . . . . .3A **100**
Rayners Ter. E14 . . . . . . .5A **66**
  (off Carr St.)
Rayner Towers E10 . . . . . .2C **38**
  (off Albany Rd.)
Raynes Av. E11 . . . . .2E **41**
Raynham *W2* 5A **60**
  (off Norfolk Cres.)
Raynham Ho. *E1* 3F **65**
  (off Harpley Sq.)
Raynham Rd. W6 . . . . . . .5D **71**
Raynor Pl. N1 . . . . .4E **49**
Ray St. EC1 . . . .4C **8** (3C **62**)
Ray St. Bri. EC1 . . . . .4C **8**
Ray Wlk. N7 . . . . .4B **34**
Reachview Cl. NW1 . . . . .4E **47**
Reader Ho. *SE5* 4E **91**
  (off Badsworth St.)
Read Ho. *SE11* 2C **90**
  (off Clayton St.)
Reading Cl. SE22 . . . . . . .4C **106**
Reading Ho. SE15 . . . . . .2C **92**
  (off Friary Est.)
  W2 . . . . .5C **59**
  (off Hallfield Est.)
Reading La. E8 . . . . .3D **51**
Ream Apartments
  SE23 . . . . .2E **121**
  (off Clyde Ter.)
Reapers Cl. NW1 . . . . . . .5F **47**
Reardon Ho. *E1* 2D **79**
  (off Reardon St.)

Reardon Path E1 . . . . . . .2D **79**
  (not continuous)
Reardon St. E1 . . . . .2D **79**
Reaston St. SE14 . . . . . . .3F **93**
Rebecca Ho. *E3* 3B **66**
  (off Brokesley St.)
Reckitt Rd. W4 . . . . .1A **84**
Record St. SE15 . . . . .2E **93**
Recovery St. SW17 . . . . .5A **116**
Recreation Rd.
  SE26 . . . . .4F **121**
Rector St. N1 . . . . .5E **49**
Rectory Chambers
  SW3 . . . . .2A **88**
  (off Old Church St.)
Rectory Cres. E11 . . . . . . .1E **41**
  (not continuous)
Rectory Field 3D **97**
Rectory Fld. Cres.
  SE7 . . . . .3E **97**
Rectory Gdns. SW4 . . . . .1E **103**
Rectory Gro. SW4 . . . . . .1E **103**
Rectory La. SW17 . . . . . .5C **116**
Rectory Orchard
  SW19 . . . . .4A **114**
Rectory Rd. N16 . . . . .4B **36**
  SW13 . . . . .5C **84**
Rectory Sq. E1 . . . . .4F **65**
Reculver Ho. *SE15* 2E **93**
  (off Lovelinch Cl.)
Reculver Rd. SE16 . . . . . .1F **93**
Redan Cl. SW3 . . . . .2F **87**
Redan Pl. W2 . . . . .5D **59**
Redan St. W14 . . . . .4F **71**
Redan Ter. SE5 . . . . .5D **91**
Redberry Gro. SE26 . . . . .3E **121**
Redbourne Ho. *E14* 5B **66**
  (off Norbiton Rd.)
Redbourn Ho. *W10* 3E **57**
  (off Sutton Way)
REDBRIDGE 1F **41**
Redbridge Gdns. SE5 . . . .3A **92**
Redbridge La. E.
  IG4: Ilf 1F **41**
Redbridge La. W.
  E11 . . . . .1D **41**
REDBRIDGE RDBT. . . .1F **41**
Redburn St. SW3 . . . . . . .2B **88**
Redcar St. SE5 . . . . .3E **91**
Redcastle Cl. E1 . . . . .1E **79**
Redchurch St.
  E2 . . . . .3F **11** (3B **64**)
Redcliffe Cl. *SW5* 1D **87**
  (off Old Brompton Rd.)
Redcliffe Ct. E5 . . . . .5D **37**
  (off Napoleon St.)
Redcliffe Gdns.
  SW10 . . . . .1D **87**
Redcliffe M. SW10 . . . . . .1D **87**
Redcliffe Pl. SW10 . . . . . .2E **87**
Redcliffe Rd. SW10 . . . . .1E **87**
Redcliffe Sq. SW10 . . . . .1D **87**
Redcliffe St. SW10 . . . . . .2D **87**
Redclyffe Rd. E6 . . . . .5E **55**
Redclyf Ho. *E1* 3E **65**
  (off Cephas St.)
Red Cow La.
  EC1 . . . . . . .3F **9** (3E **63**)
Red Cross Cotts. *SE1* . . .3A **26**
  (off Ayres St.)

Redcross Way
  SE1 . . . . . . .3A **26** (3E **77**)
Redding Ho. SE18 . . . . . .4F **83**
Redding Rd. SE15 . . . . . .2C **92**
Redenham Ho.
  SW15 . . . . .5C **98**
  (off Ellisfield Dr.)
Rede Pl. W2 . . . . .5C **58**
Redesdale St. SW3 . . . . . .2A **88**
Redfern Ho. *E13* 5B **54**
  (off Redriffe Rd.)
  NW8 . . . . .5F **45**
  (off Dorman Way)
Redfern Rd. NW10 . . . . . .4A **42**
  SE6 . . . . .5E **109**
Redfield La. SW5 . . . . . . .5C **72**
Redfield M. SW5 . . . . . . .5D **73**
Redford Wlk. *N1* 5E **49**
  (off Popham St.)
Redgate Ter. SW15 . . . . . .4F **99**
Redgrave Rd. SW15 . . . . .1F **99**
Redgrave Ter. *E2* 2C **64**
  (off Derbyshire St.)
Redhill Ct. SW2 . . . . .2C **118**
Redhill St.
  NW1 . . . . .1E **5** (1D **61**)
Red Ho. Sq. N1 . . . . .4E **49**
Redington Gdns.
  NW3 . . . . .1D **45**
Redington Ho. *N1* 1B **62**
  (off Priory Grn. Est.)
Redington Rd. NW3 . . . . .5D **31**
Redlands Way SW2 . . . . .5B **104**
Red Lion Cl. *SE17* 2F **91**
  (off Red Lion Row)
Red Lion Ct.
  EC4 . . . . . . .3C **16** (5C **62**)
  SE1 . . . . .1A **26** (2E **77**)
Red Lion Row SE17 . . . . . .2E **91**
Red Lion Sq. SW18 . . . . .3C **100**
  WC1 . . . . . . .1F **15** (4B **62**)
Red Lion St.
  WC1 . . . . .5F **7** (4B **62**)
Red Lion Yd. W1 . . . . .1C **20**
Redlynch Ct. *W14* 3A **72**
  (off Addison Cres.)
Redlynch Ho. SW9 . . . . . .4C **90**
  (off Gosling Way)
Redman Ho. *EC1* 5B **8**
  (off Bourne Est.)
  SE1 . . . . .4A **26**
  (off Borough High St.)
Redman's Rd. E1 . . . . . . .4E **65**
Redmead La. E1 . . . . .2C **78**
Redmill Ho. *E1* 3D **65**
  (off Headlam St.)
Redmond Ho. *N1* 5B **48**
  (off Barnsbury Est.)
Redmore Rd. W6 . . . . . . .5D **71**
Red Path E9 . . . . .3A **52**
Red Pl. W1 . . . . .4B **12** (1C **74**)
Red Post Hill SE21 . . . . . .2F **105**
  SE24 . . . . .2F **105**
Red Post Ho. E6 . . . . .4F **55**
Redriffe Rd. E13 . . . . .5B **54**
Redriff Est. SE16 . . . . .4B **80**
Redriff Rd. SE16 . . . . .5F **79**
RED ROVER 2C **98**
Redrup Ho. *SE14* 2F **93**
  (off John Williams Cl.)

Redruth Rd. E9 . . . . .5E 51
Redshank Ho. SE1 . . . . .1B 92
   (off Avocet Cl.)
Red Sq. N16 . . . . .5F 35
Redstart Cl. E6 . . . . .4F 69
SE14 . . . . .3A 94
Redvers St. N1 . . . . .1E 11
Redwald Rd. E5 . . . . . . .1F 51
Redwing Cl. SE1 . . . . . . .4A 26
   (off Swan St.)
Redwing M. SE5 . . . . . . .5E 91
Redwood Cl. E3 . . . . . . .1C 66
SE16 . . . . .2A 80
Redwood Ct. N19 . . . . . .2F 33
NW6 . . . . .4A 44
Redwood Mans. W8 . . . .4D 73
   (off Chantry Sq.)
Redwood M. SW4 . . . . .1D 103
Redwoods SW15 . . . . . .1C 112
Reece M. SW7 . . . . .5F 73
Reed Cl. E16 . . . . .4C 68
SE12 . . . . .3C 110
Reedham St. SE15 . . . . . .5C 92
Reedholm Vs. N16 . . . . . .1F 49
Reed Ho. SW19 . . . . . . .4D 115
Reed Pl. SW4 . . . . .2F 103
Reed's Pl. NW1 . . . . .4E 47
Reedworth St.
   SE11 . . . . .5C 76
Reef Ho. E14 . . . . .4E 81
   (off Manchester St.)
Rees St. N1 . . . . .5E 49
Reets Farm Cl. NW9 . . . .1A 28
Reeves Av. NW9 . . . . . . .2A 28
Reeves Ho. SE1 . . . . . . .4B 24
   (off Baylis Rd.)
Reeves M.
   W1 . . . . . . .5B 12 (1C 74)
Reeves Rd. E3 . . . . .3D 67
Reflection Ho. E2 . . . . . .3C 64
   (off Cheshire St.)
Reform St. SW11 . . . . . . .5B 88
Regal Bldg. W10 . . . . . . .2F 57
Regal Cl. E1 . . . . .4C 64
Regal Ct. NW6 . . . . .1B 58
   (off Malvern Rd.)
SW6 . . . . .3C 86
   (off Dawes Rd.)
Regal House, The
   SW6 . . . . .5E 87
Regal La. NW1 . . . . .5C 46
Regal Pl. E3 . . . . .2B 66
SW6 . . . . .3D 87
Regal Row SE15 . . . . . . .4E 93
Regan Way
   N1 . . . . . .1D 11 (1A 64)
Regatta Point E14 . . . . . .3C 80
   (off Westferry Rd.)
Regency Ct. E3 . . . . .1B 66
   (off Norman Gro.)
E9 . . . . .5E 51
   (off Park Cl.)
SE8 . . . . .3B 94
   (off Glenville Gro.)
Regency Ho. E16 . . . . . . .2C 82
   (off Pepys Cres.)
SW1 . . . . .5F 75
   (off Regency St.)
SW6 . . . . .4E 87
   (off The Boulevard)

Regency Lawn NW5 . . . .5D 33
Regency Lodge NW3 . . . .4F 45
   (off Adelaide Rd.)
Regency M. NW10 . . . . .3C 42
SW9 . . . . .3D 91
Regency Pde. NW3 . . . . .4F 45
   (off Finchley Rd.)
Regency Pl. SW1 . . . . . . .5F 75
Regency St.
   NW10 . . . . .3A 56
SW1 . . . . .5F 75
Regency Ter. SW7 . . . . . .1F 87
   (off Fulham Rd.)
Regeneration Rd.
   SE16 . . . . .5F 79
Regent Ct. NW6 . . . . . . .4B 44
   (off Cavendish Rd.)
NW8 . . . . .2A 60
   (off North Bank)
W8 . . . . .1C 73
   (off Wright's La.)
Regent Ho. W14 . . . . . . .5A 72
   (off Windsor Way)
Regent Pl. SW19 . . . . . .5E 115
W1 . . . . . . .4A 14 (1E 75)
Regent Rd. SE24 . . . . . .4D 105
Regent's Bri. Gdns.
   SW8 . . . . .3A 90
Regents Canal Ho.
   E14 . . . . .5A 66
   (off Commercial Rd.)
Regent's College 3A 4
Regents Ct. E8 . . . . .5B 50
   (off Pownall Rd.)
Regents Ga. Ho. E14 . . . .1A 80
   (off Horseferry Rd.)
Regents M. NW8 . . . . . . .1E 59
REGENT'S PARK
   . . . . .2E 5 (2D 61)
Regent's Pk. 1A 4 (1B 60)
Regent's Pk. Barracks . . .1E 5
Regents Pk. Est.
   NW1 . . . . .1F 5
Regent's Pk. Gdns. M.
   NW1 . . . . .5B 46
Regent's Pk. Ho.
   NW8 . . . . .2A 60
   (off Park Rd.)
Regent's Pk. Open Air Theatre
   . . . . .2B 4 (2C 60)
Regent's Pk. Rd.
   NW1 . . . . .4B 46
   (not continuous)
Regent's Pk. Ter.
   NW1 . . . . .5D 47
Regents Pl.
   NW1 . . . . . .3E 5 (3D 61)
SE3 . . . . .5C 96
Regents Plaza NW6 . . . .1D 59
   (off Kilburn High Rd.)
Regent Sq. E3 . . . . .2D 67
WC1 . . . . . .2E 7 (2A 62)
Regent's Row E8 . . . . . . .5C 50
Regent St. NW10 . . . . . . .2F 57
SW1 . . . . . .5B 14 (1F 75)
W1 . . . . . . .2E 13 (5D 61)
Regents Wharf E2 . . . . .5D 51
   (off Wharf Pl.)
N1 . . . . .1B 62
Regent Ter. SW8 . . . . . . .2A 90

Reginald Pl. SE8 . . . . . . .3C 94
   (off Deptford High St.)
Reginald Rd. E7 . . . . . . .4C 54
SE8 . . . . .3C 94
Reginald Sorenson Ho.
   E11 . . . . .2F 39
Reginald Sq. SE8 . . . . . . .3C 94
Regina Point SE16 . . . . . .4E 79
Regina Rd. N4 . . . . .3B 34
Regis Ct. NW1 . . . . .4B 60
   (off Melcombe Pl.)
Regis Ho. W1 . . . . .5C 4
   (off Beaumont St.)
Regis Pl. SW2 . . . . .2B 104
Regis Rd. NW5 . . . . .2D 47
Regnart Bldgs. NW1 . . . .3A 6
Regnas Ho. E15 . . . . .3B 54
   (off Carnarvon Rd.)
Reigate Rd.
   BR1: Brom 3B 124
Reighton Rd. E5 . . . . . . .5C 36
Reindeer Cl. E13 . . . . . . .5C 54
Reizel Cl. N16 . . . . .3B 36
Relay Rd. W12 . . . . .2E 71
Relf Rd. SE15 . . . . .1C 106
Reliance Arc. SW9 . . . . . .2C 104
Reliance Sq.
   EC2 . . . . . . .3E 11 (3A 64)
Relton M. SW7 . . . . .4A 74
Rembrandt Cl. E14 . . . . . .4F 81
SW1 . . . . .1C 88
   (off Graham Ter.)
Rembrandt Ct. SE16 . . . .1D 93
   (off Stubbs Dr.)
Rembrandt Rd.
   SE13 . . . . .2A 110
Remington Rd. E6 . . . . . . .5F 69
N15 . . . . .1F 35
Remington St. N1 . . . . . . .1D 63
Remnant St.
   WC2 . . . . . .2F 15 (5B 62)
Remsted Ho. NW6 . . . . . .5D 45
   (off Mortimer Cres.)
Remus Building, The
   EC1 . . . . .2C 8
   (off Hardwick St.)
Remus Rd. E3 . . . . .4C 52
Renaissance Wlk.
   SE10 . . . . .4B 82
   (off Teal St.)
Renbold Ho. SE10 . . . . . .4E 95
   (off Blissett St.)
Rendle Ho. W10 . . . . . . .3A 58
   (off Wornington Rd.)
Rendlesham Rd. E5 . . . . .1C 50
Renforth St. SE16 . . . . . . .4E 79
Renfrew Ho. NW6 . . . . . .1D 59
   (off Carlton Vale)
Renfrew Rd. SE11 . . . . . .5D 77
Renmuir St. SW17 . . . . . .5B 116
Rennell St. SE13 . . . . . . .1E 109
Rennie Cotts. E1 . . . . .3E 65
   (off Pernell Cl.)
Rennie Ct. SE1 . . . . .1D 25
Rennie Est. SE16 . . . . . . .5D 79
Rennie Ho. SE1 . . . . .5F 25
   (off Bath Ter.)
Rennie St.
   SE1 . . . . . .1D 25 (2D 77)
   (not continuous)

Renoir Cinema
  Brunswick Square
................................3A 62
Renoir Ct. SE16 ....1D 93
  (off Stubbs Dr.)
Rensburg Rd. E17 ......1F 37
Renters Av. NW4 ....1E 29
Renton Cl. SW2 ....4B 104
Rephidim St.
  SE1 ......5D 27 (4A 78)
Replingham Rd.
  SW18 ....1B 114
Reporton Rd. SW6 ......3A 86
Repton Ho. SW1 ......5E 75
  (off Charlwood St.)
Repton St. E14 ....5A 66
Reservoir Rd. SE4 .....5A 94
Reservoir Studios E1 ...5F 65
  (off Cable St.)
Resolution Way SE8 ....3C 94
  (off Deptford High St.)
Restell Cl. SE3 ....2A 96
Reston Pl. SW7 ....3E 73
Restoration Sq.
  SW11 ....4F 87
Restormel Ho. SE11 ....5C 76
  (off Chester Way)
Retcar Pl. N19 ....4D 33
Retford St.
  N1 ....1E 11 (1A 64)
Retreat, The SW14 ....1A 98
Retreat Ho. E9 ....3E 51
Retreat Pl. E9 ....3E 51
Reunion Row E1 ....1D 79
Reuters Plaza E14 .....2D 81
  (off The Sth. Colonnade)
Reveley Sq. SE16 .....3A 80
Revelon Rd. SE4 ......2A 108
Revelstoke Rd.
  SW18 ....2B 114
Reverdy Rd. SE1 ....5C 78
Review Rd. NW2 ....4B 28
Rewell St. SW6 ....3E 87
Rex Pl. W1 ......5C 12 (1C 74)
Reydon Av. E11 ....1E 41
Reynard Cl. SE4 ......1A 108
Reynard Pl. SE14 .....2A 94
Reynolds Gdns. SE7 ...1D 97
Reynolds Cl. NW11 ....2D 31
Reynolds Ho. E2 ......1E 65
  (off Approach Rd.)
  NW8 ....1F 59
  (off Wellington Rd.)
  SW1 ....5F 75
  (off Erasmus St.)
Reynolds Pl. SE3 ......3D 97
Reynolds Rd. SE15 ...2E 107
Rheidol M. N1 ....1E 63
Rheidol Ter. N1 ....5E 49
Rhoda St. E2 ...3F 11 (3B 64)
Rhodes Ho. N1 ....1B 10
  (off Provost Est.)
Rhodesia Rd. E11 .....4F 39
  SW9 ....5A 90
Rhodes St. N7 ....2B 48
Rhodeswell Rd. E14 ...4A 66
  (off Thomas Rd.)
Rhodium Ct. E14 ......4C 66
Rhondda Gro. E3 .....2A 66
Rhyl St. NW5 ....3C 46

Ribblesdale Ho. NW6 ...5C 44
  (off Kilburn Vale)
Ribblesdale Rd.
  SW16 ....5D 117
Ribbon Dance M. SE5 ..4F 91
Ricardo St. E14 ....5D 67
Ricards Rd. SW19 .....5B 114
Riceyman Ho. N1 ......2B 8
  (off Lloyd Baker St.)
Richard Anderson Ct.
  SE14 ....3F 93
  (off Monson Rd.)
Richard Burbidge Mans.
  SW13 ....2E 85
  (off Brasenose Dr.)
Richard Fielden Ho.
  E1 ....2A 66
Richard Ho. SE16 .....5E 79
  (off Silwood St.)
Richard Ho. Dr. E16 ...5F 69
Richard Neale Ho.
  E1 ....1D 79
  (off Cornwall St.)
Richard Robert Residence, The
  E15 ....3F 53
  (off Salway Rd.)
Richardson Cl. E8 .....5B 50
Richardson Ct. SW4 ...5A 90
  (off Studley Rd.)
Richardson Rd. E15 ...1A 68
Richardson's M. W1 ....4F 5
Richard's Pl. SW3 .....5A 74
Richard St. E1 ....5D 65
Richbell WC1 ....5E 7
  (off Boswell St.)
Richbell Pl.
  WC1 ....5F 7 (4B 62)
Richborne Ter. SW8 ...3B 90
Richborough Ho.
  SE15 ....2E 93
  (off Sharratt St.)
Richborough Rd.
  NW2 ....1A 44
Richbourne Ct. W1 ....5A 60
  (off Harrowby St.)
Richford Ga. W6 ......4E 71
Richford Rd. E15 .....5B 54
Richford St. W6 ......3E 71
Rich Ind. Est.
  SE1 ......5E 27 (4A 78)
  SE15 ....2D 93
Richland Ho. SE15 ....4C 92
  (off Goldsmith Rd.)
Rich La. SW5 ....1D 87
Richman Ho. SE8 .....1B 94
  (off Grove St.)
**Richmond,
  The American
  International University
  in London
  Kensington Campus -
  Ansdell Street** 4D 73
  (off Ansdell St.)
St Albans Grove
  ....4D 73
Young Street 3D 73
Richmond Av. N1 .....5B 48
  NW10 ....3E 43
Richmond Bldgs.
  W1 ....3B 14 (5F 61)

Richmond Cl. E17 ......1B 38
Richmond Cotts.
  W14 ....5A 72
  (off Hammersmith Rd.)
Richmond Ct. E8 ......4D 51
  (off Mare St.)
  NW6 ....4F 43
  (off Willesden La.)
  SW1 ....4A 20
  (off Sloane St.)
  W14 ....5A 72
  (off Sloane St.)
Richmond Cres. N1 ....5B 48
Richmond Gro. N1 .....4D 49
  (not continuous)
Richmond Ho. NW1 ....1E 5
  (off Park Village E.)
  SE17 ....1F 91
  (off Portland St.)
Richmond Mans.
  SW5 ....1D 87
  (off Old Brompton Rd.)
Richmond M.
  W1 ....3B 14 (5F 61)
Richmond Pk. Golf Course
................................5A 98
Richmond Rd. E7 .....2D 55
  (not continuous)
  E8 ....4B 50
  E11 ....4F 39
  N15 ....1A 36
Richmond St. E13 ....1C 68
Richmond Ter.
  SW1 ......3D 23 (3A 76)
  W12 ....3F 71
  W14 ....3F 71
Richmount Gdns.
  SE3 ....1C 110
Rich St. E14 ....1B 80
Rickard Cl. SW2 .....1C 118
Rickett St. SW6 ......2C 86
Rickman Ho. E1 ......2E 65
  (off Rickman St.)
Rickman St. E1 ....3E 65
Rick Roberts Way
  E15 ....5E 53
Rickthorne Rd. N19 ...4A 34
Rickyard Path SE9 ....2F 111
Riddell Ct. SE5 ....1B 92
  (off Albany Rd.)
Riddons Rd. SE12 ....3E 125
Ridgdale St. E3 ....1D 67
Ridgebrook Rd. SE3 ..1F 111
Ridge Ct. SE22 .....5C 106
Ridge Hill NW11 ......3A 30
Ridge Rd. N8 ....1B 34
  NW2 ....5B 30
Ridge Way SE19 .....5A 120
Ridgeway, The
  NW11 ....2A 30
Ridgeway Dr.
  BR1: Brom 4D 125
Ridgeway Gdns. N6 ...2E 33
Ridgewell Cl. N1 ......5E 49
  SE26 ....4B 122
Ridgmount Gdns.
  WC1 ....5B 6 (4F 61)
Ridgmount Pl.
  WC1 ....5B 6 (4F 61)

Ridgmount Rd.
SW18 . . . . .3D **101**
Ridgmount St.
WC1 . . . . .5B **6** (4F **61**)
Ridgway SW19 . . . . .5A **114**
Ridgway Pl.
SW19 . . . . .5A **114**
Ridgway Rd. SW9 . . . .1D **105**
Ridgwell Rd. E16 . . . . .4E **69**
Riding, The NW11 . . . .2B **30**
Riding Ho. St.
W1 . . . . . .1E **13** (4D **61**)
Ridings Cl. N6 . . . . .2E **33**
Ridley Cl. SW16 . . . . . .5A **118**
Ridley Ho. SW1 . . . . . . .5C **22**
(off Monck St.)
Ridley Rd. E7 . . . . .1E **55**
E8 . . . . .2B **50**
NW10 . . . . .1C **56**
Riffel Rd. NW2 . . . . . . .2E **43**
Rifle Ct. SE11 . . . . .2C **90**
Rifle St. E14 . . . . .4D **67**
Riga M. E1 . . . . .5C **64**
(off Commercial Rd.)
Rigault Rd. SW6 . . . . . .5A **86**
Rigden St. E14 . . . . .5D **67**
Rigeley Rd. NW10 . . . . .2C **56**
Rigg App. E10 . . . . .3F **37**
Rigge Pl. SW4 . . . . .2F **103**
Riggindale Rd.
SW16 . . . . .5F **117**
Riley Ho. E3 . . . . .3C **66**
(off Ireton St.)
SW10 . . . . .3F **87**
(off Riley St.)
Riley Rd.
SE1 . . . . . .5E **27** (4B **78**)
Riley St. SW10 . . . . . . .2F **87**
Rill Ho. SE5 . . . . .3F **91**
(off Harris St.)
Rima Ho. SW3 . . . . .2F **87**
(off Callow St.)
Rinaldo Rd. SW12 . . . .5D **103**
Ring, The SW7 . . . . .3F **73**
W2 . . . . . .4A **12** (1F **73**)
Ring Ct. SE1 . . . . .3D **77**
(off The Cut)
Ringcroft St. N7 . . . . . . .2C **48**
Ringford Rd. SW18 . . . .3B **100**
Ring Ho. E1 . . . . .1E **79**
(off Sage St.)
Ringlet Cl. E16 . . . . .4D **69**
Ringmer Av. SW6 . . . . . .4A **86**
Ringmer Gdns. N19 . . . .4A **34**
Ringmore Ri. SE23 . . . .5D **107**
Ringmore Vw. SE23 . . . .5D **107**
Ring Rd. W12 . . . . .2E **71**
(not continuous)
Ringsfield Ho. SE17 . . . .1E **91**
(off Bronti Cl.)
Ringstead Rd. SE6 . . . .5D **109**
Ringwood Gdns. E14 . . .5C **80**
SW15 . . . . .1C **112**
Ringwood Rd. E17 . . . .1B **38**
Rio Cinema
Dalston 2A **50**
(off Kingsland High St.)
Ripley Bldgs. SE1 . . . . .3E **25**
(off Rushworth St.)
Ripley Gdns. SW14 . . . .1A **98**

Ripley Ho. SW1 . . . . . . .2E **89**
(off Churchill Gdns.)
Ripley M. E11 . . . . .1A **40**
Ripley Rd. E16 . . . . .5E **69**
Ripon Gdns.
IG1: Ilf 1F **41**
Ripplevale Gro. N1 . . . .4B **48**
Risborough SE17 . . . . . .5E **77**
(off Deacon Way)
Risborough Ho. NW8 . . .3A **60**
(off Mallory St.)
Risborough St.
SE1 . . . . . .3E **25** (3D **77**)
Risdon Ho. SE16 . . . . . .3E **79**
(off Risdon St.)
Risdon St. SE16 . . . . . .4E **79**
Rise, The E11 . . . . .1C **40**
NW10 . . . . .1A **42**
Riseholme Ct. E9 . . . . . .3B **52**
Riseldine Rd. SE23 . . . .4A **108**
Risinghill St. N1 . . . . . . .1B **62**
Rising Sun Ct. EC1 . . . . .5E **9**
Rita Rd. SW8 . . . . .2A **90**
Ritches Rd. N15 . . . . . . .1E **35**
Ritchie Ho. E14 . . . . . . .5F **67**
(off Blair St.)
N19 . . . . .3F **33**
SE16 . . . . .4E **79**
(off Howland Est.)
Ritchie St. N1 . . . . .1C **62**
Ritherdon Rd.
SW17 . . . . .2C **116**
Ritson Ho. N1 . . . . .5B **48**
(off Barnsbury Est.)
Ritson Rd. E8 . . . . .3C **50**
Ritzy Picturehouse . . .2C **104**
(off Coldharbour La.)
Riva Building, The
SE13 . . . . .2F **109**
Rivaz Pl. E9 . . . . .3E **51**
Riven Ct. W2 . . . . .5D **59**
(off Inverness Ter.)
Riverbank Arena, Olympic Pk.
. . . . .2C **52**
Riverbank Rd.
BR1: Brom 3C **124**
River Barge Cl. E14 . . . .3E **81**
River Cl. E11 . . . . .1E **41**
River Ct.
SE1 . . . . . .5D **17** (1D **77**)
Rivercourt Rd. W6 . . . .5D **71**
Riverdale SE13 . . . . . . .2E **109**
Riverdale Dr. SW18 . . . .1D **115**
Riverdale Shop. Cen.
SE13 . . . . .2E **109**
Riverfleet WC1 . . . . .1E **7**
(off Birkenhead St.)
Riverford Ho. W2 . . . . . .4C **58**
(off Westbourne Pk. Rd.)
River Ho. SE26 . . . . . . .3D **121**
River Lodge SW1 . . . . . .2E **89**
(off Grosvenor Rd.)
Rivermead Ct. SW6 . . . .1B **100**
Rivermead Ho. E9 . . . . .2A **52**
River Pl. N1 . . . . .4E **49**
Riversdale Rd. N5 . . . . .5D **35**
Riverside E3 . . . . .5C **52**
NW4 . . . . .2D **29**
SE7 . . . . .4D **83**
SW11 . . . . .3A **88**

Riverside W6 . . . . .2E **85**
WC1 . . . . .1E **7**
(off Birkenhead St.)
Riverside Bus. Cen.
SW18 . . . . .1D **115**
Riverside Cl. E5 . . . . . . .3E **37**
Riverside Ct. SE3 . . . . . .2B **110**
Riverside Dr.
NW11 . . . . .1A **30**
W4 . . . . .3A **84**
Riverside Gdns. W6 . . . .1D **85**
Riverside Ho. N1 . . . . . .4E **49**
(off Canonbury St.)
Riverside Mans. E1 . . . .2E **79**
(off Milk Yd.)
Riverside Rd. E15 . . . . . .1E **67**
N15 . . . . .1C **36**
SW17 . . . . .4D **115**
Riverside Studios 1E **85**
Riverside Twr. SW6 . . . .5E **87**
(off The Boulevard)
Riverside Wlk. SE10 . . . .4A **82**
(Morden Wharf Rd.)
SE10 . . . . .3F **81**
(Tunnel Av.)
SW6 . . . . .1A **100**
W4 . . . . .2B **84**
(off Chiswick Wharf)
Riverside Wharf E8 . . . .5B **50**
Riverside Yd. SW17 . . . .4E **115**
River St. EC1 . . . .1B **8** (2C **62**)
River Ter. W6 . . . . .1E **85**
WC2 . . . . .5F **15**
Riverton Cl. W9 . . . . . . .2B **58**
Riverview Ct. E14 . . . . . .4B **80**
Riverview Gdns.
SW13 . . . . .2D **85**
River Vw. Hgts. SE16 . . .3C **78**
(off Bermondsey Wall W.)
Riverview Pk. SE6 . . . . .2C **122**
Riverview Wlk. SE6 . . . .3B **122**
River Wlk. SW6 . . . . . . .5E **87**
W6 . . . . .3E **85**
Riverwalk Ho. SW1 . . . .1A **90**
(off Millbank)
River Way SE10 . . . . . . .4B **82**
Rivet Ho. SE1 . . . . .1B **92**
(off Cooper's Rd.)
Riviera Ct. E1 . . . . .2C **78**
(off St Katharine's Way)
Rivington Ct. NW10 . . . .5C **42**
Rivington Pl.
EC2 . . . . . .2E **11** (2A **64**)
Rivington St.
EC2 . . . . . .2D **11** (2A **64**)
Rivington Wlk. E8 . . . . . .5C **50**
Rixon St. N7 . . . . .5C **34**
Roach Rd. E3 . . . . .4C **52**
Roads Pl. N19 . . . . .4A **34**
Roan St. SE10 . . . . .2E **95**
Robert Adam St.
W1 . . . . . .2B **12** (5C **60**)
Roberta St. E2 . . . . .2C **64**
Robert Bell Ho. SE16 . . .5C **78**
(off Rouel Rd.)
Robert Burns M.
SE24 . . . . .3D **105**
Robert Cl. W9 . . . . .3E **59**
Robert Ct. SE15 . . . . . . .5C **92**

Robert Dashwood Way
SE17 . . . . .5E 77

Robert Gentry Ho.
W14 . . . . .1A 86
(off Gledstanes Rd.)

Robert Jones Ho.
SE16 . . . . .5C 78
(off Rouel Rd.)

Robert Keen Cl.
SE15 . . . . .4C 92

Robert Lowe Cl.
SE14 . . . . .3F 93

Robert Morton Ho.
NW8 . . . . .4E 45

Robert Owen Ho. E2 . . .1F 11
(off Baroness Rd.)
SW6 . . . . .4F 85

Robert Runcie Ct.
SW2 . . . . .2B 104

Roberts Cl. SE16 . . . .3F 79

Roberts Ct. N1 . . . . . .5D 49
(off Essex Rd.)
NW10 . . . . .3A 42

Roberts M.
SW1 . . . . .5B 20 (4C 74)

Robertson Gro.
SW17 . . . . .5A 116

Robertson Rd. E16 . . .4C 68

Robertson St. SW8 . . .1D 103

Roberts Pl.
EC1 . . . . . . .3C 8 (3C 62)

Robert St.
NW1 . . . . . .2E 5 (2D 61)
WC2 . . . . . .5E 15 (1A 76)

Robert Sutton Ho. E1 . .5E 65
(off Tarling St.)

Robeson St. E3 . . . . . .4B 66

Robin Ct. E14 . . . . . . .3E 81
SE16 . . . . .5C 78

Robin Cres. E6 . . . . . .4F 69

Robin Gro. N6 . . . . . .4C 32

ROBIN HOOD 3A 112

Robin Hood Ct. EC4 . . .2C 16
(off Shoe La.)

Robin Hood Gdns.
E14 . . . . .1E 81
(off Woolmore St.,
not continuous)

Robin Hood La. E14 . . .1E 81
SW15 . . . . .3A 112

Robin Hood Rd.
SW19 . . . . .5C 112

Robin Hood Way
SW15 . . . . .3A 112
SW20 . . . . .3A 112

Robin Ho. NW8 . . . . . .1A 60
(off Newcourt St.)

Robin Howard Dance Theatre
. . . . .2C 6
(off Duke's Rd.)

Robinia Cres. E10 . . . .4D 39

Robins Ct. SE12 . . . . .3E 125

Robinscroft M. SE10 . . .4E 95

Robinson Cl. E11 . . . . .5A 40

Robinson Ct. N1 . . . . . .5D 49
(off St Mary's Path)

Robinson Ho. E14 . . . .4C 66
(off Selsey St.)
W10 . . . . .5F 57
(off Bramley Rd.)

Robinson Rd. E2 . . . . . .1E 65
SW17 . . . . .5A 116

Robinson St. SW3 . . . .2B 88

Robinswood M. N5 . . . .2D 49

Robinwood Pl.
SW15 . . . . .4A 112

Robsart St. SW9 . . . . .5B 90

Robson Av. NW10 . . . .4C 42

Robson Cl. E6 . . . . . . .5F 69

Robson Rd. SE27 . . . .3E 119

Roby Ho. EC1 . . . . . . .3F 9
(off Mitchell St.)

Rocastle Rd. SE4 . . . . .3A 108

Rochdale Rd. E17 . . . .2C 38

Rochdale Way SE8 . . . .3C 94
(not continuous)

Roche Ho. E14 . . . . . . .1B 80
(off Beccles St.)

Rochelle Cl. SW11 . . . .2F 101

Rochelle St.
E2 . . . . .2F 11 (2B 64)
(not continuous)

Rochemont Wlk. E8 . . . .5C 50
(off Pownall Rd.)

Rochester Av. E13 . . . .5E 55

Rochester Ct. E2 . . . . .3D 65
(off Wilmot St.)
NW1 . . . . .4E 47
(off Rochester Sq.)

Rochester Ho. SE1 . . . .4C 26
(off Manciple St.)
SE15 . . . . .2E 93
(off Sharratt St.)

Rochester M. NW1 . . . .4E 47

Rochester Pl. NW1 . . . .3E 47

Rochester Rd. NW1 . . . .3E 47

Rochester Row NW1 . . .5E 75

Rochester Sq. NW1 . . . .4E 47

Rochester St. SW1 . . . .4F 75

Rochester Ter. NW1 . . . .3E 47

Rochester Wlk.
SE1 . . . . .1B 26 (2F 77)

Rochester Way SE3 . . . .4D 97
SE9 . . . . .5C 97

Rochester Way Relief Rd.
SE3 . . . . .4D 97
SE9 . . . . .1E 111

Rochford Cl. E6 . . . . . .1F 69

Rochford Wlk. E8 . . . . .4C 50

Rochfort Ho. SE8 . . . . .1B 94

Rock Av. SW14 . . . . . .1A 98

Rockbourne M.
SE23 . . . . .1F 121

Rockbourne Rd.
SE23 . . . . .1F 121

Rock Circus 5B 14
(in Trocadero Cen.)

Rockell's Pl. SE22 . . . .4D 107

Rockfield Ho. SE10 . . . .2E 95
(off Welland St.)

Rock Gro. Way SE16 . . .5C 78
(not continuous)

Rockhall Rd. NW2 . . . .1F 43

Rockhall Way NW2 . . . .5F 29

Rockhampton Cl.
SE27 . . . . .4C 118

Rockhampton Rd.
SE27 . . . . .4C 118

Rock Hill SE26 . . . . . .4B 120
(not continuous)

Rockingham Cl.
SW15 . . . . .2B 98

Rockingham St.
SE1 . . . . .5F 25 (4E 77)

Rockland Rd. SW15 . . . .2A 100

Rockley Ct. W14 . . . . . .3F 71
(off Rockley Rd.)

Rockley Rd. W14 . . . . .3F 71

Rockmount Rd.
SE19 . . . . .5F 119

Rocks La. SW13 . . . . . .4C 84

Rock St. N4 . . . . .4C 34

Rockwell Gdns.
SE19 . . . . .5A 120

Rockwood Pl. W12 . . . .3E 71

Rocliffe St. N1 . . . . . . .1D 63

Rocombe Cres.
SE23 . . . . .5E 107

Rocque Ho. SW6 . . . . . .3B 86
(off Estcourt Rd.)

Rocque La. SE3 . . . . . .1B 110

Rodale Mans.
SW18 . . . . .4D 101

Rodborough Ct. W9 . . . .3C 58
(off Hermes Cl.)

Rodborough Rd.
NW11 . . . . .3C 30

Roden Ct. N6 . . . . .2F 33

Rodenhurst Rd.
SW4 . . . . .4E 103

Roden St. N7 . . . . .5B 34

Roderick Ho. SE16 . . . .5E 79
(off Raymouth Rd.)

Roderick Rd. NW3 . . . .1B 46

Rodgers Ho. SW4 . . . . .5F 103
(off Clapham Pk. Est.)

Rodin Ct. N1 . . . . .5D 49
(off Essex Rd.)

Roding Ho. N1 . . . . . . .5C 48
(off Barnsbury Est.)

Roding La. Sth.
IG4: Ilf 1F 41
(not continuous)

Roding M. E1 . . . . .2C 78

Roding Rd. E5 . . . . .1F 51

Rodmarton St.
W1 . . . . .1A 12 (4B 60)

Rodmell WC1 . . . . .2E 7
(off Regent Sq.)

Rodmere St. SE10 . . . .1A 96

Rodmill La. SW2 . . . . . .5A 104

Rodney Ct. W9 . . . . . . .3E 59

Rodney Ho. E14 . . . . . .5D 81
(off Cahir St.)
N1 . . . . .1B 62
(off Donegal St.)
SW1 . . . . .1E 89
(off Dolphin Sq.)
W11 . . . . .1C 72
(off Pembridge Cres.)

Rodney Pl. SE17 . . . . . .5E 77

Rodney Point SE16 . . . .3B 80
(off Rotherhithe St.)

Rodney Rd. SE17 . . . . .5E 77
(not continuous)

Rodney St. N1 . . . .1A 8 (1B 62)

Rodway Rd. SW15 . . . .5C 98

Rodwell Rd. SE22 . . . . .4B 106

Roedean Cres. SW15 . . .4A 98

ROEHAMPTON 5C 98

Roehampton Cl.
SW15 . . . . .2C **98**
Roehampton Ga.
SW15 . . . . .4A **98**
Roehampton Golf Course
. . . . .2B **98**
Roehampton High St.
SW15 . . . . .5C **98**
ROEHAMPTON LANE
. . . . .1D **113**
Roehampton La.
SW15 . . . . .2C **98**
Roehampton
Sport & Fitness Cen.
. . . . .5C **98**
Roehampton University
. . . . .4B **98**
Roehampton Va.
SW15 . . . . .3B **112**
Roffey St. E14 . . . . . . .3E **81**
Rogate Ho. E5 . . . . . . .5C **36**
Roger Dowley Ct. E2 . . .1E **65**
Roger Harriss Almshouses
E15 . . . . .5B **54**
(off Gift La.)
Rogers Ct. E14 . . . . . . .1C **80**
(off Premiere Pl.)
Rogers Est. E2 . . . . . . .2E **65**
(not continuous)
Rogers Ho. SW1 . . . . . .5F **75**
(off Page St.)
Rogers Rd. E16 . . . . . .5B **68**
SW17 . . . . .4F **115**
Roger St. WC1 . . .4A **8** (3B **62**)
Rohere Ho.
EC1 . . . . .1F **9** (2E **63**)
Rojack Rd. SE23 . . . . . .1F **121**
Rokeby Ho. SW12 . . . .5D **103**
(off Lochinvar St.)
WC1 . . . . .4F **7**
(off Lamb's Conduit St.)
Rokeby Rd. SE4 . . . . . .5B **94**
Rokeby St. E15 . . . . . . .5F **53**
Rokell Ho.
BR3: Beck 5D **123**
(off Beckenham Hill Rd.)
Roland Gdns. SW7 . . . .1E **87**
Roland Ho. SW7 . . . . . .1E **87**
(off Old Brompton Rd.)
Roland Mans. SW7 . . . .1E **87**
(off Old Brompton Rd.)
Roland M. E1 . . . . .4F **65**
Roland Way SE17 . . . . .1F **91**
SW7 . . . . .1E **87**
Rollins St. SE15 . . . . . .2E **93**
Rollit St. N7 . . . . .2C **48**
Rolls Bldgs.
EC4 . . . . . . .2B **16** (5C **62**)
Rollscourt Av. SE24 . . . .3E **105**
Rolls Pas. EC4 . . . . . . .2B **16**
Rolls Rd. SE1 . . . . .1B **92**
Rolt St. SE8 . . . . .2A **94**
(not continuous)
Roman Ct. N7 . . . . .3B **48**
Romanfield Rd.
SW2 . . . . .5B **104**
Roman Ho. EC2 . . . . . . .1A **18**
Roman Ri. SE19 . . . . . .5F **119**
Roman Rd. E2 . . . . .2E **65**
E3 . . . . .1A **66**

Roman Rd. E6 . . . . .3F **69**
NW2 . . . . .5E **29**
W4 . . . . .5A **70**
Roman Way N7 . . . . . . .3B **48**
SE15 . . . . .3E **93**
Roman Way Ind. Est.
N7 . . . . .4B **48**
(off Roman Way)
Roma Read Cl.
SW15 . . . . .5D **99**
Romayne Ho. SW4 . . . .1F **103**
Romberg Rd. SW17 . . . .3C **116**
Romborough Gdns.
SE13 . . . . .3E **109**
Romborough Way
SE13 . . . . .3E **109**
Romero Cl. SW9 . . . . . .1B **104**
Romero Sq. SE3 . . . . . .2E **111**
Romeyn Rd. SW16 . . . .3B **118**
Romford Rd. E7 . . . . . . .3A **54**
E12 . . . . .2E **55**
E15 . . . . .3A **54**
Romford St. E1 . . . . . . .4C **65**
Romilly Ho. W11 . . . . . .1A **72**
(off Wilsham St.)
Romilly Rd. N4 . . . . . . .4D **35**
Romilly St.
W1 . . . . . . .4C **14** (1F **75**)
Romily Ct. SW6 . . . . . . .5B **86**
Rommany Rd. SE27 . . . .4F **119**
(not continuous)
Romney Cl. NW11 . . . . .3E **31**
SE14 . . . . .3E **93**
Romney Ct. NW3 . . . . . .3A **46**
W12 . . . . .3F **71**
(off Shepherd's Bush Grn.)
Romney Ho. SW1 . . . . . .4F **75**
(off Marsham St.)
Romney M.
W1 . . . . .5B **4** (4C **60**)
Romney Rd. SE10 . . . . .2F **95**
Romney Row NW2 . . . . .4F **29**
(off Brent Ter.)
Romney St. SW1 . . . . . .4A **76**
Romola Rd. SE24 . . . . .1D **119**
Ronald Av. E15 . . . . . . .2A **68**
Ronald Buckingham Ct.
SE16 . . . . .3E **79**
(off Kenning St.)
Ronald Ho. SE3 . . . . . . .2E **111**
Ronaldshay N4 . . . . . . .2C **34**
Ronalds Rd. N5 . . . . . . .2C **48**
(not continuous)
Ronald St. E1 . . . . .5E **65**
Rona Rd. NW3 . . . . .1C **46**
Rona Wlk. N1 . . . . .3F **49**
Rondu Rd. NW2 . . . . . . .2A **44**
Ronver Rd. SE12 . . . . . .5B **110**
Rood La.
EC3 . . . . . . .4D **19** (1A **78**)
Roof Ter. Apartments, The
EC1 . . . . .4E **9**
(off Sutton St.)
Rookery Rd. SW4 . . . . . .2E **103**
Rookery Way NW9 . . . . .1B **28**
Rooke Way SE10 . . . . . .1B **96**
Rookstone Rd.
SW17 . . . . .5B **116**
Rook Wlk. E6 . . . . .5F **69**
Rookwood Rd. N16 . . . . .2B **36**

Roosevelt Memorial
. . . . .4C **12** (1C **74**)
Rootes Dr. W10 . . . . . . .4F **57**
Ropemaker Rd.
SE16 . . . . .3A **80**
Ropemaker's Flds.
E14 . . . . .1B **80**
Ropemaker St.
EC2 . . . . . . .5B **10** (4F **63**)
Roper La.
SE1 . . . . .4E **27** (3A **78**)
Ropers Orchard SW3 . . .2A **88**
(off Danvers St.)
Ropers Wlk. SW2 . . . . . .5C **104**
Ropery Bus. Pk. SE7 . . .5E **83**
Ropery St. E3 . . . . .3B **66**
Rope St. SE16 . . . . .5A **80**
Rope Wlk. Gdns. E1 . . . .5C **64**
Ropewalk M. E8 . . . . . . .4C **50**
(off Middleton Rd.)
Ropley St. E2 . . . . .1C **64**
Rosa Alba M. N5 . . . . . .1E **49**
Rosalind Ho. N1 . . . . . . .1A **64**
(off Arden Ho.)
Rosalind Rd. SW6 . . . . .3A **86**
Rosaline Ter. SW6 . . . . .3A **86**
(off Rosaline Rd.)
Rosamond St. SE26 . . . .3D **121**
Rosa Parks Ho. SE17 . . .5E **77**
(off Munton Rd.)
Rosary Gdns. SW7 . . . . .5E **73**
Rosaville Rd. SW6 . . . . .3B **86**
Roscoe St.
EC1 . . . . .4A **10** (3E **63**)
(not continuous)
Roscoe St. Est.
EC1 . . . . . . .4A **10** (3E **63**)
Rose All. EC2 . . . . .1E **19**
(off Bishopsgate)
SE1 . . . . .1A **26** (2E **77**)
Rose & Crown Ct.
EC2 . . . . .2A **18**
Rose & Crown Yd.
SW1 . . . . . . .1A **22** (2E **75**)
Rosebank SW6 . . . . . . .3E **85**
(not continuous)
Rosebank Gdns. E3 . . . .1B **66**
Rosebank Rd. E17 . . . . .1D **39**
Rosebank Wlk. NW1 . . . .4F **47**
Rosebay Ho. E3 . . . . . . .4C **66**
(off Hawgood St.)
Roseberry Gdns. N4 . . . .1D **35**
Roseberry Pl. E8 . . . . . .3B **50**
Roseberry St. SE16 . . . .5D **79**
Rosebery Av. E12 . . . . . .3F **55**
EC1 . . . . . . .4B **8** (3C **62**)
Rosebery Ct. EC1 . . . . . .3B **8**
(off Rosebery Av.)
W1 . . . . .1D **21**
(off Charles St.)
Rosebery Gdns. N8 . . . .1A **34**
Rosebery Rd. E16 . . . . . .1E **65**
(off Sewardstone Rd.)
Rosebery Rd. SW2 . . . . .4A **104**
Rosebery Sq. EC1 . . . . . .4B **8**
Rosebury Rd. SW6 . . . . .5D **87**
Rose Bush Ct. NW3 . . . .2B **46**
Rose Ct. E1 . . . . .1F **19**
E8 . . . . .4B **50**
(off Richmond Rd.)

Rose Ct. *N1* 5D **49**
  (off Collin's Yd.)
  SE8 . . . . .5F **79**
Rosecroft Av. NW3 . . . .5C **30**
Rosecroft Gdns.
  NW2 . . . . .5C **28**
Rosedale Ct. N5 . . . . . .1D **49**
Rosedale Ho. N16 . . . . .3F **35**
Rosedale Rd. E7 . . . . . .2E **55**
Rosedale Ter. *W6* 4D **71**
  (off Dalling Rd.)
Rosedene NW6 . . . . . . .5F **43**
Rosedene Av.
  SW16 . . . . .3B **118**
Rosedene Ter. E10 . . . .4D **39**
Rosedew Rd. W6 . . . . . .2F **85**
Rosefield Gdns.
  E14 . . . . .1C **80**
Roseford Ct. *W12* 3F **71**
  (off Shepherd's Bush Grn.)
Rosegate Ho. *E3* 1B **66**
  (off Hereford Rd.)
Rosehart M. W11 . . . . .5C **58**
Rosehill Rd. SW18 . . . .4E **101**
Rose Joan M. NW6 . . . .1C **44**
Rosekey Ct. *SE8* 3B **94**
  (off Baildon St.)
Roseleigh Av. N5 . . . . .1D **49**
Rosemary Branch Theatre
  . . . . .5F **49**
  (off Rosemary St.)
Rosemary Ct. *SE8* 2B **94**
  (off Dorking Cl.)
  SE15 . . . . .3A **92**
Rosemary Dr. E14 . . . . .5F **67**
  IG4: Ilf 1F **41**
Rosemary Ho. *N1* 5F **49**
  (off Branch Pl.)
  NW10 . . . . .5D **43**
  (off Uffington Rd.)
Rosemary Rd. SE15 . . . .3B **92**
  SW17 . . . . .3E **115**
Rosemary St. N1 . . . . . .5F **49**
Rosemead NW9 . . . . . .2B **28**
Rosemont Rd. NW3 . . . .3E **45**
Rosemoor St. SW3 . . . .5B **74**
Rosemount Point
  SE23 . . . . .3F **121**
Rosenau Cres. SW11 . . .4B **88**
Rosenau Rd. SW11 . . . .4A **88**
Rosendale Rd.
  SE21 . . . . .2E **119**
  SE24 . . . . .5E **105**
Roseneath Pl.
  SW16 . . . . .4B **118**
  (off Curtis Fld. Rd.)
Roseneath Rd.
  SW11 . . . . .4C **102**
Rosenthal Rd. SE6 . . . .4D **109**
Rosenthorpe Rd.
  SE15 . . . . .3F **107**
Rose Pl. N8 . . . . .1A **34**
Roserton St. E14 . . . . . .3E **81**
Rose Sq. SW3 . . . . .1F **87**
Rose St. EC4 . . . .2E **17** (5D **63**)
  WC2 . . . .4D **15** (1A **76**)
  (not continuous)
Rosethorn Cl. SW12 . . .5F **103**
Rosetta Cl. *SW8* 3A **90**
  (off Kenchester Cl.)

Roseveare Rd.
  SE12 . . . . .4E **125**
Rose Way SE12 . . . . . . .3C **110**
Roseway SE21 . . . . .4F **105**
Rosewood Ct. E11 . . . . .1F **53**
Rosewood Gdns.
  SE13 . . . . .5E **95**
Rosewood Ho. SW8 . . . .2B **90**
Rosewood Sq. W12 . . . .5C **56**
Rosher Cl. E15 . . . . .4F **53**
Roshni Ho. SW17 . . . . .5A **116**
Rosina St. E9 . . . . .3F **51**
Roskell Rd. SW15 . . . . .1F **99**
Roslin Ho. *E1* 1F **79**
  (off Brodlove La.)
Roslin Way
  BR1: Brom 5C **124**
Rosmead Rd. W11 . . . . .1A **72**
Rosoman Pl.
  EC1 . . . . . . .3C **8** (3C **62**)
Rosoman St.
  EC1 . . . . . .2C **8** (2C **62**)
Ross Apartments *E16* . .1C **82**
  (off Seagull La.)
Ross Ct. *E5* 1D **51**
  (off Napoleon Rd.)
  SW15 . . . . .5F **99**
Rosscourt Mans.
  SW1 . . . . .5F **21**
  (off Buckingham Pal. Rd.)
Rossdale Rd. SW15 . . . .2E **99**
Rosse Gdns. SE13 . . . . .4F **109**
Rosse M. SE3 . . . . .4D **97**
Rossendale St. E5 . . . . .4D **37**
Rossendale Way
  NW1 . . . . .4E **47**
Rossetti Ct. *WC1* 5B **6**
  (off Ridgmount Pl.)
Rossetti Gdn. Mans.
  . . . . .2B **88**
  (off Flood St.)
Rossetti Ho. *SW1* 5F **75**
  (off Erasmus St.)
Rossetti M. NW8 . . . . . .5F **45**
Rossetti Rd. SE16 . . . . .1D **93**
Rossetti Studios
  SW3 . . . . .2A **88**
  (off Flood St.)
Ross Ho. *E1* 2D **79**
  (off Prusom St.)
Rossington St. E5 . . . . .4C **36**
Rossiter Gro. SW9 . . . . .1C **104**
Rossiter Rd. SW12 . . . .1D **117**
Rosslyn Av. SW13 . . . . .1A **98**
Rosslyn Hill NW3 . . . . .1F **45**
Rosslyn Mans. *NW6* . . .4E **45**
  (off Goldhurst Ter.)
Rosslyn M. NW3 . . . . . .1F **45**
Rosslyn Pk. M. NW3 . . .2F **45**
Rossmore Cl. *NW1* 3A **60**
  (off Rossmore Rd.)
Rossmore Ct. NW1 . . . .3B **60**
Rossmore Rd. NW1 . . . .3A **60**
Ross Wlk. SE27 . . . . . . .4F **119**
Ross Way SE9 . . . . .1F **111**
Rostella Ho. SW17 . . . .4F **115**
Rostrevor Av. N15 . . . . .1B **36**
Rostrevor Mans.
  SW6 . . . . .4B **86**
  (off Rostrevor Rd.)

Rostrevor M. SW6 . . . . .4B **86**
Rostrevor Rd. SW6 . . . .4B **86**
  SW19 . . . . .5C **114**
Roswell Apartments
  E3 . . . . .4B **66**
  (off Joseph St.)
Rotary St.
  SE1 . . . . . . .5D **25** (4D **77**)
Rothay *NW1* 1E **5**
  (off Albany St.)
Rothbury Cotts. *SE10* . .5A **82**
  (off Maritius Rd.)
Rothbury Rd. E9 . . . . . .4B **52**
Rotheley Ho. *E9* 4E **51**
  (off Balcorne St.)
Rotherfield Ct. *N1* 4F **49**
  (off Rotherfield St.,
  not continuous)
Rotherfield St. N1 . . . . .4E **49**
Rotherham Wlk. SE1 . . .2D **25**
ROTHERHITHE 3E **79**
Rotherhithe Bus. Est.
  SE16 . . . . .5D **79**
Rotherhithe New Rd.
  SE16 . . . . .1D **93**
Rotherhithe Old Rd.
  SE16 . . . . .5F **79**
Rotherhithe St. SE16 . . .3E **79**
Rotherhithe Tunnel
  SE16 . . . . .2F **79**
Rother Ho. SE15 . . . . . .2D **107**
Rotherwick Ho. *E1* 1C **78**
  (off Thomas More St.)
Rotherwick Rd.
  NW11 . . . . .2C **30**
Rotherwood Rd.
  SW15 . . . . .1F **99**
Rothery St. *N1* 5D **49**
  (off St Marys Path)
Rothery Ter. SW9 . . . . . .3D **91**
  (off Foxley Rd.)
Rothesay Ct. *SE6* 2B **124**
  (off Cumberland Pl.)
  SE11 . . . . .2C **90**
  (off Harleyford St.)
  SE12 . . . . .3D **125**
Rothley Ct. *NW8* 3F **59**
  (off St John's Wood Rd.)
Rothsay Rd. E7 . . . . . . .4E **55**
Rothsay St.
  SE1 . . . . . . .5D **27** (4A **78**)
Rothsay Wlk. *E14* 5C **80**
  (off Charnwood Gdns.)
Rothschild St. SE27 . . . .4D **119**
Roth Wlk. N7 . . . . .4B **34**
Rothwell St. NW1 . . . . .5B **46**
Rotten Row NW3 . . . . . .3E **31**
  SW1 . . . . . .3A **20** (3F **73**)
  SW7 . . . . .3F **73**
Rotterdam Dr. E14 . . . . .4E **81**
Rotunda Ct.
  BR1: Brom 5D **125**
  (off Burnt Ash La.)
Rouel Rd. SE16 . . . . . . .4C **78**
  (Dockley Rd.)
  SE16 . . . . .5C **78**
  (Southwark Pk. Rd.)
Roundacre SW19 . . . . . .2F **113**
Roundel Cl. SE4 . . . . . . .2B **108**
Roundhay Cl. SE23 . . . .2F **121**

Round Hill SE26 . . . . . .2E 121
(not continuous)
Roundhouse, The 4C 46
Roundhouse La.
E20 . . . . .3E 53
(off International Way)
Roundtable Rd.
BR1: Brom 3B 124
Roundwood Ct. E2 . . . .2F 65
Roundwood Rd.
NW10 . . . . .3B 42
Rounton Rd. E3 . . . . . .3C 66
Roupell Rd. SW2 . . .1B 118
Roupell St.
SE1 . . . . . . .2C 24 (2C 76)
Rousden St. NW1 . . . .4E 47
Rouse Gdns. SE21 . . . .4A 120
Routemaster Ct. E13 . . .2D 69
Routh Rd. SW18 . . . .5A 102
Rover Ho. N1 . . . . . . .5A 50
(off Mill Row)
Rowallan Rd. SW6 . . . .3A 86
Rowan Cl. E13 . . . . . .1D 69
(off High St.)
SE15 . . . . .3B 92
(off Garnies Cl.)
SW11 . . . . .4B 102
Rowan Ho. E3 . . . . . . .5B 52
(off Hornbeam Sq.)
SE16 . . . . .3F 79
(off Woodland Cres.)
Rowan Lodge W8 . . . . .4D 73
(off Chantry Sq.)
Rowan Rd. W6 . . . . . . .5F 71
Rowans Complex 4C 34
Rowan Ter. W6 . . . . . .5F 71
Rowan Wlk. N2 . . . . . .1E 31
N19 . . . . .4E 33
W10 . . . . .3A 58
Rowberry Cl. SW6 . . . .3E 85
Rowcross St. SE1 . . . .1B 92
Rowditch La. SW11 . . . .5C 88
Rowdon Av. NW10 . . . .4D 43
Rowe Ho. E9 . . . . .3E 51
Rowe La. E9 . . . . .2E 51
Rowena Cres. SW11 . . .5A 88
Rowenhurst Mans.
NW6 . . . . .3E 45
(off Canfield Gdns.)
Rowfant Rd. SW17 . . .1C 116
Rowhill Rd. E5 . . . . . .1D 51
Rowington Cl. W2 . . . .4D 59
Rowland Ct. E16 . . . . .3B 68
Rowland Gro. SE26 . . . .3D 121
(not continuous)
Rowland Hill Ho.
SE1 . . . . . . .3D 25 (3D 77)
Rowland Hill St.
NW3 . . . . .2A 46
Rowlands Cl. N6 . . . . . .1C 32
Rowlands Gdns. N4 . . . .2E 35
Rowley Ho. SE8 . . . . . .1C 94
(off Watergate St.)
Rowley Rd. N15 . . . . . .1E 35
Rowley Way NW8 . . . . .5D 45
Rowntree Clifford Cl.
E13 . . . . .3C 68
Rowntree Cl. NW6 . . . .3C 44
Rowse Cl. E15 . . . . . . .5E 53
Rowstock Gdns. N7 . . . .2F 47

Roxburghe Mans.
W8 . . . . .3D 73
(off Kensington Ct.)
Roxburgh Rd. SE27 . . .5D 119
Roxby Pl. SW6 . . . . . . .2C 86
Roxford Ho. E3 . . . . . . .3D 67
(off Devas St.)
Roxley Ho. SE13 . . . . .4D 109
Roxwell NW1 . . . . .3D 47
(off Hartland Rd.)
Roxwell Rd. W12 . . . . .3C 70
Roxwell Trad. Pk.
E10 . . . . .2A 38
Royal Academy of Arts
(Burlington House)
. . . . .5F 13 (1E 75)
Royal Academy of Music Mus.
. . . . .4C 4
Royal Air Force Memorial
. . . . .2A 76
Royal Albert Hall 3F 73
Royal Albert Rdbt.
E16 . . . . .1F 83
(off Royal Albert Way)
Royal Albert Way
E16 . . . . .1F 83
Royal Arc. W1 . . . . . . .5F 13
Royal Archer SE14 . . . .3F 93
(off Egmont St.)
Royal Av. SW3 . . . . . . .1B 88
Royal Av. Ho. SW3 . . . .1B 88
(off Royal Av.)
Royal Belgrave Ho.
SW1 . . . . .5D 75
(off Hugh St.)
Royal Ceremonial
Dress Collection, The
. . . . .2D 73
(in Kensington Palace)
Royal Cir. SE27 . . . . . .3C 118
Royal Cl. N16 . . . . .3A 36
SE8 . . . . .2B 94
SW19 . . . . .3F 113
Royal College of Art . . .3F 73
Royal College of Music
. . . . .4F 73
Royal College of
Obstetricians &
Gynaecologists . . .3B 60
Royal College of Physicians
. . . . .3D 5
Royal College of Surgeons
. . . . .2A 16
Royal Coll. St. NW1 . . .4E 47
Royal Connaught Apartments
E16 . . . . .2F 83
(off Connaught Rd.)
Royal Ct. EC3 . . . . .3C 18
(off Cornhill)
SE16 . . . . .4B 80
Royal Courts of Justice
. . . . .3A 16
Royal Court Theatre . . .5C 74
(off Sloane Sq.)
Royal Cres. W11 . . . . .2F 71
Royal Cres. M. W11 . . .2F 71
Royal Duchess M.
SW12 . . . . .5D 103
Royal Exchange
. . . . .3C 18 (5F 63)

Royal Exchange Av.
EC3 . . . . .3C 18
Royal Exchange Bldgs.
EC3 . . . . .3C 18
Royal Festival Hall
. . . . .2A 24 (2B 76)
Royal Fusiliers Mus. . . .5F 19
(in The Tower of London)
Royal Geographical Society
. . . . .3F 73
(off Kensington Gore)
Royal Hill SE10 . . . . . .3E 95
Royal Hill Ct. SE10 . . . .3E 95
(off Greenwich High St.)
Royal Holloway
University of London
. . . . .5C 6
Royal Hospital Chelsea Mus.
. . . . .1C 88
Royal Hospital Rd.
SW3 . . . . .2B 88
Royal Institution Faraday Mus.
. . . . .5F 13 (1E 75)
Royal Langford Apartments
NW6 . . . . .1D 59
(off Greville Rd.)
Royal London Bldgs.
SE15 . . . . .2D 93
(off Old Kent Rd.)
Royal London Hospital
Archives & Museum
. . . . .4D 65
(off Newark St.)
Royal London Ind. Est.
NW10 . . . . .1A 56
Royal Mews, The
. . . . .5E 21 (3D 75)
Royal M.
SW1 . . . . . . .5E 21 (4D 75)
Royal Mint Ct.
EC3 . . . . .5F 19 (1B 78)
Royal Mint Pl. E1 . . . . .1C 78
Royal Mint St. E1 . . . . .1B 78
Royal Naval Pl. SE14 . . .3B 94
Royal Oak Ct. N1 . . . . .1D 11
(off Pitfield St.)
Royal Oak Pl. SE22 . . . .4D 107
Royal Oak Rd. E8 . . . . .3D 51
Royal Oak Yd.
SE1 . . . . . . .4D 27 (3A 78)
Royal Observatory Greenwich
. . . . .3A 96
Royal Opera Arc.
SW1 . . . . . . .1B 22 (2F 75)
Royal Opera House
. . . . .3E 15 (5A 62)
Royal Orchard Cl.
SW18 . . . . .5A 100
Royal Pde. SE3 . . . . . .5B 96
SW6 . . . . .3A 86
Royal Pde. M. SE3 . . . .5B 96
(off Royal Pde.)
Royal Pl. SE10 . . . . . . .3E 95
Royal Rd. E16 . . . . . . .5F 69
SE17 . . . . .2D 91
Royal St. SE1 . . . .5A 24 (4B 76)
Royal Twr. Lodge E1 . . .1C 78
(off Cartwright St.)
Royalty Mans. W1 . . . .3B 14
(off Meard St.)

Royalty M.
W1 . . . . . . .3B **14** (5F **61**)
Royalty Studios W11 . . .5A **58**
(off Lancaster Rd.)
Royal Veterinary College
Camden Town . . .5F **47**
Royal Victoria Docks
Watersports Cen.
. . . . .1C **82**
Royal Victoria Patriotic Bldg.
SW18 . . . . .4F **101**
Royal Victoria Pl.
E16 . . . . .2D **83**
Royal Victoria Sq.
E16 . . . . .1D **83**
Royal Victor Pl. E3 . . . . .1F **65**
Royal Westminster Lodge
SW1 . . . . .5F **75**
(off Elverton St.)
Royal Wimbledon Golf Course
. . . . .5D **113**
Roycroft Cl. SW2 . . . .1C **118**
(off Battersea Pk. Rd.)
Roydon Cl. SW11 . . . . .5B **88**
Royle Bldg. N1 . . . . . . .1E **63**
(off Wenlock Rd.)
Royley Ho. EC1 . . . . . . .3A **10**
(off Old St.)
Roy Sq. E14 . . . . .1A **80**
Royston Ct. E13 . . . . . .5C **54**
(off Stopford Rd.)
SE24 . . . . .4E **105**
W8 . . . . .2C **72**
(off Kensington Chu. St.)
Royston Gdns. IG1: IIf . .1F **41**
Royston Ho. SE15 . . . . .2D **93**
(off Friary Est.)
Royston Pde. IG1: IIf . . .1F **41**
Royston St. E2 . . . . . . .1E **65**
Rozel Cl. N1 . . . . .5A **50**
Rozel Rd. SW4 . . . . . . .1E **103**
RQ33 SW18 . . . . .2C **100**
Rubens Gdns. SE22 . . .5C **106**
(off Lordship Sq.)
Rubens Pl. SW4 . . . . . .2A **104**
Rubens St. SE6 . . . . . .2B **122**
Ruby Cl. E5 . . . . .5F **37**
Ruby Ct. E15 . . . . .5E **53**
(off Warton Rd.)
Ruby St. SE15 . . . . .2D **93**
Ruby Triangle SE15 . . . .2D **93**
Ruckholt Cl. E10 . . . . . .5D **39**
Ruckholt Rd. E10 . . . . . .1C **52**
Rucklidge Av. NW10 . . .1B **56**
Rucklidge Pas.
NW10 . . . . .1B **56**
(off Rucklidge Av.)
Rudall Cres. NW3 . . . . .1F **45**
Rudbeck Ho. SE15 . . . .3C **92**
(off Peckham Pk. Rd.)
Ruddington Cl. E5 . . . . .1A **52**
Rudge Ho. SE16 . . . . . .4C **78**
(off Jamaica Rd.)
Rudgwick Ter. NW8 . . . .5A **46**
Rudloe Ho. SW12 . . . . .5E **103**
Rudolf Pl. SW8 . . . . . . .2A **90**
Rudolph Rd. E13 . . . . . .1B **68**
NW6 . . . . .1C **58**
Rudstone Ho. E3 . . . . . .2D **67**
(off Bromley High St.)

Rudyard Ct. SE1 . . . . . .4C **26**
(off Long La.)
Rufford St. N1 . . . . .5A **48**
Rufford St. M. N1 . . . . .4A **48**
Rufus Bus. Cen.
SW18 . . . . .2D **115**
Rufus Ho. SE1 . . . . .5F **27**
(off St Saviour's Est.)
Rufus St.
N1 . . . . . . .2D **11** (2A **64**)
Rugby Mans. W14 . . . . .5A **72**
(off Bishop King's Rd.)
Rugby Rd. W4 . . . . .3A **70**
Rugby St.
WC1 . . . . . . .4F **7** (3B **62**)
Rugg St. E14 . . . . .1C **80**
Rugless Ho. E14 . . . . . . .3E **81**
(off E. Ferry Rd.)
Rugmere NW1 . . . . .4C **46**
(off Ferdinand St.)
Ruislip St. SW17 . . . . . .4B **116**
Rumball Ho. SE5 . . . . . .3A **92**
(off Harris St.)
Rumbold Rd. SW6 . . . . .3D **87**
Rum Cl. E1 . . . . .1E **79**
Rumford Ho. SE1 . . . . . .5F **25**
(off Tiverton St.)
Rumsey M. N4 . . . . .5D **35**
Rumsey Rd. SW9 . . . . . .1B **104**
Runacres Ct. SE17 . . . . .1E **91**
Runbury Circ. NW9 . . . . .4A **28**
Runcorn Pl. W11 . . . . . . .1A **72**
Rundell Cres. NW4 . . . . .1D **29**
Rundell Twr. SW8 . . . . . .4B **90**
Runnymede Ct.
SW15 . . . . .1C **112**
Runnymede Ho. E9 . . . . .1A **52**
Rupack St. SE16 . . . . . . .3E **79**
Rupert Ct.
W1 . . . . . . .4B **14** (1F **75**)
Rupert Gdns. SW9 . . . . .5D **91**
Rupert Ho. SE11 . . . . . . .5C **76**
SW5 . . . . .5C **72**
(off Nevern Sq.)
Rupert Rd. N19 . . . . .5F **33**
(not continuous)
NW6 . . . . .1B **58**
W4 . . . . .4A **70**
Rupert St.
W1 . . . . . .4B **14** (1F **75**)
Rusbridge Cl. E8 . . . . . .2C **50**
Ruscoe Rd. E16 . . . . . . .5B **68**
Ruscombe NW1 . . . . . . .5D **47**
(off Delancey St.)
Rusham Rd. SW12 . . . . .4B **102**
Rush Comn. M.
SW2 . . . . .5B **104**
Rushcroft Rd. SW2 . . . . .2C **104**
Rushcutters Ct. SE16 . . .5A **80**
(off Boat Lifter Way)
Rushey Grn. SE6 . . . . . .5D **109**
Rushey Mead SE4 . . . . .3C **108**
Rushgrove Pde. NW9 . . .1A **28**
Rush Hill M. SW11 . . . . .1C **102**
(off Rush Hill Rd.)
Rush Hill Rd. SW11 . . . .1C **102**
Rushmead E2 . . . . .2D **65**
Rushmere Pl. SW19 . . . .5F **113**
Rushmore Cres. E5 . . . .1F **51**

Rushmore Ho. SW15 . . .5C **98**
W14 . . . . .4A **72**
(off Russell Rd.)
Rushmore Rd. E5 . . . . . .1E **51**
(not continuous)
Rusholme Gro.
SE19 . . . . .5A **120**
Rusholme Rd. SW15 . . .4F **99**
Rushton Ho. SW8 . . . . . .5F **89**
Rushton St. N1 . . . . .1F **63**
Rushworth St.
SE1 . . . . . .3E **25** (3D **77**)
Ruskin Av. E12 . . . . .3F **55**
Ruskin Cl. NW11 . . . . . .1D **31**
Ruskin Ct. SE5 . . . . .1F **105**
(off Champion Hill)
Ruskin Ho. SW1 . . . . . . .5F **75**
(off Herrick St.)
Ruskin Mans. W14 . . . . .2A **86**
(off Queen's Club Gdns.)
Ruskin Pk. Ho. SE5 . . . .1F **105**
Ruskin Wlk. SE24 . . . . . .3E **105**
Rusper Cl. NW2 . . . . . . .5E **29**
Rusper Ct. SW9 . . . . . . .5A **90**
(off Clapham Rd.)
Russell Chambers
WC1 . . . . .1E **15**
(off Bury Pl.)
Russell Cl. SE7 . . . . .3E **97**
W4 . . . . .2B **84**
Russell Ct. E10 . . . . .2D **39**
SE15 . . . . .5D **93**
(off Heaton Rd.)
SW1 . . . . .2A **22**
SW16 . . . . .5B **118**
WC1 . . . . .4D **7**
Russell Flint Ho. E16 . . .2D **83**
(off Pankhurst Av.)
Russell Gdns. NW11 . . .1A **30**
W14 . . . . .4A **72**
Russell Gdns. M.
W14 . . . . .3A **72**
Russell Gro. SW9 . . . . . .3C **90**
Russell Ho. E14 . . . . . . .5C **66**
(off Saracen St.)
SW1 . . . . .1E **89**
(off Cambridge St.)
Russell Lodge SE1 . . . . .5B **26**
(off Spurgeon St.)
Russell Mans. WC1 . . . . .5E **7**
Russell Pde. NW11 . . . .1A **30**
(off Golders Grn. Rd.)
Russell Pl. NW3 . . . . . . .2A **46**
SE16 . . . . .4A **80**
Russell Rd. E10 . . . . . . .1D **39**
E16 . . . . .5C **68**
N8 . . . . .1F **33**
N15 . . . . .1A **36**
NW9 . . . . .1B **28**
W14 . . . . .4A **72**
Russell's Footpath
SW16 . . . . .5A **118**
Russell Sq.
WC1 . . . . . . .4D **7** (4A **62**)
Russell Sq. Mans.
WC1 . . . . .5E **7**
(off Southampton Row)
Russell St.
WC2 . . . . . .4E **15** (1A **76**)

Russell's Wharf Flats
W10 . . . . .3B 58
Russell Yd. SW15 . . . .2A 100
Russet Cres. N7 . . . . . .2B 48
Russett Way SE13 . . . .5D 95
Russia Dock Rd.
SE16 . . . . .2A 80
Russia La. E2 . . . . . . .1E 65
Russia Row
EC2 . . . . .3A 18 (5E 63)
Russia Wlk. SE16 . . . . .3A 80
Rusthall Av. W4 . . . . . .5A 70
Rustic Wlk. E16 . . . . . .5D 69
(off Lambert Rd.)
Ruston M. W11 . . . . . .5A 58
Ruston Rd. SE18 . . . . . .4F 83
Ruston St. E3 . . . . .5B 52
Rust Sq. SE5 . . . . .3F 91
Rutford Rd. SW16 . . . . .5A 118
Ruth Cl. E3 . . . . .1A 66
Rutherford Ho. E1 . . . . .3D 65
(off Brady St.)
Rutherford St. SW1 . . . .5F 75
Ruth Ho. W10 . . . . .3A 58
(off Kensal Rd.)
Ruthin Cl. NW9 . . . . . . .1A 28
Ruthin Rd. SE3 . . . . . . .2C 96
Ruthven St. E9 . . . . . . .5F 51
Rutland Ct. SE5 . . . . . .2F 105
SW7 . . . . .3A 74
(off Rutland Gdns.)
Rutland Gdns. N4 . . . . .1D 35
SW7 . . . . .3A 74
Rutland Gdns. M.
SW7 . . . . .3A 74
Rutland Ga. SW7 . . . . . .3A 74
Rutland Ga. M. SW7 . . . .3A 74
(off Rutland Ga.)
Rutland Gro. W6 . . . . . .1D 85
Rutland Ho. W8 . . . . . . .4D 73
(off Marloes Rd.)
Rutland M. NW6 . . . . . .5D 45
Rutland M. E. SW7 . . . . .4A 74
(off Ennismore St.)
Rutland M. Sth. SW7 . . . .4A 74
(off Ennismore St.)
Rutland M. W. SW7 . . . . .4A 74
(off Rutland Ga.)
Rutland Pk. NW2 . . . . . .3E 43
SE6 . . . . .2B 122
Rutland Pk. Gdns.
NW2 . . . . .3E 43
(off Rutland Pk.)
Rutland Pk. Mans.
NW2 . . . . .3E 43
Rutland Pl.
EC1 . . . . .5E 9 (3D 63)
Rutland Rd. E7 . . . . . . .4F 55
E9 . . . . .5F 51
E17 . . . . .1C 38
Rutland St. SW7 . . . . . .4A 74
Rutland Wlk. SE6 . . . . . .2B 122
Rutley Cl. SE17 . . . . . . .2D 91
Rutt's Ter. SE14 . . . . . . .4F 93
Ruvigny Gdns. SW15 . . . .1F 99
Ryan Cl. SE3 . . . . .2E 111
Rycott Path SE22 . . . . . .5C 106
Rycuff Sq. SE3 . . . . . . .5B 96
Rydal Dins. NW9 . . . . . .1A 28
SW15 . . . . .3A 112

Rydal Rd. SW16 . . . . . .4F 117
Rydal Water
N1 . . . . .2F 5 (2E 61)
Ryde Ho. NW6 . . . . . . .5C 44
(off Priory Pk. Rd.)
Rydens Ho. SE9 . . . . . . .3E 125
Ryder Av. E10 . . . . .2D 39
Ryder Cl.
BR1: Brom 5D 125
Ryder Ct. E10 . . . . .4D 39
SW1 . . . . .1A 22
Ryder Dr. SE16 . . . . . . .1D 93
Ryder Ho. E1 . . . . .3E 65
(off Colebert Av.)
Ryder M. E9 . . . . .2E 51
Ryder's Ter. NW8 . . . . . .1E 59
Ryder St.
SW1 . . . . . . .1A 22 (2E 75)
Ryder Yd.
SW1 . . . . . . .1A 22 (2E 75)
Ryde Va. Rd.
SW12 . . . . .2E 117
Rydons Cl. SE9 . . . . . . .1F 111
Rydon St. N1 . . . . .5E 49
Rydston Cl. N7 . . . . . . .4A 48
Ryecotes Mead
SE21 . . . . .1A 120
Ryecroft Rd. SE13 . . . . . .3E 109
SW16 . . . . .5C 118
Ryecroft St. SW6 . . . . . .4D 87
Ryedale SE22 . . . . .4D 107
Ryefield Path SW15 . . . . .1C 112
Ryefield Rd. SE19 . . . . . .5E 119
Ryegates SE15 . . . . .5D 93
(off Caulfield Rd.)
Rye Hill Pk. SE15 . . . . . .2E 107
Rye Ho. SE16 . . . . .3E 79
(off Swan Rd.)
SW1 . . . . .1D 89
(off Ebury Bri. Rd.)
Ryelands Cres.
SE12 . . . . .4E 111
Rye La. SE15 . . . . .4C 92
Rye Pas. SE15 . . . . .1C 106
Rye Rd. SE15 . . . . .2F 107
Rye Wlk. SW15 . . . . . . .3F 99
Ryfold Ho. SW19 . . . . . .3C 114
Rylandes Rd. NW2 . . . . . .5C 28
Ryland Rd. NW5 . . . . . . .3D 47
Rylett Cres. W12 . . . . . . .3B 70
Rylett Rd. W12 . . . . . . .3B 70
Rylston Rd. SW6 . . . . . . .2B 86
Rymer St. SE24 . . . . . . .4D 105
Rysbrack St.
SW3 . . . . . . .5A 20 (4B 74)

S

Saatchi Gallery 1B 88
Sabella Ct. E3 . . . . . . .1B 66
Sabine Rd. SW11 . . . . .1B 102
Sable St. N1 . . . . .4D 49
Sach Rd. E5 . . . . .4D 37
Sackville Ho. SW16 . . . .3A 118
Sackville St.
W1 . . . . . . .5A 14 (1E 75)
Saddlers M. SW8 . . . . .4A 90
Saddle Yd.
W1 . . . . . . .1D 21 (2D 75)

Sadler Ho. E3 . . . . . . .2D 67
(off Bromley High St.)
EC1 . . . . .1C 8
(off Spa Grn. Est.)
Sadlers Ga. M.
SW15 . . . . .1E 99
Sadler's Wells Theatre
. . . . .1C 8 (2C 62)
Safara Ho. SE5 . . . . . . .4A 92
(off Dalwood St.)
Saffron Av. E14 . . . . . . .1F 81
Saffron Cl. NW11 . . . . . .1B 30
Saffron Ct. E15 . . . . . . .2A 54
(off Maryland Pk.)
Saffron Hill
EC1 . . . . .5C 8 (4C 62)
Saffron St.
EC1 . . . . .5C 8 (4C 62)
Saffron Wharf SE1 . . . . .3B 78
(off Shad Thames)
Sage M. SE22 . . . . .3B 106
Sage St. E1 . . . . .1E 79
Sage Way WC1 . . . . . . .2F 7
Saigasso Cl. E16 . . . . . . .5F 69
Sailacre Ho. SE10 . . . . . .1B 96
(off Woolwich Rd.)
Sail Ct. E14 . . . . .1F 81
(off Newport Av.)
Sailmakers Ct. SW6 . . . . .1E 101
Sail St. SE11 . . . . .5B 76
Sainfoin Rd. SW17 . . . . .2C 116
Sainsbury Rd. SE19 . . . . .5A 120
Sainsbury Wing 5C 14
(in National Gallery)
St Agnes Cl. E9 . . . . . . .5E 51
St Agnes Ho. E3 . . . . . . .1C 66
(off Ordell Rd.)
St Agnes Pl. SE11 . . . . . .2C 90
St Agnes Well EC1 . . . . . .3C 10
St Aidan's Rd. SE22 . . . . .4D 107
St Alban's Av. W4 . . . . . .4A 70
St Albans Cl. NW11 . . . . .3C 30
St Albans Ct. EC2 . . . . . .1A 18
St Alban's Gro. W8 . . . . .4D 73
St Alban's La. NW11 . . . . .3C 30
St Albans Mans. W8 . . . .4D 73
(off Kensington Ct. Pl.)
St Alban's Pl. N1 . . . . . . .5D 49
St Alban's Rd. NW5 . . . . .5C 32
NW10 . . . . .5A 42
St Alban's St.
SW1 . . . . . . .5B 14 (1F 75)
St Albans Studios
W8 . . . . .4D 73
(off St Albans Gro.)
St Albans Ter. W6 . . . . . .2A 86
St Albans Vs. NW5 . . . . .5C 32
St Alfege Pas. SE10 . . . . .2E 95
St Alfege Rd. SE7 . . . . . .2F 97
St Alphage Gdn.
EC2 . . . . . . .1A 18 (4E 63)
St Alphage Highwalk
EC2 . . . . .1A 18
St Alphage Ho. EC2 . . . . .1B 18
St Alphonsus Rd.
SW4 . . . . .2E 103
St Amunds Cl. SE6 . . . . .4C 122
St Andrews Chambers
W1 . . . . .1A 14
(off Wells St.)

St Andrews Cl. NW2 . . . .5D 29
  SE16 . . . . .1D 93
  SW19 . . . . .5D 115
St Andrew's Ct.
  SW18 . . . . .2E 115
St Andrew's Gro.
  N16 . . . . .3F 35
St Andrew's Hill
  EC4 . . . . .4E 17 (1D 77)
    (not continuous)
St Andrews Ho. SE16 . . . .4D 79
    (off Southwark Pk. Rd.)
St Andrews Mans.
  W1 . . . . .1B 12
    (off Dorset St.)
  W14 . . . . .2A 86
    (off St Andrews Rd.)
St Andrews M. N16 . . . .3A 36
  SE3 . . . . .3C 96
  SW12 . . . . .1F 117
St Andrew's Pl.
  NW1 . . . . . . .3E 5 (3D 61)
St Andrew's Rd.
  E11 . . . . .1A 40
  E13 . . . . .2D 69
  NW10 . . . . .3D 43
  NW11 . . . . .1B 30
  W3 . . . . .1A 70
  W14 . . . . .2A 86
St Andrews Sq.
  W11 . . . . .5A 58
St Andrew St.
  EC4 . . . . . . .1C 16 (4C 62)
St Andrews Way E3 . . . .3D 67
St Andrew's Wharf
  SE1 . . . . .3B 78
St Anne's Cl. N6 . . . . . .5C 32
St Anne's Ct. NW6 . . . . .5A 44
  W1 . . . . . . .3B 14 (5F 61)
St Anne's Flats NW1 . . . . .1B 6
    (off Doric Way)
St Anne's Pas. E14 . . . . .5B 66
St Anne's Rd. E11 . . . . . .4F 39
St Anne's Row E14 . . . . .5B 66
St Anne's Trad. Est.
  E14 . . . . .5B 66
    (off St Anne's Row)
St Anne St. E14 . . . . . . .5B 66
St Ann's Cres.
  SW18 . . . . .4D 101
St Ann's Gdns. NW5 . . . .3C 46
St Ann's Hill SW18 . . .3D 101
St Ann's Ho. WC1 . . . . .2B 8
    (off Margery St.)
St Ann's La.
  SW1 . . . . . .5C 22 (4F 75)
St Ann's Pk. Rd.
  SW18 . . . . .4E 101
St Ann's Pas. SW13 . . .1A 98
St Ann's Rd. N15 . . . . . .1D 35
  SW13 . . . . .5B 84
  W11 . . . . .1F 71
St Ann's St.
  SW1 . . . . . .5C 22 (4F 75)
St Ann's Ter. NW8 . . . . .1F 59
St Ann's Vs. W11 . . . . . .2F 71
St Anselms Ct.
  SW16 . . . . .5A 118
St Anselm's Pl.
  W1 . . . . . .4D 13 (1D 75)

St Anthony's Cl. E1 . . . . .2C 78
  E9 . . . . .3B 52
    (off Wallis Rd.)
  SW17 . . . . .2A 116
St Anthony's Ct.
  SW17 . . . . .2C 116
St Anthony's Flats
  NW1 . . . . .1F 61
    (off Aldenham St.)
St Antony's Rd. E7 . . . . .4D 55
St Asaph Rd. SE4 . . . . .1F 107
St Aubins Ct. N1 . . . . . .5F 49
St Aubyn's Av.
  SW19 . . . . .5B 114
St Augustine's Ct.
  SE1 . . . . .1D 93
    (off Lynton Rd.)
St Augustine's Ho.
  NW1 . . . . .1B 6
    (off Werrington St.)
St Augustine's Mans.
  SW1 . . . . .5E 75
    (off Bloomburg St.)
St Augustine's Path
  N5 . . . . .1E 49
St Augustine's Rd.
  NW1 . . . . .4F 47
St Austell Rd. SE13 . . . .5E 95
St Barnabas Cl.
  SE22 . . . . .3A 106
St Barnabas M. SW1 . . .1C 88
    (off St Barnabas St.)
St Barnabas Rd. E17 . . .1C 38
St Barnabas St. SW1 . . .1C 88
St Barnabas Ter. E9 . . . .2F 51
St Barnabas Vs. SW8 . . .4A 90
St Bartholomew's Cl.
  SE26 . . . . .4D 121
St Bartholomew's
  Hospital Mus. 1E 17
St Benedict's Cl.
  SW17 . . . . .5C 116
St Benet's Cl. SW17 . . .2A 116
St Benet's Pl.
  EC3 . . . . .4C 18 (1F 77)
St Bernard's Cl.
  SE27 . . . . .4F 119
St Bernards Ho. E14 . . . .4E 81
    (off Galbraith St.)
St Bernard's Rd. E6 . . . .5F 55
St Botolph Row
  EC3 . . . . .3F 19 (5B 64)
St Botolphs Ct. E1 . . . . .2F 19
    (off St Botolph St.)
St Botolph St.
  EC3 . . . . .2F 19 (5B 64)
St Brelades Ct. N1 . . . . .5A 50
St Bride's Av. EC4 . . . . .3D 17
St Bride's Crypt Mus.
  . . . . .3D 17
  (in St Bride's, off Fleet St.)
St Bride's Ho. E3 . . . . . .1C 66
    (off Ordell Rd.)
St Bride's Pas. EC4 . . . .3D 17
St Bride St.
  EC4 . . . . .2D 17 (5D 63)
St Catherine's Apartments
  E3 . . . . .2D 67
    (off Bow Rd.)

St Catherine's Cl.
  SW17 . . . . .2A 116
St Catherine's Ct.
  W4 . . . . .4A 70
St Catherine's Dr.
  SE14 . . . . .5F 93
St Catherines M.
  SW3 . . . . .5B 74
St Cecelia's Pl. SE3 . . . .1C 96
St Chad's Pl.
  WC1 . . . . .1E 7 (2A 62)
St Chad's St.
  WC1 . . . . .1E 7 (2A 62)
    (not continuous)
St Charles Pl. W10 . . . . .4A 58
St Charles Sq. W10 . . . .4F 57
St Chloe's Ho. E3 . . . . . .1C 66
    (off Ordell Rd.)
St Christopher's Ho.
  NW1 . . . . .1E 61
    (off Bridgeway St.)
St Christopher's Pl.
  W1 . . . . . . .2C 12 (5C 60)
St Clair Ho. E3 . . . . .2B 66
    (off British St.)
St Clair Rd. E13 . . . . . . .1D 69
St Clare St.
  EC3 . . . . . . .3F 19 (5B 64)
St Clements Ct. EC4 . . . .4C 18
  N7 . . . . .3C 48
  SE14 . . . . .2F 93
    (off Myers La.)
  W11 . . . . .1F 71
    (off Stoneleigh St.)
St Clements Hgts.
  SE26 . . . . .3C 120
St Clements Ho. E1 . . . . .1F 19
    (off Leyden St.)
St Clement's La.
  WC2 . . . . . . .3F 15 (5B 62)
St Clements Mans.
  SW6 . . . . .2F 85
    (off Lillie Rd.)
St Clements Yd.
  SE22 . . . . .2B 106
St Cloud Rd. SE27 . . . . .4E 119
St Columba's Ct. E15 . . .1A 54
    (off Janson Rd.)
St Columb's Ho. W10 . . .4A 58
    (off Blagrove Rd.)
St Crispin's Cl. NW3 . . .1A 46
St Cross St.
  EC1 . . . . . .5C 8 (4C 62)
St Cuthbert's Rd.
  NW2 . . . . .3B 44
St Cyprian's St.
  SW17 . . . . .4B 116
St Davids Cl. SE16 . . . . .1D 93
    (off Masters Dr.)
St Davids M. E3 . . . . . . .2A 66
    (off Morgan St.)
St David's Pl. NW4 . . . . .2D 29
St Davids Sq. E14 . . . . .1D 95
St Denis Rd. SE27 . . . . .4F 119
St Dionis Rd. SW6 . . . . .5B 86
St Donatt's Rd. SE14 . . .4B 94
St Dunstan's All. EC3 . . .4D 19
St Dunstans Av. W3 . . . .1A 70

St Dunstan's Ct.
EC4 . . . . . .3C **16** (5C **62**)
St Dunstans Hill
EC3 . . . . .5D **19** (1A **78**)
St Dunstan's La.
EC3 . . . . .5D **19** (1A **78**)
St Dunstans M. E1 . . . .4A **66**
(off White Horse Rd.)
St Dunstan's Rd. E7 . . .3D **55**
W6 . . . . .1F **85**
St Edmund's Cl. NW8 . .5B **46**
SW17 . . . . .2A **116**
St Edmund's Ct. NW8 . .5B **46**
(off St Edmund's Ter.)
St Edmunds Sq.
SW13 . . . . .2E **85**
St Edmund's Ter.
NW8 . . . . .5A **46**
St Edward's Cl.
NW11 . . . . .1C **30**
St Edwards Ct. NW11 . . .1C **30**
St Elmo Rd. W12 . . . . .2B **70**
(not continuous)
St Elmos Rd. SE16 . . . .3A **80**
St Ermin's Hill SW1 . . . .5B **22**
St Ervan's Rd. W10 . . . .4B **58**
St Eugene Ct. NW6 . . . .5A **44**
(off Salusbury Rd.)
St Faith's Rd. SE21 . . . .1D **119**
St Fillans Rd. SE6 . . . . .1E **123**
St Francis' Ho. NW1 . . . .1F **61**
(off Bridgeway St.)
St Francis Pl. SW12 . . .4D **103**
St Francis Rd. SE22 . . .2A **106**
St Frideswide's M.
E14 . . . . .5E **67**
St Gabriel's Cl. E11 . . . .4D **41**
E14 . . . . .4D **67**
St Gabriels Mnr. SE5 . . .4D **91**
(off Cormont Rd.)
St Gabriels Rd. NW2 . . .2F **43**
St George's Av. E7 . . . .4D **55**
N7 . . . . .1F **47**
St George's Bldgs.
SE1 . . . . .4D **77**
(off St George's Rd.)
St George's Cathedral . . .1E **5**
St George's Cir.
SE1 . . . . .5D **25** (4D **77**)
St George's Cl.
NW11 . . . . .1B **30**
SW8 . . . . .4E **89**
St Georges Ct.
EC4 . . . . . .2D **17** (5D **63**)
SE1 . . . . .5D **25**
SW1 . . . . .1E **89**
(off St George's Dr.)
SW3 . . . . .5A **74**
(off Brompton Rd.)
SW7 . . . . .4E **73**
SW15 . . . . .2B **100**
St George's Dr. SW1 . . .5D **75**
ST GEORGE'S FIELD 1A **74**
St George's Flds. W2 . . .5A **60**
St Georges Gro.
SW17 . . . . .3F **115**
St Georges Ho. NW1 . . . .1F **61**
(off Bridgeway St.)

St Georges Ho. SW11 . . .4C **88**
(off Charlotte Despard Av.)
St George's La. EC3 . . . .4C **18**
St George's Mans.
SW1 . . . . .1F **89**
(off Causton St.)
St George's M. NW1 . . . .4B **46**
SE1 . . . . .5C **24**
SE8 . . . . .5B **80**
St Georges Pde.
SE6 . . . . .2B **122**
(off Perry Hill)
St George's Path
SE4 . . . . .2C **108**
(off Adelaide Av.)
St George's Pools 1D **79**
St George's RC Cathedral
. . . . . . .5C **24** (4C **76**)
St George's Rd. E7 . . . .4D **55**
E10 . . . . .5E **39**
NW11 . . . . .1B **30**
SE1 . . . . .5C **24** (4C **76**)
W4 . . . . .3A **70**
St Georges Sq. E7 . . . .4D **55**
E14 . . . . .1A **80**
SE8 . . . . .5B **80**
(not continuous)
SW1 . . . . .1F **89**
St George's Sq. M.
SW1 . . . . .1F **89**
St George's Ter. E6 . . . .2F **69**
(off Masterman Rd.)
NW1 . . . . .4B **46**
SE15 . . . . .3C **92**
(off Peckham Hill St.)
St George St.
W1 . . . . . . .3E **13** (1D **75**)
St George's Way
SE15 . . . . .2A **92**
St George's Wharf
SE1 . . . . .3F **27**
(off Shad Thames)
St George Wharf
SW8 . . . . .2A **90**
St Gerards Cl. SW4 . . . .3E **103**
St German's Pl. SE3 . . . .4C **96**
St German's Rd.
SE23 . . . . .1A **122**
St Giles High St.
WC2 . . . . .2C **14** (5F **61**)
St Giles Ho. SE5 . . . . . .4A **92**
St Giles Pas. WC2 . . . . .3C **14**
St Giles Rd. SE5 . . . . . .3A **92**
St Giles Ter. EC2 . . . . . .1A **18**
(off Wood St.)
St Giles Twr. SE5 . . . . . .4A **92**
(off Gables Cl.)
St Gilles Ho. E2 . . . . . .1F **65**
(off Mace St.)
St Gothard Rd.
SE27 . . . . .4F **119**
(not continuous)
St Helena Ho. WC1 . . . .2B **8**
(off Margery St.)
St Helena Rd. SE16 . . . .5F **79**
St Helena St.
WC1 . . . . . .2B **8** (2C **62**)
St Helen's Gdns.
W10 . . . . .4F **57**

St Helens Pl. E10 . . . . . .2A **38**
EC3 . . . . .2D **19** (5A **64**)
St Helier Ct. N1 . . . . . . .5A **50**
(off De Beauvoir Est.)
SE16 . . . . .3F **79**
(off Poolmans St.)
St Helier's Rd. E10 . . . . .1E **39**
St Hilda's Cl. NW6 . . . . .4F **43**
SW17 . . . . .2A **116**
St Hilda's Rd. SW13 . . . .2D **85**
St Hilda's Wharf E1 . . . .2E **79**
(off Wapping High St.)
St Hubert's Ho. E14 . . . .4C **80**
(off Janet St.)
St Hughes Cl.
SW17 . . . . .2A **116**
St James SE14 . . . . . . .4A **94**
St James Ct. E2 . . . . . . .2D **65**
(off Bethnal Grn. Rd.)
E12 . . . . .4E **41**
SE3 . . . . .4D **97**
SW1 . . . . .5A **22** (4E **75**)
St James Gro. SW11 . . .5B **88**
St James Hall N1 . . . . . .5E **49**
(off Prebend St.)
St James Ind. M.
SE1 . . . . .1C **92**
St James Mans.
NW6 . . . . .4C **44**
(off West End La.)
SE1 . . . . .5B **24**
(off McAuley Cl.)
St James M. E14 . . . . . .4E **81**
E17 . . . . .1A **38**
(off St James's Dr.)
St James Path E17 . . . .1A **38**
St James Residences
W1 . . . . .4B **14**
(off Brewer St.)
St James' Rd. E15 . . . . .2B **54**
ST JAMES'S 1A **22** (2F **75**)
St James's App.
EC2 . . . . . .4D **11** (3A **64**)
St James's Av. E2 . . . . .1E **65**
St James's Chambers
SW1 . . . . .1A **22**
(off Jermyn St.)
St James's Cl. NW8 . . . .5B **46**
(off St James's Ter. M.)
SW17 . . . . .2B **116**
St James's Cres.
SW9 . . . . .1C **104**
St James's Dr.
SW12 . . . . .1B **116**
SW17 . . . . .1B **116**
St James's Gdns.
W11 . . . . .2A **72**
(not continuous)
St James's Ho. SE1 . . . .5C **78**
(off Strathnairn St.)
St James's Mkt.
SW1 . . . . . .5B **14** (1F **75**)
St James's Palace
. . . . .3A **22** (3E **75**)
St James's Pk.
. . . . .3B **22** (3E **75**)
St James's Pas. EC3 . . .3E **19**
St James's Pl.
SW1 . . . . . .2F **21** (2E **75**)

St James's Rd. SE1 . . . .2C 92
  SE16 . . . . .4C 78
St James's Sq.
  SW1 . . . . . . .1A 22 (2E 75)
St James's St. E17 . . . . .1A 38
  SW1 . . . . . .1F 21 (2E 75)
St James's Ter. NW8 . . .5B 46
  (off Prince Albert Rd.)
St James's Ter. M.
  NW8 . . . . .5B 46
St James's Wlk.
  EC1 . . . . .3D 9 (3D 63)
St James Ter. SW12 . . .1C 116
St Joan's Ho. NW1 . . . . . .1B 6
  (off Phoenix Rd.)
ST JOHNS 5C 94
St John's Av. NW10 . . . .5B 42
  SW15 . . . . .3F 99
St Johns Chu. Rd. E9 . . .2E 51
St John's Cl. SW6 . . . . . .3C 86
St John's Concert Hall
  . . . . .5D 23
St Johns Ct. E1 . . . . .2D 79
  (off Scandrett St.)
  N4 . . . . .4D 35
  N5 . . . . .1D 49
  SE13 . . . . .5E 95
  SW10 . . . . .3E 87
  (off Ashburnham Rd.)
  W6 . . . . .5D 71
  (off Glenthorne Rd.)
St John's Cres.
  SW9 . . . . .1C 104
St Johns Dr. SW18 . . . .1D 115
St John's Est. N1 . . . . . .1F 63
  SE1 . . . . .3F 27
St John's Gdns. W11 . . .1A 72
St John's Gate 4D 9
St John's Gro. N19 . . . . .4E 33
  SW13 . . . . .5B 84
St John's Hill SW11 . . . .3F 101
St John's Hill Gro.
  SW11 . . . . .2F 101
St Johns Ho. E14 . . . . . .5E 81
  (off Pier St.)
  SE17 . . . . .2F 91
  (off Lytham St.)
St John's La.
  EC1 . . . . .4D 9 (3D 63)
St John's Lodge NW3 . . .4A 46
  (off King Henry's Rd.)
St John's Mans. EC1 . . . .1D 9
  (off St John St.)
St John's M. W11 . . . . . .5C 58
St John's Pk. SE3 . . . . . .3B 96
St John's Pk. Mans.
  N19 . . . . .5E 33
St John's Path EC1 . . . . .4D 9
St Johns Pathway
  SE23 . . . . .1E 121
St John's Pl.
  EC1 . . . . .4D 9 (3D 63)
St John's Rd. E16 . . . . . .5C 68
  N15 . . . . .1A 36
  NW11 . . . . .1B 30
  SW11 . . . . .2A 102
St John's Sq.
  EC1 . . . . .4D 9 (3D 63)

St John's Ter. E7 . . . . . . .3D 55
  SW15 . . . . .3A 112
  (off Kingston Va.)
  W10 . . . . .3F 57
St John St.
  EC1 . . . . .1C 8 (1C 62)
St John's Va. SE8 . . . . . .5C 94
St John's Vs. N19 . . . . . .4F 33
  W8 . . . . .4D 73
  (off St Mary's Pl.)
St John's Way N19 . . . . .4E 33
ST JOHN'S WOOD 1F 59
St John's Wood Ct.
  NW8 . . . . .2F 59
  (off St John's Wood Rd.)
St John's Wood High St.
  NW8 . . . . .1F 59
St John's Wood Pk.
  NW8 . . . . .5F 45
St John's Wood Rd.
  NW8 . . . . .3F 59
St John's Wood Ter.
  NW8 . . . . .1F 59
St Josephs Almshouses
  W6 . . . . .5F 71
  (off Brook Grn.)
St Joseph's Cl. W10 . . . .4A 58
St Joseph's College
  Sports Cen. 5D 119
St Joseph's Cotts.
  SW3 . . . . .5B 74
  (off Cadogan St.)
St Josephs Ct. SE7 . . . . .2D 97
St Joseph's Flats NW1 . . .1B 6
  (off Drummond Cres.)
St Joseph's Ho. W6 . . . . .5F 71
  (off Brook Grn.)
St Joseph's St. SW8 . . . .4D 89
St Joseph's Va. SE3 . . . .1F 109
St Jude's Rd. E2 . . . . . . .1D 65
St Jude St. N16 . . . . .2A 50
St Julian's Cl.
  SW16 . . . . .4C 118
St Julian's Farm Rd.
  SE27 . . . . .4C 118
St Julian's Rd. NW6 . . . .5C 44
St Katharine Docks 1F 27
St Katharine's Pct.
  NW1 . . . . .1D 61
St Katharine's Way
  E1 . . . . .1F 27 (2B 78)
  (not continuous)
St Katharine's Yacht Haven
  . . . . .2B 78
  (off St Katharine's Way)
St Katherine's Row
  EC3 . . . . .4E 19
St Katherines Wlk.
  W11 . . . . .2F 71
  (off St Ann's Rd.)
St Kilda's Rd. N16 . . . . . .3F 35
St Kitts Ter. SE19 . . . . . .5A 120
St Laurence Cl. NW6 . . . .5F 43
St Lawrence Cotts.
  E14 . . . . .2E 81
  (off St Lawrence St.)
St Lawrence Ct. N1 . . . . .4F 49
St Lawrence Ho. SE1 . . . .5E 27
  (off Purbrook St.)

St Lawrence St. E14 . . . .2E 81
St Lawrence Ter.
  W10 . . . . .4A 58
St Lawrence Way
  SW9 . . . . .4C 90
St Leger Ct. NW6 . . . . . .4F 43
  (off Coverdale Rd.)
St Leonard M. N1 . . . . . .1A 64
  (off Hoxton St.)
St Leonard's Ct. N1 . . . . .1C 10
St Leonard's Rd. E14 . . . .4D 67
  (not continuous)
  NW10 . . . . .3A 56
St Leonards Sq.
  NW5 . . . . .3C 46
St Leonard's St. E3 . . . . .2D 67
St Leonard's Ter.
  SW3 . . . . .1B 88
St Loo Av. SW3 . . . . .2A 88
St Loo Ct. SW3 . . . . .2A 88
  (off St Loo Av.)
St Louis Rd. SE27 . . . . . .4F 119
St Lucia Dr. E15 . . . . . . .5B 54
St Luke's 3A 10 (3E 63)
St Luke's Av. SW4 . . . . .2F 103
St Luke's Cl.
  EC1 . . . . .3A 10 (3E 63)
St Lukes Cl. E10 . . . . . . .2D 39
  (off Capworth St.)
  W11 . . . . .5B 58
  (off St Luke's Rd.)
St Luke's Est.
  EC1 . . . . .2B 10 (2F 63)
St Luke's M. W11 . . . . . .5B 58
St Luke's Rd. W11 . . . . . .4B 58
St Luke's Sq. E16 . . . . . .5B 68
St Luke's St. SW3 . . . . . .1A 88
St Luke's Yd. W9 . . . . . . .1B 58
  (not continuous)
St Margarets Cl. EC2 . . . .5F 63
St Margarets Ct.
  SE1 . . . . .2A 26 (2E 77)
  SW15 . . . . .2D 99
St Margaret's Cres.
  SW15 . . . . .3D 99
St Margaret's Gro.
  E11 . . . . .5B 40
St Margaret's Ho.
  NW1 . . . . .1B 6
  (off Polygon Rd.)
St Margaret's La.
  W8 . . . . .4D 73
St Margaret's Pas.
  SE13 . . . . .1A 110
  (not continuous)
St Margarets Rd. E12 . . .4E 41
  NW10 . . . . .2E 57
  SE4 . . . . .2B 108
  (not continuous)
St Margaret St.
  SW1 . . . . . . .4D 23 (3A 76)
St Marks Cl. SE10 . . . . . .3E 95
  SW6 . . . . .4C 86
St Marks Ct. NW8 . . . . . .1E 59
  (off Abercorn Pl.)
St Mark's Cres.
  NW1 . . . . .5C 46
St Mark's Ga. E9 . . . . . . .4B 52
St Mark's Gro. SW10 . . . .3D 87

St Marks Ho. *SE17* 2F **91**
    (off Lytham St.)
St Marks Ind. Est.
  E16 . . . . .2F **83**
St Mark's Pl.
  SW19 . . . . .5B **114**
  W11 . . . . .5A **58**
St Mark's Ri. E16 . . . . . .2B **50**
  W11 . . . . .5A **58**
St Mark's Sq. NW1 . . . .5C **46**
St Mark St. E1 . . . . . . .5B **64**
St Mark's Vs. *N4* 4B **34**
  (off Moray Rd.)
St Martin-in-the-Fields Church
  . . . . .5D **15**
  (off St Martin's Pl.)
St Martin's Almshouses
  NW1 . . . . .5E **47**
St Martin's Av. E6 . . . . .1F **69**
St Martin's Cl. NW1 . . .5E **47**
St Martins Ct. *EC4* 2F **17**
  (off Newgate St.)
  N1 . . . . .5A **50**
  (off De Beauvoir Est.)
St Martins Ho. *NW1* 1B **6**
  (off Polygon Rd.)
St Martin's La.
  WC2 . . . . . .4D **15** (1A **76**)
St Martin's Le-Grand
  EC1 . . . . . .2F **17** (5E **63**)
St Martin's Pl.
  WC2 . . . . . .5D **15** (1A **76**)
St Martin's Rd. SW9 . . .5B **90**
St Martin's St.
  WC2 . . . . . .5C **14** (1F **75**)
  (not continuous)
St Martin's Theatre 4D **15**
  (off West St.)
St Martins Way
  SW17 . . . . .3E **115**

St Mary Abbot's Ct.
  W14 . . . . .4B **72**
  (off Warwick Gdns.)
St Mary Abbot's Pl.
  W8 . . . . .4B **72**
St Mary Abbot's Ter.
  W14 . . . . .4B **72**
St Mary at Hill
  EC3 . . . . . .5D **19** (1A **78**)
St Mary Axe
  EC3 . . . . . .3D **19** (5A **64**)
Marychurch St.
  SE16 . . . . .3E **79**
St Mary Graces Ct.
  E1 . . . . .1B **78**
St Marylebone Cl.
  NW10 . . . . .5A **42**
St Mary le-Park Ct.
  SW11 . . . . .3A **88**
  (off Parkgate Rd.)
St Mary Newington Cl.
  SE17 . . . . .1A **92**
  (off Surrey Sq.)

St Mary's Av. E11 . . . . .2D **41**
St Mary's Ct. *E3* 2D **67**
  (off Bow Rd.)
  SE7 . . . . .3F **97**
  W6 . . . . .4B **70**
St Mary's Est. *SE16* 3E **79**
  (off Elephant La.)
St Mary's Flats *NW1* 1B **6**
  (off Drummond Cres.)
St Mary's Gdns.
  SE11 . . . . .5C **76**
St Mary's Ga. W8 . . . . .4D **73**
St Mary's Gro. N1 . . . . .3D **49**
  SW13 . . . . .1D **99**
St Mary's Ho. *N1* 5D **49**
  (off St Mary's Path)
St Mary's Mans. W2 . . .4F **59**
St Mary's M. NW6 . . . . .4D **45**
St Mary's Path *E1* 5C **64**
  (off White Church La.)
  N1 . . . . .5D **49**
St Mary's Pl. W8 . . . . . .4D **73**
St Mary's Rd. E10 . . . . .5E **39**
  E13 . . . . .1D **69**
  NW10 . . . . .5A **42**
  NW11 . . . . .2A **30**
  SE15 . . . . .4E **93**
  SW19 . . . . .5A **114**
St Mary's Sq. W2 . . . . .4F **59**
St Mary's Ter. W2 . . . . .4F **59**
St Mary's Twr. *EC1* 4A **10**
  (off Fortune St.)
St Mary's Wlk. SE11 . . .5C **76**
St Matthews Ct. E10 . . .2D **39**
  SE1 . . . . .5D **27**
  (off Meadow Row)
St Matthews Ho.
  SE17 . . . . .2F **91**
  (off Phelp St.)
St Matthew's Lodge
  NW1 . . . . .1E **61**
  (off Oakley Sq.)
St Matthew's Rd.
  SW2 . . . . .2B **104**
St Matthew's Row E2 . . .2C **64**
St Matthew St.
  SW1 . . . . . .5B **22** (4F **75**)
St Maur Rd. SW6 . . . . .4B **86**
St Michael's All.
  EC3 . . . . . .3C **18** (5F **63**)
St Michaels Cl. E16 . . . .4F **69**
St Michaels Cl. *E14* 4E **67**
  (off St Leonard's Rd.)
  SE1 . . . . .4A **26**
  (off Trinity St.)
St Michael's Flats
  NW1 . . . . .1B **6**
  (off Aldenham St.)
St Michael's Gdns.
  W10 . . . . .4A **58**
St Michael's M. SW1 . . .5C **74**
St Michael's Rd.
  NW2 . . . . .1E **43**
  SW9 . . . . .5B **90**
St Michaels St. W2 . . . .5F **59**
St Michaels Ter. N6 . . . .3C **32**
  (off South Gro.)
St Mildred's Ct.
  EC2 . . . . . .3B **18** (5F **63**)

St Mildreds Rd. SE6 . . .5A **110**
  SE12 . . . . .5A **110**
St Nicholas' Flats
  NW1 . . . . .1B **6**
  (off Werrington St.)
St Nicholas Glebe
  SW17 . . . . .5C **116**
St Nicholas Ho.
  SE8 . . . . .2C **94**
  (off Deptford Grn.)
St Nicholas St. SE8 . . . .4B **94**
St Norbert Grn. SE4 . . .2A **108**
St Norbert Rd. SE4 . . . .3F **107**
St Olaf Ho. SE1 . . . . . . .1C **26**
St Olaf's Rd. SW6 . . . . .3A **86**
St Olaf Stairs SE1 . . . . .1C **26**
St Olave's Ct.
  EC2 . . . . . .3B **18** (5F **63**)
St Olave's Est.
  SE1 . . . . . .3E **27** (3A **78**)
St Olave's Gdns.
  SE11 . . . . .5C **76**
St Olaves Ho. *SE11* 5C **76**
  (off Walnut Tree Wlk.)
St Olave's Mans.
  SE11 . . . . .5C **76**
St Olav's Sq. SE16 . . . .3E **79**
St Oswald's Pl. SE11 . . .1B **90**
St Oswalds Studios
  SW6 . . . . .2C **86**
  (off Sedlescombe Rd.)
St Oswulf St. SW1 . . . . .5F **75**
St Owen Ho. *SE1* 5F **27**
  (off St Saviour's Est.)
ST PANCRAS . . .2E **7** (2A **62**)
St Pancras Commercial Cen.
  NW1 . . . . .5E **47**
  (off Pratt St.)
St Pancras Way NW1 . .4E **47**
St Paul's All. *EC4* 3E **17**
  (off St Paul's Chyd.)
St Paul's Av. NW2 . . . . .3D **43**
  SE16 . . . . .2F **79**
St Paul's Bldgs. *EC1* 3E **9**
  (off Dallington St.)
St Paul's Cathedral
  . . . . .3E **17** (5E **63**)
St Paul's Chyd.
  EC4 . . . . . .3E **17** (5D **63**)
St Pauls Cl. SE7 . . . . . . .1F **97**
St Pauls Ct. SW4 . . . . .3F **103**
St Pauls Courtyard
  SE8 . . . . .3C **94**
  (off Crossfield St.)
St Paul's Cres. NW1 . . .4F **47**
  (not continuous)
St Paul's Dr. E15 . . . . . .2F **53**
St Paul's M. NW1 . . . . .4F **47**
St Paul's Pl. N1 . . . . . . .3F **49**
St Paul's Rd. N1 . . . . . . .3D **49**
St Paul's Shrubbery
  N1 . . . . .3F **49**
St Paul's Studios
  W14 . . . . .1A **86**
  (off Talgarth Rd.)
St Pauls Ter. SE17 . . . . .2D **91**
St Paul St. N1 . . . . .5E **49**
  (not continuous)

St Pauls Vw. Apartments
EC1 . . . . .2B **8**
(off Amwell St.)
St Paul's Way E3 . . . . .4B **66**
St Peter's All. EC3 . . . . .3C **18**
(off Gracechurch St.)
St Peter's Av. E2 . . . . .1C **64**
St Petersburgh M.
W2 . . . . .1D **73**
St Petersburgh Pl.
W2 . . . . .1D **73**
St Peter's Cen. E1 . . . .2D **79**
(off Reardon St.)
St Peter's Chu. Ct.
N1 . . . . .5D **49**
(off St Peter's St.)
St Peter's Cl. E2 . . . . .1C **64**
SW17 . . . . .2A **116**
St Peter's Cl. E1 . . . . . .3E **65**
(off Cephas St.)
NW4 . . . . .1E **29**
SE12 . . . . .3B **110**
WC1 . . . . .2E **7**
(off Seaford St.)
St Peter's Gdns.
SE27 . . . . .3C **118**
St Peter's Gro. W6 . . . .5C **70**
St Peters Ho. SE17 . . . .2F **91**
WC1 . . . . .2E **7**
(off Regent Sq.)
St Peters M. N4 . . . . . .1D **35**
N8 . . . . .1C **34**
St Peters Pl. W9 . . . . . .3D **59**
St Peter's Rd. W6 . . . . .1C **84**
St Peter's Sq. E2 . . . . .1C **64**
W6 . . . . .5B **70**
St Peter's St. N1 . . . . . .5D **49**
(off St Peters St.)
St Peter's St. M. N1 . . . .1D **63**
(off St Peters St.)
St Peter's Ter. SW6 . . . .3B **86**
St Peter's Vs. W6 . . . . . .5C **70**
St Peter's Way N1 . . . . .4A **50**
St Peter's Wharf W4 . . .1C **84**
St Philip Ho. WC1 . . . . .2B **8**
(off Lloyd Baker St.)
St Philip Sq. SW8 . . . . .5D **89**
St Philip's Rd. E8 . . . . .3C **50**
St Philip St. SW8 . . . . .5D **89**
St Philip's Way N1 . . . . .5E **49**
St Quentin Ho.
SW18 . . . . .4F **101**
St Quentin Av. W10 . . . .4E **57**
St Quintin Ct. W10 . . . .4E **57**
St Quintin Gdns. W10 . . .4E **57**
St Quintin Rd. E13 . . . .2D **69**
St Regis Hgts. NW3 . . . .5D **31**
St Richard's Ho. NW1 . . .1B **6**
(off Eversholt St.)
St Rule St. SW8 . . . . . . .5E **89**
St Saviour's Rd.
SE1 . . . . .5F **27** (3B **78**)
St Saviour's Rd.
SW2 . . . . .3B **104**
St Saviour's Wharf
SE1 . . . . .3B **78**
(off Mill St.)
SE1 . . . . .3B **78**
(off Shad Thames)
Saints Cl. SE27 . . . . . .4D **119**

Saints Dr. E7 . . . . .2F **55**
St Silas Pl. NW5 . . . . . .3C **46**
St Simon's Av. SW15 . . .3E **99**
St Stephen's Av. E17 . . .1E **39**
W12 . . . . .2D **71**
(not continuous)
St Stephens Cl. E17 . . .1D **39**
NW5 . . . . .2B **46**
(off Malden Rd.)
NW8 . . . . .5A **46**
St Stephens Ct. N8 . . . .1B **34**
St Stephen's Cres.
W2 . . . . .5C **58**
(not continuous)
St Stephen's Gdns.
SW15 . . . . .3B **100**
W2 . . . . .5C **58**
(not continuous)
St Stephens Gro.
SE13 . . . . .1E **109**
St Stephens Ho.
SE17 . . . . .2F **91**
(off Lytham St.)
St Stephen's M. W2 . . . .4C **58**
St Stephens Pde. E7 . . .4E **55**
St Stephen's Rd. E3 . . . .5A **52**
E6 . . . . .4E **55**
E17 . . . . .1D **39**
St Stephen's Row
EC4 . . . . .3B **18**
St Stephen's Ter.
SW8 . . . . .3B **90**
St Stephen's Wlk.
SW7 . . . . .5E **73**
(off Southwell Gdns.)
St Swithins La.
EC4 . . . . .4B **18** (1F **77**)
St Swithun's Rd.
SE13 . . . . .4F **109**
St Theresa's Cl. E9 . . . .1C **52**
St Thomas Ct. E10 . . . .2D **39**
(off Lake Rd.)
NW1 . . . . .4E **47**
(off Wrotham Rd.)
St Thomas Ho. E1 . . . . .5F **65**
(off W. Arbour St.)
St Thomas M.
SW18 . . . . .3C **100**
St Thomas Rd. E16 . . . .5C **68**
St Thomas's Gdns.
NW5 . . . . .3C **46**
St Thomas's Pl. E9 . . . .4E **51**
St Thomas's Rd. N4 . . . .4C **34**
NW10 . . . . .5A **42**
St Thomas's Sq. E9 . . . .4E **51**
St Thomas St.
SE1 . . . . .2C **26** (2F **77**)
St Thomas's Way
SW6 . . . . .3B **86**
St Vincent Cl. SE27 . . . .5D **119**
St Vincent De Paul Ho.
E1 . . . . .4E **65**
(off Jubilee St.)
St Vincent Ho. SE1 . . . . .5F **27**
(off St Saviour's Est.)
St Vincent St.
W1 . . . . .1C **12** (4C **60**)
St Williams Ct. N1 . . . . .4A **48**
Sala Ho. SE3 . . . . .2D **111**
Salamanca Pl. SE1 . . . . .5B **76**

Salamanca Sq. SE1 . . . . .5B **76**
(off Salamanca Pl.)
Salamanca St. SE1 . . . . .5B **76**
SE11 . . . . .5B **76**
Salcombe Rd. E17 . . . . .2B **38**
N16 . . . . .2A **50**
Salcott Rd. SW11 . . . . .3A **102**
Salehurst Rd. SE4 . . . . .4B **108**
Salem Rd. W2 . . . . .1D **73**
Sale Pl. W2 . . . . .4A **60**
Sale St. E2 . . . . .3C **64**
Salford Ho. E14 . . . . . . .5E **81**
(off Seyssel St.)
Salford Rd. SW2 . . . . . .1F **117**
Salisbury Cl. SE17 . . . . .5F **77**
Salisbury Ct. E9 . . . . . . .2A **52**
(off Mabley St.)
EC4 . . . . .3D **17** (5D **63**)
SE16 . . . . .4C **78**
(off Stork's Rd.)
Salisbury Ho. E14 . . . . .5D **67**
(off Hobday St.)
EC2 . . . . .1C **18**
(off London Wall)
N1 . . . . .5D **49**
(off St Mary's Path)
SW1 . . . . .1F **89**
(off Drummond Ga.)
SW9 . . . . .3C **90**
(off Cranmer Rd.)
Salisbury Mans. N15 . . .1D **35**
Salisbury M. SW6 . . . . . .3B **86**
Salisbury Pas. SW6 . . . .3B **86**
(off Dawes Rd.)
Salisbury Pavement
SW6 . . . . .3B **86**
(off Dawes Rd.)
Salisbury Pl. SW9 . . . . .3D **91**
W1 . . . . . .5A **4** (4B **60**)
Salisbury Rd. E7 . . . . . .3C **54**
E10 . . . . .4E **39**
E12 . . . . .2F **55**
E17 . . . . .1E **39**
N4 . . . . .1D **35**
Salisbury Sq.
EC4 . . . . .3C **16** (5C **62**)
Salisbury St. NW8 . . . . .3A **60**
Salisbury Ter. SE15 . . . .1E **107**
Salisbury Wlk. N19 . . . . .4E **33**
Salmen Rd. E13 . . . . . . .1B **68**
Salmon La. E14 . . . . . . .5A **66**
Salmon M. NW6 . . . . . . .2C **44**
Salmon St. E14 . . . . . . .5B **66**
Salomons Rd. E13 . . . . .4E **69**
Salop Rd. E17 . . . . .1F **37**
Saltcoats Rd. W4 . . . . . .3A **70**
Saltdene N4 . . . . .3B **34**
Salterford Rd.
SW17 . . . . .5C **116**
Salter Rd. SE16 . . . . . . .2F **79**
Salter's Ct. EC4 . . . . . . .3A **18**
Salter's Hall Ct. EC4 . . .4B **18**
Salter's Hill SE19 . . . . .5F **119**
Salters Rd. W10 . . . . . . .3F **57**
Salters Row N1 . . . . .3F **49**
(off Tilney Gdns.)
Salter St. E14 . . . . .1B **80**
NW10 . . . . .2C **56**
Salterton Rd. N7 . . . . . . .5B **34**

Saltoun Rd. SW2 . . . . . .2C 104
Saltram Cres. W9 . . . . . .2B 58
Saltwell St. E14 . . . . . . .1C 80
Saltwood Gro. SE17 . . . .1F 91
Saltwood Ho. *SE15 . . . . .2E 93*
　(off Lovelinch Cl.)
Salusbury Rd. NW6 . . . . .5A 44
Salutation Rd. SE10 . . . .5A 82
Salvador SW17 . . . . .5B 116
Salvin Rd. SW15 . . . . . .1F 99
Salway Pl. E15 . . . . .3F 53
Salway Rd. E15 . . . . . . .3F 53
Samantha Cl. E17 . . . . . .2B 38
Sam Bartram Cl. SE7 . . . .1E 97
Sambrook Ho. *E1 . . . . . .4E 65*
　(off Jubilee St.)
　SE11 . . . . .5C 76
　(off Hotspur St.)
Sambruck M. SE6 . . . . .1D 123
Samels Ct. W6 . . . . .1C 84
Samford Ho. *N1 . . . . . . .5C 48*
　(off Barnsbury Est.)
Samford St. NW8 . . . . . .3F 59
Samira Cl. E17 . . . . .1C 38
Sam Manners Ho.
　SE10 . . . . .1A 96
　(off Tuskar St.)
Sam March Ho. *E14 . . . . .5F 67*
　(off Blair St.)
Sampson Ho.
　SE1 . . . . . .1D 25 (2D 77)
Sampson St. E1 . . . . . . .2C 78
Samson St. E13 . . . . . . .1E 69
Samuda Est. E14 . . . . . . .4E 81
Samuel Cl. E8 . . . . .5B 50
　SE14 . . . . .2F 93
Samuel Ct. *N1 . . . . .2D 11*
　(off Pitfield St.)
Samuel Johnson Cl.
　SW16 . . . . .4B 118
Samuel Jones Ct.
　SE15 . . . . .3A 92
Samuel Lewis Bldgs.
　N1 . . . . .3C 48
Samuel Lewis Trust Dwellings
　E8 . . . . .2C 50
　(off Amhurst Rd.)
　N16 . . . . .1A 36
　SW3 . . . . .5A 74
　SW6 . . . . .3C 86
　(off Vanston Pl.)
　W14 . . . . .5B 72
　(off Lisgar Ter.)
Samuel Lewis Trust Est.
　SE5 . . . . .4E 91
　(off Warner Rd.)
Samuel Richardson Ho.
　W14 . . . . .5B 72
　(off North End Cres.)
Samuel's Cl. W6 . . . . . . .5E 71
Samuel St. SE15 . . . . . . .3B 92
Samuel Wallis Lodge
　SE10 . . . . .5A 82
　(off Banning St.)
Sanchia Ct. *E2 . . . . .2C 64*
　(off Wellington Row)
Sancroft Ho. NW2 . . . . . .5D 29
Sancroft Ho. *SE11 . . . . .1B 90*
　(off Sancroft St.)

Sancroft St. SE11 . . . . . . .1B 90
Sanctuary, The SW1 . . . . .5C 22
Sanctuary M. E8 . . . . . . .3B 50
Sanctuary St.
　SE1 . . . . . .3A 26 (3E 77)
Sandale Cl. N16 . . . . .5F 35
Sandall Ho. E3 . . . . .1A 66
Sandall Rd. NW5 . . . . . . .3E 47
Sandal St. E15 . . . . .5A 54
Sandalwood Cl. E1 . . . . . .3A 66
Sandalwood Mans.
　W8 . . . . .4D 73
　(off Stone Hall Gdns.)
Sandbourne NW8 . . . . . . .5D 45
　(off Abbey Rd.)
　W11 . . . . .5C 58
　(off Dartmouth Cl.)
Sandbourne Rd. SE4 . . . . .5A 94
Sandbrook Rd. N16 . . . . . .5A 36
Sandby Ct. NW10 . . . . . . .2D 57
　(off Plough Cl.)
Sandby Ho. NW6 . . . . . . .5C 44
Sandell St.
　SE1 . . . . . .3B 24 (3C 76)
Sanderling Ct. *SE8 . . . . . .2B 94*
　(off Abinger Gro.)
Sanderling Lodge *E1 . . . .1B 78*
　(off Star Pl.)
Sanders Ho. *WC1 . . . . . . .1B 8*
　(off Gt. Percy St.)
Sanderson Cl. NW5 . . . . . .1D 47
Sanderson Ho. *SE8 . . . . . .1B 94*
　(off Grove St.)
Sanderstead Av.
　NW2 . . . . .4A 30
Sanderstead Cl.
　SW12 . . . . .5E 103
Sanderstead Rd. E10 . . . . .3A 38
Sanders Way N19 . . . . . . .3F 33
Sandfield *WC1 . . . . .2E 7*
　(off Cromer St.)
Sandford Cl. N16 . . . . .3A 36
Sandford Row SE17 . . . . .1F 91
Sandford St. SW6 . . . . . . .3D 87
Sandgate Ho. E5 . . . . .2D 51
Sandgate La. SW18 . . . . .1A 116
Sandgate St. SE15 . . . . . .2D 93
Sandgate Trad. Est.
　SE15 . . . . .2D 93
　(off Sandgate St.)
Sandham Ct. SW4 . . . . . . .4A 90
Sandhills, The *SW10 . . . .2E 87*
　(off Limerston St.)
Sandhurst Ct. SW2 . . . . . .2A 104
Sandhurst Ho. *E1 . . . . . . .4E 65*
　(off Wolsy St.)
Sandhurst Mkt. *SE6 . . . .1E 123*
　(off Sandhurst Rd.)
Sandhurst Rd. SE6 . . . . . .1F 123
Sandifer Dr. NW2 . . . . . . .5F 29
Sandilands Rd. SW6 . . . . .4D 87
Sandison St. SE15 . . . . . .1C 106
Sandland St.
　WC1 . . . . . .1A 16 (4B 62)
Sandlings Cl. SE15 . . . . . .5D 93
Sandmere Rd. SW4 . . . . . .2A 104
Sandover Ho. *SE16 . . . . . .4C 78*
　(off Spa Rd.)
Sandown Ct. SE26 . . . . . .3D 121

Sandpiper Cl. SE16 . . . . . .3B 80
Sandpiper Ct. *E1 . . . . . . .1C 78*
　(off Thomas More St.)
　E14 . . . . .4E 81
　(off New Union Cl.)
　SE8 . . . . .2C 94
　(off Edward Pl.)
Sandpit Rd.
　BR1: Brom 5A 124
Sandridge St. N19 . . . . . . .4E 33
Sandringham Bldgs.
　SE17 . . . . .5F 77
　(off Balfour St.)
Sandringham Cl.
　SW19 . . . . .1F 113
Sandringham Ct.
　SE16 . . . . .2F 79
　(off King & Queen Wharf)
　W1 . . . . .3A 14
　(off Dufour's Pl.)
　W9 . . . . .2E 59
　(off Maida Va.)
Sandringham Flats
　WC2 . . . . .4C 14
　(off Charing Cross Rd.)
Sandringham Gdns.
　N8 . . . . .1A 34
Sandringham Ho.
　W14 . . . . .5A 72
　(off Windsor Way)
Sandringham Rd.
　BR1: Brom 5C 124
　E7 . . . . .2B 55
　E8 . . . . .2B 50
　E10 . . . . .1F 39
　NW2 . . . . .3D 43
　NW11 . . . . .2A 30
Sandrock Rd. SE13 . . . . . .1C 108
SANDS END 4E 87
Sand's End La. SW6 . . . . .4D 87
Sandstone La. E16 . . . . . .1D 83
Sandstone Pl. N19 . . . . . . .4D 33
Sandstone Rd.
　SE12 . . . . .2D 125
Sandtoft Rd. SE7 . . . . . . .2D 97
Sandwell Cres. NW6 . . . . .3C 44
Sandwich Ho. *SE16 . . . . .3E 79*
　(off Swan Rd.)
　WC1 . . . . .2D 7
　(off Sandwich St.)
Sandwich St.
　WC1 . . . . . .2D 7 (2A 62)
Sandy Rd. NW3 . . . . .4D 31
　NW11 . . . . .4D 31
Sandys Row
　E1 . . . . . .1E 19 (4A 64)
Sanford La. N16 . . . . .5B 36
Sanford St. SE14 . . . . .2A 94
Sanford Ter. N16 . . . . .5B 36
Sanford Wlk. N16 . . . . . . .4B 36
　SE14 . . . . .2A 94
Sangley Rd. SE6 . . . . .5D 109
Sangora Rd. SW11 . . . . . .2F 101
Sankey Ho. *E2 . . . . .1E 65*
　(off St James's Av.)
Sansom Rd. E11 . . . . .4B 40
Sansom St. SE5 . . . . .4F 91
Sans Wlk.
　EC1 . . . . . .3C 8 (3C 62)

Sant Ho. *SE17* 5E **77**
   (off Browning St.)
Santley Ho.
  SE1 . . . . . .4C **24** (3C **76**)
Santley St. SW4 . . . . . . .2B **104**
Santos Rd. SW18 . . . .3C **100**
Sapcote Trad. Cen.
  NW10 . . . . .3B **42**
Saperton Wlk. *SE11* 5B **76**
   (off Juxon St.)
Saphire Ct. *E15* 5E **53**
   (off Warton Rd.)
Sapperton Ct. EC1 . . . . . . .3F **9**
Sapperton Ho. *W2* 4C **58**
   (off Westbourne Pk. Rd.)
Sapphire Ct. *E1* 1C **78**
   (off Cable St.)
Sapphire Rd. SE8 . . . . .5A **80**
Saracens Head Yd.
  EC3 . . . . .3F **19**
Saracen St. E14 . . . . . .5C **66**
Sarah Ho. *E1* 5D **65**
   (off Commercial Rd.)
Sarah Swift Ho. *SE1* 3C **26**
   (off Kipling St.)
Sara La. Ct. *N1* 1A **64**
   (off Stanway St.)
Saratoga Rd. E5 . . . . . . .1E **51**
Sardinia St.
  WC2 . . . . . .3F **15** (5B **62**)
Sarjant Path *SW19* 2F **113**
   (off Blincoe Cl.)
Sark Wlk. E16 . . . . .5D **69**
Sarnesfield Ho.
  SE15 . . . . .2D **93**
   (off Pencraig Way)
Sarratt Ho. *W10* 4E **57**
   (off Sutton Way)
Sarre Rd. NW2 . . . . . . .2B **44**
Sarsfeld Rd. SW12 . . . .2B **116**
Sartor Rd. SE15 . . . . . .2F **107**
Sarum Ho. *W11* 1B **72**
   (off Portobello Rd.)
Sarum Ter. E3 . . . . .3B **66**
Satanita Cl. E16 . . . . . . .5F **69**
Satchwell Rd. E2 . . . . . .2C **64**
Satchwell St. E2 . . . . . .2C **64**
Sattar M. N16 . . . . .5F **35**
Saturn Ho. *E3* 5C **52**
   (off Garrison Rd.)
  E15 . . . . .5F **53**
   (off High St.)
Sauls Grn. E11 . . . . .5A **40**
Saunders Cl. *E14* 1B **80**
   (off Limehouse C'way.)
Saunders Ho. *SE16* 3F **79**
   (off Quebec Way)
Saunders Ness Rd.
  E14 . . . . .1E **95**
Saunders St. SE11 . . . . .5C **76**
Savage Gdns.
  EC3 . . . . . .4E **19** (1A **78**)
   (not continuous)
Savannah Cl. SE15 . . . . .3B **92**
Savernake Ho. N4 . . . . .2E **35**
Savernake Rd. NW3 . . . .1B **46**
Savile Row
  W1 . . . . .4F **13** (1E **75**)
Saville Rd. E16 . . . . . . .2F **83**

Savill Ho. SW4 . . . . . .4F **103**
Savona Ho. *SW8* 3E **89**
   (off Savona St.)
Savona St. SW8 . . . . . . .3E **89**
Savoy Bldgs. WC2 . . . . .5F **15**
SAVOY CIRCUS 1B **70**
Savoy Cl. E15 . . . . .5A **54**
Savoy Cl. NW3 . . . . . . .5E **31**
   (off Cromwell Rd.)
  SW5 . . . . .5C **72**
  WC2 . . . . . .5E **15** (1B **76**)
Savoy Hill
  WC2 . . . . . .5F **15** (1B **76**)
Savoy M. SW9 . . . . .1A **104**
Savoy Pl. W12 . . . . .2F **71**
  WC2 . . . . . .5E **15** (1A **76**)
Savoy Row WC2 . . . . . . .4F **15**
Savoy Steps WC2 . . . . . .5F **15**
Savoy St.
  WC2 . . . . . .5F **15** (1B **76**)
Savoy Theatre *5E **15***
   (off Strand)
Savoy Way WC2 . . . . . . .5F **15**
Sawkins Cl. SW19 . . . . .2A **114**
Sawley Rd. W12 . . . . . . .2C **70**
Saw Mill Way N1 . . . . . .1C **36**
Sawmill Yd. E3 . . . . . . .5A **52**
Sawyer Cl. NW10 . . . . . .4A **42**
Sawyer St.
  SE1 . . . . . . .3F **25** (3E **77**)
Saxby Rd. SW2 . . . . . . .5A **104**
Saxonbury Ct. N7 . . . . . .2A **48**
Saxon Chase N8 . . . . . . .1B **34**
Saxon Cl. E17 . . . . .2C **38**
Saxonfield Cl. SW2 . . . .5B **104**
Saxon Hall *W2* 1D **73**
   (off Palace Ct.)
Saxon Ho. *E1* 1F **19**
   (off Thrawl St.)
Saxon Lea Ct. *E3* 1B **66**
   (off Saxon Rd.)
Saxon Rd. E3 . . . . .1B **66**
Saxon Ter. SE6 . . . . . . .2B **122**
Saxton Cl. SE13 . . . . . .1F **109**
Sayes Ct. SE8 . . . . .2B **94**
Sayes Ct. St. SE8 . . . . . .2B **94**
Scafell *NW1* 1F **5**
   (off Stanhope St.)
Scala 1E **7**
Scala St. W1 . . . . .5A **6** (4E **61**)
Scampston M. W10 . . . . .5F **57**
Scandrett St. E1 . . . . . . .2D **79**
Scarab Cl. E16 . . . . .1B **82**
Scarba Wlk. *N1* 3F **49**
   (off Essex Rd.)
Scarborough Rd. E11 . . .3F **39**
  N4 . . . . .2C **34**
Scarborough St. E1 . . . .5B **64**
Scarlet Rd. SE6 . . . . . . .3A **124**
Scarlette Mnr. Way
  SW2 . . . . .5C **104**
Scarsbrook Rd. SE3 . . . .1F **111**
Scarsdale Pl. W8 . . . . . .4D **73**
Scarsdale Studios
  W8 . . . . .4C **72**
   (off Stratford Rd.)
Scarsdale Vs. W8 . . . . . .4C **72**
Scarth Rd. SW13 . . . . . .1B **98**
Scawen Rd. SE8 . . . . . . .1A **94**

Scawfell St. E2 . . . . .1B **64**
Sceaux Gdns. SE5 . . . . . .4A **92**
Sceptre Ct. *EC3* 5F **19**
   (off Tower Hill)
Sceptre Ho. *E1* 3E **65**
   (off Malcolm Rd.)
Sceptre Rd. E2 . . . . .2E **65**
Schafer Ho.
  NW1 . . . . . .2F **5** (2E **61**)
Schiller
  International University
  . . . . .2B **24**
Schofield Wlk. SE3 . . . . .3C **96**
Scholars Ho. *NW6* 5C **44**
   (off Glengall Rd.)
Scholars Pl. N16 . . . . . . .5A **36**
Scholars Rd. SW12 . . . . .1E **117**
Scholefield Rd. N19 . . . .4F **33**
Scholey Ho. SW11 . . . . .1A **102**
Schomberg Ho. *SW1* . . .5F **75**
   (off Page St.)
Schonfeld Sq. N16 . . . . .4F **35**
School App. E2 . . . . .1E **11**
Schoolbank Rd. SE10 . . .4B **82**
Schoolbell M. E3 . . . . . . .1A **66**
School Ho. *SE1* 5A **78**
   (off Page's Wlk.)
Schoolhouse La. E1 . . . . .1F **79**
School La. SE23 . . . . . . .2D **121**
School Rd. NW10 . . . . . .3A **56**
School Sq. SE10 . . . . . . .4B **82**
Schooner Cl. E14 . . . . . . .4F **81**
  SE16 . . . . .3E **79**
Schubert Rd. SW15 . . . . .3B **100**
Science Mus.
  Knightsbridge 4F **73**
Sclater St.
  E1 . . . . . . .3F **11** (3B **64**)
Scoble Pl. N16 . . . . .1B **50**
Scoles Cres. SW2 . . . . .1D **119**
Scoop, The 2E **27** (2A **78**)
Score Complex, The . . .5D **39**
Scoresby St.
  SE1 . . . . . . .2D **25** (2D **77**)
Scorton Ho. *N1* 1A **64**
   (off Whitmore Est.)
SCOTCH HOUSE 3B **74**
Scoter Ct. *SE8* 2B **94**
   (off Abinger Gro.)
Scotia Bldg. *E1* 1F **79**
   (off Jardine Rd.)
Scotia Ct. SE16 . . . . .3E **79**
   (off Canada Est.)
Scotia Rd. SW2 . . . . . . .5C **104**
Scotland Pl.
  SW1 . . . . . .2D **23** (2A **76**)
Scotney Ho. E9 . . . . .3E **51**
Scotsdale Rd. SE12 . . . .3D **111**
Scotson Ho. *SE11* 5C **76**
   (off Marylee Way)
Scotswood St.
  EC1 . . . . . . .3C **8** (3C **62**)
Scott Av. SW15 . . . . . . .4A **100**
Scott Ellis Gdns.
  NW8 . . . . .2F **59**
Scott Ho. *E13* 1C **68**
   (off Queens Rd. W.)
  E14 . . . . .3C **80**
   (off Admirals Way)

Scott Ho. N7 . . . . .3B 48
NW8 . . . . .3A 60
(off Broadley St.)
NW10 . . . . .4A 42
(off Stonebridge Pk.)
SE8 . . . . .1B 94
(off Grove St.)
Scott Lidgett Cres.
SE16 . . . . .3C 78
Scott Russell Pl. E14 . . .1D 95
Scotts Ct. *W12* 3E 71
(off Scott's Rd.)
Scott's Rd. E10 . . . . . . .3E 39
W12 . . . . .3D 71
Scott's Sufferance Wharf
SE1 . . . . .3B 78
(off Mill St.)
Scotts Ter. SE9 . . . . . . .2F 125
Scott St. E1 . . . . .3D 65
Scott's Yd.
EC4 . . . . . . .4B 18 (1F 77)
Scoulding Ho. E14 . . . . .4C 80
(off Mellish St.)
Scoulding Rd. E16 . . . . .5C 68
Scouler St. E14 . . . . . . .1E 81
Scout App. NW10 . . . . .1A 42
Scout La. SW4 . . . . . . .1E 103
Scovell Cres. SE1 . . . . . .4F 25
Scovell Rd.
SE1 . . . . .4F 25 (3E 77)
Screen on Baker Street
(Cinema) 5A 4
(off Baker St.)
Screen on the Green Cinema
. . . . .5D 49
(off Upper St.)
Screen on the Hill (Cinema)
Belsize Pk. 2A 46
Scriven Ct. E8 . . . . .5B 50
Scriven St. E8 . . . . .5B 50
Scrooby St. SE6 . . . . . .4D 109
Scrope Ho. EC1 . . . . . . .5B 8
(off Bourne Est.)
Scrubs La. NW10 . . . . . .2C 56
W10 . . . . .2C 56
Scrutton Cl. SW12 . . . . .5F 103
Scrutton St.
EC2 . . . . . .4D 11 (3A 64)
Scutari Rd. SE22 . . . . . .3E 107
Scylla Rd. SE15 . . . . . .1C 106
(not continuous)
Seabright St. E2 . . . . . . .2D 65
Seacole Cl. W3 . . . . .5A 56
Sea Containers Ho.
SE1 . . . . .5C 16
Seacon Twr. E14 . . . . . .3B 80
Seaford Ho. *SE16* 3E 79
(off Swan Rd.)
Seaford St.
WC1 . . . . . .2E 7 (2A 62)
Seaforth Cres. N5 . . . . . .2E 49
Seaforth Pl. SW1 . . . . . .5A 22
Seagrave Cl. E1 . . . . . . .4F 65
Seagrave Lodge *SW6* . . .2C 86
(off Seagrave Rd.)
Seagrave Rd. SW6 . . . . .2C 86
Seagry Rd. E11 . . . . .2C 40
Seagull La. E16 . . . . . . .1C 82

Seahorse Sailing Club
. . . . .4A 28
Seal Ho. *SE1* 5C 26
(off Weston St.)
Sea Life London Aquarium
. . . . . .3F 23 (3B 76)
Seal St. E8 . . . . .1B 50
Searle Ho. SW11 . . . . . .4C 88
(off Macduff St.)
Searle Pl. N4 . . . . .3B 34
Searles Cl. SW11 . . . . . .3A 88
Searles Rd. SE1 . . . . .5F 77
Searson Ho. SE17 . . . . . .5D 77
(off Canterbury Pl.)
Sears St. SE5 . . . . .3F 91
Seasalter Ho.
SW9 . . . . .4C 90
(off Gosling Way)
Seaton Cl. E13 . . . . .3C 68
SE11 . . . . .1C 90
SW15 . . . . .1D 113
Seaton Point E5 . . . . . . .1C 50
Sebastian Ho. N1 . . . . . .1D 11
(off Hoxton St.)
Sebastian St.
EC1 . . . . . . .2E 9 (2D 63)
Sebbon St. N1 . . . . .4D 49
Sebert Rd. E7 . . . . .2D 55
Sebright Ho. E2 . . . . .1C 64
(off Coate St.)
Sebright Pas. E2 . . . . . . .1C 64
Secker Ho. SW9 . . . . . . .5D 91
(off Loughborough Est.)
Secker St.
SE1 . . . . . .2B 24 (2C 76)
Second Av. E13 . . . . .2C 68
SW14 . . . . .1A 98
W3 . . . . .2B 70
W10 . . . . .3A 58
Sedan Way SE17 . . . . . .1A 92
Sedding St. SW1 . . . . . . .5C 74
Sedding Studios
SW1 . . . . .5C 74
(off Sedding St.)
Seddon Highwalk *EC2* . . .5F 9
(off Aldersgate St.)
Seddon Ho. EC2 . . . . . . .5F 9
Seddon St.
WC1 . . . . . .2A 8 (2B 62)
Sedgebrook Rd. SE3 . . . . .5F 97
Sedgeford Rd. W12 . . . . .2B 70
Sedgehill Rd. SE6 . . . . . .4C 122
Sedgeway SE6 . . . . .1B 124
Sedgmoor Pl. SE5 . . . . . .3A 92
Sedgwick Ho. *E3* 4C 66
(off Gale St.)
Sedgwick Rd. E10 . . . . . .4E 39
Sedgwick St. E9 . . . . .2F 51
Sedleigh Rd. SW18 . . . . .4B 100
Sedlescombe Rd.
SW6 . . . . .2C 86
Sedley Cl. SE26 . . . . . . .2D 121
Sedley Ho. *SE11* 1B 90
(off Newburn St.)
Sedley Pl.
W1 . . . . . .3D 13 (5D 61)
Seeley Dr. SE21 . . . . . . .4A 120
Seelig Av. NW9 . . . . .2C 28
Seely Rd. SW17 . . . . . . .5C 116

Seething La.
EC3 . . . . . .4E 19 (1A 78)
Sefton St. SW15 . . . . . . .1E 99
Segal Cl. SE23 . . . . .5A 108
Sekforde St.
EC1 . . . . . .4D 9 (3D 63)
Selbie Av. NW10 . . . . . . .2B 42
Selborne Rd. SE5 . . . . . . .5F 91
Selbourne Ho. SE1 . . . . . .4B 26
Selby Cl. E6 . . . . .4F 69
Selby Rd. E11 . . . . .5A 40
E13 . . . . .4D 69
Selby Sq. *W10* 2A 58
(off Dowland St.)
Selby St. E1 . . . . .3C 64
Selcroft Ho. *SE10* 1B 96
(off Glenister St.)
Selden Ho. SE15 . . . . . . .5E 93
(off Selden Rd.)
Selden Rd. SE15 . . . . . . .5E 93
Selden Wlk. N7 . . . . .4B 34
Seldon Ho. SW1 . . . . . . .1E 89
(off Churchill Gdns.)
SW8 . . . . .3E 89
(off Stewart's Rd.)
Selfridges 3B 12
Selhurst Cl. SW19 . . . . . .1F 113
Selina Ho. NW8 . . . . .3F 59
(off Frampton St.)
Selkirk Ho. N1 . . . . .5B 48
(off Bingfield St.)
Selkirk Rd. SW17 . . . . . .4A 116
Sellincourt Rd.
SW17 . . . . .5A 116
Sellons Av. NW10 . . . . . .5B 42
Selman Ho. E9 . . . . .3A 52
Selsdon Rd. E11 . . . . .2C 40
E13 . . . . .1B 68
NW2 . . . . .4B 28
SE27 . . . . .3C 118
Selsdon Way E14 . . . . . .4D 81
Selsea Pl. N16 . . . . .2A 50
Selsey St. E14 . . . . .4C 66
Selway Ho. SW8 . . . . . . .4A 90
(off Sth. Lambeth Rd.)
Selwood Pl. SW7 . . . . . . .1F 87
Selwoods SW2 . . . . .5C 104
Selwood Ter. SW7 . . . . . .1F 87
Selworthy Cl. E11 . . . . . . .1C 40
Selworthy Ho. *SW11* 4F 87
(off Battersea Church Rd.)
Selworthy Rd. SE6 . . . . . .3B 122
Selwyn Cl. E17 . . . . .1C 38
(off Yunus Khan Cl.)
SE3 . . . . .1B 110
Selwyn Rd. E3 . . . . .1B 66
E13 . . . . .5D 55
NW10 . . . . .4A 42
Semley Ga. E9 . . . . .3B 52
(not continuous)
Semley Ho. *SW1* 5D 75
(off Semley Pl.)
Semley Pl. SW1 . . . . .5C 74
Senate St. SE15 . . . . .5E 93
Senators Lodge *E3* 1A 66
(off Roman Rd.)

Sendall Ct. *SW11* 1F **101**
(off Winstanley Rd.)
Senior St. *W2* 4D **59**
Senlac Rd. *SE12* 1D **125**
Senrab St. *E1* 5F **65**
Sentamu St. *SE24* 1D **119**
Seraph Ct. *EC1* 1F **9**
(off Moreland St.)
Serbin Cl. *E10* 2E **39**
Serenaders Rd. *SW9* . . .5C **90**
Serenity Apartments
E17 . . . . .1D **39**
Seren Pk. Gdns.
SE3 . . . . .2A **96**
Sergeant Ind. Est.
SW18 . . . . .4D **101**
Serica Ct. *SE10* 3E **95**
Serjeants Inn
EC4 . . . . . . .3C **16** (5C **62**)
Serlby Ct. *W14* 4B **72**
(off Somerset Sq.)
Serle St.
WC2 . . . . . .2A **16** (5B **62**)
Sermon La. *EC4* 3F **17**
Serpentine, The 2A **74**
Serpentine Ct. *SE16* . . .3F **79**
(off Christopher Cl.)
Serpentine Gallery 3F **73**
Serpentine Rd.
W2 . . . . . . .2A **20** (2A **74**)
Serpentine Sackler Gallery
. . . . .2F **73**
Setchell Rd. *SE1* 5B **78**
Setchell Way *SE1* 5B **78**
Seth St. *SE16* 3E **79**
Settle Point *E13* 1C **68**
Settlers Ct. *E14* 1F **81**
Settles St. *E1* 4C **64**
Settrington Rd. *SW6* 5D **87**
Seven Dials
WC2 . . . . . .3D **15** (5A **62**)
Seven Dials Ct. *WC2* . . .3D **15**
(off Shorts Gdns.)
Seven Islands Leisure Cen.
. . . . .4E **79**
Sevenoaks Rd. *SE4* . . .4A **108**
Seven Sisters Rd. *N4* . . .5B **34**
N7 . . . . .5B **34**
N15 . . . . .4C **34**
Seven Stars Cnr.
W12 . . . . .4C **70**
Seven Stars Yd. *E1* 5F **11**
Severnake Cl. *E14* 5C **80**
Severn Av. *W10* 2A **58**
Severn Way *NW10* 2B **42**
Severus Rd. *SW11* 2A **102**
Seville Ho. *E1* 2C **78**
(off Wapping High St.)
Seville M. *N1* 4A **50**
Seville St.
SW1 . . . . . .4A **20** (3B **74**)
Sevington Rd. *NW4* 1D **29**
Sevington St. *W9* 3D **59**
Sewardstone Rd. *E2* 1E **65**
Seward St.
EC1 . . . . . .3E **9** (2D **63**)
Sewdley St. *E5* 5F **37**
Sewell St. *E13* 2C **68**
Sextant Av. *E14* 5F **81**

Sexton Ct. *E14* 1F **81**
(off Newport Av.)
Sextons Ho. *SE10* 2E **95**
(off Bardsley La.)
Seymore M. *SE14* 3B **94**
(off New Cross Rd.)
Seymour Ct. *NW2* 4D **29**
Seymour Gdns. *SE4* . . .1A **108**
Seymour Ho. *E16* 2C **82**
(off De Quincey M.)
NW1 . . . . .1C **6**
(off Churchway)
WC1 . . . . .3D **7**
(off Tavistock Pl.)
Seymour Leisure Cen.
. . . . .4B **60**
Seymour M.
W1 . . . . . .2B **12** (5C **60**)
Seymour Pl.
W1 . . . . . .2A **12** (4B **60**)
Seymour Rd. *E6* 1F **69**
E10 . . . . .3B **38**
N8 . . . . .1C **34**
SW18 . . . . .5B **100**
SW19 . . . . .3F **113**
Seymour St.
W1 . . . . . .3A **12** (5B **60**)
W2 . . . . .5B **60**
Seymour Wlk. *SW10* 2E **87**
Seyssel St. *E14* 5E **81**
Shaa Rd. *W3* 1A **70**
Shabana Rd. *W12* 2D **71**
Shackleton Cl.
SE23 . . . . .2D **121**
Shackleton Ct. *E14* 1C **94**
(off Maritime Quay)
W12 . . . . .3D **71**
(off Scott's Rd.)
Shackleton Ho. *E1* 2E **79**
(off Prusom St.)
NW10 . . . . .4A **42**
SHACKLEWELL 1B **50**
Shacklewell Grn. *E8* 1B **50**
Shacklewell Ho. *E8* 1B **50**
Shacklewell La. *E8* 2B **50**
Shacklewell Rd. *N16* 1B **50**
Shacklewell Row *E8* 1B **50**
Shacklewell St. *E2* 2B **64**
Shad Thames
SE1
. .2F **27** (2B **78**) & 3F **27**
(Anchor Brewhouse)
SE1 . . . . .3B **78**
(Jamaica Rd.)
SHADWELL 1D **79**
Shadwell Gdns. *E1* 1E **79**
Shadwell Pierhead
E1 . . . . .1E **79**
Shadwell Pl. *E1* 1E **79**
(off Sutton St.)
Shaftesbury Av.
W1 . . . . . .5B **14** (1F **75**)
WC1 . . . . . .2D **15** (5A **62**)
WC2 . . . . . .2D **15** (5A **62**)
Shaftesbury Cen.
W10 . . . . .3F **57**
(off Barlby Rd.)
Shaftesbury Ct. *N1* 1F **63**
(off Shaftesbury St.)

Shaftesbury Ct. *SE1* 5B **26**
(off Alderney M.)
SE5 . . . . .2F **105**
SW6 . . . . .4D **87**
(off Maltings Pl.)
SW16 . . . . .3F **117**
Shaftesbury Gdns.
NW10 . . . . .3A **56**
Shaftesbury Ho. *E16* 5B **68**
(off Tarling Rd.)
Shaftesbury Lodge
E14 . . . . .5D **67**
(off Upper Nth. St.)
Shaftesbury M.
SW4 . . . . .3E **103**
W8 . . . . .4C **72**
Shaftesbury Pl. *EC2* 1F **17**
(off Aldersgate St.)
W14 . . . . .5B **72**
(off Warwick Rd.)
Shaftesbury Point
E13 . . . . .1C **68**
(off High St.)
Shaftesbury Rd. *E7* 4E **55**
E10 . . . . .3C **38**
E17 . . . . .1D **39**
N19 . . . . .3A **34**
Shaftesbury Row *SE8* . . .3C **94**
(off Speedwell St.)
Shaftesbury St. *N1* 1E **63**
(not continuous)
Shaftesbury Theatre . .2D **15**
(off Shaftesbury Av.)
Shaftesbury Vs. *W8* 4C **72**
(off Allen St.)
Shafto M. *SW1* 4B **74**
Shafton M. *E9* 5F **51**
Shafton Rd. *E9* 5F **51**
Shafts Ct.
EC3 . . . . . .3D **19** (5A **64**)
Shahjalal Ho. *E2* 1C **64**
(off Pritchards St.)
Shakespeare Ct.
NW6 . . . . .4E **45**
(off Fairfax Rd.)
Shakespeare Ho. *E9* 4E **51**
(off Lyme Gro.)
Shakespeare Rd.
SE24 . . . . .3D **105**
Shakespeare's
Globe & Exhibition
. . . . .1F **25** (2E **77**)
Shakespeare Twr.
EC2 . . . . .5A **10**
Shakspeare M. *N16* 1A **50**
Shakspeare Wlk. *N16* 1A **50**
Shalbourne Sq. *E9* 3B **52**
Shalcomb St. *SW10* 2E **87**
Shalden Ho. *SW15* 4B **98**
Shalfleet Dr. *W10* 1F **71**
Shalford Ct. *N1* 1D **63**
Shalford Ho.
SE1 . . . . . .5C **26** (4F **77**)
Shamrock Ho. *SE26* 4C **120**
(off Talisman Sq.)
Shamrock St. *SW4* 1F **103**
Shandon Rd. *SW4* 4E **103**
Shand St.
SE1 . . . . . .3E **27** (3A **78**)

Shandy St. E1 . . . . .4F 65
Shan Ho. WC1 . . . . .4F 7
Shanklin Rd. N8 . . . . . .1F 33
Shannon Cl. NW2 . . . . .5F 29
Shannon Ct. N16 . . . . . .5A 36
SE15 . . . . .3B 92
(off Garnies Cl.)
Shannon Gro. SW9 . . .2B 104
Shannon M. SE3 . . . . .2B 110
Shannon Pl. NW8 . . . . . .1A 60
Shanti Ct. SW18 . . . . . .1C 114
Shard, The SE1 . . . . . . .2C 26
Shardcroft Av. SE24 . . .3D 105
Shardeloes Rd.
SE14 . . . . .5B 94
Shard's Sq. SE15 . . . . . .2C 92
Sharnbrook Ho. W14 . . .2C 86
Sharon Gdns. E9 . . . . . .5E 51
Sharp Ho. SW8 . . . . . .1D 103
Sharpleshall St.
NW1 . . . . .4B 46
Sharpley Ct. SE1 . . . . . .3D 25
(off Pocock St.)
Sharratt St. SE15 . . . . . .2E 93
Sharsted St. SE17 . . . . .1D 91
Sharwood WC1 . . . . .1A 8
(off Penton Ri.)
Shaver's Pl. SW1 . . . . . .5B 14
Shawbrooke Rd.
SE9 . . . . .3E 111
Shawbury Rd. SE22 . . .3B 106
Shaw Cres. E14 . . . . . . .4A 66
Shawfield St. SW3 . . . . .1A 88
Shawford Ct. SW15 . . . .5C 98
Shaw Path
BR1: Brom 3B 124
Shaw Rd.
BR1: Brom 3B 124
SE22 . . . . .2A 106
Shaws Cotts. SE23 . . . . .3A 122
Shaw Theatre 2C 6 (2F 61)
Shead Ct. E1 . . . . .5D 65
(off James Voller Way)
Shearling Way N7 . . . . .3A 48
Shearman Rd. SE3 . . . .2B 110
Shearsmith Ho. E1 . . . . .1C 78
(off Hindmarsh Cl.)
Shearwater Ct. E1 . . . . .1C 78
(off Star Pl.)
SE8 . . . . .2B 94
(off Abinger Gro.)
Sheba Pl. E1 . . . .4F 11 (3B 64)
Sheenewood SE26 . . . . .4D 121
Sheengate Mans.
SW14 . . . . .2A 98
Sheen Gro. N1 . . . . .5C 48
Sheepcote La. SW11 . . .5B 88
Sheep La. E8 . . . . .5D 51
Sheep Wlk. M.
SW19 . . . . .5F 113
Sheerwater Rd. E16 . . . .4F 69
Sheffield Sq. E3 . . . . . . .2B 66
Sheffield St.
WC2 . . . . . . .3F 15 (5B 62)
Sheffield Ter. W8 . . . . . .2C 72
Shelburne Rd. N7 . . . . .1B 48
Shelbury Rd. SE22 . . . .3D 107
Sheldon Av. N6 . . . . . . .2A 32
Sheldon Cl. SE12 . . . . .3D 111

Sheldon Ct. SW8 . . . . . .3A 90
(off Lansdowne Grn.)
Sheldon Ho. N1 . . . . . . .5A 50
(off Kingsland Rd.)
Sheldon Pl. E2 . . . . .1C 64
(not continuous)
Sheldon Rd. NW2 . . . . . .1F 43
Sheldon Sq. W2 . . . . . . .4E 59
Sheldrake Ho. SE16 . . . .5F 79
(off Tawny Way)
Sheldrake Pl. W8 . . . . . .3C 72
Shelduck Cl. E15 . . . . . .2B 54
Shelduck Ct. SE8 . . . . . .2B 94
(off Pilot Cl.)
Shelford Pl. N16 . . . . . . .5F 35
Shelgate Rd. SW11 . . . .3A 102
Shell Cen.
SE1 . . . . . . .2A 24 (3B 76)
Shelley Av. E12 . . . . . . .3F 55
Shelley Cl. SE15 . . . . . .5D 93
Shelley Ct. E10 . . . . .2D 39
(off Skelton's La.)
N19 . . . . .3B 34
SW3 . . . . .2B 88
(off Tite St.)
Shelley Ho. E2 . . . . .2E 65
(off Cornwall Av.)
N16 . . . . .1A 50
SE17 . . . . .1E 91
(off Browning St.)
SW1 . . . . .2E 89
(off Churchill Gdns.)
Shelley Rd. NW10 . . . . . .5A 42
Shelley Way SW19 . . . . .5F 115
Shellness Rd. E5 . . . . . .2D 51
Shell Rd. SE13 . . . . . . .1D 109
Shellwood Rd. SW11 . . . .5B 88
Shelmerdine Cl. E3 . . . . .4C 66
Shelton St.
WC2 . . . . . . .3D 15 (5A 62)
(not continuous)
Shene Ho. EC1 . . . . .5B 8
(off Bourne Est.)
Shene Sports & Fitness Cen.
. . . . .2A 98
Shenfield Ho. SE18 . . . .4F 97
(off Portway Gdns.)
Shenfield St.
N1 . . . . .1E 11 (1A 64)
(not continuous)
Shenley Rd. SE5 . . . . . . .4A 92
Shenstone Ho.
SW16 . . . . .5E 117
Shepherdess Pl.
N1 . . . . .1A 10 (2E 63)
Shepherdess Wlk.
N1 . . . . .1A 10 (1E 63)
Shepherd Ho. E14 . . . . .5D 67
(off Annabel Cl.)
Shepherd Mkt.
W1 . . . . . . .1D 21 (2D 75)
SHEPHERD'S BUSH 3E 71
Shepherd's Bush
Empire Theatre 3E 71
Shepherd's Bush Grn.
W12 . . . . .3E 71
Shepherd's Bush Mkt.
W12 . . . . .3E 71
(not continuous)

Shepherd's Bush Pl.
W12 . . . . .3F 71
Shepherd's Bush Rd.
W6 . . . . .5E 71
Shepherds Cl. N6 . . . . . .1D 33
W1 . . . . .4B 12
(off Lees Pl.)
Shepherds Ct. W12 . . . . .3F 71
(off Shepherd's Bush Grn.)
Shepherd's Hill N6 . . . . .1D 33
Shepherds La. E9 . . . . . .3F 51
Shepherd's Path
NW3 . . . . .2F 45
(off Lyndhurst Rd.)
Shepherds Pl.
W1 . . . . .4B 12 (1C 74)
Shepherd St.
W1 . . . . .2D 21 (2D 75)
Shepherds Wlk. NW2 . . .4C 28
NW3 . . . . .2F 45
Sheppard Dr. SE16 . . . .1D 93
Sheppard Ho. E2 . . . . . .1C 64
(off Warner Pl.)
SW2 . . . . .1C 118
Sheppard St. E16 . . . . . .3B 68
Shepperton Rd. N1 . . . . .5E 49
Shepton Ho's. E2 . . . . . .2E 65
(off Welwyn St.)
Sherard Ct. N7 . . . . .5A 34
Sherard Ho. E9 . . . . .4E 51
(off Frampton Pk. Rd.)
Sheraton Ho. SW1 . . . . .2D 89
(off Churchill Gdns.)
Sheraton St.
W1 . . . . .3B 14 (5F 61)
(off Agar Gro.)
Sherborne Ho. SW1 . . . .1D 89
(part of Abbots Mnr.)
SW8 . . . . .3B 90
(off Bolney St.)
Sherborne La.
EC4 . . . . . . .4B 18 (1F 77)
Sherborne St. N1 . . . . . .5F 49
Sherboro Rd. N15 . . . . . .1B 36
Sherbourne Cl. SW5 . . . .5D 73
(off Cromwell Rd.)
Sherbrooke Ho. E2 . . . . .1E 65
(off Bonner Rd.)
SW1 . . . . .4F 75
(off Monck St.)
Sherbrooke Rd. SW6 . . .3A 86
Sherbrooke Ter. SW6 . . .3A 86
(off Sherbrook Rd.)
Shere Ho. SE1 . . . . .5B 26
Sherfield Gdns.
SW15 . . . . .4B 98
Sheridan Bldgs. WC2 . . .3E 15
(off Martlett Ct.)
Sheridan Ct. NW6 . . . . . .4E 45
(off Belsize Rd.)
SW5 . . . . .5D 73
(off Barkston Gdns.)
Sheridan Hgts. E1 . . . . .5D 65
(off Watney St.)
Sheridan Ho. SE11 . . . . .5C 76
(off Wincott St.)
Sheridan M. E11 . . . . . . .1D 41
Sheridan Pl. SW13 . . . . .1B 98

Sheridan Rd. E7 . . . . . . .5B 40
Sheridan Wlk. NW11 . . .1C 30
Sheringham NW8 . . . . . .5F 45
Sheringham Ho. *NW1 . . .4A 60*
(off Lisson St.)
Sheringham Rd. N7 . . . . .3B 48
Sherington Rd. SE7 . . . .2D 97
Sherlock Ct. *NW8 . . . . . .5F 45*
(off Dorman Way)
Sherlock Holmes Mus.
. . . . .4A 4
Sherlock M.
W1 . . . . . . .5B 4 (4C 60)
Sherman Ho. E14 . . . . . .5E 67
(off Dee St.)
Shernhall St. E17 . . . . . .1E 39
Sherrard Rd. E7 . . . . . . .3E 55
E12 . . . . .3E 55
Sherren Ho. E1 . . . . .3E 65
Sherrick Grn. Rd.
NW10 . . . . .2D 43
Sherriff Ct. *NW6 . . . . . .3C 44*
(off Sherriff Rd.)
Sherriff Rd. NW6 . . . . . .3C 44
Sherrin Rd. E10 . . . . . . .1D 53
Sherston Ct. *SE1 . . . . . .5D 77*
(off Newington Butts)
WC1 . . . . .2B 8
Sherwin Ho. *SE11 . . . . .2C 90*
(off Kennington Rd.)
Sherwin Rd. SE14 . . . . . .4F 93
Sherwood NW6 . . . . .4A 44
Sherwood Cl. SW13 . . . .1D 99
Sherwood Ct. SW11 . . . .1E 101
W1 . . . . .4B 60
(off Bryanston Pl.)
Sherwood Gdns. E14 . . .5C 80
SE16 . . . . .1C 92
Sherwood St.
W1 . . . . . .4A 14 (1E 75)
Sherwood Ter. *E16 . . . . .5E 69*
(off Bingley Rd.)
Shetland Rd. E3 . . . . . . .1B 66
Shifford Path SE23 . . . . .3F 121
Shillaker Ct. W3 . . . . . . .2B 70
Shillibeer Pl. *W1 . . . . . .4A 60*
(off Harcourt St.)
Shillingford Ho. *E3 . . . .2D 67*
(off Talwin St.)
Shillingford St. N1 . . . . .4D 49
Shillingshaw Lodge
E16 . . . . .5C 68
(off Butchers Rd.)
Shillingstone Ho.
W14 . . . . .4A 72
(off Russell Rd.)
Shinfield St. W12 . . . . . .5E 57
Ship & Mermaid Row
SE1 . . . . . . .3C 26 (3F 77)
Shipka Rd. SW12 . . . . . .1D 117
Shiplake Ho. *E2 . . . . . . .2F 11*
(off Arnold Cir.)
Shipman Rd. E16 . . . . . .5D 69
SE23 . . . . .2F 121
Ship St. SE8 . . . . .4C 94
Ship Tavern Pas.
EC3 . . . . . . .4D 19 (1A 78)
Shipton Ho. *E2 . . . . .1B 64*
(off Shipton St.)

Shipton St. E2 . . . . .1B 64
Shipwright Rd. SE16 . . . .3A 80
Shipwright Yd.
SE1 . . . . . . .2D 27 (2A 78)
Ship Yd. E14 . . . . .1D 95
Shirburn Cl. SE23 . . . . . .5E 107
Shirebrook Rd. SE3 . . . .1F 111
Shirehall Cl. NW4 . . . . . .1F 29
Shirehall Gdns. NW4 . . .1F 29
Shirehall La. NW4 . . . . . .1F 29
Shirehall Pk. NW4 . . . . . .1F 29
Shire Ho. *E3 . . . . .2D 67*
(off Talwin St.)
EC1 . . . . .4B 10
(off Lamb's Pas.)
Shire Pl. SW18 . . . . .5E 101
Shirland M. W9 . . . . .2B 58
Shirland Rd. W9 . . . . . . .2B 58
Shirlbutt St. E14 . . . . . . .1D 81
Shirley Gro. SW11 . . . . .1C 102
Shirley Ho. *SE5 . . . . .3F 91*
(off Picton St.)
Shirley Ho. Dr. SE7 . . . . .3E 97
Shirley Rd. E15 . . . . .4A 54
W4 . . . . .3A 70
Shirley St. E16 . . . . .5B 68
Shirlock Rd. NW3 . . . . . .1B 46
Shobroke Cl. NW2 . . . . . .5C 29
Shoe La. EC4 . . . .2C 16 (5C 62)
Shona Ho. E13 . . . . .4E 69
Shooters Hill Rd.
SE3 . . . . .3E 97
SE10 . . . . .4F 95
SE18 . . . . .3E 97
Shoot Up Hill NW2 . . . . .2A 44
Shore Bus. Cen. E9 . . . . .4E 51
SHOREDITCH
. . . . .1D 11 (2A 64)
Shoreditch Ct. *E8 . . . . . .4B 50*
(off Queensbridge Rd.)
Shoreditch High St.
E1 . . . . .4E 11 (3A 64)
Shoreditch Ho. N1 . . . . . .2C 10
Shoreham Cl.
SW18 . . . . .3D 101
Shore Ho. SW8 . . . . .1D 103
Shore M. *E9 . . . . .4E 51*
(off Shore Rd.)
Shore Pl. E9 . . . . .4E 51
Shore Rd. E9 . . . . .4E 51
Shore Way *SW9 . . . . . . .5C 90*
(off Crowhurst Cl.)
Shorncliffe Rd. SE1 . . . . .1B 92
Shorndean St. SE6 . . . . .1E 123
Shorrold's Rd. SW6 . . . . .3B 86
Shorter St. E1 . . . . .1B 78
Shortlands W6 . . . . .5F 71
Shortlands Rd. E10 . . . . .2D 39
Short Rd. E11 . . . . .4A 40
W4 . . . . .2A 84
Shorts Gdns.
WC2 . . . . . .3D 15 (5A 62)
Short St. SE1 . . . .3C 24 (3C 76)
Short Wall E15 . . . . .2E 67
Shortwave Cinema *4A 78*
(off Bermondsey Sq.)
Short Way SE9 . . . . .1F 111
Shottendane Rd.
SW6 . . . . .4C 86

Shottery Cl. SE9 . . . . . . .3F 125
Shottfield Av. SW14 . . . .2A 98
Shottsford *W2 . . . . .5C 58*
(off Talbot Rd.)
Shoulder of Mutton All.
E14 . . . . .1A 80
Shouldham St. W1 . . . . .4A 60
Shrewsbury Ct. EC1 . . . .4A 10
Shrewsbury Ho. *SW3 . . .2A 88*
(off Cheyne Wlk.)
SW8 . . . . .2B 90
(off Kennington Oval)
Shrewsbury M. *W2 . . . . .4C 58*
(off Chepstow Rd.)
Shrewsbury Rd. E7 . . . . .2F 55
W2 . . . . .5C 58
Shrewsbury St. W10 . . . .3E 57
Shroffold Rd.
BR1: Brom 4A 124
Shropshire Pl.
WC1 . . . . .4B 6 (3E 61)
Shroton St. NW1 . . . . . . .4A 60
Shrubbery, The E11 . . . . .1D 41
Shrubbery Cl. N1 . . . . . . .5E 49
Shrubbery Rd.
SW16 . . . . .4A 118
Shrubland Rd. E8 . . . . . .5B 50
E10 . . . . .2C 38
E17 . . . . .1C 38
Shrublands Cl. SE26 . . . .3E 121
Shuna Wlk. N1 . . . . .3F 49
Shurland Gdns. SE15 . . .3B 92
Shuters Sq. W14 . . . . . . .1B 86
Shuttle St. E1 . . . . .3C 64
Shuttleworth Rd.
SW11 . . . . .5A 88
Sibella Rd. SW4 . . . . . . .5F 89
Sibthorpe Rd. SE12 . . . .4D 111
Sicilian Av. WC1 . . . . . . .1E 15
Sidbury St. SW6 . . . . . . .4A 86
Sidcup Rd. SE9 . . . . .4E 111
SE12 . . . . .4E 111
Siddons La.
NW1 . . . . . .4A 4 (3B 60)
Siddons Rd. SE23 . . . . . .2A 122
Side Rd. E17 . . . . .1B 38
Sidford Ho. SE1 . . . . .5A 24
Sidford Pl.
SE1 . . . . . . .5A 24 (4C 76)
Sidgwick Ho. *SW9 . . . . .5B 90*
(off Stockwell Rd.)
Sidings, The E11 . . . . . . .3E 39
Sidings M. N7 . . . . .5C 34
Sidlaw Ho. N16 . . . . .3B 36
Sidmouth Ho. *SE15 . . . .3C 92*
(off Lindsey Est.)
W1 . . . . .5A 60
(off Cato St.)
Sidmouth M. WC1 . . . . . .2F 7
Sidmouth Pde. NW2 . . . .4E 43
Sidmouth Rd. E10 . . . . . .5E 39
NW2 . . . . .4E 43
Sidmouth St.
WC1 . . . . . . .2E 7 (2B 62)
Sidney Boyd Ct. NW6 . . .4C 44
Sidney Est. E1 . . . . .5E 65
(Bromhead St.)
E1 . . . . .4E 65
(Lindley St.)

Sidney Godley (VC) Ho.
  E2 . . . . .2E **65**
    (off Digby St.)
Sidney Gro.
  EC1 . . . . .1D **9** (1D **63**)
Sidney Ho. E2 . . . . .1F **65**
    (off Old Ford Rd.)
Sidney Rd. E7 . . . . .5C **40**
  SW9 . . . . .5B **90**
Sidney Sq. E1 . . . . .4E **65**
Sidney St. E1 . . . . .4D **65**
    (not continuous)
Sidney Webb Ho.
  SE1 . . . . .5C **26**
    (off Tabard St.)
Sidworth St. E8 . . . . .4D **51**
Siebert Rd. SE3 . . . . .2C **96**
Siege Ho. E1 . . . . .5D **65**
    (off Sidney St.)
Siemens Rd. SE18 . . . . . .4F **83**
Sienna Ter. NW2 . . . . . . .4C **28**
Sigdon Pas. E8 . . . . .2C **50**
Sigdon Rd. E8 . . . . .2C **50**
Sigmund Freud Statue
  . . . . .3F **45**
Signal Ho. E8 . . . . .5D **47**
    (off Martello Ter.)
  SE1 . . . . .4F **25**
    (off Gt. Suffolk St.)
Signmakers Yd.
  NW1 . . . . .5D **47**
    (off Delancey St.)
Sikorski Mus. 3F **73**
Silbury Ho. SE26 . . . . . . .3C **120**
Silbury St.
  N1 . . . . .1B **10** (2F **63**)
Silchester Rd. W10 . . . . . .5F **57**
Silesia Bldgs. E8 . . . . . . .4D **51**
Silex St. SE1 . . . .4E **25** (3D **77**)
Silk Cl. SE12 . . . . .3C **110**
Silk Ct. E2 . . . . .2C **64**
    (off Squirries St.)
Silkin M. SE15 . . . . .3C **92**
Silk M. SE11 . . . . .1C **90**
    (off Kennington Rd.)
Silk Mills Pas. SE13 . . . . .5D **95**
Silk Mills Path SE13 . . . . .5E **95**
    (not continuous)
Silk Mills Sq. E9 . . . . .3B **52**
Silks Ct. E11 . . . . .3B **40**
Silk St. EC2 . . . .5A **10** (4E **63**)
Silk Weaver Way
  E2 . . . . .1D **65**
Sillitoe Ho. N1 . . . . .5F **49**
    (off Colville Est.)
Silsoe Ho. NW1 . . . . .1D **61**
Silver Birch Cl. SE6 . . . . . .3B **122**
Silverbirch Wlk.
  NW5 . . . . .3C **46**
Silverburn Ho. SW9 . . . . .4D **91**
    (off Lothian Rd.)
Silver Cl. SE14 . . . . .3A **94**
Silverdale NW1 . . . . .1F **5**
    (off Harrington St.)
  SE26 . . . . .4E **121**
Silverdale Cl. EC1 . . . . . . .3E **9**
Silverdale Dr. SE9 . . . . . .2F **125**
Silvermere Rd. SE6 . . . . . .5D **109**
Silver Pl. W1 . . .4A **14** (5E **61**)

Silver Rd. SE13 . . . . .1D **109**
  W12 . . . . .1F **71**
Silverthorn NW8 . . . . .5D **45**
    (off Abbey Rd.)
Silverthorne Loft Apartments
  SE5 . . . . .2F **91**
    (off Albany Rd.)
Silverthorne Rd.
  SW8 . . . . .5D **89**
Silverton Rd. W6 . . . . .2F **85**
SILVERTOWN 2E **83**
Silvertown Viaduct
  E16 . . . . .5B **68**
Silvertown Way
  E16 . . . . .5A **68**
    (Clarkson Rd.)
  E16 . . . . .2C **82**
    (Hanover Av.)
Silver Wlk. SE16 . . . . .2A **80**
Silvester Ho. E1 . . . . .5D **65**
    (off Varden St.)
  E2 . . . . .2E **65**
    (off Sceptre Rd.)
  W11 . . . . .5B **58**
    (off Basing St.)
Silvester Rd. SE22 . . . . . .3B **106**
Silvester St.
  SE1 . . . . .4B **26** (3F **77**)
Silvocea Way E14 . . . . . . .5F **67**
Silwood Est. SE16 . . . . . . .5E **79**
Silwood St. SE16 . . . . . . .5E **79**
    (off Rotherhithe New Rd.)
Simla Ct. N7 . . . . .4A **48**
    (off Brewery Rd.)
Simla Ho. SE1 . . . . .4C **26**
    (off Kipling Est.)
Simmonds Ct. SW5 . . . . . .5D **73**
    (off Earl's Ct. Gdns.)
Simms Rd. SE1 . . . . .5C **78**
Simnel Rd. SE12 . . . . .5D **111**
Simon Cl. W11 . . . . .1B **72**
Simon Ct. W9 . . . . .2C **58**
    (off Saltram Cres.)
Simonds Rd. E10 . . . . .4C **38**
Simone Ct. SE26 . . . . .3E **121**
Simons Ct. N16 . . . . .4B **36**
Simons Wlk. E15 . . . . .2F **53**
Simpson Dr. W3 . . . . .5A **56**
Simpson Ho.
  NW8 . . . . .3A **60**
  SE11 . . . . .1B **90**
Simpson's Rd. E14 . . . . . . .1D **81**
Simpson St. SW11 . . . . . . .5A **88**
Simrose Ct. SW18 . . . . . . .3C **100**
Sims Wlk. SE3 . . . . .2B **110**
Sinclair Gdns. W14 . . . . . .3F **71**
Sinclair Gro. NW11 . . . . . .1F **29**
Sinclair Ho. WC1 . . . . .2D **7**
    (off Sandwich St.)
Sinclair Mans. W12 . . . . . .3F **71**
    (off Richmond Way)
Sinclair Pl. SE4 . . . . .4C **108**
Sinclair Rd. W14 . . . . .3F **71**
Sinclairs Ho. E3 . . . . .1B **66**
    (off St Stephen's Rd.)
Singer M. SW4 . . . . .5A **90**
    (off Union Rd.)
Singer St.
  EC2 . . . . .2C **10** (2F **63**)

Siobhan Davis Dance Studios
  . . . . .4D **77**
    (off St George's Rd.)
Sir Abraham Dawes Cotts.
  SW15 . . . . .2A **100**
Sir Alexander Cl. W3 . . . . .2B **70**
Sir Alexander Rd.
  W3 . . . . .2B **70**
Sir Christopher France Ho.
  E1 . . . . .2A **66**
Sirdar Rd. W11 . . . . .1F **71**
Sir Francis Drake Ct.
  SE10 . . . . .1F **95**
Sirinham Point SW8 . . . . . .2B **90**
    (off Meadow Rd.)
Sirius SW11 . . . . .5B **88**
Sirius Bldg. E1 . . . . .1F **79**
    (off Jardine Rd.)
Sir James Black Ho.
  SE5 . . . . .5F **91**
    (off Coldharbour La.)
Sir John Kirk Cl. SE5 . . . . .3E **91**
Sir John Lyon Ho.
  EC4 . . . . .4F **17**
    (off High Timber St.)
Sir John Morden Wlk.
  SE3 . . . . .5C **96**
Sir John Soane's Mus.
  . . . . .2F **15** (5B **62**)
Sir Nicholas Garrow Ho.
  W10 . . . . .3A **58**
    (off Kensal Rd.)
Sir Oswald Stoll
Foundation, The
  SW6 . . . . .3D **87**
    (off Fulham Rd.)
Sir Oswald Stoll Mans.
  SW6 . . . . .3D **87**
    (off Fulham Rd.)
Sir Walter Raleigh Ct.
  SE10 . . . . .1A **96**
Sir William Powell's
Almshouses
  SW6 . . . . .5A **86**
Sise La. EC4 . . . .3B **18** (5F **63**)
Siskin Ho. SE16 . . . . .5F **79**
    (off Tawny Way)
Sispara Gdns.
  SW18 . . . . .4B **100**
Sissinghurst Cl.
  BR1: Brom 5A **124**
Sissinghurst Ho.
  SE15 . . . . .2E **93**
    (off Sharratt St.)
Sissulu Ct. E6 . . . . .5E **55**
Sister Mabel's Way
  SE15 . . . . .3C **92**
Sisters Av. SW11 . . . . .1B **102**
Sistova Rd. SW12 . . . . . . .1D **117**
Sisulu Pl. SW9 . . . . .1C **104**
Sitarey Ct. W12 . . . . .2D **71**
Sivill Ho. E2 . . . . .1F **11**
    (off Columbia Rd.)
Siward Rd. SW17 . . . . .3E **115**
Six Acres Est. N4 . . . . .4B **34**
Six Bridges Ind. Est.
  SE1 . . . . .1C **92**
    (not continuous)
Sixth Av. W10 . . . . .2A **58**

Skardu Rd. NW2 . . . . . . .2A 44
Skeena Hill SW18 . . . . .5A 100
Skeggs Ho. E14 . . . . .4E 81
   (off Glengall St.)
Skegness Ho. N7 . . . . .4B 48
   (off Sutterton St.)
Skelbrook St. SW18 . . . .2E 115
Skelgill Rd. SW15 . . . . . .2B 100
Skelley Rd. E15 . . . . .4B 54
Skelton Cl. E8 . . . . .3B 50
Skelton Rd. E7 . . . . .3C 54
Skelton's La. E10 . . . . . . .2D 39
Skelwith Rd. W6 . . . . .2E 85
Skenfrith Ho. SE15 . . . . . .2D 93
   (off Commercial Way)
Sketchley Gdns.
  SE16 . . . . .1F 93
Skiers St. E15 . . . . .5A 54
Skiffington Cl. SW2 . . . .1C 118
Skinner Pl. SW1 . . . . .5C 74
   (off Bourne St.)
Skinners La.
  EC4 . . . . . .4A 18 (1E 77)
Skinner's Row SE10 . . . .4D 95
Skinner St.
  EC1 . . . . . .2C 8 (2C 62)
Skipsea Ho. SW18 . . . . .4A 102
Skipton Ho. SE4 . . . . .2A 108
Skipwith Ho. EC1 . . . . .5B 8
   (off Bourne Est.)
Skipworth Rd. E9 . . . . . . .5E 51
Skua Ct. SE8 . . . . .2B 94
   (off Dorking Cl.)
Skylark Ct. SE1 . . . . .4A 26
   (off Swan St.)
Skyline Ct.
  SE1 . . . . . .5F 27 (4B 78)
Skyline Plaza Bldg.
  E1 . . . . .5C 64
   (off Commercial Rd.)
Skylines E14 . . . . .3E 81
Skylines Village E14 . . . . .3E 81
Sladebrook Rd. SE3 . . .1F 111
Sladen Pl. E5 . . . . .1D 51
Slade Twr. E10 . . . . .4C 38
   (off Leyton Grange Est.)
Slade Wlk. SE17 . . . . .2D 91
Slagrove Pl. SE13 . . . . . .3D 108
Slaidburn St. SW10 . . . . .2E 87
Slaithwaite Rd.
  SE13 . . . . .2E 109
Slaney Ct. NW10 . . . . . . .4E 43
Slaney Pl. N7 . . . . .2C 48
Sleaford Ho. E3 . . . . .3C 66
   (off Fern St.)
Sleaford Ind. Est.
  SW8 . . . . .3E 89
Sleaford St. SW8 . . . . . . .3E 89
Sleat Ho. E3 . . . . .1B 66
   (off Saxon Rd.)
Sleigh Ho. E2 . . . . .2E 65
   (off Bacton St.)
Slievemore Cl. SW4 . . . .1F 103
Sligo Ho. E1 . . . . .3F 65
   (off Beaumont Gro.)
Slindon Ct. N16 . . . . .5B 36
Slingsby Pl.
  WC2 . . . .4D 15 (1A 76)
Slippers Pl. SE16 . . . . . . .4D 79

Slipway Ho. E14 . . . . .1D 95
   (off Burrells Wharf Sq.)
Sloane Av. SW3 . . . . .5A 74
Sloane Av. Mans.
  SW3 . . . . .5B 74
Sloane Ct. E. SW3 . . . . . .1C 88
Sloane Ct. W. SW3 . . . . . .1C 88
Sloane Gdns. SW1 . . . . . .5C 74
Sloane Ga. Mans.
  SW1 . . . . .5C 74
   (off D'Oyley St.)
Sloane Ho. E9 . . . . .4E 51
   (off Loddiges Rd.)
Sloane M. N8 . . . . .1A 34
Sloane Sq. SW1 . . . . .5C 74
Sloane St.
  SW1 . . . . . .4A 20 (3B 74)
Sloane Ter. SW1 . . . . .5C 74
Sloane Ter. Mans.
  SW1 . . . . .5C 74
   (off Sloane Ter.)
Sly St. E1 . . . . .5D 65
Smallbrook M. W2 . . . . . .5F 59
Smalley Cl. N16 . . . . .5B 36
Smalley Rd. Est. N16 . . . .5B 36
   (off Smalley Cl.)
Smallwood Rd.
  SW17 . . . . .4F 115
Smart's Pl.
  WC2 . . . . . .2E 15 (5A 62)
Smart St. E2 . . . . .2F 65
Smead Way SE13 . . . . . .1D 109
Smeaton Ct.
  SE1 . . . . .5F 25 (4E 77)
Smeaton Rd. SW18 . . . .5C 100
Smeaton St. E1 . . . . .2D 79
Smedley St. SW4 . . . . . . .5F 89
Smeed Rd. E3 . . . . .4C 52
Smikle Ct. SE14 . . . . .4F 93
   (off Hatcham Pk. M.)
Smiles Pl. SE13 . . . . .5E 95
Smith Cl. SE16 . . . . .2F 79
Smithfield (Central Markets)
  .1D 17
Smithfield St.
  EC1 . . . . . .1D 17 (4D 63)
Smith's Ct. W1 . . . . .4A 14
Smiths Point E13 . . . . .5C 54
   (off Brooks Rd.)
Smith Sq.
  SW1 . . . . . .5D 23 (4A 76)
Smith St. SW3 . . . . .1B 88
Smiths Yd. SW18 . . . . . .2E 115
Smith Ter. SW3 . . . . .1B 88
Smithwood Cl.
  SW19 . . . . .1A 114
Smithy St. E1 . . . . .4E 65
Smokehouse Yd. EC1 . . .5E 9
   (off St John St.)
Smugglers Way
  SW18 . . . . .2D 101
Smyrk's St. SE17 . . . . . . .1A 92
Smyrna Mans. NW6 . . . . .4C 44
   (off Smyrna Rd.)
Smyrna Rd. NW6 . . . . . . .4C 44
Smythe St. E14 . . . . .1D 81
SNARESBROOK 1C 40
Snarsgate St. W10 . . . . . .4E 57
Sneath Av. NW11 . . . . . . .2B 30

Sneyd Rd. NW2 . . . . .1E 43
Snowberry Cl. E15 . . . . . .1F 53
Snowbury Rd. SW6 . . . . . .5D 87
Snowden St.
  EC2 . . . . . . .4D 11 (3A 64)
Snowdon Aviary 5B 46
   (in London Zoo)
Snowdon Dr. NW9 . . . . . . .1A 28
Snow Hill
  EC1 . . . . . .1D 17 (4D 63)
Snow Hill Ct.
  EC1 . . . . . .2E 17 (5D 63)
Snowman Ho. NW6 . . . . .5D 45
Snowsfields
  SE1 . . . . .3C 26 (3F 77)
Snowshill Rd. E12 . . . . . . .2F 55
Soames St. SE15 . . . . . . .1B 106
Soane Cl. NW1 . . . . .4E 47
   (off St Pancras Way)
Soane Ho. SE17 . . . . .1F 91
   (off Roland Way)
Sobell Leisure Cen. 5B 34
Soda Studios E8 . . . . .5B 50
   (off Kingsland Rd.)
SOHO 3B 14 (5E 61)
Soho Sq. W1 . . .2B 14 (5F 61)
Soho St. W1 . . . .2B 14 (5F 61)
Soho Theatre & Writers Cen.
  .3B 14
   (off Dean St.)
Sojourner Truth Cl.
  E8 . . . . .3D 51
Solander Gdns. E1 . . . . . .1D 79
   (off Cable St.)
  E1 . . . . .1E 79
   (The Highway)
Solar Ct. SE16 . . . . .3C 78
   (off Chambers St.)
Solar Ho. E15 . . . . .3A 54
   (off Romford Rd.)
Solarium Ct. SE1 . . . . .5B 78
   (off Alscot Rd.)
Soldene Ct. N7 . . . . .2B 48
   (off George's Rd.)
Solebay St. E1 . . . . .3A 66
Solent Ho. E1 . . . . .4A 66
   (off Ben Jonson Rd.)
Solent Ri. E13 . . . . .2C 68
Solent Rd. NW6 . . . . .2C 44
Soley M. WC1 . . . .1B 8 (2C 62)
Solna Av. SW15 . . . . .3E 99
Solomon's Pas.
  SE15 . . . . .2D 107
Solon New Rd.
  SW4 . . . . .2A 104
Solon New Rd. Est.
  SW4 . . . . .2A 104
Solon Rd. SW2 . . . . .2A 104
Solway Cl. E8 . . . . .3B 50
   (off Queensbridge Rd.)
Solway Ho. E1 . . . . .3F 65
   (off Ernest St.)
Solway Rd. SE22 . . . . . . .2C 106
Somali Rd. NW2 . . . . .2B 44
Sombourne Ho.
  SW15 . . . . .5C 98
   (off Fontley Way)
Somer Ct. SW6 . . . . .2C 86
   (off Anselm Rd.)

Somerfield Rd. N4 . . . . . . .4D 35
   (not continuous)
Somerfield St. SE16 . . . .1F 93
Somerford Gro. N16 . . . .1B 50
Somerford Gro. Est.
   N16 . . . . .1B 50
Somerford St. E1 . . . . . . .3D 65
Somerford Way
   SE16 . . . . .3A 80
Somerleyton Pas.
   SW9 . . . . .2D 105
Somerleyton Rd.
   SW9 . . . . .2C 104
Somers Cl. NW1 . . . . .1F 61
Somers Cres. W2 . . . . . . .5A 60
Somerset Ct.
   NW1 . . . . .1B 6 (1F 61)
Somerset Est. SW11 . . . .4F 87
Somerset Gdns. N6 . . . . .2C 32
   SE13 . . . . .5D 95
Somerset House
   . . . . .4F 15 (1B 76)
Somerset Ho. SW19 . . . .3F 113
Somerset Rd. E17 . . . . . .1C 38
   SW19 . . . . .3F 113
Somerset Sq. W14 . . . . . .3A 72
Somerset Pl. SW2 . . . . . .5B 104
Somers Rd. SW2 . . . . . . .4B 104
Somerston Ho. NW1 . . . . .5E 47
   (off St Pancras Way)
SOMERS TOWN
   . . . . .1B 6 (1F 61)
Somers Town Community
   Sports Cen. 1F 61
Somerton Ho. SW11 . . . . .2C 6
Somerton Rd. NW2 . . . . .5F 29
   SE15 . . . . .2D 107
Somertrees Av.
   SE12 . . . . .2D 125
Somerville Av. SW13 . . . .2D 85
Somerville Cl. SW9 . . . . .4B 90
Somerville Point
   SE16 . . . . .3B 80
Sonderburg Rd. N7 . . . . .4B 34
Sondes St. SE17 . . . . . . .2F 91
Sonesta Apartments
   SE15 . . . . .4D 93
Sonia Gdns. NW10 . . . . .1B 42
Sonning Ho. E2 . . . . .2F 11
   (off Swanfield St.)
Soper Cl. SE23 . . . . .1F 121
Sophia Cl. N7 . . . . .3B 48
Sophia Ho. W6 . . . . .1E 85
   (off Queen Caroline St.)
Sophia Rd. E10 . . . . .3D 39
   E16 . . . . .5D 69
Sophia Sq. SE16 . . . . . . .1A 80
   (off Sovereign Cres.)
Soprano Ct. E15 . . . . . . .5B 54
   (off Plaistow Rd.)
Sopwith Way SW8 . . . . . .3D 89
Sorensen Ct. E10 . . . . . .4D 39
   (off Leyton Grange Est.)
Sorrel Gdns. E6 . . . . .4F 69
Sorrel La. E14 . . . . .5F 67
Sorrell Cl. SE14 . . . . .3A 94
   SW9 . . . . .5C 90
Sotheby Rd. N5 . . . . .5D 35
Sotheran St. E8 . . . . .5C 50

Sotherby Lodge E2 . . . . .1E 65
   (off Sewardstone Rd.)
Sotheron Rd. SW6 . . . . . .3D 87
Soudan Rd. SW11 . . . . . .4B 88
Souldern Rd. W14 . . . . . .4F 71
Sounding All. E3 . . . . .5C 52
Sth. Access Rd. E17 . . . .2A 38
Southacre W2 . . . . .5A 60
   (off Hyde Pk. Cres.)
Sth. Africa Rd.
   W12 . . . . .2D 71
Southall Pl.
   SE1 . . . . .4B 26 (3F 77)
Southam Ho. W10 . . . . . .3A 58
   (off Southam St.)
Southampton Bldgs.
   WC2 . . . . .1B 16 (4C 62)
Southampton M. E16 . . . .2D 83
Southampton Pl.
   WC1 . . . . .1E 15 (4A 62)
Southampton Rd.
   NW5 . . . . .2B 46
Southampton Row
   WC1 . . . . .5E 7 (4A 62)
Southampton St.
   WC2 . . . . .4E 15 (1A 76)
Southampton Way
   SE5 . . . . .3F 91
Southam St. W10 . . . . . . .3A 58
Sth. Audley St.
   W1 . . . . .5C 12 (1C 74)
Southbank Bus. Cen.
   SW8 . . . . .2F 89
   SW11 . . . . .4B 88
Southbank Cen.
   . . . . .1A 24 (2B 76)
Sth. Birkbeck Rd.
   E11 . . . . .5F 39
Sth. Black Lion La.
   W6 . . . . .1C 84
South Block SE1 . . . . . . .4F 23
   (off Belvedere Rd.)
Sth. Bolton Gdns.
   SW5 . . . . .1D 87
Southborough Ho.
   SE17 . . . . .1A 92
   (off Kinglake Est.)
Southborough Rd. E9 . . . .5F 51
Southbourne Gdns.
   SE12 . . . . .3D 111
SOUTH BROMLEY 1E 81
Southbrook M.
   SE12 . . . . .4B 110
Southbrook Rd.
   SE12 . . . . .4B 110
Southbury NW8 . . . . .5E 45
   (off Loudoun Rd.)
Sth. Carriage Dr.
   SW1 . . . . .3A 20 (3F 73)
   SW7 . . . . .3F 73
South City Ct. SE15 . . . . .3A 92
Southcombe St. W14 . . . .5A 72
Southcote Rd. N19 . . . . . .1E 47
Southcott Ho. E3 . . . . . . .2D 67
   (off Devons Rd.)

Southcott Ho. W9 . . . . . . .3E 59
   (off Clifton Gdns.)
Southcott M. NW8 . . . . . .1A 60
South Cres. E16 . . . . .3F 67
   WC1 . . . . . . .1B 14 (4F 61)
Sth. Crescent M.
   WC1 . . . . .3A 62
Southcroft Rd.
   SW16 . . . . .5C 116
   SW17 . . . . .5C 116
Sth. Croxted Rd.
   SE21 . . . . .3F 119
Southdean Gdns.
   SW19 . . . . .2B 114
Sth. Eaton Pl.
   SW1 . . . . .5C 74
Sth. Edwardes Sq.
   W8 . . . . .4B 72
SOUTHEND 4F 123
South End W8 . . . . .4D 73
South End Cl. NW3 . . . . . .1A 46
South End Grn. NW3 . . . .1A 46
Southend La. SE6 . . . . . . .4B 122
   SE26 . . . . .4B 122
South End Rd. NW3 . . . . .1A 46
Southend Rd.
   BR3: Beck 5D 123
South Esk Rd. W8 . . . . . .4D 73
Southerngate Way
   SE14 . . . . .3A 94
Southern Gro. E3 . . . . . . .2B 66
Southern Rd. E13 . . . . . . .1D 69
Southern Row W10 . . . . . .3A 58
Southern St. N1 . . . . .1B 62
Southern Way SE10 . . . . .5B 82
Southernwood Retail Pk.
   SE1 . . . . .1B 92
Southerton Rd. W6 . . . . . .5E 71
Southey Ho. SE17 . . . . . .1E 91
   (off Browning St.)
Southey M. E16 . . . . .2C 82
Southey Rd. N15 . . . . . . .1A 36
   SW9 . . . . .4C 90
Southfield Ct. E11 . . . . . . .5B 40
Southfield Rd. W4 . . . . . . .3A 70
SOUTHFIELDS 1B 114
Southfields M.
   SW18 . . . . .4C 100
Southfields Pas.
   SW18 . . . . .4C 100
Southfields Rd.
   SW18 . . . . .4C 100
Southfleet NW5 . . . . .3C 46
Southgate Ct. N1 . . . . . . .4F 49
   (off Downham Rd.)
Southgate Gro. N1 . . . . . .4F 49
Southgate Rd. N1 . . . . . . .5F 49
South Gro. E17 . . . . .1B 38
   N6 . . . . .3C 32
   N15 . . . . .1F 35
South Gro. Ho. N6 . . . . . .3C 32
SOUTH HACKNEY 5F 51
SOUTH HAMPSTEAD . . .4E 45
South Hill M. NW3 . . . . . . .1A 46
South Hill Pk. Gdns.
   NW3 . . . . .5A 32
Southill St. E14 . . . . .5D 67
Sth. Island Pl. SW9 . . . .3B 90

SOUTH KENSINGTON
. . . . .5F 73
Sth. Kensington Sta. Arc.
SW7 . . . . .5F *73*
(off Pelham St.)
SOUTH LAMBETH 3A 90
Sth. Lambeth Pl.
SW8 . . . . .2A 90
Sth. Lambeth Rd.
SW8 . . . . .2A 90
Southlands Dr.
SW19 . . . . .2F 113
South Lodge E16 . . . . .2D *83*
(off Audley Dr.)
NW8 . . . . .1F 59
SW7 . . . . .3A *74*
(off Knightsbridge)
South London Gallery
. . . . .4A 92
South London Theatre
. . . . .3D *119*
(off Norwood High St.)
South Mall SW18 . . . . .4D 101
Southmead Rd.
SW19 . . . . .1A 114
Sth. Molton La.
W1 . . . . . . .3D **13** (5D **61**)
Sth. Molton Rd. E16 . . .5C 68
Sth. Molton St.
W1 . . . . . . .3D **13** (5D **61**)
Southmoor Way E9 . . . .3B 52
South Oak Rd.
SW16 . . . . .4B 118
Southolm St. SW11 . . . .4D 89
Southover
BR1: Brom 5C 124
South Pde. SW3 . . . . . .1F 87
W4 . . . . .5A 70
South Pk. Cres. SE6 . . .1A 124
South Pk. M. SW6 . . . .1D 101
South Pk. Rd.
SW19 . . . . .5E 115
South Pl.
EC2 . . . . . .5C **10** (4F **63**)
South Pl. M.
EC2 . . . . . .1C **18** (4F **63**)
Sth. Quay Plaza E14 . . .3D 81
Sth. Quay Sq. E14 . . . .3D 81
South Ri. W2 . . . . .1A *74*
(off St George's Flds.)
South Rd. SE23 . . . . . .2F 121
South Row SE3 . . . . . .5B 96
South Sea St. SE16 . . . .4B 80
South Side W6 . . . . . . .4B 70
Southside N7 . . . . .1F 47
Southside Comn.
SW19 . . . . .5E 113
Southside Halls SW7 . . .4F *73*
(off Prince's Gdns.)
Southside Ind. Est.
SW8 . . . . .4E *89*
(off Havelock Ter.)
Southside Shop. Cen.
SW18 . . . . .4D 101
South Sq. NW11 . . . . . .1D 31
WC1 . . . . . . .1B **16** (4C **62**)
South Stand N5 . . . . . . .1D 49
South St.
W1 . . . . . . .1C **20** (2C **74**)

Sth. Tenter St. E1 . . . . .1B 78
South Ter. SW7 . . . . . .5A 74
SOUTH TOTTENHAM . .1B 36
Southvale Rd. SE3 . . . . .5A 96
Southview Av.
NW10 . . . . .2B 42
Southview Cl.
SW17 . . . . .5C 116
Southview Rd.
BR1: Brom 4F 123
South Vs. NW1 . . . . . . .3F 47
Southville SW8 . . . . . . .4F 89
SOUTHWARK
. . . . .2D 25 (2D 77)
Southwark Bri.
SE1 . . . . . . .5A **18** (1E **77**)
Southwark Bri. Bus. Cen.
SE1 . . . . .2A 26
(off Southwark Bri. Rd.)
Southwark Bri. Rd.
SE1 . . . . . . .5E **25** (4D **77**)
Southwark Cathedral
. . . . .1B **26** (2F **77**)
Southwark Pk. Est.
SE16 . . . . .5D 79
Southwark Pk. Rd.
SE16 . . . . .5B 78
Southwark Pk.
Sports Complex . . .5E 79
Southwark St.
SE1 . . . . . . .1D **25** (2D **77**)
Southwater Cl. E14 . . . .5B 66
Southway NW11 . . . . . .1D 31
Southway Cl. W12 . . . . .3D 71
Southwell Gdns.
SW7 . . . . .5E 73
Southwell Gro. Rd.
E11 . . . . .4A 40
Southwell Ho. SE16 . . . .5D *79*
(off Anchor St.)
Southwell Rd. SE5 . . . .1E 105
Sth. W. India Dock Entrance
E14 . . . . .3E 81
Southwest Rd. E11 . . . . .3F 39
Sth. Wharf Rd. W2 . . . .5F 59
Southwick M. W2 . . . . . .5F 59
Southwick Pl. W2 . . . . . .5A 60
Southwick St. W2 . . . . . .5A 60
Southwick Yd. W2 . . . . . .5A 60
(off Titchborne Row)
SOUTH WIMBLEDON
. . . . .5D 115
Southwold Mans. W9 . . .2C *58*
(off Widley Rd.)
Southwold Rd. E5 . . . . .4D 37
Southwood Av. N6 . . . . .2D 33
Southwood Ct. EC1 . . . . .2D *9*
(off Wynyatt St.)
NW11 . . . . .1D 31
South Woodford to
Barking Relief Rd.
E11 . . . . .1F 41
IG1: Ilf 1F 41
IG4: Ilf 1F 41
Southwood Hall N6 . . . .1D 33
Southwood Hgts. N6 . . . .2D 33
Southwood Ho. W11 . . . .1A *72*
(off Avondale Pk. Rd.)
Southwood La. N6 . . . . .2C 32

Southwood Lawn Rd.
N6 . . . . .2C 32
Southwood Mans. N6 . . .1C *32*
(off Southwood La.)
Southwood Pk. N6 . . . . .2C 32
Southwood Smith Ho.
E2 . . . . .2D *65*
(off Florida St.)
Southwood Smith St.
N1 . . . . .5D 49
Sth. Worple Av.
SW14 . . . . .1A 98
Sth. Worple Way
SW14 . . . . .1A 98
Southwyck Ho.
SW9 . . . . .2D 105
Sovereign Cl. E1 . . . . . .1D 79
Sovereign Ct. W8 . . . . .4D *73*
(off Wright's La.)
Sovereign Cres.
SE16 . . . . .1A 80
Sovereign Ho. E1 . . . . . .3D *65*
(off Cambridge Heath Rd.)
Sovereign M. E2 . . . . . .1B 64
Space Arts Centre, The
. . . . .5C *80*
(off Westferry Rd.)
Spa Ct. SE16 . . . . .4C 78
SW16 . . . . .4B 118
Spafield St.
EC1 . . . . . . .3B **8** (3C **62**)
Spa Grn. Est.
EC1 . . . . . . .1C **8** (2D **63**)
Spalding Ho. SE4 . . . . .2A 108
Spalding Rd. NW4 . . . . .2E 29
SW17 . . . . .5D 117
Spanby Rd. E3 . . . . .3C 66
Spaniards Cl. NW11 . . . .3F 31
Spaniards End NW3 . . . .3E 31
Spaniards Rd. NW3 . . . .4E 31
Spanish Pl.
W1 . . . . . . .2C **12** (5C **60**)
Spanish Rd. SW18 . . . . .3E 101
Sparkes Cotts. SW1 . . . .5C *74*
(off Graham Ter.)
Sparkford Ho. SW11 . . . .4F *87*
(off Battersea Church Rd.)
Spa Rd.
SE16 . . . . . . .5F **27** (4B **78**)
Sparrick's Row
SE1 . . . . . . .3C **26** (3F **77**)
Sparrow Rd. E1 . . . . .3E *65*
(off Cephas Av.)
Sparsholt Rd. N19 . . . . .3B 34
Sparta St. SE10 . . . . . . .4E 95
Speakers' Corner
. . . . .4A **12** (1B **74**)
Speakman Ho. SE4 . . . .1A *108*
(off Arica Rd.)
Spearman Ho.
E14 . . . . .5C *66*
(off Upper Nth. St.)
Spear M. SW5 . . . . .5C 72
Spears Rd. N19 . . . . . . .3A 34
Spectacle Works E13 . . .2E 69
Spectrum Pl. SE17 . . . . .2F 91
(off Lytham St.)
Spedan Cl. NW3 . . . . . . .5E 31
Speechly M. E8 . . . . .2B 50

Speed Highwalk *EC2* 5A **10**
　(off Silk St.)
Speed Ho. EC2 . . . . . . .5A **10**
Speedwell St.
　SE8 . . . . .3C **94**
Speedy Pl. WC1 . . . . . . .2D **7**
Speke's Monument . . .2F **73**
Speldhurst Rd. E9 . . . .4F **51**
　W4 . . . . .4A **70**
Spellbrook Wlk. N1 . . .1E **49**
Spelman Ho. *E1* 4C **64**
　(off Spelman St.)
Spelman St. E1 . . . . . .4C **64**
　(not continuous)
Spence Cl. SE16 . . . . . .3B **80**
Spencer Ct. *NW8* 1E **59**
　(off Marlborough Pl.)
Spencer Dr. N2 . . . . . . .1E **31**
Spencer House 2F **21**
Spencer Ho. NW4 . . . .1D **29**
Spencer Mans. *W14* . . .2A **86**
　(off Queen's Club Gdns.)
Spencer M. *SW9* 4B **90**
　(off Lansdowne Way)
　W6 . . . . .2A **86**
SPENCER PARK 3F **101**
Spencer Pk. SW18 . . . .3F **101**
Spencer Pl. N1 . . . . . . .4D **49**
Spencer Ri. NW5 . . . . .1D **47**
Spencer Rd. E6 . . . . . . .5F **55**
　N8 . . . . .1B **34**
　(not continuous)
　SW18 . . . . .2F **101**
Spencer St.
　EC1 . . . . . .2D **9** (2D **63**)
　SW15 . . . . .2F **99**
Spencer Wlk. NW3 . . . .1F **45**
　SW15 . . . . .2F **99**
Spencer Way E1 . . . . . .5D **65**
Spencer Yd. *SE3* 5B **96**
　(off Tranquil Va.)
Spenlow Ho. *SE16* 4C **78**
　(off Jamaica Rd.)
Spenser Gro. N16 . . . . .2A **50**
Spenser M. SE21 . . . . .2F **119**
Spenser Rd. SE24 . . . .3D **105**
Spenser St.
　SW1 . . . . . .5A **22** (4E **75**)
Spens Ho. *WC1* 4F **7**
　(off Lamb's Conduit St.)
Spensley Wlk. N16 . . . .5F **35**
Spert St. E14 . . . . .1A **80**
Spey St. E14 . . . . .4E **67**
Spezia Rd. NW10 . . . . .1C **56**
Sphere, The *E16* 5B **68**
　(off Hallsville Rd.)
Spice Ct. E1 . . . . .1C **78**
Spice Quay Hgts.
　SE1 . . . . .2B **78**
Spicer Cl. SW9 . . . . . . .5D **91**
Spindrift Av. E14 . . . . . .5C **80**
Spinnaker Ho. *E14* 3C **80**
　(off Byng St.)
Spinney, The SW13 . . . .3D **85**
　SW16 . . . . .3E **117**
Spinney Gdns.
　SE19 . . . . .5B **120**
Spire Ho. *W2* 1E **73**
　(off Lancaster Ga.)
Spirit Quay E1 . . . . .2C **78**

SPITALFIELDS
　. . . . . .5F **11** (4B **64**)
Spitalfields City Farm
　. . . . . .3C **64**
Spital Sq. E1 . .5E **11** (4A **64**)
Spital St. E1 . . . . .4C **64**
Spital Yd. E1 . .5E **11** (4A **64**)
Splendour Wlk.
　SE16 . . . . .1E **93**
　(off Verney Rd.)
Spode Ho. SE11 . . . . . .5B **24**
Spode Wlk. NW6 . . . . . .2D **45**
Sporle Rd. Ct.
　SW11 . . . . .1F **101**
Sportsbank St. SE6 . . . .5E **109**
Sportsman Pl. E2 . . . . .5C **50**
Spratt Hall Rd. E11 . . . .1C **40**
Spriggs Ho. *N1* 4D **49**
　(off Canonbury Rd.)
Sprimont Pl. SW3 . . . . .1B **88**
Springall St. SE15 . . . . .3D **93**
Springalls Wharf
　SE16 . . . . .3C **78**
　(off Bermondsey Wall W.)
Springbank Rd.
　SE13 . . . . .4F **109**
Springbank Wlk.
　NW1 . . . . .4F **47**
Springdale M. N16 . . . . .1F **49**
Springdale Rd. N16 . . . .1F **49**
Springett Ho. *SW2* 3C **104**
　(off St Matthews Rd.)
Springfield E5 . . . . .3D **37**
Springfield Ct. *NW3* . . .4A **46**
　(off Eton Av.)
Springfield Gdns. E5 . . .3D **37**
　NW9 . . . . .1A **28**
Springfield Gro. SE7 . . .2E **97**
Springfield La. NW6 . . . .5D **45**
Springfield Ri.
　SE26 . . . . .3D **121**
Springfield Rd. E15 . . . .2A **68**
　E17 . . . . .1B **38**
　NW8 . . . . .5E **45**
　SE26 . . . . .5D **121**
　SW19 . . . . .5B **114**
Springfield Wlk.
　NW6 . . . . .5D **45**
Spring Gdns. N5 . . . . . .2E **49**
　SW1 . . . . . .1C **22** (2F **75**)
　(not continuous)
Spring Hill E5 . . . . .2C **36**
　SE26 . . . . .4E **121**
Springhill Cl. SE5 . . . . .1F **105**
Spring Ho. WC1 . . . . . . .2B **8**
Spring La. E5 . . . . .2D **37**
Spring M. W1 . . .5A **4** (4B **60**)
Spring Pk. Dr. N4 . . . . . .3E **35**
Spring Pas. SW15 . . . . .1F **99**
Spring Path NW3 . . . . . .2F **45**
Spring Pl. NW5 . . . . . . .2D **47**
Springrice Rd. SE13 . . . .4F **109**
Spring St. W2 . . . . .5F **59**
Spring Tide Cl. SE15 . . .4D **93**
Springvale Ter. W14 . . . .4F **71**
Spring Wlk. E1 . . . . .4C **64**
Springwater WC1 . . . . . .5F **7**
Springwell Av. NW10 . . .5B **42**

Springfield Cl.
　SW16 . . . . .4B **118**
Springwell Rd.
　SW16 . . . . .4C **118**
Springwood Cl. E3 . . . . .1C **66**
Sprowston M. E7 . . . . . .3C **54**
Sprowston Rd. E7 . . . . .2C **54**
Spruce Ho. *SE16* 3F **79**
　(off Woodland Cres.)
Sprules Rd. SE4 . . . . . . .5A **94**
Spurgeon St. SE1 . . . . .5B **26**
Spurling Rd.
　SE22 . . . . .2B **106**
Spur Rd. SE1 . .3B **24** (3C **76**)
　SW1 . . . . . .4F **21** (3E **75**)
Spurstowe Rd. E8 . . . . . .3D **51**
Spurstowe Ter. E8 . . . . .2C **50**
Square, The E10 . . . . . .5E **39**
　W6 . . . . .1E **85**
Square Rigger Row
　SW11 . . . . .1E **101**
Squarey St. SW17 . . . . .3E **115**
Squire Gdns. *NW8* 2F **59**
　(off Grove End Rd.)
Squires Ct. SW4 . . . . . .4A **90**
　SW19 . . . . .4C **114**
Squires Mt. NW3 . . . . . .5F **31**
Squirrels, The SE13 . . . .1F **109**
Squirries St. E2 . . . . . . .2C **64**
SS Robin 1C **80**
Stable Cl. *EC1* 4E **9**
　(off Clerkenwell Rd.)
Stable M. NW5 . . . . . . .3D **47**
　SE6 . . . . .1A **124**
Stables Gallery & Arts Cen.
　. . . . . .5C **28**
Stables Lodge *E8* 4D **51**
　(off Mare St.)
Stables Market, The
　NW1 . . . . .4D **47**
Stables M. SE27 . . . . . .5E **119**
Stables Way SE11 . . . . .1C **90**
Stables Yd. SW18 . . . . .4C **100**
Stable Way W10 . . . . . . .5E **57**
Stable Yd. SW1 . . . . . . .3F **21**
　SW15 . . . . .1E **99**
Stableyard, The SW9 . . .5B **90**
Stable Yd. Rd.
　SW1 . . . . . .3A **22** (3E **75**)
　(not continuous)
Stacey Cl. E10 . . . . .1F **39**
Stacey St. N7 . . . . .5C **34**
　WC2 . . . . . .3C **14** (5F **61**)
Stack Ho. *SW1* 5C **74**
　(off Cundy St.)
Stackhouse St. SW3 . . .5A **20**
Stacy Path SE5 . . . . . . .3A **92**
Stadium M. N5 . . . . .5C **34**
Stadium Rd. E. NW4 . . . .2D **29**
Stadium St. SW10 . . . . .3E **87**
Staffa Rd. E10 . . . . .3A **38**
Stafford Cl. E17 . . . . . . .1B **38**
　(not continuous)
　NW6 . . . . .2C **58**
Stafford Ct. SW8 . . . . . .3A **90**
　W8 . . . . .4C **72**
Stafford Cripps Ho.
　E2 . . . . .2E **65**
　(off Globe Rd.)

Stafford Cripps Ho.
  SW6 . . . . .2B **86**
    (off Clem Attlee Ct.)
Stafford Ho. *SE1* 1B **92**
    (off Cooper's Rd.)
Stafford Mans. *SW1* 5F **21**
    (off Stafford Pl.)
  SW4 . . . . .2A **104**
  SW11 . . . . .3B **88**
    (off Albert Bri. Rd.)
  W14 . . . . .4F **71**
    (off Haarlem Rd.)
Stafford Pl.
  SW1 . . . . . . .5F **21** (4E **75**)
Stafford Rd. *E3* 1B **66**
  E7 . . . . .4C **55**
  NW6 . . . . .2C **58**
Staffordshire St.
  SE15 . . . . .4C **92**
Stafford St.
  W1 . . . . . . .1F **21** (2E **75**)
Stafford Ter. *W8* 4C **72**
Staff St. *EC1* 2C **10** (2F **63**)
STAG LANE 2B **112**
Stag La. *SW15* 3B **112**
Stainer Ho. *SE3* 2E **111**
Stainer St.
  SE1 . . . . . . .2C **26** (2F **77**)
Staining La.
  EC2 . . . . . .2A **18** (5E **63**)
Stainsbury St. *E2* 1E **65**
Stainsby Rd. *E14* 5C **66**
Stainton Rd. *SE6* 4F **109**
Stalbridge Flats *W1* 3C **12**
    (off Lumley St.)
Stalbridge Ho. *NW1* 1F **5**
    (off Hampstead Rd.)
Stalbridge St. *NW1* 4A **60**
Stalham St. *SE16* 4D **79**
Stamford Bridge 3D **87**
Stamford Bri. Studios
  SW6 . . . . .3D **87**
    (off Wandon Rd.)
Stamford Brook Arches
  W6 . . . . .5C **70**
Stamford Brook Av.
  W6 . . . . .4B **70**
Stamford Brook Gdns.
  W6 . . . . .4B **70**
Stamford Brook Mans.
  W6 . . . . .5B **70**
    (off Goldhawk Rd.)
Stamford Brook Rd.
  W6 . . . . .4B **70**
Stamford Bldgs.
  SW8 . . . . .3A **90**
    (off Meadow Pl.)
Stamford Cl. *NW3* 5E **31**
    (off Heath St.)
Stamford Cotts.
  SW10 . . . . .3D **87**
    (off Billing St.)
Stamford Ct. *W6* 5C **70**
Stamford Ga. *SW6* 3D **87**
Stamford Gro. E.
  N16 . . . . .3C **36**
Stamford Gro. W.
  N16 . . . . .3C **36**
STAMFORD HILL 3B **36**

Stamford Hill *N16* 4B **36**
Stamford Lodge *N16* 2B **36**
Stamford Rd. *E6* 5F **55**
  N1 . . . . .4A **50**
Stamford St.
  SE1 . . . . . . .2B **24** (2C **76**)
Stamp Pl. *E2* . . .1F **11** (1B **64**)
Stanard Cl. *N16* 2C **36**
Stanborough Ho. *E3* 3D **67**
    (off Empson St.)
Stanborough Pas. *E8* . . .3B **50**
Stanbridge Rd.
  SW15 . . . . .1E **99**
Stanbury Ct. *NW3* 3B **46**
Stanbury Rd. *SE15* 5D **93**
    (not continuous)
Standard Pl. *EC2* 2E **11**
Standard Rd. *NW10* 3A **56**
Standen Rd. *SW18* 5B **100**
Standish Ho. *SE3* 2D **111**
    (off Elford Cl.)
  W6 . . . . .5C **70**
    (off St Peter's Gro.)
Standish Rd. *W6* 5C **70**
Standlake Point
  SE23 . . . . .3F **121**
Stane Gro. *SW9* 5A **90**
Stanesgate Ho. *SE15* . . .3C **92**
    (off Friary Est.)
Stane Way *SE18* 3F **97**
Stanfield Ho. *NW8* 3F **59**
    (off Frampton St.)
Stanfield Rd. *E3* 1A **66**
Stanford Ct. *SW6* 4D **87**
  W8 . . . . .4D **73**
    (off Cornwall Gdns.)
Stanford M. *E8* 2C **50**
Stanford Pl. *SE17* 5A **78**
Stanford Rd. *W8* 4D **73**
Stanford St. *SW1* 5F **75**
Stangate *SE1* 5A **24**
Stanhope Cl. *SE16* 3F **79**
Stanhope Gdns. *N4* 1D **35**
  N6 . . . . .1D **33**
  SW7 . . . . .5E **73**
Stanhope Ga.
  W1 . . . . . . .2D **20** (2C **74**)
Stanhope Ho. *SE8* 3B **94**
    (off Adolphus St.)
Stanhope M. E. *SW7* 5E **73**
Stanhope M. Sth.
  SW7 . . . . .5E **73**
Stanhope M. W. *SW7* . . .5E **73**
Stanhope Pde.
  NW1 . . . . . . .1F **5** (2E **61**)
Stanhope Pl. *W2* 1B **74**
Stanhope Rd. *E17* 1D **39**
  N6 . . . . .1E **33**
Stanhope Row
  W1 . . . . . .2D **21** (2D **75**)
Stanhope St.
  NW1 . . . . . . .1F **5** (1E **61**)
Stanhope Ter. *W2* 1F **73**
Stanier Cl. *W14* 1B **86**
Stanier Ho. *SW6* 4E **87**
    (off Station Ct.)
Stanlake M. *W12* 2E **71**
Stanlake Rd. *W12* 2D **71**
Stanlake Vs. *W12* 2E **71**

Stanley Bri. Studios
  SW6 . . . . .3D **87**
    (off King's Rd.)
Stanley Cl. *SW8* 2B **90**
Stanley Cohen Ho.
  EC1 . . . . .4F **9**
    (off Golden La.)
Stanley Cres. *W11* 1B **72**
Stanley Gdns. *NW2* 2E **43**
  W3 . . . . .3A **70**
  W11 . . . . .1B **72**
Stanley Gdns. M.
  W11 . . . . .1B **72**
    (off Kensington Pk. Rd.)
Stanley Gro. *SW8* 5C **88**
Stanley Holloway Ct.
  E16 . . . . .5C **68**
    (off Coolfin Rd.)
Stanley Ho. *E14* 5C **66**
    (off Saracen St.)
  SW10 . . . . .3E **87**
    (off Coleridge Gdns.)
Stanley Mans. *SW10* . . .2E **87**
    (off Park Wlk.)
Stanley M. *SW10* 3E **87**
    (off Coleridge Gdns.)
Stanley Rd. *E10* 1D **39**
  E12 . . . . .2F **55**
  NW9 . . . . .2C **28**
Stanley St. *SE8* 3B **94**
Stanley Studios
  SW10 . . . . .2E **87**
    (off Park Wlk.)
Stanley Ter. *N19* 4A **34**
Stanliff Ho. *E14* 4C **80**
Stanmer St. *SW11* 4A **88**
Stanmore Pl. *NW1* 5D **47**
Stanmore Rd. *E11* 3B **40**
Stanmore St. *N1* 5B **48**
Stannard Cotts. *E1* 3E **65**
    (off Fox Cl.)
Stannard Ct. *SE6* 1D **123**
Stannard Ho. *SW19* 4E **115**
Stannard M. *E8* 3C **50**
    (off Stannard Rd.)
Stannard Rd. *E8* 3C **50**
Stannary Pl. *SE11* 1C **90**
Stannary St. *SE11* 2C **90**
Stansborough Ho. *E3* . . .3D **67**
    (off Empson St.)
Stansbury Sq. *W10* 2A **58**
Stansfeld Rd. *E6* 4F **69**
  E16 . . . . .4F **69**
Stansfield Ho. *SE1* 5B **78**
    (off Longfield Est.)
Stansfield Rd. *SW9* 1B **104**
Stanstead *WC1* 2E **7**
    (off Tavistock Pl.)
Stanstead Gro.
  SE6 . . . . .1B **122**
Stanstead Ho. *E3* 3E **67**
    (off Devas St.)
Stanstead Rd. *E11* 1D **41**
  SE6 . . . . .1F **121**
  SE23 . . . . .1F **121**
Stanswood Gdns.
  SE5 . . . . .3A **92**
Stanthorpe Cl.
  SW16 . . . . .5A **118**

Stanthorpe Rd.
　SW16 . . . . .5A 118
Stanton Ho. SE10 . . . . .2E 95
　(off Thames St.)
　SE16 . . . . .3B 80
　(off Rotherhithe St.)
Stanton Rd. SE26 . . . . .4B 122
　SW13 . . . . .5B 84
Stanton Sq. SE26 . . . . .4B 122
Stanton Way SE26 . . . .4B 122
Stanway Ct. N1 . . . . . . .1A 64
　(not continuous)
Stanway St. N1 . . . . . . .1A 64
Stanwick Rd. W14 . . . . .5B 72
Stanworth St.
　SE1 . . . . . . .4F 27 (4B 78)
Stanyhurst SE23 . . . . . .1A 122
Staplefield Cl. SW2 . . . .1A 118
Stapleford Cl.
　SW19 . . . . .5A 100
Staplehurst Rd.
　SE13 . . . . .3F 109
Staple Inn WC1 . . . . . . .1B 16
Staple Inn Bldgs.
　WC1 . . . .1B 16 (4C 62)
Staples Cl. SE16 . . . . . .2A 80
STAPLES CORNER
　. . . . . .3D 29
Staples Cnr. Bus. Pk.
　NW2 . . . . .3D 29
Staples Cnr. Retail Pk.
　NW2 . . . . .3D 29
Staple St.
　SE1 . . . . . . .4C 26 (3F 77)
Stapleton Hall Rd.
　N4 . . . . .3B 34
Stapleton Ho. E2 . . . . . .2D 65
　(off Ellsworth St.)
Stapleton Vs.
　SW17 . . . . .3C 116
Stapleton Vs. N16 . . . . .1A 50
　(off Wordsworth Rd.)
Star All. EC3 . . . . .4E 19
Starboard Way E14 . . . .4C 80
Starcross St.
　NW1 . . . . .2A 6 (2E 61)
Starfield Rd. W12 . . . . .3C 70
Star La. E16 . . . . .3A 68
Starling Ho. NW8 . . . . .1A 60
　(off Charlbert St.)
Star Pl. E1 . . . . .1B 78
Star Rd. W14 . . . . .2B 86
Star St. W2 . . . . .5A 60
Star Wharf NW1 . . . . . .5E 47
　(off St Pancras Way)
Star Yd.
　WC2 . . . .2B 16 (5C 62)
Staten Bldg. E3 . . . . . . .1C 66
　(off Fairfield Rd.)
Statham Gro. N16 . . . . .1F 49
Statham Ho. SW8 . . . . .4E 89
　(off Wadhurst Rd.)
Station App. E7 . . . . . . .1D 55
　N16 . . . . .4B 36
　(off Stamford Hill)
　NW1 . . . .4A 4 (3B 60)
　NW10 . . . . .2B 56
　NW11 . . . . .2F 29
　SE3 . . . . .1D 111

Station App. SE12 . . . .4C 110
　(off Burnt Ash Hill)
　SE26 . . . . .4E 121
　SW6 . . . . .1A 100
　SW16 . . . . .5F 117
Station App. Rd.
　SE1 . . . . . .4A 24 (3C 76)
Station Arc. W1 . . . . . . .4E 5
　(off Gt. Portland St.)
Station Av. SW9 . . . . . .1D 105
Station Ct. N15 . . . . . . .1B 36
　SW6 . . . . .4E 87
Station Cres. SE3 . . . . .1C 96
Stationer's Hall Ct.
　EC4 . . . . . .3E 17 (5D 63)
Station Pde. E13 . . . . . .5E 55
　(off Green St.)
　NW2 . . . . .3E 43
　SW12 . . . . .1C 116
Station Pas. SE15 . . . . .4E 93
Station Path E8 . . . . . . .3D 51
　(off Graham Rd.)
　SW6 . . . . .1B 100
Station Pl. N4 . . . . .4C 34
Station Ri. SE27 . . . . . .2D 119
Station Rd. E7 . . . . .1C 54
　E12 . . . . .1F 55
　E17 . . . . .1A 38
　N19 . . . . .5E 33
　NW4 . . . . .1C 28
　NW10 . . . . .1B 56
　SE13 . . . . .1E 109
　SE20 . . . . .5E 121
　SW13 . . . . .5B 84
Station St. E15 . . . . . . .4F 53
Station Ter. NW10 . . . . .1F 57
　SE5 . . . . .4E 91
Station Ter. M. SE3 . . . .1C 96
Station Way SE15 . . . . .5C 92
Staton Ct. E10 . . . . .2D 39
　(off Kings Cl.)
Staunton Ho. SE17 . . . .5A 78
　(off Wansey St.)
Staunton St. SE8 . . . . . .2B 94
Stave Hill Ecological Pk.
　. . . . . .3A 80
Staveley NW1 . . . . .1F 5
　(off Varndell St.)
Staveley Cl. E9 . . . . . . .2E 51
　N7 . . . . .1A 48
　SE15 . . . . .4D 93
Staveley Gdns. W4 . . . .4A 84
Staveley Rd. W4 . . . . . .3A 84
Stavers Ho. E3 . . . . . . .1B 66
　(off Tredegar Rd.)
Staverton Rd. NW2 . . . .4E 43
Stave Yd. Rd. SE16 . . . .2A 80
Stavordale Lodge
　W14 . . . . .4B 72
　(off Melbury Rd.)
Stavordale Rd. N5 . . . . .1D 49
Stayner's Rd. E1 . . . . . .3F 65
Steadman Ct. EC1 . . . . .3A 10
　(off Old St.)
Stead St. SE17 . . . . . . .5F 77
Stean St. E8 . . . . .5B 50
Stebbing Ho. W11 . . . . .2F 71
　(off Queensdale Cres.)
Stebondale St. E14 . . . .5E 81

Stedham Pl. WC1 . . . . . .2D 15
Steedman St. SE17 . . . . .5E 77
Steele Ho. E15 . . . . .1A 68
　(off Eve Rd.)
Steele Rd. E11 . . . . .1A 54
Steele's M. Nth.
　NW3 . . . . .3B 46
Steele's M. Sth.
　NW3 . . . . .3B 46
Steele's Rd. NW3 . . . . . .3B 46
Steele's Studios
　NW3 . . . . .3B 46
Steel's La. E1 . . . . .5E 65
Steelyard Pas. EC4 . . . . .5B 18
Steen Way SE22 . . . . . . .3A 106
Steep Hill SW16 . . . . . . .3F 117
Steeple Cl. SW6 . . . . . . .5A 86
　SW19 . . . . .5A 114
Steeple Wlk. N1 . . . . . . .5E 49
　(off New Nth. Rd.)
Steerforth St. SW18 . . . .2E 115
Steers Way SE16 . . . . . .3A 80
Stelfox Ho. WC1 . . . . . . .1A 8
　(off Penton Ri.)
Stella Rd. SW17 . . . . . . .5B 116
Stellman Cl. E5 . . . . .5C 36
Stephan Cl. E8 . . . . .5C 50
Stephendale Rd.
　SW6 . . . . .1D 101
Stephen Fox Ho. W4 . . . .1A 84
　(off Chiswick La.)
Stephen M.
　W1 . . . . . . .1B 14 (4F 61)
Stephen Pl. SW4 . . . . . . .1E 103
Stephens Ct. E16 . . . . . .3B 68
　SE4 . . . . .1A 108
Stephenson Cl. E3 . . . . . .2D 67
Stephenson Ho.
　SE1 . . . . . . .5F 25 (4E 77)
Stephenson Rd. E17 . . . .1A 38
Stephenson St. E16 . . . . .3A 68
　NW10 . . . . .2A 56
Stephenson Way
　NW1 . . . . . .3A 6 (3E 61)
Stephen's Rd. E15 . . . . . .5A 54
Stephen St.
　W1 . . . . . . .1B 14 (4F 61)
STEPNEY 4F 65
Stepney C'way. E1 . . . . . .5F 65
Stepney City Apartments
　E1 . . . . .4E 65
Stepney Grn. E1 . . . . . . .4E 65
Stepney Grn. Ct. E1 . . . . .4F 65
　(off Stepney Grn.)
Stepney High St. E1 . . . . .4F 65
Stepney Way E1 . . . . . . .4D 65
Stepping Stones Farm
　. . . . . .4F 65
Sterling Cl. NW10 . . . . . .4C 42
Sterling Gdns. SE14 . . . . .2A 94
Sterling Ho. SE3 . . . . . . .2D 111
Sterling St. SW7 . . . . . . .4A 74
Sterndale Rd. W14 . . . . . .4F 71
Sterne St. W12 . . . . .3F 71
Sternhall La. SE15 . . . . . .1C 106
Sternhold Av. SW2 . . . . . .2F 117
Sterry St.
　SE1 . . . . . . .4B 26 (3F 77)

Steucers La. SE23 . . . .1A **122**
Steve Biko Ct. *W10* 3F **57**
  (off St John's Ter.)
Steve Biko La. SE6 . . . .4C **122**
Steve Biko Lodge
  E13 . . . . .1C **68**
  (off London Rd.)
Steve Biko Rd. N7 . . . . .5C **34**
Stevedore St. E1 . . . . . .2D **79**
Stevenage Rd.
  SW6 . . . . .3F **85**
Stevens Av. E9 . . . . .3E **51**
Stevenson Ct. SE6 . . . . .2B **124**
Stevenson Cres.
  SE16 . . . . .1C **92**
Stevenson Ho. *NW8* 5E **45**
  (off Boundary Rd.)
Stevens St.
  SE1 . . . . . .5E **27** (4A **78**)
Steventon Rd. W12 . . . . .1B **70**
Steward St.
  E1 . . . . . . .1E **19** (4A **64**)
Stewart Rd. E15 . . . . . . .1F **53**
Stewart's Gro. SW3 . . . . .1F **87**
Stewart's Pl. SW2 . . . . . .4B **104**
Stewart's Rd. SW8 . . . . .3E **89**
Stewart St. E14 . . . . .3E **81**
Stew La. EC4 . . . .4F **17** (1E **77**)
Stibbington Ho. *NW1* 1E **61**
  (off Cranleigh St.)
Stifford Ho. *E1* 4E **65**
  (off Stepney Way)
Stileman Ho. *E3* 4B **66**
  (off Ackroyd Dr.)
Stillingfleet Rd.
  SW13 . . . . .2C **84**
Stillington St. SW1 . . . . .5E **75**
Stillness Rd. SE23 . . . . .4A **108**
Stirling Ct. *EC1* 3D **9**
  (off St John St.)
Stirling Rd. E13 . . . . . . .1D **69**
  SW9 . . . . .5A **90**
Stockbeck *NW1* 1A **6**
  (off Ampthill Est.)
Stockfield Rd.
  SW16 . . . . .3B **118**
Stockholm Apartments
  NW1 . . . . .4C **46**
  (off Chalk Farm Rd.)
Stockholm Ho. *E1* 1C **78**
  (off Swedenborg Gdns.)
Stockholm Rd. SE16 . . . .1E **93**
Stockholm Way E1 . . . . .2C **78**
Stockhurst Cl. SW15 . . . .5E **85**
Stockleigh Hall *NW8* 1A **60**
  (off Prince Albert Rd.)
Stock Orchard Cres.
  N7 . . . . .2B **48**
Stock Orchard St. N7 . . . .2B **48**
Stocks Pl. E14 . . . . .1B **80**
Stock St. E13 . . . . .1C **68**
Stockton Ct. *SW1* 4F **75**
  (off Greycoat St.)
Stockton Ho. *E2* 2D **65**
  (off Ellsworth St.)
STOCKWELL 5B **90**
Stockwell Av. SW9 . . . . .1B **104**
Stockwell Gdns.
  SW9 . . . . .4B **90**

Stockwell Gdns. Est.
  SW9 . . . . .5A **90**
Stockwell Grn. SW9 . . . . .5B **90**
Stockwell Grn. Ct.
  SW9 . . . . .5B **90**
Stockwell La. SW9 . . . . . .5B **90**
Stockwell M. SW9 . . . . . .5B **90**
Stockwell Pk. Cres.
  SW9 . . . . .5B **90**
Stockwell Pk. Est.
  SW9 . . . . .5B **90**
Stockwell Pk. Rd.
  SW9 . . . . .4B **90**
Stockwell Pk. Wlk.
  SW9 . . . . .1C **104**
Stockwell Rd. SW9 . . . . .5B **90**
Stockwell St. SE10 . . . . .2E **95**
Stockwell Ter. SW9 . . . . .4B **90**
Stoddard Ho. SW8 . . . . .2B **90**
Stodmarsh Ho. *SW9* 4C **90**
  (off Cowley Rd.)
Stofield Gdns. SE9 . . . . .3F **125**
Stoford Cl. SW19 . . . . . .5A **100**
Stokenchurch St.
  SW6 . . . . .4D **87**
STOKE NEWINGTON . . .5B **36**
Stoke Newington Chu. St.
  N16 . . . . .5F **35**
Stoke Newington Comn.
  N16 . . . . .4B **36**
Stoke Newington High St.
  N16 . . . . .5B **36**
Stoke Newington Rd.
  N16 . . . . .2B **50**
Stoke Pl. NW10 . . . . .2B **56**
Stokesley St. W12 . . . . . .5B **56**
Stokes Rd. E6 . . . . .3F **69**
Stoll Cl. NW2 . . . . .5E **29**
Stoms Path *SE6* 5C **122**
  (off Maroons Way)
Stondon Pk. SE23 . . . . .4A **108**
Stondon Wlk. E6 . . . . . . .1F **69**
Stonebridge Cen.
  N15 . . . . .1B **36**
Stonebridge Rd. N15 . . . .1B **36**
Stone Bldgs. WC2 . . . . . .1A **16**
Stone Cl. SW4 . . . . .5E **89**
Stonecutter St.
  EC4 . . . . . .2D **17** (5D **63**)
Stonefield N4 . . . . .4B **34**
Stonefield Mans. *N1* 5C **48**
  (off Cloudesley St.)
Stonefield St. N1 . . . . . . .5C **48**
Stonefield Way SE7 . . . . .3F **97**
Stone Hall *W8* 4D **73**
  (off Stone Hall Gdns.)
Stonehall Av. IG1: Ilf 1F **41**
Stone Hall Gdns. W8 . . . .4D **73**
Stone Hall Pl. W8 . . . . . .4D **73**
Stonehills Ct. SE21 . . . . .3A **120**
Stonehouse *NW1* 5E **47**
  (off Plender St.)
Stone Ho. Ct. EC3 . . . . . .1E **19**
Stonehouse Ho. *W2* 4C **58**
  (off Westbourne Pk. Rd.)
Stone Lake Ind. Pk.
  SE7 . . . . .5E **83**
Stone Lake Retail Pk.
  SE7 . . . . .5E **83**

Stoneleigh M. E3 . . . . . . .1A **66**
Stoneleigh Pl. W11 . . . . .1F **71**
Stoneleigh St. W11 . . . . .1F **71**
Stoneleigh Ter. N19 . . . . .4D **33**
Stonell's Rd. SW11 . . . . .4B **102**
Stonemason Ct. *SE1* 4F **25**
  (off Borough Rd.)
Stonemasons Yd.
  SW18 . . . . .5F **101**
Stonenest St. N4 . . . . . . .3B **34**
Stones End St.
  SE1 . . . . . .4F **25** (3E **77**)
Stoneyard La. E14 . . . . . .1D **81**
Stoneycroft Cl.
  SE12 . . . . .5B **110**
Stoney La.
  E1 . . . . . . .2E **19** (5B **64**)
Stoney St.
  SE1 . . . . . .1B **26** (2F **77**)
Stonhouse St. SW4 . . . . .2F **103**
Stonor Rd. W14 . . . . .5B **72**
Stopes St. SE15 . . . . . . .3B **92**
Stopford Rd. E13 . . . . . . .5C **54**
  SE17 . . . . .1D **91**
Stopher Ho. *SE1* 4E **25**
  (off Webber St.)
Storehouse M. E14 . . . . .1C **80**
Storers Quay E14 . . . . . .5F **81**
Store St. E15 . . . . .2F **53**
  WC1 . . . . . .1B **14** (4F **61**)
Storey Ct. *NW8* 2F **59**
  (off St John's Wood Rd.)
Storey Ho. *E14* 1D **81**
  (off Cottage St.)
Storey Rd. N6 . . . . .1B **32**
Storey's Ga.
  SW1 . . . . . .4C **22** (3F **75**)
Stories M. SE5 . . . . .5A **92**
Stories Rd. SE5 . . . . .1A **106**
Stork Rd. E7 . . . . .3B **54**
Stork's Rd. SE16 . . . . . . .4C **78**
Stormont Rd. N6 . . . . . . .2B **32**
  SW11 . . . . .1C **102**
Storrington *WC1* 2E **7**
  (off Regent Sq.)
Story St. N1 . . . . .4B **48**
Stothard Ho. *E1* 3E **65**
  (off Amiel St.)
Stothard Pl.
  E1 . . . . . . .5E **11** (4A **64**)
Stothard St. E1 . . . . .3E **65**
Stott Cl. SW18 . . . . .4F **101**
Stoughton Cl. SE11 . . . . .5B **76**
  SW15 . . . . .1C **112**
Stourcliffe Cl. W1 . . . . . . .5B **60**
Stourcliffe St. W1 . . . . . . .5B **60**
Stourhead Cl. SW19 . . . .5F **99**
Stourhead Ho. *SW1* 1F **89**
  (off Tachbrook St.)
Stour Rd. E3 . . . . .4C **52**
Stowage SE8 . . . . .2C **94**
Stowe Ho. NW11 . . . . . . .1E **31**
Stowe Rd. W12 . . . . .3D **71**
Stracey Rd. E7 . . . . .1C **54**
  NW10 . . . . .5A **42**
Strachbole Rd. N5 . . . . . .1E **49**
Stradella Rd. SE24 . . . . .4E **105**
Strafford Ho. *SE8* 1B **94**
  (off Grove St.)

Strafford St. E14 . . . . .3C 80
Strahan Rd. E3 . . . . .2A 66
Straightsmouth
SE10 . . . . .3E 95
Strait Rd. E6 . . . . .1F 83
Strakers Rd. SE15 . . . . .2D 107
Strale Ho. N1 . . . . .5A 50
(off Whitmore Est.)
Strand WC2 . . . . .5E 15 (1A 76)
Strand Ho. SW18 . . . . . .2E 101
Strand La.
WC2 . . . . . .4A 16 (1B 76)
Strand Theatre 4F 15
(off Aldwych)
Strang Ho. N1 . . . . .5E 49
Strangways Ter. W14 . . . .4B 72
Stranraer Way N1 . . . . . . .4A 48
Strasburg Rd. SW11 . . . . .4C 88
Strata Twr. SE1 . . . . .5E 77
(off Walworth St.)
STRATFORD 4F 53
Stratford Centre, The
E15 . . . . .4F 53
Stratford Circus
(Performing Arts Cen.)
. . . . .3F 53
Stratford Eye E15 . . . . . . .3F 53
Stratford Gro. SW15 . . . . .2F 99
STRATFORD NEW TOWN
. . . . .3F 53
Stratford Office Village, The
E15 . . . . .4A 54
(off Romford Rd.)
Stratford Picture House
. . . . .3F 53
Stratford Pl. E20 . . . . .3E 53
(within Westfield Stratford
City Shopping Cen.)
W1 . . . . . .3D 13 (5D 61)
Stratford Rd. E13 . . . . . . .5B 54
(not continuous)
W8 . . . . .4C 72
Stratford Studios W8 . . . .4C 72
Stratford Vs. NW1 . . . . . . .4E 47
Stratford Workshops
E15 . . . . .5F 53
(off Burford Rd.)
Stratham Ct. N19 . . . . . . .5A 34
(off Alexander Rd.)
Strathan Cl. SW18 . . . . .4A 100
Strathaven Rd.
SE12 . . . . .4D 111
Strathblaine Rd.
SW11 . . . . .3F 101
Strathdale SW16 . . . . . . .5B 118
Strathdon Dr. SW17 . . . .3F 115
Strathearn Ho. W2 . . . . . .1A 74
(off Strearhern Pl.)
Strathearn Pl. W2 . . . . . . .5A 60
Strathearn Rd.
SW19 . . . . .5C 114
Stratheden Pde. SE3 . . . . .3C 96
Stratheden Rd. SE3 . . . . . .4C 96
Strathleven Rd.
SW2 . . . . .3A 104
Strathmore Ct. NW8 . . . . .2A 60
(off Park Rd.)
Strathmore Gdns.
W8 . . . . .2C 72

Strathmore Rd.
SW19 . . . . .3C 114
Strathnairn St. SE1 . . . . . .5C 78
(not continuous)
Strathray Gdns. NW3 . . . .3A 46
Strath Ter. SW11 . . . . . .2A 102
Strathville Rd.
SW18 . . . . .2C 114
(not continuous)
Stratton Cl. N1 . . . . .4A 50
(off Hertford Rd.)
Strattondale St. E14 . . . . . .4E 81
Stratton St.
W1 . . . . .1E 21 (2D 75)
Strauss Rd. W4 . . . . .3A 70
Streakes Fld. Rd.
NW2 . . . . .4C 28
Streamline Ct. SE22 . . . . .1C 120
(off Streamline M.)
Streamline M. SE22 . . . .1C 120
STREATHAM 3A 118
Streatham Cl.
SW16 . . . . .2A 118
STREATHAM COMMON
. . . . .5A 118
Streatham Comn. Nth.
SW16 . . . . .5A 118
Streatham Comn. Sth.
SW16 . . . . .5A 118
Streatham Ct.
SW16 . . . . .3A 118
Streatham High Rd.
SW16 . . . . .4A 118
STREATHAM HILL 2A 118
Streatham Hill SW2 . . . . .2A 118
Streatham Hub 5F 117
Streatham Kart Raceway
. . . . .5F 117
STREATHAM PARK 5E 117
Streatham Pl. SW2 . . . . .5A 104
Streatham St.
WC1 . . . . . . .2D 15 (5A 62)
Streathbourne Rd.
SW17 . . . . .2C 116
Streatley Pl. NW3 . . . . . . .1E 45
Streatley Rd. NW6 . . . . . . .4B 44
Street, The SE3 . . . . .3E 53
(within Westfield Stratford
City Shopping Cen.)
Streetfield M. SE3 . . . . .1C 110
Streimer Rd. E15 . . . . .1E 67
Strelley Way W3 . . . . .1A 70
Stretton Mans. SE8 . . . . . .1C 94
Strickland Ct. SE15 . . . . .1C 106
Strickland Ho. E2 . . . . .2F 11
(off Chambord St.)
Strickland Row
SW18 . . . . .5F 101
Strickland St. SE8 . . . . . . .5C 94
Stride Rd. E13 . . . . .1B 68
Stringer Ho. N1 . . . . .5A 50
(off Whitmore Est.)
Strode Rd. E7 . . . . .1C 54
NW10 . . . . .3C 42
SW6 . . . . .3A 86
Strome Ho. NW6 . . . . .1D 59
(off Carlton Vale)
Strone Rd. E7 . . . . .3E 55
E12 . . . . .3E 55

Stronsa Rd. W12 . . . . .3B 70
Strood Ho. SE1 . . . . .4C 26
(off Staple St.)
Stroud Cres. SW15 . . . . .3C 112
STROUD GREEN 2B 34
Stroud Grn. Rd. N4 . . . . . .3B 34
Stroudley Ho. SW8 . . . . . .4E 89
Stroudley Wik. E3 . . . . .2D 67
Stroud Rd. SW19 . . . . . . .3C 114
Strouts Pl. E2 . . . .1F 11 (2B 64)
Strudwick Ct. SW4 . . . . . . .4A 90
(off Binfield Rd.)
Strutton Ct. SW1 . . . . .5B 22
(off Gt. Peter St.)
Strutton Ground
SW1 . . . . . . .5B 22 (4F 75)
Strype St. E1 . . .1F 19 (4B 64)
Stuart Av. NW9 . . . . .2C 28
Stuart Ho. E9 . . . . .3F 51
(off Queen Anne Rd.)
E16 . . . . .2D 83
(off Beaulieu Av.)
W14 . . . . .5A 72
(off Windsor Way)
Stuart Mill Ho. N1 . . . . .1F 7
(off Killick St.)
Stuart Rd. NW6 . . . . .2C 58
SE15 . . . . .2E 107
SW19 . . . . .3C 114
Stuart Twr. W9 . . . . .2E 59
(off Maida Va.)
Stubbs Dr. SE16 . . . . .1D 93
Stubbs Ho. E2 . . . . .2F 65
(off Bonner Rd.)
SW1 . . . . .5F 75
(off Erasmus St.)
Stubbs Point E13 . . . . .3C 68
Stucley Pl. NW1 . . . . .4D 47
Studdridge St. SW6 . . . . . .5C 86
Studd St. N1 . . . . .5D 49
Studholme Ct. NW3 . . . . . .1C 44
Studholme St. SE15 . . . . . .3D 93
Studio Pl. SW1 . . . . .4A 20
Studios, The SW4 . . . . . . .2E 103
(off Crescent La.)
W8 . . . . .2C 72
(off Edge St.)
Studland SE17 . . . . .1F 91
(off Portland St.)
Studland Ho. E14 . . . . .5A 66
(off Aston St.)
Studland Rd. SE26 . . . . . . .5F 121
Studland St. W6 . . . . .5D 71
Studley Cl. E5 . . . . .2A 52
Studley Ct. E14 . . . . .1F 81
(off Jamestown Way)
Studley Dr. IG4: IIf 1F 41
Studley Est. SW4 . . . . .4A 90
Studley Rd. E7 . . . . .3D 55
SW4 . . . . .4A 90
Stukeley Rd. E7 . . . . .4D 55
Stukeley St.
WC2 . . . . . . .2E 15 (5A 62)
Stumps Hill La.
BR3: Beck 5C 122
Stunell Ho. SE14 . . . . .2F 93
(off John Williams Cl.)
Sturdee Ho. E2 . . . . .1C 64
(off Horatio St.)

Sturdy Ho. *E3* 1A *66*
   (off Gernon Rd.)
Sturdy Rd. SE15 . . . . . .5D *93*
Sturgeon Rd. SE17 . . . . .1E *91*
Sturgess Av. NW4 . . . . .2D *29*
Sturge St.
  SE1 . . . . . .3F *25* (3E *77*)
Sturmer Way N7 . . . . . .2B *48*
Sturminster NW1 . . . . . .4F *47*
   (off Agar Gro.)
Sturminster Ho. *SW8* . . .3B *90*
   (off Dorset Rd.)
Sturry St. E14 . . . . .5D *67*
Sturt St. N1 . . . .1A *10* (1E *63*)
Stutfield St. E1 . . . . .5C *64*
Stuttle Ho. *E1* 3C *64*
   (off Buxton St.)
Styles Gdns. SW9 . . . .1D *105*
Styles Ho. SE1 . . . . .3D *25*
Stylus Ho. E1 . . . . .5E *65*
Success Ho. *SE1* 1B *92*
   (off Cooper's Rd.)
Sudbourne Rd.
  SW2 . . . . .3A *104*
Sudbrooke Rd.
  SW12 . . . . .4B *102*
Sudbury Ct. *SW8* 4F *89*
   (off Allen Edwards Dr.)
Sudbury Cres.
  BR1: Brom 5C *124*
Sudbury Ho. SW18 . . . .3D *101*
Sudeley St. N1 . . . . .1D *63*
Sudlow Rd. SW18 . . . . .3C *100*
Sudrey St.
  SE1 . . . . . . .4F *25* (3E *77*)
Suffield Ho. *SE17* 1D *91*
   (off Berryfield Rd.)
Suffolk Ct. E10 . . . . .2C *38*
Suffolk La.
  EC4 . . . . . . .4B *18* (1F *77*)
Suffolk Pl.
  SW1 . . . . .1C *22* (2F *75*)
Suffolk Rd. E13 . . . . .2C *68*
  N15 . . . . .1F *35*
  NW10 . . . . .4A *42*
  SW13 . . . . .3B *84*
Suffolk St. E7 . . . . .1C *54*
  SW1 . . . . . .5C *14* (1F *75*)
Sugar Bakers Ct.
  EC3 . . . . .3E *19*
Sugar Ho. *E1* 5C *64*
   (off Leman St.)
Sugar Ho. La. E15 . . . . . .1E *67*
Sugar Loaf Wlk. E2 . . . . .2E *65*
Sugar Quay EC3 . . . . . . .5E *19*
Sugar Quay Wlk.
  EC3 . . . . . .5E *19* (1A *78*)
Sugden Rd. SW11 . . . . .1C *102*
Sulby Ho. *SE4* 2A *108*
   (off Turnham Rd.)
Sulgrave Gdns. W6 . . . . .3E *71*
Sulgrave Rd. W6 . . . . . . .4E *71*
Sulina Rd. SW2 . . . . . . .5A *104*
Sulivan Ct. SW6 . . . . . . .5C *86*
Sulivan Ent. Cen.
  SW6 . . . . .1D *101*
Sulivan Rd. SW6 . . . . . .1C *100*
Sulkin Ho. *E2* 2F *65*
   (off Knottisford St.)

Sullivan Av. E16 . . . . . . .4F *69*
Sullivan Cl. SW11 . . . . .1A *102*
Sullivan Ct. N16 . . . . . . .2B *36*
  SW5 . . . . .5C *72*
   (off Earls Ct. Rd.)
Sullivan Ho. SE11 . . . . . .5B *76*
   (off Vauxhall St.)
  SW1 . . . . .2D *89*
   (off Churchill Gdns.)
Sullivan Rd. SE11 . . . . . .5C *76*
Sultan Ho. *SE1* 1C *92*
   (off St James's Rd.)
Sultan St. SE5 . . . . .3E *91*
Sumatra Rd. NW6 . . . . . .2C *44*
Sumburgh Rd.
  SW12 . . . . .4C *102*
Sumeria Ct. *SE16* 5E *79*
   (off Rotherhithe New Rd.)
Summercourt Rd. E1 . . . .5E *65*
Summerfield Av.
  NW6 . . . . .1A *58*
Summerfield St.
  SE12 . . . . .5B *110*
Summerhouse Rd.
  N16 . . . . .4A *36*
Summerley St.
  SW18 . . . . .2D *115*
Summersby Rd. N6 . . . . .1D *33*
Summerskill Cl.
  SE15 . . . . .1D *107*
Summers St.
  EC1 . . . . .4B *8* (3C *62*)
SUMMERSTOWN 3E *115*
Summerstown
  SW17 . . . . .3E *115*
Summit Av. NW9 . . . . . . .1A *28*
Summit Cl. NW2 . . . . . . .2A *44*
Summit Est. N16 . . . . . . .2C *36*
Sumner Av. SE15 . . . . . .4B *92*
Sumner Bldgs. SE1 . . . . .1F *25*
Sumner Ct. SW8 . . . . . . .3A *90*
Sumner Est. SE15 . . . . . .3B *92*
Sumner Ho. *E3* 4D *67*
   (off Watts Gro.)
Sumner Pl. SW7 . . . . . . .5F *73*
Sumner Pl. M. SW7 . . . . .5F *73*
Sumner Rd. SE15 . . . . . .2B *92*
Sumner St.
  SE1 . . . . . .1E *25* (2D *77*)
Sumpter Cl. NW3 . . . . . .3E *45*
Sunbeam Cres.
  W10 . . . . .3E *57*
Sunbeam Rd. NW10 . . . .3A *56*
Sunbury Av. SW14 . . . . .2A *98*
Sunbury Av. Pas.
  SW14 . . . . .2A *98*
Sunbury Ho. *E2* 2F *11*
   (off Swanfield St.)
  SE14 . . . . .2F *93*
   (off Myers La.)
Sunbury La. SW11 . . . . . .4F *87*
   (not continuous)
Sunbury Workshops
  E2 . . . . .2F *11*
   (off Swanfield St.)
Sun Ct. EC3 . . . . .3C *18*
Suncroft Pl. SE26 . . . . . .3E *121*
Sunderland Ct.
  SE22 . . . . .5C *106*

Sunderland Ho. *W2* 4C *58*
   (off Westbourne Pk. Rd.)
Sunderland Mt.
  SE23 . . . . .2F *121*
Sunderland Rd.
  SE23 . . . . .1F *121*
Sunderland Ter. W2 . . . .5D *59*
Sunderland Way E12 . . . .4F *41*
Sundew Av. W12 . . . . . . .1C *70*
Sundew Cl. W12 . . . . . . .1C *70*
Sundial Ct. *EC1* 5B *10*
   (off Chiswell St.)
Sundorne Rd. SE7 . . . . . .1E *97*
Sundra Wlk. E1 . . . . .3F *65*
Sundridge Ho. *E9* 4F *51*
   (off Church Cres.)
Sundridge Pk. Golf Course
  . . . . .5D *125*
Sunfields Pl. SE3 . . . . . . .3D *97*
Sunflower Ct. NW2 . . . . .4B *30*
SUN-IN-THE-SANDS . . .3D *97*
Sun La. SE3 . . . . .3D *97*
Sunlight Cl. SW19 . . . . . .5E *115*
Sunlight Sq. E2 . . . . .2D *65*
Sunningdale Av. W3 . . . . .1A *70*
Sunningdale Cl.
  SE16 . . . . .1D *93*
Sunningdale Gdns.
  W8 . . . . .4C *72*
   (off Stratford Rd.)
Sunninghill Rd. SE13 . . .5D *95*
Sunnydale Rd.
  SE12 . . . . .3D *111*
Sunnydene St. SE26 . . . .4A *122*
Sunnyhill Cl. E5 . . . . .1A *52*
Sunnyhill Rd. SW16 . . . .4A *118*
Sunnymead Rd.
  NW9 . . . . .2A *28*
  SW15 . . . . .3D *99*
Sunny M. NW1 . . . . 4C *46*
Sunnyside NW2 . . . . . . .5B *30*
  SE6 . . . . .5B *108*
   (off Blythe Hill)
  SW19 . . . . .5A *114*
Sunnyside Ho's.
  NW2 . . . . .5B *30*
   (off Sunnyside)
Sunnyside Pl.
  SW19 . . . . .5A *114*
Sunnyside Rd. E10 . . . . . .3C *38*
  N19 . . . . .2F *33*
Sun Pas. *SE16* 4C *78*
   (off Old Jamaica Rd.)
Sunray Av. SE24 . . . . . . .2F *105*
Sun Rd. W14 . . . . .1B *86*
Sunset Lodge *NW10* 4E *43*
   (off Hanover Rd.)
Sunset Rd. SE5 . . . . .2E *105*
  SW19 . . . . .5D *113*
Sun St. EC2 . . . . .5C *10* (4F *63*)
   (Finsbury Sq.)
  EC2 . . . . . .5D *11* (4A *64*)
   (Primrose St.)
Sun St. Pas.
  EC2 . . . . . .1D *19* (4A *64*)
Sun Wlk. E1 . . . . .1B *78*
Sunwell Cl. SE15 . . . . . . .4D *93*
Sun Wharf *SE8* 3D *95*
   (off Creekside)

Supreme Court
    Westminster 3A 76
Surma Cl. E1 . . . . .3D 65
Surrendale Pl. W9 . . . . .3C 58
Surrey Canal Rd.
    SE14 . . . . .2E 93
    SE15 . . . . .2E 93
Surrey County Cricket Club
    . . . . .2B 90
Surrey Docks Farm . . .3B 80
Surrey Docks Watersports Cen.
    . . . . .4A 80
Surrey Gdns. N4 . . . . . .1E 35
Surrey Gro. SE17 . . . . .1A 92
Surrey Ho. SE16 . . . . . .2F 79
    (off Rotherhithe St.)
Surrey La. SW11 . . . . . .4A 88
Surrey La. Est.
    SW11 . . . . .4A 88
Surrey M. SE27 . . . . . . .4A 120
Surrey Mt. SE23 . . . . . .1D 121
Surrey Quays Rd.
    SE16 . . . . .4E 79
Surrey Quays Shop. Cen.
    . . . . .4F 79
Surrey Rd. SE15 . . . . . .3F 107
Surrey Row
    SE1 . . . . . .3D 25 (3D 77)
Surrey Sq. SE17 . . . . . .1A 92
Surrey Steps
    WC2 . . . . .4A 16
    (off Surrey St.)
Surrey St. E13 . . . . .2D 69
    WC2 . . . . .4A 16 (1B 76)
Surrey Ter. SE17 . . . . . .1A 92
Surrey Water Rd.
    SE16 . . . . .2F 79
Surridge Ct. SW9 . . . . .5A 90
    (off Clapham Rd.)
Surr St. N7 . . . . .2A 48
Susan Constant Ct.
    E14 . . . . .1F 81
    (off Newport Av.)
Susan Lawrence Ho.
    E3 . . . . .1A 66
    (off Zealand St.)
Susannah St. E14 . . . . .5D 67
Susan Rd. SE3 . . . . .5D 97
Sussex Cl. N19 . . . . . . .4A 34
Sussex Ct. SE10 . . . . . .2E 95
    (off Roan St.)
    W2 . . . . .5F 59
    (off Spring St.)
Sussex Gdns. N4 . . . . . .1E 35
    N6 . . . . .1B 32
    W2 . . . . .1F 73
Sussex Ga. N6 . . . . .1B 32
Sussex Ho. NW1 . . . . . .1F 61
    (off Chalton St.)
Sussex Lodge W2 . . . . .5F 59
    (off Sussex Pl.)
Sussex Mans. SW7 . . . .5F 73
    (off Old Brompton Rd.)
    WC2 . . . . .4E 15
    (off Maiden La.)
Sussex M. SE6 . . . . .5C 108
Sussex M. E. W2 . . . . . .5F 59
    (off Clifton Pl.)
Sussex M. W. W2 . . . . . .1F 73

Sussex Pl.
    NW1 . . . . . .3A 4 (3B 60)
    W2 . . . . .5F 59
    W6 . . . . .1E 85
Sussex Sq. W2 . . . . .1F 73
Sussex St. E13 . . . . .2D 69
    SW1 . . . . .1D 89
Sussex Way N7 . . . . . . .4A 34
    N19 . . . . .3F 33
    (not continuous)
Sutcliffe Cl. NW11 . . . .1D 31
Sutcliffe Pk. Athletics Track
    . . . . .3E 111
Sutherland Av. W9 . . . . .3C 58
Sutherland Ct. N16 . . . . .5F 35
    W9 . . . . .3C 58
    (off Marylands Rd.)
Sutherland Gdns.
    SW14 . . . . .1A 98
Sutherland Gro.
    SW18 . . . . .4A 100
Sutherland Ho. W8 . . . .4D 73
Sutherland Pl. W2 . . . . .5C 58
Sutherland Rd. E3 . . . . .1B 66
    W4 . . . . .2A 84
Sutherland Row SW1 . . .1D 89
Sutherland Sq. SE17 . . .1E 91
Sutherland St. SW1 . . . .1D 89
Sutherland Wlk.
    SE17 . . . . .1E 91
Sutlej Rd. SE7 . . . . .3E 97
Sutterton St. N7 . . . . . . .3B 48
Sutton Ct. Rd. E13 . . . . .2E 69
Sutton Est. EC1 . . . . . . .2C 10
    W10 . . . . .4E 57
Sutton Estate, The
    N1 . . . . .4D 49
    SW3 . . . . .1A 88
Sutton La. EC1 . . . . .4E 9
    (off Gt. Sutton St.)
Sutton Pl. E9 . . . . .2E 51
Sutton Rd. E13 . . . . .3B 68
Sutton Row
    W1 . . . . . .2C 14 (5F 61)
Sutton Sq. E9 . . . . .2E 51
Sutton St. E1 . . . . .1E 79
Sutton's Way EC1 . . . . .4A 10
Sutton Wlk.
    SE1 . . . . . .2A 24 (2B 76)
Sutton Way W10 . . . . . .3E 57
SW1 Gallery 5F 21 (4E 75)
Swaby Rd. SW18 . . . . . .1E 115
Swaffield Rd. SW18 . . . .5D 101
Swains La. N6 . . . . .3C 32
Swainson Rd. W3 . . . . . .3B 70
Swain St. NW8 . . . . .3A 60
Swallands Rd. SE6 . . . . .3C 122
    (not continuous)
Swallow Cl. SE14 . . . . . .4F 93
Swallow Ct. SE1 . . . . . .4A 26
    (off Swan St.)
    SE12 . . . . .5C 110
    W9 . . . . .4C 58
    (off Admiral Wlk.)
Swallow Dr. NW10 . . . . .3A 42
Swallowfield NW1 . . . . .2E 5
    (off Munster Sq.)
Swallowfield Rd.
    SE7 . . . . .1D 97

Swallow Gdns.
    SW16 . . . . .5F 117
Swallow Ho. NW8 . . . . .1A 60
    (off Allitsen Rd.)
Swallow Pas. W1 . . . . . .3E 13
    (off Swallow Pl.)
Swallow Pl. E14 . . . . . . .5B 66
    (off Newell St.)
    W1 . . . . . . .3E 13 (5D 61)
Swallow St.
    W1 . . . . . . .5A 14 (1E 75)
Swanage Ct. N1 . . . . . . .4A 50
    (off Hertford Rd.)
Swanage Ho. SW8 . . . . .3B 90
    (off Dorset Rd.)
Swanage Rd. SW18 . . . .4E 101
Swan App. E6 . . . . .4F 69
Swanbourne SE17 . . . . .5E 77
    (off Wansey St.)
Swanbourne Ho.
    NW8 . . . . .3A 60
    (off Capland St.)
Swan Centre, The
    SW17 . . . . .3D 115
Swan Ct. E1 . . . . .1C 78
    (off Star Pl.)
    E14 . . . . .5B 66
    (off Agnes St.)
    SW3 . . . . .1A 88
    SW6 . . . . .3C 86
    (off Fulham Rd.)
Swandon Way
    SW18 . . . . .2D 101
Swanfield St.
    E2 . . . . . . .2F 11 (2B 64)
Swan Ho. E15 . . . . .4F 53
    (off Broadway)
    N1 . . . . .4F 49
    (off Oakley Rd.)
Swan La.
    EC4 . . . . . .5C 18 (1F 77)
Swanley Ho. SE17 . . . . .1A 92
    (off Kinglake Est.)
Swan Mead
    SE1 . . . . . .5D 27 (4A 78)
Swan M. SW6 . . . . .4B 86
    SW9 . . . . .5B 90
Swanne Ho. SE10 . . . . . .3E 95
    (off Gloucester Cir.)
Swan Pas. E1 . . . . .1B 78
    (off Cartwright St.)
Swan Pl. SW13 . . . . .5B 84
Swan Rd. SE16 . . . . .3E 79
    SE18 . . . . .4F 83
Swanscombe Ho.
    W11 . . . . .2F 71
    (off St Ann's Rd.)
Swanscombe Rd. W4 . . .1A 84
    W11 . . . . .2F 71
Swan St. SE1 . . . . . .5A 26 (4E 77)
Swanton Gdns.
    SW19 . . . . .1F 113
Swan Wlk. SW3 . . . . . . .2B 88
Swanwick Cl. SW15 . . . .5B 98
Swan Yd. N1 . . . . .3D 49
Swathling Ho. SW15 . . .4B 98
    (off Tunworth Cres.)
Swaton Rd. E3 . . . . .3C 66
Swedeland Ct. E1 . . . . . .1E 19

Swedenborg Gdns.
E1 . . . . .1D 79
Sweden Ga. SE16 . . . . . .4A 80
Swedish Quays
SE16 . . . . .4A 80
(not continuous)
Sweeney Cres.
SE1 . . . . .4F 27 (3B 78)
Swell Ct. E17 . . . . .1C 38
Swete St. E13 . . . . .1C 68
Sweyn Pl. SE3 . . . . .5C 96
Swift Ho. E3 . . . . .5B 52
(off Old Ford Rd.)
Swift Lodge W9 . . . . .4C 58
(off Admiral Wlk.)
Swiftsden Way
BR1: Brom 5A 124
Swift St. SW6 . . . . .4B 86
Swinbrook Rd. W10 . . . . . .4A 58
Swinburne St. 2F 105
(off Basingdon Way)
Swinburne Ho. E2 . . . . . . .2E 65
(off Roman Rd.)
Swinburne Rd. SW15 . . .2C 98
Swindon St. W12 . . . . . . .2D 71
Swinford Gdns.
SW9 . . . . .1D 105
Swingfield Ho. E9 . . . . . .5E 51
(off Templecombe Rd.)
Swinley Ho. NW1 . . . . .1E 5
(off Redhill St.)
Swinnerton St. E9 . . . . .2A 52
Swinton Pl.
WC1 . . . . . . .1F 7 (2B 62)
Swinton St.
WC1 . . . . . . .1F 7 (2B 62)
SWISS COTTAGE 4F 45
Swiss Cottage Sports Cen.
. . . . .4F 45
Swiss Ct. WC2 . . . . .5C 14
Swiss Ter. NW6 . . . . .4F 45
Switch Ho. E14 . . . . .1F 81
Sybil M. N4 . . . . .1D 35
Sybil Phoenix Cl.
SE8 . . . . .1F 93
Sybil Thorndike Casson Ho.
SW5 . . . . .1C 86
(off Kramer M.)
Sybourn St. E17 . . . . . .2B 38
Sycamore Av. E3 . . . . . . .5B 52
Sycamore Cl. E16 . . . . . .3A 68
SE9 . . . . .2F 125
W3 . . . . .2A 70
Sycamore Ct. E7 . . . . . . .3C 54
NW6 . . . . .5C 44
(off Bransdale Cl.)
SE1 . . . . .4D 27
(off Royal Oak Yd.)
Sycamore Gdns. W6 . . .3D 71
Sycamore Gro. SE6 . . .4E 109
Sycamore Ho. SE16 . . .3F 79
(off Woodland Cres.)
W6 . . . . .3D 71
Sycamore Lodge W8 . . .4D 73
(off Stone Hall Pl.)
Sycamore M. SW4 . . . . .1E 103
Sycamore Path E17 . . . .1D 39
(off Poplars Rd.)
Sycamore Rd. SW19 . . .5E 113

Sycamore St.
EC1 . . . . .4F 9 (3E 63)
Sycamore Wlk. W10 . . .3A 58
Sydcote SE21 . . . . .1E 119
SYDENHAM 4E 121
Sydenham Av. SE26 . . .5D 121
Sydenham Cotts.
SE12 . . . . .2E 125
Sydenham Hill
SE23 . . . . .1D 121
SE26 . . . . .4B 120
Sydenham Hill Wood &
Cox's Walk Nature Reserve
. . . . .2C 120
Sydenham Pk. SE26 . . . .3E 121
Sydenham Pk. Mans.
SE26 . . . . .3E 121
(off Sydenham Pk.)
Sydenham Pk. Rd.
SE26 . . . . .3E 121
Sydenham Pl. SE27 . . .3D 119
Sydenham Ri. SE23 . . .2D 121
Sydenham Rd. SE26 . . .5F 121
Sydmons Ct. SE23 . . . .5E 107
Sydner M. N16 . . . . .1B 50
Sydner Rd. N16 . . . . .1B 50
Sydney Cl. SW3 . . . . .5F 73
Sydney Gro. NW4 . . . . . . .1E 29
Sydney M. SW3 . . . . .5F 73
Sydney Pl. SW7 . . . . .5F 73
Sydney Rd. E11 . . . . .1D 41
Sydney St. SW3 . . . . .1A 88
Sylvan Ct. NW6 . . . . .5D 45
(off Abbey Rd.)
Sylvan Gro. NW2 . . . . . . .1F 43
SE15 . . . . .2D 93
Sylvan Rd. E7 . . . . .3D 55
E17 . . . . .1C 38
Sylvan Ter. SE15 . . . . . .2D 93
(off Sylvan Gro.)
Sylvester Path E8 . . . . . .3D 51
Sylvester Rd. E8 . . . . . . .3D 51
E17 . . . . .2B 38
Sylvia Ct. N1 . . . . .1F 63
(off Wenlock St.)
Symes M. NW1 . . . . .1E 61
Symington Ho. SE1 . . . .5B 26
(off Deverell St.)
Symington M. E9 . . . . . . .2F 51
Symister M. N1 . . . . .2D 11
Symons Cl. SE15 . . . . . . .5E 93
Symons St. SW3 . . . . . . .5B 74
Symphony M. W10 . . . . .2A 58
Syon Ct. E11 . . . . .1D 41
Syon Lodge SE12 . . . .5C 110
Syringa Ho. SE4 . . . . . .1B 108

T

Tabard Ct. E14 . . . . .5E 67
(off Lodore St.)
Tabard Gdn. Est.
SE1 . . . . .4B 26 (4F 77)
Tabard Ho. SE1 . . . . .5C 26
(off Manciple St.)
Tabard St.
SE1 . . . . .3A 26 (3F 77)
Tabard Theatre 5A 70

Tabernacle, The 5B 58
(off Powis Sq.)
Tabernacle Av. E13 . . . .3C 68
Tabernacle St.
EC2 . . . . .4C 10 (3F 63)
Tableer Av. SW4 . . . . . . .3E 103
Tabley Rd. N7 . . . . .1A 48
Tabor Rd. W6 . . . . .4D 71
Tachbrook Est. SW1 . . .1F 89
Tachbrook M. SW1 . . . . .5E 75
Tachbrook St. SW1 . . . . .5E 75
Tack M. SE4 . . . . .1C 108
Tadema Ho. NW8 . . . . . . .3F 59
(off Penfold St.)
Tadema Rd. SW10 . . . . .3E 87
Tadmor St. W12 . . . . .2F 71
Tadworth Ho. SE1 . . . . .4D 25
Tadworth Rd. NW2 . . . . .4C 28
Taeping St. E14 . . . . .5D 81
Taffrail Ho. E14 . . . . .1D 95
(off Burrells Wharf Sq.)
Taft Way E3 . . . . .2D 67
Tagwright Ho. N1 . . . . . .1B 10
(off Westland Pl.)
Tailor Ho. WC1 . . . . .4E 7
(off Colonnade)
Tailworth St. E1 . . . . .4C 64
(off Chicksand St.)
Tait Ct. E3 . . . . .5A 52
(off St Stephen's Rd.)
SW8 . . . . .4A 90
(off Lansdowne Grn.)
Tait Ho. SE1 . . . . .2C 24
(off Greet St.)
Tait St. E1 . . . . .5D 65
(off Brick La.)
Taj Apartments E1 . . . . .4B 64
Talacre Community
Sports Cen. 3C 46
Talacre Rd. NW5 . . . . . . .3C 46
Talbot Ct. EC3 . . . . .4C 18
Talbot Cres. NW4 . . . . . .1C 28
Talbot Gro. Ho. W11 . . .5A 58
(off Lancaster Rd.)
Talbot Ho. E14 . . . . .5D 67
(off Girauld St.)
N7 . . . . .5C 34
Talbot Pl. SE3 . . . . .5A 96
Talbot Rd. E7 . . . . .1C 54
N6 . . . . .1C 32
SE22 . . . . .2A 106
W2 . . . . .5B 58
W11 . . . . .5B 58
(not continuous)
Talbot Sq. W2 . . . . .5F 59
Talbot Wlk. NW10 . . . . . .3A 42
W11 . . . . .5A 58
(off St Mark's Rd.)
Talbot Yd.
SE1 . . . . . . .2B 26 (2F 77)
Talcott Path SW2 . . . . .1C 118
Talfourd Pl. SE15 . . . . . .4B 92
Talfourd Rd. SE15 . . . . .4B 92
Talgarth Mans.
W14 . . . . .1A 86
(off Talgarth Rd.)
Talgarth Rd. W6 . . . . . . .1F 85
W14 . . . . .1F 85

Talia Ho. *E14* 4E **81**
 (off Manchester Rd.)
Talina Cen. SW6 . . . . . .4E **87**
Talisman Sq. SE26 . . . .4C **120**
Tallack Rd. E10 . . . . .3B **38**
Talleyrand Ho. SE5 . . . . .5E **91**
 (off Lilford Rd.)
Tallis Cl. E16 . . . . .5D **69**
Tallis Gro. SE7 . . . . .2D **97**
Tallis St.
 EC4 . . . . .4C **16** (1C **76**)
Tallis Vw. NW10 . . . . . . .3A **42**
Talmage Cl. SE23 . . . . .5E **107**
Talma Rd. SW2 . . . . . . .2C **104**
Talwin St. E3 . . . . .2D **67**
Tamar Cl. E3 . . . . .5B **52**
Tamar Ho. *E14* 3E **81**
 (off Plevna St.)
SE11 . . . . .1C **90**
 (off Kennington La.)
Tamarind Ct. SE1 . . . . . .3F **27**
W8 . . . . .4D **73**
 (off Stone Hall Gdns.)
Tamarind Ho. SE15 . . . . .3C **92**
 (off Reddins Rd.)
Tamarind Yd. E1 . . . . . .2C **78**
 (off Kennet St.)
Tamarisk Sq. W12 . . . . .1B **70**
Tamar St. SE7 . . . . .4F **83**
Tamworth *N7* 3A **48**
 (off Market Est.)
Tamworth St. SW6 . . . . .2C **86**
Tancred Rd. N4 . . . . .1D **35**
Tanfield Av. NW2 . . . . . .1B **42**
Tangerine Ho. SE1 . . . . .4C **26**
 (off Long La.)
Tangley Gro. SW15 . . . . .4B **98**
Tangmere WC1 . . . . .2F **7**
 (off Sidmouth St.)
Tanhouse Fld. NW5 . . . . .2F **47**
 (off Torriano Av.)
Tanhurst Ho. SW2 . . . . .5B **104**
 (off Redlands Way)
Tankerton Ho's. WC1 . . . .2E **7**
 (off Tankerton St.)
Tankerton St.
 WC1 . . . . . . .2E **7** (2A **62**)
Tankridge Rd. NW2 . . . . .4D **29**
Tanner Ho. SE1 . . . . .4E **27**
 (off Tanner St.)
Tanneries, The *E1* 3E **65**
 (off Cephas Av.)
Tanner Point *E13* 5B **54**
 (off Pelly Rd.)
Tanner's Hill SE8 . . . . . . .4B **94**
Tanners M. *SE8* 4B **94**
 (off Tanner's Hill)
Tanner St.
 SE1 . . . . . .4E **27** (3A **78**)
Tanners Yd. *E2* 1D **65**
 (off Treadway St.)
Tannery, The *SE1* 3A **78**
 (off Black Swan Yd.)
Tannery Ho. E1 . . . . .4C **64**
 (off Deal St.)
Tannington Ter. N5 . . . . . .5D **35**
Tannoy Sq. SE27 . . . . . .4F **119**
Tannsfeld Rd. SE26 . . . .5F **121**
Tansley Cl. N7 . . . . .2F **47**

Tanswell St.
 SE1 . . . . . .4B **24** (3C **76**)
Tantallon Rd. SW12 . . . .1C **116**
Tant Av. E16 . . . . .5B **68**
Tanza Rd. NW3 . . . . .1B **46**
Tapestry Bldg. *EC2* 1E **19**
 (off New St.)
Tapley Ho. SE1 . . . . .3C **78**
 (off Wolseley St.)
Taplow NW3 . . . . .4F **45**
SE17 . . . . .1F **91**
 (off Thurlow St.)
Taplow Ho. *E2* 2F **11**
 (off Palissy St.)
Taplow St.
 N1 . . . . . . .1A **10** (1E **63**)
Tappesfield Rd.
 SE15 . . . . .1E **107**
Tapp St. E1 . . . . .3D **65**
Tara Arts Cen. 1E **115**
Tara Ho. E14 . . . . .5C **80**
 (off Deptford Ferry Rd.)
Tara M. N8 . . . . .1A **34**
Taransay Wlk. N1 . . . . . .3F **49**
Tarbert Rd. SE22 . . . . . .3A **106**
Tarbert Wlk. E1 . . . . .1E **79**
Tariff Cres. SE8 . . . . .5B **80**
Tarleton Gdns.
 SE23 . . . . .2D **121**
Tarling Rd. E16 . . . . .5B **68**
Tarling St. E1 . . . . .5D **65**
Tarling St. Est. E1 . . . . . .5E **65**
Tarnbrook Ct. SW1 . . . . .5C **74**
 (off Holbein Pl.)
Tarns, The NW1 . . . . .1F **5**
 (off Varndell St.)
Tarn St. SE1 . . . . .5F **77**
Tarplett Ho. *SE14* 2F **93**
 (off John Williams Cl.)
Tarquin Ho. SE26 . . . . .4C **120**
 (off High Level Dr.)
Tarragon Cl. SE14 . . . . . .3A **94**
Tarragon Gro. SE26 . . . .5F **121**
Tarrant Ho. *E2* 2E **65**
 (off Roman Rd.)
W14 . . . . .4A **72**
 (off Russell Rd.)
Tarrant Pl. W1 . . . . .4B **60**
Tarrington Cl. SW16 . . . .3F **117**
Tartan Ho. E14 . . . . .5E **67**
 (off Dee St.)
Tarver Rd. SE17 . . . . . . .1D **91**
Tarves Way SE10 . . . . . .3D **95**
 (Lit. Cottage Pl.)
SE10 . . . . .3D **95**
 (Norman Rd.)
Tasker Ho. E14 . . . . .4B **66**
 (off Wallwood St.)
Tasker Lodge W8 . . . . . .3C **72**
 (off Campden Hill)
Tasker Rd. NW3 . . . . . . .2B **46**
Tasman Ct. E14 . . . . .5D **81**
 (off Westferry Rd.)
Tasman Ho. E1 . . . . .2D **79**
 (off Clegg St.)
Tasman Rd. SW9 . . . . . .1A **104**
Tasman Wlk. E16 . . . . . . .5F **69**
Tasso Rd. W6 . . . . .2A **86**

Tasso Yd. W6 . . . . .2A **86**
 (off Tasso Rd.)
Tatchbury Ho. SW15 . . . .4B **98**
 (off Tunworth Cres.)
Tate Apartments *E1* 5D **65**
 (off Sly St.)
Tate Britain 5A **76**
Tate Ho. E2 . . . . .1F **65**
 (off Mace St.)
Tate Modern 1E **25** (2D **77**)
Tatham Pl. NW8 . . . . .1F **59**
Tatnell Rd. SE23 . . . . . . .4A **108**
Tatsfield Ho. SE1 . . . . . . .5C **26**
 (off Pardoner St.)
Tatton Cres. N16 . . . . . . .2B **36**
Tatum St. SE17 . . . . .5F **77**
Tauheed Cl. N4 . . . . .4E **35**
Taunton Ho. W2 . . . . .5E **59**
 (off Hallfield Est.)
Taunton M. NW1 . . . . . . .3B **60**
Taunton Pl. NW1 . . . . . . .3B **60**
Taunton Rd. SE12 . . . . . .3A **110**
Tavern Ct. SE1 . . . . .4E **77**
 (off New Kent Rd.)
Taverners Cl. W11 . . . . . .2A **72**
Taverners Ct. E3 . . . . . . .2A **66**
 (off Grove Rd.)
Taverner Sq. N5 . . . . .1E **49**
Tavern La. SW9 . . . . .5C **90**
Tavern Quay SE16 . . . . . .5A **80**
Tavistock Cl. N16 . . . . . . .2A **50**
Tavistock Ct. WC1 . . . . . .3C **6**
 (off Tavistock Sq.)
WC2 . . . . .4E **15**
 (off Tavistock St.)
Tavistock Cres. W11 . . . .4B **58**
 (not continuous)
Tavistock Ho.
 WC1 . . . . . . .3C **6** (3F **61**)
Tavistock M. N19 . . . . . . .5A **34**
 (off Tavistock Ter.)
W11 . . . . .5B **58**
Tavistock Pl.
 WC1 . . . . . . .3D **7** (3A **62**)
Tavistock Rd. E7 . . . . . . .1B **54**
E15 . . . . .3B **54**
N4 . . . . .1F **35**
NW10 . . . . .1B **56**
W11 . . . . .5B **58**
 (not continuous)
Tavistock Sq.
 WC1 . . . . . . .3C **6** (3F **61**)
Tavistock St.
 WC2 . . . . . .4E **15** (1A **76**)
Tavistock Ter. N19 . . . . . .5F **33**
Tavistock Twr. SE16 . . . . .4A **80**
Taviton St.
 WC1 . . . . . . .3B **6** (3F **61**)
Tavy Cl. SE11 . . . . .1C **90**
 (off White Hart St.)
Tawny Way SE16 . . . . . . .5F **79**
Taybridge Rd.
 SW11 . . . . .1C **102**
Tay Bldgs. SE1 . . . . .5D **27**
Tayburn Cl. E14 . . . . .5E **67**
Tay Ct. E2 . . . . .2F **65**
 (off Meath Cres.)
SE1 . . . . .5D **27**
 (off Decima St.)

Tay Ho. *E3* 1B **66**
(off St Stephen's Rd.)
Tayler Ct. NW8 . . . . .5F **45**
Taylor Cl. SE8 . . . . .2B **94**
Taylor Ho. *E14* 1C **80**
(off Storehouse M.)
Taylor Pl. E3 . . . . .1D **67**
Taylors Grn. W3 . . . . .5A **56**
Taylor's La. SE26 . . . . . .4D **121**
Taylors Yd. *E1* 3B **64**
(off Brick La.)
Taymount Grange
SE23 . . . . .2E **121**
Taymount Ri. SE23 . . . .2E **121**
Tayport Cl. N1 . . . . .4A **48**
Tayside Ct. SE5 . . . . . . .2F **105**
Teak Cl. SE16 . . . . .2A **80**
Tealby Ct. *N7* 2B **48**
(off George's Rd.)
Teal Cl. E16 . . . . .4F **69**
Teal Cl. *E1* 1C **78**
(off Star Pl.)
SE8 . . . . .2B **94**
(off Taylor Cl.)
Teale St. E2 . . . . .1C **64**
Teal St. SE10 . . . . .4B **82**
Teasel Way E15 . . . . . . .2A **68**
Tea Trade Wharf SE1 . .3B **78**
(off Shad Thames)
Ted Roberts Ho. *E2* 1D **65**
(off Parmiter St.)
Tedworth Gdns. SW3 . .1B **88**
Tedworth Sq. SW3 . . . .1B **88**
Tee, The W3 . . . . .5A **56**
Teesdale Cl. E2 . . . . .1C **64**
Teesdale Rd. E11 . . . . . .1B **40**
Teesdale St. E2 . . . . .1D **65**
Teesdale Yd. *E2* 1D **65**
(off Teesdale St.)
Teignmouth Cl.
SW4 . . . . .2F **103**
Teignmouth Rd. NW2 . . .2F **43**
Telegraph Hill NW3 . . . .5D **31**
Telegraph Pas. *SE1* . . .2C **76**
(off New Pk. Rd.)
SW2 . . . . .5A **104**
(off New Pk. Rd.)
Telegraph Pl. E14 . . . . . .5D **81**
Telegraph Rd. SW15 . . . .5D **99**
Telegraph St.
EC2 . . . . .2B **18** (5F **63**)
Telemann Sq. SE13 . . . .2D **111**
Telephone Pl. SW6 . . . . .2B **86**
Telfer Ho. EC1 . . . . .2E **9**
Telferscot Rd.
SW12 . . . . .1F **117**
Telford Av. SW2 . . . . . . .1F **117**
Telford Cl. E17 . . . . .2A **38**
Telford Ho. *SE1* 5F **25**
(off Tiverton St.)
W10 . . . . .4A **58**
(off Portobello Rd.)
Telford Rd. NW9 . . . . . .1C **28**
W10 . . . . .4A **58**
Telfords Yd. E1 . . . . .1C **78**
Telford Ter. SW1 . . . . . . .2E **89**
Telford Way W3 . . . . .4A **56**
Tell Gro. SE22 . . . . .2B **106**
Tellson Av. SE18 . . . . . . .4F **97**

Temair Ho. *SE10* 3D **95**
(off Tarves Way)
Temeraire St. SE16 . . . . .3E **79**
Tempelhof Av. NW2 . . . . .2E **29**
NW4 . . . . .2E **29**
Temperley Rd.
SW12 . . . . .5C **102**
Templar Ct. *NW8* 2F **59**
(off St John's Wood Rd.)
Templar Ho. NW2 . . . . . .3B **44**
Templars Av.
NW11 . . . . .1B **30**
Templar St. SE5 . . . . . . .5D **91**
Temple Av.
EC4 . . . . .4C **16** (1C **76**)
Temple Bar 3B **16**
Temple Bar Gate 3E **17**
(off Paternoster Sq.)
Temple Chambers
EC4 . . . . .4C **16**
Temple Cl. E11 . . . . .2A **40**
Templecombe Rd. E9 . . .5E **51**
Temple Cl. *E1* 4F **65**
(off Rectory Sq.)
SW8 . . . . .3A **90**
(off Thorncroft St.)
Temple Dwellings *E2* . .1D **65**
(off Temple St.)

TEMPLE FORTUNE 1B **30**

Temple Fortune Hill
NW11 . . . . .1C **30**
Temple Fortune La.
NW11 . . . . .1B **30**
Temple Fortune Pde.
NW11 . . . . .1B **30**
Temple Gdns. EC4 . . . . .4B **16**
NW11 . . . . .1C **30**
Temple Gro. NW11 . . . . .1C **30**
Temple La.
EC4 . . . . .3C **16** (5C **62**)
Templemead Cl. W3 . . . .5A **56**
Templemead Ho. E9 . . . .1A **52**

TEMPLE MILLS 1D **53**

Temple Mills La.
E10 . . . . .1D **53**
E20 . . . . .2E **53**
Temple of Mithras (remains)
. . . . .3B **18**
(off Queen Victoria St.)
Temple Pl.
WC2 . . . . .4A **16** (1B **76**)
Temple Rd. E6 . . . . .5F **55**
NW2 . . . . .1E **43**
Temple St. E2 . . . . .1D **65**
Templeton Cl. N15 . . . . . .1F **35**
N16 . . . . .2A **50**
Templeton Pl. SW5 . . . . .5C **72**
Templeton Rd. N15 . . . . .1F **35**
Temple West M.
SE11 . . . . . . .5D **25** (4D **77**)
Templewood Av.
NW3 . . . . .5D **31**
Templewood Gdns.
NW3 . . . . .5D **31**
Templewood Point
NW2 . . . . .4B **30**
(off Granville Rd.)
Temple Yd. *E2* 1D **65**
(off Temple St.)

Tempus Wharf SE16 . . . .3C **78**
(off Bermondsey Wall W.)
Tenbury Cl. E7 . . . . .2F **55**
Tenbury Ct. SW2 . . . . . .1F **117**
Tenby Ho. *W2* 5E **59**
(off Hallfield Est.)
Tenby Mans. *W1* 5C **4**
(off Nottingham St.)
Tench St. E1 . . . . .2D **79**
Tenda Rd. SE16 . . . . . . .5D **79**
Tenham Av. SW2 . . . . . .1F **117**
Tenison Ct.
W1 . . . . .4F **13** (1E **75**)
Tenison Way SE1 . . . . . .2B **24**
Tenniel Cl. W2 . . . . .1E **73**
Tennis St.
SE1 . . . . .3B **26** (3F **77**)
Tennyson Av. E11 . . . . . .2C **40**
E12 . . . . .4F **55**
Tennyson Ct. *NW1* 4A **4**
(off Dorset Sq.)
SW6 . . . . .4E **87**
(off Imperial Rd.)
Tennyson Ho. *SE17* 1E **91**
(off Browning St.)
Tennyson Mans. *SW3* . .2A **88**
(off Lordship Pl.)
W14 . . . . .2B **86**
(off Queen's Club Gdns.)
Tennyson Rd. E10 . . . . . .3D **39**
E15 . . . . .4A **54**
E17 . . . . .1B **38**
NW6 . . . . .5B **44**
SW19 . . . . .5E **115**
Tennyson St. SW8 . . . . . .5D **89**
Tenterden Ho. *SE17* 1A **92**
(off Surrey Gro.)
Tenterden St.
W1 . . . . .3E **13** (5D **61**)
Tenter Ground
E1 . . . . .1F **19** (4B **64**)
Tenter Pas. *E1* 5B **64**
(off Nth. Tenter St.)
Tent St. E1 . . . . .3D **65**
Tequila Wharf E14 . . . . . .5A **66**
Terborch Way SE22 . . . .3A **106**
Teredo St. SE16 . . . . . . .4F **79**
Terence McMillan Stadium
. . . . .3E **69**
Terence Messenger Twr.
E10 . . . . .4D **39**
(off Alpine Rd.)
Terling Cl. E11 . . . . .5B **40**
Terling Ho. *W10* 4E **57**
(off Sutton Way)
Terling Wlk. *N1* 5E **49**
(off Popham St.)
Terminus Pl. SW1 . . . . . .4D **75**
Terrace, The *E2* 2E **65**
(off Old Ford Rd.)
EC4 . . . . .3C **16**
NW6 . . . . .5C **44**
SE8 . . . . .5B **80**
(off Longshore)
SE23 . . . . .5A **108**
SW13 . . . . .5A **84**
Terrace Apartments
N5 . . . . .2C **48**
Terrace Gdns. SW13 . . . .5B **84**

Terrace Rd. E9 . . . . . . .4E 51
  E13 . . . . .1C 68
Terraces, The E2 . . . . .1C 64
    (off Garner St.)
  NW8 . . . . .1F 59
    (off Queen's Ter.)
Terrace Wlk. SW11 . . . .3B 88
Terrapin Rd.
  SW17 . . . . .3D 117
Terretts Pl. N1 . . . . . . .4D 49
    (off Upper St.)
Terrick St. W12 . . . . . . .5D 57
Territorial Ho. SE11 . . .5C 76
    (off Reedworth St.)
Tesla Ct. W3 . . . . .3A 70
Tessa Sanderson Pl.
  SW8 . . . . .1D 103
    (off Daley Thompson Way)
Testerton Rd. W11 . . . .1F 71
    (off Hurstway Rd.)
Testerton Wlk. W11 . . . .1F 71
Tetbury Pl. N1 . . . . .5D 49
Tetcott Rd. SW10 . . . . .3E 87
    (not continuous)
Tevatree Ho. SE1 . . . . .1C 92
    (off Old Kent Rd.)
Teversham La. SW8 . . .4A 90
Teviot Est. E14 . . . . . . .4D 67
Teviot St. E14 . . . . .4E 67
Tewkesbury Av.
  SE23 . . . . .1D 121
Tewkesbury Cl. N15 . . .1F 35
Tewkesbury Rd. N15 . . .1F 35
    (off Southgate Rd.)
Texryte Ho. N1 . . . . . . .5F 49
Thackeray Ct. NW6 . . . .4E 45
    (off Fairfax Rd.)
  SW3 . . . . .1B 88
    (off Elystan Pl.)
  W14 . . . . .4A 72
    (off Blythe Rd.)
Thackeray Ho. WC1 . . . .3D 7
Thackeray M. E8 . . . . . .3C 50
Thackeray Rd. E6 . . . . .1F 69
  SW8 . . . . .5D 89
Thackeray St. W8 . . . . .4D 73
Thackery Ct. EC1 . . . . . .5D 9
    (off Turnmill St.)
Thakeham Cl. SE26 . . .4D 121
Thalia Cl. SE10 . . . . . . .2F 95
Thalia Ct. E8 . . . . .4B 50
    (off Albion Dr.)
Thame Rd. SE16 . . . . . .3F 79
Thames Av. SW10 . . . . .4E 87
Thames Barrier 3F 83
Thames Barrier Ind. Area
  SE18 . . . . .4F 83
    (off Faraday Way)
Thames Barrier Info. Cen.
  . . . . .4F 83
Thames Barrier Pk. 3E 83
Thamesbrook SW3 . . . .1A 88
    (off Dovehouse St.)
Thames Circ. E14 . . . . .5C 80
Thames Ct. NW6 . . . . . .1B 58
    (off Albert Rd.)
  SE15 . . . . .3B 92
    (off Daniel Gdns.)
Thames Cres. W4 . . . . .3A 84

Thames Exchange Bldg.
  EC4 . . . . .5A 18
Thames Hgts. SE1 . . . . .3F 27
    (off Gainsford St.)
Thames Ho. EC4 . . . . . .4A 18
    (off Queen St. Pl.)
  SW1 . . . . .5A 76
    (off Millbank)
Thameside Ind. Est.
  E16 . . . . .3F 83
Thames Path SE10 . . . .2A 82
Thames Pl. SW15 . . . . .1F 99
Thames Point SW6 . . . .5E 87
Thames Quay E14 . . . . .3D 81
  SW10 . . . . .4E 87
    (off Chelsea Harbour)
Thames Reach W6 . . . .2E 85
    (off Rainville Rd.)
Thames Rd. E16 . . . . . .2F 83
  E16 . . . . .3F 83
Thames Rd. Ind. Est.
  E16 . . . . .3F 83
Thames St. SE10 . . . . . .2D 95
Thames Tunnel Mills
  SE16 . . . . .3E 79
Thames Wlk. SW11 . . . .3A 88
Thames Wharf Studios
  W6 . . . . .2E 85
    (off Rainville Rd.)
Thanet Ho. WC1 . . . . . . .2D 7
    (off Thanet St.)
Thanet Lodge NW2 . . . .3A 44
    (off Mapesbury Rd.)
Thanet St.
  WC1 . . . . .2D 7 (2A 62)
Thanet Wharf SE8 . . . . .2D 95
    (off Copperas St.)
Thane Vs. N7 . . . . .5B 34
Thane Works N7 . . . . . .5B 34
Thant Cl. E10 . . . . .5D 39
Thavie's Inn
  EC4 . . . . .2C 16 (5C 62)
Thaxted Ct. N1 . . . . . . .1C 10
    (off Murray Gro.)
Thaxted Ho. SE16 . . . . .5E 79
    (off Abbeyfield Est.)
Thaxton Rd. W14 . . . . . .2B 86
Thayer St.
  W1 . . . . .1C 12 (5C 60)
The . . . .
  Names prefixed with 'The'
  for example 'The Alders'
  are indexed under the
  main name such as
  'Alders, The'
Theatre Bldg. E3 . . . . . .2C 66
    (off Paton Cl.)
Theatre-Rites 2D 115
Theatre Royal
  Stratford 4F 53
Theatre Sq. E15 . . . . . . .3F 53
Theatre St. SW11 . . . . .1B 102
Theatre Vw. Apartments
  SE1 . . . . .3C 24
    (off Short St.)
Theatro Technis 5E 47
    (off Crowndale Rd.)
Theatro Twr. SE8 . . . . . .2C 94
Theberton St. N1 . . . . . .5C 48
Theed St. SE1 . . .2C 24 (2C 76)

Thelbridge Ho. E3 . . . . .2D 67
    (off Bruce Rd.)
Thelma Gdns. SE3 . . . . .4F 97
Theobald Rd. E17 . . . . . .2B 38
Theobalds Ct. N4 . . . . . .5E 35
Theobald's Rd.
  WC1 . . . . .5F 7 (4B 62)
Theobald St. SE1 . . . . . .4F 77
Theodore Ct. SE13 . . . .4F 109
Theodore Rd. SE13 . . . .4F 109
Therapia Rd. SE22 . . . . .4F 107
Theresa Rd. W6 . . . . . . .5C 70
Therfield Ct. N4 . . . . . . .4E 35
Thermopylae Ga.
  E14 . . . . .5D 81
Theseus Wlk. N1 . . . . . .1E 9
Thessaly Ho. SW8 . . . . .3E 89
    (off Thessaly Rd.)
Thessaly Rd. SW8 . . . . .3E 89
    (not continuous)
Thesus Ho. E14 . . . . . . .5E 67
    (off Blair St.)
Thetford Ho. SE1 . . . . . .5F 27
    (off St Saviour's Est.)
Theydon Rd. E5 . . . . . . .4E 37
Theydon St. E17 . . . . . .2B 38
Third Av. E13 . . . . .2C 68
  E17 . . . . .1C 38
  W3 . . . . .2B 70
  W10 . . . . .2A 58
Thirleby Rd.
  SW1 . . . . .5A 22 (4E 75)
Thirlmere NW1 . . . . .1E 5
    (off Cumberland Mkt.)
Thirlmere Ho. N16 . . . . .1F 49
    (off Howard Rd.)
Thirlmere Rd. SW16 . . .4F 117
Thirsk Rd. SW11 . . . . . .1C 102
Thirza Ho. E1 . . . . .5E 65
    (off Devonport St.)
Thistle Ct. SE12 . . . . . .2C 124
Thistle Gro. SW10 . . . . .1E 87
Thistle Ho. E14 . . . . . . .5E 67
    (off Dee St.)
Thistlewaite Rd. E5 . . . .5D 37
Thistlewood Cl. N7 . . . . .4B 34
Thistley Ct. SE8 . . . . . . .2D 95
Thomas Baines Rd.
  SW11 . . . . .1F 101
Thomas Burt Ho. E2 . . . .2D 65
    (off Canrobert St.)
Thomas Darby Ct.
  W11 . . . . .5A 58
    (off Lancaster Rd.)
Thomas Dean Rd.
  SE26 . . . . .4B 122
Thomas Dinwiddy Rd.
  SE12 . . . . .2D 125
Thomas Doyle St.
  SE1 . . . . .5D 25 (4D 77)
    (off High St.)
Thomas Frye Ct. E15 . . .1D 67
Thomas Fyre Dr. E3 . . . .1C 66
Thomas Hollywood Ho.
  E2 . . . . .1E 65
    (off Approach Rd.)
Thomas Joseph Ho.
  SE4 . . . . .3F 107
    (off St Norbert Rd.)

Thomas La. SE6 .....5C **108**

Thomas More Highwalk
EC2 ....*1F* **17**
(off Aldersgate St.)

Thomas More Ho.
EC2 ....*1F* **17**

Thomas More Sq. E1 ...1C **78**

Thomas More St.
E1 ....1C **78**

Thomas Neal's Cen.
WC2 .....3D **15** (5A **62**)

Thomas Nth. Ter.
E16 ....*4B* **68**
(off Barking Rd.)

Thomas Pl. W8 ....4D **73**

Thomas Rd. E14 .....5B **66**

Thomas Rd. Ind. Est.
E14 ....4C **66**

Thompson Ho. *SE14* ...*2F* **93**
(off John Williams Cl.)
W10 ....*3A* **58**
(off Wornington Rd.)

Thompson Rd.
SE22 ....4B **106**

Thompson's Av. SE5 ...3E **91**

Thomson Ho. *E14* *5C* **66**
(off Saracen St.)
SE17 ....*5A* **78**
(off Tatum St.)
SW1 ....*1F* **89**
(off Bessborough Pl.)

Thorburn Ho. *SW1* *4A* **20**
(off Kinnerton St.)

Thorburn Sq. SE1 .....5C **78**

Thoresby St.
N1 ....1A **10** (2E **63**)

Thornaby Ho. *E2* *2D* **65**
(off Canrobert St.)

Thornbill Ho. *SE15* ...*3C* **92**
(off Bird in Bush Rd.)

Thornbury Cl. N16 .....2A **50**

Thornbury Ct. *W11* *1C* **72**
(off Chepstow Vs.)

Thornbury Rd. SW2 ...4A **104**

Thornbury Sq. N6 .....3E **33**

Thornby Rd. E5 ......5E **37**

Thorncliffe Rd.
SW2 ....4A **104**

Thorncombe Rd.
SE22 ....3A **106**

Thorncroft St. SW8 ...3A **90**

Thorndean St.
SW18 ....2E **115**

Thorndike Cl. SW10 ...3E **87**

Thorndike Ho. *SW1* *1F* **89**
(off Vauxhall Bri. Rd.)

Thorndike Rd. N1 .....3F **49**

Thorndike St. SW1 ...5F **75**

Thorne Cl. E11 ....1F **53**
E16 ....5C **68**

Thorne Ho. *E2* *2E* **65**
(off Roman Rd.)
E14 ....*4E* **81**
(off Launch St.)

Thorne Pas. SW13 ...5A **84**

Thorne Rd. SW8 .....3A **90**

Thorne St. SW13 ....1A **98**

Thornewill Ho. *E1* *1E* **79**
(off Cable St.)

Thorney Ct. *W8* *3E* **73**
(off Palace Ga.)

Thorney Cres. SW11 ...3F **87**

Thorney St. SW1 .....5A **76**

Thornfield Ho. *E14* *1C* **80**
(off Rosefield Gdns.)

Thornfield Rd. W12 ....3D **71**
(not continuous)

Thornford Rd.
SE13 ....3E **109**

Thorngate Rd. W9 ...3C **58**

Thorngrove Rd. E13 ...5D **55**

Thornham Gro. E15 ...2F **53**

Thornham Ind. Est.
E15 ....2F **53**

Thornham St. SE10 ...2D **95**

Thornhaugh M.
WC1 ....4C **6** (3F **61**)

Thornhaugh St.
WC1 ....4C **6** (3F **61**)

Thornhill Bri. *N1* *1B* **62**
(off Caledonian Rd.)

Thornhill Bri. Wharf
N1 ....5B **48**

Thornhill Cres. N1 ....4B **48**

Thornhill Gdns. E10 ...4D **39**

Thornhill Gro. N1 ....4B **48**

Thornhill Ho. *W4* *1A* **84**
(off Wood St.)

Thornhill Ho's. N1 ....4C **48**

Thornhill M. SW15 ...2B **100**

Thornhill Rd. E10 ....4D **39**
N1 ....4C **48**

Thornhill Sq. N1 .....4B **48**

Thornicroft Ho. *SW9* ..*5B* **90**
(off Stockwell Rd.)

Thornlaw Rd. SE27 ...4C **118**

Thornley Pl. SE10 .....1A **96**

Thornsbeach Rd.
SE6 ....1E **123**

Thornsett Rd.
SW18 ....1D **115**

Thorn Ter. SE15 .....1E **107**

Thornton Av. SW2 ...1F **117**
W4 ....5A **70**

Thornton Gdns.
SW12 ....1F **117**

Thornton Ho. *SE17* ...*5A* **78**
(off Townsend St.)

Thornton Pl.
W1 ....5A **4** (4B **60**)

Thornton Rd.
BR1: Brom 5C **124**
E11 ....4F **39**
SW12 ....5F **103**

Thornton Row SW9 ...5C **90**

Thornton Way NW11 ...1D **31**

Thorntree Rd. SE7 ...1F **97**

Thornville St. SE8 ...4C **94**

Thornwood Gdns.
W8 ....3C **72**

Thornwood Lodge
W8 ....*3C* **72**
(off Thornwood Gdns.)

Thornwood Rd.
SE13 ....3A **110**

Thornycroft Ho. *W4* ...*1A* **84**
(off Fraser St.)

Thorogood Gdns. E15 ..2A **54**

Thorold Ho. *SE1* *3F* **25**
(off Pepper St.)

Thorparch Rd. SW8 ...4F **89**

Thorpebank Rd. W12 ...2C **70**

Thorpe Cl. SE26 ....4F **121**
W10 ....5A **58**

Thorpedale Rd. N4 ....4A **34**

Thorpe Ho. *N1* *5B* **48**
(off Barnsbury St.)

Thorpe Rd. E7 ....1B **54**
N15 ....1A **36**

Thorpewood Av.
SE26 ....2D **121**

Thorsden Way SE19 ...5A **120**

Thorverton Rd. NW2 ...5A **30**

Thoydon Rd. E3 .....1A **66**

Thrale Rd. SW16 ....4E **117**

Thrale St.
SE1 ....2A **26** (2E **77**)

Thrasher Cl. E8 .....5B **50**

Thrawl St. E1 ...1F **19** (4B **64**)

Thrayle Ho. *SW9* *1B* **104**
(off Benedict Rd.)

Threadgold Ho. *N1* *3F* **49**
(off Dovercourt St.)

Threadneedle St.
EC2 ....3C **18** (5F **63**)

Threadneedle Wlk.
EC2 ....3C **18**

Three Barrels Wlk.
EC4 ....*5A* **18**
(off Queenhithe)

Three Colt Cnr. *E2* ...*3C* **64**
(off Cheshire St.)

Three Colts La. E2 ...3D **65**

Three Colts St. E14 ...5B **66**

Three Cranes Wlk.
EC4 ....5A **18**

Three Cups Yd. WC1 ...1A **16**

Three Kings Yd.
W1 .....4D **13** (1D **75**)

Three Mill La. E3 ....2E **67**
(not continuous)

Three Mills Studios
E3 ....2E **67**

Three Nun Ct. *EC2* *2A* **18**
(off Aldermanbury)

Three Oak La. SE1 ...3F **27**

Three Quays EC3 .....5E **19**

Three Quays Wlk.
EC3 .....5E **19** (1A **78**)

Threshers Pl. W11 ....1A **72**

Thriftwood SE26 ....3E **121**

Thring Ho. *SW9* *5B* **90**
(off Stockwell Rd.)

Throckmorton Av.
EC2 ....2C **18** (5F **63**)
(not continuous)

Throgmorton St.
EC2 ....2C **18** (5F **63**)

Thrush St. SE17 ....1E **91**

Thurbarn Rd. SE6 ....5D **123**

Thurland Ho. *SE16* ...*5D* **79**
(off Camilla Rd.)

Thurland Rd. SE16 ...4C **78**

Thurlby Rd. SE27 ...4C **118**

Thurleigh Av. SW12 ...4C **102**

Thurleigh Ct. SW12 . . .4C 102
Thurleigh Rd.
   SW12 . . . . .5B 102
Thurlestone Rd.
   SE27 . . . . .3C 118
Thurloe Cl. SW7 . . . . . .5A 74
Thurloe Ct. SW3 . . . . . .5A 74
   (off Fulham Rd.)
Thurloe Pl. SW7 . . . . . . .5F 73
Thurloe Pl. M. SW7 . . . . .5F 73
   (off Thurloe Pl.)
Thurloe Sq. SW7 . . . . . .5A 74
Thurloe St. SW7 . . . . . . .5F 73
Thurlow Hill SE21 . . . .1E 119
Thurlow Ho. SW16 . . . .3A 118
Thurlow Pk. Rd.
   SE21 . . . . .2D 119
Thurlow Rd. NW3 . . . . .2F 45
Thurlow St. SE17 . . . . . .1F 91
   (not continuous)
Thurlow Ter. NW5 . . . . . .2C 46
Thurlow Wlk. SE17 . . . .1A 92
   (not continuous)
Thurnscoe NW1 . . . . .5F 47
   (off Pratt St.)
Thursley Gdns.
   SW19 . . . . .2F 113
Thursley Ho. SW2 . . . .5B 104
   (off Holmewood Gdns.)
Thurso Ho. NW6 . . . . . .1D 59
Thurso St. SW17 . . . . . .4F 115
Thurstan Dwellings
   WC2 . . . . .2E 15
   (off Newton St.)
Thurston Ho. N1 . . . . . . .5B 48
   (off Carnegie St.)
Thurston Ind. Est.
   SE13 . . . . .1D 109
Thurston Rd. SE13 . . . . .5D 95
Thurtle Rd. E2 . . . . .5D 50
Thyme Cl. SE3 . . . . . . .1E 111
Tibbatt's Rd. E3 . . . . . . .3D 67
Tibbenham Pl. SE6 . . . .2C 122
Tibbenham Wlk. E13 . . .1B 68
Tibberton Sq. N1 . . . . . .5E 49
Tibbet's Cl. SW19 . . . . .1F 113
TIBBET'S CORNER 5F 99
Tibbet's Ride SW15 . . . .5F 99
Tiber Cl. E3 . . . . .5C 52
Tiber Gdns. N1 . . . . .5A 48
Ticehurst Rd. SE23 . . . .2A 122
Tickford Ho. NW8 . . . . . .2A 60
Tidal Basin Rd. E16 . . . .1B 82
   (not continuous)
Tidbury Ct. SW8 . . . . . . .3E 89
   (off Stewart's Rd.)
Tideswell Rd. SW15 . . . .2E 99
Tideway Ct. SE16 . . . . . .2F 79
Tideway Ho. E14 . . . . . . .3C 80
   (off Strafford St.)
Tideway Ind. Est.
   SW8 . . . . .2E 89
Tideway Wlk. SW8 . . . . .2E 89
Tidey St. E3 . . . . .4C 66
Tidworth Rd. E3 . . . . . . .3C 66
Tierney Rd. SW2 . . . . . .1A 118
Tiffany Hgts. SW18 . . . .5C 100
Tiger Ho. WC1 . . . . .2C 6
   (off Burton St.)

Tiger Way E5 . . . . .1D 51
Tilbrook Rd. SE3 . . . . . .1E 111
Tilbury Cl. SE15 . . . . . .3B 92
Tilbury Ho. SE14 . . . . . .2F 93
   (off Myers La.)
Tilbury Rd. E10 . . . . .2E 39
Tildesley Rd. SW15 . . . . .4E 99
Tilehurst NW1 . . . . .2E 5
   (off Lit. Albany St.)
Tilehurst Rd. SW18 . . . .1F 115
Tile Kiln La. N6 . . . . .3D 33
Tile Kiln Studios N6 . . . .2E 33
Tileyard Rd. N7 . . . . .4A 48
Tilford Gdns. SW19 . . . .1F 113
Tilford Ho. SW2 . . . . . . .5B 104
   (off Holmewood Gdns.)
Tilia Rd. E5 . . . . .1D 51
Tilia Ter. SW9 . . . . .2D 105
Tiller Ho. N1 . . . . .5A 50
   (off Whitmore Est.)
Tiller Leisure Centre, The
   . . . . .4C 80
Tiller Rd. E14 . . . . .4C 80
Tillett Sq. SE16 . . . . . . .3A 80
Tillet Way E2 . . . . .2C 64
Tilling Rd. NW2 . . . . . . .3E 29
Tillings Cl. SE5 . . . . .4E 91
Tillman St. E1 . . . . .5D 65
Tilloch St. N1 . . . . .4B 48
Tillotson Ct. SW8 . . . . . .3F 89
   (off Wandsworth Rd.)
Tilney Ct.
   EC1 . . . . . .3A 10 (3E 63)
Tilney Gdns. N1 . . . . . . .3F 49
Tilney St.
   W1 . . . . . .1C 20 (2C 74)
Tilson Cl. SE5 . . . . .3A 92
Tilson Gdns. SW2 . . . . .5A 104
Tilson Ho. SW2 . . . . . . .5A 104
Tilston Cl. E11 . . . . .5B 40
Tiltman Pl. N7 . . . . .5B 34
Tilton St. SW6 . . . . .2A 86
Timberland Cl. SE15 . . . .3C 92
Timberland Rd. E1 . . . . .5D 65
Timber Mill Way
   SW4 . . . . .1F 103
Timber Pond Rd.
   SE16 . . . . .2F 79
Timber St.
   EC1 . . . . . . .3F 9 (3E 63)
Timber Wharf E2 . . . . . .5B 50
Timberwharf Rd.
   N16 . . . . .1C 36
Timber Wharves Est.
   E14 . . . . .5C 80
   (off Copeland Dr.)
Timber Yard, The N1 . . . .2E 11
   (off Drysdale St.)
Timbrell Pl. SE16 . . . . . .2B 80
Time Sq. E8 . . . . .2B 50
Times Sq. E1 . . . . .5C 64
Timor Ho. E1 . . . . .3A 66
   (off Duckett St.)
Timothy Cl. SW4 . . . . . .3E 103
Timperley Ct. SW19 . . . .1A 114
Timsbury Wlk.
   SW15 . . . . .1C 112
Tina Ct. SE6 . . . . .5B 108
Tindal St. SW9 . . . . .4D 91

Tinderbox All. SW14 . . .1A 98
Tinniswood Cl. N5 . . . . .2C 48
Tinsley Rd. E1 . . . . .4E 65
Tintagel Ct. EC1 . . . . . . .3D 9
   (off St John St.)
Tintagel Cres. SE22 . . . .2B 106
Tintagel Gdns. SE22 . . .2B 106
Tintern Cl. SW15 . . . . . .3A 100
Tintern Ho. NW1 . . . . . . .1E 5
   (off Augustus St.)
   SW1 . . . . .5D 75
   (part of Abbots Mnr.)
Tintern Path NW9 . . . . .1A 28
   (off Fryent Gro.)
Tintern St. SW4 . . . . . .2A 104
Tinto Rd. E16 . . . . .3C 68
Tinworth St. SE11 . . . . .1A 90
Tipthorpe Rd. SW11 . . .1C 102
Tiptree NW1 . . . . .4D 47
   (off Castlehaven Rd.)
Tisbury Ct. W1 . . . . .4B 14
Tisdall Ho. SE17 . . . . . . .5F 77
   (off Barlow St.)
Tisdall Pl. SE17 . . . . . . .5F 77
Tissington Ct. SE16 . . . .5E 79
Titan Bus. Est. SE8 . . . .3C 94
   (off Ffinch St.)
Titchborne Row W2 . . . .5A 60
Titchfield Rd. NW8 . . . . .5A 46
Titchwell Rd. SW18 . . . .1F 115
Tite St. SW3 . . . . .1B 88
Titmuss St. W12 . . . . . .3E 71
Tiverton Rd. N15 . . . . . .1F 35
   NW10 . . . . .5F 43
Tiverton St.
   SE1 . . . . . .5F 25 (4E 77)
Tivoli Ct. SE16 . . . . .2B 80
Tivoli Gdns. SE10 . . . . . .5F 83
   (not continuous)
Tivoli Rd. N8 . . . . .1F 33
   SE27 . . . . .5E 119
Tobacco Dock E1 . . . . . .1D 79
Tobacco Quay E1 . . . . . .1D 79
Tobago St. E14 . . . . .3C 80
Tobin Cl. NW3 . . . . .4A 46
Toby La. E1 . . . . .3A 66
Todber Ho. W14 . . . . . . .4A 72
   (off Russell Rd.)
Todds Wlk. N7 . . . . .4B 34
Tokenhouse Yd.
   EC2 . . . . . .2B 18 (5F 63)
Token Yd. SW15 . . . . . .2A 100
Toland Sq. SW15 . . . . . .3C 98
Tolchurch W11 . . . . .5B 58
   (off Dartmouth Cl.)
Tolhurst Dr. W10 . . . . . .2A 58
Tollard Ho. W14 . . . . . . .4B 72
Tollbridge Cl. W10 . . . . .3A 58
Tollet St. E1 . . . . .3F 65
Tollgate Dr. SE21 . . . . .2A 120
Tollgate Gdns. NW6 . . . .1D 59
Tollgate Ho. NW6 . . . . . .1D 59
   (off Tollgate Gdns.)
Tollgate Rd. E6 . . . . .4E 69
   E16 . . . . .4E 69
Tollhouse Way N19 . . . . .4E 33
Tollington Pk. N4 . . . . . .4B 34
Tollington Pl. N4 . . . . . . .4B 34
Tollington Rd. N7 . . . . . .1B 48

Tollington Way N7 . . . . .5A **34**
Tolmers Sq.
  NW1 . . . . . . .3A **6** (3E **61**)
  (not continuous)
Tolpaide Ho. SE11 . . . .5C **76**
  (off Marylee Way)
Tolpuddle Av. E13 . . . . .5E **55**
Tolpuddle St. N1 . . . . . .1C **62**
Tolsford Rd. E5 . . . . . . .2D **51**
Tom Groves Cl.
  E15 . . . . .2F **53**
Tom Hood Cl. E15 . . . . .2F **53**
Tom Jenkinson Rd.
  E16 . . . . .2C **82**
Tomkyns Ho. SE11 . . . .5C **76**
  (off Distin St.)
Tomline Ho. SE1 . . . . . .2F **25**
  (off Union St.)
Tomlin's Gro. E3 . . . . . .2C **66**
Tomlinson Cl. E2 . . . . . .2B **64**
Tomlins Ter. E14 . . . . . .5A **66**
Tomlins Wlk. N7 . . . . . .4B **34**
Tom Nolan Cl. E15 . . . .1A **68**
Tompion Ho. EC1 . . . . . .3E **9**
  (off Percival St.)
Tompion St.
  EC1 . . . . . .2D **9** (2D **63**)
  (not continuous)
Tom Smith Cl. SE10 . . .2A **96**
Tomson Ho. SE1 . . . . . .5F **27**
  (off St Saviour's Est.)
Tom Williams Ho.
  SW6 . . . . .2B **86**
  (off Clem Attlee Ct.)
Tonbridge Ho's. WC1 . . .2D **7**
  (off Tonbridge St.,
  not continuous)
Tonbridge St.
  WC1 . . . . . .1D **7** (2A **62**)
Tonbridge Wlk. WC1 . . . .1D **7**
Toneborough NW8 . . . .5D **45**
  (off Abbey Rd.)
Tonsley Hill SW18 . . . .3D **101**
Tonsley Pl. SW18 . . . . .3D **101**
Tonsley Rd. SW18 . . . .3D **101**
Tonsley St. SW18 . . . . .3D **101**
Tony Cannell M. E3 . . . .2B **66**
Took's Ct.
  EC4 . . . . .2B **16** (5C **62**)
Tooley St.
  SE1 . . . . .1C **26** (2F **77**)
Toomy Cen. E16 . . . . . .2D **83**
  (off Evelyn Rd.)
TOOTING 5A **116**
TOOTING BEC 3B **116**
Tooting Bec Gdns.
  SW16 . . . . .4F **117**
  (not continuous)
Tooting Bec Lido 4E **117**
Tooting Bec Rd.
  SW16 . . . . .3C **116**
  SW17 . . . . .3C **116**
Tooting B'way.
  SW17 . . . . .5A **116**
TOOTING GRAVENEY
  . . . . .5B **116**
Tooting Gro. SW17 . . . .5A **116**
Tooting High St.
  SW17 . . . . .5A **116**

Tooting Leisure Cen.
  . . . . .4F **115**
Tooting Mkt. SW17 . . . .4B **116**
Topaz W2 . . . . .4F **59**
  (off Harbet Rd.)
Topaz Ct. E11 . . . . .3A **40**
Topaz Wlk. NW2 . . . . . .2F **29**
Topham Ho. SE10 . . . . .3E **95**
  (off Prior St.)
Topham St.
  EC1 . . . . . .3B **8** (3C **62**)
Topley St. SE9 . . . . . . .2E **111**
Topmast Point
  E14 . . . . .3C **80**
Topp Wlk. NW2 . . . . . . .4E **29**
Topsfield Cl. N8 . . . . . . .1F **33**
Topsfield Pde. N8 . . . . .1A **34**
  (off Tottenham La.)
Topsfield Rd. N8 . . . . . .1A **34**
Topsham Rd. SW17 . . . .3B **116**
Torbay Ct. NW1 . . . . . . .4D **47**
Torbay Mans. NW6 . . . .5B **44**
  (off Willesden La.)
Torbay Rd. NW6 . . . . . .4B **44**
Torbay St. NW1 . . . . . . .4D **47**
Tor Ct. W8 . . . . .3C **72**
Torcross Dr. SE23 . . . .2E **121**
Tor Gdns. W8 . . . . .3C **72**
Tor Ho. N6 . . . . .1D **33**
Tornay Ho. E9 . . . . .4E **51**
  N1 . . . . .1B **62**
  (off Priory Grn. Est.)
Toronto Ho. SE16 . . . . .3F **79**
Torquay St. W2 . . . . . . .4D **59**
Torrance Cl. SE7 . . . . . .2F **97**
Torrens Ct. SE5 . . . . . .1F **105**
Torrens Rd. E15 . . . . . . .3B **54**
  SW2 . . . . .3B **104**
Torrens Sq. E15 . . . . . . .3B **54**
Torrens St. EC1 . . . . . . .1C **62**
Torrent Lodge SE10 . . .3D **95**
  (off Merryweather Pl.)
Torres Sq. E14 . . . . . . .1C **94**
Torrey Dr. SW9 . . . . . . .5C **90**
Torriano Av. NW5 . . . . . .2F **47**
Torriano Cotts. NW5 . . .2E **47**
Torriano M. NW5 . . . . . .2E **47**
Torridge Gdns.
  SE15 . . . . .2E **107**
Torridon Ho. NW6 . . . . .1D **59**
  (off Randolph Gdns.)
Torridon Rd. SE6 . . . . .5F **109**
  SE13 . . . . .5A **110**
Torrington Ct. SE26 . . .5C **120**
  (off Crystal Pal. Pk. Rd.)
Torrington Pl. E1 . . . . . .2C **78**
  WC1 . . . . . .5B **6** (4F **61**)
Torrington Sq.
  WC1 . . . . . .4C **6** (3F **61**)
Tortington Ho. SE15 . . .3C **92**
  (off Friary Est.)
Torwood Rd. SW15 . . . .3C **98**
Tothill Ho. SW1 . . . . . . .5F **75**
  (off Page St.)
Tothill St.
  SW1 . . . . .4C **22** (3F **75**)
Tottan Ter. E1 . . . . .5F **65**
Tottenhall NW1 . . . . . . .4C **46**
  (off Ferdinand St.)

Tottenham Ct. Rd.
  W1 . . . . . . .4A **6** (3E **61**)
Tottenham La. N8 . . . . .1A **34**
Tottenham M.
  W1 . . . . . . .5A **6** (4E **61**)
Tottenham Rd. N1 . . . . .3A **50**
Tottenham St.
  W1 . . . . . .1A **14** (4E **61**)
Totterdown St.
  SW17 . . . . .4B **116**
Totteridge Ho. SW11 . . .5F **87**
  (off Yelverton Rd.)
Touchard Ho. N1 . . . . . .2C **10**
Toulmin St.
  SE1 . . . . . .4F **25** (3E **77**)
Toulon St. SE5 . . . . .3E **91**
Toulouse Ct. SE16 . . . .1D **93**
  (off Rossetti Rd.)
Tounson Ct. SW1 . . . . . .5F **75**
  (off Montaigne Cl.)
Tourist Info. Cen.
  City of London
  . . . . .3F **17** (5E **63**)
  Greenwich 2E **95**
  Hammersmith 5E **71**
  Leicester Square
  . . . . .5C **14** (1F **75**)
  Lewisham 2E **109**
Tournay Rd. SW6 . . . . .3B **86**
Tours Pas. SW11 . . . . .2E **101**
Toussaint Wlk. SE16 . . .4C **78**
Tovy Ho. SE1 . . . . .1C **92**
  (off Avondale Sq.)
Towcester Rd. E3 . . . . .3D **67**
Tower 42 . . . . .2D **19** (5A **64**)
Tower Bri.
  SE1 . . . . . .2F **27** (2B **78**)
Tower Bri. App.
  E1 . . . . . . .1F **27** (2B **78**)
Tower Bri. Bus. Complex
  SE16 . . . . .4C **78**
Tower Bri. Bus. Sq.
  SE16 . . . . .5D **79**
Tower Bridge Exhibition
  . . . . .1F **27**
Tower Bri. Plaza
  SE1 . . . . . .2F **27** (2B **78**)
Tower Bri. Rd.
  SE1 . . . . . .5D **27** (4A **78**)
Tower Bri. Sq. SE1 . . . . .3F **27**
Tower Bri. Wharf E1 . . . .2C **78**
Tower Bldgs. E1 . . . . . .2D **79**
  (off Brewhouse La.)
Tower Cl. NW3 . . . . . . .2F **45**
Tower Ct. E5 . . . . .2B **36**
  N1 . . . . .4E **49**
  (off Canonbury St.)
  NW8 . . . . .1A **60**
  (off Mackennal St.)
  WC2 . . . . .3D **15**
Towergate SE1 . . . . . . .5A **78**
  (off Page's Wlk.)
Towergate Ho. E3 . . . . .1B **66**
  (off Ordell Rd.)
Tower Hamlets Rd.
  E7 . . . . .1B **54**
TOWER HILL 1B **78**
Tower Hill
  EC3 . . . . . .5E **19** (1A **78**)

Tower Hill Ter. EC3 . . . . . .5E 19
Tower Ho. E1 . . . . .4C 64
  (off Fieldgate St.)
Tower Mans. SE1 . . . . .4B 78
  (off Grange Rd.)
Tower M. E5 . . . . .1A 52
Tower Mill Rd.
SE15 . . . . .3A 92
Tower of London, The
. . . . . . .5F 19 (1B 78)
Tower of London
Welcome Cen.
. . . . . . .5E 19 (1A 78)
Tower Pl.
EC3 . . . . . .5E 19 (1A 78)
Tower Pl. E. EC3 . . . . . . .5E 19
  (off Lwr. Thames St.)
Tower Pl. W. EC3 . . . . . . .5E 19
  (off Lwr. Thames St.)
Tower Rd. NW10 . . . . .4C 42
Tower Royal
EC4 . . . . .4B 18 (1F 77)
Tower St.
WC2 . . . . . . .3D 15 (5A 62)
Tower Wlk. SE1 . . . . .5A 78
  (off Leroy St.)
Tower Wharf SE1 . . . . .3F 27
  (off Tooley St.)
Tower Workshops
SE1 . . . . .4F 27
Town Ct. Path N4 . . . . . . .3E 35
Town Hall Rd.
SW11 . . . . .1B 102
Town Hall Wlk. N16 . . . .1F 49
  (off Albion Rd.)
Townley Ct. E15 . . . . .3B 54
Townley Rd. SE22 . . . . . . .3A 106
Townley St. SE17 . . . . . . .1F 91
  (not continuous)
Townmead Bus. Cen.
SW6 . . . . .1E 101
Townmead Rd.
SW6 . . . . .1D 101
Townsend Ho. SE1 . . . . .5C 78
  (off Strathnairn St.)
Townsend La. NW9 . . . . . . .2A 28
Townsend M. SW18 . . . . . .2E 115
Townsend Rd. N15 . . . . . . .1B 36
Townsend St. SE17 . . . . . . .5A 78
Townsend Yd. N6 . . . . .3D 33
Townshend Ct. NW8 . . . .1A 60
  (off Townshend Rd.)
Townshend Est. NW8 . . . .1A 60
Townshend Rd. NW8 . . . .5A 46
  (not continuous)
Towns Ho. SW4 . . . . .1F 103
Towpath, The
SW10 . . . . .4F 87
Towpath Wlk. E9 . . . . .2B 52
Towton Rd. SE27 . . . . .2E 119
Toynbee St.
E1 . . . . . . .1F 19 (4B 64)
Toynbee Studios 2F 19
Toyne Way N6 . . . . .1B 32
Tracey Av. NW2 . . . . .2E 43
Tracy Ho. E3 . . . . .2B 66
  (off Mile End Rd.)
Tradescant Ho. E9 . . . . . . .4E 51
  (off Frampton Pk. Rd.)
Tradescant Rd. SW8 . . . . . .3A 90

Tradewind Hgts.
SE16 . . . . .2F 79
  (off Rotherhithe St.)
Tradewinds Ct. E1 . . . . . . .1C 78
Trafalgar Av. SE15 . . . . . . .1B 92
Trafalgar Chambers
SW3 . . . . .1F 87
  (off South Pde.)
Trafalgar Cl. SE16 . . . . . . .4A 80
Trafalgar Ct. E1 . . . . .2E 79
  (off Wapping Wall)
Trafalgar Gdns. E1 . . . . . . .4F 65
W8 . . . . .4D 73
Trafalgar Gro. SE10 . . . . . .2F 95
Trafalgar Ho. SE17 . . . . . . .1E 91
  (off Bronti Cl.)
Trafalgar M. E9 . . . . .3B 52
Trafalgar Point N1 . . . . .4F 49
  (off Downham Rd.)
Trafalgar Quarters
SE10 . . . . .2F 95
  (off Park Row)
Trafalgar Rd. SE10 . . . . . . .2F 95
Trafalgar Square
. . . . . . .1C 22 (2F 75)
Trafalgar Sq. SW1 . . . . . . .2F 75
WC2 . . . . . .1C 22 (2F 75)
Trafalgar St. SE17 . . . . . . .1F 91
Trafalgar Studios 1D 23
  (off Whitehall)
Trafalgar Way E14 . . . . . . .2E 81
Trafford Ho. N1 . . . . . . .1F 63
  (off Cranston Est.)
Trahorn Cl. E1 . . . . .3D 65
Traitors' Gate 1F 27
Tralee Ct. SE16 . . . . . .1D 93
  (off Masters Dr.)
Tram Cl. SE24 . . . . . . .1D 105
  (off Milkwood Rd.)
Tramway Av. E15 . . . . .4A 54
Tramway Ct. E1 . . . . .4A 66
Tranley M. NW3 . . . . . . .1A 46
  (off Fleet Rd.)
Tranmere Rd. SW18 . . . . . .2E 115
Tranquil Pas. SE3 . . . . . . .5B 96
  (off Montpelier Va.)
Tranquil Va. SE3 . . . . .5A 96
Transenna Works N1 . . . .3D 49
  (off Laycock St.)
Transept St. NW1 . . . . . . .4A 60
Transom Cl. SE16 . . . . . . .5A 80
Transom Sq. E14 . . . . .1D 95
Tranton Rd. SE16 . . . . .4C 78
Trappes Ho. SE16 . . . . .5D 79
  (off Camilla Rd.)
Travers Ho. SE10 . . . . .2F 95
  (off Trafalgar Gro.)
Travers Rd. N7 . . . . .5C 34
Travis Ho. SE10 . . . . .4E 95
Treadgold Ho. W11 . . . . .1F 71
  (off Bomore Rd.)
Treadgold St. W11 . . . . . . .1F 71
Treadway St. E2 . . . . .1D 65
Treasury Pas. SW1 . . . . . . .3D 23
Treaty St. N1 . . . . .5B 48
Trebeck St.
W1 . . . . . . .1D 21 (2D 75)
Trebovir Rd. SW5 . . . . .1C 86
Treby St. E3 . . . . .3B 66
Trecastle Way N7 . . . . .1F 47

Tredegar Ho. E3 . . . . .2C 66
  (off Bow Rd.)
Tredegar M. E3 . . . . .2B 66
Tredegar Rd. E3 . . . . .1B 66
Tredegar Sq. E3 . . . . .2B 66
Tredegar Ter. E3 . . . . .2B 66
Trederwen Rd. E8 . . . . .5C 50
Tredown Rd. SE26 . . . . . . .5E 121
Tredwell Cl. SW2 . . . . .2B 118
Tredwell Rd.
SE27 . . . . .4D 119
Treen Av. SW13 . . . . .1B 98
Tree Rd. E16 . . . . .5E 69
Treewall Gdns.
BR1: Brom 4D 125
Trefil Wlk. N7 . . . . .1A 48
Trefoil Rd. SW18 . . . . .3E 101
Tregaron Av. N8 . . . . .1A 34
Tregarvon Rd.
SW11 . . . . .2C 102
Trego Rd. E9 . . . . .4C 52
Tregothnan Rd.
SW9 . . . . .1A 104
Tregunter Rd. SW10 . . . . . .2D 87
Treherne Ct. SW9 . . . . .4D 91
SW17 . . . . .4C 116
Trehern Rd. SW14 . . . . . . .1A 98
Trehurst St. E5 . . . . .2A 52
Trelawney Est. E9 . . . . .3E 51
Trelawney Ho. SE1 . . . . .2F 25
  (off Union St.)
Trelawn Rd. E10 . . . . .5E 39
SW2 . . . . .3C 104
Trellick Twr. W10 . . . . . .3B 58
  (off Golborne Rd.)
Trellis Sq. E3 . . . . .2B 66
Tremadoc Rd. SW4 . . . . . . .2F 103
Tremaine Cl. SE4 . . . . .5C 94
Trematon Ho. SE11 . . . . .1C 90
  (off Kennings Way)
Tremlett Gro. N19 . . . . .5E 33
Trenchard Ct. NW4 . . . . . . .1C 28
Trenchard St. SE10 . . . . . . .1F 95
Trenchold St. SW8 . . . . . . .2A 90
Trendell Ho. E14 . . . . . .5C 66
  (off Dod St.)
Trenmar Gdns. NW10 . . . . .2D 57
Trentham Ho. W3 . . . . .4A 56
Trentham St. SW18 . . . . . .1C 114
Trent Ho. SE15 . . . . .2E 107
Trent Rd. SW2 . . . . .3B 104
Treport St. SW18 . . . . .5D 101
Tresco Ho. SE11 . . . . . .1C 90
  (off Sancroft St.)
Tresco Rd. SE15 . . . . .2D 107
Tresham Cres. NW8 . . . . . . .3A 60
Tresham Ho. WC1 . . . . . .5F 7
  (off Red Lion Sq.)
Tresham Wlk. E9 . . . . .2E 51
Tresidder Ho. SW4 . . . . . . .5F 103
Tressell Cl. N1 . . . . .4D 49
Tressillian Cres.
SE4 . . . . .1C 108
Tressillian Rd. SE4 . . . . . . .2B 108
Tress Pl. SE1 . . . . .1D 25
Trevanion Rd. W14 . . . . . . .5A 72
Trevelyan Gdns.
NW10 . . . . .5E 43
Trevelyan Ho. E2 . . . . .2F 65
  (off Morpeth St.)

Trevelyan Ho. *SE5* 3D **91**
   (off John Ruskin St.)
Trevelyan Rd. E15 . . . . . .1B **54**
SW17 . . . . .5A **116**
Trevenna Ho.
  SE23 . . . . .3F **121**
   (off Dacres Rd.)
Treveris St.
  SE1 . . . . . .2E **25** (2D **77**)
Treverton St. W10 . . . . . .3F **57**
Treverton Towers
  W10 . . . . .4F **57**
   (off Treverton St.)
Treves Ho. *E1* 3C **64**
   (off Vallance Rd.)
Treville St. SW15 . . . . . .5D **99**
Treviso Rd. SE23 . . . . . .2F **121**
Trevithick Ho. *SE16* 5D **79**
   (off Rennie Est.)
Trevithick St. SE8 . . . . . .2C **94**
Trevor Pl. SW7 . . . . .3A **74**
Trevor Sq. SW7 . . . . .3B **74**
Trevor St. SW7 . . . . .3A **74**
Trevor Wlk. *SW7* 3B **74**
   (off Trevor Sq., not continuous)
Trevose Ho. SE11 . . . . . .1B **90**
   (off Orsett St.)
Trewint St. SW18 . . . . . .2E **115**
Trewsbury Rd.
  SE26 . . . . .5F **121**
Tria Apartments *E2* 2C **64**
   (off Durant St.)
Triangle, The E8 . . . . . . .5D **51**
  EC1 . . . . .3E **9**
Triangle Bus. Centre, The
  NW10 . . . . .2B **56**
Triangle Ct. E16 . . . . . . .4F **69**
  SE1 . . . . .2A **26**
   (off Redcross Way)
Triangle Est. *SE11* 1C **90**
   (off Kennington Rd.)
Triangle Ho. *SE1* 3F **27**
   (off Three Oak La.)
Triangle Pl. SW4 . . . . . .2F **103**
Triangle Rd. E8 . . . . .5D **51**
Tribeca Apartments
  E1 . . . . .4B **64**
   (off Heneage St.)
Tricycle Cinema, The
  . . . . .4B **44**
Tricycle Theatre, The
  . . . . .4B **44**
Trident Bus. Cen.
  SW17 . . . . .5B **116**
Trident Ho. *E14* 5E **67**
   (off Blair St.)
Trident Pl. *SW3* 2F **87**
   (off Old Church St.)
Trident St. SE16 . . . . . . .5F **79**
Trigon Rd. SW8 . . . . . . .3B **90**
Trilby Rd. SE23 . . . . . . .2F **121**
Trimdon NW1 . . . . .5E **47**
Trim St. SE14 . . . . .2B **94**
Trinder Gdns.
  N19 . . . . .3A **34**
Trinder Rd. N19 . . . . .3A **34**
Trinidad Ho. *E14* 1B **80**
   (off Gill St.)
Trinidad St. E14 . . . . . . .1B **80**

Trinity Buoy Wharf
  E14 . . . . .1A **82**
   (off Orchard Pl.)
Trinity Chu. Pas.
  SW13 . . . . .2D **85**
Trinity Chu. Rd.
  SW13 . . . . .2D **85**
Trinity Chu. Sq.
  SE1 . . . . . . .5A **26** (4E **77**)
Trinity Cl. E8 . . . . .3B **50**
  E11 . . . . .4A **40**
  NW3 . . . . .1F **45**
  SE13 . . . . .2F **109**
  SW4 . . . . .2E **103**
Trinity College of Music
  . . . . .2E **95**
Trinity Ct. *N1* 5A **50**
   (off Downham Rd.)
  NW2 . . . . .2E **43**
  SE7 . . . . .5F **83**
  SE8 . . . . .1A **94**
   (off Evelyn St.)
  SE26 . . . . .3E **121**
  SW9 . . . . .1B **104**
  W2 . . . . .5E **59**
   (off Gloucester Ter.)
  W9 . . . . .2B **58**
   (off Croxley Rd.)
  WC1 . . . . .3F **7**
Trinity Cres. SW17 . . . . .2B **116**
Trinity Gdns. E16 . . . . . . .4B **68**
   (not continuous)
  SW9 . . . . .2B **104**
Trinity Grn. *E1* 3E **65**
Trinity Gro. SE10 . . . . . . .4E **95**
Trinity Hospital (Almshouses)
  SE10 . . . . .1F **95**
Trinity Ho. EC3 . . . . .4F **19**
  SE1 . . . . .5A **26**
   (off Bath Ter.)
Trinity M. *E1* 4E **65**
   (off Redman's Rd.)
  W10 . . . . .4A **58**
Trinity Path SE23 . . . . . .3E **121**
  SE26 . . . . .3E **121**
Trinity Pl.
  EC3 . . . . . . .4F **19** (1B **78**)
Trinity Ri. SW2 . . . . .1C **118**
Trinity Rd. SW17 . . . . . .2E **101**
  SW18 . . . . .2E **101**
  SW19 . . . . .5C **114**
Trinity Sq.
  EC3 . . . . . . .5E **19** (1A **78**)
Trinity St. E16 . . . . .4B **68**
  SE1 . . . . . . .4A **26** (3E **77**)
   (not continuous)
Trinity Twr. *E1* 1C **78**
   (off Vaughan Way)
Trinity Wlk. NW3 . . . . . . .3E **45**
Trinity Way W3 . . . . .1A **70**
Trio Pl. SE1 . . . . . .4A **26** (3E **77**)
Tristan Ct. *SE8* 2B **94**
   (off Dorking Cl.)
Tristan Sq. SE3 . . . . . . .1A **110**
Tristram Rd.
  BR1: Brom 4B **124**
Triton Ct. *E16* 4C **68**
   (off Robertson Rd.)
Triton Ho. E14 . . . . .5D **81**
   (off Cahir St.)

Triton Sq.
  NW1 . . . . . . .3F **5** (3E **61**)
Triton St. NW1 . . . .3F **5** (3E **61**)
Tritton Rd. SE21 . . . . . . .3F **119**
Trocadero Cen.
  . . . . .4B **14** (1F **75**)
Trocette Mans. *SE1* 5D **27**
   (off Bermondsey St.)
Trojan Ct. NW6 . . . . .4A **44**
Trojan Ind. Est.
  NW10 . . . . .3B **42**
Troon Cl. SE16 . . . . .1D **93**
Troon Ho. *E1* 5A **66**
   (off White Horse Rd.)
Troon St. E1 . . . . .5A **66**
Tropical Ct. *W10* 2F **57**
   (off Kilburn La.)
Trossachs Rd. SE22 . . . .3A **106**
Trothy Rd. SE1 . . . . .5C **78**
Trotman Ho. *SE14* 4E **93**
   (off Pomeroy St.)
Trott St. SW11 . . . . .4A **88**
Trotwood Ho. *SE16* 3D **79**
   (off Wilson Gro.)
Troughton Rd. SE7 . . . . .1D **97**
Troutbeck NW1 . . . . .2E **5**
Troutbeck Rd. SE14 . . . . .4A **94**
Trouville Rd. SW4 . . . . . .4E **103**
Trowbridge Est. E9 . . . . . .3B **52**
   (off Osborne Rd.)
Trowbridge Ho. E9 . . . . . .3B **52**
   (off Felstead St.)
Trowbridge Rd. E9 . . . . . .3B **52**
Troy Ct. *W8* 4C **72**
   (off Kensington High St.)
Troy Town SE15 . . . . . . .1C **106**
Trumans Rd. N16 . . . . . . .2B **50**
Trumpington Rd. E7 . . . . .1B **54**
Trump St.
  EC2 . . . . . . .3A **18** (5E **63**)
Trundle Ho. *SE1* 3F **25**
   (off Trundle St.)
Trundle St.
  SE1 . . . . . . .3F **25** (3E **77**)
Trundleys Rd. SE8 . . . . . .1F **93**
Trundley's Ter. SE8 . . . . . .5F **79**
Truro Ho. *W2* 4C **58**
   (off Westbourne Pk. Rd.)
Truro St. NW5 . . . . .3C **46**
Truslove Ho. SE27 . . . . . .5C **118**
Trussley Rd. W6 . . . . .4E **71**
Trust Wlk. SE21 . . . . . . .1D **119**
Tryfan Cl. IG4: Ilf 1F **41**
Tryon Cres. E9 . . . . .5E **51**
Tryon St. SW3 . . . . .1B **88**
Tubbs Rd. NW10 . . . . . . .1B **56**
Tucklow Wlk.
  SW15 . . . . .5B **98**
Tudor Cl. N6 . . . . .2E **33**
  NW3 . . . . .2A **46**
  SW2 . . . . .4B **104**
Tudor Ct. E17 . . . . .2B **38**
  N1 . . . . .3A **50**
  SE16 . . . . .2F **79**
   (off Princes Riverside Rd.)
Tudor Gdns. SW13 . . . . .1A **98**
Tudor Gro. E9 . . . . .4E **51**
Tudor Ho. E9 . . . . .4E **51**
  E16 . . . . .2D **83**
   (off Wesley Av.)

Tudor Ho. *W14* 5F **71**
(off Windsor Way)
Tudor Rd. E6 . . . . .5E **55**
E9 . . . . .5D **51**
Tudor Stacks SE24 . . . . .2E **105**
Tudor St.
EC4 . . . . . .4C **16** (1C **76**)
Tudway Rd. SE3 . . . . . . .1D **111**
Tufnell Ct. *E3* 5B **52**
(off Old Ford Rd.)
TUFNELL PARK 1E **47**
Tufnell Pk. Rd. N7 . . . . . .1E **47**
N19 . . . . .1E **47**
Tufton Ct. *SW1* 5D **23**
(off Tufton St.)
Tufton St.
SW1 . . . . .5D **23** (4A **76**)
Tugela St. SE6 . . . . .2B **122**
Tullis Ho. *E9* 4E **51**
(off Frampton Pk. Rd.)
TULSE HILL 1D **119**
Tulse Hill SW2 . . . . .4C **104**
Tulse Hill Est. SW2 . . . . .4C **104**
Tulse Ho. SW2 . . . . .4C **104**
Tulsemere Rd.
SE27 . . . . .2E **119**
Tunbridge Ho. EC1 . . . . . .1C **8**
Tunis Rd. W12 . . . . .2E **71**
Tunley Grn. E14 . . . . .4B **66**
Tunley Rd. NW10 . . . . . . .5A **42**
SW17 . . . . .1C **116**
Tunmarsh La. E13 . . . . . . .2D **69**
Tunnel App. E14 . . . . .1A **80**
SE10 . . . . .3A **82**
SE16 . . . . .3E **79**
Tunnel Av. SE10 . . . . .3F **81**
(not continuous)
Tunnel Av. Trad. Est.
SE10 . . . . .3F **81**
Tunnel Rd. SE16 . . . . .3E **79**
Tunstall Rd. SW9 . . . . . . .2B **104**
Tunworth Cres.
SW15 . . . . .4B **98**
Tun Yd. *SW8* 5D **89**
(off Peardon St.)
Tupelo Rd. E10 . . . . .4D **39**
Tupman Ho. *SE16* 3C **78**
(off Scott Lidgett Cres.)
Turenne Cl. SW18 . . . . . .2E **101**
Turin St. E2 . . . . .2C **64**
Turk's Head Yd.
EC1 . . . . . .5D **9** (4D **63**)
Turk's Row SW3 . . . . .1B **88**
Turle Rd. N4 . . . . .4B **34**
Turlewray Cl. N4 . . . . .3B **34**
Turley Cl. E15 . . . . .5A **54**
Turnagain La. EC4 . . . . . . .2D **17**
Turnberry Cl. SE16 . . . . . .1D **93**
Turnberry Quay E14 . . . . . .4D **81**
Turnbull Ho. N1 . . . . .5D **49**
Turnchapel M. SW4 . . . . .1D **103**
Turner Cl. NW11 . . . . .1D **31**
SW9 . . . . .3D **91**
Turner Ct. *SE16* 3E **79**
(off Albion St.)
Turner Dr. NW11 . . . . .1D **31**
Turner Ho. *E14* 1A **80**
(off Cassilis Rd.)
NW6 . . . . .2E **45**
(off Dresden Cl.)

Turner Ho. *NW8* 1A **60**
(off Townshend Est.)
SW1 . . . . .5F **75**
(off Herrick St.)
Turner Pde. *N1* 4C **48**
(off Barnsbury Pk.)
Turner Pl. SW11 . . . . .3A **102**
Turners Ct. *E15* 1E **53**
(off Drapers Rd.)
N15 . . . . .1F **35**
Turners Rd. E3 . . . . .4B **66**
Turner St. E1 . . . . .4D **65**
E16 . . . . .5B **68**
Turners Wood NW11 . . . . .2E **31**
Turneville Rd. W14 . . . . . .2B **86**
Turney Rd. SE21 . . . . . . .5E **105**
TURNHAM GREEN 5A **70**
Turnham Grn. Ter.
W4 . . . . .5A **70**
Turnham Grn. Ter. M.
W4 . . . . .5A **70**
Turnham Rd. SE4 . . . . . . .3A **108**
Turnmill St.
EC1 . . . . . .4D **9** (3D **63**)
Turnour Ho. *E1* 5D **65**
(off Walburgh St.)
Turnpike Cl. SE8 . . . . .3B **94**
Turnpike Ho.
EC1 . . . . . .2E **9** (2D **63**)
Turnpin Cl. SE10 . . . . .2E **95**
Turnstone Cl. E13 . . . . . . .2C **68**
Turnstone Ho. *E1* 1C **78**
(off Star Pl.)
Turpentine La. SW1 . . . . . .1D **89**
Turpin Cl. E1 . . . . .1F **79**
Turpin Ho. SW11 . . . . .4D **89**
Turpins Yd. NW2 . . . . .2F **43**
SE10 . . . . .3E **95**
Turpin Way N19 . . . . .4F **33**
Turquand St. SE17 . . . . . .5E **77**
Turret Gro. SW4 . . . . .1E **103**
Turville Ho. *NW8* 3A **60**
(off Grendon St.)
Turville St. E2 . . . . .3F **11**
Tuscan Ho. *E2* 2E **65**
(off Knottisford St.)
Tuskar St. SE10 . . . . .2A **96**
Tussah Ho. *E2* 1E **65**
(off Russia La.)
Tustin Est. SE15 . . . . .2E **93**
Tuttle Ho. *SW1* 1F **89**
(off Aylesford St.)
Tweed Ho. E14 . . . . .3E **67**
(off Teviot St.)
Tweedmouth Rd. E13 . . . .1D **69**
Tweezer's All. WC2 . . . . . .4B **16**
Twelvetrees Bus. Pk.
E3 . . . . .3F **67**
Twelvetrees Cres.
E3 . . . . .3E **67**
(not continuous)
E16 . . . . .3F **67**
Twickenham Rd. E11 . . . . .4E **39**
Twig Folly Cl. E2 . . . . .1F **65**
Twilley St. SW18 . . . . . . .5D **101**
Twine Cl. E1 . . . . .1E **79**
Twine Ter. *E3* 3B **66**
(off Ropery St.)
Twisden Rd. NW5 . . . . . . .1D **47**
Twycross M. SE10 . . . . . .1A **96**

Twyford Ho. N5 . . . . .5D **35**
N15 . . . . .1A **36**
(off Chisley Rd.)
Twyford Pl.
WC2 . . . . . .2F **15** (5B **62**)
Twyford St. N1 . . . . .5B **48**
Twynholm Mans.
SW6 . . . . .3A **86**
(off Lillie Rd.)
Tyas Rd. E16 . . . . .3B **68**
Tyburn Ho. *NW8* 3F **59**
(off Fisherton St.)
Tyburn Tree (site of) 3A **12**
Tyburn Way
W1 . . . . . .4A **12** (1B **74**)
Tyers Est. SE1 . . . . .3D **27**
Tyer's Ga.
SE1 . . . . . .4D **27** (3A **78**)
Tyers St. SE11 . . . . .1B **90**
Tyers Ter. SE11 . . . . .1B **90**
Tyler Cl. E2 . . . . .1B **64**
Tyler's Ct. W1 . . . . .3B **14**
Tyler St. SE10 . . . . .1A **96**
(not continuous)
Tylney Av. SE19 . . . . .5B **120**
(not continuous)
Tylney Ho. *E1* 5D **65**
(off Nelson St.)
Tylney Rd. E7 . . . . .1E **55**
Tyndale Ct. *E9* 3A **52**
(off Brookfield Rd.)
E14 . . . . .1D **95**
(off Transom Sq.)
Tyndale Ho. *N1* 4D **49**
(off Tyndale La.)
Tyndale La. N1 . . . . .4D **49**
Tyndale Mans.
N1 . . . . .4D **49**
(off Upper St.)
Tyndale Ter. N1 . . . . .4D **49**
Tyndall Gdns. E10 . . . . . . .4E **39**
Tyndall Rd. E10 . . . . .4E **39**
Tyneham Cl.
SW11 . . . . .1C **102**
Tyneham Rd. SW11 . . . . . .5C **88**
Tynemouth St. SW6 . . . . . .5E **87**
Tyne St. E1 . . . . .5B **64**
Tynsdale Rd. NW10 . . . . . .4A **42**
Tynte Ct. *E9* 2A **52**
(off Mabley St.)
Tynwald Ho. SE26 . . . . . .3C **120**
Type St. E2 . . . . .1F **65**
Tyrawley Rd.
SW6 . . . . .4D **87**
Tyrell Ho.
BR3: Beck 5D **123**
(off Beckenham Hill Rd.)
Tyrols Rd. SE23 . . . . .1F **121**
Tyrrell Ho. *SW1* 2E **89**
(off Churchill Gdns.)
Tyrrell Rd. SE22 . . . . .2C **106**
Tyrrell Way NW9 . . . . .2B **28**
Tyrwhitt Rd. SE4 . . . . .1C **108**
Tysoe St. EC1 . . . .2C **8** (2C **62**)
Tyson Gdns. SE23 . . . . . . .5E **107**
Tyson Rd. SE23 . . . . .5E **107**
Tyssen Pas. E8 . . . . .3B **50**
Tyssen Rd. N16 . . . . .5B **36**
Tyssen St. E8 . . . . .3B **50**
N1 . . . . .1A **64**

Tytherton *E2* 1E **65**
(off Cyprus St.)
Tytherton Rd. N19 . . . . .5F **33**

U

Uamvar St. E14 . . . . . . .4D **67**
Udall St. SW1 . . . . .5E **75**
Udimore Ho. *W10* 4E **57**
(off Sutton Way)
Uffington Rd. NW10 . . .5C **42**
SE27 . . . . .4C **118**
Ufford St. SE1 . . . .3C **24** (3C **76**)
Ufton Gro. N1 . . . . .4F **49**
Ufton Rd. N1 . . . . .4F **49**
(not continuous)
Uhura Sq. N16 . . . . .5A **36**
Ujima Ct. SW16 . . . . . .4A **118**
Ullathorne Rd.
SW16 . . . . .4E **117**
Ullin St. E14 . . . . .4E **67**
Ullswater Cl. SW15 . . . .4A **112**
Ullswater Cres.
SW15 . . . . .4A **112**
Ullswater Ho. *SE15* 2E **93**
(off Hillbeck Cl.)
Ullswater Rd. SE27 . . .2D **119**
SW13 . . . . .3C **84**
Ulster Pl.
NW1 . . . . . .4D **5** (3D **61**)
Ulster Ter.
NW1 . . . . .3C **4** (3D **61**)
Ulundi Rd. SE3 . . . . . . .2A **96**
Ulva Rd. SW15 . . . . .3F **99**
Ulverscroft Rd.
SE22 . . . . .3B **106**
Ulverstone Rd.
SE27 . . . . .2D **119**
Ulysses Rd. NW6 . . . . . .2B **44**
Umberston St. E1 . . . . . .5C **64**
Umbria St. SW15 . . . . . .4C **98**
Umbriel Pl. E13 . . . . .1C **68**
Umfreville Rd. N4 . . . . . .1D **35**
Undercliff Rd. SE13 . . . .1C **108**
Underhill Ho. *E14* 4C **66**
(off Burgess St.)
Underhill Pas. NW1 . . . .5D **47**
(off Camden High St.)
Underhill Rd. SE22 . . . .3C **106**
Underhill St. NW1 . . . . . .5D **47**
Undershaft
EC3 . . . . . .3D **19** (5A **64**)
Undershaw Rd.
BR1: Brom 3B **124**
Underwood Ct. *E10* 3D **39**
(off Leyton Grange Est.)
Underwood Ho. W6 . . . .4D **71**
(off Sycamore Gdns.)
Underwood Rd. E1 . . . . .3C **64**
Underwood Row
N1 . . . . .1A **10** (2E **63**)
Underwood St.
N1 . . . . .1A **10** (2E **63**)
Undine Rd. E14 . . . . . . .5D **81**
Undine St. SW17 . . . . .5B **116**
Unicorn Bldg. *E1* 1F **79**
(off Jardine Rd.)
Unicorn Theatre 2A **78**
Union Cl. E11 . . . . .1F **53**

Union Cotts. E15 . . . . . .4A **54**
Union Ct. EC2 . . . . .2D **19**
SW4 . . . . .5A **90**
W9 . . . . .4C **58**
(off Elmfield Way)
Union Dr. E1 . . . . .3A **66**
Union Gro. SW8 . . . . . . .5F **89**
Union M. SW4 . . . . .5A **90**
Union Pk. *SE10* 1B **96**
(off Calvert Rd.)
Union Rd. SW4 . . . . .5F **89**
SW8 . . . . .5F **89**
Union Sq. N1 . . . . .5E **49**
Union St.
SE1 . . . . . .2D **25** (2D **77**)
Union Theatre 2E **25**
Union Wlk.
E2 . . . . .1E **11** (2A **64**)
Union Wharf
N1 . . . . .5E **49**
(Arlington Av.)
N1 . . . . .1E **63**
(off Wenlock Rd.)
Union Yd.
W1 . . . . .3E **13** (5D **61**)
United Ho. *SE16* 3E **79**
(off Brunel Rd.)
Unit Workshops *E1* 5C **64**
(off Adler St.)
Unity Cl. NW10 . . . . .3C **42**
SE19 . . . . .5E **119**
Unity Ct. *SE1* 1B **92**
(off Fortune Pl.)
Unity M. NW1 . . . . .1F **61**
Unity Way SE18 . . . . . . .4F **83**
Unity Wharf *SE1* 3B **78**
(off Mill St.)
University College London
Art Collections 3B **6**
(off Gower St.)
Bloomsbury Campus
. . . . .3B **6** (3F **61**)
*Department of
Geological Collections*
. . . . .4B **6**
(off Gower St.)
Institute of Neurology
. . . . .4E **7**
(off Queen Sq.)
Slade School of Fine Art
. . . . .3B **6**
(off Gower Ct.)
Windeyer Institute
. . . . .5A **6** (4E **61**)
University of East London
Duncan House 5F **53**
Stratford Campus
. . . . .3A **54**
University of Greenwich
Greenwich Campus -
King William Wlk.
. . . . .2F **95**
Maritime Greenwich Campus
. . . . .2E **95**
University of London
Birkbeck College
. . . . .5C **6** (4F **61**)
Heythrop College
. . . . .4D **73**
(off Kensington Sq.)

University of London
Institute of Education &
Institute of
Advanced Legal Studies
. . . . .4C **6** (3F **61**)
School of
Hygiene &
Tropical Medicine
. . . . .5C **6**
School of
Oriental & African Studies
. . . . .4C **6**
Senate House
. . . . .5C **6** (4F **61**)
Warburg Institute
. . . . .4C **6** (3F **61**)
University of North London
Hornsey Rd. 1C **48**
Ladbrooke House
. . . . .2E **49**
North London Campus,
Spring House 3C **48**
University of the Arts London
Camberwell College of Arts -
Peckham Rd. 4A **92**
Wilson Rd. 4A **92**
Chelsea College of
Art & Design 1F **89**
London College of Fashion -
Golden La. 4F **9**
Mare St. 4E **51**
University of Westminster
Cavendish Campus -
Hanson St.
. . . . .5F **5** (4E **61**)
Lit. Titchfield St.
. . . . .1F **13**
Marylebone Campus
. . . . .5B **4** (4C **60**)
Regent Campus -
Regent St. 2E **13**
Wells St. 2A **14**
University St.
WC1 . . . . . . .4A **6** (3E **61**)
Unwin Cl. SE15 . . . . .2C **92**
Unwin Mans. *W14* 2B **86**
(off Queen's Club Gdns.)
Unwin Rd. SW7 . . . . .4F **73**
Upbrook M. W2 . . . . .5E **59**
Upcerne Rd. SW10 . . . . .3E **87**
Upcott Ho. *E3* 2D **67**
(off Bruce Rd.)
E9 . . . . .4E **51**
(off Frampton Pk. Rd.)
Upgrove Mnr. Way
SW2 . . . . .5C **104**
Upham Pk. Rd. W4 . . . . .5A **70**
Upland M. SE22 . . . . . . .3C **106**
Upland Rd. E13 . . . . .3C **68**
SE22 . . . . .3C **106**
(not continuous)
Uplands Rd. N8 . . . . .1B **34**
Upnall Ho. SE15 . . . . . . .2E **93**
Upnor Way SE17 . . . . . . .1A **92**
Up. Addison Gdns.
W14 . . . . .3A **72**
Up. Bank St. E14 . . . . . . .2D **81**
(not continuous)
Up. Bardsey Wlk. N1 . . . .3E **49**
(off Douglas Rd. Nth.)

Up. Belgrave St.
  SW1 . . . . . . .5C **20** (4C **74**)
Up. Berenger Wlk.
  SW10 . . . . .3F **87**
  (off Berenger Wlk.)
Up. Berkeley St.
  W1 . . . . . .3A **12** (5B **60**)
Up. Blantyre Wlk.
  SW10 . . . . .3F **87**
  (off Blantyre Wlk.)
Up. Brockley Rd.
  SE4 . . . . .1B **108**
  (not continuous)
Up. Brook St.
  W1 . . . . . .4B **12** (1C **74**)
Up. Caldy St. *N1* 3E **49**
  (off Caldy Wlk.)
Up. Camelford Wlk.
  W11 . . . . .5A **58**
  (off St Mark's Rd.)
Up. Cheapside Pas.
  EC2 . . . . .3F **17**
  (off One New Change)
Up. Cheyne Row SW3 . .2A **88**
UPPER CLAPTON 4D **37**
Up. Clapton Rd. E5 . . .3D **37**
Up. Clarendon Wlk.
  W11 . . . . .5A **58**
  (off Clarendon Rd.)
Up. Dartrey Wlk.
  SW10 . . . . .3E **87**
  (off Whistler Wlk.)
Up. Dengie Wlk. *N1* . . .5E **49**
  (off Baddow Wlk.)
Upper Feilde *W1* 4B **12**
  (off Park St.)
Up. Grosvenor St.
  W1 . . . . . .5B **12** (1C **74**)
Upper Ground
  SE1 . . . . . .1B **24** (2C **76**)
Up. Gulland Wlk. *N1* . . .4E **49**
  (off Church Rd.)
Up. Hampstead Wlk.
  NW3 . . . . .1E **45**
Up. Handa Wlk. *N1* 3F **49**
  (off Handa Wlk.)
Up. Hawkwell Wlk.
  N1 . . . . .5E **49**
  (off Maldon Cl.)
UPPER HOLLOWAY 4E **33**
Up. James St.
  W1 . . . . . .4A **14** (1E **75**)
Up. John St.
  W1 . . . . . .4A **14** (1E **75**)
Up. Lismore Wlk. *N1* . .3E **49**
  (off Clephane Rd.)
Upper Lodge *W8* 2D **73**
  (off Palace Grn.)
Upper Mall W6 . . . . . .1C **84**
  (not continuous)
Upper Marsh
  SE1 . . . . . .5A **24** (4B **76**)
Up. Montagu St.
  W1 . . . . . .5A **4** (4B **60**)
Upper Nth. St. E14 . . . .4C **66**
Up. Park Rd. NW3 . . . .2B **46**
Up. Phillimore Gdns.
  W8 . . . . .3C **72**
Up. Ramsey Wlk. *N1* . . .3F **49**
  (off Ramsey Wlk.)

Up. Rawreth Wlk. *N1* . .5E **49**
  (off Basire St.)
Up. Richmond Rd.
  SW15 . . . . .2B **98**
Up. Richmond Rd. W.
  SW14 . . . . .2A **98**
Upper Rd. E13 . . . . . . .2C **68**
Up. St Martin's La.
  WC2 . . . .4D **15** (1A **76**)
Upper St. N1 . . . . .1D **63**
UPPER SYDENHAM . . .3D **121**
Up. Tachbrook St.
  SW1 . . . . .5E **75**
Up. Talbot Wlk. *W11* . .5A **58**
  (off Talbot Wlk.)
Upper Ter. NW3 . . . . . .5E **31**
Up. Thames St.
  EC4 . . . . . .4E **17** (1D **77**)
Up. Tollington Pk. N4 . .3C **34**
  (not continuous)
Upperton Rd. E. E13 . . .2E **69**
Upperton Rd. W. E13 . . .1E **69**
UPPER TOOTING 4B **116**
Up. Tooting Pk.
  SW17 . . . . .2B **116**
Up. Tooting Rd.
  SW17 . . . . .4B **116**
Up. Tulse Hill SW2 . . .5B **104**
Up. Whistler Wlk.
  SW10 . . . . .3E **87**
  (off Worlds End Est.)
Up. Wimpole St.
  W1 . . . . . . .5C **4** (4C **60**)
Up. Woburn Pl.
  WC1 . . . . . .2C **6** (2F **61**)
Upstall St. SE5 . . . . . .4D **91**
UPTON 4C **54**
Upton Av. E7 . . . . .4C **54**
Upton Cl. NW2 . . . . . . .5A **30**
Upton Hgts. E7 . . . . . .4C **54**
Upton La. E7 . . . . .4C **54**
Upton Lodge E7 . . . . . .3C **54**
UPTON PARK 5F **55**
Upton Pk. Boleyn Cinema
   . . . . .1F **69**
Upton Pk. Rd. E7 . . . . .4D **55**
Upwey Ho. N1 . . . . . . .5A **50**
Upwood Rd. SE12 . . . .4C **110**
Urban M. N4 . . . . .1D **35**
Urdang, The *2C* **8**
  (off Rosebery Av.)
Urlwin St. SE5 . . . . . . .2E **91**
Urlwin Wlk. SW9 . . . . .4C **90**
Urmston Dr. SW19 . . . .1A **114**
Urmston Ho. E14 . . . . .5E **81**
  (off Seyssel St.)
Ursula Gould Way
  E14 . . . . .4C **66**
Ursula M. N4 . . . . .3E **35**
Ursula St. SW11 . . . . . .4A **88**
Urswick Rd. E9 . . . . . .2E **51**
Usborne M. SW8 . . . . .3B **90**
Usher Rd. E3 . . . . .5B **52**
  (not continuous)
Usk Rd. SW11 . . . . . . .2E **101**
Usk St. E2 . . . . .2F **65**
Utah Bldg. *SE10* 4D **95**
  (off Deal's Gateway)
Utopia Village NW1 . . .4C **46**
Uverdale Rd. SW10 . . . .3E **87**

Uxbridge Rd. W12 . . . . .2C **70**
Uxbridge St. W8 . . . . . .2C **72**

V

Vaine Ho. E9 . . . . .3A **52**
Vaizeys Wharf SE7 . . . .4D **83**
Vale, The NW11 . . . . . .5F **29**
  SW3 . . . . .2F **87**
  W3 . . . . .2A **70**
Vale Cl. W9 . . . . .2E **59**
Vale Cotts. SW15 . . . . .3A **112**
Vale Ct. W3 . . . . .2B **70**
  W9 . . . . .2E **59**
Vale Cres. SW15 . . . . .4A **112**
Vale End SE22 . . . . . . .2B **106**
Vale Estate, The W3 . . .2A **70**
Vale Gro. N4 . . . . .2E **35**
  W3 . . . . .3A **70**
Vale Lodge SE23 . . . . .2E **121**
Valentia Pl. SW9 . . . . .2C **104**
Valentine Ct. SE23 . . . .2F **121**
  (not continuous)
Valentine Ho. *E3* 5B **52**
  (off Garrison Rd.)
Valentine Pl.
  SE1 . . . . . .3D **25** (3D **77**)
Valentine Rd. E9 . . . . .3F **51**
Valentine Row
  SE1 . . . . . .4D **25** (3D **77**)
VALE OF HEALTH 5E **31**
Vale of Health NW3 . . .5F **31**
Vale Pde. SW15 . . . . . .3A **112**
Valerian Way E15 . . . . .2A **68**
Vale Ri. NW11 . . . . .3B **30**
Vale Rd. E7 . . . . .3D **55**
  N4 . . . . .2E **35**
Vale Row N5 . . . . .5D **35**
Vale Royal N7 . . . . . . .4A **48**
Vale Royal Ho. *WC2* . . .4C **14**
  (off Charing Cross Rd.)
Vale St. SE27 . . . . .3F **119**
Valeswood Rd.
  BR1: Brom 5B **124**
Vale Ter. N4 . . . . .1E **35**
Valetta Gro. E13 . . . . . .1C **68**
Valetta Rd. W3 . . . . . . .3A **70**
Valette Ho. E9 . . . . . . .3E **51**
Valette St. E9 . . . . .3E **51**
Valiant Ho. *E14* 3E **81**
  (off Plevna St.)
  SE7 . . . . .1E **97**
Vallance Rd. E1 . . . . . .2C **64**
  E2 . . . . .2C **64**
Valley, The 1E **97**
Valleyfield Rd.
  SW16 . . . . .5B **118**
Valley Gro. SE7 . . . . . .1E **97**
Valley Rd. SW16 . . . . .5B **118**
Valley Side SE7 . . . . . .1F **97**
Valliere Rd. NW10 . . . .2C **56**
Val McKenzie Av. N7 . . .5C **34**
Valmar Rd. SE5 . . . . . .4E **91**
Valmar Trad. Est.
  SE5 . . . . .4E **91**
Valnay St. SW17 . . . . .5B **116**
Valois Ho. *SE1* 5F **27**
  (off St Saviour's Est.)
Valonia Gdns. SW18 . . .4B **100**

V&A Mus. of Childhood
. . . . .2E 65
Vanbrugh Castle
SE10 . . . . .2A 96
(off Maze Hill)
Vanbrugh Cl. E16 . . . . .4F 69
Vanbrugh Ct. SE11 . . . .5C 76
(off Wincott St.)
Vanbrugh Flds. SE3 . . .2B 96
Vanbrugh Hill SE3 . . . .1B 96
SE10 . . . . .1B 96
Vanbrugh Ho. E9 . . . . .4E 51
(off Loddiges Rd.)
Vanbrugh Pk. SE3 . . . .3B 96
Vanbrugh Pk. Rd. SE3 . .3B 96
Vanbrugh Pk. Rd. W.
SE3 . . . . .3B 96
Vanbrugh Rd. W4 . . . .4A 70
Vanbrugh Ter. SE3 . . . .4B 96
Vanburgh Ho. E1 . . . . .5F 11
(off Folgate St.)
Vancouver Ho. E1 . . . .2D 79
(off Reardon Path)
Vancouver Rd. SE23 . . .2A 122
Vanderbilt Rd.
SW18 . . . . .1D 115
Vanderbilt Vs. W12 . . . .3F 71
(off Sterne St.)
Vandervell Ct. W3 . . . .3A 70
(off Amber Way)
Vandome Cl. E16 . . . . .5D 69
Vandon Ct. SW1 . . . . .5A 22
(off Petty France)
Vandon Pas.
SW1 . . . . .5A 22 (4E 75)
Vandon St.
SW1 . . . . .5A 22 (4E 75)
Vandyke Cl. SW15 . . . .5F 99
Vandyke Cross SE9 . . .3F 111
Vandy St. EC2 . . .4D 11 (3A 64)
Vane Cl. NW3 . . . . . . .2F 45
Vane St. SW1 . . . . . . .5E 75
Vange Ho. W10 . . . . . .4E 57
(off Sutton Way)
Van Gogh Ct. E14 . . . . .4F 81
Vanguard Bldg. E14 . . . .3F 80
Vanguard Cl. E16 . . . . .4C 68
Vanguard Ct. SE5 . . . . .4A 92
Vanguard Ho. E8 . . . . .4D 51
Vanguard St. SE8 . . . . .4C 94
Vanilla & Sesame Ct.
SE1 . . . . .3F 27
(off Curlew St.)
Vanneck Sq. SW15 . . . .3C 98
Vanoc Gdns.
BR1: Brom 4C 124
Vansittart Rd. E7 . . . . .1B 54
Vansittart St. SE14 . . . .3A 94
Vanstone Ct. N7 . . . . . .3C 48
(off Blackthorn Av.)
Vanston Pl. SW6 . . . . . .3C 86
Vantage M. E14 . . . . . .2E 81
(off Coldharbour)
Vantage Pl. W8 . . . . . .4C 72
Vantrey Ho. SE11 . . . . .5C 76
(off Marylee Way)
Vant Rd. SW17 . . . . . .5B 116
Varcoe Rd. SE16 . . . . .1D 93
Vardens Rd. SW11 . . . .2F 101
Varden St. E1 . . . . .5D 65

Vardon Cl. W3 . . . . . . .5A 56
Vardon Ho. SE10 . . . . .4E 95
Varley Ho. NW6 . . . . . .5C 44
SE1 . . . . .4E 77
(off New Kent Rd.)
Varley Rd. E16 . . . . . . .5D 69
Varna Rd. SW6 . . . . . . .3A 86
Varndell St.
NW1 . . . . .1F 5 (2E 61)
Varnishers Yd. N1 . . . . .1E 7
(off York Way)
Vartry Rd. N15 . . . . . . .1F 35
Vassall Ho. E3 . . . . . . .2A 66
(off Antill Rd.)
Vassall Rd. SW9 . . . . . .3C 90
Vat Ho. SW8 . . . . .3A 90
(off Rita Rd.)
Vauban Est. SE16 . . . . .4B 78
Vauban St. SE16 . . . . . .4B 78
Vaudeville Ct. N4 . . . . .4C 34
Vaudeville Theatre 5E 15
(off Strand)
Vaughan Av. NW4 . . . . .1C 28
W6 . . . . .5B 70
Vaughan Est. E2 . . . . . .1F 11
Vaughan Ho. SE1 . . . . .3D 25
(off Blackfriars Rd.)
SW4 . . . . .5E 103
Vaughan Rd. E15 . . . . .3B 54
SE5 . . . . .5E 91
Vaughan St. SE16 . . . . .3B 80
Vaughan Way E1 . . . . .1C 78
Vaughan Williams Cl.
SE8 . . . . .3C 94
VAUXHALL 2A 90
Vauxhall Bri. SW1 . . . . .1A 90
Vauxhall Bri. Rd.
SW1 . . . . .4E 75
Vauxhall City Farm 1B 90
(off Tyers St.)
VAUXHALL CROSS 1A 90
Vauxhall Distribution Pk.
SW8 . . . . .2F 89
Vauxhall Gro. SW8 . . . .2B 90
Vauxhall St. SE11 . . . . .1B 90
Vauxhall Wlk. SE11 . . . .1B 90
Vawdrey Cl. E1 . . . . . . .3E 65
Veda Rd. SE13 . . . . . . .2C 108
Velde Way SE22 . . . . . .3A 106
Velletri Ho. E2 . . . . . . .1F 65
(off Mace St.)
Velodrome, Olympic Pk.
. . . . .2D 53
Venables St. NW8 . . . . .3F 59
Vencourt Pl. W6 . . . . . .5C 70
Venetian Rd. SE5 . . . . .5E 91
Venetia Rd. N4 . . . . . . .1D 35
Venice Ct. SE5 . . . . . . .3E 91
(off Bowyer St.)
Venice Wlk. W2 . . . . . .4E 59
(not continuous)
Venner Rd. SE26 . . . . . .5E 121
(not continuous)
Venn Ho. N1 . . . . .5B 48
(off Barnsbury Est.)
Venn St. SW4 . . . . .2E 103
Ventnor Rd. SE14 . . . . .3F 93
Venture Ct. SE1 . . . . . .1E 27
(off Bermondsey St.)
SE12 . . . . .5C 110

Venture Ho. W10 . . . . . .5F 57
(off Bridge Cl.)
Venue St. E14 . . . . .4E 67
Venus Ho. E3 . . . . .5C 52
(off Garrison Rd.)
E14 . . . . .5C 80
(off Westferry Rd.)
Vera Ct. E3 . . . . .2D 67
(off Grace Pl.)
Vera Lynn Cl. E7 . . . . . .1C 54
Vera Rd. SW6 . . . . .4A 86
Verbena Cl. E16 . . . . . .3B 68
Verbena Gdns. W6 . . . .1C 84
Verdant Ct. SE6 . . . . . .5A 110
(off Verdant La.)
Verdant La. SE6 . . . . . .5A 110
Verdi Cres. W10 . . . . . .1A 58
Verdun Rd. SW13 . . . . .2C 84
Vere Ct. W2 . . . . .5D 59
(off Westbourne Gdns.)
Vereker Rd. W14 . . . . . .1A 86
Vere St. W1 . . . .3D 13 (5D 61)
Verity Cl. W11 . . . . .1A 72
Verity Ho. E3 . . . . .2B 66
(off Merchant St.)
Vermeer Ct. E14 . . . . . .4F 81
Vermeer Gdns.
SE15 . . . . .2E 107
Vermont Rd. SW18 . . . .4D 101
Verney Ho. NW8 . . . . . .3A 60
(off Jerome Cres.)
Verney Rd. SE16 . . . . . .2C 92
Verney St. NW10 . . . . . .5A 28
Verney Way SE16 . . . . .1D 93
Vernon Ct. NW2 . . . . . .5B 30
Vernon Ho. SE11 . . . . . .1B 90
(off Vauxhall St.)
WC1 . . . . .1E 15
(off Vernon Pl.)
Vernon Mans. W14 . . . .2B 86
(off Queen's Club Mans.)
Vernon M. W14 . . . . . . .5A 72
(off Vernon Rd.)
WC1 . . . . .1E 15 (4A 62)
Vernon Ri.
WC1 . . . . .1A 8 (2B 62)
Vernon Rd. E3 . . . . .1B 66
E11 . . . . .3A 40
E15 . . . . .4A 54
SW14 . . . . .1A 98
Vernon Sq.
WC1 . . . . .1A 8 (2B 62)
Vernon St. W14 . . . . . . .5A 72
Verona Ct. SE14 . . . . . .2F 93
(off Myers La.)
W4 . . . . .1A 84
Verona Rd. E7 . . . . .4C 54
Veronica Ho. E3 . . . . . .2D 67
(off Talwin St.)
SE4 . . . . .1B 108
Veronica Rd. SW17 . . . .2D 117
Verran Rd. SW12 . . . . .5D 103
Verulam Av. E17 . . . . . .1B 38
Verulam Bldgs. WC1 . . .5A 8
Verulam Ho. W6 . . . . . .3E 71
(off Hammersmith Gro.)
Verulam St.
WC1 . . . . .5B 8 (4C 62)

Vervian Ho. SE15 . . . . . .3C 92
(off Reddins Rd.)
Verwood Ho. SW8 . . . . . . .3B 90
(off Cobbett St.)
Verwood Lodge E14 . . . .4F 81
(off Manchester Rd.)
Veryan Ct. N8 . . . . .1F 33
Vesage Ct. EC1 . . . . . .1C 16
Vesey Path E14 . . . . .5D 67
Vespan Rd. W12 . . . . . . .3C 70
Vesta Ct. SE1 . . . . .4D 27
Vesta Ho. E3 . . . . .5C 52
(off Garrison Rd.)
Vesta Rd. SE4 . . . . .5A 94
Vestris Rd. SE23 . . . . . .2F 121
Vestry Ct. SW1 . . . . .4F 75
(off Monck St.)
Vestry M. SE5 . . . . .4A 92
SW18 . . . . .3F 101
Vestry Rd. SE5 . . . . .4A 92
Vestry St. N1 . . . .1B 10 (2F 63)
Vesuvius Apartments
E3 . . . . .1B 66
(off Centurion La.)
Vevey St. SE6 . . . . .2B 122
Viaduct Bldgs.
EC1 . . . . . . .1C 16 (4C 62)
Viaduct Pl. E2 . . . . .2D 65
Viaduct St. E2 . . . . .2D 65
Vian St. SE13 . . . . .1D 109
Vibart Gdns. SW2 . . . . .5B 104
Vibart Wlk. N1 . . . . .5A 48
(off Outram Pl.)
Vibeca Apartments
E1 . . . . .4B 64
(off Chicksand St.)
Vicarage Av. SE3 . . . . . .3C 96
Vicarage Ct. W8 . . . . . . .3D 73
Vicarage Cres. SW11 . . . .4F 87
Vicarage Gdns. W8 . . . . .2C 72
Vicarage Ga. W8 . . . . . . .2D 73
Vicarage Gro. SE5 . . . . . .4F 91
Vicarage La. E15 . . . . . . .4A 54
Vicarage Path N8 . . . . . .2A 34
Vicarage Rd. E10 . . . . . .2C 38
E15 . . . . .4B 54
NW4 . . . . .1C 28
SW14 . . . . .3A 98
Vicarage Wlk. SW11 . . . .4F 87
Vicarage Way NW10 . . . .5A 28
Vicars Cl. E9 . . . . .5A 52
E15 . . . . .5C 54
Vicar's Hill SE13 . . . . . .2D 109
Vicar's Oak Rd.
SE19 . . . . .5A 120
Vicar's Rd. NW5 . . . . . . .2C 46
Vicentia Ct. SW11 . . . . .1E 101
Viceroy Ct. NW8 . . . . . . .1A 60
(off Prince Albert Rd.)
Viceroy Rd. SW8 . . . . . . .4A 90
Vicinity Ho. E14 . . . . . . .1C 80
(off Storehouse M.)
Vic Johnson Ho. E3 . . . . .5B 52
(off Armagh Rd.)
Vickery Ct. EC1 . . . . .3A 10
(off Mitchell St.)
Vickery's Wharf E14 . . . . .5C 66
Victor Cazalet Ho.
N1 . . . . .5D 49
(off Gaskin St.)

Victor Ho. SE7 . . . . .2E 97
Victoria & Albert Mus.
. . . . .4F 73
Victoria Arc. SW1 . . . . . .5E 21
(off Victoria St.)
Victoria Av. E6 . . . . .5F 55
EC2 . . . . . .1E 19 (4A 64)
Victoria Bldgs. E8 . . . . . .5D 51
(off Mare St.)
Victoria Chambers
EC2 . . . . .3D 11
(off Paul St.)
Victoria Cl.
SE22 . . . . .3C 106
Victoria Colonnade
WC1 . . . . .1E 15
(off Southampton Row)
Victoria Cotts. E1 . . . . . . .4C 64
(off Deal St.)
Victoria Ct. SE1 . . . . .5A 78
(off Hendre Rd.)
SE26 . . . . .5E 121
Victoria Cres. N15 . . . . . .1A 36
SE19 . . . . .5A 120
Victoria Dock Rd.
E16 . . . . .1B 82
Victoria Dr. SW19 . . . . . .5F 99
Victoria Emb.
EC4 . . . . . .5A 16 (3A 76)
SW1 . . . . . .3E 23 (3A 76)
WC2 . . . . . .3E 23 (3A 76)
Victoria Gdns. W11 . . . . .2C 72
Victoria Gro. W8 . . . . . . .4E 73
Victoria Gro. M. W2 . . . .1C 72
Victoria Hall E16 . . . . . .2C 82
(off Wesley Av., not continuous)
Victoria Ho. SW1 . . . . . .1D 89
(off Ebury Bri. Rd.)
SW1 . . . . .5E 75
(off Francis St.)
SW8 . . . . .3A 90
(off Sth. Lambeth Rd.)
Victoria Ind. Est. W3 . . . .4A 56
Victoria Mans.
NW10 . . . . .4D 43
SW8 . . . . .3A 90
(off Sth. Lambeth Rd.)
W14 . . . . .2B 86
(off Queen's Club Mans.)
Victoria M. SE8 . . . . .3C 50
NW6 . . . . .5C 44
SW4 . . . . .2D 103
SW18 . . . . .1E 115
Victoria Mills Studios
E15 . . . . .5F 53
Victorian Gro. N16 . . . . . .1A 50
Victorian Hgts. SW8 . . . . .5D 89
(off Thackeray Rd.)
Victoria Rd. N16 . . . . .5A 36
Victoria Palace Theatre
. . . . .5F 21
(off Victoria St.)
Victoria Pk. 5F 51
Victoria Pk. Ct. E9 . . . . . .4E 51
(off Well St.)
Victoria Pk. Ind. Cen.
E9 . . . . .4C 52
(off Rothbury Rd.)
Victoria Pk. Rd. E9 . . . . . .5E 51
Victoria Pk. Sq. E2 . . . . .2E 65

Victoria Pk. Studios
E9 . . . . .3E 51
(off Milborne St.)
Victoria Pas. NW8 . . . . . .3F 59
(off Fisherton St.)
Victoria Pl. Shop. Cen.
SW1 . . . . .5D 75
(off Buckingham Pal. Rd.)
Victoria Point E13 . . . . . .1C 68
(off Victoria Rd.)
Victoria Ri. NW6 . . . . . . .4E 45
(off Hilgrove Rd.)
SW4 . . . . .1D 103
Victoria Rd. E11 . . . . .1A 54
E13 . . . . .1C 68
N4 . . . . .2B 34
NW6 . . . . .1B 58
NW10 . . . . .4A 56
W3 . . . . .4A 56
W8 . . . . .4E 73
Victoria Sq. SW1 . . . . . . .5E 21
Victoria St. E15 . . . . .4A 54
SW1 . . . . . .5E 21 (4E 75)
Victoria Ter. N4 . . . . .3C 34
NW10 . . . . .3B 56
Victoria Way SE7 . . . . . . .1D 97
Victoria Wharf E2 . . . . . .1F 65
(off Palmers Rd.)
E14 . . . . .1A 80
SE8 . . . . .1B 94
(off Dragoon Rd.)
Victoria Works NW2 . . . . .4D 29
Victoria Yd. E1 . . . . .5C 64
Victor Rd. NW10 . . . . . . .2D 57
Victor Wharf SE1 . . . . . . .1B 26
(off Clink St.)
Victory Ct. W9 . . . . .3C 58
(off Hermes Cl.)
Victory Pl. E14 . . . . .1A 80
SE17 . . . . .5F 77
Victory Wlk. SE8 . . . . . . .4C 94
Victory Way SE16 . . . . . . .3A 80
Video Ct. N4 . . . . .2B 34
View Cl. N6 . . . . .2B 32
View Cres. N8 . . . . .1F 33
Viewfield Rd. SW18 . . . . .4B 100
View Rd. N6 . . . . .2B 32
Vigers Ct. NW10 . . . . . . .2D 57
(off Harrow Rd.)
Vigilant Cl. SE26 . . . . . . .4C 120
Vigo St. W1 . . . .5F 13 (1E 75)
Viking Cl. E3 . . . . .1A 66
Viking Ct. SW6 . . . . .2C 86
Viking Gdns. E6 . . . . .3F 69
Viking Ho. SE5 . . . . .5E 91
(off Denmark Rd.)
SE18 . . . . .5F 83
(off Pett St.)
Viking Pl. E10 . . . . .3B 38
Village, The NW3 . . . . . . .4E 31
SE7 . . . . .2E 97
Village Cl. NW3 . . . . .2F 45
(off Belsize La.)
Village Ct. SE3 . . . . .1A 110
(off Hurren Cl.)
Village Mt. NW3 . . . . .1E 45
(off Perrins Pl.)
Village Way NW10 . . . . . .1A 42
SE21 . . . . .4F 105
Villa Rd. SW9 . . . . .1C 104

Villas on the Heath
NW3 . . . . .5E **31**
Villa St. SE17 . . . . . . .1F **91**
Villa Wlk SE17 . . . . . . .1F **91**
(off Villa St.)
Villiers Cl. E10 . . . . . . .4C **38**
Villiers Ct. SW11 . . . . .4A **88**
(off Battersea Bri. Rd.)
Villiers M. NW2 . . . . . . .3C **42**
Villiers Rd. NW2 . . . . . .3C **42**
Villiers St.
WC2 . . . . . .5D **15** (2A **76**)
Vince Ct. N1 . . . .2C **10** (2F **63**)
Vincennes Est.
SE27 . . . . .4F **119**
Vincent Cl. SE16 . . . . . .3A **80**
Vincent Ct. N4 . . . . .3A **34**
SW9 . . . . .4B **90**
W1 . . . . .2A **12**
(off Seymour Pl.)
Vincent Gdns. NW2 . . . .5B **28**
Vincent Ho. SW1 . . . . . .5F **75**
(off Regency St.)
SW1 . . . . .5F **75**
(off Vincent Sq.)
Vincent M. E3 . . . . .1C **66**
Vincent Sq. SW1 . . . . . .5F **75**
Vincent Sq. Mans.
SW1 . . . . .5E **75**
(off Walcott St.)
Vincent St. E16 . . . . . . .4B **68**
SW1 . . . . .5F **75**
Vincent Ter. N1 . . . . . . .1D **63**
Vince St. EC1 . . .2C **10** (2F **63**)
Vine Cl. E5 . . . . .1C **50**
Vine Cotts. E1 . . . . .5E **65**
(off Sidney Sq.)
Vine Ct. E1 . . . . .4C **64**
Vinegar St. E1 . . . . .2D **79**
Vinegar Yd.
SE1 . . . . . .3D **27** (3A **78**)
Vine Hill EC1 . . . .4B **8** (3C **62**)
Vine La. SE1 . . . .2E **27** (2A **78**)
Vineries, The SE6 . . . . .1C **122**
Vine Rd. E15 . . . . .4B **54**
SW13 . . . . .1B **98**
Vinery, The SW8 . . . . . .3A **90**
(off Regent's Bri. Gdns.)
Vinery Row NW6 . . . . . .4D **71**
Vine Sq. W14 . . . . .1B **86**
(off Star Rd.)
Vine St. EC3 . . . .3F **19** (5B **64**)
W1 . . . . . .5A **14** (1E **75**)
Vine St. Bri.
EC1 . . . . . .4C **8** (3C **62**)
Vine Yd. SE1 . . . . .3A **26**
Vineyard Cl. SE6 . . . . . .1C **122**
Vineyard Hill Rd.
SW19 . . . . .4B **114**
Vineyard Wlk.
EC1 . . . . . .3B **8** (3C **62**)
Viney Rd. SE13 . . . . . . .1D **109**
Vining St. SW9 . . . . . . .2C **104**
Vinopolis 1A **26** (2E **77**)
Vinson Ho. N1 . . . . .1F **63**
(off Cranston Est.)
Vintner's Ct.
EC4 . . . . . .5A **18** (1E **77**)
Vintner's Pl. EC4 . . . . . .5A **18**
Viola Sq. W12 . . . . .1B **70**

Violet Cl. E16 . . . . .3A **68**
SE8 . . . . .2B **94**
Violet Ct. E15 . . . . .4A **54**
(off Victoria St.)
Violet Hill NW8 . . . . . . .1E **59**
Violet Hill Ho. NW8 . . . .1E **59**
(off Violet Hill)
Violet Rd. E3 . . . . .3D **67**
E17 . . . . .1C **38**
Violet St. E2 . . . . .3D **65**
VIP Trading Est. SE7 . . .5E **83**
Virgil Pl. W1 . . . . .4B **60**
Virgil St. SE1 . . . .5A **24** (4B **76**)
Virgin Active
Barbican 5F **9**
(off Aldersgate St.)
Cricklewood 5A **30**
Crouch End 1A **34**
(off Topsfield Pde.)
Fulham 2A **86**
(within Fulham Pools)
Hammersmith 5F **71**
(off Hammersmith Rd.)
Hendon 1E **29**
Holloway 5A **34**
Islington, Essex Road
. . . . .5D **49**
Islington, Goswell Road
. . . . .1D **9**
(off Goswell Rd.)
Kensington 3D **73**
(off Old Court Pl.)
Mayfair . . .4A **12** (5C **60**)
Moorgate
. . . . . .4B **10** (3F **63**)
Notting Hill 5A **58**
Putney 2A **100**
Swiss Cottage 3E **45**
(in O2 Cen.)
The Riverside
Health & Racquets Club,
Chiswick 4A **84**
Wandsworth,
Smugglers Way
. . . . .2D **101**
Wandsworth, Southside
. . . . .3D **101**
West London 2A **70**
Wimbledon, North Rd.
. . . . .5E **115**
Wimbledon, Worple Rd.
. . . . .5B **114**
Virginia Ct. SE16 . . . . . .3F **79**
(off Eleanor Cl.)
WC1 . . . . .3C **6**
(off Burton St.)
Virginia Ho. E14 . . . . . . .1E **81**
(off Newby Pl.)
Virginia Rd.
E2 . . . . . . .2F **11** (2B **64**)
Virginia St. E1 . . . . .1C **78**
Virginia Wlk. SW2 . . . . .4B **104**
Viridian Apartments
SW8 . . . . .3E **89**
Visage NW3 . . . . .4F **45**
(off Winchester St.)
Viscount Ct. W2 . . . . . . .5C **58**
(off Pembridge Vs.)
Viscount St.
EC1 . . . . . . .4F **9** (3E **63**)

Vista, The SE9 . . . . . . .4F **111**
Vista Bldg. E3 . . . . .2B **66**
(off Bow Rd.)
Vista Dr. IG4: IIf 1F **41**
Vista Ho. N4 . . . . .4C **34**
Vitae Apartments W6 . . .4C **70**
Vitali Cl. SW15 . . . . .4C **98**
Vittoria Ho. N1 . . . . .5B **48**
(off High Rd.)
Vivian Av. NW4 . . . . .1D **29**
Vivian Comma Cl.
N4 . . . . .5D **35**
Vivian Ct. NW6 . . . . .1D **59**
Vivian Mans. NW4 . . . . .1D **29**
(off Vivian Av.)
Vivian Rd. E3 . . . . .1A **66**
Vivian Sq. SE15 . . . . . . .1D **107**
Vixen M. E8 . . . . .4B **50**
(off Haggerston Rd.)
Vogans Mill SE1 . . . . . . .3B **78**
Vogler Ho. E1 . . . . .1E **79**
(off Cable St.)
Vollasky Ho. E1 . . . . . . .4C **64**
(off Daplyn St.)
Voltaire Rd. SW4 . . . . . .1F **103**
Volt Av. NW10 . . . . .2A **56**
Voluntary Pl. E11 . . . . . . .1C **40**
Vorley Rd. N19 . . . . .4E **33**
Voss St. E2 . . . . .2C **64**
Voyager Bus. Est.
SE16 . . . . .4C **78**
(off Spa Rd.)
Voyager Ct. E16 . . . . . . .4C **68**
(off Hammersley Rd.)
Vue Cinema
Finchley Rd. 3E **45**
(in O2 Cen.)
Fulham Broadway
. . . . .3C **86**
Islington 1C **62**
Leicester Sq. 4C **14**
(off Cranbourn St.)
Shepherds Bush
. . . . .3F **71**
The O2 . . . . .2A **82**
(in The O2)
Westfield 2E **71**
Vulcan Rd. SE4 . . . . .5B **94**
Vulcan Sq. E14 . . . . .5D **81**
Vulcan Ter. SE4 . . . . .5B **94**
Vulcan Way N7 . . . . .3B **48**
Vulcan Wharf E15 . . . . . .1D **67**
(off Cook's Rd.)
Vyner Rd. W3 . . . . .1A **70**
Vyner St. E2 . . . . .5D **51**

W

Wadding St. SE17 . . . . . .5F **77**
Waddington Rd. E15 . . . .2F **53**
Waddington St. E15 . . . . .2F **53**
Wade Ho. SE1 . . . . .3C **78**
(off Parkers Row)
Wadeson St. E2 . . . . . . .1D **65**
Wade's Pl. E14 . . . . .1D **81**
Wadham Gdns. NW3 . . . .5A **46**
Wadham Rd. SW15 . . . .2A **100**
Wadhurst Rd. SW8 . . . . .4E **89**
W4 . . . . .4A **70**

Wadley Rd. E11 . . . . . .2A **40**
Wager St. E3 . . . . .3B **66**
Waghorn Rd. E13 . . . . .5E **55**
Waghorn St. SE15 . . . .1C **106**
Wagner St. SE15 . . . . .3E **93**
Wainford Cl. SW19 . . . .1F **113**
Wainwright Ho. E1 . . . .2E **79**
    (off Garnet St.)
Waite Davies Rd.
 SE12 . . . . .5B **110**
Waite St. SE15 . . . . . . .2B **92**
Waithman St. EC4 . . . .3D **17**
   (off Black Friars La.)
Wakefield Cl. SE26 . . . .5E **121**
Wakefield Gdns.
 IG1: Ilf 1F **41**
Wakefield Ho. SE15 . . .4C **92**
Wakefield M.
 WC1 . . . . . .2E **7** (2A **62**)
Wakefield Rd. N15 . . . .1B **36**
Wakefield St. E6 . . . . . .5F **55**
 WC1 . . . . . .2E **7** (2A **62**)
Wakeford Cl. SW4 . . . .3E **103**
Wakeham St. N1 . . . . . .3F **49**
Wakehurst Rd.
 SW11 . . . . .3A **102**
Wakeling St. E14 . . . . .5A **66**
Wakelin Ho. N1 . . . . . . .4D **49**
    (off Sebbon St.)
Wakelin Rd. E15 . . . . . .1A **68**
Wakeman Ho. NW10 . . .2F **57**
   (off Wakeman Rd.)
Wakeman Rd. NW10 . . .2E **57**
Wakley St.
 EC1 . . . . . . .1D **9** (2D **63**)
Walberswick St. SW8 . .3A **90**
Walbrook EC4 . .4B **18** (1F **77**)
    (not continuous)
Walbrook Ct. N1 . . . . . .1A **64**
   (off Hemsworth St.)
Walbrook Wharf EC4 . .5A **18**
    (off Cousin La.)
Walburgh St. E1 . . . . . .5D **65**
Walcorde Av. SE17 . . . .5E **77**
Walcot Gdns. SE11 . . . .5C **76**
   (off Kennington Rd.)
Walcot Sq. SE11 . . . . . .5C **76**
Walcott St. SW1 . . . . . .5E **75**
Waldeck Gro. SE27 . . . .3D **119**
Waldemar Av. SW6 . . . .4A **86**
Waldemar Rd.
 SW19 . . . . .5C **114**
Walden Cl. SW8 . . . . . .4F **89**
Walden Ho. SW1 . . . . . .5C **74**
   (off Pimlico Rd.)
 SW11 . . . . .4C **88**
   (off Dagnall St.)
Waldenshaw Rd.
 SE23 . . . . .1E **121**
Walden St. E1 . . . . .5D **65**
    (not continuous)
Waldo Cl. SW4 . . . . . . .3E **103**
Waldo Ho. NW10 . . . . . .2D **57**
    (off Waldo Rd.)
Waldo Rd. NW10 . . . . . .2C **56**
    (not continuous)
Waldram Cres.
 SE23 . . . . .1E **121**
Waldram Pk. Rd.
 SE23 . . . . .1F **121**

Waldram Pl. SE23 . . . .1E **121**
Waldron M. SW3 . . . . . .2F **87**
Waldron Rd. SW18 . . . .3E **115**
Walerand Rd. SE13 . . . .5E **95**
Waleran Flats SE1 . . . . .5A **78**
Wales Cl. SE15 . . . . . . .2D **93**
Wales Farm Rd.
 W3 . . . . .4A **56**
Waley St. E1 . . . . .4A **66**
Walford Ho. E1 . . . . . . .5C **64**
Walford Rd. N16 . . . . . .1A **50**
WALHAM GREEN 4C **86**
Walham Grn. Ct.
 SW6 . . . . .3D **87**
   (off Waterford Rd.)
Walham Gro. SW6 . . . . .3C **86**
Walham Yd. SW6 . . . . . .3C **86**
Walker Ho.
 NW1 . . . . . . .1B **6** (1F **61**)
 SE16 . . . . .4B **80**
    (off Redriff Est.)
Walker M. SW2 . . . . . . .3C **104**
Walker's Ct. W1 . . . . . .4B **14**
Walkerscroft Mead
 SE21 . . . . .1E **119**
Walkers Lodge E14 . . . .3E **81**
   (off Manchester Rd.)
Walkers Pl. SW15 . . . . .2A **100**
Walkinshaw Ct. N1 . . . .4E **49**
   (off Rotherfield St.)
Walkynscroft SE15 . . . .5D **93**
    (off Caulfield Rd.)
Wallace Bldg. NW8 . . . .3F **59**
    (off Penfold St.)
Wallace Collection
  . . . . . . .2C **12** (5C **60**)
Wallace Ct. NW1 . . . . . .4A **60**
  (off Old Marylebone Rd.)
Wallace Ho. N7 . . . . . . .3B **48**
   (off Caledonian Rd.)
Wallace Rd. N1 . . . . . . .3E **49**
Wallace Way N19 . . . . .4F **33**
   (off St John's Way)
Wallbutton Rd. SE4 . . . .5A **94**
Wallcote Av. NW2 . . . . .3F **29**
Wall Ct. N4 . . . . .3B **34**
   (off Stroud Grn. Rd.)
Waller Rd. SE14 . . . . . .4F **93**
Waller Way SE10 . . . . . .3D **95**
Wallflower St. W12 . . . .1B **70**
Wallgrave Rd. SW5 . . . .5D **73**
Wallingford Av. W10 . . .4F **57**
Wallis All. SE1 . . . . .3A **26**
Wallis Cl. SW11 . . . . . .1F **101**
Wallis Ho. SE14 . . . . . .4A **94**
Wallis Rd. E9 . . . . .3B **52**
Wallis's Cotts. SW2 . . .5A **104**
Wallorton Gdns.
 SW14 . . . . .2A **98**
Wallpaper Apartments, The
 N1 . . . . .4C **48**
    (off Offord Rd.)
Wallside EC2 . . . . .1A **18**
Wall St. N1 . . . . .3F **49**
Wallwood Rd. E11 . . . . .2F **39**
Wallwood St. E14 . . . . .4B **66**
Walmer Ho. W10 . . . . . .5F **57**
   (off Bramley Rd.)
Walmer Pl. W1 . . . . .4B **60**
    (off Walmer St.)

Walmer Rd. W10 . . . . . .5E **57**
 W11 . . . . .1A **72**
Walmer St. W1 . . . . . . .4B **60**
Walm La. NW2 . . . . .3E **43**
Walney Wlk. N1 . . . . . . .3E **49**
Walnut Cl. SE8 . . . . .2B **94**
Walnut Ct. W8 . . . . .4D **73**
    (off St Mary's Ga.)
Walnut Gdns. E15 . . . . .2A **54**
Walnut Ho. E3 . . . . .5B **52**
    (off Barge La.)
Walnut Rd. E10 . . . . . . .4C **38**
Walnut Tree Cl.
 SW13 . . . . .4B **84**
Walnut Tree Cotts.
 SW19 . . . . .5A **114**
Walnut Tree Ho.
 SW10 . . . . .2D **87**
   (off Tregunter Rd.)
Walnut Tree Rd.
 SE10 . . . . .1A **96**
    (not continuous)
Walnut Tree Wlk.
 SE11 . . . . .5C **76**
Walpole Ct. NW6 . . . . . .4E **45**
    (off Fairfax Rd.)
 W14 . . . . .4F **71**
    (off Blythe Rd.)
Walpole Ho. SE1 . . . . . .4B **24**
   (off Westminster Bri. Rd.)
Walpole M. NW8 . . . . . .5F **45**
Walpole Rd. E6 . . . . . . .4E **55**
 SW19 . . . . .5F **115**
Walpole St. SW3 . . . . . .1B **88**
Walsham Cl. N16 . . . . . .3C **36**
Walsham Ho. SE14 . . . .5F **93**
 SE17 . . . . .1F **91**
   (off Blackwood St.)
Walsham Rd. SE14 . . . .5F **93**
Walsingham NW8 . . . . .5F **45**
Walsingham Lodge
 SW13 . . . . .4C **84**
Walsingham Mans.
 SW6 . . . . .3D **87**
    (off Fulham Rd.)
Walsingham Pl.
 SW4 . . . . .4C **102**
Walsingham Rd. E5 . . . .5C **36**
Walston Ho. SW1 . . . . .1F **89**
   (off Aylesford St.)
Walter Besant Ho. E1 . .2F **65**
    (off Bancroft Rd.)
Walter Grn. Ho. SE15 . .4E **93**
   (off Lausanne Rd.)
Walter Ho. SW10 . . . . . .3F **87**
    (off Riley St.)
Walter Langley Ct.
 SE16 . . . . .3E **79**
    (off Brunel Rd.)
Walter Savil Twr. E17 . .1C **38**
   (off Colchester Rd.)
Walters Cl. SE17 . . . . . .5F **77**
    (off Brandon St.)
Walters Ho. SE17 . . . . .2D **91**
    (off Otto St.)
Walter Sickert Hall N1 . .1F **9**
    (off Graham St.)
Walter St. E2 . . . . .2F **65**
Walters Way SE23 . . . . .4F **107**
Walter Ter. E1 . . . . .5F **65**

Walterton Rd. W9 . . . . . .3B 58
Waltham Ho. NW8 . . . .5E 45
WALTHAMSTOW 2B 38
Walthamstow Marsh
   Nature Reserve . . .2D 37
Walton Cl. E5 . . . . .5F 37
   (off Orient Way)
  NW2 . . . . .4D 29
  SW8 . . . . .3A 90
Walton Ct. NW6 . . . . . .4E 45
   (off Fairfax Rd.)
Walton Dr. NW10 . . . . .3A 42
Walton Ho. E2 . . . . .3F 11
   (off Montclare St.)
  NW1 . . . . .3E 5
   (off Longford St.)
  SW1 . . . . .4B 74
   (off Walton St.)
Walton Pl.
  SW3 . . . . . .5A 20 (4B 74)
Walton Rd. E13 . . . . . . .1E 69
Walton St. SW3 . . . . . . .5A 74
Walton Vs. N1 . . . . .4A 50
   (off Downham Rd.)
Walt Whitman Cl.
  SE24 . . . . .2D 105
WALWORTH 1E 91
Walworth Pl. SE17 . . . . .1E 91
Walworth Rd. SE1 . . . . .5E 77
  SE17 . . . . .5E 77
Wanborough Dr.
  SW15 . . . . .1D 113
Wandle Ho.
  BR1: Brom 5F 123
  NW8 . . . . .4A 60
   (off Penfold St.)
Wandle Meadow Nature Pk.
  . . . . .5E 115
Wandle Recreation Cen.
  . . . . .4D 101
Wandle Rd. SW17 . . . . .2A 116
Wandle Way SW18 . . . .1D 115
Wandon Rd. SW6 . . . . .3D 87
WANDSWORTH 3D 101
Wandsworth Bri.
  SW6 . . . . .1D 101
Wandsworth Bri. Rd.
  SW6 . . . . .4D 87
WANDSWORTH COMMON
  . . . . .1B 116
Wandsworth Comn. W. Side
  SW18 . . . . .3E 101
WANDSWORTH GYRATORY
  . . . . .3D 101
Wandsworth High St.
  SW18 . . . . .3C 100
Wandsworth Mus. 3C 100
Wandsworth Plain
  SW18 . . . . .3D 101
Wandsworth Rd.
  SW8 . . . . .1D 103
Wangford Ho. SW9 . . . .2D 105
   (off Loughborough Pk.)
Wanless Rd. SE24 . . . . .1E 105
Wanley Rd. SE5 . . . . . . .2F 105
Wanlip Rd. E13 . . . . . . .3D 69
Wansbeck Rd. E9 . . . . . .4B 52
Wansdown Pl. SW6 . . . .3D 87
Wansey St. SE17 . . . . . .5E 77
WANSTEAD 1D 41

Wanstead Gdns.
  IG4: Ilf 1F 41
Wanstead Golf Course
  . . . . .2E 41
Wanstead La.
  IG1: Ilf 1F 41
Wanstead Leisure Cen.
  . . . . .1E 41
Wanstead Pk. Av.
  E12 . . . . .3F 41
Wanstead Pk. Rd.
  IG1: Ilf 1F 41
Wanstead Pl. E11 . . . . .1C 40
Wantage Rd. SE12 . . . .3B 110
WAPPING 2D 79
Wapping Dock St. E1 . . .2D 79
Wapping High St. E1 . . .2C 78
Wapping La. E1 . . . . . . .1D 79
Wapping Wall E1 . . . . . .2E 79
Warbeck Rd. W12 . . . . .3D 71
Warburton Cl. N1 . . . . . .3A 50
   (off Culford Rd.)
Warburton Ho. E8 . . . . .5D 51
   (off Warburton St.)
Warburton Rd. E8 . . . . .5D 51
Warburton St. E8 . . . . . .5D 51
Wardalls Ho. SE8 . . . . . .2B 94
   (off Staunton St.)
Wardell Ho. SE10 . . . . . .2E 95
   (off Welland St.)
Warden Rd. NW5 . . . . . .3C 46
Wardens Gro.
  SE1 . . . . . .2F 25 (2E 77)
Wardle St. E9 . . . . .2F 51
Wardley St. SW18 . . . . .5D 101
Wardo Av. SW6 . . . . . . .4A 86
Wardour M. W1 . . . . . . .3A 14
Wardour St.
  W1 . . . . . .2A 14 (5E 61)
Ward Point SE11 . . . . . .5C 76
Ward Rd. E15 . . . . .5F 53
  N19 . . . . .5E 33
Wardrobe Pl. EC4 . . . . . .3E 17
Wardrobe Ter. EC4 . . . . .4E 17
Wardroper Ho. SE1 . . . .5D 25
   (off St George's Rd.)
Wards Wharf App.
  E16 . . . . .2F 83
Wareham Ct. N1 . . . . . . .4A 50
   (off Hertford Rd.)
Wareham Ho. SW8 . . . .3B 90
Warehouse Way E16 . . .1D 83
Warfield Rd. NW10 . . . . .2F 57
Warfield Yd. NW10 . . . . .2F 57
   (off Warfield Rd.)
Wargrave Av. N15 . . . . .1B 36
Wargrave Ho. E2 . . . . . . .2F 11
   (off Navarre St.)
Warham Rd. N4 . . . . . . .1C 34
Warham St. SE5 . . . . . . .3D 91
Waring St. SE27 . . . . . .4E 119
Warley Cl. E10 . . . . .3B 38
Warley St. E2 . . . . .2F 65
Warlingham Ct.
  SE13 . . . . .4E 109
Warlock Rd. W9 . . . . . . .3B 58
Warlters Cl. N7 . . . . .1A 48
Warlters Rd. N7 . . . . . . .1A 48
Warltersville Mans.
  N19 . . . . .2A 34

Warltersville Rd.
  N19 . . . . .2A 34
Warmington Cl. E5 . . . . .5F 37
Warmington Rd.
  SE24 . . . . .4E 105
Warmington St. E13 . . . .3C 68
Warmsworth NW1 . . . . .5E 47
   (off Pratt St.)
Warndon St. SE16 . . . . .5F 79
Wareford St. E9 . . . . . . .5D 51
Warner Cl. E15 . . . . .2A 54
  NW9 . . . . .2B 28
Warner Ho.
  BR3: Beck 5D 123
  NW8 . . . . .2E 59
  SE13 . . . . .5D 95
   (off Russett Way)
Warner Pl. E2 . . . . .1C 64
Warner Rd. SE5 . . . . . . .4E 91
Warner St.
  EC1 . . . . .4B 8 (3C 62)
Warner Ter. E14 . . . . . . .4D 67
   (off Broomfield St.)
Warner Yd. EC1 . . . . . . .4B 8
Warnford Ct. EC2 . . . . . .2C 18
   (off Throgmorton Av.)
Warnford Ho. SW15 . . . .4A 98
   (off Tunworth Cres.)
Warnham WC1 . . . . .2F 7
   (off Sidmouth St.)
Warnham Ho. SW2 . . . .5B 104
   (off Up. Tulse Hill)
Warple M. W3 . . . . .3A 70
Warple Way W3 . . . . . . .3A 70
   (not continuous)
Warren, The SE7 . . . . . .2E 97
Warren Av. E10 . . . . . . .5E 39
Warren Cl. SE21 . . . . . .5E 105
Warren Ct. NW1 . . . . . . .3A 6
   (off Warren St.)
Warrender Rd. N19 . . . . .5E 33
Warren Drive, The
  E11 . . . . .2E 41
Warren Gdns. E15 . . . . .2F 53
Warren Ho. E3 . . . . .2D 67
   (off Bromley High St.)
  W14 . . . . .5B 72
Warren M. W1 . . . .4F 5 (3E 61)
Warren Pl. E1 . . . . .5F 65
   (off Pitsea St.)
Warren Rd. E10 . . . . . . .5E 39
  E11 . . . . .1E 41
  NW2 . . . . .4B 28
Warren St. W1 . . . .4F 5 (3E 61)
Warren Wlk. SE7 . . . . . .2E 97
Warriner Gdns.
  SW11 . . . . .4B 88
Warrington Cres. W9 . . . .3E 59
Warrington Gdns. W9 . . .3E 59
   (not continuous)
Warrior Cl. SW9 . . . . . .1D 105
   (off Coldharbour Rd.)
Warspite Ho. E14 . . . . . .5D 81
   (off Cahir St.)
Warspite Rd. SE18 . . . . .4F 83
Warton Ct. E1 . . . . .1F 79
   (off Cable St.)
Warton Ho. E15 . . . . . . .5E 53
   (off High St.)
Warton Rd. E15 . . . . . . .5E 53

Warwick W14 . . . . .5B 72
(off Kensington Village)
Warwick Av. W2 . . . . . . .3E 59
W9 . . . . .3D 59
Warwick Bldg. SW8 . . . .2D 89
Warwick Chambers
W8 . . . . .4C 72
(off Pater St.)
Warwick Cl. W8 . . . . . . .4B 72
(off Kensington High St.)
Warwick Ct. EC4 . . . . . . .3E 17
(off Warwick La.)
WC1 . . . . .1A 16 (4B 62)
Warwick Cres.
W2 . . . . .4E 59
Warwick Dr. SW15 . . . .1D 99
Warwick Est. W2 . . . . . .4D 59
Warwick Gdns. N4 . . . . .1E 53
W14 . . . . .4B 72
Warwick Gro. E5 . . . . . .3D 37
Warwick Ho. E16 . . . . . .2C 82
(off Wesley Av.)
SW9 . . . . .5C 90
Warwick Ho. St.
SW1 . . . . .1C 22 (2F 75)
Warwick La.
EC4 . . . . .2E 17 (5D 63)
Warwick Mans. SW5 . . . .5C 72
(off Cromwell Cres.)
Warwick Pas. EC4 . . . . . .2E 17
(off Old Bailey)
Warwick Pl. W9 . . . . . . .4E 59
Warwick Pl. Nth.
SW1 . . . . .5E 75
Warwick Rd. E12 . . . . . .2F 55
E15 . . . . .3B 54
SW5 . . . . .5B 72
W14 . . . . .5B 72
Warwick Row
SW1 . . . . .5E 21 (4D 75)
Warwickshire Path
SE8 . . . . .3B 94
Warwickshire Rd.
N16 . . . . .1A 50
Warwick Sq.
EC4 . . . . .2E 17 (5D 63)
SW1 . . . . .1E 89
(not continuous)
Warwick Sq. M. SW1 . .5E 75
Warwick St.
W1 . . . . . .4A 14 (1E 75)
Warwick Ter. E17 . . . . . .1F 39
(off Lea Bri. Rd.)
Warwick Way SW1 . . . .1D 89
Warwick Yd.
EC1 . . . . .4A 10 (3E 63)
Wasdale NW1 . . . . .2D 61
(off Cumberland Mkt.)
Washbourne Rd.
NW10 . . . . .5A 42
Washington Bldg.
SE10 . . . . .4D 95
(off Deal's Gateway)
Washington Cl. E3 . . . . .2D 67
Washington Ho. SW3 . . .4A 20
(off Basil St.)
Washington Rd. E6 . . . . .4E 55
SW13 . . . . .3C 84
Wastdale Rd. SE23 . . . .1F 121
Waterbank Rd. SE6 . . . .3D 123

Water Brook La.
NW4 . . . . .1E 29
Watercress Pl. N1 . . . . .4A 50
Waterden La. W11 . . . .2A 72
Waterer Ho. SE6 . . . . . .4E 123
Waterfall Cotts.
SW19 . . . . .5F 115
Waterfall Rd. SW19 . . . .5F 115
Waterfall Ter. SW17 . . . .5A 116
Waterford Ho. W11 . . . .1B 72
(off Kensington Pk. Rd.)
Waterford Rd. SW6 . . . . .3D 87
Waterford Way
NW10 . . . . .2D 43
Waterfront W6 . . . . . . .2E 85
Waterfront Ho. E5 . . . . . .4E 37
(off Harry Zeital Way)
Waterfront M. N1 . . . . . .1E 63
Waterfront Studios Bus. Cen.
E16 . . . . .2B 82
(off Dock Rd.)
Water Gardens, The
W2 . . . . .5A 60
Water Gdns. Sq.
SE16 . . . . .3F 79
Watergate
EC4 . . . . .4D 17 (1D 77)
Watergate St. SE8 . . . . .2C 94
Watergate Wlk.
WC2 . . . . .1E 23 (2A 76)
Waterhead NW1 . . . . .1F 5
(off Varndell St.)
Waterhouse Cl. E16 . . . .4F 69
NW3 . . . . .2F 45
W6 . . . . .5F 71
Waterhouse Sq.
EC1 . . . . .1B 16 (4C 62)
Wateridge Cl. E14 . . . . .4C 80
Water La. E15 . . . . .3A 54
EC3 . . . . .5E 19 (1A 78)
NW1 . . . . .4D 47
SE14 . . . . .3E 93
Waterline Ho. W2 . . . . . .4A 60
(off Harbet Rd.)
Waterloo Bri.
WC2 . . . . .5F 15 (1B 76)
Waterloo Cl. E9 . . . . . . .2E 51
Waterloo East Theatre
. . . . .2C 76
(off Brad St.)
Waterloo Gdns. E2 . . . . .1E 65
N1 . . . . .4D 49
Waterloo Pas. NW6 . . . .4B 44
Waterloo Pl.
SW1 . . . . .1B 22 (2F 75)
Waterloo Rd. E6 . . . . . . .4E 55
E7 . . . . .2B 54
E10 . . . . .2C 38
NW2 . . . . .3C 28
SE1 . . . . .1A 24 (2B 76)
Waterloo Ter. N1 . . . . . .4D 49
Waterlow Ct. NW11 . . . .2D 31
Waterlow Pk. Cen. 3D 33
Waterlow Rd. N19 . . . . .3E 33
Waterman Bldg. E14 . . . .3B 80
Waterman's Quay
SW6 . . . . .5E 87
Waterman St. SW15 . . . .1F 99
Watermans Wlk.
SE16 . . . . .3A 80

Waterman Way E1 . . . . .2D 79
Waterman Ho. E9 . . . . . .2A 52
Watermead Lodge
SE16 . . . . .2F 79
(off Princes Riverside Rd.)
Watermeadow La.
SW6 . . . . .5E 87
Watermead Rd. SE6 . . . .4E 123
Water M. SE15 . . . . . . .2E 107
Watermint Quay N16 . . . .2C 36
Water Polo Arena,
Olympic Pk. 4D 53
Water's Edge SW6 . . . . .4E 85
(off Palemead Cl.)
Waterside E17 . . . . .1E 37
N1 . . . . .1E 63
W2 . . . . .4F 59
(off Nth. Wharf Rd.)
Waterside Cl. E3 . . . . . . .5B 52
SE16 . . . . .3C 78
Waterside Hgts. E16 . . . .3E 83
(off Booth Rd.)
Waterside Pl. NW1 . . . . .5C 46
Waterside Point
SW11 . . . . .3A 88
Waterside Twr. SW6 . . . .5E 87
(off The Boulevard)
Waterside Way
SW17 . . . . .4E 115
Waterson St.
E2 . . . . . .1E 11 (2A 64)
Waters Pl. SW15 . . . . . .5E 85
Waters Rd. SE6 . . . . . . .3A 124
Water St. WC2 . . . . . . .4B 16
Water Twr. Pl. N1 . . . . . .5C 48
Waterview Ho. E14 . . . . .4A 66
(off Carr St.)
Waterway Av. SE13 . . . .1D 109
Waterweave W2 . . . . . . .4F 59
(off Nth. Wharf Rd.)
Waterworks Golf Course
. . . . .4A 38
Waterworks La. E5 . . . . .4F 37
Waterworks Nature Reserve
. . . . .4A 38
Waterworks Rd.
SW2 . . . . .4B 104
Waterworks Vis. Cen.
. . . . .4A 38
Watford Cl. SW11 . . . . .4A 88
Watford Rd. E16 . . . . . . .4C 68
Watford Way NW4 . . . . .1D 29
Watkins Ho. E14 . . . . . . .3E 81
(off Manchester Rd.)
Watkinson Rd. N7 . . . . . .3B 48
Watling Ct. EC4 . . . . . . .3A 18
Watling Gdns. NW2 . . . .3A 44
Watling Ho. SE17 . . . . . .5E 77
(off New Kent Rd.)
Watling St.
EC4 . . . . .3F 17 (5E 63)
SE15 . . . . .2A 92
Watlington Gro.
SE26 . . . . .5A 122
Watney Mkt. E1 . . . . . . .5D 65
Watney St. E1 . . . . .5D 65
Watson Cl. N16 . . . . . . .2F 49
Watsons Ho. N1 . . . . . . .5A 50
(off Nuttall St.)
Watson's M. W1 . . . . . . .4A 60

Watsons St. SE8 . . . . . . .3C 94
Watson St. E13 . . . . .1D 69
Watt Cl. W3 . . . . .3A 70
Wattisfield Rd. E5 . . . . . . .5E 37
Wattsdown Cl. E13 . . . . . .5C 54
Watts Gro. E3 . . . . .4C 66
Watts Ho. W10 . . . . .4A 58
    (off Wornington Rd.)
Watts Point E13 . . . . .5C 54
    (off Brooks Rd.)
Watts St. E1 . . . . .2D 79
SE15 . . . . .4B 92
Wat Tyler Rd. SE3 . . . . . .5E 95
SE10 . . . . .5E 95
Wavel Ct. E1 . . . . .2E 79
    (off Garnet St.)
Wavelengths Leisure Cen.
    . . . . .3C 94
Wavel M. NW6 . . . . .4D 45
Wavel Pl. SE26 . . . . .4B 120
Wavendon Av. W4 . . . . . .1A 84
Waveney Av. SE15 . . . . .2D 107
Waveney Cl. E1 . . . . .2C 78
Waveney Ho. SE15 . . . . .2D 107
Waverley Ct. NW3 . . . . . .3B 46
NW6 . . . . .4A 44
SE26 . . . . .5E 121
Waverley Lodge E15 . . . . .3A 54
    (off Litchfield Av.)
Waverley Pl. N4 . . . . .4D 35
NW8 . . . . .1F 59
Waverley Rd. N8 . . . . . . .1A 34
Waverton Ho. E3 . . . . . . .5B 52
Waverton Rd. SW18 . . . .5E 101
Waverton St.
    W1 . . . . . . .1D 21 (2C 74)
Wavertree Ct. SW2 . . . .1A 118
Wavertree Rd. SW2 . . . .1B 118
Waxham NW5 . . . . .2B 46
Waxlow Rd. NW10 . . . . . .1A 56
Wayford St. SW11 . . . . . .5A 88
Wayland Av. E8 . . . . .2C 50
Wayland Ho. SW9 . . . . . .5C 90
    (off Robsart St.)
Waylett Ho. SE11 . . . . . .1B 90
    (off Loughborough St.)
Waylett Pl. SE27 . . . . . . .3D 119
Wayman Ct. E8 . . . . .3D 51
Wayne Kirkum Way
    NW6 . . . . .2B 44
Waynflete Av. SE1 . . . . . .2F 25
    (off Union St.)
Waynflete Sq. W10 . . . . .1F 71
    (not continuous)
Waynflete St. SW18 . . . .2E 115
Wayside NW11 . . . . .3A 30
Weald Cl. SE16 . . . . .1D 93
Wealden Ho. E3 . . . . .2D 67
    (off Talwin St.)
Weald Sq. E5 . . . . .4C 36
Weardale Rd. SE13 . . . . .2F 109
Wearmouth Ho. E3 . . . . . .3B 66
    (off Joseph St.)
Wear Pl. E2 . . . . .2D 65
    (not continuous)
Wearside Rd. SE13 . . . . .2D 109
Weatherbury W2 . . . . .5C 58
    (off Talbot Rd.)
Weatherbury Ho. N19 . . . .5F 33
    (off Wedmore St.)

Weatherley Cl. E3 . . . . . .4B 66
Weaver Ho. E1 . . . . .1C 78
    (off Pedley St.)
Weavers Almshouses
    E11 . . . . .1B 40
    (off Cambridge Rd.)
Weavers Ho. E11 . . . . . . .1C 40
    (off New Wanstead)
Weavers La.
    SE1 . . . . . . .2E 27 (2A 78)
Weavers Ter. SW6 . . . . . .2C 86
    (off Micklethwaite Rd.)
Weaver St. E1 . . . . .3C 64
    (not continuous)
Weavers Way NW1 . . . . . .5F 47
Weaver Wlk. SE27 . . . . .4E 119
Webb Cl. W10 . . . . .3E 57
Webber Row SE1 . . . . . . .3D 77
Webber St.
    SE1 . . . . . . .3C 24 (3C 76)
Webb Est. E5 . . . . .2C 36
Webb Gdns. E13 . . . . . . .3C 68
Webb Ho. SW8 . . . . .3F 89
Webb Pl. NW10 . . . . .2B 56
Webb Rd. SE3 . . . . .2B 96
Webb's Rd. SW11 . . . . . .2B 102
Webb St.
    SE1 . . . . . . .5D 27 (4A 78)
Webheath NW6 . . . . .4B 44
    (not continuous)
Webster Rd. E11 . . . . . . .5E 39
SE16 . . . . .4C 78
Weddell Ho. E1 . . . . .3F 65
    (off Duckett St.)
Wedderburn Ho.
    SW1 . . . . .1C 88
    (off Lwr. Sloane St.)
Wedderburn Rd.
    NW3 . . . . .2F 45
Wedgewood Ho.
    SW1 . . . . .1D 89
    (off Churchill Gdns.)
Wedgwood Ct. N7 . . . . . .1B 48
Wedgwood Ho. E2 . . . . . .2F 65
    (off Warley St.)
SE11 . . . . .4C 76
    (off Lambeth Wlk.)
Wedgwood M.
    W1 . . . . . . .3C 14 (5F 61)
Wedgwood Wlk.
    NW6 . . . . .2D 45
    (off Dresden Cl.)
Wedlake St. W10 . . . . . . .3A 58
Wedmore Gdns. N19 . . . .4F 33
Wedmore M. N19 . . . . . . .5F 33
Wedmore St. N19 . . . . . . .5F 33
Weedington Rd.
    NW5 . . . . .2C 46
Weedon Ho. W12 . . . . . . .5C 56
Weekley Sq. SW11 . . . . . .1F 101
Weigall Rd. SE12 . . . . . . .3C 110
Weighhouse St.
    W1 . . . . . . .3C 12 (5C 60)
Weightman Ho. SE16 . . . .4C 78
Weimar St. SW15 . . . . . .1A 100
Weir Ho. SW12 . . . . .5E 103
SW19 . . . . .3D 115
Weir's Pas.
    NW1 . . . . . . .1C 6 (2F 61)

Weiss Rd. SW15 . . . . . . .1F 99
Welbeck Av.
    BR1: Brom 4C 124
Welbeck Ct. W14 . . . . . . .5B 72
    (off Addison Bri. Pl.)
Welbeck Ho. W1 . . . . .2D 13
    (off Welbeck St.)
Welbeck Rd. E6 . . . . .2F 69
Welbeck St.
    W1 . . . . . . .1C 12 (4C 60)
Welbeck Way
    W1 . . . . . . .2D 13 (5D 61)
Welbury Ct. E8 . . . . .4A 50
    (off Kingsland Rd.)
Welby Ho. N19 . . . . .2F 33
Welby St. SE5 . . . . .4D 91
Welcome Ct. E17 . . . . . . .2C 38
    (off Saxon Cl.)
Weld Works M.
    SW2 . . . . .4B 104
Welfare Rd. E15 . . . . .4A 54
Welford Cl. E5 . . . . .5F 37
Welford Ct. NW1 . . . . . . .4D 47
    (off Castlehaven Rd.)
SW8 . . . . .5E 89
W9 . . . . .4C 58
    (off Elmfield Way)
Welford Pl. SW19 . . . . . . .4A 114
Welham Rd.
    SW16 . . . . .5C 116
    SW17 . . . . .5C 116
Welland Ct. SE6 . . . . .2B 122
    (off Oakham Cl.)
Welland Ho. SE15 . . . . . .2E 107
Welland M. E1 . . . . .2C 78
Welland St. SE10 . . . . . . .2E 95
Wellby Ct. E13 . . . . .5E 55
Well Cl. SW16 . . . . .4B 118
Wellclose Sq.
    E1 . . . . .1C 78
    (not continuous)
Wellclose St. E1 . . . . .1C 78
Wellcome Collection 3B 6
Wellcome Museum, The
    . . . . .2A 16
    (within Royal College of
    Surgeons)
Well Cott. Cl. E11 . . . . . . .1E 41
Well Ct. EC4 . . . . .3A 18 (5E 63)
Wellday Ho. E9 . . . . .3A 52
    (off Hedger's Gro.)
Weller Ct. W11 . . . . .2B 72
    (off Ladbroke Rd.)
Weller Ho. SE16 . . . . .3C 78
    (off George Row)
Weller St.
    SE1 . . . . . . .3F 25 (3E 77)
Welles Ct. E14 . . . . .1C 80
    (off Premiere Pl.)
Wellesley Av. W6 . . . . . . .4D 71
Wellesley Cl. SE7 . . . . . . .1E 97
Wellesley Ct. NW2 . . . . . .4C 28
SE1 . . . . .5F 25
    (off Rockingham St.)
W9 . . . . .2E 59
Wellesley Ho. NW1 . . . . . .2C 6
    (off Wellesley Pl.)
SW1 . . . . .1D 89
    (off Ebury Bri. Rd.)

Wellesley Mans.
W14 . . . . .1B **86**
(off Edith Vs.)
Wellesley Pl.
NW1 . . . . . . .2B **6** (2F **61**)
NW5 . . . . .2C **46**
Wellesley Rd. E11 . . .1C **40**
E17 . . . . .1C **38**
NW5 . . . . .2C **46**
Wellesley St. E1 . . . . .4F **65**
Wellesley Ter.
N1 . . . . .1A **10** (2E **63**)
Wellfield Rd. SW16 . . .4A **118**
Wellfield Wlk.
SW16 . . . . .4B **118**
Wellfit St. SE24 . . . . .1D **105**
Wellgarth Rd. NW11 . .3D **31**
Wellington Arch
. . . . .3C **20** (3C **74**)
Wellington Av. N15 . . . .1B **36**
Wellington Bldgs. *E3* . .2C **66**
(off Wellington Way)
SW1 . . . . .1C **88**
Wellington Cl. SE14 . . .4F **93**
W11 . . . . .5C **58**
Wellington Ct. *NW8* . . .1F **59**
(off Wellington Rd.)
SW1 . . . . .3B **74**
(off Knightsbridge)
SW6 . . . . .4D **87**
(off Maltings Pl.)
Wellington Gdns.
SE7 . . . . .2E **97**
Wellington Gro. SE10 . .3F **95**
Wellington Ho. *E16* . . .2C **82**
(off Pepys Cres.)
NW3 . . . . .1B **46**
(off Eton Rd.)
SE17 . . . . .2E **91**
(off Arnside St.)
Wellington Mans.
E10 . . . . .3C **38**
SE7 . . . . .1F **97**
(off Wellington Gdns.)
W14 . . . . .2B **86**
(off Queen's Club Mans.)
Wellington M. *N7* 3A **48**
(off Roman Way)
SE7 . . . . .2E **97**
SE22 . . . . .2C **106**
SW16 . . . . .3F **117**
Wellington Monument
. . . . .3C **20**
Wellington Mus.
. . . . .3C **20** (3C **74**)
Wellington Pk. Est.
NW2 . . . . .4C **28**
Wellington Pas. E11 . . .1C **40**
Wellington Pl. NW8 . . .2F **59**
Wellington Rd. E7 . . . . .1B **54**
E10 . . . . .3A **38**
E11 . . . . .1C **40**
NW8 . . . . .1F **59**
NW10 . . . . .2F **57**
SW19 . . . . .2C **114**
Wellington Row E2 . . . .2B **64**
Wellington Sq. N1 . . . . .5A **48**
SW3 . . . . .1B **88**
Wellington St.
WC2 . . . . . .4F **15** (1B **76**)

Wellington Ter. E1 . . . . .2D **79**
W2 . . . . .1C **72**
Wellington Way E3 . . . .2C **66**
Wellmeadow Rd.
SE6 . . . . .5A **110**
SE13 . . . . .4A **110**
(not continuous)
Well Pl. NW3 . . . . .5F **31**
Well Rd. NW3 . . . . .5F **31**
Wells Ct. *NW6* 1C **58**
(off Cambridge Av.)
Wells Gdns. IG1: Ilf 2F **41**
Wells Ho.
BR1: Brom 5D **125**
(off Pike Cl.)
EC1 . . . . .1C **8**
(off Spa Grn. Est.)
SE16 . . . . .4E **79**
(off Howland Est.)
W10 . . . . .3A **58**
(off Wornington Rd.)
Wells Ho. Rd. NW10 . . .4A **56**
Wells Pk. Rd. SE26 . . . .3C **120**
Wells Pl. SW18 . . . . . . .5E **101**
Wells Ri. NW8 . . . . .5B **46**
Wells Rd. W12 . . . . .3E **71**
Wells Sq.
WC1 . . . . . . .2F **7** (2B **62**)
Wells Ter. N4 . . . . .4C **34**
Well St. W1 . . .1F **13** (4E **61**)
N4 . . . . .4C **34**
Well St. E9 . . . . .4E **51**
E15 . . . . .3A **54**
Wells Way SE5 . . . . . . .2F **91**
SW7 . . . . .4F **73**
Wells Yd. N7 . . . . .2C **48**
Well Wlk. NW3 . . . . .1F **45**
Welmar M. *SW4* 3F **103**
(off Clapham Pk. Rd.)
Welsford St. SE1 . . . . . .5C **78**
(not continuous)
Welsh Cl. E13 . . . . .2C **68**
Welsh Harp (Brent Reservoir)
Nature Reserve . . .3B **28**
Welsh Ho. *E1* 2D **79**
(off Wapping La.)
Welshpool Ho. *E8* 5C **50**
(off Welshpool St.)
Welshpool St. E8 . . . . . .5C **50**
(not continuous)
Welshside *NW9* 1A **28**
(off Ruthin Cl.)
Welshside Wlk. NW9 . . .1A **28**
Welstead Ho. *E1* 5D **65**
(off Cannon St. Rd.)
Welstead Way W4 . . . . .5B **70**
Weltje Rd. W6 . . . . .5C **70**
Welton Ct. SE5 . . . . . . .4A **92**
Welton Ho. *E1* 4F **65**
(off Stepney Way)
Welwyn St. E2 . . . . .2E **65**
Wembley Sailing Club
. . . . .4A **28**
Wembury M. N6 . . . . . . .2E **33**
Wembury Rd. N6 . . . . . .2D **33**
Wemyss Rd. SE3 . . . . . .5B **96**
Wendell Rd. W12 . . . . . .4B **70**
Wendle Ct. SW8 . . . . . . .2A **90**
Wendle Sq. SW11 . . . . . .4A **88**

Wendling NW5 . . . . .2B **46**
Wendon St. E3 . . . . .5B **52**
Wendover SE17 . . . . . . .1A **92**
Wendover Ct. *NW2* 5C **30**
W1 . . . . .1B **12**
(off Chiltern St.)
Wendover Ho. *W1* 1B **12**
(off Chiltern St.)
Wendover Rd.
NW10 . . . . .1B **56**
SE9 . . . . .1F **111**
Wenham Ho. SW8 . . . . . .3E **89**
Wenlake Ho. *EC1* 3F **9**
(off Old St.)
Wenlock Barn Est.
N1 . . . . .1F **63**
(off Wenlock St.)
Wenlock Ct.
N1 . . . . .1C **10** (1F **63**)
Wenlock Rd.
N1 . . . . .1A **10** (1E **63**)
Wenlock St.
N1 . . . . .1A **10** (1E **63**)
Wennington Rd. E3 . . . . .1F **65**
Wensdale Ho. E5 . . . . . . .4C **36**
Wentland Cl. SE6 . . . . . .2F **123**
Wentland Rd. SE6 . . . . . .2F **123**
Wentworth Ct. SW1 . . . .1D **89**
SW18 . . . . .4D **101**
(off Garratt La.)
W6 . . . . .2A **86**
(off Paynes Wlk.)
Wentworth Cres.
SE15 . . . . .3C **92**
Wentworth Dwellings
E1 . . . . .2F **19**
(off Wentworth St.)
Wentworth M. E3 . . . . . .3A **66**
W3 . . . . .3A **56**
Wentworth Rd. E12 . . . . .1F **55**
NW11 . . . . .1B **30**
Wentworth St.
E1 . . . . .2F **19** (5B **64**)
Werrington St.
NW1 . . . . . . .1B **6** (1E **61**)
Werter Rd. SW15 . . . . . .2A **100**
Wesleyan Pl. NW5 . . . . .1D **47**
Wesley Apartments
SW8 . . . . .4F **89**
Wesley Av. E16 . . . . .2C **82**
NW10 . . . . .2A **56**
Wesley Cl. N7 . . . . .4B **34**
SE17 . . . . .5D **77**
Wesley Ct. SE16 . . . . . . .4D **79**
Wesley Rd. E10 . . . . .2E **39**
Wesley's Chapel &
Museum of Methodism
. . . . .3C **10** (3F **63**)
Wesley's House
. . . . .3C **10** (3F **63**)
Wesley Sq. W11 . . . . . . .5A **58**
Wesley St.
W1 . . . . .1C **12** (4C **60**)
Wessex Gdns. NW11 . . . .3A **30**
Wessex Ho. SE1 . . . . . . .1B **92**
Wessex St. E2 . . . . .2E **65**
Wessex Way NW11 . . . . .3A **30**
Wesson Mead *SE5* 3E **91**
(off Camberwell Rd.)

West 12 Shop. Cen.
W12 . . . . .3F **71**
Westacott Cl. N19 . . . .3F **33**
W. Arbour St. E1 . . . . .5F **65**
West Av. NW4 . . . . . . .1F **29**
West Bank N16 . . . . . .2A **36**
WEST BECKTON 5F **69**
Westbere Rd. NW2 . . . .1A **44**
West Block SE1 . . . . . .4A **24**
(off York Rd.)
Westbourne Bri. W2 . . . .4E **59**
Westbourne Ct. W2 . . . .4E **59**
Westbourne Cres. W2 . .1F **73**
Westbourne Cres. M.
W2 . . . . .1F **73**
(off Westbourne Cres.)
Westbourne Dr.
SE23 . . . . .2F **121**
Westbourne Gdns.
. . . . .5D **59**
WESTBOURNE GREEN
. . . . .4C **58**
Westbourne Gro. W2 . . .5C **58**
W11 . . . . .1B **72**
Westbourne Gro. M.
W11 . . . . .5C **58**
Westbourne Gro. Ter.
W2 . . . . .5D **59**
Westbourne Ho. SW1 . .1D **89**
(off Ebury Bri. Rd.)
Westbourne Pk. Pas.
W2 . . . . .4C **58**
(not continuous)
Westbourne Pk. Rd.
W2 . . . . .4C **58**
W11 . . . . .5A **58**
Westbourne Pk. Vs.
W2 . . . . .4C **58**
Westbourne Rd. N7 . . . .3B **48**
SE26 . . . . .5F **121**
Westbourne St. W2 . . . .1F **73**
Westbourne Ter.
SE23 . . . . .2F **121**
W2 . . . . .5E **59**
Westbourne Ter. M.
W2 . . . . .5E **59**
Westbourne Ter. Rd.
W2 . . . . .4D **59**
Westbourne Ter. Rd. Bri.
W2 . . . . .4E **59**
(off Westbourne Ter. Rd.)
Westbridge Cl. W12 . . .3C **70**
Westbridge Ho.
SW11 . . . . .4A **88**
(off Westbridge Rd.)
Westbridge Rd. SW11 . .4F **87**
WEST BROMPTON 2E **87**
Westbrook Ho. E2 . . . . .2E **65**
(off Victoria Pk. Sq.)
Westbrook Rd. SE3 . . . .4D **97**
Westbury Ho. W11 . . . .4C **58**
(off Aldridge Rd. Vs.)
Westbury Pde.
SW12 . . . . .4D **103**
(off Balham Hill)
Westbury Rd. E7 . . . . . .3D **55**
Westbury Ter. E7 . . . . . .3D **55**
Westbush Ct. W12 . . . . .3D **71**
(off Goldhawk M.)

W. Carriage Dr. W2 . . . .1A **74**
(North Ride)
W2 . . . . .3F **73**
(Rotten Row)
W. Central St.
WC1 . . . .2D **15** (5A **62**)
Westcliffe Apartments
W2 . . . . .4F **59**
Westcombe Ct. SE3 . . . .3B **96**
Westcombe Hill SE3 . . . .3C **96**
SE10 . . . . .1C **96**
Westcombe Pk. Rd.
SE3 . . . . .2A **96**
Westcote Rd. SW16 . . .5E **117**
West Cotts. NW6 . . . . . .2C **44**
Westcott Cl. N15 . . . . . .1B **36**
Westcott Ho. E14 . . . . . .1C **80**
Westcott Rd. SE17 . . . . .2D **91**
Westcroft Cl. NW2 . . . . .1A **44**
Westcroft Est. NW2 . . . .1A **44**
Westcroft Sq. W6 . . . . . .5C **70**
Westcroft Way NW2 . . . .1A **44**
W. Cromwell Rd.
SW5 . . . . .1B **86**
W14 . . . . .1B **86**
W. Cross Route W10 . . .1F **71**
W11 . . . . .1F **71**
W12 . . . . .1F **71**
Westdean Av. SE12 . . . .1D **125**
Westdean Cl. SW18 . . . .4D **101**
Westdown Rd. E15 . . . . .1E **53**
SE6 . . . . .5C **108**
West Dr. SW16 . . . . . . .4E **117**
WEST DULWICH 2F **119**
W. Eaton Pl. SW1 . . . . . .5C **74**
W. Eaton Pl. M. SW1 . . .5C **74**
(off W. Eaton Pl.)
W. Ella Rd. NW10 . . . . .4A **42**
West End Av. E10 . . . . . .1F **39**
West End Ct. NW6 . . . . . .4D **45**
West End La. NW6 . . . . . .2C **44**
(not continuous)
West End Quay W2 . . . .4F **59**
(off Harbet Rd.)
Westerdale Rd. SE10 . . .1C **96**
Westerham NW1 . . . . . .5E **47**
(off Bayham St.)
Westerham Ho. SE1 . . . .5C **26**
Westerham Rd. E10 . . . .2D **39**
Westerley Cres.
SE26 . . . . .5B **122**
Western Av. NW11 . . . . .1F **29**
W5 . . . . .5A **56**
Western Beach Apartments
E16 . . . . .1C **82**
Western Ct. NW6 . . . . . .1B **58**
Western Courtyard
EC2 . . . . .2E **19**
(off Cutlers Gdns.)
Western Gateway
E16 . . . . .1C **82**
Western La. SW12 . . . . .5C **102**
Western M. W9 . . . . . . .3B **58**
Western Pl. SE16 . . . . . .3E **79**
Western Rd. E13 . . . . . .1E **69**
E17 . . . . .1F **39**
SW9 . . . . .1C **104**
Western Ter. W6 . . . . . .1C **84**
Westferry Cir. E14 . . . . .2B **80**
Westferry Rd. E14 . . . . .1B **80**

Westfield Av. E20 . . . . . .3D **53**
Westfield Cl. SW10 . . . . .3E **87**
Westfield Ct. NW10 . . . . .2F **57**
(off Chamberlayne Rd.)
Westfield Ho. SE16 . . . . .5F **79**
(off Rotherhithe New Rd.)
SW10 . . . . .3F **87**
(off Cremorne Est.)
SW18 . . . . .1D **115**
Westfield London Shop. Cen.
W12 . . . . .2E **71**
Westfields SW13 . . . . . .1B **98**
Westfields Av. SW13 . . . .1A **98**
Westfield Stratford City
Shopping Cen.
E20 . . . . .3E **53**
Westfield St. SE18 . . . . .4F **83**
Westfield Way E1 . . . . . .2A **66**
West Gdn. Pl. W2 . . . . . .5A **60**
West Gdns. E1 . . . . .1D **79**
SW17 . . . . .5A **116**
Westgate Apartments
E16 . . . . .1C **82**
(off Western Gateway)
Westgate Centre, The
E8 . . . . .5D **51**
(off Bocking St.)
Westgate Ct. SE12 . . . .1C **124**
(off Burnt Ash Hill)
SW9 . . . . .1C **104**
(off Canterbury Cres.)
Westgate M. W10 . . . . . .3A **58**
(off West Row)
Westgate St. E8 . . . . . . .5D **51**
Westgate Ter. SW10 . . . .2D **87**
West Gro. SE10 . . . . . . .4E **95**
Westgrove La. SE10 . . . .4E **95**
W. Halkin St.
SW1 . . . . . .5B **20** (4C **74**)
West Hallowes SE9 . . . .1F **125**
WEST HAM 5B **54**
West Ham La. E15 . . . . . .4F **53**
(not continuous)
WEST HAMPSTEAD 3D **45**
W. Hampstead M.
NW6 . . . . .3D **45**
West Ham United FC . . .1E **69**
W. Harding St.
EC4 . . . . . .2C **16** (5C **62**)
W. Heath Av. NW11 . . . . .3C **30**
W. Heath Cl. NW3 . . . . . .5C **30**
W. Heath Ct. NW11 . . . . .3C **30**
W. Heath Dr. NW11 . . . . .3C **30**
W. Heath Gdns.
NW3 . . . . .4C **30**
W. Heath Rd. NW3 . . . . .4C **30**
WEST HENDON 2C **28**
W. Hendon B'way.
NW9 . . . . .1B **28**
WEST HILL 4B **100**
West Hill SW15 . . . . . . .5F **99**
SW18 . . . . .5F **99**
West Hill Ct. N6 . . . . . . .5C **32**
Westhill Ct. W11 . . . . . .1B **72**
(off Denbigh Rd.)
West Hill Pk. N6 . . . . . . .4B **32**
(not continuous)
West Hill Rd. SW18 . . . .4B **100**
Westhope Ho. E2 . . . . . .3C **64**
(off Derbyshire St.)

Westhorne Av. SE9 . . . . .5C 110
    SE12 . . . . .5C 110
Westhorpe St. SW15 . . .1E 99
West Ho. Cl. SW19 . . . .1A 114
W. India Av. E14 . . . . . .2C 80
W. India Dock Rd.
    E14 . . . . .1B 80
W. India Ho. E14 . . . . . .1C 80
    (off W. India Dock Rd.)
WEST KENSINGTON . . .5A 72
W. Kensington Ct.
    W14 . . . . .1B 86
    (off Edith Vs.)
W. Kensington Mans.
    W14 . . . . .1B 86
    (off Beaumont Cres.)
WEST KILBURN 2B 58
Westlake SE16 . . . . . . .5E 79
    (off Rotherhithe New Rd.)
Westland Pl.
    N1 . . . . .1B 10 (2F 63)
Westlands Ter.
    SW12 . . . . .4E 103
West La. SE16 . . . . . . .3D 79
Westleigh Av. SW15 . . .3D 99
Westleigh Ct. E11 . . . . .1C 40
West Lodge E16 . . . . . .2C 82
    (off Britannia Ga.)
W. London Crematorium
    NW10 . . . . .3D 57
W. London Studios
    SW6 . . . . .3D 87
    (off Fulham Rd.)
Westmacott Ho. NW8 . .3F 59
    (off Hatton St.)
West Mall W8 . . . . .2C 72
    (off Kensington Mall)
Westmark Point
    SW15 . . . . .1D 113
    (off Norley Va.)
Westmead SW15 . . . . . .4D 99
W. Mersea Cl. E16 . . . . .2D 82
West M. SW1 . . . . .5D 75
    (off W. Warwick Pl.)
WESTMINSTER
    . . . . .4D 23 (3A 76)
Westminster Abbey
    . . . . .4D 23 (4A 76)
Westminster Abbey
    Chapter House . . .5D 23
    (in Westminster Abbey)
Westminster Abbey Mus.
    . . . . .5D 23
    (in Westminster Abbey)
Westminster Abbey
    Pyx Chamber 5D 23
    (in Westminster Abbey)
Westminster
    Boating Base & Pier
    . . . . .2F 89
Westminster Bri.
    SW1 . . . . . . .4E 23 (3A 76)
Westminster Bri. Ho.
    SE1 . . . . .5D 25
    (off Lambeth Rd.)
Westminster Bri. Rd.
    SE1 . . . . . . .4B 23 (3B 76)
Westminster Bus. Sq.
    SE11 . . . . .2B 90
    (off Durham St.)

Westminster Ct. E11 . . .1D 41
    (off Cambridge Pk.)
    NW8 . . . . .3F 59
    (off Aberdeen Pl.)
    SE16 . . . . .2F 79
    (off King & Queen Wharf)
Westminster Gdns.
    SW1 . . . . .5A 76
    (off Vincent St.)
Westminster Hall 4D 23
Westminster Ind. Est.
    SE18 . . . . .4F 83
Westminster Mans.
    SW1 . . . . .5C 22
    (off Gt. Smith St.)
Westminster Pal. Gdns.
    SW1 . . . . .5B 22
Westminster RC Cathedral
    . . . . .4E 75
Westmoor St. SE7 . . . . .4E 83
Westmore Ct.
    SW15 . . . . .3A 100
Westmoreland Ho.
    E16 . . . . .2C 82
    (off Gatcombe Rd.)
Westmoreland Pl.
    SW1 . . . . .1D 89
Westmoreland Rd.
    SE17 . . . . .2F 91
    (not continuous)
    SW13 . . . . .4B 84
Westmoreland St.
    W1 . . . . .1C 12 (4C 60)
Westmoreland Ter.
    SW1 . . . . .1D 89
Westmoreland Wlk.
    SE17 . . . . .2F 91
    (not continuous)
Westmorland Cl. E12 . . .4F 41
Westmorland Rd.
    E17 . . . . .1C 38
WEST NORWOOD 4E 119
West Norwood Crematorium
    SE27 . . . . .3E 119
Westonbirt Ct. SE15 . . .2B 92
    (off Ebley Cl.)
Weston Ct. N4 . . . . .5E 35
West One Ho. W1 . . . . .1F 13
    (off Wells St.)
West One Shop. Cen.
    W1 . . . . .3C 12
Weston Ho. E9 . . . . . . .5E 51
    (off King Edward's Rd.)
    NW6 . . . . .4A 44
Weston Pk. N8 . . . . . . .1A 34
Weston Ri.
    WC1 . . . . . . .1A 8 (2B 62)
Weston St.
    SE1 . . . . . . .4C 26 (3A 78)
    (not continuous)
Weston Wlk. E8 . . . . . . .4D 51
Westover Hill NW3 . . . .4C 30
Westover Rd. SW18 . . . .5E 101
Westow Hill SE19 . . . . .5A 120
West Pk. SE9 . . . . .2F 125
West Parkside SE10 . . . .3A 82
West Pl. SW19 . . . . . . .5E 113
West Point E14 . . . . . . .1B 80
    (off Grenade St.)
    SE1 . . . . .1C 92

Westport Rd. E13 . . . . . .3D 69
Westport St. E1 . . . . . . .5F 65
W. Poultry Av.
    EC1 . . . . . . .1D 17 (4D 63)
West Quarters W12 . . . .5C 56
West Quay SW10 . . . . . .4E 87
West Quay Wlk. E14 . . . .4D 81
West Reservoir Cen. . . .3E 35
West Ri. W2 . . . . .1A 74
    (off St George's Flds.)
West Rd. E15 . . . . .5B 54
    SE1 . . . . . . .3A 24 (3B 76)
    SW3 . . . . .1B 88
    SW4 . . . . .3F 103
Westrovia Ct. SW1 . . . . .1F 89
    (off Moreton St.)
West Row W10 . . . . . . .3A 58
Westrow SW15 . . . . . . .4E 99
West Side Comn.
    SW19 . . . . .5E 113
Westside Ct. W9 . . . . . .3C 58
    (off Elgin Av.)
West Smithfield
    EC1 . . . . . . .1D 17 (4D 63)
West Sq. E10 . . . . .2D 39
    SE11 . . . . .5D 25 (4D 77)
West Stand N5 . . . . .5D 35
West St. E2 . . . . .1D 65
    E11 . . . . .5A 40
    E17 . . . . .1D 39
    WC2 . . . . . . .3C 14 (5F 61)
W. Tenter St.
    E1 . . . . .3F 19 (5B 64)
West Twr. E14 . . . . .3D 81
    (off Pan Peninsula Sq.)
Westvale M. W3 . . . . . . .3A 70
Westview Cl. NW10 . . . . .2B 42
    W10 . . . . .5E 57
Westville Rd. W12 . . . . .3C 70
W. Warwick Pl. SW1 . . . .5E 75
West Way NW10 . . . . . .5A 28
Westway W2 . . . . .4B 58
    W9 . . . . .4B 58
    W10 . . . . .4B 58
    W12 . . . . .1B 70
Westway Est. W3 . . . . . .4A 56
Westway Lodge W9 . . . .4C 58
    (off Amberley Rd.)
Westway Sports Cen. . . .5F 57
Westway Travellers Site
    W12 . . . . .1F 71
    (off Stable Way)
Westwell M. SW16 . . . . .5A 118
Westwell Rd. SW16 . . . .5A 118
Westwell Rd. App.
    SW16 . . . . .5A 118
Westwick Gdns. W14 . . .3F 71
West Wintergarden 2D 81
    (off Bank St.)
Westwood Bus. Cen.
    NW10 . . . . .3A 56
Westwood Gdns.
    SW13 . . . . .1B 98
Westwood Hill SE26 . . . .5C 120
Westwood Ho. W12 . . . .2E 71
    (off Wood La.)
Westwood M. E3 . . . . . .2C 66
    (off Addington St.)
Westwood Pk. SE23 . . . .5D 107
Westwood Rd. SE26 . . . .4C 120

Westwood Rd. E16 . . . . .2D **83**
  SW13 . . . . .1B **98**
Wetherby Gdns. SW5 . .5E **73**
Wetherby Mans.
  SW5 . . . . .1D **87**
  (off Earls Ct. Sq.)
Wetherby M. SW5 . . . .1D **87**
Wetherby Pl. SW7 . . . . .5E **73**
Wetherden St. E17 . . . .2B **38**
Wetherell Rd. E9 . . . . . .5F **51**
Wevco Wharf SE15 . . . .2D **93**
Wevell Ho. *N6* 2C **32**
  (off Hillcrest)
Wexford Ho. *E1* 4E **65**
  (off Sidney St.)
Wexford Rd. SW12 . . . .5B **102**
Wexner Bldg. *E1* 1F **19**
  (off Strype St.)
Weybourne St.
  SW18 . . . . .2E **115**
Weybridge Ct. SE16 . . .1D **93**
Weybridge Point
  SW11 . . . . .5B **88**
Weydown Cl. SW19 . . .1A **114**
Weyhill Rd. E1 . . . . . . .5C **64**
Wey Ho. *NW8* 3F **59**
  (off Church St. Est.)
Weyman Rd. SE3 . . . . .4E **97**
Weymouth Ct. *E2* 1B **64**
  (off Weymouth Ter.)
Weymouth Ho. *SW8* . . .3B **90**
  (off Bolney St.)
Weymouth M.
  W1 . . . . . . .5D **5** (4D **61**)
Weymouth St.
  W1 . . . . . .1C **12** (4C **60**)
Weymouth Ter.
  E2 . . . . . . .1F **11** (1B **64**)
Weymouth St. *N4* 4B **34**
  (off Moray Rd.)
Whadcoat St. N4 . . . . .4C **34**
Whalebone Ct. EC2 . . . .2B **18**
Whalebone La. E15 . . . .4A **54**
Whales Yd. *E15* 4A **54**
  (off West Ham La.)
Wharf, The
  EC3 . . . . . .1E **27** (2B **78**)
Wharfdale Rd. N1 . . . . .1A **62**
Wharfedale St. E5 . . . . .1F **51**
Wharfedale Ho. *NW6* . . .5D **45**
  (off Kilburn Vale)
Wharfedale
  SW10 . . . . .1D **87**
Wharfedale Yd. *N1* 1A **62**
  (off Wharfedale Rd.)
Wharf La. E14 . . . . . . .5B **66**
Wharf Pl. E2 . . . . .5D **51**
Wharf Rd. N1 . . . .1F **9** (1E **63**)
Wharfside Point Nth.
  E14 . . . . .1E **81**
  (off Poplar High St.)
Wharfside Point Sth.
  E14 . . . . .1E **81**
Wharfside Rd. E16 . . . .4A **68**
Wharf St. E16 . . . . . . .4A **68**
Wharf Vw. Ct. *E14* 5E **67**
  (off Blair St.)
Wharton Cl. NW10 . . . .3A **42**
Wharton Cotts.
  WC1 . . . . . . .2B **8** (2C **62**)

Wharton Ho. *SE1* 5F **27**
  (off St Saviour's Est.)
Wharton St.
  WC1 . . . . . . .2A **8** (2B **62**)
Whatcott's Yd. N16 . . . .1A **50**
Whateley Rd. SE22 . . . .3B **106**
Whatman Ho. *E14* 5B **66**
  (off Wallwood St.)
Whatman Rd. SE23 . . . .5F **107**
Wheatfield Ho.
  NW6 . . . . .2C **58**
  (off Kilburn Pk. Rd.)
Wheatland Ho.
  SE22 . . . . .1A **106**
Wheatlands Rd.
  SW17 . . . . .3C **116**
Wheatley Ct. *E3* 2D **67**
  (off Bruce Rd.)
Wheatley Ho. *SW15* 5C **98**
  (off Ellisfield Dr)
Wheatley St.
  W1 . . . . . .1C **12** (4C **60**)
Wheat Sheaf Cl. E14 . . .5D **81**
Wheatsheaf La. SW6 . . .3E **85**
  SW8 . . . . .3A **90**
Wheatsheaf Ter.
  SW6 . . . . .3B **86**
Wheatstone Ho. *SE1* . . .4E **77**
  (off County St.)
  W10 . . . . .4A **58**
  (off Telford Rd.)
Wheatstone Rd. W10 . . .4A **58**
Wheeler Gdns. *N1* 5A **48**
  (off Outram Pl.)
Wheel Ho. *E14* 1D **95**
  (off Burrells Wharf Sq.)
Wheelwright St. N7 . . . .4B **48**
Wheler Ho. *E1* 4F **11**
  (off Quaker St.)
Wheler St.
  E1 . . . . .4F **11** (3B **64**)
Whellock Rd. W4 . . . . .4A **70**
Whetstone Pk.
  WC2 . . . . . . .2F **15** (5B **62**)
Whetstone Rd. SE3 . . . .5E **97**
Whewell Rd. N19 . . . . .4A **34**
Whidborne Bldgs.
  WC1 . . . . .2E **7**
  (off Whidborne St.)
Whidborne Cl. SE8 . . . .5C **94**
Whidborne St.
  WC1 . . . . . . .2E **7** (2A **62**)
  (not continuous)
Whidbourne M. SW8 . . .4F **89**
Whinfell Cl. SW16 . . . .5F **117**
Whinyates Rd. SE9 . . . .1F **111**
Whippingham Ho. *E3* . .2B **66**
  (off Merchant St.)
Whipps Cross E17 . . . . .1F **39**
Whipps Cross Rd.
  E11 . . . . .1F **39**
  (not continuous)
Whiskin St.
  EC1 . . . . . . .2D **9** (2D **63**)
Whistler M. SE15 . . . . .3B **92**
Whistlers Av. SW11 . . . .3F **87**
Whistler St. N5 . . . . . . .2D **49**
Whistler Twr. *SW10* 3E **87**
  (off Worlds End Est.)
Whistler Wlk. SW10 . . . .3F **87**

Whiston Ho. *N1* 4D **49**
  (off Richmond Gro.)
Whiston Rd. E2 . . . . . . .1B **64**
Whitacre M. SE11 . . . . .1C **90**
Whitbread Rd. SE4 . . . .2A **108**
Whitburn Rd. SE13 . . . .2D **109**
Whitby Ct. N7 . . . . .1A **48**
Whitby Ho. *NW8* 5E **45**
  (off Boundary Rd.)
Whitby St. E1 . . . .3F **11** (3B **64**)
  (not continuous)
Whitcher Cl. SE14 . . . . .2A **94**
Whitcher Pl. NW1 . . . . .3E **47**
Whitchurch Ho. *W10* . . .5F **57**
  (off Kingsdown Cl.)
Whitcomb Ct. WC2 . . . .5C **14**
Whitcomb St.
  WC2 . . . . . . .5C **14** (1F **75**)
Whiteadder Way E14 . . .5D **81**
Whitear Wlk. E15 . . . . .3F **53**
Whitebeam Cl. SW9 . . . .3B **90**
Whitebeam Ho. *E15* 2A **68**
  (off Teasel Way)
White Bear Pl. NW3 . . . .1F **45**
White Bear Yd. *EC1* 4B **8**
  (off Clerkenwell Rd.)
WHITECHAPEL 4C **64**
Whitechapel Art Gallery
  . . . . .5B **64**
Whitechapel High St.
  E1 . . . . .2F **19** (5B **64**)
Whitechapel Rd. E1 . . . .4C **64**
Whitechapel Sports Cen.
  . . . . .4D **65**
White Church La. E1 . . .5C **64**
White Church Pas.
  E1 . . . . .5C **64**
  (off White Church La.)
WHITE CITY 1D **71**
WHITE CITY 5E **57**
White City Cl. W12 . . . .1E **71**
White City Est. *W12* . . .1D **71**
  (off Australia Rd.)
  W12 . . . . .1D **71**
  (Havelock Cl.)
White City Rd. W12 . . . .1E **71**
White Conduit St. N1 . . .1C **62**
Whitecross Pl.
  EC2 . . . . . . .5C **10** (4F **63**)
Whitecross St.
  EC1 . . . . . . .3A **10** (3E **63**)
Whitefield Av. NW2 . . . .3E **29**
Whitefield Cl. SW15 . . .4A **100**
Whitefoot La.
  BR1: Brom 4E **123**
  (not continuous)
Whitefoot Ter.
  BR1: Brom 3B **124**
Whitefriars St.
  EC4 . . . . . . .3C **16** (5C **62**)
Whitehall
  SW1 . . . . . . .2D **23** (2A **76**)
Whitehall Ct.
  SW1 . . . . . . .2D **23** (2A **76**)
  (not continuous)
Whitehall Gdns.
  SW1 . . . . .2D **23**
Whitehall Pk.
  N19 . . . . .2E **33**

Whitehall Pl. E7 . . . . . . .2C 54
SW1 . . . . . .2D 23 (2A 76)
White Hart Ct. EC2 . . . . .1D 19
White Hart La. NW10 . .3B 42
SW13 . . . . .1A 98
White Hart St.
EC4 . . . . . .2E 17 (5D 63)
SE11 . . . . .1C 90
White Hart Yd.
SE1 . . . . . .2B 26 (2F 77)
Whitehaven St. NW8 . . .3A 60
Whitehead Cl.
SW18 . . . . .5E 101
Whiteheads Gro.
SW3 . . . . .5A 74
White Heather Ho.
WC1 . . . . .2E 7
(off Cromer St.)
White Horse All. EC1 . . . .5D 9
White Horse La. E1 . . . .4F 65
Whitehorse M.
SE1 . . . . . .5C 24 (4C 76)
White Horse Rd. E1 . . .5A 66
(not continuous)
White Horse St.
W1 . . . . . .2E 21 (2D 75)
White Horse Yd.
EC2 . . . . . .2B 18 (5F 63)
White Ho. SW4 . . . . . .5F 103
(off Clapham Pk. Est.)
SW11 . . . . .4F 87
White House, The
NW1 . . . . .3E 5
Whitehouse Apartments
SE1 . . . . .2B 76
Whitehouse Est. E10 . . .1E 39
White Kennett St.
E1 . . . . . . .2E 19 (5B 64)
Whitelands Cres.
SW18 . . . . .5A 100
Whitelands Ho. SW3 . . .1B 88
(off Cheltenham Ter.)
Whitelegg Rd. E13 . . . .1B 68
Whiteley Rd. SE19 . . . .5F 119
Whiteleys Cen.
(Shopping Cen.)
W2 . . . . .5D 59
SE15 . . . . .2E 93
White Lion Ct. EC3 . . . .3D 19
White Lion Hill
EC4 . . . . . .4E 17 (1D 77)
White Lion St. N1 . . . . .1C 62
White Lodge Cl. N2 . . . .1F 31
White Lyon Ct. EC2 . . . .5F 9
White Post La. E9 . . . . .4B 52
White Post St. SE15 . . .3E 93
White Rd. E15 . . . . . . .4A 54
White's Grounds
SE1 . . . . . .4E 27 (3A 78)
White's Grounds Est.
SE1 . . . . .3F 27
White's Row
E1 . . . . . . .1F 19 (4B 64)
Whites Sq. SW4 . . . . . .2F 103
Whitestone La. NW3 . . . .5E 31
Whitestone Wlk.
NW3 . . . . .5E 31
White Swan M. W4 . . . .1A 84
Whitethorn Ho. E1 . . . . .2E 79
(off Prusom St.)

Whitethorn Pas. E3 . . . .3C 66
(off Whitethorn St.)
Whitethorn St. E3 . . . . .4C 66
White Twr. Way
E1 . . . . .4A 66
Whitfield Ho. NW8 . . . . .3A 60
(off Salisbury St.)
Whitfield Pl. W1 . . . . . . .4F 5
Whitfield Rd. E6 . . . . . .4E 55
SE3 . . . . .4F 95
Whitfield St.
W1 . . . . . . .4F 5 (3E 61)
Whitgift Ho. SE11 . . . . .5B 76
SW11 . . . . .4A 88
Whitgift St. SE11 . . . . . .5B 76
Whitley Ho. SW1 . . . . . .2E 89
(off Churchill Gdns.)
Whitlock Dr. SW19 . . . .5A 100
Whitman Ho. E2 . . . . . .2E 65
(off Cornwall Av.)
Whitman Rd. E3 . . . . . .3A 66
Whitmore Est. N1 . . . . .5A 50
Whitmore Gdns.
NW10 . . . . .1E 57
Whitmore Ho. N1 . . . . . .5A 50
(off Whitmore Est.)
Whitmore Rd. N1 . . . . . .5A 50
Whitnell Way SW15 . . . .3E 99
(not continuous)
Whitney Rd. E10 . . . . . .2D 39
Whitstable Ho. W10 . . . .5F 57
(off Silchester Rd.)
Whittaker Rd. E6 . . . . . .4E 55
Whittaker St. SW1 . . . . .5C 74
Whittaker Way SE1 . . . .5C 78
Whitta Rd. E12 . . . . . . .1F 55
Whittell Gdns. SE26 . . . .3E 121
Whittingham Ct. W4 . . . .3A 84
Whittingstall Rd.
SW6 . . . . .4B 86
Whittington Apartments
E1 . . . . .5F 65
(off E. Arbour St.)
Whittington Av.
EC3 . . . . . .3D 19 (5A 64)
Whittington Ct. N2 . . . . .1B 32
Whittle Cl. E17 . . . . . . .1A 38
Whittlesey St.
SE1 . . . . . .2B 24 (2C 76)
Whitton NW3 . . . . .4B 46
Whitton Wlk. E3 . . . . . . .2C 66
(not continuous)
Whitwell Rd. E13 . . . . . .2C 68
Whitworth Ho.
SE1 . . . . . .5A 26 (4E 77)
Whitworth St. SE10 . . . .1A 96
Whorlton Rd. SE15 . . . .1D 107
Whychcote Point
NW2 . . . . .3E 29
(off Whitefield Av.)
Whyteville Rd. E7 . . . . .3D 55
Whytlaw Ho. E3 . . . . . . .4B 66
(off Baythorne St.)
Wickersley Rd.
SW11 . . . . .5C 88
Wickers Oake SE19 . . . .4B 120
Wicket St. E1 . . . . .5D 65
Wickfield Apartments
E15 . . . . .3F 53
(off Grove Cres. Rd.)

Wickfield Ho. SE16 . . . .3D 79
(off Wilson Gro.)
Wickford Ho. E1 . . . . . .3E 65
(off Wickford St.)
Wickford St. E1 . . . . . . .3E 65
Wickham Cl. E1 . . . . . . .4E 65
Wickham Gdns.
SE4 . . . . .1B 108
Wickham Ho. N1 . . . . . .5A 50
(off New Era Est.)
Wickham M. SE4 . . . . . .5B 94
Wickham Rd.
SE4 . . . . .2B 108
Wickham St. SE11 . . . . .1B 90
Wick La. E3 . . . . .5C 52
Wicklow Ho. N16 . . . . . .3B 36
Wicklow St.
WC1 . . . . . .1F 7 (2B 62)
Wick M. E9 . . . . .3A 52
Wick Rd. E9 . . . . .3F 51
Wicks Cl. SE9 . . . . .4F 125
Wick Sq. E9 . . . . .3B 52
Wicksteed Ho. SE1 . . . .4E 77
Wickway Ct. SE15 . . . . .2B 92
(off Cator St.)
Wickwood St. SE5 . . . . .5D 91
Widdenham Rd. N7 . . . .1B 48
Widdin St. E15 . . . . .4A 54
Widegate St.
E1 . . . . . . .1E 19 (4A 64)
Widford NW1 . . . . .3D 47
(off Lewis St.)
Widford Ho. N1 . . . . . . .1D 63
(off Colebrooke Rd.)
Widgeon Cl. E16 . . . . . .5D 69
Widley Rd. W9 . . . . .2C 58
Wigan Ho. E5 . . . . .3D 37
Wightman Rd. N4 . . . . . .1C 34
N8 . . . . .1C 34
Wigmore Hall 2D 13
Wigmore Pl.
W1 . . . . . .2D 13 (5D 61)
Wigmore St.
W1 . . . . . .2C 12 (5C 60)
Wigram Ho. E14 . . . . . .1D 81
(off Wade's Pl.)
Wigram Rd. E11 . . . . . . .1E 41
Wigston Rd. E13 . . . . . .3D 69
Wigton Pl. SE11 . . . . . . .1C 90
Wilberforce M. SW4 . . . .2F 103
Wilberforce Rd. N4 . . . .4D 35
NW9 . . . . .1C 28
Wilberforce Wlk. E15 . . .2A 54
Wilberforce Way
SW19 . . . . .5F 113
Wilbraham Ho. SW8 . . . .3A 90
(off Wandsworth Rd.)
Wilbraham Mans.
SW1 . . . . .5C 74
(off Wilbraham Pl.)
Wilbraham Pl. SW1 . . . .5B 74
Wilbrooke Pl. SE3 . . . . .4D 97
Wilby M. W11 . . . . .2B 72
Wilcox Cl. SW8 . . . . . . .3A 90
(not continuous)
Wilcox Ho. E3 . . . . .4B 66
(off Ackroyd Dr.)
Wilcox Pl.
SW1 . . . . . .5A 22 (4E 75)
Wilcox Rd. SW8 . . . . . . .3A 90

Wild Ct. WC2 . . .3F **15** (5B **62**)
(not continuous)
Wildcroft Mnr. SW15 . . . . .5E **99**
Wildcroft Rd. SW15 . . . . .5E **99**
Wilde Cl. E8 . . . . .5C **50**
Wilde Ho. W2 . . . . .1F **73**
(off Gloucester Ter.)
Wilde Pl. SW18 . . . . .5F **101**
Wilderness Local
Nature Reserve, The
. . . . .2C **88**
Wilderness M. SW4 . . . .2D **103**
Wilderton Rd. N16 . . . . . .2A **36**
Wildfell Rd. SE6 . . . . . .5D **109**
Wild Goose Dr. SE14 . . . .4E **93**
Wild Hatch NW11 . . . . . .1C **30**
Wild's Rents
SE1 . . . . .5D **27** (4A **78**)
Wild St. WC2 . . .3E **15** (5A **62**)
Wildwood Cl. SE12 . . . .5B **110**
Wildwood Gro. NW3 . . . . .3E **31**
Wildwood Ri. NW11 . . . . . .3E **31**
Wildwood Rd. NW11 . . . . .1D **31**
Wildwood Ter. NW3 . . . . .3E **31**
Wilfred Ct. N15 . . . . .1F **35**
(off South Gro.)
Wilfred Owen Cl.
SW19 . . . . .5E **115**
Wilfred St.
SW1 . . . . . . .5F **21** (4E **75**)
Wilfred Wood Ct. W6 . . . .5E **71**
(off Samuel's Cl.)
Wilkes St. E1 . . .5F **11** (4B **64**)
Wilkie Ho. SW1 . . . . .1F **89**
(off Cureton St.)
Wilkins Ho. SW1 . . . . . .2D **89**
(off Churchill Gdns.)
Wilkinson Ct. SW17 . . .4F **115**
Wilkinson Ho. N1 . . . . . . .1F **63**
(off Cranston Est.)
Wilkinson Rd. E16 . . . . . .5E **69**
Wilkinson St. SW8 . . . . . .3B **90**
Wilkin St. NW5 . . . . .3C **46**
Wilkin St. M. NW5 . . . . . . .3D **47**
Wilks Pl. N1 . . . . .1A **64**
Willard St. SW8 . . . . . . .1D **103**
Will Crooks Gdns.
SE9 . . . . .2E **111**
WILLESDEN 3C **42**
Willesden Belle Vue Cinema
. . . . .3D **43**
(off High Rd.)
WILLESDEN GREEN 3E **43**
Willesden La. NW2 . . . . . .3E **43**
NW6 . . . . .3E **43**
Willesden Section Ho.
. . . . .4F **43**
(off Willesden La.)
Willesden Sports Cen.
. . . . .5D **43**
Willesden Sports Stadium
. . . . .5D **43**
Willes Rd. NW5 . . . . .3D **47**
Willett Ho. E13 . . . . .1D **69**
(off Queens Rd. W.)
William IV St.
WC2 . . . . . . .5D **15** (1A **76**)
William Banfield Ho.
SW6 . . . . .5B **86**
(off Munster Rd.)

William Blake Ho.
SW11 . . . . .4A **88**
William Bonney Est.
SW4 . . . . .2F **103**
William Booth Ho.
E14 . . . . .5C **66**
(off Hind Gro.)
William Caslon Ho.
E2 . . . . .1D **65**
(off Patriot Sq.)
William Channing Ho.
E2 . . . . .2D **65**
(off Canrobert St.)
William Cl.
SE13 . . . . .1E **109**
William Cobbett Ho.
W8 . . . . .4D **73**
(off Scarsdale Pl.)
William Ct. NW8 . . . . .2E **59**
William Dromey Ct.
NW6 . . . . .4B **44**
William Dunbar Ho.
NW6 . . . . .1B **58**
(off Albert Rd.)
William Dyce M.
SW16 . . . . .4F **117**
William Ellis Way
SE16 . . . . .4C **78**
(off St James's Rd.)
William Evans Ho.
SE8 . . . . .5F **79**
(off Haddonfield)
William Farm La.
SW15 . . . . .1D **99**
William Fenn Ho. E2 . . .2C **64**
(off Shipton Rd.)
William Fry Ho. E1 . . . . .5F **65**
(off W. Arbour St.)
William Gdns. SW15 . . .3D **99**
William Gibbs Ct.
SW1 . . . . .5B **22**
(off Old Pye St.)
William Gunn Ho.
NW3 . . . . .2A **46**
William Guy Gdns.
E3 . . . . .2D **67**
William Harvey Ho.
SW19 . . . . .1A **114**
(off Whitlock Dr.)
William Henry Wlk.
SW8 . . . . .2F **89**
William Hunt Mans.
SW13 . . . . .2E **85**
William Margrie Cl.
SE15 . . . . .5C **92**
William M.
SW1 . . . . . . .4A **20** (3B **74**)
William Morley Cl.
E6 . . . . .5F **55**
William Morris Ho.
W6 . . . . .2F **85**
William Morris Way
SW6 . . . . .1E **101**
William Owston Ct.
E16 . . . . .2F **83**
(off Connaught Rd.)
William Pl. E3 . . . . .1B **66**
William Rathbone Ho.
E2 . . . . .2D **65**
(off Florida St.)

William Rd.
NW1 . . . . .2F **5** (2E **61**)
William Rushbrooke Ho.
SE16 . . . . .5C **78**
(off Rouel Rd.)
William Saville Ho.
NW6 . . . . .1B **58**
(off Denmark Rd.)
William's Bldgs. E2 . . . .3E **65**
Williams Cl. N8 . . . . .1F **33**
SW6 . . . . .3A **86**
Williams Ho. E3 . . . . . . .2C **66**
(off Alfred St.)
E9 . . . . .5D **51**
(off King Edward's St.)
NW2 . . . . .5E **29**
(off Stoll Cl.)
SW1 . . . . .5F **75**
(off Montaigne Cl.)
William Smith Ho.
E3 . . . . .2C **66**
(off Ireton St.)
Williamson Cl. SE10 . . .1B **96**
Williamson Ct. SE17 . . .1E **91**
Williamson Rd. N4 . . . . .1D **35**
Williamson St. N7 . . . . . .1A **48**
William Sq. SE16 . . . . . . .1A **80**
(off Sovereign Cres.)
William St. E10 . . . . .1D **39**
SW1 . . . . . . .4A **20** (3B **74**)
William Whiffin Sq.
E3 . . . . .3B **66**
William White Ct.
E13 . . . . .5E **55**
(off Green St.)
William Wood Ho.
SE26 . . . . .3E **121**
(off Shrublands Cl.)
Willifield Way NW11 . . . .1C **30**
Willingham Cl. NW5 . . . .2E **47**
Willingham Ter. NW5 . . .2E **47**
Willington Ct. E5 . . . . . . .5A **38**
Willington Rd. SW9 . . . .1A **104**
Willis Ho. E14 . . . . .1D **81**
(off Hale St.)
Willis Rd. E15 . . . . .1B **68**
Willis St. E14 . . . . .5D **67**
Willoughby Highwalk
EC2 . . . . .1B **18**
(off Moor La.)
Willoughby Ho. E1 . . . . .2D **79**
(off Reardon Path)
EC2 . . . . .5B **10**
Willoughby M. SW4 . . . .2D **103**
(off Cedars M.)
Willoughby Pas. E14 . . .2C **80**
(off W. India Av.)
Willoughby Rd. NW3 . . . .1F **45**
Willoughbys, The
SW14 . . . . .1A **98**
Willoughby St. WC1 . . . .1D **15**
Willoughby Way SE7 . . . .5D **83**
Willow Av. SW13 . . . . . . .5B **84**
Willow Bank SW6 . . . . .1A **100**
Willow Bri. Rd. N1 . . . . . .3E **49**
(not continuous)
Willowbrook Est.
SE15 . . . . .3C **92**
Willow Brook Rd.
SE15 . . . . .3B **92**

Willow Bus. Pk.
  SE26 . . . . .3E **121**
Willow Cl. SE6 . . . . .1B **124**
Willow Ct. E11 . . . . . .4A **40**
  (off Trinity Cl.)
  EC2 . . . . .3D **11** (3A **64**)
  NW6 . . . . .4A **44**
  W4 . . . . .3A **84**
  (off Corney Reach Way)
  W9 . . . . .4C **58**
  (off Admiral Wlk.)
Willowdene N6 . . . . . .2B **32**
  SE15 . . . . .3D **93**
Willow Gro. E13 . . . . .1C **68**
Willow Ho. SE1 . . . . .5B **78**
  (off Curtis St.)
  W10 . . . . .3F **57**
  (off Maple Wlk.)
Willow Lodge SW6 . . .4F **85**
Willow Pl. SW1 . . . . .5E **75**
Willow Rd. NW3 . . . . .1F **45**
Willows, The SE1 . . . .5A **78**
  (off Willow Wlk.)
Willows Ter. NW10 . . .1B **56**
  (off Rucklidge Av.)
Willow St.
  EC2 . . . . .3D **11** (3A **64**)
Willow Tree Cl.
  E3 . . . . .5B **52**
  SW18 . . . . .1D **115**
Willow Va. W12 . . . . .2C **70**
Willow Wlk. N1 . . . . .1D **63**
  SE1 . . . . .4A **78**
  W11 . . . . .1F **71**
Willow Way SE26 . . . .3E **121**
Willsbridge Ct.
  SE15 . . . . .2B **92**
Will Wyatt Ct. N1 . . . .1A **64**
  (off Pitfield St.)
Wilman Gro. E8 . . . . .4C **50**
Wilmcote Ho. W2 . . . .4D **59**
  (off Woodchester Sq.)
Wilment Ct. NW2 . . . .5E **29**
Wilmer Gdns. N1 . . . .5A **50**
  (not continuous)
Wilmer Ho. E3 . . . . . .1A **66**
  (off Daling Way)
Wilmer Lea Cl. E15 . . .4E **53**
Wilmer Pl. N16 . . . . . .4B **36**
Wilmers Ct. NW10 . . .5A **42**
  (off Lawrence Av.)
Wilmington Sq.
  WC1 . . . . . .2B **8** (2C **62**)
  (not continuous)
Wilmington St.
  WC1 . . . . . .2B **8** (2C **62**)
Wilmot Cl. SE15 . . . . .3C **92**
Wilmot Ho. SE11 . . . .5D **77**
  (off George Mathers Rd.)
Wilmot Pl. NW1 . . . . .4E **47**
  (not continuous)
Wilmot Rd. E10 . . . . .4D **39**
Wilmot St. E2 . . . . . . .3D **65**
Wilna Rd. SW18 . . . . .5E **101**
Wilsham St. W11 . . . . .2F **71**
Wilshaw Ho. SE8 . . . .3C **94**
Wilshaw St. SE14 . . . .4C **94**
Wilson Gro. SE16 . . . .3D **79**
Wilson Ho. NW6 . . . . .4E **45**
  (off Goldhurst Ter.)

Wilson Rd. E6 . . . . . . .2F **69**
  SE5 . . . . .4A **92**
Wilson's Pl. E14 . . . . .5B **66**
Wilson's Rd. W6 . . . . .1F **85**
Wilson St.
  EC2 . . . . .5C **10** (4F **63**)
Wilson Wlk. W4 . . . . .5B **70**
  (off Prebend Gdns.)
  W6 . . . . .5B **70**
  (off Prebend Gdns.)
Wiltern Ct. NW2 . . . . .3A **44**
Wilton Av. W4 . . . . . . .1A **84**
Wilton Ct. E1 . . . . .5D **65**
  (off Cavell St.)
Wilton Cres.
  SW1 . . . . . .4B **20** (3C **74**)
Wilton Est. E8 . . . . . . .3C **50**
Wilton M. E8 . . . . .3D **51**
  SW1 . . . . . .5C **20** (4C **74**)
Wilton Pl.
  SW1 . . . . . .4B **20** (3C **74**)
Wilton Plaza SW1 . . . .5E **75**
  (off Wilton Rd.)
Wilton Rd. SW1 . . . . .4D **75**
Wilton Row
  SW1 . . . . . .4B **20** (3C **74**)
Wiltons Music Hall . . .1C **78**
  (off Graces Alley)
Wilton Sq. N1 . . . . . . .5F **49**
Wilton St.
  SW1 . . . . . .5D **21** (4D **75**)
Wilton Ter.
  SW1 . . . . . .5B **20** (4C **74**)
Wilton Vs. N1 . . . . . . .5F **49**
  (off Wilton Sq.)
Wilton Way E8 . . . . . .3C **50**
Wiltshire Cl. SW3 . . . .5B **74**
Wiltshire Ct. N4 . . . . . .3B **34**
  (off Marquis Rd.)
Wiltshire Gdns. N4 . . .1E **35**
Wiltshire Rd. SW9 . . .1C **104**
Wiltshire Row N1 . . . .5F **49**
Wimbart Rd. SW2 . . . .5B **104**
WIMBLEDON 3A **114**
Wimbledon
  All England
  Lawn Tennis &
  Croquet Club 4A **114**
Wimbledon Common
  . . . . .4C **112**
Wimbledon Common
  Golf Course 5D **113**
Wimbledon Hill Rd.
  SW19 . . . . .5A **114**
Wimbledon Lawn Tennis Mus.
  . . . . .3A **114**
Wimbledon Mus. of
  Local History 5A **114**
WIMBLEDON PARK . . .3C **114**
Wimbledon Pk. Athletics Track
  . . . . .2B **114**
Wimbledon Pk. Ct.
  SW19 . . . . .1B **114**
Wimbledon Pk. Golf Course
  . . . . .3B **114**
Wimbledon Pk. Rd.
  SW18 . . . . .2A **114**
  SW19 . . . . .2A **114**
Wimbledon Pk. Side
  SW19 . . . . .3F **113**

Wimbledon Pk.
  Watersports Cen.
  . . . . .2B **114**
Wimbledon Pk.
  Women's Fitness Suite
  . . . . .3B **114**
Wimbledon Rd.
  SW17 . . . . .4E **115**
Wimbledon Stadium Bus. Cen.
  SW17 . . . . .3D **115**
Wimbledon Stadium
  (Greyhound) 4E **115**
Wimbledon Windmill Mus.
  . . . . .2D **113**
Wimbolt St. E2 . . . . . .2C **64**
Wimborne Cl. SE12 . . .3B **110**
Wimborne Ct. SW12 . . .3E **117**
Wimborne Ho. E16 . . . .1B **82**
  (off Victoria Dock Rd.)
  NW1 . . . . .3A **60**
  (off Harewood Av.)
  SW8 . . . . .3B **90**
  (off Dorset Rd.)
  SW12 . . . . .3E **117**
Wimbourne Ct. N1 . . . .1F **63**
  (off Wimbourne St.)
Wimbourne St. N1 . . . .1F **63**
Wimpole M.
  W1 . . . . .5D **5** (4D **61**)
Wimpole St.
  W1 . . . . .1D **13** (4D **61**)
Winans Wlk. SW9 . . . .5C **90**
Winant Ho. E14 . . . . . .1D **81**
  (off Simpson's Rd.)
Wincanton Rd.
  SW18 . . . . .5B **100**
Winchcomb Gdns.
  SE9 . . . . .1F **111**
Winchelsea Cl. SW15 . .3F **99**
Winchelsea Ho. SE16 . .3E **79**
  (off Swan Rd.)
Winchelsea Rd. E7 . . . .5C **40**
  NW10 . . . . .5A **42**
Winchendon Rd. SW6 . .4B **86**
Winchester Av. NW6 . . .5A **44**
Winchester Bldgs.
  SE1 . . . . .3F **25**
  (off Copperfield St.)
Winchester Cl. SE17 . .5D **77**
Winchester Ct. W8 . . . .3C **72**
  (off Vicarage Ga.)
Winchester Ho. E3 . . . .2B **66**
  (off Hamlets Way)
  SE18 . . . . .3F **97**
  (off Portway Gdns.)
  SW3 . . . . .2F **87**
  (off Beaufort St.)
  SW9 . . . . .3C **90**
  W2 . . . . .5E **59**
  (off Hallfield Est.)
Winchester M. NW3 . . .4F **45**
  (off Winchester Rd.)
Winchester Pl. E8 . . . .2B **50**
  N6 . . . . .3D **33**
Winchester Rd. N6 . . . .2D **33**
  NW3 . . . . .4F **45**
Winchester Sq. SE1 . . .1B **26**
Winchester St. SW1 . . .1D **89**
Winchester Wlk.
  SE1 . . . . . .1B **26** (2F **77**)

Winchester Wharf
SE1 . . . . .1B **26**
(off Clink St.)
Winchfield Ho. SW15 . .4B **98**
Winchfield Rd.
SE26 . . . . .5A **122**
Winch Ho. E14 . . . . . .4D **81**
(off Tiller Rd.)
SW10 . . . . .3E **87**
(off King's Rd.)
Winchilsea Ho. NW8 . .2F **59**
(off St John's Wood Rd.)
Winckworth Ct. N1 . . . .2C **10**
(off Charles Sq. Est.)
Wincott Pde. SE11 . . . .5C **76**
(off Wincott St.)
Wincott St. SE11 . . . . .5C **76**
Windermere NW1 . . . . .2E **5**
(off Albany St.)
Windermere Av. NW6 . .5A **44**
Windermere Ct.
SW13 . . . . .2B **84**
Windermere Ho. E3 . . .3B **66**
Windermere Point
SE15 . . . . .3E **93**
(off Old Kent Rd.)
Windermere Rd. N19 . .4E **33**
SW15 . . . . .4A **112**
Winders Rd. SW11 . . . .5A **88**
(not continuous)
Windfield Cl. SE26 . . . .4F **121**
Windlass Pl. SE8 . . . . .5A **80**
Windlesham Gro.
SW19 . . . . .1F **113**
Windley Cl. SE23 . . . . .2E **121**
Windmill WC1 . . . . . . .5F **7**
(off New North St.)
Windmill Cl. SE1 . . . . .5C **78**
(off Beatrice Rd.)
SE13 . . . . .5E **95**
Windmill Ct. NW2 . . . . .3A **44**
Windmill Dr. NW2 . . . . .5A **30**
SW4 . . . . .3D **103**
Windmill Hill NW3 . . . .5E **31**
Windmill Ho. E14 . . . . .5C **80**
SE1 . . . . .2C **24**
(off Windmill Wlk.)
Windmill La. E15 . . . . .3F **53**
Windmill M. W4 . . . . . .5A **70**
Windmill Pas. W4 . . . . .5A **70**
Windmill Rd. SW18 . . .4F **101**
SW19 . . . . .2D **113**
W4 . . . . .5A **70**
Windmill Row SE11 . . .1C **90**
Windmill St.
W1 . . . . . .1B **14** (4F **61**)
(not continuous)
Windmill Wlk.
SE1 . . . . . . .2C **24** (2C **76**)
Windrose Cl. SE16 . . . .3F **79**
Windrush Cl. E8 . . . . . .4C **50**
SW11 . . . . .2F **101**
Windrush Ho. NW8 . . . .3F **59**
(off Church St. Est.)
Windrush La. SE23 . . . .3F **121**
Windsock Cl. SE16 . . . .5B **80**
Windsor Centre, The
N1 . . . . .5D **49**
(off Windsor St.)
Windsor Cl. SE27 . . . .4E **119**

Windsor Cotts.
SE14 . . . . .3B **94**
(off Amersham Gro.)
Windsor Ct. E3 . . . . . .1C **66**
(off Mostyn Gro.)
NW3 . . . . .1C **44**
NW11 . . . . .1A **30**
(off Golders Grn. Rd.)
SE16 . . . . .1F **79**
(off King & Queen Wharf)
SW3 . . . . .1A **88**
(off Jubilee Pl.)
SW11 . . . . .5F **87**
W2 . . . . .1D **73**
(off Moscow Rd.)
W10 . . . . .5F **57**
(off Bramley Rd.)
Windsor Gdns. W9 . . . .4C **58**
Windsor Gro. SE27 . . .4E **119**
Windsor Hall E16 . . . . .2D **83**
(off Wesley Av.)
Windsor Ho. E2 . . . . . .2F **65**
(off Knottisford St.)
N1 . . . . .1E **63**
NW1 . . . . .1E **5**
NW2 . . . . .3A **44**
(off Chatsworth Rd.)
Windsor M. SE6 . . . . . .1E **123**
SE23 . . . . .1A **122**
Windsor Pl. SW1 . . . . .4E **75**
Windsor Rd. E7 . . . . . .2D **55**
E10 . . . . .4D **39**
E11 . . . . .3C **40**
N7 . . . . .5A **34**
NW2 . . . . .3D **43**
Windsor St. N1 . . . . . . .5D **49**
Windsor Ter.
N1 . . . . . .1A **10** (2E **63**)
Windsor Wlk. SE5 . . . . .5F **91**
Windsor Way W14 . . . .5F **71**
Windsor Wharf E9 . . . . .2B **52**
Windspoint Dr. SE15 . . .2D **93**
Windus Rd. N16 . . . . . .3B **36**
Windus Wlk. N16 . . . . .3B **36**
Windy Ridge Cl.
SW19 . . . . .5F **113**
Wine Cl. E1 . . . . .1E **79**
(not continuous)
Wine Office Ct.
EC4 . . . . . . .2C **16** (5C **62**)
Winford Ct. SE15 . . . . .4D **93**
Winford Ho. E3 . . . . . .4B **52**
Winforton St. SE10 . . . .4E **95**
Winfrith Rd. SW18 . . . .5E **101**
Wingate Ho. E3 . . . . . .2D **67**
(off Bruce Rd.)
Wingate Rd. W6 . . . . . .4D **71**
Wingate Sq. SW4 . . . . .1E **103**
Wingfield Ct. E14 . . . . .1F **81**
(off Newport Av.)
Wingfield Ho. E2 . . . . .2F **11**
(off Virginia Rd.)
NW6 . . . . .1D **59**
(off Tollgate Gdns.)
Wingfield M. SE15 . . . .1C **106**
Wingfield Rd. E15 . . . .1A **54**
E17 . . . . .1D **39**
Wingfield St. SE15 . . . .1C **106**
Wingford Rd. SW2 . . . .4A **104**
Wingmore Rd. SE24 . . .1E **105**

Wingrad Ho. E1 . . . . . .4E **65**
(off Jubilee St.)
Wingrave SE17 . . . . . .5F **77**
Wingrave Rd. W6 . . . . .2E **85**
Wingreen NW8 . . . . . .5D **45**
(off Abbey Rd.)
Wingrove Rd. SE6 . . . .2A **124**
Wing Yip Bus. Cen.
NW2 . . . . .4D **29**
Winicotte Ho. W2 . . . . .4F **59**
(off Paddington Grn.)
Winifred Ter. E13 . . . . .1C **68**
(off Upper Rd.)
Winkfield Rd. E13 . . . . .1D **69**
Winkley St. E2 . . . . . . .1D **65**
Winkworth Cotts. E1 . . .3E **65**
(off Cephas St.)
Winlaton Rd.
BR1: Brom 4F **123**
Winnett St.
W1 . . . . .4B **14** (1F **75**)
Winnington Cl. N2 . . . . .1F **31**
Winnington Ho. SE5 . . .3E **91**
(off Wyndham Est.)
W10 . . . . .3A **58**
(off Southern Row)
Winnington Rd. N2 . . . .1F **31**
Winn Rd. SE12 . . . . . .1C **124**
Winscombe St. N19 . . .4D **33**
Winsford Rd. SE6 . . . . .3B **122**
Winsham Gro.
SW11 . . . . .3C **102**
Winsham Ho. NW1 . . . .1C **6**
(off Churchway)
Winslade Rd. SW2 . . . .3A **104**
Winslade Way SE6 . . . .5D **109**
Winsland M. W2 . . . . . .5F **59**
Winsland St. W2 . . . . . .5F **59**
Winsley St.
W1 . . . . .2A **14** (5E **61**)
Winslow SE17 . . . . . . .1A **92**
Winslow Cl. NW10 . . . .5A **28**
Winslow Rd. W6 . . . . . .2E **85**
Winstanley Est.
SW11 . . . . .1F **101**
Winstanley Rd.
SW11 . . . . .1F **101**
(not continuous)
Winston Av. NW9 . . . . .2A **28**
Winston Ho. WC1 . . . . .3C **6**
Winston Rd. N16 . . . . .1F **49**
Winter Av. E6 . . . . .5F **55**
Winterbourne Ho.
W11 . . . . .1A **72**
(off Portland Rd.)
Winterbourne Rd.
SE6 . . . . .1B **122**
Winterbrook Rd.
SE24 . . . . .4E **105**
Winterfold Cl.
SW19 . . . . .2A **114**
Wintergreen Cl. E6 . . . .4F **69**
Winterleys NW6 . . . . . .1B **58**
(off Denmark Rd.)
Winter Lodge SE16 . . . .1C **92**
(off Fern Wlk.)
Winterslow Ho. SE5 . . . .5E **91**
(off Flaxman Rd.)
Winterstoke Rd.
SE6 . . . . .1B **122**

Winterton Ho. E1 . . . . . .5E **65**
(off Deancross St.)
Winterton Pl.
SW10 . . . . .2E **87**
Winterwell Rd.
SW2 . . . . .3A **104**
Winthorpe Rd.
SW15 . . . . .2A **100**
Winthrop Ho. W12 . . . .1D **71**
(off White City Est.)
Winthrop St. E1 . . . . . .4D **65**
Winton Ct. N1 . . . . .1B **62**
(off Calshot St.)
Winton Way SW16 . . .5C **118**
Wireworks Ct. SE1 . . . . .4F **25**
(off Gt. Sufolk St.)
Wirrall Ho. SE26 . . . . . .3C **120**
Wisbech N4 . . . . .3B **34**
(off Lorne Rd.)
Wisden Ho. SW8 . . . . . .2B **90**
Wiseman Rd. E10 . . . . . .4C **38**
Wise Rd. E15 . . . . .5F **53**
Wiseton Rd. SW17 . . . .1A **116**
Wishart Rd. SE3 . . . . . . .5F **97**
Wisley Ho. SW1 . . . . . . .1F **89**
(off Rampayne St.)
Wisley Rd. SW11 . . . . . .3C **102**
Wisteria Apartments
E9 . . . . .3E **51**
(off Chatham Pl.)
Wisteria Rd. SE13 . . . . .2F **109**
Wistow Ho. E2 . . . . .5C **50**
(off Whiston Rd.)
Witanhurst La. N6 . . . . .3C **32**
Witan St. E2 . . . . .2D **65**
Witchwood Ho.
SW9 . . . . .1C **104**
(off Gresham Rd.)
Witham Ct. E10 . . . . .5D **39**
SW17 . . . . .3B **116**
Witherington Rd. N5 . . . .2C **48**
Withers Pl.
EC1 . . . . . .3A **10** (3E **63**)
Withycombe Rd.
SW19 . . . . .5F **99**
Withy Ho. E1 . . . . .3F **65**
(off Globe Rd.)
Witley Ct. WC1 . . . . .4D **7**
Witley Ho. SW2 . . . . . .5A **104**
Witley Point SW15 . . . .1D **113**
(off Wanborough Dr.)
Witley Rd. N19 . . . . .4E **33**
Witney Path SE23 . . . . .3F **121**
Wittersham Rd.
BR1: Brom 5B **124**
Wivenhoe Cl. SE15 . . .1D **107**
Wiverton Rd.
SE26 . . . . .5E **121**
Wixom Ho. SE3 . . . . . .2E **111**
Wix's La. SW4 . . . . .1D **103**
Woburn Ct. SE16 . . . . . .1D **93**
(off Masters Dr.)
WC1 . . . . .4D **7**
(off Bernard St.)
Woburn Mans. WC1 . . . .5B **6**
(off Torrington Pl.)
Woburn M.
WC1 . . . . . .4C **6** (3F **61**)
Woburn Pl.
WC1 . . . . . .4D **7** (3A **62**)

Woburn Sq.
WC1 . . . . . .4C **6** (3F **61**)
(not continuous)
Woburn Wlk.
WC1 . . . . . .2C **6** (2F **61**)
Wodeham Gdns. E1 . . . .4C **64**
Wodehouse Av.
SE5 . . . . .4B **92**
Woking Cl. SW15 . . . . . .2B **98**
Wolcot Ho. NW1 . . . . . . .1A **6**
(off Aldenham St.)
Wolfe Cres. SE7 . . . . . . .1F **97**
SE16 . . . . .3F **79**
Wolfe Ho. W12 . . . . .1D **71**
(off White City Est.)
Wolffe Gdns. E15 . . . . . .3B **54**
Wolfington Rd.
SE27 . . . . .4D **119**
Wolfram Cl. SE13 . . . . . .3A **110**
Wolftencroft Cl.
SW11 . . . . .1A **102**
Wollaston Cl. SE1 . . . . . .5E **77**
Wollaton Rd. N1 . . . . . . .1C **62**
(off Batchelor St.)
Wollett Ct. NW1 . . . . . . .4E **47**
(off St Pancras Way)
Wolseley Av. SW19 . . . .2C **114**
Wolseley Rd. E7 . . . . . . .4D **55**
N8 . . . . .1F **33**
Wolseley St. SE1 . . . . . . .3C **78**
Wolsey Cl. NW6 . . . . . . .4E **45**
SW11 . . . . .4A **88**
(off Westbridge Rd.)
Wolsey M. NW5 . . . . . . .3E **47**
Wolsey Rd. N1 . . . . .2F **49**
Wolsey St. E1 . . . . .4E **65**
Wolverley St. E2 . . . . . . .2D **65**
Wolverton SE17 . . . . . . .1A **92**
(not continuous)
Wolverton Gdns. W6 . . . .5F **71**
Womersley Rd. N8 . . . . . .1B **34**
Wontner Cl. N1 . . . . .4E **49**
Wontner Rd. SW17 . . . .2B **116**
Woodall Cl. E14 . . . . .1D **81**
Woodbank Rd.
BR1: Brom 3B **124**
Woodbastwick Rd.
SE26 . . . . .5F **121**
Woodberry Down N4 . . .2E **35**
Woodberry Down Est.
N4 . . . . .3E **35**
(Spring Pk. Dr.)
N4 . . . . .2E **35**
(Woodberry Gro.)
Woodberry Gro. N4 . . . .2E **35**
Woodbine Pl. E11 . . . . . .1C **40**
Woodbine Ter. E9 . . . . . .3E **51**
Woodborough Rd.
SW15 . . . . .2D **99**
Woodbourne Av.
SW16 . . . . .3F **117**
Woodbourne Cl.
SW16 . . . . .3A **118**
Woodbridge Cl. N7 . . . . .4B **34**
NW2 . . . . .5C **28**
Woodbridge Ho. E11 . . . .3B **40**
Woodbridge St.
EC1 . . . . . .3D **9** (3D **63**)
(not continuous)
Woodburn Cl. NW4 . . . .1F **29**

Woodbury Gdns.
SE12 . . . . .3D **125**
Woodbury Ho. SE26 . . . .3C **120**
Woodbury St. SW17 . . .5A **116**
Woodchester Ho.
E14 . . . . .4D **81**
(off Selsdon Way)
Woodchester Sq. W2 . . .4D **59**
Woodchurch Rd.
NW6 . . . . .4C **44**
Wood Cl. E2 . . . . .3C **64**
NW9 . . . . .2A **28**
Woodcock Ho. E14 . . . . .4C **66**
(off Burgess St.)
Woodcocks E16 . . . . .4E **69**
Woodcombe Cres.
SE23 . . . . .1E **121**
Woodcote Ho. SE8 . . . . .2B **94**
(off Prince St.)
Woodcote Pl. SE27 . . . .5D **119**
Woodcote Rd. E11 . . . . . .2C **40**
Woodcote Vs. SE27 . . . .5E **119**
Woodcroft M. SE8 . . . . . .5A **80**
Wood Dr. BR7: Chst . . .5F **125**
Woodend SE19 . . . . . . .5E **119**
Wooder Gdns. E7 . . . . . .1C **54**
Woodfall Rd. N4 . . . . .4C **34**
Woodfall St. SW3 . . . . . .1B **88**
Woodfarrs SE5 . . . . .2F **105**
Wood Fld. NW3 . . . . .2B **46**
Woodfield Av.
SW16 . . . . .3F **117**
Woodfield Gro.
SW16 . . . . .3F **117**
Woodfield Ho. SE23 . . .3F **121**
(off Dacres Rd.)
Woodfield La.
SW16 . . . . .3F **117**
Woodfield Pl. W9 . . . . . . .3B **58**
Woodfield Rd. W9 . . . . . .4B **58**
Woodford Ct. W12 . . . . . .3F **71**
(off Shepherd's Bush Grn.)
Woodford Rd. E7 . . . . . . .5D **41**
Woodger Rd. W12 . . . . . .3E **71**
Woodget Cl. E6 . . . . .5F **69**
Woodgrange Rd. E7 . . . .2D **55**
Woodhall NW1 . . . . .2F **5**
(off Robert St.)
Woodhall Av. SE21 . . . . .3B **120**
Woodhall Dr. SE21 . . . . .3B **120**
Woodhall Ho. SW18 . . .4F **101**
Woodham Rd. SE6 . . . . .3E **123**
Woodhatch Cl. E6 . . . . . .4F **69**
Woodheyes Rd.
NW10 . . . . .2A **42**
Wood Ho. NW6 . . . . .1B **58**
(off Albert Rd.)
Woodhouse Cl.
SE22 . . . . .2C **106**
Woodhouse Gro. E12 . . .3F **55**
Woodhouse Rd. E11 . . . .5B **40**
Woodland Cl. SE19 . . . .5A **120**
Woodland Ct. E11 . . . . . .1C **40**
(off New Wanstead)
N7 . . . . .3A **48**
Woodland Cres.
SE10 . . . . .2A **96**
SE16 . . . . .3F **79**
Woodland Gro. SE10 . . .1A **96**

Woodland Hill SE19 . . .5A **120**
Woodland M. SE19 . . . .3A **118**
Woodland Rd. SE19 . . . .5A **120**
Woodlands NW11 . . . . . .1A **30**
Woodlands, The N5 . . . . .1E **49**
  SE13 . . . . .5F **109**
  SW9 . . . .*3D 91*
  (off Langton Rd.)
Woodlands Av. E11 . . . . .3D **41**
Woodlands Cl. NW11 . . . .1A **30**
Woodlands Ct. *NW10* . . .*5F 43*
  (off Wrentham Av.)
  SE23 . . . . .5D **107**
Woodlands Ga.
  SW15 . . . .*3B 100*
  (off Woodlands Way)
Woodlands Hgts. *SE3* . .*2B 96*
  (off Vanburgh Hill)
Woodlands Pk. Rd.
  N15 . . . . .1D **35**
  SE10 . . . . .2A **96**
  (not continuous)
Woodlands Rd. E11 . . . . .4A **40**
  SW13 . . . . .1B **98**
Woodlands St. SE13 . . .5F **109**
Woodland St. E8 . . . . . .3B **50**
Woodlands Way
  SW15 . . . . .3B **100**
Woodland Ter. SE7 . . . . .5F **83**
Woodland Wlk.
  BR1: Brom 4F **123**
  (not continuous)
  NW3 . . . . .2A **46**
  SE10 . . . . .1A **96**
Wood La. N6 . . . . .1D **33**
  NW9 . . . . .2A **28**
  W12 . . . . .5E **57**
Woodlawn Cl.
  SW15 . . . . .3B **100**
Woodlawn Rd. SW6 . . . .3F **85**
Woodlea Rd. N16 . . . . . .5A **36**
Woodleigh Gdns.
  SW16 . . . . .3A **118**
Woodmans Gro.
  NW10 . . . . .2B **42**
Woodman's M. W12 . . . .4D **57**
Woodmere Cl.
  SW11 . . . . .1C **102**
Woodmill Cl. SW15 . . . .4C **98**
Woodmill Rd. E5 . . . . . . .4E **37**
Woodnook Rd.
  SW16 . . . . .5D **117**
Woodpecker M.
  SE13 . . . .*2F 109*
  (off Freshfield Cl.)
Woodpecker Rd.
  SE14 . . . . .2A **94**
Woodquest Av.
  SE24 . . . . .3E **105**
Woodriffe Rd. E11 . . . . .2F **39**
Woodrush Cl. SE14 . . . . .3A **94**
Wood's Bldgs. *E1* *4D 65*
  (off Winthrop St.)
Woodseer St. E1 . . . . . .4B **64**
Woodsford *SE17* *1F 91*
  (off Portland St.)
Woodsford Sq. W14 . . . .3A **72**
Woods Ho. *SW8* 1D **89**
  SW8 . . . .*4E 89*
  (off Wadhurst Rd.)

Woodside SW19 . . . . . .5B **114**
Woodside Av. N6 . . . . . .1B **32**
Woodside Ct. E12 . . . . . .3E **41**
Woodside Ho.
  SW19 . . . . .5B **114**
Woodside M.
  SE22 . . . . .3B **106**
Woodside Rd. E13 . . . . .3E **69**
Woods M.
  W1 . . . . . .4B **12** (1C **74**)
Woodsome Rd. NW5 . . . .5C **32**
Woods Pl.
  SE1 . . . . . .5E **27** (4A **78**)
Woodspring Rd.
  SW19 . . . . .2A **114**
Woods Rd. SE15 . . . . . .4D **93**
Woodstar Rd. *SE15* *3C 92*
  (off Reddins Rd.)
Woodstock Av. NW11 . . .2A **30**
Woodstock Ct. SE11 . . .1B **90**
  SE12 . . . . .4C **110**
Woodstock Gro. W12 . . .3F **71**
Woodstock Rd. E7 . . . . .4E **55**
  N4 . . . . .3C **34**
  NW11 . . . . .2B **30**
  W4 . . . . .5A **70**
Woodstock St.
  W1 . . . . . .3D **13** (5D **61**)
Woodstock Studios
  W12 . . . .*3F 71*
  (off Woodstock Gro.)
Woodstock Ter. E14 . . . .1D **81**
Wood St. EC2 . . .2A **18** (5E **63**)
  (not continuous)
  W4 . . . . .1A **84**
Woodsyre SE26 . . . . . .4B **120**
Wood Ter. NW2 . . . . . . .5D **29**
Woodthorpe Rd.
  SW15 . . . . .2D **99**
Wood Va. N10 . . . . .1E **33**
  SE23 . . . . .1D **121**
Wood Va. Est. SE23 . . .5E **107**
Woodvale Wlk.
  SE27 . . . . .5E **119**
Woodvale Way NW11 . . .5F **29**
Woodview Cl. N4 . . . . . .2D **35**
  SW15 . . . . .4A **112**
Woodville SE3 . . . . .3D **97**
Woodville Cl. SE12 . . . .3C **110**
Woodville Ct. *SE10* *4E 95*
  (off Blissett St.)
Woodville Gdns.
  NW11 . . . . .2F **29**
Woodville Ho. *SE1* *5F 27*
  (off St Saviour's Est.)
Woodville Rd. E11 . . . . .3B **40**
  N16 . . . . .2A **50**
  NW6 . . . . .1B **58**
  NW11 . . . . .2F **29**
Woodward Av. NW4 . . . .1C **28**
Woodwarde Rd.
  SE22 . . . . .4A **106**
Woodwell St. SW18 . . . .3E **101**
Wood Wharf SE10 . . . . .2D **95**
Wood Wharf Bus. Pk.
  E14 . . . . .2D **81**
  (not continuous)
Woodyard Cl. NW5 . . . . .2C **46**
Woodyard La. SE21 . . . .5A **106**

Woodyates Rd.
  SE12 . . . . .4C **110**
Woolacombe Rd.
  SE3 . . . . .4E **97**
Woolcombes Ct.
  SE16 . . . .*2F 79*
  (off Princes Riverside Rd.)
Wooler St. SE17 . . . . . . .1F **91**
Woolf M. *WC1* *3C 6*
  (off Burton Pl.)
Woolford Ct. *SE5* *5E 91*
  (off Coldharbour La.)
Woolgar M. *N16* *2A 50*
  (off Gillett St.)
Woollaston Rd. N4 . . . . .1D **35**
Woolley Ho. *SW9* *1D 105*
  (off Loughborough Rd.)
Woollon Ho. *E1* *5E 65*
  (off Clark St.)
Woolmead Av. NW9 . . . .2C **28**
Woolmore St. E14 . . . . . .1E **81**
Woolneigh St. SW6 . . . .1D **101**
Woolridge Way E9 . . . . .4E **51**
Woolstaplers Way
  SE16 . . . . .4C **78**
Woolstone Ho. *E2* *2C 50*
  (off Whiston Rd.)
Woolstone Rd.
  SE23 . . . . .2A **122**
Woolwich Chu. St.
  SE18 . . . . .4F **83**
Woolwich Rd. SE7 . . . . .1C **96**
  SE10 . . . . .1B **96**
Wooster Gdns. E14 . . . .5F **67**
Wooster Pl. *SE1* *5F 77*
  (off Searles Rd.)
Wootton St.
  SE1 . . . . .2C **24** (2C **76**)
Worcester Cl. NW2 . . . .5D **29**
Worcester Ct. *W9* *4C 58*
  (off Elmfield Way)
Worcester Dr. W4 . . . . . .3A **70**
Worcester Gdns.
  SW11 . . . .*3B 102*
  (off Grandison Rd.)
Worcester Ho. *SE11* . . .*5B 24*
  (off Kennington Rd.)
  SW9 . . . .*3C 90*
  (off Cranmer Rd.)
  W2 . . . .*5E 59*
  (off Hallfield Est.)
Worcester M. NW6 . . . . .3D **45**
Worcester Point EC1 . . .2E **63**
Wordsworth Av. E12 . . . .4F **55**
Wordsworth Ho. *NW6* . .*2C 58*
  (off Stafford Rd.)
Wordsworth Mans.
  W14 . . . .*2B 86*
  (off Queens Club Gdns.)
Wordsworth Pl. NW5 . . .2B **46**
Wordsworth Rd. N16 . . .1A **50**
  SE1 . . . . .5B **78**
Worfield St. SW11 . . . . .3A **88**
Worgan St. SE11 . . . . . .1B **90**
  SE16 . . . . .5F **79**
Worland Rd. E15 . . . . . . .4A **54**
Worlds End Est.
  SW10 . . . . .3F **87**

World's End Pas.
  SW10 . . . . .3F 87
  (off Worlds End Est.)
World's End Pl.
  SW10 . . . . .3F 87
Worlidge St. W6 . . . . . . .1E 85
Worlingham Rd.
  SE22 . . . . .2B 106
Wormholt Rd. W12 . . . .1C 70
Wormwood Scrubs Pk.
  (Local Nature Reserve)
  . . . . .4B 56
Wormwood St.
  EC2 . . . . .2D 19 (5A 64)
Wornington Rd. W10 . .3A 58
  (not continuous)
Woronzow Rd. NW8 . . . .5F 45
Worple Rd. SW19 . . . . .5B 114
Worple Rd. M.
  SW19 . . . . .5B 114
Worple St. SW14 . . . . .1A 98
Worship St.
  EC2 . . . . .4C 10 (3F 63)
  (not continuous)
Worslade St. SW17 . . . .4F 115
Worsley Bri. Rd.
  BR3: Beck 5C 122
  SE26 . . . . .4B 122
Worsley Gro. E5 . . . . . .1C 50
Worsley Ho. SE23 . . . . .2E 121
Worsley Rd. E11 . . . . .1A 54
Worsopp Dr. SW4 . . . . .3E 103
Worth Gro. SE17 . . . . . .1F 91
Worthing Cl. E15 . . . . . .5A 54
Worthington Rd. EC1 . . . .1C 8
  (off Myddelton Pas.)
Wortley Rd. E6 . . . . . . .4F 55
Wotton Ct. E14 . . . . . . .1F 81
  (off Jamestown Way)
Wotton Rd. NW2 . . . . . .5E 29
  SE8 . . . . .2B 94
Wouldham Rd. E16 . . . .5B 68
Wragby Rd. E11 . . . . . .5A 40
Wrayburn Ho. SE16 . . . .3C 78
  (off Llewellyn St.)
Wray Cres. N4 . . . . .4A 34
Wren Av. NW2 . . . . . . .1E 43
Wren Cl. E16 . . . . .5B 68
Wren Ho. E3 . . . . .1A 66
  (off Gernon Rd.)
  SW1 . . . . .1F 89
  (off Aylesford St.)
Wren Landing E14 . . . . .2C 80
Wren Ho. SW13 . . . . . .2E 85
Wren Rd. SE5 . . . . .4F 91
Wren's Pk. Ho. E5 . . . . .4D 37
Wren St. WC1 . . .3A 8 (3B 62)
Wrentham Av. NW10 . . .1F 57
Wrenthorpe Rd.
  BR1: Brom 4A 124
Wren Vw. N6 . . . . .2E 33
Wrestlers Ct. EC3 . . . . .2D 19
Wrexham Rd. E3 . . . . . .1C 66
Wricklemarsh Rd.
  SE3 . . . . .5D 97
  (not continuous)
Wrigglesworth St.
  SE14 . . . . .3F 93
Wright Cl. SE13 . . . . . .2F 109

Wright Rd. N1 . . . . .3A 50
Wrights Grn. SW4 . . . . .2F 103
Wright's La. W8 . . . . . . .4D 73
Wright's Rd. E3 . . . . . . .1B 66
  (not continuous)
Wrotham Ho. SE1 . . . . .5C 26
  (off Law St.)
Wrotham Rd.
  NW1 . . . . .4E 47
Wrottesley Rd.
  NW10 . . . . .1C 56
Wroughton Rd.
  SW11 . . . . .3B 102
Wroxton Rd. SE15 . . . . .5E 93
Wulfstan St. W12 . . . . .4B 56
Wyatt Cl. SE16 . . . . . . .3B 80
Wyatt Dr. SW13 . . . . . .2D 85
Wyatt Ho. NW8 . . . . . . .3F 59
  (off Frampton St.)
  SE3 . . . . .5B 96
Wyatt Pk. Rd. SW2 . . . .2A 118
Wyatt Rd. E7 . . . . .3C 54
  N5 . . . . .5E 35
Wybert St.
  NW1 . . . . .3F 5 (3E 61)
Wychcombe Studios
  NW3 . . . . .3B 46
Wycherley Cl. SE3 . . . . .3B 96
Wychwood End N6 . . . .2E 33
Wychwood Way
  SE19 . . . . .5F 119
Wyclif Ct. EC1 . . . . .2D 9
  (off Wyclif St.)
Wycliffe Rd. SW11 . . . .5C 88
Wyclif St. EC1 . . .2D 9 (2D 63)
Wycombe Gdns.
  NW11 . . . . .4C 30
Wycombe Ho. NW8 . . . .3A 60
  (off Grendon St.)
Wycombe Pl. SW18 . . . .4E 101
Wycombe Sq. W8 . . . . .2B 72
Wydeville Mnr. Rd.
  SE12 . . . . .4D 125
Wye St. SW11 . . . . .5F 87
Wyfold Rd. SW6 . . . . . .4A 86
Wykeham Ct. NW4 . . . . .1E 29
  (off Wykeham Rd.)
Wykeham Ho. SE1 . . . . .2F 25
  (off Union St.)
Wykeham Rd. NW4 . . . .1E 29
Wyke Rd. E3 . . . . .4C 52
Wyldes Cl. NW11 . . . . . .3E 31
Wyleu St. SE23 . . . . . .5A 108
Wyllen Cl. E1 . . . . .3E 65
Wymering Mans. W9 . . .2C 58
  (off Wymering Rd.)
Wymering Rd. W9 . . . . .2C 58
Wymondham Ct.
  NW8 . . . . .5F 45
  (off Queensmead)
Wymond St. SW15 . . . . .1E 99
Wynan Rd. E14 . . . . . . .1D 95
Wyndcliff Rd. SE7 . . . . .2D 97
Wyndham Cres. N19 . . .5E 33
Wyndham Deedes Ho.
  E2 . . . . .1C 64
  (off Hackney Rd.)
Wyndham Est. SE5 . . . . .3E 91
Wyndham Ho. E14 . . . . .3D 81
  (off Marsh Wall)

Wyndham Ho. SW1 . . .5C 74
  (off Sloane Sq.)
Wyndham M. W1 . . . . . .4B 60
Wyndham Pl.
  W1 . . . . .1A 12 (4B 60)
Wyndham Rd. E6 . . . . . .4F 55
  SE5 . . . . .3E 91
Wyndhams Ct. E8 . . . . .4B 50
  (off Celandine Dr.)
Wyndham's Theatre 4D 15
  (off Charing Cross Rd.)
Wyndham St. W1 . . . . . .4B 60
Wyndham Yd. W1 . . . . .4B 60
Wyneham Rd. SE24 . . . .3F 105
Wynell Rd. SE23 . . . . . .3F 121
Wynford Rd. N1 . . . . . . .1B 62
Wynne Rd. SW9 . . . . . . .5C 90
Wynnstay Gdns. W8 . . .4C 72
Wynter St. SW11 . . . . . .2E 101
Wynyard Ho. SE11 . . . . .1B 90
  (off Newburn St.)
Wynyard Ter. SE11 . . . .1B 90
Wynyatt St.
  EC1 . . . . . .2D 9 (2D 63)
Wytham Ho. NW8 . . . . .3F 59
  (off Church St. Est.)
Wythburn Ct. W1 . . . . . .2A 12
  (off Wythburn Pl.)
Wythburn Pl.
  W1 . . . . . .3A 12 (5B 60)
Wythes Rd. E16 . . . . . . .2F 83
Wyvil Rd. SW8 . . . . .3A 90
Wyvis St. E14 . . . . .4D 67

Y

Yabsley St. E14 . . . . . . .2E 81
Yaldham Ho. SE1 . . . . . .5A 78
  (off Old Kent Rd.)
Yalding Rd. SE16 . . . . . .4C 78
Yale Ct. NW6 . . . . .2D 45
Yard, The N1 . . . . .1E 7
  (off Caledonia Rd.)
Yardley St.
  WC1 . . . . . .2B 8 (2C 62)
  (not continuous)
Yarmouth Pl.
  W1 . . . . . .2D 21 (2D 75)
Yarnfield Sq. SE15 . . . .4C 92
Yarrell Mans. W14 . . . .2B 86
  (off Queen's Club Mans.)
Yarrow Cres. E6 . . . . . . .4F 69
Yarrow Ho. E14 . . . . . . .4E 81
  (off Stewart St.)
  W10 . . . . .4E 57
  (off Sutton Way)
Yateley St. SE18 . . . . . .4F 83
Yatesbury Ct. E5 . . . . . .2A 52
  (off Studley Cl.)
Yates Ct. NW2 . . . . .3F 43
  (off Willesden La.)
Yates Ho. E2 . . . . .2C 64
  (off Roberta St.)
Yatton Ho. W10 . . . . . . .4E 57
  (off Sutton Way)
Yeadon Ho. W10 . . . . . .4E 57
  (off Sutton Way)
Yearby Ho. W10 . . . . . . .3E 57
  (off Sutton Way)

Yeate St. N1 . . . . .4F 49
Yeatman Rd. N6 . . . . . . .1B 32
Yeats Cl. NW10 . . . . . . .2A 42
SE13 . . . . .5F 95
Yeldham Ho. W6 . . . . . .1F 85
(off Yeldham Rd.)
Yeldham Rd. W6 . . . . . .1F 85
Yeldham Vs. W6 . . . . . .1F 85
(off Yeldham Rd.)
Yelverton Rd. SW11 . . . .5F 87
Yeoman Cl. SE27 . . . . .3D 119
Yeoman's Row SW3 . . .4A 74
Yeoman St. SE8 . . . . . .5A 80
Yeoman's Yd. E1 . . . . .1B 78
(off Chamber St.)
Yeo St. E3 . . . . .4D 67
Yeovil Ho. W10 . . . . . . .3E 57
(off Sutton Way)
Yerbury Rd. N19 . . . . . .5F 33
(not continuous)
Yetev Lev Ct. E5 . . . . . .3C 36
Yewfield Rd. NW10 . . . .3B 42
Yew Gro. NW2 . . . . . . .1F 43
Yew Ho. SE16 . . . . .3F 79
(off Woodland Cres.)
Yew Tree Cl. SE13 . . . .1E 109
Yew Tree Ct. NW11 . . . .1B 30
(off Bridge La.)
Yew Tree Lodge
SW16 . . . . .4E 117
Yew Tree Rd. W12 . . . .1B 70
Yoakley Rd. N16 . . . . . .4A 36
Yoke Cl. N7 . . . . .3A 48
Yolande Gdns. SE9 . . . .3F 111
Yonge Pk. N4 . . . . .5C 34
York Av. SE17 . . . . .1E 91
York Bri. NW1 . . .3B 4 (3C 60)
York Bldgs.
WC2 . . . . . .5E 15 (1A 76)
York Cl. SE5 . . . . .5E 91
(off Lilford Rd.)
York Ga. NW1 . . .4B 4 (3C 60)
York Gro. SE15 . . . . . . .4E 93
York Hall Leisure Cen.
. . . . .1D 65
York Hill SE27 . . . . . . .3D 119
York Ho. E16 . . . . .2C 82
(off De Quincey M.)
SE1 . . . . . .5A 24 (4B 76)
SW3 . . . . .1B 88
(off Turks Row)
W1 . . . . .5A 4
(off York St.)

York Ho. W8 . . . . .3D 73
(off York Ho. Pl.)
York Ho. Pl. W8 . . . . . . .3D 73
Yorkley Ho. W10 . . . . . .3E 57
(off Sutton Way)
York Mans. SE17 . . . . . .1E 91
(off Browning St.)
SW5 . . . . .1D 87
(off Earls Ct. Rd.)
SW11 . . . . .4C 88
(off Prince of Wales Dr.)
W1 . . . . .5B 4
(off Chiltern St.)
York M. NW5 . . . . .2D 47
York Pde. NW9 . . . . . . .1C 28
(off W. Hendon B'way.)
York Pas. W8 . . . . .3D 73
(off York Ho. Pl.)
York Pl. SW11 . . . . .1F 101
WC2 . . . . .5E 15
York Pl. Mans. W1 . . . .5A 4
(off Baker St.)
York Ri. NW5 . . . . .5D 33
York Rd. E7 . . . . .3C 54
E10 . . . . .5E 39
E17 . . . . .1F 37
SE1 . . . . .3A 24 (3B 76)
SW11 . . . . .2E 101
SW18 . . . . .2E 101
SW19 . . . . .5E 115
York Rd. Bus. Cen.
SW11 . . . . .5F 87
Yorkshire Cl. N16 . . . . .5A 36
YORKSHIRE GREY 3F 111
Yorkshire Grey Pl.
NW3 . . . . .1E 45
Yorkshire Grey Yd.
WC1 . . . . .1F 15
Yorkshire Rd. E14 . . . . .5A 66
York Sq. E14 . . . . .5A 66
York St. W1 . . . .1A 12 (4B 60)
York St. Chambers
W1 . . . . .4B 60
(off York St.)
York Ter. E.
NW1 . . . . . .4C 4 (3C 60)
York Ter. W.
NW1 . . . . . .4B 4 (3C 60)
Yorkton St. E2 . . . . .1C 64
York Way N1 . . .1E 7 (3A 48)
N7 . . . . .3F 47
York Way Ct. N1 . . . . . .5A 48
(not continuous)

York Way Est. N7 . . . . .3A 48
Young Cl. NW6 . . . . . . .4A 44
Young Rd. E16 . . . . . . .5E 69
Youngs Bldgs. EC1 . . . .3A 10
Youngs Ct. SW11 . . . . .4C 88
Young St. W8 . . . . .3D 73
Young Vic Theatre, The
. . . . .3C 24
Yoxall Ho. W10 . . . . . . .3E 57
(off Sutton Way)
Yukon Rd. SW12 . . . . .5D 103
Yunus Khan Cl. E17 . . .1C 38
Yvon Ho. SW11 . . . . . . .4C 88
(off Alexandra Av.)

Z

Zachary Ct. SW1 . . . . . .5F 75
(off Montaigne Cl.)
Zahra Ho. NW10 . . . . . .2E 57
(off Harrow Rd.)
Zampa Rd. SE16 . . . . . .1E 93
Zander Ct. E2 . . . . .2C 64
Zangwill Ho. NW6 . . . . .1B 58
(off Carlton Vale)
Zangwill Rd. SE3 . . . . . .4F 97
Zapotec Ho. SE8 . . . . . .5F 79
(off Chilton Gro.)
Zealand Ho. SE5 . . . . . .5E 91
(off Denmark Rd.)
SE18 . . . . .5F 83
Zealand Rd. E3 . . . . . . .1A 66
Zennor Rd. SW12 . . . . .1E 117
Zennor Rd. Ind. Est.
SW12 . . . . .1E 117
Zenobia Mans. W14 . . . .2B 86
(off Queen's Club Mans.)
Zenoria St. SE22 . . . . . .2B 106
Zetland Ho. W8 . . . . . . .4D 73
(off Marloes Rd.)
Zetland St. E14 . . . . . . .4D 67
Zinc Building, The
SE13 . . . . .2A 110
Zion Ho. E1 . . . . .5E 65
(off Jubilee St.)
Zoar St. SE1 . . . .1F 25 (2E 77)
Zodiac Ho. E3 . . . . .3C 66
(off Wellington Way)
Zoffany St. N19 . . . . . . .4F 33
Zona Ct. SE1 . . . . .5F 27
(off Grange Wlk.)
Zulu M. SW11 . . . . .5A 88

HOSPITALS, HOSPICES and
selected HEALTHCARE FACILITIES
covered by this atlas.

N.B. Where it is not possible to name these facilities on the map,
the reference given is for the road in which they are situated.

BARNES HOSPITAL 1A **98**
    South Worple Way
    SW14 8SU
    Tel: 020 8878 4981

BELVEDERE HOUSE (DAY) HOSPITAL . . .5C **42**
    341 Harlesden Road
    NW10 3RX
    Tel: 020 8459 3562

BLACKHEATH BMI HOSPITAL 1B **110**
    40-42 Lee Terrace
    SE3 9UD
    Tel: 020 8318 7722

BLACKHEATH BMI HOSPITAL
(OUTPATIENT DEPARTMENT) 1B **110**
    Independents Road
    SE3 9LF
    Tel: 020 8297 4500

BLACKHEATH CYGNET HOSPITAL 4E **95**
    80 Blackheath Hill
    SE10 8AD
    Tel: 020 86942111

CAMDEN MEWS DAY HOSPITAL 4E **47**
    1-5 Camden Mews
    NW1 9DB
    Tel: 020 3317 4740

CHARING CROSS HOSPITAL 2F **85**
    Fulham Palace Road
    W6 8RF
    Tel: 0203311 1234

CHELSEA & WESTMINSTER HOSPITAL
. . . . .2E **87**
    369 Fulham Road
    SW10 9NH
    Tel: 020 8746 8000

CHILDREN'S HOSPITAL, THE (LEWISHAM)
. . . . .3D **109**
    Lewisham University Hospital
    Lewisham High Street
    SE13 6LH
    Tel: 020 8333 3000

CROMWELL BUPA HOSPITAL 5D **73**
    162-174 Cromwell Road
    SW5 0TU
    Tel: 020 7460 2000

DULWICH COMMUNITY HOSPITAL 2A **106**
    East Dulwich Grove
    SE22 8PT
    Tel: 020 3299 6257

EAST HAM CARE CENTRE & DAY HOSPITAL
. . . . .4F **55**
    Shrewsbury Road
    E7 8QP
    Tel: 0208 475 2005

EASTMAN DENTAL HOSPITAL &
    DENTAL INSTITUTE 3F **7** (3B **62**)
    256 Gray's Inn Road
    WC1X 8LD
    Tel: 020 3456 7899

EVELINA CHILDREN'S HOSPITAL
. . . . .5F **23** (4B **76**)
    St Thomas' Hospital
    Westminster Bridge Road
    SE1 7EH
    Tel: 020 7188 7188

FITZROY SQUARE BMI HOSPITAL
. . . . .4F **5** (3E **61**)
    14 Fitzroy Square
    W1T 6AH
    Tel: 020 7388 4954

GATEWAY SURGICAL CENTRE 3F **69**
    Cherry Tree Way
    Glen Road
    E13 8SL
    Tel: 020 7476 4000

GENERAL MEDICAL WALK-IN CENTRE
(LIVERPOOL STREET) 5E **11** (4A **64**)
    Exchange Arcade
    Bishopsgate
    EC2M 3WA
    Tel: 0845 880 1242

GORDON HOSPITAL 5F **75**
    Bloombur g Street
    SW1V 2RH
    Tel: 020 8746 8733

GREAT ORMOND STREET HOSPITAL
    FOR CHILDREN 4E **7** (3A **62**)
    Great Ormond Street
    WC1N 3JH
    Tel: 020 7405 9200

GUY'S HOSPITAL 2C **26** (3F **77**)
Great Maze Pond
SE1 9RT
Tel: 020 7188 7188

GUY'S NUFFIELD HOUSE 3B **26**
Guy's Hospital
Newcomen Street
SE1 1YR
Tel: 020 7188 5292

HAMMERSMITH HOSPITAL 5C **56**
Du Cane Road
W12 0HS
Tel: 020 3313 1111

HARLEY STREET CLINIC 5D **5** (4D **61**)
35 Weymouth Street
W1G 8BJ
Tel: 020 7935 7700

HEART HOSPITAL 1C **12** (4C **60**)
16-18 Westmoreland St.
W1G 8PH
Tel: 020 7573 8888

HIGHGATE HOSPITAL 1B **32**
17- 19 View Road
N6 4DJ
Tel: 020 8341 4182

HIGHGATE MENTAL HEALTH CENTRE . . .4D **33**
Dartmouth Park Hill
N19 5NX
Tel: 020 7561 4000

HOMERTON UNIVERSITY HOSPITAL 2F **51**
Homerton Row
E9 6SR
Tel: 020 8510 5555

HOSPITAL FOR TROPICAL DISEASES
. . . . .4A **6** (3E **61**)
Mortimer Market
Capper Street
WC1E 6JB
Tel: 0845 155 5000

HOSPITAL OF ST JOHN & ST ELIZABETH
. . . . .1F **59**
60 Grove End Road
NW8 9NH
Tel: 020 7806 4000

JOHN HOWARD CENTRE 2A **52**
12 Kenworthy Road
E9 5TD
Tel: 0208 9198447

KING EDWARD VII'S HOSPITAL SISTER AGNES
. . . . .5C **4** (4C **60**)
5-10 Beaumont Street
W1G 6AA
Tel: 020 7486 4411

KING'S COLLEGE HOSPITAL 1E **105**
Denmark Hill
SE5 9RS
Tel: 0203 299 9000

LAMBETH HOSPITAL 1B **104**
108 Landor Road
SW9 9NT
Tel: 020 32286000

LEWISHAM UNIVERSITY HOSPITAL . . .3D **109**
Lewisham High Street
SE13 6LH
Tel: 020 8333 3000

LISTER HOSPITAL 1D **89**
Chelsea Bridge Road
SW1W 8RH
Tel: 020 7730 7733

LONDON BRIDGE HOSPITAL 1C **26** (2F **77**)
27 Tooley Street
SE1 2PR
Tel: 020 7407 3100

LONDON CHEST HOSPITAL 1E **65**
Bonner Road
E2 9JX
Tel: 020 7377 7000

LONDON CLINIC 4C **4** (3C **60**)
20 Devonshire Place
W1G 6BW
Tel: 020 7935 4444

LONDON INDEPENDENT BMI HOSPITAL
. . . . .4F **65**
1 Beaumont Square
E1 4NL
Tel: 020 7780 2400

LONDON WELBECK HOSPITAL
. . . . .1D **13** (4D **61**)
27 Welbeck St.
W1G 8EN
Tel: 020 7224 2242

MARGARET CENTRE (HOSPICE) 1A **40**
Whipps Cross University Hospital
Whipps Cross Road
E11 1NR
Tel: 020 8535 6604

MARIE CURIE HOSPICE, HAMPSTEAD . . .2F **45**
11 Lyndhurst Gardens
NW3 5NS
Tel: 020 7853 3400

MAUDSLEY HOSPITAL 5F **91**
Denmark Hill
SE5 8AZ
Tel: 020 32286000

MILDMAY HOSPITAL 2F **11** (2B **64**)
Austin Street
E2 7NA
Tel: 020 7613 6300

MILE END HOSPITAL 3F **65**
Bancroft Road
E1 4DG
Tel: 020 8223 8211

MOORFIELDS EYE HOSPITAL . . .2B **10** (2F **63**)
162 City Road
EC1V 2PD
Tel: 020 7253 3411

NATIONAL HOSPITAL FOR
NEUROLOGY & NEUROSURGERY
. . . . .4E **7** (3A **62**)
Queen Square
WC1N 3BG
Tel: 0845 155 5000

NEWHAM CENTRE FOR MENTAL HEALTH
. . . . .3F **69**
Cherry Tree Way
Glen Road
E13 8S
Tel: 0207 5404380

NEWHAM UNIVERSITY HOSPITAL 3E **69**
Glen Road
E13 8SL
Tel: 020 7476 4000

NHS WALK-IN CENTRE
(ANGEL MEDICAL PRACTICE) 1C **62**
Ritchie Street Group Practice
34 Ritchie Street
N1 0DG
Tel: 020 7527 1000

NHS WALK-IN CENTRE (CHARING CROSS)
. . . . .1F **85**
Charing Cross Hospital
Fulham Palace Road
W6 8RF
Tel: 020 8383 0904

NHS WALK-IN CENTRE
(LISTER HEALTH CENTRE) 4B **92**
101 Peckham Road
SE15 5LJ
Tel: 020 3049 8430

NHS WALK-IN CENTRE (NEWHAM) 3E **69**
Newham University Hospital
Glen Road
E13 8SH
Tel: 020 7363 9200

NHS WALK-IN CENTRE (PARSONS GREEN)
. . . . .4C **86**
5-7 Parsons Green
SW6 4UL
Tel: 020 8846 6758

NHS WALK-IN CENTRE (ST. ANDREWS)
. . . . .2D **67**
1-3 Birchdown House
Devons Road
E3 3NS
Tel: 020 8980 1888

NHS WALK-IN CENTRE (SOHO) 3B **14**
off Frith Street
W1D 3HZ
Tel: 020 7534 6500

NHS WALK-IN CENTRE
(TOLLGATE LODGE PRIMARY CARE CENTRE)
. . . . .3B **36**
57 Stamford Hill
N16 5SR
Tel: 020 7689 3140

NHS WALK-IN CENTRE (TOOTING)
. . . . .5A **116**
St George's Hospital
Blackshaw Road
SW17 0QT
Tel: 020 8700 0505

NHS WALK-IN CENTRE (VICTORIA) 4F **75**
off Buckingham Gate
SW1E 6AS
Tel: 020 7340 1190

NHS WALK-IN CENTRE
(WALDRON HEALTH CENTRE)
. . . . .3B **94**
Amersham Vale
SE14 6LD
Tel: 020 3049 2370

NHS WALK-IN CENTRE (WHITECHAPEL)
. . . . .4D **65**
Royal London Hospital
174 Whitechapel Road
E1 1BZ
Tel: 020 7943 1333

NIGHTINGALE CAPIO HOSPITAL 4A **60**
11-19 Lisson Grove
NW1 6SH
Tel: 020 7535 7700

PARKSIDE HOSPITAL 3F **113**
53 Parkside
SW19 5NX
Tel: 020 8971 8000

PEMBRIDGE PALLIATIVE CARE CENTRE
. . . . .4F **57**
St Charles Hospital
Exmoor Street
W10 6DZ
Tel: 020 8962 4410

PLAISTOW DAY HOSPITAL 1E **69**
Samson Street
E13 9EH
Tel: 020 8586 6200

PORTLAND HOSPITAL FOR
WOMEN & CHILDREN 4E **5** (3D **61**)
205-209 Great Portland Street
W1W 5AH
Tel: 020 7580 4400

PRIMARY URGENT CARE CENTRE (HACKNEY)
.................................2F **51**
Homerton University Hospital
Homerton Row
E9 6SR
Tel: 020 8510 5342

PRINCESS GRACE HOSPITAL 5B **4** (3C **60**)
42-52 Nottingham Place
W1U 5NY
Tel: 020 7486 1234

PRINCESS GRACE HOSPITAL (OUTPATIENTS)
.................................5C **4** (4C **60**)
30 Devonshire Street
W1G 6PU
Tel: 020 7908 3602

QUEEN CHARLOTTE'S & CHELSEA HOSPITAL
.................................5C **56**
Du Cane Road
W12 0HS
Tel: 020 3313 1111

QUEEN MARY'S HOSPITAL, ROEHAMPTON
.................................4C **98**
Roehampton Lane
SW15 5PN
Tel: 020 8487 6000

QUEEN MARY'S HOUSE 5E **31**
23 East Heath Road
NW3 1DU
Tel: 020 7431 5508

RICHARD DESMOND CHILDREN'S EYE CENTRE
.................................2B **10**
3 Peerless Street
EC1V 9EZ
Tel: 020 7253 3411

RICHARD HOUSE CHILDREN'S HOSPICE
.................................1F **83**
Richard House Drive
E16 3RG
Tel: 020 7540 0200

ROEHAMPTON HUNTERCOMBE HOSPITAL
.................................5C **98**
Holybourne Avenue
SW15 4JD
Tel: 020 8780 6155

ROEHAMPTON PRIORY HOSPITAL 2B **98**
Priory Lane
SW15 5JJ
Tel: 020 8876 8261

ROYAL BROMPTON HOSPITAL 1A **88**
Sydney Street
SW3 6NP
Tel: 020 7352 8121

ROYAL BROMPTON HOSPITAL (OUTPATIENTS)
.................................1F **87**
Fulham Road
SW3 6HP
Tel: 020 7352 8121

ROYAL FREE HOSPITAL 2A **46**
Pond Street
NW3 2QG
Tel: 020 7794 0500

ROYAL HOSPITAL FOR NEURO-DISABILITY
.................................4A **100**
West Hill
SW15 3SW
Tel: 020 8780 4500

ROYAL LONDON HOMOEOPATHIC HOSPITAL
.................................5E **7** (4A **62**)
60 Great Ormond Street
WC1N 3HR
Tel: 0845 155 5000

ROYAL LONDON HOSPITAL 4D **65**
Whitechapel Road
E1 1BB
Tel: 020 7377 7000

ROYAL MARSDEN HOSPITAL (FULHAM)
.................................1F **87**
Fulham Road
SW3 6JJ
Tel: 020 7352 8171

ROYAL NATIONAL ORTHOPAEDIC HOSPITAL
(CENTRAL LONDON OUTPATIENT DEPT.)
.................................4E **5** (3D **61**)
45-51 Bolsover Street
W1W 5AQ
Tel: 020 8954 2300

ROYAL NATIONAL THROAT, NOSE &
EAR HOSPITAL 1F **7** (2B **62**)
330 Gray's Inn Road
WC1X 8DA
Tel: 020 7915 1300

ST ANN'S HOSPITAL 1E **35**
St Ann's Road
N15 3TH
Tel: 020 8442 6000

ST BARTHOLOMEW'S HOSPITAL
.................................1E **17** (4D **63**)
West Smithfield
EC1A 7BE
Tel: 020 7377 7000

ST CHARLES CENTRE FOR WELL BEING
.................................4F **57**
Exmoor Street
W10 6DZ
Tel: 020 8962 4263

ST CHARLES HOSPITAL 4F **57**
Exmoor Street
W10 6DZ
Tel: 020 8206 7000

ST CHRISTOPHER'S HOSPICE 5E **121**
51-59 Lawrie Park Road
SE26 6DZ
Tel: 020 8768 4500

ST GEORGE'S HOSPITAL (TOOTING) ...5F **115**
Blackshaw Road
SW17 0QT
Tel: 020 8672 1255

ST JOHN'S HOSPICE 1F **59**
Hospital of St John & St Elizabeth
60 Grove End Road
NW8 9NH
Tel: 020 7806 4011

ST JOSEPH'S HOSPICE 5D **51**
Mare Street
E8 4SA
Tel: 020 8525 6000

ST MARY'S HOSPITAL 5F **59**
Praed Street
W2 1NY
Tel: 0203312 6666

ST PANCRAS HOSPITAL 5F **47**
4 St Pancras Way
NW1 0PE
Tel: 020 7530 3500

ST THOMAS' HOSPITAL 4F **23** (4B **76**)
Westminster Bridge Road
SE1 7EH
Tel: 020 7188 7188

SPRINGFIELD UNIVERSITY HOSPITAL
.........................2A **116**
61 Glenburnie Road
SW17 7DJ
Tel: 020 8682 6000

TRINITY HOSPICE 2D **103**
30 Clapham Common North Side
SW4 0RN
Tel: 020 7787 1000

UCH MACMILLAN CANCER CENTRE 3E **61**
Huntley Strret
WC1E 6DH
Tel: 0845 155 5000

UNIVERSITY COLLEGE HOSPITAL
.........................3A **6** (3E **61**)
235 Euston Road
NW1 2BU
Tel: 0845 155 5000

URGENT CARE CENTRE
(WHIPPS CROSS HOSPITAL) 1F **39**
Whipps Cross University Hospital
Whipps Cross Road
E11 1NR
Tel: 020 8539 5522

URGENT CARE CENTRE (WHITTINGTON)
.........................4E **33**
Whittington Hospital
Magdala Avenue
N19 5NF
Tel: 020 7272 3070

WELLINGTON HOSPITAL 1F **59**
8a Wellington Place
NW8 9LE
Tel: 020 7483 5148

WESTERN EYE HOSPITAL 4B **60**
171 Marylebone Road
NW1 5QH
Tel: 020 3312 6666

WHIPPS CROSS UNIVERSITY HOSPITAL
.........................1F **39**
Whipps Cross Road
Leytonstone
E11 1NR
Tel: 020 8539 5522

WHITTINGTON HOSPITAL 4E **33**
Magdala Avenue
N19 5NF
Tel: 020 7272 3070

WILLESDEN CENTRE FOR HEALTH & CARE
.........................4C **42**
Robson Avenue
NW10 3RY
Tel: 020 8438 7000

WOODBURY UNIT 1A **40**
178 James Lane
E11 1NR
Tel: 0844 493 0268

RAIL, TRAMLINK, DOCKLANDS LIGHT RAILWAY, RIVERBUS, CABLE CAR, UNDERGROUND AND OVERGROUND STATIONS

with their map square reference

A

Abbey Road (DLR) 1A 68
Acton Central (Overground) 2A 70
Aldgate (Underground) 3F 19 (5B 64)
Aldgate East (Underground) 2F 19 (5B 64)
All Saints (DLR) 1D 81
Angel (Underground) 1C 62
Archway (Underground) 4E 33
Arsenal (Underground) 5C 34

B

Baker Street (Underground) 4A 4 (3B 60)
Balham (Rail & Underground) 1D 117
Bank (Underground & DLR) . . .3B 18 (5F 63)
Bankside Pier (Riverbus) 5F 17 (1E 77)
Barbican (Underground) 5F 9 (4E 63)
Barnes (Rail) 1C 98
Barnes Bridge (Rail) 5B 84
Barons Court (Underground) 1A 86
Battersea Park (Rail) 3D 89
Bayswater (Underground) 1D 73
Beckenham Hill (Rail) 5E 123
Bellingham (Rail) 3D 123
Belsize Park (Underground) 2A 46
Bermondsey (Underground) 4C 78
Bethnal Green (Rail) 3D 65
Bethnal Green (Underground) 2E 65
Blackfriars (Rail & Underground)
. . . . .4D 17 (1D 77)
Blackfriars Millennium Pier (Riverbus)
. . . . .4D 17 (1D 77)
Blackheath (Rail) 1B 110
Blackwall (DLR) 1E 81
Bond Street (Underground) . . .3D 13 (5C 60)
Borough (Underground) 4A 26 (3E 77)
Bow Church (DLR) 2C 66
Bow Road (Underground) 2C 66
Brent Cross (Underground) 2F 29
Brixton (Rail & Underground) 2C 104
Brockley (Rail & Overground) 1A 108
Bromley-by-Bow (Underground) 2D 67
Brondesbury (Overground) 4B 44
Brondesbury Park (Overground) 5A 44

C

Caledonian Road & Barnsbury (Overground)
. . . . .4B 48
Caledonian Road (Underground)
. . . . .3B 48
Cambridge Heath (Rail) 1D 65
Camden Road (Overground) 4E 47
Camden Town (Underground) 5D 47

Canada Water (Underground & Overground)
. . . . .3E 79
Canary Wharf (Underground & DLR) 2C 80
Canary Wharf Pier (Riverbus) 2B 80
Canning Town (Underground & DLR) . . .5A 68
Cannon Street (Rail & Underground)
. . . . .4B 18 (1F 77)
Canonbury (Overground) 2E 49
Catford (Rail) 5C 108
Catford Bridge (Rail) 5C 108
Chalk Farm (Underground) 4C 46
Chancery Lane (Underground)
. . . . .1B 16 (4C 62)
Charing Cross (Rail & Underground)
. . . . .1D 23 (2A 76)
Charlton (Rail) 1E 97
Chelsea Harbour Pier (Riverbus) 4F 87
City Thameslink (Rail) 2D 17 (5D 63)
Clapham Common (Underground) 2E 103
Clapham High Street (Rail) 1F 103
Clapham Junction (Rail & Overground)
. . . . .1A 102
Clapham North (Underground) 1A 104
Clapham South (Underground) 4D 103
Clapton (Rail) 4D 37
Covent Garden (Underground) . . .4E 15 (1A 76)
Cricklewood (Rail) 1F 43
Crofton Park (Rail) 3B 108
Crossharbour (Underground & DLR) 4D 81
Crouch Hill (Overground) 2B 34
Custom House for ExCeL (DLR) 1D 83
Cutty Sark for Maritime Greenwich (DLR)
. . . . .2E 95

D

Dalston Junction (Overground) 3B 50
Dalston Kingsland (Overground) 2A 50
Denmark Hill (Rail) 5F 91
Deptford (Rail) 3C 94
Deptford Bridge (DLR) 4C 94
Devons Road (DLR) 3D 67
Dollis Hill (Underground) 2C 42
Drayton Park (Rail) 1C 48

E

Earl's Court (Underground) 5C 72
Earlsfield (Rail) 1E 115
East Acton (Underground) 5B 56
East Dulwich (Rail) 2A 106
East India (DLR) 1F 81
East Putney (Underground) 3A 100
Edgware Road (Underground) 4A 60
Elephant & Castle (Rail & Underground)
. . . . .5E 77

Elmstead Woods (Rail) 5F 125
Elverson Road (DLR) 5D 95
Embankment (Underground) . . .1E 23 (2A 76)
Embankment Pier (Riverbus) . . .1F 23 (2A 76)
Emirates Greenwich Peninsula
  (Emirates Air Line) 3B 82
Emirates Royal Docks (Emirates Air Line)
  . . . . .1C 82
Essex Road (Rail) 4E 49
Euston (Rail, Underground & Overground)
  .2B 6 (2E 61)
Euston Square (Underground) . . .3A 6 (3E 61)

F

Farringdon (Rail & Underground)
  . . . . .5D 9 (4D 63)
Fenchurch Street (Rail) 4F 19 (1B 78)
Finchley Road & Frognal (Overground)
  . . . . .2E 45
Finchley Road (Underground) 3E 45
Finsbury Park (Rail & Underground) . . .4C 34
Forest Gate (Rail) 2C 54
Forest Hill (Rail & Overground) 2E 121
Fulham Broadway (Underground) 3C 86

G

Gipsy Hill (Rail) 5A 120
Gloucester Road (Underground) 5E 73
Golders Green (Underground) 3C 30
Goldhawk Road (Underground) 3E 71
Goodge Street (Underground) . . .5B 6 (4F 61)
Gospel Oak (Overground) 1C 46
Great Portland Street (Underground)
  . . . . .4E 5 (3D 61)
Greenland Pier (Riverbus) 4B 80
Green Park (Underground) . . .1E 21 (2E 75)
Greenwich (Rail & DLR) 3D 95
Greenwich Pier (Riverbus) 1E 95
Grove Park (Rail) 3D 125

H

Hackney Central (Overground) 3D 51
Hackney Downs (Rail) 2D 51
Hackney Wick (Overground) 3C 52
Haggerston (Overground) 5B 50
Hammersmith (Underground) 5E 71
Hampstead (Underground) 1E 45
Hampstead Heath (Overground) 1A 46
Harlesden (Underground & Overground)
  . . . . .1A 56
Harringay (Rail) 1C 34
Harringay Green Lanes (Overground)
  . . . . .1D 35
Haydons Road (Rail) 5E 115
Hendon (Rail) 1C 28
Hendon Central (Underground) 1D 29
Herne Hill (Rail) 4D 105
Heron Quays (DLR) 2C 80
Highbury & Islington
  (Rail, Underground & Overground)
  . . . . .3D 49
Highgate (Underground) 1D 33

High Street Kensington (Underground)
  . . . . .3D 73
Hilton Docklands Pier (Riverbus) 2B 80
Hither Green (Rail) 4A 110
Holborn (Underground) 1F 15 (5B 62)
Holland Park (Underground) 2B 72
Holloway Road (Underground) 2B 48
Homerton (Overground) 3F 51
Honor Oak Park (Rail & Overground)
  . . . . .4F 107
Hoxton (Overground) 1B 64
Hyde Park Corner (Underground)
  . . . . .3C 20 (3C 74)

I

Imperial Wharf (Rail & Overground) . . .4E 87
Island Gardens (DLR) 1E 95

K

Kennington (Underground) 1D 91
Kensal Green (Underground & Overground)
  . . . . .2E 57
Kensal Rise (Overground) 1F 57
Kensington Olympia
  (Rail, Underground & Overground)
  . . . . .4A 72
Kentish Town (Rail & Underground) 2E 47
Kentish Town West (Overground) 3D 47
Kidbrooke (Rail) 1D 111
Kilburn (Underground) 3B 44
Kilburn High Road (Overground) 5D 45
Kilburn Park (Underground) 1C 58
King's Cross (Rail & Underground)
  . . . . .1D 7 (1A 62)
King's Cross St Pancras (Underground)
  . . . . .1D 7 (2A 62)
Knightsbridge (Underground) . . .4A 20 (3B 74)

L

Ladbroke Grove (Underground) 5A 58
Ladywell (Rail) 3D 109
Lambeth North (Underground)
  . . . . .5B 24 (4C 76)
Lancaster Gate (Underground) 1F 73
Langdon Park (DLR) 5D 67
Latimer Road (Underground) 1F 71
Lee (Rail) 4C 110
Leicester Square (Underground)
  . . . . .4C 14 (1A 76)
Lewisham (Rail & DLR) 1E 109
Leyton (Underground) 5E 39
Leyton Midland Road (Overground) 3E 39
Leytonstone (Underground) 3A 40
Leytonstone High Road (Overground) . . .4A 40
Limehouse (Rail & DLR) 5A 66
Liverpool Street (Rail & Underground)
  . . . . .1D 19 (4A 64)
London Bridge (Rail & Underground)
  . . . . .2C 26 (2F 77)
London Bridge City Pier (Riverbus)
  . . . . .1C 26 (2A 78)
London City Airport (DLR) 2F 83

London Eye Millennium Pier (Riverbus)
. . . . .3F 23 (3B 76)
London Fields (Rail) 4D 51
Loughborough Junction (Rail) 1D 105
Lower Sydenham (Rail) 5B 122

M

Maida Vale (Underground) 2D 59
Manor House (Underground) 2E 35
Manor Park (Rail) 1F 55
Mansion House (Underground)
. . . . .4A 18 (1E 77)
Marble Arch (Underground) . . .3A 12 (5B 60)
Maryland (Rail) 3A 54
Marylebone (Rail & Underground) . . .3B 60
Masthouse Terrace Pier (Riverbus) . .1C 94
Maze Hill (Rail) 2A 96
Mile End (Underground) 3B 66
Millbank Millennium Pier (Riverbus)
. . . . .5A 76
Monument (Underground) 4C 18 (1F 77)
Moorgate (Rail & Underground)
. . . . .1B 18 (4F 63)
Mornington Crescent (Underground)
. . . . .1E 61
Mudchute (DLR) 5D 81

N

Neasden (Underground) 2A 42
New Cross (Rail & Overground) 3B 94
New Cross Gate (Rail & Overground) . .4A 94
North Acton (Underground) 4A 56
North Dulwich (Rail) 3F 105
North Greenwich (Underground) 3A 82
North Greenwich Pier (Riverbus) 2B 82
Notting Hill Gate (Underground) 2C 72
Nunhead (Rail) 5E 93

O

Old Street (Rail & Underground)
. . . . .2C 10 (3F 63)
Oval (Underground) 2C 90
Oxford Circus (Underground) . .3F 13 (5E 61)

P

Paddington (Rail & Underground) 5F 59
Parsons Green (Underground) 4C 86
Peckham Rye (Rail) 5C 92
Penge East (Rail) 5E 121
Piccadilly Circus (Underground)
. . . . .5B 14 (1F 75)
Pimlico (Underground) 1F 89
Plaistow (Underground) 1B 68
Pontoon Dock (DLR) 2E 83
Poplar (DLR) .1D 81
Prince Regent (DLR) 1E 83
Pudding Mill Lane (DLR) 5D 53
Putney (Rail) 2A 100
Putney Bridge (Underground) 1B 100
Putney Pier (Riverbus) 1A 100

Q

Queen's Park (Underground & Overground)
. . . . .1B 58
Queens Road, Peckham (Rail) 4E 93
Queenstown Road, Battersea (Rail) . . .4D 89
Queensway (Underground) 1D 73

R

Ravenscourt Park (Underground) 5D 71
Rectory Road (Rail) 5B 36
Redbridge (Underground) 1F 41
Regent's Park (Underground) . .4D 5 (3D 61)
Rotherhithe (Underground) 3E 79
Royal Albert (DLR) 1F 83
Royal Oak (Underground) 4D 59
Royal Victoria (DLR) 1C 82
Russell Square (Underground) . . .4D 7 (3A 62)

S

St George Wharf Pier (Riverbus) 2A 90
St James's Park (Underground)
. . . . .5B 22 (3F 75)
St James Street (Rail) 1A 38
St Johns (Rail) 5C 94
St John's Wood (Underground) 1F 59
St Pancras International (Rail) . .1D 7 (2A 62)
St Paul's (Underground) 2F 17 (5E 63)
Seven Sisters (Rail & Underground) . . .1B 36
Shadwell (Overground & DLR) 1D 79
Shepherd's Bush
(Rail, Underground & Overground)
. . . . .3F 71
Shepherd's Bush Market (Underground)
. . . . .2E 71
Shoreditch High Street (Overground)
. . . . .3F 11 (3B 64)
Sloane Square (Underground) 5C 74
Snaresbrook (Underground) 1C 40
Southfields (Underground) 1B 114
South Bermondsey (Rail) 1E 93
South Hampstead (Overground) 4E 45
South Kensington (Underground) 5F 73
South Quay (DLR) 3D 81
South Tottenham (Overground) 1B 36
Southwark (Underground) 2D 25 (2D 77)
Stamford Brook (Underground) 5B 70
Stamford Hill (Rail) 2A 36
Star Lane (DLR) 3A 68
Stepney Green (Underground) 3F 65
Stockwell (Underground) 4A 90
Stoke Newington (Rail) 4B 36
Stratford
(Rail, Underground, Overground & DLR)
. . . . .4E 53
Stratford High Street (DLR) 5F 53
Stratford International (Rail & DLR) . . .3E 53
Streatham (Rail) 5F 117
Streatham Hill (Rail) 2A 118
Surrey Quays (Overground) 5F 79
Swiss Cottage (Underground) 4F 45
Sydenham (Rail & Overground) 4E 121
Sydenham Hill (Rail) 3B 120

T

Temple (Underground) 4B 16 (1B 76)
Tooting Bec (Underground) 3C 116
Tooting Broadway (Underground) 5A 116
Tottenham Court Road (Underground)
.................2C 14 (5F 61)
Tower Gateway (DLR) 4F 19 (1B 78)
Tower Hill (Underground) 4F 19 (1B 78)
Tower Millennium Pier (Riverbus)
.................1E 27 (2A 78)
Tufnell Park (Underground) 1E 47
Tulse Hill (Rail) 2D 119
Turnham Green (Underground) 5A 70

U

Upper Holloway (Overground) 4F 33
Upton Park (Underground) 5E 55

V

Vauxhall (Rail & Underground) 1A 90
Victoria (Coach) 5D 75
Victoria (Rail & Underground) 5D 75

W

Walthamstow Queens Road (Overground)
.................1C 38
Wandsworth Common (Rail) 1B 116
Wandsworth Riverside Quarter Pier (Riverbus)
.................2C 100
Wandsworth Road (Rail) 5E 89

Wandsworth Town (Rail) 2D 101
Wanstead (Underground) 1D 41
Wanstead Park (Overground) 1D 55
Warren Street (Underground) 3F 5 (3E 61)
Warwick Avenue (Underground) 3E 59
Waterloo (Rail & Underground)
.................3B 24 (3C 76)
Waterloo East (Rail) 2C 24 (2C 76)
Westbourne Park (Underground) 4B 58
West Brompton
(Rail, Underground & Overground)
.................2C 86
Westcombe Park (Rail) 1C 96
West Dulwich (Rail) 2F 119
Westferry (DLR) 1C 80
West Hampstead (Underground & Overground)
.................3C 44
West Hampstead Thameslink (Rail)
.................3C 44
West Ham (DLR) 2A 68
West Ham (Rail & Underground) 2A 68
West India Quay (DLR) 1C 80
West Kensington (Underground) 1B 86
Westminster (Underground) 4E 23 (3A 76)
West Norwood (Rail) 4D 119
West Silvertown (DLR) 2C 82
Whitechapel (Underground & Overground)
.................4D 65
White City (Underground) 1E 71
Willesden Green (Underground) 3E 43
Willesden Junction
(Underground & Overground) 2B 56
Wimbledon (Rail, Underground & Tramlink)
.................5B 114
Wimbledon Park (Underground) 3C 114
Woodgrange Park (Overground) 2F 55
Wood Lane (Underground) 1E 71